Adventure Guide

Germany

Henk Bekker

HUNTER

HUNTER PUBLISHING, INC,
130 Campus Drive, Edison, NJ 08818
☎ 732-225-1900; 800-255-0343; fax 732-417-1744
www.hunterpublishing.com

Ulysses Travel Publications
4176 Saint-Denis, Montréal, Québec
Canada H2W 2M5
☎ 514-843-9882, ext. 2232; fax 514-843-9448

Windsor Books
The Boundary, Wheatley Road, Garsington
Oxford, OX44 9EJ England
☎ 01865-361122; fax 01865-361133

ISBN 1-58843-503-2

Manufactured in the United States of America

Cover photo: Schloss Neuschwanstein (© www.romantischestrasse.de)

Back cover photo: Dresden, Zwinger (© Christoph Münch)

Spine photo: Angel, Cologne Cathedral

Maps by Toni Carbone © 2005

Index by Jan Mucciarone

4 3 2

Contents

Introduction

In this Chapter

Germany is a large country of wide contrasts. From the beaches of the North and Baltic Seas to the Bavarian Alpine peaks and from the Black Forest to the nightspots of Berlin, Germany has much of interest to the international traveler.

For centuries, culture has played an important role in German society. Large cities have opera houses and symphony orchestras, while even small villages have musical and other cultural societies. Germany is the land of Bach, Beethoven, Goethe, Schiller, and other artists that influenced Western culture. Culture is easy to enjoy in Germany with frequent performances at relatively low prices.

Germany is also a country with amazing architectural treasures. It has some minor Roman and Carolingian monuments, but it is with the Romanesque and Gothic that German building craft really came to the fore. The influence of the Renaissance was limited, but Baroque and Rococo are well represented. More modern styles, including Art Nouveau, Bauhaus, Modern, and Post-Modern, can also be found, especially in German cities. Air raids in World War II ruined most German cities. Many rebuilt the damaged buildings while others opted to rebuild in modern style. Half-timbered houses (*Fachwerk*) make some of the most romantic townscapes and are often seen as typically German and typically medieval – though most half-timbered buildings are from the 16th to 18th century.

The long tradition of dividing inheritances gave Germany literally hundreds of small states and principalities, each with its own palaces and residences. More than 20,000 castles and castle ruins are scattered throughout the country. Often the largest palaces and churches are found in what are now small and insignificant towns.

Germany is more than arts and culture. It is also a paradise for outdoor enthusiasts. Hiking is the most popular activity in Germany, with thousands of marked trails throughout the country. Cycling is also popular, with many dedicated cycling routes. Canoeing and kayaking are done on many rivers and lakes. Skiing and other winter sports are possible in the Bavarian Alps and many parts of the Mittelgebirge. Germany also has amazing natural beauty, with the Bavarian Alps, the Black Forest and the Harz Mountains.

This book starts in Berlin and then follows a geographical Baroque "S," with a few extra curls at the top end, first through eastern, then northern Germany, before passing through the western states to end in Bavaria and Baden-Württemberg in the south.

Eastern Germany

Berlin, Germany's capital and largest city, is also the most interesting destination. It has more than 170 museums, three opera houses, enormous cultural variety, and a gripping modern history.

Brandenburg surrounds Berlin. It is the largest of the former East German states that joined West Germany after the *Wende* (the Change, as the end of the Communist regime is commonly called). It is also one of the poorest. The most popular destination here is Potsdam, which, due to its close proximity to Berlin, is more often than not visited on a day-trip from the capital.

Saxony (*Sachsen*) is one of the most densely populated states in Germany, but has natural beauty, especially in the Saxon Switzerland area south of Dresden. Its two major cities, Dresden and Leipzig, are tourist magnets. Dresden is restoring its pre-1945 Baroque appearance and, in addition to the marvelous architecture, it has some excellent museums and art collections. The immediate appeal of Leipzig is less obvious but it is a great city to visit – giving the impression of a lived-in city rather than an artificial tourist attraction.

Thuringia (*Thüringen*) is closely associated with German literature through the

Weimar classical movement led by Goethe and Schiller. In addition to Weimar, Erfurt has a wonderfully preserved medieval town center and Eisenach has the Wartburg, the most German of castles. The Thuringian Forest is a lovely wooded low-rise mountain range of outstanding natural beauty with the Rennsteig, Germany's most popular long-distance hiking trail, at its crest.

Saxony-Anhalt (*Sachsen-Anhalt*) is a predominantly rural state. A large part of the beautiful Harz Mountain range is in the southern part of the state and has lovely half-timbered villages including Quedlinburg and Wernigerode. The state also has three major sights associated with Martin Luther in Wittenberg, Eisenach, and Mansfield. Saxony-Anhalt is a magnet for Romanesque architecture enthusiasts as well.

Mecklenburg-Western Pomerania (*Mecklenburg-Vorpommern*) is the northernmost part of the former East Germany. It has the lowest population density of any state in Germany and unspoiled nature is still easy to find. Highlights include the Baltic Coast, with the island of Rügen especially popular among well-heeled travelers. In the former Hanseatic cities it is the brick Gothic churches and town halls that are especially impressive. Many country roads are tree-lined *allées*.

■ Northern Germany

Schleswig-Holstein is in the north of the former West Germany, mostly on the Jutland peninsula that ends in Denmark. Few foreign tourists travel here, but the town of Lübeck, for centuries the queen of the Hanseatic League, is worth a journey. It has marvelous examples of brick Gothic architecture.

Hamburg, a city-state, is Germany's second-largest city and premier port. It is a spread-out city with mostly modern, low-rise buildings and much water and greenery. Especially popular are harbor cruises, the Alster Lake, and the elegant shopping arcades.

Bremen, another city-state, is Germany's second-largest harbor. It has an impressive historic center but many modern attractions are being created to appeal to younger visitors.

Lower Saxony (*Niedersachsen*) is the original home of the Saxons. Its North Sea coast is popular with German families, but for most foreign travelers the south is more interesting. It has many small villages with wonderful half-timbered buildings such as Celle and Hann. Münden (Hannoversch Münden). The Weser Renaissance architecture of towns such as Hameln is also interesting. Hildesheim and Goslar were important towns at the foundation of the Holy Roman Empire a millennium ago and have interesting Romanesque structures as well as lovely half-timbered buildings in the old sections.

■ Western Germany

North Rhine Westphalia (*Nordrhein-Westfalen*) is densely populated, with the Ruhr district, the former powerhouse of German industry, having the highest concentration of large cities in the country. More interesting is Cologne, with its enormous Gothic cathedral, numerous Romanesque churches, excellent museums, and the most refreshing beer in the country. Bonn has important museums and Beethoven-related sights. Düsseldorf is a modern city with high fashion and modern art, while Aachen was the preferred capital of Charlemagne.

Rhineland-Palatinate (*Rheinland-Pfalz*) boasts the most romantic stretches of the Rhine Valley, with castles or castle ruins every two km (1.2 miles). It also has the equally beautiful Mosel Valley with the meandering river in a steep, narrow valley. Speyer, Worms and Mainz have interesting Romanesque cathedrals, while Trier has the largest collection of Roman monuments in Germany. Saarland is well off the beaten track and seldom visited by foreign tourists.

Hesse (*Hessen*) is geographically at the center of Germany with an excellent transportation network, including Frankfurt Airport, the busiest airport in continental Europe. Frankfurt is a mostly modern city but with a couple of interesting historic buildings and a number of excellent museums. The Lahn Valley is a gem, with wonderful castles and cathedrals along Germany's most popular canoeing river.

■ Southern Germany

Bavaria (*Bayern*) is the largest state in Germany and the most popular holiday destination for domestic and foreign travelers alike. In the north of the state is Franken, with important historic cities such as Würzburg, Bamberg, and Nürnberg. Regensburg and Passau are on the banks of the Danube and both cities have interesting historic centers that escaped damage during the World War II. The Romantic Road is a popular holiday route that passes romantic sites, including Rothenburg ob der Tauber, the most romantic of all Germany's medieval towns.

Apart from Berlin, **Munich** (*München*) is the most interesting German city. It has a vast range of cultural offerings, including excellent art museums and spectacular, mostly Baroque, royal palaces. It is the home of beer, with many historic beer halls, beer gardens and, of course, Oktoberfest. The Bavarian Alps have the most spectacular scenery in Germany. Their natural beauty is enhanced by castles, churches, monasteries, and historic towns.

Baden-Württemberg is also popular with tourists. Heidelberg, with its majestic castle ruin, is a must-see for most foreign visitors to Germany. Stuttgart, a major industrial city, is surprisingly beautiful and has several interesting museums and galleries. The Black Forest is the largest forested area in Germany, and contains many picture-perfect towns and valleys. It is hugely popular with hikers and cyclists. Baden-Baden is the most elegant town in Germany. The Bodensee (Lake Constance) is a popular holiday area, with the Swiss Alps providing a constant backdrop to the sights along the lakeshore. In addition to picturesque villages, it has historically significant sights, including the historic old town of Konstanz and the Romanesque churches on the island of Reichenau.

■ History

HISTORY CHEAT SHEET

German history is complex and somewhat confusing. Use this cheat sheet to keep important events in context.

100 BC-AD 400: Romans occupy parts of Germany, mostly west of the Rhine and south of the Danube.

800: Charlemagne is crowned Roman Emperor.

9th to 12th centuries: Romanesque (*Romanik*) architecture.

962: Otto II is crowned German Roman Emperor. The entity later known as the Holy Roman Empire of the German Nation lasted until 1806.

13th to 16th centuries: Gothic (*Gotik*) architecture. The oldest surviving half-timbered (*Fachwerk*) houses are from this period, although many of these "medieval" buildings actually date from the 16th to 18th centuries.

1518: Martin Luther's 95 Theses initiates the Lutheran Reformation.

1555: Peace of Augsburg allows rulers to select the state's religion.

1520-1620: Renaissance architecture.

1618-48: Thirty Years' War devastates and depopulates large areas of Germany. Peace of Westphalia (1648) left Germany with around 350 independent political entities.

17th and 18th centuries: Baroque (*Barok*) and Rococo (*Rokoko*) architecture.

1688-97: Palatine War of Succession sees French troops destroy most towns and castles in the Rhineland and Palatinate.

1756-63: Seven Years' War confirms the rise of Prussia as the fifth European power.

1792-1815: Napoleon redraws the European and German political map. The Holy Roman Empire of the German Nation comes to a formal end in 1806. Germany is reduced to 25 political entities.

19th century: Romanticism (*Romantik*) and Historicist architecture. After 1871, "Founding time" (*Gründerzeit* / *Wilhelmine*) architecture, followed by Art Nouveau (*Jugendstil*).

1866: Prussian-Austrian war confirms Prussia as the preeminent power in Germany.

1870-71: Franco-Prussian war ends with the foundation of the (Second) German Empire dominated by Prussia.

1914-18: First World War ends with Germany defeated and the end of the monarchy.

1919-1933: The ill-fated Weimar Republic fails to cope with economic and political upheaval.

1933-1945: The Nazi era ends in the carnage of World War II. Germany is totally defeated, occupied, partitioned, and reduced in size.

1949-1989: Germany divided into a democratic West Germany and a communist East Germany.

1989: A peaceful revolution ends the East German regime.

1990: Germany re-unites and Berlin again becomes the capital.

Prehistory

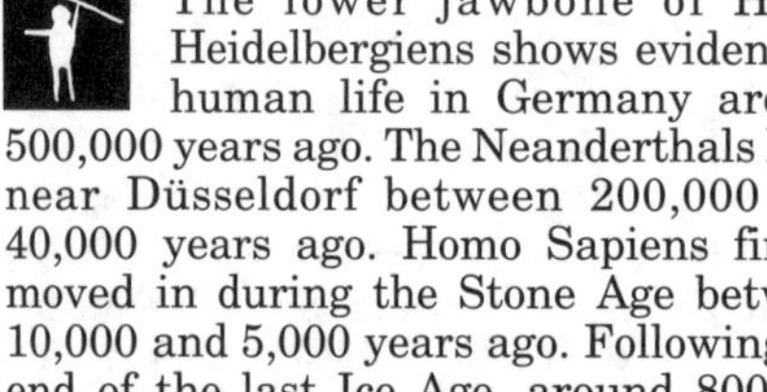

The lower jawbone of Homo Heidelbergiens shows evidence of human life in Germany around 500,000 years ago. The Neanderthals lived near Düsseldorf between 200,000 and 40,000 years ago. Homo Sapiens finally moved in during the Stone Age between 10,000 and 5,000 years ago. Following the end of the last Ice Age, around 800 BC, Celtic tribes came into southern Germany. They formed the Haltstatt (800-400 BC) and the La-Tène (500-50 BC) cultures. Although both were settled in southern Germany, their influence spread as far as the Jutland Peninsula. Roman pressure from the south and German tribes from the northeast destroyed these cultures.

The Romans

The oldest written reference to "Germania" is from the Roman writer Poseidonius, writing in the first century BC. Julius Caesar also referred to Germans that he had come in contact with during his conquest of Gaul (58-51 BC). The left bank of the Rhine became part of Rome and initial military bases became the first German cities (e.g. Trier, Cologne, Koblenz, and Mainz).

Attempts to penetrate all the way to the Elbe failed after the Germanic tribes defeated three divisions of the Roman army in AD 9. During the first century, the Limes was built, a 550-km (330-mile) defensive line to protect the new Roman territories on the right of the Rhine and north of the Danube. During the Early Middle Ages, areas that were previously under Roman rule tended to develop faster than the barbarian-held areas to the north.

Pressure from the *Völkerwanderung* (migration of the peoples), especially after the Huns had penetrated the area of the East Goths, led to the end of the Roman Empire around AD 375. Germany, like much of the rest of Europe, spent several centuries in political chaos.

The Frankish Empire

At the end of the fifth century, the Merovingian ruler **Clovis** (Clodwig in German, 482-511), succeeded in uniting most of the Frankish tribes under his rule. He converted to Christianity in 498, which changed the composition of society. Cathedrals and monasteries became the central institutions. At the end of the sixth century, Irish missionaries worked in many parts of Germany and established monasteries that would become centers of learning and culture.

After Clovis's death, his sons split up the empire and it remained divided until Karl Martell succeeded in uniting it again during the eighth century. The Anglo-Saxon missionary, **St Boniface** (672-754) reorganized the church in southern Germany, establishing new religious centers and converted large areas of central Germany to Christianity. In 751, he crowned Martell's son **Pippin** as king. This was the end of the Merovingian dynasty and the start of the Carolinian one, named after Pippin's son Karl.

Karl der Große (Charles the Great, 768-814) is in English better known under his French name, **Charlemagne**. He became king of the Franks in 768 and was crowned Roman Emperor by the Pope on Christmas day in 800. He thus was seen as the legal successor of the Roman emperors. He ruled over an empire that included most of present-day France, Germany, Switzerland, Belgium, the Netherlands, and northern Italy. After a 30-year battle, he finally defeated the northern German Saxons and enforced Christianization. Charlemagne had no fixed capital; instead, he erected several *Pfalzes*, or Imperial Palaces, and Imperial Monasteries throughout the empire and constantly traveled between them to keep control of the empire.

The Treaty of Verdun (843) divided Charlemagne's empire among his three grandsons. By the end of the ninth century, a permanent east-west division of the Frankish empire was agreed upon. In 911, the East Franks elected **Konrad I** (911-918) as king, to firmly set Germany on a separate development course from France.

Holy Roman Empire of the German Nation

What followed is a rather complicated history – Germany as a single political entity would only be established in 1871. In the meantime, a loose confederation of mainly German-speaking states continued the tradition of the East-Frankish Empire. Up to the 13th century, this empire included at least the claim to rule over northern Italy too. Different names were used for this empire, but the misnomer of Holy Roman Empire of the German Nation was the most persistent, even though it was neither holy, nor Roman, and not much of an empire. The empire had an elective monarchy with some elements of hereditary rights. Once the German king was elected, he was usually crowned emperor by the Pope – although this separate requirement fell away in later years.

On his deathbed, Konrad I took the highly unusual step of advising that his rival, rather than his brother, be elected the next king. This led to the election of the first Saxon king, **Heinrich I**. He secured the borders of the empire and succeeded in establishing his family as the rulers of the empire up to 1024 – usually referred to as the Ottonian period, since three emperors were called Otto. **Otto II**, the Great, revived the notion of Empire when he was crowned German Roman Emperor by the Pope in 962.

The Ottonians were followed by the Frankish Salians, who ruled from 1024 to 1125. They initially succeeded in strengthening the power of the king against the dukes. However, the emperor fell out with the Pope over who had the right to invest bishops. The Investiture Controversy culminated in King Heinrich IV begging for forgiveness from the pope during several snowy days in Canossa (1077). The dispute ended in the Concordat of Worms (1122), which saw bishops becoming princes and vassals of the empire. Bishoprics, which did involve division of lands and titles among sons, as was common with other nobles, increasingly enlarged their land holdings versus other political entities.

From 1138 to 1254, the Hohenstaufen family ruled the empire. This period saw a continuous power struggle with the Welfen family (in English often written as Guelph). **Friedrich I Barbarossa** (1152-1190) introduced the title Holy Roman Empire in an attempt to achieve equal status with the Pope and to reduce papal influence over religious institutions in Germany. This period also saw the conquest and incorporation of areas to the east of the Elbe.

The late 13th century saw a period of lawlessness in much of the kingdom with a range of kings and anti-kings competing for power. The claim to rule northern Italy ended. This interregnum ended with the election of the powerful **Rudolph of Habsburg** as king in 1273. He succeeded in restoring order in Germany. However, during this period many northern German cities formed the Hanseatic League, which would in effect be the most powerful economic and political force in medieval Germany.

The Golden Bull of 1356 was the first attempt at a constitution for the empire. It specified the electors of the king as the archbishops of Trier, Mainz, and Cologne, as well as the king of Bohemia, the margrave of Brandenburg, the duke of Saxony, and the duke of the Palatinate. (The composition would change after the Reformation.) The elections were to take place in Frankfurt, the coronation in Aachen, and the first Reichstag (Imperial Diet) of each emperor would take place in Nürnberg. Up to 1452, the king still had to travel to Rome to be crowned emperor by the Pope. From 1493, the king assumed the title emperor directly after coronation and avoided the long, dangerous, and expensive trip to Rome.

From 1438 until the dissolution of the Empire in 1806, the Austrian Habsburger family would provide the emperor, with only one exception. However, the power of the emperor was already weak at the start of the period and his influence eroded further as the power of the individual nation states increased.

Reformation & the Thirty Years' War

On 31 October 1517, the monk **Martin Luther** questioned the practices of the Roman Catholic Church in his famous 95 Theses (Wittenberg). What started as a seemingly minor squabble soon involved the whole of Germany. Gutenberg's invention of the moveable press in the mid-15th century ensured that Luther's Theses were soon known throughout the empire.

Luther refused to recant, was excommunicated by the Pope, and banned by the emperor following the Diet of Worms (1521). However, his ideas spread and gathered support. Soon the German states were at war. The Peace of Augsburg (1555) established Lutheran Protestantism as an equal to Roman Catholicism in so far as rulers of each territory could select the religion all nationals had to follow.

However, the question of whether a ruler can change his religious affiliation and force the population to follow, remained open. In 1618, the Protestant Bohemian Estates refused the Catholic Archduke Ferdinand von Habsburg as king. Instead, they elected Protestant Elector Friedrich V of the Palatinate as king. Soon Germany was at war and most of Europe joined in.

The Thirty Years' War that lasted from 1618 to 1648 was the most devastating war in German history. Around a third of the total population died during this period – most of hunger as warring parties destroyed without mercy harvests and cities. The war started badly for the Protestants, who were early on defeated by the Imperial army. However, the Danes joined at the side of the Protestant states and later the Swedes joined too. Spain sided with the Catholic Emperor and eventually France joined the Protestants against the Habsburgers. Peace negotiations in Osnabruck and Münster lasted four years – working out the protocol for order of precedence took up around half the time. The Peace of Westphalia (1648) redrew the maps of Europe and established most of the nation-states of Western Europe as it is known today.

The Rise of Prussia

During the late 17th and 18th century, Germany was characterized by *Kleinstäterei* (small state-ism). The Peace of Westphalia left Germany divided into 350 states, ranging from European powers such as Austria to minor, powerless but fully entitled entities. This allowed foreign powers such as France and Sweden to interfere in German affairs without having to face serious consequences. French King Louis XIV claimed the left bank of the Rhine and, during the War of Palatinate Succession (1688-97), French troops destroyed most of the cities in the region as well as virtually all castles along the Rhine and Mosel. While the European nation states such as Britain, France, Spain, and the Netherlands were building colonial empires, German princes built palaces.

However, from the mid-17th century, Brandenburg-Prussia increasingly improved its military power. By the mid-18th century, **Friedrich II der Große** (Frederick the Great, 1740-1786) felt strong enough to challenge Austria. Following the War of Austrian Succession (1740-48) and the Seven Years' War (1756-63), Prussia was seen as the fifth European power. The struggle between Prussia and Austria for supremacy in the German nation would last another century.

The German Empire

During the Napoleonic Era, Germany paid for the last time the price of its internal division. The Peace of Lunéville (1801) saw all territories west of the Rhine lost to France. Soon after, **Napoleon** redrew the map of Germany: he made an end to the small states, created new larger entities, ended the independence of most Free Imperial Cities, and forced secularization on most religious entities. In 1806, the Holy Roman Empire of the German Nation formally came to an end. Although large parts of Germany suffered from the Napoleonic wars and occupation, the ideas of nationhood were planted.

Prussia, which played a major role in the defeat of Napoleon, was the clear winner of the Congress of Vienna (1815). It vastly increased its territory in all directions. Baden, Württemberg, and Bavaria, which sided with Napoleon but switched sides in time, kept the territorial gains made under Napoleon's command. Bavaria alone doubled in size. Saxony supported Napoleon to the end and had half its territory annexed by Prussia.

The former Holy Roman Empire was replaced by the German Confederation (Deutscher Bund). It had around 40 member states, but never achieved much. It was a very loose confederation and the attempts in Frankfurt from 1848 to draw up a constitution and form a liberal parliamentary democracy failed. Although it was agreed to form a small German solution with Prussia as the anchor, rather than a larger German solution led by Austria, the Prussian king refused the terms under which he was offered the crown.

In 1862, **Otto von Bismarck** became Minister-President of Prussia – in eight years, he created the German Empire. He knew Austria and France were the main obstacles to a united Germany. In 1866, he defeated Austria and solved the struggle for supremacy in Germany for good in Prussia's favor. All German states north of the River Main joined Prussia in the North German Alliance (Norddeutscher Bund) and in a secret treaty Bavaria, Baden, and Württemberg agreed to place their troops under Prussian command in times of war.

France, alarmed by the growing power of Prussia, used a minor diplomatic incident in 1870 as a reason to declare war. France expected Bavarian and Austrian support, but miscalculated. For the first time in history, France, used to picking off small German states, had to face a united Germany, and suffered an embarrassing defeat. In 1871, the German Empire was proclaimed and **Wilhelm I** crowned Emperor in the Hall of Mirrors in Versailles.

Bismarck's empire was in theory a confederation of around 25 states, but it was dominated by Prussia and the central government like no other in German history. It also saw an unprecedented time of peace and rapid economic development.

But the empire concentrated too much power in the hands of the Emperor. While Bismarck was in control, he could use this power to ensure peace and prosperity. However, in 1888 Wilhelm I died, his son Friedrich II died after 99 days in office, and his son **Wilhelm II** became emperor. Wilhelm II was conservative and of limited intellectual ability. He was extremely vain. Wilhelm I could not stand Bismarck, but knew he needed his intellectual abilities. Wilhelm II thought he could do without the chancellor and in 1890 Bismarck was forced to resign.

Germany's geopolitical location has always been unfavorable – it is in the heart of Europe surrounded by potential enemies. In 1866, Bismarck ended the war with Austria as soon as victory for Prussia was possible and promptly made Austria a valuable ally. He knew the war with France, and especially the enormous war reparations, would made France a belligerent enemy, so he concluded a friendship treaty with Russia. Through his careful diplomacy, Bismarck ensured that France was the only potential enemy, and France alone was too weak to take on a united Germany.

Soon after Bismarck's dismissal, his carefully nurtured diplomacy was in tatters. Kaiser Wilhelm spurned the Czar's approaches to renew the treaty of friendship, allowing a Franco-Russian alliance in 1893. A decade later, Great Britain ended its isolation from the continent and concluded the Entente Cordiale with France. Early-20th-century Europe was in a nationalistic and jingoistic mood and spoiling for a fight.

In June 1914, Austrian Archduke Franz Ferdinand was assassinated in Sarajevo. A diplomatic crisis ensued and spun out of control. Germany faced enemies on two sides and, when Russia started to mobilize, Germany declared war. Fearing an attack from France, Germany ignored Belgium's neutrality and moved its armies through Belgium to attack France first. Britain, a guarantor of Belgian neutrality since 1839, came to her aid. A devastating war lasting four years ensued. The opposing armies in France found themselves entrenched, making little headway in either direction. In 1917, a separate peace with Russia allowed Germany to send more troops to the French front, but by the end of the year, American assistance had arrived in Europe to aid the Anglo-French armies. By the end of 1918, an exhausted Germany was defeated. On 9 November 1918, a republic was proclaimed and Kaiser Wilhelm II was informed that he had abdicated. He ignored a suggestion that he lead a counter-attack and die a hero on the front, instead packing his bags for exile in the Netherlands. All other German nobles lost their titles and claims at the same time.

The Weimar Republic & the Nazi Era

In the chaos of the aftermath of the First World War, Germany experienced several regional revolutions and major cities such as Berlin and Munich were at times in the hands of Bolsheviks. A very liberal constitution was drawn up by the National Convention meeting in the town Weimar.

The so-called Weimar Republic came into being in 1919. It never had popular support and was immediately saddled with hefty war reparations in the Treaty of Versailles. On average, the government changed every eight months. Parties were very small and it was impossible to form coalitions for effective government.

RUNAWAY INFLATION

The Weimar Republic had to deal with runaway inflation as an immediate result of the war and the high war reparations. The price of bread increased from 1 mark in December 1919 to 3.90 marks two years later. In December 1922, a loaf of bread cost 163 marks, and a year later 399,000,000,000 marks. At one stage, workers were paid daily by the wheelbarrow load and then ran to shops as the value of the currency would drop too much when walking!

From 1924 to 1929, the Weimar Republic did remarkably well, but then the worldwide recession did it in. In these desperate times, the Nazi party of Adolf Hitler seemed to many the only solution. It increased its support drastically between 1930 and 1932, and became the largest party in the Reichstag elections of November 1932. President **Von Hindenburg**, who previously resisted appointing Hitler, whom he dreaded, had to appoint him Chancellor on January 30, 1933. On February 27, 1933, the Reichstag burned down under circumstances that have never been satisfactorily explained. Whether the Nazis did it or not, they knew how to use the event. The Communist Party was blamed and banned. A week later, new elections saw Hitler and his allies in control. On March 23, 1933 the *Ermächtigungsgesetz* (Enabling Law) was passed – it allowed Hitler to ignore parliament and the president in an emergency.

The emergency was almost immediate. From April 1, Jewish shops were officially boycotted. Trade Unions were dissolved on May 2. Undesirable books were burned from May 10 onwards. In June and July, all parties other than the Nazis were banned. When Von Hindenburg died in 1934, Hitler became Führer (leader) and Chancellor of the Reich. Internally the Nazis took total control and established a police state via its secret police apparatus formed by the SS, Gestapo, and other organs of state. Opponents were thrown in concentration camps. Although the Jews were harassed even before the Nazis took power, the Nuremberg laws of 1935 legally took away their citizenship rights. On Reichskristallnacht (9 November 1938) a pogrom started and Jews were stripped of property and chased into concentration camps.

THE THREE REICHS (EMPIRES)

The Nazis frequently referred to their regime as the Third Reich that would last a thousand years. The Second Reich was the German Empire from 1871-1918. The First Reich was the Holy Roman Empire of

German Nations. It ended in 1806, but different interpretations are possible as to its origins. Usually 962, the crowing of Otto II, is considered the start of this empire, but if the crowning of Charlemagne in 800 is used, the first Reich lasted a thousand years. In the end, the Third Reich lasted about 12 years but the damage to Germany's reputation may continue for a thousand years.

Hitler rearmed and prepared for war, while the rest of Europe longed for peace. He first illegally remilitarized the Rhineland (1936), annexed Austria (1938), then Sudentenland (1938) and the whole of Czechoslovakia (1939). In August 1939, in a secret pact with the Soviet Union, Poland was divided and, in September 1939, Germany invaded Poland. France and Britain declared war. Using Blitzkrieg and an annihilation war, Germany soon occupied all of Western Europe and after failing to subdue Britain, invaded the Soviet Union instead. In 1942, Hitler was at the peak of his power. Germany occupied Europe from the Atlantic to deep into Russia. At the Wannsee Conference (1942) it was decided to mass-murder all the Jews of occupied Europe in gas chambers. An estimated six million Jews were killed by the end of the war.

American entry into the war turned the tide. Furthermore, Hitler needlessly sacrificed the German Sixth Army at Stalingrad and from 1943 the Germans were in retreat. However, the war dragged on until May 1945. In addition to the destruction brought to other countries, Germany lost control of its own skies in the last years of the war and most cities suffered air raids. The ample use of wood in construction saw many cities burned to cinders. The bombing of cities, more than anything else, explains the strong anti-war rhetoric in post-war German literature and an abhorrence of war among the population in general that lasts to the present day.

Two Germanys

Hitler committed suicide on April 30, 1945 and Germany capitulated unconditionally on May 8. The country was divided into four zones of occupation and Berlin into four sectors occupied by the USA, Britain, France and the Soviet Union. The Soviet Union stripped their zone of everything that could be carted away.

Early in 1948, the occupying forces clashed on how to administer Germany. The Soviet Union left the Allied Controlling Council and blocked western access to Berlin, which was an island in the Soviet zone. The Cold War began and the western allies supplied West Berlin via airlift until Stalin relented in May 1949.

However, the die was cast and in 1949, the three western sectors were united to form the Bundesrepubik Deutschland (Federal Republic of Germany) with Konrad Adenauer as Chancellor and sleepy, provincial Bonn as temporary capital. In the East, the Soviet Union created the Deutsche Demokratische Republik (German Democratic Republic) as part of its East European sphere of influence.

West Germany experienced an economic boom, partly though American financial assistance and partly through hard work. The borders of East Germany were increasingly closed to prevent refugees fleeing to the west. The most dramatic moment was the erection of a wall around West Berlin starting on August 13, 1961. Tension between rich, prosperous, democratic, and capitalist West Germany and its impoverished, communist counterpart increased until **Willy Brandt** became chancellor of West Germany. In contrast to previous governments, he was prepared to accept the fact that East Germany functioned as a separate state and concluded a treaty of friendship with East Germany in 1972.

The end of East Germany happened incredibly fast. Following Mikhail Gorbachov's policies of Glasnost and Perestroika, Hungary opened its border with Austria. East Germans started to travel to Hungary and cross over to the West. Peaceful demonstration started in East Germany, led by the Monday protest meetings in Leipzig. On the night of November 9, 1989, the inner German border was opened. Less than a year later, on October 3, 1990, the two Germanys were united. This moment is often referred to as the *Wende* (the Change).

In 1991, it was decided to move the federal capital back to Berlin and by the end of the decade the Presidency, Parliament, and Chancellor's Office opened in swanky new buildings in Berlin.

■ Culture

Germany has a long tradition of producing high culture, with many famous composers and writers. The huge number of small states in centuries past ensured that there were ample patrons and courts that needed musicians and other performers. Classical music and theater remain very popular in modern-day Germany and attending cultural events is very much part of middle class life. Ticket prices are often astonishingly low.

During summer, most regions arrange a summer concert season with many open-air events. Castles, monasteries, palaces, and churches are popular venues in addition to dedicated concert halls. Regional tourist offices have details on events and often make reservations too.

Although German art, music, and literature go back to the earliest beginnings of the empire, the post-Reformati on works are of greatest interest to most foreign travelers. The following is only a brief summary of the most important artists in the German-speaking world.

Dürer Self-Portrait at age 22

Artists

■ 15th Century

Stefan Lochner, leading master of the Cologne School (*Adoration of the Magi* in the Kölner Dom).

Veit Stoß, sculptor and painter (*Angel's Greeting* in the Lorenzkirche, Nürnberg, and *Reredos of the Nativity* in Bamberg Cathedral).

Tilman Riemenschneider, sculptor and woodcarver (Tomb of Heinrich II in Bamberg Cathedral and *Adam and Eve* in Mainfränkische Museum in Würzburg).

■ 16th Century

Albrecht Dürer, the painter who brought the Renaissance to Germany, is one of the all time greats in German art. Major works are in the Alte Pinakothek in Munich, Gemäldegalerie in Berlin, and *Charlemagne* in the Germanisches Nationalmuseum in Nürnberg.

Lucas Cranach the Elder, the master painter of the Reformation, left a huge collection of works spread though Germany. The most famous work is probably the painting of Martin Luther now in the Germanishes Nationalmuseum in Nürnberg.

■ 17th Century

Elias Holl, an important Renaissance architect (Rathaus, Augsburg).

■ 18th Century

Matthäus Daniel Pöppelmann, architect, and Balthasar Permoser, sculptor, both worked on Baroque projects for Augustus the Strong in Dresden (Zwinger, Dresden).

Dominikus Zimmermann (Wieskirche) and the **Assam brothers** (Asamkirche, Munich) were Rococo virtuosos who left their marks as architects and artists on many Bavarian churches. The **Dientzenhofer** family erected several Baroque churches in Würzburg and Bamberg.

■ 19th Century

Caspar David Friedrich – German Romantic painter, best known for fanciful landscapes.

Max Liebermann – German Impressionist painter.

■ 20th Century

Bauhaus School of Design – forced out of conservative Weimar and eventually out of Germany by the Nazis. The Bauhaus in Dessau is famous, but the best works are in the USA.

The Expressionists saw several movements develop, including Die Brücke (The

Bridge) in Dresden and the Blaue Reiter (Blue Rider), founded by Kandinsky and Marc and later joined by Klee and others. The Lenbach Museum, Munich, has many Blue Rider works.

Neue Sachlicheit (New Objectivity) included some Bauhaus and Dada artists, among others. One of the most famous proponents was Otto Dix (*War* in Albertinum, Dresden).

Post Second World War art can be seen in the Pinakothek der Moderne in Munich, the Kunsthalle in Hamburg, New Masters Gallery in Berlin, and the Museum Ludwig in Cologne.

Music

■ Middle Ages

Music in Germany has a long and rich tradition. From the 12th century onwards, the **Minnesänger** (troubadours) were famous entertainers and included masters such as Walther von der Vogelweide and Wolfram von Eschenbach. In the 15th century, the **Meistersinger** (Mastersingers) formed a guild – the most famous proponent was Hans Sachs from Nürnberg – the inspiration for Wagner's *Meistersinger von Nürnberg* opera.

The **Lutheran Reformation** boosted German music as new religious music sung in German, rather than Latin, was required. Martin Luther wrote some choral works himself including *Ein feste Burg ist unser Gott* and *Vom Himmel hoch*, two songs still very popular in modern-day Germany.

■ Baroque

Johann Sebastian Bach (1685-1750) is considered by many the greatest composer of all time. He left an incredibly large collection of works, mostly but not exclusively religious. His range was restricted by his rather conservative employers who wanted no opera or drama in the church service.

Other famous composers from the period include **Georg Friedrich Händel**, who spent most of his working life in London, and **Georg Philipp Telemann**.

■ Wiener Klassik

Under **Joseph Haydn** and **Wolfgang Amadeus Mozart**, working mostly in Vienna, classical music reached a high point. Mozart left more than 600 works, including 41 symphonies. They were followed by **Ludwig von Beethoven**, who was born in Bonn but spent most of his productive live in Vienna. He was the first major composer who financed himself through concerts rather than being employed by a court or writing on commission. His nine symphonies and other works set the stage for the Romantics.

■ Romantics

The Romantics of the 19th century wrote a wide range of music ranging from *Lieder* (songs) to operas, symphonies to chamber music and piano sonatas. Famous composers from this era include **Franz Schubert**, **Carl Maria von Weber**, **Felix Mendelssohn-Bartholdy**, **Robert Schumann**, **Franz Liszt**, and **Johannes Brahms**.

Probably the most famous composer from this period was **Richard Wagner**. His epic operas included the *Meistersinger von Nürnberg*, *Parsifal*, and the *Ring* (*Rheingold, Walküre, Siegfried*, and *Götterdämmerung)*. His popularity with the Nazis probably limited his international appeal more than the strong German themes of his works.

■ 20th-Century Classical

Richard Strauss (*Also sprach Zarathustra*) and **Carl Orff** (*Carmina Burana*) wrote some innovative pieces early in the century before World War II interfered. **Kurt Weil** cooperated with **Bertold Brecht** on *The Threepenny Opera*.

Germany continues the classical music tradition with world-class orchestras and opera houses. Even medium-size German cities have symphony orchestras and music societies are very popular even in the smallest villages.

Literature

■ Early Literature

The ninth-century ***Hildebrandlied*** is generally considered the first German literary work. It was followed in the 12th and 13th century by the works of the ***Minnesänger*** (troubadours).

The first work in modern German was **Luther's translation of the Bible**. It standardized German and most works written since can be read by anyone with a decent knowledge of German.

The first major German novel was **Grimmelshausen's *Simplicissimus***, a picaresque novel inspired by the misery of the Thirty Years' War.

The Age of Enlightenment (*Aufklärung*) saw works by philosophers such as **Gottfried Leibnitz** and **Emanuel Kant**. **Gotthold Lessing** is best known for his tragedies, following the example of Shakespeare and the ancient Greeks. **Christoph Wieland**'s novels are often also grouped as part of this era

■ Sturm und Drang & Classicism

Goethe

The short *Sturm und Drang* (Storm and Stress) period lasted only from 1767 to 1785. It broke away from the rationalism of the Enlightenment in favor of freedom, nature, and emotions. The best-known works from this period are Johann Wolfgang von **Goethe**'s novella *Die Leiden des jungen Werthers* and **Friedrich Schiller**'s play *Die Räuber.*

Both writers soon found inspiration from the Greek and Roman ideals and wrote some of the best works ever produced in German. At the top of the list is Goethe's *Faust*, a two-part drama in verse. Schiller's plays such as *Wilhelm Tell*, *Maria Stuart*, and *Don Carlos* are still popular and often performed.

■ 19th Century

As in much of the rest of Europe, Romanticism took hold in German 19th-century literature. One of the most popular poets was **Friedrich Hölderlin**, while **Hegel** is the best-known philosopher from the era. The **Brothers Grimm**, although serious scholars of the German language and literature, are best known for the fairy tales that they collected on their travels through Germany.

Natural and political realism followed in the middle of the 19th century, in part as reaction to the failed revolutions in Europe in 1830 and 1848. **Heinrich Heine** wrote several romantic works but increasingly turned to political satire. Also in this period, **Karl Marx** and **Friedrich Engels** wrote the *Communist Manifesto*.

Karl Marx

Many German writers preferred the novella, which caused their works to be taken less seriously than those of writers in other languages who produced longer works during this period.

Friedrich Nietzsche's denouncement of the decadence of humanity, extoling freedom from accepted morality came at the end of the century, but his ideas already belonged to the modern era.

■ 20th Century

Some of the best-known modern German writers wrote mostly prior to the Second World War. Novelists from this era include 1929 Nobel Prize winner **Thomas Mann** (*Death in Venice, The Beloved Returns, Buddenbrooks*), 1946 Nobel Laureate **Hermann Hesse** (*Steppenwolf*), and Czech-born **Franz Kafka** (*The Metamorphosis* and *The Trial*). Dramatist **Bertold Brecht** wrote famous pieces in this period including *The Three Penny Opera* and the *Caucasian Chalk Circle*. Like many other authors, he fled Germany during the Nazi era, but, unlike most others, he established himself after the war in East, rather than West Berlin.

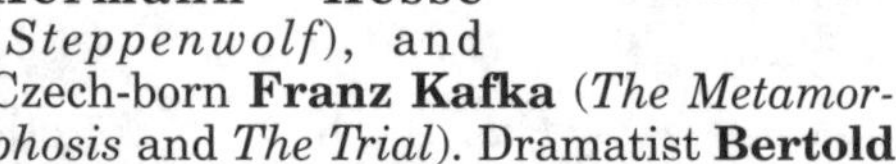

Hesse

Brecht

German writers produced a wealth of anti-war literature following the Second

World War. The best-known post-1945 German writers are 1972 Nobel Laureate **Heinrich Böll** (*The Clown, Billiards at Half Past Nine*) and 1999 Nobel Laureate **Günther Grass** (*The Tin Drum*).

Germany continues to be a nation of readers with among the highest book sales and books read per capita in the world.

■ Geography

Germany is a central European state with an area of 356,978 square km (138,000 sq miles). It measures at most 880 km by 640 km (528 by 384 miles).

The highest region is the Bavarian Alps in the south. The highest mountain peak is the Zugspitze at 2,962 m (9,478 feet) near Garmisch Partenkirchen. Most of Bavaria is made up of hills that roll up to the River Danube – the only major river in Germany that drains to the south rather than northwards.

Much of Germany from the Black Forest to the Harz is covered by the *Mittelgebirge* (Middle Mountains), a series of minor massifs that are mostly under 500 m (1,600 feet). Although *Wald* means forest, attached to a regional name, it usually means a forest in a hilly area. The most famous are the Black Forest, the Bavarian Forest, and the Thuringian Forest, all mountainous, forested areas of outstanding natural beauty.

The Harz is the highest and northernmost of the Mittelgebirge. From here to the North and Baltic Sea most of Germany is a flat plain. Despite the lack of geographic features, the area is beautiful, very green, and many minor roads often are tree-lined. Berlin is in the heart of these plains.

The North and Baltic (in Germany referred to as the East) Sea coasts can be rather windswept. It is a popular vacation area for young families and retirees as the summer heat is less severe than the Mediterranean. The island of Rügen is Germany's sunniest place, but the wind is almost constant.

Germany has several major rivers. The most famous is the **Rhine**, which forms part of the natural border with Switzerland and France. The Rhine valley between Rüdesheim and Koblenz is the land of legends and castles. The Rhine flows fairly straight, but its tributaries tend to meander wildly. The **Neckar** curls through Baden-Württemberg and passes by Stuttgart and Heidelberg before flowing into the Rhine at Mannheim. The **Main** makes several wild S-curves through Franken and Hesse before its confluence with the Rhine at Mainz near Frankfurt. The **Mosel** is similarly a meandering stream with a valley as dramatic and full of sagas as the much larger Rhine.

The **Weser** River drains most of central Germany along its way to the North Sea at Bremen. The **Elbe** is a mighty, slow-flowing river. It enters Germany near Dresden where the Saxon Switzerland area has some of the wildest, most bizarre mountain landscapes in Germany. The Elbe drains most of eastern Germany before flowing into the North Sea at Cuxhaven, downstream from Hamburg. The **Oder** and **Neise** rivers form Germany's post-1945 border with Poland.

■ Climate

Germany has a moderately cool, but temperate climate. The plains in the eastern parts of the country can get cold and windswept, but conditions are more moderate than in countries farther east. The northern coastal regions tend to be windy year-round. The central parts can be snow-covered for long stretches in winter, but have generally mild summers. The south experiences more extremes, with the Black Forest particularly sunny and the Rhine Valley usually warmer than surrounding areas.

Rainfall is fairly evenly divided throughout the year and ranges from an annual 500 mm (20 inches) in the north to triple that in the center and south. Some parts of the Alps receive more than 2,000 mm (80 inches) per year.

The most pleasant months to travel are generally May and June or September and October. In some years, July and August get uncomfortably hot, especially since German buildings are usually designed with winter in mind and lack air conditioning.

■ Flora & Fauna

Germany's natural vegetation can be surprisingly lush for a country with such a temperate climate. The most typical tree is the oak, found all over the country. Natural oak and beech forests are common in the Mittelgebirge area, with pine trees mostly on the higher slopes of the Black Forest, Harz Mountains, and the Bavarian Forest, as well as in the poorer soil of northern Germany. Wild berries and mushrooms are generally poisonous.

For a European country, Germany has a wide variety of wildlife. The largest animals are deer and wild boar. Animals such as wolfs, lynxes, and wild cats only survive in natural parks and are rarely seen.

Birdlife is more common, especially species that live in the ample forested areas. Others, such as storks, are seen in the sparsely populated northern regions. Eagles are sometimes seen at the coasts of Mecklenburg-Vorpommern and in the Alps.

Decades of strict environmental regulations led to an improvement in water quality in most German rivers and lakes. In response, the number of species living in the waters has also increased in recent years, with salmon again flourishing in the Rhine.

■ Government

Germany is a federal democracy consisting of 16 states (*Länder*). Parliament consists of the directly elected *Bundestag* (Lower House) and the *Bundesrat* (Upper House) that represents the *Länder*. The President (Bundespräsident) is elected by the *Bundesversammlung* (*Bundesrat* plus representatives from the *Länder*) and is a largely ceremonial role. The *Kanzler* (Chancellor) has the real power and is elected by the Bundestag. The Chancellor can only be removed through the appocintment of his replacement – that prevents a potential power vacuum should parties of opposite sides of the political spectrum try to remove the government. This happened only once when Helmut Kohl took power from Helmut Schmidt in 1982.

Around half the *Bundestag* is directly elected to represent specific constituencies while the rest are elected based on parties' national popularity. A party needs a minimum of 5% of the national vote to be represented in parliament (a lesson learned from the Weimar Republic where a plethora of minor parties and independent representatives made government impossible.)

Post-1945 politics have been dominated by two major parties: the left-leaning Social Democratic Party (SPD) and the right-leaning Christian Democratic Union (CDU). Most governments ruled in coalition with the Free Democrats (FDP), a generally pro-business, liberal party. However, from 1998 to the time of writing, the SPD has been in coalition with the environmentally friendly Green Party.

■ The Economy

Germany is the world's third-largest economy and the second-largest trading nation in the world. Following World War II, Germany experienced an economic boom – the *Wirtschaftswunder* – that saw annual growth of 8% between 1951 and 1961.

Manufacturing still contributes around a third of the economy with the so-called *Mittelstand* – companies, often family-run, with fewer than 100 employees – especially important. Around two-thirds of the economy consists of service industries. Agriculture, fisheries, and mining are vocal but comparatively unimportant to the economy.

The integration of the Communist East German economy into the market-orientated West German one has progressed slowly. Even to the casual visitor, East Germany is still clearly poorer. National unemployment levels are just below 10%, but hover around 18% in much of the former East.

■ Top Attractions

Top Destinations

Berlin is Germany's largest and most interesting city. It has something for everyone, from its excellent museums to its risqué nightlife. It has high culture and a vibrant underground music scene.

Munich (Bavaria) is an interesting city with many historic venues, beer gardens, and a high quality of life. It has excellent art galleries and one of the largest technology museums in the world.

Dresden (Saxony), once known as Florence on the Elbe, is recovering some of its original Baroque charm. In addition to the excellent museums, and the Semper Opera

House, the city is also convenient for day-trips into the beautiful Saxony Switzerland area.

Leipzig (Saxony) is an interesting city unwilling and unable to hide its Communist-era buildings. It is less tourist-orientated than many others but has excellent museums and cultural offerings. The revolution against the Communist regime started here and the Forum of Contemporary History is one of the most interesting museums in Germany.

The **Romantic Rhine Valley** (Rhineland-Palatinate) is a popular destination with a castle or castle ruin every few miles in the Loreley Valley. Whether traveling the valley on boat, by road, or on foot, it is a region sure to impress with its natural beauty and cultural delights.

The **Romantic Road** (Bavaria) is Germany's most popular holiday route, passing numerous small and very romantic towns and locations. Rothenburg ob der Tauber is chronically overcrowded but remains Germany's most beautiful wall-enclosed medieval town.

The **German Alpine Route** (Bavaria) offers Germany's most beautiful natural scenery. It runs the full length of the Bavarian Alps from Lindau on the Bodensee to Berchtesgaden near Salzburg. En route it passes several famous sights, including Mad King Ludwig's castles, the Wieskirche, and Kloster Ettal.

The **Black Forest** (Baden-Württemberg) is Germany's largest forested area, with superb natural beauty and ample outdoor adventure options. Hiking is particularly popular, but the area can be enjoyed without stepping out of a car as well. The spa town of Baden-Baden is one of Germany's most elegant.

The **Harz Mountains** (Saxony-Anhalt, Lower Saxony, and Thuringia), in central Germany, have natural beauty as well as some interesting towns, which played a major role in the foundation of the Holy Roman Empire of the German Nation a thousand years ago. It is also the traditional haunt of witches.

The **Hanseatic Baltic Ports** – among others Lübeck (Schleswig-Holstein), Wismar, Rostock, and Stralsund (Mecklenburg-Vorpommern) – were once united by membership in the Hanseatic League. Nowadays, the main interest for visitors is the marvelous examples of brick Gothic buildings in these cities.

Cologne (North Rhine Westphalia), for a thousand years the largest city in Germany, has the world's largest Gothic church, a dozen Romanesque churches, excellent art museums, and the most refreshing beer in the country.

Great Museums

The **Gemäldegalerie** (Berlin) has an incredible collection of mostly German, Dutch and Italian painters. A highlight is the 16 works by Rembrandt.

The **Pergamonmuseum** (Berlin) is one of the most popular in Germany, with large exhibits including the Pergamon Altar, the Ishtar Gate and Processional Way, and the Gateway to the Millet Market.

The three **Pinakothen** art galleries (Munich) give a good overview of European art from the Middle Ages to the present.

Wallraf-Richartz-Museum (Cologne) is an excellent collection of paintings from the Middle Ages to the 19th century. The Museum Ludwig, which is part of it, gives a fine overview of 20th-century art.

The **Deutsches Museum** (Munich) is one of the world's greatest technology museums. Large displays and working models are the most popular, but pure science is not ignored.

The **Zwinger** (Dresden) has several great museums, none more so than the Old Masters Picture Gallery – a collection of mainly Renaissance and Baroque paintings. The Green Vault treasury in the Residenzschloss is worth seeing too.

The **Forum of Contemporary History** (Leipzig) is the museum of modern German history that many visitors unsuccessfully look for in Berlin. It is an excellent multimedia exhibition on a divided and re-united Germany.

The **Federal Art Space** (Bonn) has no permanent collection, but houses world-class exhibitions on various themes from all over the world.

Two surprise entries from the provinces complete the list. The **Rheinisches Landesmuseum** (Trier) has the largest collection of Roman artifacts in Germany and complements a visit to the largest collection of Roman ruins in the entire country.

The recently re-opened **Luther Museum** (Lutherstadt Wittenberg) is a laudable effort – very interesting, professional displays explain the events and the background of the Reformation without preaching. All descriptions are in English too.

At the time of writing, the **Zeughaus** (Berlin) was still closed for restoration. It is due to reopen in 2005. This history museum does have a collection that warrants inclusion on any list of major museums.

Great Churches & Cathedrals

The Gothic cathedral in **Cologne** is the largest Gothic building and third-largest church in the world. It was 800 years in the making and is worth a journey.

The pure Romanesque cathedral in **Speyer** is the largest Romanesque structure in Germany and, unlike most others, is free of later Gothic additions.

Dom, Trier

The Dom in **Trier** is an amazing piece of architecture. It has elements of all styles from the Roman period onwards, not necessarily all blending harmoniously. It was once the largest church in the Roman Empire and, although now much smaller, still impressive. Adjacent is one of the first Gothic chapels in Germany.

The Marienkirche in **Lübeck** is one of the finest examples of brick Gothic in northern Germany. Further excellent examples are in Wismar, Rostock, Bad Doberan, and Stralsund.

The cathedral in **Passau** has an interesting Gothic choir and rather plain Baroque exterior. The interior is High Baroque and has the largest church organ in the world – 17,388 pipes and 231 stops.

The cathedral in **Regensburg** is the largest Gothic building in Bavaria. Its tower should have been much higher, but finances interfered before the laws of physics could.

The Late Romanesque cathedral in **Limburg** already shows the spirit of the Gothic style to come. It was repainted inside and out in its original bright colors.

The **Wieskirche** represents the pinnacle of the Bavarian Rococo. This masterpiece is in the middle of the meadows far removed from any major town.

The Baroque Frauenkirche in **Dresden**, erected in the 18th century, collapsed following air raids at the end of World War II. Reconstruction was delayed until the 1990s. It is fast reaching completion

In a small, otherwise unremarkable Black Forest town is the marvelous **St Blasien** church. It has the third-largest cupola in Europe.

Great Castles

The German term *Burg* can be translated as castle or fortress, while *Schloss* means castle or palace. In this guide, a *Schloss* that can laugh off a few cannonballs is referred to as a castle. A *Schloss* where cannonballs would ruin the porcelain and stuccos is called a palace.

Burg Eltz (Rhineland-Palatinate), near the Mosel Valley is the most beautiful of Germany's medieval castles. In 800 years, it was never defeated or significantly damaged by enemy fire. It is still family-owned and -occupied.

The **Wartburg** (Thuringia) outside Eisenach has been described as the most German of all German castles. It is a magnificent sight. While in hiding here, Martin Luther translated the New Testament into German.

Marksburg (Rhineland-Palatinate, above) is perched high on a hill on the shores of the Rhine above Braubach. It is

the only castle in this romantic stretch of the Rhine Valley that has never been destroyed or taken violently. This castle is the real thing, no 19th-centujry romanticism.

Schloss Heidelberg (Baden-Württemberg) is mostly in ruins, but it is still one of the most popular and romantic sights in Germany. Tourists come in droves and rightly so.

The seventh-century **Meersburg Alte Burg** (Baden-Württemberg), with unspoiled views of the Bodensee, is the oldest inhabitable castle in Germany. It was started by Dagoberth, a Merovingian king, and long served as the residence of the bishop of Konstanz.

Festung Königstein (Saxony), near Dresden, is the largest fortress in Germany. During World War II, it housed senior French prisoners of war as well as Dresden's best artworks.

Schloss Neuschwanstein (Bavaria) is 19th-century Romanticism pure. The highlight of Mad King Ludwig's building fantasies, it inspired Disney. Ludwig's other palaces – Herrenchiemsee and Linderhof – are worth seeing too.

Schloss Braunfels (Hesse), in the Lahn Valley, is another 19th-century folly. It has an 800-year history, but was mostly rebuilt in the 19th century in a Neo-Gothic style. It looks the part and the lines are much shorter than at Neuschwanstein.

Schloss Sanssouci (Brandenburg), Frederick the Great's Rococo summer residence in Potsdam, is surprisingly small but a masterpiece from the Baroque period. The other lavish palaces in the direct vicinity are interesting too.

The **Residenz** (Bavaria), in Munich, was the principle residence of the Wittelsbach ruling family for over 500 years. It is a massive complex, lavishly decorated. Other royal residences in the Munich area such as Schloss Nymphenburg and Schloss Schleißheim are worth seeing too.

Amazing Small Towns

Rothenburg ob der Tauber (Bavaria) is everybody's favorite medieval town. It is still completely surrounded by its defensive town wall with many towers and other buildings intact. Although swamped by tourists on weekends and in the high season, it is a town absolutely worth seeing.

Quedlinburg (Saxony-Anhalt), north of the Harz Mountains, is filled with half-timbered houses and has a marvelous Romanesque church built shortly after the foundation of the Holy Roman Empire of German States. It is a great town to simply stroll around aimlessly.

Celle (Lower Saxony) has an amazing old town center with half-timbered houses in perfect condition. Most are from the 16th to 18th century.

Hildesheim (Lower Saxony) is mostly modern, but its Market Square is surrounded by some of the most impressive half-timbered buildings in Germany. The town also has a couple of excellent Romanesque churches.

In nearby **Goslar** (Lower Saxony), the half-timbered buildings are mostly authentic. It has an impressive reconstructed Romanesque *Pfalz* (Imperial Palace).

Hann. Münden (Lower Saxony) is a lovely small town where the Rivers Wera and Fulda converge to form the Weser. It has many half-timbered buildings and a Weser Renaissance town hall.

Lübeck (Schleswig-Holstein) is not small by any definition, but its amazing old town on an island in the River Trave is. It has marvelous examples of brick Gothic architecture.

Marburg (Hesse) has a lovely old town with half-timbered buildings and the first Gothic church on German soil. The castle towers over the town and the River Lahn.

Limburg (Hesse), farther down the River Lahn, is another town with an historic, half-timbered center and a marvelous Late Romanesque Cathedral.

Berchtesgaden (Bavaria) is a lovely town. With the Alps on three sides, the natural setting and surroundings lift it above the average.

Travel Information

In this Chapter

■ Fast Facts

Population

Around 9% of the population, or 82 million people, are foreign. The largest minorities are Turks, often German-born to Turkish parents who came as guest workers to Germany in the 1960s, and Serbo-Croats. Two-thirds of Germans are at least nominally Christian with equal numbers Protestant (Lutheran) and Roman Catholic.

Location

Germany is in central Europe bordering Denmark and the North and Baltic Seas in the north; the Netherlands, Belgium, Luxemburg, and France in the west; Switzerland and Austria in the south; and the Czech Republic and Poland in the east.

Major Cities

Almost 90% of Germans live in cities, but the cities are relatively small. The 10 largest cities are:

Berlin – 3.4 million
Hamburg – 1.7 million
Munich – 1.3 million
Cologne – 960,000
Frankfurt am Main – 660,000
Essen – 617,000
Dortmund – 606,000
Stuttgart – 584,000
Düsseldorf – 572,000
Bremen – 556,000

Time Zone

Central European time (Greenwich Mean Time plus one hour, or Eastern Standard Time plus six hours).

■ Orientation

When to Go

Germany is best visited between May and October. The school holiday season in July and August is best avoided as prices increase and popular sights are crowded. One week before or after the high season can make a major difference in the number of visitors but not much in terms of weather. However, the holiday season is a good time to visit major cities as the locals go to the countryside or beaches and hotel prices can drop to mid-winter levels.

Winters can be bleak and grey and much of the natural beauty of the country will be hidden. Many non-winter sports regions may close down for the winter season. However, Advent is a beautiful time of the year with all towns lit up and Christmas markets a major draw. A wide range of concerts is also scheduled in the weeks leading up to Christmas.

Customs & Immigration

US and Canadian citizens may enter Germany for up to 90 days with a valid passport.

Germany is part of the Schengen Agreement, allowing travel across European borders without further customs or immigration controls. However, you may at any time, inside Germany and other Schengen states, be requested to produce proof of identity. (Switzerland, the Czech Republic, and Poland are not members of the Schengen Agreement and have full border controls with Germany.)

Penalties for smuggling illegal drugs are severe. If carrying prescription drugs, it is sensible to bring the prescription along and do not bring more than actually needed for the duration of the vacation.

■ Transportation

Getting Here

By Rail: Germany has good railway connections to neighboring countries. From France, the easiest entry is via Strasbourg, while high-speed trains from Paris currently pass through Belgium to Cologne. A direct high-speed link between Paris and Frankfurt is due for completion in 2006. High-speed rail connections are also available from Brussels, Amsterdam, Switzerland, and various parts of Austria. Connections from the Czech Republic and Poland are improving, but mostly on slower trains. The Eurostar from London connects with other high-speed trains in Brussels.

By Bus: Bus services are available from many European cities and are often the cheapest way to travel to Germany. One of the largest operators is **Deutsche Touring**, Am Römerhof 17, 60486 Frankfurt am Main, ☎ 069-790-350, www.deutsche-touring.de, which operates in cooperation with **Eurolines**, www.eurolines.
com. It is usually only possible to take international journeys.

Berlin Linienbus, www.berlinlinienbus.de, has many services from European cities to various destinations in Germany. It is usually possible to interrupt the journey inside Germany, but not while in another country.

By Air: Germany is well served by many airlines, with Frankfurt International Airport the busiest on continental Europe. Most intercontinental flights arrive in Frankfurt, while Munich Airport has the largest number of European destinations. Lufthansa has the largest number of direct and non-stop flights from the USA and Canada, but many American and Canadian carriers have direct flights. Discounts are often available on European airlines but require a stopover in another capital. Most larger cities have European and domestic connections.

A growing number of German budget airlines are taking to the skies but many are also expected to go bust soon. Always double-check the airports used by budget airlines – they are often less convenient and farther away than the main airports. Frankfurt-Hahn Airport, for example, is a 90-minute bus ride from Frankfurt, while Frankfurt International is 15 minutes from downtown.

On Water: A ferry service from Harwich (Britain) to Cuxhaven is available a few times per week – see the Lower Saxony chapter for details.TAXI

Several ferry services are available from Scandinavia and other Baltic Sea ports – see the Mecklenburg-Vorpommern and Schleswig-Holstein chapters for details.

Getting Around

By Rail: Germany has a well developed railway network with comfortable, high-speed trains often the best way to travel between cities. Although it is no longer possible to set your watch according to a German train's arrival time, trains generally do run on time.

German trains can be classed in two categories: *Fernverkehr* (Long Distance) and *Nahverkehr* (Local). This distinction is important for discount tickets. Long Distance trains are faster, usually more luxurious, and cost more. They have the prefixes ICE (InterCity Express), IC/EC (InterCity/EuroCity – the trains are the same but the latter crosses the German border), and D (Schnell/Fast trains).

The *Nahverkehr* (local trains) carry the prefixes (listed in order of speed – the further down the list the more stops!) IRE (InterRegioExpress), RE (RegionalExpress), RB (Regionalbanh), and S (S-Bahn). In some cases the U-Bahn, trams, and buses are also included in rail tickets.

Tickets can be bought on board most trains, though never on the S- or U-Bahn, but no discounts are available. It is generally best to buy tickets from the Internet, ticket counters, or machines prior to boarding.

Several options are available to save on German railway tickets.

- **Internet**: It is possible to book and print virtually all German rail tickets online at www.bahn.de. The site is also an invaluable tool for planning journeys and calculating budgets. At time of writing, seat reservations usually costing €3 are free when booking online, or at a ticket machine.

Last-minute deals are often available on the Internet.

- **Children**: Children under 15 always travel free when accompanied by at least one parent or grandparent. Children older than six must be added for free to the adult ticket at time of booking. Otherwise, they pay half the adult price. A seat can be reserved for the children as well at the normal rate of €3.
- **Rail Passes**: For international travelers, several rail passes are available. Passes can be a good deal, especially if one-way travel is used for which normal discounts are not available. Ticket prices are available on www.bahn.de, making both time and budget planning easier.

  If the travel involves only Germany, the best deal is the German Rail Pass. It is available from four to 10 days within any month and is available in first and second class, with twin passes for two traveling together and youth passes for under 25s slightly cheaper. Eurail passes in all variations are also valid in Germany. Passes are best bought outside Europe – most are available locally but at a surcharge and only from select railway stations.
- **Sparpreis**: Sparpreis tickets are available for round-trip journeys only and must be booked at least three days in advance to obtain a discount of 25%. If a Saturday night stay is included, the discount becomes 50%. Additionally, the exact trains for both journeys must be booked in advance. When reservations are made at the same time, the first passenger pays the normal price (with discount) and up to four additional passengers pay only half of what the first one pays. Cancellation options are limited. The discounts are available for all classes of service but the number of tickets per train is restricted.
- **Schönes-Wochenende Ticket**: Schönes-Wochenende (Nice Weekend) tickets cost €30 per day and are valid either on Saturday or on Sunday from midnight to 3 am the following morning. They cost €30 and allows up to five passengers unlimited travel nationwide on Nahverkehr trains in Second Class.
- **Länder-Tickets**: Länder-Tickets are available in the separate federal states and allow for unlimited travel on Nahverkehr trains in Second Class *inside* the different states. They are available on weekdays from 9 am to 3 am the following day. They cost between €21 and €26 and allow up to five people traveling together. Available for all states, but Saxony, Saxony-Anhalt, and Thuringia use a single ticket and similarly for Schleswig-Holstein, Hamburg, and Mecklenburg-Vorpommern. (Single tickets for individual travelers can be purchased for some of the states and cost around €15.)

By Bus: Bus services operate between many cities in Germany, but the operators are often small, making it hard to book seats from a distance. One of the largest is **Berlin Linienbus**, www.berlinlinienbus.de. Although most buses end up in Berlin, it is also possible to book shorter distances on these buses.

By Car: Trains are often the best choice if only cities are visited, but having a car is a pleasurable way of seeing more of the country. It is usually cheapest to reserve a car from abroad. Rental cars picked up from airports and stations carry a surcharge.

Driving in Germany presents little difficulty. The road signs are generally internationalized and drivers receive ample training. Roads are mostly in very good condition and well-signposted. However, bear in mind that, although all roads are numbered, many road signs only refer to the next town without giving the road numbers.

SAVING ON GAS

Gas (Benzin) in Germany is expensive. At time of writing a liter of Diesel cost €94 and Super Premium fuel €1.20. (An American gallon equals 3.9 liters.) Around 80% of the price of fuel is taxes. To get the most gas out of your euro bear the following in mind:

- Fuel is generally cheaper in northern Germany than in the south – always fill up when passing through Rostock (it has a huge refinery).
- Fuel is more expensive on highways.
- Fuel is more expensive from recognizable international brands – independent gas stations and supermarkets are always cheaper.

Travel Information

- Gas stations on commuter routes often change prices three times per day – more expensive during the rush hours.
- Fill up on Monday, never on Wednesday – it is a statistical fact that fuel is cheapest on Monday and most expensive on Wednesday. Tuesday is also best avoided. Statistically unproven, but common knowledge holds that fuel prices increase before and during long weekends.
- Rent a diesel – the fuel is cheaper and the fuel consumed significantly less.

Virtually all gas stations (*Tankstelle*) are self-service – fill up and pay at the cashier before moving your car. Most, but not all, accept credit cards.

Germany has the largest highway network after the USA. The famous Autobahnen (Highways) sometimes are without speed restriction, but are often so crowded that speeds automatically drop to a crawl. Speed restrictions on Autobahnen are generally between 100 and 130 km/h (60-78 mph) and well-signposted. Autobahnen have the prefix A before the number (the more correct prefix BAB is seldom seen) and use blue road signs.

Dual-lane roads that are not official Autobahnen use yellow road signs and have a speed restriction of 120 km/h (72 mph) if not otherwise restricted. These roads usually have a prefix B (Bundes/Federal road). On other country roads that have the prefix B or L (Länder/State road), the speed restriction is 100 km/h (60 mph), but often a lower speed is imposed.

In town, the speed restriction is 50 km/h (30 mph), if not otherwise stated. The restriction applies as soon as the town is entered – yellow signs are posted with the town name – without any further announcement of the speed limit. In residential areas, the speed limit is often 30 km/h (18 mph).

When arriving in towns, follow the directions to the Historische Altstadt (historic old town) or Zentrum (center). It is usually best to park in parking garages on the edges of the old town area.

TRAFFIC FINES

Speed cameras are few and far between – atlases with the fixed camera positions are available and radio stations announce the location of moveable cameras when spotted. Exceeding the speed limit by up to 19 km/h outside towns, the fine is a mere €30 and the chances of being caught are limited. Around 60% of German drivers, including almost 50% of female drivers, admit to speeding on a clear road on a regular basis.

On the other hand, it is illegal to try to hurry any other driver. Flashing and honking on the Autobahn as well as driving with too short a following distance can result in heavy fines. Hogging the left lane is illegal and passing cars on the right on an Autobahn results in very heavy fines per car passed, usually resulting in a license suspension. Road rage is considered a serious misdemeanor – showing someone the finger can be very expensive.

Parking fines are low, but if a car is towed away, and many cities do this, the costs and time required getting the car back spiral.

Traffic fines are payable on the spot – receipts are always given – and are usually less than when paid later. Never argue or swear at the police – the fine per insult can be as high as €1,500 and each insult is added separately.

Never drive without insurance. After an accident, costs are usually apportioned and it is rare for one party to carry 100% of the costs. The first rule of driving in Germany is the responsibility to avoid an accident. The party that had the right of way but behaved like an idiot defending his position can generally expect to carry the heavier financial burden.

By Air: Flying inside Germany is seldom a sensible option. It is possible to cover long distances that are not well served by the high-speed railway network, but few tourists would want to go from say Rostock to Munich in an hour. Domestic flights are generally expensive, with discount flights widely advertised but very hard to actually book.

By Boat: Most major rivers and lakes have boat trips. These are mostly day excursions and operators are listed in the relevant chapters.

Longer multi-day trips are available with one- to two-week cruises particularly popular on combinations of the Rhine, Main, and Danube, and on the Elbe. Two large, multi-day riverboat cruise operators are **Viking River Cruises**, 21820 Burbank Boulevard, Woodland Hills CA 91367, ☎ 1-877-668-4546, www.vikingrivercruises.com, and **Peter Deilmann Cruises**, 1800 Diagonal Rd, Suite 170, Alexandria VA 22314, ☎ 01-800-348-8287, www.deilmann-cruises.com.

In Urban Areas: Germany generally has a very good, if pricey, public transportation network and, in cities, virtually every place can easily be reached without a private car. In most cities, tickets need to be validated before boarding trains and usually on board buses and trams. The validation stamp must be on the front of the ticket; when in doubt stamp both sides. Some cities, including Frankfurt, require single tickets to be bought shortly before boarding and do not require revalidating. Riding without a ticket results in on-the-spot fines of at least €30 and eviction from the train at the next station. Most cities have day tickets that are bargains if the system is used more than twice.

By Taxi: In Germany, taxis generally do not roam the streets and are either taken from a taxi stand or ordered by telephone. Almost any shop, restaurant, or hotel will be willing to order one. Taxis can be expensive but often make sense for groups of three or four. The fare is always per meter in city limits but a price is often agreed upon if traveling outside city limits or long distances. With very few exceptions, taxis are beige so as to cut down on potential illegal operators. Although the percentage of operators using Mercedes Benz cars is declining, it is still common to find yourself in the back of a new three-pointed-star limousine when using a taxi.

EMERGENCY NUMBERS

For the police dial 110 or to reach the fire brigade and ambulance dial 112.

■ Embassies & Consulates

USA

American travelers in need of consular assistance should contact the **Embassy of the United States**, Neustädtische Kirchstr. 4-5, 10117 Berlin, ☎ 030-83-050. The Consular Section is at Clayallee 170, 14195 Berlin. For American Citizen Services, ☎ 030-832-9233 or, in emergencies only, ☎ 030-83-050.

The **American Consulate General** in Frankfurt also deals with most consular matters. It is currently at Siesmayerstraße 21, 60323 Frankfurt, ☎ 069-75-350, but is due to move out of the center of the city during 2005. The American consulates general in Düsseldorf, Munich, Leipzig, and Hamburg offer more limited services.

Canada

The **Canadian Embassy** is in the Internationalen Handelszentrum, Friedrichstraße 95, 10117 Berlin, ☎ 030-203-120, www.kanada.de. Canada has consulates in Düsseldorf, Hamburg, Munich, and Stuttgart, but in emergencies it is best to contact the Embassy in Berlin first.

■ Money Matters

Currency

Germany uses the euro (€), which is divided into 100 cents (c). The euro comes in €5, 10. 20, 50, 100, 200, and 500 notes and in €1 and €2 coins. Coins are available in 1, 2, 5, 10, 20, and 50c.

EXCHANGE RATES

€1 = US$1.30 = Can$1.60 = £0.69
US$1 = €0.77
Can$1 = €0.62
£1 = €1.49

Former German Marks (DM) and pfennigs can only be exchanged at a branch of the German Bundesbank (Federal Reserve).

Money

In Germany, the normal bank cash card is also a debit card and the preferred way of paying. Credit cards can be used in most shops, hotels, and restaurants but some, especially in rural areas, may insist on cash. Using ATMs generally gives the best exchange rates and the lowest costs. Check with your bank before leaving as to whether your card and PIN are valid abroad. Some foreign banks have agreements with German banks allowing for lower service charges.

Following the introduction of the euro, exchange bureaus have declined dramatically in number, but are available at main stations and airports. Traveler's checks are seldom used in Germany and often incur hefty service fees.

Avoid the €100, €200, and €500 notes – they are often refused in smaller establishments, especially when trying to use them for small payments. The €50 note is the most frequently forged – they often enter circulation at vending machines when fellow travelers help out with smaller notes. Hold on to €1 and €2 coins – although most vending machines accept notes, people using coins experience the urge to kick the machines less often.

All Germans have EC (Electronic Cash) cards. They work like a debit card but are not the same as a credit card. Establishments that accept EC cards do not necessarily accept Visa, MasterCard, or American Express.

Taxes

Value Added Tax (Mehrwertsteuer/MWST) is usually 16% but is always added to the advertised prices. Non-European travelers can reclaim some tax when departing from the European Union for goods purchased in shops participating in the VAT refund scheme. These stores have an English brochure explaining the finer details – note that the goods must be shown at customs on departure before the tax can be reclaimed. Frankfurt and Munich airports have desks where the tax can be reclaimed in cash on departure. VAT on hotels, food, and services consumed while in Europe is not refundable.

In Germany, all prices advertised must include all taxes. In some spa towns, a spa tax may be added to the hotel price, but this seldom exceeds €2 per adult per night.

A deposit may be charged separately on drinks sold in plastic bottles or cans – this is currently between 15c and 25c. The system is still in flux and sometimes this deposit can only be reclaimed at the shop where the bottle was purchased. However, it is increasingly possible to reclaim the deposit at any shop selling the same kind of drinks.

Tipping

Tipping is less frequent than in most Anglo-Saxon countries. In restaurants, service is generally included and rounding up to the next euro or round number is often acceptable. Tipping 10%, except in upscale international places, is generous but appreciated. Give the tip directly to the server or, when you want the server to keep the change, say, "Thank you" or "Danke schön" when handing over the payment. Leaving money on the table is sometimes considered rude, but not the ultimate insult as it is in some other parts of Europe.

Similarly, for taxi drivers round up to the next euro or round number. Tip bellhops in hotels around €1 per bag – often it will be refused in embarrassment. Don't tip anyone else.

■ Food & Drink

German food and drink are generally not strange to the western palate. The food is not particularly fattening although it can be hearty, especially in rural areas.

Although the trend is toward a standard three-meal day, the traditional five-meal day is still popular. This involves breakfast, usually eaten at home, of bread or cereal with yogurt, cheese, eggs, etc. A second breakfast is often enjoyed around 9 or 10 am, shortly after hitting the desk or shops and usually involving a sweet pastry. Lunch is usually between noon and 2 pm and is often the main meal of the day. *Kaffee und Kuchen* (coffee and cake) is an almost sacred tradition and enjoyed around 3 pm. Dinner is usually fairly early, between 6 and 8 pm. It is usually cooked if it's the main meal of the day; otherwise it is mainly bread.

Beer is still hugely popular in Germany and every town has its own breweries and specialties. The number of national brands is limited and ones with an international presence especially so. *Apfelsaftschorle*, a mixture of apple juice and soda water, is probably the most popular non-alcoholic drink served in Germany. It is low in calories and socially acceptable on any occasion. Although other soft drinks and colas are generally available, they are seldom had with a meal. Although all municipal water is safe to drink, and actually has higher safety requirements than bottled water, many Germans prefer bottled water. Do not expect tap water to be served in restaurants. Water, beer, soft drinks, and *Schorle* usually cost about the same in restaurants, with beer often slightly cheaper. Wine, both domestic and imported, is also available by the glass in most establishments.

■ Electricity

Electricity is 230V, 50 Hz. Plugs with two round pins are used, with grounding possible in all plugs. Some hotels may have 110V flat pin plugs for shavers, but do not count on it.

■ Media

Surprisingly little is published inside Germany in English. In major cities, English magazines and newspapers are generally available from bookstores – the main station is a good place to look. The *International Herald Tribune* is fairly easy to obtain.

English radio and television are also rare. Many satellite and cable services carry BBC News and CNN at most. Even in top hotels, it is unlikely that non-news programs will be available.

■ Medical

Germany has an excellent health care system, with more doctors than the country actually requires. The system is relatively expensive though. Medical insurance is a precondition for entering Germany – it is best to check first with your own insurance company on whether international travel is included in existing policies.

Doctors and pharmacists generally speak English. Consultation hours are short and it is advisable not to get sick on Wednesday afternoons, weekends, or at night. Emergency services are, of course, available 24 hours.

All medicine, even aspirin and cough syrup, can only be bought from pharmacies (Apotheke). Price controls were recently relaxed but in general, prices are still virtually the same everywhere. Pharmacies are very common and always identified by a large, red letter "A."

It is wise to bring prescription medicine, as well as the original prescription with you, but do not carry more medicine than actually needed for the duration of a holiday.

■ Restrooms

German restrooms are invariably clean, well-equipped, and often have an attendant present. You will often pay to access restrooms in fast-food restaurants, shopping malls, and gas stations. *Gebührenpflichtig* means the charge is compulsory; otherwise, it is up to the discretion of the user. A minimum of 25c is usually requested, but most people give more.

According to German law, any restaurant where people can sit down must have at least three restrooms – one each for staff, women, and men. This helps to explain the popularity of *Stehcafés* (literally "standing cafés"), where patrons can stand and eat but not sit down. Restaurants usually do not charge for the use of restrooms by patrons.

Restrooms in museums and hotels are invariably free and very clean.

International symbols are usually used, but otherwise "*Herren*" means gents and "*Damen*" means ladies.

■ Shopping

Germany's famously restrictive shopping hours have been relaxed in recent years. Shops are generally allowed to open from 8 am to 8 pm, but are closed on Sunday. Only bona fide souvenir shops are allowed to open on Sundays – washing machines and vacuum cleaners adorned with "Souvenir from Berlin" stickers have thusfar failed to impress any judge. Shops in railway stations are not bound by the same restrictions. Shops in rural areas sometimes close for lunch and are unlikely to open on Saturday afternoon.

■ Telephones

Cellular phones bought outside Europe generally do not function in Germany. Public phones are available but many require a charge card rather than cash. Many hotels still impose enormous surcharges on telephone use, including fixed charges for otherwise toll-free numbers.

It is usually worth using an international carrier such as AT&T when phoning international. For the best savings, buy discount telephone cards from telephone shops, usually in the station area. The line quality is sometimes not the best but the savings can be huge.

Telephone numbers vary in length and use an area code followed by the specific number. The telephone number of a major business is often shorter than its fax number. When dialing from abroad, use country code 49 and drop the first zero of the regional code. If not using a discount carrier, dial 00 from inside Germany to make international calls.

■ Mail

Stamps can be bought from post offices, many hotels, and often from souvenir shops. For postcards the standard rate for German and European destinations is €0.45 and for all other destinations €1.

German addresses are typically three lines: person/company name, street name with number, ZIP code (PLZ) and town name. If the addressee's name is not on the mailbox, the mail will not be delivered. If sending mail to someone staying with friends or family, ensure that the house occupant's name is also on the envelope.

■ Dates & Time

In Germany, time is always written using the 24-hour clock, e.g. 8:30 is always in the morning and 20:30 at night. In spoken German, the 12-hour clock is more common.

Dates are written as year.month.day, or day.month.year, or day.month. Therefore, 2004.08.06, 06.08.2004, and 06.08 are all August 6, 2004. The names of the months are close to English – Januar, Februar, März, April, Mai, Juni, Juli, August, September, Oktober, November, and Dezember.

■ Costs

Accommodations

The following scale is used throughout the book. It is the charge per double room including all taxes. The rate refers to the rate the average guest can expect on non-event nights, rather than the rack rate.

German hotels are generally lower-priced than in other Western European countries. Major cities are much cheaper than, for example, Paris or London.

German hotel prices are often quoted per person rather than per room. Fortunately, the quoted price always includes all taxes, with the exception of spa taxes, which are usually charged only in small towns and rarely exceed €2 per person per night. Except for luxury hotels, breakfast is usually offered for free. Not taking breakfast gives no discount. In cities, parking is generally charged separately and usually around €16, but more at some top hotels.

Hotel prices are lowest in November as well as January to March, except of course in winter sports areas. In many cities, four nights for the price of three are offered during this period. Major cities also have hotel bargains in July and August when Germans tend to travel to the countryside and coast. Hotel prices in cities are often the highest in September and October, months favored for visits to cities when the weather may be fine, but where bad weather is less disastrous than in the countryside. Hotels that cater mostly for business travelers often have spectacular discounts over weekends. Sometimes that applies to the entire city, but often different hotels in the same area have different target clienteles and are priced accord-

HOTEL PRICE CHART	
Rates per room based on double occupancy, including taxes.	
€	Under €50
€€	€50-€100
€€€	€101-€150
€€€€	Over €150

ingly. Avoid visiting cities for tourism purposes while major conferences or shows (*Messe*) are on – prices may quadruple.

The official star rating system for hotels is rather useless for travelers and is based on factors like the size of the room and number of rooms with private bathrooms. It gives little indication of the quality of the establishment or service. Major hotel reservation services such as the German-based Hotel Reservation Service (HRS), www.hrs.com, use their own ratings instead. It is worth checking directly with hotels to see if they will match the price of discount agencies – often it may result in a better room if directly booked with the hotel.

In addition to well-known international brands such as Intercontinental, Marriott, Hilton, and Crown Plaza, there are several German- and European-based chains. At the top of the range is the **Kempinski Group**, www.kempinski.com, with a small range of superb hotels, often behind historic facades, that include the Adlon in Berlin and the Atlantic in Hamburg. The **Steigenberger Group**, www.steigenberger.de, has a wide range of well managed, up-market hotels that include the flagship Frankfurter Hof in Frankfurt am Main and the Europäischer Hof in Baden-Baden. The same group also manages the **Intercity Hotels**, www.intercityhotel.de, that are in major cities and always close to the railway station. The **Romantik Hotels**, www.romantikhotels.com, have a wide variety of very pleasant hotels, often in smaller towns, with romantic settings and usually good restaurants. (However, note that this group charges full price for children over three years old.) The **Dorint Group**, www.dorint.com, has a large portfolio of mostly modern, well-managed hotels with stylish, elegant interiors. It recently became part of the French **Accor Group**, www.accorhotels.com, and some hotels may be re-branded. The Accor group also includes the Sofitel, Mercure, and Novotel brands, but the most noteworthy, as far as Germany is concerned, are the **Ibis** hotels, www.ibishotel.com. These are low-priced hotels mostly close to the railway stations in major cities. Facilities are modern and clean but without frills. A very safe budget choice without nasty surprises.

Germany also has a wealth of family-run hotels that range from large, luxury establishments to small, hotel pensions. These generally offer more personality than chain hotels.

A *hotel garni* is a hotel without a restaurant. However, breakfast is almost always available on premises.

In some cities and in most typical vacation areas, apartments and holiday homes (*Ferienwohnung/Haus*) can be rented. The minimum rental period is usually a week, but sometimes only three days are required. This is a cost-effective and convenient form of accommodation, especially for families and small groups.

A pleasant way to save on accommodation is to rent a room (*Zimmer*) in a private house. Rooms can usually be had for €20 per night and sometimes for less than €10 – a big eater can make a profit on the invariably included breakfast alone. However, do note that extra charges sometimes apply for taking a shower or bath.

Holidays on farms are popular in many parts of Germany and can involve either a rented room in the farmhouse or a separate vacation home on the farm. Prices are generally low and hospitality high.

Rooms and vacation homes are often easiest booked in advance through the local tourist information office. Sometimes it is possible on-line, but more often it is still done via a non-automated system. It is, however, easier to leave the details to the tourist office rather than contact many individual establishments to inquire about vacancies. Both rooms and vacation homes can often be rented at a moment's notice – watch for the "frei" (vacant) signs in holiday areas.

Youth hostels and campgrounds are common in Germany, often very well situated, and well-equipped.

Restaurants

Germany has a wide range of restaurant types. At the bottom end of the scale is the *Imbiss* where take-out snacks such as sandwiches, sausages, and *Döner Kebab* can be bought. One step up is the *Stehcafé* (€) – literally standing cafés, as high tables are provided but no chairs. These are usually linked to bakeries or delis and a convenient place for a fast and often cheap meal or coffee.

Fast food restaurants (€) such as McDonalds and Burger King are also popular and generally look just like back

DINING PRICE CHART	
Price per person for an entrée, including water, beer or soft drink.	
€	Under €10
€€	€10-€20
€€€	€21-€35
€€€€	Over €35

home. Self-service restaurants are usually found in department stores.

The most popular restaurants in Germany are termed *Gaststätte* (€-€€) – a mix of restaurant, inn, and bar. These are generally informal, serving mostly local dishes and offering the best value. The daily specials advertised outside on blackboards are usually the best deals and served fastest. In rural areas, as well as along country roads and hiking trails, *Gaststätten* are found with great frequency.

Coffee shops (€-€€) in all shapes and sizes are popular in Germany. Coffee is usually served strong. Formal restaurants (€€-€€€€) are mostly found in cities and the better ones are often in hotels.

RESTAURANT TIPS

Service in German restaurants can sometimes be shockingly bad. Upon arrival, find your own seat. Never wait to be seated – the servers are way too busy ignoring the patrons who are already seated to pay attention to new arrivals. It is quite common to share a table with strangers at busy times – no small talk except *bon appétit* (*Mahlzeit*) and goodbye is required.

At the end of a meal, tell the server *Bitte zahlen!* (Bill, please). It often takes an astonishingly long time for the bill to be produced. When in a hurry, ask for the bill when the coffee arrives.

Restaurants are generally open from 11 am to late at night. It is not uncommon, especially in rural areas, for restaurants to close between 2:30 and 5 pm. In rural areas, *Gaststätten* are open throughout the day on Sunday to cater for hikers and other visitors on day excursions.

With the notable exception of Berlin, service in the former East German states is actually much better than in the former West German ones!

Sightseeing & Events

Sightseeing and cultural events in Germany can be surprisingly cheap. Top museums seldom cost more than €5 and discount tickets are usually available to tourists who plan to see several sights in the same area. Paying €10 or more to enter is the absolute exception and more common for high-technology, multimedia shows rather than traditional museums and cultural venues.

The admission fees listed in this guide are the maximum payable. This is what healthy, solo travelers generally between 25 and 55 can expect to be charged. Discounts are usually available for children, scholars, students, the legally unemployed, disabled, senior citizens, and families – proof of status is required and the discount should be asked for when purchasing the tickets. The specific rules for *Ermäßigt* (reduced) prices vary.

Holidays

Public Holidays

In Germany, vacation days are a matter for the individual states. Most vacations are linked to the religious calendar, with the southern states generally following Catholic holidays and the northern states Protestant ones. Southern states generally have more holidays. On holidays, the opening hours for Sunday are usually followed, but that is not always the case and not for all holidays. Expect most places to be closed over Christmas and New Years and often over Easter as well. (Holidays listed without dates annually move according to the church calendar.)

January 1 – New Year's Day

January 6 – Three Kings' Day/Epiphany (only in Baden-Württemberg, Bavaria, and Saxony-Anhalt)

Good Friday

Easter Monday

May 1 – May Day

Asuncion (Thursday, the 40th day after Easter)

Pentecost (Monday, 50 days after Easter, 10 days after Asuncion)

Corpus Christi (the Thursday following the Sunday after Pentecost, only in

Baden-Württemberg, Bavaria, Hesse, North-Rhine-Westphalia, Rhineland-Palatinate, and Saarland)

October 3 – Day of National Unity

October 31 – Reformation Day (only in Brandenburg, Mecklenburg-Vorpommern, Saxony, Saxony-Anhalt, and Thuringia)

November 1 – All Saints' Day (only in Baden-Württemberg, Bavaria, North-Rhine-Westphalia, Rhineland-Palatinate, and Saarland)

December 25 & 26 – Christmas

Festivals & Major Events

Germany's celebratory year starts just seconds after midnight on 1 January with an incredible amount of fireworks and runs through the year to Christmas Eve.

January and **February** see Carnival-related celebrations in the mostly Roman Catholic parts of the country, with celebration especially jovial in the Rhineland. Festivities in the Black Forest are almost pagan. Parades are held in many towns and cities on *Fasching Dienstag* (Shrove Tuesday/Mardi Gras) or the preceding weekend.

In **March**, the strong beer season celebrates the end of Lent and the reopening of many beer gardens.

Religious parades during **Easter** and **Pentecost** are common in the mainly Roman Catholic areas with processions in Bavaria particularly colorful.

On **Walpurgis Nacht**, the night of **30 April**, witches traditionally met in the Harz Mountains. Nowadays every Harz town has its festivities but the largest events are at Hexentanz and on Mt Brocken. The average witch is more likely to arrive by BMW rather than by broom or on the back of a goat.

From **May to October** an amazing number of summer cultural festivals are arranged throughout Germany. Open-air performances are particularly popular. Large fireworks displays are common, with the **Rhine in Flames** series the best known.

In **June**, the **Kieler Woche** is the largest sailing regatta in the world.

On the second weekend in **July**, Berlin is invaded by the **Love Parade**, the world's largest techno-music festival. Despite a decline in attendance in recent years, those over 25 would be wise to avoid the capital for the weekend.

In **August**, the **Wagner Festival** in Bayreuth has around 65,000 tickets available, giving applicants a 10% chance of success.

The **Museumuferfest** (Museum Bank Holiday) in Frankfurt, the last weekend of **August**, is one of the largest in the country and combines popular entertainment with cultural events.

Wine harvest festivals are scheduled, mostly in **August** and **September**, throughout the wine-producing areas (many other cities happily participate too).

Munich's famous three-week **Okotberfest** is mainly held in September and ends the first Sunday in **October**.

Stuttgart's **Folk and Beer Festival** held the same period is similar but attracts fewer international visitors.

On **November** 11 , **St Martin's Festival**, children parade throughout the country in honor of Germany's patron saint.

Advent, the four weeks leading up to Christmas, is one of the loveliest seasons in Germany. Christmas decorations, often remarkably tasteful, are seen in all shops, many towns, and private residences. Most towns have Christmas markets at least on weekends and many cities have markets running the whole Advent period. Musical concerts, not all religious or even classical music, are scheduled throughout the month.

Christmas is celebrated on the evening of December 24. Expect most businesses, shops, and restaurants to close around noon, if they open at all that day. Rooms in large hotels in major cities often go for a song, while smaller establishments may be closed for the season or insist on reservations from Christmas through New Year's.

■ Adventures

Germany is a country rich in history and culture. But there is a pristine natural side to the country as well and outdoor activities are popular.

Hiking (*wandern*) is the most popular activity in Germany after reading. It is particularly popular on Sundays, when half the population seems to be rambling through the woods. On a Sunday, you'll never walk alone. *Gaststätten* have espe-

Travel Information

cially long hours on Sunday, with warm meals available at all hours. Hiking maps are available from all bookshops and tourist information offices. Public transportation often makes circular routes unnecessary. Long-distance hikes are also popular, with luggage transfers possible.

Cycling is also popular, with many dedicated cycling routes and most roads open to cyclists. Cycling maps are available from all bookshops and tourist information offices. Bicycles can usually be rented from shops close to train stations. Cyclists have the same rights and obligations as drivers and can also be fined for ignoring traffic rules. Mountain biking is increasingly popular but often restricted to special paths wider than two m (6½ feet) to limit environmental damage.

Canoeing and kayaking are possible on most German rivers. The River Lahn is particularly popular, but many picturesque options exist throughout Germany. In many states, licenses are required for boats with motors larger than 5 horsepower.

■ Special Interest

Senior Citizens: Germans are generally frequent travelers and few age groups are more actively on the road than senior citizens, generally aged over 55. They can expect all kinds of discounts when traveling in Germany. However, note that the discount should be requested when paying or making reservations and proof of age may be required.

More often than not, senior citizens qualify for reduced admission fees (*Ermäßigt*), which can mean a saving of 30-50% at many sights. Some hotels and other service providers also provide discounts.

Senior citizens frequently use the railways. Young Germans tend to respect the aged and few old people ever have to haul their own luggage into a train or up to the overhead bins. It is rare that you would have to actually ask for help.

Children: For many reasons, Germans have famously few children, but the tourism industry is not to blame. Children under 15 travel for free on German railways when accompanied by a parent or grandparent. Children and students pay reduced admission everywhere. Most hotels allow children up to 16 to stay free in their parents' room. (International franchises generally have the most liberal policies.) Separate rooms are often available at a steep discount. Many hotels have family rooms. Most restaurants have child seats, although baby-changing tables are not always guaranteed.

Disabled: Facilities for disabled travelers range from excellent to very limited. Many historic sights are completely inaccessible to the disabled. Many towns and regions made considerable efforts to improve accessibility. It is a good idea to contact the local tourist information offices and inquire about options – many have special brochures with information on the accessibility of sights, restaurants, and hotels.

■ Information Sources

Tourist Information: Tourist information is available form the German National Tourist Board (Deutsche Zentrale für Tourismus), Beethovenstrasse 69, 60325 Frankfurt am Main, Germany, www.germany-tourism.de. In the USA, contact the German National Tourist Office, 122 East 42nd Street, New York NY 10168-0072, ☎ 212-661-7200 or ☎ 800-651-7010, fax 212-661-7174, www.cometogermany.com.

It is also useful to contact the tourist office of the state, listed in each relevant chapter, before narrowing it down to relevant smaller regions and towns. Not all tourist offices are prepared to mail information internationally, but most have useful websites.

Internet: Most German towns have official websites, usually as www.*townname*.de. A dash (-) is usually, but not always, used in town names with spaces, e.g. www.bad-homburg.de. The German characters ä, ö, ü, and ß are written as ae, oe, ue, and ss in Internet addresses.

■ Language

English is widely understood in Germany even if many Germans are unable to express themselves in English. In most hotels and restaurants English-speaking staff can be found. In particularly popular tourist areas such as Bavaria, English is widely spoken. Guided tours are mostly in German, but ask for an English-language sheet when buying tickets, not at the start of tours. This is especially important if the best German speaker in a group is delegated to purchase the tickets.

Although English and German are sister languages, many English-speakers find German grammar and pronunciation difficult. German words can be famously long, as a single concept is usually written as a single word. Nouns are always written with a capital.

German is a phonetic language and all letters are pronounced. The *Umlauten* ä, ö, and ü change the sound of the vowel, while ß is pronounced like a single "s." These letters can also be written as ae, oe, ue, and ss, but the reverse is not true. Not all instances of "ss" can be written as ß and Goethe, for example, is never written as Göthe.

In this guide, the 1998 language rules are followed. However, these are not universally accepted yet, and even when they are, it will take some time before all Schloß, etc. signs are changed to Schloss.

A Few Useful Words

The following is not intended as a travelers' phrasebook, but rather a few useful words that will help in reading signs and maps while sightseeing.

Ausgang .... Exit
Auto .... Car
Bahn .... Train/railway
Bahnhof .... Station
Benzin .... Gas/fuel for a car
Berg .... Mountain
Bitte .... Please
Brücke .... Bridge
Burg .... Castle/fortress
Danke (schön) .... Thank you
Denkmal .... Memorial
Dom .... Cathedral
Eingang .... Entrance
Fachwerk .... Half-timbered
Fähre .... Ferry
Fahrrad .... Bicycle
Flughafen .... Airport
Fluss .... River
Frei .... Free
Gaststätte .... Restaurant (Inn)
Geschlossen .... Closed
Hauptbahnhof .... Main Railway Station
Ja (wohl) .... Yes
Kein Zutritt .... No admission/do not enter
Kirche .... Church
Kloster .... Monastery
Kreuz .... Cross
Markt .... Market (square)
Meer .... Sea/ocean
Nein .... No
PKW .... Car
Platz .... Square
Rathaus .... Town Hall
Schloss .... Castle/palace
See .... Lake
Straße .... Street
Straßenbahn .... Tram
Tankstelle .... Gas station
Weg .... Way
Zug/Züge .... Train/trains

■ Suggested Reading

Nonfiction

Two lovely German histories that were published in 2004 are pleasures to read despite the academic credentials of the authors. The easier read is Robert Cole's *A Traveller's History of Germany,* which is comprehensive without being overwhelming and cleverly uses appropriate quotes. It very much has the traveler in mind and offers useful listings and indexes for quick references. Despite the title, Steven Ozments's *A Mighty Fortress* is more formal, but still a good read. Both cover German history from the earliest beginnings to the present.

Mary Fullbrook's *A Concise History of Germany* gives a short, scholarly overview of German history.

Alan Bullock's *Hitler: A Study in Tyranny* is a scholarly work that reads like a (disturbing) novel. A classic work.

John Ardagh's *Germany and the Germans* gives a relatively unbiased view of Germany and German society in the 20th century. It was recently updated.

Traveling Journals

Mark Twain's *A Tramp Abroad* may be late-19th century but is still as relevant and enjoyable as ever.

Jerome K Jerome's early 20th-century *Three Men on a Bummel* is typical of the author, full of wit and interesting observations.

Heinrich Heine's *Deutschland: A Winter's Tale* and *The Harz Journey* give an interesting view of Germany from this popular mid-19th-century poet.

Johann Wolfgang von Goethe's *Poetry and Truth* is an autobiographic work, but he traveled so much it becomes very much a travel journal as well.

Fiction

English fiction seldom uses the interesting backdrop provided by Germany's colorful past. Some of the most famous works are spy novels including several James Bond books and movies as well as John Le Carré's *The Spy Who Came in from the Cold* (Berlin) and *A Small Town in Germany* (Bonn).

Almost anything written by Johann Wolfgang von Goethe is worth reading to set the atmosphere for a trip to Germany, but particularly relevant is his autobiographical work *Poetry and Truth*, *The Sorrows of Young Werther* (set in Wetzlar in Hesse), and *Wilhelm Meister.* If time is limited, at least read his masterpiece, *Faust*.

Jakob and Wilhelm Grimm are probably the most read German writers – although serious scholars of German and literature, their collection of fairy tales is their best-known and most loved work.

Also popular are several legends, including that of *Till Eulenspiegel* and the monumental epic the *Niebelungenlied*. Both original works are by unknown authors.

Germany produced four Nobel Laureates for Literature and works by all four are worth reading. Heinrich Böll (*The Clown, Billiards at Half Past Nine*) and Günther Grass (*The Tin Drum*) are very much post-1945 writers. Thomas Mann (*Buddenbrooks, Death in Venice,* and *The Beloved Returns*) and Hermann Hesse (*Steppenwolf* and *Narziss and Goldmund*) are clearly earlier writers.

Berlin

In this Chapter

Berlin emerged from the shadows of the Cold War with a lot to offer the visitor. Half a century of division left the city with an overabundance of museums, galleries, entertainment, and general visitors' facilities. Although this contributes to the city's current state of near-bankruptcy, it is a source of undiluted joy for visitors to the capital.

Berlin is the most interesting and diverse of all German cities. It is probably most famous for its division during the Cold War and seeing related sights such as the Brandenburg Gate, Checkpoint Charlie, and a few surviving pieces of the Berlin Wall are priorities for many visitors. Berlin has more than 170 museums covering all genres. After four decades of division, some collections are now again united into world-class presentations. Highlights include the superb Gemäldegalerie (Paintings Gallery) and the excellent Pergamon Museum.

The return of the federal government to Berlin in the 1990s led to several grandiose building projects, such as the huge, modern Chancellery and the very popular, domed Reichstag that houses the German parliament. While many modern buildings sprang up in the former no-man's land, several historic buildings are finally being restored. Most of the fabulous Museum Island is either just restored or will be over the next couple of years. The luxury Adlon Hotel was rebuilt to resemble its pre-War appearance. Unter den Linden, Friedrichstraße, and the Gendarmenmarkt are again vying for the heart and soul of the city.

Berlin is easy to enjoy. It is not all museums, galleries, and history. It is a great city to stroll in and enjoy the monuments and monumental structures. It is also a city that caters for all tastes in culture. There are three opera houses and 135 theaters. Its nightlife is recouping some of the fame of the twenties and thirties. Everything, from Mahler to underground heavy metal, is available in this city. It also plays host to the annual Love Parade – the world's largest technotronic music festival.

Berlin is a large city. With around 3.4 million inhabitants, it is twice the size of Hamburg, Germany's second-largest city. Geographically it is huge – 38 km (23 miles) from north to south, and 45 km (27 miles) east to west. The city is about nine times the size of Paris. However, tourist Berlin is much smaller and easily manageable on foot or with public transportation.

Berlin can be enjoyed in all seasons, although winters can be a bit cold and bleak. The most popular seasons are spring and autumn. Summer can be hot and slightly humid. July and August are excellent months to visit the city – as Germans prefer to head to the coasts or countryside for summer vacations, the hotel prices drop dramatically and sights can be enjoyed, with a bit of luck, in glorious sunshine and without entrance lines.

History

Brandenburg

The margrave (*Markgraaf*) of Brandenburg was lord of the March or border area here, with the town of Brandenburg as the center of government. It became part of the Holy Roman Empire of the German Nation during the 10th century. Berlin's origins can be traced back to a settlement in Cölln, around the present day Nikolaiviertel, which was first mentioned in 1237, Berlin on the opposite bank of the river, was mentioned seven years later. By 1389, the two towns had formed a union, joined the Hanseatic League, and achieved some prosperity as a trading and fishing town.

In 1411, the emperor awarded Brandenburg to Count Friedrich von Hohenzollern, who decided to continue residing in the much more civilized Nuremberg. However, his son Friedrich II, established his court in Berlin. The Berliners were less than amused, correctly fearing that this would end some of the city's liberties, violently opposed the building of a castle in the town. It took two years and the assistance of 600 soldiers before the building could actually make progress. The building became the Stadtschloss or town castle, which remained the primary residence of the Hohenzollerns until the forced abdication of Wilhelm II in 1918. Soon after, Berlin was expelled from the Hanseatic League and the city council lost most of its powers to the absolute rule of the margrave.

Brandenburg adopted the Reformation early on and the margrave took the opportunity to enrich himself from the properties of the church. Brandenburg suffered tremendously during the Thirty Years' War, with many battles fought on its territory and huge areas scorched repeatedly. By the end of the war, Berlin was an insignificant town of around 6,000 inhabitants.

Berlin's fortunes changed during the rule of Friedrich Wilhelm, the Great Elector (1640-88). He expanded Berlin's population dramatically by welcoming religious refugees including French Huguenots, Dutch Protestants, and rich Viennese Jewish families.

Prussia

The Hohenzollern family somehow managed to create several sons and fathers who thought and acted in direct opposition to each other. The Great Elector's son, Friedrich III, was less able and more known for his love of the good life. Although he somewhat emptied the treasury, he also created a cultured Berlin. In 1701, he united the territories of Brandenburg and Prussia and had himself crowned Friedrich I, King of Prussia. His son, Friedrich Wilhelm I, shunned all glamour and culture. He was a true miser and lived a barren life, but spent lavishly on the army. He became known as the Soldier King, as under his rule conscription was introduced. He increased the standing army and established the firm Prussian military tradition that, to the dismay of Germans from other regions, would be considered by many foreigners as typical German. Ironically, the Soldier King avoided war.

BERLIN WALL - FIRST VERSION

In the early 18th century, King Friedrich Wilhelm I had a wall built around the city of Berlin. This may seem odd, as by this time the use of cannon made city walls a useless defense measure. However, the purpose of this Berlin wall was to prevent young male Berliners from fleeing the city to avoid military conscription. Ironically, the more famous Berlin wall of 1961 was also built to prevent Berliners fleeimg to a softer and better life in the West. To the king's disgust, his own art-loving son tried to flee for that very purpose. The king was planning to execute him but was persuaded otherwise by his court. The prince, later referred to as Frederick the Great, was sent to jail while his accompanist faced the firing squad.

In contrast to his father, Frederick the Great was a cultured, educated man who made Berlin a center of enlightened thought. His father would have been surprised and proud of his record – he did not shy away from battle and brought Prussia some glorious victories on and off the battlefield. During his rule, Prussia became the fifth power in Europe – the only German state that could rival Austria.

During the Napoleonic wars, Prussia was initially defeated and suffered the ignominy of occupation. Limits were set on the size of the standing army and major art treasures were transported to Paris. However, Prussia played a major role in the defeat of the French at the Battle of the Nations in Leipzig in 1813. Prussian Field Marshall Blucher pursued Napoleon across the Rhine and contributed again at the Battle of Waterloo in 1815 to his final defeat. The Congress of Vienna, which arranged the peace settlement following the wars, made Prussia the clear winner. It greatly expanded in size, gaining the rich and strategic Rhineland among others. Attempts to annex the Kingdom of Saxony were blocked by Austria, which attempted to keep the northern competition weak. It took a half-century of diplomatic rivalry before that argument would be settled through war in Prussia's favor.

The glory of Prussia was portrayed in the growing importance of Berlin. Around 1800, Berlin, with 200,000 inhabitants, became the third-largest city in Europe (after London and Paris).

Germany

In 1871, Berlin became the capital of a united German Empire, and in contrast to the Holy Roman Empire of the German Nation, this was a true empire with Berlin the undisputed capital. Berlin expanded rapidly and became the world's largest tenement city. Growth continued until interrupted by the First World War (1914-18). In 1918, at the end of the war, the Emperor was forced to abdicate and a republic was proclaimed.

In the heady 1920s, after the disasters of the war, its violent aftermath, and the runaway inflation of 1923, Berlin became the life of Europe with nightlife and revues on a par with Paris. During the 1930s, the Nazis took power and instantly started to transform Berlin to portray its power. Despite the general intolerance of the Nazis, Berlin's famous and at times seedy nightlife survived well into the Second World War.

Hitler launched his plans for German expansion from Berlin until it culminated in the attack on Poland, which started World War II in September 1939. For a few more years, Berlin would be the center of the world, the city to be in, until the first allied air raids started. By the end of the war, 75% of central Berlin was destroyed. It was called the eyeless city, as there seemed to be no windowpane intact by the time the Russians took Berlin in April 1945.

For Berlin, the war did not stop in 1945. The three sectors of Berlin occupied by the American, British, and French forces became West Berlin, a capitalist island surrounded by the sea of Communist-dominated East Germany. Berlin would be at the heart of the Cold War. In 1948, the Russians tried to force the surrender of West Berlin by closing the land routes from the West – for a year the West, led by the United States, supplied Berlin through three air corridors. At the height of the crisis, an airplane would take off and land at West Berlin's two airports every minute.

In 1961, the East Germans started to build a wall around West Berlin to finally close off the border through which countless East German citizens were seeping to find a better life in the West. In 1963, American President John F Kennedy assured the people of West Berlin that the world would not surrender the city to Communism in his famous proclamation: *Ich bin ein Berliner*! (The fact that a small grammatical error had him in fact saying "I am a jam donut" was never stressed by Berliners.)

For the next quarter-century, Berlin would be at uneasy peace with its neighbor. The West poured massive subsidies into West Berlin to make it a beacon of capitalist prosperity in a sea of impoverished Communism. West Berlin became a popular place for young German men, as men resident here at age 15 were exempted from compulsory military service. At the same time, East Berlin would draw the best talent and excessive funds from the rest of the countryside in an attempt to compete with the West.

On November 9, 1989, after weeks of pressure and warnings of impending crisis, the East German people finally had enough, bridged the border, scaled the wall, and entered the West. Chipping away on the wall with hammers and chisels became instantly popular, but the quality of construction was such that bulldozers were needed to really make an impact. On October 3, 1990, East and West Germany were finally united again, almost half a century after the end of World War II. Soon after, the German Parliament decided with a narrow majority to move the capital from sleepy Bonn back to Berlin. In 1999, the German Parliament and several other departments of state finally started to operate from Berlin.

Berlin saw tremendous growth and decline since unification. Subsidies from the West declined in line with the normalization of the city's status. This was to some extent countered by massive investment in new government buildings, such as the conversion of the Reichstag, the new chancellery and various new museums. Leading companies such as Daimler-Chrysler,

Siemens, and Sony invested in Berlin. However, at the same time, many jobs, especially in the East, disappeared. By 2002, the city of Berlin was bankrupt. Fortunately for tourists, the fear of being branded philistines ensures that many of the excellent museums and cultural facilities are being maintained properly.

■ Getting Here

By Rail: There are frequent fast rail links to all major German centers. At least hourly trains are available to Hamburg (two hours 20 minutes), Leipzig (1½ hours), Dresden (two hours), Frankfurt (four hours), and Munich (six-seven hours). Journey times are steadily shortened as more of the former East German railways are upgraded to the high-speed network. The most dramatic changes in coming years should be on the link to Munich, while Hamburg will soon be only 90 minutes away.

Zoologischer Garten Station, mostly simply referred to as Zoo, was the main station in West Berlin and still functions in that capacity. Most intercity trains arrive here, although many also continue to the Ostbahnhof. A new main station is being constructed at Lehrter, and is due to open by the end of 2006. It will be the largest rail station in Europe.

By Road: Good Autobahns allow for easy and fast traveling times from all parts of Germany. The AVUS part of the Autobahn southwest of Berlin was Germany's first stretch of Authobahn.

Often the cheapest way to reach Berlin is by bus. The **Berlin Linienbus**, www.berlinlinienbus.de, has a vast network to many parts of Germany and the rest of Europe. The **Zentrale Omnibusbahnhof** (ZOB), Central Bus Station, is at the Messe exhibition grounds and convenient to S-Bahn station Witzleben, as well as several bus lines.

By Air: Despite being the capital of a united Germany for more than a decade there still are surprisingly few direct flights to Berlin – most intercontinental flights to Germany still go to Frankfurt. At the time of writing there were no direct flights from the USA to Berlin, although Lufthansa was planning to reintroduce flights from Washington.

Berlin has three airports, sharing the same information line, ☎ 0180-500-0186, and www.berlin-airport.de. Most flights from Western Europe arrive at **Tegel** (TXL), eight km (4.8 miles) north of the city. Bus transfers cost €2.20, with X9 taking 20 minutes to Zoo station and TXL 25 minutes to Unter den Linden. Taxis to the center cost around €20.

Most other flights, including budget airlines, fly to the less conveniently located **Schönefeld** (SXF), 18 km (11 miles) southeast of the City. A free shuttle bus transfers passengers to the nearby railway station with connections to the center taking around 40 minutes. Often more convenient is express bus SFX, which runs every 30 minutes between 6 am and 8 pm to Wittenbergplatz (near Zoo Station) and Potsdamer Platz. Schönefeld is expanding and will eventually be the only airport in Berlin.

■ Information Sources

Tourist Information: Berlin Tourist Information, ☎ 030-250-025, www.btm.de, has three major locations in Berlin: Europa Center, Budapester Straße close to the Zoologischer Garten station, inside the Brandenburg Gate, and in the basement of the Fernsehturm at Alexanderplatz. All are open daily from 10 am to 6 pm, making reservations for hotels, excursions, and cultural events. Maps and brochures are available free or at a minimal charge.

Magazines such as ***Ex-Berliner*** (in English), ***zitty*** (some English) and ***Prinz*** have good information on the current in places and the cultural scene.

BERLIN WELCOMECARD

The tourist office, S-Bahn ticket offices, and many hotels sell the WelcomeCard. It allows three days of unlimited travel on public transportation in Berlin and Potsdam for €19. It also gives discounts to many attractions. A spectacular deal is the ***Schaulust Museum pass*** *– free entry on three consecutive days to 50 top museums for a mere €10.*

■ Getting Around

Public Transportation: Berlin has an excellent public transportation network combining buses, trams, underground (U-Bahn), and commuter trains (S-Bahn) into a single ticket system. Most lines have no services between 1 and 4 am, but some do on weekends, and night buses with restricted schedules run all week.

Tickets can be bought from machines (most have English) or from the driver at stops without machines. Tickets must be validated before boarding trains or onboard buses and trams. A *Kurzstrecke* (three train or six bus stops) costs €1.20. A single ticket costs €2.20 and is valid for two hours in zone AB – transfers, interruptions and round-trips are allowed. It is generally worth buying a *Tageskarte* (unlimited day ticket) at €5.60 should you plan to use the system more than twice. The honor system is used, but buses must be boarded in the front and tickets shown after 8 pm. Plainclothes inspectors are common. Riding without a validated ticket results in a €40 fine – payable on the spot, or a time-consuming trip to the police station.

Sightseeing Tour by Public Bus

Of particular note are bus lines 100 and 200. These were very much designed with tourists in mind, offering grand views from the top of the double-decker buses. Both routes start at Zoo Station, with Route 100 running through Tiergarten via the Reichstag, past the Brandenburg Gate, down Unter den Linden, across Museum Island, past the Television Tower, and terminating soon after Alexanderplatz. Bus 200 also departs from Zoo Station but runs south of the Tiergarten via the Kulturforum and Potsdamer Platz to join Route 100 at Unter den Linden at Friederichstraße. It continues deeper into East Berlin than does Route 100. Virtually all the sights of Berlin are within a few minutes walk of either route.

By Car: Although driving in Berlin is not particularly problematic, finding parking is. It is best to leave a car parked at the hotel – generally at around €15 per day (€23 at the Adlon). Berlin drivers are reputed to be among the most aggressive and rude in Germany.

Taxis have a fairly good reputation but can be pricey. The base rate is €2.50. When going only a short distance – up to two km or five minutes, whichever comes first – it costs €3, but only if you tell the driver *Kurzstrecke* (short distance) when boarding. Taxis can be hailed, but are easier to find at stands near stations or hotels. You can also ask any shop, restaurant, or hotel to call a taxi for you. There are several cab companies, but **Würfel-Funk** has a toll free number, ☎ 0800-222-2255.

■ Sightseeing

Berlin is geographically a large city – nine times the size of Paris. For the last 50 years or so, it has been without a real center, making it difficult to get a grip on the layout of the city. The city is officially divided into five districts, but these are too large to be of much use to the short-term visitor. The one exception is Mitte (Center), which encompasses most of the area around Unter den Linden and forms the heart of the new Berlin.

For the sake of simplicity, the sights below are grouped into six geographic areas: the areas around Zoo Station and Tiergarten in the former West Berlin, Unter den Linden, Museum Island, and Friederichstraße in the former East Berlin, and Potsdamer Platz, mostly in no-man's land during the Cold War.

Bear in mind that distances in Berlin can be large. Walking is not a realistic option from Zoo to Unter den Linden, for example, but it is the best option once you are in a specific area.

Berlin has more than 170 museums. Some are mentioned under the specific geographical areas, but are described in more detail in the special museum section that follows.

Zoo Station Area

The Zoologischer Garten Station area, more often simply referred to as Zoo Station, used to be the commercial heart and life of West Berlin. It is still a bustling area at all hours, but some of the glamour has faded as most investments during the 1990s were ploughed into the newly fashionable areas of East Berlin. However, in recent years, the area again experienced growth, with new hotels and upgraded shopping facilities.

Zoo Station is still the central transportation hub of Berlin. It is the busiest in Berlin, with most long distance trains

Berlin

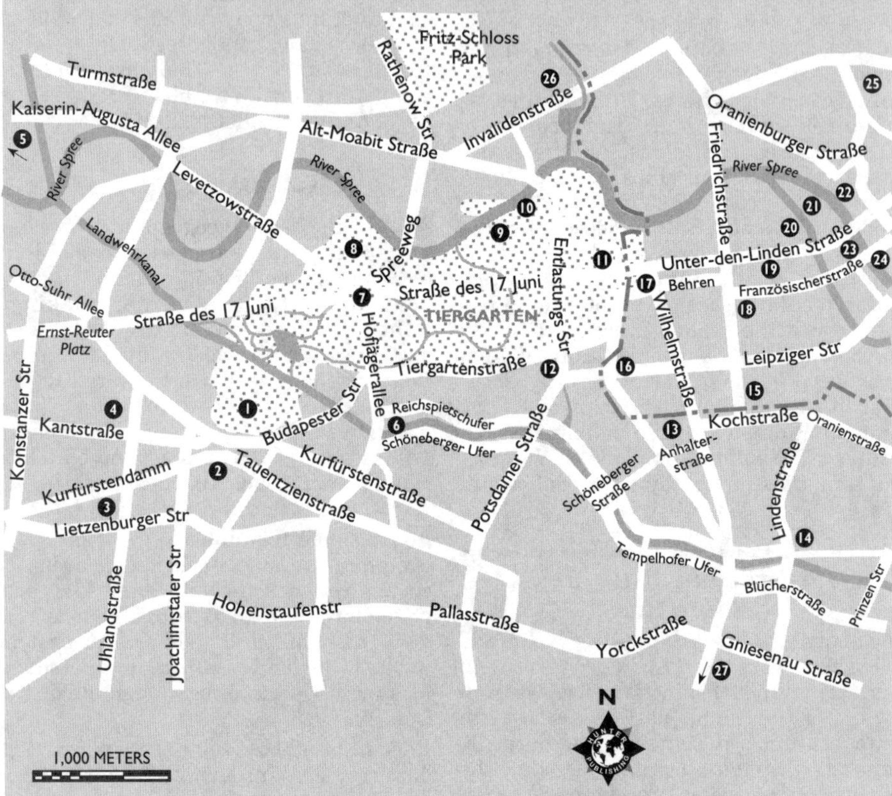

1. Zoological Garden
2. Europa Center, Breitscheidplatz; Kaiser Wilhelm I Gedächtniskirche
3. Story of Berlin
4. Savigny Platz
5. To Schloss Charlottenburg
6. Bauhausarchiv Museum für Gestaltung
7. Grossestern (Great Star) & Siegessäule (Victory Column)
8. Schloss Bellevue
9. Glockenspiel
10. Bundeskanzleramt
11. Reichstag (Parliament)
12. Kulturforum: Gemäldegalerie, Kunstgewerbemuseum, Kupferstichkabinett, Neue Nationalgalerie, Philharmonie
13. Topography of Terror Exhibit
14. Jüdisches Museum
15. Checkpoint Charlie, Mauermuseum
16. Potsdamer Platz, Sony Center & Filmmuseum Berlin
17. Brandenburg Gate, Hotel Adlon, Pariser Platz
18. Gendarmenmarkt, Deutscher Dom, Französischer Dom, Konzertsaal, Quartier 206, Galeries Lafayette
19. Deutsche Guggenheim Berlin, Bebelsplatz, St Hedwigskatedrale, Staatsoper
20. Humboldt University, Zeughaus (German History Museum)
21. Museum Island: Altes Museum, Neues Museum, Alte Nationalgalerie, Bode Musuem, Pergamonmuseum
22. Hackesher Museum
23. Berliner Dom
24. Nikolaiviertel
25. Fernsehturn
26. Hamburger Bahnhof (Hamburg Train Station)
27. To Airport (Flughafen Tempelhof)

Location of Berlin Wall, 1961-1989

Chinese Tea House at Schloss Sanssouci, Brandenburg (© TMB/Boettcher)

Above: The Schauspielhaus, Berlin

Below: Berlin's Brandenburg Gate

(both Berlin Tourism © www.berlin-tourist-information.de/Koch)

Above: The Zwinger, Dresden

Below: Semper Opera House, Dresden (*both © Christoph Münch*)

Above: The Fürstenzug, Dresden

Below: Hofkirche and Schloss from across the Elbe, Dresden

(both © Christoph Münch)

arriving here, most S-Bahn lines passing through, and many buses departing from here.

Right in front of Zoo station is **Breitsheidplatz**, a popular meeting and hangout place for people of all ages. From here, two of Berlin's busiest shopping streets spread out, the wide tree-lined **Kurfürstendamm** to the west and **Tauentzienstraße**, with the famous Kadewe store, to the east. The Kurfürstendamm was laid out as a four-lane boulevard similar to the Champs Elysées by Otto von Bismarck. Although Germany has more memorials to Bismarck than any other single figure, Berlin – typically – has denied him a statue on the one street where he really wanted one!

One of the enduring symbols of West Berlin, the **Kaiser Wilhelm Gedächtniskirche** (Emperor William Memorial Church), Breitscheidplatz, ☎ 030-218-5023, www.gedaechtniskirche.com, was built at the end of the 19th century and almost completely destroyed during World War II. After the war, it was decided to leave the bombed-out tower as a warning of the destructiveness of war. A small, very modern church and tower of blue glass bricks were built next to it between 1959 and 1961. English services are held Sundays, usually at 10 am. The modern church is open daily from 9 am to 7 pm. The bell tower houses a Third World Shop and the tower cannot be ascended. The Memorial Hall in the bombed-out tower, which has some remarkably intact mosaics depicting events in the life of the Kaiser, is open Monday to Saturday from 10 am to 4 pm. Admission is free. The bombed tower is known locally as the hollow tooth, while the modern church and tower are known as the lipstick and powder box.

Behind the Memorial Church is the 1960s **Europa Center**, the glitziest shopping center in town when the city was still split. Nowadays, it appears a bit dated, although some of the almost 100 boutiques and other small shops are still popular, especially with the younger crowd. Inside is a 13-m (33-foot) high water clock; the revolving Mercedes Benz star on the roof is a meter/three feet taller. The **Berlin Information Office** is located in the center – entrance from Budapester Straße.

The **Zoologischer Garten** (Zoological Gardens), Hardenberger Platz, ☎ 030-254-010, is home to more than 1,400 species, including pandas. It is large by European standards and a pleasant diversion. The main entrance is directly opposite Zoo station with a side-entrance across the road from the Europa Center. It is open daily from 9 am until dark (latest entrance 6:30 pm). Admission is €9.

The **Story of Berlin**, Kurfürstendamm 207-208, ☎ 030-8872-0100, www.story-of-berlin.de, is a privately run 90-minute multimedia show on the history of Berlin – a good introduction to the city's 800-year history, but, with an admission charge of €9.30, rather pricy compared to more traditional museums. It has the only original nuclear bunker open to the public in Berlin. Open daily from 10 am to 6 pm.

Tiergarten

Tiergarten is a 714-acre park in the heart of Berlin. In the 17th century, it was the hunting ground of the Elector, but during the 19th century, it was converted to its present English landscape-style park. It is a popular venue for outdoor activities of all kinds.

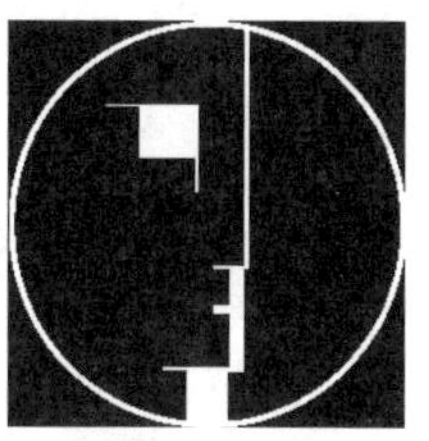

Just south of the park is the **Bauhaus Archive-Berlin**, Klingelhöferstraße 14, ☎ 030-254-0020, www.bauhaus.de. The Berlin archives cover all stages of the Bauhaus School of Design from 1919 until its forced demise in 1933. Collections from the estates of Walter Gropius, Georg Muche, and Herbert Bayer are housed here. The museum is open Wednesday to Monday from 10 am to 5 pm. Admission is €4. (See also *Dessau* in the *Saxony Anhalt* chapter, page 150, and *Weimar* in the *Thuringia* chapter, page 120, for more on Bauhaus.)

A wide boulevard cuts through the park, ending at the Brandenburg Gate. It is called **Straße des 17 Juni** – Street of 17 June – to commemorate the 1953 uprising of East German workers against the Communist regime. The uprising received no backing from the Western powers and was brutally put down by the Soviet forces. In the center of a large roundabout is the almost 70-m (224-foot) **Siegessäule** (Victory Column) at Großer Stern, ☎ 030-391-2961, with a gold-plated statue of Victory, completed in 1873 shortly after

Siegessäule statue

the unification of Germany. It originally stood in front of the Reichstag, but the Nazis had it moved to the middle of the Tiergarten in anticipation of victory parades to come. Open daily from 9:30 am to 6:30 pm. Admission is €1.20.

Schloss Bellevue in Spreeweg was built in the 18th century by the younger brother of Frederick the Great. It is the official residence of the president of Germany and not open to the public. The gardens may be visited when the president is not in residence.

Nearby, in John Foster Dulles Allée, is a **Glockenspiel** (Carillon) with 68 bells, one of the largest in Europe. It plays daily at noon and 6 pm. Free concerts are held Sundays at 3 pm between May and 3 October, and at 2 pm on Advent Sundays and Christmas Day.

The **Bundeskanzleramt** (Chancellery) is an enormous, modern square building on the banks and even crossing the River Spree. It was designed during the governing period of Helmut Kohl but was first occupied by his successor, Gerhardt Schröder. It is a bit of an embarrassment of riches but a very impressive sight, in stark contrast to the low-key federal structures previously used in Bonn.

Built between 1884 and 1894 to house the Imperial parliament, the **Reichstag**, Platz der Republik, ☎ 030-2273-2152, www.bundestag.de, burned down in 1933. Hitler blamed the Communists and used the opportunity to ban them, as well as several other groups, from parliament, thereby obtaining a majority and seizing power. Since 1998, the restored building, with a new larger glass dome designed by Sir Norman S Forster, housed the Deutscher Bundestag (German Federal Parliament). Two spiral walkways lead to the top of the glass dome, offering wonderful views of Berlin. A mirrored glass cone makes it possible to look into the Bundestag, the lower house of the German parliament. The hugely popular dome is open daily from 8 am to midnight. Mornings before 9 am and afternoons around 5 pm are generally less crowded. Admission is free, but expect airport-style security. Although currently still a must-see in Berlin, if time is limited and the lines long, you might rather spend your time elsewhere.

Unter den Linden

The **Brandenburger Tor** (Brandenburg Gate), Pariser Platz, is the symbol of Berlin. Built between 1788 and 1791, it was damaged, but not destroyed, during World War II. It has since been restored various times – the last restoration, to repair the damage done by the previous three restorations, was completed in 2002. It is the only remaining gate of the original 14 that provided access to the city.

GODDESS OF PEACE OR VICTORY?

The bronze Quadriga of four horses and Irene, the goddess of peace, by Gottfried Schadow, was placed on the Brandenburg Gate in 1794. In 1806, Napoleon had the bronze dismantled and carted to Paris as war bounty. In 1814, the work returned, a staff and iron cross were added, and Irene became Nike, the goddess of victory. During World War II, the Quadriga was damaged. It took a rare instance of East-West cooperation to replace the Quadriga because the casts of the original were in West Berlin, while the Brandenburg Gate was in the East. The Communist regime considered the iron cross a symbol of German militarism and left it out. During restoration work in 1991 the iron cross was returned.

After years of quibbling over the site and design of the **Holocaust Memorial**, corner of Behren and Ebertstraße, ☎ 030-2639-4311, www.holocaustmahnmal.de, building has finally begun on a site south of the Brandenburg Gate. The memorial, designed by Peter Eisenman, will consist of huge concrete slabs – some as high as five meters/15 feet – placed in close proximity to each other so walking solo will be the only way through. (A handy brochure, "Discover Jewish Berlin," is available from the tourist office.)

In 1647, the Great Elector planted six rows of lime trees along the road connecting his city palace and the Tiergarten. The road, just over a kilometer (.6 mile), soon became known as **Unter den Linden** (Under the Lime Trees). It has been the heart of the town ever since. The Nazis once cut the trees down, planning to replace them with Nazi banners, but protests were so livid even the masters of the Third Reich had to yield and replaced the trees. Unter den Linden stretches from the Brandenburg Gate to the Museum Island. Several cafés and restaurants of all price ranges line the street, together with embassies, fashionable shops, souvenir stalls, and luxury car showrooms.

Berlin Wall

After the war, the West Berlin border was 155-km (93 miles) long, of which 106 km (64 miles) was occupied by the infamous Berlin Wall. Construction of this steel re-enforced concrete wall started on August 18, 1961, and it was maintained until November 9, 1989. During this period, 5,075 persons succeeded in escaping over or underneath the wall, while 176 died during escape attempts. The wall's height ranged from 3.5 m to 4.2 m (11 to 13 feet) and had 302 guard towers.

One of the enduring images of the Cold War is the Brandenburg Gate, isolated in no-man's land behind the impregnable Berlin Wall. Nowadays, only four sections of the wall remain, none near the Brandenburg Gate. The longest piece is the 1.3 km (.8 mile) stretch, now called the **East Side Gallery**, in Mühlenstraße near the Ostbahnhof. It was painted by famous artists after the *Wende*.

Did you know? The *Wende*, or change, is the name for the major political shift that East Germany made when it joined democratic, capitalist West Germany.

More accessible is the stretch at the Topographie des Terors near Checkpoint Charlie, and a very small piece at Stresemannstraße near Potsdamer Platz.

Probably the most interesting part is in **Bernauerstraße**, near Nordbahnhof. Here parts of the defenses behind the wall are also preserved. The **Berlin Wall Documentation Center**, Bernauerstraße 111, ☎ 030-464-1030, www.berliner-mauer-dokumentationszentrum.de, has interesting multimedia displays on the history of the wall. It is open Wednesday to Sunday from 10 am to 5 pm. Admission is free.

Hotel Adlon faces the Brandenburg Gate at Pariser Platz. It originally opened in the presence of Kaiser Wilhelm II in 1907 as the first grand hotel of international standard in Berlin and soon became the residence of choice for visiting royalty, politicians, entertainers, and other wealthy visitors. Marlene Dietrich was discovered here. Greta Garbo desired to be left alone here. Einstein was a guest. Hitler and the Nazis generally shunned it and, as a result, it became known as Little Switzerland during the Nazi era. It miraculously survived the bombings of World War II, but burned down shortly afterwards under still unsatisfactorily explained circumstances. Shortly after the fall of the Wall, the Kempinski Group acquired the site and successfully erected a copy of the original. It opened in 1996 and again became the best temporary address in town. Staff are known and expected to be snooty and camera-toting sightseers are generally not welcomed.

The new French and British **Embassies** are nearby. The new American one, supposed to be constructed in between the Adlon and the Brandenburg Gate, is still in a planning phase while its exact location is being pondered. However, the most interesting embassy building on Unter den Linden is the Russian Embassy at Number

63-65. It is in a Neo-Classical monumental Stalinist style and was one of the first major buildings erected in East Berlin after the end of the World War II. Nowadays the red-white-blue Russian standard is flown, but the hammer and sickle can still be seen on some detailing.

The **Deutsche Guggenheim Berlin** at Unter den Linden 13-15, 10117 Berlin-Mitte, ☎ 030-202 09 30, www.deutsche-guggenheim-berlin.de, houses alternating exhibitions from classical Modernism to current art. It has no permanent collections and is closed between exhibitions. The museum is open daily from 11 am to 8 pm (10 pm on Thursdays). Daily guided tours are at 6 pm. Admission is €3; free on Monday.

Berlin has three major universities, four academies of arts, and 10 universities of applied sciences, but the most famous and oldest is **Humboldt University**, Unter den Linden 7. More than 20 Nobel Prize winners studied here. Famous students included Marx, Engels, Lenin, and the Grimm brothers. Einstein taught here. The original buildings were erected during the reign of Fredrick the Great. His equestrian statue in front of the main building was banished to Sanssouci Park in Potsdam by the Communist regime, but returned after the *Wende*.

Bebelsplatz was one of the sites where the Nazis burned books by undesirable authors. To commemorate the event a small window in the floor in the center of the square looks down on a room with empty bookshelves. Nearby, signs quote the famous words by German poet Heinrich Heine, whose works were also banned due to his Jewish heritage, that where books are burned soon people will also burn.

St Hedwigskatedrale (St Hedwig's Cathedral), Bebelsplatz, ☎ 030-203-4810, was built 1747 and 1773 as a Roman Catholic church following Frederick the Great's annexation of Catholic Silesia. It was the only church constructed by him – he was very much in favor of freedom of religion as well as the freedom of paying for your own house of prayer. It is built in a style resembling the Pantheon in Rome. Opening hours are weekdays from 10 am to 5 pm and Sundays from 1 to 5 pm.

The **Staatsoper**, Unter den Linden 7, was constructed in 1742 and is considered by many the most beautiful building that Frederick the Great erected in Berlin. Early in World War II it burned down after an air raid, but was rebuilt in a rush to restore morale and the new Oper was ready for bicentennial celebrations. It was bombed again in 1945 but rebuilt. Of the three opera houses in Berlin, this one is the oldest and most popular.

Across the road is the Classical **Neue Wache**, Unter den Linden 4. It changed designations several times but is currently the official German memorial for the victims of war and tyranny worldwide. It has a copy of a famous sculpture by Käthe Kollwitz of a mother mourning over her dead child.

The 1695 **Zeughaus** (Armory) is the oldest building on Unter den Linden. It will house the **German Historical Museum** – due to re-open early 2005.

Museuminsel

Museum Island was the center of Berlin during the Hohenzollern era. It housed not only their principal residence and church, but also, from the mid-19th century onwards, five large Neo-Classical museum buildings. (See *Museums* below for more on these.)

The **Berliner Dom** (Berlin Cathedral), Am Lustgarten, ☎ 030-2026-9119, was constructed between 1894 and 1905 in a Neo-Renaissance style and is the largest 19th-century Protestant building in Germany. The vault, hardly worth seeing, contains the sarcophagi and gravestones of 100 Hohenzollerns. Short organ concerts are offered on some afternoons – schedules are posted at the entrance. The church is open from April to September, Monday to Saturday from 9 am to 8 pm, Sundays and public holidays from noon to 8 pm. From October to March it closes at 7 pm. Admission is €5.

Across the road from the Dom was the location of the **Stadtschloss** (Town Palace), the principal residence of the Hohenzollern family since the 15th century. The palace survived the World War II with remarkably little damage, but was demolished by the East German regime in 1950. Plans are currently afoot to rebuild the palace.

Across the Spree River is the gleaming copper **Palast der Republik** (Palace of the Republic). This amazing building housed the East German parliament from 1975 onwards. It was a true people's palace with cultural forums and even a fitness center. Shortly after the *Wende* the building was closed to clean up asbestos used during construction. It has since been finally decided to destroy the building in 2005.

The origins of Berlin are in the **Nikolaiviertel** (Nicholas Quarters). Many of the buildings here were already restored during the Communist era. The **Nikolaikirche** (Nicholas Church), Poststraße 13, ☎ 030-2400-2162, dates back to 1220, although it was altered to Late Gothic style in the 15th century. This is the oldest church in Berlin. It is open Tuesday to Sunday from 10 am to 6 pm. Nearby is the red-brick Berlin Rathaus (Town Hall).

Berlin's highest construction is the 368-m (1,178-foot) **Fernsehturm** (Television Tower), Panoramastraße 1A, ☎ 030-242-3333, www.berlinfernsehturm.de. It was built using Swedish technology and opened in 1969. The rotating restaurant **Telecafé** at 207 m (662 feet) offers the best aerial views of Berlin with a complete turn every half-hour. It also lets you time-travel to East Germany of the '70s. The observation platform is open from March to October daily from 9 am to 1 am, and November to February from 10 am to 12 pm. Admission is €6.50.

With the pre-war hotspots of Unter den Linden and Friedrichstraße being too close to the Wall for comfort, the government of the German Democratic Republic planned **Alexanderplatz** as the life and soul of East Berlin. Today this huge square and the large socialist-style buildings in the immediate vicinity are often devoid of human life and a depressing sight. A few blocks away are examples of the huge, low-rise apartment blocks known as *Plattenbau*, which were favored by the Communist-era central planners.

Friedrichstraße

Gendarmenmarkt is one of Berlin's most beautiful public squares. It has two similar-looking cathedrals dating from the early 18th century, as well as the 1818 **Konzerthaus** (Concert Hall), home of the Berlin Philharmonic Orchestra. A statue of Friedrich Schiller stands in front of the hall.

The **Deutscher Dom** (German Cathedral), Gendarmenmarkt 1, ☎ 030-2273-0431 was destroyed during World War II but rebuilt in the 1990s. The outside followed the original design, but the inside is thoroughly modern and used as an exhibition space by the German Parliament. The current exhibition explains the development of parliamentary democracy in Germany. Admission is free and English-language audio guides are available. The exhibition is open on Tuesdays from 10 am to 10 pm, Wednesdays to Sundays 10 am to 6 pm (7 pm in June, July and August).

The French Cathedral (**Französischer Dom**), ☎ 030-229-1760, www.franzoeisischer-dom-berlin.de, shown above, was built for the Huguenots who had fled France and were welcomed in Prussia in the late 17th century. The tower houses a Huguenot museum and a lookout platform. The cathedral and lookout are open daily from

9 am to 7 pm, the museum Tuesday to Saturday from noon until 5 pm, Sunday from 11 am to 5 pm.

The presence of the Huguenots also gave rise to the lovely **Quartier** area between the square and Friedrichstraße. These three blocks house upmarket stores, including a Galleries Lafayette, and are well worth seeing even if you're not on a shopping spree.

Checkpoint Charlie gained notoriety as one of the places where the Cold War was at its hottest. Although not the only crossing point, it was the best-known. The famous scene of a Russian tank speeding up and breaking sharply to stop barely inches from the borderline occurred here. Today the guard house of the West is still in place but as a monument and background prop for tourist pictures. The large signboard, "You are leaving the American Sector," is a copy – the original is in the Museum Haus am Checkpoint Charlie. (See *Museum* section below for details.)

A good 15 minutes walk from here, but absolutely worth it, is the **Berlin Jüdisches Museum** (Jewish Museum). (See *Museum* section for details.)

Potsdamer Platz

Potsdamer Platz was the densest traffic point in pre-war Berlin. It had the first traffic light in Germany – a copy can be seen. It was heavily bombed during the war, afterwards was in no-man's land for four decades, and only again developed in the 1990s. It is very modern and has the tallest buildings in Berlin. Some consider it to be without a heart and soul, but it is popular, especially with the younger crowd.

The **Sony Center** is the most impressive building, housing not only Sony's European headquarters but also several restaurants and the impressive **Berlin Film Museum**. The magnificent roof has been described as tent- and sail-like, but actually represents Mt Fuji.

Nearby is the **Kulturforum** (Cultural Forum) with several museums and concert halls. The most worthwhile are the superb **Gemäldegalerie** (Picture Gallery) and the 1960s **Philharmonie**, home of Germany's most famous symphony orchestra, the Berlin Philharmonie.

It is possible to follow the line of the former Berlin Wall from Potsdamer Platz toward Checkpoint Charlie. En route is an interesting open-air exhibition, **Topographie des Terrors** (Topography of Terror), Niederkirchnerstraße 8, 10963 Berlin (Kreuzberg), ☎ 030-2548-6703. It documents the history of the Nazis' Secret Police, the SS, and other security instruments of the Third Reich. The exhibition is at the recently rediscovered foundations of the notorious Prince Albrecht headquarters of the terror organizations. The exhibition is mainly photos and a permanent museum will eventually be built. Behind the exhibition is a large remnant of the Berlin Wall. The site is open daily, October to April from 10 am to dusk (6 pm at the latest), the rest of the year, 10 am to 8 pm. Admission and English-language audio guides are free. (The nearby Finanzamt is the only Nazi-era building in Berlin that survived virtually intact.)

Museums & Galleries

Berlin has more than 170 museums and art galleries ranging from prehistoric archeological finds to contemporary art. The most important collections are in the 16 National Museums but some others are also well worth a visit. Split for more than half a century, the various collections of East and West Berlin are again being united into world-class collections.

MUSEUMPASS

Admission charges for museums in Berlin are pleasantly low, with only some of the private ones costing more than €6. The Schaulust Museen Berlin card, more commonly known simply as the Museumpass, offers entry to 50 museums on three consecutive days for only €10. The list includes all the National Museums in Berlin and all museums listed below unless otherwise noted. It is available from the museums, tourist office, and some hotels.

National Museums in Berlin

The 16 Staatliche Museen zu Berlin (SMB museums) are in different areas but all share the same visitors' contact information: Berlin State Museums, ☎ 030-20 90 55 55, www.smpk.de, and are open Tuesday to Sunday, 10 am-6 pm. (Minor exceptions noted where applicable.)

Admission to the larger ones is €6, which gives access to all 16 museums for the rest of the day. Some special exhibitions require a surcharge. Note the museum pass above for access on consecutive days. Some of the smaller ones can also be seen alone for €3 as noted.

If time or interest is limited, give priority to the **Pergamonmuseum** and the **Gemäldegalerie**.

The 16 SMB venues are clustered in four major geographical centers: Museum Island, Kulturforum, Charlottenburg, and Dahlem.

Museum Island

The traditional location of museums in Berlin is on the northern half of Museum Island, recently declared a UNESCO World Cultural Heritage Site. Up to 70% of the buildings here were destroyed during World War II and major construction work is being undertaken to repair and refurbish the museums. All museums here are either closed or will be closed for reconstruction work during the next five years.

MUSEUM REBUILDING

These major museums will be closed during the following periods:

- Bode Museum – until mid-2006
- Neues Museum – until end 2009
- Altes Museum – from 2008 to 2010
- Pergamonmuseum – from 2008 to 2010

Missed deadlines will surprise no one. Parts of museums may also be closed for shorter periods and during reconstruction parts of some collections may be displayed in other venues, in some cases even in other cities.

The oldest museum here is the appropriately named **Altes Museum** (Old Museum), Lustgarden, which has been in existence since 1830. The permanent collection consists mainly of Greek and Roman art and sculptures. The main attraction – Etruscan art – will only be on display after completion of the rebuilding. The **Neues Museum** (New Museum) was virtually destroyed during World War II and has been under reconstruction since 1986. Once completed, it will ironically house collections even older than those of the Old Museum – the Egyptian collections from both Charlottenburg and the Bode Museum, as well as the Museum of Pre- and Early History, currently in Charlottenburg.

The **Alte Nationalgalerie** (Old National Galley), Bodestraße, houses a collection of 19th- and early 20th-century art, including paintings by Edouard Manet, Claude Monet, Paul Cezanne, and sculptures by Auguste Renoir, Hans von Marees, and Louis Corinth. German artists from this period are also well represented.

The Neo-Baroque building of the **Bode Museum**, entrance from Monbijou Bridge, is due to reopen after renovations in mid-2006. It will house the Museum of Late Antiquity and Byzantine Art, the Numismatic Collection, a collection of painting and sculptures from the Middle Ages to the late 18th century, and a children's gallery. Parts of the Numismatic Collection are currently on display in the nearby Pergamon Museum and the Museum for Pre- and Early History in Charlottenburg.

The monolithic building of the **Pergamonmuseum**, Am Kupfergraben, opened in 1930 and currently houses several museums and collections – all are included on the same admission ticket. These are the true jewels in the crown of Berlin's vast collections. Complete temples, market gates, and processional streets are rebuilt here. The **Classical Antiquities Collection** includes the Pergamon Altar with a second-century BC Hellenic frieze depicting the battle between the gods and the giants. An outstanding example of Roman art is the Market Gate of Miletus. The **Museum of Islamic Art** includes, in addition to

Pergamon Altar

smaller applied arts, large works such as the Mschatta Façade from eighth-century Jordan, the 17th-century Aleppo Room of painted wood paneling, and wall ceramics such as prayer niches from Kashan and Konya. The **Museum of Ancient Near Eastern Antiquities** includes the Ishtar Gate, a magnificent blue tiled Processional Way, and the facade of the throne hall of King Nebuchadnezzar II (604-562 BC). Further exhibits of Sumeria, Babylonia, Assyrian, Iraq, Syria, and Turkey complete this display of 6,000 years of history. Admission to the Pergamonmuseum includes an excellent free audio guide in English. If you have time for only one museum in Berlin, make it this one; 750,000 annual visitors can't be wrong.

Kulturforum

At the southeast corner of the Tiergarten, a mere two blocks from the ultramodern high-rise buildings of Potsdamer Platz, is the Kulturforum. This area houses among others the Philharmonie concert hall, the State Institute of Musicology, together with the Museum of Musical Instruments, the Berlin branch of the National Library, as well as several National Museums.

The largest and most important here is the superb **Gemäldegalerie** (Picture Gallery), Matthäikirchplatz, which opened in 1998 to display works from previously divided collections. It is one of the largest and most impressive collections of European paintings from the 13th to 18th centuries in the world. The 1,500 paintings include works by Bruegel, Dürer, Rembrandt, Vermeer, Rubens, Rafael, Titian, and Caravaggio. The main gallery has 72 rooms divided into two sections: Italian paintings and Dutch-German paintings. An octagonal room is at the center of the museum, displaying some of the 16 works by Rembrandt. Early German works are also well represented with several works by Lucas Cranach as well as eight by Albrecht Dürer. Comfortable footwear is recommended – seeing all the rooms involves a 2.2-km (1.3-mile) walk. Thursdays open until 10 pm.

In the same building as the Gemäldegalerie are the **Kunstgewerbemuseum** (Applied Arts) and the **Kupferstichkabinett** (Museum of Prints and Drawings). The former exhibits European art and crafts from the Middle Ages to the present day, including costumes, furniture, porcelain, and gold and silversmith work. In the basement is an exhibition of 20th-century industrial products. The Kupferstichkabinett is a graphic collection with 80,000 drawings and more than 500,000 printed graphic sheets. The collection includes works by Dürer, Breughel, Rembrandt, and Picasso. If seen separately from other museums, admission is €3 for each of these. On weekends, both are open only from 11 am.

The oldest building in the Kulturforum is the 1968 **Neue Nationalgalerie**, Potsdamer Straße 50. The building was designed by Mies van de Rohe of the Bauhaus school and houses 20th-century art, including Expressionists, Bauhaus, New Objectivity, and postwar art. On weekends, it is open only from 11 am and Thursday it closes at 10 pm.

Not in Kulturforum itself, but just a short ride away, is the **Hamburger Bahnhof Museum for Contemporary Art**, Invalidenstraße 50-51 near S-Bahn station Lehrter. It exhibits post-1960s works ranging from paintings, sculptures and graphics to multimedia, room and light installations. Featured artists include Andy Warhol, Roy Lichtenstein, Anselm Kiefer, and representatives of minimalist art. The bookshop is impressive too. On weekends open only from 11 am and Thursdays open until 10 pm.

Charlottenburg

While the city was divided, the Baroque Palace Charlottenburg was a major attraction in West Berlin. However, since *Die Wende,* it has lost much of its appeal to the more elaborate palaces in Potsdam and some of its collections have moved to other parts of the city as well. The area still houses several major national museums, although in coming years two more are heading Museum Island's way.

Schloss Charlottenburg, Luisenplatz, ☎ 0331-969-4202, below, is the largest remaining Hohenzollern palace. It represents court art and culture in the Brandenburg-Prussian monarchy from the 17th to 19th centuries.. The Old Palace is open Tuesday to Friday from 9 am to 5 pm, and weekends from 10 am to 5 pm. Admission of €8 includes a compulsory guided tour. The New Wing is open Tuesday to Friday from 10 am to 6 pm and weekends from 11 am to 6 pm. Admission is €5.

The **Museum für Vor- und Frühgeschichte** (Pre- and Early History), Langhans Building next to Charlottenburg Palace, houses a major collection of European and Ancient Near East artifacts up to the early Middle Ages. A highlight of the collection is works of gold, ceramics, and weaponry from the legendary city of Troy, rediscovered by Heinrich Schliemann in 1870. The display of Germanic jewelry of the migration period is also impressive. Part of the Numismatic Collection from the Bode Museum is on temporary display here. The entire museum will move to Museum Island around 2009.

Located directly opposite Schloss Charlottenburg is the **Ägyptisches Museum und Papyrussammlung** (Egyptian Museum and Papyrus Collection), Östlicher Stülerbau, Schlossstraße. It is a collection of royal ancient Egyptian art from around 3000 BC up to the Roman Period. The works of art from the time of King Akhenaton (around 1340 BC) are internationally famous. The half-meter (1½-foot) high limestone and plaster bust of Queen Nefertiti, with its original bright untouched colors, is a continuous source of fascination and arguably the most famous Egyptian piece in Germany. The museum draws half a million visitors annually, a number that is sure to increase after the collection moves to Museum Island around 2009.

In the same building is the **Heinz Berggruen Collection**, Westlicher Stülerbau, Schlossstraße. It consists of paintings and sculpture from the classical modernist period. More than 70 pieces by Picasso form the center of the exhibition that also includes works by Klee, Cezanne, Matisse, and Van Gogh. On weekends, it is open only from 11 am.

Dahlem

The third-largest museum complex in Berlin is somewhat off the beaten track in Dahlem, in the southwestern corner of the city. The focus here is on non-European cultures. The first three museums are housed in the same complex at Lansstraße 8, close to U-Bahnstation Dahlem Dorf.

The **Museum für Indische Kunst** (Indian Art) covers more than 3,000 years of Indian art and culture with sculpture and reliefs in bronze, stone, and terracotta documenting the different religions from the subcontinent. In addition, a large collection of wall paintings and sculpture from Buddhist cave monasteries and temples along the Silk Road is on display.

In the **Museum für Ostasiatische Kunst** (East Asian Art) fine and applied arts from China, Korea, and Japan are exhibited in three individual country-specific galleries surrounding a central hall with Buddhist items common to all three cultures. The museum has an outstanding collection of calligraphy as well as Japanese woodcut prints.

With more than a half-million items, the **Museum für Völkerkunde** (Ethnology) has one of the largest collections of its kind in the world. The focus is on pre-industrial cultures, mainly outside Europe. Permanent displays are augmented by frequently changing temporary exhibitions. The museum also has a large collection of sound recordings and documentary photographs taken by European explorers at the end of the 19th century.

In contrast to the other museums in Dahlem, the nearby **Museum Europäischer Kulturen** (European Cultures), Im Winkel 6-8, focuses on Europe itself. The emphasis is on themes common to different cultures in Europe. Pictures play a major role in the exhibits, especially the way pictures moved away from religious and official institutions into common people's homes and everyday lives.

Other Museums

The **Zeughaus Historisches Museum** (German History), Unter den Linden 2, ☎ 030-20 30 40, www.dhm.de, will house a permanent exhibition on German history from the Middle Ages to the present. The museum is due to reopen in 2005 – several years behind schedule. It has a collection of over 700,000 items, including historic documents and photographs, military uniforms, paintings, posters, and pamphlets. Excellent temporary exhibitions on a wide range of topics are housed in the newly opened I.M. Pei-designed annex. Exhibitions here are open daily from 10 am to 6 pm and admission is generally around €2, but sometimes free. The Annex and small parts of the Zeughaus itself, including the vast museum shop, are already open to the public.

Parts of the new **Deutsches Technikmuseum Berlin** (Museum of Technical Cultural History), Trebbinger Straße 9, ☎ 030-90 25 40, www.dtmb.de, opened in 2003. (The complete museum will be finished during 2005.) Exhibition highlights include a submarine, a JU57 – the first German passenger plane, and a C47 used during the Berlin airlift in 1948. Opening hours are Tuesday to Friday from 9 am to 5:30 pm, Saturday and Sunday from 10 am to 6 pm. Admission is €3.

The **Filmmuseum Berlin**, Sony Center am Potsdamer Platz, Potsdamer Straße 2, ☎ 030-300-9030, www.filmmuseum-berlin.de, explains the history of the German film industry with a strong emphasis on the early days when Berlin could still challenge Hollywood. The permanent collection includes the estate of Marlene Dietrich – several dresses as well as her travel luggage (not up to modern aviation limits!) are on display. The exhibition offers a time journey through German film history and includes many short excerpts from famous films. *Das Kabinett des Dr Caligaris* is screened non-stop and part of Leni Riefenstahl's brilliant documentaries, used to great effect by the Nazi propaganda machine, are shown. Opening hours are Tuesday to Sunday from 10 am to 6 pm (Thursday until 10 pm). Admission is €6 and free English audio guides are available. The Museumpass is not valid here.

At the famous Checkpoint Charlie, is the very interesting and popular **Mauermuseum** (Wall Museum), Friedrichstr. 43-45, ☎ 030-253-7250. It focuses on the Berlin Wall and the role of Berlin in the Cold War but newer exhibitions concentrate on non-violent struggles for human rights throughout the world. The most popular exhibits are items including radios, cars, and wind surfers used during escape attempts from East Germany. The original sign, "You are leaving the American sector," is inside the museum – the one outside is a copy. Opening hours are very convenient: daily from 9 am to 10 pm. Admission is a rather high €9.50 and museum passes are not valid. The museum is interesting and very popular but, given the steep admission price, you may leave wondering if it was worth it. That feeling is enhanced if you have visited the excellent free Forum of Contemporary History in Leipzig.

Jüdisches Museum (Jewish), Lindenstraße 9, ☎ 030-2599-3300, www.jmberlin.de, is the largest of its kind in Europe and drew over a million visitors in its second year of existence. The zinc-plated building was designed by Daniel Libeskind. This is not primarily a Holocaust museum, but rather covers all aspects of Jewish history and culture in Germany. It is open daily from 10 am to 8 pm (until 10 pm on Mondays). Admission is €5 and expect airport-style security. A small kosher restaurant is on the premises.

■ Cultural Events

No German city has more cultural offerings than Berlin. The half-century of division left many parallel structures and, despite the city's dire finances, no politician dares touch cultural institutions for fear of being branded a philistine.

Berlin is the only city in the world with three large and well-reputed opera houses. A further 135 theaters offer entertainment ranging from high culture to stand-up comedy.

Musicals, revues, varieté, cabaret, comedy, opera, classical music, and theater are staged all over Berlin. The most famous high culture venues in the former West are the **Philharmonie** and **Kammermusiksaal**, Herbert von Karajanstraße 1, ☎ 030-2548-8132 – the home of the famous Berlin Philharmonic Orchestra, and the Deutsche Oper Berlin, Bismarckstraße 35, ☎ 030-343-8401. In the former East, in lovely restored historic venues are the **Konzerthaus Berlin**, Gendarmenmarkt 2, ☎ 030-20309-2101 – home of the Berlin Symphonic Orchestra, the **Staatsoper**, Unter den Linden 5, ☎ 030-2035-4555, and the **Komische Oper Berlin**, Behrenstraße 55, ☎ 030-4799-7400.

Tickets are reasonably priced, but a surcharge is often required for prior bookings. The Tourist Office can make reservations, often at no fee, either in person or at ☎ 030-250-025. Reservations can also be made at www.ticketonline.de.

Listings of events are available from the tourist office; free publications are available in most hotels, as well as dedicated city guides.

Brandenburg Summer Concerts

In 1990, shortly after the *Wende*, a group of West Berliners, long physically isolated from their provincial neighbors, started to organize concerts in historic Brandenburg venues. The Brandenburg Summer Concerts are held on Sundays from June to September and usually accompanied by a sightseeing program. Bus transfers are available from Berlin to the respective venues. For reservations, contact the Kartenbüro der Brandenburgischen Sommerkonzerte, Tempelhofer Weg 39-47, 10829 Berlin, ☎ 030-7895-7940, www.brandenburgische.sommerkonzerte.de.

Since 1951, Berlin has hosted the Berlinale, one of Europe's largest film festivals. However, seeing a movie in Germany in English is often a challenge as virtually all movies are dubbed into German. Berlin is, fortunately, one of the few German cities where English movies can be seen fairly regularly. Listings with OmU mean the movie has original sound with German subtitles and OF means original version. The best bet for English movies is **CineStar** in the Sony Center, Potsdamer Platz, ☎ 030-2606-6400, www.cinestar.de.

Virtually all theater and shows are in German only, but English stand-up comedy is scheduled every third Tuesday of the month in Kookaburra, Schönhauser Allée 184, ☎ 030-4862-3186, www.comedy-club.biz.

■ Shopping

Berlin has good shopping opportunities with the newly fashionable shops in the old East especially popular among the well-heeled. Some of the best shops are still in the former West.

West

The **Europa Center**, Tauentzienstraße 9, ☎ 030-2649-5851, www.24ec.de, used to be the glitziest shopping center in West Berlin, but has grown a bit stale of late. It has around 100 businesses, including many small boutiques and restaurants.

KaDeWe (Kaufhaus des Westens), Tauentzienstraße 21-24, ☎ 030-21-210, www.kadewe.de, is a large department store dating back to the early 1900s. It sells almost 400,000 items in the largest department store in continental Europe. It has the largest food department in Europe as well, selling 33,000 items, including 400 kinds of bread. Around 80,000 visitors per day ensure that it is always crowded.

Lined with restaurants and shops selling mainly clothes, books, and jewelry, **Kurfürstendamm**, www.kurfuerstendamm.de, is the most famous shopping street in West Berlin, but **Wilmersdorfer Straße** actually has a longer tradition and is the place where Berliners themselves are most likely to shop.

Mitte

For all its fame and beauty, **Unter den Linden** itself has surprisingly few shops. The largest shop here is **Automobile Forum**, ☎ 030-2092-1200, the massive showroom of the Volkswagen group, that includes not only VW, but also Skoda, Seat, Bugatti, and Bentley. Around the corner is

Audi Forum, Friederichstraße 83, ☎ 030-2063-5200.

The best shops are in the side-streets, especially in Friederichstraße, www.friederichstrasse.de, and the Gendarmenmarkt area. **Quartier 206**, Friederichstraße 71, ☎ 030-2094-6240, is a lovely three-block shopping center. It has high-class boutiques and equally stylish marble furnishing – worth seeing even if you're not shopping. It is connected through basement passages to **Galleries Lafayette**, Friedrichstraße 76, ☎ 030-209-480, which has some small bistros in the basement in addition to the more traditional department store on the upper floors.

Potsdamer Platz has many shopping opportunities, including the **Sony Style Store**, Potsdammer Straße 4, as well as **Arkaden**, ☎ 030-255-9270, a mall with more than 120 shops and restaurants.

The area around Hackesche Markt on the north bank of the Spree River is newly fashionable and a popular meeting place. In addition to the many restaurants and bars, the recently restored Art Nouveau **Hackescher Höfe** complex is particularly popular. The cheerful, green figure used in East Germany at traffic lights, the Ampelmännchen, has a cult following. The **Ampelmann Gallerie Shop**, Hackesche Höfe 5, Rosenthaler Straße 40, ☎ 030-4404-8809, www.ampelmann.de, sells souvenirs of all kinds adorned with this figure.

The **Nikolaiviertel**, near Museum Island, has many small shops selling mainly clothes and art. The area, the oldest in Berlin, has been beautifully restored and is a pleasant place to stroll in even when not on a shopping spree.

Antiques

Berlin has a surprising number of **antique shops** offering fair prices due to the concentration of competition in the same geographic areas. In Charlottenburg, some 30 shops are located in Suarezstraße (U-Bahn station Sophie-Charlotte-Platz). Many antique shops are in the side-streets around Nollendorfplatz. In Mitte, in the covered arches of the S-Bahn railway at Friederichstraße, 60 dealers take part in an antiques market, ☎ 030-208-2655. In contrast to most other shops, this market is also open on Sunday but closed on Tuesday.

Flea Markets

Flea markets (*Trödelmarkten*) are popular in Berlin and mostly held on weekends. The **Kunst und Nostalgiemarkt** (Art and Nostalgia Market) at the Kupfergraben near the Pergamon Museum has mostly arts and crafts. The **Trödelmarkt** at Straße des 17 Juni, near Tiergarten S-Bahn stop, sells anything from art to second-hand clothes. Both markets are open weekends from 11 am to 5 pm.

If the above two markets are too mainstream, try the one at **John F. Kennedy Platz** in Schöneberg. However, the funkiest market is deeper in the old east at **Boxhagener Platz**, near U-Bahn station Frankfurter Tor. Both markets are open Sundays from 9 am to 4 pm.

■ Adventures

On Foot

City Walks: Berlin Insider, ☎ 030-692-3149, www.insidertour.com, and **Berlin Walks**, ☎ 030-301-9194, www.berlinwalks.com, offer daily four-hour walks, with native English-speaking guides, to Berlin's most famous sights. Both operate similar schedules and routes. Reservations are not required. The tours start at Zoo Station at 10 am and 2:30 pm (from November to March, mornings only) for €12 per person. Insider meets in front of the McDonalds, or 20 minutes later at Hackescher Markt S-Bahn station in front of Coffee Mamas. Berlin Walks meets at the Taxi Stand at Zoo Station or 20 minutes later at the Irish Pub inside Hackescher Markt S-Bahn Station.

In addition, theme tours are offered during the summer such as tours related to the Third Reich and Nazis, the Soviet occupation and Cold War, as well as Jewish Berlin. Night walks and individual itineraries are also available. Berlin Walks has tours to Sachsenhausen Concentration Camp north of Berlin – see *Oranienburg* in the *Brandenburg* chapter for details.

Stattreisen Berlin, Malplaquetstraße 5, ☎ 030-455-3028, www.stattreisen.berlin.de, has a much wider range of walking tours on offer, often focusing on narrow areas or themes. The tours are in German only.

Jogging: Berlin is a comfortable city to jog in. It is flat and 30% of the city is park or woodland. Many streets are tree-lined. The huge Tiergarten in the center of the city has more than 20 km (12 miles) of paved routes and paths for jogging away from traffic. Dogs (Berlin famously has one for every three trees) are more likely to be a problem.

Rock Climbing: Rock climbing is currently in fashion in Germany. Although Berlin is devoid of mountains, there are rock-climbing centers. **T-Hall**, Thiemannstraße1, Neukölln, ☎ 030-6808-9864, www.t-hall.de, is the newest climbing center with 130 routes of varying difficulty. **Magic Mountain Climbing Center**, Böttgerstraße 20-26, S-Bahn Gesundbrunnen, claims to be Europe's largest rock climbing park with 200 routes.

On Wheels

By Bicycle: Berlin is a pleasant cycling city. It is relatively flat, roads and sidewalks are wide and often shady, and the number of cycling paths is increasing steadily. Although motorists may be less bicycle-friendly, cyclists usually have the law on their side. Bicycles may be taken on the S and U-Bahn as well as on trams, but they require an additional **Fahrradticket** (bicycle ticket).

Bicycle rentals start from as low as €5 depending on duration and model. Apart from the places listed below, also check with your hotel – some rent or even loan bicycles for free to hotel guests.

Fahrradstation, ☎ 0180-510-8000 or 030-2045-4500, has several rental shops scattered through Berlin. Generally the most convenient are in the Hackeschen Höfen, ☎ 030-2838-4848, and in Bahnhof Friedrichstraße, ☎ 030-2045-4500. The shops are open weekdays from 8 am to 8 pm, weekends from 10 am to 4 pm.

Berlin Insider, ☎ 030-692-3149, www.insidertour.com, conducts four-hour cycling tours of Berlin's most famous sights. From May to September, the tour starts at 10:30 am (July and August also at 3 pm) from Friedrichstraße Station's Fahrradverleih-shop. The tour price of €20 includes the bicycle rental fee. Reservations are recommended, as the group's size is restricted.

A pleasant do-it-yourself cycling tour is the 18-km (11-mile) **Mauerradweg** (Wall Cycling Route). It follows part of the route of the former Berlin Wall from U-Bahn station Bornholmer Straße to U-Bahn station Schlesisches tour. En route are remaining pieces of the wall at the Bernauer Straße memorial, Topographie des Terrors, and the East Side Gallery, as well as famous sights such as the Brandenburg Gate and Checkpoint Charlie. The route is in the process of being signposted and a free pamphlet with the route is available from the tourism office.

Velo taxis operate on four routes: Kurfürstendamm, Tiergarten, Unter den Linden, and Potsdamer Platz. Simply flag one down, or pre-book at ☎ 0172-328-8888, www.velotaxi.com. The fare is €2.50 per kilometer.

Inline Skating & Skateboarding: Inline skating is popular all over Germany and skaters may use bicycle routes. The large Tiergarten is popular, allowing for routes with views of famous buildings such as the Reichstag, Brandenburg Gate, Victory Column, and the new Government buildings.

A list of skateboard complexes with pipes and ramps is available from the Tourist Office.

By Bus: Several companies offer typical bus sightseeing tours of Berlin. Tickets can often be purchased on the bus, or from the tourist office or most hotels. Most depart from the vicinity of the Europa Center near Zoo Station. Prices and itineraries differ little.

City Circle Tour covers a circular route in two hours with 14 hop-on/hop-off points en route. Buses run every 15 or 30 minutes. Day tickets cost €18 and commentary is available in eight languages. Combinations with Spree River cruises are possible.

Berolina, ☎ 030-8856-8030, www.berolina-berlin.com, and **Severin & Kühn**, ☎ 030-880-4190, www.severin-kuehn-berlin.de, arrange bus trips of Berlin as well as nearby areas such as the Spreewald and Potsdam. Tours that include entrance to Schloss Sanssouci require prior reservations.

Trabi Safari: Trabi, the nickname of the Trabant, was the most "popular" car produced in East German – popular not due to demand, but because it was often the only one available. The smoking, polluting, two-stroke engine, plastic-bodied cars disappeared from the roads of East Germany as soon as people could get their hands on second-hand Golfs and Opels from the West.

However, **Trabi Safari**, ☎ 030-2759-2273, www.trabi-safari.de, has 15 available for rent for 45- and 90-minute "Trabi Safaris" through Berlin. An experienced driver shows the ropes – there is more to driving one than turning the key – and then the 15 proceed in convoy from Gendarmenmarkt through Berlin. Trips are scheduled daily from 10 am to midnight and cost €12 and up per person. (Dresden in Saxony can be polluted in a similar way.)

By Rail: On weekends, it is possible to take 80-minute tours of Berlin in a special **Panorama S-Bahn**, ☎ 030-2974-3333, www.s-bahn-berlin.de. The train has large glass windows, comfortable seats, and a bar service. It departs from Ostbahnhof Platform 9 at 11:06 am, 1:06, and 3:06 pm. Tickets are €14.50 and must be bought before boarding.

On Water

Berlin is a water-rich city with several lakes, canals, and the confluence of the Spree and Havel rivers inside the city borders. It has 200 km (120 miles) of waterways and almost a thousand bridges, more than any other European city including Amsterdam and Venice. In addition to regular pleasure cruises and commercial traffic, most of these waters are open to private watersports activities.

Pleasure Cruises: Several companies offer sightseeing cruises on the rivers and canals of Berlin. Although different tours and routes are offered, virtually all stop at the Schlossbrücke at Museum Island and/or Haus der Kulturen der Welt. Prices range from €5 upwards, but there is little price variation between companies for tours of equal length. Unless you have a specific itinerary in mind, simply board the first boat to depart. Most have night and dinner cruises as well.

The better-known companies include **Stern und Kreis Schiffahrt**, ☎ 030-536-3600, www.sternundkreis.de; **Reederei Bruno Winkler**, ☎ 030-349-9595, www.ReedereiWinkler.de, and **Reederei Riedel**, ☎ 030-691-3782, www.reederei-riedel.de.

BWTS Berliner Wassertaxi-Stadtrundfahrten, ☎ 030-6588-0203, has one-hour trips on original Amsterdam canal boats. Departure station: Zeughaus/Dom.

Sailing & Houseboats: Houseboats can be rented in Berlin for cruises in the city as well as through the water-rich surrounding areas. Private charter boats are allowed to moor up to 24 hours at 14 public areas of Berlin for free. For all of Berlin, and for some parts of Brandenburg State, a sports boat license is required for boats stronger than 5 HP – it is best to clear with the rental agents the acceptance of foreign licenses prior to reservations.

Several sailing schools are located on the lakes inside Berlin. Many rent out sailboats as well as motorboats by the hour or day. If required, most can arrange for a skipper and crew. The organizations listed below are all located in the west of Berlin, where 20 km of the Havel River and lakes can be sailed unhindered by bridges or sluices between Spandau and Potsdam. (Companies listed under *Potsdam* in the *Brandenburg* chapter are also convenient to this area.)

- **Marina Lanke-Berlin**, Scharfe Lanke 109-131, 13595 Berlin, ☎ 030-3620-0990, www.marina-lanke.de.
- **Segelschule Havel**, Am Pichelssee 9 B,13595 Berlin, ☎ 030-362-6020, www.segelschule-havel.de.
- **Segelschule Hering**, Bielefelder Straße 15, 10709 Berlin, ☎ 030-861-0701, www.segelschule-hering.de.
- **Yachtcharter Martin**, Nauheimer Straße 43, 14197 Berlin, ☎ 0171-544-6131, www.yachtcharter-martin.de.
- **Yachtsportschule Michael Weber**, Niebuhrstraße 41, 10629 Berlin, ☎ 030-324-0739, www.segelschule-weber.de.
- In Köpenick, in the southeast of Berlin, **Solar Water World**, Dreysestraße 3, 10559 Berlin, ☎ 0160-630-9997, www.solarwaterworld.de, operates under the logo "Loud is Out!" All boats here, including houseboats for up to eight, are either peddled or operating on solar energy. Most do not require special licenses.

On Snow

Although Berlin receives a fair amount of white stuff each winter, it is hardly the winter sports paradise of Germany. However, there is a large ski center in Pankow. **Der Gletscher, Ski Anlage**, Berliner Straße 21, Pankow, ☎ 030-479-9813, www.der-gletscher.de, is open daily from 10 am to 10 pm. Reservations are essential. S and U-Bahn stations Pankow.

In the Air

Air Service Berlin, ☎ 030-5321-5321, www.air-service-berlin.de, has several off-beat choices, including the only seaplane in Berlin, a single engine "Duck 01" that takes off from the Spree River and then circles the sights of Berlin. Flight duration is around 30 minutes and it costs €120. From Berlin-Schönefeld airport, 45-minute flights in a Rosinenbomber (DC3) that was used during the Berlin Airlift of 1948 cost around €130. Helicopter flights range from €50 to €120. A few small Zeppelin aircraft fly throughout Germany. When in Berlin, 45-minute flights cost around €300 and 70-minute flights €400.

From **Fehrbellin Airport**, the same company offers hot-air balloon flights costing about €190 per person. From March to October, Tuesday to Sunday, from 9 am to dark, tandem parachuting can be done for €180. Jumps are done from 4,000 m (12,800 feet), requiring no special clothing. Reservations two weeks in advance are recommended. Fehrbellin Airport is northwest of Berlin in Brandenburg, directly next to Autobahn A24, and are best reached by private transportation.

Berlin High Flyer, located in Ebertstraße close to Potsdamer Platz, is one of the world's largest helium balloons. Every 15 minutes, if the wind is fairly calm, it shoots 150 m (480 feet) up in the air, giving fantastic views of Berlin. No reservations are taken, but ☎ 030-2266-8811 for the wind report. In summer, the balloon is in operation from Sunday to Thursday, 10 am to 10 pm; in winter from Sunday to Thursday, 11 am to 6 pm, Friday and Saturday from 11 am to 7 pm. Each ride is €20.

■ Where to Stay

Berlin has no shortage of hotels and, with the exception of major events, hotel rooms are generally discounted throughout the year. Hotel prices are about half of what a similar room would cost in London and at least a third less than in Paris.

Following the unification of Berlin, new luxury hotels have sprung up in Mitte, with supply far outstripping demand most of the time. It is far harder to find a decent mid-price hotel in Mitte, while cheap basic accommodation with limited services and comfort levels can be found nearby in former East Berlin neighborhoods. For tourists it is often most feasible to stay in the old West Berlin areas around Zoologischer Garten Station and Charlottenburg, where hotel prices are lower, services better, and all the sights of Berlin are within easy reach. After a decade of neglect, many hotels in this area have refurbished in recent years.

Mitte & East Berlin

The **Adlon Kempinski**, right next to the Brandenburg Gate, is the best temporary address in Berlin. The original Adlon miraculously survived World War II, but burned to the ground soon after. Following the reunification of Germany, the Kempinski group bought the property and rebuilt the hotel in the original style. It reopened in 1996 to great acclaim. The famous, rich, and beautiful stay and eat here. Bedrooms are spacious and very luxurious; the more expensive ones have views of the Brandenburg Gate. Camera-toting sightseers are generally not welcome. Unter den Linden 77, 10117 Berlin, ☎ 030-226-10, fax 030-2261-2222, www.hotel-adlon.de. (€€€€)

The **Grand Hyatt** is a modern design in harmony with the ultra-modern buildings

HOTEL PRICE CHART	
Rates per room based on double occupancy, including taxes.	
€	Under €50
€€	€50-€100
€€€	€101-€150
€€€€	Over €150

Berlin

of Potsdamer Platz. Rooms are luxurious and stylish with a minimalist look. The swimming pool, on the top floor, has superb views. The hotel is popular with film stars, as befits its close location to the Berlin Film Museum. Marlene Dietrich Platz 2, 10785 Berlin, ☎ 030-2553-1234, fax 030-2553-1235, www.hyatt.com. (€€€€)

The **Westin Grand** is in the heart of Berlin at the corner of Unter den Linden and Friedrichstraße. The high glass roof impresses, as does the pleasant ambiance. Rooms are luxurious. The hotel is very popular with American visitors. Friedrichstraße 158, 10117 Berlin, ☎ 030-20-270, fax 030-2027-3362, www.westin.com. (€€€€)

The **Hilton** is beautifully located next to the Gendarmenmarkt with many rooms offering views of the square. Good deals are available during the off-season. Mohrenstraße 30, 10117 Berlin, ☎ 030-20-230, fax 030-2023-4269, www.hilton.com. (€€€-€€€€)

The **Maritim proArte** is a modern avant-garde designer hotel in the heart of central Berlin. It offers an interesting modern-look alternative to the more traditional luxury hotels in the area. Friedrichstr. 151, 10117 Berlin, ☎ 030-203 35, fax 030-2033-4209, www.maritim.de. (€€€/€€€€)

The **Madison** is a very comfortable apartment hotel at Potsdamer Platz. All rooms have kitchens and a shopping service is available. Not in the mood for cooking? On the fifth floor, the elegant **Restaurant Facil** (€€€€) has a Michelin star. Potsdamer Straße 3, 10785 Berlin, 030-590-051-234, fax 030-590-052-222, www.madison-berlin.de. (€€€-€€€€).

WOMEN ONLY

Conveniently located between the Brandenburg Gate and Potsdamer Platz is **Intermezzo**, a hotel for women and for boys under 12. Rooms are simply furnished, but prices are hard to match in this area. Gertrud-Kolmar-Straße 5, 10117 Berlin, ☎ 030-2248-9096, fax 030-2248-9097, www.hotelintermezzo.de. (€€, singles €).

Art'otel Berlin-Mitte, across the water at the south end of Museum Island, combines a modern wing with a historic patrician house. The interior is exclusively designed for the hotel. The café is on a barge on the Spree. Wallstr. 70-73, 10179 Berlin, ☎ 030-240-620, fax 030-2406-2222, www.artotel.de. (€€€/€€€€)

The **Mercure Hotel & Residenz am Checkpoint Charlie** combines modern architecture with a classical sandstone building. Rooms are large and well furnished; some have balconies. Checkpoint Charlie and the Mauermuseum are just two blocks down the road. Schutzenstr. 11, 10117 Berlin, ☎ 030-206-320, fax 030-2063-2111, www.mercure-checkpoint-charlie.de, €€€/€€€€.

Honigmond Garden Hotel, near Nordbahnhof, offers comfortable rooms at reasonable prices. The hotel has a large garden. Noise can be a problem in summer for rooms facing the street. Invalidenstraße 122, 10115 Berlin, ☎ 030-2844-5577, fax 030-2844-5588, www.honigmond-berlin.de. (€€€)

Hotel Honigmond, is a popular, small pension around the corner from the Garden Hotel. Not all rooms have private bathrooms. Tieckstraße 12, 10115 Berlin, ☎ 030-2844-550, fax 030-2844-5511, www.honigmond-berlin.de. (€€)

CHILDREN ONLY

Need a break from the kids? **Kinderisland** can take care of children under 14, from three hours to a week. Overnight stays, from 7 pm to 9 am, cost €59 per child. A 24-hour service is available. Children can be picked up by limousine with bodyguard anywhere in Berlin. Baby-sitting can also be arranged at your hotel or residence. Sightseeing tours for children and children's parties are also available. The staff is conversant in 12 languages. The institution is supported and monitored by the Berlin authorities. Two further children's hotels are planned for Frankfurt and Munich and should open in 2006/7. Eichendorfstraße 17, 10115 Berlin, ☎ 030-4171-6928, fax 030-4171-6948, www.kinderinsel.de. (€€)

The **Künstlerheim Luise**, close to the Reichstag, offers an interesting alternative to cookie-cutter chain hotels. Even in a city where designer and art hotels are in vogue, the Künstlerheim Luise is refreshingly different. Each room is designed by a different artist, resulting in décor that ranges from ultra-modern to rather kitschy. Rooms on the third floor are more basic, with shared toilet facilities. The hotel is next to a busy railway line, but noise is less of a problem in the new annex building. Luisenstraße 19, 10117 Berlin, ☎ 030-284-480, fax 030-2844-8448, www.kuenstlerheim-luise.de. (€€/€€€; €/€€ for more basic rooms).

Hotel Unter den Linden is the only tourist-class hotel on Berlin's most famous boulevard. Despite having been renovated since the Wall came down, it still offers some of the dubious charm of a Communist-era establishment. Staff has been described as indifferent and uninterested. Still, the hotel offers a brilliant location at a reasonably low price. Unter den Linden 14, 10117 Berlin, ☎ 030-238-110, fax 030-23811-100, info@hotel-unter-den-linden.de, www.hotel-unter-den-linden.de. (€€/€€€)

The **Intercity Hotel**, at the Ostbahnhof, offers comfortable, well-equipped rooms at reasonable prices. Rooms are not particularly large, but modern and furnished in an uncluttered, businesslike fashion. Am Ostbahnhof 5, 10243 Berlin, ☎ 030-293-680, fax 030-2936-8599, www.steigenberger.de. (€€-€€€)

Nearby, the **Ibis Ostbahnhof** offers excellent value for money. The hotel is modern, with clean, functional rooms and furniture. An der Schillingbrücke 2, 10243 Berlin, ☎ 030-257-600, fax 030-2576-0333, www.accor-hotels.com. (€-€€)

West

The **Grand Hotel Esplanade** is the top hotel in the former western part of Berlin. The privately run hotel was completely refurbished in 2000. The building is a thoroughly modern design and the hotel is filled with modern art. Lützowufer 15, 10785 Berlin, ☎ 030-254-780, fax 030-254-788-222, www.esplanade.de. (€€€€)

The **Palace Hotel** is a very luxurious hotel next to the Europa Center. Rooms are individually furnished, and many have views of the adjacent zoo or Kaiser Wilhelm Gedächtniskirche. The hotel was recently refurbished to the latest standards and is once again one of Berlin's top addresses. Budapester Straße 45, 10787 Berlin, ☎ 030-250-20, fax 030-2502-1119, www.palace.de. (€€€€)

The **Swissôtel** is a high-rise, postmodern design facing Berlin's most famous shopping boulevard. While many new luxury hotels opened in the former eastern parts of Berlin, this hotel completed in 2001 is one of very few new luxury hotels in the former West Berlin. The location is superb and the glass exterior impresses as much from the outside as from the inside. Augsburger Straße 44, 10789 Berlin, ☎ 030-220-100, fax 030-220-102-222, www.swissotel.com. (€€€€)

The **Kempinski Hotel Bristol** is a West Berlin institution that during the Cold War hosted most famous visitors ranging from President Kennedy to film stars. The original hotel was destroyed during the war but rebuilt in the 1950s. It was recently refurbished to the most modern standards. Kurfürstendamm 27, 10719 Berlin, ☎ 030-884-340, fax 030-883-6075, www.kempinski.com. (€€€€)

The **Inter-Continental** is a favorite with politicians and entertainers. The location is quiet, next to the Berlin Zoo and close to public transportation. The east wing is more modern, but all rooms are elegant and luxuriously furnished. Budapester Straße 2, 10787 Berlin, ☎ 030-260-20, fax 030-2602-2600, www.ichotelsgroup.com. (€€€/€€€€)

The **Brandenburger Hof** is a very pleasant, luxury hotel in a former 19th-century palace with a classicist façade. The luxurious bedrooms are furnished with Bauhaus-look furnishings. This privately run hotel is part of the Relais & Châteaux group. Eislebener Straße 14, 10789 Berlin, ☎ 030-214-050, fax 030-2140-5100, www.brandenburger-hof.de. (€€€-€€€€)

Slightly farther afield, the superb **Regent Schlosshotel** is between the Kurfürstendamm area and Potsdam. The hotel is in a former 1914 palace and much of the interior decorations have been designed by Karl Lagerfeld, a stickler for detail. The hotel has a lovely garden and top restaurants. The elegant **Vivaldi** (€€€€) is considered the most French of all restaurants in Germany. Although many guests are driven, the top sights of central Berlin are only minutes away by public transportation. Brahmsstr. 10, 14193 Berlin-Wilmersdorf, ☎ 030-895-840, fax 030-8958-4800, www.regenthotels.com. (€€€€)

Despite an anonymous exterior, the **Crowne Plaza Berlin City Center** has comfortable rooms and very friendly, competent staff. Rooms are modern and spacious with individual air conditioners, bar fridges, coffee makers, and irons. The breakfast buffet offers a wide selection in two large connected rooms. Non-smoking rooms are available. The location is conveniently close to Berlin Zoologischer Garten station, bus lines, and underground stations. Kadewe and the Kaiser Wilhelm Memorial Church are a block away. Nurnbergerstr. 65, 10787 Berlin, ☎ 030-210-070, fax 030-213-2009, www.cp-berlin.com (€€/€€€)

The **Best Western Hotel Boulevard** is a block from Zoologischer Garten station and has simple but comfortable rooms. The rooftop breakfast room has views of the Kaiser Wilhelm Gedächtniskirche. Kurfürstendamm 12, 10719 Berlin-Charlottenburg, ☎ 030-88 42 50, fax 030-88 42 54 50, www.hotel-boulevard.com. (€€/€€€)

In the **Hollywood Media Hotel**, the décor is very much Hollywood and films. Rooms are very comfortably furnished. Apartments are also available. The hotel has its own movie theater. Kurfürstendamm 202, 10789 Berlin, ☎ 030-889-100, fax 030-8891-0280, www.filmhotel.de. (€€€)

The **Ku'Damm 101** is a designer hotel with sleek, modern furnishings. Rooms have large windows and the seventh floor breakfast room offers grand views over Berlin. Kurfürstendamm 101, 10719 Berlin-Charlottenburg, ☎ 030-520-0550, fax 030-520-055-555, www.kudamm101.com. (€€-€€€)

The designer hotel **Art'otel Berlin City Center West** opened in 2002. It has a modern, bright interior with Andy Warhol artworks. The bedrooms use a white, light green, and purple color scheme, while red dominates the public spaces. Rooms are large and comfortably furnished. Lietzenburgerstr. 85, 10719 Berlin, ☎ 030-8877-770, fax 030-8877-7777, www.parkplazaww.com. (€€/€€€)

Nearby, at the end of Kurfürstendamm, is the popular **Holiday Inn Garden Court**. The hotel is somewhat sterile, but well-appointed and highly regarded in this price class. Reservations well in advance are recommended. Bleibtreustr. 25, 10707 Berlin, ☎ 030-880-930, fax 030-8809-3939, www.holiday-inn.com. (€€)

Camping

There are several camping grounds in the outskirts of Berlin. However, most are inconvenient for public transporation. Facilities are generally good, but nothing exciting.

Camping Gatow is southwest of the city. It has 80 spaces for tourists and 80 for long-term campers. Open year-round. Kladower Damm 213-217, 14089 Berlin-Gatow, ☎ 030-365-4340, fax 030-3680-8492.

The **Else-Eckert-Platz** is 25 km (15 miles) from downtown Berlin and not far from Potsdam. It has only 140 spaces for tourists, but 660 for long-term rentals. Open year-round. Krampnitzer Weg 111, 14089 Berlin-Kladow, ☎ 030-365-2797, fax 030-365-1245.

DCC Camping am Krossinsee is 30 km (18 miles) southeast of Berlin in a wooded area next to a lake. It has 288 spaces for tourists and around 200 for long-term campers. Open year-round. Wernsdorfer Straße 38, 12527 Berlin-Schmöckwitz, ☎ 030-675-8687, fax 030-675-9150, www.dccberlin.de.

■ Where to Eat

Berlin has some 6,000 restaurants and bars catering to all tastes and price classes. Unfortunately, with the exception of the pricier establishments, Berlin restaurants have a well earned reputation for indifferent and generally mediocre service. Service has improved in recent years, but it is still best to have low expectations.

Ich bin ein Berliner

When US President John F Kennedy proclaimed in 1963 "Ich bin ein Berliner," he effectively said "I am a jelly donut." The inclusion of the article "ein" (a) changed the noun from a citizen of Berlin to its most famous baked item. Ironically, while most of Germany calls it a Berliner, in Berlin it is simply a donut. In some parts of Germany, jam donuts also masquerade under the name *Kreppel* and *Krapfen*.

DINING PRICE CHART

Price per person for an entrée, including water, beer or soft drink.	
€	Under €10
€€	€10-€20
€€€	€21-€35
€€€€	Over €35

Local specialties are often hard to find – many, including locals, do not consider that a particularly bad thing either. Well-known Berlin dishes include knuckle of pork, fried herring, pickles, pea soup, and fried liver with apple rings. A favored local drink is the *Berliner Weiße* – a dry, wheat beer fermented in the bottle. It is commonly served *mit Schuss* – a shot of sweet raspberry or woodruff syrup.

In recent years Starbucks has invaded, but the local competition, often lower key, and offering much better quality coffee, is also plentiful. Kaffee Einstein, with several branches in Berlin, has excellent coffee. There are several McDonalds, Pizza Huts, and Burger King franchises in Berlin and the numerous bakeries and delicatessens also offer tasty food at reasonable prices. Döner Kebab is available, especially in the vicinity of stations and nightlife areas. It consists of grilled meat combined with salad and dressing in a lightly toasted bread pocket.

CURRYWURST

Currywurst is a Berlin specialty. It came into being after World War II and is basically a sausage served with a curry sauce. The sausage is usually cut into bite-size pieces so it can be eaten with a small plastic fork. Extra curry powder is often available to make it more spicy. It was long the preferred working-class snack and many dedicated stalls are still available in Berlin and in much of Germany. However, in recent years, currywurst has lost some popularity in favor of Döner Kebab. (Heartburn is *Sodbrennen* in German and medication is only available from pharmacies.)

As in many other German cities, most of the top restaurants are located in the best hotels. In contrast to most German cities, Berlin has no official closing time and each establishment can set its own hours.

Mitte

Unter den Linden

Unter den Linden, Berlin's grandest boulevard, runs from the Brandenburg Gate to Museum Island and en route offers both top-end and basic restaurants. For a full view of the Brandenburg Gate, the Pariser Platz **Starbuck's**, across the road from the famed Adlon Hotel, is impossible to beat and will be easier on the wallet than anything else in the direct vicinity.

The **Lorenz Adlon**, Unter den Linden 77, ☎ 030-2261-1960, in the majestic Adlon Hotel, is arguably the best restaurant in Berlin. This small, elegant restaurant is on the second floor and has views of the Brandenburg Gate. The predominantly French food is served on Wedgewood porcelain accompanied by Christoffle silver. The wine list is extensive and service first-class. The restaurant is open for dinner only and closed on Sunday and Monday. Reservations are advisable. (€€€€)

The **Quarré**, Unter den Linden 77, ☎ 030-2261-1555, is an elegant, luxury restaurant with a terrace on the ground floor of the Adlon Hotel. Food is international and features the new light German cuisine. It is more accessible than the Lorenz, but with similar views and an equally extensive wine list. (€€-€€€€)

Also on Pariser Platz, next to the French Embassy, is **Margaux**, Unter den Linden 78, ☎ 030-2265-2611, www.margaux-berlin.de. (Entrance from Wilhelmstraße.) This elegant, modern restaurant serves French cuisine ranging from classic dishes to the avant-garde. The extensive wine list betters that of the Adlon and apparently includes bottles over €10,000. (€€€€)

Café Einstein, Unter den Linden 42, ☎ 030-204-3632, is a branch of the famous similarly named Viennese-style coffee shop in West Berlin. Although the food is good, it is really the coffee and cakes that make for a great mid-morning or late-afternoon break. (€-€€)

Inside a building used by the German parliament is **Lindenlife**, Unter den Linden 44, ☎ 030-206-290-333, www.lindenlife.de. The cuisine is light, new German and a large variety of wine from the Rhineland Palatinate is available. It is popular with politicians and the media. A good choice for a quick, but upscale lunch. (€€)

Brasserie No 12, Unter den Linden 12, ☎ 030-2061-9999, is a little brasserie serving small meals in addition to drinks at very low prices. Most of the food seems pre-cooked but the location is grand and the prices minimal. (€)

The best choice for food in the immediate vicinity of the Museum Island is the **Kaiserstuben**, Am Festungsgraben 1, ☎ 030-2061-0548. The modern restaurant serves nouvelle cuisine. With only 16 seats, reservations are usually required. (€€€€)

Adjacent is the equally elegant **Die Möwe**, Am Festungsgraben 1, ☎ 030-2061-0540, www.restaurant-moewe.de. It serves nouvelle cuisine and classic dishes. Live music on Monday nights. (€€-€€€)

A generally more affordable, but still pleasant, alternative is the **Operncafé im Opernpalais**, Unter den Linden 5, ☎ 030-202-683. It is on the side of the Opera house in a former palace of the crown princess and has one of the largest cake selections in Berlin. The terrace is popular in summer, the interior spacious and elegant at all times. The Sunday brunch (€€€) is accompanied by live jazz. (€-€€)

Farther down Karl Liebknecht Straße toward Alexanderplatz, the heart of the former East Berlin, is the **Fernsehturm**, the highest structure in Berlin. The revolving **Telecafé**, Panoramastraße 1, ☎ 030-242-3333, is on the viewing platform of the television tower. Food is only average and overpriced, but the continuously changing views are the best in town. (€-€€)

Zur Letzer Instanz, Waisenstraße 14-16, ☎ 030-242-5528, serves Berlin and Brandenburg specialties. It claims to be the oldest guesthouse in Berlin and therefore draws many tourists, although the chancellor also uses it occasionally to entertain foreign dignitaries with traditional food. (€€)

Gendarmenmarkt Area

Refugium, Gendarmenmarkt 5, ☎ 030-229-1661, www.refugium-bln.de, is the only restaurant on the Gendarmenmarkt itself. Although in the vaulted cellars of the French Cathedral, the cuisine is light German. The outdoor seating is particular popular. (€€-€€€)

Brasserie am Gendarmenrmarkt, Taubenstraße 30, ☎ 030-2045-3501, www.brasserieamgendarmenmarkt.de, is a popular brasserie across the road from the Concert Hall. *Flammkuchen*, a specialty from Alsace, are popular, as is the frequently varying lunch menu. Outdoor seats give an excellent view of the Gendarmenmarkt. (€€-€€€)

The **Hilton Hotel**, Mohrenstraße 30, has several dining options. **Fellini**, ☎ 030-202-30, is an elegant Italian restaurant with an extensive wine list. (€€-€€€)

Trader Vic's, ☎ 030-2023-4605, also at the Hilton, serves Polynesian, Asian, and French cuisine. (€€-€€€)

Lutter und Wegner, Charlottenstraße 56, ☎ 030-2029-5410, www.lutter-wegner-gendarmenmarkt.de, serves excellent German and Austrian cuisine. The wine list is about a thousand labels strong. According to legend, *Sekt*, the German term for sparkling wine, was coined here. (€€€-€€€€)

The elegant French department store **Galleries Lafayette**, Französische Straße 23, ☎ 030-209-480, has several small bistros in its basement. Most serve French food but an international selection is also available. (€-€€)

In the adjacent, even more luxurious mall, the **Café and Bistro Quartier 206**, Friederichstraße 71, ☎ 030-202-9540, serves small meals in the basement as well as at a few tables on the ground floor. Meals are simple but tasty. The stylish black leather seats and elegant surroundings belie the pleasantly low prices. (€-€€)

Potsdamer Platz

Facil, Potsdamer Straße 3, ☎ 030-590-051-234, www.facil-berlin.de, on the fifth floor of the Madison Hotel, is an elegant, modern restaurant serving Mediterranean cuisine. Light floods in from the large windows and glass roof. Reservations are recommended. (€€€€)

In the Grand Hyatt is the equally upmarket **VOX**, Marlene Dietrich Platz 2, ☎ 030-2553-1772. It has an open show kitchen serving international cuisine with strong Mediterranean influences. It also has a sushi bar. (€€€-€€€€)

The Sony Center has several restaurants, but always popular is the **Lindenbräu**, Bellevuestraße 3, ☎ 030-2575-1280. This beer garden serves Bavarian brew and food. (€€)

Diekman im Weinhaus Huth, Alte Potsdamer Straße 5, ☎ 030-2529-7529, is located in the only pre-World War II building on Potsdamer Platz. This elegant restaurant serves French and nouvelle cuisine. (€€-€€€)

Tony Romas, Marlene Dietrich Platz 2, ☎ 030-2529-5830, specializes in spare ribs and other American steak house specialties. It is popular with both tourists and locals. (€€-€€€)

Hackescher Markt

Hackesher Markt is the new "in" area in Berlin Mitte. It has numerous restaurants, bars, and clubs.

Fridas Schwester, Neue Schönhauser Straße 11, ☎ 030-2838-4710, is a non-typical Tex-Mex restaurant with elements from many Latin-American countries and other parts of the world. It is popular with the in-crowd. (€€-€€€)

Hackescher Hof, Rosenthaler Straße 40, ☎ 030-283-5293, is a popular coffee shop in this recently restored complex. Only small meals are served. (€€-€€€)

Sponsored by the state of Bavaria, **Weihenstephaner**, Neue Promenade 5, ☎ 030-2576-2871, serves Bavarian specialties in a historic, vaulted cellar. (€-€€)

Mojito, Monbijoupark, S-Bahnbögen 157, ☎ 030-2838-6706, is a Mexican restaurant without kitsch décor and serves traditional Mexican rather than Tex-Mex food. The open-air seating area has views of the Museum Island. (€€-€€€)

Farther Afield

Paris-Moskau, Alt-Moabit 141, ☎ 030-394-2081, www.paris-moskau.de, is a simple restaurant but with excellent food. It serves mainly nouvelle cuisine and classical dishes. It is located in a half-timbered house – seldom seen in Berlin – near the residence of the chancellor. The atmosphere is generally relaxed despite the high prices. Open for dinner only and reservations are recommended. (€€-€€€€)

Honigmond, Borsigstraße 28, ☎ 030-2844-5512, serves hearty German and French cuisine. It was a popular meeting place of the opposition during the Communist era and thus forced to close in 1987. It reopened during the 1990s. Particularly popular are the lunch buffet and Sunday brunch (€-€€).

West

Top-End Restaurants

The elegant, luxurious restaurant **First Floor**, Hotel Palace, Budapester Straße 45, ☎ 030-2502-1020, serves mainly French food. Despite the somewhat uninspired name, this is one of the highest-rated restaurants in Berlin, with a wine list to match. (€€€€)

Hugos, Budapester Straße 2, ☎ 030-2602-1263, is a first-class restaurant on the 13th floor of the Hotel Intercontinental offering splendid views of the city. The restaurant is modern and elegant, serving nouvelle cuisine with French flair. It has an excellent wine list. Reservations recommended. (€€€€)

The Grill in the Kempinski Hotel Bristol, Kurfürstendamm 27, ☎ 030-884-340, serves international cuisine with large selections of German and French food. The restaurant is elegant and luxurious as befits the famous location. (€€€€)

The Prussian-style **Die Quadriga**, Eislebeener Straße 14, ☎ 030-2140-5650, is an elegant and luxurious restaurant in the Hotel Brandenburger Hof. The restaurant has Frank Lloyd Wright-designed furniture and uses porcelain from the Königlichen Manufaktur Berlin. The cuisine is mainly French. *Gault Millau* praised the wine list as one of the best in Germany. The restaurant is only open on weekday nights and reservations are recommended. (€€€€)

Kurfürstendamm

Kurfürstendamm is lined with shops and eateries. The better restaurants are just off the main drag and often inside luxury hotels. For people-watching the cafés and outdoor restaurants on the main street itself are hard to beat.

There are several dining options in the Europa Center – like the center itself, several seem past their prime. **Daitokai**, Tauentzienstraße 9 -12, ☎ 030-261-8090, www.daitokai.de, is clearly one of the exceptions. It is a first-class Japanese restaurant, specializing in Teppan-yaki prepared at the table, but sushi is of course also available. Servers wear kimonos. (€€€-€€€€)

Also in the Europa Center, but several notches lower on the price scale is the **Mövenpick**, ☎ 030-264-7630, part of the Swiss gastronomic group. It has mainly Swiss specialties but also a large selection of steaks and a good fresh salad bar. (€-€€)

A few blocks down the road, belonging to the same Swiss group, is **Marché**, Kurfürstendamm 14, ☎ 030-8827-5789. Food is served canteen-style but is much better than the décor suggests. Cuisine is international with a strong Swiss and Central European influence. (€-€€)

Leysieffer, Kurfürstendamm 218, ☎ 030-885-7480, is in the first instance a cake and chocolate shop, but it has a few tables and chairs in a small dining area across the narrow alley. In summer, it has more outdoor seating. The cakes served are excellent and a small bistro-style menu is available. (€-€€)

Although there are some Starbucks branches in Berlin, Germans generally prefer their coffee strong and similar local competition is all over the Ku-Damm. The best is **Kaffee Einstein** with branches at Kurfürstendamm 50, Savigny Platz, and inside the Peek and Cloppenburg store in Tauentzienstraße 19.

In the passage behind Kranzler is a branch of **Tony Romas**, Kurfürstendamm 22, ☎ 030-88877-3648. It is very much like back home, with English-speaking servers and English menus available on request. It's a good alternative if you feel like a burger but Berlin's plethora of McDonalds and Burger King franchises simply won't do. There is also a Tony Romas at Potsdamer Platz. (€€)

The **Kadewe** department store, Tauentzienstraße 21-24, ☎ 030-21-210, www.kadewe.de, is a gourmet's delight. It has the largest gourmet food selection in Europe and many small, bar-style bistros serving delicacies from all over the world. The cafeteria-style restaurant on the top floor serves excellent food and other traditional, but pricier options are also available inside the shop. (€-€€€)

Savigny Platz

The streets around Savigny Platz have long been popular for their restaurants and bars.

Jules Verne, Schlüterstraße 61, ☎ 030-3180-9410, is a pleasant restaurant two blocks from Savigny Platz. The décor is limited and the furniture simple but the food is great. The menu changes weekly and a wide range of international fare is offered. Portions are big, the food tasty, prices moderate to low, and the service is friendly. Recommended by many guidebooks, it is no longer a well-kept secret, making reservations for dinner advisable. (€€-€€€)

Epoque, Knesebeckstraße 76, ☎ 030-8867-7388, is a small French restaurant near Savigny Platz. In summer, the terrace is particularly pleasant. (€€-€€€)

To the north of Savigny Platz is **Brunello**, Knesebeckstraße 18, ☎ 030-312-9381, a small Italian restaurant with a large menu and friendly personnel. Italian dining here is on a higher level than the multitude of Italian restaurants and pizzerias that litter much of Berlin. (€€-€€€)

Next to Savigny Platz S-Bahn station, **Zwölf Apostel**, Bleibtreustraße 49, ☎ 030-312-1433, serves some of the best pizzas in Berlin. It is justifiably popular, making reservations for dinner advisable. Prices are low, with business lunches starting from €5. Outside are mainly long tables with benches, making table sharing for pairs and smaller groups common. (€-€€)

Brandenburg

In this Chapter

Brandenburg is geographically the largest of the former East German states that joined the Federal Republic of Germany in 1990 after the *Wende*. As mentioned earlier, the *Wende*, or change, refers to the major political shift that East Germany made when it joined democratic, capitalist West Germany.

It is mainly a rural state and agriculture still plays a major role in the local economy and employment. Berlin is an island in the center of Brandenburg and often blamed for sucking the life out of the state. The best talent and especially the younger people tend to move to the city. Similarly, most tourists stay in Berlin and only visit a few sites in Brandenburg on daytrips.

Apart from Potsdam, most parts of Brandenburg are firmly off the beaten track for both international and domestic tourists. As a result, many parts of the state still suffer from a lack of suitable tourist infrastructure and accommodations.

Brandenburg is mostly flat, but rich with forests. It has more water than any other German state with 33,000 km of rivers and 3,087 lakes of various sizes. Watersports opportunities are plentiful with around 6,500 km of waterways open to paddlers and a fourth of that can be traveled by motor and houseboats. On land, Brandenburg has 2,400 km (1,400 miles) of designated cycling routes and an equal distance available on marked pathways for countryside rambling.

The main sights in Brandenburg are in Potsdam, the state capital. The favored residences of the Prussian prince electors and later kings were here and these are the main destinations for tourists. Most tourists are day-trippers, as Potsdam can be reached in 20 minutes by train from the center of Berlin.

Other sights within easy reach from Berlin include the former Nazi Concentration Camp Sachsenhausen in Oranienburg to the north, and the water labyrinth of the Spreewald to the south. Rheinsberg, in the north of the state, is another lake-rich area and closer in character to the neighboring state of Mecklenburg-Vorpommern.

History

Modern-day Brandenburg encompasses most of the historic Mark (Margrave) of Brandenburg that has been part of the Holy Roman Empire of German States since the 10th century. From 1415 until the abolition of the monarchy in 1918, the area was ruled by the Hohenzollern family. The Duchy of Prussia, now part of Poland, was added to the Hohenzollern domains in the early 17th century and the total area ruled by the Hohenzollerns converted into the Kingdom of Prussia in 1701.

A series of excellent, though not necessarily popular, rulers saw a largely destroyed and depopulated Prussia rising from obscurity at the end of the Thirty Years' War (1618-48) to become the fifth major power in Europe at the end of the Seven Years' War (1756-63). A century later Prussia was the undisputed leader in Germany and succeeded in uniting the German states into the Prussian-dominated German Empire (1871-1918). During the post-1945 Communist regime, all things Prussian were officially out of favor, but democratic Germany has fewer hangups about honoring the achievements of the Hohenzollern rulers.

For more on the history of Brandenburg see the Berlin chapter.

Getting Around

Most parts of Brandenburg are easily reached from Berlin by either rail or road.

By Rail: Most long-distance railways in Brandenburg lead to Berlin, making changeovers there necessary when traveling cross-state or arriving on long-distance journeys. Do note that some long-distance trains terminate in Berlin Ost station and others in Berlin Zoologischer Garten, or even lesser stations, requiring connections via local trains or the S-Bahn. This situation should improve once the new Berlin-Hauptbahnhof opens sometime in or after 2006.

By Road: A vast network of highways allows for short traveling times to most parts of the state. Local roads are in good condition but much slower. Most highways through Brandenburg lead to Berlin, which is encircled by Autobahn A10.

By Air: See the Berlin chapter for arrivals by air and train from other parts of Germany.

On Water: The vast waterway network in Brandenburg allows for boat trips to many scenic parts of the state. Regular boat trips are scheduled on many lakes and rivers. Charter boats, with or without a special crew, are also available and, in contrast to Berlin, usually do not require a license.

■ Information Sources

Reiseland Brandenburg, Am Neuen Markt 1, 14467 Potsdam, ☎ 0331-200-4747, www.reiseland-brandenburg.de, is responsible for tourism promotion of the whole state. It has a vast collection of information and can make reservations for accommodations, events, and package deals. Many local tourist offices also offer such services in addition to information.

Brandenburg Summer Concerts

In 1990, shortly after the *Wende*, a group of West Berliners, long physically isolated from their provincial neighbors, started to organize concerts in historic Brandenburg venues. The Brandenburg Summer Concerts are held on Sundays from June to September and are usually accompanied by a (not compulsory) sightseeing and dining program. Bus transfers are available from Berlin to the respective venues. For reservations, contact the **Kartenbüro der Brandenburgischen Sommerkonzcrte**, Tempelhofer Weg 39-47, 10829 Berlin, ☎ 030-7895-7940, www.brandenburgische-sommerkonzerte.de.

■ Potsdam

The most important tourist attractions are in Potsdam, capital of the state of Brandenburg. Potsdam's fortune, and misfortune, is its location less than 20 minutes by train from central Berlin. As a result, many visitors come but most are only on a day-trip to see the major sights. If it were located anywhere else, visitors would spend the night.

Internationally, Potsdam is best known for the Potsdam Conference, held here at the end of World War II to decide the fate of a defeated Germany. However, in Germany the conference is better known as the Prussian Versailles. The town has been the favored royal residence of the Hohenzollern family since the 17th century and 17 of their palaces survived. Although the town suffered war damage, and some areas were sadly neglected during the Communist years, it has many sights worth seeing.

DAY-TRIP TIP

If visiting Potsdam on a day-trip, restrict yourself to Park Sanssouci. A full day is not enough to see all the sights here, so give preference to ***Schloss Sanssouci****, the* ***Orangerie****, and* ***Neues Palais****. During the high season, tickets for Schloss Sanssouci sell out in minutes. Seriously consider reserving in advance by joining the Information Office's guided tour.*

Information Sources

Tourist Office: The tourist information office is at Alten Markt, Friedrich-Ebert-Straße 5, 14467 Potsdam, ☎ 0331-275-580, www.potsdam-tourismus.de. It is open weekdays from 10 am to 6 pm, weekends from 10 am to 4 pm (closing 2 pm on weekends from November to March). The information office can make hotel reservations and arrange city tours.

Transportation

Potsdam can be reached from Berlin Zoologischer Garten station in 15 minutes on the twice-hourly Regional Express or less frequent InterCity trains. S-Bahn S1 runs from central Berlin to Potsdam in 40 minutes. Potsdam is part of the larger Berlin public transportation network –

day tickets for Zone C are required and are valid on the S-Bahn, but *not* on the other trains.

In Potsdam, Bus 695 runs from the Hauptbahnhof to Park Sanssouci and stops behind Schloss Sanssouci, Orangerie, and Neues Palais, among others. Bus 694 is convenient to Park Babelsberg and Bus 692 runs along the western edges of Neuer Garten. It is a fair walk from the station to the parks so using public transportation is sensible, as a lot of leg work will be required inside the parks themselves.

Sightseeing

Sanssouci Park & Palaces

The main sights in Potsdam are concentrated in Park Sanssouci – a huge 740-acre park originally laid out by Frederick the Great, with several palaces and other buildings of note. Most of the park and palaces are UNESCO World Cultural Heritage sites.

VISITOR'S INFORMATION

The park itself is open during daylight hours and admission is free. Picnicking is not allowed on the lawns but there are many benches. Food and drink is not generally available inside the park, but there are vendors close to the main parking areas on its edges – it is best to bring a picnic lunch with you from the station. The park is most easily reached by Bus 695 from the main station. Parking lots are behind the Orangerie and Neues Palais.

The individual prices at the various sights quickly add up, making one of the bewildering arrays of combination tickets worthwhile. A **Premium Day Ticket**, only available from the Sanssouci Palace ticket counter, for €15, allows access on *two* consecutive days to all the buildings in Sanssouci Park, as well as all others managed by the Prussian Palace and Gardens Foundation Berlin-Brandenburg. These include virtually all sights in Potsdam as well as Charlottenburg Palace in Berlin, and Oranienburg and Rheinsberg Palaces elsewhere in Brandenburg State. A €12 **Day Ticket**, available from all ticket offices, gives the same privileges but excludes visiting Sanssouci Palace.

All the palaces are managed by Stiftung Preußische Schlösser und Gärten Berlin-Brandenburg, Besucherzentrum, Postfach 60 14 62, 14414 Potsdam, ☎ 0331-969-4202, www.spsg.de.

The guided tour by the Potsdam Information Office is the only English-language tour allowed in Sanssouci and the only way to guarantee entry into the palace.

The most import construction in the park is the small, but magnificent, Rococo summer residence erected by Frederick the Great in 1747. He called it **Schloss Sanssouci** – French, which was his preferred language, for "without a care." Here, Frederick hoped to leave the problems of state behind and pursue his own personal interests, especially in music and philosophy. Although the business of state soon followed him here, he increasingly preferred Potsdam to Berlin. He spent time here entertaining enlightened thinkers such as Voltaire and he lured musicians, including Johann Sebastian Bach's son Carl Emmanuel, to his court. During Frederick's time only men stayed at the court during summer; a Ladies' Wing was added about a century later.

Schloss Sanssouci, ☎ 0331-969-4190, is open all year Tuesday to Sunday, 9 am to 5 pm, but closes at 4 pm from November to March. Visitors are restricted to 2,000 per day and the palace can only be seen on a guided tour in German. (For the only English-language option, see *Town Walks* below). Reservations must be made in person on the given day. Admission is €8. The Ladies Wing as well as the Palace Kitchen can be seen solely on weekends from mid-May to mid-October, 10 am to 5 pm. Frankly, neither is worth the time or minimal €1 charge each.

Strolling through the park or visiting the nearby **Bildergalerie** (Picture Gallery), ☎ 0331-969-4181, is a better way to spend time while waiting for a tour. It was also built by Frederick the Great, as the first museum building in Germany. The collection consists mainly of Baroque paintings of the Dutch, French and Italian schools and includes works by Rubens, Van Dyck, and Caravaggio. The gallery is open mid-May to mid-October from Tuesday to Sunday, 10 am to 5 pm. Admission is €2.

The **Orangerie**, ☎ 0331-969-4280, same opening hours as the Picture Gallery, was built in 1851-64. It is best approached from the center of the park. The walk is long, with numerous steep stairs, but the views are rewarding. In the park, at the edges of the palace grounds, is an equestrian statue of Frederick the Great – it is a copy of the one on Unter den Linden in Berlin. During the Communist regime, Frederick and all things Prussian were out of fashion and the original Berlin statue was banished to this park. The palace requires another short guided tour (€3) that includes the Raphael Rooms – unfortunately only copies. The tower has an observation platform with magnificent views of Potsdam and is visited without a tour, €1 per person.

Nearby is the **Historic Windmill**, originally erected 1787-1791, but burned down in 1945. It was rebuilt in 1993 to house a museum on milling, a lookout tower, and the Sanssouci Visitors' Center. According to legend, the mill's noise irritated Frederick the Great and he had it shut down until a court overruled him.

Strolling from Schloss Sanssouci to the **Neues Palais** (New Palace), ☎ 0331-969-4255, requires about half an hour. The municipal bus running along the northern edge of the park provides a viable alternative. The Baroque Neues Palais, built 1763-1769, was Frederick the Great's most opulent palace and is considered one of the most beautiful in all of Germany. It

has 400 rooms behind a façade over 200 m (656 feet) long. It was built at the end of the costly Silesian War, at great expense to Prussian taxpayers, to prove that the war had not bankrupted Prussia. (The war, combined with the palace, nearly did, however.) The palace is open all year, Saturday to Thursday, 9 am to 5 pm, but closing at 4 pm from November to March. Admission is €5. During the summer period, the €1 German guided tour is optional and an English audio guide is available. The Royal Chambers (*Königswohnung*) of Frederick the Great can only be seen during the summer season for an additional €5 on a compulsory guided tour (in German only).

In the south of the park are three more royal sights – all three are open mid-May to mid-October, from Tuesday to Sunday, 10 am to 5 pm. Arguably the most interesting is the richly gilded **Chinesisches Haus** (Chinese Teahouse), ☎ 0331-969-4222, shown below. It was built by Frederick the Great as a summer dining room and is a good example of European *chinoiserie* during the late 18th century. Admission is €1. Although the Romans never made it this far, faux **Roman Baths**, ☎ 0331-969-2224, were constructed between 1829 and 1840. This

complex consists of the Roman baths, the residence of the court gardener, a tea pavilion, and an Arcade hall with rotating exhibitions. Admission is €2 or €3 during exhibitions. **Schloss Charlottenhof**, ☎ 0331-969-4228, was built between 1826 and 1829 as a residence for Crown Prince Friedrich Wilhelm. The interiors are original and the garden is famous for its roses. Admission is €4, which includes the obligatory tour in German.

Other Royal Sights in Potsdam

Just north of the old town is the **Neues Garten** (New Garden), the first English landscape garden in Prussia, which houses the last palace constructed by the Hohenzollern family. **Schloss Cecilienhof**, ☎ 0331-969-4244, was built during the First World War for the last German Crown Prince Wilhelm and his wife Cecilie. However, the palace, in the style of an English country house, is most famous as the site of the historic Potsdam conference where Harry Truman, Winston Churchill (soon to be replaced by Clement Atlee), and Josef Stalin decided the fate of Germany at the end of World War II. The three leaders only met here; they stayed in three separate villas along the nearby Lake Griebnitz. Opening hours are Tuesday to Sunday from 9 am to 5 pm, but closing at 4 pm from November to March. Admission in summer is €4 without a guided tour and €1 additional for the German-only tour. In the winter season, admission is €4 and includes a compulsory tour. A small luxury hotel operates in part of the palace.

Also in the park is the small square **Marmorpalais** (Marble Palace), ☎ 0331-969-4246. Friedrich Wilhelm II commissioned this summer residence in 1787, as he considered himself unworthy to stay in Frederick the Great's Schloss Sanssouci. The richly decorated early classical interior was only completed in 1845, almost half a century after his death. A large Wedgwood collection is on display. Opening hours are similar to Schloss Cecilienhof and admission is €3 in summer with tour, €2 without a tour, and €2 in winter with free compulsory German tour.

Park Babelsberg is another large English-style landscaped park with royal residences. **Schloss Babelsberg**, ☎ 0331-969-4250, was built as a summer residence for Crown Prince Wilhelm, later King of Prussia and Emperor of Germany. His favored residence, used for more than 50 years, it is built in the style of an English castle and country house. The interior is Neo-Gothic, as was favored during the mid-19th century in Germany. The palace is open from April to October, Tuesday to Sunday, 10 am to 5 pm. Admission is €2.

Also in the park is the mid-19th-century **Flatow Tower**, ☎ 0331-969-4249, based on the design of the Eschenheimer Tower, a medieval city gate in Frankfurt am Main. The 46-m (147-foot) tower, with majestic views of the park, surrounding lakes and the old town, can be climbed on summer weekends from 10 am to 5 pm. Admission is €2.

Potsdam Old Town

Although Potsdam suffered war damage in World War II, several historic buildings survived to the present day. It is a short walk across the Havel River from the main and S-Bahn stations to the Old Town.

The **Alter and Neuer Markt** (Old and New Market Squares) are at the heart of Potsdam's Old Town. The **Nikolaikirche** (Nicholas Church), Am Alten Markt, ☎ 0331-270-3168, is a favorite venue for concerts. The early 19th-century church, with a huge cupola, is molded on the example of St Paul's in London. The church is open May to October from 10 am to 5 pm, Sunday from 11:30 am and Monday from 2 pm. From November to April, it is open from 2 to 5 pm, from 11:30 am on Sunday and 10 am on Saturday. Admission is free.

The **Brandenburger Tor** (Town Gate) at Luisenplatz in Potsdam's Old Town is 20 years older than its famous and more illustrious namesake in Berlin. It was completed in 1770 with some of the decorative statues based on personal drawings by Frederick the Great. Nearby is the **Jägertor**, the oldest surviving city gate. Bus 695 passes both gates en route to Park Sanssouci.

The **Holländisches Viertel** (Dutch Quarter) consists of Dutch-style brick and gabled houses. The area was created by Friedrich Wilhelm, the Great Elector, who attempted to draw Dutch citizens to repopulate Brandenburg after the devastating effects of the Thirty Years' War. During the Communist years, this area suffered

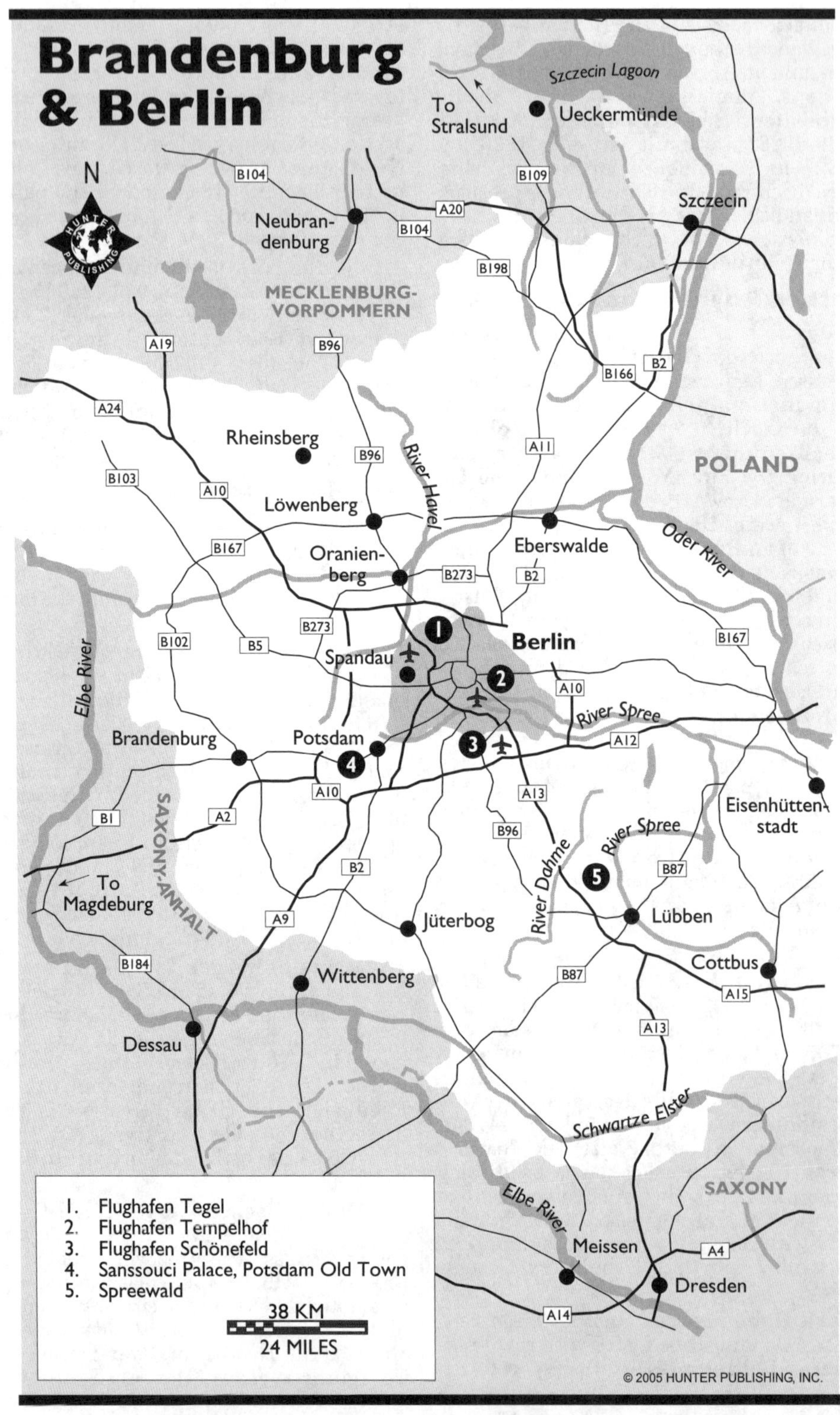
Brandenburg & Berlin
N
HUNTER PUBLISHING
Szczecin Lagoon
To Stralsund
Ueckermünde
Szczecin
Neubrandenburg
MECKLENBURG-VORPOMMERN
Rheinsberg
Löwenberg
Oranienberg
Eberswalde
River Havel
POLAND
Oder River
Berlin
Spandau
Elbe River
River Spree
Brandenburg
Potsdam
Eisenhüttenstadt
SAXONY-ANHALT
To Magdeburg
River Dahme
Lübben
Jüterbog
Cottbus
Wittenberg
Dessau
Schwartze Elster
SAXONY
Meissen
Dresden
B104
B109
A20
B198
A19
B96
A24
B166
B2
A11
B103
A10
B167
B273
B102
B5
A12
A13
A2
B1
B87
A9
B184
A15
A4
A14
1. Flughafen Tegel
2. Flughafen Tempelhof
3. Flughafen Schönefeld
4. Sanssouci Palace, Potsdam Old Town
5. Spreewald
38 KM
24 MILES
© 2005 HUNTER PUBLISHING, INC.

deprivation and restoration work was only started after re-unification. The most beautiful area is Mittelstraße, which has 128 gabled houses built around 1740.

Frederick the Great saw the beautiful fountains in Park Sanssouci in action only once. It was only in 1842 that the Berlin engineering firm Borsig managed to build a steam engine able to pump the necessary waters to the fountains on a regular basis. The **Dampfmachinenhaus** (Pump Station), at Breitestraße, ☎ 0331-969-4248, is housed in a rather politically incorrect Mosque-like building. It is open weekends from mid-May to mid-October, 10 am to 5 pm. Admission is €2 and includes the compulsory guided tour.

Cultural Events

Potsdam has a busy cultural calendar, often using historic buildings as stage. The Tourist Information office can provide information on events where we don't specify contact details.

The second half of June draws music lovers to the **Musikfestspiele Potsdam Sanssouci** (Music Festival), ☎ 0331-288-8828. Classical music concerts are staged in Frederick the Great's theater in the Neues Palais, or open-air in Sanssouci Park.

Once a year, in mid-August, the **Potsdamer Schlössernacht** (Night of the Mansions) is held. On this night, Sanssouci Park is bathed in light and the palaces illuminated. Concerts and theater are staged throughout the park and the night ends with fireworks set to music.

Bach's Brandenburg Concertos are probably the most famous music associated with this region. The **Bachtage Potsdam** (Bach Days), ☎ 0331-270-6222, www.bachtage-potsdam.de, are held annually for two weeks in August and September. Bach is played in all forms and variations, ranging from jazz versions to those using original period instruments.

The **Hofkonzerte** (Court Concerts), ☎ 0331-245-609, www.potsdamer-hofkonzerte.de, are staged throughout the year in different palaces in Potsdam.

The **International Festival for Contemporary Dance**, ☎ 0331-280-0314, www.fabrikpotsdam.de, is spread over two weeks in May and June. Major international soloists and companies participate in this festival, often referred to as Tanztage. Fabrik Potsdam stages dance performances throughout the year.

Adventures

On Foot

Town Walks: The tourist information office arranges a combination bus and walking tour of historic Potsdam in English and German. Tours take place Tuesday to Sunday from April to October at 11 am. The rest of the year tours are arranged from Friday to Sunday by special request only. The 3½-hour tour includes a guided tour of Schloss Sanssouci, making this the only way to guarantee entry into the palace. The tour costs €26, but includes admission fees. Reservations are highly recommended. Other tours are available but in German only.

Country Walks: For a longer walk, which combines the UNESCO World Cultural Heritage Sites of Potsdam with its beautiful forest and lake-rich surroundings, attempt the 35-km (21-mile) walk around the Potsdam Havel Lakes. The route leads from Potsdam to Ferch via Caputh along the Westside of the Templin Lake and returns via the East Side. Prussian palaces can be seen along the way in both Caputh and Petzow. Like most of Brandenburg, the route is practically flat. Local transportation options are available to shorten the actual walked part of the route.

On Wheels

By Bicycle: Potsdam is a particularly pleasing city to cycle in. A special cycling route named "Alter Fritz," after the nickname of Frederick the Great, leads to all the major old town and royal sights.

A longer, 82-km (50-mile) route follows the Havel from Potsdam to Brandenburg town, passing several more palaces. Most of this route is on dedicated bicycle tracks.

Bicycles can be rented at the main station from **Cityrad Radstation Potsdam**, Babelbergerstraße 14, ☎ 0331-620-0606. The shop is open daily from 9 am to 8 pm.

By Bus: The **Hamburger Hummelbahn**, Rudolf-Breitscheid-Straße 15, ☎ 0331-740-0650, www.hummelbahn.de, operates three daily tours with red double-decker buses. Tours depart from the

Hauptbahnhof and journeys may be interrupted and rejoined at any stop.

Tours on a Hummelbahn (motorized train) are offered daily on the hour by **Potsdam-Sanssouci-Express**, Eichenring 12, ☎ 0331-505-3542, www.Potsdam-Sanssouci-Express.de. The 90-minute tours depart from the Historical Mill, behind the Sanssouci Visitors Center.

Stadttourismus/Schlösserrundfahrten S. Lang, Carl-von Ossietzky-Straße 25, ☎ 0331-974-376, www.schloesserrundfahrten.de, offers 2½-hour guided tours in German. Most of the tour is by bus but three short walks are included at the major sights. Tours depart daily from mid-March to October at 11 am and 2 pm from the Hauptbahnhof.

On Horseback

Horseback riding is very popular in this mainly rural state. Brandenburg has 5,000 marked paths for riding, many leading through national parks and forests. Two wide circular routes around Berlin are already partly completed and many other long-distance routes are operational.

Most riding stables are small operations, so it is best to contact either the local tourist information office, or **Pro Agro**, Arthur-Scheunert-Allee 40-41, 14558 Bergholz-Rehbrücke, ☎ 03300-89-232, www.land-urlaub-brandenburg.de. Pro Agro has information on riding stables in the whole of Brandenburg as well as on farms open for visits and overnight stays.

In the Air

Ballooning: Ballonhafen Berlin, Pflügerstraße 2, 12047 Berlin ☎ 030-694-4158, www.ballonhafen-berlin.de, usually starts from Linthe, about 20 km (12 miles) south of Potsdam, but flights are sometimes offered from the Volkspark in Potsdam itself.

On Water

Potsdam's location on the River Havel and a series of connected lakes is ideal for water activities. Houseboat cruises that include not only Potsdam but also Brandenburg and Berlin are popular.

For all of Berlin, and for some parts of Brandenburg State, a sports boat license is required for boats stronger than 5 HP – it is best to make sure with the rental agents that foreign licenses will be accepted prior to reservations.

Day Cruises: Several companies offer cruises on the waters in and around Potsdam. Cruises range from one hour to day-trips to Berlin and elsewhere in Brandenburg.

Die Weiße Flotte, ☎ 0331-275-9210, and the **Havel Dampfschiffahrt**, ☎ 0331-275-9233, both operate from Lange Brücke 6, www.schiffahrt-in-potsdam.de, in front of the Mercure hotel close to the main station. Various daily departures are available.

Houseboats: Several companies rent houseboats in and around Potsdam. **Yachthafen Potsdam**, Kastanienallee 10, 14471 Potsdam, ☎ 0331-974-729, www.yachthafenpotsdam.de, has boats of various sizes, including some that do not require licenses. One-way rentals are also possible in combination with Crown Blue Line – see Rheinsberg section below.

Near Potsdam, boats can be rented from **Yachtcharter Heinzig**, Ringstraße 31, 26689 Apen, ☎ 04489-6500, www.heinzig.de, or from **Wassersportfachgeschäft Krüger & Till**, Unter den Linden 17, 14542 Werder, ☎ 03327-42-424, www.wassersport-werder.de.

The companies listed in the Berlin chapter are generally also convenient for Potsdam.

Where to Stay & Eat

Although the state of Brandenburg generally lacks sufficient hotel accommodation of international standards, this is definitely not the case in Potsdam. The town has some excellent hotels and offers a viable alternative to staying in Berlin.

The small, luxury **Relexa Schlosshotel Cecilienhof** recently opened in Schloss Cecilienhof, the last palace built by the Hohenzollerns, and site of the Potsdam Conference in 1945. The décor and furnishings of the large comfortable rooms follow the English country house style of the palace. The elegant **Schlossrestaurant** (€€-€€€€), with a terrace, serves light regional and international dishes with a decent vegetarian selection. Neuer Garten, 14469 Potsdam, ☎ 0331-37-050, fax 0331-292-498, www.relexa-hotel.de. (€€€-€€€€)

The **Hotel am Luisenplatz** is a 25-room privately owned and managed luxury hotel

– no risk of running into tour groups here. Located in a restored city palace, the hotel offers modern comfort and a stylish interior. Nearby, it also manages a bed and breakfast building, which offers excellent value for money. Apartments are also available. The hotel is ideally situated at the Brandenburg Gate and within easy walking distance of the shops and restaurants of Brandenburger Straße. Bicycle rentals can be arranged. Luisenplatz 5, 14471 Potsdam, ☎ 0331-971-900, fax 0331-971-9019, www.hotel-luisenplatz.de. (€€/€€€ for hotel, €/€€ for bed-and-breakfast)

Conveniently located across the road from the Brandenburg Gate, the **Steigenberger Hotel Sanssouci** is within easy walking distance of the Old Town and Park Sanssouci. This is slightly ironic since the hotel key serves as a free pass for all local public transportation. Rooms are comfortable and in the style of 1930s America. Allée nach Sanssouci 1, 14471 Potsdam, ☎ 0331-90-910, fax 0331-909-1909, www.steigenberger.de. (€€€)

Apartment Hotel im Holländerhaus is a small hotel in the Dutch Quarter. It has a quiet location with comfortable, well-appointed rooms. Kurfürstenstraße 15, 14467 Potsdam, ☎ 0331-279-110, fax 0331-279-111, www.hollaenderhaus.de. (€€€/€€€€)

The **Mercure Hotel** is across the Havel River, a few minutes walk from the train station and the old town. Bedrooms are reasonably large and comfortably furnished. It offers comfort and value for money rather than personality. The restaurant (€€) serves regional cuisine as well as more international fare. Lange Brucke, 14467 Potsdam, ☎ 0331-2722, fax 0331-272-0233, www.mercure.de. (€€-€€€)

One of the best restaurants in Potsdam is **Specker's Gaststätte zur Ratswaage**, Am Neuen Markt 10, ☎ 0331-280-4311, www.zur-ratswaage.de. The modern, but simply furnished restaurant has been in operation since 1763. International and classic recipes are served. (€€-€€€)

Built in 1736, **Der Klosterkeller,** Friedrich Ebertstraßes 94, ☎ 0331-291-218, www.klosterkeller.potsdam.de, is the oldest restaurant in Potsdam. It is in the center of the old town, close to the Holländer Viertel and serves mainly German food. The vaulted cellar has more than 120 seats and 300 seats in the courtyard, making the restaurant popular with large bus tour parties. (€-€€)

Juliette, Jägerstraße 39, ☎ 0331-270-1791, www.restaurant-juliette.de, is completely different in atmosphere. Located in a lovely half-timbered house, it is up-market, small, and intimate. It has a large wine cellar and is an excellent choice for French cuisine. Reservations recommended. (€€-€€€)

Camping

Campingpark Sanssouci-Gaisberg is south of Potsdam on the Templiner Lake. It has modern facilities and 240 spaces. An der Pirschheide /Templiner See 41, 14471 Potsdam, ☎ 033327-55-680, www.campingpark-sanssouci-potsdam.com.

■ Spreewald

The Spreewald (Spree Forest), 100 km (60 miles) south of Berlin, is a unique landscape of pristine ancient forest, protected in a UNESCO World Natural Heritage biosphere reserve. This swamp-like area has a labyrinth of almost 1,000 km (600 miles) of waterways, of which around 400 km (240 miles) are open to paddlers. Traditionally, travelers come here to go punting, but for the more energetic, canoeing and kayaking options are also numerous.

The region is famous as the home of the Sorbians, a Slavic people that settled here in the sixth century and maintained their own language and traditions centuries after the area was conquered by German groups. The picturesque towns of Lübbenau, Lübben, Lehde, and Burg are the main destinations.

Information Sources

Tourist Office: Information on the region is available from Tourismusverband Spreeewald, Lindenstraße 1, 03226 Raddusch, ☎ 035433-72-299, www.spreewald.de.

Transportation

By Train: Lübbenau is an hour by hourly train from Berlin Ostbahnhof. Lübben is another 10 minutes by train from Lübbenau.

By Car: The Spreewald is less than an hour's drive from Berlin via the Autobahn A15.

Adventures

On Foot

Hiking: The best-known and most popular hike in the Spreewald is the hour-long walk from Lübbenau to the Gaststätte (Restaurant) Wotschowska. It is an easy, well-marked route and has been in use since 1911.

On Wheels

By Bicycle: The Spreewald is traditionally explored on water, with punting especially popular. However, there are also many cycling options. The **Gurkenradweg** (Pickled Cucumber Cycling Route) is a 250-km (150-mile) circular route through the larger Spreewald area. It is named and signposted after the most famous food from the area. The 360-km (216-mile) **Spreeradweg** leads from Saxony to Berlin and passes through the Spreewald. A pleasant section of these routes, ideal for a day-trip, is the 25 km (15 miles) from Burg to Lübben.

Rental bikes are available from most hotels in the area, or in Burg from **Die Radler Scheune**, corner of Ringchaussee 155 and Zweite Kolonie, ☎ 035603-13-360, www.radler-scheune.de, and in Lübbenau from **Kowalsky's Fahrradservice**, Poststraße 6, ☎ 03542-2835.

On Water

Canoeing & Kayaking: The Spreewald is ideal for paddling. The water is slow-flowing and much of the area is a biosphere reserve closed to motorized boats. Punting boats always have the right of way. A good map is essential to explore the canals off the main flow. Canals marked with a red-white-red sign are off-limits.

A popular two-day, 25-km (15-mile) paddling route is from Burg via Lübbenau to Lübben. This route follows the main flow of the Spree and is most picturesque on the first stretch. Rental boats are available from:

- **Spreewaldhotel Stephanshof**, Lehnigksberger Weg 1, 15907 Lübben, ☎ 03546-27-210, www.spreewaldreisen.de. Bicycle rental and punting is also available from this hotel.
- **Bootsverleih Gebauer**, Lindenstraße 18, 15907 Lübben, ☎ 03546-7194, www.spreewald-bootsverleih.de.
- **Kahnfahrten und Bootshaus am Leineweber**, Hauptstraße 1, 03096 Burg, ☎ 035603-60096, www.spreewald-paddeln.de, also has houseboats and punting available.
- **Hafen Waldschlösschen**, Waldschlöss chenstraße 29, 03096 Burg, ☎ 035603-536, www.spreewaldhafen-online.de.

Punting: The Spreewald is famous for *Kahnfahrten* (punting or barge-trips). Often the barge is pushed by strong-armed local women dressed in typical regional costume. Lübbenau has the largest selection of service providers – often single-family concerns – but rides are also offered in most other towns. Trips can be up to a full day, but some may find trips over two hours tedious.

In the high season, especially on weekends, reservations are recommended, but as little distinguishes the trips, simply seeing what is available on arrival allows for more flexibility. (A full list of service providers is available from the tourist office.)

In Lübbenau, reservations are possible at **Kahnfährmann Karl-Heinz Wendland**, Kaupen 3, ☎ 03542-405-081, www.kahnfahrt.de, or at **Karl-Heinz Marschner**, Kleine Poststraße 1, ☎ 03542-2075, www.kahnfahrten-luebbenau.de.

In Burg, punting and other boat rentals are available from **Kahnfahrten und Bootshaus am Leineweber**, Hauptstraße 1, ☎ 035603-60-096, www.spreewald-paddeln.de, or from **Hafen Waldschlösschen**, Waldschlöss chenstraße 29, ☎ 035603-536, www.spreewaldhafen-online.de.

■ Oranienburg

Oranienburg is a small town north of Berlin. It was long famous as the home of the first Baroque palace in Brandburg, but, since the Nazi era, it is better known for the notorious Sachsenhausen concentration camp. Due to its proximity to Berlin, it is more often than not visited on a day-trip from the capital.

Information Sources

Tourist Office: The Touristen-Information, Bernauer Straße 52, 16515 Oranienburg, ☎ 03301-704-833, www.oranienburg.de, is open weekdays only from 8:30 am to 5 pm.

Transportation

By Train: Oranienburg can be reached from Berlin-Lichtenberg on Regionalbahn RB12 in around 30 minutes. The S-Bahn S1, taking 50 minutes from Berlin-Friederichstraße, is often more convenient.

Sightseeing

The main reason to travel to Oranienburg is to see the **Gedenkstätte Sachsenhausen** (Memorial), Straße der Nationen 22, 16515 Oranienburg, ☎ 03301-20 00, www.gedenkstaette-sachsenhausen.de.

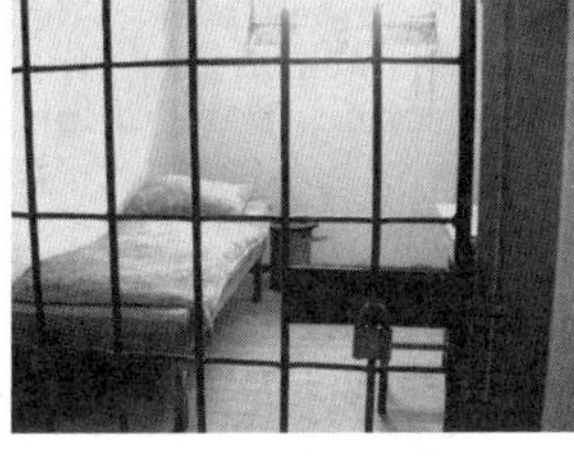

Already in 1933, the Nazis built a concentration camp in the center of Oranienburg, in an unused factory, to "house" opponents of the Nazi regime in Berlin. The town camp was soon closed and eventually replaced by **Concentration Camp Sachsenhausen**. This camp, with 100 smaller branch camps, housed some 200,000 people while used by the Nazis (1936-45) and 60,000 when used by the Soviets as an internment camp (1945-50). The Nazis saw Sachsenhausen as a model camp, used it for training purposes, and it eventually housed the central administration of all concentration camps in the Reich.

Sachsenhausen Tower A

From 1961 to 1992, the site was used as a memorial with severely skewed historical explanations. The killing of for example Jews and Gypsies was blamed on capitalist demands rather than racism and anti-Semitism. However, since 1993, serious attempts have been made to restore parts of the camp and to present a more balanced view of history. Several buildings have been restored, barracks rebuilt, and excellent exhibitions created.

The huge, triangular walled-in site is open daily from mid-March to mid-October, 8:30 am to 6 pm, closing at 4:30 pm the rest of the year. The museum and all buildings are closed on Monday. Admission is free and audio guides in English are available. The site is about 20 minutes walk from the station – the route is well marked. Alternatively, take Bus 804 from the station in the direction of Malz (stop is at Gedänkstätte).

Also in town is **Schloss Oranienburg** (Palace), Schlossplatz 2, ☎ 03301-537-437, the oldest Baroque palace in Brandenburg. It was built for Louise-Henriette of Orange, the Dutch-born first wife of the Great Elector, in 1651. It became the favored residence of Elector Frederick III (later Frederick I, King of Prussia. During the 19th and 20th centuries, it saw duty as a residence, factory, conference center, and military camp. Open to the public are the reception rooms as well as private apartments of the King and other nobles. Most of the decorations are in the style of the late 16th century and show life in the Prussian court around 1700. Quality art is on display, including paintings and sculptures. Opening hours are April to October, Tuesday to Sunday, 10 am to 6 pm; November to March on weekends only, 10 am to 5 pm. Admission is €4. In summer, the guided tour (€1) is optional; in winter the tour is compulsory, but free.

Adventures

Berlin Walks, ☎ 030-301-9194, www.berlinwalks.com, conducts guided walking tours of the Sachsenhausen Concentration Camp. The six-hour tours depart from Berlin Zoologischer Garten Station, meeting at the Taxi Stand, on Tuesday and Saturday at 10:15 am. From May to September, additional tours are offered on Thursday and Sunday. The tour cost is €15, plus €5 for the train ticket.

■ Rheinsberg

Rheinsberg is in the Ruppinerland region about 75 km (45 miles) northwest of Berlin. It is an area rich in lakes and waterways, similar to the lakes area of adjacent Mecklenburg-Vorpommern. The main cultural sights are in Rheinsberg, where Frederick the Great lived as a student.

Information Sources

Tourist Office: Tourist Information, Kavalierhaus/Markt, 16831 Rheinsberg, ☎ 033931-2059, www.rheinsberg.de, can make reservations for accommodations, concerts, bicycle and boat rental.

Transportation

By Train: Rheinsberg can be reached from Berlin-Charlottenburg by infrequent direct train in just over two hours. Trains requiring changeovers range from less than two hours to around three.

By Car: Ruppinerland is just off the busy A24 to Hamburg, or on the slower B96 via Oranienburg en route to Neubrandenburg and Mecklenburg-Vorpommern.

By Boat: Ruppingerland can also be reached from Berlin or Oranienburg by houseboat. See section below for details.

Sightseeing

Apart from the lakes, the main sights in Rheinsberg are the **Schloss (Palace) and Park Rheinsberg**, ☎ 033931-7260, www.spsg.de. Frederick the Great spent four years here before being crowned King of Prussia in 1740. The Schloss was adapted for the crown prince's use and the interior has excellent examples of early Frederican Rococo as well as early Classical elements.

Rheinsberg Park was laid out by Frederick in a late Baroque style, but his brother Heinrich, who lived here from 1752 until his death in 1802, expanded the garden and modeled it as one of the first sentimental landscape gardens in Germany.

A tour of the palace includes five of the rooms designed by Frederick and left unchanged by his brother. The hall of mirrors and the anterooms with painted ceilings are particularly worth seeing. A small museum dedicated to the nationalist writer Kurt Tucholsky, whose works were banned by the Nazis, is located inside the palace.

Schloss Rheinsberg is open year-round from Tuesday to Sunday, April to October from 9:30 am to 5 pm, and November to March from 10 am to 4 pm. Admission is €4. A guided tour (€1) is optional during the summer season; compulsory but included in the admission price in winter.

Cultural Events

Culture has played a major role in Rheinsberg at least since the time of Frederick the Great. The **Rheinsberg Music Academy** offers frequent performances in the Schlosstheater, www.schlosstheter-rheinsberg.de. Also popular are the operas staged during July and August by the **Kammeroper Schloss Rheinsberg**, www.kammeroper-rheinsberg.de.

Adventures

On Wheels

By Bicycle: The area is most popularly explored by boat, but bicycle routes also abound and cycling is generally easy on the mostly flat landscape. Most hotels rent bicycles to guests. Bicycles are also available from **Fahrrad-Centrale Ristau**, Pfarrstraße 3, 16798 Fürstenberg, ☎ 033093-32-533.

In the Air

See Berlin chapter for adventures offered from Fehrbellin Airport.

On Horseback

There are several riding stables in the vicinity offering riding opportunities in this beautiful lake-filled countryside. For details contact the Information Office or **Pro Agro**, Arthur-Scheunert-Allee 40-41, 14558 Bergholz-Rehbrücke, ☎ 03300-89-232, www.land-urlaub-brandenburg.de.

On Water

Canoeing & Kayaking: The quiet, usually calm waters of the region are ideal for canoeing and kayaking. Boats can be rented in downtown Rheinsberg from **Reederei Halbeck**, Kurt-Tucholsky-Straße, ☎ 033931-39-390, www.schifffahrt-rheinsberg.de. Boats can also be rented in the town of Warenthin on the Rheinsberger See, from **Kanuverleih Rheinsberger Seenkette**, Seestraße 6, 16831 Rheinsberg-Warenthin, ☎ 033931-2131, www.kanuverleih-rheinsberg.de.

In the south of Rheinsberg, **Kanuverleih Berger Tours**, Untermühle 2, 16831 Rheinsberg, ☎ 033931-20 42, www.bergertours.de, rents boats to individuals. Berger Tours also arranges day- and multi-day trips that include transportation of the boats and accommodations if required.

Charter Boats: Houseboats, fully equipped for two to 10 persons, can be rented without license in many parts of this lake-rich area. On the Rheinsberger Lake, boats are available from **Marina Wolfsbruch** – reservations through **Crown Blue Line**, Marktplatz 4, 61118 Bad Vilbel, ☎ 06101-501-033, www.crownblueline.com. One-way rentals are sometimes available between here and Potsdam. **Locaboat** operates from Dorfstraße 26 in Fürstenberg an der Havel – reservations through Locaboat, Postfach 867, 79008 Freiburg, ☎ 0761-207-370, www.locaboat.de.

Houseboat tours from Berlin to the Ruppiner lake area are popular. Various routes are available ranging from 170-km (102-mile), three-day round-trips to 120-km (72-mile), or longer, one-way, two-day trips. Much longer trips can include the Mecklenburg Lakes. If three weeks, or more, are available, consider a 600-km (360-mile) circular route that includes Schwerin, the Elbe, Brandenburg, Potsdam, and Berlin.

For all of Berlin, and for some parts of Brandenburg State, a sport boat license is required – it is best to clear with the agents the acceptance of foreign licenses prior to reservations.

Boat Trips: For travelers not interested in navigating the waters on their own, **Reederei Halbeck**, Markt 11, 16831 Rheinsberg, ☎ 033931-38-619, www.schifffahrt-rheinsberg.de, offers several trips per day on the lakes, rivers, and canals of the Rheinsberg region. Cruises on 150-passenger boats range from two hours to full-day trips.

Where to Stay & Eat

The small, 20-room **Hotel Der Seehof** is located in-town a mere three minutes walk from Schloss Rheinsberg. Rooms are comfortable and individually furnished. Several dining options are available on-site ranging from a casual bistro to the formal restaurant. The stylish gourmet restaurant **Der Seehof** (€-€€€) offers fireside dining in winter with a view of the lake. Regional specialties are served according to season, for example deer schnitzel in winter and fish from the lake in summer. Seestraße 18, 16831 Rheinsberg, ☎ 033931-4030, fax 033931-40399, www.seehof-rheinsberg.com. (€€/€€€)

Saxony

In this Chapter

Saxony is one of the smaller German federal states but one with a complex history and many historic and natural sights of interest to the foreign visitor. The main drawing cards are the great cities of Dresden and Leipzig. Dresden is famous for its Baroque architecture, forming one of the most beautiful city panoramas in Europe. Leipzig is architecturally less harmonious but an interesting city to visit. Both cities have a number of outstanding museums and galleries. The culture calendar in both is also nothing short of astonishing.

Saxony was one of the first German states to industrialize during the 19th century and heavy industry still plays a major role in the regional economy. Despite severe environmental damage during the Communist era and a high population density, Saxony has some areas of outstanding natural beauty – none more than the Sächsiche Schweiz (Saxon Switzerland) area near Dresden.

This chapter is divided into the three sightseeing areas of most interest to the foreign visitor: Dresden, the Dresden area, and Leipzig.

History

The modern federal state of Saxony has little in common with the more illustrious Anglo-Saxons that went on to invade Britain and from there spread all over the globe. Around 800 AD the Saxons who stayed on in Germany were a formidable tribe and it took Charlemagne over 30 years of war to repress them and force conversion to Christianity. These Saxons lived mainly in areas of the modern states of Lower Saxony and Saxony-Anhalt.

Saxony developed out of the Mark (March, or border area) Meißen, which was founded in 965 AD. From 1089 until 1918 it was ruled by the House of Wettiner, who managed to expand the state to include much of what is modern Thuringia, Saxony Anhalt and parts of Brandenburg – only to lose it all through war, deceit, pure treachery, bad diplomacy and family squabbles. At the end, the state was no bigger than the original March.

Saxony's history, like that of so many German states, is complex and much of it ultimately fairly irrelevant. It is sufficient to stick to a few high and low points. In 1423, the Wettiners became Electors and the area under their rule formally became Saxony. In 1485, two Wettiner brothers split the area: the Albertine line would rule Meißen and the Ernistine, much of what is Thuringia. The latter would keep the elector title until some first-degree treachery by a cousin saw it permanently return to the Albertines in 1547.

Much of the Reformation under Martin Luther took place in Saxon territory with Saxony one of the first states to have decided for the Reformation. However, during the Thirty Years' War (1618-1648), Saxony first supported the Emperor against the Protestants, then changed sides and, as a result, the state was devastated by battles and attacks from both sides.

Augustus the Strong (1718)

Early in the 18th century under Augustus the Strong, who simultaneously was also King of Poland, and his son Frederick Augustus II, Saxony had a golden age, which saw many of Dresden's Baroque buildings erected and Saxony becoming a center of culture and art in Europe.

However, their rule was followed by a run of incredibly bad diplomacy. Being squeezed between Prussia, Bavaria, and Austria, Saxony had a hard time maintaining its independence and influence. In the Seven Years' War (1756-63), Saxony supported Austria but Prussia eventually won and taxed Saxony heavily. It then allied with Napoleon. As reward, the Saxon ruler was made a king but after the fall of Napoleon, it was only Russian and Austrian intervention that forced Prussia to annex only half and not the entire kingdom. In 1866, the Saxon king supported his father-in-law, the Austrian Emperor, in the war against Prussia. The victorious Prussian King Wilhelm wanted to annex Saxony and was furious at his chancellor, Otto von Bismarck, who prevented him.

From the late 19th century, Saxony, as part of the German Empire, was without political power but its rapid industrialization gave it economic might. It also led to a Marxist textbook proletariat and capitalist division. At the end of the First World War Saxony briefly became a Communist republic and although this was swiftly suppressed Saxony would have mostly left-leaning governments ever since.

At the end of World War II, Russian and American troops met in Torgau at the River Elbe. The Americans soon withdrew as per prior agreement and Saxony remained part of East Germany and the German Democratic Republic until 1989.

During the Communist regime, some areas of Saxony, especially around Dresden, had trouble receiving Western radio and television. As a result, the area was known as the "valley of the clueless." However, in 1989 it was in Leipzig and not Berlin that the opposition against the Communist regime began, leading to the peaceful revolution and the unification of Germany in 1990. This process is often referred to as the *Wende* (the change).

■ Transportation

Excellent transportation links make Saxony easy to visit. Its central location between Bavaria and Berlin makes it a natural stopover en route between these major attractions.

By Rail: Leipzig has traditionally been an important railway hub in Germany and, with the largest railway station in Germany, it is aiming to reclaim that position. Major railway construction is taking place in the former East Germany to bring the railways up to the latest standards and traveling times continue to decrease as new high-speed lines are opened.

Hourly **InterCity Express** (ICE) trains connect Dresden (four hours 30 minutes) and Leipzig (just over three hours) with Frankfurt am Main via Weimar, Erfurt, Eisenach and Fulda. ICE trains from Munich via Nuremberg to Leipzig take five hours and continue to Berlin (90 minutes) via Lutherstadt Wittenberg. ICE trains to Hamburg take around four hours.

From Dresden to Berlin takes two hours on the InterCity. These trains stop at Berlin-Schönefeld Airport before continuing to Berlin Ost and Zoologischer Garten (and eventually Hauptbahnhof, once it opens around 2006). The same trains also connect Dresden with Prague in just over two hours. Vienna can be reached twice daily in seven hours. Most other trains to Dresden pass through, or require a change, in Leipzig.

Dresden and Leipzig are connected by fast hourly InterCity Express (ICE) trains as well as cheaper but slower alternatives. The rest of the state is also well-served by a combination of local trains and buses.

By Road: Saxony has a well-developed road network with the cities Leipzig and Dresden connected by a fast Autobahn (highway). Leipzig is on the A9, which connects Berlin and Munich, and Dresden can be reached from Berlin on the A13.

A highway is under construction between Dresden and Prague (Czech Republic) with traveling times decreasing as new sections are opened. The distance is 150 km (90 miles).

Although Dresden and Leipzig are best explored on foot, driving in these cities presents no major hassles. Do note however that both cities have more than the average number of speed cameras in operation. Street-side parking is limited, but sufficient parking garages are available.

By Air: Both Dresden and Leipzig have airports but have only a limited number of mainly domestic flights and destinations. Flying into one of the airports in Berlin is often a more realistic option for the international traveler.

Dresden Airport, Flughafenstraße, ☎ 0351-881-3360, www.dresden-airport.de, is easily reached from the city center. By train, the S-Bahn (S2) runs twice per hour taking 22 minutes from the Hauptbahnhof. Some trains require a change at Neustadt, from where it takes less than 15 minutes. The fare is €1.50. The airport is also easily reached by car and located at the junction of highways A4 and A13. Taxis cost around €15 for the 20-minute ride.

Leipzig-Halle Airport, ☎ 0341-2241155, www.leipzig-halle-airport.de, is halfway between Leipzig and Halle. It has more flights from European destinations than Dresden. From downtown Leipzig it is easiest to reach the airport via the Flughafen Express, a train that runs half-hourly during peak times. The journey time is only 14 minutes and costs €3,20 one-way. By car, it is about 30 minutes from downtown Leipzig along the A14. Taxi fares are about €30.

Discount airline **Ryanair**, www.ryanair.com, uses miniscule **Altenburg Airport**, www.flugplatz-altenburg.de, for flights from London-Stansted. From here, it is an 80-minute journey by bus (€12) to Leipzig. The bus schedule is very limited and arranged around the departure and arrival times of this flight.

On Water: The Elbe River flows through Saxony, making arrival by boat in Dresden and Meißen possible. Cruises ranging from a few hours to several days are popular along the Elbe from Prague in the Czech Republic to Hamburg and Cuxhaven where the Elbe enters the North Sea. See the *Adventure* section for details.

■ Information Sources

Responsible for the whole of Saxony is the Tourismus Marketing Gesellschaft Sachsen, Bautzner Straße 45-47, 01099 Dresden, ☎ 0351-491-700, www.sachsen-tourismus.de. (Regional tourism offices are listed with the individual towns below.)

■ Dresden

Although Dresden has an 800-year history, its finest moments came during the four-decade rule of Augustus the Strong (1694-1733). He was rather vain and autocratic but backed it up with good taste and built most of the Baroque structures that would transform Dresden from a provincial backwater to one of the most beautiful cities in Europe. His alchemist, Böttger, failed to produce gold but managed to produce the first porcelain in Europe, giving Augustus and his successors the funds to amass a wealth of art, which still forms the base of Dresden's impressive State Art Collection. Dresden became known as Florence on the Elbe (Elbflorenz) and an essential stop on any European tour.

On the night of 13 February 1945, allied air raids destroyed most of Dresden's Baroque core, killing at least 35,000 people in the process. (Dresden was crowded with refugees fleeing the advancing Russian army, leading to credible claims that the exact number could have been significantly higher.) The destruction of this Baroque city, which was a purely civilian target, just days before the Russians would conquer it, caused a bitter reaction that has lasted up to the present.

Some restoration work was done under the Communist regime, notably the rebuilding of the Semper Opera, but the real restoration work only started in earnest after *Die Wende*. This allows Dresden to claim the unveiling of a "new" historic building almost every year. It is hoped that most of the historic Baroque panorama will be in place by 2006 when the city will celebrate its 800-year anniversary.

MONEY SAVING TIPS FOR DRESDEN

Dresden offers several opportunities for visitors to see more for less.

All the major museums forming part of the State Art Collection can be seen for €10 per day or € 20 for the whole year. If you're staying two days, the **Dresden City Card** offers virtually all the museums as well as local public transportation for €18. For three days, the **Dresden Regio Card** is the best option at €29. It includes all the benefits of the City Card, but also commuter transport in the whole region. This includes the S-Bahn to Meißen, Sächsische Schweiz and all other destinations listed under day-trips from Dresden. These tickets allow you to enter the museums directly without having to queue for an additional ticket from the cashier.

Many hotels also offer stay-three-nights-but-pay-only-for-two deals in the off-season, which includes July and August as well as January to March. In some cases, the offer is valid all year round, although some require a Sunday arrival.

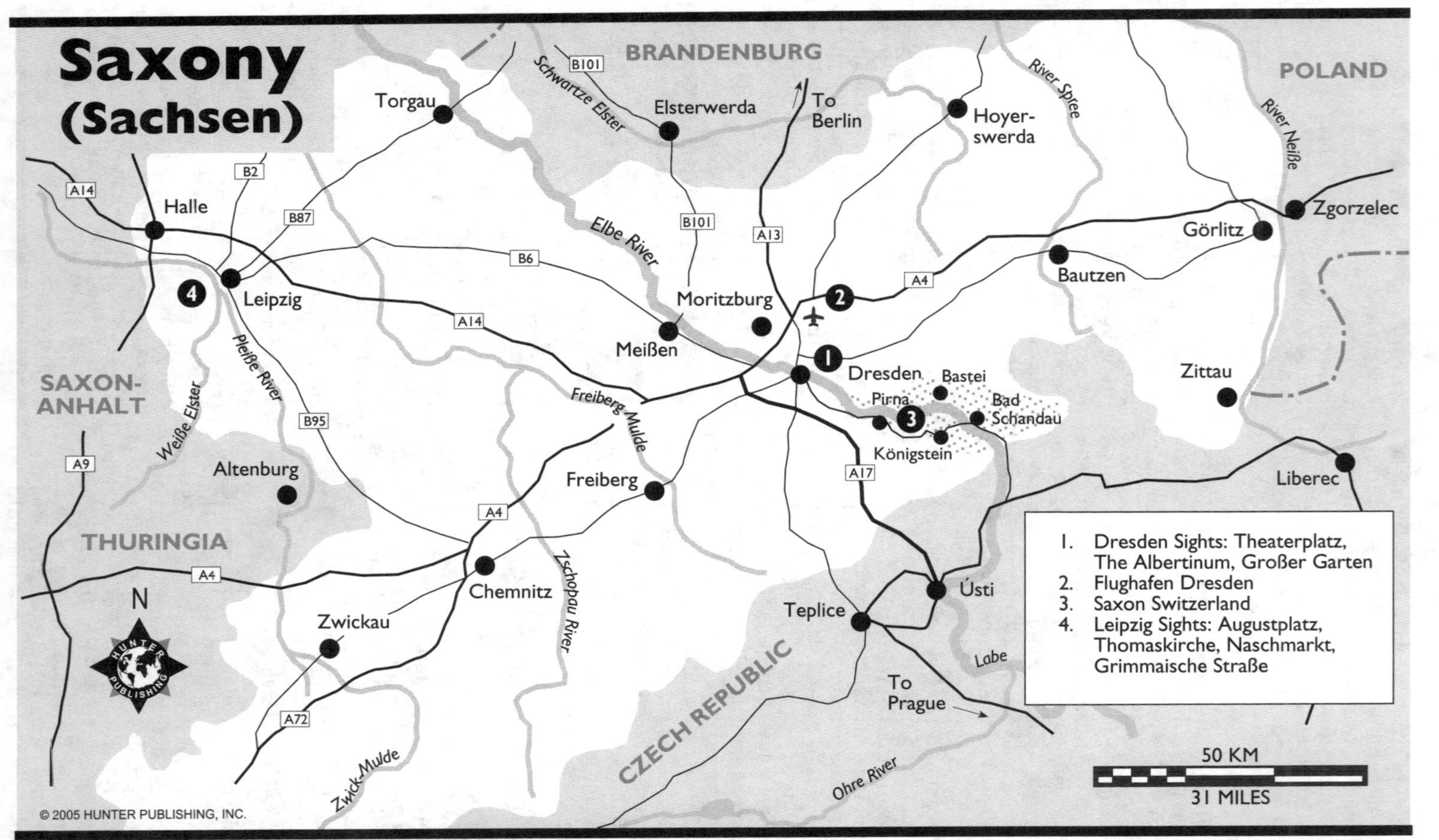
Saxony
(Sachsen)
BRANDENBURG
POLAND
SAXON-ANHALT
THURINGIA
CZECH REPUBLIC
Torgau
Elsterwerda
To Berlin
Hoyer-swerda
Halle
Leipzig
Moritzburg
Meißen
Dresden
Bastei
Pirna
Bad Schandau
Königstein
Görlitz
Zgorzelec
Bautzen
Zittau
Liberec
Altenburg
Freiberg
Chemnitz
Zwickau
Teplice
Ústi
To Prague
Schwartze Elster
Elbe River
River Spree
River Neiße
Pleiße River
Weiße Elster
Freiberg Mulde
Zschopau River
Zwick-Mulde
Ohre River
Labe
A14
B2
B87
B6
B101
A13
A4
A17
B95
A9
A72
1. Dresden Sights: Theaterplatz, The Albertinum, Großer Garten
2. Flughafen Dresden
3. Saxon Switzerland
4. Leipzig Sights: Augustplatz, Thomaskirche, Naschmarkt, Grimmaische Straße
50 KM
31 MILES
N
HUNTER PUBLISHING

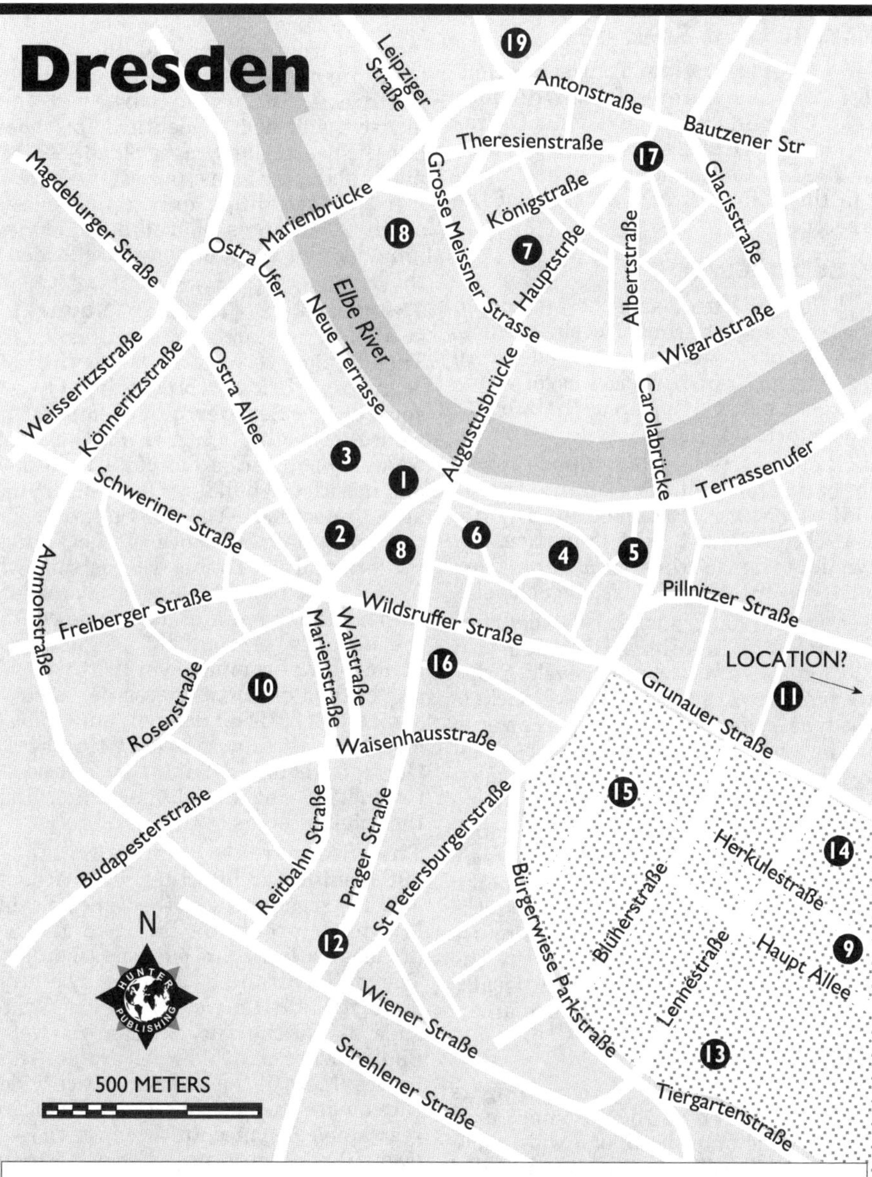

1. Theaterplatz
2. Zwinger
3. Semperoper
4. Frauenkirche
5. Albertinum
6. Brühlsche Terrasse
7. Neustadt: Dreikönigskirche, Markthalle, Museum für Volkskunst, Goldener Reiter (statue of Augustus the Strong)
8. Residenzschloss (Royal Palace), Johanneum, Hofkirke, Fürstenzug
9. Großer Garten: Palais, Park Theater, puppet theater, boathouse, playground
10. Altstadt
11. Schloss Pillnitz
12. Wienerplatz, Hauptbahnhof, Filmtheater
13. Zoologischer Garten
14. Gläserne VW Manufaktur (Transparent VW Factory)
15. Blüher Park, Hygiene Museum
16. Altmarkt
17. Albertplatz
18. Japanese Palace
19. Neustadt Station

Information Sources

Tourist Office: Tourist information is available from Dresden-Werbung und Tourismus, Ostra-Allee, 01067 Dresden, ☎ 0351-491-920, www.dresden-tourist.de. It also has an office in the Schinkelwache in front of the Semperoper.

Transportation

Central Dresden is best explored on foot. The historic old town is compact, with mostly pedestrian zones. Public transportation is of value only to get from outlying areas to the edges of the historic core.

Dresden has a well-developed public transportation network using trains (S-Bahn), trams (Strassenbahn), and buses. The S-Bahn Line 1 is particularly convenient for tourists and runs from Meißen via Dresden to Sächsiche Schweiz.

Tickets allow for transfers between bus and tram and in central Dresden cost €1.60 for up to an hour's travel. A day ticket is €4 or €13 for seven days. Tickets are bought from vending machines prior to boarding and must be validated on board.

Dresden's Hauptbahnhof (main station) is small and was flooded in 2002 when the Elbe burst its banks and caused much damage in Dresden and other riverside towns. The station is currently being rebuilt, but while the work continues, it is in a real mess. It is often advisable to use the Dresden-Neustadt station on the opposite bank of the Elbe, which is also convenient to the Baroque old town area.

Sightseeing

Most of Dresden's tourist sights are concentrated in a small area on the outer bank of a wide curve in the River Elbe. The best view is afforded by crossing the Elbe on the Augustus Bridge from Neustadt. (It is worth repeating the crossing at different times of the day as well as at night to appreciate the different lighting conditions.) Viewed from the bridge, right to left, are the Semper Opera, the Zwinger, the Hofkirche and George Gate of the Schloss, the Brühl Terrace with the Art Academy, the newly rebuilt Frauenkirche and finally the Albertinum.

The contrast with approaching from the Main Station could not be greater. Apart from the chaos of the Hauptbahnhof, the views en route to the Old Town are less than inspiring. Huge Communist-era buildings, including three adjacent massive and nearly identical Ibis hotels, line the pedestrian Prager Straße. This is a major shopping street but the first view of Baroque buildings only appears after about 20 minutes of walking and never provides the clear panorama afforded by the bridge.

Theaterplatz (Theater Square): A good place to start a tour of Dresden is at Theater Square (or even better from the Augustus Bridge proceeding to the square). The **Semperoper** (Semper Opera House), Theaterplatz 2, ☎ 0351-491-1496, www.semperoper.de, one of the best-known and most loved buildings in Dresden, manages to dominate Theater Square despite the immediate presence of the Zwinger, Schloss and Hofkirche. This is somewhat ironic, as it is High Renaissance in style rather than Baroque and much newer than the façades erected by Augustus the Strong. It was completed in 1878, replacing its burned-down predecessor, also designed by Gottfried Semper, only to be destroyed in the air raids of 1945. The East German regime rebuilt the Semper between 1977 and 1985 largely according to the original plans.

The Semper is a masterpiece of 19th-century architecture, with acoustics said to exceed those of the famed Scala in Milan. The outside has two floors of arcades with a third one recessed on top. The main entrance is adorned by a bronze quadriga. Sculptures of literary giants such as Goethe and Schiller, as well as Shakespeare and Molière, are set in the niches. Most of the interior is richly decorated, with the opera hall itself displaying restrained elegance. It is well worth seeing even if you don't attend a performance. The Semper is generally open weekdays from 10 am to 6 pm with guided tours costing €5. The exact schedule is posted weekly at the entrance as it depends on rehearsal and performance times.

DRESDEN STATE ART COLLECTION

Dresden's most famous and grandest museums and galleries are part of the Dresden State Art Collection. Most of the collection was built up by the Prince Electors, with several spending lavishly on objets d'art.

The collection is spread out over three buildings: the **Zwinger**, Theaterplatz 1, the **Albertinum**, Georg-Treu-Platz 2, and the **Residenzschloss**, Taschenberg 2. All share the same information telephone and website: ☎ 0351-491-4619, www.skd-dresden.de. Pick up an information pamphlet on the collections from the tourist information office or any of the museums – it shows the entrances to the museums. The buildings are large and the entrances can be hard to spot.

The opening hours for all are daily from 10 am to 6 pm, with the Zwinger closed on Monday; the Albertinum and the Residenzschloss are closed on Tuesday. Admission is paid separately for each exhibition but €10 gives admission to all for a day and €20 for a year. A photography permit for private use costs €5 per day for all museums. Also note the Dresden City Ticket which gives access to all and more.

Tip: *If time is limited, make the **Gemäldegalerie Alte Meister** and the **Grünes Gewölbe** top priorities – not that any of the other collections disappoints.*

Zwinger: Augustus the Strong planned an *Orangery* but his talented architect **Matthäus Pöppelmann** gave him a Baroque masterpiece of galleries, arcades and pavilions instead. The resulting Zwinger became a glorious pavilion for entertainment purposes and a highlight of any visit to Dresden. It never served as a residence and it was never intended as such. Although damaged in World War II, it was largely restored by the mid-1960s. It currently houses several major museums and galleries. Admission is charged for the museums but not for the exterior, arcades, or courtyard. The museums are open Tuesday to Sunday from 10 am to 6 pm.

The four pavilions of the Zwinger form a large rectangular courtyard with two semi-elliptical extensions. The courtyard garden has a simple Baroque layout. The entrance to the courtyard is via four distinct gates in the center of each of the four wings. Approaching from the Semper Opera, the **Semperbau** is the newest of the four wings. It was only completed in the mid-19th century in a High Renaissance style to the design of Semper. Most of the rest of the Zwinger was completed between 1709 and 1732 in a Baroque style.

Directly opposite the Semperbau is the main entrance, the **Kronentor** (Crown Gate). It is adorned by a large crown carried by four Polish eagles symbolizing the dual role of Augustus as Prince Elector of Saxony and King of Poland.

While facing Kronentor, to the right is the **Wallpavillon** (Rampart Pavilion), which serves as a staircase to the upper arcades. It is a fine symbiosis of architecture and sculpture and more art than construction. The numerous statues are from Greek mythology and include Herkulus Saxonicus carrying the globe and the weight of the world on his shoulders. From here, it is possible to access the upper arcades of most of the three older wings. To the right of the Wallpavilion is the French Pavilion housing the **Nymphenbad** (Bath of the Nymphs) with a grotto, fountains, and several sensuous feminine sculptures.

In the opposing semi-elliptical wing is the **Glockenspielpavillon** (Carillon Pavilion). Its carillon of Meißen porcelain, although envisioned by Pöppelmann, was only completed in 1936.

The largest gallery in the Zwinger and by far the most impressive museum in Dresden and all of Saxony is the **Gemäldegalerie Alte Meister** (Old Mas-

Raphael, Sistine Madonna

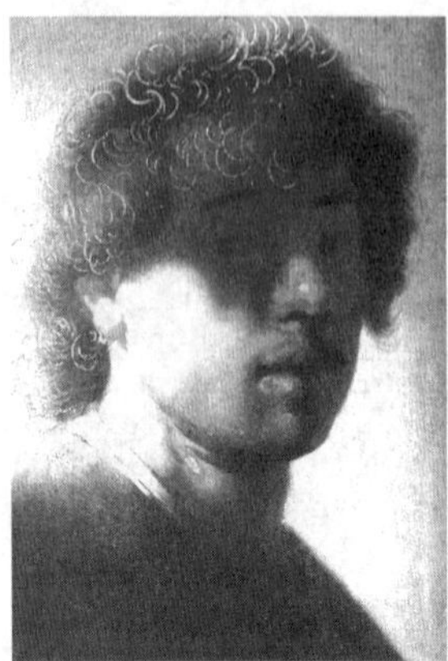
Rembrandt, Self-Portrait as a Young Man (1634)

ters Picture Gallery). Despite losing 206 works during World War II, and having most of the collection detour to Russia for a decade, it remains one of the richest archives of European paintings of the 15th to 18th century. Most of the collection was acquired during the reign of Elector Augustus the Strong (1694-1733) and that of his son Augustus II (1733-63). It reflects the taste of that period. The emphasis is on Italian paintings from the Renaissance and Baroque periods with works by Giorgione, Titian, Botticelli, Parmigianino, and Veronese. Probably the most famous work on display is Raphael's *Sistine Madonna*, featuring two adorable little angels also seen on postcards, kitsch trinkets, and wrapping paper all over town. Several large photograph-clear paintings of the Dresden panorama done by the famous Canaletto (Bernardo Bellotto) are prominently displayed.

The second main emphasis in the Gemäldegalerie is 17th-century Dutch and Flemish art, including works by Rubens, Van Dyck, Rembrandt, Jordaens, and Vermeer. The collection of German, French, and Spanish paintings is smaller but includes good examples by Dürer, Holbein, Cranach, Murillo, and Poussin. In most halls the paintings are displayed as intended by Semper in a double row with Bordeaux red backgrounds for Italian works, green for Dutch and German, and grey for Spanish and French works. Entrance to the museum is via the archway leading from the Semper. Admission is €6. (The gallery may be open on some Mondays on an experimental basis.)

The second major museum in the Zwinger is the **Porzellansammlung** (Porcelain Collection). The collection was started by Augustus the Strong in 1717. He intended to convert the Japanese Palace in Dresden-Neustadt to display his Asian porcelain collection, which comprised more than 14,500 pieces. The collection survived World War II undamaged but was transported to Russia and only returned in 1958. The core of the original collection was Chinese ceramics from the third to 17th centuries as well as Japanese Imari Porcelain from around 1700. Also on display are the Dragoon Vases – large blue and white vases that Augustus obtained from Prussia's King Friedrich Wilhelm I in exchange for 600 Saxon Dragoons (soldiers). The current collection has 8,000 Meißen pieces including some of the earliest examples produced by Johann Friedrich Böttger, the first European to produce porcelain. A complete room is dedicated to large animal figures produced by Meißen. Entrance to the museum is from the Glockenspielpavillon. Admission is €5.

The **Rüstkammer** (Armory) is one of the world's best collections of parade weapons and costumes. It contains over 1,300 pieces displaying the pageantry of the Dresden court, knights' tournaments, and hunting. In contrast to many similar collections most of the items here are not small obscure pieces of weaponry, but rather large, including several pieces of full body armor for both men and horses. A lovely collection of small children's body armor produced for the princes of Saxony is also interesting to see. Even for those with limited interest in weaponry this museum is worth a few minutes detour. The entrance is directly across the archway from the Gemäldegalerie. Admission is €3.

Jewel-handled sword (1698), Dresden State Art Collection

It would be an error to dismiss the **Mathematisch-Physikalischer Salon** (Mathematics and Physics Saloon) as boring or too specialized. This small museum hidden in a corner of the Zwinger is dedicated to clocks and scientific instruments from the 16th to 19th centuries. Even the briefest of visits will be rewarding. The pieces on display are more art than science and reflect a time when the two disciplines were not strictly divided. The collection includes the largest collection of big globes in Germany and several richly decorated measuring, optical, and meteorological instruments. On display is the world's oldest calculator, developed by Blaise Pascal in 1642. A large collection of clocks in all forms and shapes are exhibited on the second floor. The entrance to the salon is in the corner between Wallpavillon and Kronentor. Admission is €3.

Residenzschloss: Crossing Theaterplatz from the Semper or Zwinger towards the royal residential area, one passes the 1831-erected **Altstädter Wache**, which currently houses a tourist information office as well as the ticket office for the Semper Opera and other entertainment venues. Across the road is the pale yellow Baroque façade of the **Taschenberg Palace** designed by Pöppelmann and given by Augustus the Strong to his mistress the Countess Cosel. It was destroyed in 1945

Residenzschloss

and only restored in 1995 to house the luxurious Kempinski hotel.

One of the most important examples of Renaissance architecture in Germany is the **Residenzschloss** (Residence Castle). Although its history goes back to the 13th century, most of the castle dates from the 16th century. It was mainly left in ruins after the destruction of 1945 but reconstruction was recently completed and several museums moved back into the castle during 2004. All museums in the Schloss are open Wednesday to Monday from 10 am to 6 pm.

The most prominent tower of the castle is the 101-m (323-foot) **Hausmannturm**. Originally built in 1676 and damaged in 1945, it was rebuilt in 1991. The viewing platform is open from April to October. Admission is €2.50.

After decades as the main draw in the Albertinum, the **Grünes Gewölbe** (Green Vaults) returned to the Schloss in September 2004. It is named after its original place of safekeeping and thus nothing in the name hints that this is one of the largest and most magnificent treasury museums in the world. Most of the items were collected or commissioned by Augustus the Strong and his son. In contrast to most other rulers, they actually had the treasury on public display and it has been popular ever since, drawing in recent years around half a million visitors annually. The number may well increase as the move back to the Schloss will again put the full treasure on display and not only half of it as was the case in the Albertinum. The collection includes goldsmithery mainly from the 16th and 17th centuries, works of ivory and amber, pieces commissioned by the electors as well as a vast collection of jewelry. The public's favorite is the 1708 work by Johan Melchior, *Dinglinger's Hofstaat zu Delhi am Geburtstag des Großmoguls Aureng-Zeb* (Court State on the Grand Moghul's Birthday). This diorama has 137 golden and enamel figures adorned with 4,909 diamonds, 160 rubies, 164 emeralds, and 16 pearls. It cost more than the construction of Schloss Moritzburg. From an artistic point of view, Dinglinger's *Diana Bathing* and a gilded coffee service are rated even higher. You may linger and admire the jewelry and other treasures for as long and as close up as you wish. This is fortunate, as some pieces are more than you can take in at first glance

Amazing: *A cherry stone dating from 1589 is carved with 185 human heads – a strong magnifying glass shows it all.*

Most of the collection is exhibited on the second floor of the Schloss while a smaller part will be exhibited from 2006 onwards in the original green vaults in the basement. Admission is €6.

The two other museums in the Schloss are both highly regarded in their fields but are more specialized in nature and of lesser interest to the average visitor. The **Kupferstich-Kabinett** (Collection of Prints and Drawings) has drawings and photos dating from the 15th century to the present. The **Münzkabinett** (Coin Cabinet) displays only a selection of its 280,000 pieces. It consists of not only coins but also historic bonds, notes, decorations, and seals. Admission to these two museums is €3 each.

In between the Elbe and Schloss is the Roman Catholic Cathedral of St Trinitatis (formerly and still commonly known as the **Hofkirche** or Court Church), the largest church in Saxony and the last major Baroque work in Europe. The Reformation started in Saxony and it was one of the first states formally to accept Lutheranism as official religion. The electors of Saxony had long played a prominent role among protestant groupings in the German states but in 1697 Elector Augustus the Strong converted to Roman Catholicism, a condition for accession to the Polish throne. This left the elector without a suitable church to practice his newly adopted religion. It was only during the reign of his son, Friederich Augustus II, that the Hofkirche was erected. It was completed in 1755, severely damaged in 1945, but restored soon after. The tower is 86 m (272 feet) and richly decorated with statues. The 4,800-m² (53,820-square-foot) interior is mainly white with surprisingly few decorations. Of special note is the processional ambulatory between the nave and side aisles – this was essential as outdoor Catholic processions, whether the ruler took part in person or not, were forbidden in Protestant Saxony. A large painting of the *Ascension* by Anton Raphael Mengs hangs above the altar and the organ is the last masterpiece of Gottfried Silbermann. The organ was recently restored and free concerts are occasionally given – schedule at the main entrance. The tombs of the last electors and kings of Saxony can only be seen during a guided tour. Admission is free.

From the Hofkirche towards Neumarkt along Augustusstraße, the outside wall of the Schloss is decorated by a massive mosaic of 24,000 tiles of Meißen porcelain. The 102-m (326-foot) **Fürstenzug** (Procession of the Dukes) depicts all 35 rulers of the House of Saxe-Wettin on horseback, from the first Margrave of Meißen to the Dukes, Electors and finally Kings of Saxony in chronological order from 1125 to 1918. The mosaic survived the bombings of 1945.

Fürstenzug

Behind the wall is the Langer Gang (Long Hall), with a series of 22 Tuscan round-arch arcades connecting the castle with the **Johanneum**. The courtyard, **Stallhof**, was formerly the royal stables and site for knights' tournaments. Nowadays it is used for cultural events, including the medieval Christmas market – Germany's oldest. The Johanneum houses the **Verkehrsmuseum** (Tranport Museum), Augsutusstraße 1, ☎ 0351-86-440, www.verkehrsmuseum.sachsen.de; entrance next to the imposing Renaissance double staircase. The museum has an extensive collection of bicycles and the oldest tram in Germany. Admission is €6.

Frauenkirche: The Frauenkirche (Church of Our Lady), Neumarkt, ☎ 0351-498-1131, www.frauenkirche-dresden.de, is the true symbol and pride of Dresden. It is a High Baroque masterpiece designed by George Bähr, showing the first signs of the pending Classical revival. The foundations were laid in 1726 but the church was not completed until 1742. It is 95 m (311 feet) high and is built of Saxon sandstone, but its true architectural uniqueness is in the 23.5-m (75-foot) diameter stone dome weighing 5,800 tons and

Frauenkirche

nicknamed the stone bell. The Gottfried Silbermann organ was tuned and first played by Johann Sebastian Bach. During the Seven Years' War, the church survived three days of Prussian artillery fire. It withstood the initial air raid in 1945, but collapsed two days afterwards as the heat of the fires cracked the eight sandstone pillars carrying the weight of the dome. After the war, it was left in ruins as a symbol of the destructiveness of war. Reconstruction only started in 1993 and is due to be completed in 2005. In the meantime, guided tours are offered on the hour from 10 am to 4 pm. Concerts are frequently held to help finance the reconstruction. Admission to the church is free.

Frauenkirche: Symbol of Dresden

Historic records show that already in the 11th century a church stood on the site of the Frauenkirche. Several alterations followed until the Dresden town council in 1722 decided to erect a completely new church. Officially, a larger church was needed, but no doubt the main intention was as a snub by the Protestant citizens in the direction of Elector Augustus I the Strong, who converted to Roman Catholicism in order to ascend to the throne of Poland. The new church was of monumental proportions, with a large stone dome of a type virtually unknown north of the Alps. For two centuries and long after the House of Saxe-Wettin lost the Polish crown it remained the symbol of Dresden.

The church survived the bombing of Dresden but collapsed on February 15, 1945 due to cracks in the pillars caused by the extreme heat of the fires. Even before the end of World War II, attempts were made to start rebuilding the church but the postwar political situation made reconstruction impossible. The collapsed church was left as a symbol of the destructiveness of war. The decision to rebuild was only made in 1993.

The exterior of the new church are virtually true to the original but modern technology is employed beneath the surface to strengthen the building. Around 10,000 historic photographs were compared with 90,000 digital images of the ruins in order to use as many of the original stones as possible. A combination of 18th-century vanity and good bookkeeping helped – masons initialed carved blocks and accurate bookkeeping made it possible to determine which stones were used at particular phases of the original construction. A total of 7,000 original stones were reused, with the largest complete piece weighing 95 tons. For the next few years these darker old stones will be clearly visible in contrast to the bright new ones, but eventually pollution will wipe away the reminders of the past.

The Frauenkirche is due to be consecrated on October 30, 2005, but most of the building should be accessible long before then.

The Albertinum: Behind the Frauenkirche, the **Coselpalais**, residence of the illegitimate son of Countess Cosel and Augustus the Strong, was recently restored and now houses restaurants and offices. Further buildings in this area are being restored, some completely from the foundations upwards.

Two blocks farther past the enormous Police Presidium, on the banks of the Elbe, is the **Albertinum**, Georg-Treu-Platz 2, ☎ 0351-491-4619, www.skd-dresden.de. This former arsenal was converted in 1884 to a magnificent four-wing Neo-Renaissance museum. In 2004, it lost some of its main draws, including the Grünes Gewölbe (Green Vault collection of jewelry and goldsmith art), to the renovated Schloss, but the remaining two galleries are still worth a visit and displays will expand into the newly available space. Opening hours are Wednesday to Monday from 10 am to 6 pm. Admission to the Albertinum is €4 and includes entrance to both galleries.

The **Galerie Neue Meister** (Modern Masters Gallery) is a collection of 2,500 paintings from the 19th and 20th centuries. The gallery is famous for its collection of German Romantic painters, such as Caspar David Friedrich and Ludwig Richter, as well as German Impressionists such as Lovis Corinth, Max Slevogt and Max Liebermann. The French Impressionists are represented by single works of famous artists such as Gauguin, Monet, Manet and Degas. However, the Nazis removed and sold on international markets several pieces from the collection, especially Expressionist and Cubist works that did not comply with the Nazi vision of art. Two triptychs by local painters survived the Nazis' wrath: Otto Dixe's *War*, illustrating the cruelty of warlike mentalities, and Hans Grundig's *The Thousand Year Reich*, a prophesy and parody of the Nazi dreams. The collection continues to expand mainly through acquisitions of local and contemporary artists.

The **Skulpturensammlung** (Sculpture Collection) has suffered from a lack of exhibition space, which will now be solved with the move of other collections to the Schloss. The collection ranges from early Egyptian cultures to the present. Augustus the Strong acquired a large collection of antiquities in Rome in 1728 to add to treasures from the Renaissance and Baroque. Newer works, including a Rodin *Thinker*, are exhibited in the Galerie Neue Meister.

Brühlsche Terasse: Returning to the Hofkirche from the Albertinum, the Brühlsche Terasse affords fantastic views of the Elbe and the neighborhood of Neustadt on the opposite bank. It is especially atmospheric in the early evening when most of the buildings are lit up. Goethe called it the "Balcony of Europe" but several of the buildings from his day were replaced at the end of the 19th century. The view is still impressive though.

Across the entrance to the Albertinum is the pleasure garden laid out by Count Brühl. Only the Dolphin Fountain and a group of sphinxes remain of his famous summerhouse, the **Belvedere**. An image in Meißen porcelain commemorates Johann Friedrich Böttger, who was imprisoned under orders to produce gold but discovered the secrets of porcelain production instead.

The steps at the monument for the architect Gottfried Semper lead to the remains of the **Festung Dresden** (Dresden Fortress), George-Treu-Platz, ☎ 0351-491-4786, www.schloesser-dresden.de. This shows the bastions of the medieval city defenses. Opening hours are daily from 10 am to 5 pm (until 4 pm from November to March). Admission is €3.10.

The most beautiful building on the current Brühl Terrace is undoubtedly the **Art Academy**, with a distinctive glass cupola that is lit at night. It is locally known as the "lemon press." Close by is the cream-colored **Sekundogenitur**, former residence of the second-born son to the ruling couple. It now houses a pleasant coffee shop. A monumental staircase, with bronze sculptures representing the four times of day, leads down to the Hofkirche and to the right the Augustus Bridge crossing the Elbe to Neustadt.

Neustadt: One of the most pleasant walks in Dresden is crossing the Elbe on the **Augustusbrücke** (Bridge). The bridge offers the most magnificent views of the Baroque panorama that made Dresden famous. The crossing is especially pleasant at night when the buildings are lit in different colors. A stone bridge was built across the Elbe at this location as far back as 1275 but the current bridge follows the 1731 designs of Pöppelmann.

Market square in Halle, with the Marktkirche, Roter Turm and a statue of Handel (© Halle-Tourist)

Stralsund – brick Gothic facade of the Rathaus (© TZ Stralsund)

Stralsund's medieval walls (© TZ Stralsund)

Above: Schloss Schwerin viewed from the Schlossgarten
(© J. Kreuschmer / www.schwerin.com)
Below: Bremen's romantic Schnoor Quarter (© BTZ)

On the right bank of the Elbe is the Dresden suburb of Neustadt. It suffered less war damage and, although it has few major sights, it does have pleasant Baroque, Neo-Classical, and *Gründerzeit* neighborhoods. **Hauptstraße**, www.neustadt-dresden.de, leads from the 1736 gilded, oversized equestrian statue of Augustus the Strong at the end of the bridge to Albertplatz. It is lined with shops, the courtyards and passages on the left-hand side being particularly favored by artists and with intimate bars and cafés.

A bit to the right behind a large Communist-era apartment block, is the **Museum für Sächsiche Volkskunst** (Saxon Folk Art), Köpckestraße 1, www.skd-dresden.de. It is housed in the Jägerhof, one of very few buildings in Dresden that predates the Baroque era. The collection is of rustic furniture, traditional costumes, toys and Erzgebirge woodcarvings, intended mainly as Christmas decorations. Opening hours are Tuesday to Sunday from 10 am to 6 pm. Admission is €3.

The **Dreikönigskirche**, Hauptstraße 23, was destroyed during the war but repaired in 1994 to resemble the exterior designed by Pöppelmann and Bähr in the 1730s. The interior is modern, but also contains one of the most important Renaissance works in town – the *Dresden Death Dance*, designed by Christoph Walter in 1536 and originally part of the George Gate at the Castle.

A few steps off the main road in the Market Hall is the **Automobilemuseum Dresden**, Markthalle, Metzer Straße 1, ☎ 0351-811-3860. On the second floor is a small collection of cars produced in the German Democratic Republic – the variety on sale was never large. Many have plastic bodies and polluting two-stroke engines. Opening hours are Monday to Friday from 10 am to 5 pm. Admission is €3.80.

From the Albertplatz, Königstraße leads back to the Elbe. This street has some of the classiest shops in Dresden and it is worth looking into the passages and courtyards in the vicinity. At the end of the street is the **Japanese Palace**, originally intended to house Augustus the Strong's Far Eastern porcelain collection. It currently houses two specialized museums. The **Landesmuseum für Vorgeschichte** (Pre-History), Palaisplatz 11, ☎ 0351-892-6927, has temporary exhibitions on Saxon and European archeology. It is open Tuesday to Sunday from 10 am to 6 pm. Admission is €3. The **Museum für Völkerkunde** (Ethnology), Palaisplatz 11, ☎ 0351-814-4860, displays ethnological pieces. It is open Tuesday to Sunday from 10 am to 5 pm. Admission is a rather expensive €8.

Großer Garten Area: To the east of the Old Town is a large English-style garden, the **Großer Garten**. Its history dates back to 1676 but the current layout is late 19th century. It is a favored place of relaxation and includes a zoo, botanical garden, open-air stage, and a pleasure palace.

Across the road from the main entrance to the park is the **German Hygiene Museum**, Lignerplatz 1, ☎ 0351-48-460, www.dhmd.de. It was founded in 1911 by the manufacturer of Odol mouthwash and has serious scientific displays on human biology, medical progress, and a healthy lifestyle. Many displays are hands-on and popular with children as well. Opening hours are Tuesday to Friday from 9 am to 5 pm, weekends from 10 am to 6 pm. Admission is €2.50.

In a corner of the park is one of Dresden's prestige investment projects, the **Gläserne Manifaktur**, (Transparent Factory), Lennéstraße 1, ☎ 0180-589-6268, www.glaesernemanufaktur.de. In this glass cube some 800 workers produce Volkswagen's prestige car, the Phaeton. Customers taking delivery of their new vehicles have priority on the tours, which must be reserved in advance. The factory is open Monday to Saturday from 8 am to 8 pm.

Pillnitz: To the south of Dresden along the Elbe is the Schloss Pillnitz (Pillnitz Palace). It was the summer residence of the Saxon court. The River and Hillside Palaces were completed in 1722. It currently houses the **Kunstgewerbemuseum** (Museum of Decorative Arts) and is open May to October, daily from 10 am to 6 pm. Admission is €3. A major attraction in the garden is an over 200-year-old camellia.

Cultural Events & Festivals

The main cultural draw is inevitably the **Semperoper**, but no less impressive is the modern **Kulturpalast** (Civic Center), home of the Dresdner Philharmonic Orchestra, and the Schauspielhaus next to the Zwinger. For reservations, contact **Dresden Tourist**, ☎ 0351-491-920, www.dresden-tourist.de.

Dresden hosts various annual and one-time festivals ranging from flamenco dancing to mass playing of street organs. The largest is the **Dresdner Musikfestspiele** (Musical Festival) during the first half of June. It has around 170 events in 70 locations. A three-day **Dixieland Festival** in May also draws a large audience. In the Frauenkirche, Georg-treu-Platz 3, ☎ 0351-656-0680, www.frauenkriche-dresden.org, concerts are held most Saturdays at 8 pm to help finance the reconstruction of the church.

The **Striezelmarkt in Dresden** can claim to be the oldest Christmas market in Germany. It has been in existence since 1434 and has increased in size to cover more than a mile from the Hauptbahnhof all the way to the heart of Neustadt across the Elbe. The best part is inside the walls of the castle at the Stallhof. Here the market resembles one from the Middle Ages, with typical food and drink served in appropriately primitive containers. Even the lights are dimmed, leaving it fairly dark in places. *Stollen*, the most popular German Christmas cake, originally came from Dresden and is on sale everywhere – boxed and gift-wrapped if you prefer.

Shopping

The main shopping streets in Dresden are the **Prager Straße** leading from the main station toward the old town and the **Wilsdruffer Straße**, which crosses the Prager at the Altmarkt. On these streets, all the major shopping chains and department stores are represented.

More interesting are the higher-end boutiques and small shops in the **Neustadt** area across the Elbe. The 1899 **Markthalle** (market hall), Metzer Straße 1, ☎ 0351-810-5445, www.markthalle-dresden.de, has been renovated and now hosts a range of small shops and a car museum rather than a normal market. High-quality food and cheese are available here, but more useful to the foreign visitor is the **Weinkontor**, ☎ 0351-810-5455, which sells wine from five continents, including local Saxon wine. **Amida Spielzeuge**, ☎ 0351-810-5405, sells old-fashioned wooden and tin toys for children of all ages.

Nearby **Königstraße**, www.koenigstrasse-dresden.de, has the high-class shops of Dresden. This street, as well as the smaller streets and courtyards leading from it, has maintained its original Baroque character. Most popular are boutiques for both men and women, jewelers, antiques and fine arts.

A popular **flea market** is held Saturday from 7 am to 2 pm on the banks of the Elbe between Carola and Albert Bridges.

Adventures

On Foot

Town Walks: A wide range of guided old-town walks is available. Request details from the Tourist Office.

On Wheels

By Bicycle: In Dresden, both major train stations rent bicycles by the day. The shop in Dresden Hauptbahnhof, ☎ 0351-461-3262 is open daily from 6 am to 10 pm. At Dresden-Neustadt, ☎ 0351-461-5601, the opening hours are weekdays from 6 am to 8 pm and weekends from 8 am to 8 pm.

By Train: Ever since the first steam engine connected Leipzig and Dresden in 1839, Saxony has been a paradise for fans of steam engines and narrow-guage trains. Dresden annually hosts the largest **Dampflokfest** (Steam Engine Festival) in Germany, attracting 30,000 visitors each May. Contact the Dresden Tourist Office for exact details.

The **Lilliputian Park Train**, ☎ 0351-445-6795, www.liliputbahn.de, in Dresden's Grosser Garten, operates from April to October. This five-km (three-mile) route is very much aimed at children, while the other lines are historic ones that carried freight and passengers from the 19th century to the present.

Another popular route just south of Dresden is the 26-km (16-mile) **Weißeritztalbahn** from Freital-Hainsberg across 40 bridges through the romantic Rabenau Gorge to Kipsdorf in the Erz Mountains. This route was severely damaged by the floods of 2002 but should again be in service from 2005.

For information on other routes, which are more off the beaten track, contact **Sachsen Tourism & Marketing**, Bautzner Straße 45-47, 01099 Dresden, ☎ 0351-491-700, www.sachsen-tour.de.

By Bus: Dresden's Baroque heart is small and best seen on foot but the buses do take routes to outlying sights of lesser fame. Personally, I have my doubts whether these tours add anything of value that the average visitor cannot see on foot. However, for day-trips farther afield, bus and other organized trips make more sense, especially if time is limited and you want to combine more than one sight into a day-trip.

The **Hamburger Hummelbahn Dresden**, Feldschlösschenstraße 8, ☎ 0351-494-0404, www.hummerlbahn.de, offers several sightseeing tours of Dresden and the region, ranging from 90 minutes to three hours. Tours are either with a double-decker bus or a small "Hummelbahn" motorized train. Some tours can be combined with a tour of the Semperoper when the latter is open.

From Dresden several companies arrange tours to the historic and natural attractions in the vicinity. In addition to an array of city tours, the **Dresdner Verkehrsvertriebe (DVB)**, Trachenberger Straße 40, ☎ 0351-8570, www.dvbag.de, offers tours to Schloss Wackerbarth on the Saxon Wine route as well as to Schloss Mortizburg.

Rollerblading: Up to 3,000 skaters meet from April to October on Friday nights at 9 pm to skate through the streets of Dresen. The start and finish is from Halfpipe, St Petersburger Straße, near the Hauptbahnhof, and follows alternating routes of 30 km (18 miles) through Dresden. The exact schedule and routes are posted at www.nachtskaten-dresden.de or by phone at ☎ 0351-484-8794. Rollerblades and safety equipment can be rented for around €5 on a first-come, first-served basis.

Trabi Safari: Cars produced in the former East Germany are not only exhibited in Dresden museums. The Trabi, short for Trabant, was one of the most widely produced cars. It has a plastic body and noisy polluting twin-stroke engine. For most people there was simply no other choice. After the *Wende*, Trabis disappeared from the streets of Germany as fast as locals could get their hands on second-hand Golfs and Opels. However, **Trabi Safari**, Theatherplatz/Schenklwache, ☎ 0351-899-0066, www.trabi-safari.de, allows you to explore Dresden while you're driving one. In a convoy of up to eight cars, with a guide communicating via radio, you can wind through town at speeds up to 30 km/h (18 mph) – it feels a lot faster! This car is not modern so each driver gets instructions on how to operate it first and, if you do not crash it, a Trabi "driving license" is awarded afterwards. Two tours departing from Theaterplatz are available: 45 minutes cost €12 to €18 per person and 90 minutes are €20 to €30. Trips are run daily between 10 am and 6 pm. From March to November, additional night tours are scheduled between 8 pm and midnight. If you cannot fit this fun tour into your Dresden schedule the same company helps to pollute Berlin air in a similar way. Prior reservations are required should you need an English-speaking guide.

On Horseback

Although Saxony has more than 300 riding farms, most are very small. It is therefore easiest to contact **Landurlaub in Sachsen**, Friederichstraße 24, 01067 Dresden, ☎ 0351-471-5261, www.land-urlaub.de, who can arrange riding excursions all over Saxony. Landurlaub can also arrange accommodation on farms, if desired, independent of riding.

In the Air

Hot-Air Ballooning: Several companies offer flights from Dresden and the competition helps to keep prices down. Sometimes it's possible to start from the banks of the Elbe across from Dresden's Baroque center – a more magnificent urban start is hard to imagine. **Ballonfahrten Dresden**, ☎ 0351-416-1700, www.ballon-dresden.de, takes off from central Dresden as well as several other locations in Dresden and vicinity, including Moritzburg and Meißen.

Also offering flights from central Dresden is **Ballon-Crew Steina**, ☎ 03578-774-361, www.ballon-crew-steina.de. Discounts apply to morning starts on weekdays and children's discounts are larger than from most other companies. Evening flights are also available.

On Water

Canoeing & Kayaking: Canoeing is allowed on the Elbe and many options of various lengths are available. Also contact the tourist offices in the various towns; boat rentals are available in practically every town near water.

From Dresden northwards, **Augustustours**, Bischofsweg 64, 01099 Dresden, ☎ 0351-803-3280, www.augustustours.de, offers half-day and full-day paddling tours on the Elbe near Dresden. Both tours end in Meißen, with the full-day (around six hours paddling) starting from Dresden and the half-day (two hours paddling) from Radebeul. Packages include all equipment, bicycle, and luggage transfers if required.

Riverboats: The **Sächsische Dampfschiffahrt**, Hertha-Lindner-Straße 10, 01067 Dresden, ☎ 0351-866-090, www.saechsische-dampfschiffahrt.de, has eight historic paddle steamers, the largest and oldest collection in the world. They operate on the Elbe in the vicinity of Dresden. From April to October there are daily departures from Dresden's Terassenufer in front of the Brühlsche Terasse. Most but not all cruises are on steam ships. There is usually one ship going north, reaching Meißen within two hours; the round-trip is three hours. Cost is €10.50 one-way. Around 10 ships go south operating between various stations. Dresden to Königstein takes 5½ hours, but is two hours faster coming back (€14.50 one-way). Round-trip fares are heavily discounted but using the train or bus one way will save time. Several theme tours operate mostly on weekends from Dresden. On May 1 a **steamship parade** is held and at end of August a two-day **steamship festival** – written reservations are required during this period.

Where to Stay

Dresden Altstadt

Dresden has a large selection of hotels representing all standards and prices. All hotels listed here are within comfortable distance from the major sights, with the first two right in the middle of Dresden's Baroque heartland.

HOTEL PRICE CHART	
Rates per room based on double occupancy, including taxes.	
€	Under €50
€€	€50-€100
€€€	€101-€150
€€€€	Over €150

The Kempinski group often operates the best hotels in the few cities where it has a presence. In Dresden, the **Kempinski Hotel Taschenbergpalais** opened in 1994 as the best hotel in town. The Baroque Taschenberg Palace, destroyed in World War II, had originally been built by Augustus the Strong for his mistress, the countess of Cosel. It was rebuilt by Kempinski. The exterior is pure Baroque and close to the original, while the interior is modern and furnished to the highest standards. Rooms are large and tastefully decorated. The better rooms have a view of the Zwinger. In winter, an ice skating rink operates in the hotel's courtyard. Taschenberg 3, 01067 Dresden, ☎ 0351-49-120, fax 0351-491-2812, www.kempinski-dresden.de. (€€€€)

The **Hilton Dresden** has an almost perfect location between the Frauenkirche and the Brühlsche Terasse. This large modern hotel has all the expected comforts, although rooms are not particularly large. Lines are mostly straight and the combination of dark wood, chrome, and grey gives a modern, clean atmosphere. Despite its central location, the views from most rooms are not exactly exciting; the better ones will, however, soon face the newly rebuilt Frauenkirche without the dust and noise of reconstruction. The Hilton operates several restaurants and coffee shops in the vicinity, assuring good quality and service, but at a price. An der Frauenkirche 5, 01067 Dresden, ☎ 0351-86-420, fax 0351-864-2725, www.hilton.com. (€€€-€€€€)

The luxury five-star **Radisson SAS Gewandhaus** was completely renovated in 1997 and is within easy reach of the old town. Its location on the edge of the old town is convenient for private or public transportation but also for walking to the sights. The large rooms are luxuriously furnished in warm colors. A large atrium with natural light is the focal point in the hotel and several dining options are available. Ringstraße 1, 01067 Dresden, ☎ 0351-49-490, fax 0351494-9490, www.radissonsas.com. (€€€-€€€€)

As the name promises, the **Art'otel Dresden** oozes art, but mostly post-modern art, not the Baroque that seems to dominate much of Dresden. More than 600 paintings and sculptures by local artist A Penck decorate the hotel. Rooms are very comfortable, furnished with mostly neutral colors. Some may find the decoration a bit over-styled but for the in crowd it is all cutting edge here. Service is first-class. Not surprisingly, there is an art gallery inside the hotel as well. Ostra-Allee 33, 01067 Dresden, ☎ 0351-49-220, fax 0351-492-2777, www.artotel.de. (€€€-€€€€)

Just outside the old town, on the banks of the Elbe, is **Am Terrassenufer**, a comfortable midrange hotel. A curve in the Elbe gives some rooms a view of the Semperopera and Schloss, while many have clear views of the Elbe. All visitors can enjoy these views from the modern bar. Terassenufer 12, 01069, Dresden, ☎ 0351-440-9500, fax 0351-440-9600, www.hotel-terrassenufer.de. (€€€)

The Dorint group has a reputation for well-managed middle class hotels and the Dresden **Dorint** is no exception. Located a few blocks from the Frauenkirche it is just outside the historic district but still within easy walking distance. The hotel was built in 1994 to a modern design. Rooms are comfortably furnished and the fitness area is well-equipped. Grunauer Straße 14, 01069 Dresden, ☎ 0351-49-150, fax 0351-491-5100, www.dorint.com/dresden. (€€€)

There are three Mercure hotels in Dresden but the **Mercure Newa** has the advantage of being close to the main station. Rooms are well-appointed and more luxurious than the Ibis hotels, making this a more comfortable option should you need an address close to the main station. St Petersburger Straße 34, 01069 Dresden, ☎ 0351-481-4109, fax 0351-495-5137, www.mercure.com. (€€-€€€)

Close to the Hauptbahnhof are three massive 1960s-style buildings owned by the **Ibis** hotel group. The three almost identical hotels offer close to a thousand rooms. There is little to distinguish the three, the rooms, or personnel. The rates are the same too. Approaching from the station, they are the **Bastei**, **Königstein** and **Lilienstein**. The location close to the station and in the heart of Dresden's main shopping street is convenient. The rooms may be uninspiring and small but so is the price. Small single rooms (€) go for a song. Prager Straße, 01069 Dresden, ☎ 0351-48-560, fax 0351-4856-6667, www.ibishotels.com. (€€)

Neustadt

Dresden's Neustadt neighborhood on the opposite bank of the Elbe has several pleasant hotels still within easy reach of the historic center.

Some consider the **Bülow Residenz** as still the best hotel in Dresden. Less famous and much smaller than the Kempinski Hotel Taschenberg, it does not have to give it an inch in terms of luxury or quality of service. It occupies a 1730 Baroque manor house that was completely renovated in 1993. The 30 rooms are large and comfortably furnished. The hotel is in a quiet neighborhood between König and Hauptstraße. It also has the best restaurant in Dresden – one of only two Michelin star establishments in all of Saxony. Rähnitzgasse 19, 01097 Dresden, ☎ 0351-80-030, fax 0351-800-3100, www.buelow-residenz.de. (€€€-€€€€)

The modern and not particularly inspiring exterior of the **Westin Bellevue** dates from the Communist era but was completely refurbished in 2000. Rooms are comfortably furnished and reasonable large. For once, Bellevue in the name does not refer to what was destroyed but rather what is available. The better rooms have spectacular views across the Elbe towards Dresden's Baroque skyline. Similar views can be enjoyed from the fitness area, which has a large pool. Unfortunately, the view for cheaper rooms is of a busy street, but double-glazing successfully keeps the noise out. Very good deals are available during the off-season. Große Meißner Straße 15, 01097 Dresden, ☎ 0351-8050, fax 0351-805-1609, www.westin.com/bellevue. (€€-€€€€)

The **Bayerischer Hof** is a small but pleasant hotel close to Dresden-Neustadt train station. Rooms are comfortably furnished and stylish. The restaurant offers both Saxon and Bavarian cuisine. However, special deals at the Westin are better value when available. Antonstraße 33-35, 01097 Dresden, ☎ 0351-829-370, fax

0351-801-4860, www.bayerischer-hof-dresden.de. (€€-€€€)

The **Mercure Albertbrücke** is in the heart of the new governmental area of Dresden. Most guests are on government-related business, opening the way for good deals in the off-season. Excellent public transportation connections mean the major sights are just minutes away. Furnishings are comfortable rather than grand but all rooms are fully air-conditioned. Melanchthonstraße 2, 01099 Dresden, ☎ 0351-80-610, fax 0351-806-1444, www.accor-hotels.com. (€€-€€€)

Camping

A very pleasant site is **Camping & Freizeitpark LuxOase** just north of Dresden near Radeberg. It has been in operation since 1997 with excellent sanitation and other facilities. It is idyllically located at the Stausee Lake with ample entertainment options. Closest public transportation: 800 m (2,560 feet) to bus line 305, three km (1.8 miles) to S-Bahn line Arnsdorf-Dresden. The site is open March to October. It has space for 120 tents, caravans, or campers. Arnsdorfer Straße 1, 01900 Kleinröhrsdorf/Dresden, ☎ 035952-56-666, fax 035952-56-024, www.luxoase.de.

Where to Eat

Dresden offers many dining options in the historic old town area, with a strong concentration of establishments in the vicinity of the Frauenkirche and Hilton Hotel as well as some pricy options close to the Zwinger and Semperoper. Neustadt also has pleasant dining, with fewer foreign tourists. Most of the restaurants listed here are popular and reservations for dinner are highly recommended. For most, simply phoning half an hour ahead to jump the waiting lines would be sufficient.

Zwinger - Semperoper area

In German cities, the best gourmet restaurants are often in the top hotels and Dresden is no exception. The luxurious Kempinski Hotel Taschenbergpalais hosts the restaurant **Intermezzo**, Taschenberg 3, ☎ 0351-49-120, www.kempinski-dresden.de. Like the hotel, the restaurant is elegant but modern, with first-class food and service to match. The cuisine is light Mediterranean inspired with seasonal variations. (€€€€)

DINING PRICE CHART

Price per person for an entrée, including water, beer or soft drink.

€	Under €10
€€	€10-€20
€€€	€21-€35
€€€€	Over €35

Behind the Semperoper in a former studio of the Zwinger is the **Alte Meister**, Theaterplatz 1a, ☎ 0351-481-0426, www.altemeister.net. The cuisine hints of French but the chef loves to experiment and create new innovations. The menu selection is small but varied. The restaurant itself has only 30 seats but in summer the outdoor terrace accommodates 120 more with a free view of the Semper, Zwinger, and Hofkirche. (€€-€€€€)

Also on Theaterplatz is the elegant **Italienische Dörfchen**, Theaterplatz 3, ☎ 0351-498-160, www.zugast.de/id. The name, meaning Little Italian Town, is derived from the Italian artisans who resided here while working on the Hofkirche. In contrast, the cuisine is mostly Saxon and international with not much emphasis on Italian at all. The restaurant has several sections, with the second floor the most elegant. In summer, the outdoor seating is particularly pleasant with some of the best views in town. Generally, having a drink and snack here is more rewarding than a complete meal. (€-€€€)

Saxon Cuisine

It is often difficult to find traditional German restaurants in the centers of major German cities but Dresden's historic district has a surprisingly large number of restaurants offering Saxon cuisine.

Three very popular restaurants share the same concept of regional cuisine in the setting of historic vaulted cellars. The décor recalls Saxony of old and the staff wears 18th-century period costume. Suckling pig is on the spit. The tables are mainly large and smaller groups may have to share. It all contributes to a jovial atmosphere. The food is pretty good and service is fast and friendly too. Reservations are highly recommended and, even then, parties of less than four may have to share a table with others.

The largest of the three, with space for up to 400 diners, is the **Sophienkeller**, in the basement of the lofty Kempinski Hotel Taschenbergerpalais, Taschenberg 3, ☎ 0351-497-260, www.sophienkeller-dresden.de. (€€-€€€)

The other two are in the Frauenkirche district, with the **Pulverturm**, An der Frauenkirche 12, ☎ 0351-262-600, www.pulverturm-dresden.de (€-€€), in the cellar of the Coselpalais, a building with a close connection to the Taschenbergpalais. The **Festungsmauern**, Am Brühlschen Garten 4, ☎ 0351-262-032, www.festungsmauern-dresden.de (€-€€), is inside the former city fortifications in an incredible large barrel vault.

Slightly more upmarket, but still unashamedly Saxon, is the wine restaurant **Wettiner Keller**, Hilton Hotel, An der Frauenkirche 5, ☎ 0351-864-2860, www.hilton.com. The emphasis here is on good Saxon wine to accompany traditional hearty Saxon food. The décor is rustic and, in summer, the terrace has Elbe views. Although part of the Hilton, the entrance is across the street at the back of the Hilton in Terassengasse or via a covered walkway from the second floor of the hotel. Closed on Sunday and Monday. (€€-€€€)

Around Frauenkirche & Brühlsche Terasse

The Hilton hotel is perfectly located next to the Frauenkirchen in the heart of Dresden's traditional gastronomic district. Although most of the restaurants in this area now squarely aim at the tourist market, the variety is still good. Many of the best belong to the **Hilton Hotel**, An der Frauenkirche 5, www.hilton.com, assuring English menus, good quality, and service, but at a markup. The **Rossinni**, ☎ 0351-864-2855, (€€-€€€€), on the second floor of the Hilton, is one of the best Italian restaurants in the region. The good kitchen is backed up by excellent service and views of the Frauenkirche. Underneath this splendid restaurant on the ground floor is the more informal **Bistro**, ☎ 0351-86-420, (€-€€), offering an international menu of smaller meals. The following cafés serve better food and have better surroundings.

At the back of the Hilton in Terassengasse is the very pleasant **Café Antik Kunst**, Terassengasse, ☎ 0351-498-9836, which combines an antique shop with a café. You actually sit on some antiques here. The menu includes not only coffee but also small meals. (€-€€)

Inside the Sekundogenitur, the Hilton operates two cafés that more or less share the same menu and the same kitchen. The **Café Vis-à-Vis**, ☎ 0351-86-420, (€-€€), is an elegant establishment with stylish furniture and decoration in keeping with the lovely exterior of the former palace. On the far right is the small **Splendid Espresso Bar**, ☎ 0351-86-420, (€-€€), with modern red leather seats. The atmosphere here is more relaxed, although the surroundings are still very much up-market and a bit formal. The staff is friendly and relaxed though. Coffee and food comes at a slight premium but the quality is excellent.

Like the Taschenbergpalais, the Coselpalais was rebuilt in the 1990s. It now has office space and two noteworthy restaurants. In the cellar is the Pulverturm, described above, but on the ground floor is the stylish **Restaurant & Grand Café Coselpalais**, An der Frauenkirche 12, ☎ 0351-498-9803. The cuisine is mostly Saxon and the surroundings elegant. (€€-€€€€)

The **Münzgasse** has traditionally been the place for bars and restaurants in Dresden but the fare now on offer is more international. Two interesting options are the Australian restaurant and bar, **Ayers Rock**, Münzgasse 8, ☎ 0351-490-1188, and the Spanish **Las Tapas**, Munzgasse 4, ☎ 0351-496-0108, www.las-tapas.de. (€-€€)

Großer Garten

In the middle of the Großer Garten near the Carola Lake is the **Carola-Schlösschen**, Karcherallee 29, ☎ 0351-472-7374, www.carolaschloesschen.de.

In keeping with the up-market image of the Phaeton that is manufactured in VW's Gläserne Manufaktur, the **Lesage**, Lennéstraße 1, ☎ 0351-420-4250, offers quality Mediterranean food supervised by the Hotel Kempinski. The atmosphere is high-tech architecture but comfortable and stylish. (€€-€€€)

Neustadt

The Neustadt area has some pleasant restaurants where you are less likely to meet up with fellow foreigners. There are several small restaurant-bars hidden in courtyards and passages with the higher end restaurants concentrated, like the classier shops, in Königstraße.

The two top gourmet restaurants are located in the two top hotels of the district. The **Caroussel**, in the Hotel Bülow Residenz, Rähnitzgasse 19, ☎ 0351-80-030, www.buelow-residenz.de, is one of the best in Saxony and proudly carries its Michelin star. The cuisine is new German with Mediterranean touches. A la carte is available but the set menus are the connoisseur's choice to appreciate fully the award-winning chef's skill. The décor is elegant Baroque. The restaurant is closed on Sunday and Monday. (€€€€)

The **Canaletto** in the Westin Bellevue, Große Meisner Straße 15, ☎ 0351-8050, www.canaletto-dresden.de, is named after the Italian painter whose panoramas of Dresden have pride of place in the Old Masters Gallery in the Zwinger. Like the better rooms of the hotel, the restaurant offers views of the Dresden Baroque panorama. Once again, the cuisine is light German with a Mediterranean touch. (€€€€)

The Königstraße has several pleasant restaurants scattered between the stylish shops and boutiques. For Saxon and international cuisine, try **Kö 5**, Königstraße 5a, ☎ 0351-802-4088, www.koe5.de. (€€-€€€)

French cuisine is served at **La Marechal de Saxe**, Königstraße 15, ☎ 0351-810-5880. (€€-€€€)

Just off Königstraße near Palaisplatz is **New California**, Wallgässchen 4, ☎ 0351-811-3510, www.newcalifornia.de, a bar-restaurant combination. (€€-€€€)

Similar places are scattered through the area but, as they all seem to cater to the same clientele, many go out of business as fast as new ones open.

Prague is a mere 150 km (90 miles) from Dresden, but if you are not heading that way you can still enjoy some traditional Czech cuisine at **Wenzels Prager Bierstuben**, Königstraße 1, ☎ 0351-804-2010, www.wenzel-prager-bierstube.de. The atmosphere is informal. (€€-€€€)

■ Day-Trips from Dresden

Saxon Switzerland (Elbsandsteingebirge)

Just south of Dresden the Sächsische Schweiz (Saxon Switzerland) is one of Germany's most beautiful and strangest landscapes. The name is a bit of a misnomer as the highest peak here is only 561 m (1,795 feet) high. The alternative name Elbsandsteingebirge (Elbe sandstone mountains) is a better indication of what is on offer. The drenching of lakes millions of years ago combined with centuries of erosion left a landscape of strange peaks, sheer cliffs and deep canyons not found elsewhere in Germany. Most of the area is protected in the Saxon Switzerland National Park.

The area is a haven for outdoor fanatics, offering 1,200 km (720 miles) of marked hiking trails, 384 km (220 miles) of cycling routes, the Elbe, smaller streams, and lakes for boating, a fantastic natural theater, and a wealth of fauna and flora. In addition, there are pretty towns and mighty fortresses to explore. All this is within easy reach of Dresden with half-hourly S-Bahn suburban trains reaching deep into the area. Annual visitors are 2½ million making early reservations in the peak season advisable.

Information Sources

Tourist Office: For information on the whole area as well as booking of hotels and package deals, contact Tourbu, Am Bahnhof 6, 01814 Bad Schandau, ☎ 035022-4950, www.saechsische-schweiz.de.

Transportation

The area is easily reached from Dresden on the S-Bahn line S1. It runs every 30 minutes from Meißen via Dresden to Bad Schandau and beyond. All stations are on the left bank of the Elbe with convenient ferries to the opposite bank in towns without bridges. The region is also well-served by bus as well as narrow-guage railways – see *Adventures* for details. It can also be reached by boat – see page 98, *Elbe Steamers* in the *Dresden* section.

Pirna

Pirna considers itself the gateway to Saxon Switzerland and it has useful transport connections to the rest of the region. It also has a beautifully preserved medieval town center still resembling almost unchanged a 1753 painting by Canaletto. The town hall is the symbol of Pirna but equally famous is the **Marienkirche**. It has a 60-meter (195-foot) tower, but the interior is the most impressive. Built in the early 16th century, it is a hall church with three naves and beautifully decorated pillars and roof paintings. The pillars never give the functional impression of supporting the roof – some look like tree trunks and others twist like corkscrews.

Where to Stay & Eat

The **Romantik Hotel Deutsches Haus**, Niedere Burgstraße 1, 01796 Pirna, ☎ 03501-443-440, fax 03501-528-104, www.romantikhotels.com/pirna, is a pleasant small hotel in the heart of the historic old town. The hotel is elegant and rooms are furnished with solid wood furniture. It has been under management of the Riedel family since 1922. The restaurant (€€-€€€) is famous for its Saxon wines as well as for cuisine ranging from hearty local dishes to Italian and French. (€€)

Bastei

The **Kurort Rathen**, a town with only 500 inhabitants, is famous for two natural wonders made somewhat more famous through human interference. The Bastei area has some of the most spectacular scenery, including a 305-m (976-foot) peak and a deep narrow valley. This was made easily accessible by construction of the seven-m (22-foot) **Basteibrücke** (Bastei Bridge), offering fabulous views 200 m (656 feet) above the valley. The bridge was built in 1851 with local sandstone, replacing the 1826 wooden construction and resulting in less visual interference than one normally would have expected. The bridge is reached by a 30- to 45-minute walk from Rathen – the route becomes steep close to the bridge, with many stairs. Even higher, at 305 m (976 feet), is the viewing platform on the Bastei peak itself. On a really busy summer day up to 50,000 people come to the bridge.

An alternative way to get there is by bus from Stadt Wehlen. Buses operated by **Bastei-Kraxler**, Dresdner Straße 1, 01824 Königstein, ☎ 035021-67614, leave from the Marktplatz every hour and reach the parking area near the Bastei in 20 minutes. From here it is just a few minutes walk to the bridge. Round-trips to Wehlen depart on the half-hour. It is also possible to take the bus four times per day from the Bastei to Königstein via Hohnstein and Bad Schandau. Journey time is just over an hour.

Also in Rathen is the **Rathen Felsenbühne** (Rock Stage), Amselgrund 17, 01824 Rathen, ☎ 035024-7770, one of the most beautiful natural theaters in Europe. It stages operas, musicals and other shows annually from May to September. During daytime, it is open to visitors for free.

Transportation

In Rathen, the S-Bahn stops on the left bank while the sights are on the right bank. A historic **Gierseilfähre** ferry operates between the two banks. It uses a cable on the riverbed and the kinetic energy of the river itself to make the crossing without any other outside energy sources.

Where to Stay & Eat

Very close to the most famous viewing point in the area, the Bastei Bridge, is the modern **Berghotel und Panorama Restaurant Bastei**, 01847 Lohmen-Bastei, ☎ 035024-7790, www.bastei-berghotel.de. This modern hotel was erected in grand style during the Communist era and offers magnificent views of the area. It is under private management now and comfortably furnished but, apart from the view, offers nothing special. Staying here allows parking access closer than day-visitors have. In contrast to the approach from Rathen, the hotel is on the higher level, allowing easier access to the viewing bridge (though you will still have to climb some steps). (€€)

Königstein

On a hilltop 240 m (750 feet) above the Elbe towers Germany's largest fortress – **Festung Königstein**, 01824 Königstein, ☎ 035021-64-607, www.festung-koenigstein.de. Its history dates back to the early 13th century and it has been part of the Mark Meißen, later Saxony, since 1459. Its main purpose from then on was as a refuge for the Saxon court and art treasures in times of crisis. This role it performed masterfully and it was never conquered. During the Seven Years' War with Prussia and during the revolutionary events of 1848/49 the court hightailed it here. It also served as a prison, with the most famous inmate Johann Böttger, inventor of European porcelain, from 1706 to 1707. Due to the presence of much of Saxony's ammunition in the castle, he was not allowed to experiment here using fire. In World War II, it served as a prison for captured senior officers, mainly French. Probably unknown to them, they shared the castle with the best museum pieces from Dresden – many pieces were to detour via Russia before returning home in the mid-1950s. More willing overnight guests included Czar Peter I and Napoleon Bonaparte (Saxony was a French ally, with disastrous consequences.)

It is a mighty fortress, consisting of 30 buildings surrounded by an outside wall over a mile long. The well is 152.5 m (487 feet) deep – literally drilled through sandstone. In summer months, the 1912-installed technology to draw water is demonstrated. The barracks, dating from 1589, are the oldest in Germany. Other buildings are furnished with period furniture from the late 19th century and some house museums on military and local history. Several dining options are available, including a theme restaurant in the casemates.

The castle is located on the B172 between Pirna and Königstein. It is a short walk from the parking lot. Bus 241 operates between the two towns; the castle is a short walk from bus stop Abzweig Festung. The classic approach is the half-hour walk from the town center of Königstein. The incline is steep but ultimately rewarding. Alternatively, Bastei-Kraxler, Dresdner Straße 1, 01824 Königstein, ☎ 035021-67614, operates the Festung Express, one of those goofy motorized trains found in European tourist areas, April to October every 30 minutes, from Königstein Reißiger Platz to the fortress parking lot.

The castle opens daily year-round at 9 am but closes April to September at 8 pm, October at 6 pm, and November to March at 5 pm. Small parts and some shops and restaurants are closed from October to March. Admission is €4. Guided tours on special themes are €1.50 in German or €2 should an English one be available.

Where to Stay & Eat

Most visitors to Königstein stop over just long enough to find the route to the castle. **Hotel Lindernhof**, Gohrischer Straße 2, 01824 Königstein, ☎ 035021-68-243, fax 035021-66-214, www.lindenhof-koenigstein.de, is a pleasant small hotel with comfortable rooms. It offers views of the Elbe Valley from Lilienstein to the fortress. (€-€€)

There are several dining options in the fortress but the most popular is the enormous theme restaurant **In der Kasematten**, Festung Königstein, 01824 Königstein, ☎ 035021-64-444, www.kasematten.de. Here guests can dine as in the time of Augustus the Strong, meaning opulent portions of Saxon cuisine served by staff in period costume. The restaurant is closed November, and January to March, but other dining facilities at the castle remain open. (€€-€€€)

Camping: Located between the railway line and Elbe River, **Camping Königstein** has views of both the river and the castle. The sanitation facilities are modern and well-equipped. Closest public transportation: one km (.6 mile) to S-Bahn station Königstein. The site is open April to October. Schandauer Straße 25e, 01824 Königstein, ☎/fax 035021-68-224, www.camping-königstein.de.

In the beautiful Kirnitzschtal Valley is **Campingplatz Ostrauer Mühle**. The Kirnitzschtal tram as well as the public bus stop at the campsite offering easy connections to the S-Bahn station in Bad Schandau four km (2.4 miles) away. The site is open all year. Kirnitzschtal, 01814 Bad Schandau, ☎ 035022-42-742, fax 035022-50-352, www.ostrauer-muehle.de.

Adventures

■ On Foot

Countryside Hikes: Some of the best walks are in the Saxon Switzerland area with around 1,200 km (720 miles) of marked paths. Despite the name, the peaks are not that high and the winters not that cold. Most paths are accessible year-round without any special equipment. A popular 40-minute walk is from Rathen to the Bastei, with marvelous views from the Bastei Bridge. A circular route leads back to Rathen via the Schwedische Löcher (Swedish holes), where the local population hid from the Swedish troops during the Thirty Years' War, and the Rathen Felsenbühne (Rock Theater).

Good options for those not willing to walk around on their own, are the free daily guided walks with Saxon Switzerland National Park officials from April to October. Schedules and destinations vary but the walks are generally around four hours long. Although the tour will be in German, non-German speakers are free to go along and in the process see areas they would have been unlikely to find on their own. If the guides do not speak English, some fellow-hikers almost certainly will.

Rock Climbing: Rock climbing is currently very popular in Germany with most larger cities offering a couple of indoor climbing opportunities. Saxony is no exception, but the Saxon Switzerland area offers excellent outdoor opportunities. In fact, it is claimed that free climbing has its origin here. More than a thousand peaks can be scaled in over 16,000 different ways.

Several companies offer lessons ranging from one to several days and rent equipment. Prices vary little and are mostly between €40 and €60 per day per adult. Cheaper tours do not include equipment while more expensive ones do, meaning the price is about equal should you need to rent. Many have indoor walls for training purposes in case the weather turns bad.

- **Outdoor Tours**, Hauptstraße 27, 01855 Kirnitzschtal/OT Ottendorf, ☎ 035971-56-907, www.klettern-sachsen.de.
- **Adventure Service**, Niederweg 10, 01814 Bad Schandau, ☎ 035022-43-253, www.adventureservice.de.
- **Bergsport Arnold**, Obere Strasse 2, 01848 Hohnstein, ☎ 035975-81-246, www.bergsport-arnold.de.
- **Bad Schandauer Tourismus**, Elbsandstein Reisen, Marktplatz 12, 01814 Bad Schandau, www.elbsandstein-reisen.de.
- **Rock-Trail**, Götzingerstraße 3, 01855 Sebnitz, ☎ 035971-80-300, www.rock-trail.de.

■ On Wheels

The Elbe Cycling Route: One of the longest and most popular long-distance cycling paths in Germany is the 860-km (516-mile) Elbe Cycling Route, www.elberadweg.de, marked by a blue "e." It runs the full distance of the Elbe from where it enters Germany in Saxony south of Dresden to where it finally flows into the North Sea at Cuxhaven beyond Hamburg.

The full route is usually done over a period of two weeks. The altitude difference is a mere 60 m (192 feet), meaning cycling upstream is as easy as following the downstream route.

Nowhere is the scenery more beautiful and hugs the route of the Elbe itself more closely than the 76 km (46 miles) between Schöna and Meißen.

Although it is of course possible to make your own arrangements for a long-distance cycling tour, many companies specialize in it and can arrange individual tailor-made tours, including suitable accommodation along the way and luggage transfers if necessary. The prices of many are very reasonable and often work out cheaper than making individual arrangements. In addition, it is much easier having to deal with only one institution than to arrange things separately with every service provider.

Often the local or regional tourism offices arrange special packages. For the Elbe Cycling Path in Saxony the **Tourismusverband Sächsiches Elbland**, ☎ 03521-76-350, fax 03521-763-540, www.elbland.de, arranges cycling packages ranging from three to 15 nights. Packages can also be combined with canoeing, hiking, rock climbing, and other activities.

By Train: Visitors to German cities are familiar with trams but from Bad Schanday to the Lichtenhainer waterfalls a tram, the **Kirnitzshtalbahn**, actually runs through a valley in the national park. The tram has been in operation since 1898 and currently runs daily every half-hour between 8 am and 8 pm. Hiking opportunities abound from every stop.

Also departing from Bad Schandau, the **Sächsischer Semmering** train runs through some of the most spectacular scenery to Sebnitz. From here, it is possible to return to Dresden via Neustadt and

Stolpen or continue into the Czech Republic.

■ On Horseback

In **Bad Schandau** the tourist office, Elbsandstein Reisen, Marktplatz 12, 01814 Bad Schandau, ☎ 035022-90-051, www.elbsandsteinreisen.de, arranges horseback riding through this beautiful region. Prices are from €10 per hour.

■ On Water

Canoeing & Kayaking: South of Dresden, **Elbe Kanu Aktiv Tours**, Elbpromenade Schandauer Straße 17-19, 01824 Königstein, ☎ 035022-50-704, www.kanu-aktiv-tours.de, offers daily boat rental and complete packages for longer trips. The classic route is Königstein to Pirna, which takes 3½ hours. Starting from Bad Schandau adds an hour and no extra charge. Several longer, and shorter, options, are available with boat drop-off points in most towns along the Elbe.

In the vicinity of Rathen and the Bastei is the small **Amselsee**. This lake was artificially created in 1934, mainly for collecting ice blocks, but since the 1960s it has been used for leisure purposes. Rowboats can be rented from April to October. On some summer weekends, evening rowing is popular. It takes about half an hour to do a round-trip on the small but beautiful lake. In winter, ice-skating is permitted when the ice is thick enough.

Riverboats: Elbe steamers operate throughout the region – see *Dresden* (page 90) for details.

Cultural Events

In the nearby Sächsische Schweiz, the annual **Sanstein & Musik Festival**, www.sandstein-musik.de, schedules events from March to November. The open-air **Rathen Felsenbühne**, ☎ 035024-7770, www.dresden-theater.de, has performances ranging from opera to children's theater from April to October.

Moritzburg

Transportation

From Dresden, Mortizburg is most easily reached by Bus 326 or 328 (direction Radeburg/Großenhain) running from Dresden-Neustadt station. Far more interesting though is the narrow-gauge steam train via Radebeul – see page 170 for details. The Meißen tourist office arranges programs allowing a same-day visit to both Meißen and Moritzburg.

Sightseeing

One of the most popular daytrip destinations in Saxony is to the magnificently located **Jagdschloss Moritzburg** (Moritzburg Hunting Palace), ☎ 035207-8730, www.schloss-moritzburg.de, about 15 km (nine miles) north of Dresden. The ocher and white Baroque palace was built on an island in an artificial pond. The current building

Jagdschloss Moritzburg

was completed in 1736 to the design of Augustus the Strong's favorite architect, Mattäus Pöppelmann, but some parts of the building are 200 years older. The symmetrical palace with four massive round towers in the four corners never fails to impress. Inside the palace is the **Baroque Museum**, with period furniture, paintings, porcelain, and the world's largest collection of Baroque leather wall coverings. The palace also has a large collection of hunting trophies, mostly antlers. Opening hours are 10 am year-round but closing from April to October at 5:30 pm; November, December, and March at 4:30 pm; January and February at 4 pm. Admission is €4.10. Guided tours are €2.

Just north of the palace is the small French-style **Schlosspark** (Palace Park), but the real treat is the large **Waldpark** (Forest Park) that lies beyond. It is a fine place to stroll around and has a few interesting historic sights. The Rococo **Fassanenschlösschen** was built in the late 18th century for Elector Friedrich

Augustus II and is a good example of the *chinoiserie* that was popular all over Europe at the time. Nearby is the harbor where the nobles started boating parties. Ruins were constructed on the edge of the large pond and miniature frigates were built to stage "naval battles" for entertaining members of court.

There are six natural lakes and 25 artificial ponds in the Moritzburg area. This makes it a haven for birdlife, with around 200 species as well as other small animals. The area is popular for hiking and cycling.

Käthe Kollwitz, Child & Sick Mother

The artist **Käthe Kollwitz** was persecuted by the Nazis and spent the last days before her death in 1945 at Moritzburg on the invitation of Prince Ernst Heinrich von Saxen. After the war her house was converted into a Gedenkstätte (Memorial Site), Im Rüdenhof, Meißner Straße 7, ☎ 035207-82-818, www.kollwitz-moritzburg.de. Opening hours are April to October daily from 11 am to 5 pm (opening at 10 am on weekends) and November to March weekdays from noon to 4 pm and weekends from 11 to 4 pm. Admission is €2. (Larger collections of her works are displayed in several German cities, including Berlin and Cologne.)

Adventures

■ On Wheels

Several narrow-gauge trains operate in Saxony but the 16-km (9.6-mile) **Loßnitzgrundbahn** between Radebeul Ost and Radeburg via Moritzburg near Dresden is easily accessible and particularly popular. It crosses 17 bridges and stops at 11 stations but many passengers embark at Moritzburg to admire the hunting palace of Augustus the Strong. Depending on the season, there are around eight trains daily, taking an hour for the trip, with Moritzburg about halfway. Round-trip for the full route is €8,60. Radebeul Ost can be reached in 15 minutes from Dresden Hauptbahnhof by S-Bahn Line 1. For more information contact **Oberelbe Tours**, Leipzigerstraße 120, 01127 Dresden, ☎ 0351-852-6529, www.oberelbetours.de.

About once a month, the route is covered by the **Traditionsbahn** (Traditional Train), Bahnhof Radebeul Ost, Sidonienstraße 1a, ☎ 0351-4614-8001, www.traditionsbahn-radebeul.de, which has 19th-century style wagons complete with wooden seats and staff in period costume. Round-trip fare for the full route is €11 or €8 up to Moritzburg. Reservations at no additional charge are recommended.

■ On Horseback

Moritzburg has been associated with noble horses for at least 200 years. **Moritzburg Tourism Information**, ☎ 035207-8540, arranges one-hour carriage rides through the beautiful pond and forest area of this small town with its famous Baroque castle.

Where to Stay & Eat

The small but comfortable Hotel and Restaurant **Churfürsteliche Waldschanke**, Große Fasanenstraße, 01468 Moritzburg, ☎ 035207-8600, fax 035207-86-093, www.churfuerstliche-waldschaenke.de, is beautifully located inside the forest and within easy walking distance of the palace and all other local sights. It dates from 1770 and was originally a gamekeeper house for the royal forest, but converted into a hotel in the 1990s. Some walls have hunting trophies and the original leather wall coverings. The rooms are comfortably furnished with stylish furniture. The restaurant offers local cuisine, including venison, fowl, and Saxon wine. (€€-€€€)

Inside the palace itself the **Restaurant im Barockschloss**, Im Schloss, Mortizburg, ☎ 035207-89-390, www.schlossrestaurant-moritzburg.de, offers several dining options ranging from a simple café to a stylish restaurant. (€-€€€)

Meißen

Meißen is an interesting town north of Dresden. It is most famous as the site of the Meissen Porcelain factory but it is also the cradle of Saxony itself, with a written history dating back to AD 929. In 1089, the Wettiner family obtained the Mark (March or border area) Meißen and the family would rule it (from 1423 all of Saxony), until the abolition of the monarchy in 1918.

Meißen is interesting to visit not only for its history and porcelain but also for the town itself. Parts of Meißen are beautiful, with historic houses in excellent condition. However, right next to well-maintained buildings there are often uninspired ones from the Communist era and older structures suffering from bad maintenance. All this can be seen on a 15-minute walk from the station to the market square.

Information Sources

Tourist Office: Tourist Information, Markt 3, 01662 Meißen, ☎ 03521-41-940, www.touristinfo-meissen.de.

Transportation

Meißen is easiest reached by S-Bahn line S2 that runs every 30 minutes from Dresden Hauptbahnhof and Neustadt. A more leisurely way is by boat on the Elbe or by bicycle on the Elbe Cycle Route – see *Adventures* for details.

Sightseeing

The Meißen skyline is dominated by the **Burgberg** (Fortress Mountain) with the historic **Albrechtsburg Meißen**, Domplatz 1, ☎ 03521-47-070, www.albrechtsburg-meissen.de. The castle, which was the first of its kind in Germany, is more a residence palace than a fortress. It was commissioned in 1464 by the brothers Ernst and Albrecht Wettiner, who jointly ruled what is mostly modern-day Saxony and Thuringia. However, in 1485, shortly before the castle's completion, the brothers split up the land and Albrecht moved the residence to Dresden. As a result the castle was seldom used.

The castle, designed by Arnold von Westfalen, is in a Late Gothic style showing some influence from French châteaux.

It has a masterful staircase that conveys a sense of lightness despite its size. Renouncing the use of flying buttresses, the outside walls were made thicker to support the weight of the building – from two to four meters (six-12 feet) between the ground and third floor. The architectural techniques and final appearance were considered very modern at the time. Parts of the interior have some of the best wall paintings in Germany, but they date from the late 19th century when the castle was restored in the spirit of historicism.

Although the Albrechtsburg seldom served its purpose as a residence, it did play a role in history. The Meißen porcelain factory was located here from 1710 to 1863. Initially Böttger and some staff were virtual prisoners here as King Augustus attempted (unsuccessfully) to keep the manufacturing secrets out of the hands of other European states. On 3 October 1990, the Free State of Saxony was officially proclaimed from the castle.

Despite its role in the history of Meissen porcelain, very little of it is seen in the castle. The permanent exhibitions cover the history of the castle, Böttger and the manufacturing of porcelain. There are also medieval statues on loan from the State Art Collection in Dresden. Opening hours are March to October from 10 am to 6 pm and November to February from 10 am to 5 pm. Admission is €3.50.

Next to the castle is the **Dom zu Meißen** (Cathedral), Domplatz 7, ☎ 03521-452-490, www.dom-zu-meissen.de. The current building was constructed between 1250 and 1400 in a pure Gothic style to replace the previous Romanesque structure. Of special note are the bronze funerary plaques based on designs by Albrecht Dürer and Lucas Cranach, as well as the Lay Brothers' Altar and Benefactors' statues from the studio of Cranach. Opening hours are April to October from 9 am to 6 pm and November to March from 10 am to 4 pm. During the summer months 20-minute organ concerts are held daily, except Sundays, at noon, with longer concerts on Saturday at 6 pm. Admission to the cathedral is €2.

There are many dining options at the Dom square and also at the **Marktplatz** at the bottom of the hill in the center of the old town. In 1472, the town ordered a new **Rathaus** (town hall) in order to keep up with the Wettiners. The resulting building still dominates the market square. In this building was a large hall, 20 by 37 m (64 x 118 feet), where the entire town could gather to discuss business. At the height of absolutism in the mid-18th century, the hall was divided into many small rooms. The current restoration project plans to bring the hall back to its former glory.

About 10 minutes walk from the Marktplatz is the **Staatliche Porzellanmanufaktur Meissen** (State Porcelain Manufactory), Talstraße 9, ☎ 03521-468-208, www.meissen.de.

Did you know? *Unlike the town name, Meissen porcelain is always spelled with a regular double "s."*

Visits to the manufactory do not include the actual factory itself but rather the Schauwerkstatt (demonstration workshop) and the Schauhalle (Exhibition Hall). The collection consists of 20,000 pieces, of which 3,000 are selected annually for display in the exhibition. The exhibition always includes a large variety ranging from animal figures to dinner sets. A 3½-m (11.2-foot) centerpiece made for the court table of King Augustus III in 1749 never fails to impress.

During the tour of the demonstration workshop, four subjects are covered: turning and molding, embossing, under glaze painting and over glaze painting. The tour is via recordings available in 12 languages and they last just over 30 minutes. Opening hours are May to October from 9 am to 6 pm; November to April from 9 am to 5 pm. Admission is €4.50 for the exhibition and €3 for the workshop.

MEISSEN PORCELAIN

The blue crossed swords in the trademark of Meissen porcelain have been a sign for handmade quality ever since their start at the start of the 18th century. Meissen porcelain is precious and expensive. There is, of course, a shop at the factory itself where pieces immediately available range from around €80 to items such as a large porcelain elephant that cost as much as a new BMW (a company that incidentally also uses a famous blue and white trademark). For pieces on special order, the sky is the limit. Children on the demonstration tour often get small samples like a doll's head for free – unglazed and unsigned but Meissen nonetheless.

Meissen has their own shops in all major German cities and the porcelain is on sale at all better department stores.

Cultural Events

Porcelain Painting: Meissen State Porcelain Manufactory, Talstraße 9, 01662 Meißen, ☎ 03521-468-700, www.meissen.de, offers porcelain painting courses in several languages, ranging from three to nine days at its plant in Meißen. The course includes one piece of Meissen "Hobby Collection" porcelain with the plate identified as your own paintwork. Courses are offered throughout the year and are limited to between five and 10 participants.

Wine Tasting: Germany's smallest, a mere 2,000 acres in total, and easternmost wine growing region is in Saxony between Dresden and Meißen. The average production per acre is about a third of that for other German production areas, giving Saxon wine scarcity and a higher price. The 55-km (33-mile) **Saxon Wine Road**, www.elbland.de, winds through the picturesque area connecting villages, palaces and vineyards. Wine has been produced on the southern slopes of the Elbe for the past 800 years. The better wines are good, the cheaper ones headache-inducing.

One of the larger estates belonging to the state of Saxony is **Schloss Wackerbarth**, Wackerbarthstraße 1, 01445 Radebeul, ☎ 0351-89-550, which can be seen from the S-Bahn and Elbe en route to Meißen from Dresden. It offers guided tours in German only as well as wine tasting for €9 per person. Open daily from 10 am to 7 pm (4:30 pm from October to April). Reservations are essential.

Adventures

On Water: See Dresden section – many canoeing and steamer trips originating from Dresden end in Meißen.

Shopping

Meissen porcelain can be bought at two official shops and many antique shops in town. The main shop is in the factory at Talstraße 1, ☎ 03521-458-015, with a branch office in town at Burgstraße 6, ☎ 03521-468-332.

Local Meißner Wein (wine) also makes a good souvenir, as the production volume is limited. Two shops offering local wines both for sale and for tasting are **Der Weinladen**, Burgstraße 18, ☎ 03521-402-544, and **Original Meißner Weine Küfertheke**, Markt 5, ☎ 03521-453-615.

Two local entrepreneurs attempt to show that Meißen offers more than just Meissen. The **Meissener Bleikristall**, Kalkberg 15, ☎ 03521-732-613, produces carved lead crystal in all forms, shapes and colors. The workshop can be visited weekdays between 8 am and 3 pm. **Glasskunst Meissen**, Rauhentalstraße 38, produces copies of famous Tiffany-designed Art Nouveau windows and lamp shades at a fraction of the price of the originals.

Where to Stay & Eat

The **Mercure Grand Hotel**, Hafenstraße 27-31, 01662 Meißen, ☎ 03521-72-250, fax 03521-722-904, www.mercure.de, is located inside a park on the opposite bank of the Elbe. The restaurant, terrace, and the better rooms offer grand views of the Albrechtsburg and Cathedral. The heart of the hotel is a beautiful Art Nouveau villa, but rooms are generally modern and comfortably furnished. The highly regarded restaurant **Die Villa** offers regional as well as international dishes. (€€-€€€)

Inside the Porcelain Manufaktur is the small but pleasant **Café Meißen**, Talstraße 9, ☎ 03521-452-472. It offers mainly drinks and snacks, but small delicious meals are available during lunchtime too. Food and drink are served on Meißen porcelain but do not be tempted – any attempted theft is either reported to the police or involves a €150 per item "administrative" fee. (€)

A pleasant place to stay in the old town is at **Am Markt Residenz**, An der Frauenkirche 1, 01662 Meißen, ☎ 03521-41-510, fax 03521-415-151. Rooms are comfortably furnished and decorations are mostly Italian. The restaurant (€€) serves a wide range of dishes with a well-stocked wine list. Also on the ground floor is the very informal **Café Cappuccino** (€), with great coffee and small snacks at very low prices. The view of the church and market square is free as well. (€€)

Nearby, behind the church, is the legendary **Vincenz Richter Romantik Restaurant**, An der Frauenkirche 12, Meißen, ☎ 03521-453-285, www.vincenz-richter.de. It is a museum, wine bar, and restaurant combination. Guests can tour the torture chambers before enjoying some of the best food on offer in the town. The original villa dates from 1523 and looks the part. Cuisine is classical regional dishes with some new creations. (€€-€€€)

On the Burgberg on the Domplatz in front of the cathedral are several dining options. **Café am Dom**, Domplatz 5, ☎ 03521-404-486, is a modern café inside an historic vault but the real draw is the lovely garden with panoramic views over the town. (€)

The oldest restaurant in town and in operation since 1470 is the **Domkeller**, Domplatz 9, ☎ 03521-457-676, www.domkeller.com. It is located in a historic cellar but also offers outdoor seating with grand views. The cuisine is mainly Saxon and the wine list is the same. (€-€€)

■ Leipzig

Some observers consider Dresden's Baroque old town as beautiful, while some find it a bit over the top. Since World War II Leipzig has never been accused of either. Few cities can offer such a contrast within such a small area as the Leipzig old town presents. Within 15 minutes walk you can see the enormous early-20th-century Hauptbahnhof, huge Communist-era apartment blocks, the modern glass box art gallery, the Renaissance town hall, Gothic and Baroque churches, modern shopping centers, shopping passages dating back to the Middle Ages, concert halls from the 1960s, new buildings being erected, old ones being restored to their former glory while some equally impressive old ones are simply going to waste. Although much has been done since the *Wende* to restore Leipzig's historic buildings, much still needs to be done. Architecturally, this city is one scrambled egg that will not be unscrambled anytime soon. For the visitor, it is one incredibly interesting experience.

Leipzig became part of the German empire during the eastern expansion in 1015 but only received town and market privileges banning competing markets within a radius of 15 km (nine miles) in 1165. The name is derived from the Slavic Lipzk, meaning "place of the lime trees (*Linden*)." The town was firmly placed on the route to wealth after Emperor Maximilian I in 1497 designated the trade fair here as an Imperial Fair, guaranteeing safe passage and imperial protection to all traders traveling to the fair. A Fair Privilege issued in 1507 was even more helpful. It banned competing trade fairs within a radius of 225 km (140 miles). Leipzig became a wealthy city with a rich cultural life dominated by civilians rather than the nobles, unlike Dresden.

Leipzig was heavily damaged by air raids in World War II and the scars left can still be seen – the city is a real mix of old and new with seemingly little planning. As a result, the visitor gets the feeling that this is a city where people actually live rather than the somewhat artificial impression that the tourist areas of Dresden and Berlin leave.

Leipzig played a major role in the peaceful German revolution of 1989 that led to the end of Communist East Germany. It was here, rather than in Berlin, where the peaceful protest movements against the Communist regime started.

Leipzig's environment suffered terribly during Communist rule when huge polluting factories and large open mines – mainly lignite – poisoned the atmosphere and countryside. Although the scars can still be seen when traveling to and from the city, the rapid pace of recovery has pleasantly surprised even experts. Closing these polluting industries left major unemployment and, despite investments by blue chip companies such as BMW and Porsche, employment levels are still far below those of the West.

Information Sources

Tourist Office: Leipzig's tourist information office is across the road from the Hauptbahnhof at Richard-Wagner-Straße 1, ☎ 0341-710-4260, www.leipzig.de. They have information on the sights as well as what is on at all the main venues. Staff can also make reservations for hotels and tour packages and cultural events.

Two free magazines in German only but available all over the city and on the web have listings of cultural and popular events: *Zeitpunkt*, www.zeitpunkt-kulturmagazin.de, and *Fritz*, www.fritz-leipzig.de.

Transportation

Leipzig has a very well-developed public transportation system combining trains, trams, and buses. Due to the compactness of the old town, it is quite possible to visit without using public transportation at all. The Völkerschlachtdenkmal and the Göhlis areas are the only places described below that are not within walking distance from the main station.

Tip: *Fares depend on the distance but most are around €1.50. Day tickets are €4.40. The* ***Leipziger Card****, which allows unlimited transportation and discounts at many sights, is €7.40 per day or €15.50 for three days. However, should you not make extensive use of public transportation, it is much harder to make this card pay than it is for the Dresden counterpart.*

Driving in most of Leipzig is not a problem but the historic center is best avoided due to pedestrian zones and one-way roads. Street-side parking can be cumbersome to find and has strictly enforced maximum parking limits. It is best to leave the car at the hotel if central or to use one of the ample parking garages.

Sightseeing

Leipzig's historic center is compact and best explored on foot. The area is flat and, once inside the ring road area, traffic is light. Most sights are within easy walking distance from the main station.

Hauptbahnhof Area

Leipzig's **Hauptbahnhof** (Central Station), Willy-Brandt-Platz 7, ☎ 0180-599-6633, with 26 platforms, is the largest terminus in Germany. The building dates from 1915 and was restored to its original condition in the 1990s. It is colossal: the front façade is almost 300 m (960 feet) long and the huge glass roof larger than three soccer fields. Back in 1915, it served the Saxon and Prussian railway companies together but separately, meaning the facilities are doubled, from waiting rooms to grand staircases. With 150 shops and restaurants, it is also the largest shopping center in town. All major buses and trams depart from Willy Brandt Platz in front of the station.

Close by, at Sachsenplatz, a huge glass cube 34 m (110 feet) high is due to become the new location of the **Museum der Bildenden Künste** (Fine Arts Museum), one of the world's great collections of European art. Highlights include early German and Dutch works, Dutch art of the 17th century, Italian art from the 15th to 18th centuries, and German art from the 18th century to the present. The new gallery was due to open early in 2004 but work is way behind schedule. In the meantime the 140 most important works are on display in the **Handelshof**, Grimmaische Straße 1-7, ☎ 0341-216-990. Opening hours are Tuesday to Sunday from 10 am to 6 pm; Wednesday from 1 to 8 pm.

Across the road in Katherinenstraße are a few surviving Baroque houses. The most interesting is the **Romanushaus** (1704), at the corner with Brühl. It was built by the mayor Romanus, who financed its construction with uncovered notes and spent over four decades in Königstein jail as punishment for this and other cases of corruption. At No 11 is the **Fregehaus**, which belonged to a rich banker. It is based on a 16th-century building but was reconstructed in the early 18th century. In contrast to these, the huge Communist-era apartment blocks and second-hand shops in the area remind you that this is very much a living city and not a purely tourist destination.

Markt Area

The **Markt** (Market Square) is dominated by one of the most beautiful Renaissance edifices in Germany, the **Altes Rathaus** (Old City Hall), Markt 1. It was built over a record-breaking nine months in 1556 by Mayor Hieronymus Lotter, but required major renovations less than 150 years later. Locals still refer to rushed, below-standards work as a Lotter-job. It was due to be demolished early in the 20th century after the New Town Hall was built but instead was renovated and used for shops and the town museum. Markt is the center of all festivals and is still used on Tuesday and Friday for the farmers' fresh produce market.

To the south is the magnificent **Königshaus** (Kings' House), where the Saxon rulers resided when in town. It was converted into a Baroque house in 1707 and famous guests, in addition to the Saxon rulers, include Czar Peter the

Great, Frederick the Great, and Napoleon, who said farewell from the balcony to his Saxon allies after losing the Battle of the Nations. On the opposite end of the square only the façade with sundial remain of the **Alte Waage** (Old Weigh house). Here items were weighed, tested, and taxed during the fairs.

Leipzig has been an important city in Germany for centuries and it therefore comes as no real surprise that the **Stadtgeschichtliches Museum Leipzig** (City History Museum), Markt 1, ☎ 0341-965-130, www.t-online.de/home/stadtmuseum.leipzig/ has several interesting displays. The pride of the museum are the several imperial edicts related to the trade fair privileges granted to the city. The term Messe, meaning trade fair in German and several other languages, was first used with reference to the Leipzig fair. As in most city museums, the council silver and other treasures are on display and Leipzig's is impressive, as befitted a rich city.

The largest hall is 53 m (170 feet) long and has a large scale model of Leipzig made in 1823. Most of the rooms maintain the Renaissance style but there is also a Baroque room with rich wall paintings. Leipzig drew many musicians in the 19th century and a special room is dedicated to the more famous as well as to instruments from the period. A famous 1746 painting by Elias Gottlob Haussmann shows a 62-year-old Johann Sebastian Bach. It hangs in the Ratstube where Bach received his commission in 1723. Several Lucas Cranach paintings are on display as well as some of the 24,000 prints featuring Leipzig panoramas.

Opening hours are Tuesday to Sunday from 10 am to 6 pm and Tuesday from 2 to 8 pm. Admission is €2,50 but free on the first Sunday of the month.

Naschmarkt Area & Grimmaische Straße

Behind the Altes Rathaus is the **Naschmarkt**, with a statue (1903) of a young Goethe in front of the **Alte Börse** (Old Commodities Trading Exchange). The building was completed in 1687 as the first major Baroque structure in Leipzig. The beautifully decorated façade is in perfect restored condition. The large former trading hall can be rented for private functions, but the interior is not open for general viewing.

Alte Börse

Goethe's stare is fixed on the **Mädler-Passage**, www.maedlerpassage.de, Leipzig's most magnificent passage. Here are several stylish shops and restaurants. The most famous is the **Auerbachs Keller**, a drinking hall and restaurant that is the setting of a key scene in Goethe's most famous work, *Faust*. Goethe himself was a frequent visitor and it is still the destination of many visitors to Leipzig. Large statues of Mephisto and Dr Faust mark the entrance to the cellars. This is Leipzig – despite the glamour of the establishments in the Mädler-Passage, in an adjacent and directly linked passage cheap socks and underwear can be bought from stalls.

One of the most interesting museums in all of Germany is the **Zeitgeschichtliches Forum Leipzig** (Forum of Contemporary History), Grimmaische Straße 6, ☎ 0341-22-200, www.hdg.de. The museum displays the history of the two post-World War II Germanys, with special emphasis on the history of dictatorship, opposition, and resistance in the Soviet Occupation Zone and in the German Democratic Republic during 40 years of German division. In addition to contemporary items, there is also a very impressive range of multimedia presentations. Particularly interesting is video footage showing how the same events were portrayed on news programs in the former East and West. Several audio recordings of famous speeches are available to complement the hundreds of photos and documents on display. Most of the information is in German, but English audio guides are available. This museum is far more impressive and interesting than any of the more widely advertised, and often pricey, competition in Berlin. Opening hours are Tuesday to

Friday from 9 am to 6 pm, weekends from 10 am to 6 pm. Admission is free.

Less famous but older and larger than the Thomas Church (see below) is the **Nikolaikirche**, Nikolaikirchhof 3, ☎ 0341-960-5270, www.nikolaikirche-leipzig.de. The Gothic chancel and west towers date from the 14th century, while the triple nave and galleries are early 16th century. The central tower was completed in 1555. The classical interior dates from the late 18th century and is currently being restored. The slender white pillars resemble palm trees and end in light green leaves. The rest of the ceiling is coffered in light pink stucco flowers. The organ is one of the largest in Germany. Opening hours are Monday to Saturday from 10 am to 6 pm. Admission is free.

Nikolaikirche

WIR SIND DAS VOLK!

The Nikolai Church's finest moment came in 1989. Since 1982 peace prayers were held every Monday but on October 9, 1989, two days after uniformed police fired on protesters, 70,000 people gathered at the church armed only with candles. They then marched around the old town to protest against the SED (the East German Communist Party) chanting – "Wir sind das Volk" (We are the people/nation). A week later, it was 100,000 people and two days after that General Secretary Erich Honecker resigned. Less than a year later East Germany became part of the Federal Republic of Germany, an event often referred to as *Die Wende* (the change). After the *Wende* a senior SED member remarked that they were prepared for everything but not for candles and prayers.

Augustusplatz Area

Augustusplatz is in the heart of the University of Leipzig, known as the Karl Marx University during the Communist period. On the south end, the **Gewandhaus**, Augustusplatz 8, ☎ 0341-12-700, www.gewandhaus.de, opened in 1981 as the third building to house the famous Gewandhaus Orchestra, which has been in existence since 1743. Its Grand Hall has seating for 1,900. On the opposite end of the square is the controversial **Opera House**, Augustusplatz 12, ☎ 0341-126-1261, www.oper-leipzig.de, which was built in a stark Communist style during the 1950s. It stages operas and ballets and can accommodate 1,426.

Behind the Gewandhaus is Leipzig's most popular cultural center, the **Moritzbastei**, Universitätstraße 9, ☎ 0341-702-590, www.moritzbastei.de. It is located in three stories of the former city fortifications that were dug out by students in the mid-1970s. It is used for theater performances, films, and concerts. Although the audience is mainly students, older visitors are more than welcome.

The **Ägyptisches Museum** (Egyptian), Schillerstraße 6, ☎ 0341-973-7010, www.uni-leipzig.de/~egypt/, has a rich collection with around 8,000 pieces on display. The collection spans five millennia, from 4000 BC to the early Christian period. In addition to the usual statues and sarcophagi, the museum also has an impressive display of Nubian ceramics and smaller artworks. The pride of the collection is a cedar wood sarcophagus of Hedeb-bastet-iru with delicate relief carvings and still partly untranslated inscriptions. Opening hours are Tuesday to Saturday from 1 to 5 pm and Sunday from 10 am to 1 pm. Admission is €2. (While the museum building is being renovated, the collection will temporarily be housed in Burgstraße 21 near the Thomaskirche.)

The **International Mendelssohn Stiftung** (Foundation), Goldschidtstraße 12, ☎ 0341-127-0294, www.mendelssohn-stiftung.de, is located in the house where Felix Mendelssohn Bartholdy lived the last two years of his short life. It is the only house of his that has survived and is the only museum dedicated to this musician. In addition to his own compositions, his great contribution to music was his effort to reintroduce to a wider audience the music of Bach. The house is furnished in the Biedermeier style and left largely as it was when the composer lived there. Mendelssohn founded the first German conservatoire and concerts are still frequently held here. Opening hours are daily from 10 am to 6 pm.

Leipzig's highest concentration of museums is in the **Grassi Museum** complex at Johannesplatz, www.grassimuseum.de. This complex was erected in the 1920s in the Expressionist style with hints of Art Deco. It was extensively damaged during World War II and is currently under reconstruction. The three museums are due to reopen here in stages during 2005 and 2006. In the interim, parts of the collections of the museums are on display elsewhere in the city.

The **Museum für Kunsthandwerk** (Arts and Crafts), ☎ 0341-213-3719, www.grassimuseum.de, has a collection of mainly European arts and crafts dating from the beginnings to the present. A special focus is items collected during the 1920s and 1930s at the Leipzig fairs. German ceramics from the post-war period also are featured. Of special interest is the furniture and goldsmith work from the late Middle Ages onwards. Opening hours are Tuesday to Sunday from 10 am to 6 pm; Wednesdays until 8 pm. Admission is €4. (Until the move back to the Grassi the museum will be housed at Am Neumarkt 20.)

The **Museum für Völkerkunde** (Ethnography), ☎ 0341-268-9568, www.grassimuseum.de, with 220,000 items and around 100,000 photographs, is one of the oldest and largest collections of its kind in Europe. It displays the cultures and ways of life of people from all continents outside Europe. In the new museum, the display will allow a historical and cultural tour through the world. Opening hours are Tuesday to Friday from 10 am to 6 pm; weekends from 10 am to 5 pm. Admission is €2 but free the first Sunday of the month. In the interim, the museum is housed in the Mädlerpassage, Grimmaische Straße 2-4.

The third museum offers pleasure for both eye and ear. The **Musikinstrumentenmuseum** (Musical Instruments), ☎ 0341-687-0790, www.grassimuseum.de, displays about a quarter of the 4,000 historic musical instruments belonging to the University of Leipzig. The collection is considered to be the second-most important in Europe, after Brussels, and spans five centuries. The collection ranges from small instruments such as mouth harmonicas to a self-playing zither and other mechanical instruments popular in the 19th century. Opening hours are Tuesday to Saturday from 10 am to 5 pm; Sundays and public holidays from 10 am to 1 pm. Admission is €3. The museum is temporarily housed at Thomaskirchhof 20.

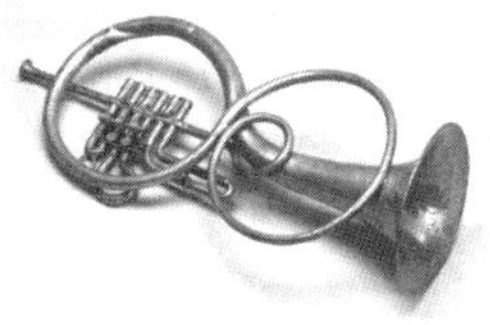

A few blocks from the Grassimuseum is the **Schumann-Haus**, Inselstraße 18, ☎ 0341-393-9620, www.schumann-verein.de. It was the residence of Robert and Clara Schumann during the first four years (1840-1844) of their marriage. It is one of the few remaining classical buildings in Leipzig. Most of the painted interior was found undamaged under layers of newer paint and wallpaper. The layout resembles that of the time when the Schuhmanns lived here. The permanent exhibition is on the life and work of the two musicians, with temporary exhibitions focusing on contemporaries that were guests in the house, such as Wagner, Liszt, Mendelssohn, Berlioz, and Hans Christian Andersen. Opening hours are short and only from Wednesday to Saturday from 2 to 5 pm.

Thomaskirche Area

From 1723 until his death in 1750 Johann Sebastian Bach was cantor of the **Thomaskirche**, Thomaskirchhof 18, ☎ 0341-960-2855, www.thomaskirche.org. Most of his cantatas, oratorios, and passions were first performed here. Martin Luther preached here in 1539 and Felix Mendelssohn Bartholdy performed Bach's St. Matthew Passion here to reintroduce his work to the general public in 1841. During Bach's time, the church interior was

Baroque and richly decorated with colorful paintings and biblical verses. However, it was remodeled in a Neo-Gothic style during 1884-89, leaving the interior rather bare. After a detour in the local graveyard and the now-destroyed Johanniskirche, Bach's body was finally buried here in the chancel after World War II. A statue of Bach was erected in front of the church in 1908. The church is open daily from 9 am to 6 pm and admission is free.

Thomasner Chor (St Thomas Boys Choir)

Bach led the Thomasner Chor and they first performed many of his works. The choir is still considered one of the best in Germany. When not on holiday or traveling, the choir performs during the motet services on Friday at 6 pm and Saturday with cantata at 3 pm. Admission is €1 and reservations are not possible – doors open 45 minutes before the service starts. Other concerts, for which reservations are possible and indeed recommended, are held throughout the year with many around Easter and Christmas. Tickets for the Christmas Oratorio generally sell out long before the posters are hung.

Johann Sebastian Bach Museum in the Bose Haus, Thomaskirchhof 15-16, ☎ 0341-913-7200, www.bach-leipzig.de, is a bit disappointing. Bach became nationally and then internationally famous only long after his death and consequently few items remained that could be directly attributed to his life. The Museum is on the second floor and consists mainly of information and copies of documents relating to the great composer's life. All information is in German only, but audio guides are available in English. Apart from the information panels, there are a few pieces of furniture and a Bible that belonged to Bach as well as an exhibition of period instruments. A video on Bach and a collection of CDs with a discussion in German of some of his works can be listened to in comfortable chairs with high quality earphones. The library and archives on the premises have a vast collection of music and documents relating to Bach. Opening hours are daily from 10 am to 5 pm. Admission is €3.

The **Neues Rathaus** (New Town Hall), Martin Luther Ring 4-6, ☎ 0341-1230, was built at the start of the 20th century and still serves as the seat of the local government. The building was extensively restored in the 1990s and has richly decorated façades and roof structures.

A building closely resembling the original Reichstag in Berlin is the former **Reichsgericht** (Supreme Court of the Empire). From 1879, the highest court of the German Empire resided in Leipzig and from 1895 in this building. Its most spectacular ruling was the "not guilty" verdict for Georgij Dimitroff, who was accused by the Nazis, with Hermann Goering leading the case in person, of instigating the burning of the Reichstag in 1933. After the war, it housed the Museum of Fine Arts, then, since 2002, the Bundesverwaltungsgericht (Federal Administration Court).

One of Leipzig's most interesting museums is the **Museum in der "Runden Ecke"** (literally Museum in the Round Corner), Dittrichring 24, ☎ 0341-961-2443, www.runde-ecke-leipzig.de. It is housed in the former Leipzig head office of the feared and despised Stasi, the secret police of the German Democratic Republic. The site was known as the Round Corner due to the curvature of the building. The Stasi managed to know a lot of what the citizens were up to through a wide network of spies, the illegal opening of mail, and wiretapping of phones. On display are some of the machines designed to open and close letters – up to 2,000 per day – as well as ones designed to read the contents of some without having to open the actual envelope. Money was routinely stolen from the mail and suspect letters routinely photographed onto microfiche. The technology to spy on their own citizens was highly developed and several small cameras and listening devices designed to be hidden in bags and clothes are on display. The Stasi's ability to fake documents, both domestic and foreign, was impressive, as was the makeup and the planning that went into secret sting operations. The paranoia reached far and near: after the fall of the regime, a permanently staffed telephone listening post was found inside the Stasi building itself. Thousands of files that were kept on ordinary citizens are on display. An enormous pile of shredded paper bears testimony to the attempts to destroy as much as possible in the final days of the regime. Probably the oddest item on display is a collection of bottles with people's smells! The Stasi was convinced that they could develop reliable technology to identify people by smell and collected swabs and pieces of clothing for record keeping. Information in the museum is in German only, but an English folder with a room-by-room description is available at the entrance. Opening hours are daily from 10 am to 6 pm. Admission is free.

The coffee shop **Zum Arabischen Coffe Baum**, Feine Fleischergasse 4, ☎ 0341-961-0060, www.coffe-baum.de, opened in 1694 and has been in continuous operation ever since. It therefore is the oldest coffee shop in the world, although a Parisian establishment disputes this. It has three coffee shops and three restaurants on the premises, as well as a Coffee Museum (free entry) on the second and third floors. On display are all sorts of paraphernalia associated with coffee since its introduction to Europe from the East. The Coffe Baum has been popular with high society for centuries and frequent guests included literary figures such as Goethe and Lessing, as well as composers such as Liszt, Wagner and the Schumanns. A lesser-known work by the great composer Johann Sebastian Bach, the Coffee Cantata, is played constantly in the museum. According to legend, the Baroque sculpture above the front door featuring a sultan, a small cupid, and a coffee tree (*Coffe Baum*) was a gift from none other than Saxony's King Augustus the Strong, who presented it to the landlady with whom he supposedly had secret amorous liaisons.

Farther Afield: Völkerschlachtdenkmal Area

To commemorate the centenary of the allied victory over Napoleon at the Battle of the Nations, the German Empire erected the **Völkerschlachtdenkmal** (Battle of the Nations Monument), Prager Straße, ☎ 0341-878-0471, www.t-online.de/home/stadtmuseum.leipzig. The 91-m (270-foot) colossus of Saxon porphyry took 15 years to build and is still undisputedly the largest monument in Germany. (It is also a strong contender for the titles of ugliest and most overdone!) The monument has a Hall of Honor with 324 equestrian soldiers in the cupola. A further 12 huge soldiers guard the outside of the building together with an enormous archangel Gabriel. Around 500 steps lead to the viewing platform with marvelous views of Leipzig and the surrounding countryside. The hall has fantastic acoustics, making it a popular venue for concerts. The **Forum 1813** right next to the monument has exhibitions on the battle, the developments in Europe leading up to the battle, as well as the suffering of soldiers during the period. Around 350 original items relating to the battle are on display and multimedia is used to bring across the horrors of the event. Beyond the reflecting pool is the **Napoleonstein** (Napoleon Stone), marking the spot where Bonaparte stood during the battle. Reenactments of the battle are staged annually in mid-October. Opening hours are daily April to October from 10 am to 6 pm, November to March daily from 10 am to 4 pm. The area is best reached by Tram No 15, running from the Hauptbahnhof.

THE BATTLE OF THE NATIONS

In October 1813, Napoleon Bonaparte with an army of 165,000 men faced the 225,000 men of the allied armies of Prussia, Russia, Austria, and Sweden south of the city of Leipzig. Saxony was officially an ally of France but many soldiers changed sides during the battle. One of the largest battles in history, the Battle of the Nations, often simply referred to as the Battle of Leipzig, ensued. Initially France won and on October 16 Napoleon rung victory bells. However, with fresh reserves the allies attacked again and scored a clear victory on October 18. Around 130,000 soldiers lost their lives during the battle and thousands more during Napoleon's hasty and chaotic retreat to France. The Battle of Leipzig finally broke Napoleon's power and hold on much of Europe.

Leipzig

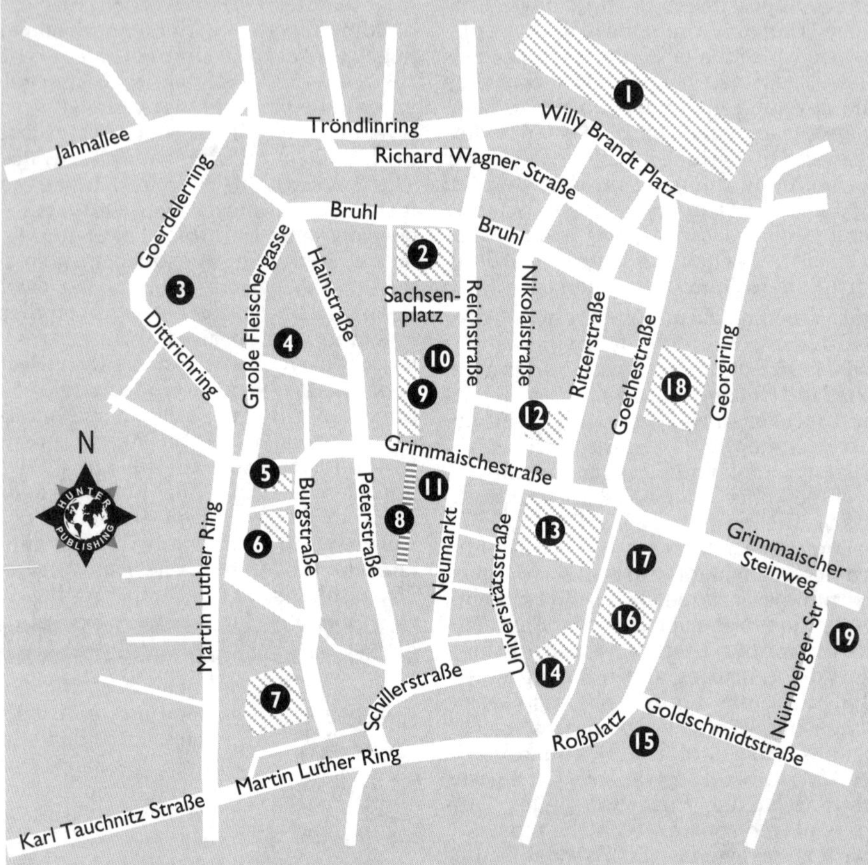

Jahnallee
Tröndlinring
Willy Brandt Platz
Richard Wagner Straße
Goerdelerring
Bruhl
Bruhl
Große Fleischergasse
Hainstraße
Sachsen-platz
Reichstraße
Nikolaistraße
Ritterstraße
Goethestraße
Georgiring
Dittrichring
Grimmaischestraße
Burgstraße
Peterstraße
Neumarkt
Universitätsstraße
Martin Luther Ring
Grimmaischer Steinweg
Nürnberger Str
Schillerstraße
Roßplatz
Goldschmidtstraße
Martin Luther Ring
Karl Tauchnitz Straße
N
HUNTER PUBLISHING

1. Hauptbahnhof
2. Museum der Bildenen Künste
3. Museum in der Runden Ecke
4. Zum Arabischen Coffe Baum
5. Thomaskirche
6. Bosehaus, Bach Museum
7. Neues Rathaus
8. Mädlerpassage
9. Altes Rathaus, Stadtgeschichtliches Museum
10. Alte Handelsbörse, Naschmarkt
11. Zeitgeschichtliches Forum
12. Nikolaikirche
13. Leipzig University
14. Moritzbastei
15. Mendelssohnhaus
16. Neues Gewandhaus
17. Augustusplatz
18. Opernhaus
19. Grassi Museum

Buildings

NOT TO SCALE

The Russian **Gedächtniskirche St Alexei's** (Memorial Church) opened the same day as the monument to honor the 22,000 Russian soldiers as well as 16,000 Germans, 12,000 Austrians and 300 Swedish allies who died in the battle. It is a copy of the 16th-century Kolomenskoye Church of the Ascension near Moscow and used by the Russian Orthodox community. Of special note are the icon walls in the upper part of the church.

Nearby, at the edge of the old fair grounds, is the **Deutsche Bücherei** (German National Library), Deutscher Platz 1, ☎ 0341-22-710, which from 1913 served as the depository for all German publications. Due to the separated German states after World War II this role is now shared with Frankfurt am Main. It has seven reading halls – admission is free, but requires prior permission. Also on the premises is the **Deutsche Buch und Schriftmuseum** (German Museum of Books and Literature) emphasizing the important role Leipzig played over 500 years in terms of book publishing and trade. The first book printed in Leipzig was in 1481 and the world's first newspaper in 1650. Although books always had been part of the fairs from 1594 they became important enough to warrant an annual catalog. Opening hours are Monday to Saturday from 9 am to 4 pm.

Leipzig-Göhlis

The **Schillerhaus Leipzig-Gohlis**, Menckestraße 42, ☎ 0341-566-2170, www.t-online.de/home/stadtmuseum.leipzig/, was the residence of Friederich Schiller during his stay in Leipzig in during the summer of 1785. He worked here on his *Ode to Joy* that was incorporated into Beethoven's Ninth Symphony. The house has been restored to what it was like in Schiller's time and is the oldest literary memorial in Germany. Opening hours are April to October from Tuesday to Sunday from 10 am to 6 pm; November to March Wednesday to Sunday from 10 am to 4 pm. The museum is most easily reached by Tram No 4 (stop Menckestraße) or Tram No 12 (stop Fritz-Seger-Straße.

Cultural Events

Leipzig is the city of Bach, Mendelssohn, Schumann, Wagner, and many others ensuring that there is always a wide variety of musical performances on offer throughout the year. In Advent, the number of concerts is particularly high, as it is in summer when open-air performances are popular. Leipzig has an amazing amount of theater ranging from classical pieces to cabaret – unfortunately all in German. It is easiest to contact the tourist office, Richard-Wagner-Straße 1, ☎ 0341-710-4260, www.leipzig.de, which has information on all the main venues.

Tip: *Two free magazines in German only, but available for free all over the city, have listings of cultural and popular events:* ***Zeitpunkt****, www.zeitpunkt-kulturmagazin.de, and* ***Fritz****, www.fritz-leipzig.de.*

A special annual event is the **Bachfest**, a two-week festival of around 70 concerts held in mid-May. The emphasis is obviously on Bach, but music of others is also performed. Tickets and information are available from the Bach Archive, ☎ 0341-913-7333, www.bach-leipzig.de.

The St Thomas Boys' choir sings Bach during Motet services on Friday and Saturday. See Sightseeing section, page 108, for details.

Mendelssohn's music can be heard every Sunday at 11 am in the Mendelssohn-Haus, Goldschmidtstraße 12, ☎ 0341-127-024, www.mendelssohn-stiftung.de.

Festivals

The center of the Christmas market is on the Market Square. However, more interesting is the small market on the adjacent Naschmarkt. Here, the market resembles that of the Middle Ages with old-fashioned stalls and fare far removed from the sausages and potato cakes offered at the main market.

Shopping

Leipzig's best-known shopping center is the **Promenaden** with around 150 shops inside the main station. In contrast to other areas where shops have to close at 8 pm, most here are open until 10 pm. Shops range from electronics to clothing and supermarkets.

The major department stores are found on Neumarkt and Petersstraße. The more interesting smaller shops are found in the

historic passages, which abound in the area around the Markt. Most famous is the Mädler-Passage, but with fame came high prices. Better deals are found in the adjacent passages.

Antique and flea markets are popular in Leipzig. Flea markets are held the first weekend of the month: Saturday at the Hauptbahnhof Platform 24 and Sunday at the Alte Messe Hall 13. Arguably, the best market is the large antique and flea market held usually the last weekend of the month at the agra-exhibition ground (Tram Line 11 from the main station) in Leipzig-Markkleeberg, www.agra-markkleeberg.de. This market is "ohne Neuwaren" (without new goods), meaning no cheap plastic junk and discounted socks and underwear. For exact times and location, ☎ 0341-980-4817, or 0172-968-7629 on the day of the market itself.

Adventures

On Foot

Town Walks: The tourist office arranges frequent guided walking-tours of the old town area.

Rock Climbing: Indoor rock climbing can be practiced at the **Leipziger Fitness-Studio Aerobbis Wellfit Park**, Forststr. 9, 04229 Leipzig, ☎ 0341-124-8530, www.kletterausflug.de. Not surprisingly, the outdoor climbing is done in Saxon Switzerland.

On Wheels

By Bus: Several companies offer bus tours of Leipzig. **Leipzig Erleben**, www.leipzig-erleben.de, and **Elke's Oldtimer**, www.elkes-oldtimer-tours.net, operate in cooperation with the Tourist Information Office from Richard-Wagner-Straße 1, ☎ 0341-710-4230. Leipzig Erleben has several daily tours to various destinations in and around the town. Elke's Oldtimer offers an interesting alternative: daily at 11 am and 2 pm it uses 1930s Parisian buses for 90-minute city tours.

Departing from Augustusplatz, **Treffpunkt Leipzig**, Friedrich-Ebert-Straße 33, ☎ 0341-149-7879, www.treffpunkt-leipzig.de, has several daily bus and walking tours. For some tours, a red London double-decker bus is used. Night tours are also available.

An alternative to bus tours is the **Leipziger Gläserner**, a tram with panorama windows. It departs daily at 11 am and 2 pm from the west side of the Hauptbahnhof on two-hour sightseeing tours. Tickets are available in the tram or in advance from the Mobilitätszentrum at the Hauptbahnhof, ☎ 0341-492-1748, www.lvb.de.

In the Air

Hot-Air Ballooning: Sachsen Ballooning, ☎ 0341-521-5315, www.sachsen-ballooning.de, offers flights from the Völkerschlachtdenkmal and several other places in the vicinity.

The annual **Saxonia International Balloon Fiesta** takes place at the end of July. It is one of the largest hot-air balloon gatherings in Europe. Contact the tourist office for exact dates and schedules.

On Water

From May to September **Leipzig Verkehrsbetriebe**, www.lvb.de, offers on Sunday at 2:30 pm a two-hour bus tour of the southern parts of the city, including an hour-long cruise on the Cospunder Lake. Tours depart from the west side of the Hauptbahnhof.

Where to Stay in Leipzig

Leipzig has a wide variety of hotels in all price categories. All the hotels listed here are close to the Hauptbahnhof and within easy walking distance of the major sights. Do not be put off by the rather bleak exteriors of almost all the hotels – inside they are comfortable, warm and a world away from the Communist-era designs.

The best temporary address in Leipzig is the elegant **Hotel Fürstenhof**. It has just under 100 rooms in a renovated patrician house dating from 1770. It was originally renovated by the luxury Kempinski hotel

HOTEL PRICE CHART	
Rates per room based on double occupancy, including taxes.	
€	Under €50
€€	€50-€100
€€€	€101-€150
€€€€	Over €150

group in the early 1990s, but has been part of the Sheraton Luxury Collection since 2000. Rooms are very comfortable and stylish with lots of natural light. The spa is large and well-equipped. **Restaurant Fürstenhof** (€€€€) is one of the best in Leipzig with light international and nouvelle cuisine. The ***Vinothek*** has a large selection of Saxon, German, and international wines on offer as well as lighter meals. Tröndlinring 8, 04105 Leipzig, ☎ 0341-1400, fax 0341-140-3707, www.arabellasheraton.com. (€€€€)

The **Westin Leipzig** occupies the top 15 floors of a 27-floor building two blocks from the station. All rooms are comfortably furnished. Most have stylish modern furniture, although some still have older and slightly worn furnishings clearly dating from the previous owners. The hotel was part of the Intercontinental group until recently and the "I" emblems can still be seen on some of the detailing. All rooms offer spectacular views, allowing you to study from the comfort of your own bedroom the architectural mix of old, Communist era, and new that make up central Leipzig. The restaurant, **Yamato** (€€€-€€€€), is one of the best Japanese dining options in Saxony. **Panorama XXVII** (€€€) on the 27th floor offers a buffet dinner by candlelight and live piano music on Friday and Saturday from 6:30 pm. On Sunday from 11 am to 2 pm, a brunch buffet is available. The food is mainly international and the view one of the best in town. Reservations are recommended. The health club in the basement has the largest hotel pool in Leipzig. Gerberstraße 15, 04105 Leipzig, ☎ 0341-9880, fax 0341-988-1229, www.westing.com/leipzig. (€€-€€€€)

Across the wide ring road from the Hauptbahnhof is the comfortable **Leipzig Marriott**. Rooms are large and luxuriously furnished in typical Marriott style. The target clientele is clearly on business rather than on a romantic weekend. The hotel offers several international dining options, including a sports bar. Am Hallischen Tor 1, 04109 Leipzig, ☎ 0341-965-30, fax 0341-965-3999, www.marriott.de/lejdt. (€€-€€€€)

In the same block is the historic **Seaside Park Hotel**. It was the first grand hotel in Leipzig and opened in 1913. It reopened in 1995 as a modern hotel behind a listed façade. The rooms are decorated in an Art Deco style that some may find a bit too impersonal but is well-equipped for the business and leisure traveler. The **Oriental Express** restaurant serves dishes from the menu of the legendary train. Richard-Wagner-Straße 7, 04109 Leipzig, ☎ 0341-98-520, fax 0341-985-2750, www.seaside-hotels.de. (€€-€€€)

In the same area is the **Ibis Leipzig Zentrum**. It is a typical Ibis with few frills but reasonable prices for well-maintained, modern, and clean rooms. Rooms are without mini-bars and without mini-bar markups. Prices remain sane during the high season. Brühl 69, 04109 Leipzig, ☎ 0341-218-60, fax 0341-218-6222, www.ibishotel.com. (€-€€)

The closest hotel to the main station, across the street from the west entrance, is the ever-popular **Holiday Inn Garden Court Leipzig City Center**. From the outside, it looks a bit grim, but inside it is stylish and modern, designed by London-based Ezra Attia. The bedrooms are small, but careful design and good space utilization give a much larger impression. A combination of location and low prices make early reservations usually a necessity. Kurt-Schuhmacher-Straße 3, 04105 Leipzig, ☎ 0341-125-10, fax 0341-125-1100, www.holiday-inn.com. (€€-€€€)

About 200 m (640 feet) farther down the road, the **Mercure Vier Jahreszeiten** (previously Am Hauptbahnhof) offers an alternative should the Holiday Inn be fully booked. It is a modern city hotel with elegant and stylish furnishings. There is a Greek restaurant on the premises. Kurt-Schuhmacher-Straße 23-29, 04105 Leipzig, ☎ 0341-985-10, fax 0341-985-122, www.mercure.com. (€-€€)

The large **Renaissance Leipzig** is a modern mid-1990s hotel a few blocks from the main station in a quieter area close to the Opera Haus. The emphasis is on business travelers and conferences, but facilities for vacationers also abound. Rooms are reasonably large and comfortably furnished. The restaurant (€€-€€€) is highly rated and offers international and regional dishes. Großer Brockhaus 3, 04103 Leipzig, ☎ 0341-12-920, fax 0341-129-2800, www.marriott.de/lejrn. (€€-€€€)

The **Mercure am Augustusplatz** shares the square with the Opera House and Gewandhaus concert hall, making it the ideal location for visitors to these cultural icons. It is also convenient to all the major sights in the old town. Rooms are comfortable if not particularly luxurious or large. Augustusplatz 5-6, 04109 Leipzig, ☎ 0341-21-460, fax 0341-960-4916, www.hotel-mercure-leipzig.de. (€-€€)

A few blocks away in a quiet neighborhood is the modern but very elegant **Dorint Hotel Leipzig**. Rooms are stylishly furnished and comfortable. The restaurant offers international and Saxon dishes. Stephanstraße 6, 04103 Leipzig, ☎ 0341-977-90, fax 0341-977-9100, www.dorint.de. (€€-€€€)

Camping

Camping Am Auensee is a pleasant site in a forest northwest of Leipzig. It has excellent facilities and 130 spaces. Open year-round. Gustav-Esche-Straße 5, 04159 Leipzig, ☎ 0341-465-1600, fax 0341-465-1617.

Where to Eat

Leipzig has no shortage of restaurants offering local as well as international cuisine. Coffee has been popular in Leipzig for centuries and the local coffee shops are as pleasant, if not more so, than the more illustrious competition in Berlin. All the better hotels have restaurants serving international fare, but the restaurants in the old town generally offer better value and more atmosphere.

Markt & Naschmarkt Areas

In the Altes Rathaus, the large restaurant **Café Brasserie Lotter & Widemann**, Markt 1, ☎ 0341-149-7901, is a pleasant place for anything from coffee to a full dinner. The restaurant is divided into three sections: brasserie, restaurant, and gourmet restaurant. The latter clearly rubs off even on the simplest dishes in the brasserie section, making for pleasant dining with a view of the passersby on the often-busy Market Square. Regional dishes and fare that is more international are served. Service is fast and friendly. (€-€€€)

DINING PRICE CHART	
Price per person for an entrée, including water, beer or soft drink.	
€	Under €10
€€	€10-€20
€€€	€21-€35
€€€€	Over €35

The Mädlerpassage, www.maedlerpassage.de, has one of the most famous restaurants in Germany, the **Auerbachs Keller**, Mädlerpassage, Grimmaischestraße 2-4, ☎ 0341-216-100. A young Wolfgang von Goethe frequented it as a student and used it as the setting of a scene in his most famous work, *Faust*. It still serves good food, but with a tourist surcharge. The restaurant has two distinct parts. The **Großer Keller** (€€-€€€) is open daily from 11:30 am to midnight. The **Historische Weinstube** (€€€-€€€€) is open only from 6 pm to midnight and offers more upscale food at upscale prices. Reservations for dinner are highly advisable.

Also in the Mädlerpassage but at ground level are two good French bistros. **Mephisto**, ☎ 0341-216-1050, is close to the Auersbachkeller, with the **Kümmel Apotheke Bistro**, ☎ 0341-960-8705, set deeper into the building. Both offer the same fairly authentic French bistro-style food with good service and similar prices. Kümmel seems to attract more French-speaking customers. (€-€€)

On the Naschmarkt itself, the Swiss chain **Mövenpick**, Am Naschmarkt 1-3, ☎ 0341-211-7722, www.moevenpick.com, has a large restaurant. The menu has mainly Swiss and German specialties. The food is fairly good, but more or less the same as any other Mövenpick in any other major German city. The salad bar is large, with fresh produce. (€-€€)

Kaiser Maximilian, Neumarkt 9-19, ☎ 0341-998-6900, www.kaiser-maximilian.de, is considered one of the best restaurants in Leipzig. It offers light international and Mediterranean cuisine in a stylish environment. Chairs are black leather, the walls are virtually undecorated and the ceilings high. As for quality of food, it is clearly the best choice in the area. Prices of the lunch menu can be surprisingly low. (€-€€€)

Nikolaikirche Area

Across the courtyard from the Nikolaikirche is the very modern steel and glass **Medici**, Nikolaikrichhof 5, ☎ 0341-211-3878, www.medici-leipzig. The restaurant is airy, with designer chairs, small round tables, and a relaxed atmosphere. The predominantly Italian food is first-class, but high-priced. (€€€-€€€€)

In stark contrast is the more traditional and very pleasant **Café Riquet**, Schuhmachergässchen 1, ☎ 0341-961-0000. It is three places in one: a wine cellar in the basement, a coffee shop on the ground floor and a very nice Viennese-style café to linger in on the first floor. Outside, it is instantly recognizable by the carved elephants above the door. Inside, it is comfortably furnished but lightly decorated, with wood paneling providing warmth. (€-€€)

Farther down the road toward the station is **Classico**, Nikolaistraße 16, ☎ 0341-211-1355, another stylish Italian restaurant. It's an elegant place with classic Italian cuisine and high prices. (€€€€)

Thomaskirche Area

Across the road from the Thomaskirche are several coffee shops. **Café Concerto** (€) is a smart café with stylish red-covered chairs. It offers mainly drinks and cakes. Next door is the **Bachstübl**, ☎ 0341-960-2382, also offering mostly drinks and cakes, but small snacks as well. Its interior is more elaborately decorated and aims at a faux-Baroque style. (€)

Other establishments in the area also use Bach's name but visitors can almost certainly do better elsewhere. A good option is the **Thüringerhof**, Burgstraße 19, ☎ 0341-994-4999, www.thueringer-hof.de, a Leipzig institution since 1454. It is the oldest restaurant in the city and can count Martin Luther as a former patron. The cuisine is a combination of Thuringian and Franconian specialties. Dishes tend to be hearty, prices surprisingly low. (€-€€)

After the *Wende*, Paulaner, the Munich brewery giant, was quick to move back to its original pre-war premises in Leipzig. In between the Thomaskirche and the Barfußgässchen, the **Paulaner Leipzig**, Klostergasse 3-5, ☎ 0341-211-3115, www.paulaner-leipzig.de, has a typical Bavarian operation going: an informal beer hall, a slightly more formal and much quieter restaurant and, when the weather cooperates, a beer garden. The food is a combination of Bavarian specialties and international dishes. The beer is Bavarian and only Paulaner brand. (€-€€)

Paulaner has a second establishment at the **Mückenschlösschen**, Waldstraße 86, ☎ 0341-983-2051, www.mueckenschloesschen.de, in a large Gründerzeit building at the edge of the Rosental Park. It has Leipzig's biggest beer garden, with 700 outdoor seats and 130 indoors. There is a petting zoo on the premises giving fathers a valid excuse to linger. The cuisine is German, ranging from typical Bavarian to Saxon. Tram No 4 stops right in front of the restaurant.

Drallewatch Area

The Drallewatch, Saxon for "going out," has traditionally been in the narrow alleys and passages along Brühl and Fleischergasse. It still is crowded with small bars and pubs as well as higher-end restaurants.

On the edge of the area is the historic **Zum Arabischen Coffe Baum**, Kleine Fleischergasse 4, ☎ 0341-961-0060, www.coffe-baum.de, with a wide range of cafés and restaurants. It has been in continuous operation since 1694. On the ground floor are two rustic restaurants (€-€€): **Lehmannschen Stube** and the **Schumann-Zimmer**, the latter named after the musical couple who frequented it. Both share the same menu, consisting mainly of hearty Saxon dishes. On the first floor is the more stylish restaurant **Lusatia** (€€-€€€€), offering Saxon cuisine and international dishes. On the second floor are three separate cafés (€) in Viennese, Arabian, and French style; the cakes are good and the coffee naturally superb. Contrary to popular belief, Coffe Baum has been serving tea and alcohol since 1720, and continues to do so, but having your alcohol here any way other than in your coffee would be a shame.

Barthels Hof, Hainstraße 1, ☎ 0341-141-310, www.barthels-hof.de, has been in the gastronomical business since 1497 and is the only surviving drive-through courtyard in Leipzig. (These types of courtyards were once very popular in Leipzig and used during the fairs, as they allowed wagons to be loaded and driven out of the building without the need to turn around.) The complex is divided into three establishments: the **Barthel's Weinschäncke** (wine bar), **Weber's Speisestube** (informal restaurant or inn), and the **Tollhardt's Zechgewölbe** (vaults). Cuisine is local Saxon fare, ranging from light to hearty. Between 7 am and 9 am the breakfast buffet is a bargain at €6, including Sekt (sparkling wine). (€-€€)

Thuringia (Thüringen)

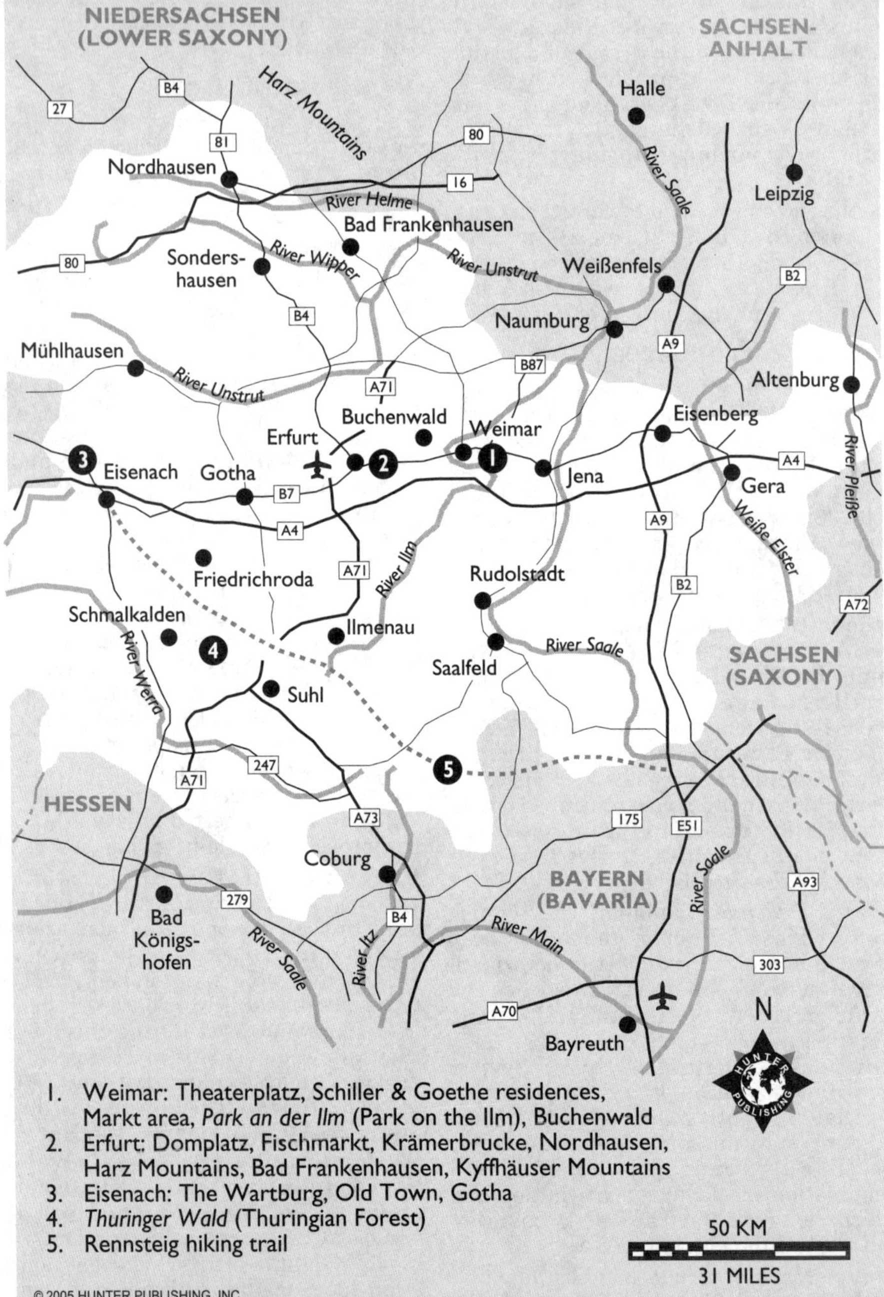

1. Weimar: Theaterplatz, Schiller & Goethe residences, Markt area, *Park an der Ilm* (Park on the Ilm), Buchenwald
2. Erfurt: Domplatz, Fischmarkt, Krämerbrucke, Nordhausen, Harz Mountains, Bad Frankenhausen, Kyffhäuser Mountains
3. Eisenach: The Wartburg, Old Town, Gotha
4. *Thuringer Wald* (Thuringian Forest)
5. Rennsteig hiking trail

Thuringia

In this Chapter

Thuringia is the smallest of the former East German states that joined the Federal Republic of Germany in 1990. Its central location at the geographical heart of Germany allows easy access from all regions.

During East German times, Thuringia, with its lovely forested mountains and important cultural cities, was very popular with tourists from the East Block. After the *Wende* (the *change*, as the end of the Communist regime in 1990 is often called), Western tourists streamed in to see the same sights, long forbidden or difficult to visit for outsiders.

Thuringia, despite its small area, has more than 400 fortresses, castles, and palaces, including the magnificent Wartburg – often referred to as the German national monument. Weimar, seat of classicist German artists such as Goethe and Schiller, is still as important a cultural site as it was in the early 19th century. Erfurt, with 204,000 inhabitants the largest city in the state, has one of the best-preserved medieval city centers in Germany. The Thuringian Forest is a low, tree-covered mountain range that offers adventures ranging from hiking and cycling to winter sports.

History

Around 400 BC Thuringia was a powerful Germanic nation. However, attacks from the north by the Saxons and from the south by the Franks led to the territory being split between these two stronger nations. Most of Thuringia become part of the Frankish Empire.

Thuringia's most powerful position was in the early years of the German Kingdom. The Ludovingian family, which built the Wartburg around 1067, became the counts of Thuringia from 1131 and ruled most of the land that constitutes modern-day Thuringia. Their rule ended in 1247 when the family died out. A war of succession followed and the Margrave of Meißen (later Saxony) took over most of the territory.

Three centuries later, Martin Luther sojourned in the Wartburg and translated the New Testament into German. A few years later, in 1525, Thuringia saw the bloody end of a Peasants' War led by Thomas Müntzer.

From the 16th century onwards, Thuringia became a textbook example of German *Kleinstaaterei* (small state-ism). The territory was continuously divided into smaller states to ensure that all sons inherited land and titles. In 1920, eight sovereign small states united to form Thuringia, a free state in the German Republic.

The small states prevented Thuringia from playing a major role in power politics, but culture and architecture flourished as counts vied to outdo their neighbors. Many splendid residences were built, which nowadays often house museums and art collections.

Weimar is the most famous town in Thuringia and is considered the cradle of German classical literature. At the turn of the 18th century, it had enlightened rulers and, under the influence of Johann Wolfgang von Goethe, became the cultural capital of Germany. After the First World War, the National Assembly gathered here to approve the new ultra-liberal constitution of the ill-fated Weimar Republic.

After World War II, Thuringia was part of Communist-ruled East Germany and again divided into smaller administrative regions. These parts reunited after the *Wende* and formed the Free State of Thuringia. It is the smallest of the five former East German states but in the early 21st century its economy was the best.

Transportation

Thuringia is geographically small and in the center of Germany with good transportation links to all areas of the country.

By Rail: The major Thuringian cities are stops on the fast, luxurious ICE network, allowing fast travel times to other German cities. From Frankfurt to Eisenach requires just under two hours. From here, it is 10 minutes to Gotha and a further 20 minutes to Erfurt, which is only 15 minutes from Weimar and an hour from Leipzig. Not every ICE train stops in each city on every run, but the frequent local trains are not much slower, occasionally even faster, and always significantly cheaper.

Money Saving Tickets in Saxony Anhalt

The **HopperTicket** allows round-trip journeys on any regional train in Saxony Anhalt and Thuringia for distances up to 50 km (30 miles) each way. It costs only €4.50 per person. (Erfurt to Weimar one-way would be €4.20!) The HopperTicket is valid weekdays after 9 am and all day weekends. Thuringia's small size makes the HopperTicket especially attractive.

By Road: Autobahn A4 cuts through the southern part of Thuringia, giving fast access to the cities of Eisenach, Gotha, Erfurt, Weimar, Jena, and Gera. At the east end, this autobahn connects to the A9 with access to Berlin and Leipzig in the north, as well as Bavaria to the south. Just west of Thuringia, the A4 crosses the A5 with access to Frankfurt, and the A7 with access to Hamburg in the north and Bavaria to the south. Do not be tempted to take the B7, which runs parallel to the A4. Distances may be shorter, but this road is as slow as molasses, overcrowded, and runs mainly through industrial areas.

Minor roads in Thuringia are generally in good condition, well-signposted, but slow. Most roads still pass through, rather than around, towns. Do not expect to cover more than about 60 km (36 miles) in an hour. Driving and parking in Eisenach is easy, but in Erfurt and Weimar, park at the edge of the historic town and explore on foot.

By Air: Erfurt Airport, Flughafenstraße 4, 99092 Erfurt, ☎ 0361-656-2200, www.flughafen-erfurt.de, is a minor regional airport with mainly charter flights. Some scheduled flights are available to domestic destinations as well to London-Stansted on Ryanair. The airport is only five km (three miles) from the city center and can be reached in 16 minutes with Bus 99 from the main bus station, or around 10 minutes by taxi.

A more realistic option is to use **Leipzig-Halle Airport** – see Saxony chapter, page 77 – or **Frankfurt International Airport** – see Hesse chapter, page 312.

■ Information Sources

Tourist Office: Many tourism offices in Thuringia make reservations for accommodation and events, and some even put together their own package deals. It is easiest to first contact the statewide agency and from there narrow it down to cities and regions.

Handling tourism promotion for the whole of Thuringia is Thüringer Tourismus, Postfach 100519, 99005 Erfurt, ☎ 0361-37-420, www.thueringen-tourismus.de. Reservations for accommodations and package deals can also be made.

THE THÜRINGEN CARD

The Thüringen Card, www.thueringencard.info, is available from most tourist offices as well as participating venues. It gives free access and discounts to many sights and forms of transportation. Conditions vary each year, but it generally saves money when visiting more than two major participating sights per day. The card is €13 for 24 hours, €29 for three consecutive days, and €50 for six freely elected days in a calendar year.

Local tourism offices, listed under the relevant sections below, can provide information on all kinds of cultural events, and in Thuringia the cultural calendar can be busy. Two free magazines, in German only, with a web presence, also provide information on cultural and popular events in the major cities: *Blitz!*, www.blitz-world.de, and *t.akt*, www.takt-magazin.de.

■ Weimar

Weimar is a pretty, small town of around 60,000 inhabitants, but its fame stretches far beyond the borders of Thuringia. Foreigners generally associated Weimar with the ill-fated Weimar Republic; founded here in 1919, but ruled from Berlin where it floundered in the early 1930s after the Nazis came to power.

For Germans, and the average tourist, visiting Weimar is all about classicism. Although never a large town, and never of real strategic importance, Weimar attracted artistic talent for centuries. During the late 18th century, under the reign of the talented Duchess Anna Amalia and later her son Carl August, the Duchy Saxe-Weimar-Eisenach reached its classical period and for a few decades, this town of less than 5,000 was the center of intellectual thought in Germany. The Duchess came to power in 1758, and acquired the services of **Christoph Martin Wieland** to educate her son. The greatest coup was inviting the brilliant young, but upcoming, writer **Johann Wolfgang von Goethe**. He would stay in Weimar from 1775 until his death in 1832, playing a major role not only in the arts but also in the administration of the duchy. He attracted other writers such as the dramatist **Friederich von Schiller** and the theologian **Gottfried Herder**. These four elevated German literature to an unknown level, leading to the period generally referred to as the classical. For most German tourists, and students of German, visiting Weimar is primarily a pilgrimage to the sites associated with these writers.

Germany's Foremost Poet

"*Die beste Bildung findet ein gescheiter Mensch auf Reisen.*" ("An intelligent person obtains the best education while traveling.") - J W von Goethe

Johann Wolfgang Goethe (1749-1832) was born in Frankfurt am Main into a rich and well-educated, middle-class family. He trained as a lawyer in Leipzig and Strasbourg but lost interest in law long before his father forced him to complete his training in Wetzlar. His experiences there led to *Die Leiden des Jungen Werther* (*The Sorrows of Young Werther*), the biggest-selling work in his lifetime. It brought him European fame – Napoleon carried a copy on his Egyptian campaign and said he read it seven times.

In 1776, he visited the court of Duke Karl August in Weimar and ended up staying here the rest of his life. The Duke had him elevated into the nobility – thus allowing the "von" in his surname. In addition to his writings, he was an avid scientist and geologist. As de facto prime minister, he did much to improve the administration and finances of the Duchy of Saxe-Weimar-Eisenach.

It is of course on his writing that his reputation is built. Initially he belonged to the *Sturm und Drang* movement but later turned classical. He wrote numerous plays, poems, and books. He traveled frequently and his traveling notes are in books such as *Die Italienische Reise* (*Italian Journey*) and his autobiography *Dichtung und Wahrheit* (*Poetry and Truth*). His most famous work is the epic drama *Faust* – a tragedy with a happy ending and the most likeable devil ever. It was published in two parts. *Faust I* was published in 1808. He completed *Faust II* shortly before his death, refused to show it to anyone, and only had it published posthumously (1832).

Through the centuries Weimar also attracted other talents such as **Lucas Cranach the Elder**, who died here. **Johann Sebastian Bach** was organist and choirmaster in Weimar from 1708 to 1717. From 1848, **Franz Liszt** filled the same position and created a famous musical school that currently bears his name.

In the 20th century, Weimar played a major role in the foundation of modern architecture and design. From 1902, **Henri van de Velde**, the Belgian exponent of Art Nouveau, worked in Weimar. After the First World War, the **Bauhaus** was founded in Weimar under the leadership of **Walter Gropius**. However, the ideas of the Bauhaus were too radical for the conservative town and by 1925 Bauhaus moved to Dessau.

A mere 10 km (six miles) north of Weimar, the Nazis constructed **Buchenwald**, a notorious labor concentration camp.

Information Sources

Tourist Office: The tourist information office is at Markt 10, 99423 Weimar, ☎ 03643-240-00, www.weimar.de. Some information is also available at the Hauptbahnhof.

Visitor Information

Virtually all tourist sights in Weimar are managed by the **Stiftung Weimarer Klassik** (Weimar Classics Foundation) and share the same contact details: Besucherinformation, Frauentorstraße 4, 99423 Weimar, ☎ 03643-545-401, www.weimar-klassik.de.

The interiors of many of the former houses of artists are not lit, which makes visiting on bright days desirable. In these houses, the atmosphere of a home rather than a museum is preserved, meaning very few descriptions and only a few chained-off spaces. A guided tour, or adequate guidebook, is essential for visitors interested in more than just seeing the houses and furniture. Out of conservation concerns, the number of visitors is sometimes limited during the high season. The signs on the building exterior are often very low key, and just because the front door is closed, does not mean it is necessarily locked. Audio guides in English are available in most.

Unless otherwise noted, opening hours for all the sights are Tuesday to Sunday, April to October from 9 am to 6 pm, November to March from 9 am to 4 pm.

Admission fees vary. An annual ticket, giving multiple accesses to all, is available at €30. A combination ticket with single entries to 15 houses, excluding the Goethehaus, is €20.

Transportation

Weimar is best explored on foot. Cars and even public transportation are mostly banned from the city center. Parking is scarce and it is best to park in the parking lots at the edge of the historic center, or at the hotel if convenient.

The main station is about 20 minutes walk from the historic center – taking a bus to Goetheplatz is more sensible. Bus 6 is particularly convenient, running past the Nietzsche Archive, Goetheplatz, and the Hauptbahnhof to Buchenwald.

Sightseeing

At first glance, Weimar may seem like one big celebration of Goethe and Schiller. This is true to some extent, as Goethe especially played a dominant role in establishing Weimar as a cultural center. Weimar does not have large structures, cathedrals, or castles. The sights here are more subtle and it takes more time to appreciate them. However, even for visitors with no interest in German literature, a visit to Weimar can be enjoyable.

Weimar is best explored on foot. Goetheplatz, with good bus connections, is a good place to start. From here, follow the crowds down the pedestrian mall to the classical sights of Weimar.

Theatherplatz

The Neo-Classical **Deutsches Nationaltheater** (German National Theater), Theaterplatz, ☎ 03643-755-334, is the third theater built on this site. The current building was erected in 1948, following the plans of the 1908 theater, which was destroyed during World War II. Goethe and Schiller were directors here; Liszt and Wagner conducted here. In 1919, after the collapse of the German Empire at the end of the First World War, the National Assembly met here to write Germany's first democratic constitution. This ultraliberal constitution almost faltered in the early 1920s, but it was the consequences of the Depression that exposed its limitations, allowing Hitler to grab power.

In front of the theater is the **Goethe-Schiller statue**, showing the two literary giants in period dress. This 1857 work by Ernst Rietschel is arguably Germany's most famous and most photographed statue. Copies of the statue are found in San Francisco, Cleveland, and Milwaukee.

Bauhaus in Weimar

The Bauhaus was founded in Weimar in 1919 under the leadership of Walter Gropius. The group's interdisciplinary interaction between artist and artisans laid the foundation for modern architecture and design. Cubicle architectural design was not acceptable to conservative Weimar and the Bauhaus moved to Dessau in 1925. In 1932, the Nazis closed the Bauhaus, accusing leading members of being Communist. Some, led by Mies van de Rohe, tried to set up studios in Berlin, but they were soon forced to close there as well. Most went abroad to find more acceptance of their ideas, especially in the USA.

Reflecting the original rejection of the Bauhaus ideas, Weimar has only four Bauhaus sights – the Bauhaus Museum, the former Arts and Crafts School, the former School of Fine Arts, and the Haus am Horn. The latter three are UNESCO World Cultural Heritage sites.

The **Bauhaus-Museum**, Am Theaterplatz, ☎ 03643-546-961, is located, somewhat ironically, inside a Classical building. The museum exhibits around 500 items at a time from its vast Bauhaus collection, as well as a number of Art Nouveau works by Henri van de Velde and his followers. Admission is €4.

The adjacent **Wittumspalast** (Widow's Palace), Am Theaterplatz, ☎ 03643-545-377, dates from the mid-18th century and was the town residence of Duchess Anna Amalia from 1775 until 1807. On display are living and reception rooms typical of that period. The main draw is the *Tafelrundezimmer*, a drawing room where Goethe and other luminaries met for social and intellectual discussions. The palace opens at 10 am. Admission is €3.50.

The **Weimar Haus**, Schillerstraße 16, ☎ 03643-901-890, www.weimarhaus.de, is the first multimedia experience museum in Germany. It explains 5,000 years of local history in 30 minutes. English audio is available. It offers an introduction to Weimar and the important local characters, but at a price. It is not managed by the Weimar Classics Foundation. Opening hours are daily from 10 am to 7 pm, closing at 6 pm from October to March. Admission is €6.50.

The Schiller & Goethe Residences

Friederich von Schiller came to Weimar in 1799 and rented various properties before acquiring, in 1802, a yellow Baroque house on the Esplanade (since renamed Schillerstraße). After renovations, the house cost 5,000 *talers*, a large sum for the time, but he managed to pay off all his debt prior to his death in 1805. The house was converted into a museum, **Schillers Wohnhaus** (Schiller's Residence), Schillerstraße 12, ☎ 03643-545-401.

Schiller's House

Although the museum was created only in 1847, 20 years after his widow's estate sold the property, family members returned much of the original furniture. The complete house is furnished and decorated as it was in Schiller's time. The museum is closed on Tuesday but open on Monday. Admission is €3.50.

Germany's Foremost Playwright

Johann Christoph Friedrich Schiller was born on 10 November 1759 in Marbach on the Neckar River. He had a rebellious youth and intensely disliked the military positions forced upon him by the Duke of Württemberg. His first play, *Die Räuber* (The Robbers), was published anonymously and first performed in 1782, at Mannheim. In the same year, he fled Württemberg and soon found his skills appreciated elsewhere. He was made an honorary citizen of the French Republic in 1792, although he continued to live and work in Germany.

He first met Goethe in 1787 and the two eventually became lifelong friends – some say rivals – and cooperated intensively after Schiller settled in Weimar in 1799. In 1802, he was granted a noble title, allowing "*von*" to be added to his name. He died in Weimar on May 9, 1805.

In contrast to Goethe, Schiller wrote plays to be performed, rather than just read. He took into consideration the limitations of the theater as well as the actors, things Goethe famously ignored. During their lifetime, Schiller was performed more than Goethe was, and he remained popular.

His famous plays include *Don Carlos*, *Maria Stuart*, *Wallenstein*, *Maid of Orleans*, and *Wilhelm Tell*. In the English-speaking world, his most famous work is *Lied an der Freude* (*Ode to Joy*), set to music by Ludwig von Beethoven in his monumental Ninth Symphony.

Two blocks away is Weimar's most popular attraction, the **Goethe-Nationalmuseum**, Frauenplan 1, ☎ 03643-545-300, which encompasses Goethe's house and a permanent exhibition. Although Goethe preferred living in his small cottage in the Park an der Ilm, his stature and status grew to such an extent that Duke Carl August bought him a large Baroque house in town. In 1792, Goethe moved into the house Am Frauenplan and lived there until his death in 1832. It remained in the hands of the Goethe family until it was opened as a permanent museum in 1885. The **Goethes Wohnhaus** (Goethe's Residence) is furnished almost exactly as it was in Goethe's days – he kept meticulous records and described parts of the house in detail in letters to friends and family. Many pieces are original. Goethe left an art collection of 26,511 pieces, 5,400 books, and some 22,000 scientific specimens; only a very small part is on display. The house is elegantly, although simply furnished. Bear Goethe's observation in mind that excessively beautiful and over-decorated rooms are for people without their own thoughts or new ideas. Note the high desks – he preferred to write standing up. Admission is €6.

In the adjacent houkse is a moderately interesting **Permanent Exhibition** on the members of the Weimar Classical period, 1759-1832. The exhibition consists of art works and items associated with the various artists who worked in Weimar during the period. Admission is €2.50.

Markt Area

On thc **Markt** (Market) are the Neo-Gothic **Rathaus** (Town Hall), the Renaissance **Cranachhaus**, where Lucas Cranach died in 1553, and the mid-1930s exterior of the famed **Hotel Elephant**. In addition to the tourist information office, Markt also has an information office for Buchenwald Concentration Camp, Markt 5, ☎ 03646-747-540.

Nearby is the **Herzogin Anna Amalia Bibliothek** (Duchess Anna Amalia Library), Platz der Demokratie 1, ☎ 03643-545-200. Although this library dates back to the early 16th century, it was under Goethe's leadership that it expanded to 80,000 catalogued volumes, one of the largest collections in Germany at the time. Currently the library has more than a million items, including the libraries of Liszt and Nietzsche. The main attraction is the magnificent Rococo Hall. The library and reading room are open to all. A devastating fire in September 2004 severely damaged the library. The Rococo Hall will be restored but will be closed for several years.

Two blocks north of Markt is the triple-nave **Stadtkirche**, Herderplatz. The oldest parts of the church date back to the 15th century, but most parts are Baroque. The high, steep roof is particularly impressive. The church was virtually destroyed during World War II, but was largely restored to its original condition. The church is also commonly known as the Herderkirche, since Johann Gottfried Herder, above,

preached here during Goethe's time. A large statue of Herder is on the square in front of the building. Bach and Liszt were organists here. The main sight in the church is the splendid Cranach triptych. Originally started by Lucas Cranach the Elder, it was finished after his death by his son. It features the crucifixion of Christ, with other scenes from the Bible. Luther and Cranach himself are also depicted in the picture. The church is open Monday to Saturday, from April to October, 10 am to noon and 2 pm to 4 pm, and November to March, 11 to noon and 2 to 3 pm.

Although Goethe played a major role in the construction of the palace, in the **Schloßmuseum** (Palace Museum), Burgplatz 4, ☎ 03643-546-960, the focus for once is not on Goethe but on fine art. The museum has a large collection, spread over three floors, with works from the Middle Ages to the early 20th century. Especially noteworthy are the Cranach gallery and the ceremonial rooms. A few rooms are dedicated to the Classical writers, with wall paintings illustrating scenes from their works. Admission is €4.50.

Park an der Ilm

The lovely Park an der Ilm, sometimes referred to as Goethe Park, stretches from the Schloss southwards along both banks of the River Ilm. On the east bank is the best-known structure in the park, **Goethes Gartenhaus** (Goethe's Garden Cottage), Im Park an der Ilm, ☎ 03643-545-375. It is a simple, small house with a remarkable high steep roof. Goethe lived here from 1776 to 1782. Even after moving to town, he frequently stayed here during summer to work in the peaceful surroundings. It is one of the most painted, sketched, and photographed structures in Weimar. The sparsely furnished house is open daily and admission is €3.

On the edge of the park, the **Haus am Horn**, Am Horn 6, ☎ 03643-904-054, is the only original Bauhaus-designed house in Weimar. It was built in 1923 as part of what should have become a complete Bauhaus neighborhood. In 1999, it was restored to its original shape and is used for exhibitions. Opening hours are Wednesday and weekends from 11 am to 5 pm.

In the park, near the bridge to Goethe's Garden Cottage, is a **Shakespeare** statue. It was erected in 1904 as the first statue to honor Shakespeare on the European continent. Nearby is the **Liszt-Haus**, Marienstraße 17, where Franz Liszt lived most summers from 1869 to 1886. The house is open Tuesday to Sunday from April to October, 10 am to 1 pm and 2 to 6 pm. Closed on Monday and during the winter season. Admission is €2.

The **Bauhaus University**, Geschwester Scholl Straße 8, has two UNESCO World Cultural Heritage buildings that were used by the original Bauhaus. Both were designed by Henri van de Velde around 1904 and became the seat of the Bauhaus in 1919. The university is open weekdays from 8 am to 9 pm and Saturdays from 8 am to 3 pm.

Both Goethe and Schiller found their final resting place in the mausoleum of the ducal family, the **Fürstengruft**, Historischer Friedhof, Am Poseckschen Garten, ☎ 03643-545-380. The mausoleum and adjacent Russian Orthodox church are open Tuesday to Sunday from April to October, 10 am to 1 pm and 2 to 6 pm, closing at 4 pm during the winter season. Admission is €2.

About 15 minutes walk from the center is the **Nietzsche-Archiv**, Humboldstraße 36, ☎ 03643-545-159. Friederich Nietzsche spent his final years, from 1897 to 1900, here with his sister. After his death, she had Henri van de Velde design an archive to house his works. Under the Communist regime, Nietzsche was ignored. His writings are now in the Goethe-Schiller archive and his library in the Duchess Anna Amalia Library, but the Art Nouveau interior can be visited. The museum is open Tuesday to Sunday from April to October, 3 to 6 pm. Closed on Monday and during the winter season. Admission is €2. From here, Bus 6 is convenient to return to Goetheplatz, the main station, or to Buchenwald.

Near Weimar: Buchenwald

A mere 10 km (six miles) from the spiritual home of German humanism, the Nazis constructed the notorious **Buchenwald Concentration Camp**. Between 1937 and 1945, 250,000 people were interned here and around 50,000 died. Buchenwald was a work camp and not purely an extermination center. Between 1945 and 1950, the Soviet occupation forces used parts of the camp as an internment center for both Nazis and arbitrarily arrested persons. During this period, 7,000 of 28,000 prisoners died. This fact was hidden until the discovery of the mass graves during the 1990s.

Former SS Barracks & Parade Ground

The **Gedenkstätte Buchenwald** (Memorial), ☎ 03643-4300, www.buchenwald.de, is located at the original camp. Most of the camp was demolished while establishing a memorial to anti-Fascist resistance. Only the foundations of most buildings are still visible. The gate still displays the original message: "*Jedem das Seine*" ("To each what he deserves"). A museum is inside the former storehouse. Other buildings that survived include the crematorium, prisoners' canteen, the arrest cells, and the disinfection building.

The museum and exhibition rooms are open Tuesday to Sunday from May to September, 9:45 am to 6 pm, and from October to April, 8:45 to 5 pm. The campgrounds are open daily until nightfall. Detailed maps and information in English are available at the information office. The camp can be reached from Weimar by Bus no 6 if marked Buchenwald – usually one per hour. Admission is free.

See also Norhausen in the Harz, page 129, for Dora concentration camp, the extension of Buchenwald that was used for missile production.

Cultural Events & Festivals

Weimar has a rich cultural tradition and many events are scheduled throughout the year. Virtually all plays are performed in German only, but musical and dancing events, ranging from contemporary to classical, are also frequently scheduled. The Tourist Information office has details and can make some reservations.

The Weimar **Kunstfest (Art Festival)**, www.kunstfest-weimar.de, is a cultural highlight from mid-August to mid-September. Music and plays are performed on most public squares and in all theaters, including the famed German National Theater.

Weimar also arranges events during the **Thuringian Bach Weeks**, www.bachwochen.de, staged during March and April.

The largest folk festival in Thuringia is the three-day Weimar **Zwiebelmarkt (Onion Market)** in mid-October. Apart from onions, loads of food and drink are available and live music is performed on most squares and public spaces. Reserve hotel accommodation months in advance and do not even think about going by car.

Shopping

Weimar is a good place to buy German literature. The town breathes literature and classical works are available from many bookshops as well as most museum shops. Classical works in paperback are surprisingly cheap but prices rise fast as soon as photographs and color are added. **Stiftung Weimarer Klassik** (Weimar Classics Foundation), Frauentorstraße 4, ☎ 03643-545-401, www.weimar-klassik.de, has a vast selection of books and other paraphernalia associated with the Weimar Classicists.

Adventures

On Foot

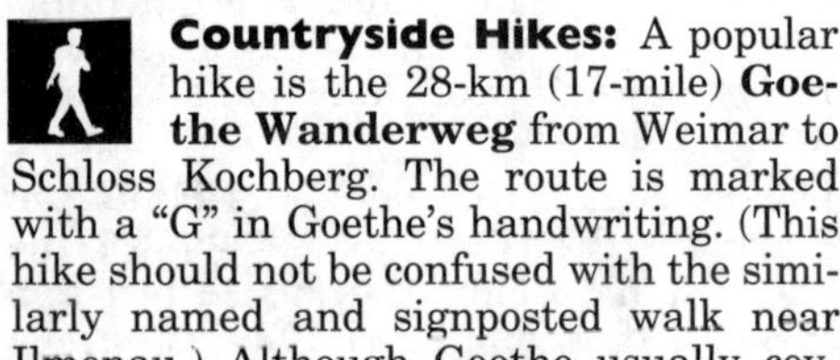

Countryside Hikes: A popular hike is the 28-km (17-mile) **Goethe Wanderweg** from Weimar to Schloss Kochberg. The route is marked with a "G" in Goethe's handwriting. (This hike should not be confused with the similarly named and signposted walk near Ilmenau.) Although Goethe usually covered the route on horseback to visit his close confidant Charlotte von Stein, he also famously walked the route in around four hours. Most hikers take significantly longer, spending time en route enjoying the scenery and visiting inns and beer gardens. A popular stop is the 39-m (124-foot) covered bridge over the River Ilm at Buchfahrt. Parts of this wooden bridge and the adjacent watermill date from the 17th century.

On Wheels

By Bicycle: The **Ilmtal cycling route** runs for 125 km (75 miles) in the Ilm Valley from the Thuringia Forest to where the Ilm flows into the Saale near Bad Sulza. This route is easy and mostly asphalt. It is marked by a cyclist and a blue and green wave. An interesting side-route is the 28-km (17-mile) **Feininger route**. It makes a circle from Weimar and passes sites frequented and sketched by the Bauhaus artist Lyonel Feininger in the 1920s.

In **Weimar** bicycles can be rented from **Fahrradverleih Grüne Liga**, Goetheplatz 9b, ☎ 03643-492-796, or from **Fahrrad Hopf**, Untergraben 2, ☎ 03643-202-120. In **Bad Sulza** from **Hotel an der Therme**, Wunderwaldstraße 2, ☎ 036461-92-888, or **Gästeinformation**, Kurpark 2, ☎ 036461-82-110.

By Minibus: Sightseeing Tour Weimar, Am Brühl 9, ☎ 03643-59-526, conducts two-hour guided tours in English of Weimar and vicinity in eight-seater minibuses. The price is €20 and tours depart at 10 am, noon, 2 and 4 pm. Individualized tours and excursions to other sights in the vicinity can be arranged.

Where to Stay & Eat

Weimar has hotels of all price classes, reflecting the importance this small town accords to tourism. In the off-season luxury hotels, especially major chains, often drop their prices to below those of much lesser establishments.

The most famous hotel in Weimar, and one of the best known in Germany, is the **Hotel Elephant**, centrally located on the Market Square. From the outside, it looks like nothing special, but inside it oozes sheer class. It is part of the Sheraton's *Luxury Collection* and has a history as a restaurant going back to 1696. The first paying guests slept here in 1741 and since then luminaries such as Goethe, Schiller, Bach, Clara Schumann, Felix Mendelssohn-Bartholdy, Franz Liszt, Richard Wagner, and Tolstoy have spent the night. Thomas Mann used it as the setting for *Lotte in Weimar* (translated as *Beloved Returned*). Hitler stayed and apparently did not like it much as the Nazis had the upper floors rebuilt in the style that survived to the present. The comfortable rooms are furnished with Bauhaus and Art Deco furniture. The restaurant **Anna Amalia** (€€€-€€€€) is arguably the best in town and the **Elephantenkeller** (€€-€€€) the most famous. The Anna Amalia offers nouvelle cuisine, mixing German and Mediterranean dishes, while the Elephantenkeller has more traditional regional food on the menu. Markt 19, 99423 Weimar, ☎ 03643-8020, fax 03643-802-610. (€€€€)

The most comfortable hotel in town is the **Hilton Weimar**. This thoroughly modern hotel was built by the former East German regime and completed around the time of the *Wende*. It was refurbished in 1999. Rooms are comfortably furnished and bright with light woods. It may have less tradition and history than some of the competition, but it's first-class in terms of comfort and service. The restaurant **Esplanade** (€€-€€€) serves international cuisine with a large selection of local and Italian dishes. The Hilton is at the edge of the Park an der Ilm, about 10 minutes walk from the old town. Belvederer Allee 25, 99425 Weimar, ☎ 03643-7220, fax 03643-722-741, www.hilton.com. (€€-€€€)

The **Dorint am Goethepark** is conveniently located between the Goethehaus and the Park an der Ilm. It successfully combines two historic houses with modern architecture to create a thoroughly modern interior. Rooms are comfortable and spacious. The hotel has a large exercise area with free sauna, whirlpool, and fitness center. Massages and beauty treatments can be arranged. Beethovenplatz 1-2, 99423 Weimar, ☎ 03643-8720, fax 03643-872100, www.dorint.de. (€€-€€€€)

In a quiet residential neighborhood, about 15 minutes walk south of the old town, is the stylish **Wolff's Art Hotel**. This designer hotel is furnished in a postmodern Bauhaus style with art works and designer furniture. Rooms are well-equipped despite the minimalist look. It has a large fitness area with numerous related options. The restaurant (€€-€€€) serves international cuisine, with a strong leaning towards Mediterranean food. Freiherr-vom-Stein-Allee 3a/b, 99425 Weimar, ☎ 03643-540-60, fax 03643-540-699. (€€€-€€€€)

In Weimar, only the Elephant has a longer tradition and more impressive guest list than the **Grand Hotel Russischer Hof**. The building dates back to 1797 and, in contrast to the Elephant, the exterior here looks the part. It is on Goetheplatz near the National Theatre and Bauhaus Museum. In 1999, the hotel was completely renovated to modern standards. Rooms are comfortable with French style period furniture. The restaurant **Anastasia** (€€-€€€€) is equally luxurious and stylish. The cuisine is international, with a large selection of Austrian and Thuringian dishes. Goetheplatz 2, 99423 Weimar, ☎ 03643-7740, fax 03643-774-840. (€€€€)

Across the road from the main station, behind a historic façade, is the modern interior of the **Intercity Hotel**. Like other hotels in this chain, the hotel is well-equipped and especially popular with business travelers. Rooms are not particularly large, but comfortable with stylish dark furniture. The room key gives free access to local public transportation. Spectacular deals are sometimes on offer in the off-season. Carl-August-Allee 17, 99423 Weimar, ☎ 03643-2340, fax 03643-234-444, www.intercityhotel-weimar.de. (€€)

Located in a quiet neighborhood about 10 minutes walk from the old town is the small **Hotel Liszt Garni**. The hotel consists of 23 apartments of varying sizes, each with a small kitchen. The furnishings are comfortable rather than luxurious, reflected in the low rates. Lisztstraße 1, 99423 Weimar, ☎ 03643-540-80, fax 03643-540-830, www.hotel-liszt.de. (€€)

About 10 minutes south of the old town, in a lovely early-19th-century villa restored in the 1990s, is the small **Hotel Villa Hentzel**. Rooms are comfortable and individually furnished. Rates include a large breakfast buffet. Bauhausstraße 12, 99423 Weimar, ☎ 03643-865-80, fax 03643-865-819, www.weimar.de/hentzel. (€€)

Only a block from the Goethehaus is the **Hotel Amalienhof**. This small hotel is in a restored classical villa dating from 1826. Rooms are comfortable, with stylish furniture, more reminiscent of a private house than a hotel. Amalienstraße 2, 99423 Weimar, ☎ 03643-549-0, fax 03643-549-110, www.amalienhof-weimar.de. (€€-€€€)

Apart from the Elephantenkeller, the most famous restaurant in Weimar is **Gasthaus Zum Weißen Schwan**, Frauentorstraße 23, ☎ 03643-202-521. It is literally around the corner from the Goethehaus, which is not surprising given that it was one of Goethe's favored restaurants for entertaining guests. The cuisine consists of hearty local specialties and the prices are surprisingly moderate for such a well-known establishment. (€-€€).

Just off the Market Square is **Shakespeares**, Windischenstraße 4, ☎ 03643-901-285. It is a large, modern bistro-style restaurant with its own stage. The food is both good and reasonably priced. Open only for dinner. (€-€€)

Camping

Near Weimar, in the Ilm Valley, is the campsite called **Ilmtal-Oettern**. It has 100 spaces but facilities are rather basic. It is open from mid-April to October. Campingplatz Ilmtal, 99438 Oettern, ☎ 036453-80-264.

■ Erfurt

Erfurt, the capital of Thuringia, is a lovely, unpretentious town. It receives far fewer visitors than nearby Weimar, but is easier to enjoy. Much of the Erfurt experience is simply strolling through the beautiful streets, many dating back to the Middle Ages, and enjoying one of Germany's most authentic medieval cities.

In 742, Erfurt was founded as a bishopric by St Boniface. Its heyday was in the 14th and 15th centuries, when trade in the woad plant, used for blue dye before the introduction of indigo, made it a rich city. Martin Luther lived here from 1501 to 1511, first as a student and then as a monk. In 1808, Napoleon Bonaparte met Czar Alexander I here for a congress lasting 17 days. Napoleon failed in his attempts to turn the Czar against Austria. During this stay, Napoleon met Goethe several times and subsequently made him a member of the League of Honor.

Erfurt's historic town center survived both World War II and the Communist regime without major damage. After the *Wende*, Erfurt became the capital of the Thuringia.

Information Sources

Tourist Office: The Tourismus Gesellschat Erfurt, Benediktsplatz 1, 99084 Erfurt, ☎ 0361664-0110, www.erfurt-tourismus.de, is between the Krämerbrücke and the Fischmarkt. It can make reservations for accommodations, tours, packages, and cultural events. Opening hours are April to December on weekdays from 10 am to 7 pm, Saturday from 9 am to 6 pm, and Sunday from 10 am to 4 pm; January to March, Monday to Saturday from 10 am to 6 pm, Sunday 10 am to 4 pm.

Transportation

The main train station is about five minutes walk south of Anger, the main shopping area at the edge of the old town. Frequent trains to Weimar take between 11 and 20 minutes. Trams 3, 4, and 6 run from the station through the old town to Domplatz and beyond.

Sightseeing

Erfurt's historic center is fairly large, but the numerous beautifully decorated buildings make the city easy to enjoy and a pleasure to stroll in. A good place to start is from the massive Domplatz, the size of four football fields. It is about half an hours' walk from the station – well worth it to see the interesting decorated buildings – or it can be reached in minutes by tram.

Domplatz

The most impressive sight in Erfurt is from the Domplatz towards Cathedral Hill. A wide flight of 70 stairs leads from the square to the top of the hill where the cathedral and an abbey are set in close proximity.

The **Dom St Marien** (St Mary's Cathedral), Domberg, ☎ 0361-646-1265, was originally a Romanesque basilica, constructed in 1154. The High Gothic choir was added in the 14th century and, from 1455, the original nave was replaced by a Late Gothic construction. One of the largest free-swinging bells in the world, the 1497 "Gloriosa" rings on special occasions from the central tower. The main entrance is through an interesting High Gothic portal – two doors are set obliquely to form a rare triangular portal. The current interior is mostly Baroque. The Wolfram, a bronze statue candelabra dating from 1160, is considered the oldest freestanding bronze sculpture in Germany. The stained-glass windows in the choir are 14th-century originals. In 1507, Martin Luther was ordained as a Roman Catholic priest in this cathedral. The church is open May to October from Monday to Saturday, 9 to 11:30 am and 12:30 to 5 pm, closing at 4:30 pm on Saturdays; from November to April, Monday to Saturday, 10 to 11:30 am and 12:30 to 4 pm. On Sunday, it's open from 2 to 4 pm, year-round. Admission is free and information boards in English are available.

The Wolfram

The Wolfram

Across the road is the **St Severikirche** (St Severus Church), Severihof 2, ☎ 0361-576-960, a five-nave early Gothic hall church. Its towers have tall, sleek spire roofs – the cathedral once had similar ones – that must be any thunderbolt's dream. The interior is mostly Baroque, but the real treasures are Gothic: the 1,360 sarcophagi of St Severus and the 15-m (48-foot) baptismal font created in 1467. The church is only open on weekdays, from May to October, 9 am to 12:30 pm and 1:30 to 5 pm, and November to April, 10 am to 12:30 pm and 1:30 to 4 pm.

The narrow road in front of the church, Severihof, leads to the **Zitadelle Petersberg** (Petersberg Citadel), the only largely intact Baroque town fortifications in central Europe. The view from here on a clear day is magnificent. The interesting underground passages can be seen on guided tours conducted by the tourist information office.

Fischmarkt

From the Domplatz, Marktstraße leads to the Fischmarkt (Fish Market) with its Neo-Gothic Rathaus (Town Hall). The early 14th-century **Heiligengeistkirche** (Holy Ghost Church) is on the way. Interestingly, it has a triangular shape that follows the lay of the land. From the church, look down Große Arche road to see the lovely yellow Baroque façade of the **Haus zum Sonnenborn**, Große Arche 6. It is used as a wedding registry and not open to the general public.

In addition to the Rathaus, there are several imposing facades on the Fischmarkt, including the lovely Renaissance **Zum breiten Herd** (1584) and the **Zum roten Ochsen** (1562). On the square is a statue of St Martin, Germany's patron saint, oddly dressed as a Roman soldier.

Nearby is the **Predigerkirche**, Predigerstraße 4, ☎ 0361-562-6214, erected between 1270 and 1400 by the Order of the Mendicant Friars. In summer, it has organ concerts on most Wednesday afternoons. The church is open April to October from Tuesday to Saturday, 10 am to 6 pm, and Sunday, noon to 4 pm. From November to March, it is open Tuesday to Saturday, 10 am to noon, and 2 to 4 pm.

Across the stream is the **Barfüßerkirche**, Barfüßerstraße 20, ☎ 0361-554-560. It was left in ruins after World War II but the choir is a small museum of medieval art. It is open April to October from Tuesday to Sunday, 10 am to 1 pm, and 2 to 6 pm. Admission is €2.

Krämerbrucke

A block from the Rathaus is the **Krämerbrücke** (Shopkeepers' Bridge), one of Erfurt's best-known sights. It is the only bridge north of the Alps with inhabited houses. It is 120 m (384 feet) long and lined by two rows of houses that completely cover both sides of the bridge. It dates back to 1325 and currently spans the River Gera with six arches. It has 33 buildings including a church at the far end. It nowadays houses mostly antique shops and small boutiques.

The best views of the bridge are from Horngasse, which spans the river slightly north. Nearby is the **Augustinerkloster** (Augustine Monastery), Augustinerstraße 10, ☎ 0361-576-600, www.augustinerkloster.de, where Martin Luther lived from 1505 until 1511. The original 13th-century buildings were completely destroyed in 1945, but rebuilt in recent years. Most of it is used as a conference center, but the reconstructed Martin Luther cell, the lovely library, and other parts of the monastery can be seen. It is open from April to October, Monday to Saturday, 10 am to noon and 2 to 4 pm, and Sunday from 11 am to 2 pm. From November to March, it is open Monday to Saturday from 10 am to noon, and 2 to 4 pm, Sunday from 11 am to 2 pm. Admission is €3.50 and €2 for a photography permit.

Krämerbrücke leads into Futterstraße, where at No 15 Napoleon entertained the Czar in what is now known as the **Kaisersaal** (Emperor's Hall). The building houses several restaurants and conference facilities and is not open to the general public.

The **Anger** is a large square near the main station and is the heart of commercial Erfurt. It is also a major hub of the tram network. At the north end of the square is the Kaufmannskirche, where Martin Luther preached and Bach's parents were married. The shops on the square are all housed in large, grand buildings and the post office building here must be one of the best looking in Germany.

The **Angermuseum**, Anger 18, ☎ 0361-554-560, is in a lovely yellow Baroque building. The museum has a collection of art ranging from the Middle Ages to the present but is closed indefinitely for renovations.

Excursions from Erfurt

Nordhausen in the Harz Mountains:

Nordhausen used to be a very pretty town,

but aerial bombing during World War II destroyed most of the town center. Neglect during the Communist period did not help either.

The main reason for stopping over here is to see the former **KZ Gedänkstatte Dora** (concentration camp) Kohnsteinweg 20, 99734 Nordhausen, ☎ 036-313-636, just off the main road north at the edge of the Harz Mountains. This was where the V2 missiles that rained on London at the end of World War II were produced by prisoners, inside tunnels carved into the Harz Mountains. Dora was a subdivision of the notorious Buchenwald camp near Weimar. Opening hours are daily from April to September, 10 am to 6 pm, and from October to March, 10 am to 3 pm. Note that the buildings, including the tunnels and museum, are closed on Monday.

Nordhausen is the south terminus of the **Harzquerbahn**, a narrow-gauge steam engine train that runs 60 km (36 miles) through the Harz Mountains to Wernigerode. Departing from Nordhausen, the best seats are in the rear on the left. See chapter on Saxony Anhalt for details.

By car, Nordhausen is about an hour north of Erfurt. By hourly train, it takes between 75 and 105 minutes. Nordhausen is best visited en route to towns north of the Harz in Saxony Anhalt.

Bad Frankenhausen in the Kyffhäuser Mountains: The Kyffhäuser Mountains is a lovely low range, often described as a mini-Harz. It is popular with hikers and cyclists who enjoy the often gentle slopes and fine views.

Bad Frankenhausen has the largest oil painting in the world in the **Panoramamuseum**, Am Schlachtberg 9, ☎ 034671-6190, www.panorama-museum.de. A 1975 round building, known locally as the elephant toilet, houses this painting measuring 14½ by 123 m (46 x 394 feet), entitled *Early Bourgeois Revolution in Germany*. It was painted by Werner Tübke between 1976 and 1987, and depicts the Peasants' Revolt of the early 16th century. The realistic painting features 75 major scenes and around 3,000 people. The revolt was led by Thomas Müntzer, a one-time ally of Martin Luther. However, he was condemned by Luther after demanding full social revolution, including the overthrow of nobles, and the destruction of monasteries and other religious centers. He led peasants into a one-sided battle against the armies of the nobles. The peasants were slaughtered at the battle of Schlachtberg in 1525. Müntzer was captured, tortured, and executed. Not surprisingly, Thomas Müntzer became a hero in the German Democratic Republic, while Martin Luther was initially viewed as a traitor of the people. Luther was only rehabilitated in the late 1950s. Opening hours are April to September from Tuesday to Sunday, 10 am to 6 pm, in July and August also on Monday, 1 to 6 pm. From October to March opening hours are Tuesday to Sunday, 10 am to 5 pm. Admission is €5.

Nearby, on the road to Kelbra, are the ruins of the former imperial castle of **Kyffhausen** with the **Kaiser Wilhelm-Nationaldenkmal** (Emperor Wilhelm National Monument), ☎ 034671-71-716, www.kyffhaeuser-tourismus.de. According to legend, Emperor Friederich I Barbarossa, who drowned in a river while on a crusade in 1190, never really died, but was merely resting inside the hill of Kyffhausen, waiting to return to the throne when the time was right. The never-modest Hohenzollern regime of the late 19th century, decided that the restoration of the Empire by Prussia in 1871 clearly implied that the popular Barbarossa had risen in the form of the new emperor. A bombastic 81-m (259-foot) high monument was erected in 1896 featuring an enormous imperial crown and a 10-m (32-foot) high equestrian statue of Kaiser Wilhelm I. Just over 230 stairs lead to a viewing platform with grand views. The monument is open daily from 9 am to 5 pm, 7 pm from May to September. Admission is €4.

These sights are best reached by private transportation and are about a 45-minute drive from Erfurt and half an hour from Nordhausen.

Cultural Events

A highlight on the Erfurt cultural calendar is the **Thuringia Bach Weeks**, www.bach-wochen.de, staged during March and April. The main theme is obviously music by Bach but music by other composers is also played.

The **Domstufenfestpiele** (Cathedral Steps Festival), www.domstufen.de, is staged from mid-August to early September on the famous steps at Erfurt's cathedral. The events range from operettas to plays.

In summer, the **Predigerkirche**, Predigerstraße 4, ☎ 0361-562-6214, has organ concerts on most Wednesday afternoons.

Shopping

The **Krämerbrücke** has a number of small antique shops and art galleries. In many studios, the artists can be observed at work. Although the bridge is a popular tourist destination, prices remain sane. Erfurt's main shopping area is at nearby Anger, where many new department stores and other major outlets are located.

Erfurt's wealth was built on the **woad** trade and products made from it can still be bought. Apart from blue printed fabrics, cosmetics (*Waidkosmetik*) are also available from many outlets, including the Tourist Office, Benediktplatz 1, Erfurt, ☎ 0361-664-0240. The woad blue fabric printing workshop of Sigritt Weiss, Mühlburgweg 32, 99094 Erfurt-Hochheim, can be visited by appointment.

Adventures

On Foot

Town Walks: Erfurt's old town is best explored on foot. Most of it is flat and many streets are for pedestrians only. The tourist office conducts guided tours in German only.

On Wheels

By Bicycle: Bicycles may be rented from **ADFC Fahrradverleih**, Espachstraße 3a, ☎ 0361-225-1732.

Where to Stay & Eat

Erfurt has several convenient and comfortable hotels of international calibre. However, for true luxury it is necessary to stay in nearby Weimar, where the top hotels exceed most superlatives.

The **Dorint Hotel** is a safe choice in the center of town, close to the Krämerbrücke. It combines restored 16th-century buildings and a new wing into a modern, comfortable hotel. Rooms are well-equipped. The stylish **Restaurant Zum Rebstock** (€€-€€€) has international and local cuisine. Meienbergstraße 26-27, 99084 Erfurt, ☎ 0361-594-90, fax 0361-594-9100, www.dorint.de. (€€-€€€)

Nearby is the **Sorat Hotel Erfurt**, a designer hotel with modern furnishings. Each room is individually decorated with furniture designed exclusively for the hotel by French designer Didier Gomez. Some rooms have views of the Krämerbrücke. The **Restaurant Zum Alten Schwan** (€€-€€€) has a long tradition, but is rendered totally modern in the refurbished hotel. International cuisine and a large vegetarian selection are available. Gotthardstraße 27, 99084 Erfurt, ☎ 0361-674-00, fax 0361-674-0444, www.sorat-hotels.com. (€€€-€€€€)

Hotel Zum Norde am Anger is a small, privately run hotel, offering a pleasant alternative to the chain hotels in the region. It is near the Anger Museum in the old town. Rooms are comfortably furnished and service is first-class. The hotel has a huge roof garden. The **Restaurant Zum Norde** (€€-€€€) serves light, regional cuisine in an authentic Art Nouveau setting. Anger 50-51, 99084 Erfurt, ☎ 0361-568-00, fax 0361-568-0400, www.hotel-zumnorde.de. (€€-€€€€)

Close to the main station is the comfortable **Best Western Hotel Excelsior**, a modern hotel behind a restored Art Nouveau façade with a large glass cupola. Rooms are comfortably furnished with pastel and light-colored wood furniture. The **Restaurant Zum Bürgerhof** (€€-€€€) has an open kitchen and offers modern international cuisine. Bahnhofstrße 35, 99804 Erfurt, ☎ 0361-567-00, fax 0361-567-0100, www.bestwestern.de. (€€-€€€).

Even closer to the station is the very modern **InterCity Hotel**. As always with the Intercity group, the focus is on the business traveler, but vacationers will also enjoy the comfortable rooms and convenient location. Rooms are not particularly large, but they are stylish and well-equipped. Willy-Brandt-Platz 11, 99084 Erfurt, ☎ 0361-560-00, fax 0361-560-0999, www.intercityhotel.de. (€€-€€€).

The **Hotel Ibis** is in the center of the old town, just minutes from the Dom. Rooms are modern and well-equipped for this price class. As usual, an Ibis is unexciting but safe, a clean and well-run, no-frills establishment. Barfüßerstraße 9, 99084 Erfurt, ☎ 0361-664-10, fax 0361-664-1111, www.accorhotels.com. (€€)

Erfurt's best restaurant is not inside a hotel but rather in the much more lavish Kaisersaal. The gourmet restaurant **Alboth's**, Futterstraße 15, ☎ 0361-568-8207, www.alboths.de, is located at the splendid Kaisersaal, where Napoleon and the Czar engaged in diplomacy. On offer is nouvelle cuisine as well as light regional dishes. The wine list is extensive. (€€€-€€€€).

In one of the town's loveliest buildings, with a view of the equally impressive Rathaus, is **Paganini im Gildenhaus**, Fischmarkt 13-16, ☎ 0361-643-0692. Food is mainly Italian with some regional specialties and international dishes as well. (€-€€€)

Camping

About 25 km (15 miles) from Erfurt, in the small town of Mühlberg, is the campsite known as **Drei Gleichen**. It has 150 spaces. A golf course and riding stables are adjacent to the site. It is open year-round but advance reservations are required from November to March. Am Gut Ringhofen, 99869 Mühlberg, ☎ 036256-22-715, fax 036256-86-801, www.campingplatz-muehlberg.de.

■ Eisenach

The old town of Eisenach suffered major damage during World War II. Under Communist rule, little was spent on upkeep and many historic buildings were torn down. Things changed dramatically after the *Wende*. The most famous sights have been restored and all over town restoration and preservation work is continuing.

The main attraction in Eisenach is undoubtedly the Wartburg castle. The fortress perched high on a hill has been described as the most German of all castles and is often considered the national monument of Germany. In town, the main draws are the Luther Museum and the Bachhaus. Most museums in Eisenach are open seven days a week.

Information Sources

Tourist Office: Tourist Information, Markt, 99817 Eisenach, ☎ 03691-79-230, www.eisenach.de.

Transportation

The Hauptbahnhof is a few minutes walk from the Nikolaitor and the start of the historic old town. Eisenach is a frequent stop of the ICE trains and has convenient regional train connections.

Bus No 10 runs from the station to the Wartburg. Bus No 11 is convenient for hikes starting at Hohe Sonne and the bottom parking lots of the Wartburg.

Sightseeing

The Wartburg

History: The Wartburg's history goes back to around 1067 and the time when the Ludovingian family ruled Thuringia. The family was powerful enough to consider it proper to add a third floor to the main Romanesque palace building, something that was generally done only for a residence of the German king. St Elizabeth (see Marburg in Hesse chapter, page 330) also lived at the Wartburg, shortly before the Ludovingian family died out in 1247.

The next period of interest came in 1521, when Elector Friedrich the Wise of Saxony, right, had Martin Luther kidnapped on his way back to Saxony, after Luther had been declared an outlaw at the Diet of Worms. For 10 months, Luther lived in the Wartburg, disguised as a monk called Junker Jörg. In only 10 weeks, he translated the New Testament from Greek into German. The Wartburg has been a drawing card for tourists ever since and pilgrims carried away his original desk splinter by splinter. The current desk on display replaced the paltry remains of the original.

As the Wartburg lost its strategic importance due to changing military technology, the counts moved to more comfortable quarters in town and the castle was left to waste away. It was through the influence of Goethe, who was more impressed by the natural beauty of the Wartburg, rather than its architecture or history, that attempts were made to restore the castle to its former glory. In contrast to other similar castle reconstructions in the Historicist style of the 19th century, the Wartburg followed the original plans to a larger extent.

The Nazis loved the Wartburg and all the symbolism surrounding it. They had the golden Christian cross replaced by a swastika. However, at the end of the war the Wartburg hoisted the white flag to prevent it being damaged by the advancing American troops. It was declared a UNESCO World Cultural Heritage Site in 1999.

LEGENDS OF THE WARTBURG

There are several famous legends connected to it, all illustrated somewhere inside the castle walls. According to legend, the castle was founded and named by count Ludwig der Springer (Louis the Jumper), who saw the rocky hill and proclaimed "***Wart**! Berg, du sollst mir eine **Burg** werden!*" (Wait Mountain, you should become my fortress!) He was not the owner of the land, but that minor problem was overcome by carting some of his own ground to the top of the hill. That allowed his servants to swear with a clear conscience, when the real owner took the case to the emperor, that they had dug into their master's soil when building the castle.

St Elizabeth spent most of her childhood here – see Marburg in the Hesse chapter for more on her life, page 330.

A popular sight on the Wartburg is the wood-paneled quarters where Martin Luther resided for almost a year, while disguised as a simple monk. Apart from translating the New Testament into German, Luther was a prolific writer producing numerous letters and manuscripts. Soon after he left the Wartburg, it became an important pilgrim's station and one of the famous sights was the ink stain on the wall. Martin Luther wrote that he had to fight the devil with ink. Although he meant fighting with writing, it soon became legend that an ink stain on the wall of his room was caused when Martin Luther threw an inkpot at the devil. For centuries, pilgrims scraped the ink of the wall and the authorities re-inked it when necessary. Although that practice ended at the end of the 19th century, the legend survives to the present day.

The most famous legend, however, is that of the competition of the Meistersänger (troubadours) in 1206 and 1207. According to legend, six troubadours competed here in a singing competition, with the loser to lose his head. In the end the power of music triumphed and all survived. Whether the competition really took place is uncertain, but it is known that the count at that time, Hermann I, was a great supporter of cultural life and that Wolfram von Eschenbach wrote part of his 25,000-line *Parzival* here. The competition was made famous by Wagner's opera *Tannhäuser und der Sängerkreig auf Wartburg.*

Visiting the Wartburg: There are three distinct parts when visiting the Wartburg – the palace, the museum and the Luther quarters. The **palace** can only be seen on a guided tour in German. (English leaflets are available.) The 45-minute tour includes some of the historic rooms dating back to the origin of the castle, such as the knight's hall, dining room, as well as more modern 19th-century decorated ones, including roof paintings, tributes to St Elizabeth, and the music hall that is used for concerts.

At the end of the tour, visitors are guided straight into the **museum**, which contains period pieces from the region but not actually from the Wartburg itself. Displays

Luther's Father, by Lucas Cranach

include crockery, silverware, time-keeping instruments, a closet produced by Dürer, and several famous paintings by Lucas Cranach, including two of Martin Luther's parents. At the end of the museum, cross over to the **Lutherstube** (Luther's Room), where Martin Luther worked and slept during his 10-month sojourn at the Wartburg. Visitors not taking the guided tour of the castle enter the museum and Lutherstube at intervals of 15 minutes to limit the numbers inside the somewhat cramped space.

The Wartburg is a very popular destination for Germans of all age groups. Even in the off-season, expect school groups and, during vacation time, families. It is highly advisable to arrive at opening time and to take the first tour of the day – seeing the crowds in the courtyard when emerging from the first tour will make you glad you did.

The Wartburg, Schlossbergweg 2, ☎ 03691-77-073, www.wartburg-eisenach.de, is open daily from March to October, 8:30 am to 8 pm (last tour at 5 pm), and November to February, 9 am to 5 pm (last tour at 3:30 pm). Admission to the palace, museum and Lutherstube is €6.50 or €3.50 without the palace. Reservations are not possible.

The castle is a few minutes drive south of the Old Town. When the parking lot at the castle itself is full, cars are directed to parking lots at the bottom of the hill and a shuttle bus, or a steep 20-minute walk, must be taken to the castle terminus. During the high season children weighing less than 60 kg (132 lbs) can take the traditional donkey ride, ☎ 03691-210-404, to the top castle terminus. Bus No 10 runs from the Hauptbahnhof in Eisenach to the top of the hill; Bus 11 stops at the parking lots at the foot of the hill.

From the castle parking lot, donkey, and bus terminus it is still a good 10 minutes of stair climbing or a 500-m (1,600-foot) steep walk to reach the first gate of the Wartburg. In summer, an infrequent bus service is available for the infirm. Unfortunately, the Wartburg itself is completely inaccessible to wheelchair users.

Old Town Sights

The old town of Eisenach is not particularly pretty, but there are a few interesting sights well worth seeing. Continuing restoration works are improving the attractiveness of the old town. Most attractions are within easy walking distance from the main train station, with the exception of the Wartburg, which is at least half an hour's walk, including steep hills.

Close to the main train station is the **Nikolaitor** (Nicholas Gate). This huge Romanesque town gate is the only one of the original five that survived. Next to the gate is the **Nikolaikirche**, Karlsplatz, the last Romanesque church built in Thuringia (around 1180), but altered at the end of the 19th century. Opening hours are daily May to October from 10 am to noon and 3 to 5 pm. On the small Karlsplatz is an oversized statue (1895) of **Martin Luther** with three reliefs illustrating scenes from his sojourns in Eisenach.

The recently pedestrianized and major shopping street Karlstraße leads to **Markt** (Market Square), where a fountain with a golden statue of St George slaying the dragon forms the focal point. The main building at the square is the huge **Georgenkirche** (George Church), Markt, ☎ 03691-79-230. It dates back to 1180, but most of the current church, with three levels of galleries, and the tower are Baroque. Johan Sebastian Bach was baptized here on March 23, 1685 and several of his family members were the organists here, a position the great composer never held in his hometown. Opening hours are daily from 10 am to noon and 2 to 4 pm.

Two other important buildings on Markt are the Late Renaissance **Rathaus** and the Baroque **Stadtschloss** (Town Palace), erected around 1750 by the Dukes of Saxe-Weimar-Eisenach. It houses the

Thuringian Museum, which is indefinitely closed due to restoration work. The adjacent **Marstall**, Markt 24, ☎ 03691-670-450, houses temporary exhibitions. Opening hours are Tuesday to Sunday from 10 am to 5 pm.

Lutherhaus

Nearby, in a neat, 14th-century half-timber building is the **Lutherhaus**, Lutherplatz 8, ☎ 03691-29-830, www.lutherhaus-eisenach.de. Martin Luther stayed here from 1498 to 1501 with the Cotta family, while studying Latin. The house has a museum with an exhibition on Luther's life and the history of the Reformation. Opening hours are April to October daily from 9 am to 5 pm, and November to March from 10 am to 5 pm. Admission is €2.50.

Farther up the road is the **Bachhaus**, Frauenplan 21, ☎ 03691-79-340, www.bachhaus.de. This museum is dedicated to Eisenach's most famous son, the composer Johan Sebastian Bach (1685-1750). It was originally thought that this house was his place of birth, but arguments still rage over whether that was an honest mistake or the truth was hidden until the real birth house could be destroyed and the land used for other commercial purposes. Although the first museum in the world dedicated to Bach, it only opened in 1906 and has little that was used by Bach himself. Most of the exhibits are documents and prints on his life and work, with descriptions in German only. Furniture and musical instruments on display date from Bach's time. Behind the lovely garden in the back of the house is a modern glass and steel hall used for temporary exhibitions. The Bach statue in front of the house dates from 1884 and was moved here from Markt in 1938. Admission is €4 and includes a 20-minute program of Bach music, with some pieces played on period instruments. Concerts are sometimes held in the museum. Opening hours are daily from 10 am to 6 pm.

Bachhaus

In the direction of the station, at Johannisplatz 9, is the **Schmale Haus** (Narrow House). This building, erected around 1750, is 8½ m (27 feet) high, but only 2.05 m (6½ feet) wide and is thus considered the narrowest half-timber house in Germany. Visits in the interior, not really worth it, can be arranged in advance through the tourism office.

Higher up the hill, close to the access road to the Wartburg, is the **Reuter-Wagner-Museum**, Reuterweg 2, ☎ 03691-743-293. A popular German poet, Fritz Reuter, had the Neo-Renaissance villa built in 1866. In addition to rooms dedicated to Reuter, the villa houses the second-largest archive on Wagner works, which in contrast to the larger archive in Bayreuth, is actually open to the public. Opening hours are Tuesday to Sunday from 10 am to 5 pm. Admission is €3.

Side Trips from Eisenach

Gotha

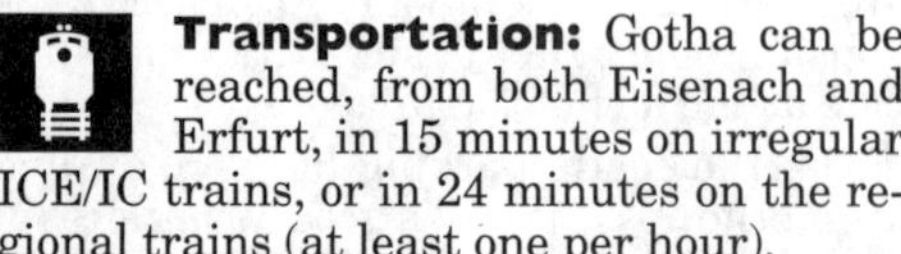

Transportation: Gotha can be reached, from both Eisenach and Erfurt, in 15 minutes on irregular ICE/IC trains, or in 24 minutes on the regional trains (at least one per hour).

Sightseeing: Gotha – another Thuringian town, another duchy, and another palatial

Above: Rathaus and Cathedral in Bremen (© BTZ)
Below: Celle's geranium market in May (© Tourismus Region Celle)

Above: Celle's Neue Straße

Below: Herzogschloss, Celle (both © Tourismus Region Celle)

Above: The Breite Tor, Goslar

Below: Goslar's Market Square and Rathaus (*both © www.goslar.de*)

Above: Boppard, on the Rhine

Below: St. Goarshausen, with Burg Katz in the background

(both © Rheinland-Pfalz Tourismus/Piel Media)

ducal residence! **Schloss Friedenstein**, Schlossstraße, ☎ 03621-8234-14, the largest Early Baroque palace in Germany – a room for every day – was constructed in 1643-55 as the residence of the dukes of Saxe-Gotha. The exterior is relatively simple, but inside the rooms are richly decorated in Baroque, Rococo, and Classical styles. The palace houses several museum collections. The art gallery specializes in German paintings of the 15th and 16th centuries but also has some Dutch paintings from the 17th century. The most famous is *The Gotha Lovers* (1484), the oldest German double portrait. The Egyptian Collection is one of the oldest in Germany. Further collections include coins, glasswork, porcelain and ceramics, and prints

The Gotha Lovers

In 1681, Duke Friederich I von Saxe-Coburg-Altenburg changed the ballroom into what is now known as the **Ekhoftheater**. In 1775 the first permanent court theater in Germany was established here, paving the way for society's acceptance of actors as an honorable profession. The original stage machinery and footlights are still in use. Concerts are mainly scheduled in July and August for the Ekhof Festival, www.ekhof-festival.defestival.de. The palace is open May to October from Tuesday to Sunday, 10 am to 5 pm and closing at 4 pm from November to April. Admission is €4 for the palace and museums and an additional €2 for the theater.

Cultural Events

Eisenach, with its important links to the talented Bach family, plays a central role in the **Thuringia Bach Weeks**, www.bach-wochen.de, staged during March and April. Music by Bach is the focus of these culture weeks but music by other composers is also staged.

Concerts are often held in the Festival Hall of the Wartburg, with performances by the excellent ensembles of Deutschlandradio Berlin and the MDR particularly popular. Most concerts are scheduled between May and September.

Near Eisenach are the **Burgruine Brandenburg** (castle ruins), 99819 Lauchröden, ☎ 036927-90-619. Although the ruins have nothing to do with Bach's famous Brandenburg Concertos, open-air Brandenburg concerts are held in June and July.

Adventures

On Foot

Countryside Hikes: A popular three-hour, 10-km (six-mile) walk, is from Hohe Sonne (Bus 11 from Eisenach Station) to the Wartburg. The most beautiful part of the route is the first hour, around 3.5 km (two miles), leading through the dramatic landscape of the narrow **Drachenschlucht** (Dragon's Gorge) to Großes A. This part has many stairs, making the route dangerous when iced over.

In the opposite direction, and continuing beyond Hohe Sonne, is the **Pummpälzweg**, www.pummpaelz.de, connecting the Wartburg with Frankenstein 28 km (17 miles) away. Part of this hiking and cycling route is along the Rennsteig – see Thuringia Forest section, page 138. En route several large, often grotesque wooden sculptures of fairy tale characters are on display. Guided tours in German are occasionally offered by Pummpälzweg eV, Truft 15, 36433 Moorgrund OT Gumpelstadt, ☎ 03695-620-580.

Where to Stay & Eat in Eisenach

Since 1913, the **Hotel auf der Wartburg** has been the preferred temporary address in Eisenach. The hotel was constructed in the style of a Thuringian castle just below the entrance to the Wartburg castle. This recently refurbished luxury hotel has only 26 double rooms and nine singles, making early reservations essential. All rooms are luxurious, individually furnished, and with views of the Wartburg, Eisenach or the Thuringian Forest. The restaurant **Landgrafenstube** (€€€-€€€€) serves regional Thuringian dishes with seasonal variations and a large vegetarian selection. The restaurant and terrace have views of the forest. Reservations are advisable. Smaller meals can be enjoyed on the terrace of **Café Wintergarten**, which has views of Eisenach. Hotel guests may drive up to the hotel on arrival and departure but have to park, like the restaurant guests and castle visitors, in the Wartburg parking lot 10 minutes walk downhill. Auf der Wartburg, 99817 Eisenach, ☎ 03691-7970, fax 03691-797-100, www.wartburghotel.de. (€€€€)

In town, several hotels have a longer tradition. The luxurious **Steigenberger Hotel Thüringer Hof** is in a restored building dating back to 1807. The interior was completely renovated in 2002 after its acquisition by the Steigenberger group. Rooms are very comfortable, well-appointed, and with city or forest views. The fitness area is on the top floor. In addition to the café, the elegant **Galerie Restaurant** (€€-€€€) serves regional cuisine with a large seafood selection – something rare in a region best-known for its sausages. Karlsplatz 11, 99817 Eisenach, ☎ 03691-280, fax 03691-281-900, www.steigenberger.de. (€€€)

Nearby, next to the Nikolai Gate, is the very pleasant **Best Western Hotel Kaiserhof**. Rooms are comfortably furnished in a romantic style, reflecting that the hotel was previously part of the Romantik Hotel group. Many rooms face a busy road and although double-glazing keeps most street noise out, rooms in the back are quieter. A special treat is the hotel's gourmet restaurant, **Turmschäncke** (€€€-€€€€), inside the Nikolaitor, the only surviving medieval city gate. Regional and international dishes are complemented by a long wine list. The menu changes weekly and the restaurant is open for dinner only. Reservations are recommended. The **Zwinger** restaurant (€€-€€€) serves Thuringian and Bavarian cuisine in a relaxed atmosphere. Wartburgallee 2, 99817 Eisenach, ☎ 03691-213-513, fax 03691-203-653, www.bestwestern.de. (€€-€€€)

On a busy shopping street, between Karlsplatz and Markt, is **Café-Restaurant Alt Eisenach**, Karlstraße 51, ☎ 03691-746-088. Although it has Viennese charm, the food is mostly Thuringian but with sufficient international offerings to keep unadventurous foreigners happy. It is less formal than the restaurants located in hotels, but still much more pleasant than other budget establishments preying on the tourist market. (€-€€)

Near the Lutherhaus is the **Schlosshotel**, a modern hotel partly set in a former Franciscan Monastery, which has a history dating back to the 13th century. Rooms are comfortable, with solid wood furniture. The large 17th-century vaulted cellars of the monastery are the setting for the very pleasant and atmospheric **Schlosskeller** (€€), which serves international and local food. Markt 10, 99817 Eisenach, ☎ 03691-214-260, fax 03691-214-259, www.schlosshotel-eisenach.de. (€€-€€€)

Nearby, also in a vaulted cellar but this time part of a former castle, is the **Brunnenkeller** restaurant, Markt 10, ☎ 03691-212-358, www.brunnenkeller-eisenach.de. The food is predominantly home-style regional cuisine at low prices. (€)

Also centrally located, very close to Bach's supposed place of birth, is the **Hotel am Bachhaus**. It is run by the Schindler family and has an informal, relaxed atmosphere. Rooms are large and comfortable rather than luxurious. Families are most welcome and double rooms with a separate sleeping area for small children are available for young families. Marienstraße 7, 99817 Eisenach, ☎ 03691-204-70, fax 03691-204-7133, www.hotel-am-bachhaus.de. (€€)

Several dining options are available on the square in front of the Bachhaus. At **Café Konditorei Brüheim**, Marienstraße 1, ☎ 03691-203-509, at the bottom end of the square, the quality of the cakes and sweets is good enough to draw in clientele. The Bachhaus and statue are within visual range if you choose your seat well. The café is smoke-free – a rarity in this part of the world. (€)

A very pleasant alternative to staying directly in the old town is **Villa Anna**. It is on a hill opposite the Wartburg, in a quiet residential neighborhood of mainly *Gründerzeit* villas. From the hotel, it is about 15 minutes walk, involving steep slopes and stairs, to the Bachhaus. Rooms are spacious, very modern, and flooded with natural light from large windows that offer wonderful views of the valley. The focus is on business travelers but families and vacationers are also heartily welcomed. Apart from a cold breakfast buffet, only small snacks are served. Villa Anna, Fritz-Koch-Straße 12, 99817 Eisenach, ☎ 03691-23-950, fax 03691-239-530, www.hotel-villa-anna.de. (€€)

Camping

The closest campsite to Eisenach is the very pleasant **Altenberger See Campinpark Eisenach** on the banks of the Altenberger Lake, offering not only watersports opportunities but also hiking in the nearby forests. It has 240 spaces, of which 120 are available for short-term campers. It is open from December to October. Campingpark Eisenach, 99819 Wilhelmsthal, ☎ 03691-215-637, fax 03691-215-607, www.campingpark-eisenach.de.

■ Thuringian Forest

The Thuringian Forest is a lovely mountain range, mostly covered by forests, and one of Germany's favorite leisure centers.

Germany's most famous hiking trail, the 160-km (96-mile) **Rennsteig**, runs through the length of the forest and ends close to Eisenach. This route runs along the crest of the mountains and is popular with hikers and mountain bikers alike.

Although hiking is the foremost activity, the area was also the center for East German winter sports and still produces an extraordinary number of top athletes. The small town of **Oberhof** is the center of winter sports activities.

The lovely university town of **Ilmenau** is known to all readers of Goethe. He loved the small town and visited it several times, often on foot. The 18-km (11-mile) **Goethe Hiking Trail** starts in the town.

Information Sources

Tourist Office: Information is available by mail or Internet from the Tourismusverband Thüringer Wald, Postfach 300124, 98501 Suhl, ☎ 03681-394-511, www.thueringer-wald.de, or from any of the local tourist offices in towns in the region.

Transportation

Eisenach itself is in the Thuringian Forest but other cities such as Erfurt, Gotha, and Weimar are within easy reach too. Trains are convenient for getting to the larger towns but an extensive bus service is available, making circular hiking routes unnecessary. Many parking lots are available in the woods, with bus services often stopping nearby.

Adventures

On Foot

Hiking: Thuringia's best hiking routes are in the beautiful hills of the Thuringian Forest. Although Eisenach is in the northwestern corner of the forest, it is also easily reached from Erfurt and Weimar. Guided tours, more often than not aimed at senior citizens, are always in German, but being in a group does offer some security and many fellow hikers may well be able to converse in English. Hiking maps are sold in bookshops all over Germany – hikers like to plan before leaving home – with the best selection, of course, available in the immediate region.

Germany's most famous hiking trail is the 168-km (100-mile) **Rennsteig**, www.rennsteig.de, that runs along the highest parts of the Thuringian Forest. It has been in use as a trade route since 1330. The total route is between 700 and 900 m (2,300-2,950 feet) above sea level. Most of the route is surprisingly level, but with steep inclines at both ends. The way is clearly marked with a white "R" and is fairly busy from April to September. The total walk is traditionally done in six days, hiking west-to-east, starting from Hörschel, near Eisenach, and ending in Blankenstein. Hiking shorter sections is also popular, as parking lots, bus services, and restaurants are scattered along the way, making flexible options possible. Most hotels on the path offer a luggage forwarding service.

Many tourist offices in the region arrange packages of various lengths for hikers. Some offer guided tours although solo hiking is also popular. **Wirthweins Wander Welt**, Goethestraße 39, 99817 Eisenach, ☎ 03691-72-3540, wirthweins-wanderwelt@web.de, arranges several tours of varying lengths on the Rennsteig and other areas in the region.

The **Goethewanderweg** (Goethe Hiking Trail) from Ilmenau to Stützerbach should not be confused with the similarly named trial from Weimar. Both are hikes that Goethe enjoyed and are marked with a white "g" using his handwriting. The 18-km (11-mile) route can be done in around five hours. It starts in Ilmenau from the town museum, which has displays on Goethe's work as chairman of the Mining Commission. Popular stops en route are the Goethehäuschen (Goethe Cottage), the viewing tower on Mount Kickelhahn, and the Jagdhaus Gabelbach (hunting house), with a museum on Goethe's nature studies. The route ends at the Goethe Wohnhaus in Stützerbach. During the second hour of the walk, the climb is around 350 m (1,148 feet) to the peak of Mount Kickelhahn, 861 m (2,824 feet), with fantastic views.

On Wheels

By Bicycle: Cycling in the Thuringia Forest is often challenging, with many tough mountain biking trails rather than the easy, leisurely rides along slow-flowing rivers. A new cycling path, separate from the more famous hiking trail, runs the full length of the **Rennsteig**. The cycling route is 195 km (117 miles), with two-thirds suitable only for mountain bikes. The altitude ranges from 196 to 911 m (643-2,988 feet) above sea level. The route is mostly medium to difficult and is marked by a cyclist and a green "R."

By Car: The natural beauty of the area is not available to hikers and cyclists alone. Much of it can also be seen while driving. A popular route is the B88, which runs along the edge of the forest and into the foothills of the mountains from Eisenach to Ilmenau. Most routes crossing the mountains are beautiful drives, such as the road connecting Schmalkalden – famous from the Reformation wars – and Friedrichroda, or the route from Suhl to Ilmenau.

By Train: One of Germany's most interesting train journeys is on the **Schwarzatalbahn**, www.oberweissbacher-bergbahn.de, in the beautiful Schwarza Valley of the Thuringian Forest. The route has three sections. The longest is the 25 km (15 miles) on a fairly normal train section from Rottenbach to Katzhütte. The most interesting part is from Obstfelderschmiede to Lichtenhain. On this stretch, the train wagon is loaded on a special platform, which allows the train to remain level despite the up to 25% incline. The 1,387-m (4,438-foot) journey takes 18 minutes. Lichtenhain to Cursdorf is again a normal train and a bus service is available to Katzhütte, making a circular journey possible. Several hiking routes are available in this beautiful area. For information on the region, contact the **VG Mittleres Schwarzatal**, Friederich-Ebert-Platz 2a, 07427 Schwarzburg, ☎ 036730-22-350, www.mittleres-schwarzatal.de.

On Snow

Although most foreign visitors would rather head for the Bavarian Alps, or even farther south, for winter sports, skiing has been popular in the Thuringian Forest since the late 19th century. Snow is not guaranteed, but the **Thuringian Snow Telephone**, ☎ 036870-53-399, and the **Oberhof Snow Telephone**, ☎ 036842-26-921, can be dialed to find out about current and predicted snow conditions.

The small town of **Oberhof**, with 1,800 inhabitants, has traditionally been the center of East German winter sports. It has two ski slopes, both easy and floodlit at night. At Fallbach is an 800-m (2,560-foot) ski slope. At the Alten Golfwiese, is a 500-m (1,600-foot) slope, as well as opportunities for ice skating, snow tubing, and tobogganing. Oberhof has 25 km (15 miles) of cross-country skiing courses and 60 km (36 miles) of winter hiking routes. Equipment can be rented from **Sport Luck**, Gräfenrodaer Straße 2, Oberhof, ☎ 036842-22-212, www.sportluck.de.

Bobsleigh: The **Gästebobteam Oberhof**, Alpinhang Oberhof, ☎ 0173-390-1564, www.gaestebob.de, gives visitors the opportunity to go down the 1,130-m (3,616-foot) bobsleigh track at speeds of up to 75 km/h (45 mph). From April to September, a pilot and up to 10 guests go down the hill in a summer bob with wheels. From October to February, the real thing is available – a bobsleigh with pilot and brakeman accompanied by two guests speeds down the ice tunnel. The charge in both summer and winter is €11 per person.

Shopping

Blown and hand-painted **glass** has a long tradition in Thuringia. **Glas Studio Risch**, Jägerstraße 16, 98544 Zella-Hehlis, ☎ 03682-483-298, www.glas-studio-risch.de, allows visits to the workshop with demonstrations. A branch at Dr Theo-Neubauer-Straße, Oberhof, ☎ 036842-52-400 sells works from the workshop as well as from other producers in Thuringia and the Erz Mountains.

The small town of Gräfenroda claims to be the original producer of terra cotta **garden gnomes**. The **Griebel family**, Ohrdrufer Straße 1, ☎ 036205-76-470, allows visits to the workshop and has a museum explaining the 130-year tradition. It is open weekdays from 10 am to 5 pm, and weekends from 10 am to 2 pm.

Where to Stay & Eat

The Thuringian Forest was extremely popular with families and groups during the Communist rule, but saw a huge decline in visitors after the *Wende*. The natural beauty of the area remained and the hotels improved their image in recent years by concentrating on the fitness craze in Germany. The better ones offer beauty treatments and additional relaxation and health options. Barebones establishments also survived. In general, hotels in the area still aim mainly at active vacationers, with hotel rooms comfortable and functional rather than luxurious.

In **Oberhof**, the 400-room **Treff Hotel Panorma** is one of the best-known vacation hotels in the region. It has a characteristic triangular shape and all rooms have great views of the forest. Rooms are modern and comfortable. The hotel restaurants serve local specialties and international food. Theodor-Neubauer-Straße 29, 98559 Oberhof, ☎ 036842-500, fax 036842-22-551. (€€-€€€)

Ilmenau has several good accommodation options. The Lindenhof is a recently renovated hotel dating from the 19th century. Inside, it is modern and comfortably furnished, pleasantly quiet despite its location in the heart of town. The bistro serves good food. Lindenstraße 5-11, 98693 Ilmenau, ☎ 03677-680-00, fax 03677-680-088, www.hotel-lindenhof.de. (€€)

Farther down the road is the modern **Hotel Tanne**. Although it has a 550-year tradition in the gastronomical sector, the current hotel is thoroughly modern and rooms are bright and comfortably furnished. The restaurant has an informal atmosphere. Lindenstraße 38, 98693 Ilmenau, ☎ 03677-6590, fax 03677-659-503, www.hotel-tanne-thueringen.de. (€€)

The most pleasant hotel and dining option in the region is just under five km (three miles) south of Ilmenau. The **Romantik Berg und Jagdhotel Gabelbach** has a lovely location above town. Rooms are comfortably furnished, some with antiques. The restaurant **La Cheminée** (€€-€€€) is small and intimate but has an excellent reputation. International dishes as well as local specialties are served. It is open for dinner only. Waldstraße 23a, 98693 Ilmenau, ☎ 03677-8600, fax 03677-860-2222. (€€-€€€)

Camping

Near Oberhof, at the Lütsche dam, is the **Oberhof Campsite**. It is open year-round and an ideal location for both water- and winter-sports fans. It has 350 spaces, of which 160 are available to short-term campers. Boats and bicycles can be rented on the site. Oberhof Camping, Lütsche Stausee, 99330 Frankenhain, ☎ 036205-76-518, fax 036205-71-768, www.oberhofcamping.de.

Am Schwimmbad is a small campsite in the Georgenthal with space for 35 RVs or mobile homes and 20 tents. Convenient for excursions to Gotha and Erfurt, it is open from April to October. Am Steiger 3, 99887 Georgenthal, ☎ 036253-41-314, fax 036253-25-207, www.campingplatz-georgenthal.de.

Near Ilmenau is **Intercamping Großbreitenbach**, with 160 mostly shady spaces. Open year-round. 98701 Großbreitenbach, ☎/fax 036781-42-398, www.intercamping-grossbreitenbach.com.

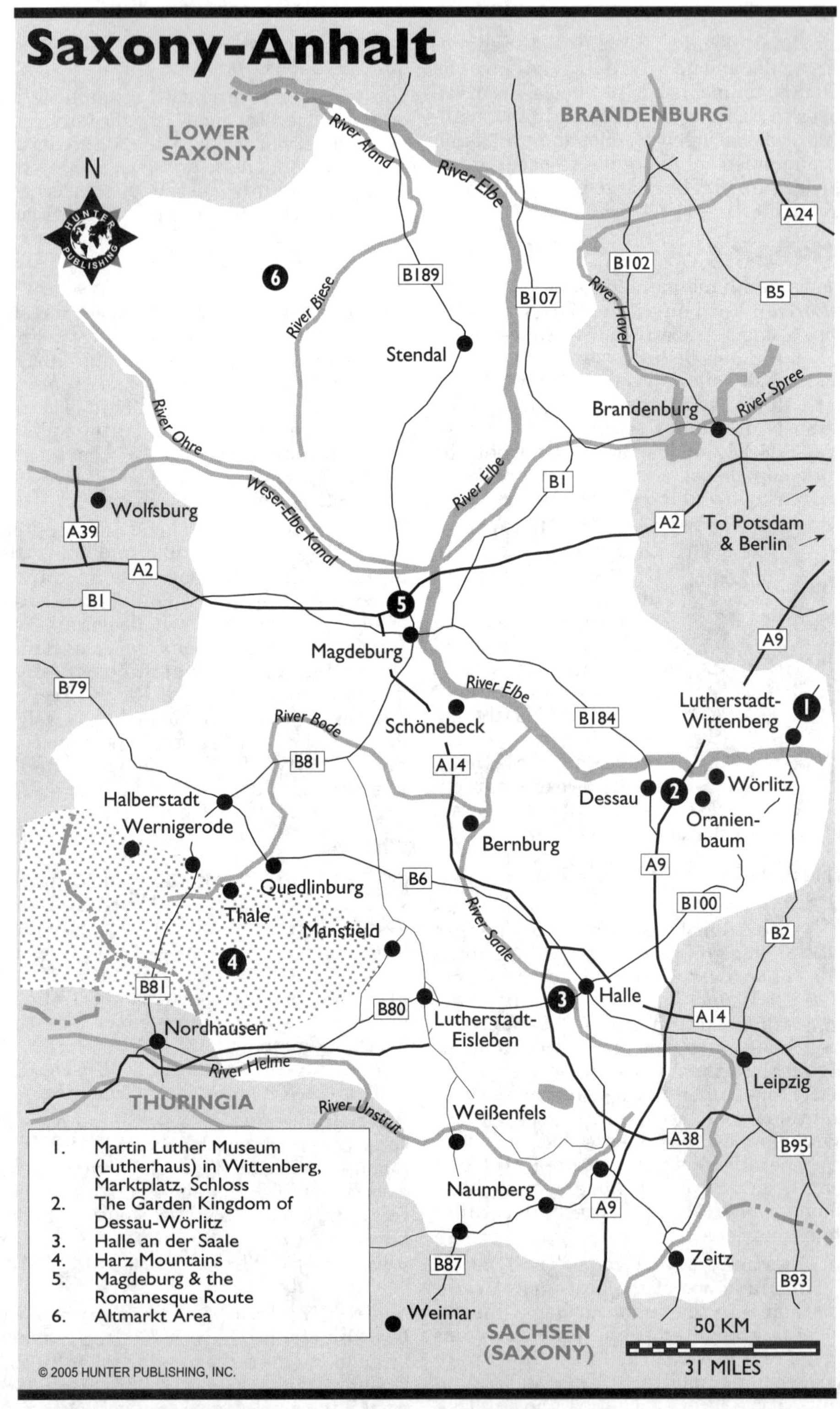

Saxony-Anhalt
LOWER SAXONY
BRANDENBURG
N
HUNTER PUBLISHING
River Aland
River Elbe
River Biese
River Havel
River Spree
River Ohre
Weser-Elbe Kanal
River Bode
River Saale
River Helme
River Unstrut
THURINGIA
SACHSEN (SAXONY)
Stendal
Brandenburg
Wolfsburg
To Potsdam & Berlin
Magdeburg
Schönebeck
Lutherstadt-Wittenberg
Dessau
Wörlitz
Oranienbaum
Halberstadt
Wernigerode
Quedlinburg
Thale
Mansfield
Bernburg
Halle
Lutherstadt-Eisleben
Nordhausen
Leipzig
Weißenfels
Naumberg
Zeitz
Weimar
A24
B102
B5
B189
B107
B1
A2
A39
A9
B79
B184
B81
A14
B6
B100
B2
B80
A38
B95
B87
B93
50 KM
31 MILES
1. Martin Luther Museum (Lutherhaus) in Wittenberg, Marktplatz, Schloss
2. The Garden Kingdom of Dessau-Wörlitz
3. Halle an der Saale
4. Harz Mountains
5. Magdeburg & the Romanesque Route
6. Altmarkt Area
© 2005 HUNTER PUBLISHING, INC.

Saxony-Anhalt

In this Chapter

Saxony-Anhalt is in the center of Germany. In contrast to neighboring states with great cities such as Leipzig and Berlin, the sights in Saxony-Anhalt are more understated and in small towns. It is a predominantly rural area with only two cities having more than 90,000 inhabitants. In the south and southwestern areas are hills and mountains, but the rest of the state is part of the plains that characterize most of northern Germany.

For foreign visitors the most famous town is Lutherstadt Wittenberg where Martin Luther initiated the Protestant Reformation in the early 16th century. Nearby, in Dessau and Wörlitz, is a marvelous collection of English-style landscape parks as well as famous Bauhaus buildings. Halle, birthplace of Georg Friedrich Händel, has an historic town center despite the destruction caused by World War II and magnified by bad Communist-era city and industrial planning. The Harz Mountains are the most beautiful parts of the state, with the historic towns from the foundation of the German Empire complementing the beautiful landscape. Saxony-Anhalt also has the largest collection of Romanesque buildings in Germany, testifying to the important role this area played a millennium ago.

■ History

At the foundation of the German Kingdom in the early 10th century, the area north of the Harz Mountains, which was a royal hunting area in the time of Charlemagne, suddenly assumed a central strategic position in the power politics of the new empire. The first two ruling families, the Ottonians and the Salians, resided in the here. As the German kings had no permanent residence, they tended to move around and built a series of castles – referred to as Palatinate or *Pfalz* – in several towns in the region.

Their patrimony saw the region develop rapidly and remain at the forefront of German politics, culture, and architecture for more than three centuries. During this era, the magnificent Romanesque buildings were erected. However, by 1250, the influence of the area started to fade, never to be at the forefront of German power politics again.

In the early 16th century, Wittenberg, then still a part of Saxony, was the center of the Reformation led by Martin Luther. However, the Germanic habit of continuously splitting areas up among inheriting sons meant that most principalities were too small to influence events much. In addition, Prussia increasingly annexed parts of the region to its kingdom.

After the division of Germany in 1945, Saxony-Anhalt became a border state, and the Iron Curtain severed contact with West Germany. Towns near the border were suddenly cut off from their natural markets. It was a serious blow to the region as tourism was increasing in importance from the end of the 19th century. Although the mining of brown coal and other minerals was no longer economical, mining continued and even expanded under the Communist rulers in an attempt to reduce foreign exchange needs.

It was only after the *Wende* (the change, as the end of the Communist regime in 1990 is usually referred to) that the separate parts of Saxony-Anhalt united into a state. Massive investment in tourism infrastructure ensured that old and beautiful but long-neglected towns such as Quedlinburg, Wernigerode, and Lutherstadt Wittenberg could freely attract visitors from the West and abroad. In other cities, especially Halle and Magdeburg, the polluting industries were closed down, leading to massive unemployment but a vastly improved environment.

■ Transportation

Saxony-Anhalt's central location in the heart of Germany makes it easily accessible to travelers.

By Rail: Although few major rail links run through the state itself, connections are easily made to major lines. Hourly trains connect Magdeburg with Hannover (80 minutes) and Berlin (around 90 minutes). Hannover is an important stop on the very busy north-south routes between Frankfurt and Hamburg, as well as between Frankfurt and Berlin. Leipzig, with its excellent rail connections, can be reached in half an hour from Lutherstadt Wittenberg, which is a stop on the Berlin-Leipzig line, and Halle, which has excellent connections to the rest of the state.

Local public transportation is well-organized and extensive.

Tip: *A route planner is available at www.nasa.de.*

By Car: The state has a limited number of Autobahns, meaning traveling by car on back roads can take longer than is customary in some other states. Two major highways do run through Saxony-Anhalt, with the A2 connecting the Ruhr area via Hannover and Magdeburg with Berlin. The A9 connects the south of Germany via Leipzig with Berlin and passes between the towns of Dessau and Wörlitz. An Autobahn connects Magdeburg and Leipzig via Halle.

Major roads are in good condition and fairly quiet. Traveling Saxony-Anhalt by car is a joy and probably the easiest way to get around and see more than the major cities.

By Air: Leipzig-Halle Airport is the most convenient for travelers to Saxony-Anhalt – see Saxony chapter, page **, for details. The airport is 15 minutes by train both from Halle, with at least one train per hour, and from Leipzig, with a train every half-hour. Destinations in Anhalt-Wittenberg are best reached via Leipzig, other areas via Halle.

It is possible to check-in at Magdeburg station for flights departing from Leipzig-Halle. By train, it takes 75 minutes or around an hour by car.

By Boat: A boating license is required in Saxony-Anhalt in order to operate a boat with an engine exceeding 5 HP. In some cases, foreign licenses are accepted. Chartering, where only a brief introduction is given on how to operate the boat, is not allowed in Saxony-Anhalt, but is very popular in the neighboring states of Brandenburg and Mecklenburg-Vorpommern. Boats can be rented in virtually any riverbank town – contact the relevant tourist authorities for listings other than the selection given below.

Most riverbanks in Saxony-Anhalt are under special protection orders. The entire Elbe in this state is a biosphere reserve with the area around Dessau a UNESCO World Natural Heritage Site.

■ Information Sources

Many tourism offices in Saxony-Anhalt do more than just provide information. Many book hotels as well as complete packages for adventure trips. Those not offering their own packages can usually provide details on companies that do.

Responsible for tourism promotion of the whole state is **Landesmarketing Sachsen-Anhalt**, Am Alten Theater 6, 31904 Magdeburg, ☎ 0391-567-7080, fax 0391-567-7081, www.sachsen-anhalt-tourismus.de.

Two regional offices that cover the main destinations of interest to the foreign traveler are **Tourismus Verband Anhalt-Wittenberg**, Albrechtstraße 48, 06844 Dessau, ☎ 0340-220-0044, fax 0340-240-0334, www.anhalt-wittenberg.de, and **Harzer Verkehrsverband**, Marktstraße 45, 38640 Goslar, ☎ 05321-34-040, fax 05321-340-466, www.harzinfo.de.

■ Cultural Events

Post-medieval Saxony-Anhalt has been described as so much culture, so little power, and that is still very much a fact of life here today. The area may have been far removed from true political or military power for centuries, but the magnificent architecture and wide range of cultural events constantly remind you of its rich heritage. Local tourism offices are good sources for schedules of events and often make reservations as well.

MDR, the public broadcaster of Saxony, Saxony-Anhalt and Thuringia, schedules various classical music concerts throughout the region. The summer concerts held in churches and castles are particularly popular. Schedules are available from www.mdr.de/musiksommer or ☎ 0341-141-414.

■ Anhalt-Wittenberg

Lutherstadt Wittenberg

The major reason for visiting Lutherstadt Wittenberg is to see the sights associated with Martin Luther. Although the town itself is pretty, it is only the Luther connection that lifts it above the average and makes it a major tourist destination for foreigners and German travelers alike.

Wittenberg has a written history reaching back to 1180, but only received township rights in 1293. Like so many other towns and regions in Germany, it belonged to several rulers through the centuries. During Luther's time, it was part of Saxony-Wittenberg but became part of Prussia after the Napoleonic wars. It suffered tremendous damage during the Thirty Years' and Seven Years' wars. After his disastrous loss at the Battle of Leipzig, Napoleon turned Wittenberg into a fortress to halt the advancing Prussian army in January 1814. This resulted in a major artillery assault, but the town has known relative peace ever since.

The Prussians started to conserve the Luther memorials in the late 1800s. In the 1930s, Lutherstadt was officially added to the name to increase tourism potential. Under Communism, Luther was initially out of vogue but made a strong comeback after his rehabilitation in the 1950s. Wittenberg has again become a major attraction since the unification of Germany and all sights are in magnificent condition. In 1996 the Luther House, Melanchthon House, Stadtkirche and Schlosskirche were declared UNESCO World Cultural Heritage Sites.

MARTIN LUTHER SIGHTS

The most important towns associated with great church reformer Martin Luther are in modern-day Saxony-Anhalt. Lutherstadt Wittenberg is where he lived from 1508 until his death in 1546. Many sights in this town call to mind Luther's life and work. He was born and coincidently died in Lutherstadt Eisleben. Several sights in both towns are UNESCO World Cultural Heritage Sites. He spent his childhood in Mansfeld Lutherstadt, but the attractions there are of lesser interest.

Thuringia also has important Luther sights and museums. He studied in both Erfurt and Eisenach and, after his banning in 1521, spent time in the Wartburg. He traveled extensively, and virtually every town where he sojourned, and usually preached, from Worms to Dresden and Augsburg to Magdeburg, is quick to remind visitors of this fact.

Information Sources

Tourist Office: The Tourist Information Office, Schlossplatz 2, 06886 Lutherstadt Wittenberg, ☎ 03491-498-610, www.wittenberg.de, is somewhat inconveniently located for those arriving by train. It is on the far side of the old town right across the road from the Schlosskirche. As virtually all the sights are located down the street, you have basically seen it all by the time you get there. They do make reservations for accommodations and adventures.

Getting There

The station, with the oldest surviving station building in Germany on one side and a very modern design on the other side of the railway line, is about 10 minutes walk from the Lutherhaus.

Wittenberg is a stop for the ICE trains, 30 minutes from Leipzig and an hour from Berlin. ICE trains run every two hours. The more frequent but slower regional train reaches Leipzig in an hour.

It is important to buy tickets for *Lutherstadt* Wittenberg and not for Wittenberge. The similarly named town is also on the Elbe but a few hundred km downstream in Brandenburg. Although it has the largest tower clock in Europe, it also sees its fair share of tourists searching in vain for Luther sites!

Martin Luther (1483-1546)

Martin Luther was born on November 10, 1483 in Eisleben. Shortly afterwards he moved to nearby Mansfeld, where he spent most of his childhood. From 1488 to 1501, he attended schools here as well as in Magdeburg and Eisenach. Thereafter he studied law in Erfurt, but after narrowly escaping a thunderbolt during a severe thunderstorm, he entered the Augustine Monastery in Erfurt. He was ordained in

Martin Luther & Katherine Bore, his wife, by Lucas Cranach (1529)

1507 and a year later started teaching at the university in Wittenberg.

Sometime during the 1510s, Luther concluded that the only way to eternal salvation was through faith. The selling of indulgences outraged him as his flock increasingly relied on indulgences rather than confession and a Christian lifestyle. On October 31, 1517 he wrote to his superiors deploring the practice and suggested 95 theses for debate by the church. The 95 theses became public knowledge and copies spread through Germany in a matter of weeks.

Originally, Luther intended to change practices inside the church. He did not intend to start a new church. In 1521, Luther was excommunicated by the Pope and declared an outlaw at the Diet of Worms, but allowed to flee. The famous words he supposedly uttered in front of the Diet: "Here I stand for I cannot do otherwise," were added later by Luther for more emphasis. He received protection from the Saxon Elector Frederick the Wise, even though he did not agree with Luther. While disguised as a monk in the Wartburg, he translated the New Testament into German. Apart from its influence on religion, Luther's German New Testament finally united the various regional dialects into a High German still understood and used by all German speakers.

He returned to Wittenberg in 1522, and after that there was no return to the old ways. Germany became split between his supporters and those of the Roman Catholic Church. Several battles were fought, some intellectual and some physical. It was only in 1555 that Emperor Charles V, the same emperor who banned Luther at Worms, agreed to freedom of religion – meaning freedom to choose either Lutheran or the Roman Catholic faith – in the German states.

Luther died while on business in Eisleben on February 18, 1546. He was buried in the Schlosskirche in Wittenberg. In 1547, according to legend rather than fact, Emperor Charles V meditated at his grave, saying afterwards: "He has found his judge. I only fight the living, not the dead."

In Germany, the Lutheran church is mostly referred to as the Evangelical (*Evangelsiche*) church. Members of this church follow the teachings of the Bible as interpreted by Luther, and thus do not consider themselves as followers of Luther, but rather followers of Christ.

Sightseeing

Sightseeing in Wittenberg is easy as all the major sights are in a straight line in Collegienstraße, which turns into Schlossstraße after the Market Square. The places below are described assuming arrival from the station, about 10 minutes walk away, and then moving uphill in Collegienstraße from east to west.

Martin Luther in Wittenberg: The **Luthereiche** (Luther Oak) is in a small park on the corner of Collegien and Lutherstraße. In 1520, Luther burned a copy of the papal bull that excommunicated him along with books by his opponents here. (Through the years, he burned various other copies in other towns as well. The original bull is in the state archives in Dresden.) The original oak died long ago and the current one dates from 1830.

Up the street, past the park and parts of the former city walls is the stately **Collegium Augusteum** (Augustus College). Dating from the mid-16th century, it currently houses the Evangelical Seminary and Library.

Directly behind it is the **Lutherhaus** (Luther House), Collegienstraße 54, ☎ 03491-42-030, www.martinluther.de, where Luther lived from 1508, first as a monk and, from 1525 until 1544, with his wife, Katharina von Bora. The building was converted into a museum in the late 19th century and was completely renovated in 2003. The museum is one of the most interesting in Germany and, for a change, virtually all descriptions are also in English. The museum gives a good overview of the life of Luther as well as the reasons for the spread of the Reformation. In addition, the museum is about the only place in Wittenberg where it is openly acknowledged that Luther never nailed his 95 Theses to the church door.

The most interesting exhibitions are on the ground and first floor. In 11 rooms, Luther's life and his move from critic to outright reformer are illustrated with more than a thousand exhibits. In the Lutherstube on the first floor, the original wood paneling survived in the room that Luther and his family used as dining and reception room for his numerous guests. Note the "Petr" scratched on a doorsill – graffiti left by Czar Peter the Great in 1702. The top floor has mainly coins and newer items, with the library visible through glass panes. The cellar has exhibitions on daily life in Luther's time that are mainly aimed at younger children.

The museum has more than 15,000 prints dating from the 15th to 18th century and 11,000 manuscripts from the 11th to 19th century. The library has 30,000 books, a complete collection of Luther's works including 90% of his first editions. Paintings include several from the Cranach studio of leading Reformation figures as well as a large panel painting of the 10 Commandments that used to hang in the courtroom of the local town hall. Of particular relevance and interest are numerous indulgences from all over Germany – the items that sparked Luther's protest in the first place.

The Lutherhaus is open April to October daily from 9 am to 6 pm, and November to March, Tuesday to Sunday, from 10 am to 5 pm. Admission is €5. (A combination ticket with the Melanchthonhaus valid for two days is available for €6)

Nearby is the **Melanchthonhaus**, (Melanchthon House), Collegienstraße 60, ☎ 03491-403-279, with its characteristic gable. Philipp Melanchthon (1497-1560), one of Luther's closest friends and strongest supporters, lived here from 1536 until his death. His role in building the Evangelical church as well as an education system gave him the nickname "Teacher of Germany." The house has an interesting interior with mainly prints and panels on his life. All information is in German only. Behind the house, facing the Elbe, is his famous garden. Opening hours are the same as the Lutherhaus. Admission is €2.50.

Philipp Melanchthon, by Albrecht Dürer (1526)

Practically next door is the **Alte Universität** (Old University) that existed from 1502 to 1817. This institution drew both Luther and Melanchthon to Wittenberg as teachers of Philosophy and Greek respectively.

Marktplatz Area: Like most similar towns, the **Marktplatz** (Market Square) is still the heart of the town. Most festivals are centered here and many restaurants are on the square or in the immediate vicinity. On the square is a Luther statue (1821) and one of Melanchthon (1865). The large Renaissance **Rathaus** (Town Hall) was completed in 1535. Opposite is the birthplace of **Lucas Cranach the Younger**, Markt 6. Lucas Cranach the Elder lived and worked here from 1505 to 1547. The house was severely damaged by bombardments during the Seven Years' War. It was repaired and the Baroque façade added in 1760.

Clearly visible from the Marktplatz but accessible from here only through a narrow alley is the **Stadtkirche St Marien** (Town Church of St Mary), Kirchplatz, ☎ 03491-403-201. It is the oldest building in town and has a famous Cranach Reformation altarpiece. Most of this Gothic church dates from the early 1400s, but parts of the towers are from the 13th century. The adjacent chapel is from 1370. Opening hours are May to October from Monday to Saturday, 9 am to 5 pm; Sunday from 11:30 am to 5 pm. November to April opening hours are Monday to Saturday, 10 am to 4 pm, Sunday from 11:30 am to 4 pm.

The **Cranach Höfe** (Cranach Courtyards), Schlosstraße 1, ☎ 03491-432-817, dates from 1506 and has around 100 rooms in which Cranach the Elder lived and worked up to 1550. Major work in recent years restored the building to what it used

Lucas Cranach the Elder, Self-Portrait (1550)

to be like in Cranach's time. It is used as a museum, with a historic printing press and gallery. It is open Monday to Saturday from 10 am to 5 pm, but closed on Monday from November to April. On Sunday it is open from 1 to 5 pm. Admission is €3 for some exhibitions but free to most parts of the building.

Furniture and other consumer items from the former German Democratic Republic are currently in vogue in Germany. The **Haus der Geschichte** (House of History), Schlossstraße 6, ☎ 03491-660-366, is a small museum dedicated to life in the former GDR. The focus is on everyday life and the articles that were used by ordinary people. Living rooms of every decade from the 1940s to 1970s show how fashion changed even in the Communist era. It also has kitchens, bathrooms, and toys from various eras. On the ground floor is an exhibition of bulky radios and televisions, some with modifications to receive western broadcasts. Information displays are very limited as the explanations are done live, in German only, by local residents. Opening hours are Tuesday to Friday from 10 am to 5 pm and weekends from 11 am to 6 pm. Admission is €3.

The Schloss Area: At the far end of the old town on the Schlossplatz are the Schloss (Castle) and more famous Schlosskirche (Castle Church). Both were built by Elector Frederick the Wise around 1500 but were damaged during wars and rebuilt differently from the originals.

The **Schloss** was changed into a citadel in 1819 after Prussia annexed Saxony-Wittenberg as punishment for Saxony's alliance with Napoleon. It currently houses a not particularly interesting Nature and Ethnology Museum. Of more interest is the restaurant in the cellar, the views from the garden, and the plaques in the courtyard with names of famous people associated with Wittenberg.

The **Schlosskirche Allerheiligen**, ☎ 03491-402-585, is a major tourist draw. It is on the doors of this church that Martin Luther was supposed to have nailed his 95 Theses on October 31, 1517. The church, and said door, burned down in 1760 during the Seven Years' War. The current church was reconstructed in 1892 and incorporated one of the original castle towers as a church tower. In 1855, the 95 Theses were cast in bronze and are seen on the door facing the square. Inside the church are the graves of several Askanian counts who ruled the area from 1157 until 1422, but generally of more interest are the graves of both Luther and Melanchthon in the front of the church. Also of note are the bronze epitaph (1527 by Peter Vischer) of Fredrick the Wise and an alabaster statue (1537) of him kneeling in knight's armor. The pulpit, altar, baptism font, and most other decorations date from 1892, although most are made to look older. Openings hours are the same as for the Stadtkirche. On most Tuesdays from May to October at 2:30 pm, half-hour organ concerts are held here or in the Stadtkirche.

Elector Frederick the Wise, by Albrecht Dürer (1496)

DID HE OR DID HE NOT?

It was long believed that Martin Luther started his protest against the Roman Catholic Church on October 31, 1517 when he nailed his 95 Theses to the door of the Schlosskirche. This act was confirmed by his close friend Philipp Melanchthon, who claimed to have witnessed the event.

It is now generally accepted by most historians that this event never took place. Luther's 95 Theses were written in Latin. Only the educated at the university could read Latin, thus excluding even the nobles in town, making the Schlosskirche less than a suitable choice for a protest notice. Furthermore, Melanchthon, the chief witness, only arrived in town six months after the event. In addition, Martin Luther at this stage, and for several years afterward, was more interested in reforming the church than in creating a separate church.

Historians now accept that on October 31, 1517, Luther wrote to his church superior in Magdeburg complaining about the fact that people were buying indulgences rather than confessing their sins. He included his 95 Theses intended for theological debate with the letter. However, it became public knowledge and transcripts were distributed in less than two months throughout Germany. With the notable exception of the Lutherhaus museum, virtually all of Wittenberg prefers and accepts only the version with the Theses on the door.

Farther Afield: About 15 minutes walk from the historic old town area is a very surprising, architecturally unique school building. The **Martin Luther Gymnasium**, Straße der Völkerfreundschaft 130, ☎ 03491-881-131, www.gym-luther-wittenberg.bildung-lsa.de, was built in 1975 in a typical square GDR fashion according to a standard floor plan known as Erfurt Type II. It looked as exciting as it sounded, and after the *Wende* the school requested ideas on making it less depressing. Nothing exciting came forth, but upon request the Viennese artist Friedensreich Hundertwasser took up the cause. In 1999, the school was changed into a typical Hundertwasser design, complete with multiple bright colors and mosque-like towers. The school building can be visited on weekday afternoons from 1:30 to 5 pm (4 pm from November to March), and weekends from 10 am to 4 pm all year round.

Cultural Events & Festivals

Town Festivals: The two largest town festivals in Wittenberg both honor Martin Luther. On June 13, 1525, Martin Luther married Katharina von Bora, against the advice of many friends and supporters who thought it would leave the impression that his protests were simply to break his celibacy vows. Since 1994, the second weekend in June has been the **Luthers Hochzeit** (Luther's Wedding), with the festival spread all over the old town. In addition to the usual eating and drinking, some 50 cultural events are held. The highlight of the festival is the parade on Saturday at 2 pm, with about 800 people participate in period costume.

In most of Protestant Germany October 31, is a public holiday in honor of Martin Luther's protest on that day in 1517. In Wittenberg, this is the highlight of the four-day **Reformation Festival**. Although the emphasis is more on formal cultural events, much of the festivities of the Wedding festival are repeated. Some church services and lectures are in English.

Organ Concerts: From May to October, 30-minute organ concerts are held on Tuesday from 2:30 in either the Schlosskirche or Stadtkirche. The same two venues also host **summer concerts** at 5 pm every second Saturday of the month.

Adventures

On Wheels: Almost half of the over 800-km (480-mile) **Elbe Radweg (Elbe River Cycling Route)** is in Saxony-Anhalt. The route, marked by a blue "e," runs through Wittenberg. Information on this part of the route is available at www.elberadweg-r2.de or from the state tourism agency, but also see the chapter on Saxony for a fuller description of the route, page ***.

More popular for day-trips, is cycling the 13 km (eight miles) from Wittenberg to Wörlitz to see the parks and the further 18 km (11 miles) to see the Bauhaus and other parks in Dessau.

In addition to most hotels, the following two shops in Wittenberg will also deliver the bicycle for a nominal fee within city limits: **Mobiler Service**, Rental station in the Stadthotel Schwarzer Bär, Schlossstraße 2, 03491-877-099, or for a larger selection, **M&B**, Coswiger Straße 21, ☎ 03491-402-849.

On Water: Watersports are possible on the River Elbe that flows slowly through the area. Various kinds of boats can be rented from **Marina Camp Elbe**, Brückenkopf 1, 06888

Lutherstadt Wittenberg, ☎ 0178-601-7665, www.marina-camp-elbe.de.

From Lutherstadt Wittenberg, **Schiffsagentur Mittelelbe**, An der Elbe 11, ☎ 03491-660-231, juengek@kleinwittenberg.de, arranges day-trips on riverboats mainly to Dessau and Magdeburg. The schedule is irregular and cruises are not available every day.

Shopping

In Wittenberg the **Cranach Höfe** (Cranach Courtyards), Schlosstraße 1, ☎ 03491-432-817, is a good source for traditional prints and copies of old books produced in the historic printing studio. The shop is open daily from 9 am to 5 pm, but only 10 am to 2 pm from March to October.

Where to Stay & Eat

Wittenberg has a large selection of comfortable middle-range and budget hotels. For luxurious accommodations, it is best to stay in one of the larger cities in the region.

The most pleasant accommodation is at the **Best Western Stadtpalais Wittenberg**. The hotel opened in 1999 in a restored mansion. Rooms are large with all modern comforts. The public rooms are equally stylish. The hotel is near the Lutherhaus. Colegienstraße 56-57, 06886 Lutherstadt Wittenberg, ☎ 03491-4250, fax 03491-425-100, www.stadtpalais.bestwestern.com. (€€-€€€)

The restaurant **Wittenberger Hof** (€-€€€) is the town's best choice for international cuisine although regional specialties are also available.

The Schwarzer Baer

Martin Luther & Swiss students in the Schwarzer Baer, by Otto Schwerdtgeburth (1522)

A pleasant alternative close to the Market Square is the **Stadthotel Wittenberg Schwarzer Baer**. It claims to be the oldest inn and newest hotel in town. It has been serving food since 1520 and Luther, Melanchthon and Cranach were obvious patrons. It only branched out into accommodation in the past two years. Rooms are comfortable, rather than luxurious, but still well-appointed and spacious. All rooms have Internet access. Free parking is available. Schlossstraße 2, 06886 Lutherstadt Wittenberg, ☎ 03491-420-4344, fax 03491-420-4345, www.stadthotel-wittenberg.de. (€€)

The historic restaurant **Schwarzer Baer** (€-€€) serves snacks and full meals.

Many dining options are available on the Market Square and its direct vicinity. An excellent option is the **Brauhaus Wittenberg im Beyerhof**. It is a brewery and patrons are welcome to observe the brewmaster at work. The courtyard transforms into a 250-seat beer garden when the weather is good and is also the setting for frequent concerts. Indoors, space is available for a further 150 guests in two rooms. The food ranges from local specialties to Mediterranean cuisine. The beer is local only and fresh. In addition, 14 large and comfortable rooms are available for overnight guests. Markt 6, 06886 Lutherstadt Wittenberg, ☎ 03491-433-130, fax 03491-433-131, www.brauhaus-wittenberg.de. (€-€€)

For cheap regional food in the Market Square area, try **Tante Emma's Bier & Café Haus**, Markt 9, ☎ 03491-419-757.

Near the St Marienkirche is the very pleasant **Eiscafé Dolce Vita**, Collegienstraße 11, ☎ 03491-410-986. It serves good coffee and delightful sweet snacks. (€)

Inside the cellars of the castle is the restaurant **Schlosskeller Lutherstube**, Schlossplatz, ☎ 03491-580-805. The walls here are several yards thick and tables are set in all kinds of nooks and crannies. The food is unashamedly old German and regional. Portions are large. Local beer and wine from the Saale region are available. Service is fast and friendly. (€-€€)

In sharp contrast to the more traditional locations mentioned above is the very modern **Acron Hotel**. It has clean spartanly furnished rooms but at equally reasonable prices. As can be expected, it has little soul or character, but everything is in good working order. All rooms have showers and color televisions, but telephones only upon request. The hotel is close to the Luthereiche, 300 m (330 yards) from the station. Am Hauptbahnhof 3, 06886 Lutherstadt Wittenberg, ☎ 03491-433-20, fax 03491-433-218, www.wittenberg-acron.de. (€€)

Camping

The **Marina-Camp Elbe** is on the banks of the Elbe in Wittenberg across from the Lutherhaus. It is newly built and in excellent condition with all the latest comforts. There are 100 spaces for visitors. Boat and bicycle rental, as well as simple holiday homes, are available on the site. Internet access is available to guests. Open from March to November. Brückenkopf 1, 06886 Lutherstadt Wittenberg, ☎ 0178-601-7665, fax 03491-454-199, www.marina-camp-elbe.de.

On the banks of the clean Bergwitzsee Lake, 11 km (six miles) south of Wittenberg, is the large **Camping und Water Sports Park Bergwitzsee**. It has space for 220 long-term and 265 short-term campers. The location is right next to the lake with its own beach and boating facilities. Boat and bicycle rentals are available on site. Open year-round. Bergwitzsee, 06773 Bergwitz, ☎/fax 034921-28-228, www.bergwitzsee.de.

For anglers and nature lovers, campsite **Königsee**, less than 10 km (six miles) away, is a good choice. It is smaller, with 200 long-term and only 50 short-term spaces available. In a forested area, it's five km (three miles) from the nearest town, between three small forest lakes. Bicycle rental is available. Open year-round. Campingplatz Königsee, 06773 Uthausen, ☎ 034921-21-060, fax 034921-21-250.

Dessau-Wörlitz Area

Internationally, Dessau is best known for the Bauhaus architectural school located here from 1925 until closed down by the Nazis in 1932. The town still has several Bauhaus structures – two are UNESCO World Cultural Heritage Sites.

In addition, the area is famous for the largest English-style landscape gardens on the European continent. They were created in the late 18th century and somehow managed to survive to the present day. Six are UNESCO World Cultural Heritage sites.)

Information Sources

Information Office: The tourist offices in Wörlitz and Dessau have information on the sights as well as a cultural program that is especially full in the summer months. The contact details are **Tourist Information Dessau**, Zerbster Straße 2c, 06844 Dessau, ☎ 0340-204-1442, www.dessau.de, and **Wörlitz-Informationen**, Neuer Wall 103, 06786 Wörlitz, ☎ 034905-20-216, www.woerlitz.de.

Information on the Garden Kingdom is also available from **Kulturstiftung DessauWörlitz**, Schloss Großkühnau, 06846 Dessau, ☎ 0340-64-6150, www.gartenreich.de.

Transportation

The A9, a major Autobahn connecting Munich and Berlin, passes between Dessau and Wörlitz, allowing fast connections to Berlin (100 km/60 miles) as well as Leipzig (70 km/42 miles) and Leipzig-Halle airport.

Dessau can be reached from Halle by frequent trains, taking between 30 and 50 minutes; Magdeburg is about an hour away. Hourly trains from Lutherstadt Wittenberg take 36 minutes, although cycling this route is very popular. Wörlitz is only 20 km (12 miles) from Lutherstadt Wittenberg.

Good bus services are available for transportation in the region as well. On weekends only, Dessau and Wörlitz are connected by train, but Bus 333, which stops at Oranienbaum and Wörlitz Park, is often more convenient.

Sightseeing

Bauhaus in Dessau: The Bauhaus school of design moved to Dessau in 1925 after its ideas were rejected by the conservative town council of Weimar. For seven years, members of the school, such as Walter Gropius and Lyonel Feininger, had the opportunity to put their ideas of form following function into practice before the Nazis forced them out of Dessau in 1932. Some members led by Mies van der Rohe briefly set up in Berlin but were soon forced to close their studios permanently. Many members found fame and much more acceptance abroad.

The best-known building is the Walther Gropius-designed **Bauhaus Dessau**, Gropiusallee 38, ☎ 0340-650-8251, www.bauhaus-dessau.de, which was erected in 1925-26 as head office for the school. It is a synthesis of glass, steel, and concrete and a prime example of the philosophy of the Bauhaus school, having served as studios, workshop, school, and a stage. It is open daily from 10 am to 6 pm and is a few minutes walk from the station or can be reached by Bus 10 and 11, stop Bauhausplatz. Admission is €4.

About five minutes walk away are the **Meisterhäuser** (Masters' Houses), Ebertallee 69/71, ☎ 0340-661-0934, www.meisterhaeuser.de, a community of buildings that served as housing and studios for the masters of the school. After the Nazis forced the masters out, the buildings were sold to the Junkers factory on condition that the exteriors be sufficiently altered to remove the alien building from from the cityscape.

Threc semi-detached buildings survived and are in excellent condition. The **Feininger House** currently houses a museum for the Dessau-born composer Kurt Weill. In this house, 40 different colors were used to paint the walls, ceilings, etc. The **Kandinsky/Klee House** was restored in 2000. During the process, it was found that the artists used 170 different colors to color their living environment. The house has extensive documentation and information on the lives of the two artists. The **Meisterhaus Muche/Schlemmer** was only restored in 2002. The Meisterhäuser are open mid-February to October, Tuesday to Sunday from 10 am to 6 pm; November to mid-February, Tuesday to Sunday from 10 am to 5 pm. Admission is €5.

Paul Klee

Several other Bauhaus buildings survived in Dessau. The largest concentration is in **Gropius-Siedlung Dessau-Törten**, south of Dessau. The buildings here can only be seen on a guided tour. Contact the Tourist Office for more information.

The historic **Arbeitsamt** (Employment Office), August-Bebel-Platz 16, ☎ 0340-204-2136, is currently used by the Department of Traffic. It has appropriately impossible bureaucratic opening hours. Admission is free. It can be reached by Bus 11, stop Museum West, or Tram 1, 3 or 4, stop Museum Nord.

To the north of the town is the **Gaststätte Kornhaus**, Kornhaustraße 146, ☎ 0340-640-4141, www.kornhaus.de. See *Where to Eat* section below for details of this restaurant in a Bauhaus.

The Garden Kingdom of Dessau-Wörlitz: The principality of Anhalt Dessau was fortunate to have had several able rulers. Prince Leopold III Friedrich Franz (1740-1817), commonly known as Fürst Franz, was an enlightened and talented ruler who loved to combine the beautiful with the useful. Under his rule, the first and still the largest English-style landscape gardens on the European continent were laid out in the Dessau-Wörlitz area. He combined existing structures and parks and added new ones until the entire **Gartenreich** (Garden Kingdom) stretched over 25 km (14 miles) on the south bank of the Elbe.

VISITORS INFORMATION

The parks of the Garden Kingdom are always open for free – the absence of fences necessitates continuation of this tradition begun by Prince Franz. Unless otherwise noted, all the buildings are open May to September from Tuesday to Sunday, 10 am to 6 pm; in April and October, the same days but from 10 am to 5 pm. Admission is €4.50 to each, including compulsory guided tours, usually available in German only. Guided tours of the parks are also available but in German only.

Schloss Wörlitz

Parks in Wörlitz: The oldest of the gardens is the **Wörlitzer Anlagen**, which occupies an area of 112 hectares (314 acres). It has canals and bridges, castles and temples, sculptures and grottos. The scenery changes frequently and almost 20 lines of sight have been identified that give the visitor unique and different perspectives. Two buildings inside the park are of particular note: both the Neo-Classical **Schloss Wörlitz** (Palace) and the Neo-Gothic **Gotisches Haus** (Gothic House) were the first two buildings of these styles in Germany. The Gothic House has a Venetian-church look facing the canals but a Gothic Tudor façade toward the garden. Water is an integral part of the park, and regular ferries transport visitors for a minimal charge across the lake and to islands. Longer gondola rides are also available. A large restaurant is located inside the kitchen buildings of the Schloss. The park is at northern edge of the town and can be reached by Bus 333, stop Wörlitz-Neue Reihe.

About six km (3.6 miles) south of Wörlitz on the B-185 is the park and palace of **Oranienbaum** (Orange Tree), ☎ 034904-20-259. The palace was built as a widow's residence in the late 17th century in a Dutch Baroque style reflecting the tastes of the Dutch-born Princess Henriette Catharina von Nassau-Oranien. The existing palace was incorporated into the Garden Kingdom and Fürst Franz added English-Chinese elements including a pagoda, the only surviving one in Germany from that period. The present Orangerie, at 180 m (590 feet) one of the longest in Europe, was built in the early 19th-century and has again been used for citrus farming since 1989. The park can be reached by Buses 331 and 333, stop Oranienbaum.

Oranienbaum

Parks in Dessau: Three more parks and palaces are located in and near Dessau. The largest, and second only to Wörlitz in size, is the **Georgium**. It was constructed by Prince George, brother of the ruling Prince Franz. The park starts just two blocks from the Bauhaus and stretches over 56 acres all the way to the River Elbe. The garden has several small classical structures and sculptures that blend in harmoniously with the surroundings. The Georgium Palace houses the **Anhaltische Gemäldegalerie Dessau** (Anhalt Picture Gallery), Puschkinallee 100, ☎ 0340-613-874, www.georgium.de, with a fine collection of German painters from the 15th to 19th centuries and Dutch painters from

The Daughters of Friedrich Heinrichs von Oranien, by Jan Mijtens (1666)

the 15th to 17th centuries. It has single works by Pieter Breughel, Lucas Cranach, and Peter Paul Rubens. The gardens and palace are within easy walking distance from the station or can be reached by buses 10, 11, or 17 (the stop is Puschkinallee). In contrast to the other parks, the gallery here is open year-round, Tuesday to Sunday from 10 am to 6 pm. Admission is €3.

About 10 km (six miles) southwest of Dessau is **Schloss Mosigkau**, Knobelsdorffallee 3, ☎ 0340-521-139, www.mosigkau.de. This Rococo castle was built in 1757 from first drafts by the designers of Sanssouci in Potsdam for Princess Anna Wilhelmina, who never married. After her death, she donated the property to a monastery. It remains one of the best examples of Rococo in central Germany. Inside, the palace is richly furnished with original furniture, mirrors, porcelain, and vases, complementing the marble stuccowork. It also has a small but rich collection of paintings, including works by Peter Paul Rubens, Jordaens, and Van Dyck. The Orangerie has a collection of rare and, in some cases, centuries-old potted plants. The park can be reached by Bus 16 or 17 (stop Schloss Mosigkau).

Four km (2.4 miles) east of Dessau is **Schloss Luisium**, ☎ 0340-218-370, built by Prince Franz for his wife Luise. The palace is small but attractive in a Neo-Classical style. The interior has stark clean lines with elegant ceiling and wall paintings as well as marble stuccos. Scattered through the park are mainly Greco-Roman structures and sculptures but also a small orangerie and a Chinese bridge. The park is best visited in the morning or around sunset when light conditions are optimal. The Neo-Gothic Schlangenhaus (Snake House) can be rented by the night – see *Where to Stay* section below. The Luisium can be reached by Bus 13 (stop Vogelherd).

Cultural Events: Dessau and Wörlitz have a wide range of cultural events. Annual favorites include the **Kurt Weill Festival** (first week of March) in Dessau and the **Seekonzerte** (Lake Concerts), which are held Saturdays from May to September on the Wörlitzer See. Also, the large modern **Anhaltisches Theater Dessau**, Friedensplatz 1a, ☎ 0340-251-1333, www.anhaltisches-theater.de, has events ranging from modern pop concerts to classical ballet and opera.

Adventures

On Foot: The Garden Kingdom invites strolling and hiking is also popular between the parks. Large parts of the banks of the Elbe are part of a UNESCO Biosphere and ideal for walking. Here, as throughout Germany, parks are generally not fenced off, so leaving the marked paths and trails is strictly forbidden. The routes described for cycling below are also open to hikers.

On Wheels: The **Fürst-Franz-Weg** is a 45-km (27-mile) circular route between Dessau and Wörlitz. It starts from the Kühnau Park and passes by the Georgium and Luisium en route to Wörlitzer Park. On summer weekends, when trains operate between Dessau and Wörlitz, the round-trip journey can be made by train allowing more time for sightseeing. The route is marked by an orange band on a white background.

If staying in the area, first inquire from the hotel about bicycle availability. Rentals can normally be found at **Dessauer Verkehrs**, Erich Klöckert Straße 48, ☎ 0340-213-366.

On Water: The slow-flowing River Elbe offers plenty of watersports possibilities.

Feriendorf am Flämingbad, Zieckner Landstraße 4, 06869 Coswig, ☎ 034903-59-260, on the opposite bank from Wörlitz, rents canoes and kayaks. They also arrange longer tours such as a week of canoeing from Pretzsch to Magdeburg, with appropriate accommodation. Tours can also be combined with cycling.

In Dessau, kayaks and rubber ducks can be rented from **Bootsport-Center Königer**, Ludwighafener Straße 73, 06842 Dessau, ☎ 0340-850-5075.

On Horseback: In Wörlitz, the **Pferdehof zur Elbaue**, An der Seespitze, ☎ 034905-20-048, is next to Rousseau Island in the Wörlitz Park. It offers coach rides as well as pony and horse rides in this lovely region.

Where to Stay & Eat

The best hotel and restaurant in the region is the **Fürst Leopold**, a modern Bauhaus-styled hotel in the city center close to the main station. The hotel has 204 rooms of which, surprisingly, 148 are single rooms but with oversize beds. Rather uncommon for a German hotel, 50% of the rooms are for non-smoking guests. Rooms are well-equipped with stylish modern furniture. Bicycles are available for rent directly from the hotel. The fitness area is large. The elegant restaurant (€€-€€€) has a wide-ranging menu that changes monthly. Regional specialties are naturally on offer as is international fare ranging from Mexican to Italian food. The vegetarian selection is extensive. Friedensplatz, 06844 Dessau, ☎ 0340-251-50, fax 0340-251-5177, www.fuerst-leopold.de. (€€€)

Although the **nh Hotel** (formerly Astron) aims squarely at the business traveler, it is also a pleasant and economical choice for the leisure traveler. It is about a kilometer (.6 mile) from the station in the pedestrian zone of the city center. Although the rooms are comfortably furnished, mostly in light modern colors, they lack the individuality of the competing (more expensive) non-chain hotels. The restaurant (€€) serves local and international dishes. Zerster Strasse 29, 06844 Dessau, ☎ 0340-251-40, fax 0340-251-4100, www.nh-hotels.com. (€€)

Sleeping in the Garden Kingdom

Although rental homes are scattered throughout the area, two are simply a cut above the rest. In recent years, it has been possible to rent two historic properties inside or on the edge of the parks. The **Schlangenhaus** (Snake House) is in the Luisium and the **Elbpavillion** in Dessau is close to the Georgium and other parks. The serene setting is enhanced by the absence of telephones, television, and radio. Both are luxuriously furnished and non-smoking. The bedroom is on the second floor, but the lounge can also be used to sleep a maximum of four people per unit. Two bicycles are available, and all extras except food are included in the quoted prices. (€€€-€€€€)

Reservations are made through the Kulturstiftung DessauWörlitz, Schloss Großkühnau, 06846 Dessau, ☎ 0340-646-150, fax 0340-646-1210, www.gartenreich.com.

The **Kornhaus**, Kornhaustraße 146, ☎ 0340-640-4141, www.kornhaus.de, is a restaurant located in an original Bauhaus building designed by Carl Flieger, an assistant of Gropius. The food is typical for a countryside *Gaststätte* (inn): regional and hearty home-style cooking. Prices are small, portions big. The Kornhaus is in the north of Dessau on the edge of the Kuhnau Park and can be reached by Bus 11 (stop Kornhaus). (€-€€)

Wörlitz has two comfortable hotels with good restaurants. The **Landhaus Wörlitzer Hof** is perfectly located right at Schloss Wörlitz. Standard rooms are bright and comfortable, but a few *Komfortzimmer* are available and worth the slight surcharge. The restaurant serves local specialties and in summer has a pleasant terrace and beer garden under the lime trees. Markt 96, 06786 Wörlitz, ☎ 034905-4110, fax 034905-41-122, www.woerlitzer-hof.de. (€€-€€€)

Slightly more upmarket is the **Ringhotel Zum Stein**, which has been managed by the Pirl family since 1914. (The founder was headwaiter in the famed Berlin Adlon hotel.) The standard rooms are comfortably furnished, but it is worth paying around €10 extra per night for a *Komfortzimmer* that has better furnishings, a larger living area, a balcony, and garden views. The fitness area, with Roman bathhouse styling, has a large indoor pool and ample natural light. The restaurant (€€-€€€) is elegant, serves mainly regional cuisine according to the season and has a long wine list. Erdmannsdorffstraße 228, 06786 Wörlitz, ☎ 034905-500, fax 034905-50-199, www.hotel-zum-stein.de. (€€€)

■ Saale-Unstrutt Region

Halle an der Saale

Although the largest city in Saxony-Anhalt, Halle was passed over when Magdeburg became the state capital in 1990. Similarly, many tourists also pass Halle by en route to the more famous destinations. This is not completely unjustified. A thousand-year history originally built on the salt trade was ruined in the 20th century. Although Halle has an interesting town center, much of the city lay in ruins after World War II. In addition, the Communist-era construction of the area Halle-Neustadt received the not exactly complimentary nickname of Hanoi. Halle was an important industrial city during GDR times and, being the center of the chemical industry, had terribly polluted air. Although the environment is improving rapidly, the scars will remain for some years to come.

Information Sources

Information Office: The tourist information is in the Rote Turm, Marktplatz 1, 06100 Halle, ☎ 0345-221-1115, www.halle.de.

Transportation

Halle is easily reached by train from Leipzig – two to four trains per hour taking around half an hour. Trains to Berlin take two hours and to Magdeburg just over an hour.

Halle's station is unfortunately not in the best part of town, about a km (.6 mile) from the Markt. Avoid using the Tunnel leading from the station to Leipziger Straße, and eventually to Markt, at quiet times after dark.

Halle had the first electrical tram in Germany and public transportation is still good. Trams are generally more useful than the bus. Both Markt and the main station are major intersection points for trams. Fares start at a reasonable €1.40 for short journeys.

Sightseeing

Most of the major sights in Halle are within easy walking distance from the enormous **Markt** (Market Square), adorned by a statue of Halle's most famous son, the composer baptized Georg Friederich Händel. After becoming an English citizen in 1727, he was known as George Frederic Handel. Also on the square is the tourist information office, housed in the **Roter Turm** (Red Tower), a freestanding 84-m (269-foot) tower constructed between 1418 and 1506. Its 84-bell carillon is the largest in Germany.

Handel

The most interesting structure on the Markt is the **Marienkirche**, right, An der Marienkirche 2, ☎ 0345-517-0894. Its four tall, slim towers dominate the skyline. The current Late Gothic, triple-nave hall church was completed in 1554, replacing two Romanesque churches. Händel was baptized here and learned to play the organ on the smaller of the two instruments in the church. Johann Sebastian Bach introduced the larger Reichel organ in 1716, even though his application was rejected three years earlier for the position of organist, a post one of his sons filled three decades later. The church also has a death mask of Luther, made while his body stayed overnight en route to Wittenberg. The church is open Monday to Saturday from 10 am to noon and daily from 3 to 5 pm. Half-hour organ concerts are held most Tuesdays and Thursdays from 4 pm. Admission is free.

Next to the church is the Late Renaissance **Marktschlösschen** (Little Market Palace), Markt 13, ☎ 0345-202-5977, which has a non-commercial gallery with exhibitions of contemporary art, mostly from the region. It is open daily from 10 am to 6 pm, closing at 5 pm on weekends. Admission is free. (A collection of historic musical instruments previously housed here is now at the Händelhaus.)

Although Händel (1685-1759) left Halle in 1703 and eventually found fame in London, Halle has not forgotten him. In addition to the statue on Markt and an annual Händel festival, his birth house was turned into a museum. The **Händelhaus** (Händel House), Große Nikolaistraße 5, ☎ 0345-500-900, www.haendelhaus.de, is devoted to the composer and has a large collection of musical instruments and documents from the period. Information on some displays is available in up to 23 languages. Händel is played in most rooms. The museum is open Wednesday to Monday from 9:30 am to 5:30 pm; until 7:30 pm on Thursday. Admission is €2.60.

The nearby **Dom**, ☎ 0345-202-1379, is surprisingly without a tower or an impressive façade as one would expect from a cathedral. It is, however, the largest church in

Halle and originally served as a monastery church. It has three aisles, with the central one only slightly higher than the narrow side ones. It dates back to the 13th century, but the original Gothic church was converted to a more Renaissance style during the Reformation. The church has excellent acoustics and is thus a favored venue for concerts.

Schloss Moritzburg, Friedemann-Bach-Platz 5, ☎ 0345-212-590, www.moritzburg.halle.de, should not be confused with the similarly named and also round-towered palace near Dresden. This Late Gothic castle was built by the archbishop of Magdeburg during the 15th century. It was destroyed during the Thirty Years' War, which was also a turn for the worse for Halle's power, and only partly restored. It currently houses the **Staatliche Galerie Moritzburg** (National Gallery), which has a fine collection of 19th- and 20th-century art, including Rodin's *The Kiss*, at left. There is a special emphasis on German art from Romanticism to Impressionism and Expressionism. The Nazis considered much of the latter as degenerate and had it removed, though some original works have returned. The gallery is considered the best in Saxony-Anhalt, but then again the competition is not very strong given that the magnificent collections in nearby Leipzig, Dresden, and Berlin are across state borders. The castle also has a fine numismatics collection and display of glassware, porcelain, and ceramics from the Middle Ages to the present. Opening hours are Tuesday from 11 am to 8:30 pm, Wednesday to Sunday from 10 am to 6 pm. Admission is €4, but half-price after 5 pm and free the first Sunday of the month.

Cultural Events

In Halle the main cultural event of the year is the 10-day **Händel Festspiele** in early June. The highlight of the festival is the performance of one of Händel's 40 operas, but a range of his other works is also performed. In addition, frequent concerts are held in the 130-seat chamber music room of the Händelhaus or in the courtyard during summer. For more information, see www.haendelfestspiele.halle.de. (Händel festivals are also held in Göttingen and Karlsruhe.)

Near Querfurt is the **Goethe Theater**, Parkstraße 18, 06246 Bad Lauchstädt, ☎ 034635-7820, www.goethe-theater.com. It was built in 1802 as a summer theater in close cooperation with Johann Wolfgang von Goethe, who was the chief director for 20 years. Performances range from rock classics to symphonies, opera to plays. The latter are only in German. Particularly popular are Goethe, Schiller, Mozart and Händel. Reservations well in advance are recommended.

Adventures

On Wheels: Bicycles can be rented from **Fa Bike-Insider**, Mansfelder Straße 44, ☎ 0345-209-0932.

In the Air: Two companies offer hot-air balloon flights near Halle. **Bareiku Touristik**, Stedtener Straße 11, 06318 Wansleben/See, ☎ 0177-749-1004, www.bareiku.de, starts from various points in Halle and vicinity. **Ballonteam Weissenfels**, Weissenfels, ☎ 03443-232-234, www.ballonteam-weissenfels.de, offers balloon flights in the beautiful Saale-Unstrut area near Naumburg.

On Water: Three companies operating from Halle rent canoes, kayacks, and 5 HP boats. **Boot-Center Halle**, Hansastraße 99, 06118 Halle, ☎ 0645-532-1228, north of the city, also has party boats available for large groups. **Bootsverleih Halle**, K Liebknecht Straße 16, 06114 Halle, ☎ 0345-523-7424, is south of the city and also has paddle boats. Nearby is **Wassertouristik Saaletal**, Lerchenweg 6, 06198 Brachwitz, ☎ 0034606-29-160, which also rents rowing and sailing boats.

Where to Stay & Eat

Halle has a wealth of hotels in all price categories. All the establishments listed here are within easy walking distance to the sights. The amount of competition leads to very reasonable prices. For once, a Kempinski hotel can be described as almost affordable.

The **Kempinski Hotel Rotes Ross** opened in 1997 behind a renovated 265-year-old façade. The inside is modern, comfortably equipped, and very stylish. A new less charming wing was added in 1999. The restaurant (€€-€€€) is elegant, with an international menu, while the rustic wine cellar (€€) offers more local dishes. The hotel is conveniently located close to the main station en route to the old town center. Leipziger Straße 76, 06110 Halle, ☎ 0345-233-430, fax 0340-2334-3699, www.kempinski.com. (€€€-€€€€)

In the same area is the thoroughly modern **Dorint Charlottenhof**, for many the best choice in Halle. Rooms are bright and very comfortable. Art Nouveau furniture provides an interesting touch. The restaurant (€-€€) has a wide range of international and local dishes. Dorotheenstraße 12, 06108 Halle, ☎ 0340-292-30, fax 0340-292-3100, www.dorint.de/halle. (€€-€€€)

Even closer to the station is the **Maritim-Hotel Halle**, also a modern building with very comfortable rooms. It is the only hotel in Halle with a swimming pool. The restaurant has international and regional dishes. Riebeckplatz, 06009 Halle, ☎ 0345-5101-0, fax 0345-5101-777, www.maritim.de. (€€-€€€)

The tourist class **Europa Hotel** offers good value but is on the "wrong" side of the station. (It was formerly part of the Best Western group.) The rooms are clean and comfortable, rather than luxurious, although the elegance of the interior belies the low prices. It is popular with business travelers due to its location a block from the station, but it's also family-friendly. Delitzscher Straße 17, 06112 Halle, ☎ 0345-571-20, fax 0345-571-2161, www.europa-halle.de. (€€)

The pedestrian zone has many street cafés and informal restaurants are easy to find near all tourist attractions. A particularly pleasant restaurant is the **Mönchshof**, Talamstraße 6, ☎ 0345-203-0699, across the road from the Marienkirche. The name means Monks' Courtyard and the food is, not surprisingly, hearty local cuisine. The locale has high ceilings, rustic charm, and reasonable prices. (€-€€)

One of the best restaurants in town is **San Luca**, Universitätsring 8, ☎ 0345-200-3587, not far from the Moritzburg. The cuisine is Mediterranean with an emphasis on Italian. The vegetarian selection is also large. The restaurant is elegant with a pleasant terrace. Prices are fairly high for the region, but not for the quality of food. (€€€-€€€€).

Camping

In Halle itself, a short-term campsite for mobile homes and RVs is at the **Deutsche Campingplatz-Nummer 33**, Pfarrstraße, 06118 Halle, ☎ 0345-523-4085. It is behind the Nordbad swimming pool on the banks of the Saale. Facilities are limited but the showers of the adjacent pool may be used between 8 am and 9 pm. Open from May to mid-September.

Lutherstadt Eisleben

Two towns closely associated with Martin Luther are near Halle.

The center of Eisleben, the town of Martin Luther's birth and death, is unfortunately a bit rundown and somewhat depressing. The area near the main square is well-restored and very pretty, but step two blocks away and buildings are dilapidated, broken windows go unrepaired and even inhabited buildings are left unpainted. The main problem is that what is unique to Eisleben is not unique to Germany and thus funds are often not available to restore half-timbered houses considered of lesser architectural value to the nation as a whole. The town is a bit grey and therefore best visited on a sunny day. Lutherstadt was added to the town name in 1946. For travelers not interested in Luther, time is better spent elsewhere.

Information Sources

Tourist Office: The tourism office is at Bahnhofstraße 36, 0695 Lutherstadt Eisleben, ☎ 03475-602-124, www.eisleben.de, between the station and the Geburtshaus. There is also an information office near the Sterbeshaus at Andreaskirchplatz.

Transportation

Lutherstadt Eisleben is 40 minutes from Halle by at least hourly local trains. From Lutherstadt Wittenberg the journey takes between an hour and 40 minutes and 2½ hours;

changeovers are required at Halle. From Quedlinburg it can be reached in two hours, requiring multiple changeovers. In all instances traveling time by car is significantly less.

Sightseeing

Eisleben's main draws are the two museums dedicated to Martin Luther – both UNESCO World Cultural Heritage Sites. In both museums, information is almost exclusively in German.

Martin Luther was born on November 10, 1483 in what is now known as the **Martin Luther Geburtshaus** (Place of Birth), corner of Luther and Seminarstraße 16, ☎ 03475-714-780. His father was a mine inspector and rented part of the house considered one of the best in the area. The house was severely damaged by a neighborhood fire in 1689. Thereafter the town council acquired the property and restored it mostly to its original condition. The museum is spread over two floors and has sacred art, copies of paintings, and documents related to Luther's life. Behind the house is a former school now used for temporary exhibitions. In the direct vicinity is the Church of St Petri und Paul, Petrikirchplatz, where Luther was baptized the day after his birth. Opening hours are April to October, daily from 10 am to 6 pm. From November to March, Tuesday to Friday, 10 am to 4 pm and weekends from noon to 4 pm. Admission is €2.

The museum in the **Luthers Sterbehaus** (Death House), Andreaskirchplatz 7, ☎ 03475-602-285, also has descriptions almost exclusively in German. Luther died in this house on February 18, 1546. The museum has some period furniture as well as death masks on display. Opening hours are April to October, daily from 9 am to 5 pm; from November to March, Tuesday to Friday, 10 am to 4 pm and weekends from noon to 4 pm. Admission is €2.

Directly opposite the museum is the **Kirche St Andreas** (church), Andreasplatz, ☎ 03475-602-285 where Luther held his last sermon. The current church was constructed in 1498 after a town fire gutted the original 13th-century one. Of particular artistic value is the magnificently carved Gothic wing altar by Joseph Wackerle (1520). Luther preached from the Lutherkanzel (Luther pulpit) two

Marktplatz with Kirche St Andreas in background

days before his death. The church has the graves of some counts of Mansfeld and busts of Luther and Melanchthon were added in 1817.

The buildings of the **Marktplatz** (Market Square) are very well-restored. The Rathaus dates from 1530 but most of the façade facing the square is from 1874. The statue of Luther was added in 1883. Also on the square are the three former palaces belonging to the three lines of Mansfeld counts. A dispute between them was the purpose of Luther's final visit to Eisleben and it was settled shortly before he died.

Adventures

In the Air: Near **Lutherstadt Eisenleben**, Ballon '94, Feldstr. 7f, 06311 Helbra, ☎ 034772-27-752, www.ballon94.de, takes passengers on 60- to 90-minute hot air balloon rides. Occasionally, three- to four-hour flights across the full length of the Harz are offered, costing only €160 per person. The same company also offers flights in light planes costing from €40 for 20 minutes to €150 for 90 minutes.

Where to Stay & Eat

The four star **Hotel Graf von Mansfeld** is in one of the 500-year-old town palaces of the former counts of Mansfeld. All 50 rooms are individually furnished with antique-looking furniture. It is worth paying slightly more for one of the larger rooms. The pleasant restaurant serves mainly regional cuisine. The hotel is at the top end of the Market Square near the Rathaus and many rooms offer views of the restored historic buildings. Markt 56,

06295 Lutherstadt Eisleben, ☎ 03475-66300, fax 03475-250-723, www.hotel-eisleben.de. (€€)

At the lower end of the market square is **Eiscafé Madeira**, Markt 49, ☎ 03475-680-057. It is similar to thousands of other *Eiscafés* in Germany but offers splendid value for money compared to similar ones in former West Germany. Small meals are also available in addition to the large selection of cakes, pastries, and ice creams. Even if you prefer to sit outside and enjoy the view of the square, the Luther statue and the Rathaus, do go inside to see the large photos on the walls showing what the square looked like before World War II. (€)

Mansfeld Lutherstadt

Information Sources

Tourist Office: The information center is inside the Luther Schule, Junghuhnstraße 2, 06343 Mansfeld, ☎ 034782-90-342, www.mansfeld-lutherstadt.de.

Transportation

Mansfeld is easiest to visit by car, but can be reached from Eisleben in around 40 minutes by an hourly bus.

Sightseeing

Within months after his birth, Martin Luther's family moved to the nearby town of Mansfeld, which added Lutherstadt to the name only in the 1990s. Compared to Wittenberg, Eisleben, and Eisenach, the Luther sights here attract far fewer visitors.

Martin Luther's mother, by Lucas Cranach the Elder (1527)

Luther spent his childhood in this town until he moved in 1497 to study in Magdeburg. His parents' house was partly destroyed in 1805 but largely reconstructed in 1883. It has been converted into a museum devoted to Luther's childhood. The **Museum Luthers Elternhaus** (Luther's parents' home), Lutherstraße 26, ☎ 034782-20-320, has relatively short opening hours, reflecting the fact that this town is only visited by the truly devout. From mid-April to October it is open Tuesday to Friday, 11 am to 4 pm; the same hours apply on the first and third weekends of the month. From November to mid-April, it is open only Tuesday to Friday from 11 am to 3 pm. Alternative opening hours can be arranged in advance. Admission is €1.

Luther first worshipped in the **Talkirche St Georg** (Municipal Church of St George), Lutherstraße 7, ☎ 034782-20-320. However, the current church was built right after Luther left the town. Its present layout is single-aisled Gothic and most of the decorations date from the early 16th century. Opening hours are the same as for the Museum.

Across the road is the **Luther Schule** where Martin Luther first attended school. His bad experiences there are credited for the interest he showed in reforming the education system later in his life. The original school was destroyed, but a modern copy was constructed in 2000 and is used as an information center with multimedia displays.

Farther down Lutherstraße, close to the Rathaus, is the **Lutherbrunne** (Luther Fountain). It was created in 1913 and has a statue of a 13-year-old Martin Luther.

Naumburg

Naumburg is an ideal center to explore the beautiful and interesting valleys of the Rivers Saale and Unstrut. The Saale valley is particularly impressive, with rugged natural surroundings from Jena in Thuringia to Naumburg. The Unstrut River is smaller and calmer, and an ideal canoeing river for the inexperienced. The Unstrut flows into the Saale in Naumburg.

Naumburg is best known for its beautiful cathedral, and the region is the northernmost wine growing area in Germany. The two valleys are also littered with castles – most are in ruins but they make for a welcome break from physical adventures.

Information Sources

Tourist Office: For information on Naumburg contact the **Tourist und Tagungservice**, Markt 6, 06618 Naumburg, ☎ 03445-201-614, www.naumburg.de. Information on the Saale-Unstrutt region is available from **Saale-Unstrutt Tourismus**, Grochlitzer Straße 55, 06618 Naumburg, ☎ 03445-233-790, www.saale-unstrut-tourismus.de.

Sightseeing

Naumburg was long divided into religious and secular sections. It was a bishopric from 1028 until 1564, but the two sections operated independently until 1832. For that reason the cathedral is a few blocks from the town center. The secular part of town grew rich from trade, but after Leipzig received its trade fair privilege in 1506, preventing Naumburg from competing in this area, the town rapidly declined in wealth and importance.

Naumburg is well-known for its amazing **Dom St Peter und Paul** (above), Domplatz, ☎ 03445-230-10. The church combines Late Romanesque and Early Gothic elements, with the oldest parts dating from 1042. It has choirs at both ends of the nave, with the mid-13th-century west choir the most interesting. Here are 12 lifesize stone statues of the benefactors, who donated the funds for the construction of the cathedral. The statues were crafted in the 13th century by an unknown artist and are considered some of the best examples of art from that period. The best known are the statues of Margrave Ekkehard and his wife Uta. However, do not overlook the statue of Reglindis (right), the wife of Margrave Hermann; her smile has been described as the most beautiful of the Middle Ages. The church is open daily, but Sundays and holidays only from noon, from April to September, 9 am to 6 pm, March and October, 9 am to 5 pm, and November to February, 9 am to 4 pm. Admission is €4.

The **Marktplatz** (Market Square) is surrounded by beautiful, mostly Renaissance and Baroque buildings. However, the Rathaus (Town Hall) is Late Gothic and the Ratskeller dates from the 14th century. The **Stadtkirche St Wenzel** (Town Church), Markt, ☎ 03445-775-940, was the main church of the secular part of town. The exterior is Late Gothic, but the interior mainly Baroque. It has a magnificent Hildebrandt organ that was first tuned by Johann Sebastian Bach and two paintings by Lucas Cranach. Except for services, the church is closed from November to March.

The controversial late 19th-century philosopher Friederich Nietzsche lived in Naumburg as a child and again later in life when his mental health started to deteriorate. The **Nietzsche-Haus Naumburg**, Weingarten 18, ☎ 03445-703-503, was opened in 1994 – he was largely ignored during the Communist regime – as a museum with a permanent exhibition on his life and time in Naumburg. Opening hours are Tuesday to Friday from 2 to 5 pm and weekends from 10 am to 4 pm. Admission is €1.50.

Wine Tasting: The Saale-Unstrut region is the farthest north of Germany's wine growing regions. It has a wine tradition of over a thousand years, with typical terraced vineyards along the steep valley banks. Although some red wines are produced, the dry whites are best.

Many wine producers and wine shops offer wine tasting at a nominal fee but most do not accept individual visitors. The following do, and often have English speaking personnel on premises.

- **Weingut Familie Fuchs**, Im Dorfe 47a, 99518 Darnstedt, ☎ 036461-20-855 (near Bad Sulza), is the smallest winery in Thuringia and follows strict ecological policies.
- **Weinbau Rittergut**, Dorfstraße 8, 06636 Weischütz, ☎ 034462-601-901, www.weinbau-rittergut-weischuetz.de , is on the Unstrut near Laucha. It has a 700-year wine-producing tradition and is open weekends from 2 to 8 pm. Wine from here, as well as other farms, is also available for sale and tasting at **Gutausschank Herbert Pawis**, Ehrauberge 12, 06632 Freyburg, ☎ 034464-27-433.

Little Red Riding Hood Sparkling Wine

During the Communist era, no decent celebration in East Germany went without *Rottkäppchensekt* (Little Red Riding Hood sparkling wine). The main reason, of course, was that it was produced here and was therefore often available. It is still drunk when people want to remember the good old days, but nowadays other brands are more popular. The wine is available in all shops in the region and in most other parts of Germany as well. It can cost as little as €3 in supermarket sales.

Rottkäppchen Sektkellerei, Sektkellereistraße 5, 06632 Freyburg, ☎ 034464-340, www.rotkaeppchen.de, has been in the sparkling wine business since 1856 and the wine is not bad, but not particularly good either. It does make a novel gift and conversation piece. Although the cellars cater mainly for groups, individuals are welcome at 2 pm, and on weekends also at 11 am.

Cultural Events

Short organ concerts, known as *Orgel punkt 12*, are held in the Wenzlerkirche, ☎ 03445-775-940, at noon on Wednesday, Saturday, and Sunday from May to October. Admission is €2. In August and September, the magnificent Hildebrandt organ is played in more concerts in the *Orgelsommer* program.

Adventures

On Wheels: The **Saale Cycling Path**, www.saale-radwanderweg.de, follows the Saale River for 427 km (256 miles), 152 km (91 miles) in Saxony-Anhalt, 180 km (108 miles) in Thuringia, and the rest in Bavaria. Despite the rapidly changing scenery, the path itself closely follows the flow of the river. The part of the route through Thuringia can be challenging and is better described as medium to difficult, rather than easy, as with many riverbank routes such as the Elbe cycling route. The route is marked by a cyclist and a blue horizontal bar.

The route combines well with the 190-km (114-mile) **Unstrut path**, www.unstrutradweg.de. Although most of the river is in neighboring Thuringia, it is the 42 km (25 miles) in Saxony-Anhalt that have the most exciting scenery. A popular stop is at the **Vinothek Saale-Unstrut**, Volkmar-Kroll-Straße 22, 06642 Memleben, www.vinothek-saale-unstrut.de, which offers wine for sale and tasting inside the ruins of the Romanesque monastery. Wine tasting is also available from many other vineyards en route, although not all welcome individual travelers.

In the Saale-Unstrut region an excellent option for renting a bicycle is **Regio-Bike Fahrrad Fiedelak**, Bahnhofstraße 4, 06632 Freyburg and der Unstrut, ☎ 034464-7080, fax 034464-70-825, www.regiobike.de. This company has 15 centers in the region and one-way rentals between stations are possible without additional charges.

On Water: On the **Unstrut**, canoes and kayaks can be rented from **Kanuverleih Laucha**, Hallesche Straße 25, 06636 Laucha, ☎ 034462-22-957, ikoeppel@web.de. From here to Freyburg is less than three hours paddling. Farther upstream, boats can be rented from **Kanustation Titteburg**, An der Pension Schluese, 06556 Ritteburg, ☎ 03445-202-051, www.saale-unstrut-tours.de.

The Unstrut flows into the Saale at **Naumburg** from where **Kanustation Blütengrund**, 06618 Naumburg, ☎ 03445-202-051, www.saale-unstrut-tours.de, rents out boats and arranges active trips combining cycling, hiking, canoeing, and wine tasting in the region. It also has a campsite. In summer, guided torchlit canoe tours are sometimes available at night.

Operating river boats on the two rivers from Naumburg is **Saale Unstrut Schifffahrtsgeschellschaft**, Blütengrund 8, ☎ 03445-202-830, www.froehliche-doerte.de. Boats depart on the one-hour cruise to Freyburg, at the center of the wine trade in the beautiful Unstrutt valley, three times daily from May to August, as well as from Wednesday to Sunday in April, September, and October. Individuals may often join special cruises if seats are available.

Where to Stay & Eat

Hotel Stadt Aachen is in a lovely restored house directly on the Market Square. Rooms are furnished with stylish dark furniture and are comfortable rather than luxurious. Markt 11, 06618 Naumburg, ☎ 03445-2470, fax 03445-247-130, www.hotel-stadt-aachen.de. (€€)

The two restaurants on the premises serve mostly local specialties in a historic milieu: the **Carolus Magnus** (€€-€€€) is more upscale, while the **Ottonenkeller** (€-€€) provides a medieval atmosphere.

Nearby is the historic **Ratskeller**, Markt 1, ☎ 03445-202-063, inside a 14th-century vaulted cellar. The food is mostly regional, but a large selection of international dishes is also available. In summer, the street cafés on the Markt may be more appealing, but in winter, the lovely cellar is hard to beat. (€-€€)

Camping in the Saale-Unstrutt Region

The better camping facilities in this region are concentrated in the Saale and Unstrut valleys. The **Naherholungszentrum Laucha** is in the beautiful Unstrut valley, with easy access to historic and viniculture sites. Across the river is the Laucha Airport, offering sightseeing and balloon flights. A large outdoor swimming pool is available to campers. Boat rental is offered. Open from May to October. Krahwinklerstraße, 06636 Laucha an der Unstrut, ☎ 034462-202-75, nez-Laucha@web.de.

Near Naumburg, at the foot of vine-covered slopes, is the **Blütengrund campsite**. It has 100 spaces for long-term and 200 for short-term campers. The location is ideal for excursions, whether on foot, water or with wheels. Boat rental is available on site. Boat excursions up the Unstrut are offered from the town. Open all year. Campingplatz Blütengrund, 06618 Naumburg, ☎ 03445-202-711, fax 03445-200-0571, www.campingnaumburg.de.

■ Harz Mountains

The Harz is a small mountain range of only about 100 by 40 km (60 x 24 miles). However, it is the northernmost of the German Mittelgebirge, a generally low mountain range spread over most of Central Germany. From here to the North and East (Baltic) seas, Germany is a low-lying plain. Mount Brocken, at 1,142 m (3,746 feet), is the highest peak in the Harz and easily accessible, confirming that this is not exactly the Alps. However, it is an area of outstanding natural beauty, blending with historic small towns. The Harz spreads over three states – also see the Thuringia and Lower Saxony chapters for additional information.

The most interesting towns are Quedlinburg – a UNESCO World Cultural Heritage Site – and Wernigerode in the north of the Harz. Lutherstadt Eisleben can also easily be visited from here. A thousand years ago, Quedlinburg was at the heart of the German Kingdom and, although most buildings are somewhat newer, it still is a place where time seems to have stood still for a few centuries. The towns deeper into the mountains are small, and it is nature rather than history or culture that takes center stage.

The Iron Curtain cut through the Harz Mountains – and the remaining cleared border area with a patrol road on the East German side is nowadays a favored walking and biking route. Due to the proximity of the border, much of the Harz was off-limits to tourists after 1960, but that changed quickly after the *Wende*. Massive Western investment poured into the Harz area to safeguard the old half-timbered towns and other cultural treasures that were neglected by the East German regime. Tourism continues to increase, with the Harz being popular year-round.

BEWITCHED

The Harz has been considered the haunt of witches since time immemorial. On Walpurgis Night – the night from April 30 to May 1 – witches from all over Germany arrive, mostly with broom, though not exactly riding one, to dance the night away on the peak of Brocken or at Hexentanzplatz. Nowadays it is one big party with most Harz towns offering some kind of parade or show of witches to pull the crowds in.

During the Inquisition, the Harz was known for its excess of witches. Exact figures were not kept, but in 1589 some 133 people were burned at the stake in Quedlinburg alone. Although witches can be of any sex, around 80% of cases involved females.

Quedlinburg

According to legend, in AD 916 Heinrich, Duke of Saxony, was out catching birds (finches) near Quedlinburg castle when a delegation bearing the imperial insignia arrived to inform him that he had been elected King of Germany. For the next two centuries, this part of the world, and Quedlinburg in particular, would be the center of political power in Germany. During this period, Quedlinburg was considered one of the four most important cities in Germany. However, the center of power gradually moved away – first to nearby towns such as Goslar and Magdeburg, but eventually farther south. Heinrich I left much of Quedlinburg to his wife Mathilda, who founded a convent that determined the history of the town until 1802.

Quedlinburg's tourism appeal lies mainly in the beautiful town panorama, with some 1,400 half-timbered houses dating from the 15th to 19th centuries. Virtually all buildings in the old town are half-timbered, while the newer areas on the outskirts are Communist-era flat and square buildings. For Quedlinburg the *Wende* came just in time – it allowed restoration of buildings that were on the verge of collapsing due to neglect and prevented the planned destruction of large parts of the old town by the Communist regime. Apart from tourism, Quedlinburg is famous for its flower and seed industries.

The old town and the castle mountain, with the Stiftkirche St Servatius' treasure, are UNESCO World Heritage Sites. It is a popular destination year-round, and although many visitors are day-trippers, it is a very pleasant and romantic town to spend the night.

Information Sources

Tourist Information: The tourist information office is in the Rathaus, Markt 1, 06484 Quedlinburg, ☎ 03946-90-550, www.quedlinburg.de.

Transportation

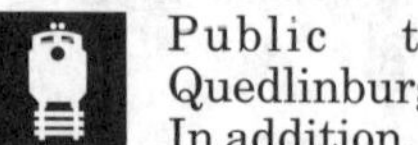

Public transportation to Quedlinburg is somewhat limited. In addition, the train station is not in the best part of town, but is still within 10 minutes walking distance from the old town down Bahnhofstraße. Magdeburg can be reached by hourly trains in 70 to 90 minutes. Wernigerode is an hour away by frequent trains, requiring a changeover in Halberstadt.

A **Bimmelbahn**, ☎ 03946-91-8888, www.quedlinburger-bimmelbahn.de, runs hourly past the sights from April to October between 10 am and 4 pm from Carl Ritter Platz.

Sightseeing

For sightseeing purposes, the town can be divided into two areas: Schlossberg, with the castle and monumental church, and the Markt area, with the market, town hall, and endless half-timbered houses.

Schlossberg: The castle and, more impressively, the church on **Schlossberg** (Castle Hill) can be seen from most parts of town. The hill is a sandstone rock on which Heinrich I constructed his favorite *Pfalz* (imperial residence) next to an even older Carolingian church. Of this castle, only some of the vaults can still be seen in the cellar of the restaurant on the hill. The most magnificent views of old town Quedlinburg are from the terrace of the restaurant and the garden of the former abbess. The areas that have free access are open daily May to October from 6 am to 10 pm, and close at 8 pm the rest of the year.

The current **Schloss** (Castle), Schlossberg 1, ☎ 03946-2730, is a Renaissance palace dating mainly from the 16th to 18th centuries. It has a museum explaining the history of the town and castle. Most furniture is from the Renaissance. A very popular item is the Robber Baron Box – a wooden crate in which Count Albrecht von Regenstein was publicly held prisoner on grounds of breaking the peace of the land – stealing and maiming in modern parlance. Opening hours are April to October daily from 10 am to 6 pm and the rest of the year Saturday to Thursday from 10 am to 4 pm.

The most impressive building on the hill and indeed in the whole region is the **Stiftskirche St Servatius** (Collegiate Church), Schlossberg 1, ☎ 03946-709-900. The current church is one of the most important and best-preserved examples of High Romanesque architecture in Germany. It was constructed around 1100 to replace the earlier Carolingian church, which was damaged by fire in 1070. The interior is decorated with statues and carvings done by highly skilled Italian artists. The choir was reconstructed in the

mid-14th century in a Gothic style and the south towers only completed in the 19th century. During the 1930s, the Nazis considered the church to have special significance as it contained the grave of Heinrich I, founder of the first *Reich*. The grand staircase dates from the Nazi period, as well as walls, built to return the Romanesque look of the choir, leaving the Gothic only visible from the exterior. Underneath the choir is the crypt, a three-aisle basilica with original Romanesque wall paintings. It had the graves of Heinrich I and his wife Mathilda. However, after she became a saint, his bones were removed to the church itself where they probably burned to ashes in the fire of 1070. (It was practice at the time that the graves of spouses could not be together if only one was declared a saint.)

The two small rooms of the **treasury** contain one of the most valuable church treasures of the Middle Ages.

The treasure contains numerous reliquaries adorned with gold and jewels (see above), a codex from the ninth century, the Servatius staff, a golden comb used by Heinrich I, and a knotted carpet dating from 1200. The treasure can only be seen on a guided tour.

Opening hours are May to October, Tuesday to Saturday from 10 am to 5:30 pm, Sunday and holidays from noon to 5:30 pm. In April, closing time is 4:40 pm and from November to March 3:30 pm. Combination tickets for the castle museum, church, and treasury are €5, or €4 without the museum.

The $3 Million Finder's Fee

Twelve of the most valuable pieces of the treasure disappeared shortly after World War II. Although this part of Germany was occupied by Russia, it was first liberated by the US army. An American lieutenant stole several items and mailed them home to Texas. Only after his death did it become known when his inheritors tried to cash in and sell the pieces. Germany paid a controversial "finder's fee" of around $3 million for the stolen goods and the treasure was returned to Quedlinburg in 1993. (Two pieces stolen in 1945 are still missing.)

At the square in front of the access road leading up to the castle is the birth house of Friedrich Gotlieb Klapstock (1724-1803), one of the most important German writers, who initiated the classical period. The **Klapstock-Haus**, Schlossberg 12, ☎ 03946-2610, has a museum dedicated mainly to Klapstock but also has a display on Dorothea Erxleben (1715-1762), another Quedlinburg native who was the first qualified female medical doctor in Germany. Opening hours are April to October from Wednesday to Sunday, 10 am to 5 pm. Closing time from November to March is at 4 pm. Admission is €2.

Nearby is the **Finkenherd**, a row of narrow half-timbered houses. According to legend, this is the place where Duke Heinrich was informed of his election as German King. Several other towns claim the same honor, but Quedlinburg's claim is generally the strongest. The **Lyonel Feininger Gallery**, Finkenherd 5a, ☎ 03946-2384, www.feininger-galerie.de, a modern gallery set behind the historic houses, is a large collection of drawings and watercolors by this American-born artist who had to leave the Bauhaus school and eventually Germany due to opposition by the Nazis. A friend of Feininger in Quedlinburg hid the works from the Nazis, and these form the basis of the exhibition, which is complemented by temporary exhibitions of works by contemporaries. Opening hours are Tuesday to Sunday from 10 am to 6 pm. Admission is €6.

Markt Area: Eight streets end in the huge triangular Markt (Market Square), which has been in use since the 10th century. The fountain of musicians was erected in 1979. Several outdoor cafés enhance the Markt's appeal as do two of the best hotels in town.

The **Rathaus** (Town Hall, below) is a Renaissance building dating from 1619. Inside the Rathaus, the Festhalle has large frescos commemorating the town's glorious history. (Many visitors go up the flight of stairs directly into the council meeting room and leave unimpressed. The Festhalle is around the corner and down the passage!)

In front of the Rathaus is a sandstone statue of the knight **Roland**. Roland was a symbol of a city's independence and privileges and can still be seen in 26 European cities. (The largest is in Bremen.) It was erected in the early 15th century when the citizens of Quedlinburg increasingly sought to free themselves from the rule of the convent on the hill by joining the Hanseatic League. Unfortunately, the abbess Hedwig was not pleased with having her powers eroded and called in the help of her brothers. They just happened to be the

Dukes of Saxony and two of the most powerful men in the kingdom. After a battle in 1477, the citizens had to give up privileges and all alliances with other towns. The Roland was destroyed and only re-erected in 1867 after its chance discovery under rubble in the old Rathaus cellars.

To the right of the Rathaus, the narrowest alley in Quedlinburg leads to the **Schuhhof** (Shoe Courtyard). This was the area of cobblers, and on some of the small houses the wooden boards that were lifted up to form a shop table in front of the windows can still be seen.

Behind the Rathaus is the Gothic **St Benedikti Marktkirche** (Market Church). It dates from the mid-13th century and is decorated with sculptures, Late Gothic wooden crucifixes, and altars. A graveyard used to be next to the church but only the 1727 chapel for the Gephardt and Goetze families survived.

Two blocks down Marschlinger Hof is a large remaining section of the **town wall**, complete with several watchtowers. The highest is the 40-m (128-foot) Schreckensturm. The wall is best seen from outside the city walking along Wall Street. Many buildings in this area have not yet been restored and give an idea of what the town must have looked like at the end of the Communist era.

Walking through the streets of Quedlinburg is like strolling through a giant open-air museum of medieval architecture. Streets with particularly interesting half-timbered buildings include Lange Gasse, Fleischhof, Marktstraße, Breite Straße, and Steinweg. However, a more formal treatment of the subject is possible in the **Fachwerkmuseum** (Half-Timbered Museum, below), Ständerbau, Wordgasse 3, ☎ 03946-3828. The museum is in the oldest house in town (1310), and it was occupied until 1965. The techniques of half-timbered architecture are explained with the aid of sketches, photos, and models. Opening hours are April to October from Friday to Wednesday, 10 am to 5 pm. (Closing at 4 pm from November to March.) Admission is €3.

Near Quedlinburg: North of the Harz are several rock formations that resemble a giant wall. According to legend, this is the work of the devil and thus is known as **Teufelmauer** (Devil's Wall). Hiking to parts of the wall is popular, but when driving along the minor road connecting Thale with Quedlinburg via Neinstedt, a large piece of the Teufelmauer can be seen right next to the road.

Lovers of the Romanesque should visit the **Stiftkirche St Cyriakus** (Collegiate Church of St Cyriacus) in the small town of **Gernrode** about seven km (4.2 miles) south of Quedlinburg. This church is one of the best examples in Germany of Romanesque architecture dating from the Ottonian period (10th century). Construction begun around 959, but the building was altered early in the 12th century. It has three aisles and a flat ceiling as was common in the period. In the south aisle is a rare example of an Ottonian sculpture. The baptismal font is from the 12th century. The east and west choirs are not perfectly in line due to ground movements through the centuries that also severely damaged the long aisles, which were restored in the 19th century. The church is open weekdays from 9 am to 5 pm, Saturdays from 10 am to 2:30 pm, and Sundays after the service until noon.

Adventures

In the Air: From Ballenstedt, near Quedlinburg, balloon flights, as well as small plane and glider flights, are possible. Contact **Ballenstedt Aeroclub**, ☎ 039487-662, www.ballenstedt-harz.de, for exact details and flying times.

Where to Stay & Eat

Quedlinburg is popular with tourists and although many are day-trippers, several good hotels and restaurants are available for those interested in spending the night in this most romantic of towns.

There are a number of restaurants and cafés on the market square, but the two inside the hotels are especially pleasant. **Hotel Zum Bär** is at the far end of the square away from the town hall and church. The hotel has a tradition going back 250 years and was restored in 1997 to its former glory. It was Goethe's chosen abode. Rooms are comfortable, with stylish furniture and an eye for detail. Markt 8-9, 06484 Quedlinburg, ☎ 03946-77-70, fax 03946-700-268, www.hotelzumbaer.de. (€€-€€€)

The restaurant **Bärenschencke** (€-€€) in the hotel spills out onto the square if the weather is good, while the indoor room is small with simple yet elegant décor. The menu is mainly regional dishes and portions are fairly large. Saale-Unstrut wines and local beers are available.

Also on the Markt but pricier and more upmarket is the **Romantik Hotel Theophano**. The hotel opened recently in two restored 350-year old houses and is tastefully decorated. Rooms are comfortable and aimed at travelers on a romantic break. Markt 13-14, ☎ 03946-96-300, fax 03946-963-036, www.hoteltheophano.de. (€€-€€€)

Open for dinner only, the hotel's rustic **Weinkeller Theophano** (€€-€€€€) is a highly recommended, upscale restaurant. The menu combines new international cuisine with more traditional regional dishes.

THEOPHANO & EDITH

The wife of Otto II was Theophano, a Byzantium princess. When Otto II died in 983 AD his son, Otto III, was only three years old. His mother, Theophano and, after her death his grandmother Edith, ruled the empire and skillfully too – the only time in the Empire's 900-year history that a female was at the helm.

On the opposite side of the Schlossberg from the Markt is the very pleasant **Romantik Hotel am Brühl**. It is family-owned and ensconced in historic buildings that the owners reclaimed after the end of the Communist period. Rooms are comfortable and furnished with high quality furniture. The non-smoking rooms in the newer wing are the best. In contrast to the hotels on the Market Square, the hotel has a quiet location, yet is only a few minutes from the castle and about 15 minutes walk from the Markt. Parking is free. The excellent restaurant **Weinstube** (€€-€€€€) is open for dinner only. The menu is mainly local dishes. The high prices reflect the taste and quality of the food. Billungstraße 11, ☎ 03946-96-180, fax 03946-961-8246, www.hotelambruehl.de. (€€-€€€)

A more modern and cheaper alternative is the **Acron Hotel**. It is thoroughly modern and located conveniently for drivers at the edge of the town but still only 200 m (650 feet) from the Old Town. Rooms are simply furnished but clean and all equipment is in good condition. Breakfast is the only meal served, but a bar is open at night. Gartenstraße 44a, 06484 Quedlinburg, ☎ 03946-770-20, fax 03946-770-230, www.quedlinburg.de/acron. (€-€€)

Behind the castle gate, at the same level as the entrances to the castle and the cathedral, is **Schlosskrug am Dom**, Am Schlossberg 1, 06484 Quedlinburg, ☎ 03946-2838, a pleasant restaurant with a 100-seat beer garden. The food is simple local dishes, including beer garden standards such as bratwurst auf sauerkraut, eisbein, and baked potatoes, offering great value. Service is fast. The beer garden has splendid views of the roofs of the old town. The restaurant also has a few simple bedrooms available. (€)

Camping: Near Quedlinburg, in the picturesque town of Gernrode, is **Harz Camp Bremer Teich**. The camp is next to a large pond where swimming is allowed. Bicycles can be rented on site and hot-air balloon trips can be arranged. In addition to 150 long-term campers, the site has space for 100 vacationers. A further 40 mobile homes and 40 hostel beds are available. Open year-round. Campingplatz Harz Camp Bremer Teich, 06507 Gernrode, ☎ 039485-60-810, fax 039485-50-055, www.harz-camp-gernrode.de.

Deeper into the Harz is the **Panoramablick campground**. The site has space for only 40 campers, but they do get luxuries unknown in the average campsite. Every space is about 120 m² (430 square feet) and has its own private bathroom. Unfortunately, the trees are still small and shade limited. A few rooms are available in the guesthouse. Bicycles can be rented on site. Open year-round. Gasthaus Zur Linde, Hinterdorf 79, 06493 Dankerode, ☎ 03984-2140, fax 039484-42-341, www.hotelcamping-ludwig.de.

Thale

Thale is not a pretty town. It made its fortune from the mining and refining of iron, which during the Communist era employed around 8,000 workers but fewer than 500 10 years after the *Wende*. However, Thale is blessed with some amazing natural beauty nearby – as long as you can manage to overlook the industrial parts of the town.

HARZ LEGEND

On the Rosstrappe is a rock which looks as if it has the imprint of a large horseshoe. According to legend, this imprint was left when Princess Brunhilde's horse prepared to jump the valley to the Hexentanzplatz while being chased by a giant. Her crown fell in the river and the giant changed into a black dog guarding the crown for the rest of his life. According to other versions, the mark was made when she landed while fleeing in the opposite direction from an uncouth bridegroom, whose fate was the same as that of the giant.

Two of the most famous Harz natural sights, the Hexentanzplatz and the Rosstrappe, are within easy reach from Thale. These two high rock outcrops with sheer drops guard the Bode valley.

The **Hexentanzplatz** (Witches' Dancing Place) is a rock 514 m (1,644 feet) high, with marvelous views of the Bode Valley and the Rosstrappe. It can be reached from Thale by hiking, by car, or via a four-minute cable car ride. It is a popular venue, with a lot of kitsch souvenir shops, anything witch-related, and restaurant facilities, but the view is worth braving the commercial excesses. During the pre-Christian era, the rock was a favored place for pagan rituals. On Walpurgis Night, the night of 30 April, witches gather here and it is a haven for all sorts of modern-day neo-pagans. Also on the cliff is the 1,400-seat **Bergtheater**, ☎ 03947-2324, one of Germany's loveliest natural theaters, an animal park, summer toboggan-run, and other garish entertainment options.

On the opposite side of the valley is the **Rosstrappe**, 403 m (1,290 feet) high, with similar sheer cliffs and magnificent views. Things are quieter here, making it a more pleasant alternative. It can be reached by either hiking or taking the single-seat six-minute chairlift from Thale.

Cultural Events

The Harz region is more than just natural beauty and, especially in summer, cultural events abound. The **Harzer Bergtheater** (Mountain Theater), Hexentanzplatz near Thale, ☎ 03947-2324, www.harzer-bergtheater.de, is one of Germany's most spectacularly located open-air theaters. From April to September its program includes opera, operettas, children's plays, musicals, and popular music.

All over the Harz **Walpurgis Night**, the night of April 30, is celebrated. Most towns have parades and cultural events. The best festivals are on Brocken and Hexentanzplatz.

Adventures

Country Hikes: Walks through an area of outstanding natural beauty are found in the **Bodetal** (Bode Valley). One of the best walks is the three-hour, 10-km (six-mile) walk, marked by a blue triangle, from Thale to Treseburg. It is possible to take a bus from Thale and walk back, mostly in the bottom of the valley next to the river and enjoying the best views. Alternatively, you can make a round-trip and return via the Hexentanzplatz on a trail marked with a red dot. Shorter walks, but with steep slopes, are possible in the region, including Hexentanzplatz and Rosstrappe. Several inns are available en route.

Summer Tobogganing: Tobogganing is popular in Germany, and special summer runs eliminate the need for snow. The longest summer run in Germany at 1,000 m (3,200 feet), with speeds up to 40 km/h (24 mph) and four jumps, is the **Harzbob** at Hexentanzplatz, ☎ 03947-2500, www.seilbahnen-thale.de. No maximum age; two-seaters are available. Open year-round from 9:30 until dark, February to April, only on weekends.

Where to Stay & Eat

High up the cliffs, with overwhelming views of the Bode Valley, is the **Berghotel Hexentanzplatz**. Rooms are comfortable rather than luxurious, but the views are superb. The hotel has several restaurants (€-€€), all serving hearty local fare. The views of the valley are particularly good from the terrace. However, thousands of tourists visit the Hexentanzplatz entertainment complex daily, making the setting less serene for most of the day. Hexentanzplatz, 06502 Thale, ☎ 03947-4730, fax 03947-47-338. (€€)

Wernigerode

Although Wernigerode has an 875-year history, it has never been in the same powerful political position as Quedlinburg. Its glory years were in the 14th and 15th centuries, when trade in cloth, beer, and spirits brought immense wealth. The plague and the Thirty Years' War reduced the town to a shadow of its former self. Today it is lovely, with many colorful half-timbered houses and a mighty castle set high on a hill on the outskirts of the town.

Information Sources

Information Office: The **Wernigerode Tourist Office**, Nikolaiplatz 1, 38855 Wernigerode, ☎03943-633-03, www.wernigerode-tourismus.de, is a short walk from the Marktplatz down Breite Straße.

Transportation

Wernigerode has good regional public transportation links, making it an ideal base for travelers not relying on private cars. Most sights in town are easiest reached on foot, with the exception of the Schloss, which is a 1½-km (one-mile) walk up the hill. An alternative to walking is the Wernigerode **Bimmelbahn**, ☎ 03943-604-000, www.wernigerode-bimmelbahn.de, which departs from the Marktplatz, or the **Schlossbahn**, ☎ 03943-625-493, which departs from the Anger parking lot and the Krummelsches Haus. From May to October, departures are every 25 minutes between 9:30 am and 6:10 pm, and every 45 minutes between 10 am and 4 pm in winter.

The **Harzquerbahn** departs from Wernigerode, giving easy access to Mount Brocken and Nordhausen. See *Adventures, Narrow-Gauge Trains***.

By train, Wernigerode can be reached directly from both Hannover and Halle in just under two hours. Buses from Wernigerode offer easy access to most towns in the region.

Sightseeing

Old Town: The heart of the old town is the **Markt** (Market Square). The most beautiful building here is the **Rathaus**, below, which dates mostly from 1544, but parts go back to 1277. It has a unique design with two small towers flanking the ceremonial external staircase. Of particular interest are the carved wooden figures of clowns, dancers, and saints that adorn the crossbeams and joists. Also on the Markt are two impressive half-timbered hotel buildings: the façade of the luxury **Gothisches Haus** dates from 1425 and the **Weißer Hirsch** from at least 1760.

From Markt, the narrow Klint alley leads to the oldest part of town. The **Schiefes Haus** (Leaning House), Klintgasse 5, was erected in 1680 as a mill for the cloth makers, but the stream eroded the foundations until it came to rest on solid rock. Currently the gable leans over 1.2 m (3.8 feet), more than the tower of Pisa. In the narrow streets around the Gothic **Silvestrikirche** (St Sylvester Church) are several impressive half-timbered houses, especially at Oberpfarkirchhoff numbers 6, 7, 12, and 13.

Das Kleinste Haus (the Smallest House), Kochstraße 43, ☎ 03943-654-454, is a tiny Baroque half-timbered house from the mid-18th century. It is 4.2 m (14 feet) high but only 2.95 m (9.7 feet) wide, with a front

Das Kleinste Haus

door of 1.7 m (5½ feet). It has only a front and back wall, using the adjacent houses for sidewalls. The house has three levels, with the largest room being only 10 square m (32 square feet). In the 1920s, a train conductor lived here with his wife and seven children! The last inhabitant died in 1976, and since then it has been used as a museum. Open hours are daily from 10 am to 5 pm. Admission is €1. Several houses in the vicinity are also pretty small – some have signs in the windows pointing visitors to the *real* smallest house.

From Markt, Breite Straße, now a busy shopping street, leads eastwards. At No 4 is the 1583 building housing **Café Wien** since 1897. It is not only a pleasant place for coffee and cake but also the oldest building in the vicinity, as a major town fire in 1848 stopped here. Much farther down the street, at No 72, is the **Krummelsches Haus**, erected in 1674, with a richly carved façade. The **Krellsche Schmiede** (1678) is a former blacksmith workshop decorated with a horsehead and shoe. It currently houses the small **Schmiedermuseum** (Blacksmith Museum), Breite Straße 95, ☎ 03943-601-772, www.schmiedemuseum-wernigerode.de. Opening hours are Wednesday to Saturday from 10 am to 4 pm. Admission is €2.50.

Schloss Wernigerode: Apart from the magnificent half-timber buildings in the old town, the major attraction is the knight's castle Schloss Wernigerode, Am Schloss 1, ☎ 03943-553-030, www.schloss-wernigerode.de. It is on a 350-m (1,148-foot) hill outside the town and can be reached by walking up (1½ km/one mile) or taking the Bimmelbahn from the town center.

The origins of the castle go back to the 12th century, but only a few cellar vaults remain from that period. Around 1500, the castle was updated and served as residence for the Counts of Stolberg, who had to flee their own castle during the peasants' war. Lack of water never made the castle much of a defensible proposition, although it again served as a Baroque residence for the counts of Ilsenburg. Its current knight's castle look dates from 1885, when Count Otto zu Stolberg-Wernigerode, for years Otto von Bismarck's vice chancellor of the German empire, rebuilt the castle in the Historicist style. It combined all architectural styles from the Gothic to Baroque into a fairy tale castle.

Schloss Wernigerode

The East German Government confiscated the castle and turned it into a museum in 1949. Only around 40 of the 250 rooms are open and have displays of furniture and art illustrating the life of nobility of the late 19th century. The **Schlosskirche** (Castle Church) was consecrated in 1880, replacing the previous Baroque chapel. It has a marble altar and pulpit. The terrace offers superb views of Wernigerode and on a clear day Mount Brocken can be seen.

Opening hours are May to October daily from 10 am to 6 pm; November to April from Tuesday to Friday, 10 am to 4 pm, and weekends from 10 am to 6 pm. Admission is €4.50.

Mount Brocken: Close to Wernigerode is the highest peak in the Harz, the 1,142-m (3,654-foot) Mount Brocken. The view from the top can stretch 125 km (74 miles), but as the mountain is surrounded by clouds or mist 300 days a year, the view is by no means guaranteed.

During the Cold War, the Brocken – being at the inner German border – was a major spying point for the Russians to monitor events in the West. The whole region was off-limits for tourists from the early 1960s until 1989. Some areas were so sensitive the Russian army apparently even forbade their East German allies from entering. As a result of these activities, a road was built to the peak. The road is still closed to private traffic but gives an easy if somewhat boring access for hikers. The Brockenbahn gives rail access to the peak.

Shopping

Glasswork has been produced in the Harz area for around 2,000 years. **Staatliche Glasmanufaktur Harzkristall**, Im Freien Felde 5, 38895 Derenburg, ☎ 039453-68-071, www.glasmanu.de, near Wernigerode, is one of the largest producers. Its range stretches from glasses to vases in all shapes and sizes.

In Wernigerode, several artists belonging to the **Wernigerode Kunst und Kulturverein**, Marktstraße 1, ☎ 03943-260-693, have studios near the Rathaus. Works range from modern paintings to woodcarvings and statues. A large selection of wooden toys produced in the Harz Mountains is available. It is often possible to see artists at work.

Hütter Porzellan, Mittelstraße 6, 38855 Wernigerode, ☎ 03943-32-991, produces excellent porcelain, with some magnificently crafted artistic pieces. Hütter may be less famous than Meissen, but prices are lower and the buyer can claim to buy based on personal taste rather than on brand name.

Adventures

On Foot: Quedlinburg Tourism Office, Markt 2, ☎ 03946-905-6245, www.quedlinburg-info.de, is the only place in the region that offers regular English guided walking tours to individuals. The 90-minute guided walks take place May to September on Tuesday and Saturday at 2 pm. Tours in German are more frequent. The charge is €5 per person.

The Harz Mountains offer ample opportunities of all lengths and difficulties for hikers. The region has 8,000 km (4,800 miles) of marked walkways.

A popular hiking area is around the **Brocken**, the highest peak inside a national park. It can be assailed from all directions. The most frequent starting point is from the town of Schierke. From here, one can simply stroll along the **Brockenstraße**, the road built by the Soviet military and not open for private vehicles, but the route is best described as boring.

More strenuous is the shortest route from Schierke through the Eckerloch, an 11-km (6.6-mile) route with steep inclines. The **Goethe Route** is the 18-km (11-mile) path the writer used on December 10, 1777. It starts in Torfhaus, which was beyond the border during the Cold War.

One of the most picturesque routes is the **Heinrich Heine Route**. In 1824, Heine used this 22-km (13-mile) approach from Insenburg. (The Brockenbahn, see below, offers an easier descent, or ascent.) Guided tours of around five hours on the Goethe Route are organized by **Altenau Tourismus**, ☎ 05328-80-222, www.harztourismus.com, from May to October on Thursdays, departing at 9:30 am from Altenau.

On Wheels: The 350-km (210-mile) **Harzrundweg cycling route** leads around the Harz Mountains. The route is marked by a black witch on a bicycle – broom on the carrier! The route is in the low hills and without difficult inclines, but for more adventurous cyclists the opportunities to turn into the mountain valleys are numerous and some routes very challenging. Cycling in the Harz itself is generally strenuous but it is possible for example to take a bicycle by train to the top of Brocken and basically free-wheel all the way down. Bicycle rental shops are rare in the Harz as most hotels, holiday homes, and campsites rent bicycles to patrons.

The Harz Mountains have Europe's highest density of **narrow-guage steam train** routes, which was in the GDR a valuable source of foreign exchange income from tourists. All lines are operated by the **Harzer Schmallspurbahnen**, Friederichstraße 151, 38855 Wernigerode, ☎ 03943-5580, www.hsb-wr.de. The longest route of 60 km

(36 miles) crosses the Harz from **Wernigerode** in the north to **Nordhausen** (see Thuringia chapter) in the south. The total route, which has been in operation since 1896, takes around three hours.

It is popular to change trains in Drei Annen Hohne, 50 minutes from Wernigerode, and take the Brockenbahn (50 minutes) via Schierke to **Mount Brocken**, the highest peak in the Harz. From Wernigerode to Drei Annen Hohen, the train climbs 300 m (984 feet) in 14 km (8.4 miles) and, from here to Brocken, 582 m (1,908 feet) in 19 km (11.4 miles). The traditional starting point is from the historic Wernigerode Westbahnhof, but in order to grab the best seats it is wiser to board four minutes earlier at the Hauptbahnhof.

Where to Stay & Eat

There are several hotels, restaurants and coffee shops on and near the Marktplatz, Wernigerode's historic town center. As in many other German towns, the town hall has a restaurant in the basement, offering mainly hearty local cuisine. The restaurant **Ratskeller**, Marktplatz 1, ☎ 03943-632-704, is in this historic building and the food is very good. (€€)

More interesting though are the places offering a view of the Rathaus. The **Ringhotel Weißer Hirsch** is inside a large building dating from at least 1760. It was refurbished in the 1990s and the half-timbered façade restored to its original beauty. Rooms are large and comfortably furnished, with the better ones offering views of the square and Rathaus. Marktplatz 5, 38855 Wernigerode, ☎ 03943-602-020, www.hotel-weisser-hirsch.de. (€€-€€€)

The hotel has an elegant up-market restaurant (€€-€€€) with a large terrace facing the market square and historic Rathaus. The menu features mainly classical regional cuisine, including a menu with food as cooked in the restaurant a century ago.

The **Travel Charme Hotel Gotisches Haus** is a thoroughly modern luxury hotel behind a beautifully preserved Renaissance façade. Rooms are large and furnished to a high standard. Rooms with a view require a surcharge. Am Marktplatz 2, 38855 Wernigerode, ☎ 03943-6750, fax 03943-675-555, www.tc-hotels.de. (€€-€€€€)

The hotel has four restaurants, with the **Winkeller 1360** (€€-€€€), open for dinner only, especially recommended. Four wood-carved statues dating from 1480 enhance the atmosphere.

For a more casual approach and lighter meals, try the **Konditorei & Café am Markt**, Marktplatz 6–8, % 03943-604-030, www.cafe-wiecker.de. Inside it has a large multi-level space, but the real treat is outside with views of the square and town hall. The selection of cakes and pastries is large, as one would expect from a confectioner, but the meal options are also vast. (€-€€)

Around the corner is **Café Wien**, Breite Straße 4, ☎ 03943-632-409, in the oldest house (1583) on the street (the 1848 town fire was finally extinguished at the house next door). It has been in business since 1897. The views are rather limited. Fortunately, the choice of Viennese delicacies is not. (€-€€)

The **Ramada-Treff Hotel** offers a completely modern package only about 100 m (328 feet) from the old town. It is in a quiet neighborhood with easy access by car. Rooms are stylishly furnished and comfortable. Pfarrstraße 41, 38855 Wernigerode, ☎ 03943-9410, fax 03943-941-555, www.ramada-treff.de. (€€€)

Camping: Near Wernigerode is **Camping am Brocken**, in the town of Elbingerode, at the foot of the Brocken peak. The campsite is right next to the forest and away from through-traffic. The site has space for 150 tourists and 30 long-term campers. Open year-round. Camping am Brocken, Schützenrigg 6, 38875 Elbingerode, ☎/fax 039454-42-589, www.elbingerode.de.

Border Museum & Monument

A bit off the beaten track, north of the Harz, near the A2 Autobahn connecting Magdeburg and Hannover, is the **Grenzdenkmal Hötensleben** (Border Monument), ☎ 05351-17-178, www.grenzdenkmaeler.de. While most parts of the border dividing the two Germanys were destroyed in 1990 at the pace that a bulldozer could drive, a small part was kept intact near the town of Hötensleben on the road to Schöningen. The border was an incredible feat of technology and included two concrete walls up to 3.4 m (10 feet) high, fences, anti-tank spikes, patrol roads, search lights, watch towers and, in some places, automatic guns.

The **Zonengrenz-Museum Helmstedt** (Border Museum), Südertor 6, 38350 Helmstedt, 05351-121-248, is in the nearby town and explains the history of the internal border with scale models and equipment used during escape attempts. Opening hours are a bit of a strain: Tuesday and Friday from 3 to 5 pm, Wednesday from 10 am to noon and 3 to 5 pm, Thursday from 3 to 6:30 pm and weekends from 10 am to 5 pm. Admission is free.

■ Magdeburg & the Romanesque Route

Saxony-Anhalt's unique position at the heart of power of the early German kingdom saw a range of buildings constructed in the Romanesque style of the period. In contrast to many other areas such as the Rhinelands, the loss of power and political significance during the 13th century prevented many from being converted to the Gothic style. The monuments of Saxony-Anhalt thus are not only unique in number but also in purity of style.

ROMANIKSTRAẞE

A thousand km long (600 miles), the Romanikstraße (Romanesque Route), cuts a figure-eight shape through Saxony-Anhalt. It connects 72 Romanesque buildings in 60 often isolated and rural locations. The crossing point is in Magdeburg, with the southern route including Quedlinburg, Naumburg, and Halle the most popular. The northern route goes through the Altmarkt region (very much off the beaten track) with the brick monastery in Jerichow being especially noteworthy. It served as model for the brick Gothic churches farther north.

Magdeburg, the state capital, has a population of 245,000 and a history going back 1,200 years. Otto I the Great, King of Germany from 936-973 and first emperor of the Holy Roman Empire from 962, made Magdeburg his de facto capital. He also made Magdeburg a bishopric and started the construction of several Romanesque buildings. Despite severe damage by several town fires and the Thirty Years' War, Magdeburg remained a beautiful city until a 40-minute air raid on January 16, 1945 destroyed 90% of the city. Magdeburg was rebuilt in the ugly style of the Communist era. Although the city is beautifully located on the banks of the Elbe, with several large parks, only a very limited number of historically significant buildings survived.

Otto I the Great

Information Sources

Tourist Office: The Tourist Information, Ernst-Reuter-Allee 12, 39104 Magdeburg, ☎ 0391-540-4900, fax 0391-540-4930, www.magdeburg-tourist.de, can make reservations for hotels and package deals.

For more information on the *Romanikstraße* contact **Landesmarketing Sachsen Anhalt**, Am Alten Theater 6, 39104 Magdeburg, ☎ 0391-567-7080, fax 0391-567-7081, www.sachsen-anhalt-tourismus.de. For the northern circle and information in general on the rural Altmarkt area north of Magdeburg, contact **Tourismusverband Altmarkt**, Marktstraße 13, 39590 Tangermünde, ☎ 039322-3460, fax 03922-43-233, www.altmarkttourismus.de.

Sightseeing

The most famous sight in Magdeburg is the **Dom St Mauritius und St Katharina** (Cathedral), Am Dom 1, ☎ 0391-543-2414. It was originally constructed by Otto I, but his church was destroyed by a town fire in 1207. The current cathedral built between 1209 and 1520 claims to be the first Gothic style cathedral in Germany. (Both Marburg in Hesse and Trier along the Mosel claim the first Gothic church.) Small parts of the Romanesque are still visible. The statues of the wise and foolish virgins, as well as the graves of Otto I and his wife Editha, date from the mid-12th century.

Opening hours are Monday to Saturday from 10 am to 6 pm, Sunday from 11:30 am to 6 pm; closing daily at 4 pm from October to April. Admission is free.

The oldest building in Magdeburg and the symbolic crossing point of the two circular Romanikstraße routes is the **Kloster Unser Lieben Frauen** (Monastery of Our Dear Ladies, below), Regierungsstraße 4-6, ☎ 0391-565-020. Most of the building dates from 1064. Although Gothic vaults were added in 1220, the buildings are among the best-preserved samples of Romanesque architecture in Germany. The convent moved out in 1632 and the building was then used as a school until 1945. Since the 1970s, the church has been used as the Georg Philipp Telemann concert hall and the school as an art gallery. Telemann (1681-1767) was born in Magdeburg and his music is played at concerts held the first Sunday of most months. Opening hours are Tuesday to Sunday from 10 am to 5 pm. Admission is €2.

In front of the Baroque **Rathaus** (Town Hall) is the **Magdeburger Reiter** (Magdeburg Knight), a golden equestrian statue. It dates from around 1240 and is considered the oldest freestanding equestrian sculpture north of the Alps. (The one on the market square is a copy – the original is in the Cultural History Museum.)

Adventures

On Wheels

The **Elberadweg trail** goes through Magdeburg. Many hotels have bicycles available for guests, or they can be rented from the **Herrenkrug Parkhotel**, Herrenkrug 3, ☎ 0391-85-080, or from the **Zweirad-Schutz**, Breiter Weg, ☎ 0391-531-4545.

On Water

Elbe Steamers: Day-trips on steamers on the Elbe are less popular in Saxony-Anhalt than in Dresden. Trips are less regular but the best options are from Magdeburg.

Magdeburger Weiße Flotte, Petriförder 1, ☎ 0391-532-8890, www.weisseflotte-magdeburg.de, has day-trips from Magdeburg to varying destinations on most days between April and September. Shorter 90-minute to three-hour trips are also available in the Magdeburg region.

Waterskiing: In the north of Magdeburg on the Neustädter See Lake, **Wasserskilift Magdeburg**, Barleber Straße, 39126 Magdeburg, ☎ 0391-253-5927, www.wasserski-magdeburg.de, has five pole lifts, allowing up to 18 persons to water-ski simultaneously at up to 60 km/h (36 mph). From May to September the lifts operate daily from noon to 7 pm, April and October only on weekends from 1 to 6 pm. Prices start from €5 for three runs. The Neustädter See can be reached by Tram 8 or 9.

In the Air

Hot-Air Ballooning: Balloon flights are arranged by **Balloninsel im Elbepark**, Osterweddinger Straße 35, 39116 Magdeburg, ☎ 0391-636-0476. Departures are from the Elbauepark, north of the city center.

In summer, usually mid-August, at the **Ballon-Magie-Tage** up to 80 balloons take part in flights, including a night display.

On Horseback

Horseback riding is popular in Saxony-Anhalt, with the off-the-beaten-track area in the north – the **Altmark** – being particularly popular with riders. Riding stables are numerous but the operations relatively small. The Tourismusverband Altmarkt, Marktstraße 13, 39590 Tangermünde, ☎ 039322-3460, fax 03922-43-233, www.altmarkttourismus.
de, can supply details.

In Magdeburg, the **Reitpark Herrenkrug**, ☎ 0391-818-380, just north of the city center, offers riding opportunities. The tourism office can also supply details on other companies taking advantage of the vast parks in this city for riding.

Where to Stay & Eat

Magdeburg is blessed with numerous good hotels at reasonable prices. **Herrenkrug Parkhotel**, inside a large park on the banks of the Elbe, is the nicest place to stay. It is a bit outside the town center but worth the short tram ride (final stop of Tram 6) if you're not driving. It combines Art Nouveau rooms with a lovely newer building. Rooms are large and luxuriously furnished. The fitness options are extensive and there is a mini-golf course. Bicycle rental is available on the premises. Next door is a racetrack and horseback riding opportunities. Herrenkrug 3, 39114 Magdeburg, ☎ 0391-850-80, fax 0391-850-8501, www.herrenkrug.de. (€€-€€€)

The restaurant **Die Saison** (€€-€€€) in the Parkhotel offers international and regional cuisine in a luxury Art Nouveau setting. Less formal are the **Historische Eiskeller** (€€) and the terraces.

The centrally located **Maritim Hotel**, a short block from the main station and close to the Dom and Rathaus, is the best in-town option. The hotel is modern with a large glass atrium. Rooms are luxurious. The Maritim's elegant restaurant (€€-€€€) has light German and Mediterranean cuisine. The fitness area has a very large pool. Otto-von-Gerricke-Straße 87, 39104 Magdeburg, ☎ 0391-594-90, fax 0391-594-9990, www.maritim.de. (€€€-€€€€)

Aiming more at business travelers, but still welcoming to tourists, is the modern **Intercity Hotel**, next to the main station. Rooms are not particularly large but are comfortable and well-equipped. The room key gives access to local public transportation. Bahnhofstraße 69, 39104 Magdeburg, ☎ 0391-596-20, fax 0391-596-2499, www.intercityhotel.de. (€€-€€€)

The **Ratskeller**, Alter Markt, ☎ 0391-568-2323, in the cellars of the Town Hall, offers good local cuisine at reasonable prices. The vaults date from 1230 and are an excellent place to try some local wine and beer. (€€)

Mecklenburg-Vorpommern

In this Chapter

Mecklenburg-Vorpommern is a large, mostly rural, state in the north of the former East Germany. It is about the size of Hesse, but a population of only 1.8 million gives it by far the lowest population density of any German state. It has large unspoiled natural areas with 20% of the state occupied by forests.

The Baltic harbors were traditionally of economic and cultural importance and are the focus of this chapter. These cities mostly reached their zenith during the late Middle Ages as part of the Hanseatic League. A typical architectural feature, constantly repeated in each of these cities, is the use of brick as primary construction material. The monumental brick Gothic churches and occasional secular buildings are a true highlight of any visit to this region.

The state is a watersports haven. In addition to the 340-km (200-mile) Baltic coast, it has 1,800 lakes, many rivers and is particularly popular with domestic tourists, especially young families. The seaside resorts have mostly white, soft sand beaches and generally calm, shallow seas. Rügen island, Germany's largest, claims the highest number of annual sunshine hours in Germany. However, the swimming season is short and even in the middle of summer the water will not be confused with the tropics or Mediterranean.

Most domestic tourists spend a week or more at a beach resort, usually in vacation homes, and visit the large towns on day-trips. However, as it is unlikely that the average international visitor will select the German Baltic coast for a beach vacation, this chapter is arranged according to the larger towns rather than the coastal resorts. The chapter starts with Stralsund in the northeast and moves westward along the coast to Rostock, the largest city in the state, then Wismar, before turning slightly inland to Schwerin, the state capital.

History

Human settlements in Mecklenburg and Vorpommern date back to the Stone Age. However, written history starts in the 10th century, when the area was mostly populated by Slavic people. Saxon traders had successful commercial dealings deep into the territory, but missionaries had little initial success. During the 11th century, Emperor Friedrich I Barbarossa decided to Christianize the area and a campaign led by Saxon Duke Heinrich I der Löwe (the Lion) conquered most of the area. Schwerin was founded in 1160 as the first German town east of the Elbe.

Friedrich I Barbarossa

Due to the German custom of dividing territory among male sons, the area in subsequent centuries was repeatedly split and rejoined. Several cities became Free Imperial Cities and the foremost at the time formed the Hanseatic League in 1281. Although the League is most famous for monopolizing trade, it also fought some wars and in 1367 forced the Danish Kingdom out of the Eastern Baltic region.

The wealth and the power of the Hanseatic League lasted for three centuries and was finally broken during the Thirty Years' War. Mecklenburg and Pomerania accepted the Lutheran Reformation early on and fought against the imperial troops. At the Peace of Westphalia (1648), Sweden gained control of Wismar and most of Vorpommern. During the Nordic War (1700-20), Prussia gained parts of Vorpommern and, after the Napoleonic Wars, took control of all previous Swedish territories. Mecklenburg remained independent until it became part of the German Empire in 1871.

During World War II, the port cities suffered from air raids. Shortly after the war the population in the area doubled due to refugees and German people transported from Pomerania and other areas that were lost mainly to Poland. (Vorpommern is usually translated as Western Pomerania, but literally means Before Pomerania, as distinct from Pomerania itself, which was long Prussian but now part of Poland.)

In the Communist era, Rostock was the gateway to East Germany for the rest of the world and the harbor was expanded. Shipping became the major industry and, following the *Wende*, massive unemployment resulted as bloated Socialist institutions could not compete with Western industries. Fifteen years after joining the Federal Republic of Germany, the area still has unemployment levels well over 20%. Tourism has taken over as the main industry and, as in most former East German states, the population is declining due to a declining birthrate and people leaving to seek employment.

■ Transportation

By Rail: Mecklenburg-Vorpommern has good railway connections although high-speed trains to the rest of Germany usually require transfers in Hamburg or Berlin – each is two hours from Rostock by an hourly train.

The northern towns, described in this chapter, have at least hourly rail connections. Schwerin to Wismar takes 40 minutes, Wismar to Rostock, Schwerin to Rostock, and Stralsund to Rostock, each takes an hour, mostly on local Regional Express trains.

By Road: Since the *Wende*, major Autobahns are being constructed in Mecklenburg-Vorpommern and new stretches are opened to traffic regularly. However, many segments are still incomplete, leading to severe bottlenecks at places – driving the 25 km (15 miles) from Lübeck to where the A20 starts, for example, can take well over an hour.

The A20 connects the towns in the northern part of the state. The stretches between Wismar and Rostock are complete, with an extension to Stralsund due for completion later this decade. The excellent A24 connects Hamburg and Berlin and has completed highway connections to Schwerin (A241) and Rostock (A19).

Most of the pleasures and beauty of the state are off the highways on country lanes. Although the roads are generally in good condition, traveling in Mecklenburg-Vorpommern by road tends to be slow, as most roads pass through small villages rather than around them. In addition, many country roads are *allées* (tree-lined boulevards) where overtaking is difficult and often impossible for long stretches. Speed restrictions are often in place and strictly enforced – all those trees provide excellent hiding places for speed cameras. It is sensible to drive with lights switched on, even on a sunny day.

CYCLING

Mecklenburg-Vorpommern is rather flat and easy cycling territory. A popular cycling route is the Ostseeküsten-Radweg (Baltic Coast Cycling Route) along the coast from Lübeck to Stralsund. It can easily be done in a week with stages ranging from 35 to 60 km (21-36 miles) per day. Many tourism offices arrange packages that include accommodation and luggage transfers.

By Air: The largest airport in the state is **Rostock-Laage**, Parkstraße 105, 18299 Weitendorf, ☎ (038454)31-323, www.rostock-flughafen.de. It is served mainly by charter flights, but has some flights by **Cirrus Airlines** (www.cirrus-world.de) to Munich. It is 35 km (21 miles) south of Rostock and best reached by private transport. A limited bus service is available. Taxis cost around €35 from the airport to Rostock station. For most travelers, coming into Hamburg or Berlin is more feasible.

By Boat: Mecklenburg-Vorpommern has excellent car ferry connections to Scandinavia and the Baltic states. **Scandlines** vessels (☎ 0381-543-5309, www.scandlines.de) depart mostly from Rostock, although some also sail from Sassnitz-Neu Mukran on Rügen Island.

Between seven and nine ships sail daily on the two-hour route from Rostock to Gedser in Denmark. Three ships per day do the Rostock to Trelleborg, Sweden route in just under six hours. Five departures per day sail from Sassnitz to Trelleborg in under four hours. A twice-weekly ferry sails from

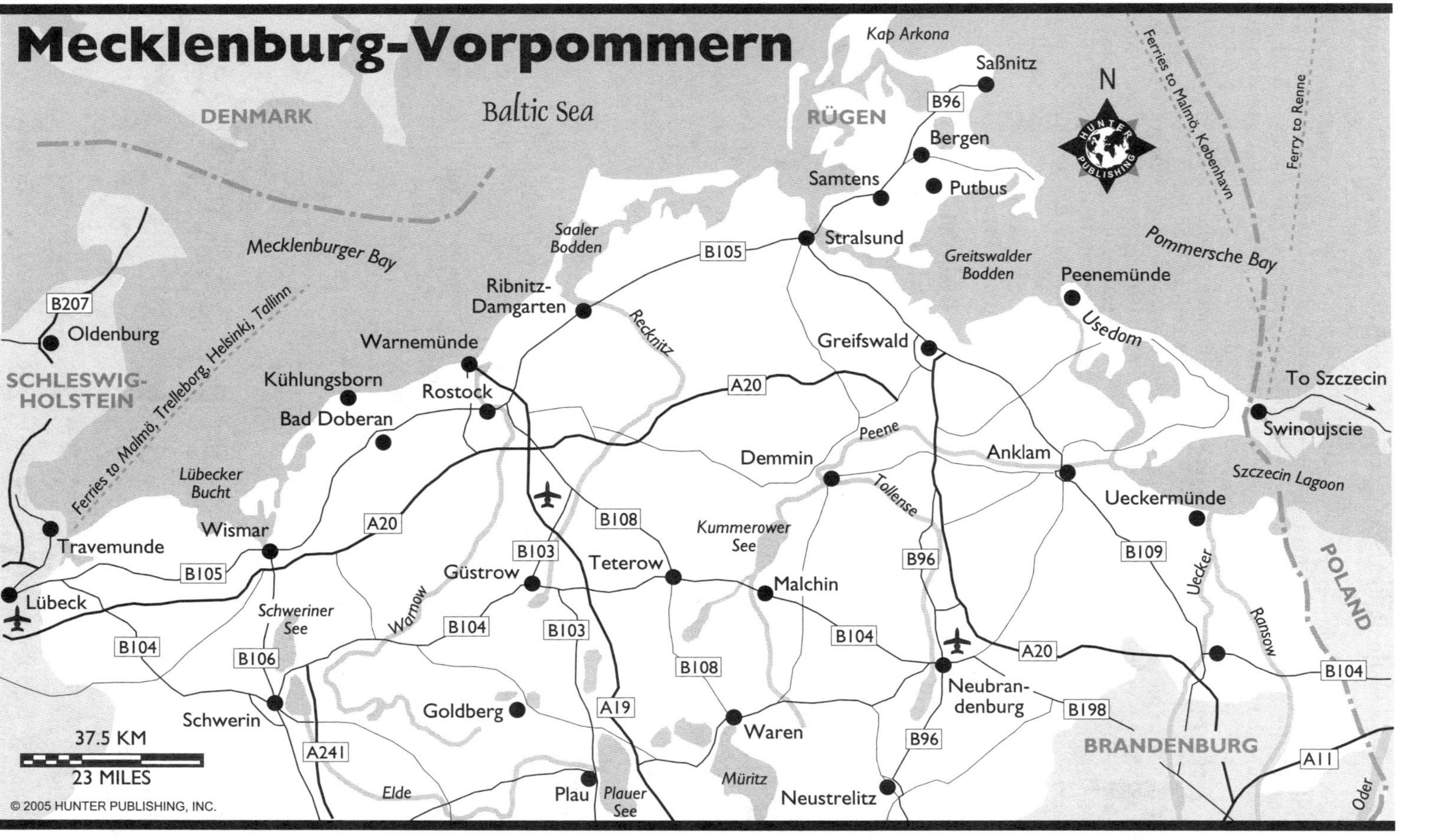

Mecklenburg-Vorpommern

Rostock to Liepaja in Letland, taking about 24 hours.

In the summer season, ferry services are available from Sassnitz on Rügen to Ronne on Bornholm (Denmark). The journey is just under four hours.

■ Information Sources

Tourismusverband Mecklenburg-Vorpommern, Platz der Freundschaft 1, 18059 Rostock, ☎ 0381-403-0500, www.auf-nach-mv.de, is responsible for the entire state. They can make reservations for accommodation, events, and all kinds of package deals.

The Mecklenburg-Vorpommern Festival

This Festspiele (Festival) annually arranges about 100 concerts at some 60 venues in the state. The emphasis is on classical music. Tickets and schedules are available from Festspiele MV, Graf-Schack-Allee 11, 19053 Schwerin, ☎ 0385-591-8585, www.festspiele-mv.de.

■ Stralsund

Of all the large towns in Mecklenburg-Vormpommern, Stralsund is arguably the most interesting and most beautiful. It has several brick Gothic buildings, which bear testimony to the wealth and power this town once enjoyed as a leading member of the Hanseatic League. Its strategic position, surrounded by water on all sides, made it the envy of many rivals, but also allowed it to beat off all comers while the Hanseatic League was operational. Nowadays, the water enhances the beauty of the town and allows for many water-related activities.

Stralsund received town rights in 1234 and in 1293 joined Lübeck, Wismar, Rostock, and Greifswald in forming the Hanseatic League. The town experienced three centuries of prosperity, with its greatest moment also that of the Hanseatic League – the Peace of Stralsund in 1370 by which the Danish Kingdom was forced to give up all rights in the eastern Baltic areas.

During the Thirty Years' War, Stralsund was unsuccessfully besieged by the Imperial armies led by Wallenstein and, in the Peace of Westphalia, it was awarded to Sweden. It became Prussian in 1815. During the Communist era, the town gained importance due to the loss of competing harbors such as Stettin to Poland.

Despite neglect during Communist rule, it managed to preserve many historic buildings and, since the *Wende*, massive efforts have been made to restore buildings of historical value. Although Stralsund's old town was added to the UNESCO World Cultural Heritage list in 2002, the general state of repair of many areas is still a far cry from the pristine condition of former West German cities such as Lübeck.

Information Sources

Tourist Office: Tourist information is available from **Stralsund Information**, Alter Markt 9, 18439 Stralsund, ☎ 03831-24-690, www.stralsund.de.

Transportation

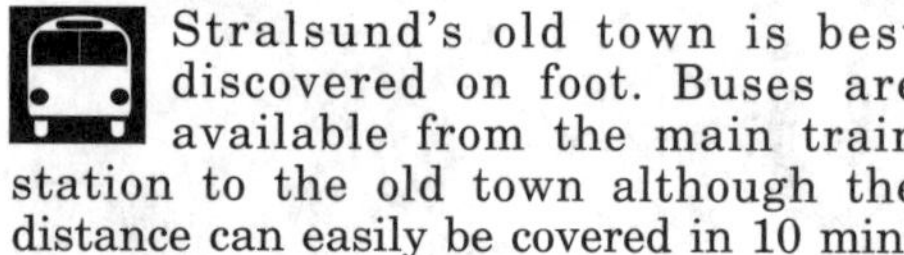

Stralsund's old town is best discovered on foot. Buses are available from the main train station to the old town although the distance can easily be covered in 10 minutes on foot.

Sightseeing

Stralsund's old town is compact and can easily be explored on foot. A good place to start is at the Alter Markt and then move along to Neuer Markt. From here stroll to the harbor via the Heilgeistkirche if interested.

Rathaus

Alter Markt

The large Alter Markt (Old Market Square) is dominated by the Rathaus and the Nikolaikirche. The early 13th-century **Rathaus** (Town Hall), ☎ 03831-2520, is a brick Gothic masterpiece. The brick façade facing the market square was added around 1400 and is adorned by the shields of the foremost Hanseatic members. The Renaissance staircase was added in 1579. Behind the arcades that served as market hall is a lovely 17th-century gallery, now with a protective glass roof.

Nikolaikirche doorway

Closely integrated with the Rathaus is the **Nikolaikirche** (St Nicholas Church), Alter Markt, ☎ 03831-297-199, the oldest church in Stralsund. It was erected between 1270 and 1360 following the example of the Marienkirche in Lübeck. Following a fire in 1662, the 104-m (310-foot) south tower received a Baroque roof, while that of the north tower remained flat. The brick Gothic church has no transept and the side aisles are low, in contrast to the high nave. Some of the original colorful wall paintings survived. The church has a wealth of art treasures – of particular note are the St Anne figure dating from before 1280, the crucifix of the high altar dating back to 1360, and an astronomical clock. Opening hours are Sunday, year-round from 11:15 am to noon, and 2 to 4 pm. From Monday to Saturday, it is open from April to September, 10 am to 5 pm, and from October to March, 10 am to noon and 2 to 4 pm.

St Anne, Nikolaikirche

On the north side of the square, is the interesting façade of the **Wulflamhaus**. This brick Gothic house dates from 1380. It has a high gable with turrets and candlesnuffer rooftops, blending well with the design of the Rathaus. On the east side of the square is the Baroque **Commandanten-Hus**, the residence of the town commander during Swedish rule.

Neuer Markt

The shortest way from the Alter Markt to the Neuer Markt is via the Rathaus and the pedestrian zone, which is lined with shops. If time is available, turn left into Böttcherstraße to see the **Jakobikirche** (St James' Church), Jakobiturmstraße, ☎ 03831-290-446, built during the 14th century. It was severely damaged by a thunderbolt in 1662 and the reconstruction was almost completely destroyed by air raids in 1944. The interior is rather bare and in the process of a rather leisurely reconstruction.

Following the pedestrian route automatically leads you to the former **Katharinenkloster** (St Catherine's Monastery), Katherinenberg 14-20, which was founded in the 13th century as a Dominican monastery. Since 1951, the former monastery has housed the **Deutsches Meeresmuseum** (German Maritime Museum), ☎ 03831-265-010, www.meeresmuseum.de. The museum is the largest of its kind in central Europe and has exhibitions on fisheries and sea life in general. The monastery's originally 73-m (234-foot) triple nave hall church is the heart of the museum with a 50,000-liter (11,000-gallon) tank in the former crypt filled with tropical fish. Opening hours are daily from 10 am to 5 pm, but closing at 6 pm from June to September.

Also in the monastery, but enter from Mönchstraße 25, is the **Kulturhistorisches Museum** (Cultural History), ☎ 03831-28-790. It has been in existence since 1859 and focuses on the archeological finds, arts, crafts, and culture of Vorpommern. It is open Tuesday to Sunday from 10 am to 5 pm.

The monumental **Marienkirche**, Neuer Markt, ☎ 03831-298-965, was built between 1384 and 1478. It is the largest medieval church in the town and the last major brick Gothic basilica built in northern Europe. It has a precious Baroque organ. The 104-m (330-foot) tower

Marienkirche interior

can be scaled for superb views. Organ music is played at 11 am on Tuesday and Thursday. The church is open daily from May to October, 10 am to 5 pm, and from November to April, 10 am to noon and 2 to 4 pm.

Cultural Events & Festivals

Most Baltic harbor cities have annual sail **regattas**. Stralsund's, held in mid-June, is one of the smaller ones. Races include courses around the islands Rügen and Hiddensee.

End July sees the three-day **Wallensteintage**. The name commemorates Wallenstein's unsuccessful siege of the town during the Thirty Years' War. It comprises arts and crafts markets, cultural events, and ample food and drink. The Alter Markt is the main location, but stalls stretch all the way to the yacht harbor.

Like most German towns, Stralsund also has a lovely **Christmas Market**, with the main part around the Rathaus. However, note that this market breaks up after the second weekend of December.

Both the Nikolaikirche and Marienkirche are venues for frequent concerts. Organ concerts are scheduled on Wednesdays at 8 pm, alternating between these two churches. In the Marienkirche, organ music is played at 11 am on Tuesday and Thursday. The Nikolaikirche has frequent additional organ and choral concerts; schedules are available from the Nikolaikantor, ☎ 03831-298-371, st.nikolai@t-online.de.

Adventures

On Foot

Town Walks: The tourism office conducts guided walking tours of the old town from May to October daily at 11 am and 2 pm. The meeting point is at the tourism office near the Rathaus. The tourism office has handy free flyers with a map for a self-guided walking tour too.

On Wheels

By Bicycle: The flat land of Stralsund makes it ideal bicycling country. The network of dedicated cycling routes is steadily increasing. Bicycles can be rented from **SIC Fahrradverleih** on Neue Badenstraße 4, ☎ 03831-280-155, near the harbor, or from **Tribseer Damm**, ☎ 03831-306-185, near the main station.

By Hummelbahn: The Hanse-Bahn, Zudarerweg 18, ☎ 03831-49-0372, operates a motorized train with 40-minute city and harbor tours from end April to late October from the Neuer Markt near the Marienkirche. Note that the service only operates if enough people board.

On Water

Boat Rental: Rowing and pedal boats can be rented from **Bootsklause**, Knieperdamm 80a, ☎ 03831-392-862.

Yacht Charter: Yachts can be chartered from several institutions in Stralsund, including:

- **Yachtcharter am Klabautermannac**, Am Querkanal, ☎ 03831-293-628.
- **Yachtcharterservice K Küstner**, Rudenstraße 2, ☎ 03831-280-117.
- **Hansecharter**, Seestraße 3, ☎ 03831-348-953.

Harbor Cruises: The **Weiße Flotte**, Fährstraße 16, ☎ 03831-268-116, www.weisee-flotte.com, arranges one-hour harbor cruises that also go around Dänholm island. Departures are from the yacht harbor (Yachthafen).

Where to Stay & Eat

The most pleasant hotel in Stralsund is the **Steigenberger Hotel Baltic**. It is near the Heilgeistspital on the edge of the old town area. Rooms are stylish and comfortably furnished with views of the old town or across the harbor toward Rügen island. The Steigenberger's restaurant (€-€€) serves light regional cuisine with a strong emphasis on seafood. Frankendamm 22, 18439 Stralsund, ☎ 03831-2040, fax 03831-204-999, www.steigenberger.de. (€€-€€€)

In the old town, at Neuer Markt, is the luxurious privately managed **Hotel Zur Post**. It opened in 1995 in a new building in this historic area. Rooms are modern and comfortable. The restaurant at the Zur Post (€-€€) serves hearty local dishes. Am Neuer Markt, Tribseer Straße 22, 18439 Stralsund, ☎ 03831-200-500, fax

03831-200-510, www.hotel-zur-post-stralsund.de. (€€-€€€)

The **Intercity Hotel** was constructed in 1999 and offers modern rooms and facilities. Rooms are well-equipped and, although the focus is on the business traveler, leisure travelers will also appreciate its convenient location in between the station and the old town. It is linked to the Hansecenter office and shopping complex. The room key gives free access to local transportation. Tribeer Damm 76, 18437 Stralsund, ☎ 03831-2020, fax 03831-202-599, www.intercityhotel.de. (€€-€€€)

Also constructed in 1999 is the luxury **Dorint im HanseDom**. It is about two km (1.2 miles) from the old town and integrated into the large Hansedom water fun park. Rooms are elegant and comfortable. Grünhufer Bogen 18-20, 18437 Stralsund-Grünhufe, ☎ 03831-37-730, fax 03831-377-3100, www.dorint.de. (€€€-€€€€)

The **Tafelfreuden im Sommerhaus**, Jungfernsteig 8a, ☎ 03831-299-260, is an upscale restaurant in a Swedish summer-house building across the Knieper pond from the old town. Light Mediterranean cuisine is served. Open only for dinner during the week, but also for lunch over weekends. (€€-€€€)

On the Alter Markt is the pleasant **Goldener Löwe**, Alter Markt 1, ☎ 03831-306-390. It serves mainly Mediterranean and regional dishes. The large windows and terrace seats allow good views of the square and Rathaus. (€-€€)

■ Rügen Island

Rügen is Germany's largest island. Its area is 926 km² (358 square miles), but with a population of only 77,000. It is a popular holiday destination for Germans of all ages but seems to attract especially large numbers of retirees and young families. During the high season in July and August it can be uncomfortably crowded but a month earlier or later parts can be deserted and prices much lower.

Information Sources

Tourist Office: Tourismuszentral Rügen, Markt 4, 18528 Bergen, ☎ 03838-80-770, www.ruegen.de.

Transportation

Rügen is connected to the mainland at Stralsund by a 2½-km (1½-mile) road and rail bridge that gets crowded during the season. Railway connections are available from Stralsund to the major towns.

A narrow-gauge steam engine, the Rasende Roland (see *Adventures* below), connects Putbus with the resort towns of Binz, Sellin, Baabe, and Göhren. Bus services are available to most parts of the island.

Travelling on Rügen is slow even by Mecklenburg-Vorpommern standards. Around 80% of the roads are tree-lined *allées*, making overtaking hazardous and often impossible for long stretches. The island has an unusually large number of speed cameras – many brochures handed out at hotels have maps with the positions of the cameras clearly marked.

Ferries to Scandinavia depart from Sassnitz.

Sightseeing

The main attraction at Rügen is the white, sandy beaches but there are a few places worth seeing as well as enough minor sights to keep visitors busy during a rainy spell. However, Rügen does claim the highest number of sunshine hours in Germany.

Resort Towns

The main beach resort towns are on the east coast. The largest and most elegant town is **Binz** – cars from all parts of Germany line the streets on sunny weekends and during the summer season. The town has the longest seaside promenade on the island. It also has the largest collection of **Bäderarchitektur** (resort architecture) buildings that survived from the late 19th century. Often Art Nouveau, these buildings are characterized by corner towers, gables, and balconies.

FKK & NUDIST BEACHES

Freikörperkultur (FKK), literally free body culture, used to be popular in the former East Germany. In a country where freedom of expression was strictly repressed, the freedom to go nude at the beach, swimming pool, or wherever was treasured and frequently practiced. Immediately following the *Wende*, East Germans got tired of being laughed at by West German tourists and nude beaches disappeared almost overnight. However, in recent years, nude beaches have made a comeback and most Baltic Sea resorts have nude beaches, usually at the far ends of the regular beach areas. Nude beaches are denoted as FKK and non-nude beaches as "Textil." Still, many locals can't be bothered to schlep themselves to the far edges before stripping.

One of the most popular destinations on the island is the **Jagdschloss Granitz** (Hunting Castle), ☎ 038393-2263, a few km south of Binz. It was erected by Prince Malte (see Putbus** below) in 1836 in a Neo-Gothic Tudor style. It is on the highest point in this part of the island – the 107-m (351-foot) Tempelberg, offering grand views of the surroundings. From Binz, it is best approached by walking or public transportation. Drivers have to pay for parking as well as for the shuttle bus from the parking lot to the castle itself. Opening hours are daily from 9 am to 6 pm.

South of Binz are the resort towns of Sellin, Baabe and Göhren. All are much smaller and less elegant than Binz – they do offer more peace and quiet though. It's worth stopping in **Sellin** to see the impressive 400-m (1,280-foot) pier with its two-level restaurant. Here the beach is 70 m (220 feet) lower than the town – an elevator is available.

Putbus

The most interesting town on the island is Putbus, also known as the "white town" as all buildings here were painted white. The center of the town was laid out from 1808 in a Neo-Classical style by Prince Wilhelm Malte. His palace was destroyed in the 1960s but many of the oddities he created here survived.

At the heart of the town is the **Circus**, a huge roundabout surrounded by large, white, mid-19th-century Neo-Classical buildings. A high obelisk with the prince's crown on top is in the center of the circus. Some of the buildings once housed an elite school but it has moved downmarket from the end of the 19th century and currently houses a special needs school.

From the Circus, Alleestraße leads to the **Markt**, where the 1819 Classical Theater has pride of place. It is the only true theater on Rügen and its excellent acoustics are appreciated mostly by visitors during summer performances.

Across Alleestraße is the 185-acre **Schlosspark** (Palace Park). It was laid out as an English-style landscape garden in the early 19th century. During summer, several cafés are open inside the park.

Prora

Four km (2.4 miles) north of Binz is Prora, one of the oddest places on this island. Here a building 4½ km (2.7 miles) long, six stories high runs parallel to the lovely white, soft sand beach. This monstrosity, known as the **Koloss** (colossus) of Prora was erected between 1936 and 1939 by the Nazis as a vacation resort for up to 20,000 party members at a time. The outbreak of World War II meant that the Nazis never used it. After the war, the East German army used the grounds for training purposes.

Since the *Wende*, debate has been raging on what to do with this eyesore. It is now a protected building, so property developers cannot tear it down, but it is still searching for a purpose. At the moment it houses among other things a disco and several museums, best left for rainy days. The museum themes include railways, the East German Army, a touch-and-feel science exhibition, a documentation center, a water world, and a graphic art gallery. The museums are generally open daily from 10 am to 5 pm. Some close during the winter season.

The beach is popular with locals – it is less crowded than the resort towns and more beautiful, provided eyes are directed toward the sea.

Prora can be reached by private car or by frequent shuttle services from Binz and other coastal resort towns.

Königstuhl

A popular hiking area is the **National Park Jasmund**, www.koenigsstuhl.com, just north of Sassnitz. The top destination is the chalk cliffs at Stubbenkammer. The most famous viewing point is Königstuhl, a 117-m (384-foot) cliff projecting over the

Burg Maus, St. Goarshausen (© Rheinland-Pfalz Tourismus/Piel Media)

Above: The Marksburg at Braubach, the only undamaged medieval castle on this stretch of the Rhine

Below: Boppard – the Rhine's sharpest hairpin curve

(both © Rheinland-Pfalz Tourismus / Piel Media)

View of the Dom at Trier (© *Rheinland-Pfalz Tourismus/Piel Media*)

Above: Reichsburg Castle, Cochem

Below: Mainz, the Romanesque Cathedral (both © Rheinland-Pfalz Tourismus/Piel M

sea. No less impressive, and generally a lot more peaceful, is the view from nearby Victoria-Sicht (Victoria's View). To reach the area by car, park in Hagen – the parking area is well-signposted. From here, it is an easy three-km (1.8-mile) hike through a thick forest along a clearly marked trail. Alternatively, take the shuttle bus, which runs every 10 minutes. Admission is charged to enter Königstuhl (€1) but it's free to Victoria-Sicht. The best views are early in the morning when the white cliffs change color with the rising sun and before the hordes of bus tour groups arrive. However, bear in mind that these cliffs are fairly small in comparison to other parts of Europe such as Normandy or Dover.

Cultural Events & Festivals

Most evenings at 8 pm, Binz has free, open-air concerts of varying quality at the Kurhaus.

A cultural highlight is the **Störtebeker Festival**, Am Bodden 100, Ralswiek, ☎ 03838-31-100, www.stoertebeker.de, held annually in July and August. It recalls the life of Klaus Störtebeker, below, a famous Rügen pirate, cum Robin Hood of the Seas, who was executed in 1401 at Hamburg. The performance in a huge, open-air natural theater in Ralswiek involves around 20 actors, 120 extras, 30 horses, and several ships.

Adventures

On Foot

Countryside Hikes: Hiking is popular on Rügen. A favored area is the **National Park Jasmund**, which has several well-marked routes including the three-km (1.8-mile) direct route from the parking lot to the Königsstuhl and longer routes leading to other viewing points.

Several routes lead from the popular seaside resort town of Binz through the Granitz Forest. The Hochuferweg (High Water Route) runs along the beach from Binz to Sellin – about six km (3.6 miles). Also popular is the seven-km (4.2-mile) route through the forest via the Jagdschloss Granitz.

On Wheels

By Bicycle: In Binz, bicycles can be rented from **Pauli's Radshop**, Hauptstraße 9a, ☎ 038393-66-924. Many hotels also rent bicycles but usually only to overnight guests.

By Train: A narrow-gauge steam railway operates between Putbus and Göhren via Binz, Sellin, and Baabe. The so-called **Rasender Roland**, Binzer Straße 12, 18581 Putbus, ☎ 038301-80-112, www.rasender-roland.de, runs about 12 times per day and completes the full journey in just over an hour.

In the Air

Sightseeing Flights: To see Rügen from the air, contact **Ostsee Flug Rügen**, Flugplatz Güttin, 18573 Güttin, ☎ 038306-1289, www.flugplatz-ruegen.de. Flights range from 12 to 60 minutes and from €20 to €100.

On Water

Being an island, watersports opportunities abound.

Fishing: Deep sea fishing can be arranged by **Wünscher**, Kapitänsweg 4, 18546 Sassnitz, ☎ 038392-32-180, www.kalinin-sassnitz.de.

Canoeing & Kayaking: Canoes and catamarans can be rented from **Wasersportschue Timpeltu**, Strandpromenade, 18528 Lietzow, ☎ 0180-584-673-588, www.timpeltu.com.

Sailing & Yacht Charters: Yachts and other sailing vessels can be chartered from several companies, including:

- **IM Jaich**, Am Yachthafen, 18581 Lauterbach, ☎ 038301-8090, www.im-jaich.de (motorboats and sea kayaks are also available).
- **Windjammer Reederei Rügen**, Puddemin Nr 1, 18574 Poseritz, ☎ 0170-381-7513, www.yachtcharter-ruegen.de.

Coastal Cruises: Several boats connect the coastal resorts of east Rügen by boat. Many also offer cruises to see the white cliffs at Königsstuhl from the sea.

- **Reederei Lojewski**, Schlossallee 4, 18546 Sassnitz, ☎ 038392-35-136, www.reederei-lojewski.de, has several cruises per day from Sassnitz to the cliffs.

- **Reederei Ostsee-tour**, Hafenstraße 12j, 18546 Sassnitz, ☎ 038392-3150, www.reederei-ostsee-tour.de, has various cruises connecting the east coast resorts and continuing to the white cliffs.

Where to Stay & Eat

Generally, the nicest town to stay in is Binz. The town has accommodation and restaurant facilities in all price classes. Most hotels listed below are on the pedestrians-only beach promenade. However, the town is long and narrow, meaning even inland accommodation is within five blocks from the beach.

The **Travel Charme Hotel Kurhaus Binz** has one of the best locations in town. It is in the Kurhaus close to the pier and all the major restaurants and other attractions. Rooms are luxurious with bright colors. Strandpromenade 27, 18609 Binz, ☎ 038393-6650, fax 038393-665-555, www.tc-hotels.de. (€€€€)

The restaurant **Surf'n Turf** (€-€€€) is at the promenade level of the Travel Charme Hotel and has several budget options, especially during lunch time.

The super-luxurious **Kempinski Resort Hotel Bel Air** is some distance from the heart of the town. The hotel is spread over several connected buildings. Rooms are large and posh. The beauty spa area is enormous and exclusively for hotel guests. Strandpromenade 7, 18609 Binz, ☎ 038393-150, fax 038393-555, www.kempinski-ruegen.de. (€€€€)

The elegant **Ruiani** (€€-€€€), serving international and nouvelle cuisine, is the best of the three restaurants at the Kempinski.

The **Dorint Strandhotel** is in a new, modern building. Rooms are large and stylish with south European style furniture. The hotel often has good deals in the shoulder season. Strandpromenade 58, 18609 Binz, ☎ 038393-430, fax 038393-43-100, www.dorint.de (€€-€€€€).

The restaurant **Olivio** (€€-€€€) at the Dorint serves Mediterranean cuisine.

The **Loew Hotel**, a few blocks inland, offers good value. Bedrooms are large and modern with elegant bathrooms. The hotel is in the main shopping and restaurant street just minutes from the beach. Hauptstraße 22, 18609 Binz, ☎ 038393-390, fax 038393-39-444, www.loew.de. (€-€€)

Camping

Rügen has several large campgrounds. Some of the better ones include:

Regenbogen Resort Nonnevitz is huge, with 600 spaces in the north of the island near Kap Arkona. It has lots of natural vegetation and is only a dune away from a two-km (1.2-mile) beach. It has excellent facilities and is open from April to October. 18556 Dranske, ☎ 038391-89-032, fax 038391-8765, www.regenbogen-resorts.de.

Camping Gross Banzelvitz is at the center of the island next to the Jasmunder lagoon. It is in a forested area with good facilities and has 180 spaces for tourists. Open from March to October. 18528 Rappin, ☎ 03838-31-248, fax 03838-31-260, www.banzelvitzer-berge.de.

Ostsee Camping Göhren is at the south of the island with 400 tourist and 500 long-term spaces. It is next to the beach about a km from the center of town. 18586 Göhren, ☎ 038308-90-120, fax 038308-2123, www.regenbogen-resorts.de.

■ Rostock

With just over 200,000 inhabitants, this is by far the largest city in Mecklenburg-Vorpommern. It has the fifth-largest port in Germany, and during the Communist era served as East Germany's main trading port. After the *Wende,* it suffered the ignominy of being passed over in the choice of state capital in favor of Schwerin, only half its size.

Rostock received town rights in 1218 and developed into a prosperous and strong city during the Hanseatic League era. It bought the small town of Warnemünde in 1323 to ensure control of the mouth of the Warnow River. Its university, founded in 1419, is the oldest in northern Europe. Following the Thirty Years' War, Rostock experienced a decline until renewed sailing ship activities on the Baltic Sea led to renewed growth in the 18th century.

Rostock's major shipbuilding industries made it a prime target during World War II. Air raids from 1942 onwards reduced most of the historic old town to rubble. During the Communist rule, little was spent on maintenance and several eyesores were erected. The outskirts of Rostock are still littered with Communist-era square buildings, but since the *Wende,* much of the old town has been restored and beautified, making it worth a stopover. Warnemünde is a popular beach resort, packed with visitors on weekends and during the summer season.

Information Sources

Tourist Office: Tourist information is available from **TI Stadtzentrum**, Neuer Markt 3, 18055 Rostock, ☎ 0381-381-2222, www.rostock.de.

Transportation

The old town is best explored on foot, but buses and trams operate inside the city and are convenient from the old town to Warnemünde. Driving through Rostock is slow, street parking limited and time restricted, but ample parking garages are available.

Sightseeing

Rostock was heavily bombed during the Second World War and suffered more damage than other Baltic harbors. Neglect and socialist-style planned developments did not enhance the cityscape either. Since the *Wende*, much has been done to restore the historically significant buildings that survived. The major sights can be seen in half a day.

ROSTOCK MONEY SAVING CARDS

The Rostock card costs €8 per person and is valid for 48 hours. It gives free access to all local transportation and a free city tour, as well as discounts to many other sights. It only pays off if public transportation is used. The card is available from the tourist office, museums, many hotels, and bus ticket machines. Admission to Rostock's museums is €4 to each per person, or €7.50 for all museums.

Neuer Markt Area

The monumental **Marienkirche** (St Mary's Church), Am Ziegenmarkt, ☎ 0381-492-3396, www.marienkirche-rostock.de, is one of the most interesting

examples of brick Gothic in northern Germany. The original hall church of 1260 was converted to a basilica in 1290 following the example of the Marienkirche in Lübeck. The church was only completed in the mid-15th century. The multiple changes in floor plans during the long building period gave it somewhat odd proportions – the nave seems too short for the 31-m (102-foot) ceiling. The church has several art works of note, including a bronze baptismal font (1290), a huge astrological clock (designed in 1472 but altered in 1643) that has a calendar up to 2017, and a magnificent Baroque organ (1769). The church is often used for concerts. It is open from May to September, Monday to Saturday, 10 am to 6 pm, and Sunday from 11:15 am to 5 pm. From October to April, it is open Monday to Saturday, 10 am to 12:15 pm and 2 to 4 pm, but Sunday only from 11:15 am to noon.

The huge **Neuer Markt** has several fine gabled buildings. The most interesting is the **Rathaus**, ☎ 0381-3810, which was formed in the 13th century by joining three existing houses. Only a small part of the original brick façade can be seen, as a Baroque façade was added in the early 18th century. Most of the buildings on the south and north sides of the square were destroyed in the war, but some modern ones were built to blend in with the traditional style. The Alte Post building, which houses the post office and tourism office, was built in the mid-1950s.

Steinstraße leads from the Neuer Markt to **Steintor**, one of only four of the original 22 city gates that survived. This Reniassance gate was erected in 1577. The surviving part of the city's defense wall to the left leads to the oldest gate, the 13th-century **Kuhtor**.

Near Steintor is the interesting **Schifffahrtsmuseum** (Shipping/Naviga-

Steintor

tional Museum), corner of Augsut-Bebl-Straße & Richard-Wagner-Straße, ☎ 0381-492-2697. It uses models, paintings, photographs, and original shipping-related items to illustrate the history of shipping from the Vikings up to the *Wende*. In addition to several scale models, it also has a full-size bridge from a trading vessel. The displays are often a bit old fashioned, but that in itself is interesting from a cultural-historical standpoint. Opening hours are Tuesday to Sunday from 10 am to 6 pm. Admission is €4.

The Best Views

The best views of Rostock are from the top of the 117-m (386-foot) tower of the **Petrikirche** (St Peter's Church), Alter Markt, ☎ 0381-21-101. This 14th-century basilica was severely damaged during the war but rebuilt. The interior is rather bare and the main draw is the tower – still the highest construction in town. It can be ascended by elevator in 26 seconds or via 196 stairs. The Petrikirche is at the Alter Markt – 15 minutes walk northeast of the Neuer Markt. Opening hours are daily from 10 am to 5 pm, but closing at 4 pm on weekdays between November and March.

Kröperliner Straße

Most of Rostock's sights are along or near **Kröpeliner Straße**, which runs from Neuer Markt westward to Köpeliner Tor. The street is for pedestrians only and is lined with shops of all kinds. Most of the gabled houses here date from the 17th to 19th centuries, but a few are older and some modern ones added gables to blend in harmoniously with the historic character of the area. The most interesting is the 15th-century brick Gothic **Haus Ratschow** at No 82 – currently the town library.

The triangular **Universitätsplatz** (University Square) is a popular meeting place. On its south side are the Baroque **Saalgebäude** (1750) and the adjacent former **ducal palace** (1712). Nearby, in a former monastery, is the interesting **Kulturhistorisches Museum** (Cultural History), Kloster zum Heiligen Kreuz, Klosterhof, ☎ 0381-203-590. The former monastery church, dating from the 13th century, now houses the best pieces from the religious art collection. In addition to items from the town's history, the museum also has a noteworthy collection of Dutch paintings and drawings. Opening hours are Tuesday to Sunday from 1:30 to 6 pm. Admission is €4.

Kröpeliner Straße ends at the imposing 14th-century brick **Kröpeliner Tor** (Gate). It houses the **Stadtgeschichtliches Museum** (Local History), Kröpeliner Straße, ☎ 0381-454-177. The section of the town wall leading from here towards Schwaansche Straße still has some half-round guardhouses from the 14th century. Opening hours are Tuesday to Sunday from 10 am to 1 pm. Admission is €4.

Warnemünde

Warnemünde, bought by Rostock in 1323, is a small seaside resort 11 km (six miles) to the north. It is popular with vacationers as well as with luxury cruise ships – up to 50 stop here annually.

Apart from the beach and promenade, the main sights are along the pedestrian street Am Strom. As the German name indicates, this road is next to the river and lined with gabled houses now used as restaurants and bars. In the vicinity are the yacht harbor, the 1898 lighthouse, and the Westmole, a pier extending 500 m (1,640 feet) out into the sea, allowing splendid views of the ocean-going vessels entering the canal en route to Rostock harbor.

Cultural Events & Festivals

The **Hanse Sail Rostock** is the largest maritime event along the coast of Mecklenburg-Vorpommern. During the second weekend of August, around 200 large and historic sailing boats participate in regattas drawing a million spectators. It is possible to sail as passenger on a tall ship or to follow the spectacle from a seaplane. For reservations contact **Tall-Ship Buchungszentrale Hanse Sail Verein**, Warnowufer 65, 18057 Rostock, ☎ 0381-208-5226, www.hansesail.com.

The **Marienkirche** is often used for concerts with organ, choral, and trumpet concerts particularly popular. Most concerts are scheduled during the summer or in Advent.

Adventures

On Foot

Town Walks: The tourist office arranges Old Town guided walking tours starting from its offices on Neuer Markt. From November to April, the tour is on Saturday at 2 pm, from May to October, Monday to Saturday at 2 pm and Sunday at 11 am.

Similar tours of Warnemünde start from the tourist office in Am Strom 59, April to October on Thursday at 11 am.

On Wheels

By Bicycle: Bicycles can be rented from the Hauptbahnhof, Konrad-Adenauer-Platz 1, ☎ 0381 2523990. A pleasant cycling route is along the Baltic Sea coast from Warnemünde to Kühlungsborn via Bad Doberan and Heiligendamm.

By Train: Molli, Am Bahnhof, Bad Doberan, ☎ 038203-4150, www.molli-bahn.de, is a popular narrow-gauge steam train that runs from Bad Doberan to the seaside resort town of Kühlungsborn. The 15-km (nine-mile) route takes 40 minutes and makes various stops en route, including at the picturesque Heiligendamm. Parts of the line date back to 1886 and it has been in constant use since 1910. Three of the engines have been in use since 1932. Bad Doberan can be reached by at least hourly trains from Rostock in 19 minutes.

On Water

Fishing: For fishing on the Baltic Sea, contact **Angel- und Seetouristik**, Am Bahnhof 1, 18119 Warnemünde, ☎ 0381-519-2012, www.angeltouristik-mv.net. In addition to full boat charters, single seats on fishing boats are also available.

Canoeing & Kayaking: A popular five-day canoeing route is the 112 km (67 miles) along the Warnow River from Barnin, near Schwerin, to Rostock.

Wanderer, Dorfstrasse 16, 18276 Oldenstorf, ☎ 038458-8011, fax 038458-8012, www.wanderer-kanu-outdoor.de, arranges canoe and cycling trips along the Warnow River and its tributaries. A wide range of equipment is available for rent, including a hydro-bike.

Riverboats & Harbor Cruises: Several companies offer harbor and river cruises from either Rostock or Warnemünde. Most have several daily departures from Easter to October. In winter, cruises are available on weekends if the River Warnow is ice-free.

The **Blaue Flotte**, Wossidlostraße 8, ☎ 0381-686-3172, has daily departures from Rostock Stadthafen and Warnemünde Alter Strom. The **Gelbe Flotte**, Hinrichsdorf 1 B, ☎ 0381-669-980, www.gelbde-flotte.de, sails from Warnemünde Alter Strom. In addition to pleasure cruises, **Rostocker Personenschifffahrt**, Wossidlostraße 5, ☎ 0381-699-962, operates a shuttle service between Rostock and Warnemünde.

Many boats only depart if enough passengers are on board – companies operating from Warnmünde tend to sail more according to the time, rather than the number of passengers, but on a quiet day, it is best to check before boarding.

Sailing: Windsurfers and catamarans can be rented from **Wassersportschule Rostock**, Dünenweg, 18146 Markgrafenheide, ☎ 0381-200-9555, www.wassersportrostock.de. Kite surfing is also possible.

Windsurfers and catamarans can also be rented from **Wassersport Center**, Anglersteig 2, ☎ 038293-14-026, www.wassersport-center.de, in Kühlungsborn, the largest resort town in Mecklenburg-Vorpommern, a few km from Rostock. Waterskiing can be arranged.

Where to Stay & Eat

Rostock

The **Steigenberger Hotel Sonne** is on the Neuer Markt in the heart of Rostock's old town. Rooms are modern, stylish, and comfort-

HOTEL PRICE CHART	
Rates per room based on double occupancy, including taxes.	
€	Under €50
€€	€50-€100
€€€	€101-€150
€€€€	Over €150

able. Neuer Markt 2, 18055 Rostock, ☎ 0381-49-730, fax 0381-497-3351, www.steigenberger.de. (€€-€€€)

The elegant restaurant **Reuters** (€€-€€€) at the Sonne serves international and local dishes. The wine and beer pub "**Alte Apotheke**" has furniture from an old English pharmacy.

Equally convenient in the old town, but at Universitätsplatz in the pedestrian zone, is the **Courtyard by Marriott**. Although in a historic part of town, the hotel is modern with large stylish and comfortable rooms. Schwaansche Straße 6, 18055 Rostock ☎ 0381-49-700, fax 0381-497-0700, www.marriott.com. (€€-€€€)

The restaurant **Fischers Fritze** (€€-€€€) at the Marriott serves mainly seafood.

The **Intercity Hotel** is at the main station, which is south of the old town. The hotel has modern, well-equipped rooms aimed at the business traveler. The room key allows free local public transportation. Herweghstraße 51, 18055 Rostock, ☎ 0381-49-500, fax 0381-459-0999, www.intercityhotel.de. (€€)

Warnemünde

Warnemünde offers a number of alternatives to what is available in Rostock itself.

The **Neptun Hotel** is a modern high-rise building directly on the beach. Rooms are modern and comfortable with unbeatable sea views. The hotel has the only thalasso-therapy center in Germany. The restaurant (€€-€€€) at Neptun serves nouvelle cuisine and local specialties. Seestraße 19, 18119 Rostock-Warnemünde, ☎ 0381-770, fax 0381-54-023, www.hotel-neptun.de. (€€€-€€€€)

DINING PRICE CHART	
Price per person for an entrée, including water, beer or soft drink.	
€	Under €10
€€	€10-€20
€€€	€21-€35
€€€€	Over €35

The nearby **Strand-Hotel Hübner** is another comfortable hotel but closer to the harbor and lighthouse. Rooms are well-furnished with lightwood furniture; many have sea views. The Hübner's restaurant (€€) has a frequently varying menu that includes local and international dishes, often with strong Asian influences. Seestraße 12, 18119 Rostock-Warnemünde, ☎ 0381-54-340, fax 0381-543-4444, www.hotel-huebner.de. (€€-€€€)

Il Restorante, Am Strom 107, ☎ 0381-52-674, serves, not surprisingly, mostly Italian cuisine but also local specialties. The location on the second floor allows for good harbor views. (€€-€€€)

Camping

Campingpark Kühlungsborn near Rostock is a huge park with 300 spaces for tourists in addition to the 130 long-term ones. It has good facilities and is next to the beach at the edge of the town and is open from April to October. Waldstraße 16, 18225 Kühlungsborn, ☎ 038293-7195, fax 038293-7192, www.topcamping.de.

Excursions in the Bad Doberan Area

The main draws out of Rostock are the Münster in Bad Doberan, the Molli narrow-guage steam train (see *Adventures* above), and the coastal resorts of Heiligendamm and Kühlungborn.

Bad Doberan can be reached by an hourly train from Rostock in 19 minutes. Cycling, especially from Warnemünde along the coastal cycling path, is also popular.

Bad Doberan

The main sight in Bad Doberan is the **Münster**, Klosterstraße 2, 18209 Bad Doberan, ☎ 038203-62-716, www.doberanermuenster.de. This brick Gothic church was part of a 14th-century Cistercian monastery and has a largely original interior. It is one of the loveliest brick Gothic churches in Germany and worth a detour. The gilded high altar dates from around 1310 and is one of the oldest

wing altars in Germany. Some of the carved choir stalls (below) date from the early 14th century. The church also has several graves, including many of the dukes of Mecklenburg as well as the grave of Queen Margarete of Denmark (1282). During summer, concerts, especially organ, are held most Fridays at 7:30 pm – bus services are available afterwards to Rostock and Kühlungsborn. From May to September, on Wednesday at 11:45, short organ recitals are given. Opening hours are May to September from 9 am to 6 pm; March, April and October from 10 am to 5 pm; and November to February from 10 am to 4 pm. On Sundays, it is only open after morning services end, around 11:30 am. Admission is €2. The Münster is in a park inside the original walled monastery complex, an easy 10-minute walk from the town center.

There is not much else of interest in town, apart from the Molli narrow-guage steam train to the coast.

Where to Eat: A pleasant place to eat is

in the restaurant **Weisser Pavillon**, Auf dem Kamp, ☎ 038203-648-799, in a park halfway between the Molli line and the Münster. It serves a wide variety of dishes as well as good coffee and great cakes. (€-€€)

Heiligendamm

In 1793, Duke Friedrich Franz I of Mecklenburg established Heiligendamm as the first beach resort on the German Baltic coast. It soon established itself as a summer holiday town for the nobility. Even today, with many buildings still showing the signs of neglect from the Communist era, it is still obvious that this resort catered to the rich. All buildings are painted white.

About half the town is owned by the Kempinski hotel group. Their buildings and lawns are in pristine condition. However, many other buildings are left unpainted and in dire need of repair. Still, this sleepy town is peaceful and beautiful, with many walking paths in forested areas in addition to the beach promenade and pier.

Heiligendamm is a popular stop on the Molli steam train or on cycling tours of the region.

Where to Stay & Eat: One of the best

resort hotels in Germany is the **Kempinski Grand Hotel Heiligendamm**. The hotel comprises six buildings, all white and in the classic resort style of the 19th century. Rooms are spacious and luxurious. The hotel has a large fitness area. 18209 Heiligendamm, ☎ 038203-7400, fax 038203-740-7474, www.kempinski-heiligendamm.de. (€€€€)

The excellent **Kurhaus Restaurant** (€€-€€€€) at the Kempinski serves international and regional dishes.

Kühlungsborn

Nearby Kühlungsbronn is the largest beach resort in the state and very much alive. It has accommodations in all price classes but the majority of visitors rent apartments or holiday homes. Many buildings here date from the late 19th century and are in a Classical Historicism or Art Nouveau style. The town has a large beechwood forest.

The main attraction is the long beach, which is well-maintained. As with most other German beaches, a small admission fee is payable and FKK (nude) beaches are on both far ends of the town.

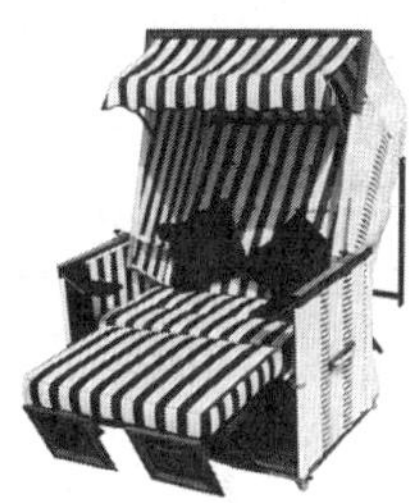

The town can claim a world first – the Strandkorb (above), so popular with German beachgoers, was invented here in 1882. These rattan seats can be rented on all German beaches and are useful not only for shade, but more important to cut the wind that often blows mercilessly.

The Molli steam train terminus in Kühlungsborn-West has a small exhibition on the steam train. The Kühlungsborn-Ost part of town is more alive and more interesting. It also has a pier over 200 m (660 feet) long, where boat cruises to nearby towns depart during the high season.

Kühlungsborn is only minutes by car from Heiligendamm or can be reached via the Molli steam train. It is a six-km (3.6-mile) walk (about 90 minutes) or you can cycle along the coastal road from Heiligendamm.

■ Wismar

Wismar is an interesting town halfway between Rostock and Lübeck. It shares with them a seafaring and trading tradition. Once a rich city, as several recently restored buildings testify, it somehow fell a bit behind and, with 55,000 inhabitants, is only a quarter the size of Rostock. It's a pleasant city to visit, with one of the largest market squares in Germany and a couple of interesting brick Gothic buildings. The old town has an unaltered medieval layout and was added to the UNESCO World Cultural Heritage list in 2002.

Wismar was founded in the late 11th century. It served as residence of the princes of Mecklenburg from 1256 until their move to Schwerin just over a century later. Its golden age coincided with that of the Hanseatic League and, like the league, suffered a decline in the 16th century. Following the Peace of Westphalia (1648), Schwerin became part of Sweden, which fortified the town as a strategic post in the heart of the Duchy of Mecklenburg-Schwerin. In 1803, Sweden leased Wismar in a hundred-year treaty to the duchy. With tiny Mecklenburg part of the powerful and belligerent German Empire, Sweden made little attempt to recover the town in 1903.

Wismar suffered severe damage during World War II and general neglect during the Communist era further ruined many historic buildings. The market square has been restored to pristine condition, but walk one block away in any direction and you will be in no doubt that this is the former East Germany and not Lübeck. However, even in unrestored areas architectural treasures lurk.

Information Sources

Tourist Office: The Tourist Information, Am Markt 11, 23966 Wismar, ☎ 03841-251-3025, www.wismar.de, has useful information and maps in English. Several self-guided walking tours are available. The office is on the market square in the southwest corner towards St Marien.

Transportation

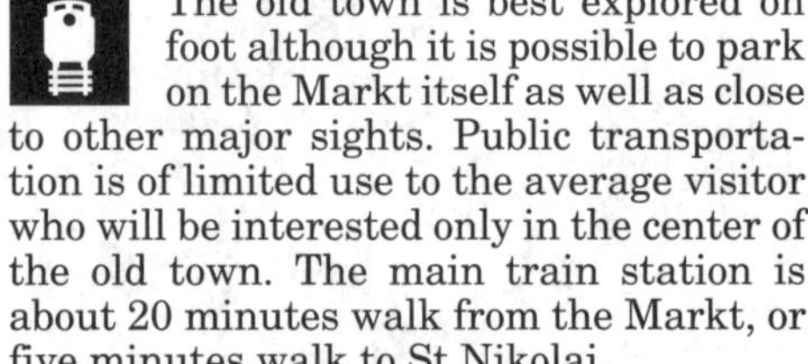

The old town is best explored on foot although it is possible to park on the Markt itself as well as close to other major sights. Public transportation is of limited use to the average visitor who will be interested only in the center of the old town. The main train station is about 20 minutes walk from the Markt, or five minutes walk to St Nikolai.

Sightseeing

Wismar's major sights are its huge market square and the brick Gothic St Nikolaikirche. Other sights of lesser interest are scattered through the city. The old town is relative compact and the sights can be seen in less than half a day.

Markt

Wismar's main attraction is its huge 100 by 100 m (328 x 328 feet) Markt or Market Square. It is lined on all four sides by gabled buildings, mostly three or four stories high, of varying styles. This part of town has been magnificently restored since the *Wende*.

In the southeastern corner of the square is the **Wasserkunst** (literary Water Art). This beautiful Dutch Renaissance pavilion was completed in 1602 to cover a waterworks system that for centuries supplied parts of Wismar with water through wooden pipes.

The largest building on the square is the 19th-century Neo-Classical **Rathaus** (Town Hall), which stretches almost the full length of the north side of the square. Parts of the original Gothic Rathaus are incorporated in the new building, including the vaulted cellars with patches of the original 14th-century wall paintings.

The oldest unaltered façade is the lovely brick Gothic **Alter Schwede** dating from 1380. It has housed a restaurant since 1878. Adjacent to the right is the Reuterhaus, housing a hotel and restaurant, and to the left an Art Nouveau building showing clear medieval influences in its design. Baroque and Renaissance façades round out the hodgepodge of architectural styles. The huge market square itself is used as a handy, if somewhat unattractive parking lot.

Two blocks to the west of Markt is **St Marienkirche** (St Mary's Church), or more accurately the remaining tower of the former early 13th-century church. The church was largely destroyed in an air raid and only the 80-m (264-foot) tower survived further destruction during the Communist era. The clock has a diameter of five m (16.4 feet) and the 14-song carillon chimes daily at noon, 3, and 7 pm.

Nearby is the **Fürstenhof** (Princes' Court). Parts of this building are Gothic, but more interesting is the richly decorated mid-16th-century Renaissance façade. The building originally housed the princes of Mecklenburg and during the Swedish period served as the highest tribunal for Swedish territories in Northern Germany.

Across the road is the **St Georgen-Kirche** (St George's Church). This early 13th-century brick Gothic church was left in ruins after World War II. A complete reconstruction started in 1990, but is not due for completion for several more years.

Nikolaikirche Area

The **Nikolaikirche** (St Nicholas Church), Speiegelberg 14, ☎ 03841-213-624, is a good 10 minutes walk from the Markt in the general direction of the Hauptbahnhof.

The present brick Gothic church dates mostly from the 14th century and is of monumental proportions – the nave is the fourth-highest in Germany, at 37 m (122 feet). The west tower was only completed in 1508. The collapse of its slender ridge turret during a storm in 1703 led to the introduction of several Baroque elements on the repaired church. The interior is filled with art – many pieces from the destroyed St Georgen and St Marienkirche found a new home here after 1945. The 1430 carved Gothic high altar is one of the largest in the region and over nine m wide (30 feet) when opened. The bronze baptismal font is about a century older. Opening hours are daily from May to September, 8 am to 8 pm, in April and October, 10 am to 6 pm, and from November to March, 11 am to 4 pm.

Nearby is the **Schabbelhaus**, built in the late 16th century. It was one of the first Renaissance houses in the Baltic region and uses brick with decorative elements cut from sandstone. It currently houses the **Stadtgeschichtliches Museum** (Local History), Schweinsbrücke 8, ☎ 03841-282-350. On display are items

Wassertor

Mecklenburg-Vorpommern

related to Wismar and the immediate region as well as a large collection on the history of medicine. Opening hours are Tuesday to Sunday from November to April, 10 am to 5 pm, closing at 8 pm from May to October. Admission is €2.

In front of the church flows the **Grube**, an artificial waterway laid out in 1255 and used for doing laundry well into the 20th century. The waterway leads to the Alter Hafen (Old Harbor), which is nowadays mostly used for leisure and fishing vessels. Also here, the brick Gothic **Wassertor** (Water Gate, see above) is the only gate surviving from the medieval town fortifications.

Cultural Events & Festivals

The cultural highlight of the year is the **Hafentage** (Harbor Days), held on the second weekend of June. This involves parades, multiple cultural events, and lots of food and drink. The **Schwedenfest** (Swedish Festival), a similar festival, is held on the third weekend of August and recalls the connection with Sweden.

Shopping

Karstadt, one of the largest department store chains in Germany, has its origins in Wismar. The firm opened its first shop in 1881 on the corner of Lübsche and Krämerstraße, behind the Rathaus. In 1991, after the *Wende*, Karstadt reclaimed the land and reopened in the Art Nouveau building. More shops of all kinds are found in the immediate region.

Adventures

On Foot

Town Walks: The tourist office conducts guided town walks daily from Easter to October at 10:30 am. On weekends, an additional tour is available at 2 pm.

On Wheels

By Bicycle: Bicycles may be rented from **Wismar Rad**, ☎ 03841-224-670, inside the Hauptbahnhof. A pick-up service can be arranged within a 50-km (30-mile) radius.

On Water

Fishing: Angling on the high seas is possible from Wismar. Several companies operate from Wismar and can provide equipment and arrange necessary permits. Companies operating from Wismar include:

- **Hotel New Orleans**, Runde Grube 3, ☎ 03841-26-860.
- **HSC Sea Charter**, Lübsche Straße 32, ☎ 038423-54-832.
- **Seetourismusservice Ziemer**, An der Dünung 61a, ☎ 03841-205-028.

Sailing & Charter Boats: Yachts and sailing vessels with skipper may be rented for a day or multiple days.

- **Alter Hafen Wismar**, Blüffelstraße 3-5, ☎ 03841-205-305, www.alterhafenwismar.de, as well as **Oldtimer Segel-Club**, 23999 Kirchdorf/ Insel Poel, ☎ 0171-712-4756, operate historic sailing vessels.
- **Segelschule Cipra**, Klußer Damm1, ☎ 03841-212-596, www.cipra-segelschule.de, has sailing courses but also charters out yachts and other boats.
- **Poeler Forellenhof**, Wismarsche Straße 13, 23999 Niendorf, ☎ 038425-4200, charters motor boats from the Island Poel.

Where to Stay & Eat

The **Steigenberger Hotel Stadt Hamburg** opened in 1993 inside a modern building behind a listed Baroque façade. It is directly on the Markt in the heart of the old town. Rooms are modern, stylish, and comfortable. Am Markt 24, 23966 Wismar, ☎ 03841-2390, fax 03841-239-239, www.steigenberger.de. (€€-€€€)

The restaurant (€-€€) at the Steigenberger serves international cuisine with strong Italian influences.

On the same square is the **Reuterhaus**. It has 10 large bedrooms furnished with Italian furniture. Am Markt 19, 23966 Wismar, ☎ 03841-22-230, fax 03841-222-324. (€€)

The Reuterhaus is best known for its restaurant (€-€€€), which serves excellent international and local dishes, either on its terrace with views of the square, or in the lovely interior with stone floors and dark, Baroque wood-paneled walls and furniture up to 300 years old.

Adjacent to the Reuterhaus is the restaurant **Alter Schwede**, Am Mark 19, ☎ 03841-283-552, one of the most famous buildings in Wismar. It serves local specialties, meaning a large fish selection but meat dishes are also available. (€€-€€€)

Camping

Ostsee Camping Zierow is on the coast six km (3.6 miles) northwest of Wismar. It has good facilities but limited shade. There are 450 spaces for tourists and 150 more for long-term stays. It is open year-round. 23968 Zierow, ☎ 03841-642-377, fax 03841-642-374, www.ostsee-camping.de.

■ Schwerin

After the *Wende*, Schwerin (population 100,000) became the capital of the state of Mecklenburg-Vorpommern, aiding its claim to be the cultural capital of the region. In contrast to the other major towns in the region, Schwerin is not a coastal town but mostly surrounded by freshwater lakes.

In the 11th century, Slavs settled in what is now Schloss Island. They were expelled by Heinrich the Lion, Duke of Saxony, who founded the first German town east of the Elbe here in 1160. From 1358 to 1918, Schwerin was the capital of the Duchy of Mecklenburg. Schwerin was also the ducal residence, except for 1756 to 1837, when the dukes resided in nearby Ludwigslust.

Schwerin escaped World War II virtually unscathed. However, the brick Gothic cathedral is the only significant surviving medieval building – several town fires ensured that most major buildings are Baroque, Neo-Renaissance, and Neo-Classical.

Information Sources

Tourist Office: The Tourist Information office is in the Rathaus, Am Markt 14, 190555 Schwerin, ☎ 0385-592-5212, www.schwerin.com.

Information on events and the nightlife scene is also available from two free publications – *Piste*, www.piste.de, and *Nachtlichter*, www.nachtlichter.com.

MONEY SAVING TICKET

*The **Schwerin-Ticket** costs €6 per day or €8 for two days and allows unlimited local transportation, a guided city tour, and reductions on admission fees at many sights. It is available from the tourist office, bus ticket offices, and many hotels.*

Transportation

Schwerin's old town is compact and easiest to navigate on foot. Street parking is time-restricted but ample parking garages are available. A bus service is available and useful for getting to outlying sights such as the open-air museum.

Schwerin is 30 km (18 miles) south of Wismar along the busy, and slow, B106, running along the west bank of Lake Schwerin. Once the Autobahn 241 along the east bank is completed, probably in 2006, the situation should improve.

Sightseeing

Schloss Area

A good place to start a tour of Schwerin is at its most famous building, the Neo-Renaissance **Schloss** (Palace). It was built in 1843-57 on a small island in Lake Schwerin when the Dukes of Mecklenburg returned from almost a century in nearby Ludwigslust. The architects, Demmler and Stüler, were inspired by Chambord in the Loire Valley and the influence is obvious although this Schloss is of course much smaller. The Schloss houses the Landstag (Parliament) of Mecklenburg-Vorpommern as well as the **Schloss Museum**, Lennéstraße 1, ☎ 0385-525-2920. The museum includes the staterooms from the 19th century, fur-

niture, Meissen porcelain, and court paintings. The 16th-century Schlosskirche (Palace Chapel) at the north of the building is Renaissance, with lovely galleries and intricate vaulting. Opening hours are daily from 10 am to 5 pm, closing at 6 pm from mid-April to mid-October. Admission is €4.

On Schloss Island is the small **Burggarten** (Castle Garden), with an Orangery, statues, viewing points, and a grotto. More interesting is the lovely 17th-century Baroque **Schlossgarten** (Palace Garden) on the south shore of the lake and connected by bridge to Schloss Island. At its center is a canal in the form of a cross. The statues are copies of the Balthasar Permoser originals. Elements such as the pavilion were added in the 19th century. Both gardens are unfenced and freely accessible.

The second bridge from the island leads to Schlossstraße, with several mostly Neo-Classical public buildings. The **Staatliches Museum** (National Museum), Alter Garten 3, ☎ 038559-580, www.museum-schwerin.de, has a noteworthy collection of Dutch and Flemish paintings (Hals, Brueghel, Jordaens) from the 17th century. It also has some 3,000 paintings, 35,000 drawings, and a rich collection of sculpture and furniture from the 18th century to the present. Opening hours are Tuesday, 10 am to 8 pm, and Wednesday to Sunday, 10 am to 5 pm, closing at 6 pm from mid-April to mid-October. Admission is €3.

To the left of the museum is the 19th-century Neo-Renaissance and Neo-Baroque state theater and to its left the half-timber **Altes Palais** (Old Palace), which served as the dowager residence. The Neo-Classical buildings along Schlossstraße are mostly used by government departments.

Markt Area

A right turn in Puschkinstraße leads to the **Markt** (Market Square). The core of the Rathaus dates from the 14th century, but the Tudor Gothic façade was only added in the mid-19th century. Four half-timber houses from the 17th century have recently been restored. The **Neues Gebäude** (New Building), a Classical building with Doric columns on the north side of the square, was erected in the late 18th century – the first in an uncompleted project to enlarge and improve the market square. It currently houses a reasonably priced café – see below. In front of the building is a copy of the Braunschweig Lion that commemorates the founder of the town.

Behind the Neues Gebäude towers the majestic brick Gothic **Dom** (Cathedral) Am Dom 4, ☎ 0385-565-014. The current church was completed between 1280 and 1420 as a triple-nave basilica. Only the Paradise Gate survived from a previous Romanesque structure. The slender 118-m (389-foot) tower was only added in the 19th century. It offers the best views of Schwerin and its beautiful surroundings. The interior is surprisingly bright. A Neo-Gothic restoration project during the 19th century destroyed most of the original medieval interior; however, some original 13th- and 14th-century wall paintings can be seen in the Maria Asuncion Chapel at the north end of the transept. Nearby is an early 14th-century bronze baptismal

font. The magnificent Neo-Gothic organ was installed in 1871. The Dom is a frequent venue for concerts. It is open from April to September, Monday to Saturday, 11 am to 5 pm, and Sunday from noon to 5 pm. From October to March, it is open weekdays, 11 am to 2 pm, Saturday, 11 am to 4 pm, and Sunday from noon to 3 pm.

Two blocks to the north is the **Pfaffenteich** – a small lake that has been compared to the Binnenalster in Hamburg. Most of the buildings on its shores are in the Historicist style of the late 19th century. A ferry has been operational between the west and east sides since 1879. Mecklinburgstraße, Schwerin's foremost shopping street, leads from the lake back to the old town.

Farther Afield

The **Mecklenburgisches Volkskundemuseum**, Alte Crivitzer Landstraße 13, Schwerin-Mueß, ☎ 0385-208-410, an open-air museum in the southern suburbs of Schwerin, opened in 1970. At its heart is the town center of Mueß that dates back to 1304. The museum focuses on the life of rural communities from the 18th to early 20th centuries and has a dozen typical houses from the period. Frequent demonstrations are held. Opening hours are Tuesday to Sunday, 10 am to 5 pm, closing at 6 pm from May to September. Admission is €2.50. The museum can be reached by Bus 6 from Schwerin station.

Cultural Events & Festivals

Schwerin, as state capital, has a full cultural program ranging from classical music to theater and popular music. The tourist office has schedules and more information.

The largest festival is the annual **Schlossfestspiele**, held from end June through July. At its center is a major opera, performed on an open-air stage with the lake and Schloss as backdrop.

On most Mondays, at 2 pm, a free 20-minute organ recital is given in the Dom. The Dom is also the venue for frequent organ concerts, sometimes accompanied by trumpet, and choral music – the schedules are available from the Dom or tourist office.

Shopping

Mecklinburgstraße, at the west of the old town, is Schwerin's foremost shopping street. It has a wide range of small and chain stores. For typical produce from Mecklenburg-Vormpommern visit **Kiek ins Land** on the Markt. It sells mainly arts and crafts produced locally.

Adventures

On Foot

Town Walks: The tourist office arranges guided city walks of the old town, departing daily at 11 am from its offices on the Market Square.

From May to September, walking tours with the night watchman take place on Thursday and Saturday at 8:30 pm – reservations at ☎ 0385-392-3092.

On Wheels

By Bicycle: Bicycles can be rented from **Strandhotel Zippendorf**, Am Strand 3, ☎ 0385-208-380, or from **Räder und Radreisen-Center Andreas Brolle**, Schusterstraße 3, ☎ 0385-500-7630.

By Bus: Petermännchen, Carl-von-Linde-Straße 2, ☎ 0385-65-800, www.petermaennchen-stadtrundfahrten.de, operates bus and motorized train city tours from the Martkt. Tours are available several times per day from April to October and on weekends only, from November to March.

Stadtrundfahrten, Semmelweissstraße 1, ☎ 0172-312-6507, has similar city tours that depart daily from the Schloss. On Tuesday and Saturday, tours are available to Wismar – reservations required and hotel pick-ups possible.

On Horseback

Horseback riding is popular in the region. The tourist office has details on stables offering riding opportunities to casual visitors.

On Water

Lake Schwerin extends 21 km (13 miles) to the north and is between three and five km (1.8 to three miles) wide. It is a mecca for watersports.

Canoeing & Sailing: Several types of boats, including canoes, motorboats, and sailboats can be rented from **Segelschule Petermännchen**, Seestraße 18, 19053 Pinnow bei Schwerin, ☎ 0385-734-383.

Lewitzboot, Unter den Linden 22a, 19079 Mirow, ☎ 03861-7234, www.lewitzboot-foese.m-vp.de, arranges canoe and cycling tours in the Lewitz area – a natural protected region between Schwerin and Ludwigslust.

Riverboats: The **Weisse Flotte**, Werderstraße 140, ☎ 0385-557-770, www.weisseflotteschwerin.de, operates several routes on the Schwerin Lake. From April to October, boats depart several times per day from near Schloss Island, on various routes ranging from one to two hours.

Waterskiing: A waterski and wakeboard lift, ☎ 038859-6010, operates on Lake Zachun near Badenitz. The total course is 800-m (2,640 feet) long and takes about 100 seconds to complete. Equipment can be rented on site and courses for beginners are available.

Where to Stay & Eat

In contrast to nearby Wismar, Schwerin has a larger selection of hotels with international standards. The most luxurious is the **Crowne Plaza Hotel** just over a km south of the old town area. The hotel is modern, with large, comfortable, well-equipped rooms. It is also a good choice for drivers – the hotel operates one of the largest parking garages in town and is therefore well-signposted. Bleicher Ufer 23, 19053 Schwerin, ☎ 0385-57-550, fax 0385-575-5777, www.ichotels.com. (€€€)

The restaurant **Marco Polo** (€€-€€€) at the Crowne Plaza is modern and bright and serves wide ranging international cuisine.

Just north of the old town, near the Pfaffenteich lake, is the elegant **Hotel Niederländischer Hof**. It is in a protected, but recently completely renovated, building. Rooms are comfortable and individually furnished to a high standard. The small restaurant (€€-€€€) at Niederländischer Hof serves nouvelle cuisine and regional specialties. Karl-Marx-Straße 12, 19053 Schwerin, ☎ 0385-591-100, fax 0385-591-1099, www.niederlaendischer-hof.de. (€€-€€€)

Nearby, close to the main station, is the **Intercity Hotel**. As usual with this chain, it is in a slick, modern building with well-equipped rooms aimed mostly at the business traveler. The room key allows for free local transportation. Grunthalplatz 5-7, 19053 Schwerin, ☎ 0385-59-500, fax 0385-595-0999, www.intercityhotel.de. (€€)

Near the center of the old town is the **Hotel Mercure Marienplatz**. It is a modern hotel behind an old façade offering good value at a convenient location. Breakfast can be had on the roof terrace. Wismarsche Straße 107, 19053 Schwerin, ☎ 0385-59-550, fax 0385-595-559, www.mercure.de. (€€)

Arguably the best restaurant in town is the elegant **Schröter's**, Schliemannstraße 2, ☎ 0385-550-7698, just north of the old town area. It serves nouvelle cuisine as well as classic dishes, but it seats only 30, making reservations advisable. (€€-€€€€)

In the heart of the old town is **Weinhaus Uhle**, Schusterstraße 15, ☎ 0385-562-956. It serves international and regional dishes and has a long wine list. There is a terrace, but the grand vaulted room is also appealing. (€€-€€€)

Schwerin has several pleasant cafés in historic venues. **Café Prag**, Schlossstraße 17, ☎ 0385-565-909, in a Rococo building, is the oldest with a tradition dating back to 1755. **Classic Café Röntgen**, Am Markt 1, ☎ 0385-521-3740, is in the Classical columned building on the Market Square. **Orangerie-Café**, Lennéstraße 1, ☎ 0385-525-2915, is in the Orangerie underneath the Schloss – enter from the Burggarten. All three offer small meals in addition to coffee and cakes. (€-€€)

Camping

Ferienpark Seehof is a highly rated campsite with good facilities on the banks of the Schwerin Lake. Hourly bus connections are available to downtown Schwerin. Boat and bicycle rentals are offered. It has 270 spaces for tourists and 150 for long-term stays. It is open year-round. 19069 Seehof, ☎ 0385-512-540, fax 0385-581-4170, www.ferienparkseehof.de.

Schleswig-Holstein

In this Chapter

Schleswig-Holstein is Germany's northernmost state. It is on the Jutland peninsula that ends in Denmark and the proximity to the sea influenced its development and character. Fisheries and trade have traditionally been the main industries but agriculture and tourism are also major contributors to its economy.

Although the coasts of the state are popular with German families, Schleswig-Holstein is of limited interest to the foreign traveler. However, the lovely town of Lübeck, at the southern edges of the state close to Hamburg, is worth a journey. It has a historic town center that is a UNESCO World Cultural Heritage site.

Kieler Woche

Several Baltic Sea ports stage sailing festivals each summer, but none is larger or more famous than the Kieler Woche (Kiel Week) held annually in late June. It draws more than 5,000 yachtsmen from more than 50 countries to the biggest sailing event in the world. For hotel reservations, boat charters, and seats on the accompanying boats, it is best to contact Tourist Information Kiel, Neues Rathaus, Andreas-Gayk-Str. 31, 24103 Kiel, www.kiel.de.

■ History

Although first united in 1460 under Danish rule, Schleswig-Holstein has frequently changed rulers and allegiances. In 1864, a powerful Prussia settled squabbles in Germany's favor. The territory remained part of Germany ever since with the exception of a small Danish-speaking area that reverted to Denmark after the First World War.

Following World War II, the area saw a large influx of refugees from Germany's lost eastern provinces. Lübeck, for example, doubled in size through this influx.

One of the most powerful and richest cities in medieval Germany, Lübeck was a Free Imperial City from 1226 onwards. It only became part of Schleswig-Holstein during the Nazi era. After the Second World War, Lübeck failed to regain independence.

■ Getting Here

By Rail: Most long-distance trains to Lübeck require a change-over in Hamburg. Hamburg and Lübeck are connected at least hourly by trains taking 45 minutes.

By Road: Lübeck is an easy 45-minute drive from Hamburg along the excellent Autobahn A1. The A20, completed in 2005, gives easy access to Wismar, Rostock, and Berlin.

A twice-daily bus service from Berlin to Lübeck is operated by **Berlin Linien Bus**, Bunsenstraße 2, 24145 Kiel, ☎ 0431-666-2222, www.berlinlinie.de. The journey takes four hours – traveling times should decrease as more sections of the new highway are opened. One bus daily continues to Kiel, another two hours drive.

By Car Ferry: Lübeck has traditionally been an important link between Western Europe and Scandinavia. This role is gradually being eroded as the former East German ports offer shorter connection times. However, several car ferries still operate from Lübeck or Travemünde:

- **Finnlines**, Einsiedelstraße 43-45, 23554 Lübeck, ☎ 0451-150-7443, www.finnlines.de, sails daily from Helsinki to Travemünde.
- **TT-Line**, 20422 Hamburg, ☎ 04502-80-181, www.TTLine.com, sails daily from Trelleborg to Travemünde
- **Latlines**, ☎ 0451-709-9697, operates from Riga in Letland to Lübeck.

By Air: For travelers arriving by air, **Hamburg Airport (HAM)** is usually the most logical point of entry. **Trave-Liner**,

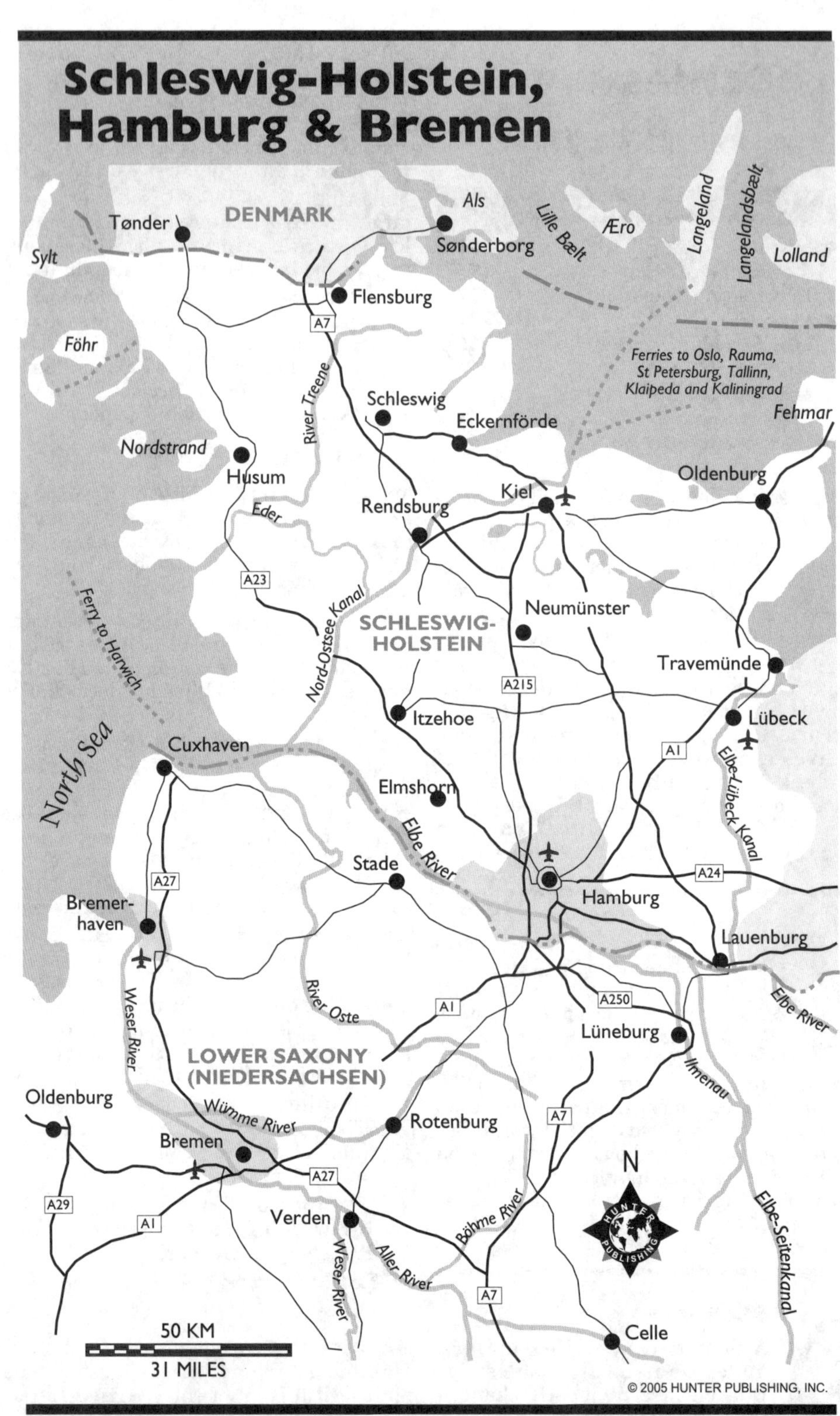

Schleswig-Holstein, Hamburg & Bremen
DENMARK
Tønder
Als
Sønderborg
Lille Bælt
Æro
Langeland
Langelandsbælt
Lolland
Sylt
Flensburg
A7
Föhr
River Treene
Ferries to Oslo, Rauma, St Petersburg, Tallinn, Klaipeda and Kaliningrad
Schleswig
Eckernförde
Fehmar
Nordstrand
Husum
Kiel
Oldenburg
Rendsburg
Eder
A23
Neumünster
Ferry to Harwich
Nord-Ostsee Kanal
SCHLESWIG-HOLSTEIN
Travemünde
A215
Itzehoe
Lübeck
North Sea
Cuxhaven
A1
Elbe-Lübeck Kanal
Elmshorn
Elbe River
Stade
A27
A24
Bremerhaven
Hamburg
Lauenburg
River Oste
A1
A250
Elbe River
Weser River
Lüneburg
LOWER SAXONY (NIEDERSACHSEN)
Ilmenau
Oldenburg
Wümme River
Rotenburg
A7
Bremen
N
A27
A29
A1
Verden
Böhme River
HUNTER PUBLISHING
Weser River
Aller River
A7
Elbe-Seitenkanal
50 KM
31 MILES
Celle

☎ 0451-888-1078, operates buses directly from Lübeck to Hamburg Airport, cutting out the need to connect by train through Hamburg Hauptbahnhof.

Lübeck Airport (LBC), Blankenseer Straße 101, ☎ 0451-583-010, www.flughafen-luebeck.de, is used mostly by low-cost carriers such as Ryanair. It is about half an hour south of Lübeck with Bus 6 connecting to the main station every 20 minutes. Shuttle buses to Hamburg are available to coincide with flight arrivals.

■ Information Sources

Information on the whole state is available from **Tourismus-Agentur Schleswig-Holstein**, Walkerdamm 17, ☎ 0431-600-5840, www.sh-tourismus.de.

■ Lübeck

Lübeck is by far the most interesting city in Schleswig-Holstein and for foreign visitors the only one really worth visiting. It is a popular daytrip from Hamburg, but few would regret staying longer. The main sight is the historic town center, which is a UNESCO World Cultural Heritage Site because it kept its original medieval layout and has about 1,000 listed buildings.

Historic Lübeck was founded in 1143 on a strategic and relatively safe island in the River Trave. It became a free imperial city as early as 1226 and soon after became the center of the Hanseatic League. For the next 400 years, up to the league's demise at the time of the Thirty Year's War, Lübeck was one of the richest and most powerful cities in Northern Europe. From the 17th century the city was in decline, a process only halted after the completion of the Elbe-Lübeck canal in 1900. During World War II, the town suffered from air raids as early as March 1942. Following the war, the influx of refugees from the eastern provinces of Germany doubled the town's population to 200,000.

As with other cities in northern Germany, the main building material in Lübeck is brick. The massive brick structures, especially churches, are the main draw. Also interesting are the narrow alleys reminiscent of medieval times. Lübeck remains Germany's most important Baltic Sea port and water activities abound. At the mouth of the Trave, 20 km (12 miles) north of Lübeck itself, is the town of Travemünde, a popular seaside resort.

THE HANSEATIC LEAGUE

The Hanse (Hanseatic League) started as a guild of traders in the 13th century, but eventually turned into a loose confederation of cities. It had no written constitution or even fixed rules, but when a city came under the rule of a noble family it was usually forced out, e.g. Berlin after the Hohenzollerns moved in. The Hanseatic cities were by no means democratic – decisions were made by a small elite that often acted like born nobles – lower classes were often violently suppressed. When a city needed the support of others a Hansetag (Hanseatic Meeting) was called – the member towns would send delegations to the meeting, usually held in Lübeck, where decisions were made by unanimous vote.

The main aim of the Hanseatic League was to facilitate trade and to keep it in the hands of the members. During the 14th and 15th century, the Hanseatic League was the most powerful political and economic force in Germany and much of northern Europe. At its height, it had over 200 member cities. Although it tried to preserve peace, because peace is good for trade, it did not shy away from war either. A glorious moment was when the Hanseatic League defeated Denmark in 1370 and ended Danish interference in the East Baltic region.

The Hanseatic League was undone during the 16th century when its power was increasingly challenged by upcoming nation states such as England and the Netherlands. It finally fell apart during the ravaging Thirty Years' War. The last Hansetag was held in 1669 – although nine cities attended, the League was a spent force and never recovered.

Lübeck, the third-largest city in Germany during the 14th century, was known as the Queen of the Hanse, as the Hansetage were usually held here. During the late 20th century, many former East German cities restored Hanse to the town name, mainly for tourism purposes. Hamburg, however, has used the title since 1806 and still is officially the Free and Hanseatic City of Hamburg.

Information Sources

Tourist Office: Tourist information is available from **Lübecker Verkehrsverein**, Am Bahnhof/ Linden Arcaden, Konrad-Adenauer-Straße 6, 23558 Lübeck, ☎ 0451-72-300, www.luebeck.de. The tourist office arranges accommodation as well as reservations for most cultural events.

Transportation

Lübeck is best explored on foot. Traffic is banned from many streets and the one-way street system is developed in a way to discourage driving. Street parking is limited but ample parking garages are available with electronic boards indicating the available spaces.

The main train station is a few minutes walk from the Holstentor. Long distance buses stop near the station and local buses run from the station to the old town and Travemünde. Trains connect Lübeck and Travemünde at least hourly for the 15-minute trip.

Sightseeing

The main sights in Lübeck can be seen by walking from the Holstentor into the old town and along Breite Straße.

Holstentor Area

The massive brick, twin-tower **Holstentor** (Holsten Gate), the symbol of Lübeck, was erected in 1464-78. It was actually constructed before the city walls and clearly more intended to flaunt the city's power and wealth rather than serve for defensive purposes. The less frequently photographed façade facing the city is artistically more impressive. It houses the **Holstentor-Museum** (Local History Museum), ☎ 0451-122 -4129. Opening hours are daily from 10 am to 5 pm, closing at 6 pm from April to October. Admission is €4. The large brick buildings south of the gate date from the 16th to 18th centuries and once served as salt stores (Salzspeicher).

A flight of stairs from Kolkstraße leads to the **Petrikirche** (St Peter's Church), Schmiedestraße, ☎ 0451-397-730. This original triple-nave, mid-13th-century Romanesque church was altered to the Gothic style in the 14th century and two additional naves were added in the following two centuries. It was virtually destroyed during World War II but rebuilt. More interesting than the church itself, is the view from the top of the tower. It is reached by elevator and thus one of the most popular viewing platforms in the region. The church is a popular venue for concerts. Opening hours are daily from March to September, 9 am to 7 pm.

Rathaus Area

Lübeck's two most impressive brick buildings, the Rathaus (Town Hall) and Marienkirche (St Mary's Church), are adjacent to each other along Breite Straße.

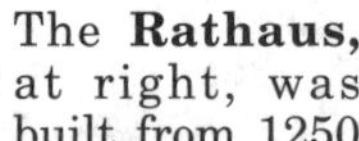

The **Rathaus,** at right, was built from 1250 onwards. It is mostly of glazed, dark brick and built in an L-shape on two sides of the Marktplatz. It has characteristic high protective walls decorated with slender turrets. On ground level, it has Gothic arcades, still used by local traders for their intended purpose. On Breite Straße, it has a wonderful late 16th-century Dutch Renaissance external staircase. Up to 1669, the representatives of the Hanseatic League usually met at Lübeck in the Hansasaal. The interior can only be seen on a German guided tour, weekdays at 11 am, noon, and 3 pm. Admission is €2. Across the road is the famous Café Niederegger – see below**.

The monumental **Marienkirche**, Schüsselbuden 13, ☎ 0451-397-700, served as a prototype for all northern Germany's

brick Gothic churches. The church was constructed between 1250 and 1350. It is the third-largest church in Germany and its 80-m (262-foot) central nave is the highest brick nave in the world, at 38½ m (126 feet), The spires are 125-m (410-feet) high. The church was damaged during an air raid in 1942. During the ensuing fire, most of the interior was lost but long-forgotten medieval wall paintings were laid bare and restored with the rest of the church. At the rear, two bells lie where they fell as reminders of the destructiveness of war. Two-hour guided tours of the towers and vaulting are conducted on Saturday from April to October at 3:15 pm, and during July and August also on Wednesday at 3:15 pm. Opening hours are daily from 10 am to 6 pm.

St John the Evangelist (wood, 1500)

Across the road from the church is the 1758 Baroque **Buddenbrookhaus** at Mengstraße 4. It belonged to the Mann family from 1841 to 1891 and Lübeck's most famous sons, the writers Thomas and Heinrich Mann, spent several summers here. Thomas Mann, Nobel laureate for literature in 1929, used the house as the setting for his novel *Die Buddenbrooks*, which described the life and fall of a rich patrician family. The house was virtually destroyed during the war but the façade was restored. The modern interior houses the **Heinrich and Thomas Mann Center**, ☎ 0451-122-5407, with displays on the two writers' lives and works. Opening hours are daily from April to October, 10 am to 6 pm, and from November to March, 11 am to 4 pm. Admission is €5. (Combination tickets with the Günther Grass-Haus are €7.)

Thomas Mann, by Marianne Kühnel

Northern Altstadt Area

At the far end of Breite Straße is the 1535 **Schiffergesellschaft** (Seamen's Guild) house with a Renaissance exterior and a beautiful preserved interior. It is mostly wood paneled with rough wooden furniture and brass fittings as befits a seamen's tavern. It houses a popular restaurant – see below.

Across the road is the small, Gothic triple-nave **Jakobikirche** (St James's Church), Jakobikirchhof 5, ☎ 0451-308-0115. More interesting than the mostly 14th-century church are the magnificently carved 16th-century organ lofts. A chapel with a damaged lifeboat commemorates the sinking of the training vessel *Pamir*, lost with all hands in 1957. The church is open daily from 10 am to 6 pm, but from September to April and on Monday closing at dusk.

The **Heiligen-Geist-Hospital** (Holy Ghost Hospice), Am Koberg, ☎ 0451-122-2040, founded in 1280, is one of the oldest social institutions in Europe. It originally served as an institution to take care of the sick, but gradually turned into an almshouse and later a house for the aged. Of special note are the Late Gothic wall paintings in the chapel as well as the large Gothic Langes Haus (Great Hall). It is open Tuesday to Sunday from April to October, 10 am to 5 pm, and from November to March, 10 am to 4 pm.

The **Museumskirche St. Katharinen**, (St Catharine's Church Museum), Königstraße, ☎ 0451-122-4180, houses modern statues inside the 14th-century church. Some wall paintings from the 14th and 15th centuries survived. Opening hours are April to September from Tuesday to Sunday, 10 am to 1 pm, and 2 to 5 pm. Admission is €1.

Günther Grass

Nearby is the **Günther Grass-Haus**, Glockengießerstraße 21, ☎ 0451-122-4192, www.guenter-grass-haus.de. Here the emphasis is not only on the 1999 Nobel Laureate for Literature's written work, but also on his less well-known fine art works, including drawings, paintings, and sculptures. Opening hours are daily from April to October, 10 am to 6 pm, and from November to March, 11 am to 4 pm. Admission is €4. (Combination tickets with the Buddenbrookhaus are €7.)

Farther down Glockengießerstraße are several courtyards and passages (Höfe und Gänge) that housed social institutions. In the 17th century, several buildings here were erected for the poor and elderly. Of special note is the 1636 Baroque façade of the **Füchtingshof** (no 25).

Southern Altstadt

The southern parts of the old town generally receive fewer visitors but two sights here are worth the slight detour.

The **St Annen-Museum**, St-Annen-Straße, ☎ 0451-122-4134, is in a former monastery dating back to 1502. The monastery dissolved after the Reformation. Since 1915, the building has been used as a museum for religious art and cultural objects. The selection of carved altars is huge and includes a late 15th-century altar painted by Hans Memling. Opening hours are Tuesday to Sunday, 10 am to 5 pm, closing at 4 pm from October to March. Admission is €4.

The **Dom** (Cathedral), Mühlendamm 2-6, ☎ 0451-74-704, is the oldest building in town. It was founded in 1173 by the illustrious Heinrich the Lion but the original Romanesque church was converted and enlarged in a Gothic style during the 14th century. The Paradise Portal dates from 1260. The Late Gothic crucifix is a 15th-century masterpiece. Opening hours are daily from April to September, 10 am to 6 pm, closing at 3 pm from October to March.

Heinrich the Lion

Travemünde

Travemünde (literally Trave's Mouth) is a small town 20 km (12 miles) north of Lübeck. It was bought by Lübeck in 1329 to ensure the town's control over the entry of the Trave River into the Baltic Sea. Nowadays, it is mostly visited for its lovely long sandy beach and its casino.

Its most prominent sight is the Maritim Hotel, a highrise looming up 158 m (518 feet), but the old town is charming and filled with with half-timbered houses. This has been a popular resort since the 19th century and can still get crowded over weekends and during the summer season.

The **Priwall** area, on the right bank of the Trave estuary, can be reached from Vorderreihe on the west bank by car ferry and, during the season, by pedestrian ferry, ☎ 04502-2249, from Nordermole. A popular sight here is the ***Passat***, ☎ 04502-5287, a four-masted ship built in Hamburg in 1911. It can be viewed from mid-May to mid-September

Timmendorfer Strand, a resort a few miles north, is also popular, especially with the well-heeled. It has two piers, a yacht harbor, grand parks, and many expensive holiday homes. It also has **Sea-Life**, Kurpromenade 5, ☎ 04503-358-888, www.sealife.de, a popular park with several fish tanks, a walk-through undersea glass tunnel, and several displays on maritime themes, especially as they relate to the Lübeck area. Opening hours are daily from 10 am.

The Travemünde area is popular for watersports activities. Several ferries depart from here to Scandinavia.

Cultural Events

Lübeck's magnificent brick churches are frequently used for concerts. Organ music is particularly popular, but other classical music concerts are also arranged. Many church services include extensive musical recitals. The schedules are available from the **Kirchenkreis Lübeck**, Bäckerstraße 3-5, 23564 Lübeck, ☎ 0451-790-2127, www.kirchenmusik-luebeck.de. Most concerts are held during summer and in December.

The **Schleswig-Holstein Music Festival**, www.shmf.de, stretches over seven weeks in July and August. During this period, some 40 classical music concerts are scheduled at various venues in Schleswig-Holstein, with several in Lübeck itself. A special theme is selected each year.

This festival is complemented by the **Theater Sommer Lübeck** – a series of concerts, theater, and musical productions held during the summer months. For the past decade, operettas, www.luebecker-sommeroperette.de, have been an integral part of this festival and increasingly its most popular events.

Festivals

Sand World Travemünde, www.sand-world.de, is Germany's largest sand sculpture festival with works up to 11-m (36 feet) high. It is held annually for eight weeks from July to early September on the beach at Primwall.

Baltic Sail Travemünde is held during the second half of August. It draws windjammers, sail boats, and old craft from around the world to this three-day extravaganza. You can participate on some of the large sail vessels. A similar event is held in Rostock

The **Travemünde Woche**, www.travemuender-woche.de, is held at the end of July and early August. Around 3,000 yachtsmen and more than 850 sailboats participate in this annual event with a tradition dating back 115 years.

The largest festival of Nordic films is not in Scandinavia, but rather at Lübeck in early November. At the **Nordische Filmtage**, www.nordische-filmtage.de, new Scandinavian and Baltic films of all genres as well as classics are presented.

Most German towns have Christmas markets. Lübeck is no exception and its already splendid market has been enhanced by an ice and snow sculpture festival. For eight weeks, from mid-December to the end of January, **Ice World Lübeck**, www.iceworld.de, transforms Lübeck to a land of winter fairytales.

Shopping

Konditorei-Café Niederegger, Breite Straße 89, ☎ 0451-530-1126, is a Lübeck institution. The firm is most famous for producing marzipan. Its products are sold all over Germany, but only here does the selection exceed 300 items. A museum, on the second floor, explains the almond delicacy's journey from the Orient to Lübeck and from here to the rest of Germany.

Adventures

On Foot

Town Walks: The tourist office arranges guided two-hour walking tours of the city. The tours are available year-round on Sunday at 11 am. From May to October, additional tours take place from Monday to Saturday at 11 am, and also at 2 pm from July to September. Participation is €4 per person or €6 if you include the Rathaus.

On Wheels

By Bicycle: In Travemünde, bicycles can be rented from **Beitsch**, Kurgartenstraße 67, ☎ 04502-6622; Bruders, Mecklenburger Landstraße 14, Priwall, ☎ 04502-5340; or **Oske**, Kurgarten 86, ☎ 04502-777-990.

On Horseback

Riding opportunities for riders of all ages are available at **Reiterhof Travemünde-Priwall**, Fliegerweg 11, Travemünde, ☎ 04502-302-400, www.reiterhof-travemuende.de.

On Water

Fishing: This requires a license – details are available from the tourism office. For angling on the high seas contact **Peter Tuchtenhagen**, Mecklenburger Landstraße 54, Travemünde-Priwall, ☎ 04502-26-089.

Beaches: The main reason for traveling to Travemünde is to visit the beaches. The most popular are in the vicinity of the Maritim Hotel. Entering the beach area costs €2.60 (€1.50 after 3 pm) for most beaches on the city side, and €1 for beaches on the Priwall side. The Grünstradt and Brodtener Ufer are free. Nudist beaches

(FKK) and areas where dogs are allowed to run freely are at the far ends of town. Beach baskets, popular two-seat rattan beach benches, can be rented for €7.50 per day. Lifeguards are on duty at all beaches from Söhrmanndamm to Mecklenburg, mid-May to mid-September.

Charter Boats: It is possible to charter a single- or two-mast sailboat with crew for the day. Alternatively, it is also possible to sail on one of these beauties and participate in hoisting the sails. The cost is about €50 per person for a full seven-hour cruise. Depending on wind conditions, the boat sails along the Mecklenburg coast or towards Holstein. Reservations can be made through the tourism office.

Riverboats: Lübeck's old town is on an island and water has always played a major role in the town's development. It is no surprise that the boating options for tourists are vast.

- **Maak-Linie**, ☎ 0451-706-3859, www.maak-linie.de, operates short cruises around the island, canals, and harbor of Lübeck. Cruises depart daily every half-hour from 10 am from Untertrave, near the Holsentor.
- **Quandt Linie Lübeck**, Willy-Brandt-Allee 13, ☎ 0451-77-799, www.quandt-linie.de, has similar tours departing from the Holstentorterrassen and from the Wallhalbinsel.
- The Lübeck-Travemünde route is done by **Könemann Schiffahrt**, Teerhofinsel 14a, ☎ 0451-280-1635, www.koenemann-schiffahrt.de.
- The Lübeck-Rothenhusen cruise takes just under two hours. **Wakenitz-Schiffahrt Quandt**, Wakenitzufer 1c, ☎ 0451-793-885, and **Personenschiffahrt Maiworm**, Roeckstraße 50, ☎ 0415-35-455, www.maiworm-schiffahrt.de, operate on this route.

Sailing: Sailing courses and boat rental with skipper are available in Travemünde from:

- **Wasserfahrschule Schött**, teutendorfer Weg 2, ☎ 04502-4504, www.wasser-fahrschule.de.
- **Segelschule Mövenstein**, Kaiserallee 40-42, ☎ 04502-2452, www.moevenstein.de.
- **Jutta Stute Charteryachten**, Achterdeck 21a, ☎ 04502-6013, www.jutta.stute.charteryachten.de.
- **Park & Sail**, Am Fischereihafen, ☎ 04502-1300.

On Ice

Ice-skating: Ice-skating is possible in the Altstadt in December and January. It is referred to as "Hals- und Beinbruch" (literally neck and leg breaking). Rental skates are available.

Where to Stay & Eat

Lübeck

The best temporary address in Lübeck is the **Radisson SAS Senator Hotel**. It is in a mode'rn building just outside the Holstentor, offering great views of the Trave and the old town. Rooms are comfortable and stylishly furnished. The **Nautilo** restaurant (€€-€€€) at the Radisson serves international and nouvelle cuisine and the **Restaurant Kogge** (€€-€€€) offers mostly fish and Nordic specialties. Willy-Brandt-Allee 6, ☎ 23554 Lübeck, ☎ 0451-1420, fax 0451-142-2222, www.senatorhotel.de. (€€€-€€€€)

Nearby, with equally good views, but this time in the old town itself, is the simpler **Ringhotel Jensen**. It is in a patrician house dating back to 1307. However, rooms are modern and comfortably furnished. The **Yachtzimmer** restaurant (€€-€€€) at Ringhotel Jensen recalls Lübeck's seafaring tradition and serves regional specialties. An der Obertrave 4, ☎ 23552 Lübeck, ☎ 0451-702-490, fax 0451-73-386, www.ringhotel-jensen.de. (€€)

The **Ibis Hotel** is close to the main station. As is usual with this chain, rooms are bright but simple, with no frills. Fackenburger Allée 45, 23554 Lübeck,

HOTEL PRICE CHART	
Rates per room based on double occupancy, including taxes.	
€	Under €50
€€	€50-€100
€€€	€101-€150
€€€€	Over €150

☎ 0451-40-040, fax 0451-400-4444, www.ibishotel.com. (€-€€)

Lübeck's best and priciest restaurant is the **Wullenwever**, Beckergrube 71, ☎ 0451-704-333. It serves Mediterranean and nouvelle cuisine in elegant surroundings. (€€€-€€€€)

For a more local flavor, it is hard to beat the historic **Schiffergesellschaft**, Breite Straße 2, ☎ 0451-76-776. Even if not dining here, take a look inside to see the traditional wood-paneled seamen's tavern. The building dates back to 1535. The food is mostly local specialties. Reservations are advisable. (€€-€€€)

A similar local option is **Zimmermann's Lübecker Hanse**, Kolkstraße 7, ☎ 0451-78-054, near the Holstentor. Wood beams and wooden floors add to the charm of the venue. The offerings are mainly seafood, but meat and a large vegetarian selection are also available. Reservations are advisable. (€€-€€€)

Another Lübeck institution is the pleasant **Konditorei-Café Niederegger**, Breite Straße 89, ☎ 0451-530-1126 – across the road from the Rathaus. This firm made marzipan famous in Germany and the marzipan is used in many dishes. The café serves small meals, including several breakfast options, and tasty cakes. It is elegant and spread over multiple levels. Prices are pleasantly reasonable. (€-€€)

Travemünde

In keeping with its seaside resort tradition, Travemünde has several grand hotels – none more so than the **Vier Jahreszeiten Casino Travemünde**, which is on the beach promenade. The hotel has a tradition dating back to 1833, but the complex reopened in 2003 after a complete renovation. Rooms are large and luxuriously furnished in classic, modern, or country-house style. There are five restaurants (€-€€€€) on the premises and, as the name suggests, a casino as well. Kaiserallee 2, 23570 Lübeck-Travemünde, ☎ 04502-3080, fax 04502-308-333, www.vier-jahreszeiten.de. (€€€-€€€€)

DINING PRICE CHART

Price per person for an entrée, including water, beer or soft drink.

€	Under €10
€€	€10-€20
€€€	€21-€35
€€€€	Over €35

Nearby is the modern, 35-story **Maritim Strandhotel**. It has comfortably furnished, elegant rooms with wonderful views. Trelleborgalee 2, 23570 Lübeck-Travemünde, ☎ 04502-890, fax 04502-892-020, www.maritim.de. (€€€-€€€€)

The **Café Über den Wolken** (€-€€) is on the 35th floor of the Maritim Strandhotel, with unbeatable views.

Camping

Camp Lübeck-Schönbröcken is three km (1.8 miles) from Lübeck's historic town center. It has 70 spaces for tourists, with limited shade. A direct bus service is available to Lübeck. The site is open from April to October. Steinrader Damm 12, ☎/fax 0451-893-090.

RVs may park at **Park & Sail**, Am Fischereihafen, ☎ 04502-1300.

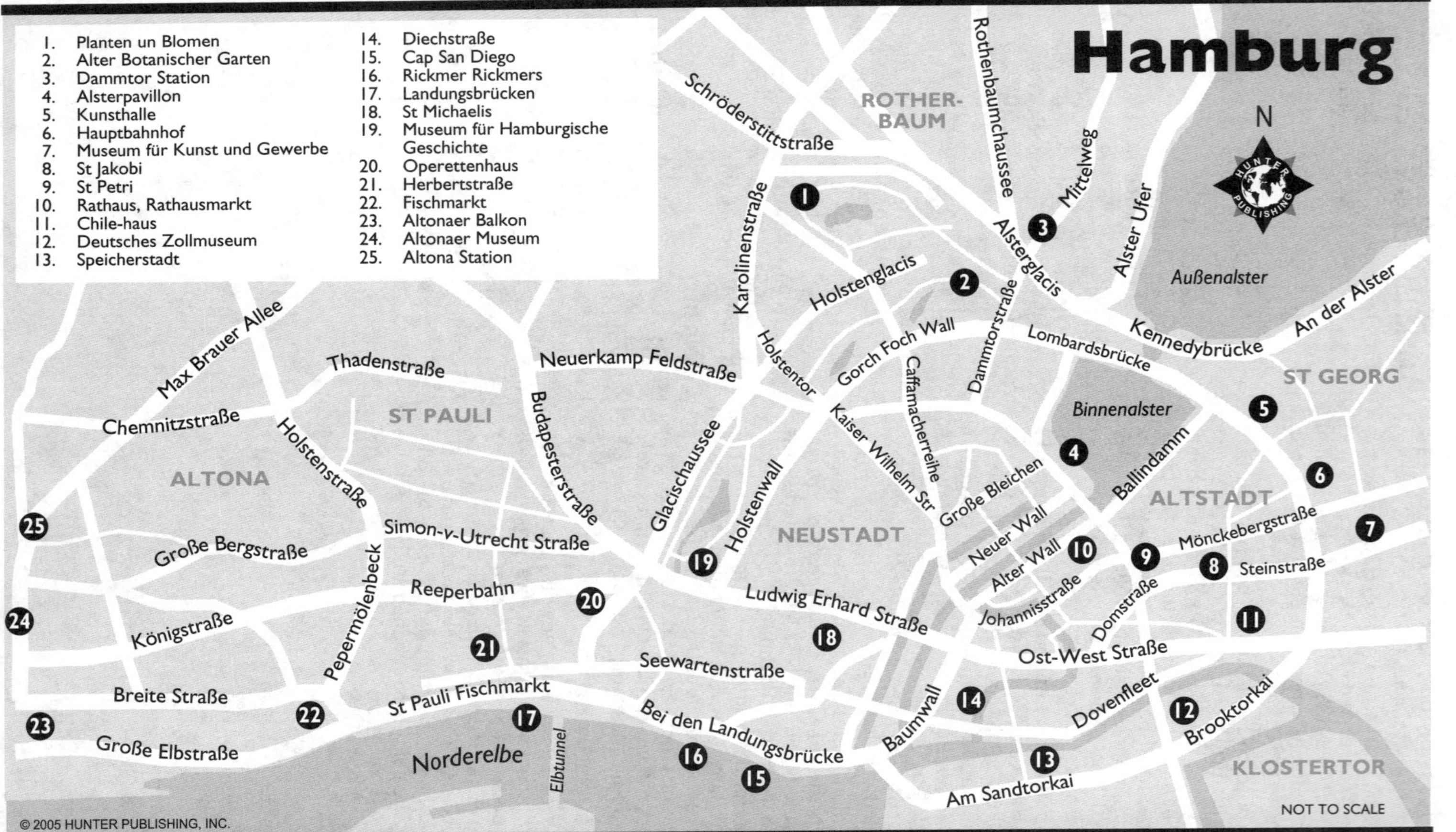
Hamburg
1. Planten un Blomen
2. Alter Botanischer Garten
3. Dammtor Station
4. Alsterpavillon
5. Kunsthalle
6. Hauptbahnhof
7. Museum für Kunst und Gewerbe
8. St Jakobi
9. St Petri
10. Rathaus, Rathausmarkt
11. Chile-haus
12. Deutsches Zollmuseum
13. Speicherstadt
14. Diechstraße
15. Cap San Diego
16. Rickmer Rickmers
17. Landungsbrücken
18. St Michaelis
19. Museum für Hamburgische Geschichte
20. Operettenhaus
21. Herbertstraße
22. Fischmarkt
23. Altonaer Balkon
24. Altonaer Museum
25. Altona Station
N
HUNTER PUBLISHING
ROTHER-BAUM
ST GEORG
ST PAULI
ALTONA
NEUSTADT
ALTSTADT
KLOSTERTOR
Außenalster
Binnenalster
Norderelbe
Elbtunnel
Schröderstiftstraße
Rothenbaumchaussee
Mittelweg
Alster Ufer
Alsterglacis
Kennedybrücke
An der Alster
Lombardsbrücke
Dammtorstraße
Holstenglacis
Karolinenstraße
Gorch Foch Wall
Holstentor
Caffamacherreihe
Kaiser Wilhelm Str
Große Bleichen
Ballindamm
Mönckebergstraße
Steinstraße
Neuer Wall
Alter Wall
Johannisstraße
Domstraße
Ost-West Straße
Max Brauer Allee
Thadenstraße
Neuerkamp Feldstraße
Chemnitzstraße
Holstenstraße
Budapesterstraße
Glacischaussee
Holstenwall
Simon-v-Utrecht Straße
Große Bergstraße
Pepermölenbeck
Reeperbahn
Ludwig Erhard Straße
Königstraße
Seewartenstraße
Breite Straße
St Pauli Fischmarkt
Bei den Landungsbrücke
Baumwall
Dovenfleet
Brooktorkai
Große Elbstraße
Am Sandtorkai
NOT TO SCALE

Hamburg

In this Chapter

Hamburg is Germany's second-largest city and premier port. It is mostly a modern city with liberal and independent attitudes. Hamburgers are often considered rather reserved and formal. The elegant city similarly seems to hide its best features. Most sights are low-key and not as upfront and in your face as in other parts of Germany.

Hamburg is famous for its relationship to water. The mighty River Elbe flows through the city and provides the largest harbor in Germany. In addition, the Alster is a huge artificial lake in the middle of the city. The city is very green with many large parks in the city center.

Hamburg was destroyed in 1842 by a huge town fire and again a century later during World War II by air raids. Most buildings are therefore fairly new, although some historic ones have been restored. Several major churches with high spires fill the skyline from all directions. The 19th-century Neo-Renaissance Rathaus is the most impressive of these buildings.

As a harbor city, Hamburg has a reputation for seedy nightlife. Even though the Reeperbahn, the traditional red-light district, is a shadow of its former self, it is still internationally the best-known aspect of Hamburg. Nowadays, more respectable family entertainment options, such as musicals, are a major attraction in this area.

History

In AD 808, shortly after defeating the Saxons and forcing their conversion to Christianity, Hamburg was founded by Charlemagne as Hammaburg. Its main purpose was to support missionaries operating in Schleswig-Holstein, Denmark, and Scandinavia. The town developed slowly until it came under the control of the Schaumburgs. Under their rule, the population increased and trade became important. On May 7, 1189, Duke Adolf III managed to obtain from Emperor Friedrich I Barbarossa an Imperial guarantee of free trade along the Elbe, from its mouth to Hamburg. From this moment onwards, Hamburg would be an important trading city.

Hamburg's path to wealth began when it joined the Hanseatic League in 1321. It became a partner town with the fabulously rich Lübeck. During the Middle Ages, light loads were unloaded in Lübeck and transported overland to Hamburg, where the journey continued by sea rather than risk sailing around Denmark.

Hamburg became a Free Imperial City in 1510. It adopted the Lutheran Reformation early on and attracted religious refugees from all parts of Europe. Its population doubled to 40,000 between 1550 and 1600. After the collapse of the Hanseatic League, Hamburg increasingly turned its access to the Atlantic Ocean to advantage in trade. However, French occupation during the Napoleonic Wars and the continental system, which banned trade with Britain, left the city in financial ruin. Its sovereignty was guaranteed at the Congress of Vienna and Hamburg has been known officially as the Free and Hanseatic City of Hamburg ever since.

The Great Fire of 1842 destroyed most of the old town, including 71 city blocks and 1,749 houses. However, for most of the 19th century it saw tremendous growth as trans-Atlantic trade increased in importance. In 1871, it joined the new German Empire led by Prussia. To counter the effects of the customs union, it founded the free port system still in existence today. A large part of Hamburg's port is a tax-free zone allowing for cheaper re-exports – taxes are only payable should the goods enter Germany itself.

Shortly before the First World War, Hamburg was the world's third-largest port (behind London and New York). However, the war cost the lives of 40,000 Hamburgers, interrupted trade, and the war reparations cost Hamburg virtually its entire commercial fleet.

The town was severely affected by the Nazi regime. The temporary loss of "Free" from its name was the least serious. Shortly before the war, Hamburg had the largest Jewish community in Germany, and they suffered the same terrible fate as other Jews in Nazi-controlled areas. The city itself suffered air raids early on, with the most severe in July 1943. Air raids killed 55,000, destroyed more than half of all houses and 80% of port facilities. Around 70,000 Hamburgers died on the front. During the war, the population declined from 1.7 million to 1.1 million.

At the foundation of the Federal Republic of (West) Germany in 1949, Hamburg joined as a city-state. As before, it relied on trade to recover and it became one of the wealthiest cities in Germany. Currently, the port is still Hamburg's lifeline, but other industries are important too. It is a major media city and controls a significant part of Germany's printed media.

■ Transportation

By Rail: Although it is in the far north of Germany, many other centers can be reached quickly by high-speed train. At least hourly connections are available to Berlin (two hours 20 minutes), Frankfurt (3½ hours), Cologne (four hours) and Munich (six hours). The traveling time to Berlin should drop to 90 minutes in the near future.

AREAS TO AVOID

If possible, at night avoid the eastern exit of the Hauptbahnhof and especially nearby Hanseplatz – the area is a known hangout for drug dealers and other unsavory characters.

By Car: Major highways from all parts of Germany lead to Hamburg. The roads are generally in good condition. The A7 runs from Denmark via Hamburg to Hannover and eventually to Bavaria in the south. The A1 leads from Lübeck past Hamburg via Bremen to the Rühr. The A24 connects Berlin and Hamburg.

Driving in most of Hamburg is not challenging and easier than in most other large German cities. In central Hamburg, a car is not particularly useful but, for outlying areas, it is a viable option. Street parking in downtown Hamburg is limited, but parking garages with electronic space-availability displays are available.

By Bus: Hamburg can easily be reached from Berlin by bus. The **Berlin Linien Bus** departs daily at least every two hours between 7 am and 9 pm from Berlin ZOB am Funkturm to Hamburg ZOB am Hauptbahnhof. The journey takes just over three hours. Round-trip tickets are as low as €35.

Hamburg has an excellent public transportation system, which combines buses, trains, and ferries. Do note that some express buses are classified First Class and require more expensive tickets. (The Hamburg Card includes the surcharge for first class.)

Particularly useful for tourists is Bus 36. It runs from Rathausmarkt past most of the attractions, down the Reeperbahn, and continues via Altona to Blankenese. Bus 112 connects the Hauptbahnhof with Altona via the Landungsbrücke.

By Air: Hamburg Airport, Flughafenstr. 1-3, 22335 Hamburg, ☎ 040-50-750, www.ham.airport.de, is close to the city center. It is the fifth-largest airport in Germany and has flights to over 130 destinations, mainly inside Europe. The **Airport Express Bus** line 110 connects the airport every 10 minutes with Ohlsdorf station. From here U1, S1, and S11 run to downtown Hamburg in 20 minutes. (The S-Bahn will be connected to the airport in 2007.) Several other bus services are available to various parts of Hamburg, including the Airport Express to the Hauptbahnhof. Taxis from the airport to downtown Hamburg take 30 minutes and cost about €20 (according to meter). Fixed fares to other towns can be agreed upon prior to departure.

By Boat: Despite its famous harbor, no international ferry services serve this port. Ferries from Britain calls at Cuxhaven (see Lower Saxony chapter, page **) and from Scandinavia at Lübeck (see Schleswig-Holstein chapter, page**).

■ Information Sources

Tourist Office: Tourism information is available from **Hamburg Tourismus**, Postfach 102249, 20015 Hamburg, ☎ 040-300-51-333, www.hamburg-tourismus.de. In addition to information, the organization also books all kinds of accommodations and events. It has offices at the Hauptbahnhof and at the Landungsbrücke in St Pauli.

Hamburg Führer, www.hamburg.fuehrer.de, a free publication, lists what is on in Hamburg and has tips on sightseeing, restaurants, shopping, and events.

MONEY-SAVING TIP

The **Hamburg Card** (often simply HH-Card), allows free local transportation and reduced entrance to many museums and attractions, as well as city tours and harbor cruises. It comes in two versions: the single ticket (€7 for one day or €14.50 for three consecutive days) and a group ticket for up to five (€13 per day or €23 for three consecutive days). It is quite a good value – a bus trip and entry to the interesting Museum of Art and Crafts pays the cost of a single day ticket. The card is sold at tourism offices, hotels, and vending machines at many stations.

Visitors under 30 can save even more with the **Power-Pass**. It offers the same discounts as the HH-Card plus further discounts at movies, restaurants, clubs, and discos. It is €6.70 for the first day and can be extended up to seven days for €3 per day.

A **transportation-only card** is available at €4.45 per person or €7.40 for a group ticket for up to five. The card is valid only after 9 am.

■ Sightseeing

Hamburg has fewer high-profile sights than other large German cities such as Berlin and Munich. Like its inhabitants, Hamburg itself seems to enjoy being a bit reserved, formal, elegant, and stylish – never vulgar or showy.

The city is large and spread-out, but the tourist area is mainly concentrated in the area bound by the Hauptbahnhof and Binnenalster, St Pauli and the River Elbe. It is generally a pleasant city to stroll in but it is a long haul from for example the Hauptbahnhof to St Pauli, or even from the Rathaus to Speicherstadt. It is often best to use buses or trains to move between major sightseeing areas.

Rathausmarkt

Rathausmarkt is the heart of Hamburg and the place where most festivals and protests take place. Gotttfried Semper and Alexis de Chateauneuf used Venice's St Marks Square as inspiration when designing the Rathausmarkt in the 1840s, following the Great Fire. This is clearly seen in the Renaissance-style, white-pillared Alster Arcades. At the Kleinen Alster is a memorial for the fallen soldiers of the First World War. This monument, showing the misery of war, did not please the Nazis, who erected a more belligerent monument near Dammtor station. At the south end is a memorial for the poet Heinrich Heine that replaced a memorial destroyed by the Nazis.

However, the square is dominated by the magnificent Neo-Renaissance **Rathaus** (Town Hall), ☎ 040-428-312-063, built 1886-97. It has 647 rooms – for some reason the Hamburgers seem proud that this is apparently six more than in Buckingham Palace. The building is 111 by 70 m (364 x 230 feet) with a 112-m (368-foot) campanile. The façade facing the square is decorated with the bronze statues of 20 former emperors. The building rests on over 4,000 piles. The fountain in the courtyard commemorates the cholera epidemic of 1892 when almost 9,000 people were killed in just over two months. The interior of the Rathaus can only be seen on guided tours. Even if not taking a tour, stroll into the first rooms to see some of the splendor of this building. English tours are conducted from Monday to Thursday at 10:15 am and 3:15 pm, and from Friday to Sunday at 10:15 am and 1:15 pm. German tours are more frequent. Admission is €1.50.

Alster

The Alster is a 500-acre lake in the heart of Hamburg formed when the River Alster was dammed. The lake is divided into the Binnenalster (Inner Alster) and the much larger Aussenalster (Outer Aster). The division is formed by the Lombard rail bridge and the Kennedy road bridge.

The Binnenalster is lined on three sides by elegant buildings that form a beautiful backdrop to the water. In summer, a fountain sprays up to 35 m (115 feet) into the air. Walking around the Binnenalster takes just over half an hour. The most famous part is the Jungfernstieg, which is lined by expensive shops.

The Aussenalster is mostly lined by parks and a popular relaxation area. The lake itself is at most two m (6½ feet) deep and popular for all kinds of watersports. The shore is suitable for walking and cycling, but even a car trip is rewarding as several points allow views of the skyline with the four church towers and the Rathaus tower, all over 100 m (328 feet) high. (Drive clockwise for the best views and easier parking.) In summer, ferries operate on the lake, while pleasure cruises are available as long as the lake remains ice-free.

Hauptbahnhof

Mönckebergstraße, a major shopping street, leads from the Rathausmarkt to the Hauptbahnhof. In addition to the numerous department stores, two of Hamburg's main churches are along this boulevard.

St Petri Kirche (St Peter's Church), Speesort 10, ☎ 040-325-7400, first mentioned in 1195, is the oldest parish church in Hamburg. The Gothic church of the 14th century was destroyed during the Great Fire of 1842 and rebuilt in a Neo-Gothic style. The tower is 132 m (435 feet) high. The church suffered relatively minor damage during World War II and has many old artworks that were rescued from the fire. The lion door knob on the left door of the main portal dates from the 14th century and is considered the oldest artwork in Hamburg. The Madonna with Child dates from 1470. Concerts of religious music are scheduled on most Wednesdays at 5:15 pm. The church is open Monday to Saturday from 10 am to 6:30 pm, closing at 5 pm on Saturday. On Sunday it is open from 9 am to 9 pm.

The nearby **Jacobikirche** (St Jacob's), Jakobikirchhof 22, ☎ 040-303-7370, has a slightly shorter history, but parts of the 1340 brick Gothic basilica survived as the oldest actual church building in Hamburg. The church was frequently changed and has elements from every century in its design. The tower is 123 m (405 feet) high. The church was severely damaged during World War II but most of the art treasures were saved. Of special note are three early 16th-century altars and a marble pulpit from 1610. The 1693 Arp Schnitger organ, with 3,880 pipes, is the largest Baroque organ in Northern Germany. Opening hours are Monday to Saturday from 10 am to 5 pm.

Two blocks south of the church is the **Kontorhausviertel** (Counting House Buildings Quarter). Here, several huge brick office buildings were built in the 1920s. The best known is the 10-story **Chilehaus**, Buchardsplatz, which was erected in 1924 for the successful trader Henry B. Sloman, who traded sulfur with Chile. Its decorative façade serves as a prime example of the versatility of brick.

Nearby, just south of the Hauptbahnhof, is the excellent **Museum für Kunst und Gewerbe** (Arts & Crafts), Steintorplatz 1, ☎ 040-428-542-732, www.mkg-hamburg.de. It opened 1877 and established itself as one of Europe's leading museums for cultural history, decorative arts, design, and photography. In addition to the large collection of European items, it also has objects from the Middle East, China, and Japan. It has an impressive collection of keyboard instruments – an audio guide with music samples is included in the admission price. The instruments are played on special guided tours, usually on Thursday at 6:30, Saturday at 3, and Sunday at 4. Opening hours are Tuesday to Sunday from 10 am to 6 pm (closing at 9 pm on Thursday). Admission is €8.20.

Hamburg Kunsthalle (Art Gallery), Glockengiesserwall, ☎ 040-428-131-200, has art from Renaissance to modern. It has lesser-known works from all the major artists, as well as a large modern art collection displayed in a post-modern cubic building. Although the largest collection in Northern Germany, the old masters' section is not of the same quality and depth that is available in Berlin, Dresden, and Munich. The modern art collection is large, and especially strong in late 20th-century art. Opening hours are Tuesday to Sunday from 10 am to 6 pm (closing at 9 pm on Thursday). Admission is €8.50.

St Michaelis

St Michaelis (St Michel's Church), Englische Plancke 1a, ☎ 040-3767-8100, locally known as the Michel, is the symbol of Hamburg. The church had a rather eventful history. The first large church built here in 1647-61 was struck by lightening and burned down in 1750. Its replacement, completed in 1762, was a Baroque masterpiece. However, soldering work in 1906 caused the wooden tower to catch fire and the entire church burned down. Its replacement, completed in 1912, was severely damaged during World War II. The current church was completed in 1952 to the designs of 1750, but used more modern building techniques, including a convenient elevator to the top of the tower. The tower is 132 m (435 feet) high with a viewing platform at 82 m (264 feet). The church clock, with a diameter of eight m (26 feet), is the largest in Germany. The hands are five m (16 feet) and 3.6 m (11.8 feet) respectively.

The lovely Baroque interior seats 2,500 and is frequently used for organ concerts. The church has three organs, including a 1962 Steinmeyer organ with 6,665 pipes, a 1912 Marcussen organ with 3,562 pipes, and a Grollmann organ with 224 pipes. All three can be heard daily at noon. From Monday to Saturday at 10 am and 9 pm, Sunday at noon only, the tower trumpeter plays a hymn from the tower platform in all four wind directions.

The church is open from May to October, Monday to Saturday, 9 am to 6 pm, and Sunday from 11:30 am to 5:30 am. From November to April, it is open Monday to Saturday, 10 am to 4:30 pm and Sunday from 11:30 am to 4:30 pm. Admission to the church is free, but €2.50 for the tower.

Speicherstadt

When Hamburg lost its free trade status at the end of the 19th century, it responded by creating the world's largest free harbor to facilitate trade. In the process the Speicherstadt was built. Here, huge brick buildings formed the largest warehouses in the world. Up to 20,000 Hamburgers had to move to make way for these buildings that became the economic lifeline of the city. Many of these buildings, as well as large sections of the former port – the so-called HafenCity (Harbor City) – are currently being converted into office space and apartments in what is the largest building project in Europe. Several popular tourist spots are still open but note that the building activity makes navigation difficult in the area and signposting is presently poor to non-existent.

The **Hamburg Dungeon**, Kehrwieder 2-3, ☎ 040-3005-1512, offers a multimedia trip through the trials and tribulations of Hamburg's past. Themes include the great Hamburg fire, the Black Plague, the Inquisition, the floods of 1717, plundering Vikings, and the execution of the pirate Störtebeker. Opening hours are daily from 11 am to 6 pm. Admission is €13.45. Advance reservations are possible, and recommended in the high season. (The show is not recommended for children under 10, and children under 14 must be accompanied by an adult.)

Miniature Wonderland, Kehrwieder 2, ☎ 040-3005-1505, has one of the largest miniature train sets in the world. The display has models from many parts of the world using 500 trains, 5,000 m (16,400 feet) of rails, 50,000 lights, and 60,000 figures. Opening hours are weekdays from 10 am to 6 pm (Tuesday until 8 pm) and weekends from 9 am to 8 pm. Admission is €9.60.

Spicy's Gewürzmuseum (Spice Museum), Am Sandtorkai 31, ☎ 040-367-989, claims to be the only spice museum in the world. It has 800 displays including 50 spices that can be touched, smelled, and tasted. Opening hours are Tuesday to Sunday from 10 am to 5 pm. Admission is €3 (including some free samples).

Some distance away in the Baakenhafen is the **U-Bootmuseum Hamburg** (U-Boat Museum), Versmannstraße 23c, ☎ 040-

3200-4934, www.u-434.de. On display is a decommissioned Russian U-434, built in 1976 and in use until 2002. Guided tours of 45 minutes are available in multiple languages. Opening hours are daily from 10 am to 6 pm. Admission is €8.

The **Deutsches Zollmuseum** (German Custom Museum), Alter Wandrahm 16, ☎ 040-300-876, has exhibitions on customs in Germany and the world. On display are customs receipts dating back to Roman times as well as confiscated goods. Some original smuggling methods are also illustrated. The museum is appropriately located at the edge of the free port area. Opening hours are Tuesday to Sunday from 10 am to 5 pm. Admission is free.

Some of the loveliest early buildings in Hamburg are in the **Deichstraße**. The street has been in existence since at least 1304 but most houses here actually date from the 17th to 19th centuries. Many buildings were destroyed in the Great Fire of 1842 but rebuilt on the original foundations.

Planten und Blomen

Dammtor Bahnhof (station), Dag-Hammarskjöld-Platz, is in a 1903 Art Nouveau, glass and steel building. On the approach from downtown are a series of memorials for victims of World War II – a dispute between the Senate and the artist ended with only two of the works completed. Also in the region is the 1936 Kriegerdenkmal (War Memorial), erected by the Nazis who found the Hamburg First World War memorial at the Rathausmarkt too pacifist and defeatist.

In the 1930s, a large park called **Planten und Blomen** (Plants and Flowers) was laid out on the land of the former city defenses. It stretches as a wide green belt, a half-circle from the Alster to the Elbe. Close to Dammtor is the botanical garden as well as the largest Japenese garden in Europe. A Wasserlichtorgel (water and light organ) plays summer evenings at 10 pm (9 pm in September). It also performs at 2, 4, and 6 pm without light effects.

Still in the park, but close to St Pauli, is the **Museum für Hamburgische Geschichte** (Hamburg History), Holstenwall 24, ☎ 040-428-132-2380, www.hamburgmuseum.de. It is the largest city history museum in Germany and has several scale models in addition to historic items. Particularly popular are the models of the harbor and the railway system. It is housed in a 1922 building. Opening hours are Tuesday to Sunday from 10 am to 5 pm (closing at 6 pm on Sunday). Admission is €7.50.

St Pauli

St Pauli is Hamburg's most (in)famous neighborhood. From St Pauli U-Bahn Station, the 600-m (660-yard) **Reeperbahn** stretches westwards towards Altona. The Reeperbahn and Große Freiheit have traditionally been the red-light district of Hamburg. In addition to sex-related shops, they have 500 bars and restaurants. The area attracts 15 million visitors each year. Recent years have seen a gradual gentrification, with musical shows doing well in theaters at both ends of the Reeperbahn – *Cats* played nonstop for 15 years in the 1980s and 1990s. Sex still sells, but middle-class and family entertainment clearly brings in bigger profits.

PROSTITUTION

Prostitution is perfectly legal in Germany, although pimping and many related activities are not. Prostitutes have their own labor unions that set working hours, rates, and work practices. They are supposed to pay tax, but politicians frequently lament about the low amount of both income and value added tax that is actually forked over. However, even in this legal framework, prostitution remains very much an underworld culture with dubious practices and frequent complaints – especially about east European women being forced into prostitution through illegal contracts. Red light districts, sex shops, and related businesses are usually found in the vicinity of train stations.

During the day, the area is quiet – it only comes to life after 8 pm and then knows no official closing time. A huge police presence means that the area is pretty safe at all hours. Halfway down the Reeperbahn is the **Davidwache** – Germany's best-known police station. In addition to being busy, it also features frequently in German films and television programs. Nearby is the **Herbertstraße**, since 1900 a closed-off street that basically turned into a huge brothel district. Since the mid-1980s, the street has been open to men only. (The prostitutes working here got tired of troops of school and pensioner bus parties strolling through with cameras in hand.)

The Landungsbrücke

The Reeperbahn runs parallel to the River Elbe, which is only a few minutes walk downhill. In between St Pauli and the Landungsbrücke U-Bahn stations is a 14.8-m (50-foot) high statue of Otto von Bismarck. It was erected in 1906 and depicts the protective power of Bismarck's mighty German Empire over the trade interests of Hamburg.

Otto von Bismarck

The **Landungsbrücke** is Europe's largest floating island – it is a pontoon bridge that is a popular hangout spot with ample benches and restaurants to sit and watch the world go by. Many future Americans departed from here to the New World. Nowadays, virtually all harbor cruises leave from here. The Art Nouveau reception halls were constructed in 1909, with archways to the pontoon, two corner towers, and cupolas.

At the west end is the **Alte Elbtunnel** (Old Elbe Tunnel). It was completed in 1911 and connects St Pauli with the opposite bank via two tiled tunnels. Elevators on both ends are used to lower cars and pedestrians by 23 m (75 feet). Cars have to pay a toll and may only use the tunnel from Monday to Saturday. The **New Elbe Tunnel**, part of the Autobahn A7, is three km (two miles) west of the old one and opened in 1975. It currently has four passageways and is used by 100,000 cars per day.

At the east end is the **Rickmer Rickmers**, St Pauli Landungbrücke Pier 1, ☎ 040-319-5959, a former East Indies windjammer. A museum is housed inside this green and red vessel. Built in Bremerhaven in 1896 and confiscated off the Azores in 1916, it served the Portuguese navy up to 1962 as a training vessel and opened as a museum following restoration in 1987. Opening hours are daily from 10 am to 6 pm. Admission is €3. There is a restaurant on board.

Slightly farther upstream is the **Überseebrücke**. Visiting naval vessels often anchor here – opening hours are listed at the gangway. Permanently anchored here is the **MS *Cap San Diego***, Überseebrücke, ☎ 040-364-209, built in Hamburg in 1962 to serve the trade route to South America. The ship remained in service up to 1986 but the changeover to containers made it outdated. It is one of the last ships built of this type. Opening hours are daily from 10 am to 6 pm. Admission is €5.

Altona

Altona is about four km (three miles) west of downtown Hamburg. It only became part of Hamburg in 1937 and previously often acted as a rival. The town was under Danish control from 1640 until 1867 and, during this period, was a constant thorn in Hamburg's side. At times it allowed more liberal drinking hours within easy strolling distance from the often more conservative Hamburg. Far more seriously, it also tried to compete in trade and shipping.

The **Altona Museum/Norddeutsches Landesmuseum** (North German Museum), Museumstraße 23, ☎ 040-42-811-3582, www.altonaer-museum.hamburg.de, has exhibitions on North German art and cultural history. The importance of the fishing and shipping industries is tracked as well. The museum also has a large collection of ships' figureheads. Opening hours are Tuesday to Sunday from 11 am to 6 pm. Admission is €6.

South of the Rathaus is the so-called **Altonaer Balkon** (Altona's Balcony). This terrace allows views of large stretches of the Elbe and is one of the best spots to admire the incredible number of ships passing through to the harbor. Cruise ships dock nearby in the Altona Harbor when visiting Hamburg. From here the Elbchaussee runs parallel with the Elbe River and passes some of the largest and most expensive houses in Germany en route to the suburb of Blankenese.

The most famous sight in Altona is the **Fischmarkt** (Fish Market) – see *Shopping: Flea Markets,* page** for details.

■ Cultural Events

Hamburg has a full cultural calendar with concerts of all types scheduled throughout the year. Classical music is popular and concerts are held in many dedicated halls and churches. Theater and cabaret are also available but always in German only.

In recent years, Hamburg has become famous as the city in Germany to see musicals. Although the names are instantly recognizable, all lyrics are sung in German. These musicals are a huge source of income for the city and tourism operators with trips from all over Germany scheduled around seeing a musical while in Hamburg. For example, at the time of writing *The Lion King* was sold out more than a year in advance.

The tourism office has information on most events and can make reservations for many at a charge similar to that of all advance ticket booking services.

■ Festivals

The **Hafengeburtsdag** (literally Harbor's Birthday) is one of Hamburg's greatest festivals. It celebrates the founding of the harbor on May 7, 1188, when Emperor Friedrich I Barbarossa guaranteed tax-free entry for all ships from the North Sea down the River Elbe to Hamburg. The festival has many cultural and gastronomic events, but the highlight is the parade of ships, including everything from historic windjammers to modern cruise ships.

Dom usually translates as "Cathedral" and a Dom at the Heiligengeistfeld (Holy Ghost Field) seems fitting. However, this particular **Dom** refers to the largest fun fair in Northern Germany. It is held three times a year in Hamburg for about a month on each occasion. It opens daily at 3 pm.

■ Shopping

Passages

Hamburg is famous for its large number of "passages," or covered malls. Most are in the triangle formed by Jungfernstieg, Fuhlentwiete, and Alsterfleet. Most top brand name shops are here, while Mönckebergstraße near the Hauptbahnhof has the top department stores (the Karstadt is the largest department store in Hamburg). Peek & Cloppenburg has upmarket, mainly European-made clothes.

For top international brands such as Hermès, Giorgio Armani, and Hugo Boss, head to Neuer Wall. Other top brands are found in the immediate vicinity.

Antiques Market

A few minutes walk from the Hauptbahnhof is **Antik-Center**, Klosterwall 9-21. Here, there are 39 small shops selling all kinds of antiques. With so many dealers in close proximity, bargains are not likely, but neither are outrageous prices. Opening hours are Tuesday to Friday from noon to 6 pm, and Saturday from 10 am to 2 pm and 4 to 6 pm.

Flea Market

The most famous flea market in Hamburg is the **Fischmarkt** in Altona, held Sunday mornings from 5 am to 10 am (mid-November to mid-March from 7 am). It is a huge market with live music and eating and drinking. The market is favored by late night revelers, who come here straight from nightspots, and by early risers as well. Fish is actually still sold on the sidelines, but now of lesser importance.

■ Adventures

On Foot

Town Walks

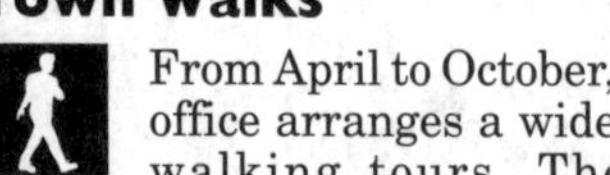

From April to October, the tourism office arranges a wide selection of walking tours. The two-hour walks are mostly on weekday afternoons from 4 pm or Saturday from 2:30. The schedule, with starting points for the various walks, is available from the tourism office.

Stattreisen Hamburg, Bartelsstraße 12, ☎ 040-430-3481, www.statttreisen-hamburg.de, has more specialized tours in a season that runs from February to November. Some tours are in English. Prior reservations are generally not required but are essential for the popular Beatles in St Pauli tour.

Jogging

Innovative Sport Organisation, Goesta Gerd Dreise, Schanzenstr. 41a, ☎ 0178-660-6604, www.touristjogging.de, guides joggers through Hamburg on four routes ranging from seven to 10 km (four to six miles), taking 45 to 80 minutes. The jogging tours generally start at 8 am or 6 pm.

On Wheels

By Bicycle

Hamburg is a pleasant city to cycle in, at least away from the busiest roads. Popular cycling areas are around the Alster and along the Elbe. Outside rush hours, bicycles may be taken for free on subways and all day on Elbe ferries.

Bicycles can be rented from **DB Service**, Hachmannplatz at the Hauptbahnhof, ☎ 040-319-850-475.

Several companies offer guided cycling tours to various parts of Hamburg. **Sightcycling (SD-Bikes)**, Jarrestraße 29, ☎ 040-278-008-00, www.sightcycling.de, has eight different tours. Your own bicycle is required.

Bikestation, Burmesterstrasse 34a, ☎ 0178-640-1800, www.bikestation-hamburg.de, is run by a local who conducts four- to five-hour cycling tours – bicycle rental and a coffee is included in the price.

Stattreisen Hamburg, Bartelsstraße 12, ☎ 040-430-3481, www.stattreisen-hamburg.de, is famous for themed walking tours, but also conducts a few bicycle tours per year. Your own bicycle is required.

By Bus

Three bus tours operate in cooperation with the Hamburg tourism office. The **Top Tour**, www.top-tour-hamburg.de, uses open-top double-decker buses on a circular route with several hop-on, hop-off points. During the high season, buses depart every 30 minutes from 9:30 am. The **Gala-Tour**, www.gala-tour.de, is a standard 50-km (30-mile) bus tour taking in all the major sights in 2½ hours. Departures are daily at 10 am and 2 pm. **The Scene Night Tour** includes a walking tour of the Reeperbahn area and a visit to a bar. It departs Friday and Saturday at 9 pm. The principal departure point for all three tours is the Hauptbahnhof/Kirchenallee. Tickets are available on the bus or from many hotels.

In the Air

Hot-Air Ballooning

Ballons Über Hanburg, Schrammsweg 25, ☎ 040-484-577, www.ballons-ueber-hamburg.de, offers hot-air balloon flights over Hamburg at sunrise and sunset. Prices are around €210 per person over the weekend and slightly cheaper during the week. Morning flights are usually cheaper too.

Seaplane

A seaplane, operated by **Himmelschreiber**, ☎ 040-378-341, www.himmelsschreiber.de, takes off from the River Elbe at the City Sporthafen on Baumwall. Flights depart every 45 minutes, Tuesday to Sunday from 10 am until dark. Flights last 20 minutes plus taxi time and cost €85. Children under three or weighing less than 15 kg (33 lbs) fly for free.

Historic Plane

Flights over Hamburg in a JU52 depart from Hamburg Airport. Flights of 30 minutes cost €160 per person, and 60 minute flights are €260. Reservations at ☎ 040-5070-1717

Helicopter Flights

Helicopter Service Wasserthal, ☎ 040-5075-2114, offers helicopter flights and transfers from Hamburg Airport.

On Water

Boat Rentals

Segelschule Pieper Sohn, An der Alster at the Hotel Atlantic, ☎ 040-247-578, rents sail- , pedal- , and rowboats daily, 10 am to 9 pm from April to early October.

Canal & Harbor Cruises

Boat trips in Hamburg can be divided into two distinct categories: cruises of the harbor and cruises on the Alster Lake and canals. When in Germany's largest port city, a harbor tour is considered a must. However, touring the *fleets*, the traditional canals that led to the warehouses and other sites, is also interesting.

Harbor Cruises: Virtually all harbor cruises depart from the Landungsbrücke. There is little to distinguish the cruises, either in content or price. It is generally best to simply select the next cruise that departs, unless a particular ship is desired. Smaller boats can go deeper into canals, while larger boats usually have better views from the top deck. Buying tickets when boarding allows for flexibility but can lead to disappointment in the high season.

The largest operator is **HADAG**, St Pauli Fischmarkt 28, ☎ 040-311-7070, www.hadag.de. In addition to the river and harbor cruises, HADAG also runs ferry or waterbus services. These are much cheaper than the regular harbor cruises. On some routes, the Hamburg Card or other transportation cards are valid. Particularly popular is Route 62 that runs from Sandtorhöft near the Altstadt via Landungsbrücke and Altona to Finkenwerder. From here, connections to Blankenese are available via Teufelsbrück. Route 73 is also popular – it goes from Landungbrücke via the Theater im Hafen deeper into the harbor.

Kapitän Prüsse, Bei den St Pauli Landungsbrücke, Brücke 3A, ☎ 040-313-130, www.kapitaen-pruesse.de, is another large organization. In addition to standard cruises, it also operates a Mississippi-style boat that departs from the Überseebrücke.

Alster & Fleet Cruises: Boats operate on the Alster Lake and the waterways (*fleet*) of old Hamburg. **ATG**, Anleger Jungfernstieg, ☎ 040-357-4240, www.alstertouristik.de, has several boat trips daily. The main season is from May to September but cruises are available all year. There are several cruises on the lake itself but more interesting are the ones on the *fleets*. The boats are narrow and small enough to enter canals inaccessible to the larger vessels operating harbor cruises. From April to September, a ferry service connects several stations on the Alster.

■ Where to Stay & Eat

Raffles Hotel Vier Jahreszeiten is a grand hotel, perfectly located on the Binnenalster. Its core is an 1897 Gründerzeit building, but rooms are modern, large, elegant, and luxurious. It has a large, exclusive spa area. Raffles' elegant **Haerlin** restaurant (€€€-€€€€) is one of the best in Hamburg, serves mainly French cuisine, and offers great views of the Binnenalster. **Doc Cheng's** (€€-€€€) serves Euro-Asian food in a faux 1920s Shanghai-style locale. Neuer Jungfernstieg 9, 20354 ☎ 040-34-940, fax 040-3494-2600, www.raffles-hvj.de. (€€€€)

Kempinski Hotel Atlantic has been known as the Weiße Riese (White Giant) since it opened its doors in 1909. This elegant luxury hotel is close to the Hauptbahnhof on the banks of the Außenalster. Rooms are modern, luxurious, and elegant – some with lake views. The Kempinski's **Atlantic** restaurant (€€€-€€€€) serves nouvelle cuisine with French and Italian influences, while the **Atlantic-Mühle** (€€-€€€) serves local specialties. An der Alster 72, 20099 Hamburg, ☎ 040-28-880, fax 040-247-129, www.kempinski.de. (€€€€)

Dorint Am Alter Wall is a luxurious designer hotel that opened in 2000 in a converted former post office building close to the Rathaus. It is stylish and modern with wood, concrete, and marble surfaces. Rooms are comfortable and modern. Alter Wal 40, 20457 Ha,burg, ☎ 040-369-500, fax 040-3695-1000, www.dorint.de. (€€€€)

The red brick **Steigenberger Hotel** is ideally situated between the Rathaus and harbor area. The modern bedrooms are large and elegant. Large windows allow ample natural light, although the views from some rooms are better than from others. The hotel has its own two docks on the Alsterfleet waterway. The **Calla** restaurant (€€€-€€€€) at the Steigenberger serves Euro-Asian food and is open for dinner only. **Bistro am Fleet** (€€) is a modern restaurant serving a wide range of international dishes. Heiligengeistbrücke 4, 20458 Hamburg, ☎ 040-368-060, fax 040-3680-6777, www.steigenberger.de. (€€€€)

The **Intercontinental Hotel** is on the Außenalster with views of the lake and the city skyline. This luxury hotel has comfortable, well-equipped rooms. It is open for dinner only. The Hamburg Spielbank (Casino) is inside the hotel. **Windows** restaurant (€€€€) in the Intercontinental serves international cuisine with a view – it is on the ninth floor facing the lake and city. Fontenay 10, 20354 Hamburg, ☎ 040-41-420, fax 040-4142-2999, www.interconti.com. (€€€€)

The **Renaissance Hamburg Hotel** is a modern hotel behind a historic brick façade in the heart of the shopping area. It is connected to the Hanse-Viertel shopping mall. Rooms are comfortable and decorated in shades of yellow and red. The Renaissance's modern **Esprit** restaurant (€€-€€€) serves nouvelle cuisine with strong north German influences. Große Bleichen, 20354 Hamburg, ☎ 040-349-180, fax 040-3491-8919, www.renaissancehotels.com. (€€€-€€€€)

Hotel Elysée is a few minutes from the Dammtor station. It is a luxury hotel with comfortable rooms. The library has a wide range of international newspapers. **Piazza Romana** restaurant (€€-€€€) at the Elysée serves international cuisine with strong Mediterranean influences. The **Bourbon Street Bar** has live music. Rothenbaumchaussee 10, 20148 Hamburg, ☎ 040-414-120, fax 040-4141-2733, www.elysee-hamburg.de. (€€€-€€€€)

The modern **SIDE** designer hotel opened in 2001 near the Staatsoper. Rooms are luxurious and modern. **Fusion** (€€-€€€) is equally modern and serves Euro-Asian food. Drehbahn 49, 20354 Hamburg, ☎ 040-309-990, fax 040-3099-9399, www.side-hamburg.de. (€€€€)

Hotel Europäischer Hof is Hamburg's largest privately managed hotel and has been in operation since 1925. It is at the Hauptbahnhof. Rooms are large and comfortable. The hotel has a large spa area with a 150-m (500-foot) waterslide that goes down six stories. The room key gives access to three days of public transportation and a harbor cruise. Kirchenallee 45, 20099 Hamburg, ☎ 040-248-248, fax 040-2482-4799, www.europaeischer-hof.de. (€€€-€€€€)

The 26-floor **Hotel Radisson SAS** is Hamburg's tallest hotel. It is inside the Planten und Blomen park and connected to the Congress Center and the Dammtor Station. Rooms are well-equipped and have grand views. The restaurant **Trader's Vic's** (€€-€€€) serves Polynesian and French cuisine (open for dinner only). Marseiller Straße 2, 20355 Hamburg, ☎ 040-35-020, fax 040-3502-3440, www.radissaonsas.com. (€€€-€€€€)

The **Intercity Hotel Hamburg Hauptbahnhof** opened in 2004 across the road from the Hauptbahnhof near the Mönckestraße shopping area. The hotel is modern, with well-equipped and comfortable rooms, aimed mainly at the business traveler. The room key gives free access to local transportation. Glockengießerwall 14/15, 20095 Hamburg, ☎ 040-248-700, fax 040-2487-0111, www.intercityhotel.de. (€€€)

The **Intercity Hotel Hamburg-Altona** opened next to the Altona ICE station in 1995. It has modern, well-equipped rooms. The location allows easy access to local attractions in Altona as well as to downtown Hamburg. The room key gives free access to local public transportation. Paul-Nevermann-Platz 17, 22765 Hamburg-Altone, ☎ 040-431-6026, fax 040-439-7579, www.intercityhotel.de. (€€-€€€)

Hotel Hafen is on a hill above the Landungsbrücke with grand views of the Elbe from most rooms. The hotel has three wings and the oldest keeps its seafaring tradition with many maritime decorative items. The newer wing has rooms that are more comfortable. The best option, but pricier, is the elegant Classic Residenz. The close proximity of the Landungsbrücke and the Reperbahn makes the hotel a popular destination for those attending the musicals performed on the Reperbahn and across the Elbe. The restaurant (€€-€€€) serves international dishes and offers lovely views of the Landungsbrücke area. Limited free parking is available on a first-come, first-park basis. Seewartenstraße 9, 20459 Hamburg, ☎ 040-311-130, fax 040-3111-3755, www.hotel-hamburg.de. (€€-€€€)

Privately run **Hotel Baseler Hof** is between the Alster and the botanical garden. Rooms are comfortably furnished. The **Restaurant Kleinhuis** (€-€€) serves new German cooking in a bistro-style locale. Esplanade 11, 20354 Hamburg, ☎ 040-359-060, fax 040-3590-6918, www.vch.de. (€€-€€€)

Nearby is the **Alster Hof**, another privately run establishment. Rooms have functional furniture, with some rooms recently refurbished. Esplanade 12, 20354 Hamburg, ☎ 040-350-070, fax 040-3500-7514, www.alster-hof.de. (€€-€€€)

Best Western St Raphael is a few blocks from the Hauptbahnhof. It was the first designer hotel in Hamburg and rooms are still modern, comfortable, and in a range of different styles. The restaurant **Le Jardin** (€€) serves international cuisine. Adenauerallee 41, 20097 Hamburg, ☎ 040-248-200, fax 040-2482-0333, www.bestwestern.com. (€€-€€€)

Hotel Kronprinz is next to the Hauptbahnhof and has neat rooms furnished with high-quality solid wood furniture. Some antiques are used in the public areas. Kirchenallee 46, 20099 Hamburg, ☎ 040-271-4070, fax 040-280-1097, www.kronprinz-hamburg.de. (€€)

The **Ibis** chain has several hotels in Hamburg, of which three are well-located for tourists. As is usual with this chain, there are few thrills, no minibars but clean rooms at low prices in attractive locations. (All €€ even during event times.) The **Ibis Hamburg Alster**, Holzdamm 4-12, 20099 Hamburg, ☎ 040-248-290, fax 040-2482-9734, is near the Hauptbahnhof on the banks of the Alster. The **Ibis Altona**, Königstraße 4, 22767 Hamburg, ☎ 040-311-870, fax 040-3118-7304, is at the far end of the Reeperbahn and popular with tour groups visiting the nearby musical theater. The **Ibis St Pauli**, Simon-von-Utrecht-Straße 63, 20359 Hamburg, ☎ 040-650-460, fax 040-6504-6555, is at the east end of the Reeperbahn near St Pauli U-Bahn station.

Farther Afield

Hamburg has a few hotels that are unique and worth going the extra distance for. Some are extraordinarily luxurious, while others simply offer interesting variations on the hotel theme.

Gastwerk Hotel Hamburg is west of Altona in a former gasworks plant. The building style has been described as Industrial Design. The rooms are huge and loft-like with ample use of natural wood and attention to details. Beim Alten Gaswerk 3/Ecke Daimlerstraße, 22761 Hamburg-Bahnrenfeld, ☎ 040-890-620, fax 040-890-220, www.gastwerk-hotel.de. (€€€€)

About 20 km (12 miles) west of Hamburg, with Elbe views, is the **Hotel Louis C Jacob**. Many consider this luxury hotel not only the best in the region, but the best in Germany. It is typical of Hamburg – elegant, but restrained, with great attention to detail. The furniture is of the best quality and carpets are handmade. Rooms have marvelous views of the Elbe and the harbor. The Michelin star restaurant (€€€€) serves international nouvelle cuisine. It has an excellent wine list. As does the **Kleines Jacob** (€-€€€), a wine bar across the road that serves hearty local and Mediterranean cuisine. Elbeschausee 401, 22609 Hamburg-Nienstedten, ☎ 040-822-550, fax 040-8225-5444, www.hotel-jacob.de. (€€€€)

Clipper Hotels, www.clipper-hotels.de, have two luxury apartment buildings in central Hamburg. They basically function as a luxury hotel, but have the space and convenience of apartments. Both facilities are elegant and some apartments have excellent views. These are mainly aimed at business visitors – as a result, the prices drop over weekends. On long weekends, the discerning traveler can move into the grand suite at a fraction of the normal price. The **Clipper Elb Lodge**, Carsten-Rehder-Straße 71, 22767 Hamburg, ☎ 040-809-010, fax 040-8090-1999, is the more luxurious, with elegant designer furniture and harbor views. The **Hanse Clipper Haus**, Ditmar-Koel-Straße 1, 20459 Hamburg, ☎ 040-376-960, fax 040-3769-6194, is close to the Landungsbrücke. (€€-€€€€)

Hotel Nippon, as the name indicates, is Japanese-style with straight lines, clear colors, and restrained elegance. Bedrooms have tatami mats and shoji screens. The hotel is a few blocks from the Außenalster. The **Wa Yo** restaurant (€€-€€€) serves Japanese food in a typical modern Japanese ambiance. Hofweg 75, 22085 Hamburg, ☎ 040-227-1140, fax 040-2271-1490, www.nippon-hotel-hh.de. (€€€)

25 hours Hotel Hamburg welcomes visitors of all ages, but those under 25 receive about 40% discount. Rooms are furnished with stylish, modern furniture. Paul-Dessau-Straße 2, 22761 Hamburg, ☎ 040-855-070, fax 040-5550-7100, www.25hours-hotel.de. (€€-€€€)

Other Restaurants

In addition to the hotel restaurants mentioned above, Hamburg has many other excellent places to eat in all price classes scattered through the city.

Anna, Bleichenbrücke 2, ☎ 040-367-014, is a rustic locale with terrace near the Rathaus. It serves a wide range of dishes with a large selection of local specialties. (€€€)

Nearby, close to the Binnenalster on the second floor of a passage, is **Il Restorante**, Große Bleichen 16, ☎ 040-343-335. It serves nouvelle cuisine with Italian flair. The restaurant is favored by local VIPs. (€€€)

Across the road from the Michaelskirche is **San Michele**, Englische Plancke 8, ☎ 040-371-127. It serves Italian food, mostly from the Naples region. A good choice in a neighborhood that otherwise lacks decent dining spots. (€€-€€€)

Ratsweinkeller, Große Johannisstraße 2, ☎ 040-364-153, is in the historic vaults underneath the impressive Rathaus. The restaurant is stylish and decorated with ship models and maritime items. The menu has a large selection of local specialties, but also more international fare. (€€-€€€)

Îlot, ABC-Straße 46, ☎ 040-3571-5885, is a modern restaurant with large windows and a terrace. It serves Mediterranean cuisine with strong French and North African influences. There is a large vegetarian selection. (€-€€€)

Le Plat du Jour, Dornbuschstraße 4, ☎ 040-321-414, is a bistro-style restaurant serving excellent French food at reasonable prices. It is near the Rathaus in the Altstadt area. (€€)

Casse Croute, Büschstraße 2, ☎ 040-343-373, is another bistro-style restaurant serving mainly French food. It is near the Gänsemarkt. (€€)

Nearby is **Matsumi**, Colonnaden 96, ☎ 040-343-125, an excellent Japanese restaurant. It serves classic Japanese dishes in an authentic setting. There are some 50 types of sushi and sashimi, as well as classic Japanese dishes such as teppenyaki, sukiyaki, and shabu shabu. (€-€€€)

Jena Paradies, Klosterwall 23, ☎ 040-327-008, is at the south end of the Hauptbahnhof inside a former art academy. A wide variety of dishes, ranging from French to Austrian, are served inside this Bauhaus-style building. Lunch menus are particularly good value. (€-€€€).

There are many informal coffee shops and restaurants in the downtown area, but none has a better view than **Alex im Alsterpavillon**, Jungfernstieg 54, ☎ 040-350-1870. Located in the elegant pavilion on the banks of the Binnenalster, it offers the best views of the lake. (€-€€)

The **Arkaden Café**, Alsterarkaden 9-10, seems to have all the elements of a tourist trap. It is in the Alster Arcade with wonderful views of the Rathaus from the terrace, or the Alsterfleet from the basement rooms. However, prices show no tourist markup, service is fast and friendly, and the bistro-style food is good. It has great breakfast options from 8 am – two hours before anything else in the vicinity opens for the day. (€-€€)

Camping

Camping Buchholz is within easy walking distance from U-Bahn station Hagenbecks Tierpark. Facilities are rather basic as it is mostly considered a one-night transit campground, with only 30 spaces for tourists. Open year-round. Kielerstraße 374, ☎ 040-540-4532, fax 040-540-2536, www.camping-buchholz,de.

Camping Schnelsen Nord is 15 km (10 miles) north of Hamburg. It is directly next to the A7 highway (and the local Ikea) but noise levels are acceptable due to sound reduction walls. Facilities are good. There are 150 tourist spaces. Open from April to October. Wunderbrunnen 2, ☎ 040-559-4225, fax 040-550-7334, www.campingplatz-hamburg.de.

Bremen

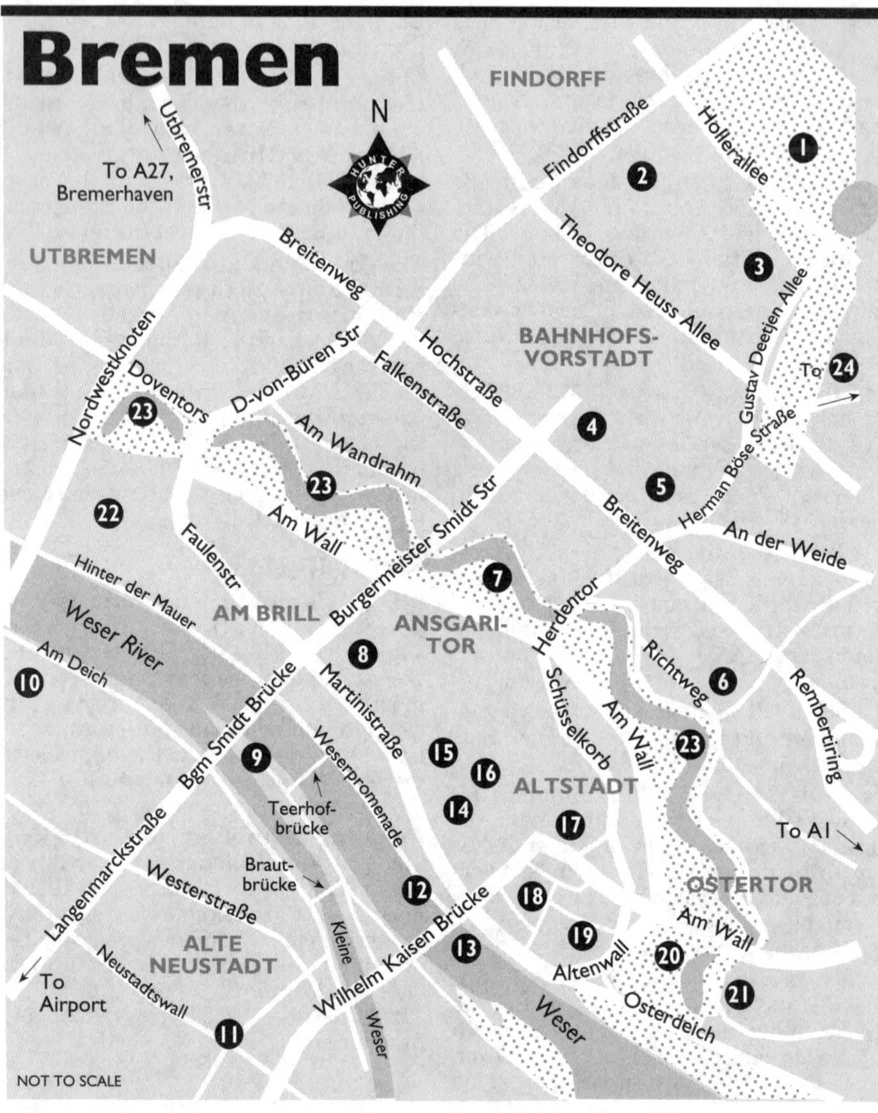

1. Bürgerpark
2. Bürgerweide Park, Schlachthof Arts Center
3. Bremen Exhibition Center
4. Übersee Museum
5. Hauptbahnhof, Tourist Information
6. Bremen Musical Theater
7. Windmill am Wall
8. Gewerbehaus (crafts center)
9. Neues Museum Wesenburg Bremen
10. Beck's Brewery Visitors Center
11. Bremen Shakespeare Co.
12. Martini Landing Stage (river cruise dock), St Martini Kirche
13. Bremen Theater Ship
14. Böttcherstraße: Glockenspiel, Paula Modersohn-Becker Museum, Roselin Museum
15. Stadtwaage Museum
16. Rathaus, statues of Knight Roland and Brementown Musicians, Cathedral of St Petri, Unser Liebfrau Kirche
17. Die Glocke Concerthall
18. St Johann Kirche
19. Schnoor Quarter: Travesty Theater, St Jacobus Warehouse
20. Kunsthalle (Bremen Art Museum), Gerhard Marcks House, Wagenfeld Design Museum
21. Theatre on Goetheplatz, Schauspielhaus Theater, MOKS im Brauhaus Theater
22. St Stephani Kirche, Seemannsheim
23. Stadtgaben (moat/park)
24. Bremen University, Rhododendron Park & Botanika, Focke Museum

Bremen

In this Chapter

Bremen is the smallest state in Germany. It has a population of 660,000 and consists of two territories: Bremen City and Bremerhaven, which is 65 km (39 miles) downstream at the mouth of the River Weser.

Bremen's tourism appeal is based on a combination of old and new. It has some beautiful historic buildings and neighborhoods that form the traditional tourist attractions. However, in recent years some high-technology sites were added that appeal especially to younger visitors. Bremerhaven in contrast is not a beautiful town. Its major draw is its harbor and maritime life, with the German Maritime Museum worth the journey.

History

Bremen entered written history in 787 when Charlemagne elevated the town to a bishopric. It became an archbishopric in 847 and experienced a golden age in the 11th century. It joined the Hanseatic League in 1358 and in 1646 became a Free Imperial City. Despite major damage during World War II, parts of Bremen's old town survived or were restored to their former condition. Bremen managed to remain a separate state when the Federal Republic of Germany was founded in 1949 and is, together with Bavaria, the oldest continuous political entity in the German-speaking world.

The harbor with its related trade and fisheries has been the lifeline for Bremen for most of its existence. Currently, it is the second-largest in Germany and mainly used for the importation of raw materials. More glamorously, it is also the main conduit of German-built cars to intercontinental destinations – 700,000 cars pass through the harbor annually. Half of all coffee consumed in Germany is imported through Bremen – coffee shops were fashionable here in the late 17th century, long before they were opened in Leipzig or Vienna. Decaffeinated coffee was first made here by Ludwig Roselius, who subsequently used his wealth to promote art projects in Bremen; some are still major attractions.

Getting Here

By Rail: Bremen has good rail connections to the rest of Germany, usually requiring changeovers at Hamburg or Hanover, each around an hour by trains that depart hourly or even more often. Berlin is just under three hours away and Frankfurt around four.

Bremerhaven can be reached by twice-an-hour trains in 34-52 minutes, and Cuxhaven in 90-120 minutes – usually requiring a changeover in Bremerhaven.

By Road: Bremen is easily reached by road. The A27 connects Bremen with Bremerhaven and Cuxhaven. The A1 runs east to Hamburg and west to Osnabrück and the Rhinelands. The A27 connects to the A7 near Hanover.

By Air: Bremen Airport, Flughafenallee 20, ☎ 0421-55-950, www.airport-bremen.de, has mostly domestic and low-cost carriers serving European destinations. **Hamburg Airport** is often a more realistic option. The airport can be reached by taxi in 20 minutes (€10), or Tramline 6 – running every 10 minutes from downtown. It costs less than €2, and stops only 22 m (72 feet) from the check-in counters!

By Boat: Bremen and Bremerhaven are major ports, but they see few non-freight arrivals. Passenger ferries to Harwich in England use Cuxhaven – see the Lower Saxony chapter.

Information Sources

Tourist Office: Tourist information is available from the Bremer Touristik-Zentrale, Findorffstraße 105, 28215 Bremen, ☎ 0180-510-1030, www.bremen-tourism.de. The office also makes reservations for accommodations, events, and all adventures listed below.

DISCOUNT TICKETS

*The **EntdeckerCard Nordwest**, www.entdeckerdard.de, is valid for 72 hours and allows free local transportation and entry to 120 sights in a large area around Bremen. It is valid from Osnabrück to Cuxhaven. The cost is €39.*

■ Getting Around

Bremen's old town is compact and easily explored on foot. Outlying destinations are usually easiest to reach by tram.

■ Sightseeing

The port plays a much smaller role in tourism than in Hamburg. Bremen combines an historic core with several modern, high-technology attractions slightly farther afield.

Marktplatz

Bremen's huge **Rathaus** (Town Hall) is one of the loveliest civic buildings in Germany. It was constructed as a Gothic building in 1410, but received its Weser Renaissance façade (see page **) during the 17th century. The statues of Charlemagne and the seven electors are copies – the original Gothic works are in the Focke-Museum. At the west wing is a 1951 Gerhard Marcks bronze of the Street Musicians of Bremen. The interior of the Rathaus has impressive historic rooms. Guided tours are given Monday to Saturday at 11 am, noon, 3 and 4 pm, and Sunday at 11 am and noon. Admission is €4.

THE STREET MUSICIANS OF BREMEN

The Street Musicians of Bremen (*Bremer Stadtmusikanten*) is one of the fairy tales recorded by the Brothers Grimm. According to this tale, a donkey, dog, cat, and cockerel fled their original homes when the onset of old age made them useless to their owners and thereby threatened their continued survival. The four decided to go to Bremen and try their luck at being street musicians. En route, their terrible singing scared thieves from their robbers' nest and the four moved in and lived happily ever after. Although they never actually made it to Bremen itself, Bremen is happy to celebrate them nonetheless.

At the west wing is the entrance to the **Ratskeller** (Council Cellar), Am Markt, ☎ 0421-321-676, which has been in operation for 600 years. There are magnificent vaults, huge pillars, ornate wine vats, and quaint drinking cubicles. It sells exclusively German wine sourced from 650 estates and is open daily from 11 am to midnight.

The huge 5.55-m (18-foot) statue of **Roland** has been a sign of the town's civic freedom and independence since 1404. It is the tallest of the 26 Roland statues still in existence in Germany. (The real significance of these Roland statues is still being debated.)

The modern 1966 **Haus der Bürgerschaft** houses the city and state parliaments. Arguments still rages as to whether it blends in harmoniously or entirely ruins the historic square. In sharp contrast is the nearby **Haus Schütting**. This 1537 Renaissance building is the former guild house of Bremen traders and has housed the Chamber of Commerce since 1849. The elaborate entrance was added in the 19th century.

The **St Petri-Dom** (St Peter's Cathedral), Marktplatz, was erected in the 11th century, but the exterior drastically altered in the 13th and 16th centuries. The tall spires were rebuilt in the late 19th century. Inside, the original Romanesque capitals and bronze baptismal font can be seen in the western crypt. There is also a small, Gottfried Silberman organ – the only one outside Saxony. The Bleikeller (Lead Cellar) has mummified bodies in eight glass coffins that for unknown reasons did not decompose. Opening hours are weekdays from 10 am to 5 pm, Saturday from 10 am to 2 pm, and Sunday from 2 to 5 pm. The spires (€1) and Lead Cellars (€1.40) are open weekdays only.

The **Dom Museum** (Cathedral Museum) has mainly vestments on display but also a number of noteworthy altarpieces and paintings by Lucas Cranach. Opening hours are weekdays from 10 am to 5 pm (11 am to 4 pm, November to March), Saturday from 10 am to 1:30 pm, and Sunday from 2 to 5 pm. Admission is €2.

Unser Liebfrauen Kirche (Church of Our Dear Lady) is a 13th-century Gothic hall church, built on the site of an 11th-century parish church. The interior is rather bare but the crypt murals are 14th century. Opening hours are weekdays from 11 am to 4 pm.

Böttcherstraße & Schoon Viertel

Böttcherstraße is a 110-m (330-foot) pedestrian street leading from the Marktplatz to the River Weser. It was transformed between 1923 and 1931 by Ludwig Roselius, inventor of decaffeinated coffee. He employed various architects – some working with local styles as inspiration, but Bernhard Hoetger used Expressionist ideas to create Art Nouveau and Art Deco masterpieces. The Nazis hated it and wanted to tear down the degenerate art. The street survived when Roselius somehow convinced the Nazis to preserve the street as warning to others of what not to build. The Meissen porcelain carillon chimes daily between January and April at noon, 3, and 6 pm, and the rest of the year hourly between noon and 6 pm. St Martini-kirche at the end of the street is a 1960 copy of the 1229 original that was destroyed during World War II.

The **Kunstsammlungen Böttcherstraße** (Art Collections), Böttcherstraße 6-10, ☎ 0421-336-5077, comprise two museums. The **Paula Modersohn-Becker Museum** was the first museum dedicated to works of a single female artist. Her work helped paved the way for Expressionists in Germany. The **Roselius Museum**, in sharp contrast, has late medieval art that belonged to Ludwig Roselius. It includes works by Lucas Cranach as well as period furniture. Opening hours for both are Tuesday to Sunday from 11 am to 6 pm. Admission is €5.

The **Schnoor Viertel** consists mostly of 15th- and 16th-century gabled houses (above). It is the oldest surviving neighborhood in Bremen and a popular place for artists' studios and galleries. It also has a huge number of cafés and restaurants.

At the far end of the area is the **Kunsthalle Bremen** (Art Museum), Am Wall 207, ☎ 0421-329-080. The collection ranges from old masters to the present. Of particular note are the German and French Impressionists of the 19th and 20th centuries. The museum also has a large Kupferstichkabinett (Prints Room) with a quarter of a million mostly German and French drawings and lithographs from the late Middle Ages to the present. Opening hours are Tuesday to Sunday from 10 am to 5 pm, closing at 9 pm on Tuesday. Admission is €5.

Farther Afield

The **Übersee Museum** (Overseas Museum), Bahnhofplatz 13, ☎ 0421-1603-8101, www.uebersee-museum.de, is close to the Hauptbahnhof. It is an ethnological museum with items from all over the world. Opening hours are Tuesday to Friday from 9 am to 6 pm and weekends from 10 am to 6 pm. Admission is €6.

The **Focke-Museum**, Schwachhauser Heerstraße 240, ☎ 0421-361-3575, is a local history museum with displays from pre-history to the present. It emphasizes themes that were important in the development of Bremen, especially seafaring, trade, and religion. Opening hours are Tuesday to Sunday from 10 am to 5 pm, closing at 9 pm on Tuesday. Admission is €4. It can be reached by Tramline 4 (stop Focke Museum).

Beck's, Am Deich 18, ☎ 0421-5094-5555, www.becks.com, one of Germany's largest breweries and one of the few with an international presence, offers two-hour guided tours of its factory. Hourly tours are available Tuesday to Saturday from 10 am to 5 pm, and Sunday from 10 am to 3 pm. Advance phone bookings are required. Admission is €3 and includes some sampling. It can be reached by tramlines 2 and 3 (stop Am Brill) or lines 1 and 8 (stop Westerstraße).

TRAVELING WITH TEENAGERS

Bremen has a couple of ultra-modern museums, cum entertainment centers. These are a far cry from stuffy museums of old and invite active participation.

The **Space Center Bremen**, Space Park Plaza 1, ☎ 0421-840-000, www.space-center-bremen.de, opened in 2004 as the largest indoor theme park in Europe. It combines some space science with science fiction and a strong emphasis on popular futuristic movies. It is open Tuesday to Thursday from 10 am to 6 pm and Friday to Sunday from 9 am to 6 pm. The center can be reached from the Hauptbahnhof in 20 minutes by Tramline 3 (stop Use Akschen/Space Park), or by boat from Martini Landing Stage. Admission is €22.

The **Universum Science Center,** Wiener Straße 2, ☎ 0421-33-460, www.universum-bremen.de, is in a modern building that looks like a UFO. It has huge exhibits and uses some 250 models to explain the sciences relating to earth, man, and the cosmos. Active participation is required in many exhibits. Opening hours are weekdays from 9 am to 6 pm, open to 9 pm on Wednesday, and weekends from 10 am to 7 pm. Admission is €10. The center can be reached in 15 minutes from the Hauptbahnhof on Tramline 6 (stop Universität/NW1).

The **Packhaus im Schnoor**, Wüste Stätte 11, ☎ 0421-277-2780, www.packhaus.de, has no physical exhibits. It is a multimedia experience using three-dimensional animation and computer-supported exhibits to bring alive the history of Bremen, especially its merchant past. Opening hours are daily 11 am to 6 pm, closing at 7 pm from April to October. Admission is €6.

Bremerhaven

Bremerhaven is 65-km (39 miles) downstream at the mouth of the River Weser. It is not an attractive town, but it has an interesting maritime museum, the **Deutsches Schiffahrtsmuseum** (German Maritime Museum), Hans-Scharoun-Platz 1, ☎ 0471-82-070, www.dsm.de. It documents the development of the German shipping industry from Roman times to the present. A huge museum with large displays, it is easy to enjoy even if you are not particularly interested in shipping. The prize possession is the 1388 *Hansekogge* – a merchant ship discovered in the 1960s during harbor excavations. Other items of interest include staterooms from ocean liners, bridges, large-scale models, and navigational instruments. From April to October, eight historic vessels can be inspected in the open-air museum area. Opening hours are daily April to October from 10 am to 6 pm. From November to March, it is open Tuesday to Sunday, 10 am to 6 pm. Admission is €5. The museum is just under two km (1.2 miles) from Bremerhaven station and can be reached on bus lines 502 or 506 (stop Hochschule Bremerhaven).

■ Cultural Events & Festivals

Bremen has many cultural events ranging from classical music to modern jazz. The tourism office has details and can make bookings for most.

The **Musikfest** (Musical Festival) is held annually in September and presents a month of music in many locations throughout the city. The festival opens on the illuminated Marktplatz.

The **Petrikirche** has concerts on Thursday at 7 pm – mostly choral, organ, or chamber music.

Carnival is usually held only in the Roman Catholic parts of Germany. However, the **Bremer Karneval**, held at the end of January, includes the largest samba parade in Germany.

■ Shopping

A **flea market** is held Saturday mornings at the Schlacht Promenade. In recent years this whole area has developed into a popular venue for cafés, restaurants, and pleasure boats.

■ Adventures

On Foot

The tourism office conducts two-hour guided walking tours of the old town daily at 2 pm, from mid-May to early October, as well as on Saturday at 11 am. English-speaking guides are sometimes available.

On Wheels

Bicycles may be rented from **Cycle Station**, Hauptbahnhof Eastern Side, ☎ 0421-302-114, or from **Cycle Depot**, between the Hauptbahnhof and Übersee Museum, ☎ 0421-178-3361. Guided tours are arranged by the local branch of the **German Bicycle Association** (ADFC), ☎ 0421-701-179.

In the Air

Seaplane Center, Zum Lakenauer Höft, ☎ 0421-558-013, offers **seaplane flights** of Bremen. Flights last 20 minutes and cost €100.

On Water

Cruises of the Weser River and the Bremen harbor are available daily from March to October and on weekends from November to February. Departure times and reservations are available from the tourism office. All boats depart from the Martini Landing, west of the old town. From here to the Space Center takes 15 minutes and to Bremerhaven 3½ hours.

■ Where to Stay

Park Hotel Bremen is a luxury grand hotel in the middle of the large Bürgerpark about two km (1.2 miles) from the Hauptbahnhof. Rooms

HOTEL PRICE CHART	
Rates per room based on double occupancy, including taxes.	
€	Under €50
€€	€50-€100
€€€	€101-€150
€€€€	Over €150

are as opulent as the building itself. The very elegant **Park Restaurant** (€€€-€€€€) serves international cuisine with strong French influences. It has a noteworthy wine list. **Restaurant Fontana** (€€-€€€) serves nouvelle cuisine with strong Mediterranean influences. Im Bürgerpark, 28209 Bremen, ☎ 0421- 34-080, fax 0421-340-8602, www.park-hotel-bremen.de. (€€€-€€€€)

Maritim Hotel is a luxury hotel close to the Hauptbahnhof across from the Bürgerpark. It is connected to the Congress Center, allowing for good discounts in the off-season. The hotel and rooms are modern and elegant. **Restaurant L'Echalote** (€€-€€€) serves mostly Mediterranean cuisine in elegant surroundings. Hollerallee 99, 28215 Bremen, ☎ 0421-37-890, fax 0421-378-9600, www.maritim.de. (€€€-€€€€)

The **Hilton Hotel** is in the old town close to the River Weser. It has elegant, comfortable rooms. The building is modern, but the design fits in easily with the original character of the area. The public spaces are very elegant. The hotel has several restaurants but **L'Olivia** (€€-€€€), serving Mediterranean cuisine, is the most elegant. **Captain Sushi** (€-€€€) is a modern Japanese restaurant. Böttcherstraße 2, 28195 Bremen, ☎ 0421-36-960, fax 0421-369-6960, www.hilton.com. (€€€-€€€€)

Nearby, at Market Square is the **Ramada Treff Überseehotel**. Rooms are large, comfortable, and individually furnished. The restaurant **Friesenhof** (€€) serves North German specialties. Wachtstraße 27, 28195 Bremen, ☎ 0421-36-010, fax 0421-360-1555, www.ramada-treff.de. (€€-€€€)

The **InterCity Hotel** is, as usual with this group, close to the Hauptbahnhof. The hotel opened in 2003 and has elegant, well-equipped rooms aimed mainly at the business traveler. The room key gives free access to local transportation. Bahnhofplatz 17, 28195 Bremen, ☎ 0421-16-030, fax 040-160-3599, www.intercityhotel.de. (€€-€€€)

In contrast, the **Ibis Hotel Bremen Altstadt** is some distance from the station and a km (.6 mile) from the Marktplatz. It has simple, clean rooms at low prices. Faulenstraße 45, 28195 Bremen, ☎ 0421-30-480, fax 0421-304-8600, www.ibishotel.com. (€€)

Camping

The **Freie Hansestadt Bremen** campsite is five km (three miles) north of the center of Bremen. It has space for 100 casual visitors. Facilities are good and clean, but shade is limited. It is open year-round. Am Stadtwaldsee 1, 28359 Bremen, ☎ 0421-212-002, fax 0421-219-857.

■ Where to Eat

The Market Square is a good place to dine. At the top end of the scale is the **L'Orchidée in Bremer Ratskeller**, Am Markt, ☎ 0421-334-7927. It is in the 16th-century reception rooms of the town hall – an elegant wood-paneled room with wall paintings and Rococo details. Nouvelle cuisine is on offer and the wine list is vast. Reservations are advisable. (€€€-€€€€)

In the same building is the more rustic **Historische Halle in Bremer Ratskeller**, Am Markt, ☎ 0421-321-676. Food is mostly hearty local dishes; the wine list has 650 labels. The vaulted room is pleasant and so is the terrace. (€-€€)

Also on the Markt, but this time in the cellar of the Schütting, is **à point – das Restaurant im Club**, Am Markt 13, ☎ 0421-364-8458. This very modern restaurant serves nouvelle cuisine. (€€-€€€)

DINING PRICE CHART	
Price per person for an entrée, including water, beer or soft drink.	
€	Under €10
€€	€10-€20
€€€	€21-€35
€€€€	Over €35

Lower Saxony

In this Chapter

Lower Saxony is the second-largest state in Germany and very popular with German vacationers. However, for the foreign tourist, the attractions are less than the size of the state would suggest. The sights here are often low-key and less well known than those in other parts of Germany.

The greater part of the state comprises relatively flat, but water-rich land. It does not make for the most exciting landscape but the area is green and beautiful. Many country roads are tree-lined *allées* and most towns relatively small and picturesque. The parts south of Hanover are more varied with hills and a small section of the Harz Mountains.

Major highways and railroads run through the state and most of the sights described in this chapter are along the Autobahn A7 that runs from the north of Germany through Lower Saxony to the south.

Celle has a lovely historic old town with half-timbered buildings and a large palace. The area is typical of northern Germany with tree-lined roads and much greenery to compensate for the rather flat landscape.

Hannover is a large city but with limited tourist appeal beyond its gardens and a few first-class museums. Nearby **Hildesheim** and **Goslar** were major cities during the first centuries of the Holy Roman Empire of German States and still have several Romanesque reminders of that period in addition to some marvelous half-timbered buildings.

Hamelin and the **Weser Valley** are at the heart of the Fairy Tale Route and have many sights reminiscent of children's stories. Weser Renaissance buildings, unique to this region, are also interesting to see. This style features ram's horn scrollwork, masks and gargoyle reliefs.

History

Lower Saxony came into being only after World War II when the British occupational forces created the land out of the former territories of Hanover, Oldenburg, Schaumburg-Lippe, and Braunschweig. The southern parts of the state played an important role in the first centuries of the Holy Roman Empire and many Romanesque buildings survived from this period. Although the ruler of Hanover became the ninth elector of the emperor in 1692, the area mostly failed to play much of a role in German power politics. From 1714 until 1837, the Hanover and British crowns were carried by the same persons, but both countries failed to exploit fully the potential advantages of the union.

Hanover lost its independence after it disastrously supported Austria in the 1866 war against Prussia. The other territories remained independent parts of the German Empire and later the German Republic until the end of World War II.

Getting Here

By Rail: Lower Saxony is easily accessible by high-speed railways from most parts of Germany. Hanover is a major crossing point of north-south and east-west routes, including the busy Hamburg-to-Frankfurt, Berlin-to-Frankfurt, and Berlin-to-the-Ruhr routes.

Hourly trains connect Frankfurt and Hanover in under 2½ hours and Berlin and Hanover in 90 minutes. Around three trains per hour run from Hamburg to Hanover in 1¼ hours.

By Road: The roads in Lower Saxony are generally in excellent condition. Two major Autobahns cross at Hanover: the A7 from northern Germany and Hamburg to the south, and the A2 from Berlin to the industrial Ruhr area. The A27 connects Cuxhaven and Bremen with the A7. Country roads are more interesting but slower. Some, especially in the north, are tree-lined *allées*.

By Air: Flughafen Hannover Langenhagen, Petzelstrasse 84, 30669 Hannover,

☎ 0511-9770, www.hannover-airport.de, has mainly European flights, including several by low-cost carriers. It is easily reached by car – a taxi from downtown Hanover costs around €20 for the 20-minute ride. The S-Bahn Line 5 connects the airport and Hauptbahnhof every half-hour, taking 12 minutes for €2.40.

Frankfurt Airport (see Hesse) is convenient for intercontinental travelers as well as for travel to the southern parts of the state. **Hamburg Airport** offers alternatives, especially to the northern areas.

By Boat: A regular car and passenger ferry service operates between Cuxhaven in the far north of the state (near Hamburg and Bremen) and Harwich in England. **SeawaysDFDS**, Van-der-Smissen-Strasse 4, 22767 Hamburg, ☎ 040-389-030, www.dfdsseaways.co.uk, has four sailings per week, each taking 15 hours.

■ Information Sources

Information on the whole state is available from **Tourismus Marketing Niedersachsen**, Theaterstraße 4-5, 30159 Hannover, ☎ 0511-2704-8888, www.reiseland-niedersachsen.de. Information on events is available from tourist information offices. The free ***Niedersachsen Vorschau***, www.niedersachsenvorschau.de, is a magazine with useful listings about what is on in the state.

■ Celle

Celle has a beautifully preserved old town with some 500 half-timbered buildings. Most date from the 16th to 18th century and show conformity in style. In addition, it has a Schloss (palace) that served as ducal residence for 700 years and a few interesting museums. Celle is at the southern edge of the Lüneburger Heide (Heaths) and a good starting point for excursions into this natural wonder. The area is also famous for horse stud farming.

Celle can trace its history back to 993, but only received town rights in 1248. Parts of the Schloss and church date to 1292 when Duke Otto der Strenge (Otto the Strict) moved the town center three km downstream for strategic reasons. It was the seat of the Duke of Braunschweig-Lüneburg until the family died out in 1705. The town became part of Hannover until the Prussians took over in 1866. Celle survived World War II undamaged. The largest concentration camp on German soil was set up near the town of Bergen, a few km to the north.

Information Sources

Tourist Office: The Tourist-Information, Markt 14, 29221 Celle, ☎ 05141-1212, www.celle.de, has useful maps and can make reservations for accommodations and adventures.

Getting Here

If driving from the north, leave the Autobahn A7 at Solltau-Süd and follow the B3 to Celle. En route, the road passes near the Bergen-Belsen Concentration Camp (signposted as KZ Gedenkstätte). From Celle, continue on the B3 to where it rejoins the A7 north of Hannover. Most of the B3 is a tree-lined *allée* – beautiful but rather slow.

TRAVELING WITH CHILDREN

At Soltau, next to the Autobahn A7, is the huge **Heide Park**, 29614 Soltau, ☎ 0180-591-9101, www.heide-park.de. It is a pleasure park with 50 rides and attractions, open daily, April to October from 9 am to 6 pm. Admission is €25.

If arriving by train, do not confuse the French-style palace near the station with the Schloss. This building is actually the oldest jail still in use in Germany – it was erected in a French château style in 1717. The station is a pleasant 15 minutes walk to the west of the old town.

Sightseeing

The main sight in Celle is its beautiful old town. Most of the 500 preserved half-timbered houses date from the 16th to 18th century and are still used as houses, shops, and other businesses. In contrast to most other towns in the region, the A-shape gable of most houses faces the street front, and not to the side as is more common elsewhere. Also note the high number of corner houses with small towers and turrets – this was a building requirement until the church tower was erected in 1913.

The oldest dated house in town is at Am Heiligen Kreuz 26, built in 1526 with a

Gothic gable. The Hoppenerhaus (1532), corner of Post and Rundestraße, is the most impressive house in town. All the streets of the old town are lined with half-timbered buildings but the Zöllner and Neue Straße have particularly good samples.

The **Stadtkirche St Marien** (St Mary's Town Church) is a Gothic building dating partly from the 13th century. The rich Baroque interior with stuccos was done in the late 17th century. The Fürstengrub (Prince's Vault), underneath the chancel, contains the graves of many members of the Welfen (Guelph) ruling family. The high tower was added in 1913 – 234 steps lead to the viewing platform with grand views of the region. A trumpet sounds from here daily at 8:15 am and 5:15 pm.

The **Stechbahn**, a wide road leading from the Schloss into the old town, was formerly used as a tournament course. The **Alte Rathaus** has a vaulted Gothic cellar and a Renaissance façade. Across the road is a Glockenspiel (Carillon) that sounds each hour.

The **Bomann Museum**, Schlossplatz 7, ☎ 05141-12-544, is a large regional museum with mainly displays on local history and folklore. A complete farmer's house interior and an inn are displayed. A recent addition is the 24-Stunden-Kunstmuseum (24-Hour Art Gallery) with modern art sculptures, paintings, and light displays. Some of the lights can be seen from outside the building leading to the claim that it is the first 24-hour gallery in the world. Opening hours are Tuesday to Sunday from 10 am to 5 pm. Admission is €3.

The **Herzogschloss** (Ducal Palace), Schlossplatz 1, ☎ 05141-12-373, is set inside a park. Parts of the Schloss date back to 1292, but the present Baroque appearance is mostly 17th century. The Schloss has the oldest Baroque theater (1674) still regularly in use in Germany. The interior can only be seen on guided tours that include the private apartments of Queen Caroline Mathilde, the Renaissance Hofkapelle (Court Chapel), and the theater. Guided tours are conducted from Tuesday to Sunday, April to October, on the hour from 11 am to 3 pm; from November to February tours are at 11 am and 3 pm only. Admission is €3.50.

Queen Caroline Mathilde

The Schloss in Celle served as principal residence of the dukes of Braunschweig-Lüneburg from 1378 to 1705. However, the most famous resident was Queen Caroline Mathilde of Denmark (1751-75). She was the sister of British King George III. Her husband, King Christian VII of Denmark, was schizophrenic. When his queen was discovered having an affair with his doctor and principle advisor, Dr Struensee, the doctor was executed and his body carved up. Caroline Mathilde was jailed but at the request of George III banished to Celle in 1772. (George was simultaneously Duke of Hannover.) He refused her requests to return to England and she died in Celle three years later.

Bergen Belsen

About 25 km (15 miles) north of Celle is the **KZ Gedenkstätte Bergen-Belsen** (Concentration Camp Memorial), 29303 Berge, ☎ 05051-6011, www.bergenbelsen.de. This former prisoner of war and later concentration camp was the largest Nazi such camp on German soil. Between 1940 and 1945, 70,000 people died here – the most famous, Anne Frank. The British liberated the camp on April 15, 1945 and burned the

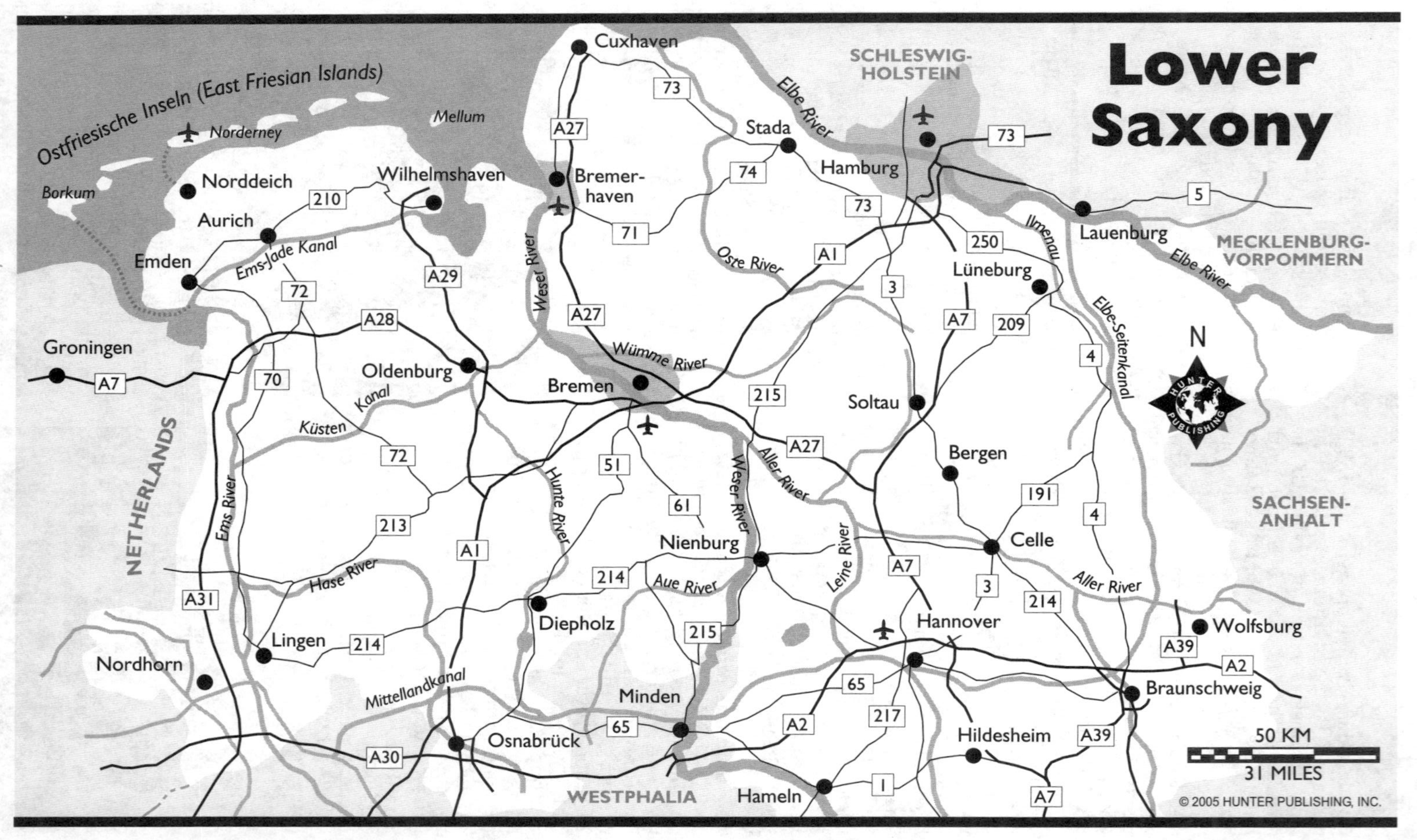
Lower Saxony
Ostfriesische Inseln (East Friesian Islands)
Borkum
Norderney
Mellum
Norddeich
Aurich
Emden
Wilhelmshaven
Ems-Jade Kanal
Groningen
Oldenburg
Küsten Kanal
Cuxhaven
Bremer-haven
Weser River
Bremen
Wümme River
Stada
Hamburg
SCHLESWIG-HOLSTEIN
Elbe River
Oste River
Lauenburg
MECKLENBURG-VORPOMMERN
Ilmenau
Lüneburg
Elbe-Seitenkanal
Soltau
Bergen
Celle
Aller River
Leine River
Hunte River
Hase River
Aue River
Ems River
Mittellandkanal
NETHERLANDS
SACHSEN-ANHALT
WESTPHALIA
Nienburg
Diepholz
Lingen
Nordhorn
Osnabrück
Minden
Hameln
Hannover
Hildesheim
Braunschweig
Wolfsburg
N
HUNTER PUBLISHING
A1
A2
A7
A27
A28
A29
A30
A31
A39
1
3
4
5
51
61
65
70
71
72
73
74
191
209
210
213
214
215
217
250
50 KM
31 MILES
© 2005 HUNTER PUBLISHING, INC.

Above: Mainz Cathedral

Below: Speyer's Dom – the largest Romanesque structure in Germany

(both © Rheinland-Pfalz Tourismus/Piel Media)

Above: The Alte Oper in Frankfurt
Below: The Rathaus, Römer district, Frankfurt
(both © Seifert, Frank / Tourismus+Congress GmbH Frankfurt am Main)

Above: Canoeing on the Lahn in Weilburg

Below: Schloss Weilburg *(both © Tourist-Information Weilburg)*

Above: Füssen seen from the air

Below: The Zügspitze, Germany's highest peak (both © *www.romantischestrasse.d*

Anne Frank

remains to the ground a month later to prevent the spread of disease. The memorial site is park-like and strangely peaceful, as only the foundations of the former buildings remain. A documentation center has exhibitions on the horrors that occurred here. A chilling half-hour video is played – children under 12 are not allowed in the theater. The site is open daily from 9 am to 6 pm. It is best reached by private transportation. Admission is free.

Cultural Events

The **Schlosstheater**, Markt 14, 29221 Celle, ☎ 05141-12-713, www.schlosstheater-celle.de, is the oldest Baroque theater still in use in Germany. Classical music, theater, musicals, and modern productions are staged year-round except in August.

Adventures

On Foot

Town Walks: The tourism office arranges guided walking tours. From May to October, tours are Monday to Saturday at 2:30 pm and Sunday at 11 am. In April and November, tours are on weekends only. Further thematic tours, including one conducted by the night watchman, are also available.

Countryside Hikes: Hiking and cycling tours of the Heiden (heaths) area are conducted by the Tourism Office of Müden, Unterlüßer Straße 5, 29328 Faßberg, ☎ 05053-989-222, www.mueden-oerze.de.

On Wheels

By Bicycle: Guided countryside cycling tours in the Lüneberg Heath are arranged by tourism offices of two towns near Celle: **Touristinformation Hermannsburg**, Harmsstraße 3a, 29320 Hermannsburg, ☎ 05052-8055, and **Verkehrsverein**, Am Amtshof 4, 29308 Winsen, ☎ 05143-912-212.

Bicycles can be rented in Hermannsburg from **Hans Georg Rüge**, Lotharstraße 7, ☎ 05052-3702, or from **Reinhard Könemann**, Lindenweg 11, ☎ 05052-1415. Both also rent out kayaks.

On Horseback

On July 27, 1735, Prince Elector George II of Hannover founded a horse stud farm that would produce race winners of fame. The **Hengstparade** (stallion parade) is held the last two weekends of September and the first weekend of October. The **Niedersächsische Landgestüt**, Spörckenstraße 10, ☎ 05131-92-940, www.landgestuetcelle.de, is open from early July to mid-February on weekdays from 8:30 am to noon, 1 to 3:30 pm, and Saturday from 8:30 am to noon. Admission is free but €25 on parade weekends.

Schubotz, Westerceller Straße 34, ☎ 05141-98-790, offers horse-drawn carriage tours of Celle's old town. The 35-minute tours are available daily from 10 am to 6 pm. Departure point is from the Schloss. Horse-drawn carriage rides through the heaths can be arranged through the Celle Tourism Office or through the tourism office in Hermannsburg, Harmsstraße 3a, 29320 Hermannsburg, ☎ 05052-8055.

Horseback riding is popular in Lower Saxony. As most stables are small, it is best to first approach the statewide agency, which has a special website for riding: www.pferdeland-niedersachsen.de, or contact local tourist information offices. Some, such as the Hannover Regional Tourismusverband, Prinzenstraße 12, 30159 Hannover, ☎ 0511-366-1990, www.tourismus-hannover-region.de, make reservations too.

Where to Stay & Eat

The **Hotel Fürstenhof Celle** is in a 300-year old former palace. Bedrooms are luxurious and opulently furnished. Public rooms are equally elegant and fit for a prince. The hotel is at the edge of the old town near the Schloss. The luxurious **Restaurant Endtenfang** (€€€-€€€€) serves French cuisine good enough to have earned it a Michelin star. The rustic **Palio Taverna & Trattoria** (€€-€€€) serves rustic Italian dishes. Hannoversche Straße 55, 29221 Celle, ☎ 05141-2010, fax 05141-201-120, www.fuerstenhof.de. (€€€€)

Under the same management as the Fürstenhof is the much simpler **Hotel**

Borchers. It is in the heart of the old town, surrounded by streets of historic half-timbered houses. However, the rooms are modern and comfortable. Guests may use the indoor pool and sauna of the Fürstenhof. Schuhstraße 5, 29221 Celle, ☎ 05141-911-920, fax 05141-911-9244, www.residenzhotel.de. (€€-€€€)

Also in the heart of the old town and managed by the Fürstenhof is the **Hotel Celler Hof**. It has the longest hotel tradition in town and is close to the Schloss at the edge of the pedestrian zone. Rooms are simple but neat and well-maintained. Guests may use the indoor pool and sauna of the Fürstenhof. Stechbahn 11, 29221 Celle, ☎ 05141-911-960, fax 05141-911-9644, www.residenzhotel.de. (€€-€€€)

At the edge of the old town is the **Inter-City Hotel Celle** (previously Steigenberger Esprix), a modern hotel inside and out with elegant bedrooms. It is mainly popular with business travelers, allowing for bargain rates over weekends. Nordwall 20, 29221 Celle, ☎ 05141-2000, fax 05141-200-200, www.intercityhotel.de. (€€-€€€)

The rustic **Restaurant Historischer Ratskeller**, Markt 14, ☎ 05141-29-099, serves hearty international and local cuisine. It has been in business since 1378. In addition to the Gothic, vaulted cellar rooms it also has a pleasant terrace. Locally produced moorland mutton is a specialty. (€€-€€€)

The **Restaurant Zum Ältesten Haus**, Neue Straße 27, ☎ 05141-487-399, serves mainly hearty local dishes. Service is fast and friendly and portions large. (€-€€).

Camping

Camping Silbersee is four km (2½ miles) north of Celle and has good facilities. It has 160 spaces for tourists and 240 for long-term rentals. It is open year-round. Zum Silbersee 19, 29229 Celle-Vorwerk, ☎ 05141-31-223, fax 05141-33-758, www.celler-land.de.

■ Hannover

Hannover (in English usually written as Hanover), the state capital, is a city of just over 500,000 people. It is a great city to live in with lots of greenery and cultural events. It also has Germany's newest and by far most reliable suburban rail system. However, for foreign tourists, the attractions are less obvious and many will pass the city by with few regrets. Still, it does have some excellent gardens and a few outstanding museums.

Hanover's written history goes back to at least 1150, but the glory days were between 1636 and 1866, when it served as residence of the dukes of Calenberg and later the kings of Hanover. The town became a major cultural capital in the late 17th and early 18th centuries. In 1692, the principality became the Electorate of Brunswick-Lüneburg and two decades later it controlled the British throne. Hanover became a kingdom in 1814, but in 1866 backed Austria in war against Prussia and was subsequently annexed by Prussia. Hanover remained a provincial capital in Prussia until it became capital of the new federal state of Lower Saxony in 1946. During World War II, up to 85% of the old town was destroyed. Hanover rebuilt in modern style and very few old buildings survived.

The House of Hanover & the Court of St James

In 1658, Duke Ernst-Augustus married the Palatine Princess Sophia, granddaughter of King James I of England. This gave the House of Hanover a distant claim to the English crown, which unexpectedly saw Sophia's son, Elector Georg-Ludwig, ascend the English throne as George I. The King of England and the Elector of Hanover (after 1814 its King as well) remained the same person until Queen Victoria ascended to the British throne. German law did not allow female succession and her uncle Ernest-Augustus became King of Hanover. The Kingdom of Hanover ceased to exist after it was annexed by Prussia in 1866.

Information Sources

Tourist Office: Tourist information is available from the Tourist Information Office, Ernst-August-Platz 2, 30159 Hannover, ☎ 0511-1234-5111, www.hannover.de.

Getting Around

Walking is generally the easiest way to get around the center of Hanover. From the Hauptbahnhof to the Rathaus is about 20 minutes stroll.

The Herrenhäuser Gartens are four km (2½ miles) from the center of town and can be reached by walking or on Tram Lines 4 and 5.

Sightseeing

The main attractions in Hanover are the museums, mostly in the vicinity of the Rathaus, and the Herrenhausen Gardens to the west of the city.

Rathaus Area

The **Rathaus** (Town Hall), Trammplatz 2, ☎ 0511-1684-5333, erected in 1901-13 in a Wilhelmine style, is the symbol of Hanover. Built on 6,026 pilings, it is best seen from across the Masch pond. The best view of town is from the cupola, reached by elevator. Note the models of Hanover in the entrance portals. Opening hours are mid-March to October daily from 10 am to 6:30 pm, opening at 9:30 am on weekdays. From November to mid-March, it is open daily, 11 am to 4 pm. Admission is €3.

In front of the Rathaus is the **Kestner Museum**, Trammplatz 3, ☎ 0511-1684-2120. It has large collections on four themes: Egypt, Art of Antiquity, Decorative Art, and Numismatics. The latter two collections focus mainly on Europe with special emphasis on the area that covers modern-day Lower Saxony. Opening hours are Tuesday to Sunday from 11 am to 6 pm, closing at 8 pm on Wednesday. Admission is €1.50.

The **Niedersächsisches Landesmuseum** (Lower Saxony National Museum), Willy-Brandt-Allee 5, ☎ 0511-980-7620, www.nlmh.de, is the largest and most popular museum in the state. It has a huge collection of European paintings from the 12th to 20th century. Its prehistoric department is also popular, with articles and models displaying the early history of the region. Opening hours are Tuesday to Sunday from 10 am to 5 pm, closing at 8 pm on Thursday. Admission is €4.

The **Sprengel-Museum**, Kurt-Schwitters-Platz, ☎ 0511-1684-3875, www.sprengel-museum.de, houses one of the largest 20th-century art collections in Germany. It has representative works by all major artists of all genres. Opening hours are Tuesday to Sunday from 10 am to 6 pm, closing at 8 pm on Tuesday. Admission is €4.

Markt Area

Hanover rebuilt after World War II and the few remaining old buildings are west of the Markt. The 14th-century brick Gothic **Marktkirche** (Market Church), Hanns-Lilje-Platz 2, ☎ 0511-364-370, was rebuilt true to the original in the 1950s. The 97-m (320-foot) tower seems strangely short but is similar to the original, which was completed prematurely due to a lack of funds. The interior has a remarkable 14th-century wood-carved altar and a 15th-century bronze baptismal font. Some of the stained-glass windows are original. The doors are from 1957 and illustrate scenes from modern German history. Opening hours are daily from 10 am to 4 pm, closing at 6 pm on weekends.

The nearby **Altes Rathaus** (Old Town Hall, right) is another example of north Ger-

Lower Saxony

man brick Gothic. It was built over a period of a century, starting in 1410.

Kramer and Burgstraße are lined by rebuilt half-timbered buildings. Some of the original town defenses survived at Hohen Ufer, but the area is dominated by the modern **Historisches Museum am Hohen Ufer** (Local History Museum), Pferdestraße 6 (Entrance in Burgstraße), ☎ 0511-1684-
3052. It has an interesting eclectic collection illustrating the city's sometimes turbulent history. In addition to the usual range of arts and applied arts it has a collection of small German cars produced locally in the 1920s. It is a great museum for children as well. Opening hours are Tuesday to Sunday from 10 am to 5 pm, closing at 7 pm on Tuesday and Thursday. Admission is €3.

Herrenhäuser Gärten

In the northwestern part of the city was the former summer residence of the rulers of Hanover. The palace was destroyed during World War II but the severely damaged gardens were restored to their former glory. The **Herrenhäuser Gärten** (Royal Gardens), ☎ 0511-1684-9734, www.hannover.de/herrenhausen, are among the largest and most impressive in Germany and consist of three parts: the Großer Garten (Large Garden), the Berggarten (Mountain/Rock Garden), and the Georgengarten (George Garden). They are open daily from 9 am, closing between 4:30 and 8 pm according to light conditions. Admission is €4 to the Großer Garten and Berggarten, or €2 for the Berggarten only.

The **Großer Garten** was started by Elector Johann Friedrich in 1666, but it was his wife Princess Sophia, who really dictated much of its design. It is a formal Baroque garden with strong French influence spread over 140 acres. It has strong geometric features, sculptures, a maze, cascades, grottos, and an open-air theater. The **Große Fontäne** (Great Fountain) can blast water up to 82-m (270 feet) in the air – the highest such spout in Europe. It functions from April to early October, daily from 11 am to noon, and 3 to 5 pm.

To the north is the **Berggarten**, initially a kitchen garden for the royal court but now a botanical garden with 11,000 plants. The greenhouses have the largest collection of orchids on the European mainland and an impressive display of cacti. The mausoleum houses the remains of many members of the House of Hanover.

The **Georgengarten** is an English-style landscape park laid out in the 1830s. The two-km (1.2-mile) Herrenhäuser Allee is lined by a double row of lime trees on both sides and leads though this garden to the entrance of the other two. The Georgengarten is unfenced and always open.

AUTOSTADT WOLFSBURG

Wolfsburg is 100 km (60 miles) east of Hanover on the busy highway and railroad to Berlin. It was founded in the 1930s to produce what would later be called the Beetle. The town is still completely dominated by Volkswagen, which has the largest motor manufacturing plant in Europe, producing 2,700 cars per day, in this town. The town is sometime also known as Golfsburg and it is said that being a car dealer here for Ford or Opel is the hardest job in Germany.

In recent years, Volkswagen opened Autostadt, Stadtbrücke, 38435 Wolfsburg, ☎ 0800-288-678-238, www.autostadt.de – a huge theme park on automobiles. Modern glass and steel pavilions for each of the Volkswagen family brands (including Audi, Bentley, and Lamborghini) are set in a 70-acre park. Tours of parts of the factory are available. Around a thousand customers per day prefer to pick up their cars from the factory, thereby saving the delivery charges. Two glass towers house 400 cars each waiting to be picked up. The Swiss Mövenpick group has six restaurants in the park covering all price ranges, but for real elegance head to the Ritz Carlton.

Opening hours are daily from 9 am, closing at 6 pm, November to March, and at 8 pm from April to October. Admission is €14, but for the last two hours of the day it drops to €6 that can be refunded at the restaurants. Autostadt is a short walk from the Hauptbahnhof and has ample parking.

Where to Stay in Wolfsburg

The **Ritz-Carlton Hotel** is at the far end of the park. It opened in 2000 and is considered one of the best hotels in Germany. It is modern and luxurious with several huge suites. The Vision restaurant (€€-€€€) serves Euro-Asian cuisine in elegant surroundings. The Michelin-star **Aqua** restaurant (€€€-€€€€) serves nouvelle cuisine and European dishes. It is open only for dinner. Stadtbrücke, 38440 Wolfsburg, ☎ 05361-706-000, fax 05361-608-000, www.ritzcarlton.com. (€€€€)

Cultural Events

During summer months a wide range of concerts are staged in the open-air theater of the Herrenhäuser Gärten. Although there is an emphasis on Baroque music, many events are much more modern.

On most nights, classical music can be heard in several venues, including churches and the State Opera House. More modern music, such as jazz, is also popular. The tourism office has details and can make reservations for most events. Two German-language websites have information on modern music events: www.in-your-face.de and www.rockszene.de.

Adventures

On Foot

The **Roten Faden** is a four-km (2½-mile) route marked on the street with a red line that leads to 36 sights in the center of town. Starting point is the tourist information office at the Hauptbahnhof. A comprehensive brochure on this route is available from the tourist office.

On Wheels

Bicycle rentals are available from **Hannover Fahrradstation**, Fernroderstraße, ☎ 0511-353-9640, and from **Werkstatt Treff Vahrenheide**, Ikarusallee 2, ☎ 0511-633-293.

In the Air

Several companies operate hot-air **balloon** flights from Hanover and vicinity.

Perspektive, Steinbrink 2, 31863 Coppenbrügge, ☎ 0511-450-1112, www.ballon-perspektive.de, starts from several locations in the Hanover region, including Celle, Hamelin, and Hildesheim.

Others include **BASYS-Ballonsysteme**, Scheibenstandsweg 5, Hannover-Anderten, ☎ 0551-517-673, www.basys-ballonsysteme.de, and **bab-Ballonwerbung**, Oldekopstraße 68, ☎ 0511-905-5040, www.bab-ballonwerbung.de.

On Horseback

Horse-drawn carriage rides are available in the Georgengarten from May to October. Departure is from the Infopavillion in the Großer Garten. Reservations are not possible.

On Water

Boating is a popular activity in Hanover. In addition to the Leine River that flows through the city, the artificial Lake Maschsee offers several watersports options. **Fahr mit Üstra Reisen**, Nordmannpassage 6, ☎ 0511-700-950, arranges boat rides on the Maschsee Lake daily from mid-May to October.

Where to Stay & Eat

The **Kastens Hotel Luisenhof** is the top choice in Hannover. No hotel in this city has a longer tradition or is more elegant. Rooms are well-equipped and luxurious. The hotel is near the Hauptbahnhof and within easy walking distance of downtown attractions. The elegant restaurant (€€€-€€€€) serves international and local dishes. Luisenstraße 1, 30159 Hannover, ☎ 0511-30-440, fax 0511-304-4807, www.kastens-luisenhof.de. (€€€-€€€€)

Another luxury option at the edge of the old town is the **Maritim Grand Hotel**. It has luxurious rooms and excellent service. The elegant **L'Adresse** restaurant (€€-€€€) serves international cuisine with strong Mediterranean influences, while the **Brasserie** (€€) is more casual. Friedrichswakk 11, 30159 Hannover, ☎ 0511-36-770, fax 0511-325-195, www.maritim.de. (€€€-€€€€)

Close to the station is the comfortable **Crowne Plaza Schweizerhof**. It is in a modern building with large atrium. Rooms are comfortable and well-equipped with the business traveler in mind. The restaurant **Gourmet's Buffet** (€€-€€€) serves Mediterranean cuisine. Hinüberstraße 6, 30175 Hannover, ☎ 0511-34-950, fax 0511-349-5102, www.chhof.de. (€€€-€€€€)

Also near the Hauptbahnhof is the privately managed **Grand Hotel Mussmann**. Rooms are comfortable and tastefully furnished, with either carpets or wooden floors. Ernst-August-Platz 7, 30159 Hannover, ☎ 0511-36-560, fax 0511-365-6145, www.grandhotel.de. (€€€-€€€€)

The **Central Hotel Kaiserhof** is in the same area. The hotel was recently renovated. Rooms are comfortable with country-house furniture. The elegant restaurant **Brunnenhof** (€-€€€) serves international cuisine, while the **Wiener Café** (€-€€) has mostly Austrian specialties. Ernst-August-Platz 4, 30159 Hannover, ☎ 0511-36-830, fax 0511-369-3114, www.centralhotel.de. (€€€)

Camping

Camping Arnumer See is 10 km (six miles) south of Hanover. It has lush vegetation and modern facilities. There are only 75 spaces for tourists and 350 for long-term rentals. It is open year-round. Osterbruchweg 3, 30966 Hemmingen-Arnum, ☎ 05101-3534, fax 05101-584-254, www.camping-hannover.de.

■ Hildesheim

Hildesheim, a town of 100,000 people, is 30 km (18 miles) southeast of Hannover. It is famous for its Early Romanesque buildings (two are UNESCO World Cultural Heritage sites), as well as a beautifully restored market square. Although many visitors come on daytrips, it is a pleasant town to spend the night.

In AD 815, King Louis the Pious established a bishopric in Hildesheim. The town rapidly developed from a small trading village into one of the most important religious centers in the German-speaking world. Its true golden age was from 993 to 1038 when Bishops Bernward and Godehard started the construction of the Romanesque churches. Somehow, the town failed to maintain its importance in subsequent centuries. In 1945, most of the historic town center was destroyed by air raids. Much of the town was rebuilt in modern style, but the magnificent Marktplatz was restored in the 1980s.

Information Sources

Tourist Office: The Tourist Information Office is at Rathausstraße 20, 31134 Hildesheim, ☎ 05121-17-980, www.hildesheim.de.

Transportation

Hildesheim has easy access to the Autobahn A7 that runs through the eastern part of town. It is also a stop on the ICE rail network, allowing for fast connections to all of Germany.

Walking is the easiest way to explore the old town. The main station is about 10 minutes walk north of the old town. Parking garages are on the edges of the old town. Street parking is available near some of the outlying churches, making driving a feasible option on quiet days.

Sightseeing

The main attractions in Hildesheim are the beautiful Marktplatz and the Romanesque churches. The Brühl area has some original half-timbered buildings.

Markt Area

On March 22, 1945, air raids destroyed virtually the entire historic center of town. Hildesheim was known for its beautiful half-timbered buildings, but the ample use of wood was their undoing when fires raged after the bombing raid. After the war, Hildesheim rebuilt in modern and ugly style. However, in the 1980s, the buildings at the Markt were restored to their former glory. They now serve as reminder of what was lost in the war, not only here but also in many other German cities.

On the west side is the eight-storey, High Gothic **Knochenhaueramthaus** (Butchers' Guild Hall, shown at right), often considered the most beautiful half-timbered building in the world. The building is a copy of the 1529 original and has interesting Renaissance decorations. The reconstruction

required 400 m² (4,280 square feet) of oak timber. It currently houses the **Stadtmuseum** (Local History Museum), Markt 7, ☎ 05121301-163, on the upper five floors – entrance from the rear of the building. Opening hours are Tuesday to Sunday from 10 am to 6 pm. Admission is €1.50.

Adjacent is the much smaller **Bäckeramthaus** (1800). The three buildings on the north side are joined inside to form Le Méridien Hotel. The **Rokokohaus** (1757) in the middle is flanked by the **Stadtschäncke** (1666) and the Wollenwebergildehauses (Weavers' Guild Hall, from about 1600).

The Gothic **Rathaus** (Town Hall) dates to 1268 but it has been altered often in subsequent years and the current restoration is a simplified version of the original. Its carillon plays daily at noon, 1, and 5 pm, as well as at 9 am on Wednesday and Saturday. The fountain is a copy of the 1540 original.

On the south side is the oriental-looking 14th-century **Tempelhaus**, above. Its most interesting feature is the Renaissance oriel or bay window (1591). The Renaissance **Wenekindhaus** (1598) has lovely bay windows running almost the full length of the building. The adjacent **Lüntzelhaus** dates from the mid-18th century. The 14th-century **Rolandhaus** has a Baroque porch added in 1730.

Just south of the Markt is the 14th-century Gothic **St Andreaskirche** (St Andrew's Church), Andreasplatz, 05121-12-434. The church was destroyed in 1945 but reconstructed soon after. The interior is rather bare but it has one of the largest organs in Northern Germany. The 114.35-m (378-foot) tower is the highest church tower in Lower Saxony. A viewing platform at 75 m (246 feet) can be reached via 364 steps. The view is worth the effort. Opening hours are from April to September on weekdays, 9 am to 6 pm, Saturday from 9 am to 4 pm, and Sunday from 11:30 am to 4 pm. From October to March, opening hours are Monday to Saturday, 10 am to 4 pm, and Sunday, 11:30 am to 4 pm. During the summer the tower is only open from 11 am to 4 pm. Admission to the tower is €1.50.

Michaelishügel

St Michael, shown below, Michaelisplatz, ☎ 05121-34-410, constructed between 1010 and 1033, is an excellent example of Early Romanesque or Ottonian architecture. The basilica has a triple nave, double chancels, and alternates the use of columns and pillars. It was severely damaged during World War II but restored soon after to its original condition. In addition to the marvelous architecture itself, note the flat, painted ceiling. It is the 12th-century original and uses 90 figures to illustrate the *Family Tree of Jesus Christ*. The Angel Screen is late 12th century and the cloisters date from 1250. The church was added to the UNESCO World Cultural Heritage list in 1985. Opening hours are daily from April to

October, 8 am to 6 pm, and from November to March, 9 am to 4 pm. On Sunday it is only open from noon.

Downhill from St Michael is the **Dom** (Cathedral), Domhof, ☎ 05121-179-1760. It dates to 872, but had major alterations between the 11th and 14th centuries. There was severe damage in 1945 but it was restored to its original condition. This is a prime example of Ottonian Romanesque style, with alternating pillars and columns. Although the interior retains much of the simplicity of the original, it does have some excellent art works. Particularly noteworthy are the

Bernwardinischen Bronzegüsse (Bishop Bernward's bronze doors, details shown above) dating from 1015. These large doors are now in the west front porch and illustrate biblical scenes. Also, note the large 11th-century chandelier over the transept crossing. At the east end is a rare, original two-storey Romanesque **cloister**. From here the legendary rose growing along the east apse can be seen. Inside the cloister is the small, but bright Early Gothic **Annenkapelle** (St Anne's Chapel). Opening hours are November to mid-March on weekdays, 10 am to 4 pm, Saturday, 9:30 am to 4:30 pm, and Sunday from noon to 5 pm. From mid-March to October, opening hours are Monday to Saturday, 9:30 am to 5 pm, and Sunday, noon to 5 pm. Admission to the cloister is €0.50.

The **Dom Museum**, Domhof 4, ☎ 05121-179-1640, houses the cathedral treasure. It is open Tuesday to Saturday, 10 am to 1 pm and 1:30 to 5 pm; Sunday from noon to 5 pm. Admission is €3.50.

THE 1,100-YEAR-OLD ROSE TREE

According to legend, Louis the Pious, left, hid his personal reliquary in a rose bush while out hunting. According to one version, it disappeared and he saw this as a sign from heaven. Other versions have him forgetting about the reliquary, and when he returned he found it stuck in the rose tree. Either way, he promptly ordered the construction of a chapel, which was followed by the cathedral soon after. During the air raids of World War II, the by-now 1,100-year-old rose tree burned with the rest of the cathedral. However, miraculously, a few weeks later it was found growing again.

Just west of the Dom, is the **Roemer-Pelizaeus-Museum**, Am Steine 2, ☎ 05121-93-690, www.rpmuseum.de, with an important Egyptian and Peruvian collection. (Roemer here refers to the name of the founder and not to Romans!) The museum annually stages world-class special exhibitions. Opening hours are daily from 10 am to 6 pm. Admission is €6.

Brühl Area

In contrast to the town center, the half-timbered buildings in the Brühl area are originals that were spared the devastation of the air raids and subsequent fires in 1945. Good examples can be seen in Hinterer Brühl, Brühl, Gelber Stern, and Keßlerstraße. Especially noteworthy is the **Wernerhaus** (1606) at the lower end of Hinterer Brühl.

In the same area is the 12th-century Romanesque **St Godhardikirche** (St Gothard's Church), Godehardsplatz, ☎ 05121-34-578. This basilica is one of the few in Germany that kept its original Romanesque style unaltered. The silhouette has clean lines emphasizing its three towers with slender spires. It is open daily from 9 am to 5:30 pm, and from noon only on Sunday.

The World's Largest Small Car Museum

A few km southwest of Hildesheim, along the B243 en route to Bockenem, is the **Automuseum Störy**, 31167 Bockenem-Störy, ☎ 05067-759. It has 130 mini-cars and an equal number of motorcycles, mostly from the 1950s. Many of these cars, including the miniscule BMW Isetta (above), the Goggo, and the Messerschmitt, are the vehicles that made Germans mobile again after the devastation of World War II – a far cry for the powerful cars seen on the Autobahns these days. Opening hours are weekends, mid-March to October from 10 am to 6 pm.

Cultural Events

In summer, a special program combines visiting several of the old town churches with organ music being played during the visit. The program is available from the tourism office.

Adventures

On Foot

The tourism office arranges guided walking tours of the **old town**. It starts from the tourist office on the Markt, daily from April to October at 2 pm, as well as Saturday at 9:30 am. From November to March, the tour is available only on weekends at 11 am. Special thematic tours with guides in period costume are also available.

The **Hildesheimer Wald** (Hildesheim's Forest) southwest of the town is a popular hiking area. It has at least 14 well-marked trails ranging from four to 10 km (2.4 to six miles).

The **Hildes Ring** is a 47-km (28-mile) walking route that encircles the town. It is divided into eight stages ranging from less than four to 12 km (2.4 to 7.2 miles). A free brochure with public transportation options to different starting points is available from the tourism office.

On Wheels

In the vicinity of Hildesheim are several interesting **cycling** routes. The **Art, Culture, and Nature route** is 64 km (38 miles) and leads past sites that fit its name. It can be done in four different stages.

The **ADFC Hildesheim**, Am Ratsbauhof 1c, ☎ 05121-130-666, www.adfc-hildesheim.de, arranges guided cycling tours in the area ranging from 20 to over 80 km (12 to 48 miles). Non-members pay a nominal €2 participation fee.

The **Go-Kart-Hallenbahn**, Cheruskerring 51, ☎ 05121-52-789, www.gokartbahn-hildesheim.de, is an indoor go-cart track where anyone taller than 1.2 m (3.9 feet) can try their hand at racing. It is open Tuesday to Friday from 4 to 11 pm, Saturday, 2 to 11 pm, and Sunday, noon to 10 pm.

In the Air

Hot-air balloon flights are available from **Skyline Ballooning**, Verkaufsbüro Hildesheim, ☎ 05121-997-105, www.skyline-ballooning.de.

Where to Stay & Eat

The best place to stay in Hildesheim is **Le Méridien**, a modern hotel behind a restored historic façade on the lovely Marktplatz. Rooms are comfortable, with stylish furniture. The better rooms have views of the square. The **Restaurant Gildehaus** (€-€€€) is the best choice on a square with plenty of competition. It has a wide range of international and local cuisine with a large selection of vegetarian dishes. The restaurant has rustic décor but even more pleasant are the seats on the square. Markt 4, 31134 Hildesheim, ☎ 05121-3000, fax 05121-134-298, www.meridien-hildesheim.com. (€€-€€€€)

The **Dorint Sülte Hotel** is closer to the station, about 10 minutes walk from the Markt, but it is such a pleasant hotel that it makes a good alternative to Le Méridien. Completed in 1999, it integrates historical buildings in an otherwise modern design. Rooms are large, well-equipped, and stylish, with a quiet understated elegance that the Dorint group generally does so well. The hotel is in large park-like grounds with a pleasant garden café in service when weather allows. Bahnhofsallee 38, 31134 Hildesheim, ☎ 05121-17-170, fax 05121-171-7100, www.dorint.de. (€€-€€€€)

Camping

About two km (1.2 miles) from the old town is **Camping Am Müggelsee**. It is next to a small lake, with swimming possible. Services are rather basic. The site is open from May to October. Am Müggelsee4, 31135 Hildesheim, ☎ 05121-53-151, fax 05121-514-018.

■ Goslar

Goslar is a lively small town at the northwestern edge of the Harz Mountains. In contrast to most other Harz towns, it remained part of West Germany during the Communist era. It is interesting to compare the state of restoration between Goslar and towns such as Quedlinburg and Wernigerode – especially the state of buildings in back alleys. It shows the neglect these towns suffered after World War II.

Goslar owes its fame and wealth to the rich mines (silver, lead, and copper) in the Rammelsberg just south of town. Although mining took place here in Roman times, it was the rediscovery of the ores in the 10th century that led to Goslar's rapid development. Early in the 11th century, Emperor Heinrich II moved his primary Pfalz (Palace) here, giving the city political importance in addition to its economic might. Up to 1219, 23 Reichstage (Imperial Parliaments) met in Goslar.

In the 14th century, Goslar became a member of the Hanseatic League and its metal sources played an important role in this loose confederation. In the 15th century, Goslar took temporary control of the mines and the town benefited tremendously from its riches. However, it lost the mines again less than a century later and the town stagnated as a provincial backwater of little influence. This decline was only halted in the late 19th century by industrialization and the development of tourism. The Rammelsberg mines stayed in operation up to 1988.

Information Sources

Tourist Office: Tourist information is available from the **Kur- und Fremdenverkehrsgesellschaft Goslar-Hahnenklee**, Markt 7, 38640 Goslar, ☎ 05321-78-060,, www.goslar.de.

Getting Around

Walking is the best way to get around the old town area. Parking garages are mostly at the edges of the old town, which has limited street parking and several pedestrian zones. The station is north of the town near the Neuwerkkirche.

Sightseeing

Goslar has a lovely old town with many buildings dating from medieval times. It was once a rich city and maintained its beauty despite the centuries of economic decline since the Middle Ages. The most impressive area is around the Marktplatz, but the Kaiserpfalz is also interesting and for drivers an easy place to park and start a city tour.

Kaiserpfalz Area

The largest secular Romanesque building in Germany is the **Kaiserpfalz** (Imperial Palace), Kaiserbeek 6, ☎ 05321-704-358, originally built around 1015 by Heinrich II. It was favored by several Ottonian and Salian emperors – Henry III stayed here 17 times and his heart is buried in a sarcophagus in the St Ulrich Chapel. (His body lies in Speyer near Heidelberg.) A total of 23 imperial diets were held here, the last under the Staufer Emperor Friederich II in 1219. The Staufers moved away from the Harz region and Goslar's political preeminence ended.

The current building is not original. It is a reconstruction dating from the late 19th century. In front of the palace are two huge equestrian statues of Emperors Friedrich Barbarossa and Wilhelm I (below, entitled Wilhelm der Grosse – William the Great).

The vaulted cellar houses a museum with exhibits about the traveling Imperial court during the Middle Ages as well as Romanesque and Gothic architectural ornaments. Of special note are the Romanesque Kaiserstuhl (Emperor's Chair) and the 13th-century Goslar Reichsadler (Imperial Eagle). A copy of the eagle is on the Markt. On the main floor of the palace is the huge Kaisersaal (Imperial Hall). It has a series of paintings illustrating the glory days when the Emperors frequented the town. It also has a smaller series of paintings illustrating the fairy tale *Dornröschen* (*Sleeping Beauty*). A door at the far end of this hall leads to the St Ulrich Chapel – once private chapel of the emperor and still housing the heart of Heinrich III. Opening hours are daily from 10 am to 5 pm (4 pm from November to March). Admission is €4.50.

Nearby is the **Domvorhalle** (left, Cathedral Portal) of the opulent former Imperial cathedral. It was added in the 12th century to the church built by Heinrich III in 1050 and survived the demolition of the rest of the church in 1820. A copy of the Kaiserstuhl is kept here – the original is now in the museum of the Kaiserpfalz.

Hoher Weg leads from the Kaiserpfalz to the Marktplatz. En route is the **Großes Heiliges Kreuz** – a former almshouse dating from 1254. It now houses a couple of interesting arts and crafts studios. The workshops are worth seeing even if you aren't buying.

In the same area is the **Goslarer Museum**, Königstraße 1, ☎ 05321-43-394. It has displays of local arts, culture, and history from medieval times to the present. There are art treasures from the former Imperial Church, a large coin collection, and an early pharmacy. Opening hours are Tuesday to Sunday from 10 am to 5 pm, but closing at 4 pm from November to March. Admission is €3.

Markt Area

Goslar has a magnificent, mostly original, Marktplatz (Market Square). Due to the economic decline of the town from the 16th century onwards, most buildings in the area kept their medieval character. At the center of the square is a 13th-century fountain with a copy of the Imperial Eagle (looking a bit like a fat hen). The lower basin of the fountain dates from the 12th century and was the largest bronze casting of the time. The upper basin and the eagle's body is 100 years younger, while its crowned head is from the 18th century.

The Gothic **Rathaus** (Town Hall), Markt 1, ☎ 05321-704-241, was constructed from 1450 onwards. It has an arcaded gallery opening to the square. An external staircase leads to the staterooms, including the magnificent **Huldigungssaal** (Hall of Allegiance) featuring paintings of Roman emperors, Renaissance dignitaries, and the coming of Christ as envisioned in the early 1500s. The walls, window sills, and ceiling are covered by paintings. The room can only be seen through a Perspex screen. Opening hours are April to October from 11:30 am to 3 pm. Admission is €2.

The **Glockenspiel** (Carillon) at Market Square was donated to the city by Preussag on June 7, 1968 to commemorate the thousand-year anniversary of the founding of the mines at Rammelsberg. The bells and figures play daily at 9 am, noon, 3, and 6 pm, illustrating four different tales from the mines' and city's past.

Kaiserworth

The most impressive building on the square is the red Gothic **Kaiserworth**. The building dates from 1494, with later Baroque additions. The stone figures of

Hercules and Abantia are original, while the carved wooden ones are copies of originals dating from 1684. Note the grotesque **Dukatenmännchen** (Ducat Man) that symbolizes Goslar's right to mint coins. The building currently houses a hotel and restaurant with a terrace facing the square.

Behind the Rathaus is the **Marktkirche** (Market Church), ☎ 05321-22-922. It dates partly from 1151, but was altered in the 14th and 15th century. It has two high towers of unequal height and contrasting styles. The interior has windows dating from the 13th century, wall paintings from around 1440, and a carved Baroque altar. Opening hours are daily, April to October from 10 am to 5 pm, but closing at 4 pm from November to March. The north tower can be climbed Friday to Sunday from 11 am to 4 pm.

Goslar has a thousand half-timbered and stone houses. Some prime examples can be seen at Schuhhof and along the Münzstraße. Two famous early 16th-century buildings are across from the Marktkirche: the **Brusttuch** (1526) and the **Bäckergildehaus** (Baker's Guild). At the crossing of Markt and Bäckerstraße are Renaissance houses with friezes.

Nearby, is the **Siemenshaus**, Schreiberstraße 12, ☎ 05321-23-837, the ancestral home of the Siemens family that later founded the Siemens industrial giant. The wood timber and brick house is a rare sample of Baroque building artistry in Goslar. The hall, courtyard, and beer-brewing house are open to the public on Tuesday and Thursday from 9 am to noon. Admission is free.

The **Mönchehaus Museum für Moderne Kunst** (Modern Art), Monchestraße 3, ☎ 05321-29-570, exhibits modern art in a large house dating from 1528. The museum annually awards the Kaiserring prize and exhibits works from the recipient of this prestigious art award. Opening hours are Tuesday to Saturday, 10 am to 5 pm, Sunday, 10 am to 1 pm. Admission is €3.

About 400 m (1,300 feet) north of the Marktplatz, but well worth the stroll, is the **Neuwerkkirche**, Rosentorstraße, ☎ 05321-22-39. This former chapter church is a Romanesque basilica with parts dating from 1186. It has lovely octagonal Romanesque towers. The interior has well-preserved Late Romanesque wall paintings. Adjacent to the church is a Romanesque garden with 70 different types of plants. Opening hours are April to October, Monday to Friday, 10 am to noon and 2:30 to 4:30 pm; Saturday, 10 am to noon.

Town Walls & Defenses

Due to its obvious riches, Goslar was envied by many and had to fortify itself. The town walls were two km (1.2 miles) long with 50 guard towers, some with walls eight m (26 feet) thick. The defenses were maintained up to the Thirty Years' War. The largest remaining parts of the defenses are near the Kaiserpfalz.

The **Zwinger**, a round tower built in 1517, has walls up to six m (19 feet) thick. The tower has a diameter of 26 m (85 feet) and could house up to 1,000 men on four levels. It is worth climbing to the top for views of the old town. Inside the tower is the **Museum des Späten Mittelalters** (Late Middle Ages Museum), Thomasstraße 2, ☎ 05321-43-140, with displays on medieval life, including armory, weapons used by peasants during the Peasants' Revolt and, inevitably, implements of torture. The museum is open daily in March from 10 am to 4 pm, and April to mid-November daily from 9 am to 5 pm. Admission is €2.

The best-preserved town gate is the mighty **Breites Tor** (Broad Gate). Originally built in the 13th century, it was enlarged around 1500. It was in reality a fortress functioning as a gateway and is as impressive now as it was 500 years ago.

Farther Afield

Goslar owed its riches and fame to the Rammelsberg mines, about a km south of the Kaiserpfalz. In 1992, parts of the mine were converted into the **Museum und Besucherbergwerk Rammelsberg** (Museum and Visitors' Mine), Bergtal 19, ☎ 05321-7500, www.rammelsberg.de. The museum has exhibits on the history and workings of the mine. More interesting, though, is a tour of the mine itself – these last an hour each and are available several times per day. A four-hour tour called Abenteuer Mittelalter (Medieval Adventure) requires reservations. Note that the average temperature underground is a chilly 12°C/54°F. Opening hours are Tuesday to Sunday from 9 am to 6 pm (last tour at 4:30 pm). Admission is €6 for the museum, €10 for museum plus one tour, and €60 for the museum and Medieval Adventure tour. Free parking is available at the museum, or use Bus Line C/803 from the Hauptbahnhof.

Shopping

The medieval **Großen Heiligen Kreuz Spital**, Hoher Weg 7, ☎ 05321-21-800, a former almshouse, has been converted into an interesting center with active arts and crafts workshops and shops. The crafts include woodwork, goldsmith and silversmith work, blown glass, paper, ceramics and leather works. The center is well worth seeing even if you're not planning to buy anything. The building is open daily from November to March, 11 am to 4 pm, April to October, 11 am to 5 pm. The shops set their own individual opening hours during these times.

Adventures

On Foot

The tourist office conducts two-hour guided walking tours of the **old town** daily at 10 am. From May to October, additional thematic tours are available daily at 2:30 pm. All tours start at the tourism office on the Marktplatz.

On Wheels

Bicycles can be rented from **Harz-Bike**, Bomhardt Straße 3-5, ☎ 05321-82-011.

From mid-April to October, **bus tours** are offered daily at 11 am, 12:30, 2, and 3:30 pm in the open-roof **Cabrio-Bus**, ☎ 05321-553-134, www.stadtbus-goslar.de. The one-hour tour departs from the Marktplatz.

The **Goslarer Bimmelbahn**, Ahornweg 4, ☎ 05321-21-661, departs hourly from the Marktplatz with **train tours** lasting just over half an hour.

Where to Stay & Eat

Goslar's hotels are not particularly luxurious, reflecting the fact that many visitors are only on daytrips, but there are sufficient comfortable ones in the old town area.

The **Hotel Der Achtermann** is partly ensconced in the former city defensive walls at the edge of the old town near the Hauptbahnhof. It combines early and modern elements. Bedrooms are comfortable and come in a range of sizes and furnishings. The spa area has a large pool. The restaurant **Altdeutsche Stube** (€€) serves international cuisine. It is in a former defensive tower and has an impressive painted wood ceiling. Rosentorstraße 20, 38640 Goslar, ☎ 05321-70-000, fax 05321-700-0999, www.der-achtermann.de. (€€€-€€€€)

Hotel Niedersächsischer Hof is in the same area close to the Hauptbahnhof. It has modern, comfortably furnished rooms. The hotel exhibits modern art in cooperation with the Mönckehaus Museum. International and regional dishes are available in the elegant restaurant (€€-€€€) or the more informal **Pieper's Bistro** (€€). Klubgartenstraße 1, 38640 Goslar, ☎ 05321-3160, fax 05321-316-444. www.alemannia-hotels.de. (€€€)

Hotel Kaiserworth is in the loveliest building on the Marktplatz. Rooms come in five different categories with prices depending on location and size. Some are more comfortable and modern than others. The **Worth** restaurant (€€-€€€) serves local specialties and international cuisine. It has an elegant dining room with vaulted ceilings or you can dine on the terrace facing the market square. Markt 3, 38640 Goslar, ☎ 05321-7090, fax 05321-709-345, www.kaiserworth.de. (€€-€€€)

The **Treff-Hotel Das Brusttuch** is an equally lovely and famous building. It is opposite the Marktkirche in a former Late Gothic patrician house from 1526. The bedrooms are modern and comfortable. Hoher Weg 1, 38640 Goslar, ☎ 05321-34-600, fax 05321-346-099, www.treff-hotels.de. (€€€)

Camping

Camping Sennhütte is a pleasant campground but facilities are limited. It is three km (1.8 miles) south of Goslar. There are 170 spaces for tourists and it's open year-round. Clausthaler Straße 28, 38644 Goslar, ☎ / fax 05321-22-498.

■ Hameln

Hameln, often translated to Hamelin in English, is most famous for the *Pied Piper* fairy tale. The historic old town has several interesting sights, but the famous Rat Catcher is still the main selling point.

The Pied Piper or Rat Catcher

The *Rattenfänger* (Rat Catcher) is one of the most famous German fairy tales. According to the story, in the year 1284 a strangely dressed man appeared in Hameln claiming he could rid the town of a rat plague. He was promptly hired. He played on a small flute and all the rats and mice followed him into the River Weser, where the vermin died. The town, happy to be rid of the mice, decided not to pay the promised sum. The piper left in anger but returned on June 26. Again he played his flute, but this time all the town's children followed him, never to return.

The legend was recorded by the Brothers Grimm in the 19th century and became famous in the English-speaking world as the Pied Piper of Hamelin. Like many legends, it is at least partly based on facts. At the end of the 13th century, young people, often referred to as the town's children, were recruited to populate newly colonized parts of eastern Europe – the Grimms mentioned that the children ended up in Transylvania.

Hameln keeps the legend alive with numerous rat statues, a rat-catcher museum, and frequent free performances of the sad tale.

Hameln was founded in the ninth century by monks from Fulda who established a monastery next to an existing community. A town developed by the 13th century and used its strategic position on the River Weser as a trading advantage and achieved prosperity as a member of the Hanseatic League in the Middle Ages. The 16th century saw great prosperity in the Weser Valley and most of the sights in the old town date from this period. The large, attractive buildings erected in this period are clearly Renaissance, but with a light-hearted touch termed Weser Renaissance. The style is defined by the use of ram's horn scrollwork, lavishly decorated pinnacled gables and oriels, stone bands encircling buildings, and the use of masks and gargoyle reliefs. Hameln has some prime samples.

Information Sources

Tourist Office: Tourist information is available from **Hameln Marketing and Tourismus**, Postfach 101144, 31761 Hameln, 05151-957-824, www.hameln.de, or in person from Deisteralle 1 – Am Bürgergarten.

Getting Around

Parking garages at the edge of the old town are well-signposted. Most streets in the old town are closed to traffic.

The train station is about a km (.6 mile) along Deisterstraße to the east of the old town. The S-Bahn connects Hameln with Hannover every half-hour and takes 43 minutes.

Sightseeing

Hameln is most famous for the Pied Piper and the town uses large painted rats, small rat-shaped breads, and rats everywhere to keep the legend alive. The main sights in the town, however, are the pretty buildings erected mostly in the 16th century when Hameln's strategic position on the River Weser led to a long period of prosperity.

The attractions below are described in order, starting from Ostertor (10 minutes walk from the station) along Osterstraße, turning left into Bäckerstraße at the Markt. The main sights can be seen in a bit over an hour.

Osterstraße

Just inside the former town walls is the **Rattenfängerhaus** (Rat Catcher's

House). This 1602 Weser Renaissance house has a lavishly decorated façade with small ornaments. The name derives from an inscription about the fairy tale on the wall facing Bungelosenstraße. The building now houses a restaurant.

The **Stiftherrenhaus**, Osterstraße 8, is a half-timbered building dating from 1558 and has lovely wood-carved, mostly biblical figures on the slanted brackets (cleats).

The **Leisthaus**, Osterstraße 9, was built in 1589 as another prime sample of the Weser Renaissance. It has a lovely two-storey oriel or bay window and richly decorated gable. Inside are the **Städtische Museum** (Local History), ☎ 05151-202-215, and a pleasant café. The museum recalls the tale and has displays of other local history and cultural objects. Opening hours are Tuesday to Sunday from 10 am to 4:30 pm. Admission is €3.

The **Hochzeithaus** (Wedding House), Osterstraße 2, a beautiful Weser Renaissance building, was erected in 1610-17. Constructed as a huge reception hall (43 m/142 feet long) for the community, it has three gables and typical stone band work.

Markt & Bäckerstraße

The Markt (Market Square) is the heart of the old town. The Early Gothic **Marktkirche St Nicolai** (Market Church of St Nicolas), was destroyed in World War II by artillery fire but rebuilt. The golden boat on its tower reminds viewers that this was once the church of the shipping guild. Note the Pied Piper mosaic window on the south side.

The **Dempterhaus**, Am Markt, is another Weser Renaissance building. It was built in 1607 and has two stone floors, plus a half-timbered third storey and gable.

The **Löwenapotheke** (Lion's Pharmacy), corner of Bäcker and Wendenstraße, is a Gothic building from around 1300. The nearby **Rattenkrug** (Rat's Tankard), Bäckerstraße 16, houses the oldest restaurant in town. Parts of the building date from 1250 but it was converted into a Weser Renaissance structure with a five-floor gable in 1568.

The **Münster St Bonifatius**, Münsterkirchhof, is where the original monastery was built. A 12th-century Romanesque basilica was converted into the present Gothic hall church in the 13th century. The huge polygonal tower affords great views of the region – ask for the key at the cashier. The crypt underneath the choir dates from 1120.

Cultural Events

From mid-May to mid-September, the tale of the **Pied Piper** is performed Sunday at noon on an open-air stage in front of the Hochzeithaus. This free 30-minute performance by 80 actors in period costume draws on average 3,500 spectators per performance. During the same period, on Wednesday at 4:30 pm the same story is performed, also for free, as the musical *Rats*.

The carillon with figures on the same building recalls the tale daily at 1:05, 3:35, and 5:35 pm (9:35 and 11:35 am has bells only). Other fairy tales are performed during the same period in nearby towns:

In Bodenwerder, the **Münchhausen Play** is performed the first Sunday of the month at 3 pm.

In Polle, **Aschenputtel (Cinderella)** is performed every third Sunday of the month at 3 pm on the open-air stage at the Burgruine Polle.

In Höxter, **Hänsel und Gretel** is performed on the Marktplatz the first Saturday of the month at 3 pm.

More formal concerts and theater are staged, especially during summer, in various halls and churches in the region. Request a schedule from the tourism office.

Adventures

On Foot

The tourism office arranges one-hour guided walking tours of the **old town** starting from the tourism office in Deisterallee. From April to October, the tour is daily at 2:30 pm and additionally on Sunday at 10:15 am. From November to March, the tour is only on Saturday at 2:30 pm and Sunday at 10:15 am. Longer 90-minute tours on different themes are available from May to September on the first Friday of the month at 6 pm.

The **Weser Valley** is a popular hiking area, with the **Weserberglandweg**, www.weserbergland.de, the favored long-distance route. It is 200 km (120 miles) and leads from Porta Westfalica via Hameln to Hann. Münden. The full route is usually done in eight days in stages. **Kurverwaltung Bad Karlshafen**, Hafenplatz 8, 34385 Bad Karlshafen, ☎ 05672-999-922, arranges multi-day trips with luggage transfers. Many hotels in the region can arrange luggage transfers too.

The **Rattenfängerpfad** (Rat Catcher's Route) is an almost 80-km (48-mile) walking route around Hameln – usually divided into three stages.

On Wheels

Several **cycling** routes are available in the region. The best known is the 500-km (300-mile) **Weserradweg** (Weser Cycling Route) that connects Hann. Münden and Cuxhaven via Hameln and Bremen. The route is mostly on special cycling roads and suitable to families as well. Luggage forwarding can be arranged. Long-distance cyclists can safely park their bicycles and luggage for a minimal charge at the parking garages at Rattenfängerhall and Kopmanshof.

Bicycles can be rented from **Fa. Anderas Troche**, Kreuzstraße 7, ☎ 05151-13-670, near the station.

Near Hameln, from Rinteln-Süd to Alverdissen is a **Draisinenbahn** (cycling on a railway trolley). Two cyclists are required per trolley and two additional passengers are possible. The 18-km (11-mile) route requires about three hours uphill and 90 minutes coming downhill. Reservations through **Pro Riteln**, Verein für Stadtmarketing, 31737 Rinteln, ☎ 05751-958-255, www.draisinen.de. The tracks are open from April to October.

In the Air

Balloon flights in the region are offered by **Ballonteam Perspektive**, ☎ 05151-7179, www.ballon-perspektive.de.

On Water

The River Weser is a popular rowing venue. **Kayaking** trips from several days to a few hours are possible in the Hameln area. The Weser in this region is slow-flowing and suitable for beginners as well. The Emmer tributary offers conditions that are slightly more challenging. Kayaks and canoes can be rented from **Kanu Tours Hameln**, Lohstraße 4, ☎ 05151-924-107, www.kanu-tours-hameln.de.

The **Flotte Weser**, Deisterallee 1, ☎ 05151-939-999, www.flotte-weser.de, operates hour-long **cruises** on the Weser from Tuesday to Sunday from late April to early October. From May to early October, it also has cruises from Hameln to Polle on Wednesday, Friday, and weekends.

Where to Stay & Eat

The **Dorint Hotel** is just outside the old town in a modern building. Rooms are elegant and comfortable. The sauna on the ninth floor has views of the old town. The restaurant **Safran** (€€) serves international cuisine. 164er Ring 3, 31785 Hameln,

☎ 05151-7920, ☎ 05151-792-191, www.dorint.com. (€€€-€€€€)

The **Best Western Hotel Stadt Hameln** is at the southern edge of the old town on the banks of the River Weser. The building, originally a prison, was converted into an elegant hotel in the early 1990s. Rooms are bright with large windows and elegant furnishings. The restaurant **Stadt Hameln** serves new light German cuisine. Münsterwall 2, 31787 Hameln, ☎ 05151-9010, fax 05151-901-333, www.stadthameln.bestwestern.de. (€€€)

Hotel Zur Börse is in the heart of the old town. It is in a modern building with modern, functionally furnished rooms. Osterstraße 41a, 31785 Hameln, ☎ 05151-7080, fax 05151-25-485, www.hotel-zur-boerse.de. (€€)

Also in the old town is the modern **Hotel Zur Post**. Rooms are modern and size depends on the price paid – some have small balconies. Am Posthof 6, 31785 Hameln, ☎ 05151-7630, fax 05151-7641. (€€)

Many cafés and restaurants are available in Oster and Bäckerstraße, but the following are in historic or noteworthy buildings. The **Museums-Café**, Osterstraße 8, ☎ 05151-21-553, is inside the same building as the town museum. It has excellent cakes in addition to small meals. The **Restaurant im Rattenfängerhaus**, Osterstraße 28, ☎ 05151-3888, serves hearty local cuisine – no matter what the menu says, no rats are used in the actual food. The **Paulaner im Rattenkrug**, Bäckerstraße 16, ☎ 05151-22-731, serves Bavarian beer and food in the oldest restaurant in town. (€-€€)

Camping

The campground **Zum Fährhaus an der Weser** is a mere 10-minute walk from the town center. It is peacefully located on the left bank of the Weser, has 100 spaces and is open year-round. Uferstraße 80, 31787 Hameln, ☎ 05151-61-167, www.campingplatz-fährhaus-hameln.de.

The **Capingplatz am Waldbad** is five km (three miles) from the center of Hameln. It has modern facilities, including electric outlets at each of the 200 spaces, and is open from April to October. Pferdeweg 2, 31787 Hameln-Halvestorf, ☎/fax 05158-2774, www.campingamwaldbad.de.

Excursions in the Upper Weser Valley

The Upper Weser Valley between Hameln and Hann. Münden is a lovely area to explore by car, boat, bicycle, or walking. Several small towns have interesting samples of Weser Renaissance as well as lovely half-timbered buildings. Many towns claim to be the origin of Grimms' fairy tales and, although not all can prove the claims, the towns are so picturesque that they may well be. To make the most of this journey, it is necessary to turn off for the smaller villages and sights that the main road bypasses.

THE FAIRY TALE ROUTE

One of the more recent additions to Germany's many themed vacation routes is the Märchenstraße (Fairy Tale Route). It retraces the steps of the Brothers Grimm and the places that claim to be the settings of their collection of fairy tales. Starting from their town of birth, Hanau east of Frankfurt, it winds its way north to Bremen. The total route, including turnoffs, is 600 km (360 miles). Many of the sights are terribly romantic and not for children only. Some of the best-known tales and sights are in the Upper Weser Valley between Hameln (Pied Piper) and Hann. Münden (Dr Eisenbart).

More information is available from any tourist office along the route or from **Deutsche Märchenstraße**, Königsplatz 53, 34117 Kassel, ☎ 0561-707-707, www.german-fairy-tale-route.com.

Hämelschenburg

Ten km (six miles) south of Hameln is the **Schloss Hämelschenburg**, Schlossstraße 1, 31860 Emmerthal, ☎ 05155-951-690, www.haemelschenburg.de. Construction started in 1588 on this excellent example of Weser Renaissance architecture. The Schloss is surrounded by a water moat and has a bridge gate with a statue of St George dating from 1608. The interior can only be seen on a guided tour. Opening hours are April to October, Tuesday to

Sunday, 10 am to noon and 2 to 5 pm. Tours once every hour.

Höxter

The **Reichsabtei Corvey** (Imperial Abbey, shown below) is a few km north of Höxter. It was founded in 822 by Louis the Pious and remained a monastery until secularization in 1803. The only part remaining of the original Carolingian building is the Westwerk. An ancient copy of Tacitus' history annals was discovered here in the 16th century. Heinrich Hoffman von Fallerleben, who worked here as a librarian, wrote *Das Deutschlandlied*, which, set to music by Haydn, became Germany's national anthem. The original first verse, which has Germany's boundaries at prewar levels, is now banned in Germany. The **Höxter-Corvey Museum** explains the role of the area in early German politics. The **Schlossrestaurant**, ☎ 05271-8323 (€-€€) is a pleasant place to lunch, with seating under the trees in summer.

The old town of Höxter has many half-timber buildings from the 16th century with excellent samples in Markstraße and Westerbachstraße. The Weser Renaissance **Rathaus** (Town Hall) was built in 1610-13. The 12th-century Romanesque **Kilianikirche** has two visibly unequal towers and an interesting Renaissance pulpit. The town claims to be the original setting for *Hansel and Gretel*.

Sababurg

Sababurg, a castle that goes back to the 14th century, claims to be the authentic **Dornröschenschloss (Sleeping Beauty Castle)**. It certainly looks the part with turrets, thick forests, and, of course, roses. The castle was rebuilt as a

hunting lodge for the counts of Hesse and c/schloss Sababurg. Rooms are comfortable, with the tower room particularly romantic. The restaurant (€-€€) serves local specialties, including venison and other game. Im Reinhardswakd, 34369 Hofgeismar-Sababurg, ☎ 05671-8080, fax 05671-808-200, www.sababurg.de. (€€€-€€€€)

■ Hann. Münden

Ha9nn. Münden used to be the abbreviation for Hannoversch (Hanoverian) Münden, to distinguish it from a similarly named town in Prussia. However, in the 1970s the town adopted the abbreviated version as its official name. The town has lovely half-timber buildings and is often the starting point for trips by car, bicycle, walking, or by boat in the Weser Valley. This is where the Wera and Fulda rivers join to form the Weser.

The town was founded in 1155 and in 1247 received trade privileges that forced all traders passing through to offer all goods for sale to locals for three days before being allowed to move on. The town prospered, as is confirmed by the large half-timbered and Weser Renaissance buildings, until railways surpassed shipping as the main method for transporting goods.

Information Sources

Tourist Office: Tourist information is available from **Touristik Naturpark Münden**, Rathaus, 34346 Hann. Münden, ☎ 05541-75-313, www.hann.muenden.de. The office can book accommodations and most of the adventures listed below.

Getting Around

Hann. Münden is best explored on foot. The town is a few minutes drive from the Autobahn A7.

The train and bus stations are about 10 minutes stroll along Bahnhofstraße to the east of the old town. Hann. Münden is reachable by hourly train from Kassel (16 minutes) or Göttingen (36 minutes).

Sightseeing

Hann. Münden has a lovely, small old town with impressive half-timbered buildings. It can be seen in just over an hour.

The Weser Renaissance-style **Rathaus** (Town Hal) was erected in 1603-19. It has three decorative gables, a two-storey oriel, and an interesting center portal. The Doctor Eisenbart-Glockenspiel (carillon) plays daily at noon, 3, and 5 pm. Inside is the Hochtiedshus (Wedding Hall) where countless couples nailed wooden hearts to the beams. The tourist information office is in the building – entrance from Lotzestraße. The Rathaus is open daily from 8 am to 8 pm.

The choir and east portals of the **St Blasius-Kirche** date from the 13th century, while the rest is mostly 15th and 16th century. Parts of the original Romanesque basilica can be seen inside the church. Opening hours are daily from May to September, 11 am to 4 pm.

In 2000, the town erected six water fountains in the public spaces surrounding the Rathaus and St Blasius-Kirche. Children are welcome to play in all.

The **Alte Werrabrücke** (Old Wera Bridge), constructed around 1250, is one of the oldest stone bridges in northern Germany. It is still in daily use. The **Sydekumstraße** that leads from here to the palace has several impressive buildings and decorated entrances.

The **Welfenschloss** (Palace of the Guelph family) is a Weser Renaissance building erected in 1562-84 to replace its burned predecessor. The interior can only be seen on a guided tour. The palace also houses the **Städtisches Museum**, which has exhibits on local history as well as in impressive collection of locally produced porcelain from 1753 to 1854 by the Mündener Fayence-Manufaktur. Opening hours are Wednesday to Saturday, 10 am to noon and 2:30 to 5 pm, and Sunday, 10 am to 12:30 pm. Admission is € 1.02 (!).

Doctor Eisenbart

Hann. Münden's most famous son was Dr Johan Andreas Eisenbart (1663-1727). This legendary quack doctor claimed many miracles and, of course, legends exaggerated them even more. He used sledgehammers for anesthetics and shot a bad tooth out of his own mouth with a pistol, among other feats. A leaflet from 1692 advertising his services is shown above. A popular German song hails that he made the blind walk and the lame see. Free comic plays are staged on summer Sundays at 11:15 in front of the Rathaus to commemorate his feats.

Cultural Events

In summer, a series of concerts is held in the Romanesque Bursfelder Monastery, about 20 km (12 miles) north of Hann. Münden. The schedule is available from the tourism office.

Shopping

An **antiques market** is held at Gimte im Weserpark, usually on the third weekend of the month. It is open Saturday from 1 to 5 pm and Sunday from 9 am to 5 pm.

Adventures

On Foot

From May to October, guided **walking tours** of town depart from the Tourism Office daily at 2 pm. A free brochure with suggested self-guided walks is also available.

A pleasant half-hour hike from the old town is to the **Tillyschanzenturm** (Tilly's Tower). The 25-m (82-foot) tower is on a low hill to the west of town and offers great views of the town and the confluence of the rivers. The viewing tower is open from April to October daily, 9 am to 8 pm, and from November to March daily, 11 am to 8 pm, closing at 1 pm on Monday. Admission is €1.10.

On Wheels

Hann. Münden is at the center of three long-distance **cycling** routes running along the three rivers: the Weser (450 km/270 miles), the Werra (300 km/180 miles), and the Fulda (196 km/118 miles). All three follow the flow of the rivers closely, meaning relatively even ground.

The tourism office can arrange multi-day trips with accommodation and luggage transfers. On weekends, usually from Easter to October, a bus with bicycle transportation options runs in the Fulda Valley between Kassel and Hann. Münden. Get details from ☎ 0561-200-9833 or the tourism office. Fahrradtransfer, ☎ 05541-75-343, arranges bicycle transportation in the region.

Bicycles can be rented from **Campingplatz Hann. Münden**, ☎ 05541-12-257; **Frank's Radhaus**, ☎ 05541-73-954; or from **Hotel Schlossschänke**, ☎ 05541-70-940.

On Water

Fishing is possible on all three rivers. The necessary permits and equipment are available from **Angelshop S Fiedler**, Zieglerstraße 4, ☎ 05541-6569.

The rivers around Hann. Münden are ideal for **rowing**. Boats can be rented from **Busch Freizeitservice**, Campingplatz Hann. Münden, ☎ 05541-12-257, or from **Campingplatz Hann. Münden-Hemeln**, ☎ 05544-1414.

From May to September, **riverboats** operate in the rivers around Hann. Münden. One-hour cruises to see the three rivers depart several times per day, except on Monday. Limited services are also offered to Bad Karlshafen, Bursfelde, and Kassel. Schedules and tickets are available from the tourist office.

Where to Stay & Eat

Hotel Alter Packhof opened in 2000 in a storage house built in 1837 on the bank of the River Fulda. Rooms are elegant with solid wood furniture and marble baths. The restaurant (€€) serves light German cuisine and regional specialties. Bremer Schlagd 10, 34346 Hann. Münden, ☎ 05541-98-890, www.hotel-alter-packhof.de. (€€€)

Berghotel Eberburg has a peaceful location on the slopes of Reinhard's Forest at the edge of town. Rooms are comfortable and some have balconies with views of the valley and the old town. The restaurant (€€-€€€) serves Mediterranean cuisine. (Open for dinner only.) Tillyschanzenweg 14, 34346 Hann. Münden, ☎ 05541-5088, fax 05541-4685, www.berghotel-eberburg.de. (€€)

Hotel Schmucker Jäger is at the edge of town. It has simple, practically furnished rooms with balconies. The restaurant (€-€€) serves game and local specialties. Wilhelmhäuser Straße 45, 34346 Hann. Münden, ☎ 05541-98-100, fax 05541-981-033, www.hotel-schmucker-jaeger.de. (€€)

Camping

Grüne Insel Tanzwerder is ideally located on an island in the River Fulda right next to the old town. Boat and bicycle rentals are available on site. Busch Freizeit Service, 34346 Hann. Münden, ☎ 05541-12-257, fax 05541-660-778, www.busch-freizeit.de.

About 10 km (six miles) north of the old town is **Camping Hemeln**, a quiet campground with good facilities and 100 spaces. It is on the bank of the Weser River and next to the Weser Cycling Route. Boat rental is available on site. It is open year-round. Unterdorf 34, 34346 Hann. Münden-Hemeln, ☎ 05544-1414, ☎ 05544-1414, www.wesercamping.de.

North Rhine Westphalia

North Rhine Westphalia (*Nordrhein-Westfalen*) is Germany's most heavily populated state, with 18 million people, more than a fifth of the total population. Although the majority of people live in cities of more than half a million people, 75% of the state is covered by greenery or water.

The most popular destination in the state is **Cologne**, with its magnificent Gothic cathedral and excellent museums. Nearby **Bonn** may have lost its status as federal capital of Germany, but is still worth a visit to see some of the museums and sights associated with Beethoven. **Aachen** is the cradle of German nationhood and has some reminders from the times of Charlemagne and the early Holy Roman Empire of the German Nation. **Düsseldorf**, in sharp contrast, is a modern city famous for its fashion and modern art scene.

The industrial Ruhr area was long the heart of German mining and heavy industries and this image lingers. Nowadays, the Ruhr is more accurately associated with modern high technology and clean industries. It is a pleasant area to live in, with excellent infrastructure and an astonishing number of cultural events, but seldom visited by foreign tourists.

History

North Rhine Westphalia was formed after World War II by the British occupation forces mainly by combining the areas of the Rhineland with Westphalia. It found itself with the provisional capital of Germany in sleepy Bonn, while progressive Düsseldorf became the state capital. During the early postwar period, the Ruhr area was the industrial engine of Germany's *Wirtschaftswunder* (Economic Miracle) that led economic growth in the 1950s.

Much of the Rhinelands were settled by the Romans, while the east bank of the Rhine was left to the German "barbaric" tribes. In the fourth and fifth centuries, the Franks took over most of the area and at the end of the eighth century, Charlemagne founded his preferred residence in Aachen, which would remain an important symbolic seat of power up to the 16th century. For much of the Middle Ages, large parts of the area were ruled by the powerful Archbishop of Cologne, who as an elector also had huge temporal powers.

France long considered the Rhine as her natural border and, during the Napoleonic years, the Rhinelands west of the Rhine were indeed part of France, while Westphalia was created on the east bank as a new kingdom and at times ruled by Jerome Bonaparte. After Napoleon's defeat, Prussia took most of the area as reward, retaining it up to World War II.

Getting Here & Getting Around

By Rail: North Rhine Westphalia has excellent rail connections inside the state itself as well as to other parts of Germany and Western Europe.

At least three ICE trains per hour connect Cologne and Frankfurt's Airport or Hauptbahnhof in just over an hour. Connections to northern Germany usually require a change in Hanover – just over an hour away. Berlin is a bit more than four hours away on hourly trains.

Cologne has good connections to Amsterdam and Brussels, taking 2½ hours. Thalys trains to Brussels continue to Paris, taking four hours in total.

At least nine trains per hour connect Düsseldorf and Cologne , taking between 20 minutes (ICE) and 50 minutes (S-Bahn). Best value is the Regional Express, taking 30 minutes. Five trains per hour connect Bonn and Cologne; the ICE takes 20 minutes and the Regional Express 30 minutes. Five trains per hour connect Aachen and Cologne – the high-speed trains continuing to Brussels and Paris stop here after 40 minutes. Regular trains take an hour.

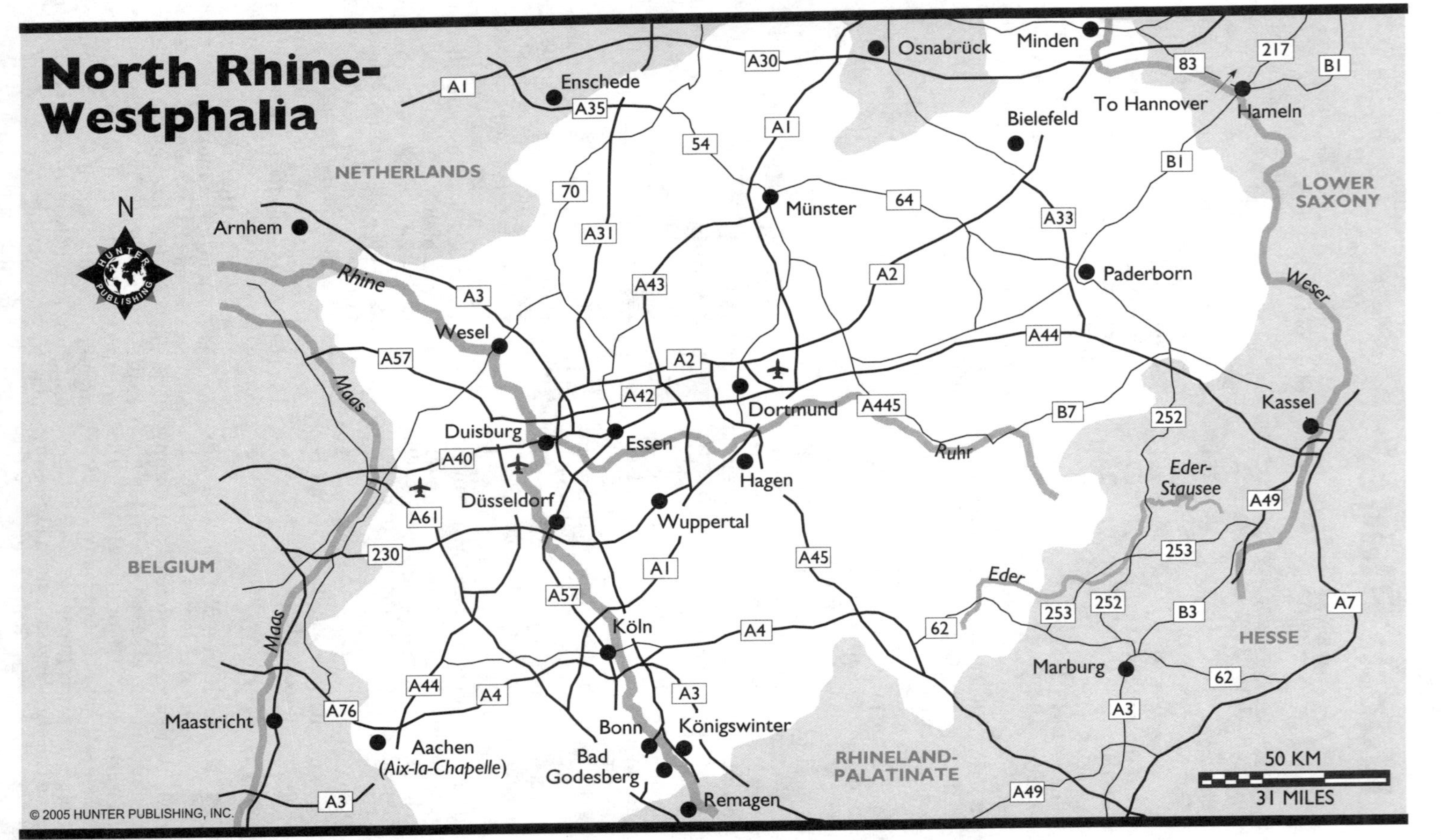

North Rhine-Westphalia
N
HUNTER PUBLISHING
NETHERLANDS
BELGIUM
LOWER SAXONY
HESSE
RHINELAND-PALATINATE
Arnhem
Enschede
Osnabrück
Minden
Bielefeld
To Hannover
Hameln
Münster
Paderborn
Wesel
Duisburg
Essen
Dortmund
Hagen
Düsseldorf
Wuppertal
Kassel
Eder-Stausee
Köln
Bonn
Bad Godesberg
Königswinter
Remagen
Marburg
Aachen
(Aix-la-Chapelle)
Maastricht
Rhine
Maas
Ruhr
Eder
Weser
A1
A30
A35
54
70
A31
A43
A2
A3
A57
A42
A40
A61
230
A44
A4
A76
A445
A45
B7
64
A33
B1
83
217
252
253
A49
B3
62
A7
50 KM
31 MILES
© 2005 HUNTER PUBLISHING, INC.

High-Speed Trains & Köln-Deutz Station

The Hohenzollern Bridge, which connects Cologne's Hauptbahnhof (Main Station) and the east bank of the Rhine, is crossed by trains at a rate of two per minute. Due to this bottleneck, many high-speed ICE trains stop at Köln-Deutz station on the east bank. From here, it is only two minutes on the local train to the Hauptbahnhof, but if carrying luggage bear in mind that it is a bit of a walk from the ICE to the S-Bahn platforms.

By Road: The state has excellent Autobahns but, being the most densely populated area of Germany, its roads can get crowded and slow during rush hour.

By Air: The airports in North Rhine Westphalia are mostly served from European cities and are popular with low-cost carriers.

Köln-Bonn Airport, ☎ 02203-404-001, www.koeln-bonn-airport.de, is southeast of Cologne. It can be reached by at least twice-hourly trains from Cologne Hauptbahnhof – the 21-minute journey costs €2. Taxis to Cologne take 15 minutes (€25) and to Bonn 20 minutes (€40). Bus services are available to several parts of Cologne, Bonn, and Aachen. **Düsseldorf Airport**, Flughafenstraße 120, ☎ 0211-4210, www.duesseldorf-airport.de, is north of the city and similarly has mainly European connections. Several bus services are available but the fastest is the S-Bahn Line S7 that makes the journey to the Hauptbahnhof in just 12 minutes. Taxis to the center of town take 20 minutes (€16).

The frequent high-speed train connections between **Frankfurt Airport** and Cologne, taking only an hour, make flying into Frankfurt often the preferred option for intercontinental travelers.

By Boat: The Rhine River and several tributaries and canals continue to play an important role in trade and transportation for most of the state. The Rhine is also popular for tourist boat trips lasting from less than an hour to several days, with Switzerland and the Netherlands popular starting points in addition to the ports in Germany.

The largest tourist boat operator on the Rhine is **Köln-Düsseldorfer** (usually abbreviated simply to KD), Frankenwerft 35, ☎ 0221-208-8319, www.k-d.com. It has boats in virtually all Rhine towns and operates local sightseeing cruises as well as rides between towns. Most towns have smaller competitors, which usually charge slightly less but often have fewer departures.

■ Information Sources

i For information on the whole state contact **Nordrhein-Westfalen Tourismus**, Worringer Str. 22, 50668 Köln, ☎ 0221-179-450, www.nrw-tourismus.de.

The Ruhr Area & the Industrial Culture Route

The Ruhr area was once the engine of German industry with large mining operation and heavy industrial plants. This situation was dramatically changed by the end of the 20th century with a move toward high-technology and cleaner industries. Many giant industrial plants were left behind to rot and rust.

The **Route der Industriekultur** (Industry Cultural Route) connects 52 former major industrial sites in the Ruhr area. Included in the route are mines, former factories, and gasworks. It started as something for specialists, but proved surprisingly popular and other areas have set up their own industry routes since. More information on the route is available from the **Visitor Center Zeche Zollverein XII**, Gelsenkirchener Straße 181, 45309 Essen, ☎ 0180-400-0086, www.route-industriekultur.de,

■ Cologne (Köln)

Cologne (Köln) is a popular destination for foreign tourists and Germans alike. It is a city known for its easy attitude to life, its relaxed atmosphere, and the ability to have a good time. It might have been part of Prussia from 1866 to 1945, but it never took on much of the Prussian militarism or the Protestant work ethic. Karneval (carnival), starting at 11:11 am on the 11th day of the 11th month, is nowhere celebrated with more passion or by larger numbers. At the same time, Cologne has the largest Gothic cathedral in the world,

12 surviving Romanesque churches, and some of the best museums in Germany.

Cologne was formally founded in AD 50, when Emperor Claudius' wife Agrippa attached her name to her place of birth. The former military camp became a city known back then as Colonia Claudia Ara Agrippinensium (CCAA) – Colonia eventually became Köln in German, Cologne in French, but survived in several Latin languages. In the fourth century, Emperor Constantine made Cologne a bishopric, placing it firmly on the path to become a major religious center.

After the Romans left, Cologne came under the control of the Franks. Charlemagne upgraded it to an archbishopric and more than 150 churches were built here during the Middle Ages – the most famous, the magnificent Gothic Dom that took 600 years to complete. After Emperor Friedrich Barbarossa had confiscated the relics of the Magi in Milan, he donated them to Cologne in 1164. This started Cologne's role as pilgrimage center, second only to Rome for much of the Middle Ages.

The temporal powers of the archbishop were broken in the 13th century and after that Cologne developed rapidly as a trade and commercial center. In the Hanseatic League, it was second only to Lübeck. In terms of population, it was the largest city in Germany for more than a millennium until Berlin surpassed it in the late 19th century.

Cologne became a Free Imperial City in 1475 and remained independent until the French occupied the city from 1794 to 1814. Thereafter it became part of Prussia. During World War II, 90% of the old town and 70% of the surrounding area were destroyed by air raids. Like St Paul's in London, the Dom somehow survived with relatively minor damage. The city's population dwindled from more than 800,000 at the outset of war to only 45,000 directly afterward as people fled the city.

Cologne rapidly recovered after the war as one of the leading industrial cities in Germany. It also houses media giants, such as the broadcasters RTL and WDR, as well as several publishers. It is a vibrant city with a diverse cultural life and art scene. For many diplomats, Cologne made life bearable when they were posted to sleepy Bonn nearby during the Cold War era.

Information Sources

Tourist Office: Tourist information is available from **Köln Tourismus**, Unter Fettenhennen 19, 50667 Köln, ☎ 0221-221-30400, www.stadt-koeln.de. It is directly opposite the Dom and has handy free maps.

Listings about what is on in Cologne are also available in the free *Live! Magazine*, www.livemagazine.de. Another free magazine, *Känguru*, www.kaenguru-colonia.de, has listings aimed at families and children.

Getting Around

The old town area of Cologne is best explored on foot. The Hauptbahnhof is north of the old town, right next to the Dom and the River Rhine. Although most areas are easily reached on foot, the city has a reliable network of buses and underground trains. Street parking in the old town is limited, but parking garages are available and well-signposted.

Sightseeing

The most popular tourist sights in Cologne are all concentrated in the old town and easily reached on foot. The principle sight is the Dom with most other attractions in the immediate vicinity. The Rathaus and many museums are slightly to the south, while St Gereon church to the west is worth the few minutes walk. If time is limited, give priority to the Dom and the Wallraf-Richartz-Museum, or the Ludwig Museum if you prefer modern art.

The Dom

The most important site in Cologne is the magnificent High Gothic **Dom St Peter und Marien** (Cathedral of St Peter and Mary) that dominates the skyline from virtually any place in town. The Dom is right next to the Rhine and Hauptbahnhof, making it an easy destination for travelers even on the briefest of stopovers. It is a UNESCO World Cultural Heritage site that attracts six million visitors annually – by far the highest number for any monitored sight in Germany.

Construction of the High Gothic cathedral started in 1248 to replace a Romanesque predecessor. The chancel was completed by 1300, but the rest followed slowly, with

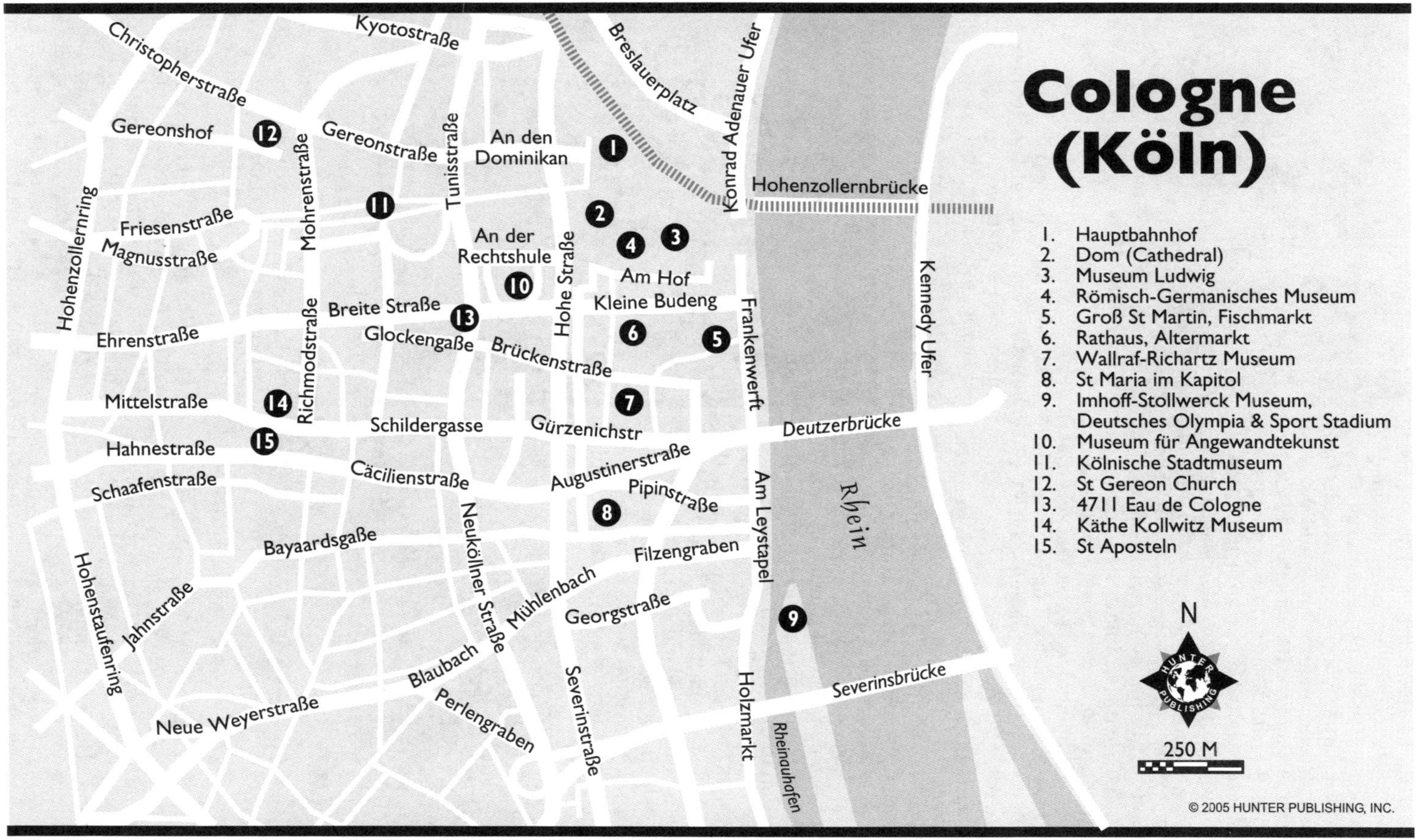

Cologne
(Köln)
1. Hauptbahnhof
2. Dom (Cathedral)
3. Museum Ludwig
4. Römisch-Germanisches Museum
5. Groß St Martin, Fischmarkt
6. Rathaus, Altermarkt
7. Wallraf-Richartz Museum
8. St Maria im Kapitol
9. Imhoff-Stollwerck Museum, Deutsches Olympia & Sport Stadium
10. Museum für Angewandtekunst
11. Kölnische Stadtmuseum
12. St Gereon Church
13. 4711 Eau de Cologne
14. Käthe Kollwitz Museum
15. St Aposteln
Christopherstraße
Kyotostraße
Breslauerplatz
Konrad Adenauer Ufer
Hohenzollernbrücke
Gereonshof
Gereonstraße
An den Dominikan
Tunisstraße
Mohrenstraße
Friesenstraße
Magnusstraße
Hohenzollernring
An der Rechtshule
Hohe Straße
Am Hof
Kleine Budeng
Frankenwerft
Kennedy Ufer
Breite Straße
Glockengaße
Ehrenstraße
Brückenstraße
Richmodstraße
Mittelstraße
Schildergasse
Gürzenichstr
Deutzerbrücke
Hahnestraße
Cäcilienstraße
Augustinerstraße
Pipinstraße
Schaafenstraße
Am Leystapel
Rhein
Bayaardsgaße
Filzengraben
Neuköllner Straße
Mühlenbach
Georgstraße
Hohenstaufenring
Jahnstraße
Blaubach
Perlengraben
Neue Weyerstraße
Severinstraße
Holzmarkt
Rheinauhafen
Severinsbrücke
N
HUNTER PUBLISHING
250 M
© 2005 HUNTER PUBLISHING, INC.

only parts of the south wall and tower completed by 1560, when construction was suspended. For the next three centuries, an enormous wooden crane on the uncompleted Dom tower would be the symbol of Cologne. Construction resumed in 1842 when German Romantics considered Gothic a pure German style – ironically the original commission for the Dom clearly called for a church in the *French* style – and completion of the Dom became a matter of national honor. In 1880, the Dom was finally consecrated – the presence of the bombastic Protestant Emperor Wilhelm I led to accusations that God had to occupy second place during the ceremony and the archbishop stayed away in protest.

The cathedral's twin-towered western façade is the largest in the world and completed according to the original 13th-century plan. The exterior of the church is decorated with statues, gables, and buttresses. The twin towers are 157 m (518 feet) high – on completion, it was the tallest building in the world, as was the intention in the 13th century. In the south tower, 509 steps lead to a viewing platform at 97 m (320 feet). On the way up, note the bells, including the 24-ton Petersglocke (St Peter's Bell), the world's largest swinging bell, which rings only on major religious holidays. Admission to the south tower is €2. Combination tickets with the Treasury are €5.

Dom, arches of the Cathedral crossing

The church's interior is the third-largest in the world – the nave is 144 m (475 feet) long and 43.5 m (143 feet) high. More than a hundred pillars and columns keep it all together. During a papal visit in 1980, 8,500 visitors were packed into the interior but normally just under 4,000 are allowed in for special occasions. The huge stained

Dom, Three Apostles

glass windows – altogether larger than a football field – let in ample light. The oldest were installed in 1265 in the Achskapelle (also known as the Three Kings' Chapel). This chapel is painted, as the complete cathedral would have been in the Middle Ages.

Dom, stained glass window

The most important artwork is the **Dreikönigenschrein** (Shrine of the Three Magi) in the choir behind the high altar. This bejeweled, golden shrine is a masterpiece of medieval goldsmithing. It is in the form of a 2.2-m (seven-foot) long basilica. In the Marienkapelle (St Mary's Chapel) is the **Altar der Stadtpatrone** (Altar of the City's Patrons) painted in 1440 by Stephan Lochner. It illustrates the *Adoration of the Magi* and has such detail that many herbs and other plants, as well as a stag beetle, can be recognized in the grass. The left wing shows St Ursula and the right St Gereon – the two patron saints of Cologne. In the Kreuzkapelle (Cross Chapel) is the AD 980 **Gerokreuz** (Gero Crucifixion) – a rare sample of Ottonian art. The choir, only open to guided tours, has 104 seats and is the largest in Germany.

Opening hours are daily from 6 am to 7:30 pm. Sightseeing is not allowed during the frequent services – the daily schedule is posted at the door. Guided tours in English are available daily at 11 am and 2:30 pm (Sundays in the afternoon only). German tours are more frequent. Information on the Dom and tours are available from the Domforum, Domkloster 3, ☎ 0221-9258-4720, www.domforum.de.

The **Schatzkamer** (Treasury), ☎ 0221-1794-0530, is at the north of the church. It houses a large collection of religious paraphernalia, shrines, and reliquaries. Opening hours are daily from 10 am to 6 pm. Admission is €4. A combination ticket with tower access costs €5.

Dom Area

Immediately north of the Dom is the **Hauptbahnhof** (Main Station). It has an impressive glass roof and houses a large number of shops not subject to normal closing hours. The **Hohenzollernbrücke** is a busy rail and pedestrian bridge across the Rhine – some of the best vistas of the Dom and the old town can be had from here. Between the bridge and the Dom is a square named after 1972 Nobel Prize for Literature laureate Heinrich Böll (1917-85).

The **Museum Ludwig**, Bischofsgartenstraße 1, ☎ 0221-2212-6165, www.museum-ludwig.de, opened after Peter and Irene Ludwig donated the largest Pop Art collection outside the USA to the Wallraf Richartz Museum. In addition to the original 350 Pop Art paintings, the museum also has a large collection of Russian avant-garde works, and a major collection of works by Picasso. The museum continuously adds new works and some are only months old. On the ground floor is the **Agfa Photo-Historama** – a collection of photos and photographical equipment from the 1840s to the present. Opening hours are Tuesday to Sunday from 10 am to 6 pm, but open on Friday only at 11 am. The first Friday of the month it is open from 11 am to 11 pm. Admission is €7.50.

The **Römisch-Germanisches Museum** (Roman-Germanic Museum), Roncalliplatz 4, ☎ 0221-2212-4438, www.museenkoeln.de, houses articles from the Roman and early Frankish periods. Cologne served as the capital of the Roman province of Lower Germania and was an important trading post with the barbaric Germanic tribes. The magnificent glass and jewelry collections show that these "barbarians" knew how to produce first-class items. The museum is built on the foundations of a former Roman villa that was discovered in 1941 during the construction of an air-raid shelter. The pride of the museum is the second-century Dionysius Mosaic, comprised of more than 1.5 million pieces. It is well preserved and can actually be seen from outside the museum through a huge window. Another large display is the reconstruction of the Mausoleum of Lucius Poblicius – a first-century tomb. Other themes in the museum include Roman statues, architecture, coins, trade, religious objects, and funerary practices. The museum is best visited in the afternoon, or on weekends, to avoid ever-present school groups. Opening hours are Tuesday to Sunday from 10 am to 5 pm. Admission is €4.30.

Roman bust in Römisch-Germanisches Museum

The **Museum für Angewandte Kunst** (Museum of Applied Arts, An der Rechtschule, ☎ 0221-2212-6714, www.museenkoeln.de, is one of the principle collections of its kind in Germany, with items from the Gothic era to the present. Articles range from furniture and clothes to jewelry and tableware. Although the emphasis is on German items, European and

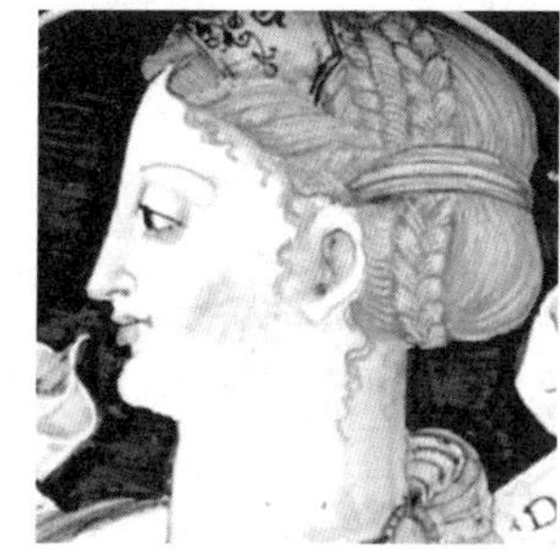

Faience from Museum für Angewandte Kunst

Asian objects are also on display. Opening hours are Tuesday to Sunday from 11 am to 5 pm, closing at 8 pm on Wednesday. Admission is €4.20.

Southern Altstadt

Groß St Martin

Until the completion of the Dom, **Groß St Martin**, An Groß St Martin, ☎ 0221-1642-5650, was the largest church in Cologne. Originally built from 1150 to 1250, this Romanesque church with its fortress-like square tower and four octagonal turrets, still is a major feature on the Cologne skyline. It was originally a Benedictine monastery church built on what was then an island in the Rhine. The church was virtually destroyed during World War II and the reconstruction has a stark, almost naked interior. Opening hours are Tuesday to Friday, 10:15 am to 6 pm, Saturday, 10 am to 12:30 pm and 1:30 to 6 pm, and Sunday, 2 to 4 pm.

The **Historisches Rathaus** (Historic Town Hall) was severely damaged during World War II, but rebuilt soon after. It has a lovely Renaissance pavilion and a 60-m (198-foot) Gothic tower, erected in 1407, with a carillon playing at noon and 5 pm. The impressive Gothic Hansesaal and the rest of the interior can only be seen in conjunction with a guided tour. The area was part of a Jewish ghetto stormed in 1349. A **Mikwe** (Jewish Bath) from around 1170 can be seen under a glass pyramid in front of the Rathaus.

The **Wallraf-Richartz-Museum – Foundation Corboud**, Martinstraße 39, ☎ 0221-2212-1119, www.museenkoeln.de, is the oldest museum in Cologne. It was started with a major art collection donated by Wallraf Richartz in 1824 and has since grown to one of the largest collections of classical paintings in Germany. Highlights include an impressive medieval painting collection, paintings by Rubens and Rembrandt, and paintings and sculpture by Romantic, Realist, and Impressionist artists. The large graphic arts collection (75,000 items) can be seen on special request. The museum was housed for decades in the same building as the Ludwig Museum, next to the Dom, but recently moved to its own modern building between the Rathaus and the Gürnzenich. If time is limited in Cologne, make this gallery a priority. Opening hours are Tuesday to Friday from 10 am to 6 pm, closing at 8 pm on Tuesday, and weekends from 11 am to 7 pm. Admission is €5.80.

Behind the museum is the **Gürzenich**, a 15th-century Gothic hall used for celebrations. The annual Karneval celebrations start from here.

St Maria Im Kapitol, detail of carved wooden door

A few blocks farther south is the **St Maria Im Kapitol**, Kasinostraße, ☎ 0221-214-615. It was constructed in 1040-65 and is an excellent example of Ottonian-Romanesque architecture. This triple nave basilica was the first to use a trefoil chancel – this cloverleaf-like feature is typical of Cologne Romanesque. The crypt runs almost the full length of the nave and is the second-largest in Germany after Speyer. The interior is richly decorated – particularly note the original wooden doors from 1060 at the west end of the south aisle and the 1523 Renaissance choir screen. Opening hours are daily from 9 am to 6 pm.

Nearby, on a peninsula in the Rhine, is the **Imhoff-Stollwerck-Museum**, Rheinauhafen 1a, ☎ 0221-9318-880, www.schokoladenmuseum.de, a hugely popular museum devoted to chocolate. In addition to an interesting display on chocolate and its role in society, it has a scaled-down, operational chocolate manufacturing plant with demonstrations. Free sampling opportunities, however, are limited. Opening hours are Tuesday to Friday from 10 am to 6 pm and weekends from 11 am to 7 pm. Admission is €6.

Adjacent is the **Deutsches Sport und Olympia Museum** (German Sport and Olympics Museum), Rheinauhafen 1, ☎ 0221-336-090, www.sportmuseum.info, with an exhibition on the development of sports over the past 2,500 years. Naturally, the emphasis is on German sports and athletes of the 20th century. Opening hours are Tuesday to Friday from 10 am to 6 pm and weekends from 11 am to 7 pm. Admission is €5.

Western Altstadt

Local history museums can be a bore, but the **Kölnische Stadtmuseum** (Cologne City Musum), Zeughausstraße 1-3, ☎ 0221-2212-5789, www.museenkoeln.de, is everything but. It has an eclectic collection of items related to Cologne's history from the Middle Ages to the present. Items include armor, scale models and paintings, religious objects, and cars – Ford has a major factory in Cologne. The museum is housed in the Renaissance Zeughaus with red and white window shutters – large windows allow some displays to be seen from the street and they draw many in. It's an enjoyable experience for all ages. The admission fee includes a handy English audio guide. Opening hours are Tuesday to Friday from 10 am to 6 pm, closing at 8 pm on Tuesday, and weekends from 11 am to 7 pm. Admission is €4.20.

A few block farther west is the fascinating **St Gereon Church**, Geronsdriesch (entrance in Christopherstraße), ☎ 0221-124-922. It combines Late Roman, fourth-century oval building style elements with a Late Romanesque, 13th-century decagon cupola. The monumental cupola was the largest built between the construction of Hagia Sophia in Istanbul and the Renaissance Duomo in Florence. The 13th-century baptismal chapel has some original wall paintings of St Gereon. Following reconstruction after World War II, modern stained glass windows by Georg Meistermann and Wilhelm Buschulkte were added to the cupola. Opening hours are daily, 9 am to 12:30 and 1:30 to 6 pm; Sunday open in the afternoon only.

The **Käthe Kollwitz Museum Köln**, Neumarkt 18-24, ☎ 0221-227-2363, www.kollwitz.de, opened in 1985 as the first museum dedicated to this 20th-century artist. It has the largest collection in the world of her works. Special exhibitions are regularly held with works from artists associated with her work and ideas. Käthe Kollwitz (1867-1945) was the first female art professor at the Prussian Academy in Berlin and dedicated her life and works to the causes of peace and social justice. (See also Berlin and Dresden for more on this remarkable artist that fell afoul of the Nazi regime**page.) Opening hours are Tuesday to Friday, 10 am to 6 pm, and weekends, 11 am to 7 pm. Admission is €3.

Käthe Kollwitz

St Aposteln, Apostelnkloster at Neumarkt, ☎ 0221-92-587, is another typical Rhineland Romanesque church with trefoil chancel. The latter was probably added around 1200 after a fire destroyed part of the original 11th-century church. It has an octagonal tower above the transept and a lovely gallery with blind arcading. Opening hours are Wednesday to Sunday, 10 am to noon and 3 to 5 pm.

Cultural Events & Festivals

Cologne has a full cultural calendar, with many music halls and theaters in addition to the more than 150 museums, galleries, and art spaces. On offer is everything from old classics to contemporary music, theater, and art. The tourist bureau has details on events – prior reservations are generally advisable.

North Rhine Westphalia

Karneval (Carnival) is known as the fifth season in Cologne and in much of the Rhinelands. It starts at 11:11 am on the 11th day of the 11th month and continues until lent. Apart from the first day, a highlight is also the parade on Rosenmontag (Rose Monday) – an interesting event and usually high-spirited, though many consider it as an excuse to get drunk. Many shops and even museums close down completely during Karneval.

Shopping

4711 EAU THE COLOGNE

France has long considered the Rhine as its natural eastern border, so when French troops occupied Cologne in 1794, they had every intention of staying. Up to then, buildings worth identifying were known by name only. For taxation purposes, the French started to number all buildings consecutively. This rather messy system was replaced by normal street names and numbers in 1811. But one became world-famous – 4711 was the number of the house where Eau de Cologne was produced.

Cologne entered the English language as a term for perfumed water thanks to the Miracle Water produced in Cologne. The French put a stop to the drinking of Eau de Cologne and from the early 19th century, it was appreciated for its smell rather than its supposedly medicinal qualities. Products of 4711, the Original Eau de Cologne, can be bought all over Cologne, and Germany for that matter, but the Traditionshaus 4711, Glockengasse, ☎ 0221-925-0450, www.4711.com, once housed the factory. The shop is not particularly attractive, but stocks a wide range of 4711 products. The Carillon outside plays the *Marseillaise* hourly from 9 am to 8 pm.

Adventures

On Foot

More than 120 guided **tours** are available to Cologne, its museums, and other sights. The tourist office has information on schedules. Guided tours of the various churches and religious themes are frequently scheduled – contact the **Domforum**, Domkloster 3, ☎ 0221-9258-4720, www.domforum.de, for schedules.

Jogging is popular in Cologne along the Rhine and in the parks. **Good Friends Jog Together**, ☎ 0700-1231-2322, www.laufeninkoeln.de, lists groups that regularly jog with open invitations for visitors to join in.

On Wheels

A **Bimmelbahn** (motorized train), ☎ 0177-418-5659, departs daily every half-hour between 10 am and 6 pm from the Dom/Roncalliplatz. **Cologne Coach Service** runs regular bus tours of the city several times per day. Reservations can be made through the tourist office.

The Cologne area is relatively flat and easily explored on **bicycle**. **Fahrrad Verleihservice**, Markmannsgasse/Altstadt, ☎ 0171-629-8796, www.koelner-fahrradverleih.de, rents out bicycles and from April to October conducts three-hour cycling tours daily at 1:30 pm.

On Water

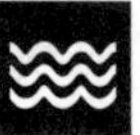

One of the largest **riverboat** operators in Gemany has its home in Cologne. **Köln-Düsseldorfer** (usually abbreviated simply to KD), Frankenwerft 35, ☎ 0221-208-8319, www.k-d.com, has several hour-long cruises daily as well as services to other towns along the Rhine. Lunch, dinner, and thematic cruises are also available.

Where to Stay & Eat

For well over a century, the **Excelsior Hotel Ernst** has been the leading grand hotel in the region. This luxury hotel is close to the Dom and the Hauptbahnhof. Rooms are stylish and luxurious. The elegant **Hanse Stube** restaurant (€€€-€€€€) serves international cuisine and is one of the best restaurants in the region. The modern **Taku** (€€€-€€€€) serves Asian food. Domplatz, 50667 Köln, ☎ 0221-2701, fax 0221-135-150, www.excelsiorhotel.de. (€€€€)

The **Hyatt Regency Hotel** is on the opposite bank of the Rhine, giving many rooms a splendid view of the Cologne Dom and old town. This luxurious hotel was erected in the late 1980s and has impressive public spaces. The rooms are extremely well furnished and equipped. The elegant restaurant **Graugans** (€€€-€€€€) serves Euro-Asian food. Kennedy-Ufer 2a, 50679 Köln-deutz, ☎ 0221-8281-1771, fax 0221-828-1370, www.hyatt.de. (€€€€)

Hotel Im Wasserturm is an exclusive luxury hotel that recently opened inside the 130-year-old former water tower (Wasserturm). At its initial construction, it was the largest such tower in Europe and now is among the most extravagant hotels in Germany. Rooms are modern, elegant, and luxurious. The Michelin star restaurant **La Vision** (€€€€) serves French cuisine and has lovely views from its location on the 11th floor. The restaurant **d^blju "W"** (€€€-€€€) is modern, serving international and nouvelle cuisine (yes, that really is their name). Although a bit south of the old town, this hotel is a fantastic place to stay or eat. Kaygasse 2, 50676 Köln, ☎ 0221-20-080, fax 0221-200-8888, www.hotel-im-wasserturm.de. (€€€€)

The **Dom Hotel** is another grand institution with a tradition going back more than a century. It has a perfect location on the square in front of the Dom and within minutes of most old town attractions. Rooms are comfortable and individually furnished. Some rooms have antique furniture and the better ones have views of the Dom. The restaurant **Le Merou** (€€€) serves international cuisine and has a terrace with views of the Dom. Domkloster 2a, 50667 Köln, ☎ 0221-20-240, fax 0221-202-4444, www.dom-hotel.com. (€€€€)

The luxury **Maritim Hotel** is on the banks of the Rhine at the south of the old town near the Stolwerck-Imhoff Museum. Rooms are comfortable and large but the 100-m (328-foot) long glass-roof lobby attracts the most attention. The restaurant **Bellevue** (€€€) serves international cuisine and offers views of the old town and region. Heumarkt 20, 50667 Köln, ☎ 0221-20-270, fax 0221-202-7826, www.maritin.de. (€€€-€€€€)

The **Hilton Cologne** opened in 2002 close to the Dom and Hauptbahnhof. It is a modern building with modern, straight lines throughout. Rooms have wooden floors and are well-equipped. The hotel caters mostly for business travelers allowing for good deals on non-conference weekends. The bar top at the **Ice Bar** is made of ice. Marzellenstraße 13-17, 50668 Köln, ☎ 0221-130-710, fax 0221-130-720, www.hilton.com. (€€€-€€€€)

The **Hotel Dorint im Friesenviertel** is close to St Gereon in the western part of the old town. It has modern, comfortable rooms, although some are a bit small. Friesenstraße 44, 50670 Köln, ☎ 0221-16-140, fax 0221-161-4100, www.dorint.de. (€€€)

Best Western Hotel Lyskirchen is close to the Rhine near the Imhoff-Stollwerck Museum. The hotel is about a century old but rooms are modern, elegant, and comfortably furnished. Filzengraben 26-32, 50676 Köln, ☎ 0221-20-970, fax 0221-209-7718, www.lyskirchen.bestwestern.de. (€€€)

Senats-Hotel, near the Rathaus, combines historic elements with modern features. Rooms are comfortable and individually furnished. Unter Goldschmied 9-17, 50667 Köln, ☎ 0221-20-620, fax 0221-206-2200, www.senats-hotel.de. (€€-€€€)

Classic Hotel Harmonie is in a former monastery a few minutes walk from the Hauptbahnhof. The peaceful past continues, with harmonious warm Mediterranean colors and a relaxed atmosphere. Rooms are comfortably furnished with tasteful decorations. Ursulaplatz 13-19, 50668 Köln, ☎ 0221-16-570, fax 0221-165-7200, www.classic-hotels.com. (€€-€€€)

The nearby **Cristall Hotel** is a modern hotel with hand-built designer furniture. Rooms are comfortable and bright. Ursulaplatz 9, 50668 Köln, ☎ 0221-16-300, fax 0221-163-0333, www.hotelcristall.de. (€€€)

Hotel Königshof is a pleasant, centrally located spot close to the Dom and Museum für Angewandte Kunst. Rooms are modern and functionally furnished. Richardtzstraße 14, 50667 Köln, ☎ 0221-257-8771, fax 0221-257-8762, www.hotelkoenigshof.de. (€€-€€€€)

Antik Hotel Bristol is west of the old town near St Gereon. The hotel uses stylish antique furniture from various periods to combine old with modern comforts – an interesting alternative to standard hotels. Kaiser-Wilhelm.Ring 48, 50672 Köln, ☎ 0221-120-195, fax 0221-131-495, www.antik-hotel-bristol.de. (€€-€€€€)

CityClass Hotel Caprice is a new hotel in the middle of the old town just south of Groß St Martin. It has modern rooms furnished to high standards. Auf dem Rothenberg 7, 50667 Köln, ☎ 0221-920-540, fax 0221-9205-4100, www.cityclass.de. (€€-€€€)

Hotel Ibis am Dom is typical of this chain – not much thrill or personality but decent, clean, and reasonably furnished rooms. It is perfectly located right next to the station. Prices remain sane even during congress or exhibition season. Bahnhofvorplatz, 50667 Köln, ☎ 0221-912-8580, fax 0221-912-858-199, www.ibishotel.de. (€€)

Brewery Restaurants

The refreshing local beer, *Kölsch*, can be enjoyed everywhere, but doing so in one of the traditional breweries is of course particularly pleasing. **Früh am Dom**, Am Hof 12, ☎ 0221-261-3211, recently celebrated its centenary at this location just south of the Dom. It is spread over three floors with slightly different menus – it gets grander and more expensive as you move up in the building. Traditional brewery fare is served in the vaulted cellars and the ground floor, while the upper floor offers more elaborate food, including game. On the street-side terrace, only beer and small snacks are available. The place is hugely popular, making reservations sensible for groups. (€-€€)

Nearby is another famous brewery, **Brauhaus Sion**, Unter Taschenmacher 5, ☎ 0221-257-8540. Traditional food is served in the former brewery decorated with paraphernalia used for beer-making in years gone by. The brewery has its own bowling alley. (€-€€)

Alt Köln am Dom, Trankgasse 7, ☎ 0221-137-471, is between the Dom and the Hauptbahnhof. It is spread over three floors and offers cheap food in a traditional locale. (€-€€)

Camping

Camping Berger is south of Cologne on the banks of the Rhine. It has good facilities and offers 125 spaces each for tourists and long-term campers. It is open year-round. Uferstraße 53a, 50996 Köln-Rodenkirchen, ☎ 0221-935-5240, fax 0221-935-5246, www.camping-berger-koeln.de.

■ Bonn

After World War II, Bonn suddenly found itself catapulted from a provincial backwater to the capital of what was soon to be one of the richest democracies in the world. It was never a natural capital and, although the new status brought huge spending on public works, Bonn would always be considered a provincial town. In German, it was often referred to as the *Bundeshauptdorf* (federal capital town) rather than *Bundeshauptstadt* (federal capital city).

Shortly after the re-unification of Germany in 1990, the decision was made to move the capital back to Berlin and by 2004 only six government departments remained in Bonn. The sudden departure of thousands of bureaucrats and diplomats brought a drop in property prices but the quality of life in Bonn remains high. For tourists, the main attractions are the excellent museums set up during the federal capital years, as well as pleasantly low hotel prices. All the sights can be seen on a daytrip from Cologne, which is a 30-minute drive or train ride north.

Bonn has a written history going back to the foundation of Castra Bonnensia as a Roman military base in 11 BC – celebrations of its 2,000-year history were concluded just months before the Berlin Wall came down. The town served as a summer residence for the archbishops of Cologne and has several pretty Baroque buildings in addition to an impressive Romanesque church. Apart from its role as provisional federal capital from 1949 to the 1990s, Bonn is famous as the birthplace of Ludwig von Beethoven.

Beethoven as a young man

Information Sources

Tourist Office: The Tourist Information Office, Windeckstraße 1, 53103 Bonn, ☎ 0228-775-000, www.bonn.de, is at the Münsterplatz near the Hauptbahnhof.

BONN REGIO WELCOME CARD

The tourism office sells the Bonn Regio Welcome Card, www.bonn-region.de, which allows unlimited local public transportation and free entry at many museums and attractions. It costs €9 for 24 hours, €14 for 48 hours, and €19 for 72 hours. The one-day ticket pays for itself with two museum visits. The card is available from the tourism office, many hotels, the Kunsthalle, and the Beethovenhaus.

Getting Around

The old town is best explored on foot but to reach the Museum Mile it is better to take the U-Bahn. Although the U-Bahn continues all the way to Cologne, regular trains are faster. Bonn is also a pleasant town to cycle in with many cycling routes, including both sides of the Rhine promenades.

Sightseeing

Sightseeing in Bonn can be divided into two main areas: the old town, with several interesting buildings, and the Museum Mile a few km south, with a number of museums. On the east side of the Rhine is the Siebengebirge – an area with dramatic hills and a few castles to see.

Old Town

A top priority for many visitors is **Beethovenhaus** (Beethoven's Birthplace), Bonngasse 20, ☎ 0228-981-7525, www.beethoven-haus-bonn.de. Ludwig von Beethoven (1770-1827) was born here. He spent his early years in Bonn until he left for Vienna in 1792. The museum covers Beethoven's entire life with exhibitions of original manuscripts and items used by him, including some hearing pipes and his last grand piano. Museum staff is generally friendly and a free comprehensive English pamphlet is available. Opening hours are Monday to Saturday, 10 am to 5 pm, closing at 6 pm from April to October, and year-round on Sunday, 11 am to 4 pm. Admission is € 4.

The Rococo **Rathaus** (Town Hall), Markt, was completed in its current form in 1737. It is a pretty pink and grey-blue building with elaborate decorations. The building was damaged during World War II, but rebuilt in its original form. During Bonn's time as federal capital, most state visitors came here. Several, including John F Kennedy (1963) and Michael Gorbachev (1989), received a warm welcome when addressing the public from the external double-flight staircase. The inside, which is still in daily use, can only be seen between May and October on the first Saturday of the month, noon to 4 pm. Admission is free.

The **Münsterbasilika** (Minster Basilica), Münstreplatz, ☎ 0228-985-880, is a lovely example of Rhineland Romanesque with some Gothic additions blending in harmoniously. It was built mostly in the 11th century, although much of the interior is Baroque or 19th century. The 11th-century Romanesque cloister is one of the best-preserved examples in Germany from this period. Opening hours are daily for the church from 7 am to 7 pm and for the cloister from 9:30 am to 5:50 pm.

At the north end of the Münsterplatz is the **Beethoven Memorial** – it was erected in 1845 as the first memorial to honor the composer. In the base of the memorial is the original score of the Ninth Symphony.

The Baroque **Poppelsdorfer Schloss** (Palace), Meckenheimer Allee 171, is about a km (.6 mile) down the lovely chestnut tree-lined Poppelsdorf Allee. It was built as a summer residence by the archbishop of Cologne, but has been part of the university since 1818. The palace is generally not open to the public, but the surrounding botanical gardens are.

Museum Mile

The Museum Mile is about three km (1.8 miles) south of the Bonn old town in the federal government buildings area. It is best reached by U-Bahn or buses 16, 63, or 66. Heussallee/Museummeile stop is the most convenient to all three museums listed below.

The **Haus der Geschichte der Bundesrepublik Deutscland** (House of History of the Federal Republic of Germany), Willy-Brandt-Allee 14, ☎ 0228-91-650, www.hdg.de, is an exhibition of post-World War II German history. It has 7,000 items ranging from Konrad Adenauer's official Mercedes to the original arrest warrant for Erich Honecker. It uses modern technology to make displays interesting and to illustrate the background for events. Opening hours are Tuesday to Sunday from 9 am to 7 pm. Admission is free.

Bonn was fortunate that a very impressive exhibition space was already under construction when the decision came to move the capital back to Berlin. The **Kunst- und Ausstellungshalle der Bundesrepublik Deutschland** (Art and Exhibition Hall of the Federal Republic of Germany), Friedrich Ebeert Allee 4, ☎ 0228-9171-200, www.bundeskunsthalle.de, which for obvious reasons is usually shortened to just **Bundeskunsthalle** (Federal Art Space), is a huge modern exhibition space that can be used simultaneously for up to five temporary exhibitions. The institution has no permanent collection, but hosts rotating world-class exhibitions. Admission fees depend on the specific exhibition, but a recent Mexican exhibition here charged 30% less than the same one cost in Berlin and less than 50% of the price in London. Furthermore, two adults with a child qualify for a family ticket that costs less than two adults alone! Opening hours are Tuesday and Wednesday from 10 am to 9 pm and Thursday to Sunday from 10 am to 7 pm. Admission is €7 per day, €9.50 for two consecutive days, and €10.50 for a family ticket. A combination ticket with the Kunstmuseum is available for €10.50.

The adjacent **Kunstmuseum Bonn** (Museum of Art), Friedrich-Ebert-Allee 2, ☎ 0228-776-260, www.bonn.de/kunsthalle, is in an equally impressive modern building. It features 20th-century art with a special emphasis on post-World War II German artists. Temporary exhibitions are usually of international artists used to place the German works in context. Opening hours are Tuesday to Sunday from 10 am to 6 pm, closing at 9 pm on Wednesday. Admission is €5 or €10.50 when combined with the Kunsthalle.

Siebengebirge

On the opposite bank of the Rhine are the Siebengebirge Mountains, with dramatic scenery more reminiscent of the Loreley Valley farther upstream between St Goar and Rüdesheim. This area is Germany's oldest nature conservation area and popular for hiking.

The most famous sight here is the **Drachenfels** (Dragon Rock), a 321-m (1,055-foot) peak with marvelous views of the Rhine Valley. According to the Nibelungen legend, Siegfried slew the dragon here and bathed in his blood to become invincible. The peak can be reached by walking, or via Germany's oldest *Zahnrad* (cogwheel) cable car, below. The ruins at the top are from a 12th-century castle that was destroyed in the 17th century.

En route to the top, the Neo-Gothic late 19th-century **Schloss Drachenburg**, Drachenfelsstraße 118, 53639 Königswinter, ☎ 02223-901-970, is passed – it has a large, panoramic terrace. The interior can only be seen on a guided tour. It is open from April to October, Tuesday to Sunday from 11 am to 6 pm.

Excursion to Remagen

Remagen is just over 20 km (12 miles) south of Bonn. It is most famous for its former rail bridge that fell undamaged into the hands of the advancing American forces on March 7, 1945. This allowed the Americans to establish a bridgehead on the east side of the Rhine. According to General Eisenhower, the bridge was worth its weight in gold. It collapsed 10 days later under the weight of tanks, but by then a suitable pontoon bridge was already in place.

The rest of the bridge was torn down, as it hindered navigation on the Rhine, but the towers on both sides of the river survived. They now house a Peace Museum with displays on the history of the bridge. The Museum is open daily from March to November from 10 am to 5 pm.

The bridge is best reached by car. Follow the rather small Brücke von Remagen signs. The first turnoff from the main road is south of the town in Gewerbegebiet-Süd.

Cultural Events

Bonn has a busy cultural calendar not restricted to Beethoven and classical music. Information on all events is available from the tourist office, but reservations should be made through **BonnTicket**, ☎ 0180-500-1812, www.bonnticket.de.

The **International Beethovenfest Bonn** (Beethoven Festival), www.beethovenfest.de, is held annually from mid-September to mid-October. Various venues in and around Bonn are used to stage some 50 concerts.

On summer weekends, from May to September, free open-air concerts are scheduled on the Marktplatz in front of the Rathaus. During the same period, concerts ranging from classical music to rock are held in the space between the Bundeskunsthalle and the Kunstmuseum.

Festivals

The **Rhein in Flammen** (Rhine in Flames) is a festival combined with a huge fireworks display that takes place the first Saturday in May between Bonn and Linz. The Rhine banks and many historic buildings are lit and live music shows are staged. The fireworks are best observed from a Rhine boat, but early reservations are essential.

Adventures

On Foot

A free pamphlet is available from the tourist office for a self-guided tour of Bonn's Beethoven sights. As theses include most of the **old town** sights, it is quite useful for non-Beethoven lovers too.

Bonn is a green city with many parks and green areas to stroll in. Particularly nice are the Rhine promenades on both sides of the river. The **Alter Zoll** offers great views of the Rhine and the old town. The huge **Freizeitpark Rheinaue** has 45 km (27 miles) of walkways, including six km (3.6 miles) along the Rhine alone. It has a small Japanese garden and numerous art works.

A popular hiking route that can easily reached by train from Bonn is the **Rotweinwanderweg** (Red Wine Hiking Route), www.wohlsein365.de, in the Ahr Valley, just past Remagen. Many vineyards along the route allow wine tasting and serve meals. A cycling route also runs in the valley.

On Wheels

Bonn is an ideal **cycling** city with plenty of cycling paths in the city and in the parks on both sides of the Rhine. Many cycling routes in the region can easily be combined with public transportation options.

The Bonn cycling club, **ADFC Bonn**, ☎ 0228-630-015, www.adfc-bonn.de, arranges cycling tours of Bonn on every second Saturday of the month, starting at 2 pm from the Poppelsdorfer Schloss. The tour is aimed at new residents, but all are welcome. The club also has regular tours of the region.

Bicycle rentals are available from **Radstation Bonn**, Quantiusstraße 26, ☎ 0228-981-4636, and from **Fun Bikes**, Annaberger Straße 164, ☎ 0228-317-957.

Where to Stay & Eat

The sudden departure of much of the government and the entire diplomatic corps left Bonn with several good hotels that have rooms often available at bargain prices. The best ones are slightly out of town, but absolutely worth going the distance, especially if you are driving.

The luxury **Dorint Venusberg** is five km (three miles) southwest of the old town on a hill inside a protected forested park. It is in the style of a French country house with luxurious and comfortable rooms. The hotel offers great views of the Rhine valley. The excellent restaurant **L'Orquivit** (€€€-€€€€) serves nouvelle cuisine in modern, elegant surroundings. An der Casselsruhe 1, 53127 Bonn-Kessenich, ☎ 0228-2880, fax 0228-288-288, www.dorint.de. (€€€-€€€€)

A pleasant hotel with superb views of the Rhine valley is the **Steigenberger Gästehaus Petersberg**. It is 20 km (12 miles) from Bonn on the left bank of the Rhine on Peters Mountain. This elegant building was used as the official guest-house of the government until the capital moved back to Berlin. Rooms are luxurious and stylishly furnished. The restaurant **Rheinterrassen** (€€€-€€€€) serves international cuisine. It is open for dinner only and reservations are recommended. In summer, a **bistro** (€€) serves lighter meals on the terrace with grand views. It is a favorite stopover on several hiking trails. Auf dem Petersberg, 53639 Königswinter, ☎ 02223-740, fax 02223-74-443, www.steigenberger.de. (€€€€)

The **Maritim Hotel** in Bad Godesberg is in the heart of the government area and used to be the favorite of many diplomats and visiting politicians. A modern hotel with luxurious rooms, it has views of the Rhine and a driving range on the roof for golfers. The restaurant **La Marée** (€€€) serves international cuisine with strong Mediterranean influences. Godesberger Allee, 53175 Bonn-Bad Godesberg, ☎ 0228-81-080, fax 0228-810-8811. (€€€-€€€€)

The **Hilton Hotel** opened a year before Germany re-united and rooms here can go for a song during quiet periods. It is conveniently located next to the Kennedy Bridge near the heart of Bonn. Rooms are modern and comfortable – some have Rhine views. Berliner Freiheit 2, 53111 Bonn, ☎ 0228-72-690, fax 0228-726-9700, www.hilton.com. (€€-€€€)

Günnewig Hotel Residence is near the station at the Kaiserplatz. Rooms are functionally furnished and comfortable. The hotel has a lovely swimming pool with Mediterranean atmosphere. The restaurant **Kaisergarten** (€-€€) serves international cuisine. Kaiserplatz 11, 53113 Bonn, ☎ 0228-26-970, fax 0228-269-7777, www.guennewig.de. (€€-€€€)

The **Consul Hotel** is near the Beethoven Museum, just north of the old town. The comfortable rooms with large desks are clearly aimed at business travelers. Oxfordstraße 12, 53111 Bonn, ☎ 0228-72-920, fax 0228-729-2250, www.consul-bonn.de. (€€-€€€)

Sternhotel with its historic façade is on the Market Square next to the Altes Rathaus. Rooms are comfortably furnished. Most sights and many restaurants are in the immediate vicinity. Markt 8, 53111 Bonn, ☎ 0228-72-670, fax 0228-726-7125, www.sternhotel-bonn.de. (€€-€€€)

Ibis Hotel is at the edge of the old town. It has functional rooms with bright furniture. There are few thrills but prices are low. Vorgebirgsstraße 33, 53119 Bonn, ☎ 0228-72-660, fax 0228-726-6405, www.ibishotel.com. (€-€€)

Right next to the Rathaus is a pleasant traditional restaurant, **Em Höttche**, Markt 4, ☎ 0228-690-009. It serves local cuisine with some international dishes in a locale with a history going back to 1389. Inscriptions on the wooden beams commemorate historic dates and events: in 1628, Elizabeth Kurzrock was burned here as a witch! A young Ludwig von Beethoven also danced here with his sweetheart. (€-€€)

■ Düsseldorf

Düsseldorf, a city of 600,000, is the capital of North Rhine Westphalia. It is a modern city with a tourist appeal completely different from the other Rhine cities in this guide. Its old town sights are limited, but it has good art galleries, modern architecture, and the best fashion shopping in all of Germany.

Düsseldorf has a history going back to at least 1288, but it was during the reign of Elector Johann Wilhelm (1679-1716), locally known as Jan Wellem, that the city came to prominence. He attracted artists to his court and transformed the town. A century later, it was briefly the capital of the French-created Grand Duchy of Berg, ruled by Jerome Bonaparte, but became part of Prussia from 1815.

During World War II, Düsseldorf was bombed almost out of existence. After the war, the town rebuilt in a modern and generally more elegant style than many other cities that made a similar decision not to restore the old buildings. Only a small part of the old city survived or was restored in later years.

Düsseldorf is known internationally as a fashion city – the world's largest annual fashion trade fair is held here. The Königsallee is lined with fashion houses and stylish malls; even the locals are known to dress more beautifully than is common in other German cities. It is also a major business center with much of the financing of the Ruhr industrial area flowing through the city. Furthermore, it is the preferred location for Japanese and other Asian companies establishing European head offices. In recent years, it has also become an important media center.

Information Sources

Tourist Office: Tourist information is available from **Düsseldorf Marketing Tourismus**, Postfach 102163, 40012 Düsseldorf, ☎ 0211-172-020, www.duesseldorf.de. Information offices are in Immermannfhof across from the Hauptbahnhof and in the Kö-Gallerie, Berliner Allee 33.

Getting Around

Düsseldorf has a good public transportation system combining buses, trams, and trains. Most sights are within easy walking distance. Street parking is limited but parking garages are well-signposted.

Sightseeing

The Rhine is generally a straight-flowing river, but it literally meanders through Düsseldorf giving the city a natural beauty advantage over others such as Cologne or Bonn. The Rhine averages 300 m (980 feet) wide here. In the 1990s, a major road was diverted through a tunnel, giving pedestrians free access to the two-km (1.2-mile) **Rhine Promenade** at the edge of the old town. It is a popular area to walk and cycle, with views of the Rhine, the opposite bank, and the old town.

Along the Rhine Promenade is the round, white **Schlossturm** (Castle Tower), the only part of the former Elector's palace that survived World War II. Behind it is the 14th-century Gothic **St Lambertuskirche** (St Lambert's Church). It was severely damaged during the war, but rebuilt true to the original – the famous twisted spire included. The twisted spire came into being when wet wood was used during the original construction – amazingly the whole spire twisted without collapsing.

On the **Marktplatz** (Market Square) is an equestrian statue of Jan Wellem made in 1711. Behind it is the 16th-century Altes Rathaus (Old Town Hall). The rest of the old town consists mainly of bars, cafés, and restaurants.

A few blocks inland is the **Königsallee**, often simply referred to as the Kö. It has some of the most expensive shops in Germany. Most well-known fashion houses have shops here, or in various elegant malls leading from the street. The street is about a km (.6 mile) long and runs on both sides of the former water-filled moat. It is lined with chestnut trees and was known up to 1851 as Chestnut Street. However, in 1848, when much of Europe and Germany saw popular uprisings, someone threw horse manure here at King Friedrich Wilhelm IV of Prussia and, to restore goodwill, the street was renamed in his honor. At the north end of the street are the Triton Fountains.

HEINRICH HEINE

The popular German poet Heinrich Heine (1797-1856) was born in Düsseldorf. A plaque in **Bolkerstraße** marks the house. Heine was born Jewish, but converted to Roman Catholicism in order to enter the university. In addition to poems, he also wrote pamphlets and political protest notices, which forced him to spend years in exile in France. He is best known for his *Loreley-Lied*, which tells the story of the singing mermaid mesmerizing shippers until they ran their boats aground at the Lorelei rock near St Goar. During the Nazi period, his works were banned.

Bebelsplatz in Berlin, site of one of the first and largest book-burning events scheduled by the Nazis, now carries his immortal words: "Where books are burned, soon people will also burn."

In addition to his birthplace, there is also a **Heinrich Heine Memorial** at Schwanenmarkt and the local university is named after him. The **Heinrich Heine Institute**, Bilkerstraße 12, ☎ 0211-899-5571, has an exhibition of manuscripts, letters, and his death mask. Opening hours are Tuesday to Sunday from 11 am to 5 pm, opening at 1 pm on Saturday. Admission is €2.

Art Museums

Düsseldorf is proud of its well-developed arts scene and, in addition to many galleries and studios, has several excellent art museums.

The **Kunstmuseum** (Museum of Fine Arts), Ehrenhof 5, ☎ 0211-899-2460, has art from the Middle Ages to the present. Particularly impressive is the collection of Dutch paintings and works by local artists. The museum also has a large collection of glassware ranging from Roman times to the present. Opening hours are Tuesday to Saturday, 11 am to 6 pm. Admission is €2.50.

The impressive **Kunstsammlung Nordrhein-Westfalen** (Art Collection of North Rhine Westphalia), www.kunstsammlung.de, is spread over two buildings at opposite ends of the old town. The **K20**, Grabbeplatz 5, ☎ 0211-828-1130, exhibits 20th-century paintings. It has a noteworthy Paul Klee collection of 92 paintings shown in rotation. The **K21**, Ständehausstraße 1, ☎ 0211-838-1600, exhibits 21st-century art. Both museums are open from Tuesday to Friday, 10 am to 6 pm, and weekends from 11 am to 6 pm. On the first Wednesday of the month, it is open from 10 am to 10 pm. Admission is €6.50 to each or €10 to both on the same day. Free bicycles are available to cycle between the two.

Tunisian Gardens, Paul Klee

Near the K20 is the **Kunsthalle** (Art Hall), Grabbeplatz 4, ☎ 0211-899-6243, www.kunsthalle-duesseldorf.de, which has temporary exhibitions, mostly of modern art. Opening hours are Tuesday to Saturday from noon to 7 pm, and Sunday from 11 to 6 pm. Free guided tours are available on Sunday at 12:30. Admission is €5.50.

The **Hetjens-Museum Deutsches Keramik-Museum** (German Ceramics Museum), Schulstraße 4, ☎ 0211-899-4210, www.duesseldorf.de/hetjens, is the only museum in the German-speaking world dedicated exclusively to ceramics. It uses its collection of 12,000 items to explain the use and development of ceramics over 8,000 years in different regions and cultures. Opening hours are Tuesday to Sunday from 11 am to 5 pm, closing at 9 pm on Wednesday. Admission is €3.

Cultural Events & Festivals

As befits a state capital, Düsseldorf has several concert venues, including the Deutsche Oper am Rhein and several theaters. Information on events is available from the tourist office, but for reservations contact **Düsseldorf Ticket**, ☎ 01805-664-332, or from outside Germany, ☎ 49211-172-0228, www.dticket.de.

The Düsseldorfers enjoy a good party. In addition to the normal festivals such as Karneval, the **St Martin's parades**, and the **Christmas market**, it also has **Japanese Fireworks on the Rhine** (May), celebrates the **French National Day** (14 July), and schedules the largest fun fair on the Rhine during the second weekend of July. Festivals are usually centered on the Marktplatz and the Rhine Uferpromenade.

Shopping

Düsseldorf has more high-end clothing stores than any other German city. Most international and domestic brands have stores here, mostly on the Königsallee, Schadowstraße, or in the classy malls.

Bargains av re hard to find at the top addresses, but that's no problem at **Magazzino**, Mittelstraße 19, ☎ 0211-869-3027, www.designermode.com. This outlet store at Karlsplatz, between the Kö and the old town, sells designer labels at up to 70% discount.

For discounts on golfing wear, equipment, and paraphernalia, try **Golf Discount**, Bahnstraße 3, ☎ 0211-398-2887.

Adventures

In the Air

Balloon flights are arranged in the Düsseldorf region by **Ballonclub Barbarossa**, Grafenbergerallee 239, ☎ 0211-666-619, www.mps.de/balloon.

On Water

Köln-Düsseldorfer (usually abbreviated simply to KD), Frankenwerft 35, ☎ 0221-208-8319, www.k-d.com, has several hour-long cruises daily as well as services to other towns along the Rhine. Lunch, dinner, and thematic cruises are also available.

Where to Stay & Eat

The **Steigenberger Parkhotel** is at the top end of Königsallee on the edge of the Hofgarten and the old town. It has a classic façade and elegant public rooms with marble floors. Rooms are modern, stylish, and luxurious. The elegant restaurant **Menuett** (€€€-€€€€) serves nouvelle cuisine. Corneliusplatz 1, 40213 Düsseldorf, ☎ 0211-13-810, fax 0211-138-1592, www.steigenberger.de. (€€€€)

Düsseldorf hosts more European headquarters of Japanese companies than any city. It also has a Japanese school, a cherry blossom festival, and a **Nikko Hotel**. This luxury Japanese hotel is halfway between the Königsallee and the Hauptbahnhof. Rooms are luxurious. The fitness center, with swimming pool on the 11th floor, offers grand views of the city. The hotel has a branch of famed Japanese department store Mitsukoshi. The **Benkay** restaurant (€€€-€€€€) serves Japanese cuisine. Immermannstraße 41, 40210 Düsseldorf, ☎ 0211-8340, fax 0211-161-216, www.nikko-hotel.de. (€€€€)

Hotel Dorint am Stresemannplatz is in a historic building near the Hauptbahnhof. Rooms are modern and comfortable but available in a wide range of sizes and comfort levels. Some compare price-wise with lesser hotels. Stresemannplartz 1, 40210 Düsseldorf, ☎ 0211-35-540, fax 0211-354-120, www.dorint.de. (€€-€€€€)

Hotel Ibis am Hauptbahnhof is conveniently located inside the station building. Rooms are simply furnished but are clean and have air conditioning. Prices remain sane during exhibition weeks. (The hotel will be booked solid though!) Konrad-Adenaurplatz 14, 40210 Düsseldorf, ☎ 0211-16-720, fax 0211-167-2101, ww.ibishotel.com. (€€)

Just off the Kö is the **Victorian Bistro** (€€-€€€), Königstraße 3a, ☎ 0211-865-5020, a modern restaurant serving regional and Mediterranean dishes. Upstairs is the Michelin star **Restaurant Victoria** (€€€-€€€€). This English-style restaurant serves nouvelle cuisine with strong Mediterranean influences.

Nearby, is **La Terazza**, Königsallee 30, ☎ 0211-327-540. It serves Italian cuisine in a modern setting with huge panorama windows. (€€€)

In addition to the Nikko, two more Japanese restaurants are of interest. The **Nippon Kan** (€€-€€€€), Immermannstraße 35, ☎ 0211-173-470, is near the Nikko. It serves Japanese food in a traditional setting with low tables and pillows on the floor, Ikebana, and tatami mats. The **Daitokai** (€€€-€€€€), Mutter-Ey-Straße 1, ☎ 0211-325-054, serves prepared-at-the-table teppanyaki and sushi.

Many restaurants, bars, and cafés are in the old town. For a cut above the rest, try **Brauerei Zum Schiffchen**, Hafenstraße 5, ☎ 0211-132-421. This rustic spot has an almost 400-year tradition and serves typical local cuisine. (€-€€€).

Gourmet's Choice

Gourmets don't mind driving north to the suburb of Kaiserswerth to dine in the **Im Schiffchen**, Kaiserwerther Markt 9, ☎ 0211-401-050. In a historic brick building, it serves mainly nouvelle and classic French cuisine. Many consider this Michelin three-star restaurant as the best French kitchen in Germany. (€€€€)

North Rhine Westphalia

Camping

Camping Unterbacher See is north of Düsseldorf next to the Unterbach lake – campers have free access to the beach and lake area. The site has good facilities but the best spaces are reserved for the almost 300 long-term campers. For tourists, 100 spaces are available. It is open from mid-April to late October. Kleiner Torfbrüch 311, 40608 Düsseldord-Unterbach, ☎ 0211-899-2038, fax 0211-892-9132, www.unterbachersee.de.

Camping Düsseldorf-Lörick is northwest of Düsseldorf next to the Rhine. It has reasonable facilities and 85 spaces. Open from March to October. Lütticher Straße, Düsseldorf-Lörick, ☎ / fax 0211-591-401.

■ Aachen (Aix-la-Chapelle)

Most people visit Aachen, close to the border with Belgium and the Netherlands,to see the Dom, which partly dates from Charlemagne's time. It makes an interesting daytrip from Cologne and is also a convenient stopover on the high-speed trains from Brussels and Paris to Cologne. (In English, the French name Aix-la-Chapelle, which Charlemagne would have recognized, is often used for Aachen.)

The Celts and later the Romans already enjoyed the *Aquae Granni*, the hottest springs north of the Alps, but Aachen's fame came when Charlemagne (742-814) made it his preferred residence. Over a period of 600 years, 32 German kings were crowned here, starting with Otto I in 936. Many Reichstage (Imperial Diets) met here. After Charlemagne had become a saint in 1165, the town rapidly developed as one of the premier pilgrimage sites in Europe.

The city's decline started in the late Middle Ages. From the 16th century, the coronations took place in Frankfurt and in 1656 a town fire destroyed 80% of the town. It suffered severe damage during World War II and, as the westernmost city in Germany, was the first to be liberated by American troops. The most important cultural sites were restored soon after.

Information Sources

Tourist Office: Tourist information is available from the **Verkehrsverein**, Informationsbüro Elisenbrunnen, Friedrich-Wilhelm-Platz, ☎ 0241-180-2960, www.aachen-tourist.de.

Getting Around

Walking is generally the best option in the compact old town. Bus services are available and are useful from the station, which is about 15 minutes walk southeast of the old town, and to some of the outlying museums.

Sightseeing

The main sights are concentrated in a small area near the Dom and Rathaus. Two noteworthy art galleries are farther afield and can be reached in about 15 minutes on foot.

KARL DER GROßE (CHARLEMAGNE)

Charlemagne crowned by Pope Leo II, December 25, 800

Karl der Große (742-814), or Charles the Great, is in English usually known by his French name, Charlemagne. He succeeded in forming an empire in Europe from the chaos that followed the fall of the Roman Empire. He became king of the Franks in 768. In a relatively short time he forged together most of what is modern-day France, Germany, Switzerland, Austria, Belgium, the Netherlands, and Northern Italy into a true empire. On Christmas Day 800, he was crowned Emperor of the Roman Empire by Pope Leo III. Strong links between church and state would continue for centuries.

Although Charlemagne could neither read nor write, he assembled the best minds in arts, science, and culture in his court and his reign is often referred to as the Carolingian Renaissance. In a time when there was hardly a brick house north of the Alps, he erected cathedrals, monasteries, and palaces. He had no fixed capital, but continuously traveled between different *Pfalzen* (Imperial Palaces) to keep control of his empire. After his death, his inheritors split the empire among them and, by the end of the ninth century, France and Germany were developing as separate entities.

Dom Area

The Cathedral or **Dom**, Münsterplatz, ☎ 0241-477-090, www.aachendom.de, is the highlight of any visit to Aachen. At its core is the octagonal Pfalzkapelle (Palatine Chapel) erected by Charlemagne around 800. A Gothic chancel and choir were added between 1355 and 1414, with further additions made up to the present. Large sections of the original Carolingian structure can be seen from Münsterplatz (south side). The 16-sided cupola is 17th century. The bronze doors with lions' heads are original.

The Carolingian structures are more obvious inside, although more modern elements were added through the centuries. The marble throne of Charlemagne is on the upper floors of the west yoke and can only be seen on guided tours. Between 936 and 1531, 32 kings were crowned here. All of them brought gifts to the cathedral. One of the most impressive is the huge copper wheel chandelier donated by Friedrich I Barbarossa in 1165. It hangs in the center of the dome. (The mosaics of the dome are 19th century.) The gilded silver shrine of Charlemagne was donated by Friedrich II in the early 13th century. Also note the 11th-century gilded copper pulpit with precious stones donated by Heinrich II. The Carolingian high altar has an early 11th-century golden altar front with scenes from the passion of Christ.

Reliquary containing part of Charlemagne's skull

Opening hours are daily from 7 am to 7 pm. As no sightseeing is allowed during services that means tourist access begins at 11 am on most days and at 12:45 on Sunday. The choir performs on Sunday during the 11:30 am service. Concerts are held Wednesday at 7 pm from April to October.

The **Domschatzkammer** (Cathedral Treasury), Klostergasse, ☎ 0241-4770-9127, is one of the most important church treasuries in northern Europe. It has over a hundred artworks, with especially fine pieces from the Carolingian, Ottonian, and Hohenstaufen periods. The 14th-century silver and gold bust reliquary of Charlemagne, donated by Karl IV, actually contains a part of Charlemagne's skull. Another highlight is the Lothar Cross (990) – a golden cross encrusted with

Lothar Cross

Ivory font, Dom, ca 1000

precious stones. Opening hours are daily from 10 am to 6 pm, but closing at 1 pm on Monday and at 9 pm on Thursday. Admission is €2.50.

The **Rathaus** (Town Hall), Markt, ☎ 0241-432-7310, was built in the 14th century on the site of Charlemagne's Aula – the Granus tower at Krämerstraße is part of the original palace. The façade has statues of the 32 kings crowned in Aachen. On the ground floor is the Baroque White Room, used as a formal reception room. The Gothic Krönungssaal (Coronation Hall) on the upper floor was used for the feast following coronations. Five of the original eight 19th-century Charlemagne frescoes by Alfred Rethel survived World War II. The room has copies of the imperial insignia – the originals are in the Hofburg in Vienna. Opening hours are daily from 10 am to 1 pm, and 2 to 5 pm. Admission is €2.

The nearby **Couven-Museum**, Hühnermarkt 17, ☎ 0241-432-4421, www.couven-museum.de, has a display of domestic life in middle-class Aachen between 1740 and 1840. It consists mainly of furniture and decorative items. Opening hours are Tuesday to Sunday from 10 am to 5 pm. Admission is €3.

Farther Afield

Peter Ludwig, one of the greatest art collectors of the 20th century, endowed two museums that bear his name in Aachen, his hometown, with a large number of works. (See also the Ludwig-Museum in Cologne.)

The **Ludwig Forum für Internationale Kunst** (Forum for International Art), Jülicher Straße 97-109, ☎ 0241-180-7104, www.heimat.de/ludwigforum, is in a Bauhaus-style building that once housed the largest umbrella factory in Europe. It exhibits modern art and is also used for temporary exhibitions and theatrical performances. Opening hours are Tuesday to Sunday from noon to 6 pm. Admission is €3. Free guided tours Sunday at noon.

MUSEUM COMBINATION TICKET

A museum combination ticket (Museen-Kombikarte) costs €5 and includes admission to the Ludwig Forum, Suermondt-Ludwig Museum, Couven-Museum, as well as the Zeitungsmuseum and Burg Frankenberg. It is available from the named museums and pays for itself after the second museum visited.

The **Suermondt-Ludwig-Museum**, Wilhelmstraße 18, ☎ 0241-479-800, www.suermondt-ludwig-museum.de, has displays of art ranging from the present to antiquity. In contrast to most galleries, the display here starts with the modern and then goes back in time. Highlights include paintings and statues from the late Middle Ages and paintings of the 17th century. Opening hours are Tuesday to Sunday, noon to 6 pm, but closing at 9 pm on Wednesday. Admission is €3.

Adventures

On Foot

Guided **walking tours** of the city are arranged by the tourist office on weekends at 11 am and, from April to October, on weekdays as well at 2 pm.

On Wheels

Bicycle rental is available from **Debo Sport**, Martinstraße 2, ☎ 0241-34-354.

In the Air

Balloon flights are offered by **Euregio Ballooning**, Weststraße 24c, ☎ 0241-8944-9555, www.euregio-ballooning.de, and by **Montgolfiera**, Emmi-Welter-Straße 18, ☎ 0241-701-8924, www.montgolfiera.de. **Pleasure flights** are available in small aircraft from **Westflug Aachen**, Flugplatz Merzbrück, 52146 Würselen-Merzbrück, ☎ 02405-48-510, www.westflug.de. For **helicopter** rides, contact **HeliTeam Aachen**, Auf der Maar 6, ☎ 0800-4354-8326, www.heliteamac.de.

On Horseback

Pony rides are available from **Ponyverleih Meisel**, Kornelimünsterweg 1, ☎ 0241-604-072.

Where to Stay & Eat

The **Dorint Quellenhof** is a grand hotel with a tradition dating back to the early 19th century. It is near the casino north of the old town. Rooms are luxurious and beautifully furnished. The **Lakmé** restaurant (€€€) serves international cuisine with an emphasis on Euro-Asian dishes. The **Brasserie** (€€-€€€) has a terrace and serves international cuisine with a large vegetarian selection. Monheimsallee 52, 52062 Aachen, ☎ 0241-91-320, fax 0241-913-2100, www.dorint.de. (€€€-€€€€).

Best Western Hotel Regence is at the edge of the old town. This modern hotel has comfortable rooms with designer furniture. The **Edo** (€€-€€€€) is the only Japanese restaurant in town. Peterstraße 71, 52068 aachen, ☎ 0241-47-870, fax 0241-39-055, www.bestwestern.de. (€€€-€€€€)

The nearby **Hotel Mercure Aachen City** is a modern city hotel. It was built in 1990 and refurbished in 2002. All rooms are the same but relatively spacious and comfortably furnished. Jülicher Straße 10, 52070 Aachen, ☎ 0241-51-060, fax 0241-501-180, www.accor-hotels.com. (€€-€€€)

The **Dorint am Graben** is in the heart of the old town close to the Dom and Rathaus. It is modern, with comfortable rooms clearly aimed at the business traveler. Holzgraben 6, 52062 Aachen, ☎ 0241-91-320, fax 0241-913-2100, www.dorint.de. (€€-€€€)

A pleasant option in the heart of the old town close to the Dom is **Hotel Brülls am Dom**. It has only nine rooms but is comfortable and stylishly furnished. Rommelgasse 2, 52062 Aachen, ☎ 0241-31-704, fax 0241-404-326. (€€-€€€)

Two Ibis hotels close to the station offer the chain's familiar combination of good value and clean and decent, if simple, rooms. **Ibis Marschiertor**, Friedlandstraße 6, 52064 Aachen, ☎ 0241-47-880, fax 0241-478-8110, www.ibishotel.com. (€€) **Ibis Normaluhr**, Zollernstraße 2, 52070 Aachen, ☎ 0241-51-840, fax 0241-518-4199, www.ibishotel.com. (€-€€)

Camping

RVs may park at Branderhofer Weg 11 in Aachen-Burstscheid. For information, contact the **Haus des Gastes**, Burstscheider Markt 1, 52066 Aachen-Burtscheid, ☎ 0241-608-8057, www.aachen-camping.de.

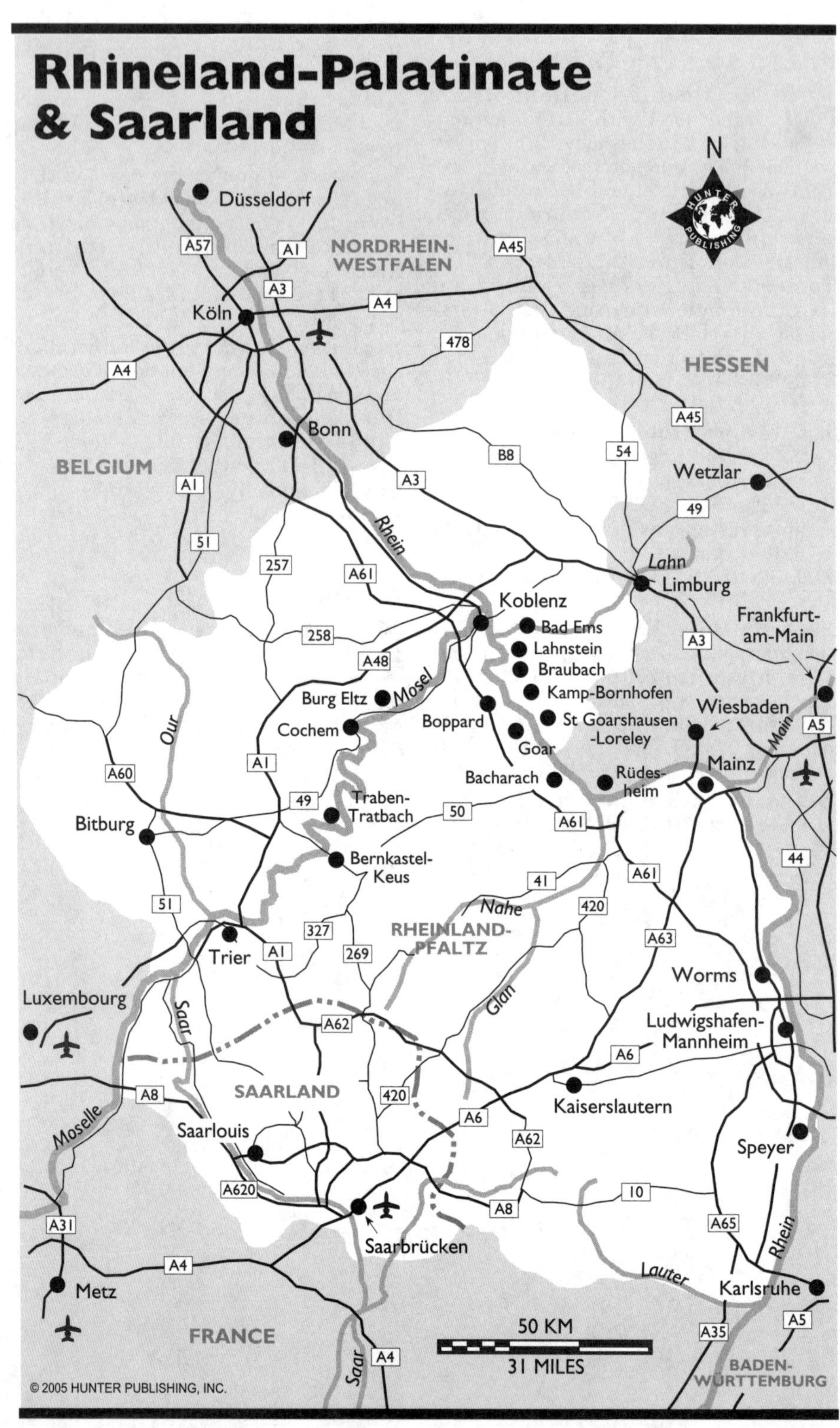
Rhineland-Palatinate
& Saarland
N
HUNTER PUBLISHING
Düsseldorf
A57
A1
NORDRHEIN-
WESTFALEN
A45
A3
Köln
A4
478
HESSEN
A4
Bonn
A45
BELGIUM
B8
54
Wetzlar
A1
A3
Rhein
49
51
257
A61
Lahn
Limburg
Koblenz
Frankfurt-
am-Main
258
Bad Ems
Lahnstein
A3
A48
Braubach
Kamp-Bornhofen
Burg Eltz
Mosel
Wiesbaden
Cochem
Boppard
St Goarshausen
-Loreley
Main
A5
Our
Goar
A60
A1
Bacharach
Rüdes-
heim
Mainz
49
Traben-
Tratbach
50
Bitburg
A61
44
Bernkastel-
Keus
A61
41
51
Nahe
420
327
RHEINLAND-
PFALTZ
A63
Trier
A1
269
Worms
Luxembourg
Saar
Glan
Ludwigshafen-
Mannheim
A62
A6
A8
SAARLAND
420
Kaiserslautern
Moselle
A6
Saarlouis
A62
Speyer
A620
10
A8
A31
Saarbrücken
A65
Rhein
A4
Lauter
Karlsruhe
Metz
50 KM
A5
A35
FRANCE
31 MILES
Saar
A4
BADEN-
WÜRTTEMBURG

Rhineland-Palatinate

In this Chapter

The Rhineland-Palatinate was created mostly out of the Palatinate (Pfalz) and the Rhineland (Rheinland) that were occupied by France after World War II. The state has huge wine-producing areas, of which the Pfalz, Rhine, and Mosel Valleys are the best known.

The Rhine Valley is one of the most popular holiday destinations for visitors to Germany. The most interesting part of the Rhine is from Rüdesheim to Koblenz – a castle or castle ruin can be seen every two km. The valley is at its narrowest and the river flowing at its fastest pace here. The villages are small, romantic, and picturesque. Restaurants and outdoor cafés abound.

Farther upstream are the cathedral cities of Speyer, Worms, and Mainz. All three are dominated by their Romanesque cathedrals. Speyer's remained true to the original, while the cathedrals in Worms and Mainz received Gothic additions.

The Mosel Valley is for many an even more spectacular destination than the Rhine. The valley is narrower, the hills steeper, and the river meanders constantly. Villages are mostly small and picture-perfect. Castles and castle ruins line the banks of the river. Burg Eltz, a castle that was never destroyed in eight centuries, is arguable the best-looking medieval castle in Germany. Trier, the largest town on the Mosel, is the oldest city in Germany and has the largest collection of Roman ruins on German soil.

History

The Romans first produced wine on the riverbanks of the area that forms modern-day Rhineland-Palatinate. Remains of Roman occupation can still be seen in Mainz and Trier.

During the Middle Ages, the region was also of economic, political, and religious importance. Romanesque cathedrals such as the Speyer, Worms, and Mainz trio, bear testimony to that. Up to 1803, the archbishop of Mainz was one of the most powerful political figures in Germany. The archbishop of Trier was also rich and powerful.

During the Middle Ages, various castles were built along the Rhine and Mosel to enforce tolls. When French King Louis IV invaded the area during the War of Palatinate Succession (1688-97), his main aim was to obtain some of this income. The Rhine was the largest single source of taxation in Europe at that stage. His troops destroyed most castles and many towns in the area.

During the Napoleonic years, France realized an old dream of making the Rhine its eastern border. After Napoleon's defeat, much of this area fell to Prussia. In contrast to Protestant Prussia, most of the Rhineland was Catholic and it was always an uneasy union.

After World War II, the area was joined together by the French occupying forces. It had never been under a single administration before. The state has major industries, especially around Ludwigsburg in the south of the state, but also some of the most spectacular natural scenery along the major rivers flowing through the state. Rhineland-Palatinate currently produces some two-thirds of all German wines.

Transportation

By Rail: Although a car makes traveling easier, there are more than adequate public transportation options as well. However, most trains are not part of the super-fast ICE network.

There are railway lines on both sides of the Rhine, with the left bank (Mainz to Koblenz) carrying slightly more traffic than the right bank (Wiesbaden via Rüdesheim to Lahnstein and Koblenz). Frankfurt am Main to Mainz or Wiesbaden takes about 45 minutes and Koblenz to Cologne about an hour, bringing the Rhine Valley into reach for daytrips from these larger cities. The trains between Koblenz and Mainz take one to two hours depending on the number of stops. Do note that the luxurious and fast Intercity Express (ICE) trains no longer run through the Rhine Valley – the frequent Mainz and Frankfurt to Cologne connections now use a much faster direct route. Most trains allow bicycles for a nominal amount.

In the Mosel Valley, at least hourly trains run from Koblenz to Trier. The faster trains take 90 minutes and the local trains two hours. All stop in Cochem.

By Road: The state has good highways for fast traveling times, but the main sights in the valleys are on smaller, slower roads with little commercial or through traffic.

Mainz at the south and Koblenz at the north of the romantic Rhine Valley are both major transportation hubs, with fast Autobahn connections to all part of Germany. The fastest road from Mainz to Koblenz is the Autobahn A61, which runs parallel to the Rhine but in the hills out of view of the river. Similarly, the Koblenz-to-Trier Autobahn is north of the Mosel with few views.

By Air: **Frankfurt Airport** (see Hesse chapter) is the most convenient access point. It is about half an hour by road or frequent trains to Mainz or Wiesbaden.

Hahn Airport, ☎ 06543-509-200, www.hahn-airport.de, is mainly used by budget carriers. Ryanair currently uses Hahn as a hub, with flights to London-Stansted and several European destinations. From Hahn, buses take about half an hour to Koblenz, an hour to Mainz, and 90 minutes to Frankfurt Airport. A pre-booked rental car is a good idea.

By Boat: Boat trips are a slow but enjoyable way of traveling the Rhine and Mosel valleys. Boats operate mostly between April and October with the main season from May to September. Multi-day trips are also popular and usually combine with other tributaries of the Rhine such as the Main or the Neckar and even with the Danube.

■ Information Sources

i Information on the whole state is available from **Rheinland-Pfalz Tourismus**, Löhrstraße 103-105, 56068 Koblenz, ☎ 0261-915-200, www.rlp-info.de.

The Rhine Valley

The Rhine River is arguably Europe's most famous and most important waterway, from its source in Switzerland to its end in the Netherlands, with the stretch from Basel downriver completely navigable. However, the romantic Rhine of castles, robber barons, and legends is concentrated between Mainz and Koblenz, where the scenery is at its most dramatic. At first, the 450-m/1,480-foot wide Rhine flows slowly through a broad open valley, then narrows dramatically from the Bingen Loch to its narrowest point at the Loreley rock. Here the river is only 130 m (420 feet) wide and flows at 10 km/h (six mph).

Unfortunately, most of the small towns along the banks of the Rhine have been ruined by mass tourism. The towns are still pretty, but they are flooded with tacky souvenir stores and overpriced restaurants often offering mediocre food. During July and August, it can become uncomfortably busy, but it can be surprisingly quiet just weeks prior or after the main holiday season. During spring and autumn, when the Rhine Valley is at its prettiest, even weekends can be quiet, except during the frequent festivals held in towns along the river. In winter, many sights and towns close down for the season and the valley is often filled with fog, which can be hauntingly beautiful, but hides much of the scenery and the castles that most visitors came to see.

Most of the famous castles along the Rhine, and there are many, have been ruined twice. First by invading French troops, who blew most of them up in the 17th century, and then by Rhine Romanticism, when many were rebuilt and restored during the 19th century in a false romantic notion of what medieval castles should have looked like. However, they are still pretty and worth seeing. Statistically, there is one every two km (1.2 miles).

Despite roads and railways running along both banks of the river, much of the natural beauty remains unspoiled. This is especially true for the section from Rüdesheim to Boppard where the valley is steep. The views can be enjoyed from river level or from various viewpoints at the top of the hills.

A good introduction to the area is via Speyer, Worms, and Mainz, where three of the most magnificent Romanesque cathedrals still dominate the skyline. Wiesbaden (see Hesse chapter) is a newer and elegant city. The scenery from here changes to much smaller towns and vineyards. Rüdesheim is the quintessential Rhine tourist town offering all the facilities associated with mass tourism. From here, the character of the Rhine changes to a narrow stream flowing rapidly through a steep valley. Castles seem to spring up everywhere and the natural beauty of the valley seems more impressive with every twist and turn of the river. At the Loreley Rock, the river is at its narrowest, fastest, and most treacherous. Soon after, the pace slows again as it makes its sharpest turn, shortly after Boppard. The river is reinforced by the confluence of the Lahn River in Lahnstein and the meandering Mosel in Koblenz. Here bridges again span the river and the best part of Rhine romanticism is over.

■ Speyer

Speyer is an interesting town close to the more popular and famous Heidelberg. The huge cathedral, Germany's largest Romanesque structure, is worth the journey. In addition, Speyer has a lovely old town area and a large technology museum with full-size aircraft.

Speyer was an important city at the turn of the first millennium. It was especially favored by the Salian Emperors (1024-1125) of the Holy Roman Empire, who sponsored the construction of a monastery and other buildings. From here, Emperor Heinrich IV set out in 1076 to apologize in person to the Pope in Canossa. The imperial diet met over 50 times in Speyer, including the momentous 1526 to 1529 meeting, which prepared the division of the Empire into Roman Catholic and Protestant areas. In 1689, French armies destroyed much of the medieval town. As a result, most of the buildings date from the Baroque period. Like Mainz and Worms, Speyer also had a flourishing Jewish community, which suffered from persecution during several episodes over the past 900 years.

Information Sources

Tourist Office: Verkehrsamt Speyer, Maximilianstraße 11, 67346 Speyer, ☎ 06232-142-392, www.speyer.de.

Transportation

Speyer can be reached by frequent local trains from Heidelberg in 40 minutes and from Worms in 30 minutes. It is a 20-minute drive by car from either town.

Sightseeing

The main sight in Speyer is the domed, four-tower **Kaiserdom St Maria and St Stephan** (Imperial Cathedral of St Mary and St Stephan), the largest Romanesque building in Germany. Constructed between 1030 and 1061, it withstood most of the trials and tribulations of the centuries, although it did suffer some war damage. Recent restoration work returned it to its original Romanesque condition with an airy, almost bare interior, emphasizing the natural beauty of the architecture. Different color stones break the monotony and wall paintings color the areas above the high Romanesque arches. The large crypt houses the graves of eight German emperors and kings. The octagonal cupola is best viewed from the raised transept. The cathedral is 134 m (440 feet) long in total; the nave 105 m (330 feet) long and 33 m (105 feet) high, with the towers looming up

Speyer Marktplatz

71 m (230 feet). The basilica was made a UNESCO World Cultural Heritage site in 1981. It is open Monday to Friday, 9 am to 7 pm, Saturdays, 9 am to 6 pm, and Sundays, 1:30 to 6 pm. From November to March, it closes at 5 pm.

The **Altpörtal** (old west tower, above) of the original 13th-century city walls survives to the present day. At 55 m (180 feet), it is one of the highest medieval city towers built in Germany. The lower parts date from 1230, but the highest floors were added later and the Baroque roof in 1708. It is possible to climb the 154 stairs to the top for spectacular views of Speyer, the Rhine, and the surrounding countryside. The tower is open from April to October on weekdays, 10 am to noon and 2 to 4 pm, weekends from 10 am to 5 pm. Admission is €1.

Maximillianstraße connects the Altpörtal with the Cathedral. Along this route, considered one of the most impressive medieval roads in Germany until it was destroyed by the French, the imperial court trekked in splendor and it is often referred to as the **Via Triumphalis**. Today, the Via Triumphalis is mostly for pedestrians only and lined with appealing cafés, outdoor restaurants, and large, mostly Baroque buildings.

Around 1090, the Bishop of Speyer invited Jews to settle near the cathedral. Today, little is left of the former Jewish Quarter, but the ritual Jewish bath, **Mikwe**, Judengaße, ☎ 06232-291-971, is still preserved. A barrel-vaulted staircase leads to this bath, which is 10 m (33 feet) below the surface. It is the oldest bath and best preserved of its type in Central Europe. Open daily from April to October, 10 am to 5 pm. Admission is €1.

About 10 minutes stroll, a world away from the Cathedral and centuries past, is the **Technik Museum** (Technology Museum), Am Technik Museum 1, ☎ 06232 67080 www.technik-museum.de. The most popular exhibits relate to transportation, ranging from old cars to locomotives and airplanes that can be seen close up and in some cases even entered for closer inspection. The crowds' favorite is a Lufthansa Boeing 747. Also popular is the cramped interior of a 46-m (150-foot) German submarine dating from the late 1960s. An IMAX theater forms part of the complex. The museum is open daily from 10 am to 6 pm. Admission is €10.50.

Adventures

On Foot

The tourist office arranges guided **town walks** from April to November on weekends at 11 am and on the first Friday of the month at 7 pm.

Where to Stay & Eat

The **Domhof Hotel** opened in 1990 in several connected old buildings near the Dom. Rooms are comfortable and functional. The hotel has its own brewery and guests are welcome to watch the brewing process. Bauhof 3, 67346 Speyer, ☎ 06232-13-290, fax 06232-132-990, www.domhof.de. (€€€)

The **Goldener Engel Hotel** is near the Altpörtel in the heart of the old town. It uses a combination of antique and designer furniture in comfortable rooms. The **Wirstshcaft Zum Alten Engel** restaurant (€-€€€) is in the vaulted cellars and serves hearty local specialties. Mühlturmstraße 5-7, 67346 Speyer, ☎ 06232-13-260, fax 06232-132-695. (€€)

The **Restaurant Backmülde**, Karmeliterstraße 11, ☎ 06232-71-577, is a block from the Altpörtel. It offers nouvelle cuisine with strong Mediterranean overtones. The wine list features 600 labels – mostly from the Palatinate. (€€€)

The **Ratskeller**, Maximilianstraße 12, ☎ 06232-78-612, serves local specialties in the vaulted, 16th-century cellars of the Rathaus. (€-€€)

■ Worms

Like Speyer, Worms was favored by the Salian Emperors but the town today is best remembered for the 1521 Diet of Worms. Here, Martin Luther was invited to appear before the Imperial Parliament to explain and revoke his opposition to the excesses of the Roman Catholic Church. He refused and claimed to have uttered the immortal words: "Here I stand for I

Above: The medieval walled town of Dinkelsbuehl
Below: Nördlingen, Germany's only town with its surrounding wall intact
(both © www.romantischestrasse.de)

Nördlingen's church tower (© www.romantischestrasse.de)

Würzburg's Baroque Residenz (© www.romantischestrasse.de)

Rothenburg ob der Tauber, with the Markusturm (© www.romantischestrasse.d

cannot do otherwise. So help me God! Amen." The Diet's decision to outlaw Martin Luther had probably the most devastating consequences of any conference decision up to the 20th century.

Most of medieval Worms was destroyed by the French in 1689 during the wars of the Palatinate succession. As a result, from the time of Martin Luther only the cathedral and a plaque recall the momentous events of 1521. The main reason to visit Worms is to see the cathedral.

Information Sources

Tourist Office: Information is available from the Tourist Information, Neumarkt 14, 67547 Worms, www.worms.de.

Carolingian Königshalle in Lorsch

For drivers, Lorsch makes an interesting stop before joining the A67 or A5 back to Mainz or Frankfurt. Its Königshalle is the oldest complete monument in Germany. Constructed in 767 during the reign of Charlemagne, as part of the Monastery at Lorsch, its exact purpose remains unclear. However, the elaborate Franco-Merovingian outside decorations are considered some of the best examples of Carolingian architecture in Germany. Inside, some of the original wall paintings can still be seen. The roof is a late Renaissance, early Baroque addition. Currently the inside can only be seen on a guided tour, which is in German at irregular intervals – ☎ 06251-103-820 for exact times.

Sightseeing

The **Kaiserdom St Peter und St Paul** (Imperial Cathedral of St Peter and St Paul), Domplatz 1, ☎ 06241-6115, is a mainly Romanesque cathedral in magnificent condition following restoration work after World War II. It was originally erected between 1000 and 1025, but most of what you see now dates from the early 12th century. It is considered one of the best examples of Late Rhine Romanesque, despite some Gothic and Baroque additions. The cathedral, together with those in Mainz and Speyer, had a unique position in early German history. Opening hours are daily from 9 am to 5 pm, closing at 6 pm from April to October.

For centuries after the start of the Reformation, Worms remained a multi-religion area. As a result, it was only in 1868 that the **Luther monument** was erected in a park laid out after the destruction of the city walls. It is the largest monument in the world to honor the Reformation. At its center stands Martin Luther surrounded by statues of followers and supporters and the names of cities and regions that played a major role in the Reformation.

LIEBFRAUMILCH

Liebfraumilch originates from the Worms region. Originally a highly respected white wine, mass production for export saw the name decline to become a byword for sweet, headache-inducing plonk. The original is still available under the producer name Liebfrauenstift Kirchenstück.

One of the most famous medieval German poems is the *Nibelungenlied*. Many people are surprised that this is based at least partly on fact. The Burgundian Kingdom was established early in the fifth century in the Worms' area. The legend is filled with action heroes and betrayal of the worst kind. A famous scene in the poem has Hagen throwing the treasure of the Nibelungen in the Rhine – a statue of Hagen caught in the act is on the Nibelungen Bridge. A **Nibelungen Museum**, Fischerpförtchen 12, ☎ 06241-202-120, www.nibelungen-museum.de, opened recently in two medieval towers and part of the town wall. It uses multimedia techniques to explain the legend. English audio guides are available.

Opening hours are Tuesday to Sunday from 10 am to 5 pm, closing at 10 pm on Friday. Admission is €5.50.

Where to Sleep & Eat

Hotel Asgard is a modern hotel at the edge of the inner city. It has comfortable, bright rooms with tasteful furniture. Some rooms with kitchenettes are available. Gutleutstraße 4, 67547 Worms, ☎ 06241-86-080, fax 06241-860-8100, www.asgard-hotel.de. (€€)

The **Dom Hotel** is near the Luther Memorial in the heart of the pedestrian zone. Rooms are quiet, with high-quality furniture. The restaurant (€€-€€€) serves international and regional dishes. Obermarkt 10, 67547 Worms, ☎ 06241-9070, fax 06241-23-515, www.dom-hotel.de. (€€-€€€)

The pleasant **Landhotel Bechtel** is just under 10 km (six miles) west of Worms. It is in the small village of Heppenheim and the owner is also a wine producer. Rooms are modern, comfortable, and stylish. All have balconies with views of the countryside. The restaurant (€-€€) serves hearty local cuisine. Pfälzer Waldstraße 98, 67551 Worms-Heppenheim, ☎ 06241-36-536, fax 06241-34-745. (€)

■ Mainz

Mainz has a population of 180,000 and is the capital of the state of Rhineland-Palatinate. It is on the left bank of the Rhine across from the confluence of the River Main with the Rhine and thus has been of strategic importance for most of its more than 2,000 years of recorded history.

Mainz was founded in 39 BC by the Romans as *Mogontiacum*, later the capital of the province *Germania Prima*. Throughout the Roman period, it remained an important city, housing at times up to 16,000 Romans. In AD 27, a bridge was built over the Rhine, which was a much narrower river at that time. This bridge was protected on the other side of the Rhine by a castle, which gave the town of Mainz-Kastel its name. Through an oddity of post-World War II political geography, Mainz-Kastel is now part of the city of Wiesbaden, which is the capital of the state of Hesse, while the wine-growing area surrounding Mainz is known as Rheinhesse, but part of the state of Rhineland-Palatinate.

At times, the Roman borders extended well beyond the Rhine, and there were attempts to conquer most of what is contemporary Germany in order to extend the border to the Elbe River. However, attacks from German tribes increased and, by the end of the third century, the Rhine was again the final frontier of the Roman Empire. On New Year's Eve 406, the Rhine froze over and the German tribes crossed the river. Mainz was sacked and the Romans abandoned the city, which was eventually to be settled by the Franks.

By 750, Mainz was regaining importance after St Boniface, the Anglo-Saxon missionary who brought Christianity to the Germans, settled here. The reign of Bishop Willigud, from 975 to 1011, brought Mainz special glory, as he was not only one of the electors of the German king but also the chancellor of the realm. The archbishopric of Mainz remained one of the most powerful and wealthiest posts in the German-speaking world up until secularization in the early 19th century. The archbishop owned large tracts of land stretching way past Frankfurt, most of the monasteries in the area were under his control, and he earned tolls at several strategic trading points.

Around 1440, Johannes Gutenberg invented the first printer with movable type in Mainz. However, through his lack of business acumen, others benefited most from it. Mainz did become an important center for the press, a position that continued into the modern era with Germany's second public television broadcaster (ZDF) and several publishing houses in the city.

Napoleon passed by several times and made *Mayence* a privileged city in his empire. He also secularized the monasteries and came close to destroying the Mainz cathedral as well. In the chaos following collapse of the Napoleonic regime, Mainz briefly became a republic – the first in Germany.

Although most of the Old Town was destroyed during World War II, Mainz was rebuilt sympathetically, combining older and modern styles. The cathedral was largely restored to its former state.

Information Sources

Tourist Office: Information is available from the **Verkehrsverein Mainz**, Brückenturm am Rathaus, 55116 Mainz, ☎ 06131 286-210, fax 06131 286-2155, www.mainz.de.

Transportation

Mainz offers good transport connections and serves as a hub for long-distance trains and traffic on the Rhine. It is within half an hour from Frankfurt International Airport and several major highways pass and intersect in the region.

The sights of Mainz are concentrated in the compact Old Town, which consists mostly of pedestrian zones. The Dom is about 20 minutes walk from the main train station while the passenger lines of the Rhine embark almost in the heart of the old town. Street parking is limited but several parking garages are available and well-signposted.

Sightseeing

The **Dom St Martin and St Stephan**, Markt 10, ☎ 06131-253-412, was begun under the auspices of Archbishop Willigud during the reign of Emperor Otto II in 975. Through the next millennium, it burned down seven times, the first time the day before its consecration in 1009. What remains today is mostly from the 12th and 13th centuries. Despite added Gothic features, the dominant style, especially noticeable in the dark interior, remains Romanesque. Seven German kings were crowned in the cathedral, including Heinrich II, the last Saxon Emperor, and Konrad II, the first Salian (Frankish) emperor. Most of the Mainz archbishops from the past millennium are buried here, with many memorial tombstones adoring the pillars of the church. The east choir is the oldest part of the church, with two-meter-thick (6½-foot) walls. None of the original stained glass and wall paintings survived the seven fires, but the bronze doors of the main entrance are the originals from Willigud's time. The two lion doorknobs are about 200 years younger. Opening hours are April to September on weekdays from 9 am to 6:30 pm, Saturdays, 9 pm to 4 pm, and Sundays, 12:45 to 3 pm and 4 to 6:30. During winter months, the Dom closes at 5 pm, and 4 on Saturdays.

The nearby **Gutenberg Museum**, Liebfrauenplatz 5, 55116 Mainz, ☎ 06131-122-640, www.gutenberg.de, commemorates Mainz's most famous son – Johannes Gensfleisch zu Gutenberg, who invented the moveable type press around 1440. The display includes two Gutenberg bibles as well as other books and scriptures of the past two millennia. Several presses and other equipment used in printing are on display, along with explanations of different papers and processes. Live demonstrations are frequently held in the basement. A short film with amateurish marionettes gives an introduction to Gutenberg's work and life, of which little is known. All descriptions in the museum are in German only – English audio guides are available. The museum shop is small but has a wide variety of trinkets in addition to lots of books. Opening hours are Tuesday to Saturday, 9 am to 5 pm, Sundays, 11 am to 3 pm; closed on Mondays and all official holidays. Admission is €3.

The facades of the building on **Marktplatz**, across from the Dom, are copies of the originals. However, on the south side of the Dom, stroll south along Leichhof and Augustinerstraße to see some parts of the Old Town that escaped war damage.

The **Museum für Antike Schifffahrt** (Ancient Ships), Neutorstraße 2, ☎ 06131-286-630, opened in 1994 at the southern edge of the old town. In 1981, while digging foundations for an extension of the Hilton Hotel, five well-preserved Roman ships were discovered under almost eight m (26 feet) of rubble. After treating the wood to prevent further decay, these ships were put on display in the brightly lit former Market Hall. Two full-size replicas of Roman river battleships are on display together with wrecks of the original five boats and three boats discovered elsewhere. The ship building techniques are illustrated as well as the expansion plans of the Roman Empire. The ships are assumed to date from around 407 when the Romans had to abandon Mainz, following successful attacks by Germanic tribes from across the Rhine. All descriptions are in German only, but English audio guides (€4) provide a 45-minute tour. Admission is free. The museum is open Tuesday to Sunday from 10 am to 6 pm.

On the highest hill of old Mainz is **St Stephankirche** (Church of St Stephan), Kleine Weißgasse 12, ☎ 06131-231-640. The first church was erected here in 990 by Bishop Willigis. He was also buried here in 1011, as the Dom was still undergoing repair at the time of his death. The current Gothic church dates from the early 14th century. The church was severely damaged after a nearby gunpowder depot blew up in 1857. It was hit in three air raids during World War II and only the outer walls remained. Attempts were made to restore the church to its Gothic origins and they largely succeeded, although a lack of money necessitated a flat ceiling rather than vaults. Few of the 200,000 annual visitors notice this, as the main attractions are the stained glass windows. In the last years of his life Marc Chagall, who never visited Mainz, created the windows for the apse and the transept and his colleague of 28 years, Charles Marq, did the rest. The predominant color is blue, to create an atmosphere for meditation, with Chagall using up to 18 tones of blue while Marq restricted himself to 10 for the north and only eight for the south windows. This is the only church in Germany with Chagall windows and it is also the largest single work by Chagall. The church is open daily from 10 am to 12 pm and 2 to 5 pm (4:30 in December and January); Sunday mornings it's open only for services. For the best light conditions, visit in the morning. Limited parking and a labyrinth of cul-de-sacs and one-way streets make visiting on foot or by public transportation the better options.

Cultural Events & Festivals

Under the umbrella title **Cultural Summer Rhineland-Palatinate** a range of events is presented throughout the state. This program includes 40 jazz concerts held mostly on wine estates and 70 choral and other vocal concerts, For exact details contact Kultursommer Rheinland-Pfalz, Kaiserstraße 26-30, 55116 Mainz, ☎ 06131-288-380, www.kultursommer.de.

Villa Musica, Auf der Bastei 3, ☎ 06131-925-1800, www.villamusica.de, organizes concerts right through the year, mainly in castles and fortresses. The schedule is not restricted to the Rhineland area.

Mainz also arranges a special summer program of mainly classical music in historic settings such as churches, museums, and castles. A similar program is arranged in winter, with special concerts in the Christmas season. For more information, contact the Mainz tourism office, or Ticketbox, ☎ 06131-211-500, www.ticketbox-mainz.de.

Karneval is celebrated enthusiastically in Mainz. The traditional parades are usually held at the end of February or early March. The tourist office has details on the exact dates and route.

Adventures

On Foot

The Mainz Tourist Office conducts two-hour English guided walks of the **old town** sights on Saturday and, from April to end October, also on Wednesday and Friday. Time of departure is 2 pm from the Tourist Office at Brückenturm am Rathaus, 5516 Mainz, ☎ 06131-286-2127. More frequent tours in German are also available.

On Wheels

Bicycles can be rented from **ASM Parkhaus Cityport**, ☎ 06131-225-699. There are pleasant cycling stretches along the Rhine but also see Frankfurt (page xx) for the **Mainuferradweg**, a cycling route along the Main River.

For an alternative to ordinary cycling, a **Fahrraddraisine (cycling rail trolley)** is available in the Glan valley, west of Mainz. On an otherwise unused railroad, the trolley is powered by two cyclists with two or more passengers on stretches of either 20 or 40 km (12 or 24 miles). For more information contact **Naheland-Touristik** at Bahnhofstraße 37, 55606 Kirn, ☎ 06752-2055, fax 06752-3170, www.naheland.net. Combinations with cycling and walking and luggage transfers are possible.

On Water

On the Nahe, and its tributary the Glan, **kayaking** is possible. **Naheland-Touristik** at Bahnhofstraße 37, 55606 Kirn, ☎ 06752-2055, fax 06752-3170, www.naheland.net, arranges kayaking tours, which can also be combined with cycling or hiking, including luggage transportation.

Köln-Düsseldorfer (KD), Adenauerufer, ☎ 06131-232-800, www.k-d.de, operates **cruises** on the Rhine from in front of the Rathaus. If time is limited, start a cruise farther downstream for more interesting views.

Where to Stay & Eat

The fabulous **Hyatt Regency Hotel** is on the banks of the Rhine in a building that successfully combines parts of the historic Fort Malakoff and a modern glass and steel design. It is close to the Ancient Ship Museum, about 10 minutes stroll from the Dom. Rooms are large and luxurious. The **Bellpepper** restaurant (€€-€€€) uses an open kitchen to produce fresh Mediterranean dishes. Malakoff-Terrasse 1, 55116 Mainz, ☎ 06131-731-234, fax 06131-731-235, www.hyatt.com. (€€€€)

The **Mainz Hilton**, on the banks of the Rhine adjacent to the Rheingoldhalle conference and entertainment center, has the best location close to tourist attractions. Rooms are luxurious. The **Brasserie** (€€) serves international cuisine with strong French influences and has excellent views of the Rhine. Rheinstrasse 68, 55116 Mainz, ☎ 06131-2450, fax 06131-245-589, www.hilton.com. (€€€- €€€€)

The **Mainz City Hilton** is at the western edge of the pedestrian zone close to the Hauptbahnhof. It may lack the views of its namesake on the banks of the Rhine, but it's equally modern and luxurious. Münsterstraße 11, 55116 Mainz, ☎ 06131-2780, fax 06131-278-567, www.hilton.com. (€€€-€€€€)

Hotel Hammer is close to the Hauptbahnhof. Rooms are modern and comfortable. Bahnhofsplatz 6, 55116 Mainz, ☎ 06131-965-280, fax 06131-965-2888, www.hotel-hammer.com. (€€)

The **Ibis Hotel** is close to the Südbahnhof at the southern edge of the old town. Rooms are modern and functional. Holzhofstraße 2, 55116 Mainz, ☎ 06131-2470, fax 06131-234-126, www.ibishotel.com. (€€)

Camping

Camping Maaraue is idyllically located at the confluence of the Rivers Rhine and Main. It has 100 spaces, many with views of Mainz and the Dom, and is open from mid-March to October. Auf der Maaraue, 55246 Mainz-Kostheim, ☎ 06134-4383, www.krkg.de.

■ Rheingau

Rheingau is the region roughly bordered by Hofheim am Main east and the Rhine River up to Lorch in the west. It is one of the most famous wine producing areas in Germany with some of the oldest and most respected vineyards in the country. To the south of Rheingau, the Rhine flows as a broad stream and at a leisurely pace through a wide valley. The southern slopes of the low hills of Rheingau facing the Rhine are covered with vineyards, mostly Riesling, as temperatures here are more moderate than the higher Taunus Mountains farther north.

The sights of Rheingau are mostly related to wine, with several picturesque towns active in wine production and the wine trade on the banks of the Rhine. On top of the hills are famous vineyards and castles such as Schloss Johannisberg and Schloss Vollrath. In the valleys are former monasteries such as Kloster Eberbach, nowadays a museum, wine institute and the largest single vineyard in Germany, and Kloster

Marienthal, where church services are still held and a peaceful retreat is offered.

Information Sources

Tourist Office: In contrast to other parts of the Rhine Valley, Rheingau is in the state of Hesse. Information is available from **Hessen Touristik Service**, Postfach 3165, 65021 Wiesbaden, ☎ 0611-778800, www.hessen-tourismus.de.

Transportation

A rail service is available from Frankfurt via Wiesbaden and/or Mainz to most parts of the Rheingau region. Buses run to outlying areas. Boats on the Rhine also connect most towns at a more leisurely pace. Cycling and hiking are popular in the region.

Eltville

In 1136, in a remote valley above Eltville-Kiedrich, Cistercian monks founded **Kloster Eberbach** (Monastery), 65343 Eltville, ☎ 06723-4228, www.kloster-eberbach.de. On a large estate, the monks not only built one of the best-preserved monasteries in the region, but also excelled in farming. The monks, who were strict vegetarians, concentrated on agriculture and were particularly successful in viniculture. At one stage, the monks even owned their own fleet of ships for transporting the produce down the Rhine. The monastery was secularized in 1803, but most of it has been preserved as a museum. The Romanesque church was stripped of its art in earlier wars and remains bare, which emphasizes the stark straight lines of the style. The Gothic monks' dormitory, at 73 m (240 feet) long, is one of the largest halls of the period. A few Baroque elements also found their way into later additions, but only the refectory with its stucco ceiling is truly representative of that style. It is surrounded by a wall five m (16 feet) high, just over a km (.6 mile) long, which has been preserved from the 13th century. The monastery is nearing the end of a 25-year restoration project and is in excellent condition.

Eberbach is, at 560 acres, the largest single vineyard in Germany and belongs to the state of Hesse. A wine academy is housed in the estate. Kloster Eberbach wines are highly rated and for sale on the premises. The Monastery is open daily from April to September, 10 am until 6 pm, and from October to March, weekdays, 10 am to 4 pm, and weekends, 11 am to 4 pm. Admission to see the inside of the buildings is €3.50.

Where to Stay & Eat

The **Kloster Eberbach Guesthouse** offers the chance to experience some of the peace and tranquility at night that the monks must have valued centuries ago. This small hotel has 20 well-appointed double rooms with simple stark lines and a grayish color scheme in accordance with the Cistercian ideals of simplicity. The hotel is in a 16th-century building formerly used as a mill. Breakfast is included. It is rated as a three-star, deluxe hotel – the monks never had it this good. Gastronomiebetriebe, Kloster Eberbach, 65346 Eltville ☎ 06723-993-0, fax 06723-993-100, www.klostereberbach.com. (€€€, singles €€)

The **Klosterschänke**, ☎ 06723-9930, at Kloster Eberbach, offers regional cuisine in a rustic setting with outdoor seating when sunny. Open daily, 11:30 am until 10 pm (longer hours on concert nights). The extensive menu offers mainly regional specialties as well as wine from the award-winning local cellar. Specialties of the house include Cistercian Bread (a meat loaf with plum-bacon sauce) and Rheingauer Speckkuchen (a thin baked quiche with bacon, onions, and sour cream). (€-€€)

Much more luxurious is the **Schloss Reinhartshausen Kempinski Hotel**. It is on the banks of the Rhine in a palace erected in 1801 for a Prussian Princess. Rooms are luxurious – some have Jacuzzis and fireplaces. The **Schlosskeller** (€€-€€€) serves mostly regional cuisine and is open for dinner only. The Michelin-star **Marcobrunn** restaurant (€€€€) serves classic cuisine with French and Austrian influences. Hauptstraße 43, 65346 Eltville-Erbach, ☎ 06123-6760, fax 06123-676-400, www.kempinski.de. (€€€€)

Johannisberg

Closer to Rüdesheim, in Geisenheim, is one of Germany's best-known wine estates. **Schloss Johannisberg's** winemaking tradition goes back to the 12th century, when Benedictine monks planted vines here on the south-facing slopes.

DID YOU KNOW?

The most famous moment for the Schloss came in 1775. A messenger bringing the permission to harvest from the owner, the prince-abbot of Fulda, was delayed for unknown reasons and the grapes eventually rotted on the vines. They were harvested nonetheless and noble rot was discovered – the resulting sweet wine, *Spätlese*, or Late Harvest, has been popular ever since.

The estate was also the first to produce *Eiswein* (Ice Wine), where grapes are harvested after having frozen on the vine. The estate was given to Austrian Chancellor Fürst von Metternich for his services at the Congress of Vienna (1815). The *Sekt* produced here bears his name and his family still owns part of the estate. A vinothek on the estate allows sampling and purchasing. The Baroque palace, which was damaged during the war but rebuilt, is not open to the public but much of the grounds and the church are.

Where to Stay & Eat

The **Gutausschank Schloss Johannisberg,** ☎ 06722-96-090, www.schloss-johannisberg.de, is a pleasant restaurant with marvelous views of the Rhine Valley. It serves mainly regional cuisine. The atmosphere is generally relaxed and unpretentious, despite the noble name of the estate. (€-€€€)

Rüdesheim

Rüdesheim is the most popular tourist town in the Rheingau and caters well for the estimated three million visitors that come here from early spring to late autumn. Up to the middle of the 19th century, the fast and treacherous rapids of the Bingen Gorge made the Rhine unnavigable between Bingen and Lorch. As a result, cargo was carted overland between Rüdesheim and Lorch. Rüdesheim did well out of this and, since much of the cargo involved wine, soon established itself as the center of the wine trade. By the time the rapids were blasted to submission in the mid-19th century, tourists, mainly led by the British, had discovered the *Romantic Rhine* and Rüdesheim swiftly established itself as the premier tourist town in the area.

Information Sources

Information is available from **Tourist-Information Rüdesheim** and Assmannshausen, Geisenheimerstraße 22, 65385 Rüdesheim, ☎ 06722-19433, fax 06722-3485, www.ruedesheim.de.

Transportation

Although walking is generally the best way to get around Rüdesheim, and walks up the vineyard-covered hills above the town are especially rewarding, a motorized mini-train is available for tours up the hills and through the nearby vineyards. The **Winzerexpress**, www.winzerexpress.de, shown above, departs from Oberstraße in front of the Musikkabinett. Adults €4.30, children €2.

Parking on the Rhine Promenade is expensive. The parking lots a few blocks inland are much cheaper and a better place to park, especially if planning to take a Rhine cruise from here.

Sightseeing

Eating, drinking, and having a good time is the essential Rüdesheim experience. The most famous street is the **Drosselgasse** leading from the Rhine Promenade uphill. On both sides, this narrow alley is lined with bars and restaurants. Live music is expected on weekends from noon until around midnight and sometimes during the week as well. Weekends, and especially Sunday afternoons, can be crowded. German guidebooks often snigger that the garish mixture of faux Gothic and Rhine Romantic style buildings here are what Japanese and American tourists demand, but more German than English is heard.

Rüdesheim has several cultural sights to offer apart from the festivities. The

Rheingauer Weinmuseum Brömser burg (Rheingau Wine Museum), Rheinstraße 2, ☎ 06722-2348, www.rheingauer-weinmuseum.de, is inside the Brömserburg, one of the oldest castles along the Rhine, dating from the ninth century. Apart from information on wine making, the museum has a collection of more than 2,000 wine glasses on display, ranging from Roman times up to the present. The museum is open daily from mid-March until end October, 9 am to 6 pm. Admission is €3.

Siegfried's Mechanisches Musikkabinett, Im Brömserhof, Oberstraße 27-29, ☎ 06722 49217, www.siegfrieds-musikkabinett.de, was the first musical cabinet museum in Germany. It has one of the largest collections in the world of self-playing musical instruments from the past three centuries. Some of the more than 350 instruments are played during the 45-minute tours. The museum is open daily from March to December, 10 am to 6 pm. Admission is €5.

The **Mittelalterliches Foltermuseum** (Medieval Torture Museum) Oberstraße 49-51, ☎ 06722-47510, www.foltermuseum.com, demonstrates the judicial history of medieval Germany with special emphasis on witch-hunts. The museum is open daily from April to November, 10 am to 6 pm. Admission is €5 for adult. (For a far more formal treatment of the subject, see the Museum of Medieval Justice in Rothenburg ob der Tauber.)

High on the hills above Rüdesheim is the **Niederwalddenkmal**. This monument, featuring a huge bronze statue of Germania, was completed in 1883. It is dedicated to the soldiers who died in the struggle for German unity in the latter half of the 19th century. More rewarding than the monument are the views from here across the Rhine Valley. Walking from here through the vineyards down to Rüdesheim can be done in 30 minutes via the straightest route, but there are many options and making a detour via the ruins of Ehrenfels Castle is popular as well. From here, there is a lovely view of the Mäuseturm, a little fortress on a small island near the opposite bank of the Rhine.

MOUSE TOWER?

According to legend, a particularly unpopular Archbishop of Mainz, Hatto, hoarded wheat in a tower on a small Rhine island during a famine, hoping to further increase the price. Hungry mice were drawn to the bountiful tower and devoured everything in sight including the despised Hatto. The tower thus became known as Mäuseturm, which translates to Mouse Tower. However, the name is most likely a corruption of Maut (meaning toll), which accords better with the tower's role in enforcing toll collection on the Rhine, and the rather inconvenient fact that it was constructed more than 300 years after the death of Hatto.

Mäuseturm

Shortly after Rüdesheim, the Rhine makes a 90-degree turn, enters the Bingen Gorge and the valley gradually gets narrower and the hills steeper. The first town is **Assmannshausen**, which administratively is part of Rüdesheim and can also be reached by walking or taking the cable cars over the hill via the Niederwalddenkmal. It is a pretty town with lovely houses but without any major sights. It is famous as the only area along the Rhine that produces red rather than white wines. The Spätburgunder produced here is one of the best-known German red wines.

A PLEASANT HALF-DAY TRIP

A half-open, two-seater Seilbahn (gondola cable car), Oberstraße 37, ☎ 06722-2402, www.seilbahn-ruedesheim.de, operates between the Niederwalddenkmal and Rüdesheim and a chair lift goes down to Assmannshausen. For adults, €4 one way, €6 roundtrip or combination ticket with the chairlift, children (five-18) and big dogs ride at half-price.

Take the cable car from Rüdesheim to Niederwalddenkmal, and then a pleasant stroll parallel to the Rhine for the views and to see the castle ruins at Ehrnefels. Then take the chairlift down to Assmannshausen. From here, return to Rüdesheim by boat via Mäuseturm and Bingen. Combination tickets including cable car, chairlift and boat trip are on sale at €9 for adults, half-price for children.

Where to Stay & Eat

Breuer's Rüdesheimer Schloss Hotel is in a 1729 building. However, the rooms are modern and comfortable, with designer furniture. The restaurant (€-€€) is typical Drosselgasse in design but the food is good and the wine selection excellent. Steingasse 10, 65385 Rüdesheim, ☎ 06722-90-500, fax 06722-47-960, www.ruedesheimerschloss.de. (€€€)

Hotel Trapp is in the center of the old town. Rooms are comfortable, with rustic or lightwood furniture. The restaurant **Entenstube** (€€) serves classic dishes and regional specialties. Kirchstaße 7, 65385 Rüdesheim, ☎ 06722-91-140, fax 06722-47-715, www.ruedesheim-trapp.de. (€€-€€€)

The fourth-generation, family-owned restaurant **Winzerkeller**, Oberstraße 33, ☎ 06722-2324, is in a half-timbered house dating back to 1609 at the top end of the Drosselgasse. It serves both local and international cuisine. A play corner for smaller children provides peace for parents and grandparents. (€-€€)

Assmannshausen has several good hotels and restaurants and is generally a more pleasant part of town to sleep in.

The **Hotel Krone Assmannshausen** is in a 16th-century half-timbered building with interesting towers and other architectural features. Rooms are luxurious, with antique furniture. The **Krone** restaurant (€€€-€€€€) serves international and regional cuisine. Rheinuferstraße 10, 65385 Rüdesheim-Assmannshausen, ☎ 06722-4030, fax 06722-3049, www.hotel-krone.com. (€€€-€€€€)

Even older is the **Alte Bauernschänke Nassauer Hof**. The hotel is spread over five buildings, with the oldest dating from 1408. Rooms are furnished in rustic or modern style. The rustic restaurant (€-€€) has a pleasant terrace and serves mostly regional specialties. Niderwaldstraße 18-23, 65385 Rüdesheim-Assmannshausen, ☎ 06722-49-990, fax 06722-47-912, www.altebaurenschänke.de. (€€-€€€)

High above Rüdesheim is the **Jagdschloss Niederwald**, a comfortable hotel in the former hunting lodge of the princes of Nassau. Rooms are stylishly furnished. The restaurant (€€-€€€), with terrace, serves fish and game as well as other local specialties. Auf dem Niederwald, 65385 Rüdesheim, ☎ 06722-71-060, fax 06722-710-6666, www.nierderwald.de. (€€€)

Camping

Camping Am Rhein is on the banks of the Rhine, less than a km from the Drosselgasse. With good facilities and over 200 spaces, it is open from May to September. Kastanienallee, 65385 Rüdesheim, ☎ 06722-2528, fax 06722-406-783, www.campingplatz-ruedesheim.de.

Camping Ebentaler Hof is inland, close to the Nierderwalddenkmal. It has reasonable facilities and is surrounded by a forest and next to a pony farm. It has 100 spaces and is open from March to mid-November. 65385 Rüdesheim, ☎ 06722-2518, fax 06722-3006, www.herrliche-natur.de.

Lorch

Lorch, a small town active in viniculture since at least 1085, marks the end of the Rheingau. The town became rich from the off-loading of ships, but unlike Rüdesheim, tourism never penetrated to the same extend. Lorch was a favored town among nobles as the size of some of the medieval and half-timbered buildings testifies. At

Lorch, the Wisper flows into the Rhine – a beautiful winding route for cyclists and drivers runs up the narrow Wisper Valley. It is a particularly nice way to return to Wiesbaden via thick forests and pristine nature.

Camping

Naturpark Camping Suleika is about three km (1.8 miles) from Lorch on the hills, with wonderful views of the Rhine Valley. With good facilities and about 100 spaces. It is open from mid-March to October. 65382 Lorch, ☎ 06726-9496, fax 06726-9440, www.suleika-camping.de.

Cultural Events

The **Rheingau Musik Festival**, Rheinallee 1, 65375 Oestrich-Winkel, ☎ 06723-91770, www.rheingaufestival.de, is an annual music and cultural festival arranged in summer in various castles, churches, and monasteries in the Rheingau region.

Kloster Eberbach (Monastery), 65343 Eltville, ☎ 06723-4228, www.kloster-eberbach.de, frequently schedules classical concerts at the monastery.

Wine Tasting

Unfortunately, most wine estates offer wine tasting only for groups. Notable exceptions where individuals are also welcome include:

In Rüdesheim, **Weingut & Vinothek Georg Breuer**, Grabenstraße 8, ☎ 06722-1027, www.georg-breuer.com, has wine tasting for individuals from March to November daily, 10 am to 6 pm. Out of season by arrangement. English-speaking personnel are generally available.

Kloster Eberbach's wine tasting is generally for groups only, but on Friday nights during the summer season, a two-hour tasting is conducted for individuals (in German only). For details contact Kloster Eberbach, 65346 Eltville im Rheingau ☎ 06723-91780, www.kloster-eberbach.de.

At **Schloss Johannisberg**, where the original Spätlese came from, individuals are welcome to sample in the Weinshäncke, Schloss Johannisberg, ☎ 06722-96-090, www.schloss-johannisberg.de. The adjacent restaurant is a pleasant place to try the wine with a full meal.

Adventures in Rheingau

On Foot

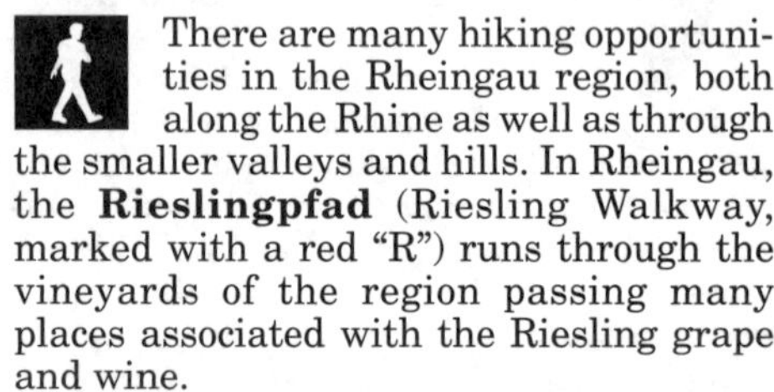

There are many hiking opportunities in the Rheingau region, both along the Rhine as well as through the smaller valleys and hills. In Rheingau, the **Rieslingpfad** (Riesling Walkway, marked with a red "R") runs through the vineyards of the region passing many places associated with the Riesling grape and wine.

Popular starting points for hikes are from Kloster Eberbach, Schloss Johannisberg, and Rüdesheim – all with ample parking space and public transportation options that make circular routes unnecessary.

On Wheels

The hills of Rheingau are ideal for **cycling**, as the slopes are generally not too steep. Cycling along the Rhine is popular, but best done on the left bank where a dedicated cycling route is available almost the entire length of the river from Bingen to Koblenz. The stretch from Rüdesheim to Assmannshausen is on a dangerous public road and best avoided.

Radkranz Rent a Bike, Oberstrasse 42-44, 65385 Rüdesheim, ☎ 06722 48336, www.rad-kranz.com, rents out various types of bicycles. It also offers guided tours and luggage transfers.

On Horseback

Ebentaler Hof Ponyland, ☎ 06722-2518, www.ebental.de, has 50 ponies for riding and also offers farm tractor rides and demonstrations for children.

On Water

Rüdesheim is a popular starting point for Rhine **cruises** through the Loreley Valley. The most interesting part of the valley, from Rüdesheim to St Goarshausen, takes two hours downstream and three hours round-trip. Going all the way to Koblenz takes four hours, six hours round-trip.

Several companies operate from Rüdesheim, including **KD** (see Loreley Valley for special offers); **Bingen-Rüdesheimer**, Rheinkai 10, 55411

Bingen, ☎ 06721-14140, www.bingen-ruedesheimer.com; and **Rössler-Linie**, ☎ 06722-2353, www.roesslerlinie.de.

Wildlife

The **Adlerwart Niederwald** (falconry), ☎ 06722-47-339, is right next to the Niederwalddenkmal. Here eagles and other birds can be observed in large cages, with demonstrations, depending on weather conditions.

■ The Loreley Valley

The Rhine Valley from Kaub to Boppard is often called the Loreley Valley. Here the river is at its narrowest, flows fastest, and the valley is at its steepest, with the most dramatic scenery and several castles. The whole stretch of the Rhine from Rüdesheim and Bingen to Koblenz and Lahnstein are a UNESCO World Cultural Heritage site.

Information Sources

Tourist Office: Information is available from **Tourist Information**, Bahnhofstraße 8, 56346 St Goarhausen, ☎ 06771-9100, www.loreley-touristik.de, or from **Rheintouristik**, Heerstraße 86, 56329 St Goar, ☎ 06741-1300, www.talderloreley.de.

DISCOUNT MULTIPLE CASTLE TICKET

The Burgenticket (Castle Ticket), www.burgen-am-rhein.de, allows for one-time entry into the 10 participating castles. It is valid for 24 months after purchase and is transferable. It costs €14 and is available from all participating castles.

Transportation

The B42 connects Rüdesheim and Koblenz on the left bank of the Rhine and the B9 Bingen and Koblenz on the right bank. Both roads are in excellent condition and follow the flow of the river closely. No bridges cross the Rhine between Mainz and Koblenz, but car ferries are available between Rüdesheim and Bingen, Lorch and Niederheimbach (Bacharach), Kaub and Oberwesel, St Goarhausen and St Goar, Kamp-Bornhofen and Boppard, and Oberlahnstein and Stolzenfels.

Frequent rail services are available on both sides of the Rhine. Riverboats connect virtually all towns as well.

Kaub (Right Bank)

The small town of Kaub is most famous for **Pfalzgrafenstein**, a small fortress that was built on an island in the Rhine in 1327 by Ludwig of Bavaria. Ludwig's spectacularly successful entry into the Rhine toll extortion business through this venture enraged even the Pope. Most of what is seen today dates from 1607 when the fortifications were strengthened. Visits to the castle, which is sparsely furnished, are possible but frankly not worth the effort. It is best seen from the distance of the riverbank. Open daily from 9 am to 12 and 2 to 5 pm, except closed on Monday and in December.

Along the main road through Kaub is a statue of Prussian Field Marshall Blücher, built to commemorate the crossing of the Rhine via pontoon bridge of the Prussian and Russian armies on New Year's Eve 1813/14. Napoleon, who was in Mainz at that stage, was caught off-guard and soon after departed for Elba. The small **Blüchermuseum**, Hotel Stadt Mannheim, Metzgergasse 6, ☎ 06774-222, is in the former headquarters of Blücher. It has mainly 19th-century military memorabilia and information on the historic crossing. It is open Monday to Sunday from April to October, 11 am to 4 pm, and from November to March, 2 to 5 pm. Admission is €2.

Other buildings along the Metzgerstraße are also beautifully preserved.

Where to Stay & Eat

Hotel Zum Turm is in a 300-year-old building next to a medieval tower. It is primarily known for its excellent rustic restaurant (€€-€€€), which serves nouvelle cuisine with French and Swiss influences, as well as local specialties. The hotel has only six bedrooms, which are large and comfortably furnished. Zollstraße 50, 56349 Kaub, ☎ 06774-92-200, fax 06774-922-011, www.rhein-hotel-turm.de. (€€)

Bacharach (Left Bank)

Bacharach on the left bank played an important role in the Rhine wine trade, but somehow managed to remain a small town. During the Thirty Years' War, Bacharach changed hands no fewer than eight times. It withstood the occupations and plundering, but in 1689 the French destroyed most of the town. The main road and railway cut the town off from the Rhine to some degree and the visitor has to access the town via narrow tunnels that connect the town with the parking areas at several points on the main road. It is strongly advised that you not drive into the town if on a short visit. It is possible to walk on the city fortifications next to the railway line but the view is somewhat disappointing.

St Peter's Church is a beautiful example of Late Rhine Romanesque. Although the nave is only 11-m (33 feet) long, it has a height of 17 m (56 feet). However, more interesting are the skeletal remains of the Gothic **Wernerkapelle** right behind and about 100 steps above the church. The history of this chapel goes back to 1287 when a young man, Werner, was found murdered on this spot. His death was blamed on a ritual killing by the local Jews and a pogrom followed. The chapel was built to house Werner's bones and became a pilgrimage chapel. About a century after the event, it was acknowledged that the evidence was faked and Werner was scrapped from the church calendar. High on the hill is **Burg Stahleck**. When the French blew up the castle in 1689, falling rock destroyed the Wernerkapelle, which was never restored. The castle was rebuilt in the 1920s and currently houses what must be one of the most beautiful youth hostels in Germany. It is worth climbing the steep stairs from the Wernerkapelle to the castle for the view. It is also possible to drive up to the castle – drive through the town towards Rheinböllen and then follow the signposting.

Where to Stay & Eat

The **Hotel Altkölnischer Hof** is in a half-timbered building near the Markt. Rooms are attractively furnished with natural wood. Some rooms have balconies. The wood-paneled restaurant (€€-€€€) serves local specialties. Blücherstraße 2, 55422 Bacharach, ☎ 06743-1339, fax 06743-2793, altkoelnischer-hof@t-online.de. (€€)

An interesting alternative is the **Landhaus Delle Hotel** in the hills above the town with excellent views. It is a modern designer-type hotel with only seven rooms. Rooms are comfortable, with elegant furniture and marble baths. The restaurant (€€€€) is only open to houseguests and serves gourmet food. The wine list has a thousand labels. Gutenfeldsstraße 16, Bacharach-Henschhausen, ☎ 06743-1765, fax 06743-1011, www.landhaus-delle-hotel.com. (€€€€)

Camping Sonnenstrand is about half a km from Bacharach on the banks of the Rhine. Facilities are limited and not the most modern, but the location is convenient. 55422 Bacharach, ☎ 06743-1752, fax 06743-3192, www.camping-sonnenstrand.de.

Oberwesel (Left Bank)

Oberwesel maintains 16 medieval towers and large sections of the original town walls. The two Gothic churches at the opposite ends of town are worth seeing. The early 14th-century Gothic

Liebfrauenkirche (Church of Our Dear Lady) has a characteristic red exterior. It has some interesting art works, including a Baroque organ and an early 14th-century wing altar. The **St Martinkirche** (St Martin's Church) is on a small hill. It is light in color and has interesting painted vaulting.

Where to Stay & Eat

The **Burg Hotel auf Schönburg** is one of the best hotels in the Rhine Valley. It is in the Schönburg Castle that dates back to the 11th century, with wonderful views of Kaub, Pfalz, and Burg Gutenfels. Rooms are comfortable and stylish. The restaurant (€€€-€€€€) serves international and regional cuisine. It is divided into several rooms and has a pleasant terrace. Reservations are recommended. Auf Schönburg, 55430 Oberwesel, ☎ 06744-93-930, fax 06744-1613, www.hotel-schoenburg.co, (€€€-€€€€)

Back in town, the 10-room **Hotel Weinhaus Weiler** is in a lovely half-timbered house. Rooms are comfortable and individually furnished in country-house style. The rustic restaurant (€-€€€) serves hearty local cuisine. Marktplatz 4, 55430 Oberwesel, ☎ 06744-7003, fax 06744-930-520, www.weinhaus-weiler.com (€€)

Also on the market square is the **Römerkrug** restaurant (€€-€€€) in a 15th-century half-timbered building and serving a wide range of dishes, including a good vegetarian selection. It also is a hotel, with seven simple bedrooms. The décor features exposed beams and solid furniture. Marktplatz 1, 55430 Oberwesel, ☎ 06744-7091, fax 06744-1677, roemerkrug@web.de. (€€-€€€)

St Goarhausen & the Loreley (Right Bank)

Shortly before reaching St Goarhausen, the Rhine turns sharply to the left and narrows to 113 m (370 feet), a third of its normal width. Here, a mighty rock, the Loreley, looms up 132 m (430 feet) and blocks the flow of the river, creating dangerous rapids that caused the demise of many a shipper and boat.

RHINE LEGEND - THE LORELEY

According to legend, the Loreley, a beautiful mermaid, sang from the rock, mesmerized navigators, and led them onto the rocks. Heinrich Heine, one of Germany's favorite romantic poets, wrote a poem about the Loreley, which was set to music by Friedrich Silchers and became one of the best-known, if slowest, of German folksongs. It is particularly popular in Japan, but known in many languages. Souvenir shops in the region sell postcards with the English translations – most of them terrible!

Just past the rock is a small parking lot and a winter harbor. At the far end of this land finger protruding into the Rhine is a small statue of the mermaid, with no artistic significance, erected in the 1960s as a commercial exercise. It is an uncomfortable walk to the end of the harbor and not really recommended – she can be seen well from the edge of the road farther downriver. It is possible to climb up via steep stairs to the top of the **Loreley rock**, but the less energetic can drive up via a well-marked road in St Goarhausen. The view from the top is splendid and highly recommended. The top of the rock is in private hands, but open at no charge to visitors, with a pleasant café-hotel available. The €1 parking fee is waived for patrons. The nearby Loreley Visitor's Center, a remnant of the ill-fated Expo2000, is best avoided.

Originally, St Goarhausen was just a couple of houses for the fishermen who caught mainly salmon for the market in St Goar. However, at the end of the 13th century the area came into the hands of the mighty Katzenelnbogen family through marriage. In 1371, they constructed Burg Neu-Katzenelnbogen, better known as

Burg Katz (Cat Castle) – the twin towers actually resemble the ears of a cat. The main purpose of this castle was to counter the newly constructed Burg Peterseck, built downriver by the archbishop of Trier. The mighty Burg Katz showed up the power relationship between the mighty and rich Katzenelnbogens and the rather weak archbishop, whose castle became known as Burg Maus (Mouse Castle). Burg Katz was destroyed by Napoleon in 1806, but rebuilt in the late 19th century. It is in private hands and currently a very exclusive hotel, ☎ 06771-1870.

Although the privately owned **Burg Maus**, ☎ 06771-7669, seems like a ruin, the interior is restored, furnished and well worth a visit. In addition, a falconry is in the castle with demonstrations during the summer season (see *Falconries* below).

Stranger than Fiction

Wine is important in most Rhine towns but in St Goarhausen it is taken to a new extreme. In the suburb Ehrenthal, the small Roman Catholic Church and a bar share the same roof! In fact, at one stage the only way to enter the church was through the bar. The local priest claimed there was no change in the congregation after the church obtained a separate entrance.

A lovely view is from the **Drei Bürgenblick** (Three Castles View) on the hill above St Goarhausen. From here, it is possible to see Burg Maus, Burg Katz, and Burg Rheinfels, as well as the Rhine Valley, of course. It is a 15-minute walk from the station or you can drive up to the viewing point.

St Goar & Burg Rheinfels (Left Bank)

Shortly before arriving in St Goar by car, the road makes a sharp turn to the left. At that point a large parking area and a garish collection of souvenir shops appear. This is the place to view and photograph the Loreley Rock on the opposite side of the river.

St Goar is a small town and suffers from Rhine mass tourism. Many restaurants are overpriced, with questionable quality food and most souvenir shops sell the same kind of junk. According to a major distributor of souvenirs, the Americans prefer decorative beer mugs and cuckoo clocks, although the latter are actually from the Black Forest region, the French and Italians prefer wine glasses, and the British want tea towels, which are in fact mostly produced in Britain. The largest cuckoo clock in the world, over three m (10 feet) high and two m (six feet) wide, hangs in the main road of St Goar. This cuckoo clock, dating from 1973, has two faces with cuckoos popping out on both sides every 30 minutes.

High above St Goar are the castle ruins of **Burg Rheinfels**, Schlossberg Straße, ☎ 06741-383, the mightiest fortress ever constructed on the banks of the Rhine. The original was built by Graf Dieter V von Katzenelnbogen in 1245. On completion, he did the obvious thing and increased toll charges. In response, 26 Rhine towns raised an army of 8,000 men and 1,000 knights, encircled the fortress for a year and 14 weeks before retreating in defeat. When the Katzenelnbogen family died out in 1479, the castle came into the hands of the Hessen family, who continued building work and constructed the mine tunnels, which allowed enemies to be surprised from below ground. These tunnels can still be visited, but require a flashlight. The French failed to conquer the castle in 1692 when a force of 18,000 with 10,000 backups faced a garrison of 3,000. Despite 10 days of artillery bombardments, the French had to retreat, with 4,000 dead and 6,500 wounded – eight times more than the Germans. A century later, in 1794, the coward commander fled before the advancing French army and the castle fell without a shot being fired. It was systematically blown up in following years, but reconstruction commenced in 1818.

Today the castle is still mostly in ruins, but well worth a visit. It houses an interesting museum with a large scale model of the original castle. Maps for self-guided tours are available at the entrance. The view from the castle over the Rhine Valley is absolutely stunning. The small restaurant at the castle serves excellent food, but for eating with a view, try the upmarket restaurant in the adjacent castle hotel. The castle is open daily from April to end October, 9 am to 6 pm. Admission is €3.

The parking lot at the castle is small and the hill very steep, making the motorized train, Burg-Express, that travels up the hill about four times per hour, well worth the expense. While waiting for the train in St Goar, check out the houses that mark the high-water levels of various Rhine floods.

Where to Stay & Eat

Schlosshotel and Villa Rheinfels is high above the town, attached to the ruins of the castle. The views of the Rhine Valley are incredible from both the bedrooms and restaurant. The rooms are individually furnished to a very high standard. The restaurant (€€-€€€) serves international and regional cuisine – reservations are recommended if you want a window seat. Schlossberg 47, 56329 St. Goar, ☎ 06741-8020, fax 06741-802-802, www.schlosshotel-rheinfels.de. (€€ single, €€€ double, €€€ suite)

Three km (1.8 miles) north of St Goar is the pleasant **Hotel Landsknecht**. It is right next to the Rhine and some of the comfortable bedrooms have river views. The rustic restaurant (€€-€€€) serves hearty local specialties. An der Rheinufer-Straße (B8), 56329 St Goar-Fellen, ☎ 06741-2011, fax 06741-7499, www.hotel-landknecht.de. (€€-€€€)

Camping

Camping Loreleyblick is on the banks of the Rhine, a km (.6 mile) south of the town with views of the Loreley rock. It is a bit old fashioned and has limited facilities. There are 200 spaces and it's open all year. 56329 St Goar, ☎ 06741-2066, fax 06741-7233, www.camping-loreleyblick.de.

Kamp-Bornhofen & the Enemy Brothers Castles (Right Bank)

Shortly before Kamp Bornhofen are two castles: **Burg Liebenstein**, ☎ 06773-308, and **Burg Sterrenberg**, ☎ 06773-323. These are commonly known as the enemy brothers' castles (*Feindlichen Brüder Schlösser*). A wall was built between the two to improve defenses. However, legend soon had it that the two brothers had a fight and built the wall, as they could not bear seeing each other. According to one version, one brother betrayed their sister, but more popular is the tale of a beautiful lady and an inevitable love-triangle. Both castles have cafés and excellent views.

Boppard (Left Bank)

Boppard is a lovely town – from the opposite bank of the river, it forms a beautiful panorama, as most of its buildings facing the Rhine are white.

The fourth-century Roman **Kastell** (Fort, above), Angertstraße, is the best-preserved Roman fort in Germany. Here, 55 m (170 feet) of the wall and two towers survive. The original structure was 308 by 154 meters (1,102 by 508 feet) and had 28 fortified towers. The site is freely accessible.

The two-tower, triple-nave **St Severuskirche** (St Severus Church), Marktplatz, from the 12th and 13th centuries, has fine Romanesque wall paintings. It is a good example of Late Rhineland Romanesque. Opening hours are daily, 10 am to 6 pm.

The **Local History Museum** is in the tower of the former **Kurtrierische Burg** (Trier Prince Electors' Fortress), An der Fähre, ☎ 06742-10-369. It has displays on local history as well as a large collection of wood furniture by Michael Thonet (1796-1871). The fortress was erected in the early 14th century by the archbishop of Trier to enforce his rule on the town and to enhance tolls collected on the Rhine. In contrast to other Rhine castles, this one is at river level and not in the hills. Opening hours are from April to October, Tuesday to Sunday, 10 am to noon and 2 to 5 pm. Admission is free.

A chairlift north of the town takes visitors in 20 minutes from the Mühltal to the Gedeonseck viewing point. From here, the Rhine's biggest horseshoe bend can be taken in. It is an easy walk to the so-called **Vierseenblick** (Four Lakes View). From this viewing point, the curves and hills make the Rhine appear like four lakes. The Sesselbahn (chairlift), ☎ 06742-2510, operates daily from April to October, 10 am to 5 pm, and from 9:30 am to 6:30 during the summer vacation season.

Where to Stay & Eat

The **Best Western Hotel Bellevue** is a grand hotel dating from 1887. This Art Nouveau building is on the banks of the Rhine in the heart of Boppard. Rooms are comfortable and most have river views. The **Chopin** (€€€-€€€€) is a gourmet restaurant, while **Le Bristol** (€€) serves mostly local specialties. Rheinallee 41, 56154 Boppard, ☎ 06742-1020, fax 06742-102-602, www.bellevue-boppard.de. (€€€)

The Marksburg (Right Bank)

The Marksburg castle is an impressive sight. It can be seen from afar perched on a small steep hill. The defense possibilities are obvious even to the untrained eye. This is the only castle along the Middle Rhine that was never conquered or destroyed. If you have time to visit only one castle along the Rhine, make it this one.

The Marksburg, 56338 Braubach, ☎ 02627-206, was erected mainly between the 12th and 14th centuries. It was intended as a refuge in times of war and was seldom occupied during peacetime. The building is generally in good, authentic condition. When entering, note how the main gate was made smaller so no man on a horse could enter. The view from the battery is phenomenal. The large herb garden has 170 different species, including poisonous ones. The impressive armory collection has items from 500 BC to the 15th century. A small 1450 breech-loader is one of the oldest cannons in Germany.

The interior can only be seen on a guided tour – ask for an English-language brochure when buying tickets. Opening hours are daily from Easter to October, 10 am to 5 pm, and November to Easter, 11 am to 4 pm. Admission is €4.50.

It is a rewarding walk from Braubach up to the Marksburg. Driving up is easier, but from the parking lot it is still quite a climb – either stairs or a steep access road – to reach the castle itself.

Koblenz

Koblenz is a town of 110,000 at the confluence of the Rhine and Mosel rivers. The Romans erected a castle here to defend this spot. From 1018 to 1798, Koblenz belonged to the archbishop of Trier, who often resided here. Koblenz was virtually destroyed during World War II, but partly rebuilt in the original style soon after.

The most famous sight is the **Deutsches Eck** (German Corner). It is the land tongue at the meeting of the Rhine and Mosel rivers, which is banked in concrete to resemble a battleship. A huge equestrian statue of Emperor Wilhelm I was erected here in 1897. At the end of World War II, this statue was destroyed and the pedestal left empty as a symbol of German division. After unification, a statue of Wilhelm I was again placed here. Pieces of the Berlin Wall are placed at the start of the Mosel Promenade. The name of this corner has nothing to do with 19th-century nationalism – it refers to the Teutonic Knights (Deutsche Orden) who constructed a seat here in 1216.

The **St Kastorkirche** (St Castor Church), Kastorhof, is a Romanesque basilica from 836. Its most famous moment was in 842 when Ludwig der Fromme (Louis the Pious) negotiated here the finer points of the Treaty of

Verdun that split Charlemagne's empire into what is now modern-day France and Germany. Most of the present building is from the 12th century, with elegant Gothic vaulting on top of squat Romanesque pillars. Opening hours are daily from 9 am to 6 pm.

The **Liebfrauenkirche** (Church of Our Dear Lady), Am Plan, is at the highest point of the old town. The church has Roman foundations, a Romanesque structure, a fine Gothic choir, and Baroque towers. It was mostly destroyed during World War II, but soon after rebuilt. Opening hours are daily from 8 am to 6 pm.

The mighty **Festung Ehrenbreitstein** (Fortress), ☎ 0261-974-2440, perched on a hill on the right bank of the Rhine, has been the most prominent building in town since the first castle was erected here a thousand years ago. The French destroyed the fortress during the Napoleonic era. After the town fell to Prussia in 1815, the fortress was expanded to one of the largest ever erected in Europe. It last saw military action in 1945 and is currently only used for peaceful purposes. There is a **Landesmuseum** (Local History Museum), ☎ 0261-97-030, with exhibitions on history and culture. The fortress affords the best views of the Koblenz old town, the Deutsches Eck, and the confluence of the two rivers. Opening hours for the museum and fortress are mid-March to mid-November daily, 9:30 am to 5 pm. Admission is €1.10 to the fortress and grounds or €3.30 for the grounds and museum. The fortress can be reached on Bus 9 from the old town. It can also be ascended by chairlift from Ehrenstein.

Schloss Stolzenfels (Castle), Koblenz-Stolzenfels, ☎ 0261-51-656, is in the southern suburbs of Koblenz. It is one of the best examples of Rhine Romanticism. The original castle was erected in the mid-13th century but destroyed by the French in 1689. The ruins were given to the Prussian crown prince in 1823. He had it reconstructed in a Neo-Gothic style with elements of all fashions since visible in the interior. It has period furniture, armor, and decorations. Opening hours are Tuesday to Sunday from 9 am but it closes at 4 pm from January to March, 6 pm from April to September, and 5 pm from October to November. Admission is €2.60, which includes the compulsory guided tour. The castle can be reached from Koblenz on Bus 6050. It is 15 minutes walk from the Rhine bank to the castle.

Where to Stay & Eat

Hotel Mercure is a modern hotel next to the conference center a few minutes stroll south of the old town. Rooms are comfortable and well-appointed – some have Rhine views. Julius-Wegeler-Straße 6, 56068 Koblenz, ☎ 0261-1360, fax 0261-136-1199, www.mercure.com. (€€-€€€)

On the opposite bank of the Rhine is the comfortable **Diehls Hotel**. Rooms are stylish and some are large. All have Rhine views. The **Clemens** restaurant (€€-€€€) serves international and regional cuisine and offers wonderful views of the river. Am Pfaffendorder Tor 10 (access from the B10 via Emser Straße), 56068 Koblenz-Ehrnebreitstein, ☎ 0261-97-070, fax 0261-970-7213, www.diehls-hotel.de. (€€-€€€)

The modern **Continental-Pfälzer Hof** is at the Hauptbahnhof. Rooms are comfortable and well-equipped, with the business traveler in mind. The restaurant **Bossa Nova** (€€) serves German and Brazilian cuisine. Bahnhofplatz 1, 56068 Koblenz, ☎ 0261-30-160, fax 0261-301-610, www.contihotel.de. (€€-€€€)

The nearby **Hohenstaufen Hotel** shares the same convenient location. Rooms are comfortable and furnished in either rustic or modern style. Emil-Schüler-Straße 41, 56068 Koblenz, ☎ 0261-30-140, fax 0261-301-4444, www.hohenstaufen.de. (€€)

The **Ibis Hotel** is in the same area but even closer to the old town. Rooms are modern and functionally furnished. Rizzastraße 42, 56068 Koblenz, ☎ 0261-302-40, fax 0261-302-4240, www.ibishotel.com. (€-€€)

The Loup De Mer restaurant, Neustadt 12, ☎ 0261-16-138, is in the Schlossrondell. It serves mainly fish. (€€-€€€€)

Camping

Camping Rhein-Mosel is ideally located across the Rhine River from Festung Ehrenbreitstein and across the River Mosel from the Deutsche Eck. It has reasonably good facilities and many shady spots. There are 200 spaces and it's open from April to late October. A passenger ferry service is available to the old town area.

Schartwiesenweg, 56070 Koblenz, ☎ 0261-82-719, fax 0261-802-489.

Cultural Events

Concert Series

The **Mittelrhein Musik Momente** (Middle Rhine Music Moments), www.musikmomente.de, is a series of concerts held during summer in the Loreley Valley. Many events are staged in open-air venues. Information and reservations are available from most tourist information offices in the valley.

The **Loreley Freilichtbühne** (Open Air Theater), www.loreley-klassik.de, Tickethotline ☎ 0180-500-0511, is one of the best-known in Germany. It offers a wide range of events, ranging from rock to opera.

Knights' Tournament

Many of the castles of the Rhine were occupied by knights during the Middle Ages and served as dens for robber barons. A special knights' tournament (Rittertournier) and market is held at Burg Rheinfels at the end of May and beginning of June.

Fireworks - Rhein in Flammen

Each year, huge fireworks displays are held along the Rhine in events known as "Rhine in Flames." Reservations for seats on the flotilla of up to 70 boats must be made months in advance and thousands of spectators line the banks of the river. The schedule is as follows:

- First Saturday in May: Linz to Bonn – Night of the Bengal Lights
- First Saturday in July: Bingen and Rüdesheim – Magic Fire-Lit Night
- Second Saturday in August: Spay/Braubach to Koblenz – The Mega-night – eight fireworks displays in 90 minutes stretched over 17 km (10 miles)
- Second Saturday in September: Oberwesel – Night of a Thousand Fires – music accompanies the fireworks display
- Third Saturday in September: St Goar and St Goarhausen – Loreley Night

Adventures in the Loreley Valley

On Foot

Boppard has guided **old town walks** on Tuesday at 2 pm from April to October. English-language tours are available in July and August at 3 pm on Wednesday.

Hiking paths abound on both sides of the Rhine and in the surrounding hills and valleys. A special pedestrian and cycling way runs practically the full length of the Rhine from Bingen to Koblenz. On the left bank long stretches of walkways and cycling routes exist but these are not completely continuous.

The **Rhein-Wein-Wanderpfad** (Rhine Wine Walking Route, marked with "RP") is 52 km (31 miles) from Kaub to Bornhofen along the edge of the Rhine Valley hills.

On Wheels

Like walking, **cycling** has been popular in the Rhine Valley for decades. Lots of hotels participate in a scheme where luggage is forwarded to your next destination for a nominal fee. Many cycling and walking routes share the same road space

On the left bank of the Rhine, a cycling route runs the full distance from Bingen to Koblenz, with only a minimal part on public roads. Cycling distances are as follows:

From Bingen (left bank):

15 km/nine miles . . . . Bacahrach
seven km/4.2 miles. . . . . Oberwesel
11 km/6.6 miles. . . . . St Goar
five km/three miles. . . . . Bad Salzig
19 km/11 miles . . . . Boppard
19 km/11 miles. . . . . Koblenz

From Rüdesheim (right bank):

seven km/4.2 miles. . . . . Lorch
nine km/5.4 miles . . . . Kaub
11 km/6.6 miles . . . . St Goarhausen
12 km/7.2 miles. . . . . . . Kamp-Bornhofen
14 km/8.4 miles . . . . Braubach
four km/2.4 miles . . . . Lahnstein

Much of the right bank cycling is on public roads, with the stretch near Rüdesheim particularly dangerous.

In addition to the Rhine Valley, the adjacent hills and valleys are also popular cycling territory. A particularly popular option is to take the **Hunsrückbahn**, the steepest normal train route in Germany, from **Boppard** to **Emmelshausen** and cycle along a 10-km/six-mile almost flat road on the top of the Hunsrück mountain range to **Pfalzfeld**. Return via the same route or cycle down to the Rhine along steep curves.

Bicycles can be rented in most towns, often from the station or from many hotels. In Rhineland-Palatinate, bicycles can be taken for free on local trains after 9 am on weekdays and all day on weekends plus for free on most boats. The KD lines offer two for the price of one on Tuesdays for one-way tickets if both travelers have bicycles with them.

On Water

Fishing is allowed along some stretches of the Rhine, but requires a license. Currently, 63 species are recorded in the Rhine and, as water quality improves, the number is increasing. In St Goarhausen, contact **Opticus Schmidt** at Marktplatz 3, ☎ 06771-7577. In St Goar, **Nagelschmidt**, An der Loreley 9, ☎ 06741-7737. In other areas, inquire at the local tourist office.

FACTS STRANGER THAN FICTION

Up to the 18th century, St Goarhausen, where the Rhine was once 94 feet deep, was considered one jof the best places to catch fresh-water salmon. The fish was so plentiful and cheap that household servants made it an employment condition that they were not forced to eat salmon more than three times a week. Salmon only recently returned to the Rhine with almost 2,000 adults recorded at Koblenz.

Years of strict environmental rules in Germany saw the Rhine's water improve to bathing quality. That said, swimming in the Rhine is not encouraged and is rather dangerous, especially in the Loreley Valley, due to the strong currents and sudden deepening of the water. However, in summer when the water levels are at their lowest, sand banks emerge that are used by locals as **beaches**. None of them are officially marked, but a sudden group of cars parked along the road is a clear sign.

Pleasure **cruises** on the Rhine have been popular since the 19th century. Although it is possible to take cruises lasting several days, more popular and affordable are day-trips lasting from less than an hour to a full day. Boats operate generally from April to October, with the main season between May and September. Several companies ply the Rhine route but the most established is **Köln-Düsseldorf**, better known simply as **KD**, Frankenwerft 35, 50667 Cologne, ☎ 0221-208-8318, www.k-d.com. It is sometimes possible to do the whole route from Mainz to Cologne, but the stretch between Rüdesheim and Koblenz is particularly popular, with many daily departures. If time is limited, the best part of the route is between **Kaub** or **Oberwesel** and **St Goar** or **St Goarhausen** – this part includes the Loreley. KD has several special rates, including free trips on birthdays, half-price for over 60s on Monday and Friday, and two for the price of one on Tuesday if two bicycles are taken with you. (Bicycles are always transported for free.) Passengers arriving on DB railways receive 20% discount.

Local companies are often slightly cheaper than KD, but they have fewer departures and fewer stops where journeys may be interrupted.

Wildlife

Although some of the castles along the Rhine were bought by Prussian nobles in the 19th century as hunting lodges, wildlife along the Rhine is limited despite the thick-forested areas. However, **Burg Maus** in St Goarhausen-Wellmich, ☎ 06771 7669, www.burg-maus.de, has an interesting **falconry**. From mid-March until early October, one-hour demonstrations are held of sea and stone eagles, kites, and falcons flying freely over the Rhine Valley. Flying demonstrations take place daily at 11 am and 2:30 pm as well as 4:30 pm on Sundays and holidays. Entry is €6.50. It is 20-minute walk from the parking lot to the castle.

The Mosel Valley

The 545-km (325-mile) Mosel River is one of the longest tributaries of the

Rhine. It is a meandering river with a steep valley often more dramatic than the wider Rhine. Like the Rhine, its valleys are planted with vines and castles lurk at every twist and turn. Driving through the valley is slow, due to all the river curves, but rewarding. The natural beauty of the valley is awesome and many picture-perfect villages are strewn along the way.

Close to the confluence of the Mosel and the Rhine in Koblenz, is **Burg Eltz**, the loveliest castle in Germany. **Cochem** is a famous town with an impressive Historicist castle. The wine towns **Zell**, **Traben-Trarbach**, and **Bernkastel-Kues** are several twists and turns farther upriver.

Trier is at the far end of the Mosel, where the river enters Germany from France and forms part of the German-Luxemburg border. It is 192 river km (115 miles) from Koblenz. The city was founded by the Romans and has the largest collection of Roman monuments in Germany. Apart from Koblenz, Trier is the only large city on the banks of the Mosel. It is slightly off the main tourist routes but easy to reach and well worth the effort.

■ Information Sources

Tourist Office: Information on the Mosel is available from **Mosellandtouristik**, Postfach 1310, 54463 Bernkastel-Kues, ☎ 06531-2091, www.mosellandtouristik.de.

■ Transportation

In the Mosel Valley, hourly or more frequent **trains** run from Koblenz to Trier. The faster trains take 90 minutes and the local trains two hours. All stop in Cochem but only the Regional Bahn (RB) trains stop in Moselkern and other smaller towns. The trains follow the flow of the river from Koblenz to Cochem, but after that, Trier is the next Mosel town on the main line. **Buses** are available to smaller towns

Driving is a pleasant option – keep following the main route as it crosses the river several times. The meandering of the Mosel and the wide curves make for slow progress. If in a hurry, use the Autobahn A48 between Koblenz and Trier, but do not expect any river views en route.

Boat excursions are popular and are the best way to enjoy the valley. Progress is slow, however, and boats are used for excursions rather than actual transportation. See *Adventures* below for details.

■ The Lower Mosel Valley

Burg Eltz

The most beautiful medieval castle in all of Germany is Burg Eltz, 56204 Burg Eltz, Münstermaifeld, ☎ 02672-950-500, www.burg-eltz.de. It is in a small side-valley near Moselkern. Parts of the castle date back to 1160, but building work continues to the present day. Three branches of the Eltz family built their dwellings in the castle complex, but the whole castle has been owned by the Golden Lion branch of the family since 1815. In the courtyard, the three buildings in different architectural styles can easily be distinguished.

The castle is full of period furniture and decorations. In contrast to other castles, Burg Eltz has 20 flushable toilets that date back to the 15th century. (The splendid Palace of Versailles, by contrast, has none.) Parts of the building are Gothic with original ornamentation. The late medieval kitchen also survived. The interior can only be seen on a guided tour (usually in German only, but an excellent flyer in English is available.) The treasury has some family heirlooms and can be seen without a tour. Opening hours are daily from April to October, 9:30 am to 5:30 pm. Admission is €6 and €2.50 for the treasury.

Getting to the castle can be challenging. The easiest is by car. If approaching from the Autobahn A48, take the Mayen off-ramp towards Münstermaifeld. From the Mosel road B416, turn off at Hatzneport. From Münstermaifeld, follow the signs to the Schloss – a parking lot is available at the Antoniuskapelle past Wald Wierschem. From here, it is an 800-m (2,900-foot) walk. A shuttle bus is available for part of the journey. Although the inclines are steep, the route is on a paved road.

A more interesting approach is from the small town of Moselkern on the Mosel River. Use the parking lot Ringelsteiner Mühle and hike through the lovely Eltzbachtal (Eltz Stream Valley) – an easy 35-minute walk. This is also the standard approach when arriving by train or boat.

Cochem

Cochem is a picture-perfect Mosel town, with lovely half-timbered houses, a few surviving medieval defense towers and city gates, as well as a huge castle. It is hugely popular with tourists and can get busy during the summer and Advent.

The main sight is the **Reichsburg Cochem**, Schlossstraße 36, ☎ 02671-255, www.reichsburg-cochem.de, which towers over the old town. Its history dates back to around AD 1000, but only a small part of the original keep survived. It was an imperial property (*Reichsgut*) up to 1294, when the emperor pawned it to the bishop of Trier. The French destroyed it in 1689 and the current Neo-Gothic building with ample towers and turrets was constructed in the late 19th century. Opening hours are mid-March to mid-October daily from 9 am to 5 pm. The 40-minute guided tour in German (leaflets in English are available) is the only way to see the interior. Admission is €4.

Where to Stay & Eat

The **Hotel Alte Thorschenke** is at the start of the pedestrian zone in an interesting building dating from 1332. Rooms are comfortable and use period furniture, including some four-poster beds. The wood-paneled restaurant (€€-€€€€) serves international and regional cuisine. Brückenstraße 3, 56812 Cochem, ☎ 02671-7059, fax 02671-4202, www.castle-thornschenke.de. (€€-€€€)

The **Moselromantik-Hotel Thul** is in the vineyards above the town. It is a modern hotel with comfortable rooms, some with balconies and views of the Reichsburg. The rustic restaurant (€€) serves classical and local dishes. Brauselaystraße 27, 56812 Cochem-Cond, ☎ 02671-914-150, fax 02671-9141-5144, www.hotel-thul.de. (€€-€€€)

Two km (1.2 miles) northwest of Cochem is the **Moselromantik-Silencehotel Weißmühle**. It is partly in an old mill. Rooms are in either country-house style or more rustic, with farmhouse-type furniture. A thick forest surrounds the hotel, a world away from the crowds that sometimes clog the Mosel towns. The restaurant (€€-€€€) serves classic and local cuisine. Im Enderttal, 56812 Cochem, ☎ 02671-8955, fax 02671-8207, www.weissmuehle.de. (€€-€€€)

In town, a great place to dine is the **Lohspeicher – L'Auberge du Vin**. This elegant restaurant (€€€) serves nouvelle cuisine with strong Mediterranean influences. It also has nine comfortable, modern rooms. Obergasse 1, 56812 Cochem, ☎ 02671-3976, fax 08671-1772, www.lohspeicher.de. (€€-€€€)

Camping

Camping am Freizeitzentrum is a pleasantly located campsite about 1.2 km (.7 mile) upstream from Cochem, with many shady spots and good sports facilities nearby. It is open from April to October and has about 300 spaces. 56812 Cochem-Cond,

☎ 02671-4409, fax 02671-910-719, www.campingplatz-cochem.de.

Bernkastel-Kues

Bernkastel-Kues is a small town with beautiful half-timbered houses. It is also the largest single wine-growing region in Germany. Some 95% of the grapes are Riesling.

Bernkastel is on the right bank. The most picturesque sight is the **Marktplatz** with the 17th-century Michaelsbrunnen (Michael Fountains) and Renaissance Rathaus (Town Hall). The ruins of **Burg Landshut** tower over the town. This 11th-century castle belonged to the archbishop of Trier, but has been in ruins since the French destroyed it in the 17th century. The views are worth the climb.

On the left bank is Kues. The 15th-century **St Nikolaus Hospital** is here, with a chapel and cloisters. It also houses the the **Weinkulturelles Zentrum** (Wine Cultural Center), Cusanusstraße 2, ☎ 06531-4141, www.mosel-vinothek.de, with the Mosel-Weinmuseum (Mosel Wine Museum) and a vinothek in the original vaulted cellars. The vinothek allows visitors to sample some 130 local labels. Opening hours are daily from November to mid-April, 2 to 5 pm, and from mid-April to October, 10 am to 5 pm. Admission is €2 for the museum and €9, including sampling, for the vinothek.

Where to Stay & Eat

Hotel Zur Post is close to the center of Bernkastel. Rooms are comfortable and elegant. Some rooms have views of the ruins of Burg Landshut. The **Poststube** restaurant (€-€€) serves mostly regional cuisine and has a long wine list. Gestade 17, 54470 Bernkastel-Kues, ☎ 06531-6531, fax 06531-967-050, www.hotel-zur-post-bernkastel.de. (€€)

The **Hotel Panorama** is in a quiet neighborhood in Kues next to the forest. Rooms are comfortable and well-equipped, with attention to detail. Rebschulweg 48, 54470 Bernkastel-Kues, ☎ 06531-3061, fax 06531-94-214. (€-€€)

There are many restaurants and cafés in the region, but for excellent food try the **Rotisserie Royale**, Burgstraße 19, ☎ 06531-6572. This rustic restaurant serves nouvelle cuisine with strong Mediterranean influences. It seats only 30, making reservations advisable. (€€-€€€)

Camping

Camping Schenk is a small site with 50 tourist and 50 long-term spaces. It has many shady spots and is surrounded by vineyard-covered hills. Wine from the owner's own estate is available. Facilities are good. It is open from mid-April to October. 54470 Bernkastel-Wehlen, ☎ 06531-8176, fax 06531-7681, www.camping-schenk.de.

Cultural Events & Festivals

The **Moselfestwochen** (Mosel Music Festival), Im Kurpark, 54470 Bernkastel-Kues, ☎ 06531-30000, www.moselfestwochen.de, takes place from May to October at various venues in the Mosel Valley. The music ranges from medieval to modern, but the preferred venues are historic locations in the Mosel Valley.

A **medieval festival** is held in the Reichsburg in Cochem, usually on the first weekend of August. Medieval handcrafts, cooking, fighting, and fashion are demonstrated. Dress medieval for reduced admission fees.

Adventures

On Foot

The Mosel is a popular hiking area. The **Moselhöhenweg (Mosel Heights Trail)** goes the full length of the German Mosel on both banks through the hills rather than the valley. The views are generally breathtaking.

Multi-day trips including accommodations and luggage transfers can be arranged by **Mosellandtouristik**, Gestade 18a, Bernkastel-Kues, ☎ 06531-3075, www.mosellandtoursitik.de.

On Wheels

Many **long-distance cycling** routes are in the direct vicinity of the Mosel. Very popular is the route in the valley itself – the 275-km (165-mile) **Moselradweg** (Mosel Cycling Route) is from Thonville in France to Koblenz. It is mostly on dedicated, level cycling routes. Public transportation connections make cycling short parts of the route easy. Full seven-day cycling trips on this route can be arranged by **Mosellandtouristik**, Gestade 18a, Bernkastel-Kues, ☎ 06531-3075, www.mosellandtoursitik.de.

Three challenging **mountain biking** routes are in the Traben-Trarbach region. The **Weinberg-Steillagen-Tour** (Wine Hills) is 12 km (7.2 miles) with a 400-m (1,300-foot) altitude difference. The **Zwei-Täler-Tour** (Two Valleys Tour) is 20 km (12 miles) with a 550-m (1,810-foot) altitude difference. Even more challenging is the 40-km (24-mile) **Drei-Täler-Tour** (Three Valleys Tour). All have breathtaking views and pass medieval castles, ruins, pretty towns, and other cultural sights. Four-hour guided mountain biking tours are arranged from March to October on Sunday at 10 pm by **Fahrradladen Camphausen Bikes & More**, ☎ 06541-3276, for details.

Many hotels have bicycles available for guests, but rentals are also available from **Fahrradshop Kreutz**, Ravenéstraße 42, Cochem, ☎ 02671-91-131, and **Fun Bike Team**, Schanzstraße 22, Bernkastel-Kues, ☎ 06531-94-024.

In the Air

Hot-air balloon flights in the Mosel Valley can be arranged by **Moseltouristik**, Gestade 18a, Bernkastel-Kues, ☎ 06531-3075, www.mosellandtoursitik.de. Weekday and morning flights are cheaper than afternoon and weekend flights.

On Water

Fishing is allowed in the Mosel and in much of the surrounding waters. A permit is required and generally available from the local tourist offices.

Motor boat rentals are available from **Angela Medilinger & Robert Mattern**, Moselstraße, 54347 Neumagen-Dhron (near Bernkastel-Kues), ☎ 06507-701-670. Some, but not all, boats require sport boat licenses.

Kayaks and **canoes** can be rented from **Moseltourts Kanu-Charter**, Königstraße 3, 54538 Kinheim, ☎ 06532-94-320, www.kanu-xxl.de, and from **Edgar Welter**, Römerstraße 38, 54498 Piesport, ☎ 06507-5558.

Several companies arrange **riverboat excursions** on the Mosel. The season is generally from May to October. Most operate only on certain parts of the river. Due to the meandering of the river and several locks, a complete cruise from Koblenz to Trier would take 16 hours and no company currently provides a complete one-day trip.

- **Hans Michels & Mosel-Schiffstoursitik**, Goldbachstraße 52, ☎ 06531-6897, www.mosel-schiffstouristik.de, has up to five daily cruises from Bernkastel-Kues to Traben-Trarbach. The journey takes two hours each way, with several stops en route.
- **Gebr. Kolb**, 56820 Briedern, ☎ 06673-1515, has up to six daily excursions between Bernkastel-Kues and Traben-Trarbach. It also has frequent services from Traben-Trarbach to Cochem – four hours. Services to Trier are also available.
- **Köln-Düsseldorfer (KD)**, ☎ 02671-980-023 (Cochem) or ☎ 0261-31-030 (Koblenz), www.k-d.com, has one daily excursion between Koblenz and Cochem, taking five hours each way. Mosselkern (Burg Eltz) is three hours from Koblenz.

■ Trier

Trier is Germany's oldest city. Archeological finds of Celtic settlements show people living here as far back as 2000 BC. Even in terms of written history, it is the oldest, having been founded in 16 BC by the Romans as *Augusta Treverorum*.

Trier was mainly a residential city at the start and was overrun in 274 AD by invading Germanic tribes. It was re-conquered by the Romans, rebuilt in an even grander style, leading to its description as a Second Rome. Trier became an imperial residential city under Constantine (306-337) and functioned as the capital of Germany, Gaul, Spain and Britain. Continued waves of attacks by Germanic tribes forced the

Imperial family to return to Italy and the city itself finally succumbed to the Franks by the end of the fifth century.

Constantine made Trier the first See in Germany (314) and, about 500 years later, Charlemagne upgraded it to a full archbishopric. The archbishop of Trier was a Prince Elector and therefore an important religious and political figure in the Holy Roman Empire. Trier briefly became French in the aftermath of the French Revolution, but has been part of Prussia, and then modern Germany, since 1815.

The most impressive sights in Trier are the Roman ruins, with the most extensive collection north of the Alps, but there are some architectural treasures from later periods as well. The town's most famous son is the economist and philosopher Karl Marx.

Modern Trier is a city of 100,000 inhabitants on the banks of the Mosel River. It is close to the border with the Grand Duchy of Luxemburg and the proximity to France also influenced local cuisine, style, and language. Trier is a major exporter of wine, but the tourist-oriented wine trade here is much less in your face than in other Mosel Valley towns.

Information Sources

Tourist Office: Tourist Information Trier, An der Porta Nigra, 54290 Trier, ☎ 0651-978-080, www.trier.de.

Transportation

Trier is a bit off the beaten track but not difficult to get to. By **car**, it can be reached via Autobahns from Koblenz, but the local roads on the banks of the Mosel are much more pleasant, if slow. **Trains** usually require a changeover at Koblenz or Saarbrücken. If arriving by **air**, it is only 30 minutes to Luxemburg's airport or an hour by car from Frankfurt-Hahn. Many **boats** also call here.

Trier has a good public transportation network using both trains and buses. Although all the main sights are within walking distance, buses are useful for reaching the outlying sights. From Easter to October, the **Trier Tour** runs half-hourly buses to 16 of the main sights. It costs €5.60.

DISCOUNT TICKETS

Day passes for the Trier bus network are €4.15 for the inner city and €5.55 for the entire network.

The **Trier Card** gives unlimited access to inner city buses for three days and discounts to museum and other admissions. It costs €9, or €15 for two adults with children.

Sightseeing

The four-story **Porta Nigra** (Black Gate) is the largest Roman building in Germany and one of the best-preserved. It dates back to 180 AD and is a UNESCO World Cultural Heritage site. As part of the city's defenses, it has a set of double gates with an inner courtyard, leaving potential attackers exposed to assault from above and from all sides. The building is constructed out of sandstone blocks, weighing up to six tons each, colored black from centuries of pollution. It was built without mortar and some of the original iron clamps attached with lead to the stone can still be seen. Note the holes in the stones where clamps were dug out during the Middle Ages when people recycled the lead.

Did you know? The Porta Nigra owes its survival to a Greek monk, Simeon, who lived as a hermit in the gate. After he was declared a saint, two churches were constructed in the gate in the 11th century, thereby preventing locals from recycling the building material as had happened at many other ruins. Both churches were torn down and the gate restored on the orders of Napoleon, but traces of the church decorations can still be seen on some upper floors. A spiral staircase leads all the way to the fourth floor, which has fine views of the city and surrounding hills.

ROMAN SITES IN TRIER

Trier has the largest collection of Roman ruins north of the Alps. The five major sites are the **Porta Nigra**, the **Amphitheater**, the **Imperial Baths**, the **Thermal Baths** under Viehmarkt, and the **Barbara Baths**. Admission is €2.10 to each or €6.20 for a combination ticket valid for one year. The superb Landesmuseum is unfortunately not included and entry to the Basilika is free. Opening hours are daily from 9 am to 6 pm (closing 5 pm from October to March). The Thermal Baths under Viehmarket always close at 5 pm and remain closed on the first working day of the week. If time is limited, give preference to the first three sites. For more information, contact the tourist office, ☎ 0651-978-0820 or www.burgen-rlp.de.

Next to the Porta Nigra is the **Städtisches Museum Simeonstift** (Municipal Museum in the Simeon's College), Simeonstiftplatz, ☎ 0651-718-1450, www.museum-trier.de. Parts of the building date back to the 11th century, with the original oak floor of 1060 still being used in the cloisters. The museum mainly features exhibits relating to Trier from the Middle Ages to the present. It also has more than 300 Coptic textiles dating from the third to the ninth century. The museum is open daily from April to October, 9 am to 5 pm. From November to March, it is open Tuesday to Friday, 9 am to 5 pm and 9 am to 3 pm on weekends. Admission is €2.60.

From here, stroll down Simeonstraße, a major shopping street, to the **Hauptmarkt**. En route, note the Early Gothic **Dreikönigenhaus** (1230), now a café. The cross in the center of Hauptmarkt dates from 958 when the town obtained the right to hold a market. The magnificent gables of buildings facing the market are from all ages. On the corner with Dietrichstraße are two medieval-looking buildings rebuilt in 1970 after being destroyed during World War II. The older building with arcades is the **Steipe**, a former town hall, and adjacent is the **Rotes Haus** (Red House) still bearing its 17th-century inscription: "ANTE ROMAM TREVIRIS STETIT ANNIS MILLE TRECENTIS – There was life in Trier 1,600 years before Rome even existed." Also on Hauptmarkt is the early 15th-century **St Gangolf** church. Its 62-m (200-foot) tower was once the highest in town but one of the towers of the nearby cathedral was raised one story to regain that status. The **Löwen-Apotheke** has a Baroque façade but, founded in 1241, it is the oldest pharmacy in Germany.

The fortress-like **Dom** (Cathedral, above), Domfreihof, ☎ 0651-979-0790, www.trierer-dom.de, was built on the site of the former Constantinian Palace. The palace was destroyed in 330 after the Emperor's last visit and replaced by the largest Christian church in antiquity, which was about four times the size of the current cathedral. Note the large pillar, the Domstein, at the main entrance, which was part of the Roman church. The Roman church was destroyed in the fifth and ninth centuries, but the central sections can still be seen with some parts of the original Roman walls, up to 26 m (85 feet) high, incorporated into the 11th-century Romanesque building. Although most of the current structure is Romanesque, the cathedral incorporates, not always smoothly, 1,650 years of architectural styles. Most of the somewhat restrained interior decorations are Baroque, with interesting altarpieces. The cathedral has a small treasury with gold and silver works and ivory carvings. The prize relic is Christ's seamless robe.

When the cathedral is busy with visitors, the **cloisters** can offer a remarkable respite – partly because entry is the last of a series of no-entry doors at the right front of the cathedral. It has a few panels illustrating the floor plans and development through the centuries of the cathedral complex. The Dom is open daily from 6:30 am to 6 pm (5:30 pm from November to March). Admission is free, except for €1.50 to see the treasury.

In contrast to the dark interior of the cathedral, the adjacent **Liebfrauen-**

kirche (Church of Our Lady, to the right in the picture on previous page), ☎ 0651-979-0790, www.trierer-dom.de, shows the advances Gothic church architecture made to allow natural light into the building. It was built between 1235 and 1260 on the original southern part of the Roman church as one of the first fully Gothic churches in Germany. Its floor plan is a Greek cross with two smaller chapels between each of the larger apsidal ones. It gives the impression of a round shape, sometimes described as a rose with 12 petals. Opening hours are daily from 8 am to noon and 2 to 6 pm. Admission is free.

The Oldest Gothic Church in Germany

Many Romanesque churches in Germany had later Gothic additions in an attempt to modernize and obtain some of the allure of the newer style. The cathedrals of Mainz and Worms are good examples. Others added some Gothic elements at the time of construction but remained Romanesque in their main structure, such as the magnificent cathedral of Limburg. The title for first completely Gothic church is being disputed by St Elizabeth in Marburg (1234-85) and Liebfrau in Trier (1235-60). Construction of St Elizabeth started first, but the Liebfrau in Trier was completed earlier. In addition, its airiness is much closer to the spirit of the Gothic ideal.

North of the Dom is the **Bischöflichen Museum** (Bishop's Museum), Windstraße 6-8, ☎ 0651-710-5255, www.museum.bistum-trier.de. Not surprisingly, the main treasures here are archeological finds from the Roman church and other sites in the region. Highlights include a 60,000-stone mosaic found three m (10 feet) under the crossing of the church and presumed to have been part of Constantine's Palace. Further exhibits include sacral art from the Middle Ages to the present, including robes, gold and silversmith works, as well as original statues from the Liebfrauenkirche. Opening hours are Monday to Saturday, 9 am to 5 pm, Sundays and holidays, 1 to 5 pm; closed on Mondays from November to March. Admission is €2.

A few minutes stroll down Liebfraustraße is the second-largest single-room structure from Roman times, the **Basilika** or **Römische Palastaula**, which currently houses the Protestant church Zum Erloeser (Our Savior), Konstantinplatz, ☎ 0651-42-570. The pillar-less room was the throne room of Emperor Constantine and is an impressive 27 m (90 feet) wide, 33 m (108 feet) high, and 67 m (220 feet) long. The windows narrow progressively toward the center of the building to create the optical illusion of the hall being even bigger. The original art and hollow floor heating system was lost after the Franks invaded and settled for some time in the roofless ruin. It was later used by the archbishop of Trier, then, since the mid-19th century, after Trier became part of Prussia, as the first Protestant church in this predominantly Catholic city. Decorations are limited, but note the organ pipes in the front window and the beautifully coffered wooden ceiling. From April to October, opening hours are daily, 10 am to 6 pm, except Sunday from noon to 6 pm. Visiting the church from November to March is more of a challenge; then it is open Tuesday to Saturday, 11 am to noon and 3 to 4 pm; Sundays from noon to 1 pm. Admission is free.

Adjacent is the magnificent Rococo **Kurfürsteliche Palais** (Electoral Palace), ☎ 0651-9494-202. The north and east wings are the older parts and date from 1615, but the south wing, which was remodeled in 1756 by Johannes Seiz with sculptures crafted by Ferdinand Tietz, is the real highlight. Unfortunately, the Palace is used as administrative offices and not generally open to the public. The exterior of the south wing can be admired from the lovely Baroque palace gardens. Admission is free.

The **Rheinische Landesmuseum** (Archeological Museum), Weimarer Allee 1, ☎ 0651-97-740, www.landesmuseum-trier.de, has the largest collection of Roman artifacts in Germany and perfectly

Silver denier of Trajan, 108 AD

complements a tour of the larger ruins in the town. Highlights include several Roman burial monuments and mosaics. Rather unusual for a museum, one of the mosaics is still displayed and used as a floor, allowing visitors to admire it up close. City models explain Trier in Roman times, with several rooms dedicated to religion and ancient wine culture. A reconstruction of the 23-m high (75-foot) Iglerer Säule, a grave monument near Trier, confirms that the Roman color taste might now be considered kitsch. Some non-Roman finds, including Stone Age, Celtic and Merovingian, plus a few Renaissance and Baroque rooms, round off the display. The museum is open weekdays from 9:30 to 5 pm (but closed on Mondays from November to April) and 10:30 am to 5 pm on weekends. Free English-language audio guides are available. Admission is €5.50.

At the edge of the Baroque garden is the **Kaiserthermen** (Imperial Baths, above),

which were constructed 1,600 years ago as one of the largest such complexes in the civilized world. It is possible to descend into the subterranean labyrinth of the engineering feat that provided the hot water for one of the major social rituals of Roman life. The original hot water bath was large enough for its remains to be used for opera and theater performances, with seats for 650 spectators. Cold water was heated in six boiler rooms, of which four are still distinguishable, to 40°C/104°F. A hollow floor system was used to heat the entire complex.

A good 10 minutes walk uphill, is the Roman **Amphitheatre**, originally just outside the city, with the town walls actually running along the highest level of the west pavilion. It was used for popular entertainment such as gladiator fights and execution by wild animals. During the Middle Ages, it became a quarry but much of the original remained. It had a seating capacity of 20,000 and is still sometimes used for open-air concerts. It is possible to climb up to the highest levels for fine views, or to descend to the subterranean level in the center of the stadium where prisoners and animals were held.

Near the River Mosel, the **Barbarathermen** (Barbara Baths) were built in the second century as the largest Roman-bathing complex at that time. Its ruins were used as a castle in the Middle Ages, but torn down in the 17th century when the building material was recycled to build a college. Only the foundations and subterranean service tunnels survived to the present day. To date, about a third of the complex has been excavated.

The **Römerbrücke** (Roman Bridge) is the oldest bridge in Germany (AD 144-152)

and, amazingly, five of the seven foundations and pilings are the originals from Roman times. The arches and roadway are 18th century – the Romans used a flat wooden roadbed without arches. The black stones are local basalt and not blackened sandstone like the Porta Negra. The bridge was due to be demolished at the end of World War II, but General Patton's troops captured the bridge on March 2, 1945 before the charges were set. The empty charge chambers can still be seen from the upriver side. The bridge is still in use.

From the bridge, follow Karl-Marx-Straße until it changes to Brückenstraße. The first part of this road was not renamed in order to preserve the historic address of where Karl Marx was born. The **Karl-Marx-Haus**, Brueckenstrasse 10, ☎ 0651-970-680, www.fes.de/marx, is a lovely 18th-century patrician house. It is best described as a documentation center and its prized possessions are first editions of *Das Kapital* and the *Communist Manifesto.* Trier of Marx's youth had a population of 10,000 and his first ideas were based on the exploitation of vineyard workers that he observed in the Mosel Valley. The museum is open November to

March, Tuesday to Sunday, 10 am to 1 pm and 2 to 5 pm, and on Monday, 2 to 5 pm. From April to October, it is open Tuesday to Sunday, 10 am to 6 pm, and on Monday, 1 to 6 pm. Admission is €2.

The **Thermen am Viehmarkt** (Forum Baths) were rediscovered in 1987 during excavation work for an underground parking garage. The baths were covered by a modern glass and steel box allowing passersby a peek at most of the ruins. The ruins cover a surprisingly large area with many remaining arches and tunnels. Descriptions are in German only and rather vague.

Cultural Events & Festivals

Trier has a busy cultural and festival program. From **Karneval** in March to the **Christmas Market** in December, it doesn't miss any available opportunity. Wine, good food, and culture are never far apart at these events. Information is available from www.trier-today.de or from the tourist office.

Highlights include the **Wine and Gourmet Festival**, www.wein-gourmetfestival.de, in May, and several shorter wine-related events, usually scheduled over weekends.

The amphitheater is sometimes used for major dramas and operas, while other Roman monuments serve as backdrop to concerts ranging from classics to jazz.

Adventures

On Foot

The tourist office conducts two-hour guided walking tours of the **old city** from April to October. The English tour is daily at 2 pm and in German at 10:30 am and 2:30 pm. A do-it-yourself tour using a Walkman is also available.

Trier is surrounded by beautiful countryside with many **hiking** opportunities. On weekends, the **Eifel** and **Hunsrück Hiking Clubs** conduct guided walks in the region. The schedules are available from the tourist office.

On Wheels

Several long-distance **bicycle** routes pass through Trier, including the **Moselradweg** (Mosel Cycling Route) from Koblenz all the way to Thionville in France. Some 200 km (120 miles) of mountain biking trails are available in the region. During summer weekends, **Radelbusse** (Bicycle Buses) take bikers with equipment to interesting destinations in the region.

Bicycle rentals are available from **Fahrrad-Service-Station** in the Hauptbahnhof, ☎ 0651-148-856, from April to October and year-round from **Zweiradwerkstatt TINA**, Hornstraße 32, ☎ 0651-89-555.

The motorized train **Römer Express**, Olewiger Straße 151, ☎ 0651-9935-9525, www.roemer-express.de, departs from the Porta Nigra on 35-minute tours of the city.

In the Air

Hot-air balloon flights are available from **Ballon Reisen Moselland**, Im Flürchen 7, 54338 Schwich, ☎ 06502-99-080.

Tandem **paragliding** flights are arranged by **Moselglider**, Maximstraße 11, ☎ 0172-619-1183.

On Horseback

For **carriage rides** through Trier during summer months, contact **Rudolf Alt**, Nellstraße 26, ☎ 0651-24-215.

On Water

The Mosel and tributaries are popular for **canoeing** and **kayaking**. **Mosel Tours Kanu-Charter**, Königstraße 3, Kinheim, ☎ 06532-94-320, www.moseltours.de, rents out boats and arranges multi-day trips. Boat rentals are also available from **Edgar Welter**, Römerstraße 38, Piesport, ☎ 06507-5558, and from **Ionons**, Moselstraße 4, Temmels, ☎ 06584-95-179.

Several **riverboat trips** on the Mosel start from Trier. **Personenschifffahrt Kolb**, 56820 Briedern, ☎ 02673-1515, departs from Tier-Zurlauben. From April to October, daily trips depart at 10 am for Trier-Pfalzel – a two-hour round-trip. From early May to mid-October, cruises to

Bernkastel-Kues depart from Tuesday to Sunday at 9:15 am.

Entente Touristique de la Moselle Luxembuourgeoise has **cruises** from Trier to several destinations in Luxemburg. The cruises are mostly in July and August. Information and reservations are possible through the tourist office.

Where to Stay

The **Dorint Hotel** is directly behind the Porta Nigra. It is a modern city hotel with elegant, comfortable rooms. Some are elegant with cherry-wood furniture. The local Spielbank (Casino) is in the hotel – it opens daily at 7 pm. Porta-Nigra-Platz 1, 54292 Trier, ☎ 0651-27-010, fax 0651-270-1170, www.dorint.de. (€€€)

The **Hotel Deutscher Hof** is a modern spot south of the old town between the Barbara and Kaiserthermen. It has comfortable rooms clearly aimed at the business traveler. Südallee 25, 54290 Trier, ☎ 0651-97-780, fax 0651-977-8400, www.hotel-deutscher-hof.de. (€€-€€€)

The **Hotel Aulmann** is in the heart of the old town at the Kornmarkt. Part of it is in an old building, but most of the hotel is in a building erected in the late 1990s. Rooms are comfortable and spacious. Fleischstraße 47, 54290 Trier, ☎ 0651-97-670, fax 0651-976-7102, www.hotel-aulmann.de. (€€-€€€)

The **Hotel Paulin** is close to the Porta Nigra. Rooms in the old building have rustic oak furniture, while the newer wing is better-equipped and uses modern natural wood furniture. Paulinstraße 13, 54292 Trier, ☎ 0651-147-400, fax 0651-147-4010, hotelpaulin@aol.com. (€€)

A pleasant small option with an excellent restaurant is the **Hotel Klosterschenke** in Trier-Pfalzel. It is seven km (4.2 miles) downstream and on the opposite bank of the Mosel in a former fourth-century monastery. Each of the 11 rooms is individually furnished in widely different styles. The restaurant (€€-€€€) serves Mediterranean and local dishes in a room with vaulted ceilings. Reservations are recommended. The hotel can most easily be reached by car, but it is also a stop on the riverboats from Trier, and the Mosel Cycling path passes right in front of the hotel. Klosterstraße 10, 54293 Trier, ☎ 0651-968-440, fax 0651-968-4430, www.hotel-klosterschenke.de. (€€)

Where to Eat

Trier has its fair share of cheap eateries depending on the tourist trade, with many

options in Simeonstraße and the roads leading from the Hauptmarkt. The McDonalds signs at Hauptmarkt are so low-key, it is easy to miss the entrance. However, more rewarding options are also easy to find.

With entrances from both the Hauptmarkt and the Domfreihof is the restaurant complex **Zum Domstein**, Hauptmarkt 5, ☎ 0651-74-490. Food and wine are served in several separate areas, including a restaurant, wine cellars, and a courtyard if the weather cooperates. Most interesting is the **Römischer Weinkellar**, a cellar built around AD 326 and restored in the 1970s. Dishes are local cuisine with some using recipes dating from Roman times. Reservations are recommended. (€€-€€€)

Across the road from the Liebfraukirche is the upscale **Palais Kesselstatt**, Liebfrauenstraße 10, ☎ 0651-40-204, www.restaurant-kesselstatt.de. Located in a former Baroque palace, this smart, but unpretentious, restaurant serves upscale regional dishes with a French touch. The extensive wine list contains wines from the Reichsgraf von Kesselstatt estate as well as other fine local whites and imported reds. Simpler dishes and wine tasting are available in the Weinstube. (€€€)

Another good option in the Dom area is **Schlemmereule**, Domfreihof 1b, ☎ 0651-73-616, www.schlemmereule.de, which serves light regional and French cuisine in an elegant modern setting. Ten wines are available by the glass and about 200 by the bottle. Reservations are essential. (€€€-€€€€)

Right next to the Porta Nigra in the City Museum is **Brunnenhof**, Simeonstr 60, ☎ 0651-700-295, which serves hearty German dishes. (€-€€)

An interesting option is the **Historischer Keller**, Simeonstraße 46, ☎ 0651-469-496. It is in a Gothic cellar dating from 1200, in the basement of the modern Karstadt department store. International and local dishes are served. (€-€€)

Camping

Camping Trier City is four km (2.4 miles) from the center of Trier on the banks of the Mosel, offering some shade, reasonable facilities, and 140 spaces. It is open from April to October. 54294 Trier, ☎ 0651-86-921, fax 0651-83-072.

■ Saarland

The Saarland is the smallest non-city state in Germany. Although it has natural beauty and some interesting sights, it is not generally on any foreign visitor's priority list. The area is somewhat isolated and off the normal tourist and transportation routes.

Saarland had a turbulent history. It was first occupied by the Celts and the Romans and has been disputed between France and Germany ever since. Its main assets were its coal mines and the 19th-century steelworks. After the First and Second World Wars, France tried to annex the area but on both occasions, an overwhelming majority in plebiscites voted for returning to Germany.

The coal and steel industries declined from the late 1960s and Saarland failed to restructure its economy. It became the poorest area in West Germany. Only in recent years was the economy restructured. Despite its natural beauty, tourist infrastructure is still undeveloped.

Information

Tourist information: Tourismus Zentrale Saarland, Franz-Josef-Röder-Straße 9, 66119 Saarbrücken, ☎ 0681-927-200, www.tourismus.saarland.de.

Sightseeing

The following two sights are best visited with private transportation and are 40 km (24 miles) from Trier.

The most famous sight in Saarland is the **Saarschleife**. Here, the River Saar makes a huge 180-degree hairpin loop and for a long stretch flows parallel in opposite directions. The sight is best seen from the viewpoint in Cloef and requires a 15-minute hike through the forest.

Several companies offer boat excursions from Mettlach to the Saarschleife. Round-trips take 90 minutes. Boats operate daily from Easter to October. Details are available from **Saarschleife Touristik**, Freiherr-vom-Stein-Straße 64, 66693 Mettlach, ☎ 06864-8334, www.mettlach.de.

Mettlach is famous for its **Villeroy & Boch** ceramics factory, Postfach 1120, 66688 Mettlach, ☎ 06864-811-020, www.villeroy-boch.de, which produces everything from toilet bowls to the most dainty teacups. The firm's headquarters are in a Baroque former monastery where it also has a **Keramikmuseum** (Ceramics Museum), with one of the largest private collections of porcelain in Europe. In the complex are large outlet shops selling the firm's wares at a slight discount. The best bargains are found in the *Fundgrube*, where odds and ends are sold at huge discounts. Opening hours are weekdays from 9 am to 6 pm and weekends from 9:30 am to 4 pm – shops are closed on Sunday.

Hesse

In this Chapter

Hesse (Hessen in German) is at the geographical heart of Germany. It is often referred to as a travel-through state; vacationers from the northern parts of Germany and Scandinavia often drive through it to get to the south without bothering to leave the highways. However, Hesse is a surprisingly diverse state with lots to see in addition to the excellent transportation infrastructure.

The largest city in Hesse is **Frankfurt**, the only German city with a true modern skyline. Its population of 650,000 makes it the fifth-largest city in Germany, but the larger Rhine Main Region, with nearly five million people, is the strongest economic region in the country. In recent years, Frankfurt shook off its dour, boring image and is an increasingly popular destination. More visitors spent a night here than in any other German city, although most visitors still come for the exhibitions (*Messen*) and other business trips. Frankfurt has 38 museums, 109 art galleries, and 33 theaters.

Wiesbaden, the state capital, is less than an hour west of Frankfurt. It is a pretty city with elegant boulevards, buildings, and shops. It seems to have an extraordinary number of outdoor cafés. To the north is the **Taunus** mountain range with lovely forested areas. It is a favorite place for recreation, including hiking, cycling, and other outdoor activities.

The **Lahn Valley** is one of Germany's best-kept secrets, easily accessible, but drawing few foreign tourists. It has lovely castles and churches in small, mostly half-timbered villages. Its river is the most popular in Germany for canoeing.

Fulda was an important center for the development of Christianity in Germany. The town has mostly Baroque sights, although its founding by St Boniface goes back to AD 744.

History

Like most of the other German states, Hesse has a complex history. What constitutes Hesse today is a post-World War II amalgamation of cities and territories that were previously independent for centuries.

Hesse had a definite beginning as an independent state. In 1247, Count Heinrich Raspe IV of Thuringia died without an heir and, as a result, the emperor had to reassign his properties. Several claims where made, but the most interesting and least likely to succeed was by Sophie, daughter of Ludwig IV of Thuringia and St Elizabeth, on behalf of her four-year-old son. (See Eisenach in Thuringia chapter.**) The claim prevailed and the small county of Hesse was proclaimed and initially ruled from Marburg.

That Hesse managed to prosper was no main feat as its territories were also claimed by the archbishop of Mainz, for centuries the most powerful church figure in Germany, as well as the archbishops of Trier and Cologne, and several other much stronger neighbors. Sophie started what is now known as the Landgrafenschloss or the castle of Marburg, which still towers over the town today.

Hesse was at its peak under the rule of Count Philip the Magnanimous, right, in the early 16th century. Under his rule, much of modern-day Hesse was united and adopted the Reformation. However, as with other German states, the territory was split again afterwards among the sons. Siding with the wrong side in the 1866 war between Prussia and Austria led to most of current Hesse becoming part of Prussia.

After World War II, the federal state of Hesse was proclaimed with Wiesbaden as capital. The much larger city of Frankfurt seemed destined to become the capital of

West Germany but narrowly lost out to sleepy, provincial Bonn.

■ Transportation

Hesse has been at the geographic center of Europe and Germany since the time of Charlemagne. Frankfurt has been a center of trade and commerce for centuries – a position it never lost. As a result, transportation routes of all types cross Hesse, with Frankfurt a particularly important transportation hub.

Frankfurt has the largest airport on continental Europe and the busiest train station in Germany. Some 50 million annual passengers pass through the airport and close to 100 million through the Hauptbahnhof. Daily, 1,800 trains stop at Frankfurt Hauptbahnhof and almost half of all German trains pass through the Rhine Main area. The Frankfurter Kreuz, where the Autobahns A3 and A5 intersect, is the busiest in Germany with 300,000 cars per day.

By Rail: Frankfurt's Hauptbahnhof offers excellent transportation to other cities in Germany. By train, Cologne can be reached in just over an hour (three departures per hour and more from the airport). Hourly, or more frequent, direct trains take four hours to Berlin; 3½ hours to Hamburg, Leipzig, or Munich. Amsterdam can be reached in four hours on several trains per day.

The airport has a major railway station as well, making it often unnecessary to travel to the Hauptbahnhof before continuing to your final destination. Due to the overcrowding at the Hauptbahnhof, some long-distance trains stop in Frankfurt-Süd, with S-Bahn connections to the Hauptbahnhof or elsewhere in the city.

By Road: Several major Autobahns cross Hesse. The A3 connects Cologne and the Ruhr area with Frankfurt, Würzburg, and further destinations in northern Bavaria. The A5 connects northern German destinations with the Black Forest and Switzerland via Frankfurt. The A7 from Denmark via Hamburg and Hanover runs through the eastern parts of the state to southern Germany. Minor roads are generally in good condition, more picturesque, but of course slower.

By Air: Frankfurt's **Rhein-Main International Airport**, ☎ 01805-372-4636, www.flughafen-frankfurt.de, is the busiest in continental Europe. Virtually all intercontinental flights to Germany arrive here and many scheduled European flights as well. The airport is southwest of the city and can easily be reached by public transportation. Taxis to downtown take less than 30 minutes and cost €25. The fastest way is by rail. There are two train stations at the airport. The one closest to the terminal is for local transportation: take the S-Bahn from here to downtown (Hauptbahnhof) or in the opposite direction to Wiesbaden and Mainz. The Fernbahnhof serves long-distance trains including the InterCityExpress (ICE) trains. Many airlines have check-in counters at the Fernbahnhof.

■ Information Sources

Information is available from **Hessen Touristik Service**, Postfach 3165, 65021 Wiesbaden, www.hessen-touristik.de.

■ Frankfurt

Frankfurt is mostly a modern city, but more attention to conservation, arts, and cultural projects after the 1970s has done much to improve the rather dour and boring image of the city. It has several interesting historic buildings, many skyscrapers, a lovely riverfront, many museums, and a vibrant cultural scene. Also it has had a reputation over centuries for throwing a party at the drop of a hat.

Although some parts of Frankfurt were settled in Roman times, its modern history dates from the time of Charlemagne, who erected a Pfalz (Imperial Palace) here and resided on the banks of the Main for 10 months.

Ever since, Frankfurt has occupied a strategic position on the major trade routes. Frankfurt has held trade fairs (*Messe*), which became the base of its wealth and fame, since the 11th century. From 1240 onwards, traders en route to the fair received imperial protection and guarantees. In 1372, Frankfurt became a Free Imperial City.

In 1152, Friedrich Barbarossa was elected German king. This was the first of the 33 imperial elections (out of 52) that took place here. From 1356, all elections took place in Frankfurt and, from 1562, the formal coronations were in the Frankfurt Kaiserdom, rather than the cathedral in Aachen.

After the dissolution of the Holy Roman Empire in 1806, Frankfurt remained an independent city. In 1848-49, the first German parliament congregated in Frankfurt. Attempts to draw up a liberal constitution and to form a loose German federation failed when the King of Prussia refused the offered crown.

During the 1866 Prussian-Austrian war, Frankfurt was occupied by Prussian troops and, after paying heavy war reparations, incorporated into the Kingdom of Prussia. As there was already a Frankfurt in Prussia, "am Main" (on the River Main) was added to distinguish it from Frankfurt an der Oder.

During World War II Frankfurt suffered several air raids that destroyed most of the old town and killed 6,000 people. After the war, Frankfurt narrowly missed out to provincial Bonn to become the capital of West Germany. Frankfurt's rebuilding was decidedly modern with few of the original old buildings preserved, but note the exceptions below.

Frankfurt remained the banking center of Germany and banks mainly occupy the skyscrapers that were constructed here during the last quarter of the 20th century. Frankfurt has 19 buildings higher than 50 m (164 feet), making it the only city in Germany with a skyline. The Commerzbank building, at 258.7 m (850 feet), is the tallest in Europe. These factors contributed to Frankfurt's nicknames: *Bankfurt*, an obvious reference to the banks in the city, which led to *Krankfurt*, German for "sick-furt," a reference to the city's attention to making money rather than following more noble social issues, and Mainhatten – combining *Manhattan*, high buildings, the River Main, and a lot of wishful thinking!

Information Sources

Tourist Office: Tourist information is available at Römerberg 27, ☎ 60313 Frankfurt, ☎ 069-2123-8800, www.frankfurt.de, or at the Hauptbahnhof. Useful information on the cultural scene is available at www.kultur.frankfurt.de.

Transportation

Frankfurt has an excellent public transportation system, combining S-Bahn, U-Bahn, tram, and bus networks. For sightseeing in the old town, the U-Bahn is usually the most convenient. Bus 46 runs from the Hauptbahnhof along the Schaumainkai where most of the Sachsenhausen museums are located. In contrast to most other German cities, tickets must be bought only shortly before boarding and are not separately validated.

Sightseeing

The main sights in Frankfurt are concentrated in the old town center, with several museums on the opposite bank of the Main in Sachsenhausen. There are a few more sights in the surrounding Neustadt, which was still within the old city walls. Most of the skyscrapers are in the Bankerviertel, but these are best seen from a distance, especially from the banks of the river.

If time is limited, give priority to Römer and the Kaiserdom, the view of the skyline from the Eiserner Steg (a pedestrian bridge), and the Städel Art Museum.

Altstadt

Frankfurt's main sights are close to Römerberg, the physical and spiritual heart of Frankfurt since the days of Charlemagne. This huge square is the setting for all modern day festivals. The fountain (1611) has Justice, not blindfolded, but rather facing the Town Hall, as a warning to the town council to treat the citizens fairly.

Nowadays, **Römer** refers to the whole Rathaus, which consists of 16 buildings that were connected through the centuries to form the town hall. However, the name originally referred only to the middle house, which was used by traders from Rome, rather than the Romans of empire-building fame, when visiting the annual trade fairs. The exterior is Neo-Gothic and the statues only added decades after the last emperor was crowned here. Römer was extensively damaged during World War II, but rebuilt in simplified form. The **Kaisersaal** is the only part of the building open to tourists. It has paintings of all emperors from Charlemagne to Joseph II. These portraits were

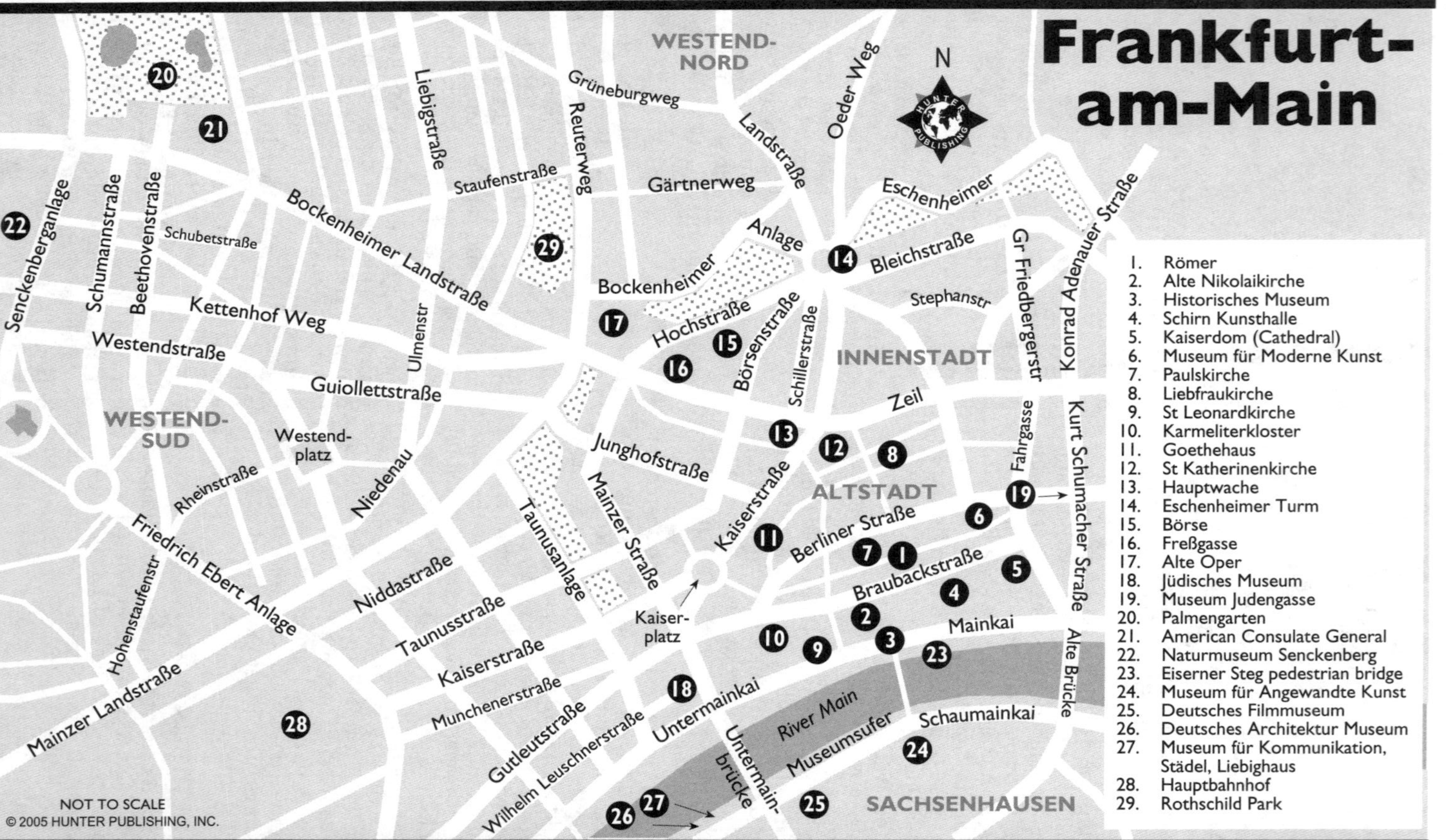
Frankfurt-am-Main
N
HUNTER PUBLISHING
1. Römer
2. Alte Nikolaikirche
3. Historisches Museum
4. Schirn Kunsthalle
5. Kaiserdom (Cathedral)
6. Museum für Moderne Kunst
7. Paulskirche
8. Liebfraukirche
9. St Leonardkirche
10. Karmeliterkloster
11. Goethehaus
12. St Katherinenkirche
13. Hauptwache
14. Eschenheimer Turm
15. Börse
16. Freßgasse
17. Alte Oper
18. Jüdisches Museum
19. Museum Judengasse
20. Palmengarten
21. American Consulate General
22. Naturmuseum Senckenberg
23. Eiserner Steg pedestrian bridge
24. Museum für Angewandte Kunst
25. Deutsches Filmmuseum
26. Deutsches Architektur Museum
27. Museum für Kommunikation, Städel, Liebighaus
28. Hauptbahnhof
29. Rothschild Park
WESTEND-NORD
WESTEND-SUD
INNENSTADT
ALTSTADT
SACHSENHAUSEN
Grüneburgweg
Oeder Weg
Landstraße
Liebigstraße
Reuterweg
Staufenstraße
Gärtnerweg
Eschenheimer
Anlage
Bleichstraße
Konrad Adenauer Straße
Gr Friedbergerstr
Stephanstr
Senckenberganlage
Schumannstraße
Beethovenstraße
Schubetstraße
Bockenheimer Landstraße
Bockenheimer
Hochstraße
Börsenstraße
Schillerstraße
Kettenhof Weg
Westendstraße
Ulmenstr
Guiollettstraße
Zeil
Fahrgasse
Kurt Schumacher Straße
Westend-platz
Junghofstraße
Mainzer Straße
Kaiserstraße
Berliner Straße
Braubackstraße
Rheinstraße
Niedenau
Taunusanlage
Friedrich Ebert Anlage
Niddastraße
Taunusstraße
Kaiserstraße
Kaiser-platz
Mainkai
Alte Brücke
Hohenstaufenstr
Munchenerstraße
Untermainkai
River Main
Schaumainkai
Museumsufer
Untermain-brücke
Gutleutstraße
Wilhelm Leuschnerstraße
Mainzer Landstraße
NOT TO SCALE

painted in the late 19th century. Note the portrait of Matthias – his coronation in 1612 is fondly remembered. Contrary to popular belief, his coronation was the only one where the fountain in the square spouted wine. Opening hours are daily from 10 am to 1 pm and 2 to 5 pm. It is often closed for official functions. Admission is €1.50.

The lovely half-timbered houses facing the Rathaus were constructed only in the 1980s as true copies of the originals destroyed during World War II. Most of the old town still looked like that in 1940. The only half-timbered building in the old town that survived the inferno following the air raids is Haus Wertheym across from the History Museum.

Römerberg in 1822, with Alte Nikolaikirche at right

At the south end of the square, dividing it from the River Main, is the 12th-century **Alte Nikolaikirche** (Old St Nicholas Church), Am Römerberg, www.alte-nikolaikirche.de. It has a surprisingly small interior given the high roof. During the Christmas Market, an orchestra often plays from the balcony. Opening hours are daily from 10 am to 6 pm, closing at 8 pm from April to September. The carillon chimes daily at 9:05 am, 12:05, and 5:05 pm.

Next to the church is the **Historisches Museum** (Local History Museum), Saalgasse 19, ☎ 069-2123-5599, www.historisches-museum.frankfurt.de. It has interesting displays, but unfortunately few English descriptions. Of particular interest is the model of the old town as well as a small part of Charlemagne's original Pfalz. It also has a huge coin collection. Opening hours are Tuesday to Saturday from 10 am to 5 pm, Wednesday from 4 to 8 pm, and Sunday from 1 to 5 pm. Admission is €4.

The ultra-modern **Schirn Kunsthalle**, Römerberg, ☎ 069-299-8820, www.schirn.de, occupies the full length from the Kaiserdom to Römerberg. Such a modern design in the heart of the old town is very much in keeping with Frankfurt's approach to life and, for once, the building was not cheaply done. It looks the part, in contrast to the rather drab Technical Rathaus directly opposite it. Opened in 1986 as the largest art exhibition space in Frankfurt, it houses rotating exhibitions of internationally recognized modern art. It commonly has two exhibitions running simultaneously for which admission has to be paid separately. Opening hours are Tuesday-Sunday from 10 am to 7 pm (Wednesday and Thursday until 10 pm). Admission depends on the exhibition but is usually about €6. The attached art bookshop has surprisingly reasonable prices and a large bargains section. The coffee shop offers brunch on Sundays with childcare from 10 am to 3 pm.

The **Kaiserdom** (Imperial Cathedral), is a bit of a misnomer as it was never the seat of the bishop, but had the honorary title added after it became the church in which the German King was crowned. Its proper name is the **Dom St Batholomäus** (Cathedral of St Bartholomew). The Gothic church was built between 1315 and 1514, but the tower was left unfinished. A major fire in 1867 destroyed parts of the cathedral, but it was rebuilt using the original plans and this time the tower was actually completed. The bombing raids of World War II left only the shell of the church but it was soon rebuilt. Major renovations are currently underway and parts of the church may be closed through 2005.

The reddish interior of the church houses several works of art. Also note the paint-on bricks where concrete was used instead of sandstone. From 1356, the election of the German emperor took place in the library south of the choir. The coronations were held here from 1562 to 1792. Opening hours are daily from 8 am to noon and from 2:30 to 6 pm, but it's open in the mornings only on Friday and Sunday. During the winter, it closes at 5 pm.

The **Dommuseum** (Cathedral Museum), Domplatz 1, ☎ 069-1337-6186, is attached to the church and houses the cathedral treasures, mainly gowns and some chalices and minor reliquaries. It is of minor interest and can be seen in a few minutes. Opening hours are Tuesday to Friday, 10 am to 5 pm, and weekends from 11 am to 5 pm. Admission is €2.

The **Museum für Moderne Kunst** (Modern Art), Domstraße 10, ☎ 069-2123-0447, www.mmk-frankfurt.de, is in a building that opened in 1991. The collection is primarily European and American art from the 1960s. Works are rotated every six months. Opening hours are Tuesday to Sunday from 10 am to 5 pm, closing at 8 pm on Wednesday. Admission is €5.

Just north of the Römer, is the round **Paulskirche**, Paulsplatz. This Classical building is a post-war copy of the original erected in 1790-1833. The first elected German parliament met here in 1848-49. The current interior is modern with a small exhibition on German parliamentary history. A plenary hall on the second floor is used for conferences and other mostly non-religious events. Opening hours are daily from 10 am to 5 pm. Admission is free.

The **Liebfrauenkirche**, (Church of Our Dear Lady), was a former monastery church. It was destroyed in 1944, but rebuilt using the original Gothic style. It has an interesting Three-Kings Tympanum, Gothic panels, and Baroque figures saved from the ruins of the former church. At the back is a Lourdes grotto and Gothic chapel entrance. It is open daily from 6:30 am to 6 pm.

The **St Leonhardkirche** (St Leonard's Church) is a Late Romanesque construction with a Gothic chancel added around 1430. Note the Romanesque spires and the Gothic frescoes and altars. Opening hours are Tuesday to Sunday from 10 am to noon and from 3 to 6 pm.

The **Karmeliterkloster** (Carmelite Monastery), Münzgasse 9, ☎ 069-2123-6276, has the largest religious mural created north of the Alps. This 140-m (460-foot) painting was done in the 15th century by Jörg Ratgeb. On the second floor are changing exhibitions, mainly photographs of early events or themes related to Frankfurt. Opening hours are weekdays from 8:30 am to 5 pm and weekends from 10 am to 5 pm. Admission is free.

Neustadt

The **Goethehaus** (Goethe House) and **Goethe Museum**, Großer Hirschgraben 23-25, ☎ 069-138-800, www.goethehaus-frankfurt.de, focus on the influences on Goethe's early years. He was born and spent his youth here. Although almost completely destroyed during World War II, the house of Goethe's youth has been restored faithfully. Inside, the 16 rooms on four floors are furnished as in Goethe's time. A gallery has works on display from artists that influenced or inspired Goethe. A free English information sheet is available. Opening hours are weekdays from 9 am to 4 pm (closing at 6 pm from April to September) and weekends from 10 am to 4 pm. Admission is € 5.

The **St Katherinenkirche** (St Catherine's Church) is a Late Gothic hall church with Baroque portals added in the late 17th century. It is open weekdays from 2 to 6 pm.

The Baroque **Hauptwache** was erected in 1729 but altered over the years. It was actually torn down to make way for the construction of the huge subway interchange underneath the square and then rebuilt in its original form. It houses a pleasant café serving mostly local cuisine at surprisingly reasonable prices. To the east of the square is the **Zeil**, Frankfurt's premier shopping street.

To the north is the **Eschenheimer Turm** (Tower), the loveliest of the few remaining pieces of the original city defenses. The tower dates from the early 15th century and was one of 42 that protected the rich city. A copy of the tower is in Potsdam near Berlin. When Frankfurt tore down the last parts of the wall in the 19th century, a large park was created that forms a green half-circle around the old town. It is a favorite recreation area for locals.

The **Börse** (Stock Exchange), Börseplatz, is in a 19th-century building. As all trading is by computer, there is not much to see except the obligatory Bull and Bear statues in front of the building.

To the west of the Hauptwache is the **Grosse Bockenheimer Straße**. Part of the street is known as the **Freßgasse** (Gluttony Alley) due to the number of food shops that traditionally traded here. Presently most businesses here are restaurants or coffee shops. In contrast to the cafés at the Paulskirche, locals outnumber tourists by far here. Parallel to the Freßgasse is the **Goethestraße** – the most expensive shopping street in Frankfurt with all the international haute couture names.

At the end of the Freßgasse is the **Opernplatz** with the Late Classic **Alte Oper** (Old Opera House), Opernplatz 1, ☎ 069-134-0400, www.alte-oper-frankfurt.de, completed in 1880 and opened in the presence of Kaiser Wilhelm I. It was bombed out in World War II and its shell was for almost 30 years the most beautiful ruin in Germany. Restored in the 1970s, it re-opened in 1981. The lovely exterior is a copy of the original, but the interior is more modern and is used for all kind of performances, though seldom for opera. (An excellent, modern opera house is a few blocks away.)

The park that leads from here to the River Main has several statues of famous German artists, including Beethoven and Schiller in the Taunusanlage and Goethe in the Gallusanlage. (Goethe may move to the renovated Goetheplatz in the near future.) The park also affords great views of the banking houses in the vicinity.

Anne Frank

Close to the Main is the Jewish Museum. Frankfurt traditionally had a large Jewish community whose financial skills were absolutely necessary for the development of Frankfurt's trade and banking industry. In addition, Jews were taxed more than other nationals and their huge tax contributions ensured that the town council opposed, usually unsuccessfully, medieval pogroms. In addition to the Rothschilds, Anne Frank was born in Frankfurt and fled with her family to Amsterdam soon afterwards. The **Jüdisches Museum** (Jewish Museum), Untermainkai 14-15, ☎ 069-2123-5000, www.juedischesmuseum.de, in the former Rothschild Palace, illustrates the history of Jewish settlements in Germany from the Middle Ages to the present. Opening hours are Tuesday to Sunday from 10 am to 5 pm, closing at 8 pm on Wednesday. Admission is €2.60.

During construction work for a utilities company building, foundations were discovered of some buildings in the former Jewish Ghetto destroyed by the Nazis. The small **Museum Judengasse - Börneplatz** (Museum Jewish Street), Kurt-Schumacher-Straße 10, ☎ 069-297-7419, www.juedischesmuseum.de, focuses on the foundations of buildings in the former Judengasse and has an exhibition on life in this street over a period of almost four centuries. Opening hours are Tuesday to Sunday from 10 am to 5 pm, closing at 8 pm on Wednesday. Admission is €1.50. (This museum is close to the Modern Art Museum.)

Westend

The Westend is to the west of the Alte Oper and the traditional area of bankers and diplomats. It has some of the most expensive residential property in Germany. It also has two sights worth seeing. Both are easiest to reach on foot from U-Bahn station Bockenheimer Warte. (The presence of increased security due to the American Consulate's location next to the Palmengarten makes the bus service less convenient.)

The **Palmengarten** (Palm/Tropical Gardens), Siesmayerstraße 43, ☎ 069-2123-3939, is a huge park and botanical garden. It has the oldest botanical building in Europe – the 1869 Palm House. And then there are the more modern glass and steel houses that have plants from different climate zones. Whatever the season, there always seem to be flowers blooming in the garden. The Goethe Garden, with famous sayings by the poet, recently opened inside the park. A large children's play area and open-air theater provides entertainment for all ages. Opening hours are daily, 9 am to 6 pm, closing at 4 pm from November to January. Admission is €3.50.

Nearby is the **Naturmuseum Senckenberg** (Natural History Museum), Senckenberganlage 25, ☎ 069-75-420, www.senckenberg.uni-frankfurt.de. It is one of the largest of its kind in Europe and has an important paleontology collection. However, the fossils and rocks are upstaged by the dinosaur displays. The museum is hugely popular with children and many displays are interactive. Opening hours are daily, 9 am to 5 pm, but closing at 8 pm on Wednesday and 6 pm on weekends. Admission is €5.

Sachsenhausen

Sachsenhausen is the section of Frankfurt on the south bank of the River Main. It was not destroyed during World War II and still has large areas with 19th-century villas. During the last two decades of the 20th century, a huge number of excellent museums were erected on the south bank of the Main. The museums are described in order, moving from the Eiserner Steg downstream. If time is limited, give preference to the Städel and the Liebieghaus.

Several bridges span the River Main but, if on foot, give preference to the **Eiserner Steg**. This pedestrian footbridge was erected in the 19th century as a private initiative to be paid from tolls. However, the city took control of the bridge soon after its completion and opened it for free to all. It offers some of the best views of the Frankfurt skyline. In addition, it is the most convenient crossing point from the Römer area to Sachsenhausen. In summer, many outdoor cafés line the Sachsenhausen bank of the Main.

The **Museum für Angewandte Kunst Frankfurt** (Museum of Applied Arts), Schaumainkai (Museumsufer) 17, ☎ 069-2123-4037, www.museumfuer-angewandte-kunst.frankfurt.de, has a collection spanning 6,000 years. The emphasis is on European applied arts from the 12th century to the present, but works from other parts of the world, especially East Asia and Islamic countries, are also on display. Opening hours are Tuesday to Sunday from 10 am to 5 pm, closing at 9 pm on Wednesday. Admission is €5.

The **Deutsches Filmmuseum** (German Cinema Museum), Schaumainkai 41, ☎ 069-2123-8830, www.deutsches-filmmuseum.de, has exhibitions on the development of cinema, both German and international. It exhibits various instruments used in filmmaking and projecting, as well as the development of the industry. At its heart is a cinema that shows mainly art films. Opening hours are Tuesday, Thursday, Friday and Sunday from 10 am to 5 pm, Wednesday, 10 am to 8 pm, and Saturday, 2 to 8 pm. Admission is €2.50.

The **Deutsches Architektur Museum** (German Architectur Museum), Schaumainkai (Museumsufer) 43, ☎ 069-2123-8844, www.dam-online.de, opened in 1984 as the only museum of its kind in Europe at the time. It has a permanent exhibition on the development of architecture from the most primitive hut to modern skyscrapers. It also houses impressive temporary exhibitions Opening hours are Tuesday to Sunday from 10 am to 5 pm, closing at 8 pm on Wednesday. Admission is €6.

The **Museum für Kommunikation** (Communications Museum), Schaumainkai (Museumsufer) 53, ☎ 069-60-600, www.museumsstiftung.de, has displays on all matters related to mail and communication. In addition to the permanent collection, it hosts temporary exhibitions and has a large space where children can experience communication through practical experience. Opening hours are Tuesday to Friday, 9 am to 5 pm, and weekends from 11 am to 7 pm. Admission is free.

The **Städelsches Kunstinstitut und Städtische Galerie** (Municipal Art Institute and Gallery), Schaumainkai (Museumsufer) 63, ☎ 069-605-0980, www.staedelmuseum.de, is usually referred to as **Das Städel**. It is Frankfurt's most impressive museum, with a huge collection covering seven centuries. The Old Masters' collection is particularly impressive and includes works by Holbein, Rembrandt, Rubens, and Van Eyck. The French Impressionists, including Renoir and Monet, as well as the German Impressionists, are well represented. Modern works by Picasso, Klee, and Feininger are complemented by contemporary art. Special exhibitions are often held in an adjacent building. The most celebrated work is a Tischbein painting of Goethe painted in 1787, shown on the previous page. The Café-Restaurant Holbein is currently fashionable. Opening hours are Tuesday to Sunday from 10 am to 5 pm, closing at 9 pm on Wednesday and Thursday. Admission is €6.

The **Liebieghaus - Museum Alter Plastik** (Museum of Ancient Sculpture), Schaumainkai (Museumsufer) 71, ☎ 069-2123-8617, www.liebieghaus.de, has an impressive range of sculpture, with works from the Egyptian, Greek, and Roman periods, medieval sculptures, works from the Renaissance and the Baroque, Classicism, and some from East Asia. It also has sculptures from the Boden Museum in Berlin on loan. Opening hours are Tuesday to Sunday from 10 am to 5 pm, closing at 8 pm on Wednesday. Admission is €4.

Cultural Events & Festivals

Frankfurt has 33 theaters, making for a busy cultural calendar. The **Alte Oper** alone hosts some 600 concerts per year. Music is also played in many of the churches. In summer, open-air concerts are popular. Schedules are available from the tourist office and they can also make reservations for many events. The **English Theater**, Kaiserstraße 52, ☎ 069-2423-1620, www.englishtheater-frankfurt.de, performs in English only.

Frankfurt has a reputation for throwing a party at any and every occasion. A recent move by a politician to ban the **Opernplatz festival** (end June, early July), since it was dedicated to eating and drinking rather than to cultural events, was shouted down from all directions.

The **Mainfest**, early August, is a folk festival with rides and food stalls, held at Römerberg and the Main quay. The **Rheingauer Weinmarkt** (Rheingau Wine Market) is held in the Freßgasse the last week of August. The last weekend of August sees the **Museumuferfest** – a huge cultural festival at the museums in Sachsenshausen.

The year ends with the best festival of all – the **Christmas market**, held from end November to just before Christmas. It is the largest Christmas market in Germany, with the largest Christmas tree standing in front of the Rathaus. The heart of the market is Römerberg, but it spreads to the Main banks, the square in front of the Paulskirche, farther up the road and down much of the Zeil.

Shopping

The high-class shops are in **Goethestraße**, which leads from the Opernplatz parallel to the Freßgasse. It has all the premier international brands.

Ordinary people shop on the **Zeil**, a huge pedestrian street, which claims to be the most valuable shopping street in the country. It has mostly department stores and fashion outlets. The **Zeilgallerie**, Zeil 112, has many small, moderately priced boutiques popular with the younger crowd.

Sachsenhausen has a major **flea market** on Saturday mornings from 8 am to 2 pm. It is held in the vicinity of the Eiserner Steg. However, quality items are few and far between.

Adventures

On Foot

Guided tours on specialized themes are conducted during weekends by **Statt-Reisen**, Rotlintstraße 70, ☎ 069-9441-5940, www.stattreisen.de.

On Wheels

Frankfurt is an easy city to **cycle** in – it is mostly flat and there are many dedicated cycling paths. A popular longer-distance cycling route is the **Mainuferweg** (Main Banks Route), which runs on both sides of the Main from Aschaffenburg to Mainz and Wiesbaden.

Bicycles can be rented from the Hauptbahnhof, ☎ 069-2653-4834.

The **Ebbelwei-Express** is a tourist tram that operates on weekend afternoons following a circular route through the old town and Sachsenhausen. A round-trip takes an hour but it is possible to disrupt the journey temporarily at any stop. It costs €5 and includes a bottle of apple wine or juice.

On Water

Primus-Linie, Mainkai 36, ☎ 069-1338-370, www.primus-linie.de, has regular **cruises** on the River Main, departing mostly from near Römer. In addition to one- to two-hour circular cruises, dinner and dance cruises, as well as day cruises up the Main are also available.

On Horseback

Just northwest of Frankfurt, in Steinbach, **Western Riding in the Fields**, ☎ 06173-67-601, offers horseback riding opportunities. The owner, Katherine Wissel, an American lady who has been in Germany forever, rides her professionally trained horses every evening in the fields and on weekends four-hour rides into the beautiful Taunus mountains are available to experienced riders.

Where to Stay & Eat

Old Town Area

Steigenberger Hotel Frankfurter Hof is the grand dame of Frankfurt hotels and the premier property in the impressive Steigenberger portfolio. Behind the Neo-Renaissance façade is a modern hotel with a stylish interior. Rooms are comfortable with impressive bathrooms. It is worth paying slightly more for a larger room. The hotel is halfway between the Hauptbahnhof and old town. It has several restaurants. The **Francois** (€€€€) serves French cuisine. The bistro-style **Oscar's** (€€-€€€) serves international fare, while **Iroha** (€€€-€€€€) offers Japanese cuisine. Do not even dream of staying here during the major exhibitions – it is booked up years in advance. Am Kaiserplatz, 60311 Frankfurt, ☎ 069-21-502, fax 069-215-900, www.steigenberger.de. (€€€€)

ArabellaSheraton Grand Hotel is at the far end of the old town at Konstabler Wache. It is a large, modern hotel, much flashier than the Frankfurter Hof or Hessishcer Hof. Décor in the spacious rooms ranges from Arabian to Asian and Post-Modern. The hotel has six restaurants. The **Peninsula** (€€€) serves nouvelle cuisine with strong Mediterranean influences. Konrad-Adenauer-Straße 7, 60313 Frankfurt, ☎ 069-29-810, fax 069-298-1810, www.arabellasheraton.de. (€€€€)

The **Hilton Hotel** is next to a large park near the Alte Oper, a modern hotel with comfortable, rooms. It has a large fitness center and a swimming pool. The **Hard Rock Café** is across the road. Hochstraße 4, 60313 Frankfurt, ☎ 069-133-8000, fax 069-1338-1338, www.hilton.com. (€€€€)

Palmenhof Hotel is between the old town and the Messe (the Fair Grounds), close to the Palmengarten. Rooms are comfortable, with a combination of modern and antique furniture. The restaurant **L'Artichoc** (€€-€€€) serves nouvelle cuisine and local specialties. Bockenheimer Landstraße 89-91, 60325 Frankfurt, ☎ 069-75-0060, fax 069-7530-0666, www.palmenhof.com. (€€€)

Miramar Hotel is one of very few hotels inside the old town itself. It is close to the Paulskirche. Rooms are functionally furnished, mostly in dark wood. Berliner Straße 31, 60311 Frankfurt, ☎ 069-920-3970, fax 069-9203-9769, www.miramar-frankfurt.de. (€€€)

Best Western Hotel Scala is close to the ArabellaSheraton in the northern reaches of the old town. The building was recently renovated and has modern, neat rooms. Schäfergasse 31, 60313 Frankfurt, ☎ 069-138-1110, fax 069-284-234, www.scala.bestwestern.de. (€€-€€€)

Hauptbahnhof Area

The **Steigenberger Hotel Metropolitan** opened in 2003 at the north side of the Hauptbahnhof. Rooms are luxurious, with all modern comforts and technology requirements for the business traveler. The health club has a sauna, solarium, and whirlpool. Poststraße 6, 60329 Frankfurt, ☎ 069-5060-700, fax 069-506-070-555, www.steigenberger.de. (€€€€)

Le Meridien Parkhotel is close to the Hauptbahnhof in an early 19th-century building with a modern wing. Rooms are comfortable. The bistro-style restaurant **Le Parc** (€€-€€€) serves international and local cuisine. Weishüttenplatz 28-38, 60329 Frankfurt, ☎ 069-26-970, fax 069-269-7884, www.lemeridien-frankfurt.com. (€€€€)

The **Intercontinental Hotel** is a modern option on the banks of the River Main close to the new opera house and theaters. It has elegant rooms, many with river views. The fitness center is large and includes a swimming pool. The restaurant **Signatures** (€€€-€€€€) serves international cuisine with a large Euro-Asian selection. Wilhelm-Leuchner-Straße 43, 60329 Frankfurt, ☎ 069-26-050, fax 069-252-467, www.frankfurt-interconti.com. (€€€€)

The **InterCity Hotel** is at the north entrance of the station. Rooms are comfortable, with lightwood furniture. Free local transportation is included in the room price. Poststraße 8, 60329 Frankfurt, ☎ 069-273-910, fax 069-2739-1999, www.intercityhotel.de. (€€-€€€€)

Nearby is the **Manhatten Hotel**. It is a modern building with modern interior. Rooms are well-designed, with modern furniture. It is close to the nightlife area. Düsseldorfer Straße 20, 60329 Frankfurt, ☎ 069-269-5970, fax 069-269-597-777, www.manhatten-hotel.com. (€€-€€€)

The **Ibis Frankfurt Friedensbrücke** is a few blocks from the Hauptbahnhof on the banks of the Main. Rooms are typically Ibis with functional furniture and few thrills. Some have good river views though. Speicherstraße 4, 60327 Frankfurt, ☎ 069-273-030, fax 069-237-024, www.ibishotels.com. (€€-€€€).

Messe Area

The Messe, or Fair Ground, area has several large hotels serving mainly visitors to exhibitions and conferences. During major fairs, expect to pay top dollar, but in the quiet season hotels, with the exception of the Hessischer Hof, offer huge discounts. The area is a mere two subway stops from the Hauptbahnhof and a good value option in the off-season.

The **Hessischer Hof** is near the Messe. The hotel uses antiques and art originally belonging to the Princes of Hesse. Rooms are luxurious. The restaurant **Sèvres** (€€-€€€) serves nouvelle cuisine with strong French influences. The Sèvres porcelain on display was a wedding gift from Napoleon Bonaparte to Princess Alix of Hesse and the Russian Czar. Friedrich-Ebert-Allee 40, 60325 Frankfurt, ☎ 069-75-400, fax 069-7540-2924, www.hessischer-hof.de. (€€€€)

The enormous **Marriott Hotel** occupies the top 19 floors of a 44-floor building across the road from the Messe. Rooms are standard Marriott luxury and style. The **Arizona** restaurant (€€-€€€) serves Arizona specialties. Hamburger Allee 2, 60486 Frankfurt, ☎ 069-79-550, fax 069-7955-2374, www.marriotthotels.com. (€€-€€€€)

The **Maritim Hotel** is right at the main entrance to the Messe. It has elegant rooms aimed at the business traveler. The higher floors have lovely views. Extra-long beds are available. The hotel has several restaurants to serve the crowds, but the **Sushisho** (€€-€€€€) is particularly pleasant, with kaiseki and other Japanese dishes available, in addition to raw fish. Theodor-Heuss-Allee 3, 60486 Frankfurt, ☎ 069-7578-1148, fax 069-7578-1000, www.maritim.de. (€€€€)

The **Hotel An Der Messe** is a small hotel close to the Messe. Rooms are individually furnished. Westendstraße 104, 60325 Frankfurt, ☎ 069-747-979, fax 069-748-349, www.hotel-an-der-messe.de. (€€€-€€€€)

Camping

City-Camp Frankfurt is northwest of the city. It is has many shady spots and good facilities. The U-Bahn station is 200 m (656 feet) from the site and reaches Frankfurt downtown in 15 minutes. It has 130 spaces and is open year-round. An der Sandelmühle 35, 60439 Frankfurt am Main-Heddenheim, ☎/fax 069-570-332, www.city-camp-frankfurt.de.

Where to Eat

The **Opéra**, Opernplatz 1, ☎ 069-134-0215, is a restaurant on the second floor of the Alte Oper. More pleasant than the elegant room is the terrace, with views of the Frankfurt skyline. The restaurant serves international nouvelle cuisine with strong French influences. Do not confuse the restaurant with the pleasant, small café bistro in front of the Alte Oper. (€€€-€€€€).

Gallo Nero, Kaiserhofstraße 7, ☎ 069-284-840, is an Italian restaurant just off the Fressgasse. (€€-€€€)

Nearby, is the more informal, hugely popular **Garibaldi**, Klein Hochstraße 4, ☎ 069-2199-7644. All servers are Italian and treat guests as if they were dining in an ultra-luxury restaurant. (€-€€)

The **Main Tower Restaurant**, Neuer Mainzer Straße 52, ☎ 069-3650-4777, is on the 53rd floor and the only restaurant open to the general public in Frankfurt's skyscrapers. The modern restaurant serves international cuisine with the best views in town. Dinner reservations are advisable. (€€-€€€).

Yours Australian Sports Bar, Rahmhofstraße 2, ☎ 069-282-100, is in the Schillerpassage near the Hilton Hotel. It is a great place for burgers and other Australian or American food – a much better choice than the Hard Rock next door. (€-€€)

Café Liebfrauenberg, Liebfrauenberg 24, ☎ 069-287-380, is an old-style café with pleasant service and a large selection of food and drink. It is close to the Liebfrauenkirche. (€)

Café Laumer, Bockenheimer Landstraße 67, ☎ 069-727-912, is a Viennese-style café in the heart of the Westend. It serves breakfast and lunch and has great cakes to accompany coffee at any hour. There is a large non-smoking section too. (€)

Sachsenhausen

Inside the Städel Art Museum is **Holbein's**, Holbeinstraße 1, ☎ 069-6605-6666, a modern restaurant serving mainly international cuisine with Mediterranean influences. It is also a pleasant place for afternoon coffee and cake. Fashionable right now, making dinner reservations advisable. (€€-€€€)

NYC, Schweizer Straße/Hans-Thomas-Straße, ☎ 069-614-818, is a good choice for American food close to the museum area. (€)

Sachsenhausen is famous for its apple wine. Apple wine (Ebbelwoi) is a local specialty, but a bit of an acquired taste. It has the same alcohol content as beer. The taverns that specialize in it usually serve only small meals and have a limited selection. The traditional places are in the area between Wall, Dreieichstraße and the Main. Two taverns with good food are closer to the Musuemufer: **Adolf Wagner**, Schweizer Straße 71, ☎ 069-612-565, and **Zum Gemahlten Haus**, Schweizer Straße 67, ☎ 069-614-559. (€)

■ Wiesbaden

Wiesbaden, the capital of the state of Hesse, is a beautiful town. It is filled with tree-lined avenues, huge well-kept parks, and stylish 19th-century villas.

The Romans already treasured the warm water springs of Wiesbaden. Although the town was briefly an imperial city in the 13th century, its real heyday came only in the 19th century. In 1806, the duke of Nassau moved his residence here and the rich and famous soon followed. Wiesbaden became famous as a spa town, with gambling allowed since 1771. Roulette started its route to fame and popularity here after the citizens of nearby Mainz were forbidden to play cards. Many famous people came here, ranging from Bismarck to Elvis Presley. However, the most famous story involved Russian novelist Fyodor Dostoyevsky who in 1865 lost 3,000 gold rubles in a single blow. Afterwards, he dictated in 26 days his famous novel *The Gambler*, in which he referred to Wiesbaden as Roulettenburg. He never managed to repay his gambling debts.

In 1866, the Prussians took over. Gambling was soon banned and, while the gambling set decamped mostly to Monaco, Kaiser Wilhelm II and other German and European nobles continued to favor the elegant spa town.

After World War II Wiesbaden became the center of the American-occupied zone. Military, especially air force, installations are still being used outside the town.

Information Sources

Tourist Office: Wiesbaden Tourist Information, Marktstraße 6, 65183 Wiesbaden, ☎ 0611-17-290, www.wiesbaden.de.

Getting Here

From Frankfurt, Wiesbaden is most easily reached on S-Bahn S1, S8, or S9. About five trains run per hour, taking 45 minutes. By car it is about 40 minutes on the Autobahn A66.

Sightseeing

For foreign visitors, the most interesting sight is the 1907 **Kurhaus**, Kurhausplatz 1, ☎ 0611-172-9290, www.kurbetriebe.wiesbaden.de. Constructed in a Belle Époque style, it has been restored to its former glory, including the over-the-top interior. It is a multipurpose building with event halls of various sizes, including a 1,350-seat theater with highly praised acoustics. It is possible to take a guided tour of the building or simply look around when the various halls are not in use.

The most famous part of the Kurhaus is used for the **Spielbank** (Casino), Kurhausplatz 1, ☎ 0611-536-100, www.spielbank-wiesbaden.de. Spielbank means casino. In Germany, most casinos enforce the rules and dress code seriously. In Wiesbaden at all hours men must wear a jacket and tie and women must be suitably dressed. Entry into the casino is €2.50 with no obligation to partake in the gambling. Photo identification is required and the minimum age is 18 years. Minimum bets range from €2 to €100, depending on the game and table. Spielbank Wiesbaden offers the highest roulette stakes in Germany: on a full number up to €1,000 can be bet and on black or red up to €50,000. Opening hours are daily from 2:45 pm to at least 4 am – longer if the going is good.

From the main entrance to the Kurhaus, a small park, sometimes referred to as the Bowling Green, flanked by two wide tree-lined boulevards, leads towards the grand hotel Nassauer Hof. More interesting than the park, however, are the two early 19th-century white colonnade buildings, at 129 m (423 feet) the longest in Europe. To the right is the **Kurhauskollonade** – it houses part of the casino where the stakes are smaller and the technology higher. Here, 170 different slot machines can be played with 50 cents the minimum stake. The maximum payout is €20,000, except for the Super Jackpot, which can exceed €100,000. Admission is €1, the minimum age 18. Open daily from 1 pm to at least 4 am.

On the other side of the park is the **Theaterkollonade**. It is attached to the rear of the Hesse State Theater and houses several top-line shops. In front of the theater is a statue of Friedrich Schiller facing the **Warmer Damm Park**. The unfenced park is well-kept, with rolling lawns, high trees, and a large pond with water birds. On the one side, it borders Wilhelmstraße, Wiesbaden's most fashionable street, lined with exclusive boutiques and a number of luxury restaurants and hotels. The large **Kurpark** behind the Kurhaus is Wiesabaden's most beautiful park and a joy to stroll in.

Most of the Old Town is a huge pedestrian zone shopping district. At the south end, it starts from the **Marktplatz** with the 1884 Neo-Renaissance **Rathaus**. This was damaged during World War II and rebuilt in a simpler form. Behind it is the **Stadtschloss**, since 1946 seat of the Parliament of Hesse (Hessischer Landstag).

The old town skyline is dominated by the 92-m (300-foot) tower of the Evangelical **Marktkirche**, Schlossplatz 4, ☎ 0611-900-1611. Built in 1853-62 in a Neo-Gothic style, this was the first brick building in the duchy of Nassau. The 50-m (165-foot) interior is decorated with classical statues. Half-hour organ recitals are offered Saturdays at 11:30. The carillon plays daily at 9 am, noon, and 5 pm.

The hot-water spring at the **Kochbrunnen**, Am Kranzplatz, has been known since at least 1366. This health water is high in sodium chloride and comes to the surface at 66°C/150°F. Nearby is the **Kaiser Friedrich Therme**, an expensive Roman-Irish spa (see *Adventures* below).

Adventures

On Foot

The tourist office conducts guided walking tours of the **old town** area from April to October on Saturday at 10 am. From November to March, the tour is only on the first and third Saturday of the month at 10 am.

On Water

The **Kaiser-Friedrich Terme**, Langgasse 38-40, ☎ 0611-172-9660, has recently been restored to its 1913 glory. It is described as an **Irish-Roman bath** with several of the rooms decorated in an Art Nouveau (*Jugendstil*) style. The spa is fed by the Adlerquelle (Eagle Spring), which has a temperature of 66°C (151°F). The Romans may well have used this spring themselves as the Roman gate behind the spa suggests. The spa includes an array of hot rooms, both dry and steam, cold rooms, warm and cold baths, and relaxation rooms with special lights and aroma conditions. The basic entry is €17.50 for four hours. To this can be added all sorts of spa treatments and massages, ranging from €8 for a sand bath to €40 for a full aroma massage. A small drinks bar and an oxygen bar are also available. Textile-free bathing is preferred – meaning clothes will be frowned upon. The spa is open daily from 10 am to 10 pm, on Tuesday for women only. The minimum age is 16 and a strict non-smoking policy is enforced.

Köln-Düsseldörfer, Rheingaustraße 145, ☎ 0611-600-995, has **boat cruises** on the Rhine from April to October. **Primus Linie**, Rheinguastraße 150, ☎ 0611-133-8370 has boat cruises on the Rhine and on the Main to Frankfurt. It operates from May to October.

Where to Stay

For well over a century, the top address in town has been the **Nassauer Hof**, across the road from the Kollonade and Spielbank. The building is a typical turn-of-the-19th-century Neo-Baroque attention-grabber in the tradition of a grand hotel. Rooms are large and lavishly furnished. Both restaurants in the hotel are excellent, with the Euro-Asian **Ente** restaurant (€€€€) considered the best in Wiesbaden. Service is excellent and the wine list vast. The **Orangerie** (€€€) offers regional cuisine in a less formal setting. Kaiser Friedrich Platz 3, 65183 Wiesbaden, ☎ 0611-1330, fax 0611-133-632, www.nassauer-hof.de. €€€€)

Close to the Kochbrunnen is the luxury **Radisson SAS Schwarzer Bock**, one of the oldest hotels in Germany. Although the building dates from 1586, it was completely renovated in the late 1990s. All rooms are comfortably furnished and have marble baths. Kranzplatz 12, 65183 Wiesbaden, ☎ 0611-1550, fax 0611-155-111, www.radissonsas.com. (€€€€)

Far more affordable, and almost next door, is one of Wiesbaden's two **Ibis** hotels. The hotel is typical Ibis with few frills but modern, clean, and reasonably comfortable. Kranzplatz 10, 65183 Wiesbaden, ☎ 0611-36-140, fax 0611-361-4499, www.ibishotels.com. (€-€€)

Where to Eat

Wiesbaden has a remarkable number of outdoor eateries – as soon as the sun is out, tables on the sidewalks fill up making parts of the old town seem like a huge open-air restaurant. But it is best to compare the daily specials and the clientele before sitting down.

Beck's am Bäckerbrunnen, Grabenstraße 28, ☎ 0611-373-409, is a pleasant, informal restaurant with outdoor seating around the Bäckerbrunnen under large green Beck's beer umbrellas. The menu is mainly modern German cuisine. Portions are large. Service can vary from just fine to a bit slow. (€-€€)

Across from the classy Art Nouveau Kaiser Friederich Therme is the modern building housing **Alex**, Langgasse 38-40, ☎ 0611-341-2740, www.alexgastro.com, a very informal restaurant. It offers good value and serves mainly smaller meals, ice creams, and cakes. The breakfast and afternoon cake buffets on weekdays and brunch buffet on Sundays are especially popular. The clientele are mainly younger people and families. (€-€€)

Near the Kochbrunnen in the former hospital are two eateries. The tiny **Bistro Karim's**, Kochbrunnenplatz 3, ☎ 0611-959-0608, offers Mediterranean cuisine sourced from Morocco to Lebanon. The menu is rather small but changes frequently. It is more a delicatessen than a restaurant and all dishes are also available for take-out. (€-€€)

Far larger and more modern is **Spital**, Kranzplatz, ☎ 0611-528-830. Located in a steel and glass building, it offers good views of the square in front. The cuisine is similarly modern and light. (€-€€)

Between the Rathaus and Marktkirche is another modern steel and glass building housing the excellent restaurant **Lumen**, Dernsches Gelände, ☎ 0611-300-200, www.lumen-gastronomie.de. The menu changes weekly. Between meals, it serves as a café and bar. (€€-€€€)

Inside the Spielbank is **Käfer's**, Kurhausplatz 1, ☎ 0611-536-200, www.kurhaus-gastronomie.de, an upscale bistro, bar with a terrace, and beer garden when weather allows. The cuisine ranges from international to nouvelle cuisine and regional specialties. The interior is Art Nouveau and blends in well with the rest of the smart Kurhaus. Live music at night. (€€-€€€€)

■ Taunus

The Taunus is a series of forested, low mountains that cover the area from north of Frankfurt to the River Lahn. Picturesque small towns, thick forests, and ample recreation options make the Taunus a favored weekend escape for urbanites.

It is easiest to travel the Taunus by car, but public transportation is available to almost all areas. The Taunus is covered by walking and cycling routes and buses are available to make circular routes unnecessary.

The Taunus has been inhabited since at least Celtic times and the Roman border, the *Limes Line*, ran through it. In the Middle Ages, about 100 castles existed in the Taunus but few remain and most are in ruins. The Taunus is not particularly suited for agriculture and the region was mostly poor until the 19th century brought wealth in the form of tourism and industry.

Information Sources

Tourist Office: Tourist-Info Hochtaunus, Ludwig-Erhard-Anlage 1-4, 61352 Bad Homburg v.d. Höhe, www.taunus-info.de.

Getting Here

Bus 917 runs from Bad Homburg station via Oberursel, Kronberg, and Königstein to Falkenstein. Bad Homburg and Kronberg are easily reached from Frankfurt by S-Bahn.

Bad Homburg vor der Höhe

Bad Homburg is in many respects similar to the larger Wiesbaden. It was also the residence of a lesser noble, it has a spa and casino and became popular with the rich and the aristocracy after the area became part of Prussia in the 19th century. Kaiser Wilhelm II used to spend a month each summer here and the Prince of Wales used to sojourn here frequently before he became King Edward VII. His favored style of hat became known as the Homburg.

The wonder waters are still used today to treat rheumatism, stomach and intestinal ailments, heart problems, and skin disease. For the healthy, there are minor historic sites and one of the loveliest spa parks in Germany.

Information Sources

Tourist Office: Tourist Information, Kurhaus, Louisenstraße 58, 61348 Bad Homburg v. d. Höhe, ☎ 06172-178-110, www.badhomburg.de.

Getting Here

Bad Homburg is most easily reached from Frankfurt on S-Bahn S5 – up to four connections per hour taking 20 minutes. Alternatively, a bus from Frankfurt's Main station runs to the casino hourly from 2 to 10 pm, and then hourly from 10:25 pm to 1:25 am. The €6 fee is refunded for visitors to the casino.

Sightseeing

There are two distinct areas for sightseeing: the Kurpark and the old town.

■ Old Town

The main attraction in the old town is **Schloss Bad Homburg**, Schulbergstraße 1, ☎ 06172-926-2148, the residence of the Counts of Hesse-Homburg from 1622-1866. Only a small part of the castle is open to the public as a museum. It mainly features art and furniture from the residence period as well as the English Rooms, the rooms used by Countess Elizabeth, an English princess. The museum is open Tuesday to Sunday from 9 am to 5 pm (November to February from 10 am to 4 pm). Admission is €3.50 and includes a German-only guided tour.

You are free to wander around the buildings, admire the view, and stroll in the pleasant garden at no charge. In the central courtyard, standing a bit awkwardly on its own, is the 48-m (158-foot) medieval

White Tower, shown below, the only part of the original fortress that survived the conversion to a Baroque palace in 1679. It is open daily from 9 am to 6 pm (to 3 pm from November to February) with free admission. A pleasant beer garden operates in its shade during summer months. To the north of the castle is the 1330 **Hexenturm** (Witches Gate), part of the former medieval town walls.

The ancient-looking Lutheran **Erlöserkirche**, Dorotheanstraße 1, was constructed in 1902-08 on order of Kaiser Wilhelm II, who favored Bad Homburg throughout his life. It combines Romanesque and Byzantine elements. Its four towers enhance the impression of size and height, despite the overall compactness of the building. The interior is another surprise, with marble walls and golden mosaics reminiscent of San Marco in Venice. The nearby Roman Catholic **Marienkirche** is only a decade older and built as a Neo-Gothic basilica.

■ Kurpark

A block down from the modern 1980s Kurhaus is the 114-acre **Kurpark**. It is filled with art – ranging from temporary modern art to statues of famous literary figures, including Dostoievsky. Seven of the hot springs that made Bad Homburg famous are inside the Kurpark. Water from the Victoria fountain tastes like liquid metal. The tennis club inside the park is the oldest on the European continent.

The late 19th-century **Kaiser Wilhelms Bad** is a grandiose sandstone and brick building typical of the period. Currently it is being used as an event space in addition to hosting the grand Kur Royal – see *Spas* below.

Nearby is the **Spielbank** (Casino), Im Kurpark, ☎ 06172-1701-0, www.spielbank-bad-homburg.de. It was designed by the Blanc brothers in 1841. They later also designed the Casino in Monte Carlo, making the move there easier for the gambling jet set after the Prussians stopped legal gambling in Germany in 1872. Currently the tables are open daily from 3 pm to 3 am and slot machines from 1:45 pm to 1:45 am. Entry to the main casino is €2.50 and €1 to the slot machines. A passport or European identification card must be shown upon first entry. The minimum age is 18. Men must wear a jacket and tie at all times and women must be dressed similarly – jeans, sport clothing, and sneakers are not welcome.

Foreign aristocracy also took to the waters in Bad Homburg and left their mark in the park. King Chulanlongkorn of Siam donated the **Thai-Sala** in 1907, with golden carvings and other rich decorations in appreciation for his cure. The czar laid the foundation stone for the small **Russian church** with typical onion domes as a place of prayer for Russian visitors to the spa. It is still used by the Russian community and the interior can only be seen on a guided tour of the Kurpark.

■ Spas

Bad Homburg has several expensive private clinics where patients can take advantage of the health benefits of the local springs. For the casual visitor the Kur Royal and Taunus Therme offer the two most attractive, if completely different, options.

The **Kur Royal** is a day spa inside the grand late 19th-century Kaiser Wilhemsbad in the Kurpark, ☎ 06172-178-178, www.kur-royal.de. Its facilities and splendor remind the visitor why Bad Homburg was the spa of choice for the royalty of Europe before the First World War. The basic Kur Royal Inclusive package goes for €25 per two hours, €40 for four, and €60 for a full day. It includes the following course: a warm saltwater relaxation pool, a stone oven bath, an aromatherapy bath, a hay steam bath, a sand and light bath (a dawn-to-dusk day on the beach simulation in 30 minutes), a high-humidity Roman steam bath and, to finish, wave dreams – cooling down with visual effects and coordinated music. To this can be added a whole range of additional baths, massages, and acupunctures costing €30 to €75 extra. Nude bathing is not allowed – towels are supplied but not bathing suits or slippers. No smoking and no under-16s. Prior reservations are required.

Just outside the Kurpark is the much more informal and cheaper **Taunus Therme**, Seedamweg, ☎ 06172-406-40, www.taunus-therme.de. It combines elements of Japanese, Finnish, and Greco-Roman culture in both its architecture and approach to the spa concept. It has an enormous outdoor pool as well as several other hot and cold pools, cascading waterfalls and bubbling hot whirlpools fed by the Victoria Luise spring (32-36°C/90-97°F). Traditional Finnish saunas add Nordic charm and some go up to 45°C/113°F and 98% humidity. Most areas require bathing suits but 150 outdoor tanning spots are available in the FKK (nude) zone. The spa is open daily from 9 am to 11 pm. Admission fees include the use of all facilities. During the week, admission is €12.50 for two hours, €17 for four hours, and €24 for a full day. On weekends and holidays, add €2 to each fee.

Excursion to Saalburg

The *Limes Line*, the border between the civilized Roman province of Germania Superior and the "barbarian" areas of Germany, ran through the Taunus. At Saalburg, ☎ 06175-93-740, a former Roman border castle has been restored to the state it was in around 200 AD when up to 3,000 soldiers and civilians lived inside the castle and the adjacent village. The outside walls are 150 by 220 m (490 by 722 feet) and the main hall measures an impressive 39 by 12 m (127 by 39 feet). The castle fell into disrepair after the Romans abandoned the Limes around 260 AD and withdrew behind the Rhine. In the late 19th century, reconstruction started with the support of Kaiser Wilhelm II, who visited the site in his youth while staying in nearby Bad Homburg. Inside the castle are various exhibition rooms on Germanic-Roman history and Roman life in general. On summer Sundays, demonstrations of Roman arts such as baking are held. The forest around the castle is a favored hiking area. A section of the Limes Wall has been restored and is about 15 minutes walk from the castle.

Bronze coin of Emperor Hadrian in Saalburg museum

The **museum** is open daily from 9 am to 6 pm (to 4 pm November to February). Admission is €2.50. The museum café **Taberna** has a small menu that includes tasty dishes originating from Roman cuisine. It has the same opening hours as the museum, but is closed from mid-November to end February.

Saalburg is a few km north of Bad Homburg along the B456 in the direction of Usingen. Alternatively, take Bus 5 from Bad Homburg direct to the castle or take the Taunusbahn to Saalburg-Lochmühle and follow the 45-minute walkway along the Limes Line to Saalburg.

Where to Stay & Eat

The luxurious **Steigenberger Hotel Bad Homburg** is in a large villa at the Kurpark. The interior has a 1920s and Art Deco feel to it. Rooms are luxurious with marble bathrooms. **Charly's Bistro** (€€-€€€) serves international and French cuisine. Kaiser-Friedrich-Promenade 69-75, 61348 Bad Homburg, ☎ 06172-1810, fax 06172-181-631, www.steigenberger.de. (€€€€)

The **Parkhotel Bad Homburg** is a privately managed hotel in three connected villas across the road from the Kurpark. Rooms are comfortably furnished and most are spacious. The restaurant **La Tavola** (€€-€€€) serves Italian cuisine and the **Jade** (€€-€€€) offers Chinese dishes. Kaiser-Friedrich-Promenade 53, 61348 Bad Homburg, ☎ 06172-8010, fax 06172-801-400. www.parkhotel-bad-homburg.de. (€€-€€€€)

Hotel Hardtwald is slightly north of the Kurpark in a forested area. Rooms are comfortable and some have balconies. The restaurant (€€€) serves Mediterranean cuisine. Philosophenweg 31, 61348 Bad Homburg, ☎ 06172-988-151, fax 06172-82-512, www.hardtwald-hotel.de. (€€-€€€€)

Kronberg

Information Sources

Tourist Office: Tourist information is available from the **Verkehrs und Kulturampt**, Katherinenstraße 7, 61476 Kronberg, ☎ 06173-703-220, www.kronberg.de.

Getting Here

Kronberg can be reached in less than 30 minutes from Frankfurt on S-Bahn S4.

Sightseeing

Burg Kronberg (Castle), Schlossstraße 10, ☎ 06173-7788, towers over the old town. The keep is early 13th century, with the rest of the castle added in the following two centuries. A small museum documents the town's history. The castle is open from Easter to October on Saturdays from 1 to 5 pm and Sundays from 11:30 am to 5 pm. Admission is €2.50.

The rest of the old town is pretty, well-maintained, and romantic, especially at night. It is highly recommended and popular with diners from Frankfurt making reservations for dinner, especially over weekends. In the late 19th century, Kronberg became a favorite place for painters from Frankfurt trying their hand at the new French Impressionist style. Ever since, Kronberg has been favored by artists, with the number of small art galleries in the old town out of proportion to the number of actual residents.

Queen Victoria of Prussia (1840-1901), the eldest daughter of the more famous Queen Victoria of Great Britain, built **Schloss Victoria** in 1889-94 after the death of her husband Kaiser Friedrich III. He was emperor for only 99 days. She was a liberal figure with views directly opposite those of her son, Kaiser Wilhelm II, whom she had little contact with during her final years. The castle is now a luxury hotel with an upscale restaurant. It is worth driving by and the park is freely open. Guided tours in small groups are available on weekends between 3 and 6 pm – inquire at the hotel.

Where to Stay & Eat

Schlosshotel Kronberg is a luxury hotel in the former palace of Empress Victoria, Queen of Prussia. The huge palace has some 50 luxurious rooms with classical furniture and original art. The hotel is in a large park with a golf course and an Italian rose garden. The restaurant (€€€€) serves international nouvelle cuisine. Hainstraße 25, 61476 Kronberg, ☎ 06173-70-101, fax 06173-701-267, www.schlosshotel-kronberg.de. (€€€€)

Concorde Hotel Viktoria is a modern hotel, its comfortable rooms equipped with the latest technology required by the business traveler. Some rooms have small kitchens. Viktoriastraße, 61476 Kronberg, ☎ 06173-92-100, fax 06173-921-050, www.concordehotel-viktoria.sw. (€€€-€€€€)

Restaurant Zum Adler, Friedrich-Ebert-Straße 13, ☎ 06173-5701, is in the heart of the old town. Despite the traditional old German tavern name, it serves Italian food. The interior feels a bit like being inside a meringue, but the pasta and pizzas taste great and prices are low. (€-€€)

Königstein

Information Sources

Tourist Office: Tourist information is available from the **Kur- und Stadtinformation**, Kurparkpassage, Haupstraße 21, 61462 Königstein, ☎ 06174-202-251, www.koenigstein.de.

Sightseeing

Königstein is a pretty town in the foothills of the Feldberg, at 880 m (2,886 feet), the highest settlement in the Taunus. The town is a *Luftkurort* (a health resort where clean air and a refreshing climate is thought to be beneficial) and a popular residence for the wealthy working in Frankfurt.

The main sight in town is the **Burgruine**, the ruins of the former fortress that used to guard the trade route from Frankfurt to Cologne between the 12th and 18th centuries. Nowadays, it is famous as the second-largest fortress ruins in Germany. Very steep staircases lead to the viewing

Passau – view of the old town from Veste Oberhaus (© Passau Tourismus)

Interior of the cathedral at Passau (© Passau Tourismus)

ove: Confluence of the Ilz, Danube and Inn rivers at Passau (© Passau Tourismus)

Below: Munich's Odeonsplatz, with the Felderhalle and Theatinerkirche (© Christl Reiter/FVA-muc)

Above: Munich's Marienplatz, with the Neues Rathaus and Frauenkirche
(© Christl Reiter / FVA-muc)

Below: Old town in Munich with Alps as backdrop *(© Rudolf Sterflinger / FVA-m*

platform on the 35-m (195-foot) tower. The view from here is spectacular and includes the Frankfurt skyline, Feldberg, and Burg Kronberg. Apart from the view, it is also a fun place for children, as there is no museum and they can run wild and climb all the remaining staircases. The ruins are open daily, November to February from 9:30 am to 3 pm, March and October until 4:30 pm and April to September from 9 am to 7 pm. Admission is €1.50.

The **Kurpark** at the foot of the castle has pleasant walks, including some that are suitable for wheelchair users.

A smaller castle ruin is in the nearby suburb of **Falkenstein**. The ruins here date from the 12th century and once again offer spectacular views. The ruins are open daily from 9 am to 4 pm. Admission is free.

The highest and most popular peak in the Taunus is the 880-m (2,886-foot) **Großer Feldberg**. The top can be reached by car or bus and is a popular hiking and mountain biking destination. A 20-m (66-foot) tower with viewing platform crowned by an eagle at the top is open daily from 9 am until dusk, except closed in November. The tower was destroyed in World War II when a German plane crashed into it in thick fog. On a clear day, the views are awe-inspiring. A large restaurant and several snack bars provide nourishment for the masses. The other buildings are used by radio and telecommunication companies and not open to the public. From Königstein follow the B8 in the direction of Limburg or use Bus 511.

Adventures in the Taunus

On Foot

The Taunus is crisscrossed by well-marked hiking routes freely open to individuals and groups. Very popular is **hiking** up the highest peak, the **Großer Feldberg**. Many options exist and hiking up and down can be done in three hours. It is also possible to take the bus to the peak and stroll down. A 13-km (7.8-mile) route leads from the Tillmannsweg parking space on the B8 (Bus 502 or 511, stop Friedhof) from Königstein to Glashütten. Bus 511 goes all the way to the top and returns to Oberursel.

Several easy walking routes through the forest without too many inclines start from the Roman castle at **Saalburg**. A popular six-km (90-minute) educational route connects the castle with the Hessenpark Open Air Museum. Along this route, 14 stations explain the history and nature of the Taunus region. Shorter routes are also available

Highly qualified guides at the **Nature Park Hochtaunus**, Pestalozzistraße 2, 61250 Usingen, ☎ 06081-2885, offer various tours between May and October. The schedule is available from April. Participation is about €8 per person.

Guided walking tours are offered by several tourist information offices and hiking clubs in the region. Although the tours will generally be in German only, English speakers, who prefer not to ramble alone, can always tag along. Many of your fellow hikers may speak English and the atmosphere on country trips is generally convivial. The charges are minimal, often only the public transportation fee to get to the starting point. Literally every town in the Taunus has a hiking club but the ones listed below offer regular, at least weekly, guided tours.

- The **Bad Homburg** tourist office conducts several country walking tours on Monday and Wednesday afternoons. The destinations and routes change weekly.
- **Bad Camberg** tourist office, ☎ 06434-202-411, offers country walks on Saturday afternoons ranging from two to three hours, depending on the route.
- An informal walking club meets every Wednesday in **Königstein** in all weather conditions for a three-hour walk in the region – contact the Königstein tourist office, ☎ 06174-202-251, www.koenigstein.de, for meeting times and more details.
- The Taunusklub 1878 **Oberursel**, ☎ 06171-26468, offers walking tours on Wednesday and Thursday mornings.

On Wheels

The Taunus area is for trained **bikers** only. There are virtually no level roads and most have steep inclines. Cycling up or down the Große Feldberg is popular for those who are in shape.

In the Air

Heissluftballon "Papa Oskar," Familie Schäfer, Wilhelm-Reuter-Straße 9, 65817 Eppstein, ☎ 06198-500-178, starts their **hot-air balloon** trips from several sites in the Taunus region.

Gliding noiselessly through the air has been the dream of many and in the Taunus region this dream can become reality. Two organizations offer guests the chance to catch a bird's-eye view of the countryside. Both are private gliding clubs that offer visitors an opportunity to fly, so the number of seats is limited and mostly available on weekends only.

- Near Feldberg, in the Oberems neighborhood of Glashütten, **Flugsportgruppe Feldberg**, ☎ 06174-61-886 or on weekends ☎ 06082-1042, www.fsg-feldberg.de, allows guests to accompany experienced pilots in two-seater gliders. Flights start at a surprisingly low €10 and €1 per flight-minute. The minimum age is six years and, although the cabin is narrow, thusfar all guests have managed to squeeze both in and out.
- In Weilburg, the **Sportfliegerclub Riedelbach**, ☎ 06144-44407 or on weekends ☎ 06083-1090, www.sfc-riedelbach.de, has both regular gliders and motorized gliders flying on weekends. Flights start at €15 for gliders and €0.80 per minute after 11 minutes, or €28 for motorized gliders and €1.30 per minute after 21 minutes.

On Snow

Hesse is not a winter sports wonderland, but there are a few options available when weather conditions are right. The target groups are clearly local residents who want to take advantage of the occasional snow when they cannot make it to the much better slopes in Bavaria. Do not expect too much in terms of rental equipment and facilities.

Downhill skiing without a ski lift is possible on the slopes of Feldberg near Schmitten. Three slopes ranging from 600 m to 1,500 m (1,968 to 4,920 feet) are available.

There are 17 cross-country ski trails in the Taunus region. Most are easy to moderately easy. Once again, the best bets are on the northern side of Feldberg. A 30-km (18-mile) trail connects Saalburg and Rod an der Weil.

For information on actual snow conditions, dial the **Taunus Snow Telephone**, ☎ 06082-2727, or see www.wintersport-in-taunus.de.

■ Lahn Valley

The Lahn Valley is one of Germany's best-kept secrets. It is an area of outstanding beauty, with many ancient towns and castles, and very few foreign tourists. This is odd as it is Germany's favorite waterway for canoeing and the valley and most towns can be reached within an hour by either car or train from Frankfurt.

All the towns described below are worth a visit, but priority should be given to **Marburg** and **Limburg** – both with outstandingly well-preserved medieval town centers, though they are completely different in character.

Information Sources

Tourist Office: Information is available from the **Lahntal Tourismus Verband**, Karl-Kellner-Ring 51, 35576 Wetzlar, ☎ 06441-407-1900, www.lahntal.de, or from any tourist information office in the valley.

Transportation

The Lahn Valley has good roads, which follow the flow of the river closely from Limburg to Lahnstein. Both Limburg and Gießen have connections to major Autobahns.

A train service is available and runs at least hourly through the valley from Gießen to Koblenz. Trains to Marburg often require a changeover in Gießen.

Adventures in the Lahn Valley

The Lahn Valley is popular for cycling, walking, and canoeing – a combination of all three activities is called a TriathLahn. Hiking and cycling routes run the full length of the river, while most of it is open to canoeists as well.

On Foot

Along the right bank of the river, the **Lahnhöhen walking route** is 300 km (180 miles) and divided into 18 stages, ranging from 12 to 37 km (seven to 22 miles) each. The route offers not only natural beauty, but also passes through the historic towns of the Lahn. The routes are marked with a white "L."

An interesting side-route from Weilburg is the 46-km (27-mile) **Weil Valley Walking and Cycling Route**, www.weiltalweg.de. The route follows the flow of the narrow Weil River through the Hochtaunuspark (www.hochtaunus.naturpark.de) from Schmitten to Weilburg, with a height difference of 460 m (1,500 feet). From April to mid-October, a bus (the Weiltalbus) operates on this route – it has a carrier for bicycles.

On Wheels

The **Lahn Valley Cycling Route** is 250 km (150 miles) and mostly on separate tracks from the regular auto roads. It is possible to cycle from Marburg to Lahnstein in three days, but longer tours are recommended in order to do some sightseeing along the way.

Cycling Distances from Lahnquelle (Lahn Source)

Marburg	66 km/40 miles
Gießen	30 km/18 miles
Wetzlar	16 km/9.5 miles
Braunfels	15 km/9 miles
Weilburg	16 km/9.5 miles
Limburg	31 km/18.6 miles
Nassau	31 km/18.6 miles
Bad Ems	10 km/6 miles
Lahnstein (confluence with the Rhine)	12 km/7.2 miles
Braubach with the Marksburg castle	5 km/3 miles

In Marburg, **Velociped**, Alte Kassler Straße 43, 35039 Marburg, ☎ 06421-24-511, www.velociped.de, specializes in cycling tours ranging from less than a day to a week or more. For multi-day trips, accommodation and luggage forwarding arrangements can be made. TriathLahn can be arranged, ranging from multi-day tours to an active seven-hour day-trip around Marburg. Near Marburg, **Lahntours**, Lahnstraße 45, 35096 Roth, ☎ 06426-92-800, www.lahntours.de, does similar trips.

On Water

The Lahn is Germany's most popular river for **canoeing**. The river is slow-flowing, not particularly wide, and passes through a beautiful valley filled with historic towns and castles. It is also easily accessible from Frankfurt. Several companies offer equipment for rent and many can also arrange a complete vacation, including accommodation and luggage forwarding. Combination packages, with alternating days of rowing, cycling, and walking, are also popular.

ROWING DISTANCES ON THE LAHN

The Lahn is navigable all year from Roth, just south of Marburg, to the confluence with the Rhine River at Lahnstein. Experienced rowers can do the whole trip in a week, but options as short as only a few hours are possible.

Rowing distances between major points are listed below. There are of course many more landing sites, including some not accessible by car. From Lahnstein to Limburg, sluice operators are on hand, but farther upstream sluices must be worked by users on their own.

Distances from Roth (near Marburg)

Gießen	21 km/12.6 miles
Wetzlar	16 km/9.6 miles
Oberbiel Sluices	8 km/4.8 miles
Solms-Braunfels	5 km/3 miles
Selters	12 km/7.2 miles
Weilburg	4 km/2.4 miles
Runkel	24 km/14.4 miles
Limburg	10 km/6 miles
Diez	7 km/4.2 miles
Laurenburg	19 km/11.4 miles
Nassau	14 km/8.4 miles
Bad Ems	9 km/5.4 miles
Lahnstein am Rhein	13 km/7.8 miles

Near Marburg, **Lahntours Aktivreisen**, Lahnstraße 45, 35096 Roth, ☎ 06426-92-800, www.lahntours.de, offers multiple options for active vacations ranging from one day to a week. The trips can start from six different stations on the Lahn and end at various places situated about every 15 km (nine miles). For multi-day trips, Lahntours can arrange accommodation including camping and luggage forwarding if desired. Rates include the return of the boat and passengers to the home station. Multiple day combination with walking and cycling can also be arranged.

Other companies renting boats include:

- **Rotana Touristik**, Talstraße 6, 35606 Solms, ☎ 06442-23-332, www.rotana.de.
- **Krumos Kanus**, Beethovenstraße 1, 35606 Solms, ☎ 06442-92-119, www.krumos-kanus.de.
- **Tourist Info Weilburg**, Mauerstraße 6-8, 35781 Weilburg, ☎ 06471-7671.
- **Biwak**, Schaumburger Straße 1, 65549 Limburg, ☎ 06431-98-280, www.biwak.com.
- **Wassersport Danner**, Koblenzer Straße 13,65582 Diez, ☎ 06432-81-389.
- **Bootsvermietung Hofmann**, Kaltbachtal 2, 56377 Nassau, ☎ 02604-942-083, www.kanucharter.de.
- **Bootsvermietung Bad Ems**, Thomas Kreutz, Auf der Au 29B, 56132 Dausenau, ☎ 02603-13-964, www.canutours.de.

Marburg

Marburg is a pretty university town of 75,000 (including some 18,000 students) built on several steep hills in the Lahn Valley. The town survived World War II undamaged and has some of the most impressive half-timbered buildings in Germany.

Visiting Marburg requires stamina. This is not a place for the infirm as most of the old town is built against the steep hills to the west of the River Lahn. Sturdy footwear is required to negotiate the slippery cobblestone streets.

The castle high on the hill above Marburg can be seen from several km down the road when arriving from the south. This is fortunate, as the first impressions of Marburg would otherwise be of a disappointingly modern and bland town. However, this is quickly forgotten once you leave the lower section and enter the medieval upper town.

Information Sources

Tourist Office: Marburg Tourism, Pilgrimstein 26, 35037 Marburg, ☎ 06421-99-120, fax 06421-99-1212, www.marburg.de.

Transportation

Marburg is about 100 km (60 miles) north of Frankfurt. By **car**, it can be reached in less than an hour via the A5; take the turnoff Gambacher Kreuz for Gießen and from Gießen on the B3 to Marburg. The route is well marked. Follow the signs to Marburg Mitte or Zentrum and park soon after crossing the Lahn River. Street parking is at a premium in the old town, making it best to steer directly to the signposted official parking garages.

By **train**, Marburg can be reached from Frankfurt in an hour on the InterCity or in 90 minutes on the at least hourly (and cheaper) Regional Express. Trains down the Lahn Valley depart at least hourly as well – some require a changeover in Gießen. The station is on the "wrong" side of the Lahn, about 10 minutes walk from the Elizabeth Church. Virtually all buses from the station pass through Rudolphplatz at the bottom of the old town, from where Bus 16 can be taken to the Marktplatz, or all the way up to the castle.

Sightseeing

The first stop in Marburg should be the **Elizabethkirche**, c/o Elizabeth & Deutschhausstraße, ☎ 06421-655-73. Erected between 1235 and 1283 this was the first completely Gothic church in all of Germany. (Some, especially Trier, claim the same honor.) Although pure Gothic in form, the thickness of the walls and pillars shows that this is an early sample of the new form with previous knowledge of the Romanesque clearly still influential. Virtually the entire interior of this church is original.

The church was built to house the remains of St Elizabeth of Thuringia and soon became a popular venue on pilgrim routes. However, a later descendant, Count Philipp the Magnanimous, a prominent figure in the Lutheran Reformation, unceremoniously removed her bones to a nearby graveyard in 1539. The original shrine remained, though, and the current evangelical church management has no qualms about charging visitors to see it. Entry to the church is free, but admission to the choirs is €2.50 (well worth it). In addition to the Elizabeth reliquaries, the graves of several of the counts of Hesse can be seen in the south transept. Also note the stained glass windows dating from the 13th and 15th centuries. At the back, to the left of the main entrance, is the grave of Paul von Hindenburg (1847-1934), a war hero and the last President of the ill-fated Weimar Republic. He had the dishonor of appointing Hitler, whom he openly despised, as chancellor in 1933.

The church is open daily from 9 am to 6 pm, April to September, 9 am to 5 pm in October, and 10 am to 4 pm from November to March. On all Sundays and religious holidays it is open from 11:15 (after the evangelical service).

Saint Elizabeth of Thuringia (1207-1231)

At age four, Princess Elizabeth, daughter of the King of Hungary, was engaged to Ludwig IV of Thuringia and sent to live in the Wartburg in Eisenach. At age 14, the prince duly married her, although by that time the alliance with Hungary had lost its strategic importance. A year later, she gave birth to a daughter, Sophie. Elizabeth was famous for assisting the poor, to the dismay and at times disgust of her in-laws. On one famous occasion, while taking bread to the local poor, she was stopped by her husband's entourage. She claimed to have been picking flowers and, when challenged, she opened her basket and the bread had turned to roses – one of the wonders that sent her on the fast track to sainthood.

After the unexpected death, according to most legends murder, of her husband during a crusade, Elizabeth was hounded from the Wartburg by her brother-in-law, Heinrich Raspe IV. She established a hospital for the poor in Marburg, where she was under the influence of her rather eccentric confessor. Here she slaved away her last few years doing menial labor among the poor and sick. Four years after her death in 1231, she was made a saint and her bones moved to the Elizabethkirche in the presence of Emperor Friedrich II. Her grandson was the first count of Hesse.

From the Elizabethkirche, follow Steinweg to the upper town, or continue on Pilgrimstein Road and use the free public elevator (across from the Sorat Hotel) to whoosh you up five stories, where you will emerge in the marvelous medieval center of town without breaking a sweat. There are several impressive half-timbered houses in Reitgasse, but the real jewels of the town are around the **Market Square**. The oldest building in town is the **Steinernes Haus** (Stone House, above) at Markt 18, which dates back to 1319. The main building of the **Rathaus** (Town Hall) dates from 1512, with the gable added in 1581. Near the Town Hall, at Hirschgasse 13, is a 1970s reconstruction of Marburg's oldest timber-framed building, originally constructed in 1321. More impressive though are the half-timbered houses at Markt 14, 16, 17, 19, 21 and 23. All date from the 16th century and most have restaurants on the ground floors.

From the market square, it is a steep but rewarding 20-minute walk along Markt and Landgraf Philippstraße to the **Marburg Castle** (Landgrafenschloss), seat of the counts of Hesse from the 13th to the 17th centuries. From the old town, follow the clearly marked directions "Zum Schloss." No less rewarding is driving up.

A series of impossibly sharp bends, steep inclines and narrow roads bring you close to the castle. However, avoid driving in the high season, as the parking lot is rather small. Alternatively, take Bus 16 that passes through the market square and goes right to the entrance of the castle.

Inside the castle is the **University Museum of Cultural History** (Gisonenweg, ☎ 06421-282-5871), which focuses on the history of Hesse. Although all descriptions are in German, the museum is well worth a short visit. The museum can be divided into three main sections. The first part on the ground floor is of ceramics, some modern, and pretty much missable. On the first floor, cross over to the 15th-century Wilhemsbau, which has five small floors of museum exhibitions. The best ones are on floors two to four, which include armories and weapons, religious objects and, most interestingly, articles from civilian life in Hesse. It is easy to picture characters from early Goethe works and later Romantics in chairs and furniture on display here. Not particularly well marked are the entrances to the knights' hall, the largest secular Gothic room in Germany, and the small chapel on the second floor of the main building. The wall painting of St Christopher in the chapel is original and dates from the 13th century. The museum is open Tuesday to Sunday, 10 am to 6 pm (November to March from 11 am to 5 pm). Admission is €2.60.

At the back of the castle is a large garden with walkways and lawns offering views of the town and Lahn Valley. Admission is free.

Many of the larger and older buildings in town, including the castle, are used by the 17 faculties of Philipps University. The Grimm brothers of fairy-tale fame studied here from 1802-5. The university was founded by Count Philipp of Hesse in 1527 as the first Protestant university in the world. The most prominent building is the Neo-Gothic **Old University Building** (1872) at Rudolphsplatz, attached to the large 13th-century Dominican church. The latter is open daily from 9 am to 5 pm.

Adventures

■ On Foot

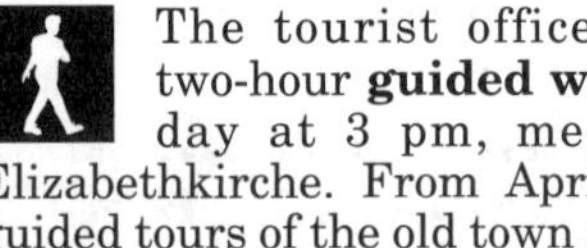

The tourist office conducts a two-hour **guided walk** on Saturday at 3 pm, meeting in the Elizabethkirche. From April to October, guided tours of the old town are also available on Wednesday at 3 pm. Further thematic tours are arranged mostly during the summer months.

■ On Wheels

Bicycle rentals are available from the parking garage **Parkhaus Pilgrimstein**, ☎ 06421-205-151, or from **Velociped**, Alte Kassler Straße 43, ☎ 06421-24-511, www.velociped.de.

Where to Stay

The **Sorat** is a comfortable luxury hotel in the lower part of town, across the road from the public elevator to the old town. The 150 rooms are comfortably furnished in a modern style. All rooms have air-conditioners and some non-smoking rooms are available. Pilgrimstein 29, 35037 Marburg, ☎ 06421-9180, fax 06421-918-444, www.sorat-hotels.com. (€€-€€€)

Close to the station, on an island in the Lahn, is the newest and most luxurious hotel in town, **Villa Vita Hotel & Residenz Rosenpark**. This five-star establishment offers 108 hotel rooms in addition to luxury apartments for longer stays. Bedrooms are large and comfortable. The hotel has an extensive fitness center and several highly acclaimed, if pricey, restaurants. Rosenstraße 18-28, 35037 Marburg, ☎ 06421-60-050, fax 06421-600-5100, www.villavitahotels.com. (€€€€)

More famous as a restaurant, **Hotel und Gasthaus Zur Sonne** offers an interesting alternative. Located in a half-timbered house on the historic Markt, it has six double and three single rooms. The rooms are simply furnished in a traditional, rustic style. Noise may drift in from the square but you will be sleeping in a guesthouse with a tradition going back to 1569. Markt 14, 35037 Marburg, ☎ 06421-17-190, fax 06421-171-940. (€€)

Where to Eat

As Marburg caters less to tourists and more to the local student population, the competition in the old town especially is cut-throat, with low to reasonable prices and good service.

Right at the market square, with views of the Rathaus and other medieval buildings from its large terrace, is **Café am Markt**, Markt 9, ☎ 06421-25-522. This café offers lighter meals as well as sweets without a markup for the location. Service is fast and friendly and a 20% discount applies if you brave it on the terrace during inclement weather. (€-€€)

Café Vetter, Reitgasse 4, can with justification claim to have the best views of the Lahn Valley. Baumkuchen is a specialty of the house. (€-€€)

In contrast to most establishments in the old town, **Alter Ritter**, Steinweg 44, ☎ 06421-62-838, www.alterritter.de, offers German and Mediterranean cuisine in an up-market, stylish restaurant. The higher prices keep the throngs of students out. The vegetarian selection is above-average for a German restaurant. (€€-€€€)

Just below the entrance to the castle is **Restaurant-Café Bückingsgarten am Schloss**, Landgraf-Philipstraße 6, ☎ 06421-12-610, www.restaurant-bueckingsgarten.de. In summer, it has a large beer garden, but in winter the long narrow building with magnificent views of the Lahn Valley provides a slightly more upscale, though still relaxed, atmosphere. Regional dishes, including venison and fish, are served. The menu selection is not particularly large; when not ordering from the daily specials, the wait for main courses can be a bit long, although worth it. (€€-€€€)

Camping

Camping Lahnaue is 1½ km (.9 mile) from the center along the banks of the Lahn. Facilities are good and it's beautifully located, but noise can be a problem. It has 60 spaces and is open from April to October. Trojedamm 47, 35037 Marburg, ☎ / fax 06421-21-331.

Wetzlar

Wetzlar is famous in Germany for three reasons: law, literature, and photography. In 1495, the Holy Roman Empire of the German Nation established the *Reichskammergericht* (Imperial Supreme Court) as the highest civil court in the Empire. The court was seated in Speyer, but in 1689, during the War of the Palatinate Succession, the court fled from the advancing French troops and the small town of Wetzlar somehow managed to have the court relocated there. It remained, with its support staff of 1,000 people, until the dissolution of the empire in 1806.

The presence of the *Reichskammergericht* not only brought prestige to the town, but also famous legal minds and other visitors – none more famous than literary genius Johann Wolfgang von Goethe. In the summer of 1772, Goethe was finishing legal training at the court. His stay would be remembered not for his legal prowess, but rather for a thin novella, *The Sorrows of Young Werther*, that caused sensation, outrage, and flocks of tourists ever since.

Lastly, Wetzlar played a major role in the development of popular photography. In 1914, Oskar Barnack developed the first small-format film camera, which would go into serial production here in 1926 as the Leica I. The town is still famous for optical industries, including Siebert microscopes and Hensoldt binoculars.

Goethe's The Sorrows of Young Werther

Goethe lost interest in his legal studies and career long before his father forced him to finish his studies at the *Reichskammergericht*. After spending time in such world cities as Strasbourg, Leipzig and Frankfurt, the small town of Wetzlar had limited appeal. However, fortunately for Goethe, Wetzlar, and German literature, he soon fell in love with a local beauty, Charlotte "Lotte" Buff. She was already engaged, liked Goethe as a friend, but ultimately spurned his affections. During the same period, a mutual lovesick friend, Karl Wilhelm Jerusalem, committed suicide.

After leaving Wetzlar, Goethe combined this event with his own experience in the 1774 novella, *Die Leiden des jungen Werthers* (The Sorrows of Young Werther). The book was a sensation – it became one of the first international bestsellers and instantly made Goethe a household name in Europe. (Napoleon carried a copy during the Egyptian campaign and claimed to have read it seven times.) It also caused a scandal because Charlotte and Wetzlar were instantly recognized and the tourist droves soon followed. Copycat suicides by lovesick youngsters in various parts of Germany led to attempts at banning the work altogether. The book consists mostly of a series of letters written by Werther to a friend explaining his life and love for Lotte. It is considered a key work of the *Sturm und Drang* movement. Although not his best work by a long shot, Goethe never had a similar sales success with any other work during his lifetime.

The old town of Wetzlar was extensively damaged during World War II and many sites were rebuilt in modern style, resulting in a center that is less harmonious architecturally than such towns as Marburg and Limburg. In addition, the newer suburbs surrounding the original core are thoroughly modern and even a bit drab.

Information Sources

Tourist Office: Tourist Information, Domplatz 8, 35573 Wetzlar, ☎ 06441-99-338, www.wetzlar.de.

Getting Here

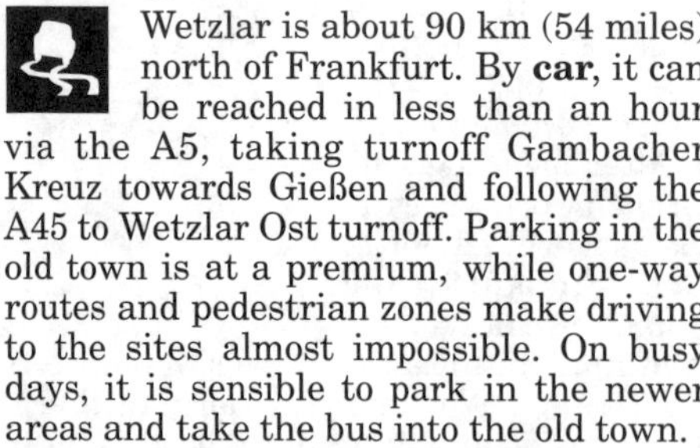

Wetzlar is about 90 km (54 miles) north of Frankfurt. By **car**, it can be reached in less than an hour via the A5, taking turnoff Gambacher Kreuz towards Gießen and following the A45 to Wetzlar Ost turnoff. Parking in the old town is at a premium, while one-way routes and pedestrian zones make driving to the sites almost impossible. On busy days, it is sensible to park in the newer areas and take the bus into the old town.

Frequent **trains** from Frankfurt take about an hour, most requiring a change at Gießen. The train station is north of the old town, not exactly within comfortable walking distance. It is far more convenient to take the City Bus, which runs from the station past all the major sights into town. Once inside the old town, all sites are within walking distance, although some slopes are steep.

Sightseeing

The symbol of Wetzlar is the **Dom** (Cathedral), Domplatz 8, ☎ 06441-99-338, an eclectic mixture of architectural styles forming a not altogether successful synthesis. The oldest parts, in dark stone, are Romanesque and date from the late 12th century. Before this church had been in use for 50 years, the more modern cathedrals in nearby Magdeburg and Limburg created the need for something similarly Gothic in Wetzlar. A new church was begun and the old one destroyed in phases to ensure that at least part of it was usable at all times. It was a sensible approach, since the new church was never completed. Wetzlar lost influence and was bankrupt by the end of the 14th century. The red sandstone south tower is Gothic with a rather awkward Late Renaissance, Early Baroque rooftop added in 1590. The high Gothic portal opens into empty space, as the north tower was never built. Most of the rest of the church is in a lighter stone in the Gothic style. Wetzlar chose the Reformation, but the church ended up being used in turns by both the Catholic and Lutheran congregations – a situation that continues to the present day, making the interior hard to see on Sunday mornings.

■ Goethe Was Here

Wetzlar has a range of almost obligatory Goethe sites – the tourist office provides a pamphlet with details. The most famous is the **Lottehaus**, right, Lottestraße 8-10, ☎ 06641-99-221, in the complex that used to belong to the Order of the Teutonic Knights. A museum was opened here in 1863 to keep alive the memory of the summer of 1772, when Goethe almost daily visited Charlotte Buff, who lived here. The museum contains items used by the Buff family as well as other period furniture. Three rooms are dedicated to *Werther*, including a rare first edition, translations, and comments from the period. One of the most famous German literary paintings hangs here: *Lotte Cutting Bread*. Open Tuesday to Sunday from 10 am to 1 pm, and 2 pm to 5 pm.

Two blocks downhill are the Kornmarkt (wheat market) and Engelsgasse, with some of the best half-timbered houses in town. Goethe resided on the second floor of the more modern **Kornmarkt 7** during his stay in Wetzlar. A memorial plaque marks the house, now partly used as a restaurant.

Farther downhill is the **Jerusalemhaus**, Schillerplatz 5, ☎ 06441-99-269, where Karl Wilhelm Jerusalem lived and committed suicide, providing Goethe with the climax for *Werther*. The two rooms on the second floor of this half-timbered house are a museum, with period documents, including the handwritten note in which Jerusalem requested the use of his pistol from a friend under false pretences. The museum is open Tuesday to Sunday, 2 to 5 pm. Admission is €1.50.

■ Other Sights

One block uphill is the **Reichskammergerichtsmuseum**, Hofstatt 19, ☎ 06441-99-612, the only legal history museum in Germany. It focuses on three centuries of the court, with several original judgments and documents. Although an English audio guide is available, this museum is only of interest to specialists. Ironically, it is housed in the regal residence of Franz von Papius, a judge equally known for his legal knowledge as his willingness to accept bribes. The museum is open Tuesday to Sunday, 10 am to 1 pm, and 2 to 5 pm.

Across the road is the **Dr Irmgard von Lemmers-Danforth Collection**, Kornblumgasse 1, ☎ 06641-99-366. It consists of European art and furniture from the Renaissance and Baroque periods, including paintings, gold and silver work, tapestries, ceramics, as well as furniture. The museum is open Tuesday to Sunday from 10 am to 1 pm, and 2 to 5 pm.

Farther uphill, toward the cathedral, are more half-timbered houses at **Eisenmarkt** (Iron Market) and **Fischmarkt** (Fish Market). Most currently serve as cafés or shops.

In the same complex as the Lottemuseum is the **City and Industry Museum**, Lottestraße 8-10, ☎ 06641-99-221. It has an eclectic collection of items related to Wetzlar, ranging from prehistoric archeological finds to more modern industrial products. On display is the Ur-Leica, above, the first one, that used 36x24 mm film. The century Wetzlar spent as seat of the Reichskammergericht left it not only with several houses seeming too large and rich for a town of this size, but also a large collection of valuable furniture and paintings. Opening hours are Tuesday to Sunday from 10 am to 1 pm, and 2 to 5 pm. Admission is €1.50.

■ Mining

Near Wetzlar is the **Besucherbergwerk Fortuna** (Visitors' Mine), Grube Fortuna, 35606 Solms-Oberbiel, ☎ 06443-82-460. It was the last iron mine in Hesse and closed in 1983. On the guided tour, in German only, visitors are taken 150 m (495 feet) below ground where mining techniques are illustrated using some of the original equipment. In the adjacent museum, more than 40 locomotives from different eras are displayed. The mine is open March to November from Tuesday to Sunday, 10 am to 4 pm (to 5 pm on weekends).

Where to Eat

Goethe used to lunch at "Zum Kronprinzen," Domplatz 17, but neither the building nor the restaurant survived to the present era. However, there are several other options available in the direct vicinity. Almost next door is the **Hauptwache**, Domplatz 3, ☎ 06441-48-504, inside a garrison building, which dates from the Prussian period in the late 19th century. This small restaurant offers mainly local dishes with a special emphasis on breakfast during weekends. (€-€€)

At the opposite side of the square is **Wirt am Dom**, Domplatz 9, ☎ 06441-42-522, which offers German and Italian cuisine ranging from fish dishes to homemade pasta and pizzas. (€-€€)

Nearby in a green-and-white half-timbered building, the **Ratsschäncke**, Fischmarkt 2, ☎ 06441-46-176, offers more traditional German dishes in one of the former town halls. (€-€€)

In an even more historic setting is the **Café am Dom**, Fischmarkt 13, ☎ 06441-32-288. It is in the former Reichskammergericht hall, but only a memorial plaque reminds of that glorious former role. Ignore the somewhat dated yellow "café" sign and squeeze by the long counter with the most appetizing cakes and confectioneries into two surprisingly large welcoming rooms. Lighter meals are available, but the real specialties are the cakes and pastries as well as a large selection of teas. Service is fast and friendly. (€-€€)

During Goethe's days, **Am Römischen Kaiser** was a newly constructed restaurant with a dance hall and is mentioned in *Werther*. Back then it was at Kornmarkt 5, but has since expanded to Kornmarkt 7, ☎ 06441-44-3754, the very house where Goethe lived himself. It offers typical German hearty meals as well as internationally popular dishes. (€-€€)

Braunfels

Braunfels is a few km inland, but the distinct profile of the Neo-Gothic Castle Braunfels can be seen from the Lahn River as well as the main roads passing through the valley. Braunfels is a *Luftkurort*, offering clean air, peace, and tranquility to the mainly elderly guests. The main sights are the castle and the half-timbered houses on the market square.

Information Sources

Tourist Office: Tourist information is available from Braunfelser Kur, Fürst Ferdinandstraße 4a, 35619 Braunfels, ☎ 06442-934-40, www.braunfels.de.

Transportation

Braunfels is easiest to reach by private car, but, of course, public transportation is also available. Change at Leun train station to Bus 180 and get off at Europaplatz, close to the castle.

Sightseeing

Schloss Braunfels, ☎ 06442-5002, www.schloss-braunfels.de, has an 800-year history, but most of the current castle dates from the mid-19th century. In 1679, a major fire destroyed the castle and most of the town. The count subsequently erected a Baroque residence. However, during the romantic period of the mid-19th century, the residence was converted into a Neo-Gothic castle and the knight's hall rebuilt according to the original plans. In 1880, the towers were added, giving the castle its characteristic silhouette and nickname as the Neuschwanstein of Hesse.

The interior of the castle can only be seen on a guided tour, which includes the knight's hall, with medieval weaponry, and several other rooms full of porcelain, paintings, and other art works. One famous painting is of a group of deer – no matter from which angle it is viewed, the groups always seem to be storming straight at the viewer. Some of the former counts are described as if you should have read about them in last week's *People* magazine, but one former resident actually did play a role in European politics: Amalie, née Countess zu Solms-Braunfels, was the mother of William II of Orange and thus the grandmother of William III, who became King of England in 1688.

The castle is open April to October daily from 9 am to 6 pm and the rest of the year on weekends only from 11 am to 5 pm. English tours are sometimes available but need to be reserved in advance. Admission is €4.

It is a few minutes stroll down the steep road and steps to the Market Square. En route, you pass through three tower gates from the mid-14th century, although the Baroque look was added after the great fire. The half-timbered houses of the **Marktplatz** (Market Square) show great conformity, which is the result of a regulation after the town fire requiring all new buildings to be 60 feet long and 40 feet wide. The 13 remaining buildings here all date from 1700 to 1720. The "new" fountain was dug in 1727, but the bronze dates from 1572.

The **Kurpark** is one block down Am Kurpark from the square. It offers the walkways, lawns, trees, fountains, gentle slopes, and kiosks that are deemed necessary to encourage the recovery and well being of visitors to a Kur resort. It is open dawn to dusk and admission is free.

Where to Stay & Eat

The **Schloss Hotel Braunfels** is in a late 19th-century building constructed like a castle. This hotel is not inside the Braunfels castle but rather a few blocks away from the Marktplatz at the edge of the Kurpark. It has been family-owned and -managed since its inception. Rooms are comfortably furnished. Hubertusstraße 2, 35619 Braunfels, ☎ 06442-3050, fax 06442-305-222, www.schloss-hotel-braunfels.de. (€€-€€€)

At the Market Square, the two restaurants on either side of the Lower Gate leading to the castle also offer rooms. Rooms are sparely furnished, but all have en suite bathrooms. Facing the gate, to the right is **Hotel Solmser Hof**, Am Marktplatz, 35619 Braunfels, ☎ 06442-4235, fax 06442-6953, www.solmserhof.de. (€€) To the left is **Gasthof am Turm**, Marktplatz 11, 35619 Braunfels, ☎ 06442-5582, www.amturm.de. (€€) Both serve mostly hearty local cuisine – select either by the advertised daily specials.

Camping

Campingpark Braunfels is on the banks of the Lahn, half a km from the center of town. It is beautifully located but can be slightly noisy. It has 80 spaces for tourists, 140 for long-term rental and is open year-round. 35619 Braunfels, ☎ 06442-4366, fax 06442-6895.

Weilburg

Goethe referred to Weilburg as "a pearl high above the River Lahn" and his observation is still true today. In contrast to the other Lahn towns described here, the emphasis in Weilburg is not on the medieval look of half-timbered houses, but rather on the more modern and elegant Baroque. The old town and castle are built high on a rock with the Lahn almost encircling it. Since the completion of the ship tunnel, the old town has in effect become an island.

Weilburg's history goes back to the founding of Germany – it was the residence of the first German king, Konrad I, who ruled with limited success from 911 to 918. However, more influential on the town's development was its role for 500 years as residence of the Nassau family. The remaining Nassau residential complex is extraordinarily large in comparison to the size of the town.

Weilburg has the only ship tunnel in Germany – a 19th-century masterpiece of civil engineering, that turned into a meaningless folly a mere 15 years after its completion. Today, it still is popular with canoeists, who consider passing through it an integral part of the River Lahn experience.

Information Sources

Tourist Office: Tourist-Information, Mauerstraße 6-8, 35781 Weilburg, ☎ 06471-7671, fax 06471-7675, www.weilburg.de.

Sightseeing

Weilburg's main sight is the Renaissance-Baroque **Schloss zu Weilburg** – the residence of the counts and princes of Nassau-Weilburg up to 1816. The residence complex is built high on a rock around which the Lahn meanders. In addition to the buildings, the complex has terraced gardens with lovely views of the Lahn Valley.

The Renaissance heart of the castle dates from 1533-72 and is preserved almost unchanged. The interior or **Castle Museum**, Schlossplatz 1, ☎ 06471-2236, can only be seen on a 50-minute, German-only, guided tour. Some 30 richly decorated rooms are seen, including popular highlights such as the modern Baroque

kitchen, the huge marble bath, and the hothouse of the upper Orangery. The castle interior is open Tuesday to Sunday, 10 am to 5 pm (to 4 pm from November to February). Admission is €3.50.

Even if not taking the guided tour of the castle interior, the **Renaissance courtyard**, which is used for concerts in summer, can be seen. It looks more like an English stage set right out of Shakespearean times than a castle in the heart of Germany.

Most of the rest of the complex is Baroque and was added or altered in the early 18th century. The French/Dutch-style **Upper Orangery** connects the main Renaissance palace with the Protestant **Schlosskirche** (Palace Church) on the elegant Baroque Marktplatz. The church shares a roof with the Rathaus and both date from around 1710.

The main entrance to the **castle gardens** is next to the church. (An alternative entrance leads directly from the Renaissance courtyard.) The views from the upper terrace are spectacular: on the east side is a sharp drop to the Lahn River and on the west the glassed-in arcades of the Upper Orangery. To the south is a lower terrace with a small, formal Baroque garden. An informal restaurant is here in the **Lower Orangery**, reminiscent of the Petit Trianon and Orangerie at Versailles. At the north end of the complex is the luxury Schlosshotel with more formal dining options. The gardens are open daily from 8 am until dark. Admission is free.

The former chancellery houses the **Bergbau- und Stadtmuseum** (Museum of Local History and Mining), Schlossplatz, ☎ 06471-379-447. The emphasis is on mining equipment and some 200 m (660 feet) of the original iron ore mining tunnels can be seen. It is especially popular with children and school groups. The museum hours are 10 am to noon and 2 to 5 pm. November to March the museum is open Monday to Friday; April to October, from Tuesday to Sunday. Admission is €3.

Weilburg's **Schiffstunnel** (shipping tunnel) is the only tunnel for ships in Germany. It was built between 1841 and 1847 as part of a plan to connect the Rhine and Elbe Rivers, but it was completed late and cost triple the original budget. The tunnel succeeded in bypassing the weirs around Weilburg, but lost its economic significance after only 15 years when the Gießen-Koblenz railroad made the shipping route superfluous. The tunnel is almost 200 m long (656 feet) and is paved with 32,000 bricks. A 4.65-m (15-foot) elevation difference required a sluice inside the tunnel. The tunnel is open to canoes and other leisure crafts and passing through it is considered an essential part of any rowing trip on the Lahn.

A DEFEATIST KING

In 1894, a statue of Konrad I, from Weilburg and ruler of Franconia, was erected in the nearby town of Villmar. He was elected king of the German states in 911. He was considered the weakest candidate and therefore a safe compromise. As expected, his rule brought little glory and on his deathbed he did the unthinkable by stating in his political testament that his greatest opponent, Heinrich Duke of Saxony, right, rather than his own brother, should be made successor. It was a wise choice, but in nationalistic Germany of the late 19th century, such defeatist thoughts were not the stuff that politics were made of. Weilburg, Konrad's hometown, was not interested in the statue and by the time opinions changed, Villmar refused to let go of its treasure.

Adventures

■ On Foot

From May to mid-October, the tourism office conducts guided walking tours of the **old town** on Saturday at 10:30 am.

When driving from the old town, a sharp right turn directly after passing through the Landtor (one of the city gates) leads to the lower exit of the Schiffstunnel. The road continues to the Taunus through the narrow, forested Weil River valley. A few km down the road is the turnoff to the **Kubacher Kristallhöhle** (Kubach Crystal Cave), Weilburg-Kubach, ☎ 06471-94-000. It was formed 350 million years ago but lost until its chance rediscovery in 1874. The cave consists mainly of limestone, crystals, and stalactites. At 30 m (99 feet), it is the highest hall of a natural cave in Germany and the largest crystal cave overall. The cave is open April to October, on weekdays from 2 to 4 pm, weekends from 10 am to 5 pm. Admission is €3.50 and includes a compulsory German-only tour.

■ On Wheels

Bicycle rentals are available from the tourist office.

■ In the Air

AX Ballooning, Mauerstrasse 6-8, 35781 Weilburg, ☎ 06471-1330, fax 06471-38-159, www.axballooning.de, offers balloon flights from Weilburg or Bad Camberg in the Taunus.

Where to Stay & Eat

The **Schlosshotel Weilburg** is in the north wing of the castle. Although this part of the building dates from the 18th century, rooms have all the comforts of the modern era. Many rooms have excellent views. The restaurant **Alte Reitshcule** (€€-€€€) serves international and regional specialties. Langgasse 25, 35781 Weilburg, ☎ 06471-50-900, fax 06471-509-0111, www.schlosshotel-weilburg.de. (€€€)

Joseph's La Lucia, Marktplatz 10, ☎ 06471-2130, is as elegant a restaurant as the Baroque exteriors in this neighborhood suggest. The excellent food is mostly Italian. (€€-€€€)

To the south of the castle garden is a lower terrace with a formal Baroque garden. In the Orangery here is the pleasant **Schlossterrassen Café Restaurant**, Im Schlossgarten, ☎ 06471-30-611. It has an eclectic menu with regional specialties but also a surprisingly large Asian selection. The terrace facing the gardens is particularly nice. (€)

■ Camping

Camping Odersbach is between the River Lahn and a forest. It is an attractive site with good facilities. There are 75 spaces for tourists and 235 for long-term campers. It is open from April to October. 35781 Weilburg-Odersbach, ☎ 06471-7620, fax 06471-379-603, www.camping-odersbach.de.

Limburg

During the Middle Ages, Limburg was an important crossing point for trade routes from Frankfurt to Cologne and from the Rhine up the Lahn Valley towards Wetzlar, Marburg, and eventually Thuringia. The construction of a stone bridge across the River Lahn from 1315-54 enhanced the town's importance.

The old part of Limburg escaped war damage and thus presents architecturally one of the most harmonious medieval old town centers in Germany. The whole of the old town, with its half-timbered houses dating from the 13th to 18th centuries, is a protected area and mostly accessible to pedestrians only. It is relatively small and perfect for a pleasant half-day excursion.

Information Sources

Tourist Office: Städtisches Verkehrsamt, Hospitalstraße 2, 65549 Limburg, ☎ 06431-6166, www.limburg.de

Transportation

Since 2002, Limburg-Süd station has been a stop for about 10 high-speed ICE **trains** per day on the Frankfurt-Cologne route and eight on the Wiesbaden-Cologne route. From Frankfurt Airport to Limburg Süd requires only 20 minutes. Limburg Süd is a free seven-minute bus ride from Limburg Station, which is near the old town. Around two trains per hour run on the normal slower Frankfurt-Limburg route, taking just over an hour. In reality, the time saved from Frankfurt Hauptbahnhof on the ICE route works out to just 10 minutes, which is negligible given the higher costs. From the Airport, howver, the time saved is an hour.

From Limburg station to the edge of the old town is about five minutes walk. All the sights in the old town are within easy walking distance from each other, although once again some of the slopes are steep.

Limburg is about 40 minutes **drive** from Frankfurt on the largely speed restriction-free A3 highway. A more scenic route is the much slower B8 via Königstein. The highway continues to Cologne, just over an hour north. The B49 runs from Limburg up the Lahn Valley and connects Weilburg, Braunfels, and Wetzlar. The B417 runs down the valley past Diez and Bad Ems towards Lahnstein on the Rhine. Parking is available in several parking garages at the edge of the old town.

Sightseeing

The main sight in Limburg is the seven-tower **Sankt Georgs Dom** (Cathedral of St George), easily the most impressive building in the Lahn Valley. Originally constructed between 1206 and 1235 as a town church in a Late Romanesque style, it already showed elements of the Early Gothic in its interior.

What set this basilica apart from so many others is its colorfully painted exterior in white, red, ocher, black, and green. Zealots in the late 19th century, when the state of Nassau became part of Prussia, refused to believe that a medieval church should be anything but bland grey stone and scraped off the painted plaster exterior. The Baroque interior, which was added in the mid-18th century, was redone in a non-authentic Romanesque style. Only during the 20th century would the church return to its medieval appearance. In 1965, the exterior was again plastered, to protect the sandstone against erosion, and painted in its original colors. The original medieval frescoes were uncovered and almost three quarters of the interior decorations visible today are original. The inside is 50 m (165 feet) long and the central nave is 21 m (69 feet) high with the cupola rising 33 m (107 feet). A clever alternation of lighter and darker areas creates the illusion of a much larger structure. The baptistery dates from the founding of the church.

The view from behind the church over the Lahn Valley is spectacular. The best views of the cathedral itself can be had from the Lahn Bridge at the edge of the old town or from the A3 highway.

The **Domschatz und Diözesanmuseum** (Cathedral Treasury), Domstraße 12, ☎ 06431-295-327, www.staurothek.de, is worth a brief visit. The two rooms in the basement contain the real treasures, with jewel-studded gold and silver works. The highlight is the Staurotek, a mid-10th-century Byzantine cross reliquary with fine gold work and jewels claiming to contain wood from Christ's cross. It was stolen from Constantinople during a crusade in 1204 and came to Limburg only in 1827 when Limburg became a bishopric. Also of note is a St Peter's staff reliquary encased in bejeweled gold made in Trier in AD 988. The five rooms on the second floor consist of church art, including tapestries, statues, a small early 14th-century St George slaying the dragon, and works by Hans Holbein the Elder. The museum is open from mid-March to mid-November, Tuesdays to Saturdays, 10 am to noon and 2 to 5 pm; Sundays from 11 am to 5 pm.

Further sights in Limburg are the various half-timbered houses in the lower parts of the old town – most currently used as restaurants or shops stocked with antiques, fine art, or other items. One of the joys of visiting Limburg is to round a corner and discover buildings even more impressive than the ones just seen minutes before. The oldest houses are in Römer, with the **Gothic House** at Römer 2-6 dating from 1289 one of the oldest freestanding half-timbered houses in Germany. **Haus Kleine Rutsche 4**, also dating from 1289, influenced transportation decisions for centuries: at this spot was the narrowest part of the trade route and carriages loaded in Frankfurt or Cologne were packed to specifications ensuring that they could pass here without unloading. Inspections were made several blocks down the road in either direction to prevent traffic jams. A particularly nice collection of half-timbered houses is at **Fischmarkt** (Fish Market), with most buildings here dating from the 14th and 15th centuries.

■ Farther Afield

If driving or cycling, cross the Alte Lahnbrücke and continue about five km (three miles) down the road towards **Dietkirchen**. In this small town, now part of Limburg, an impressive Romanesque basilica, the **Church of St Lubentius**, left, built like a fortress on a rock, towers over the Lahn. The **Michael's Chapel** north of the choir dates from 1000, while the rest of the church is from the 12th century. The golden head of the reliquary of St Lubentius is from 1270, and the rest of the statue is from 1477. The views of the Lahn from the south side of the church are impressive, but the best views are from the pedestrian bridge across the Lahn several hundred feet downstream from the church. The church can be seen from a distance, which is fortunate, as the turnoff to the church from the main road just before leaving the village is not well marked.

Where to Stay & Eat

Perfectly located on the banks of the Lahn River at the edge of the old town is the small 30-room **Hotel Nassauer Hof**. All rooms are comfortable and furnished in modern style. Many have views of the valley and/or the old town. **Der Kleine Prins** restaurant (€€-€€€) serves regional cuisine but with a refreshingly light and modern touch. The menu is not particularly large, but features various kinds of fowl, fish, meat, venison, and vegetarian dishes. Service is friendly and attentive. Open for dinner only, as well as Sundays for lunch. Brückengasse 1, 65549 Limburg, ☎ 06431-99-60, ☎ 06431-996-555, www.hotel-nassauerhof-limburg.de, (€€€)

The old town of Limburg is literally littered with coffee shops, but one claims to be the oldest. **Café Will**, Salzgasse 23, ☎ 06431-6970, has been in business for just over a century. Located in a rather modern-looking establishment with a slightly formal interior, this café is also a confectionery, making it the ideal place to indulge in coffee and excellent cakes or pastries. The food menu itself is limited and, for a meal, one can do better elsewhere. (€)

Older than Café Will, but a full restaurant is the **Werner Senger Haus**, Rüttsche 5, ☎ 06431-6942, one of the oldest restaurants in Germany. Regional cuisine complemented by a long wine list is served in a historic location with ambiance. (€€-€€€)

■ Camping

Lahn Camping is on the banks of the Lahn five minutes walk from the old town. It has good facilities but can be noisy at times. There are 200 spaces and it's open from mid-April to late October. 65549 Limburg, ☎ 06431-22-610, fax 06431-92-013, www.lahncamping.de.

Bad Ems

Bad Ems is a small town but a famous Kurort (Health Resort). It has a large number of health clinics and taking to the waters is currently as popular as it has ever been. This is also a very elegant town with much of its 19th-century charm intact. In contrast to most parts of the Lahn Valley, it is in Rhineland Palatinate and not in Hesse.

THE BAD EMS TELEGRAM

Historians are mostly aware of the name Bad Ems. During the 1860s, this spa town became the summer capital of Europe and a favorite with Prussian King Wilhelm and other royals. In 1870, when France and Prussia were spoiling for a fight, Bismarck altered a report from an informal meeting in the Bad Ems Kurpark between King Wilhelm and the French Foreign Minister and released it to the press. The so-called *Bad Emser Depesche*, made the incident appear as both an insult to the King and an affront to French national sensibilities. A few days later France declared war on Prussia. France miscalculated, as it expected support from Bavaria and Austria, but instead for the first time in history had to face the united armies of Germany. The short war ended with Paris under siege, Germany united, and the Prussian king crowned in Versailles as Emperor Wilhelm I of Germany.

Information Sources

Tourist Office: Bad Ems Touristik, Römerstraße 1, 56130 Bad Ems, ☎ 02603-94-150, www.bad-ems-touristik.de.

Sightseeing

Although the Celts and Romans lived in the area, the first written reference to the hot springs is from 1172. The counts of Nassau and Katzenelmbogen built a bathhouse in the 15th century and the lovely Baroque **Kurhaus** in 1711-20. The health waters may be sampled for free in the **Brunnenhalle**.

Nearby, the **Benedettistein**, Platz der Partnershaft, a flagstone named after the French foreign minister, marks the place of his meeting with King Wilhelm on July 13, 1870. Good views of the Classical bathhouse architecture are available from the Kurbrücke (bridge).

The **Kursaalgebäude** (Spa Hall buildings), Römerstraße 8, were erected in 1836-39. There is a lovely marble hall as well as the early 20th-century Kurtheater (Spa Theater). The **Spielbank** (Casino), Römerstraße 8, ☎ 02603-4541, is also here. It was popular from its inception in 1720 until it was closed by the puritan Prussians in 1872. It reopened in 1987. In contrast to Wiesbaden, Bad Homburg, and Baden-Baden casinos, jackets and ties are not compulsory. However, elegant dress is required – an information desk is available to clarify the definition. Roulette is popular, with bets between €2 and €10,000 possible. Opening hours are daily from 7 pm to 2 am. Admission is €2.50 for the roulette tables and €1 for machines.

Farther downstream is the **Kurpark** (Spa Park). It has a memorial to Kaiser Wilhelm I, the town's most famous visitor.

The Russian nobles discovered Bad Ems shortly after the Napoleonic era. Improved transportation networks, especially railways, saw several thousand Russians visit the spa town by 1880. They often stayed several weeks and became a good source of income. To cater for their spiritual well-being, the local population suggested the construction of a Russian Orthodox chapel, which was erected in 1876. The **St Alexandrakapelle** (St Alexandra Chapel), Wilhelmsallee 12, ☎ 02603-4491, is open from April to October, Tuesday to Sunday, from 3 to 5 pm. Admission is €1.

The **Emser Therme** (Spa Baths), Viktoriaallee 25, ☎ 02603-97-900, www.emser-therme.de, is a modern spa park with hot-water baths, a therapy and massage center, and an "oxyparc" fitness center with a high oxygen concentration.

Cultural Events & Festivals

Germany's largest flower parade, the third-largest in the world, is the **Blumenkorso**, www.blumenkorso.de, held annually in Bad Ems during the last weekend of August. The parade is four km (2.4 miles) long and includes some

30 flower-decorated caravans, marching bands, and, of course, eating, drinking, and other entertainment.

The **Jacques Offenbach Festival** is held annually over two weeks at the end of May and early June. The music of the Cologne-born composer is played by orchestras from all over the world. Information and ticket reservations are possible through the tourism office.

Kurkonzerte (Spa concerts) are held almost daily in the open-air theater in the Kurpark or in the Konzertsaal of the Gästezentrum, Römerstraße 1. The schedule is available from the tourist office.

Adventures

■ On Foot

The tourism office conducts guided walking tours of the **old town** on Friday at 2 pm from the Gästezentrum, Römerstraße 1.

The Bad Ems area has many **hiking** trails – maps are available from the tourist office, which also occasionally conducts guided hikes in the region.

The **Running-Team Bad Ems** meets Tuesday and Friday at 7 pm from April to September for **cross-country runs**. Visitors are welcome to join – dial ☎ 0261-896-7844 for the exact meeting point.

■ On Wheels

Bicycle rentals are available from **Firma Kreutz**, Wilhelmsallee, ☎ 02603-13-964; **Fahrradverleih am Quellenturm**, Wilhelmsalee, ☎ 02603-2518; or from **Fahrradverleih Sporthütte**, Römerstraße 71, ☎ 02603-919-570.

The **Kurwaldbahn** is a mountain cogwheel **cable car** that swishes guests up 130 m (426 feet) in two minutes. It operates from the Kurpark next to the Bismarckhöhe part of town daily, 6:15 am to 10:30 pm at a cost of €1.50 one-way. The car runs at an incredible incline of 78%!

■ On Water

Firma Kreutz, Wilhelmsallee, ☎ 02603-13-964, rents canoes, pedal, rowing, and electrical **boats** from April to October.

Where to Stay & Eat

Häcker's Kurhotel is a grand hotel on the banks of the Lahn in the heart of Bad Ems. It is a white Neo-Baroque building that reflects in the river and contrasts equally well with the green, forested slopes of the valley hills. Rooms are luxurious; some have balconies and Lahn views. The hotel has its own thermal baths and the large spa area has a beauty farm. The restaurant **Benedetti** (€€-€€€) serves international cuisine under stucco ceilings. Römerstraße 1-3, 56130 Bad Ems, ☎ 02603-7990, fax 02603-799-252, www.haeckers-kurhotel.com. (€€€-€€€€)

■ Fulda

Fulda is a small town in the mountains northeast of Hesse. It is best known as a religious center and mostly visited for its elegant Baroque churches and palaces.

In 744, the Anglo-Saxon monk Winfrid, better known as St Boniface, founded a monastery in Fulda. Boniface converted much of modern Thuringia and Hesse to Christianity and played a major role in strengthening the church in Germany. After his death in 754, Boniface was buried in Fulda. His grave became a major pilgrimage site.

Fulda received market rights in 1019 and a year later Emperor Heinrich II and Pope Benedict VIII visited the town. For the following seven centuries, Fulda would not be of much strategic or political importance. However, in the early 18th century much of Fulda's center, including many churches, was rebuilt as the elegant Baroque buildings that still draw visitors today.

Information Sources

Tourist Office: The Tourist Information is in **Palais Butlar**, Bonifatiusplatz 1, 36037 Fulda, ☎ 0661-102-1814, www.touristmus-fulda.de. Opening hours are weekdays from 8:30 am to 6 pm, Saturday from 9:30 am to 4 pm, and Sunday from 10 am to 2 pm.

Transportation

Fulda is a stop on the busy ICE lines between north and south Germany. It is just under an hour by ICE **train** from Frankfurt. The hourly regional train does the same journey in 80 minutes for half the price.

By **car**, it is easily reached on the A66 from Frankfurt or the A7 from Kassel or Würzburg.

Sightseeing

Most of the sights in Fulda are in a small area in the vicinity of the cathedral and palace, a few minutes walk from the station. The town is best explored on foot.

The current Baroque **Dom** (Cathedral), Domplatz, ☎ 0661-73-370, www.bistum-fulda.de, was erected between 1704 and 1712 to replace the ninth-century Romanesque church. Decorations on the exterior are limited, but the dome and other roof parts are unmistakably Baroque. The interior is bright with typical Baroque touches, but not as fussy as Bavarian Rococo. A major attraction is the tomb of St Boniface. Although his grave has been here since 819, the current Baroque tomb and altar date from 1731. Opening hours are April to October, weekdays from 10 am to 6 pm, and November to March on weekdays from 10 am to 5 pm; year-round on Saturday, 10 am to 3 pm, and Sunday, 1 to 6 pm.

Adjacent to the Dom is the **Dommuseum** (Cathedral Museum), Domplatz, ☎ 0661-87-207, www.bistum-fulda.de, with a large collection of religious art and paraphernalia. In addition to a collection of liturgical robes, the museum also has sacred vessels, reliquaries, and medieval tapestries. The sword of St Boniface, a reliquary containing his head and a codex that belonged to him are important displays. The painting collection includes *The Adulteress* by Lucas Cranach and *The Crucifixion* by Johann Tischbein. Opening hours are April to October from Tuesday to Saturday, 10 am to 5:30 pm, and Sunday, 12:30-5:30 pm. From November to March, opening hours are Tuesday to Saturday, 10 am to 12:30 pm and 1:30 to 4 pm, Sunday, 12:30 to 4 pm. The museum is closed from mid-January to mid-February. Admission is €2.10.

Michaelskirche

Michaelskirche Carolingian crypt

The **Michaelskirche** (St Michael's Church), Hinterburg 2, ☎ 0661-73-370, is a small chapel, but its Carolingian crypt, dating from 819, is one of the most significant structures from this era. The vaulted crypt rests on a single pillar, while the small rotunda is on eight pillars. The church is open daily from April to October, 10 am to 6 pm, and from November to March, 2 to 4 pm, but closed during January.

About 15 minutes walk from the Dom past the Paulustor and up the hill is **Kloster Frauenberg**, a Franciscan monastery. The Baroque church is not particularly interesting but on a clear day, the views of Fulda and the surrounding mountains are wonderful.

The Baroque **Stadtschloss/Residenz** (City Palace/Residence), was built by the prince-abbots between 1706 and 1721.

Most of the building is used as the city offices, but the original rooms, including the lavishly decorated reception rooms and private apartments of the Fulda prince-abbots, are open to visitors. A collection of Thuringian and rare Fulda porcelain, only produced between 1764 and 1789, is also on display. Opening hours are Saturday to Thursday, 10 am to 6 pm, and Friday, 2 to 6 pm. Admission is €2.10.

The **Schlossgarten** (Residence Garden) was originally Baroque, but altered to an English landscape style in the 19th century. Currently it has elements from both styles. In front of the Orangery is a beautiful Baroque garden sculpture, the *Flora Vase*, a 1728 work by Johann Humnach. Note the pineapples on the roof of the Orangery. Pineapples were the fashionable fruit of the Baroque, grown in the Orangery together with citrus; they also feature on other Baroque palaces in the vicinity.

Although the emphasis in Fulda is on the Baroque, other styles are also represented. The small **St Severikirche**, Severiberg, is the only Gothic church in town. The former **Rathaus**, (Town Hall) Marktstraße, now a clothing store, is a wonderful 16th-century half-timbered building with interesting little towers. The adjacent **St Blasiuskirche**, with its distinct red-white exterior, has a lovely restored Baroque interior.

Farther Afield

Just seven km (4.2 miles) south of Fulda is the Baroque **Schloss Fasanerie**, ☎ 0661-94-860, www.schloss-fasanerie.de. It was built between 1739 and 1754 as a summer residence for the prince-bishop, but its current interior, decorations and furnishings are due to the Prince Electors of Hesse, who took over the palace in 1816. Some 60 richly decorated and furnished rooms are accessible; guided tours (in German) are compulsory. The palace contains the largest private antique art collection in Germany. The palace is open from April to October, Tuesday to Sunday, from 10 am to 5 pm. Admission is €5 for the palace and museum or for the porcelain collection; add €3.50 to see both. The palace is on the B27, with the turnoff in Fulda-Bronzell. It can be reached by Bus 3 (stop Engelsheim) or 4 (stop Bronzell) – it is a 20-minute walk from either stop.

Cultural Events

The **Dom** (Cathedral), ☎ 0661-87-268, is a popular venue for frequent concerts of religious music. In May, June, September, October, and during Advent, 30-minute organ concerts are held on Saturdays at noon.

Adventures

On Foot

The tourism office conducts one-hour guided walks of the **old town and Dom** from April to October daily at 11:30 am and 3 pm. From November to March, the tour is only on weekends at 11:30 am. A two-hour tour is available during the summer period from Friday to Sunday at 2 pm, and during winter on Saturday at 2 pm only.

On Wheels

Bicycles can be rented from **Hahner Zweiradtechnik**, Beethovenstraße 3, ☎ 0661-933-9944. They can be delivered to hotels in Fulda.

Where to Stay & Eat

Arguably the most pleasant hotel in Fulda is the **Romantik Hotel Goldener Karpfen**, a few minutes stroll from the Dom. Rooms are furnished to a high standard. The restaurant (€€€-€€€€) offers nouvelle cuisine with Asian and Mediterranean touches. Simpliziusbrunnen 1, 36037 Fulda, ☎ 0661-868-00, fax 0661-868-0100, www.romantikhotels.com. (€€€-€€€€)

The luxury **Maritim Hotel Am Schlossgarten** is behind the Orangery. It combines a modern new wing with some Baroque rooms. Rooms are well-furnished and comfortable. Paulusprominade 2, 36037 Fulda, ☎ 0661-2820, fax 0661-282-499, www.maritim.de. (€€-€€€)

The small **Hotel Kurfürst** is in a restored Baroque palace, perfectly located directly across the road from the Stadtschloss. Rooms are well-equipped and bright. The restaurant **Zum Kurfürsten** (€€€-€€€€) has a pleasant terrace and serves nouvelle cuisine and regional specialties. Schlossstraße 2, 36037 Fulda, ☎ 0661-833-90, fax 0661-833-9339, www.kurfuerst-fulda.de. (€€€)

The **Ibis Hotel** is in a modern building near the train station. It offers value for money in clean, well-designed functional rooms without excessive luxuries. Kurfürstenstraße 3, 36037 Fulda, ☎ 0661-250-560, fax 0661-250-565, www.accor-hotels.com. (€€)

Two lovely small restaurants are in the narrow Pfandhausstraße that leads from the south end of Bonifatiusplatz. At No 8 is **Dachsbau**, ☎ 0661-74-1112, a comfortable spot in a building with an original painted façade. The interior is decorated with original prints. Nouvelle cuisine is on offer. (€€-€€€)

Across the road at No 7 & 9, is the pleasant **Alte Pfandhausstube**, ☎ 0661-22-901. The decoration is rustic and tables mostly uncovered, but service and food are first-class. Hearty regional cuisine is served. The owners also manage the adjacent wine shop, ensuring a good selection of reasonably priced wines. (€-€€)

Northern Bavaria

Franken, Eastern Bavaria & the Romantic Road

In this Chapter

Franken is in the northwestern part of Bavaria. The name derives from the Franks that lived in the area and eventually ruled most of Central Europe during the time of Charlemagne. Franconia is the English term for Franken.

Franken is often informally divided into two parts: "wine Franken" and "beer Franken." **Würzburg** is the undisputed capital of the former and even has vineyards inside the city borders. Wine has been an important industry at least since AD 777. **Nürnberg** is the capital of the beer-drinking area, with **Bamberg**, which is on the border of the two, also famous for its beer.

In addition to its natural beauty, Franken has fascinating cities to visit, including Würzburg, Bamberg, Bayreuth, and Nürnberg. The River Main snakes through the region and, since 1993, the Main-Danube Canal turned a centuries-old dream into reality, allowing boat transportation between these two important rivers. The canal passes through Bamberg and Nürnberg.

Eastern Bavaria forms part of the Bavarian heartland and contains some of the oldest parts of Bavaria. For foreign visitors, the two Danube cities of **Regensburg** and **Passau** are of most interest. Both cities escaped World War II virtually undamaged. Regensburg has a lovely medieval town center, while Passau is mostly Baroque. Both cities are popular with European travelers, but English-speakers still seem to pass them by. This is unfortunate, as both are intriguing and easy to reach from Franken, both by rail and by car.

Arguably, the most popular of Germany's 150 or so themed vacation routes is the **Romantic Road**. It connects several romantic sights along a 350-km (210-mile) route that leads through Franken to sights farther south. **Rothenburg ob der Tauber**, everybody's favorite small medieval town, is a major stop on the route.

History

The Celts settled Franken by 1000 BC and the Romans lived in parts of it around AD 100. The Franks arrived between the sixth and eighth centuries and settled around the River Main before Karl Martell and Charlemagne conquered most of Western Europe.

Christian missionaries were active in the region in the seventh century – St Kilian was murdered in Würzburg in 689. In 742, St Boniface founded the Bishopric of Würzburg, which played a dominant role in the region for just over a millennium. The Bishops of Würzburg ruled most of the area from the time of Otto I up to secularization in 1803. Bavaria annexed all Frankish lands between 1803 and 1815.

In contrast to Bamberg and Würzburg, Nürnberg played a more earthly role. It became an important palatinate of the Staufer emperors and was an essential stop for most emperors up to the Reformation. In the English-speaking world, Nürnberg is more famous for the Nazi Party Rallies before World War II and the trials of Nazi leaders afterwards.

In Eastern Bavaria, Regensburg served as ducal seat from the sixth to the 13th century. Passau was an Episcopal city and its location on the confluence of the Danube and Inn rivers long gave it strong links with present-day Austria.

Transportation

Franken has excellent transportation links to other parts of Germany. Towns in the former border area with East Germany and Czechoslovakia were in a dead-end situation for most of the latter half of the 20th century. However, since the end of the Cold War and especially after the Czech Republic joined the European Union, ancient trade routes and natural markets have been restored and many of these towns suddenly find themselves again in the heart of Europe.

By Rail: Nürnberg is a major railway junction, with excellent links to all parts of Germany. At least hourly trains connect Nürnberg with Munich (one hour, 40 minutes) and Berlin (five hours). At least every two hours, an ICE or IC train connects Frankfurt, Würzburg, Nürnberg, Regensburg, and Passau, with the traveling time between each of these cities about an hour. The train continues to Vienna. Bamberg is an hour by train from Würzburg, and Bayreuth an hour from Nürnberg.

By Road: Several major highways run through Franken. The A3 from Cologne and Frankfurt passes through Würzburg, Nürnberg, Regensburg, and Passau before continuing into Austria. The A7 from Hamburg passes through Würzburg and the western parts of the region. The A9 from Berlin goes through Bayreuth and Nürnberg en route to Munich. Other minor Autobahns also traverse Franken and smaller roads, although slower, are in good condition. With the exception of the original city centers, driving in this area is easy and a pleasurable way to enjoy the region.

By Air: Frankfurt Airport (See *Hesse*, page **) is generally the most convenient airport for travelers to Franken, although **Munich Airport** is closer to the southern parts of the region. Fast road and rail connections exist from both airports to the main towns in Franken.

Nürnberg Airport, Flughafenstraße 100, 90411 Nürnberg, ☎ 0911-93-700, www.airport-nuernberg.de, is small but it serves a growing number of European destinations. It is reached within 12 minutes by U-Bahn U2 from the Hauptbahnhof, or 15 minutes by taxi (€15).

By Boat: Two major European rivers, the **Main** and the **Danube**, flow through the region. A channel connecting the two had been contemplated for centuries but was ultimately completed in the 1990s. River cruises on both rivers, usually a week long, are increasingly popular. Passau is especially popular as a starting and finishing port for cruises into Austria and Hungary.

■ Franken

Information Sources

For information on Franken, contact the **Tourismusverband Franken**, Postfach 440453, 90209 Nürnberg, ☎ 0911-941-510, www.frankentourismus.de.

Würzburg

Würzburg is a city of 130,000 on the banks of the River Main. It was long the capital of the Duchy of Franken and, with its magnificent Baroque buildings, is an important holiday destination. The town is at the heart of the Franken wine region, which still uses flat, oval-shaped *Bocksbeutel* wine bottles.

Human settlements in Würzburg go back to at least 1000 BC when Celts erected a fort on the site of the present Marienburg. In the mid-seventh century, it became a Frankish ducal seat.

Much of Würzburg's history was determined by religion. In 689, the Irish missionary St Kilian was murdered here and in 742, the bishopric of Würzburg was founded. In the 12th century, Emperor Friedrich Barbarossa married Beatrice of Burgundy here. He also elevated the bishops to prince-bishops, who would rule the Duchy of Franken up to secularization in 1802. Würzburg became part of Bavaria in 1814.

In 1945, 90% of Würzburg was destroyed by air raids. Large parts of the old town were rebuilt true to the original.

Several important artists are closely associated with Würzburg, although none of them is native: the medieval poet Walther von der Vogelweide, sculptor and woodcarver Tilman Riemenschneider, Baroque master builder Balthasar Neuman, and the painter Giovanni Battista Tiepolo. Wilhelm Röntgen discovered X-rays here in 1895.

Information Sources

Tourist Office: Tourist information is available from Tourist Information, Falkenhaus am Markt, 97070 Würzburg, ☎ 0931-372-398, www.wuerzburg.de.

Bavaria

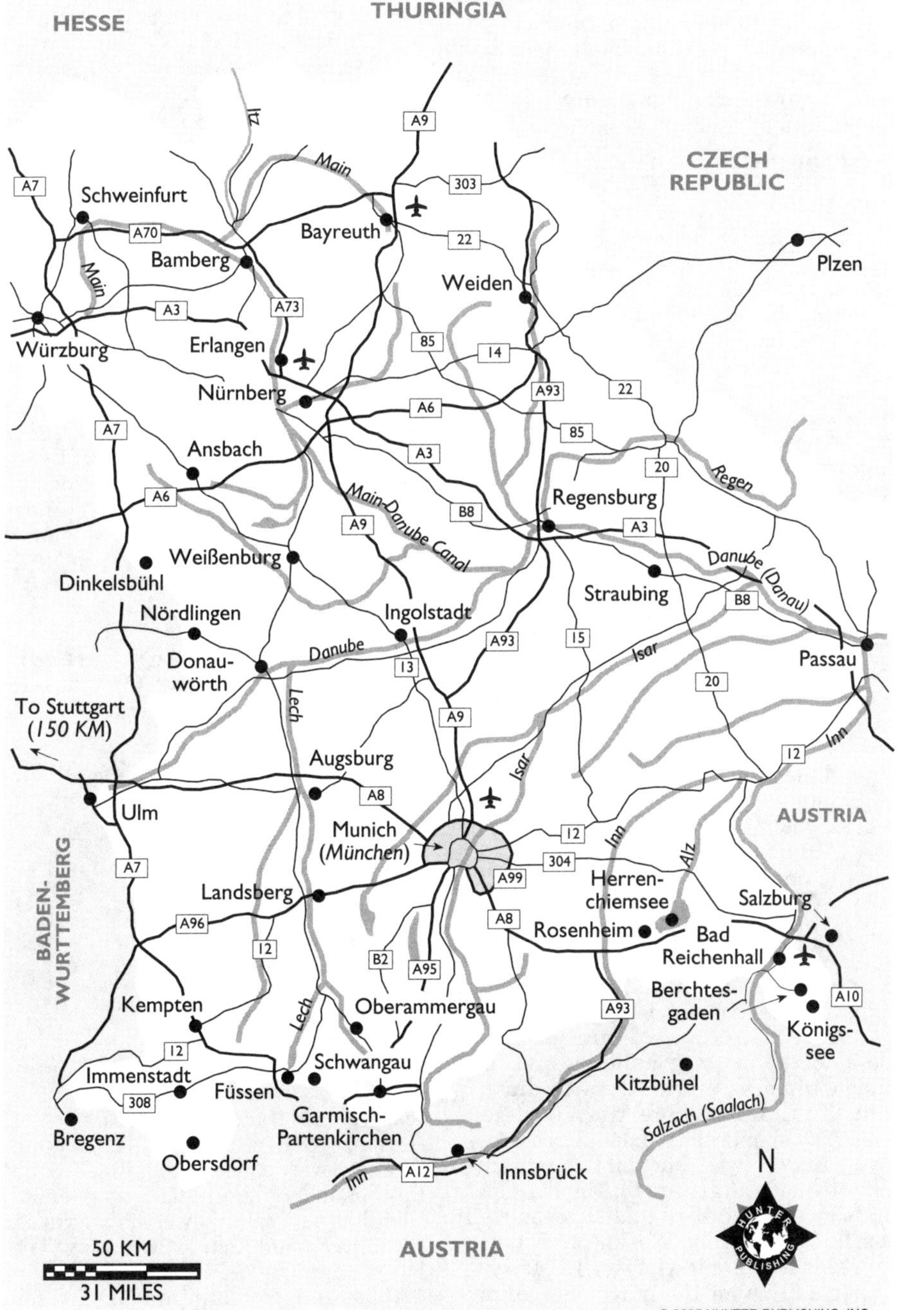

SAXONY
HESSE
THURINGIA
CZECH REPUBLIC
Schweinfurt
Bamberg
Bayreuth
Weiden
Plzen
Würzburg
Erlangen
Nürnberg
Ansbach
Regensburg
Weißenburg
Dinkelsbühl
Straubing
Nördlingen
Ingolstadt
Passau
Donau-wörth
To Stuttgart (150 KM)
Augsburg
Ulm
Munich (München)
AUSTRIA
BADEN-WURTTEMBERG
Landsberg
Herren-chiemsee
Salzburg
Rosenheim
Bad Reichenhall
Berchtes-gaden
Kempten
Oberammergau
Königs-see
Schwangau
Immenstadt
Füssen
Kitzbühel
Garmisch-Partenkirchen
Bregenz
Obersdorf
Innsbrück
Main
Main-Danube Canal
Danube
Danube (Danau)
Regen
Isar
Inn
Lech
Alz
Salzach (Saalach)
A7
A70
A3
A73
A9
303
22
85
14
A93
A6
20
B8
15
13
12
A8
304
A99
A96
B2
A95
A10
308
A12
N
HUNTER PUBLISHING
50 KM
31 MILES

Transportation

Würzburg has an excellent public transportation system using mainly trams and buses. Trams 1, 2, 3, and 5 connect the Hauptbahnhof with the old town, although the distance is only a few minutes walk. Of more use is Bus 9, which connects the Residenz and Festung Marienburg at least once per hour – it stops at Juliuspromenade, but not at the Hauptbahnhof itself.

Sightseeing

■ Residenz

The Residenz (Residence), Residenzplatz 2, ☎ 0931-355-170, ww.bsv.bayern.de, was constructed between 1720 and 1744 by Balthasar Neumann for the bishops of Würzburg. It is one of the finest Baroque palaces in Europe and is a UNESCO World Cultural Heritage site. Large parts of the Residenz were destroyed in 1945 but reconstructed. Original parts include the magnificent monumental Treppenhaus (staircase) with the vaulted ceiling containing the 600 m^2 (6,400 square foot) fresco by Tiepolo; the Weißer Saal (White Hall) with stuccos by Bossi; the Kaisersaal (Imperial Hall) with more frescoes by Tiepolo; and the Gartensaal (Garden Hall) with frescoes by Johann Zick. The rich Rococo Paradezimmer (Parade Room) was reconstructed. Opening hours are daily from April to October, 9 am to 6 pm, and from November to March, 10 am to 4:30 pm. Admission is €4.50 and includes a 45-minute guided tour – daily in English at 11 am and 3 pm, more frequently in German. (Although the tour is not compulsory, it is the only way to see the South Wing and the Mirrors Cabinet.)

The **Hofkirche** (Court Chapel) is in the South Wing of the Residenz, but visitors use a separate entrance. It was the private chapel of the bishop and a superb example of Baroque architecture. Neumann had to adapt to the existing building and used hidden windows and mirrors to draw in light. The gilding here uses real gold, although the marble is fake. The frescoes are by Rudolf Byss, but the two paintings above the side altars are by Tiepolo. Opening hours are April to mid-October, daily from 9 am to 6 pm, closing at 8 pm on Thursday. From mid-October to March, it is open daily from 10 am to 4 pm. Admission is free.

The **Hofgarten** (Court Garden) is a formal Baroque garden with Italian and French sections. The eastern part of the garden gives great views of the palace façade. The garden is open until dark. Admission is free.

The **Martin von Wagner Museum**, ☎ 0931-312-288, is in the South Wing of the Residenz. It has a fine art gallery of European paintings and statues from the 14th to 19th centuries. There is also has an interesting antiquities collection with Egyptian jewelry, Roman pottery, and Greek vases. To see the whole collection requires at least two visits as opening hours are complicated. The museum is open Tuesday to Saturday, with the art gallery open from 9:30 am to 12:30 pm and the antiquities collection from 2 to 5 pm. The two sections are open on Sunday from 9:30 am to 12:30 pm. Admission is free.

Guided tours of the **Staatlicher Hofkeller** (National Wine Cellar), Residenzplatz 2, ☎ 0931-305-0931, www.hofkeller.de, are available on weekends from March to November and end with a glass of locally produced wine. The wine estate is one of the largest in Germany.

■ East Bank & Old Town

The **Dom St Kilian** (Cathedral), Domerpfarrgasse 10, ☎ 0931-321-1830, retains its original 1188 exterior and, at 105-m (340 feet) long is the fourth-largest Romanesque church in Germany. Its interior has been changed throughout the centuries. The church burned out in 1945 and the nave collapsed a year later, but was restored to its original condition. The Baroque Schönbornkapelle (Schönborn Chapel) was constructed in 1721-36 by Balthasar Neumann. The interior of the Dom has several noteworthy works of art, including sandstone statues by Tilman Riemenschneider and 12th- to 17th-century funerary monuments for the bishops. Opening hours are Monday to

Dom St Kilian

Wilhem Von Grumbach, 1493 (Dom)

Saturday from 10 am to 5 pm, but it is closed between noon and 2 pm from November to Easter. On Sunday, it is open from 1 to 6 pm. The Schönbornkapelle can only be seen on the guided tour of the Dom taking place daily from Easter to October at 12:05 (Sunday at 12:30).

The oldest part of the **Neumünster Church**, Kürschnerhof, is a triple-aisle Romanesque basilica built in the 11th century over the place where the Irish missionary St Kilian was murdered in AD 689. However, later Baroque additions now dominate, with the impressive western façade attributed to Johann Dientzenhofer. The structural components survived the bombing of 1945, but much of the interior was destroyed. Some noteworthy works of art survived, including a *Madonna and Christ* by Tilman Riemenschneider (at right). Behind the church, in the Lusamgärtlein, is the grave of medieval troubadour Walther von der Vogelweide (1170-1230) who died in Würzburg.

The **Falkenhaus** on the Markt has the loveliest Rococo façade in Würzburg, with mid-18th-century stucco work. It currently houses the municipal library and information office.

Adjacent is the **Marienkapelle** (St Mary's Chapel), a Gothic hall church erected by the town between 1377 and 1440. The Neo-Gothic steeple has a double gilded 18th-century Madonna. The interior has noteworthy works by Tilman Riemenschneider, including the 1502 tombstone of Konrad von Schaumberg, and copies of the statues of Adam and Eve in the portal. (The originals are in the Mainfränkisches Museum). The church has the grave of the master Baroque architect Balthasar Neumann (1687-1753).

Madonna & Christ, Tilman Riemenschneider, 1490

Parts of the **Rathaus** (Town Hall) date to the 13th century, while the Renaissance façade is from 1660. The tower is 55 m (180 feet) high. Ironically, the oldest parts of the building survived the bombing of 1945, while most of the newer additions were destroyed and subsequently rebuilt.

■ West Bank & Marienberg

The **Alte Mainbrücke** (Old Main Bridge) was constructed between 1473 and 1543 to replace a previous Romanesque bridge destroyed by floods. Twelve huge Baroque statues of saints, including Charlemagne, were added in the early 18th century.

Festung Marienberg (Fortress), ☎ 0931-355-1750, www.schloesser.bayern.de, served as primary residence for the bishops from 1253 to 1719. Its history, however, is much older. Celts first built a fort here around 1000 BC. In AD 706, the first Marienkapelle (St Mary's Chapel) was erected. Construction of the fortress started about 1200. In the 17th century, it was altered to a Renaissance palace but, after the Thirty Years' War, was converted into a Baroque fortress. Opening hours are from April to October, Tuesday to Sunday,

Adam, Mainfränkisches Museum, from the Marienkapelle, Tilman Riemenschneider

9 am to 6 pm. Admission is €2. (The two museums in the fortress have separate opening hours and admission fees.)

The former Baroque Zeughaus (Arsenal) now houses the **Mainfränkisches Museum**, ☎ 0931-205-940, www.mainfraenkisches-museum.de. It has the largest collection of Tilman Riemenschneider works in the world, including the originals removed from the Dom. It also has exhibitions on local history as well as the role of wine in the regional economy and way of life. Opening hours are Tuesday to Sunday, 10 am to 7 pm. Admission is €3 or €5 with the Fürstenbaumuseum.

The **Fürstenbaumuseum**, ☎ 0931-43-838, is in the east wing. It includes the former bishops' apartments, treasury, and a section on the town's history. Opening hours are Tuesday to Sunday from 10 am to 5 pm. Admission is €4 or €5 with the Mainfränkische Museum.

It is a good 20-minute walk from the bottom of the hill or take Bus Line 9, which runs from the Residenz via the Juliuspromenade near the Hauptbahnhof to the top of the hill. Limited parking is available.

The finest views of Würzburg are from the terrace of the **Käppele**, Nikolausberg/Leutfresserweg, on a hill slightly farther upstream from the Marienfestung. This pilgrim's chapel is the last work by the Baroque master architect Balthasar Neumann. The stuccos are by Johann Feuchtmayer and Materno Bossi and the frescos by Matthäus Günther. A passage leads to the adjacent chapel of mercy. The Käppele is reached on foot via a steep walkway with many stairs and the Stations of the Cross.

Cultural Events

Contact the tourist office for information and reservations at the following festivals.

The **Mozartfest** (Mozart Festival) is the best-known musical event in Würzburg and attracts internationally renowned orchestras and conductors. It is held mainly during June, using several venues, including the Residenz.

The **Bachtage** (Bach Days) are held the last week of November. They involve several Bach performances, including a 100-voice choir. Some concerts are held in the Residenz

The **Barockfeste** (Baroque Festival) is held end of May – it involves music and fine dining in the Residenz.

The **Africa-Festival** is held end of May-early June and is the largest African music festival in Europe, attracting bands from all over Africa.

Festivals

Würzburg is at the heart of the Franconian wine lands and sees eight major wine-related festivals annually. Most are held in May or June, but a highlight is the **Wine Parade** at the Dom held the last week of July. For exact details contact the tourism office and for wine festivals in the whole area inquire with **Fränkischer Weinbauverband**, Haus des Frankenweins, Kranenkai 1, 97070 Würzburg, ☎ 0931-390-1111, www.weinland-franken.de.

Adventures

■ On Foot

The tourist office conducts 90-minute walking tours of the **old town** daily from April to October at 10:30 am. They depart from the tourist office at the Markt. Once a month, tours of 17th-century witch-hunt sights are available.

Night tours conducted by a night watchman, Wolfgang Mainka, ☎ 0931-409-356, start from the Vierröhrenbrunnen at the Rathaus. The 60-minute tour is available at 8 and 9 pm on Friday and Saturday, mid-January to March, and Wednesday to Saturday, April to shortly before Christmas.

The Main Valley is a lovely area for hiking. A popular hiking route is the 55-km (33-mile) **Franconian Red Wine Hiking Route**. It is divided into five stages and leads through the area and vineyards that produce red wine. It is downstream from Würzburg and connects Bürgstadt with Großwallstadt. At its center is the picturesque town of **Miltenberg** – one of the loveliest small towns in Germany. Information on the route is available from **Tourist Information Landkreis Miltenberg**, Brückenstraße 2, 63897 Miltenberg, ☎ 09371-501-502, www.rotweinwanderweg.de.

■ On Wheels

Cycling is popular in the Würzburg area, with a cycling route running the full length of the River Main. **Der Rad-Touren-Teufel**, Erthalterstraße 18, 97074 Würzburg, ☎ 0931-882-830, www.radtourenteufel.de, arranges multi-day cycling tours with luggage transfers, rental bicycles, accommodations, and maps.

Bicycle rentals are available from **Fahrradstation**, Am Hauptbahnhof, ☎ 0931-57-445; **Radsport Schuster**, Raiffeisenstraße 3, ☎ 0931-12-338; or **Velo-Momber**, Landwehrstraße 13, ☎ 0931-12-627.

■ In the Air

Bernhardt Ballonfahrten, Am Feller 8, 97234 Reichenberg, ☎ 09366-99-211, www.bernhardt-ballonfahrten.de, starts **balloon flights** from several sites in Franken, including Würzburg. From November to March, flights from Würzburg are discounted.

■ On Water

From April to October, several companies operate **boat cruises** on the River Main. Boats depart from the Alter Kranen near the Congress Centrum. A popular excursion is the 40-minute trip to Veitshöchheim run by **Kurth und Schiebe**, Alter Kranen, Roter Kiosk, ☎ 0931-58-573, or **Veitshöchheimer Personenschifffahrt**, Alter Kranen, Weißer Kiosk, ☎ 0931-55-631.

A 90-minute round-trip cruise is available daily at 2 pm from Volkach on a picturesque Main curve. Departures are more frequent on weekends. Contact the **Fränkische Personen-Schifffahrt**, Postfach 408, 97318 Kitzingen, ☎ 09321-91-810, www.mainschifffahrt.info.

Where to Stay & Eat

■ Old Town Center

The **Maritim Hotel** is beautifully located on the banks of the Main close to both the main station and the old town. Rooms are luxurious and spacious with some having views of the Marienberg Castle. The restaurant **Viaggo** (€€-€€€) is open for dinner only and serves international cuisine with a strong Mediterranean selection. Pleichertorstraße 5, 97070 Würzburg, ☎ 0931-30-530, fax 0931-305-3900, www.maritim.de. (€€€-€€€€)

The **Best Western Hotel Rebstock**, in the center of the town, has an early 18th-century Rococo façade and a sophisticated; interior. Comfortable rooms are furnished in different styles ranging from elegant to modern and country-house style. The restaurant (€€€-€€€€) serves classic dishes and has an excellent wine list. Neubaustraße 7, 97070 Würzburg, ☎ 0931-30-930, fax 0931-309-3100, www.rebstock.com. (€€€€)

The **Dorint Hotel** is a comfortable spot with a convenient location between the station and the Residenz. Rooms are modern and well-equipped. The rustic **Frankenstube** (€€-€€€) serves mostly local specialties. Ludwigstraße/Ecke Eichstraße, 97070 Würzburg, ☎ 0931-30-540, fax 0931-305-4423, www.dorint.de. (€€€)

In the same area are two small hotels. The **Amberger Hotel** has comfortable rooms and soundproof windows. Ludwigstraße 17, 97070 Würzburg, ☎ 0931-35-100, fax 0931-351-0800, www.hotel-amberger.de. (€€-€€€)

The **Zur Stadt Mainz** is behind an original colorfully painted façade dating from 1430. The 15 rooms are comfortably furnished with country-style furniture. The rustic restaurant (€€-€€€) has an old-Franconian atmosphere and serves regional dishes; reservations are recommended. Semmelstraße 39, 97070 Würzburg, ☎ 0931-53-155, fax 0931-58-510, www.hotel-stadtmainz.de. (€€).

■ Left Bank

The **Mercure am Mainufer** is a modern hotel completed in 1990 on the left bank of the Main and is especially popular with business travelers. Rooms are well-equipped and comfortable. Dreikronenstraße 27, 97082 Würzburg, ☎ 0931-41-930, fax 0931-419-3460, www.accor-hotels.com. (€€)

A block from here is the restaurant **Schiffbäuerin**, Katzengasse 7, ☎ 0931-42-487. It is a rustic, typical Franconian establishment serving regional dishes, with fish featuring prominently. (€€-€€€)

Just south of the Marienberg is the excellent **Bacchus Stuben**, Leistenstraße 6, ☎ 0931-883-739. This nostalgic Art Nouveau restaurant serves international dishes, including both light and hearty local specialties. (€€-€€€)

Camping

Camping Kalte Quelle is on the banks of the River Main south of Würzburg. There are rather basic facilities with 170 spaces for tourists and 130 for long-term rental. It is open from mid-March to late November. 97084 Würzburg-Heidingsfeld, ☎ 0931-65-598, fax 0931-612-611.

Bamberg

Bamberg is one of Germany's most beautiful towns. It has a long history, with architectural gems spanning a millennium. Its main attraction are the 2,300 protected buildings that led to the town being listed on the UNESCO World Cultural Heritage list.

Bamberg has a written history going back to 902, but its moment came in 1007 when Emperor Heinrich II founded a bishopric and erected an Imperial Palace in the town. As with other Episcopal towns in the region, the clergy chose the high ground and frequently came into conflict with the citizens who settled in the valley. The most impressive buildings in Bamberg are mostly Baroque and located in the former bishop's town.

Following secularization, Bamberg became part of Bavaria. After the First World War, it briefly served as capital of Bavaria while Munich was in the hands of revolutionaries. World War II left Bamberg virtually unscathed.

Tilman Riemenschneider (1460-1531), one of the most famous German sculptors, was born here. His most famous work in town is the grave for Heinrich II and his wife in the Dom. The talented Dientzenhofer family, who designed and built many a Baroque palace in Germany, also hailed from here. The Bamberg Neues Residenz is one of their masterpieces.

Information Sources

Tourist Office: Tourist Information, Geyerswörthstraße 3, 96047 Bamberg, ☎ 0951-297-6200, www.bamberg.de, can make reservations for most events and adventures as well as accommodations.

Transportation

The **train** station is about 10 minutes walk from the old town. Follow Luitpoldstraße, turn right into Obere Königstraße and then cross the Main-Danube Canal on Kettenbrücke into the old town. Alternatively, several **bus** lines run from the station to the ZOB (Central Bus Station) near the Maximiliansplatz. Most travel to Bamberg requires changeovers at Würzburg, an hour away on the hourly train.

Sightseeing

The major sights in Bamberg can be grouped into three distinct areas. The Bürgerstadt is between the Main-Danube Canal and the River Regnitz. It is here that the civilians lived while the Episcopal area, often referred to as the Bischofsstadt (Bishop's City), is the higher ground to the west of the Regnitz. The Michaelsberg is higher than the Dom area and has marvelous views of the old town.

■ Bürgerstadt

The citizens' old town area is dominated by two large squares. The **Maximiliansplatz** is surrounded by Baroque buildings – the large former priest seminary is now used as the **Rathaus** (Town Hall). The long, narrow **Grüner Markt** (Green Market) is also lined by Baroque buildings, including the **St Martins-Kirche** (St Martin's Church), another work by the talented Johann Dietzenhofer.

The **Altes Rathaus** (Old Town Hall) is, with the Dom, the most famous sight in Bamberg. It is on a small island between the civilian and religious towns. The core of the building is 15th-century Gothic but it received a Baroque exterior during the mid-18th century. Note the angel's leg sticking out at the bottom of the wall in an attempt to add some 3-D! On the south side is the Rottmeisterhaus, a half-timbered house that seems to piggyback on the main building. This 1688 building was erected on the pontoon of the bridge, but from many angles seems to float in the air. The Altes Rathaus now houses the **Sammlung Ludwig** (Ludwig Collection), Obere Brücke 1a, ☎ 0951-871-871, a mostly Baroque porcelain collection donated by the Ludwigs (see page ** for more on this art-loving couple). Opening hours are Tuesday to Sunday from 9:30 am to 4:30 pm. Admission is €3.10.

The best views of the Altes Rathaus are upstream from the bridge leading to the Geyerswörth Castle. The Unteres Brücke, on the opposite side of the Rathaus, has good views of the former fishermen's houses that are often referred to as **Klein Venedig** (Little Venice).

■ Bischofsstadt

The four-tower **Dom** (Cathedral), Domplatz, was consecrated in 1237. It replaced the original church, erected on the orders of Heinrich II in 1012, which burned down twice. The newer church is mainly Gothic but with strong Romanesque influences – the plans were altered 20 times during its construction as traditionalists argued with more progressives over the suitability of the new French style. The result is one of the most impressive medieval buildings in Germany. The Fürstenportal (Princes' Portal), facing the Domplatz, has 10 recessed arches and an interesting sculpture of the Last Judgement. The Adamspforte (Adam's Door), on the south side, is the main entrance.

Most of the interior walls are bare, as Bavarian King Ludwig I stripped off the medieval paintwork in the 19th century, but some early reliefs can still be seen in the choir. The most famous artwork in the church is the **Bamberger Reiter** (Bamberg Knight). The 13th-century equestrian statue of a king is an idealized view of the medieval world, but mystery surrounds its creator, or indeed who it is supposed to represent. It is generally assumed that it is King Stephan of Hungary, but many other theories exist. The Nazis used it as a symbol of Aryan perfection. No less impressive is **St Heinrichs-Grab** (St Henry's Tomb) in the east choir. It was carved between 1499 and 1513 by Tilman Riemenschneider as a suitable memorial to Heinrich II, founder of the cathedral and later declared a saint. Opening hours are daily from 8 am to 5 pm. The choir performs during the 8:45 am services on Sunday.

The **Diözesanmuseum** (Diocesan Museum), Domkapitelhaus, Domplatz 5, ☎ 0951-502-325, is entered through the cathedral. It has the usual collection of lapidary remains and vestments. Of special note is Heinrich II's Blue Coat of Stars and the original statues of Adam and Eve from the Adamspforte – these were the first nudes in German art. Opening hours are Tuesday to Sunday from 10 am to 5 pm. Admission is €2.

The **Alte Hofhaltung** (Old Residence) was erected mostly in the 16th century as a residence for the bishop. It was built on the site of the 11th-century Kaiserspfalz (Imperial Palace) but most of the visible facades are Renaissance. The doorway has a statue of Heinrich II and his wife Kunigunde, with a model of the cathedral. The Innenhof (Inner Courtyard) has Gothic half-timbered buildings.

The **Neue Residenz** (New Residence), Domplatz 8, ☎ 0951-519-390, is the largest building in Bamberg. It was erected by Johann Dientzenhofer in 1695-1704 for the Prince Elector of Mainz and bishop of Bamberg. The interior has a painting gallery with old German masters and Baroque paintings. The Kaisersaal (Emperor's Hall) is where Napoleon signed the declaration of war with Prussia on October 6, 1806. The Rosengarten (Rose Garden), behind the Residenz, has good views of the town. Opening hours are daily from April to September, 9 am to 6 pm, and from October to March, 10 am to 4 pm. Admission is €4.

■ The Michaelsberg

The Michaelberg is higher than the Dom and overlooks the old town. It housed a Benedictine monastery from 1015 until 1803. A fire destroyed much of the monastery and it was rebuilt in 1610 in a Gothic style.

Most of the former monastery is now a home for the aged but a small part is used for the **Fränkisches Brauereimuseum** (Franconian Brewery Museum), Michaelsberg 10f, ☎ 0951-53-016, www.bierstadt.de/museum. It has a small exhibition on the history of beer making in the region as well as models and a display of traditional equipment. Opening hours are from April to October, Wednesday to Sunday, 1 to 5 pm. Admission is €2 – no free sampling, but a beer garden is at hand.

The **Michaelskirche** (St Michael's Church), erected between the 12th and 15th centuries, has a ceiling decorated with 578 flowers and medicinal herbs. It is open daily from 9 am to 5 pm.

To get to the Michealsberg from the Domplatz, either follow the road between the two residences via Jakobsplatz, or take the walkway through the park across from the Rosengarten. Alternatively use Bus 10 from the Domplatz to the top.

Cultural Events

Information on cultural events is available from the tourist office. Bamberg has its own symphony orchestra and several theaters.

Concerts are frequently scheduled in the Dom, www.bamberger-dommusik.de. From May to October, short organ concerts are held in the Dom on Saturday at noon.

Shopping

Around 30 **antique** dealers are in the narrow alleys between the Altes Rathaus and the Domberg. This allows for variety and fair prices, but bargains are hard to find. The **Bamberger Antiquitätenwochen** (Antiques Weeks) are held annually from end of July to end of August and attract many dealers and buyers. Exact dates are available from the tourism office.

Adventures

■ On Foot

Two-hour guided walking tours of the **old town** sights are arranged by the tourist office from April to October from Monday to Saturday at 10:30 am and 2 pm, and on Sunday at 11 am.

A self-guided audio-tour on CD is also available from the tourist office. The CD is available in English or German and can be rented throughout the year.

The self-guided **Bierschmeckertour (Beer Lover's Tour)** is available for €20 from the tourist office. The fee includes a backpack, a color guide to the best beer sights, and five vouchers for a pint of beer in several restaurants.

■ On Wheels

Bamberg is not a particularly good city to **cycle** in. Cycling routes are limited and the steep slopes make cycling a less attractive option. The surrounding countryside is more appealing. The local cycling club, **ADFC Bamberg**, Postfach 1022, 96001 Bamberg, ☎ 0951-54-773, www.adfc-bamberg.de, occasionally arranges cycling tours in the region.

Bicycles can be rented from **Zweirad Shop**, Siechenstraße 3, ☎ 0951-203-477.

■ On Water

The tourism office can runs **canoe tours** of Bamberg on the River Regnitz from Fähre Pettstadt to the Konzerthalle. This five-hour tour can be booked from April to October.

The tourism office also arranges 25-minute Venetian-style **gondola rides** on the calm waters of the Regnitz and the canals of the Hain area. The rides are available from June to August, Friday to Sunday, between 2 and 7 pm. Reservations are essential.

Where to Stay & Eat

The **Hotel Residenzschloss Bamberg** is at the edge of the old town in a former hospital and the Bishop Elector's residence, combined with a modern wing. Rooms are luxurious and comfortable. The restaurants (€€-€€€) serve mainly international cuisine. Untere Sandstraße 32, 96049 Bamberg, ☎ 0951-60-910, fax 0951-609-1701, www.residenzschloss.com. (€€€€)

The **Bamberger Hof Bellevue** is a first-class hotel in the heart of the old town – the best rooms have views of the Kaiserdom. Although rooms range in style from turn of the 19th century to thoroughly modern, all are comfortabe and well-equipped. The restaurant (€€-€€€) serves French cuisine. Schönleinsplatz 4, 96047 Bamberg, ☎ 98-550, fax 0931-985-862, www.bambergerhof.de. (€€€).

A pleasant place to stay is the **Romantik Hotel Weinhaus Messerschmitt**. The hotel is in a building dating partly from 1422 and the hotel itself has a 170-year tradition. The exterior is white and yellow, while the interior makes ample use of wood. Rooms are furnished using either antique or modern furniture. The highly rated restaurant (€€-€€€) serves international and nouvelle cuisine. Lange Straße 41, 96047 Bamberg, ☎ 0951-297-800, fax 0951-297-8029, www.hotel-messerschmitt.de. (€€€).

The **Hotel St Nepomuk** is beautifully located next to the Regnitz River in the former milling quarters. Rooms are comfortably furnished. Some have exposed half-timbered beams. The restaurant (€€-€€€) serves international and local specialties and offers spectacular views of the old town. Obere Mühöbrücke 9, 96047 Bamberg, ☎ 0951-98-420, fax 0951-984-2100, www.hotel-nepomuk.de. (€€€)

The **Barock-Hotel am Dom** is next to the cathedral. Behind its beautiful façade hide 20 comfortable rooms. The stairways are Baroque; the breakfast room is Gothic. Vorderer Bach 4, 96049 Bamberg, ☎ 0951-54-031, fax 0951-54-021. (€€)

In the same vicinity, in a converted 16th-century building, is **Hotel Alt Ringlein**. Rooms are rustic but with modern comforts. The restaurant (€€) serves hearty, local dishes. Dominikanerstraße 9, 96049 Bamberg, ☎ 0951-95-320, fax 0951-953-2500, www.alt-ringlein.com. (€€)

■ Camping

Campingplatz Insel is on the banks of the River Regnitz. It has 170 spaces, with good facilities, and is open year-round. Am Campingplatz 1, 96049 Bamberg-Bug, ☎ 0951-56-320, fax 0951-56-321, www.campinginsel.de.

Bayreuth

Bayreuth is internationally famous for hosting the annual Richard Wagner Festival. Thanks to Wilhelmina, sister of Prussia's Frederick the Great, Bayreuth is also a town rich with Baroque and Rococo buildings.

Bayreuth was founded in the 12th century but reached its golden age under the influence of Wilhemina (1709-1758). This talented woman was married off to the margrave of Brandenburg-Bayreuth. She found him dull and filled her court with talented artists and intellectuals. She loved the arts and was responsible for the construction of some of Bayreuth's finest

Wilhelmina of Prussia, 1774

Baroque buildings with interiors in Bayreuth-Rococo, a style marked by dainty garlands and flowers.

Richard Wagner chose Bayreuth in 1872 as the setting for his Festspielhaus (Festival Theater), which was specially built to perform his works. The theater opened in 1876 with a performance of *The Ring* and the annual festival has been drawing crowds ever since.

Information Sources

Tourist Office: Tourist Information, Luitpoldplatz 9, 95444 Bayreuth, ☎ 0921-88-588, www.bayreuth.de. For theater tickets use the same address but ☎ 0921-69-001.

BAYREUTH CARD

The tourist office sells the Bayreuth Card for €9. It is valid for three days and allows free admission to nine museums, a free guided walking tour, a daily newspaper, and free use of local transportation. It is a good deal if public transportation is used and is available from the tourist office as well as many hotels.

Transportation

The **railway** station is a few minutes walk north of the old town. Frequent rail connections to Nürnberg take an hour.

Sightseeing

Most of the sights in Bayreuth are within easy walking distance of each other in the old town. The Wagner-Museum is south of the old town and connected to the Neues Schloss with the lovely Hofgarten (Court Garden). The Festspielhaus is about 20 minutes walk north of the old town. The Ermitage is five km (three miles) northeast of the old town on the B85.

■ Old Town

The **Markgräfliches Opernhaus** (Margraves' Opera House), Opernstraße 14, ☎ 0921-759-6922, was erected in the 18th century on orders of the Margravine Wilhelmina and is considered the best-preserved unaltered Baroque theater in Europe. It is fairly plain outside, but the interior is in Rococo splendor with no surface left unpainted or ungilded. Astonishingly, the whole interior is made of wood. The theater was the largest in Germany up to 1871. The three levels of galleries are divided into boxes, with the royal box carrying the crown of Prussia and the coat of arms of the local margraves. Apparently, this theater drew Wagner to Bayreuth but he considered it unsuitable for his greatest works – it really is more suitable to magic flutes than riding Valkyries. Opening hours are daily from April to September, 9 am to 6 pm, and from October to March, 10 am to 4 pm. Light and sound shows are every 45 minutes. No sightseeing during recitals. Admission is €5 or €7 for a combination ticket with the Neues Schloss.

The **Schlosskirche**, Schlossberglein 1-3, ☎ 0921-65-427, is a single-aisle church completed in the mid-18th century. The mighty octagonal belfry is early 17th century. The church interior is Rococo and has the graves of the Margrave Friedrich and Margravine Wilhelmina.

The **Neues Schloss** (New Palace), Ludwigstraße 21, ☎ 0921-759-6921, was erected in just two years on the orders of Margravine Wilhelmina. It combined and converted a number of existing buildings. The interior is dominated by the Rococo with the margravine's apartments particularly elaborate and in stark contrast to the more somber quarters of the margrave. Opening hours are daily from April to September, 9 am to 6 pm, and from October to March, 10 am to 4 pm. Admission is €4 or €7 for a combination ticket with the Markgräfliches Opernhaus.

■ Wagner Sights

The **Haus Wahnfried Wagner Museum**, Richard-Wagner-Straße 48, ☎ 0921-757-2816, www.wagnermuseum.de, is in the only house Wagner ever owned. Only the façade survived World War II but the rest was meticulously restored. The museum is dedicated to the life and work of Wagner as well as the history of the Festspiele. Cherished possessions include original scripts

Richard Wagner

of several operas and instruments used by Wagner. Richard and Cosima Wagner are buried in the garden. Music is played at 10 am, noon, and 2 pm; a video is played at 11 am and 3 pm. Opening hours are daily from April to October, 9 am to 5 pm, closing at 9 pm on Wednesday and Thursday. From November to March, opening hours are daily, 10 am to 5 pm. Admission is €4.

Franz Liszt

The **Franz Liszt Museum** is nearby, at Wahnfriedstraße 9, ☎ 0921-516-6488, www.wagner-museum.de. Liszt (1811-1886) died here during one of the Festspiele. He was an admirer of Wagner's work, a friend, and eventually father-in-law. The museum has mainly pictures and manuscripts. Opening hours are daily from 10 am to noon and 2 to 5 pm, in July and August from 10 am to 5 pm. Admission is €1.60.

The **Festspielhaus** (Festival Theater), Festspielhügel 1-2, 95445 Bayreuth, ☎ 0921-78-780, www.bayreuther-festspiele.de, is what many Wagner fans come to Bayreuth to see. It is a rather plain building inside and out. Wagner designed it himself and the emphasis was on the sound quality, not the aesthetics of the building or the comfort of the audience. The bare walls and uncovered, wooden seats enhance the acoustics. The orchestra plays in a pit below the stage from where the music is guided by soundboards to bounce off the wall behind the singers, so it can mix with their voices before being blasted to the audience. The acoustics even take into account the density of the audience. Guided tours are scheduled from Tuesday to Sunday at 10 and 10:45 am and 2:15 and 3 pm. No tours in November or during recitals.

■ Farther Afield

The **Eremitage Altes Schloss**, Eremitage 1, 95448 Bayreuth, ☎ 0921-759-6937, five km (three miles) outside Bayreuth, was the pleasure garden and palace of the margraves. The influence of Margravine Wilhelmine is evident in many features, including the interior of the Altes Schloss (Old Palace). Its most impressive room is the Japanese Hall, with Asian furniture and decorations typical of the chinoiserie in vogue at the time. The garden features fountains, fake grottos, and the fake ruin of a theater. The mid-18th-century **Neues Schloss** (New Palace) was destroyed during World War II but was rebuilt and has a Temple of the Sun in its center. The musical fountains play daily from May to October, 10 am to 5 pm on the hour. Opening hours for the Schloss are daily from April to September, 9 am to 6 pm. Admission is €3 and includes the obligatory tour. The park is open for free.

Cultural Events & Festivals

About 60,000 seats are annually available for the **Bayreuther Festspiele** (Bayreuth Festival), Festspielhügel 1-2, 95445 Bayreuth, ☎ 0921-78-780, www.bayreuther-festspiele.de, held from the end of July through August. Applications for tickets open a year in advance and can only be made by writing to **Kartenbüro der Bayreuther Festspiele**, Postfach 100262, 95402 Bayreuth. Telephone information – but no reservations – is available weekdays between 11 am and noon at ☎ 0921-78-780. Applicants supposedly have a 10% chance of success.

Adventures

■ On Foot

Two-hour guided **old town walks** are arranged by the tourist information office from May to October from Tuesday to Saturday at 10:30 am and from November to March on Saturday at 10:30 am only.

Bayreuth is surrounded by interesting landscapes and natural beauty. The tourist information office has maps for over 30 walks in the region ranging from 12 to 20 km (seven-12 miles) each. Public transportation is available from starting and finishing points.

Where to Stay & Eat

The **Ramada Treff Hotel Residenzschloss** is partly located in a former brewery. Rooms are well-equipped and comfortable. Erlanger Straße 37, 95444 Bayreuth, ☎ 0921-75-850, fax 0921-758-5601, www.ramada-treff.de. (€€-€€€)

Nearby is the **Ramada Treff Hotel Rheingold**, which is especially popular with business travelers. However, tourists also appreciate the large, comfortable rooms with light wood furniture and the large fitness area. Austraße 2/Unteres Tor, 95445 Bayreuth, ☎ 0921-75-650, fax 0921-756-5801, www.ramada-treff.de. (€€-€€€).

The **Hotel Goldener Anker**, near the Opera, has been managed by the Graf family since 1753. Rooms are comfortably furnished with either antiques or modern furniture and attention to details. The Art Deco restaurant (€€€-€€€) serves mainly international and French cuisine. Opernstraße 6, 95444 Bayreuth, ☎ 0921-65-051, fax 0921-65-500, www.anker-bayreuth.de. (€€-€€€).

The **Hotel Bayerischer Hof** is close to the station, near the Bayreuth Festspielhaus. Rooms are individually furnished, with the modern rooms most comfortable. The restaurant **Gendarmerie** (€€-€€€) serves bistro-style food with the front tables casual and those to the rear more formal. Bahnhofstraße 14, 95444 Bayreuth, ☎ 0921-78-600, fax 0921-786-0560, www.bayerischer-hof.de. (€€-€€€)

Nürnberg

Nürnberg (in English usually written Nuremberg), is a city of half a million people. It is the second-largest city in Bavaria and a major industrial center. Approaching the old town, the outlying areas reveal none of the gems that are in the center. It is a popular destination with German and continental tourists, but receives far fewer English-speaking visitors than it should. Many English speakers associate Nürnberg with the events before and directly after World War II, rather than the vast political and cultural role the town played over a period of 800 years.

The oldest reference to Nürnberg goes back to 1050 and eight centuries of glorious history followed. Two towns on either side of the River Pegnitz, Lorenz and Sebald, developed separately until they united in the 14th century. Emperor Konrad II built a palace in Lorenz and Emperor Heinrich III started the castle in Sebald.

In 1219, Nürnberg received a privilege called *Stapelrecht*, which forced all traders passing through to offer their wares first for sale to local merchants for three days before being allowed to continue their journeys. Nürnberg thus developed as one of the more important cities on the trade routes from Venice to the north.

The Golden Bull, forced on Emperor Karl IV in 1356, stipulated that all new emperors had to hold their first Reichstag (Imperial Parliament) in Nürnberg – a tradition that continued until 1543. The imperial jewels were kept in Nürnberg from 1424 to 1796, and again briefly during the Nazi period.

Albrecht Dürer, self-portrait

Nürnberg's golden age was in the late 15th and early 16th centuries. During this period, it was at the peak of its economic and cultural development. Several artists and scientists were based here. Albrecht Dürer (1471-1528), the man who brought the Renaissance to Germany, was born and spent most of his life in Nürnberg. The poet Hans Sachs (1494-1576); the sculptor Veit Stoß (1445-1533); Peter Henlein (1480-1542), the builder of the first pocket watch; and Martin Behaim (1459-1506), the cosmographer and creator of the first globe – all worked here during the period.

Ironically, it was the maps created in Nürnberg that helped with the discoveries of sea routes to the east. This altered trade patterns and spelled the end of wealth for the area for centuries. Additionally, Nürnberg decided for the Reformation early on and thus upset the staunchly Catholic emperors. They ceased holding parliaments in the town and, worse, favored Augsburg in southern Bavaria, which increasingly took away trade and culture. The decline continued until the area industrialized in the 19th century. The town became part of Bavaria in 1806. The first railway in Germany ran from here to nearby Fürth in 1835.

The Nazis picked Nürnberg, probably because of its location at the center of Germany, for a party rally in 1927. The symbolism of the town was not lost on the Nazis and from 1933, it was the permanent home of the annual party rallies that attracted up to 1.6 million participants. At the 1935 rally, anti-Semitic laws, often referred to as the Nuremberg Laws, were adopted that legalized the segregation of Jews – common practice since the Nazis came to power in 1933.

On January 2, 1945, an air raid destroyed 90% of the old town. Most of the buildings are therefore reconstructions, but generally faithful to the original plans. The town walls largely escaped damage.

The allies selected Nürnberg for the trial of Nazi leaders after the war. (The initial proceedings were in Berlin but due to the chaos in that city, they were moved here because of the good infrastructure provided by an American base.) This process set new international law standards and ended with some of the accused executed, some jailed, and some even pronounced innocent.

For many, Nürnberg will always be associated primarily with the Nazi rallies, the Nuremberg Laws, and the Nuremberg Trials. In contrast to Berlin and Munich, which have somewhat managed to hide their Nazi heritage, sights associated with the Nazis are large and easily accessible in Nürnberg. These are well worth seeing.

Information Sources

Tourist Office: Information is available from the **Verkehrsverein**, Postfach 4248, 90022 Nürnberg, ☎ 0911-23-360, www.tourismus-nuernberg.de. In addition to information, touring packages, including accommodations, events, and adventures are also available.

Information offices for callers are across from the Hauptbahnhof in the Künstlerhaus, Königstraße 93, ☎ 0911-233-6131, and at the Hauptmarkt, ☎ 0911-233-6135.

THE NÜRNBERG CARD+FÜRTH

The tourism office and many hotels sell the Nürnberg Card+Fürth for €18. It allows free entry into most museums and use of local transportation in Nürnberg and nearby Fürth for two days. The card is only available to visitors spending at least one night in a local hotel.

Transportation

Nürnberg has an excellent public transportation system combining, S-Bahn and U-Bahn **trains**, **trams**, and **buses**. The Hauptbahnhof, directly south of the old town, is the hub for all modes of transportation.

Walking is by far the best option as many parts of the old town are for pedestrians only and one-way streets make for difficult navigation. To reach the Nazi sights, public transportation is more convenient. Tram line 4 is convenient to reach the Kaiserburg and the far side of the old town via the road on the outside of the western town walls.

Sightseeing

Virtually all tourist sights are within the medieval town wall, which is five km (three miles) long. It is possible to cross the old town on foot from the Hauptbahnhof to the Kaiserburg in about half an hour – however, few would want to rush through it that quickly.

For the purposes of this guide, the Lorenzkirche area is from the Hauptbahnhof to the River Pegnitz and the Hauptmarkt area from the river to the Kaisersburg. From here, return to the station through the western parts of the town – the Dürer Museum area, the western town walls, the Weisser Turm area, and the marvelous German National Museum. Use public transportation to reach the Nazi sights.

If time is limited, give preference to the German National Museum, the Kaiserburg, the town fortifications, and the Reichsparteigelände. The St Lorenz, St Sebald, and Frauenkirche are also interesting.

■ St Lorenzkirche Area

The modern Hauptbahnhof is just outside the town walls. From here, the main entrance into the old town is via the **Königstor** (King's Gate), one of four remaining fat, round towers. In total, 71 of the original 130 defensive towers survived. Fine parts of the town wall can be seen at Frauengrabe, but the sections at the west of the town and below the Kaiserburg are even better. Behind the gate is the **Handwerkerhof**, Am Königstor, ☎ 01805-860-700-590, a restored medieval-looking area selling mainly arts and crafts – see *Shopping* below for details.

Not all of Nürnberg is or tries to be medieval. The city is also proud of its role in contemporary design, not only in art but also in industrial products. The **Neues Museum** (New Museum), Luitpoldstraße 5, ☎ 0911-240-200, www.nmn.de, is dedicated to contemporary fine arts, applied arts, and design. In addition to the vast permanent exhibition, large temporary exhibitions are staged. Opening hours are Tuesday to Friday from 10 am to 8 pm, and weekends from 10 am to 6 pm. Admission is €3.50 – free on Sunday.

Annunciation (detail), Veit Stoß

Königstraße leads up to the **St. Lorenzkirche** (St Laurent's Church), Lorenzer Platz, ☎ 0911-244-6990, www.lorenzkirche.de. This High Gothic church was erected over a century, starting from 1260, and enhanced in 1477 with Late Gothic elements. The second-largest church in Nürnberg, it was severely damaged in 1945, with only the towers left standing, but was rebuilt, with much of the art original. Of special note is the *Englischer Gruß* (*Annunciation*, 1517-18) by Veit Stoß, the tabernacle (1493) by Adam Krafft adorned with a crucifix by Stoß. The rose window in the west façade has a diameter of nine m (29 feet). Opening hours are Monday to Saturday from 9 am to 5 pm and Sunday from 1 to 4 pm.

At the west of the church is the **Nassauer Haus**, Karolinenstraße 2, the oldest private home in Nürnberg. The lower two floors are from the 13th century, while the choir and towers are 15th century.

The **Tugendbrunnen** (Virtues Fountain) was completed in 1589 to symbolize Nürnberg's independence as a Free Imperial City. The figures depict the virtues, with justice towering over the rest on the third level of the fountain.

The **Museumsbrücke** (Museum Bridge) crosses the River Pegnitz to the Sebald part of town. There are actually no museums near the bridge, but it affords the best views of the **Heilig-Geist-Spital** (Holy Ghost Hospice), Spitalgasse/Hans-Sachs-Platz. It is partly 14th century, but the most famous parts that span the River Pegnitz are 16th century. It now houses an old age home.

■ Hauptmarkt Area

The **Hauptmarkt** (Main Market) is the center of all markets and festivals in Nürnberg. Its beginnings are anything but celebratory. In 1349, Emperor Karl IV, right, who was constitutionally responsible for the protection of Jews in the city, was dependent on Nürnberg for financing and secretly made it known that he would not oppose the town's plans to rid themselves of debts owed to Jewish moneylenders. Following the example of Swiss and French towns, the Jews were blamed for the plague that threatened the town. The local Jews were forced into their houses, the doors cemented shut, and the whole ghetto set on fire. With the Jews dead and debts cleared, the former ghetto area was used to create the new market square.

Probably to atone for this sin, Karl IV donated the **Frauenkirche** (Church of Our Lady), Hauptmarkt, ☎ 0911-206-560. This 14th-century Gothic church was the first hall church in the area. More interesting than the church or the art is the carillon. The **Männleinlaufen** is a set of seven small metal men representing the seven Prince Electors who come out daily at noon to pay homage to the Emperor. It reflects the constitutional decree determined by the Golden Bull of 1356, which determined the seven electors, who could elect the emperor and in return swore allegiance. The symbolism is more interesting than the actual show. Opening hours are Monday to Saturday from 9 am to 6 pm and Sunday from 12:30 to 6 pm.

The **Schöner Brunnen** (Beautiful Fountain) is a century-old copy of the original late 14th-century Gothic marvel. It stands 19 m (62 feet) high and has 40 colorfully painted statues representing biblical, philosophy and liberal arts, and political figures. Note the Golden Ring, a seemingly seamless copper ring inside the fencing. Tourists turn it three times for good luck – locals know one turn is quite sufficient! (Parts of the original fountain are in the German National Museum.)

The **Altes Rathaus** (Old Town Hall) was completed in 1622 in a mixture of High Renaissance and Early Baroque. It also incorporated parts of an earlier 1340 building such as the large reception hall. This is the largest secular building in historic Nürnberg. It has copies of the imperial jewels in the foyer. The building was severely damaged in the war and much of the interior, including Albrecht Dürer's wall paintings, has not been restored

The nearby **Gänsemännchenbrunnen** (Geese Boy Fountain) dates from 1550 and shows a boy carrying a goose under each arm.

St. Sebalduskirche, Albrecht-Dürer-Platz 1, ☎ 0911-214-2500, is the largest church in town. It was initially a Late Romanesque triple-nave church, erected in 1230-40, but altered up to the 14th century with Gothic additions. The interior is far more harmonious than the somewhat odd-looking exterior. The church was severely damaged in 1945 but restored – photos with peace messages show some of the damage. The church is filled with art. A highlight is the Gothic St Sebald's tomb – a 1519 bronze by Peter Vischer. In the chancel and ambulatory are several works by Veit Stoß. The church opens daily at 9:30 am and closes at 4 pm from January to March and November, at 6 pm in October, December, April, and May, and at 8 pm from June to September.

Nürnberg has long been an important player in the toy production market and still hosts a large annual toy trade fair. Admission to this fair is strictly limited to bona fide traders and manufacturers, but open to all is the **Spielzeugmuseum** (Toy Museum), Karlstraße 13-15, ☎ 0911-231-3164, www.museen.nuernberg.de. It has displays of toys over the centuries, with historic wooden toys, dolls, mechanical toys, tin toys, and model trains. The upper floor has post-World War II toys, including Lego and Barbies. It is very much a do-not-touch museum, but a special room on the top floor has toys for children to play with while parents look at the historic ones. Opening hours are Tuesday to Friday from 10 am to 5 pm and weekends from 10 am to 6 pm. Admission is €5.

Adjacent to St Sebald is the triangular **Albrecht Dürer Platz**, with an 1840 bronze statue of the great artist. Behind the statue is the entrance to the **Nürnberger Felsengänge** (Nuremberg Rock-Cut Cellars), Bergstraße 19, ☎ 0911-227-066, huge cellars cut out of sandstone to provide cold storage for beer. The first ones were cut before 1380 and were used up to 1900. Four levels of cellars were cut and, during the air raids of World War II, up to 25,000 people hid here. As with the Art Bunker, there is not much to see other than the bare walls. Note that, even in summer, the temperature stays below 8°C/46°F. Guided tours meet at the Albrecht-Dürer-Platz behind the memorial, daily at 11 am, 1, 3, and 5 pm. Admission is €4.

The **Stadtmuseum Fembohaus** (Fembo House City Museum), Burgstraße 15, ☎ 0911-231-2595, www.museen.nuernberg.de, is in the best-preserved patrician house in town from the 16th century. Note the large sundial when walking uphill from the Hauptmarkt – Nürnberg still has 32 of its original 73 in working condition. In addition to the usual local history displays, a multimedia 50-minute show brings local history to life. Nürnberg's position at the heart of Germany and the wealth of artists that lived here during the Middle Ages insure interesting displays. Opening hours are Tuesday to Sunday from 10 am to 5 pm, closing at 8 pm on Thursday. Admission is €5.

■ Kaisersburg

The Kaiserburg is a highlight of any visit to Nürnberg. It is in this mighty fortress that the Emperor stayed while in town. Construction of the castle started in 1167.

The Holy Roman Empire of the German Nation had no permanent capital and the emperor had to move around with his entourage from palace to palace. Between 1050 and 1571, every emperor visited Nürnberg. In total some 300 imperial visits took place and several imperial parliaments met here. Karl IV visited 40 times and Ludwig the Bavarian 70 times.

It is a steep walk up from the old town to the castle. The ticket office recently moved to the deepest inner courtyard next to the **Kaiserburgmuseum** (Imperial Castle and Kaiserburg Museum), Auf der Burg 13, ☎ 0911-244-6590, www.schloesser.bayern.de. This subsidiary of the German National Museum is a good place to spend time while waiting for the guided tour of the Castle. The museum focuses on military history and practices during the Middle Ages and it has a fine collection of armor and weapons.

The interior of the castle can only be seen on a guided tour – sometimes available in English. During the tour, the palace is seen with the double chapel, the imperial reception rooms and apartments. The tour ends with a demonstration of the **Tiefer Brunnen** (deep well) – a 53-m (174-foot) well cut out of solid rock. It is worth climbing the mighty round **Sinwell Tower** for fantastic views of Nürnberg's old town.

Opening hours of the buildings are daily from April to September, 9 am to 6 pm, and October to March, 10 am to 4 pm. Some parts of the castle grounds remain open until dark. Admission to the whole complex, including guided tour is €6.

■ Dürer-Museum Area

The **Tiergärtnerplatz**, directly below the castle, is one of the loveliest medieval squares in Nürnberg. A tourist magnet and a meeting place for young people in the early evenings, it is framed by several half-timbered houses and the former town defenses. The lower, smaller gate is from the 13th century, but the wider gate had to be added in the 16th century to allow the increasingly larger carts to pass through. It is possible to walk from here to Neutor on the sentries walk. The walk is closed during winter, but the walls can also be admired from roads inside and outside the old town.

Albrecht-Dürer-Haus (Albrecht Dürer's House), Albrecht-Dürer-Straße 39, ☎ 0911-231-2568, www.museen.nuernberg.de, is a museum dedicated to the great Early Renaissance artist who lived and worked here from 1509 up to his death in 1528. The house miraculously survived the carnage of 1945. The museum is furnished mostly as it was in the time of Dürer and demonstrations of some of the printing techniques Dürer introduced are held in the upper floor studio. Some Dürer drawings are on display but, for his greatest works, visit the German National Museum. Opening hours are Tuesday to Sunday, 10 am to 5 pm, closing at 8 pm on Thursday. In July and August, as well as during the Christmas market, the museum is also open on Monday. Admission is €5 and includes an English audio guide.

The **Historischer Kunstbunker im Burgberg** (World War II Art Bunker), Obere Schmiedgasse 52, ☎ 0911-227-066, is where much of Nürnberg's art was stored during World War II. In these medieval cellars cut out of rock 24 m (78 feet) underneath the castle, the art was safe from air raids and fires. The bunker can only be seen on the daily guided tour at 3 pm – frankly, there is not much to see here except the bare bunker, some photographs, and the ingenious, simple air-circulation system. Admission is €5.

The most impressive part of the **town defenses** is the section from the castle to Spittlertor. The defenses over the River

Pegnitz can be seen from Hallertorbrücke outside the old town, or more interestingly from a hanging bridge on the inside of the walls. The area at Maxbrücke and the Henkersteg that leads to a small island in the river is particularly picturesque.

■ Weisser Turm

The Weisser Turm (White Tower) was part of the 13th-century defenses, but is now several blocks from the later walls. The area is a popular meeting place, partly because one of the two underground stations in the old town is directly underneath the tower.

Next to the tower is the 1984 **Ehekarussellbrunnen** (Wedding Carousel Fountain). It illustrates scenes from Hans Sachs' poem about the bittersweetness of marriage. The comical caricatures are graphic enough to be understood even without reading the titles.

The **St. Elisabethkirche** (St Elizabeth's Church), Jakobsplatz, ☎ 0911-940-1280, originally belonged to the Order of Teutonic Knights. In 1785, the existing simple church was replaced by a Neo-Classical building with a cupola 50 m (165 feet) high. Napoleon forced the order to disband in 1809, so the interior was only completed in 1902. It is dominated by huge statues of the apostles. Opening hours are daily from 7 am to 7:30 pm.

The 14th-century **St. Jakobkirche** (St James Church), Jakobsplatz, ☎ 0911-209-143, was severely damaged in 1945, but the exterior was rebuilt following the original plans. The inside is more modern, although the high altar is thought to be the oldest in town. Opening hours are daily, 9 am to 5 pm.

■ German National Museum

The Germanisches Nationalmusem (National Museum of German Art and Culture), Kartäusergasse 1, ☎ 0911-13-310, www.gnm.de, was founded in 1852 to collect art, cultural objects, and documents related to the German-speaking world. Currently it has some 1.2 million pieces, of which 20,000 are on display, making it the largest cultural history museum in Germany. The core of the museum complex is a medieval monastery, with the church and cloisters used to exhibit religious artworks. The rest of the museum is more modern – the layout is somewhat confusing, but free floorplans are available.

The Picture Gallery has a large number of works by Dürer, Cranach, Rembrandt, and Holbein, while the sculpture section has excellent works by Veit Stoß and Tilman Riemenschneider. The applied and decorative arts sections are impressive and include the oldest globes in the world, early clocks, pianos, other musical instruments, and even a 17th-century dollhouse. The early history and prehistory sections have jewelry from the Germanic tribes and, the oldest item, a golden cone dating from 1200 BC. Opening hours are Tuesday to Sunday, 10 am to 6 pm, closing at 9 pm on Wednesday. Admission is €5.

■ Nazi Sights

The sights associated with the Nazis are not within walking distance from the old town but can be reached easily by public transportation. The parade ground of the Nazi rallies is southeast of the old town and the court of the Nürnberg trials is to the west.

It is best to start a visit to the **Reichsparteigelände** (Nazi Party Rallying Ground) with a visit to the documentation center. The area is large and will help to explain the background and the lay of the land. (Signposting was limited at the time of writing but there were plans to improve it in time for the 2006 Soccer World Cup.) Three major structures survive to the present: the Congress Hall, the Great Road, and the Zeppelin Tribune. The area is easiest reached by Tramlines 6 and 9 (stop Dokumentations-Zentrum), or S-Bahn S2 (station Dutzenteich).

THE NAZI PARTY RALLIES

The Nazi Party held rallies in Nürnberg in 1927 and 1929, mostly due to the city's central location and easy access from all parts of Germany. But this, as well as the symbolism of Nürnberg's links to the old empire, led to the town being selected as the permanent venue for the party rallies. From 1933 to 1938, six party rallies were held here. The seventh, under the motto "Party Rally of Peace," was scheduled for September 2, 1939 but abruptly cancelled without explanation on August 26.

As the distinction between party and state became increasingly vague, the rallies served more as a show of military might. The 1938 rally was attended by 1.6 million people over a period of a week. It was a logistical nightmare – in the Documentation Center are some priceless comments of attendees on the toilet facilities, the attempts of senior party members to enter the red light district, and the fact that bars playing music seemed to be better attended than those playing Hitler's speech.

The rallies involved endless speeches, parades and sporting events. It was accompanied by a folk festival and, for a week in September, Nürnberg again felt like the center of Germany.

The increasing importance of the rallies led to plans for an entire complex specifically for the use of the rallies. It was designed by Albert Speer and construction was done largely by slave labor. Work slowed down after the outbreak of the war but never completely stopped – until 1945.

Leni Riefenstahl's Triumph of the Will

The Nazis had a fascination with new technology, especially when useful for propaganda purposes. Virtually all film footage of their crimes was shot by themselves. In 1934, Hitler asked film producer Leni Riefenstahl, right, to film the Party Rally. Her *Triumph of the Will* was an excellent documentary, which the Nazis used to brilliant effect as probably the best propaganda film ever made. Parts of this film are shown in the Documentation Center. Her filming of the 1936 Berlin Olympics also set new standards. Riefenstahl always claimed she had no evil intent and saw her films purely as art and a record of events. She was jailed for four years after the war and driven out of filmmaking forever. She went on to become an underwater photographer and once again set new standards, but her name would forever be associated primarily with Hitler. She died in 2002, aged 101.

The massive **Kongreßhalle** (Congress Hall) was designed to accommodate 50,000 delegates. It was never completed but the parts that were, were built "to last a thousand years." Nürnberg is now stuck with the building. Demolishing it would be expensive and the whole area is now under protection order. Most of the building is currently a storage warehouse, but it also houses the interesting **Dokumentationszentrum Reichsparteitagsgelände** (Documentation Center Nazi Party Rallying Grounds), Bayernstraße 110, ☎ 0911-231-5666, www.museen.nuernberg.de. The center has an excellent permanent exhibition entitled *Fascination and Terror*, which uses photos, models, audio, and video to explain the Nazi regime, with special emphasis on the events surrounding the Party Rallies. Opening hours are weekdays from 9 am to 6 pm and weekends from 10 am to 6 pm. Admission is €5.

The area and buildings are surprisingly large and it takes a good 15 minutes to walk around the Kongreßhalle to the **Große Straße** (Great Road). This road – two km (1.2 miles) long and 60 m (198 feet) wide – was to have been the central axis of the monumental area. It is paved with 60,000 slabs of granite. Immediately after the war, the American forces used it as a landing strip and currently most of it serves as a good-looking parking lot for the nearby conference center and soccer field.

Walk down the Great Road and turn left once you're across the Dutzenteich pond to reach the 300-m (990-foot) **Zeppelin Tribune**. Although the columns along the top of the main tribune were destroyed for safety reasons in 1967, the tribune is still instantly recognizable as the place from where Hitler addressed the party faithful. The main and side tribunes provided seating for 60,000, while the field could hold another 100,000. The field is fenced off but the tribune is open and freely accessible.

■ The Nuremberg Trials

The famous Nuremberg Trials took place from November 20, 1945 and continued for 218 days. In the dock were 21 top Nazi officials; 12 received the death sentence and were executed on October 16, 1946. Hermann Göring cheated the hangman by committing suicide hours before. Proceedings took place in the **Schwurgerichtssaal 600 - Nürnberger Prozesse** (International Military Tribunal, Landgericht Nürnberg-Fürth/ Schwurgerichtssaal, Fürther Straße 110, ☎ 0911-231-5421, www.museen.nuernberg.de. The court is still in use and is open weekends only and only for guided tours that depart on the hour between 1 and 4 pm. Reservations are not possible. Inquire about the availability of English tours. Admission is €2.50. (It is usually possible to look into the court on weekdays but sightseeing is not allowed when the court is in use.) The court is most easily reached by U-Bahn U1 or U11 (station Bärenschanze).

Hitler & Göring

Cultural Events

Nürnberg has a busy cultural schedule with a wide range of performances and styles. In addition to the special events, regular concerts are held in the Meistersingerhalle and inside the Kaiserburg. Information is available from the tourist office or www.tourismus.nuernberg.de if no other details are given.

Rock im Park, www.rock-im-park.de, is an open-air rock festival that attracts international stars – it is held on Pentecost weekend at the Zeppelinfield.

Klassik Open Air is an open-air classical music festival held in the Luitpoldhein Park at the end of July, beginning of August. Admission is free and picnic baskets are welcomed.

The **Internationale Orgelwoche** (International Organ Week), ☎ 0911-214-4466, www.ion.nuernberg.de, is held at the end of June, beginning of August and is the oldest and largest religious music festival in the world. In addition to organs, choral music, soloists, and orchestras are also featured in the churches and the Meistersingerhalle.

The **Tucher Ritterspiele** is a knight's tournament held in August at the Kaiserburg. It features typical medieval tournament events and a medieval market.

The **St Lorenzkirche**, ☎ 0911-2446-9937, www.kirchenmusik-st-lorenz.de, is a frequent venue for religious music. On weekdays in May, half-hour organ recitals follow the Männleinlauf at 12:15 pm. Most 10 am church services on Sunday are accompanied by choir or orchestra music. Concerts are also scheduled throughout the year with Advent a particularly busy time.

The **St Sebaldkirche**, ☎ 0911-214-2525, www.kirchenmusik-st-sebald-nbg.de, is also a popular venue for frequent concerts. About once a month, the church has a musical guided night tour of the church and its history.

Festivals

Nürnberg enjoys a couple of good annual festivals. Although the town is definitely in the middle of beer-drinking Franken, it does have a wine festival. The **Fränkische Weinfest** is held annually over two weeks at the end of June, beginning of July. The **Spargelmarkt** (Asparagus Market) is held the last week of May to welcome the start of the asparagus season. The **Altstadtfest** (Old Town Festival) is held at the end of September and claims to be the largest in Germany.

The **Nürnberger Christkindlemarkt** (Christmas Market) has a 400-year tradition and is world-famous. It is one of the best in Germany and is held annually from end of November to Christmas. It is best to arrive on a Sunday or Monday to avoid the crowds. The month is also a cultural highlight with musical concerts staged in many churches.

Shopping

A good place to buy arts and crafts is the **Handwerkerhof**, Am Königstor, ☎ 01805-860-700-590. It is a large courtyard with medieval-style small half-timbered houses selling locally made items. Even if you are not planning to buy, it is interesting to see how Nürnberg must have looked prior to 1945. Opening hours are weekdays from 10 am to 6:30 pm and Saturday from 10 am to 4 pm.

Nürnberg is famous for two edible products: the finger-size Nürnberger Bratwurst sausages and Lebkuchen. **Lebkuchen** is a gingerbread delicacy, especially associated with Christmas but available throughout the year. The best ones are baked without the use of flour. They are usually available in colorful tins that make good souvenirs. One of the most famous producers is **Lebkuchen Schmidt**, Zollhausstraße 30, ☎ 0911-896-631, www.leckuchen-schmidt.com. They are sold at Plobenhof 6 (at the Hauptmarkt), in the Handwerkerhof, and at the Christmas Market.

The **Trempelmarkt** is Germany's largest open-air flea market and is held annually in the old town in May and September.

Adventures

■ On Foot

Nürnberg has an astonishing number of competing guided **walking tours**. The tourist office conducts a two-hour, English guided walking tour of the old town daily from May to October at 1 pm, departing from the tourist office at Hauptmarkt. Audio guides in English can also be rented from the tourist office for self-guided tours.

Die Stadtführer, www.nuernberg.de, conducts a wide range of tours emphasizing history and art. The **Institute for Regional History**, Wiesentalstraße 32, ☎ 0911-307-360, www.geschichte-fuer-alle.de, has frequent tours in the city and region focusing on history

A night watchwomen, with a PhD to boot, offers night tours of Nürnberg most Friday to Sunday nights from March to December. Four different tours are available and English tours are possible on request. Contact **Dr U Jager**, Marktplatz 6, 91781 Weißenburg, ☎ 09141-997-207, www.nachtwaechterin.de.

Marco Kircher, Postfach 130248, 90114 Nürnberg, ☎ 0175-402-4148, conducts ghost tours of Nürnberg most Friday and Saturday nights from April to December.

■ On Wheels

Bicycle rentals are available from **Fahrradkiste**, Knauerstraße 9, ☎ 0911-287-9064; **Ride a Rainbow**, Adam-Kraft-Straße 55, ☎ 0911-397-337; or **Play It Again Sports**, Rennweg 7-9, ☎ 0911-538-580.

Motorized train (**Bimmelbahn**) tours of Nürnberg depart frequently from the Hauptmarkt. For details, contact **Altstadtrundfahrten**, Kreulstraße 59E, ☎ 0911-421-919, www.nuernberg-tourist.de. The tour lasts about 40 minutes.

■ In the Air

Ballonfahren Macht Spaß, Richard-Wagner-Straße 11, 91207 Lauf/Pegnitz, ☎ 09123-99-393, www.ballonfahren.de, offers balloon flights in the Nürnberg region but also has longer flights, including crossing the Alps.

Where to Stay & Eat

■ Station Area

Nuremberg has three luxury hotels within a block of the main station at the edge of the historic old town. The **ArabellaSheraton Hotel Carlton**, which opened in 2001, is the newest and the most comfortable. Rooms are spacious and modern, with straight lines and light colors. Service is friendly and efficient. Eilgutstraße 15, 90443 Nürnberg, ☎ 0911-20-030, fax 0911-200-3111, www.carlton-nuernberg.de. (€€€-€€€€)

Le Méridien Grand Hotel combines a hundred-year tradition with modern comforts. Rooms have Art Nouveau influences and marble baths. The **Brasserie** (€€-€€€) serves international and regional dishes in elegant surroundings with ample use of marble, mirrors, and carved glass. Bahnhofstraße 1, 90443 Nürnberg, ☎ 0911-23-220, fax 0911-232-2444, www.grand-hotel.de. (€€€€)

Maritim Hotel has large, beautifully furnished rooms using light wood and warm colors. The restaurant **Nürnberger Stuben** (€€-€€€) is rustic, yet luxurious and serves international cuisine in addition to regional favorites. Frauentorgraben 11, 90443 Nürnberg, ☎ 0911-23-630, fax 0911-236-3851, www.maritim.de. (€€€-€€€€)

DINING PRICE CHART	
Price per person for an entrée, including water, beer or soft drink.	
€	Under €10
€€	€10-€20
€€€	€21-€35
€€€€	Over €35

InterCity Hotel offers good value for money in the same area close to the station. Rooms are comfortably furnished and well-equipped. The room key gives free access to public transportation. Eilgutstraße 8, 90443 Nürnberg, ☎ 0911-24-780, fax 0911-247-8999, www.steigenberger.de. (€€-€€€)

The best value is offered by the two Ibis hotels close to the station. As is usual with this budget chain, little distinguishes the hotels and rooms from each other. All rooms are clean, bright, and equipped with the necessities. The **Ibis Marientor** is just outside the city walls behind the Grand Hotel. Königstorgraben 9, 90402 Nürnberg, ☎ 0911-24-090, fax 0911-240-9413, www.ibishotel.com. (€)

The new **Ibis Königstor** is just inside the old town close to the Handwerkerhof. Königstraße 74, 90402 Nürnberg, ☎ 0911-232-000, fax 0911-209-684, www.ibishotel.com (€€).

■ Old Town-Sebald Area

Although the top hotels are near the Hauptbahnhof, some pleasant hotels can also be found inside the Altstadt itself. The Sebald area is north of the river towards the castle and Lorenz to the south nearer to the station.

Two small hotels with modern rooms and facilities are near the Dürer House.

The **Hotel Agneshof** is pleasantly located in the heart of the old town. Rooms are modern and stylish. Most look out on the courtyard but some have balconies facing the Kaisersburg. Agnessgasse 10, 90403 Nürnberg, ☎ 0911-214-440, fax 0911-2144-4140, www.agneshof-nuernberg.de. (€€€-€€€€)

The **Dürer Hotel** is a thoroughly modern hotel close to its namesake's museum. Rooms are comfortable and furnished mostly with light wood. Neutormauer 32, 90403 Nürnberg, ☎ 0911-214-6650, fax 0911-2146-6555, www.altstadthotels-nuernberg.de. (€€€)

Several informal restaurants with terraces enliven the scene at the picturesque Tiergärtenplatz between the Dürer Haus and the Kaisersburg. However, nearby restaurants offer a more upscale experience.

Leading the way, with a Michelin star, is **Essigbrätlein**, Weinmarkt 3, ☎ 0911-225-131, close to the Sebaldkirche. This comfortable restaurant is in the oldest guesthouse in town; the building dates from 1550. Nouvelle cuisine and the chef's own creations are on offer. Reservations are recommended. (€€€-€€€€)

Nearby is **Goldenes Posthorn**, Glöckleingasse 2, ☎ 0911-225-153, dating back to 1498. It claims to be Germany's oldest wine cellar. Local specialties feature prominently on the menu that also includes international dishes. (€-€€€)

Similar food is available at the nearby **Zum Sudhaus**, Bergstraße 20, ☎ 0911-204-314. It is a rustic restaurant in a half-timbered building with large, copper brewery equipment as decoration. (€€-€€€).

■ Old Town-Lorenz Area

The **Victoria Hotel** is in a hundred-year-old sandstone building next to the Museum of Modern Design. Rooms are comfortable and with light wood furniture. Königstraße 80, 90402 Nürnberg, ☎ 0911-24-050, fax 0911-227-432, www.hotelvictoria.de. (€€-€€€€)

Hotel Am Jakobsmarkt is in a side-street near the Weisser Turm. Rooms are comfortably furnished and those in the attached half-timbered wings offer a rustic atmosphere, some with exposed beams. Schottengasse 5, 90402 Nürnberg, ☎ 0911-20-070, fax 0911-200-7200, www.hotel-am-jakobsmarkt.de. (€€-€€€)

HOTEL PRICE CHART	
Rates per room based on double occupancy, including taxes.	
€	Under €50
€€	€50-€100
€€€	€101-€150
€€€€	Over €150

The **Romantik Hotel Am Josephsplatz** is in a building dating back to 1675. Rooms are comfortably furnished in either a rustic or an Italian style. Josephsplatz 30, 90403 Nürnberg, ☎ 0911-90-403, fax 0911-214-470, www.romantikhotels.com. (€€€)

The **Nassauer Keller**, Karolinenstraße 2, ☎ 0911-225-967, inside Nuremberg's oldest private house, serves mainly regional specialties. The entrance door is low and the stairway down is steep, as is to be expected from such an old building. (€€-€€€)

Ishihara, Schottengasse 3, ☎ 0911-226-395, near Weisser Turm, is a good place for Japanese food. In addition to sushi, teppanyaki is prepared at the table. (€€-€€€)

■ Bratwurst Restaurants

Nürnberg's most famous contribution to German cuisine are the small finger-size grilled sausages called Nürnberger Bratwürstchen, served all over town and in many other German cities too. By law, the sausages must be between seven and nine cm (2.7-3.5 inches) long and weigh between 20 and 25 grams (.7-.9 ounces). They may only contain pork meat – no innards – encased in sheep entrails. Of course, they need to be produced inside the city limits in order to add "Nürnberg" to the name. They are a favorite in many German kitchens and at grill parties as most are sold already cooked, requiring just some grilling to warm them up and perfect the flavor.

Bratwurst is available all over town but the three places listed below are the most famous and still grill over beech wood fires. Most serve other regional dishes as well but ordering them is akin to requesting steak in a fish restaurant. The Bratwurst is traditionally served with sauerkraut and potatoes and washed down with local beer. Keep count of the bread and pretzels consumed during the meal as they are charged for separately.

Historische Bratwurstküche Zum Golden Stern, Zirkelschmiedsgasse 26, ☎ 0911-205-9288, dates from 1419 and claims to be the oldest bratwurst restaurant in town. It is close to Färbertor. (€-€€)

Das Bratwurstglöcklein, Im Handwerkerhof, ☎ 0911-227-625, is inside the picturesque Handwerkershof at Königstor. The sausages are served on bell-shaped plates by waitresses in traditional costume. (€-€€)

A personal favorite is the **Bratwursthäusle**, Rathausplatz 1, ☎ 0911-227-695, in the morning shade of St Sebaldkirche. It has a small, rustic room, where smaller parties have to share tables, and a pleasant terrace with views of the passersby. (€-€€)

■ Camping

Knaus Campingpark is at the Dutzenteich near the Nazi Party Rallying grounds four km (2.4 miles) south of central Nürnberg. It has excellent facilities, with 150, often shady, spaces and is open year-round. Hans-Kalb-Straße 56, 90471 Nürnberg, ☎ 0911-981-2717, fax 0911-981-2718, www.knauscamping.de.

■ Eastern Bavaria

Information Sources

Tourist Office: For information on Eastern Bavaria contact the **Tourismusverband Ostbayern**, Luitpoldstraße 20, 93047 Regensburg, ☎ 0941-585-390, www.otsbayern-toursimus.de.

Regensburg

Regensburg, with 140,000 inhabitants, is the fourth-largest city in Bavaria. As World War II left little damage, it has one of the most beautiful medieval city centers in Germany. The town is popular with European travelers but somehow English speakers tend to pass it by.

Regensburg is at the northernmost point of the River Danube. Its location is so pretty that, according to Goethe, such surroundings were bound to attract a city. A Celtic colony, *Radasbona*, was first located here five centuries before the Romans erected a military camp in AD 80. By AD 179, this camp had been enlarged and was called *Castra Regina*. Two centuries later, Bavarian tribes forced out the Romans. Regensburg was the ducal seat of the Bavarian rulers from the sixth up to the 13th century.

In the High Middle Ages, Regensburg, with 10,000 inhabitants, was the largest and richest city in the region. In 1245, it became a Free Imperial City. Its decline after that was gradual. By the 16th century, trade routes had shifted and talent moved to the new upcoming cities of Augsburg and Nürnberg. As a result, much of the core of Regensburg that survived is older than that of those two cities. The changing fortunes saw the traders losing business and most of the city indebted to the Jewish bankers. In 1519, the city expelled the Jews and wiped the slate clean. However, the prosperity of previous centuries would never return.

From 1663 to 1806, Regensburg had the prestige of housing the Reichstag – the first Permanent Diet or Parliament in Germany. The Napoleonic wars saw an end of the Holy Roman Empire and in 1810 Regensburg lost its independence and became a provincial backwater in an enlarged Kingdom of Bavaria.

Regensburg's economic revival waited until after World War II. New industries were founded in the region, including a BMW plant where virtually all 3-series models are produced – wait at the main station and a long train loaded with newly produced cars will pass by sooner or later.

Information Sources

Tourist Office: The Tourist Information, Altes Rathaus, 93047 Regensburg, ☎ 0941-507-4410, www.regensburg.de, has information on all attractions and events. It also makes reservations for accommodations and events and is open weekdays from 9:15 am to 6 pm and Saturday from 9:15 am to 4 pm. From April to October, it is also open on Sunday from 9:30 am to 4 pm.

Transportation

Regensburg has a well-developed **bus** system. However, tourists need only the Altstadtbus (Old Town Bus), which runs from the main station past all the most important sights in the old town. It departs every six minutes or so and costs €0.60.

If traveling by **car**, it is often best to leave the car at the hotel, if convenient, or otherwise park it in the well-marked parking garages at the edges of the old town. Street parking is limited and severely time restricted.

Sightseeing

All the sights in Regensburg are in the old town on the south bank of the River Danube. Most of the old town is a pedestrian zone. The area is about 15 minutes walk from the main station along shopping roads – the Altstadtbus is a convenient alternative. All the areas below are within easy walking distance of each other, with the Turn und Taxis Palace about 15 minutes walk from the center.

Dom, main entrance

■ Dom Area

Construction of the **Dom St Peter** (Cathedral), Domplatz 5, ☎ 0941-586-5500, www.bistum-regensburg.de, started around 1260 shortly after Regensburg became a Free Imperial City. It was a prestige project to show off the wealth of the city and it is still the most important Gothic structure in Bavaria. The new cathedral replaced its Romanesque predecessor, of which the Eselturm (Donkey Tower) above the north transept is the only remaining part. The city overestimated the size of its purse as well as the skill of the architect. His planned 160-m (520-foot) single tower could never have been constructed. In addition to the laws of physics, a shortage of funds meant that the building was only completed in 1525, sans tower. The spires, making the west towers 105 m (340 feet), were only added in the 19th century and it was a shoddy job – they had to be replaced a century later. The western façade is richly decorated.

Inside, the church has three naves and a non-projecting transept. Most of the stained glass windows, as well as the sculptures of Mary and the Archangel Gabriel, on the west transept pillars, are from the 13th century. The high altar was constructed between 1695 and 1785. Note the plaque on the south wall for Pastor Johann Maier. He was hanged on the square on April 24, 1945 for demanding that the city should surrender to the advancing American army rather than waste life and property on a lost battle. Opening hours are daily from 6:30 am to 6 pm, closing at 5 pm from November to March. Admission is free. The cloisters, the Romanesque Allerheiligenkapelle, and the Carolingian Stephanskapelle can only be seen on the guided tour of the cathedral.

The **Domschatzmuseum** (Cathedral Treasury), ☎ 0941-57-645, shows the wealth of the cathedral in goldsmith work and vestments from the 11th to the 19th century. The designs of the planned single tower for the cathedral can be seen at the entrance to the museum. Opening hours are April to October from Tuesday to Sunday, 10 am to 5 pm; from noon on Sunday. From November to March, it is open only on Friday and Saturday, 10 am to 4 pm, and Sunday, noon to 4 pm. Admission is €1.50.

The **Diözesanmuseum St Ulrich** (Diocesan Museum), Domplatz 2, ☎ 0941-51-688, has a rich collection of sculpture, paintings, and goldsmith work from the 11th century to the present. The museum is housed in the Early Gothic former church of St Ulrich. Opening hours are April to October from Tuesday to Sunday, 10 am to 5 pm. Admission is €1.50.

The **Alte Kapelle** (Old Chapel), Alter Kornmarkt, was originally a Carolingian Pfalzkapelle, but after two centuries of neglect was rebuilt as a Romanesque structure in 1002. However, in the 18th century it was transformed into a Rococo masterpiece. Its rich gilded interior decorations can be seen through the gates at the rear of the church during the same hours as the cathedral.

The **Historisches Museum** (City History Museum), Dachauplatz 2, ☎ 0941-507-2448, is in a former Minorite monastery. It has displays on local history from the Stone Age to the present. Highlights include the *Act of Foundation* – an eight-m (26-foot) stone with an inscription referring to the foundation of the Roman garrison here in AD 179. Further exhibits focus on Eastern Bavarian arts and crafts. Opening hours are Tuesday to Sunday from 10 am to 4 pm. Admission is €2.20.

The **Porta Praetoria**, Unter den Schwibbögen, is part of a gate that remained from the Roman garrison, *Castra Regina*, established here in the second century. It is part of a more modern building and was covered by plaster for centuries, but is now again uncovered. Apart from the huge monuments in Trier, this is the largest surviving Roman structure in Germany.

■ Danube

The **Steinerne Brücke** (Stone Bridge), with its 16 arches, was constructed between 1135 and 1146. Its construction greatly facilitated trading with northern areas and for eight centuries it was the only permanent crossing point of the Danube in the region. Fine views of the old town can be enjoyed from halfway across.

The 14th-century **Brückturm-Museum** (Bridge Tower Museum), Weiße-Lamm-Gasse 1, ☎ 0941-567-6015, has displays of objects and photos on the history of the Stone Bridge and shipping on the Danube. However, the main reason to visit is to enjoy the view of the old town from the top of the tower. Opening hours are April to October from Tuesday to Sunday, 10 am to 5 pm. Admission is €2.

The adjacent 1620 **Salzstadel**, with its enormous five-floor roof, was used as a salt warehouse. It currently houses a restaurant. The small, old building next to it on the banks of the Danube is the **Historische Wurstkuchl** (Historical Sausage Kitchen). The building dates from the 12th century and claims to be the oldest sausage restaurant in Germany. Goethe stayed across the road in the building that is now painted yellow and white.

A few blocks upstream is the **Kepler-Gedächtnishaus** (Kepler Memorial Center), Keplerstraße 5, ☎ 0941-507-3442. The mathematician and astronomer Johannes Kepler (1571-1630) lived and died in this house. It is now a museum, with period furniture, instruments used by him, and some functioning models. Opening hours are Tuesday to Sunday, 10 am to noon and 2 to 4 pm. From November to March, it is closed on Sunday afternoons. Admission is €2.20.

Johannes Kepler

■ Rathaus Area

The **Altes Rathaus** (Old Town Hall) was built as a prestige project to celebrate Regensburg's status as a Free Imperial City. The oldest parts date from the mid-13th century while the large Gothic additions are a century younger. The building currently houses the information office as well as the **Reichstagmuseum** (Imperial Diet Museum), which can only be seen on a guided tour. From 1663 until the dissolution of the Holy Roman Empire of the German Nation in 1806, a permanent Imperial Diet sat in Regensburg. The tour includes four sections. The **Beratungszimmer**, a discussion room for the Prince Electors, is in the oldest part of the building. Most impressive, though, is the **Reichsaal** (Imperial Hall), where the actual diet congregated according to a strict protocol, which kept the different estates apart. (Commoners were not represented.) The **Fragstatt**, literally questioning place, is in the cellars and include the original torture equipment and dark cells that were used in the disbursement of justice and injustice. The tour ends with some cannons and a huge official city scale that astonishingly can distinguish weight differences as small as five grams (.17 ounce). It is open daily, with German tours at various times from 10 am to 4 pm. English tours are available from May to September, Monday to Saturday at 3:30 pm. Admission is €3 and tickets are sold only inside the tourism office.

Nearby **Haidplatz** is a particularly picturesque square surrounded by early buildings, above. The **Neue Waage** held the official scales. The 13th-century **Zum Goldenen Kreuz**, at Number 7, was a guesthouse and for centuries the choice of the visiting emperor and kings. The **Justiabrunnen** (Fountain of Justice) is mid-17th century. **Hinter der Grieb** is a narrow alley with medieval houses leading from the square.

The **Golf Museum**, Antikhaus Insam, Tändlergasse 3, ☎ 0941-510-74, www.antikhaus-insam.de, claims to be the most important golf museum in Europe. It is a private collection inside an antique dealership. Although the collection is vast, admission prices keep visitors down to only the really interested. Opening hours are Monday to Saturday from 10 am to 6 pm. Admission is €7.50.

Schloss Thurn und Taxis

From the mid-15th century to the 19th century, the Thurn und Taxis family held a postal monopoly in much of Europe. The horn used by many European countries as symbol of the postal service originates from the family emblem. From 1748, the head of the family was also the emperor's principal representative (*Prinzipalkommissäre*) at the Permanent Diet. The former Benedictine monastery of St Emmeram was converted into one of Europe's most modern and lavish palaces for their use. It is still the principal seat of the family. In the late 1980s and early 1990s the palace frequently featured in the local gossip columns for the lavish parties that were held there. Inheritance taxes forced the family to open parts of the palace to the public.

St Emmeramskirche (St Emmerammus' Church), Emmeramsplatz 3, ☎ 0941-510-30, is a basilica dating back to the late seventh century when the region was converted to Christianity. Most of the exterior is Romanesque and Gothic. The statues at the main entrance of Jesus Christ, St Emmerammus, and St Dionysius are 11th century and among the oldest sculptures in Germany. The interior is a bit of a surprise – the Asam brothers altered the original Romanesque into Baroque with frescos and stucco work. Despite their efforts, the highest art here is still the sculpted tombstone of Queen Hemma from 1280. The crypt dates from AD 740. The church is open daily from 10 am to 4:30 pm but open only at 1 pm on Friday and at noon on Sunday. Admission is free.

Fürsterliches Schloss Thurn und Taxis (Thurn und Taxis Palace), Emmeramsplatz 5, ☎ 0941-5048-133, www.thurnundtaxis.de, is still the principal residence of the family. Three sections are open to visitors but only on guided tours. The tour of the **Schlossmuseum** (Palace Museum) includes the state apartments, the ball and throne rooms, and other rooms converted by the family in the 19th century into the Historicist style. The **Kreuzgang** (Cloisters) of the former monastery can be seen as part of the palace tour, or separately. The cloisters are a Romanesque-Gothic combination erected between the 11th and 14th centuries. From April to October, tours of the Palace Museum and Cloisters are available daily at 11 am and 2, 3, and 4 pm (on weekends also at 10 am). From November to March, tours are on weekends only at 10 and 11 am as well as 2 and 3 pm.

The **Marstall Museum** houses more than 70 coaches that were used by the Thurn und Taxis postal service. It is open April to October on weekdays from 11 am to 5 pm and weekends from 10 am to 5 pm. From November to March, it can only be seen on guided tours on weekends at 11:30 am and 2 pm. Admission is €4.50 – in winter that includes the compulsory guided tour and in summer, it includes admission to the Thurn und Taxis Museum.

The **Thurn und Taxis Museum**, Emmeramsplatz 5, ☎ 0941-504-8133, houses artwork from the family and the Bavarian National Museum. Highlights include goldsmith work, clocks, porcelain, glass, and furniture, mainly from the 17th to 19th centuries. Opening hours are April to October on weekdays, 11 am to 5 pm, weekends, 10 am to 5 pm, and from November to March only on weekends, 10 am to 6 pm. Admission in summer is €4.50 and includes the Marstall Museum. In winter, admission is €3.50 for this museum only.

■ Excursions

A popular excursion from Regensburg is downstream to **Walhalla**, Donaustauf bei Regensburg, ☎ 09403-961-680. According to Nordic mythology, the Valkyries carried the souls of fallen heroes to Walhalla to meet the god Odin. In the 19th century, King Ludwig I of Bavaria constructed a huge marble monument inspired by the Parthenon in Athens to house the hall of fame of Germany. Here 121 busts and 64 plaques commemorate the great and good from German history – mostly statesmen, scientists, and artists. A committee evaluates every six years who should be added or removed. The monument is most easily reached by car – follow the road on the northern bank of the Danube for eight km (4.8 miles) towards Donaustauf and park at the top of the hill behind the monument. A more interesting way is by boat – see *Adventures* below for details. Arriving by river requires climbing 358 marble steps to get to the top. Opening hours are daily from April to September, 9 am to 5:45 pm, in October, 9 am to 4:45 pm, and from November to March, 10 to 11:45 am and 1 to 3:45 pm. Admission is €2.50.

Another excursion, this time 30 km (18 miles) upriver, is to **Weltenburg**. The main sight in Weltenburg is the High Baroque **Stiftskirche Sts George und Martin** (Abbey Church of St George and St Martin) erected in 1720 by the famous Asam brothers. Its interior is lavishly decorated. Opening hours are daily from 9 am to dusk.

The most interesting way of approaching Weltenburg is by boat from Regensburg or Kelkheim – see *Adventures* below for details. Along a five-km (three-mile) stretch of the river, known as the **Donaudurchbruch** (Danube breakthrough), the Danube carved its way through the Franconian Jura mountains. At times, stone walls, 100 m (330 feet) high, rise from both banks of the river.

Cultural Events

Regensburg has a busy cultural calendar. Details of programs are available from the tourist office, which can also make reservations for several events.

Apart from the symphony orchestra and several theaters, many churches schedule concerts. The **Regensburger Kultursommer** (Culture Summer) has a month of events, both indoors and outdoors, mostly in August.

From June to September, on Wednesday at noon, free 20-minute organ concerts are held in the Dom. When not on tour, the *Domspatzen* (Cathedral Sparrows) boys' choir sings at the 9 am service on Sunday.

Munich, Schloss Nymphenburg (© Wilfried Hös / FVA-muc)

Baden-Baden: The Friedrichsbad (© BBM)

The Spielbank (Casino) at Baden-Baden (© BBM)

Schloss Favorite near Baden-Baden (© BBM)

Shopping

Regenburg has a wealth of antique shops. Most are in the narrow alleys in the old town near the Altes Rathaus.

From April to December, but not in August, the **Kunsthandwerkermarkt (Artisans' Market)** is held the first weekend of the month on Haidplatz.

Adventures

■ On Foot

The tourist office arranges frequent two-hour **old town walks** for individuals. English-language tours are available from May to September on Wednesday and Saturday at 1:30 pm. Thematic tours are also available but in German only.

■ On Wheels

Bicycles can be rented from **Bikehaus**, Bahnhofstraße 17, ☎ 0941-599-8193, www.bikeprojekt.de. A large selection of bicycles and equipment is available and deliveries are possible at a nominal charge.

The **Altstadtbahn**, ☎ 0941-630-8813, www.city-tour.info, is a *Bimmelbahn* (motorized train) that offers sightseeing tours of the old town from April to October. The tour last 45 minutes and departs from the Dom, close to the St Ulrichs. Commentary is in German and English. Tickets are sold at the tourism office up to 30 minutes prior to departure – remaining tickets are sold at the departure point.

■ In the Air

Balloon flights are offered by **Airsport**, Ockerweg 3, Hinterzhof, 93164 Laaber, ☎ 09498-902-460, www.airpsport.de. **Flugzentrum Bayerwald**, Schwarzer Helm 71, 93086 Wörth an der Donau, ☎ 09482-959-525, www.flugzentrum-bayerwald.de, offers balloon flights and tandem **paragliding** jumps.

■ On Water

A popular day-trip is on the River Regen from Ramspau to its confluence with the Danube in Regensburg.

Kayak and **canoe** rentals are available from **Penk an der Naab**, ☎ 09401-567-777, www.trekking-kanu-laden.de; **Kanuverleih Platzeck**, Embacher Straße 10, Niedertraubling, ☎ 09401-51-295, www.kanu-outdoor.de; or **Regental Kanu**, Am Burghof 16, Nittenau, ☎ 094326-2740, www.bootswandern.de.

Since Regensburg is situated at the northernmost point of the River Danube, it is no surprise that several boating options are available. **Regensburger Personenschifffahrt Klinger**, Werftstraße 6, ☎ 0941-55-359, has 50-minute **cruises** each hour from 10 am to 4 pm, end March to early October. Very popular are the Regensburg-to-Walhalla cruises that depart daily at 10:30 am and 2 pm. Cruising time is 45 minutes in each direction and there is an hour stop at Walhalla. Longer and specialty cruises are also available.

Personenschiffahrt im Donau und Altmühltal, Postfach 1641, 93305 Kelkheim, ☎ 09441-5858, www.schiffahrt-kelkheim.de, has daily cruises from the end of March to October on the Danube and the Altmühl. Particularly popular are cruises to the Donaudurchbruch and Kloster Weltenburg.

Where to Stay & Eat

Regensburg is a good place to break away from the chain hotels – there are not many of them and the independent hotels are in the best locations.

A top choice is the modern **Sorat Insel-Hotel**, on one of the islands in the River Danube. Rooms are comfortable, stylish and offer lovely views of the old town. The **Brandner** restaurant (€€-€€€) serves international and regional dishes in a modern setting with views of the Dom. Müllerstraße 7, 93059 Regensburg, ☎ 0941-81-040, fax 0941-810-444, www.sorat-hotels.com. (€€€-€€€€)

The **Park Hotel Maximilian** is halfway between the station and the old town in a 19th-century palace with an exquisite

Neo-Rococo façade. Rooms are attractive and some are quite spacious. No other hotel in town oozes more class. The rustic **Locanda Botticelli** (€€-€€€) serves Italian food and the cellar restaurant **High Fish** (€€-€€€) has Mediterranean cuisine. Maximiliansraße 28, 93047 Regensburg, ☎ 0941-56-850, fax 0941-52-942, www.maximilian-hotel.de. (€€-€€€€)

A romantic choice is **Bischofshof am Dom**, in a former bishop's palace adjacent to the cathedral. Romantic rooms are furnished in a country-house style. Part of the building includes the Porta Praetoria. The rustic restaurant (€-€€) with a beer garden in the romantic courtyard serves hearty local specialties. Kräutermarkt 3, 93047 Regensburg, ☎ 0941-58-460, fax 0941-584-6146, www.hotel-bischofshof.de. (€€€-€€€€)

The **Altstadthotel Arch Ringhotel** is on Haidsplatz in a huge patrician house dating partly from the 12th century. Rooms are comfortably furnished in keeping with the old tradition of the hotel. The rooms with exposed roof beams are the nicest. Haidplatz 4, 93047 Regensburg, ☎ 0941-58-660, fax 0941-586-6168, www.regensburg-ringhotels.de/arch. (€€-€€€)

The Ibis group has two modern, functionally furnished hotels near the station. The **Ibis Castra Regina**, Bahnhofstraße 22, 93047 Regensburg, ☎ 0941-56-930, fax 0941-569-3505, is north of the railway lines. South of the railway lines, across the road from the large shopping complex, is the similar **Ibis Furtmayr**, Furtmayerstraße 1, 93047 Regensburg, ☎ 0941-78-040, fax 0941-780-4509, www.ibishotel.com. (€-€€)

The modest ground-floor entrance of the Goliathhaus reveals none of the elegance of the fifth-floor **Restaurant David**, Watmarkt 5, ☎ 0941-561-858. International nouvelle cuisine is on offer. The terrace is particularly pleasant, with views of the Altstadt and the Dom. Open for dinner only. (€€€)

On the banks of the Danube, in the afternoon shadows of the Brückturm and the Salzstadel, is the **Historische Wurstkuchl**, Thundorferstraße 3, ☎ 0941-466-210, www.wurstkuchl.de. It claims to be the oldest sausage kitchen in Germany and looks the part. Sausages with sauerkraut and beer are mostly enjoyed on the Danube terrace but there is also some seating inside. The menu includes non-sausage items, but it is mostly for the famous grilled sausages that the diners come. (€)

■ Camping

Azur-camping is two km (1.2 miles) from the town center on the south bank of the Danube. It has 200 spaces. Bus 6 from the Hauptbahnhof stops in front of the campground. Weinweg 40, 93049 Regensburg, ☎ 0941-270-025, fax 0941-299-432, www.azur-camping.de.

Passau

Passau is a lovely town, beautifully located at the confluence of the Danube, Inn, and Ilz rivers on the border with Austria. The old town is mostly Baroque, although its written history stretches back to Roman times.

Celtic tribes settled in the area 4,000 years ago, but written history started after the Romans founded the military base of *Castra Batava* here in AD 200. In the eighth century, St Boniface founded a bishopric here and, by the late 10th century, Passau was as powerful as Salzburg. The bishops became princes of the empire in 1217 and controlled much of the Danube valley up to the 16th century.

Passau escaped the Thirty Years' War unscathed but a major town fire destroyed most of the town in 1662. As a result, most of the old town is Baroque, although the narrow alleys confirm that much of the Baroque splendor is erected on medieval foundations. Following the two world wars, Passau found itself a provincial backwater cut off from its natural central European commercial base. Links with Austria, of course, continued, but links with the Czech Republic were only restored in the 1990s.

Apart from its Baroque core, Passau is a popular departure point for bicycle tours and river cruises in the Danube Valley.

Information Sources

Tourist Office: Passau has two tourist offices, one at the **Hauptbahnhof** and a larger one at **Rathausplatz 3**, Neues Rathaus, 94032 Passau, ☎ 0821-955-980, www.passau.de. Opening hours are Easter to October on weekdays, 8:30 am to 6 pm, weekends from

9 am to 4 pm. From November to Easter, opening hours are Monday to Thursday, 8:30 am to 5 pm, Friday until 4 pm.

Transportation

The narrow alleys of Passau are best explored on foot. For **train** travelers, the Hauptbahnhof is about 10 minutes stroll through a shopping district to the edge of the old town and another 15 minutes to the Rathaus. The **City Bus** makes the same journey for €0.25. From the Rathausplatz, it is a steep, but rewarding, 30-minute walk up to the Veste Oberhaus. From April to October, a shuttle bus does the journey for €1.50 one-way or €2 round-trip.

For **drivers**, most parking garages are close to the station, but on a quiet day try the one near the Luitpold Bridge and the one at the top of the hill behind the Veste Oberhaus.

Sightseeing

Most of the sights are in the compact old town area on the peninsula ending at the confluence of the Danube and Inn rivers. The Ilzstadt is the area between the Danube and the Ilz and was the traditional bastion of the prince-bishops. The main sight in the Innstadt, south of the Inn River, is the Mariahilf church.

■ Dom Area

The **Dom Sankt Stephan** (Cathedral of St Stephan), Domplatz, is at the highest point of the old town. The Late Gothic east chancel and transept are the only parts that survived the 1662 town fire. The new cathedral is Baroque and has a decorated façade facing the Domplatz. The dome was only completed in the 19th century. The delicate Gothic parts can be seen from Residenzplatz.

The huge interior, the largest Baroque church north of the Alps, was designed by Carlo Lurago and he left no surface uncovered. It is overloaded with gilded stuccos and frescos. The gilded pulpit is 18th century but the high altar of silver poplar wood is a modern, 1953 design by Henselmann. However, the true highlight is the organ – originally built in the 1920s but enlarged in the 1970s. With 17,974 pipes, 233 registers, and four carillons, it is the largest church organ in the world. The cathedral has fantastic acoustics and the organ is put through its paces frequently – see *Cultural Events* below.

The church is open daily from November to April, 6:30 am to 6 pm. May to October, it is open from 6:30 am to 7 pm, but on weekdays when organ recitals are given it is closed from 10:45 until 12:30 pm. Admission for the noon concerts is from 11:20 and that gives you some time to see the interior if planning to stay for the concert. Admission is free, but €3 during the concert time.

The small **Domschatz** (Cathedral Treasure) and the **Diözesan-Museum** (Diocesan Museum), ☎ 0851-393-374, is in the 18th-century bishop's palace. The museum can be entered via a spiral staircase to the right of the choir in the cathedral, or from the Residenzplatz. Enter from the latter, if planning to see only the Baroque staircase (free). The museum itself has the usual collection of Episcopal paraphernalia as well as a lovely Baroque library. Opening hours are Monday to Saturday from May to October, 10 am to 4 pm. Admission is €1.50.

■ Rathaus Area

The **Altes Rathaus** (Old Town Hall) was erected in 1399 but the tower with clock was only added in the 19th century. Bavaria's largest carillon plays inside daily at 10:30 am, 2, 7:25, and 9 pm, and also at 3:30 pm on Saturdays. High-water levels are marked on the front of the building. The **Großer Rathaussaal** (Large Town Hall), entrance on Schrottgasse, is a Baroque hall with large wall and roof paintings depicting the Niebelungenlied and events from local history. Opening hours are daily from April to November, and December, from 10 am to 4 pm. Admission is €1.50.

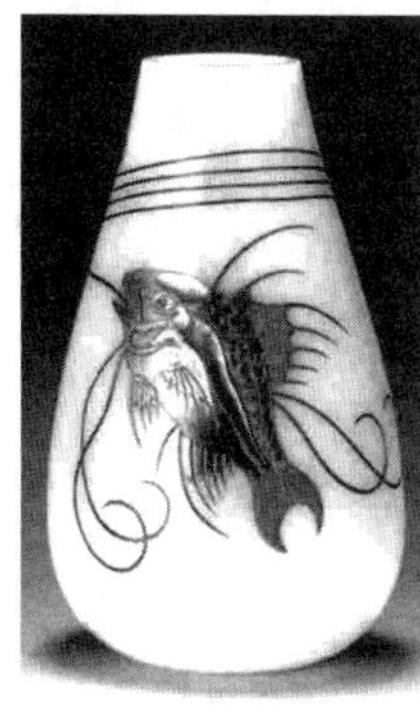

The **Passauer Glasmuseum** (Glass Museum) is inside the Hotel Wilder Mann, Am Rathausplatz, ☎ 0851-35-071, www.glasmuseumde. Its 30,000 items constitute the world's largest collection of Bohemian glass. It exhibits works of all periods of Bohemian glasswork from the 17th-century

Baroque to the modern, up to 1950. The collection also includes Bavarian and Austrian works. Opening hours are daily from 1 to 5 pm. Admission is €5.

The **Museum Moderner Kunst** (Modern Art), ☎ 0851-383-8790, www.mmk-passau.de, has a collection of lesser-known contemporary artists. A real treat for devotees, but others may find the part-Gothic, part-Baroque architecture of the building more enticing. Opening hours are Tuesday to Sunday from 10 am to 6 pm. Admission is €5.

The **Dreiflußeckspaziergang** (Three Rivers' Corner Walk) is a lovely short walk on the banks of the Danube and Inn rivers. The far end of the promontory is the only point from where all three rivers, including the Ilz, can actually be seen at the same time. Note how long the green water of the Inn and the muddy-brown water of the Danube flow next to each other before eventually mixing deep into Austrian territory. Boat trips, to observe this process up close are popular – see *Adventures* below.

■ Ilzstadt

The **Veste Oberhaus** was founded in 1219 as the residence of the prince-bishops. It is on the hill between the Danube and the Ilz and offers spectacular views of the old town and the valleys, either from the Battery Linden belvedere or from the castle tower (€1).

The complex houses the impressive **Oberhausmuseum**, ☎ 0851-493-350, www.oberhausmuseum.de. It has exhibitions on local history but, more importantly, impressive special exhibitions on Bavarian-Austrian-Czech cultural history. Opening hours are April to October, weekdays from 9 am to 5 pm and weekends from 9 am to 6 pm. Admission is €5.

■ Innstadt

The main sight in the Innstadt is the **Wallfahrtskirche Kloster Mariahilf** (Pilgrim's Church of the Monastery Maria Help). The complex can be seen from the Old Town and, in return, some of the best views of the Altstadt are from the church. The church is reached via 321 steps along the Pilgrims' Stairs. The church was erected in 1627, but achieved fame after Emperor Leopold I prayed here in 1683 requesting help to lift the Turkish siege of Vienna.

Cultural Events

Organ concerts are frequently held in the Dom. Most popular are the half-hour

concerts held at noon on weekdays from May to October. The organist ensures that the program shows off the full range of the organ's many features. Admission is €3. On Thursdays at 7:30 during the same period, longer concerts are presented. Admission is €5 for organ-only concerts and €8 if choral music is included.

The **Europäische Wochen** (European Weeks), www.ew-passau.de, is a large music festival held from mid-June to end July. Towns in Austria, the Czech Republic, and Germany host events but Passau is the center of the festival.

Shopping

Passau's narrow alleys are filled with historic buildings and interesting shops. Fine arts are particularly popular, with many galleries. An interesting shop is at the **Produzentengalerie Passau**, Ecke Bräugasse 6 Jesuitengasse 9, ☎ 08503-8250, where modern art is produced close to the Museum of Modern Art

Adventures

■ On Foot

The tourism office conducts one-hour walks of the **old town** in German only.

■ On Wheels

Passau is a major crossing point for long-distance **cycling** routes. The most famous route is the **Donau Radweg (Danube Cycling Route)** that is traditionally done over a week from Passau to Vienna, with extensions possible to Bratislava.

Bicycles can be rented from **Fahrrad-Klinik**, Bräugasse 10,

☎ 0851-33-411, www.fahrradklinik-passau.de, or at the station from **Österreichischer Tourismus-radverleih**, Bahnhof, ☎ 0851-490-5872, reisezentrum.passau@t-online.de, which gives 20% discount for travelers arriving by train.

■ In the Air

Bayernhimmel Ballonfahrt, Ludwigsplatz 4, ☎ 0851-34-600, www.bayernhimmel.de, offers **hot-air balloon flights** in the Passau region. Flights are available from €130.

Near Passau, **Pick Helicopter Tours**, Haberbühl 4, 94262 Kollnburg, ☎ 09942-902-840, www.pick-heli.de, has helicopter sightseeing tours starting from only €29.

■ On Water

Canoes and **kayaks** can be rented from **Bichlmoser Oberhofer**, Hochstraße 33, ☎ 0851-966-3603, www.wandern-klettern.de. Deliveries and pick-ups can also be arranged.

With three rivers to pick from, an above-average range of **boat trips** is available from Passau. **Wuem & Köck**, Höllgasse 26, ☎ 0851-929-292, www.donauschiffahrt.de, has several options. From March to October, 45-minute cruises to the three-river confluence depart every 30 minutes. Longer cruises are also available, including a four-hour cruise to Linz in Austria. Long weekend cruises to Vienna, with overnight stays in hotels, are also possible in the high season.

Where to Stay & Eat

The **Holiday Inn** is a modern hotel close to the main station inside a shopping center. Rooms are comfortably furnished and many have views of the Danube. Bahnhofstraße 24, 94032 Passau, ☎ 0851-59-000, fax 0851-590-0529, www.holiday-inn-passau.com. (€€-€€€)

Hotel Weisser Hase, at the edge of the old town, has a tradition going back to the 16th century but the rooms are furnished in modern style with marble bathrooms. The restaurant (€€) serves international and regional cuisine. Ludwigstraße 23, 94032 Passau, ☎ 0851-92-110, fax 0851-921-1100, www.weisser-hase.de. (€€€)

Hotel Passauer Wolf is on the banks of the Danube below the Dom. Rooms are comfortably furnished to the standards of a traditional luxury hotel. The restaurant (€€-€€€) is in a vaulted, 16th-century cellar and has views of the Danube. International and regional dishes are available. Rindermarkt 6, 94032 Passau, ☎ 0851-931-5110, fax 0851-931-5150, www.passauerwolf.de. (€€-€€€).

Hotel Wilder Mann dates back to the 11th century and has seen its share of famous guests, from emperors to Neil Armstrong. It is in a large patrician house next to the Rathaus and houses the famed Glass Museum as well. Rooms are opulently furnished with antiques or country-house-style furniture. Some cheaper rooms are a bit cramped, though. The restaurant (€€-€€€), on the fifth floor, is in a Baroque room and open for dinner only. Rathausplatz, 94032 Passau, ☎ 0851-35-071, fax 0851-31-712, www.wilder-mann.com. (€€)

A pleasant restaurant is the **Heilig Geist Stift Schenke**, Heiliggeistgasse 4, ☎ 0851-2607, a rustic, vaulted wine cellar dating from 1358. Both the terrace and wood-paneled interior are popular. Dishes are regional and include Austrian specialties. Especially recommended are the Austrian wines. (€-€€€).

■ Romantic Road

The Romantische Straße (Romantic Road) is one of Germany's oldest and most popular vacation routes. It follows backroads from Würzburg on the Main to Füssen at the foot of the Bavaria Alps. En route, it passes romantic towns, hamlets, castles, and churches. This section describes some of the stops on this route; some are worth a stopover of a few hours, while others can literally be seen in minutes.

Würzburg is described separately in the Franken section. Three popular sights at the south end, the Wieskirche, Schwangau, and Füssen, are described in the following chapter, on *Munich & the Bavarian Alps*.

Information Sources

Tourist Office: For information on the Romantic Route, contact Touristik-Arbeitsgemeinschaft Romantische Straße, Waaggässlein1, 91550 Dinkelsbühl, ☎ 09851-90-271, www.romantischestrasse.de, or any tourist information office en route.

Transportation

The 350 km (210 miles) of the route can easily be **driven** in less than a day, but the time required depends on the number of stopovers made en route. The route uses mostly backroads, but much faster parallel Autobahns are sometimes available to make up time. Tourist offices have free maps of the road, which is handy, as the route is not generally marked with signboards.

From April to October, **Deutsche Touring**, Am Römerhof 17, 60486 Frankfurt, ☎ 069-790-350, www.deutsche-touring.com, operates a daily **bus** departing from Frankfurt at 8 am, running the full route to arrive in Füssen at 8 pm. Stopovers are permitted en route and a 90-minute break in Rothenburg is included. Reservations (free) are recommended, especially during the high season. Bicycles may be taken on the bus but three days prior reservations are required.

Rail services are available to some of the towns, but they do not run along the route itself. Würzburg and Augsburg are major stops on high-speed networks, while Rothenburg, Donauwörth, and Füssen can also be reached by rail.

CYCLING THE ROMANTIC ROAD

The **Tourismusverband Ammersee-Lech**, Kohlstattstraße 8, 86899 Landsberg a Lech, ☎ 08191-47-177, www.radler-paradies.de, arranges nine-day tours along the full length of the route from Würzburg to Füssen. The tours include rental bicycles, accommodations, luggage transportation, and maps.

Rothenburg ob der Tauber

Rothenburg ob der Tauber is a medieval walled town in an excellent state of repair. The population is 12,000 but 2½ million day-trippers visit annually and just under half a million spend the night. It certainly is not the only medieval walled town in Germany but none is as attractive, or as popular. In the high season it is best to arrive in the afternoon, spend the night, and leave before lunch to avoid the crowds.

Rothenburg was founded in the 12th century and became a Free Imperial City in 1274. By 1400, Rothenburg was at the peak of its power and, with 6,000 inhabitants, one of the largest cities in the empire. Decline started in the 16th century and was hastened by its adopting the Reformation, which led to its occupation several times during the Thirty Years' War. Thereafter the town was generally too poor to rebuild, resulting in most of the town seemingly in a 16th-century time warp. It became part of Bavaria in 1802 and by the end of the century was discovered by tourists. During the Second World War, artillery fire destroyed 40% of the town, but most buildings were restored.

The Meistertrunk Legend

Rothenburg's most famous moment came during the Thirty Years' War when General Tilly threatened to destroy the town. According to legend, all pleas were rejected until the general was offered the best local wine. He offered to spare the town if a burgher could drink a hanap (six liters, or 1.6 gallons) in a single gulp. A certain Nusch, a former Burgomeister, came forward and achieved the feat. This event is commemorated annually during the Pentecost weekend with an open-air play on the market square. (Historians generally agree that a bag of cash is what really changed the general's mind).

Information Sources

Tourist Office: The tourist information office is at Marktplatz 2, 91541 Rothenburg ob der Tauber, ☎ 09861-40-492, www.rothenburg.de.

Transportation

Rothenburg is close to the Autobahn A7 and can be reached on the **Europa Bus** from Frankfurt. By **train** it is just over an hour from Würzburg (change at Steinach) or between one and two hours from Nürnberg (change at Ansbach and Steinach). The station is about a 10-minute walk to the east of the old town.

Joachim Schöbel, Rothenburgerstraße 11, 91583 Schillingsfürst, ☎ 0171-782-8022, www.shuttle-service.net, offers a convenient **airport shuttle** service to Rothenburg. Rates from Frankfurt are €120 for up to five persons. The service is also available to other towns and airports in the region.

Once at Rothenburg, walking is the only option. Street parking is scarce and time-restricted. Large, well-marked parking lots are outside the walls. Most of the old town is closed to cars on weekdays from 11 am to 4 pm and from 7 pm to 5 am. The whole old town is closed to traffic on weekends – drivers with hotel reservations may enter through Galgentor.

Sightseeing

The main attraction of Rothenburg is its medieval atmosphere and the magnificent fortifications. Large sections of the wall may be explored at will. The tourist information office and most hotels have maps with suggested walking routes to see the town from its most picturesque angles. Apart from St Jakob and the Criminal Museum, indoor attractions are best reserved for rainy days.

The Markt is a large square in the center of the old town. The Gothic parts of the **Rathaus** (Town Hall) date from the 14th century and the Renaissance additions are late 16th century. The 60-m (195-foot) tower has the best views in town. Opening hours are daily from April to October, 9:30 am to 12:30 pm. From November to March, it is open on weekends only from noon to 3 pm, but daily during December. Admission is €1.

To the north is the former **Ratstrinkstube** (City Councilors' Tavern), formerly open to council members only. It has several clocks, including a carillon that recalls the Meistertrunk daily at the full hour between 11 am and 3 pm, and 8 and 10 pm.

Käthe Wohlfahrt's Christmas ornament shops seem to be everywhere in Rothenburg, but a different approach is in the **Deutsches Weihnachtsmuseum** (German Christmas Museum), Herrngasse 1, ☎ 09861-409-365, www.weihnachtsmuseum.de. It is in the back of the main Käthe Wohlfahrt shop and has a huge exhibition of early Christmas ornaments, mostly from the late 19th century. Opening hours are daily from 10 am to 5:30 pm, but closed on Sunday from January to April. Admission is € 4.

The **St Jakobs-Kirche** (St James' Church), is a triple-nave Gothic basilica. Construction of the east chancel started in 1311, the nave was completed in 1436, and the west chancel built in 1450-71 with a

passageway underneath. The church has several remarkable art treasures from the 15th and 16th centuries. Most impressive is Tilman Riemenschneider's **Heilig-Blut Altar** (Holy Blood Altar – detail above) carved between 1499 and 1505. Its main panel shows *The Last Supper.* Opening hours are daily from April to October, 9:30 am to 5:30 pm, December from 10 am to 5 pm, November and January to March from 10 am to noon and 2 to 4 pm. Admission is €1.50.

The **Reichsstadtmuseum** (Imperial City Museum), Klosterhof 5, ☎ 09861-939-043, is in a former Dominican monastery. It has mostly exhibits on furniture, weapons, sculptures and the former 14th-century convent kitchen. Opening hours are daily from April to October, 10 am to 5 pm, and from November to March, 1 to 4 pm. Admission is €3.

St Wolfgangskirche (St Wolfgang's Church), Beim Klingentor, is an interesting 15th-century church in unaltered state just outside the Klingen Gate. The church itself actually forms part of the town defenses – note the casemates (gun openings) and parapet walk. Opening hours are daily from March to October, 11 am to 1 pm and 2 to 5 pm. Admission is €1.50.

Many German towns and castles have a torture museum, but the **Mittelalterliches Kriminalmuseum** (Medieval Crime Museum), Burggasse 3-5, ☎ 09861-5359, approaches the subject more seriously and in greater depth. It is a large display on the development of justice in Europe up to the 19th century. The instruments of torture obviously attract the most attention, but the illustrated law books and explanations of procedures are also interesting. All descriptions are in English. Opening hours are daily from April to October, 9:30 am to 6 pm, November and January to March, 2 to 4 pm, and December, 10 am to 4 pm. Admission is €3.20.

Plönlein and Spitaltor

Towards the southern part of the old town is the **Plönlein**, a picturesque little square with a fork in the road. The main road leads to the **Spitaltor**, the mightiest of the city gates. Its 16th-century bastions encircle two large inner courtyards. Walking on stretches of the wall from here to Burgtor often affords grand views of both the old town and the Tauber Valley.

Cultural Events

The **St Jakobskirche** and **Franziskanerkirche** are frequent venues for musical **concerts**, www.kirchenmusik.rothenburg.de. Reservations can be made at the tourist information office.

Festivals

Rothenburg has three major annual festivals on the Markt – the exact dates are available from the tourist information office. The **Meistertrunk Festpiel** (Master Draught play) in June recalls the events during the Thirty Years' War. The **Reichsstadt Festtage** (Imperial City Festival) in September is accompanied by theatrical performances, traditional dancing, and fireworks. The **Reiterlesmarkt** in December is a small Christmas market but with arguably the most romantic setting in all of Germany.

Shopping

Käthe Wohlfahrt is Europe's largest Christmas ornament business. It has several shops in Rothenburg, the main one is at Herrngasse 1, ☎ 09861-4090, www.wohlfahrt.com. It is Christmas here all year. Prices are high but so is the quality of the products. A small outlet shop for end-of-the-line and slightly damaged goods is across the road from the St Jakobskirche at the corner of Kirchgasse. Ignore all the shops claiming cheap Christmas decorations in the immediate vicinity – the one you want is the low-key, nameless one with just a small "Schnäppchenmarkt/Discount Store" sign. The name Käthe Wohlfahrt is never used, except when the goods are finally packed into their Wohlfahrt bags.

Adventures

■ On Foot

English-language guided walking tours of the **old town** area are conducted by the tourist information office daily between April and October at 2 pm and with the night watchman at 8 pm. (German-language tours are at 11 am, 2, and 9:30 pm.

The Tauber Valley is a popular **hiking** area. The tourist information office has details on more than 10 walks starting from the Markt into the nearby countryside, ranging from two to five hours. Hiking maps are available from the tourist office or any bookstore. On Wednesday at 2 pm, a **Wandern & Singen (Walking and Singing)** tour starts from the Markt and heads into the surrounding countryside.

Joggers meet Saturday at 4:30 pm at the Waldparkplatz Aidenau parking area for a **cross-country run**.

■ On Wheels

The Tauber Valley is a popular **cycling** area – the tourist office has maps on cycling routes. Multi-day cycling tours along the Romantic Route are popular.

Bicycles can be rented from **Rat & Tat**, Bensenstraße 17, ☎ 09861-87-984, or from **Skazel, Rad und Freizeittouristik**, Am Stadtschreiber 27, ☎ 09341-5395.

■ In the Air

Happy Ballooning, Paradiesgasse 17, ☎ 09861-87-888, www.happy-ballooning.de, has late afternoon flights starting directly south of Rothenburg. In winter, flights are usually possible all day.

■ On Horseback

For horseback riding, contact the **Reit- und Fahrverein**, Reithall am Schwanensee, ☎ 09861-3262.

Where to Stay & Eat

The hotels in Rothenburg are mainly small and family-run. Early reservations during summer and Christmas are highly advisable. Many hotels have excellent restaurants attached. All hotels listed here are within the walls of the old town, unless specifically stated otherwise.

The **Eisenhut Hotel** is the best temporary address in town. It is in four 15th-century patrician houses at the Markt. Rooms are comfortable and individually furnished to a high standard. The restaurant (€€-€€€) with wall paintings and ample use of wood serves international dishes and local specialties. Herrngasse 3, 91541 Rothenburg ob der Tauber, ☎ 09861-7050, fax 09861-70-545, www.eisenhut.com. (€€€-€€€€)

The **Romantik Hotel Markusturm** is in a former customs house with a history going back to 1264. The hotel has been run by the same family for four generations and has large, very comfortable, individually furnished rooms. The restaurant (€€-€€€) serves local specialties accompanied by local wine. Rödergasse 1, 91541 Rothenburg ob der Tauber, ☎ 09861-94-280, fax 09861-942-8113, www.markusturm.de. (€€€-€€€€)

The **Burghotel** is quietly located at the town wall near St Jakobs-Kirche. Rooms are well-appointed and furnished with good taste and attention to detail. Breakfast can be enjoyed on the town wall itself when weather allows. Klostergasse 1-3, 91541 Rothenburg ob der Tauber, ☎ 09861-94-890, fax 09861-948-940, www.burghotel.rothenburg.de. (€€-€€€)

The **Tilman Riemenschneider Hotel** is in a romantic half-timbered building. Rooms are comfortable and mostly with hand-painted country-style furniture. The rustic restaurants (€€-€€€) in the complex serve mainly local cuisine. Georgengasse 11-13, 91541 Rothenburg ob der Tauber, ☎ 09861-9790, fax 09861-2979, www.tilman-riemenschneider.de. (€€-€€€€)

Nearby is the **Flair Hotel Reichs-Küchenmeister** in an old patrician house. Rooms are individually furnished and of different styles and sizes. Kirchplatz 8, 91541 Rothenburg ob der Tauber, ☎ 09861-9700, fax 09861-970-409, www.reichskuechenmeister.com. (€€-€€€)

A good choice just outside the town walls is the **Hotel Mittermeier**. Rooms are comfortably furnished and available in completely different styles. The elegant restaurant (€€-€€€€) is one of the best in the region and serves international and local nouvelle cuisine. Am Würzburger Tor 9, 91541 Rothenburg ob der Tauber, ☎ 09861-94-540, fax 09861-945-494, www.mittermeier.rothernburg.de. (€€-€€€)

The **Gerberhaus Hotel** is in the southern part of the old town close to the Spitaltor. It is a pleasant place with bright, comfortable rooms. Spitalgasse 25, 91541 Rothenburg ob der Tauber, ☎ 09861-94-900, fax 09861-86-555, www.romanticroad.com/gerberhaus. (€€)

Just outside the city gates is **Hotel Zum Rappen**. It has comfortable, individually furnished rooms. The restaurant (€-€€) serves hearty local cuisine. Am Würzburger Tor, 91541 Rothenburg ob der Tauber, ☎ 09861-95-710, fax 09861-6076, www.hotel-rappen.com. (€€)

The small **Hotel Klosterstüble** is near the Franziskaner-Kirche. It has comfortable, individually furnished rooms; some are partly wood-paneled in the Alpine tradition. The hotel is welcoming to families with young children. The restaurant (€€) serves local cuisine. Heringsbronnengasse 5, 91541 Rothenburg ob der Tauber, ☎ 09861-6774, fax 09861-6474, www.klosterstueble.de. (€€)

At the Markt are two lovely restaurants. A pleasant place for coffee and cake, or full meals, is the **Restaurant Baumeisterhaus**, Obere Schmiedgasse 3, ☎ 09861-94-700. It is inside a 1596 Renaissance house with courtyard, wall paintings, and antique decorations – serving excellent cakes and local dishes. The adjacent **Restaurant Zum Greifen**, Obere

Schmiedgassse 5, ☎ 09861-2281, serves hearty local cuisine. (€-€€)

■ Camping

Camping Tauber-Idyll is two km (1.2 miles) outside the walled town. It has good facilities, 40 spaces and is open from early April to early November. 91541 Rothenburg ob der Tauber-Detwang, ☎ 09861-3177, fax 09861-92-848.

Camping Tauberromantik is also two km outside Rothenburg in the Tauber valley. It has good facilities, 120 spaces and is open from mid-March to October. 91541 Rothenburg ob der Tauber-Detwang, ☎ 09861-6191, fax 09861-86-899, www.camping-tauberromantik.de.

Dinkelsbühl

Information Sources

Tourist Office: Tourist information is available from **Touristik Service Dinkelbühl**, Marktplatz, 91550 Dinkelsbühl, ☎ 09851-90-240, www.dinkelsbuehl.de.

Transportation

The town is best reached by **car** or on the **Europa Bus**. It is 50 km (30 miles) southeast of Rothenburg on country roads and 10 km (six miles) from the Autobahn A7. Most of the old town is closed to private vehicles – large parking areas are on the edge of the old town.

Sightseeing

Dinkelbühl is for many an alternative to overcrowded Rothenburg. Like Rothenburg, it is entirely surrounded by a town wall and most of the old town buildings date from before the 16th century. The town was saved the ravages of war and since 1826 had the town defenses under protection order. Currently, 18 watchtowers survive. The town walls are lower and much thinner than those of Rothenburg and, although it is possible to walk around the town, it is not actually possible to walk on the walls.

Dinkelsbühl is best enjoyed by walking the old streets and seeing the interesting architecture. The **Münster St Georg** is worth entering, as it is one of the most beautiful hall churches in Germany. The church has a Romanesque tower 65 m (214 feet) high, but most of the rest of the building and interior is Gothic. Note the statues of the *Last Supper* on the outside wall of the choir. Inside, the church is filled with art, with the late 15th-century tabernacle of the sacristy and the high altar especially noteworthy.

The Weinmarkt and Marktplatz directly in front of the Münster are the most beautiful parts of the town. It has several large, half-timbered houses, including the Deutsches Haus from the 16th century. Segringer Straße that leads westward from the square also has particularly beautiful buildings.

Adventures

■ On Foot

Guided tours of the **old town** are conducted by the information office daily from April to October at 2:30 and 8:30 pm. A walk with the night watchman is possible daily during the same period at 9 pm. All tours start from the Münster St Georg. Longer walks into the **countryside** are also arranged on a less regular basis.

■ On Wheels

The tourism office rents out **bicycles** and runs half-day guided cycling tours in the region. Maps are also available for self-guided tours.

On some weekends, an old **steam train** makes three round-trips between Nördlingen and Dinkelsbühl. Occasionally, the journey continues to Harburg and Feuchtwangen. Details are available from the tourist offices or from the Bayerisches Eisenbahnmuseum, Postfach 1316, 86713 Nördlingen im Ries, ☎ 09083-340, www.bayerisches-eisenbahnmuseum.de.

■ On Horseback

Horse-drawn **wagon rides** are available from April to October. The 40-minute rides depart from the tourist office.

Horseback riding is also possible in the region – inquire from the tourist office.

■ On Water

Canoes and **kayaks** can be rented from the **Naturfreundehaus**, ☎ 09851-9565.

Where to Stay & Eat

Dinkelsbühl has several comfortable hotels and offers a good alternative to staying in Rothenburg. Prices are much lower too.

The **Hotel Deutsches Haus** is in one of the most beautiful half-timbered secular buildings in southern Germany. Rooms are comfortable and romantic, with antique furniture. The restaurant (€€) serves regional cuisine with a good local wine selection. Weinmarkt 3, 91550 Dinkelsbühl, ☎ 09851-6058, fax 09851-7911, www.deutsches-haus-dkb.de. (€€-€€€)

The **Hotel Blauer Hecht** is in a former brewery building dating back to 1648. Rooms are comfortable and romantic with all modern comforts. The old German restaurant (€€-€€€) serves regional and international dishes. Schweinemarkt 1, 91550 Dinkelsbühl, ☎ 09851-5810, fax 09851-581-170, www.hotel-blauer-hecht.de. (€€)

The **Hotel Goldene Kanne** is in a 17th-century building in the heart of the old town. Rooms are fairly modern, though, with the two bay-window suites especially nice. The **Angus** restaurant (€-€€) serves steaks and Mexican dishes. Segringer Straße 8, 91550 Dinkelsbühl, ☎ 09851-572-910, fax 09851-572-929, www.hotel-goldene-kanne.de. (€€)

■ Camping

Campingplatz Dinkelsbühl, a well-equipped campground, is just north of the town. It is at a small lake and offers fishing and pony rides on-site. There are 475 spaces and it's open year-round. Kobeltsmühle 2, 91550 Dinkelsbühl, ☎ 09851-7817, fax 09851-7848, www.campingpark-dinkelsbuehl.de.

Nördlingen

Nördlingen is even farther from the highways and attracts visibly fewer tourists than Rothenburg and Dinkelsbühl. It is once again a completely walled-in town, and the town is almost perfectly round. Its written history started in 898 and it became a Free Imperial City in 1215. The town population was halved in the Thirty Years' War and it never recovered its former important position. The town became part of Bavaria in 1803.

Did you know? A meteor struck the earth millions of years ago and left a crater of 20 km (12 miles) in diameter. Nördlingen is in the heart of this, the Ries crater, an area still without significant trees.

Information Sources

Tourist Office: Tourist information is available from the **Verkehrsamt**, Marktplatz 2, 86720 Nördlingen im Ries, ☎ 09081-4380, www.noerdlingen.de.

Transportation

Nördlingen is best reached by **car** or the **Europa Bus**. The old town can only be entered via one gate – signposting is clear. On quiet days, it is possible to park in the heart of the old town; otherwise use the parking lots just outside the town walls.

Sightseeing

The main sights are once again the interesting old houses. Here, in contrast to Rothenburg and Dinkelsbühl, it is fairly easy to see decaying and less well-maintained buildings in the back streets.

The 15th-century **St Georgskirche** (St George's Church), Am Obstmarkt, has a 90-m (295-foot) tower. This tower, virtually in the center of town, gives the best view of the Romantic Road, as the interesting circular old town and the concentric development are clearly visible. The interior of the church itself is bright and has intricate vaulting.

The nearby **Rathaus** (Town Hall) is the oldest stone building in town. Parts date from the 13th century but the building was significantly altered around 1500.

The **Stadtmauer** (Town Walls) are the only ones in Germany that are still fully accessible. It is possible to walk around the town, mostly under cover, on the wall itself, passing 11 watchtowers and five gates en route.

Adventures

■ On Foot

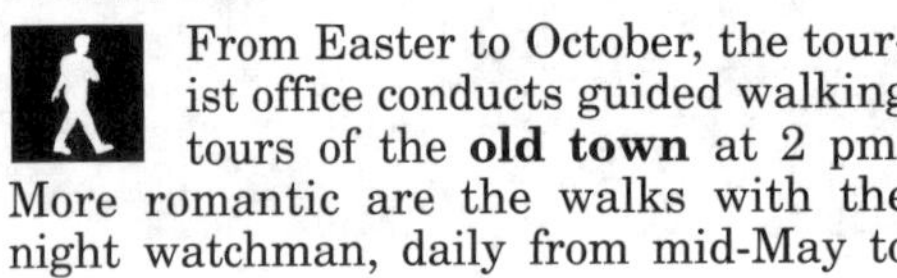

From Easter to October, the tourist office conducts guided walking tours of the **old town** at 2 pm. More romantic are the walks with the night watchman, daily from mid-May to mid-September at 8:30 pm.

■ On Wheels

Bicycle rentals are available from **Radsport Böckle**, Reimlinger Straße 19, ☎ 09081-801-040, or from **Zweirad Müller**, Gewerbestraße 16, ☎ 09081-5675.

■ On Horseback

The **Scharlachrennen**, www.scharlachrennen.de, are held annually at the end of July. This is one of the oldest horse-racing events in Europe, dating back to at least 1438. It is one of the largest riding events in south Germany and involves races and show jumping.

Where to Stay & Eat

The **Hotel Am Ring** is comfortable and outside the walled-in area. Rooms are modern and tastefully decorated. The restaurant (€€) serves regional dishes with seasonal specialties. Bürgermeister-Reiger-Straße 14, 86720 Nördlingen, ☎ 09081-290-030, fax 09081-23-170, www.hotelamring.de. (€€)

The **Kaiserhof Hotel Sonne** is in the heart of the old town. The building dates back to the 15th century and not all walls and floors are straight. Rooms are comfortable and individually furnished. The **Weinstäpfele** restaurant (€-€€) serves regional cuisine in a rustic setting with vaulting. Marktplatz 3, 86720 Nördlingen, ☎ 09081-273-8380, fax 09081-23-999, www.kaiserhof-hotel-sonne.de. (€€-€€€)

A surprisingly pleasant informal restaurant with excellent pizza and pasta is **La Fontana Pizzeria Espresso-Bar**, Bei den Kornschrannen, ☎ 09081-211-021, www.lafontana.ws. It is inside a large, red building with a terrace on the square next to a fountain recalling the town's history. Prices are low, for both the food and the long wine list. (€)

■ Camping

RVs and mobile homes are allowed to use the parking lot at the Kaiserwiese.

Donauwörth

Donauwörth is another small town with some original town walls surviving to the present. It is less interesting than Nördlingen or Dinkelsbuhl but still worth a brief stopover.

The town started as a fishing village at the confluence of the Wörnitz and the Danube. The construction of a bridge over the Danube in 977 made it an important stop on medieval trading routes. The town grew rich and became a Free Imperial City in 1301. Like the other once-important towns on the Romantic Road, changing trade routes lessened Donauwörth's importance. However, even to the present day, it has excellent transportation links to larger cities in the region.

Information Sources

Tourist Office: Tourist information is available from the **Städtische Tourist Information**, Rathausgasse 1, 86609 Donnauwörth, ☎ 0906-789-151, www.donauwoerth.de.

Transportation

In contrast to other small Romantic Road towns, Donauwörth has excellent **rail** links with direct connections to Augsburg, Munich, Nürnberg, Regensburg, and Stuttgart.

By **car**, the town is also easily reached on the new B2 road from Augsburg. Large sections of the road are two-lane and fairly busy, as many trucks use this shortcut to Nürnberg.

Sightseeing

Most of the sights are in Reichstraße, the main road through the town. Other sights are on Ried Island in the Wörnitz River, close to its confluence with the Danube. The museums are best left for a rainy day.

The wide **Reichstraße** is one of the most impressive main streets in the area. At its far end is the large **Fuggerhaus**, Pflegestraße 2, with a Renaissance gable. It belonged to the famous Augsburg banking family, the Fuggers. Nearby is the **Heilig Kreuz Kloster** (Holy Cross Monastery) with an interesting Baroque pilgrim's church. The **Münster**, Reichstraße, is a brick Gothic building with Gothic frescos and a tabernacle from 1503. The oldest house in town is **Café Engel**, Reichstraße 10, dating from 1297. The **Rathaus** (Town Hall) at the bottom of Reichstraße dates from the 13th century, but its façade is mid-19th century. The adjacent **Marienbrunnen** (St Mary's fountain) spouts potable water. Some of the original town walls, gates, and towers can be seen on the side facing the Wörnitz River as well as to the east side facing the Kallbach stream.

Käthe Kruse is famous in doll making circles. Her pretty dolls were designed to be played with by children in a time when many dolls still had porcelain heads. The **Käthe-Kruse-Puppen-Museum** (Doll Museum), Pflegestraße 2a, ☎ 0906-789-170, has a display of about 150 of her dolls. Opening hours are Tuesday to Sunday from May to September, 11 am to 5 pm; April and October, 2 to 5 pm; and November to March on Wednesday and weekends, 2 to 5 pm. Admission is €2.

Cultural Events & Festivals

End of July sees the **Schwäbischwerder Kindertag** in which over 1,000 children act out the town's history in a large open-air theater. It is followed by a processional march in period costumes through the old town.

Several summer concerts and festivals are staged annually. The **Open-Air Theater** at Mangoldfelsen, www.theater-donauwoerth.de, stages comedies, operettas, musicals, and plays from June to August. In June and July, open-air concerts of chamber music are held in the courtyard of the monastery on the island. The **Donauwörther-Kulturtage** in October involve three weeks of theater, music, literature, and art. The tourist office has information and can make reservations.

Shopping

Käthe Kruse dolls are popular souvenirs from Donauwörth and are on sale at several outlets in the town.

Adventures

■ On Foot

The tourist office conducts **guided walking tours** from May to September on weekdays at 6 pm. Meeting point is at the tourist information office.

Around 80 km (48 miles) of marked **hiking routes** are in the immediate countryside. The tourist information office has maps of suggested routes ranging from an hour to four hours. Some routes are circular and others end at convenient public transportation points.

■ On Wheels

Cycling is popular in the region and the tourism office has maps of several routes ranging from three to seven hours. In addition to the long-distance Romantic Road, the **Danube Cycling Route** also passes through the town. The tourist office can make reservations for multi-day cycling tours.

Bicycle rentals are available from **Top Bike Brachem**, Kapellstraße 25, ☎ 0906-8077, or from **Fa Mück**, Dillinger Straße 57, ☎ 0906-3468.

■ On Water

Donauwörth, founded as a **fishing** community, in 1434 received an enormous fishing concession after a local fisherman had saved Emperor Sigmund's life. In addition to the 20 km (12 miles) of the Danube and 35 km (21 miles) of the Wörnitz, several smaller streams and ponds are open to anglers. Information and licenses are available from the tourism office.

Canoeing is possible on both the Danube and Wörnitz. Boat rentals are available from **Kanu-Laden Purtec**, Alte Augsburger Straße 12, ☎ 09090-8086

Where to Stay

■ Camping

Donau-Lech Camping is about five km (three miles) from the town next to a small lake. It is open year-round and has 100 spaces. Campingweg 1, 86698 Eggelstetten, ☎ & fax 09090-4046, www.donau-lech-camping.de.

Tents may also be pitched at the **Kanu-Club Donauwörth**, An der Westspange, ☎ 0906-22-605.

Campers or mobile homes may park for free up to 24 hours at several parking spots in the town. These are signposted, or inquire from the tourism office.

Augsburg

With 265,000 inhabitants, this is the third-largest city in Bavaria after Munich and Nürnberg. The main attractions are the splendid Renaissance and Rococo buildings that reflect the wealth this town once enjoyed

Augsburg is one of Germany's oldest cities. It was founded in 15 BC by Druses and Tiberius, stepsons of Roman Emperor Augustus. According to Tacitus, it was the most splendid city in the colony and it maintained that importance as a trading center well into the 17th century. Augsburg was the first city to introduce the Italian Renaissance to Germany and later also became the home of Rococo. During the late Middle Ages, the Fugger family, based in Augsburg, served as banker for popes, kings, and emperors and much of the wealth and splendor rubbed off on surviving buildings.

Augsburg saw several milestones during the Reformation. In 1518, Cardinal Cajetanus met Martin Luther here but failed to convince him to recant his views. In 1530, the Confession of Augsburg was drawn up by Protestant delegations to the Diet. Much blood was spilled before the Protestants received the right to religious freedom in the Peace of Augsburg (1555). However, the Thirty Years' War, fought over many of the issues that were supposedly settled in 1555, finally ended the prosperity of Augsburg and many other towns in the region.

A Free Imperial City since 1276, Augsburg was forced to become part of Bavaria in 1806. The city was severely damaged during the Second World War but large parts of the old town were restored.

Information Sources

Tourist Office: Regio Augsburg Tourismus, Bahnhostraße 7, 86150 Augsburg, ☎ 0821-502-070, www.regio-augsburg.de.

Transportation

Augsburg is 40 minutes by **train** from Munich. There are at least four trains per hour – the cheaper local trains (RE and RB) are only minutes slower than the IC and ICE trains. It is a major stop on the route from Munich to Stuttgart and beyond.

By **car** it is reached in about the same time on the Autobahn A8 that connects Munich and Stuttgart. It is also easy to reach all Romantic Road destinations by road from here. The proximity to Munich makes Augsburg a feasible alternative to staying in Munich during busy periods such as Oktoberfest.

Sightseeing

The main sights of Augsburg are in a long, narrow stretch of the old town. To the north of the Rathaus are the Dom and Mozarthaus, and to the south most sights are in or near the Maximilianstraße. A walking tour of the sights described here takes about two hours, plus time spent inside the attractions.

■ Northern Old Town Area

The Renaissance **Rathaus** (Town Hall), Rathausplatz, ☎ 0821-502-072 4, replaced its Gothic predecessor in 1614. It is the most important work of Elias Holl and arguably one of the loveliest and most important secular Renaissance buildings in Germany. It was severely damaged by an air raid in 1944, but rebuilt true to the original. The **Goldene Saal** (Golden Hall) is one of the most impressive ceremonial rooms north of the Alps. The

Rathaus and Goldene Saal are open daily from 10 am to 6 pm. Admission is €1.50.

The **Perlachturm** (Tower) dates partly from 1060. Its present height of 70.4 m (231 feet) was achieved in 1616. For the best views of Augsburg, and on a clear day all the way to the Alps, climb the 258 steps to the viewing platform at the top. It is open daily from May to October, 10 am to 6 pm, and on Advent weekends from 2 to 7 pm. Admission is €1. Since 2000, a Glockenspiel (carillon) plays Mozart tunes daily at 11 am, noon, 5 and 6 pm.

Near the Rathausplatz is the **St Annakirche** (St Anne's Church), Anna-Straße. In 1321, a Carmelite monastery built the Gothic church, which was enlarged in the 15th century. Martin Luther stayed in the monastery during his 1518 visit to Augsburg. The church is famous for the Fuggerkapelle (Fugger Funeral Chapel), the first religious Italian Renaissance structure erected on German soil. It cost more than the Fuggerei (see below). Most of the church received a Rococo makeover in the 18th century. However, the 15th-century Goldschmiedekapelle (Goldsmiths' Chapel), used as Lutheran church, still has its original Gothic layout and wall paintings. It also has paintings by Lucas Cranach. Opening hours are Tuesday to Sunday from 10 am to 12:30 pm and 3 to 6 pm, Sunday from noon to 6 pm.

The playwright Bertolt Brecht (1898-1956, left) was born in what is now the **Gedenkstätte für Bertolt Brecht** (Memorial), Auf dem Rain 7, ☎ 0821-324-2779. He spent his youth in Augsburg until he moved to Munich in 1917 and during the Nazi period to Scandinavia and the USA, before settling in East Berlin. Opening hours are Tuesday to Sunday from 10 am to 5 pm. Admission is €1.50.

In 1516, Jakob Fugger the Rich (see below) donated the **Fuggerei** as home for the poor. It is the oldest social housing project still in use in the world. Even now, Augsburgers who become poor and destitute through no fault of their own, can find accommodation here. The annual rent is still a symbolic Rhenish guilder (€0.88!) *and* three daily prayers for the founder. The 104 homes here currently house some 150 people. The project is a city inside a city with eight streets and four access gates that are locked at 10 pm. Residents arriving late are fined 25-50 cents. The small **Fuggereimuseum**, Mitelgasse 13, is in an original house in the Fuggerei. It explains the history of the institution and is furnished in the style of the 17th and 18th century. It is open daily from March to December 23, 9 am to 6 pm. Admission is €1. (From the Rathaus follow Barfüßer and Jakoberstraße eastward and turn right into Herrengasse.)

The **Dom St Maria** (Cathedral of St Mary), Domplatz, is mainly 14th-century Gothic, but the core, including the crypt, is from the 10th century and is Romanesque. The church has wall paintings from the Romanesque and Gothic periods, but the altar by Hans Holbein receives the most attention. Note the five windows of the prophets on the south side. These 12th-century painted glass windows are considered the oldest of their kind in Germany.

The Mozart family worked in Augsburg from 1643 onwards. Leopold Mozart, right, father of Wolfgang Amadeus, was born in Augsburg in 1719. His place of birth is now called the **Mozarthaus**, Frauentorstraße 30, ☎ 0821-324-3894, with a museum dedicated to Mozart and his works. Wolfgang Amadeus visited Augsburg five times – both as tourist and as musician. His music is frequently performed at various venues. The museum is open Tuesday to Sunday from 10 am to 5 pm. Admission is €1.50.

■ Maximilianstraße

Maximilianstraße leads from the Rathaus southward. It is the traditional shopping street, with many elegant, gabled houses from the Renaissance and Baroque periods. The **Fuggerhäuser** (Fugger Houses), Maximilianstraße 36-38, is a group of existing houses that were united behind a Renaissance façade in 1515 to serve as city residence and offices of the Fugger family. The building is mostly in private use, but enter the Damenhof (Ladies' Courtyard) to see the colonnaded area reserved for the Fugger women.

THE FUGGER FAMILY OF AUGSBURG

At the end of the 15th century, the Fugger family owned a prominent trading firm in Augsburg. Jakob Fugger, the seventh son, was heading toward a religious career, when the death of his older brothers called him back to more worldly matters in 1478. He soon implemented ideas learned in Italy about double-entry bookkeeping and cashless trade, but it was cornering the European market for copper that made his fortune. From 1500 Jakob Fugger, by now known as The Rich, acted as banker of the pope and in 1519 financed the election of Emperor Karl V. Foundations set up by Jakob Fugger still finance the tourist magnets of the Fuggerei and the Fugger Chapel in St Anne's. He also spent lavishly on the arts, bringing the Renaissance to Germany, and had several paintings and drawings done by, among others, Albrecht Dürer (see his portrait of Jakob above).

Despite his nickname, Jakob Fugger was not the richest man in the world. His nephew, Anton Fugger, shown at right, managed that around 1546. By most accounts, he was the richest man the world has ever known, even overshadowing Bill Gates. The continuous demands for financing from the Habsburg Emperors, who never bothered to repay debts, forced the Fuggers to diversify out of financing into property. By 1658 the financing firm was dissolved. Several Fuggers still live in castles and palaces in the region.

A block farther is the magnificent Rococo **Schaezler-Palais** (Palace), Maximilianstraße 46, ☎ 0821-324-4117. It was erected in 1765-70 by the Von Liebenhofens, a wealthy banking family. It has a huge **Festsaal** (Banqueting Hall) with Rococo ceiling and wall panels. Marie Antoinette attended a ball here en route to getting married in Paris. The palace houses several galleries. The **Baroque Gallery** has mostly paintings by German artists. The **Staatsgalerie Alter Kunst** (National Old Masters' Gallery) has work by local painters, including Holbein and Dürer, as well as works by Van Dyck, Veronese, and Tiepolo. Opening hours are Tuesday to Sunday from 10 am to 5 pm. Admission is €3.

At the far end of the Maximilianstraße are the Roman Catholic **St Ulrich and St Afra**, ☎ 0821-345-560, and the Lutheran **St Ulrichskirche**. The Late Gothic church was built on the site where St Afra was martyred in AD 304. St Ulrich, whose grave is in the crypt, helped in the victory over the Hungarians in the 10th century. A Baroque preaching hall was added in the early 18th century to serve as a Lutheran church. (A similar set-up is at the Heilig-Kreuz-Kirchen.)

The **Augsburger Puppenkiste** (Marionettes) are among the most famous in the world. Presentations are held on Wednesday, Friday, Saturday, and Sunday at 2 and 7:30 pm. The schedule is available from the tourism office or at www.augsburger-puppenkiste.de. A small museum, **Die Kiste** (The Box), Spitalgasse 15, ☎ 0821-450-3450, www.diekiste.net, is dedicated to this art form. It is open Tuesday to Sunday from 10 am to 7 pm.

The 16th-century **Rotes Tor** (Red Gate) was remodeled by Elias Holl in the early 17th century. This fortified gate is most popular as a huge open-air stage.

Cultural Events

Die Fugger und die Musik (The Fuggers and Music) is a concert series arranged by the tourism office annually from May to June. It involves music played in places associated with the Fuggers, including several churches and the Goldene Saal in Augusburg, as well as in other towns, including Nürnberg.

The **Freilichtbühne am Roten Tor** (Open-Air Theater), ☎ 0821-324-4900, www.theater-augsburg.de, is the largest open-air theater in southern Germany. Its major performances are operas and musicals staged usually between June and August.

Adventures

■ On Foot

The tourism office conducts **guided walking tours** departing from the Rathaus, daily April to October at 2 pm, and on Saturday at 2 pm from November to March. Other thematic tours are also available.

■ In the Air

Pleasure flights over the Alps can be arranged by **Schwabenflug**, Flughafen Augsburg-Mühlhausen, ☎ 0821-701-098.

■ On Horseback

Riding opportunities are available from **Reit-Club Augsburg**, Paul-Eipper-Straße 5, ☎ 0821-554-118.

■ On Ice

From September to March, **ice skating** is possible in the **Curt Frenzel Eisstadion**, Senkelbachstraße, ☎ 0821-324-9752. It is open to the public on Wednesday and Friday from 8 to 10 pm, Saturday from 2 to 10 pm, and Sunday from 9:30 am to 6 pm.

Where to Stay

Steigenberger Hotel Drei Mohren is in the center of town close to the pedestrian zone – an elegant hotel with large, luxurious rooms. The upper floors are more modern. **Maximilian's** restaurant (€€-€€€) serves international cuisine with strong Euro-Asian and Mediterranean influences. Maximilianstraße 40, 86150 Augsburg, ☎ 0821-50-360, fax 0821-157-864, www.steigenberger.de. (€€€)

Hotel Augusta is at the northern edge of the pedestrian zone in the former printing factory of the local newspaper. Rooms are comfortable, with all the latest technology. The restaurant (€€), open for dinner only, serves international and regional dishes. Ludwigstraße 2, 86152 Augsburg, ☎ 0821-50-140, fax 0821-501-4605, www.hotelaugusta.de. (€€-€€€)

Romantik Hotel Augsburger Hof is the oldest in town. It has a Renaissance façade but is more modern inside. Close to the Dom, it is next to the former city walls. Rooms are comfortable and individually furnished with good taste and attention to detail. The rustic restaurant (€€-€€€) serves international cuisine but the local Swabian dishes are what regulars come for. Auf dem Kreuz 2, 86152 Augsburg, ☎ 0821-343-050, fax 0821-343-0555, www.augsburger-hof.de. (€€-€€€)

The **Dom Hotel** is a fourth-generation, family-run establishment close to the Dom. Rooms are pleasant – some have exposed beams and great views. All are quite comfortable. Frauentorstraße 8, 86152 Augsburg, ☎ 0821-343-930, fax 0821-3439-3200, www.domhotel-augsburg.de. (€€)

The **Ibis Hotel beim Hauptbahnhof** is, as the name implies, right at the main station. Rooms are simply furnished, but clean and modern. Halderstraße 25, 86150 Augsburg, ☎ 0821-50-160, fax 0821-501-6150, www.ibishotel.com. (€-€€)

Where to Eat

Die Ecke restaurant, Elias-Holl-Patz 2, ☎ 0821-510-600, is close to the Rathaus. It serves mostly regional cuisine with seasonal variations. Although the house has a 400-year tradition, it combines modern elements with a more rustic décor. (€€-€€€)

Feinkost Kahn, Annastraße 16, ☎ 0821-312-031, is primarily an upscale delicatessen. However, on the second floor is an excellent restaurant serving international and regional dishes. It is in the heart of the pedestrian zone. (€€-€€€)

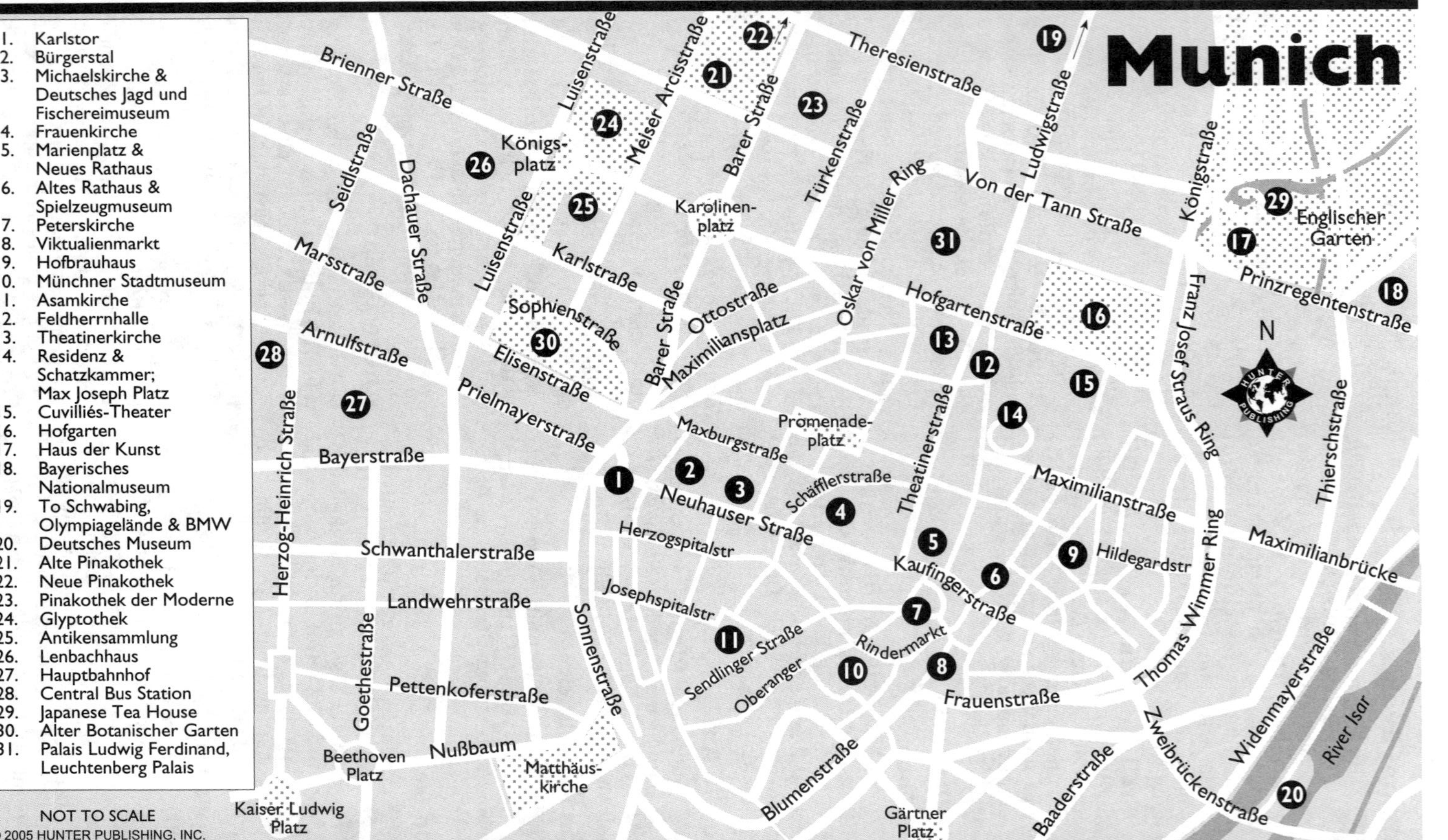
Munich
1. Karlstor
2. Bürgerstal
3. Michaelskirche & Deutsches Jagd und Fischereimuseum
4. Frauenkirche
5. Marienplatz & Neues Rathaus
6. Altes Rathaus & Spielzeugmuseum
7. Peterskirche
8. Viktualienmarkt
9. Hofbrauhaus
10. Münchner Stadtmuseum
11. Asamkirche
12. Feldherrnhalle
13. Theatinerkirche
14. Residenz & Schatzkammer; Max Joseph Platz
15. Cuvilliés-Theater
16. Hofgarten
17. Haus der Kunst
18. Bayerisches Nationalmuseum
19. To Schwabing, Olympiagelände & BMW
20. Deutsches Museum
21. Alte Pinakothek
22. Neue Pinakothek
23. Pinakothek der Moderne
24. Glyptothek
25. Antikensammlung
26. Lenbachhaus
27. Hauptbahnhof
28. Central Bus Station
29. Japanese Tea House
30. Alter Botanischer Garten
31. Palais Ludwig Ferdinand, Leuchtenberg Palais
NOT TO SCALE
© 2005 HUNTER PUBLISHING, INC.
Brienner Straße
Luisenstraße
Meiser Arcisstraße
Barer Straße
Theresienstraße
Ludwigstraße
Königsplatz
Türkenstraße
Seidlstraße
Dachauer Straße
Karolinenplatz
Oskar von Miller Ring
Von der Tann Straße
Königstraße
Englischer Garten
Marsstraße
Karlstraße
Prinzregentenstraße
Sophienstraße
Ottostraße
Hofgartenstraße
Franz Josef Straus Ring
Arnulfstraße
Maximiliansplatz
Elisenstraße
N
HUNTER PUBLISHING
Prielmayerstraße
Promenadeplatz
Maxburgstraße
Theatinerstraße
Thierschstraße
Bayerstraße
Schäfflerstraße
Maximilianstraße
Herzog-Heinrich Straße
Neuhauser Straße
Herzogspitalstr
Schwanthalerstraße
Hildegardstr
Maximilianbrücke
Kaufingerstraße
Thomas Wimmer Ring
Josephspitalstr
Landwehrstraße
Sonnenstraße
Rindermarkt
Sendlinger Straße
Oberanger
Widenmayerstraße
Goethestraße
Pettenkoferstraße
Frauenstraße
River Isar
Zweibrückenstraße
Beethoven Platz
Nußbaum
Matthäuskirche
Blumenstraße
Baaderstraße
Kaiser Ludwig Platz
Gärtner Platz

Munich & the Bavarian Alps

In this Chapter

Bavaria is Germany's largest state and the favored holiday destination of both domestic and foreign tourists. No part of the country offers more to visitors than Bavaria. It has a rich cultural heritage, natural beauty, and is a haven for outdoor enthusiasts. For many foreigners this is what Germany is all about – rolling green meadows set off against an Alpine backdrop, small villages with half-timbered houses, Baroque churches with onion-shaped domes, beer, sausages, women in traditional dresses and men in *Lederhosen*. Southern Bavaria is all that and a lot more.

Munich has a rich heritage and, despite war damage, many early buildings, including churches and palaces testify to its glorious past. It has the largest technology museum in the world and some of the best art galleries in Germany. The English Garden is the largest urban park in Europe. The beer gardens open as soon as the weather is good. The historic center is surrounded by a modern city built on high-technology industries. No other German city has a higher concentration of electronic and computer firms.

Despite its size, most areas of Bavaria can easily be reached from Munich on the excellent transportation network. Many of the lakes and mountains of southern Bavaria can be reached in an hour from the capital. The second part of this chapter concentrates on a few destinations that are especially popular with foreign visitors. Most can be visited on daytrips from Munich, but the natural beauty of the areas is such that few would regret staying over longer.

King Ludwig

In the 19th-century, mad King Ludwig planned many fantasy castles but only three became reality. For foreign visitors the most popular remains **Schloss Neuschwanstein**, the fairytale castle that inspired Disney. Both this castle and the much smaller **Schloss Linderhof** are southwest of Munich, while **Herrenchiemsee**, which tried to outdo Versailles in splendor, is on an island in a lake to the east of Munich.

Berchtesgaden, surrounded by mountains on three sides, is one of the most beautiful areas in Germany. In addition to the mountains and countryside, it is also closely associated with Hitler's Berghof mountain retreat.

Garmisch-Partenkirchen, which hosted the 1936 Winter Olympic Games, is close to Zugspitze, Germany's highest mountain. Nearby are the Rococo masterpieces of the Ettal Monastery and the Wieskirche.

History

Bavaria is the oldest political entity in Germany. Much of current Bavaria south of the Danube was occupied by the Romans from 15 BC to around AD 500 as the province of *Raetia*. Following their departure, the Bavarian tribe from Bohemia moved in. The Agilolfinger family ruled the land up to the time of Charlemagne. Christianization followed from the mid-eighth century and Bavaria would be a bastion of the Roman Catholic Church during the Middle Ages; the church is still influential now.

Up to the 12th century, ruling families changed frequently. However, in 1180, Heinrich der Löwe, duke of Saxony and of Bavaria-Munich, fell out of favor with Emperor Friedrich I Barbarossa. The Emperor gave Bavaria to Count Otto von Wittelsbach of the Palatinate. The Wittelsbach family ruled Bavaria up to the abolition of the monarchy in 1918.

As was German custom, property was divided between sons and re-united should a branch of the family die out. In Bavaria, this practice stopped after Albrecht IV the Wise, who united three parts of Bavaria under his rule, establishing the right of the first-born to the land and title in 1506.

Participation in several wars saw Bavaria grow and decline in size, but the trend was mostly upwards. Through opportunistic coalitions and side-switching during the Napoleonic wars, Bavaria doubled in size between 1800 and 1815 and upgraded to a kingdom in 1806. During this period, the areas of Franken and Allgäu were added as well as many Free Imperial Cities.

The Wittelsbach dukes of the 17th and 18th centuries generally had good taste in architecture and art and erected many buildings that are now major tourist attractions. The kings of the 19th century were enlightened rulers who continued the art and building tradition of their forebears. Although always rich, the secularization of monasteries in 1803, and Bavaria had many of them, provided the kings with funds to continue their architectural excesses.

Architectural Tastes of Bavarian Kings (1806-1918)

King Maximilian I (1806-25) favored the Classical style, while his son Ludwig I (1825-48) admired classical antiquity. Ludwig built the Pinakothek, Glyptothek, and university in Munich. He also cut the elegant Ludwigstraße through the old town. He had a gallery in Schloss Nymphenburg filled with paintings of beautiful women who caught his roving eye. One of them, Lola Montez, a Spanish dancer and opportunist, eventually cost him his throne when her involvement in politics led to a rebel movement. Maximilian II (1848-1864) continued the buildings, but his reign was overshadowed by the loss of independence when Bavaria had to join the Prussian-dominated German Empire in 1871.

His son, Ludwig II (1864-86), also known as Mad Ludwig, is probably the most famous of all Bavarian kings. He became king at age 18 and continued the family's building tradition. However, his designs were even more fanciful and included Schloss Neuschwanstein, which served as inspiration for the Disney castles, Linderhof, and Herrenchiemsee, which was inspired by Versailles. He died in mysterious circumstances days after being deposed in 1886 and was succeeded by another son of Ludwig I, Prince Luitpold (1886-1912), who built the Deutsches Museum and the monumental Prinzregentenstraße. His son, Ludwig III (1912-18), was forced to abdicate at the end of the First World War.

Lola Montez

In the chaotic aftermath of the First World War and the collapse of the Hohenzollern Empire, Bavaria briefly became a Soviet republic, before right-wingers took over power. Hitler unsuccessfully attempted a Putsch in 1923. Because the Nazi party was founded in Bavaria, it was a favorite area of many of the top leaders. Hitler had his vacation home in Berchtesgaden and Munich was declared the Capital of the Movement. Huge party rallies were annually held in Nürnberg.

Following World War II, Bavaria was occupied by American forces. It was the only state to reject the West German constitution and wrote its own to become a Free State in the Federal Republic of Germany. Although an economic powerhouse, the state is relatively conservative, with strong traditional values and traditions.

■ Transportation

By Rail: Munich has good high-speed rail connections to other parts of Germany. Most towns in Bavaria can be reached on regional trains, although transfers are often required in Munich.

From Munich Hauptbahnhof there are at least two trains per hour to Nürnberg (one hour and 40 minutes), Augsburg (40 minutes), Stuttgart (two hours and 20 minutes), Frankfurt (less than four hours, but not always direct), and Salzburg (90 minutes to two hours). At least hourly trains are available to Berlin (six to seven hours, mostly not direct) and Hamburg (six hours, mostly direct). Connections to Berlin and other East German cities will improve drastically in coming years as new high-speed rails are added to the network.

By Road: The Bavarians love their cars – it is the home of both BMW and Audi – and roads are generally in excellent condition. There are many Autobahns with large sections having no speed limits allowing for blistering fast traveling times between major centers.

A quick glance at a Bavarian map confirms that all highways lead to Munich. This allows *Münchner* (Munich residents) to get away easily for weekends and daytrips in the countryside. The A8 connects Salzburg and the Berchtesgaden area with Stuttgart, passing Munich and Augsburg en route. The A9 connects Munich and Berlin via Nürnberg. The A3 connects Passau with Frankfurt and Cologne via Regensburg, Nürnberg, and Würzburg. The A96 connects Munich with Lindau on the Bodensee and the A95 allows fast access to the excellent skiing area at Garmisch-Partenkirchen. Off the Autobahns, the going is much slower but generally more interesting.

By Air: The new **Munich International Airport**, 85356 Flughafen München, ☎ 089-97-500, www.munich-airport, has established itself as the second-largest airport in the country. It currently serves more European destinations than chronically overcrowded Frankfurt Airport. The airport is most easily reached by S-Bahn lines S1 and S8, each connecting to the Hauptbahnhof every 20 minutes. The journey takes 40 minutes and costs €8.

Many transfer services are available from the airport to all major towns in Bavaria and nearby parts of Austria. A list of the different service providers – most serve only one town – are available from the airport's website.

■ Information Sources

Tourist information on the whole of Bavaria is available from **Bayern Tourismus Marketing**, Postfach 662228, 8121 München, ☎ 0180-585-5050, www.bayern.info.

■ Munich

Munich (München in German) is Germany's third-largest city with 1.3 million inhabitants, but it is by far the city most Germans say they would prefer to live in – a relatively rich city with a high quality of life.

For tourists, Munich is, after Berlin, the most rewarding city in Germany. It has a rich history with a wide range of cultural offerings. Perhaps most famous for its Oktoberfest and beer in general, it also has fine museums. The three Pinakotheken form one of the largest art collections in Europe and the Deutsches Museum is one of the largest science and technology museums in the world. Munich has been a royal residence for seven centuries and has some of the most splendid Baroque palaces in Europe with the Residenz, Schloss Nymphenburg and Schloss Schließheim trio. The wide variety of architecture ranges from old Gothic churches to the modern glass, tent-like roof of the 1972 Olympic Games stadium and the BMW headquarters.

Munich was founded in the ninth century as a small village near a Benedictine monastery. The name is derived from the old German term for monk. In 1225, Munich became a ducal seat and from 1504 the undisputed capital of Bavaria. It remained the primary residence of the ruling Wittelsbach family up to the abolition of the monarchy in 1918. They were avid builders and created palaces and churches, as well as structures that filled whole city blocks. Bavaria was elevated to a kingdom in 1806 and the kings were generally enlightened rulers who attracted artistic talent to the city.

After the First World War, Munich briefly fell into the hands of revolutionaries and also saw the foundation of the National Socialist German Labor Party – commonly known later simply as the Nazis. In 1923, its leader, Adolf Hitler, unsuccessfully attempted a coup d'état. Once he was in power, Munich became the "Capital of the Movement" and several buildings were erected or altered to reflect the Nazi views. In 1938, the infamous meeting where Britain, France, and Italy sold out Czechoslovakia took place in Munich.

The city suffered terrible bombardments during the war but rebuilt quickly afterwards. On December 15, 1957, it officially became a city of a million inhabitants. In 1972, it hosted the summer Olympic Games and two years later Germany won the soccer world cup in the Olympic stadium. Munich's wealth is built on modern industries.

Information Sources

Tourist Office: The tourist information office has two branches for casual callers in the **Hauptbahnhof** and at the **Marienplatz**. For written or telephone inquiries contact the **Fremdenverkehrsamt München**, Sendlinger Straße 1, 80331 München, ☎ 089-2339-6500, www.muenchen.de.

MÜNCHEN WELCOME CARD

The München Welcome Card allows unlimited public transportation in central Munich and reduced admission to most museums and many attractions. It costs €6.50 for one day or €16 for three days. A partner ticket, for up to five traveling together, is available for €11 and €23.50 respectively. The card is available from the tourist office and many hotels.

Transportation

Munich has an excellent public transportation system that combines S-Bahn, U-Bahn, trams, and buses in a single network. Tickets must be validated before entering the platform of the S- and U-Bahn or on the tram or bus. Single and strip tickets are available, but day-tickets are more economical if more than two journeys are planned. A day ticket is €4.50 or €7.50 for up to five traveling together. The three-day version costs €11 and €17.50 respectively.

Sightseeing

Old Town Pedestrian Zone

Karlsplatz to Frauenkirche: Approaching the old town and pedestrian zone from the main station, the first sights that deliver some impression of what is to follow are the monumental buildings at **Karlsplatz**. The square is locally known as *Stachus*, named after an inn that disappeared long ago. It was the busiest traffic circle in Europe before World War II and there is a huge fountain which is a popular meeting spot. The old town area is entered via the

14th-century **Karlstor** (Karl's Gate, shown above in an early photograph).

The **Bürgersaal** (Citizens' Hall), Neuhauserstraße 14, ☎ 089-219-9720, has a plain exterior but a richly decorated interior. This church was erected on a citizens' initiative as a prayer hall in the early 18th century. The almost crypt-like lower church area has the grave of Priest Rupert Mayer, a fierce critic of the Nazis who spent many years in Dachau and died shortly after the war. He was made a saint in 1987 and the chapel has attracted a steady stream of pilgrims ever since. Artistically, the Baroque **Oberkirche** (Upper Church) is more interesting. It has many Rococo features, although the main decorations were not restored after World War II. This part of the church is open only from 3 to 5 pm. The rest of the church is open daily from 6:30 am to 7 pm.

Across the road is the **Augustinerbräu** beer cellars – the oldest of Munich's famous brewing houses, now home to a popular restaurant and beer garden (see *Where to Eat*).

Michaelskirche (St Michael's Church), Neuhauser-straße 52, ☎ 089-231-7060, was one of the first and is still the largest Renaissance church north of the Alps. It was erected by Duke Wilhelm V between 1583 and 1597. The impressive three-story gabled façade shows 15 of his forebears, going back to the Agilolfingers. All are overshadowed, though, by the bronze statue of the Archangel Gabriel, a masterpiece by Hubert Gerhard (1588). The single-nave interior, with a cradle vault ceiling 20 m (66 feet) wide, is mostly white and inspired many of the Baroque churches that would soon follow in southern Germany. The crypt has the graves of 41 Wittelsbach rulers. Opening hours are daily from 8 am to 7 pm.

Deutsches Jagd- und Fischereimuseum (German Hunting & Fishing Museum), Neuhauser Straße 2, ☎ 089-220-522, www.jagd-fischerei-museum.de, is in an impressive Gothic former church building. The church was secularized after 1803 and the museum moved in during the 1960s. The museum is popular and displays include stuffed animals, hunting weapons, and the world's largest collection of fishing hooks. Despite the name, many items are of non-German origin. Opening hours are daily from 9:30 am to 5 pm, closing at 9 pm on Thursday. Admission is €3.50.

Archangel, Michaelskirche, Hubert Gerhard

The two 98-m (320-foot) copper onion-domed towers of the **Frauenkirche** are the symbols of Munich. The official name Domkirche zu Unserer Lieben Frau (Cathedral of Our Dear Lady), Frauenplatz, ☎ 089-290-0820, never really caught on. The Late Gothic church was erected in 1468-88 and has a simple red brick exterior. Inside, it is bright with mostly white walls. The church is over 100 m (330 feet) long and 41 m (132 feet) wide. Although damaged in World War II, many parts, including the towers, are original. The rose windows in the choir of the Annunciation date from 1392 and were used in an earlier church. From April to October, Monday to Saturday, 10 am to 5 pm, the south tower has an elevator (€2) to a viewing platform. Do note that it is 86 steps to the elevator and that the views from St Peter are better. The church is a popular venue for concerts. Opening hours are 8 am to 7 pm.

THE DEVIL'S FOOTPRINT

Cheating the devil made for popular stories in the Middle Ages. According to legend, the architect of the Frauenkirche, Jörg von Halspach, accepted a challenge from the devil to build a church without windows. Until the current High Altar was built in the 19th century, it was impossible to see the front windows from the rear of the church. From one spot in the back of the church, the pillars obscure the side windows and the bright church appears to be windowless. At this very spot, the cheated devil stamped his foot in anger and left a small footprint with a small hooked tail at the heel. An alternative version has the devil stamping his foot in delight when visiting the church at night and laughing at the stupidity of building a church without windows. The so-called Teufelstritt (Devil's Footprint) is in the center rear of the church almost in-line with the gift shop.

An early photograph of Karlsplatz with the Frauenkirche in the distance

Marienplatz: Marienplatz (Mary's Square) is the heart of Munich. It is a large square, where most festivals and protest rallies are held. In 1638, Prince Elector Maximilian erected the **Mariensäule** (Mary's Column) to give thanks for the relief of the city from the Swedish threat during the Thirty Years' War. It has a statue of the Virgin made in 1590 by Hubert Gerhard on top of an 11-m (33-foot) Corinthian column.

The north of the square is occupied by the **Neues Rathaus** (New Town Hall). This Neo-Gothic (1867-1908) monumental building looks a bit out of place in Baroque and Rococo Munich but people got used to it. An elevator (€1.50) to the top of the

80-m (260-foot) tower is available on weekdays from 9 am to 4 pm, closing at 1 pm on Friday. Particularly popular is the famous carillon, with 43 bells the fourth-largest in Europe. At 11 am and noon, and summer at 5 pm as well, it plays a knight's tournament and local dance with 32 life-size figures. At 9 pm, the night watchman and Münchner Kindl are blessed by an angel. The huge **Ratskeller** in the cellar is a popular restaurant – see *Where to Eat*.

At the east is the **Altes Rathaus** (Old Town Hall), a Gothic building from 1474. It has a hall, still used for official receptions, above open arcades. The Rathaus was severely damaged during World War II but restored in simplified form. The Rathaus incorporated a former defense tower that now houses the **Spielzeugmuseum** (Toy Museum), Marienplatz, ☎ 089-294-001, which shows toys from the past two centuries. It is open daily from 10 am to 5:30 pm. Admission is €3.

Close by is the **Alter Hof** (Old Castle), Burgstraße 8, which was the castle of the Wittelsbach rulers from 1253 to 1474. It is currently used as local government offices but it is worth strolling into the courtyard to see the medieval oriel or bay window.

The **Peterskirche** (St Peter's Church), Rindermarkt, ☎ 089-260-4828, is the oldest church in Munich. It dates back to the 11th century but has style elements of almost every fashion since. Its main structure is a triple-nave, 13th-century Gothic basilica but the interior is mostly Baroque. It is 306 steps to the top of the tower for the best views of Munich and the Alps if the skies are clear (€1.50). Opening hours are Monday to Saturday from 9 am to 6 pm and Sunday from 10 am to 7 pm.

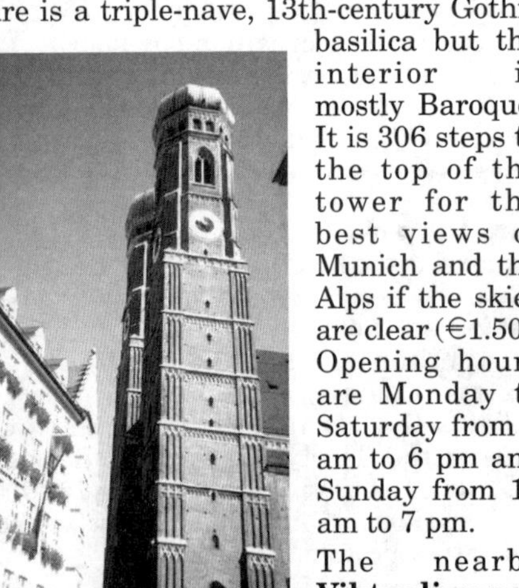

Peterskirche

The nearby **Viktualienmarkt** (Victuals Market) has been in operation since 1807. It is a popular spot with all kinds of people from businessmen to blue-collar workers who grab a quick bite to eat or buy fresh produce. The market women are famous for both quick wit and zero tolerance – no self-service here. Do not fret if your school German does not reach – most non-locals will not understand much of what's said either.

The nearby **Hofbräuhaus** is a legend too. See *Where to Eat* below.

Three blocks southwest of the Marienplatz is the **Münchner Stadtmuseum** (Municipal Museum), St.-Jakobs-Platz 1, ☎ 089-2332-2370, www.stadtmuseum-online.de. It has an eclectic collection ranging from musical instruments and rare movies to puppet theaters and home décor. A star exhibit is the collection of 10 wood-carved, painted and gilded Moriskentänzer (Moorish Dancers, below) made by Erasmus Grasser in 1480. Opening hours are Tuesday to Sunday from 10 am to 6 pm. Admission is €2.50, free on Sunday.

Nearby, close to the Sendlinger Tor, is the **Asamkirche** (Asam Church), Sendlinger Straße 32. The official name is St Johannes Nepomuk Church but nobody refers to it as other than the Asamkirche, named after the two talented Baroque master-builder Asam brothers. Both were multitalented, but Cosmas Damian (1686-1739) specialized in frescoes and his brother Egid Quirin (1692-1750) specialized in sculptures and stuccos. Their work decorated many Baroque churches in Munich and central Europe. They financed and designed the Asamkirche themselves, which helps to explain the harmony of the interior. It is over-the-top Baroque with no square inch left undecorated, but all beautifully integrated. It has been described as a combination of a fanciful grotto and a court theater, showing off the absolute skill of the two brothers and serving as a remarkable example of Bavarian Late Baroque. It is small, with only 12 rows of pews, but it has enough art to fill a cathedral. Opening hours are daily from 9 am to 5:30 pm.

Odeonsplatz: The roads on both side of the Neues Rathaus eventually lead to the Odeonsplatz. At the east side is the huge Residenz complex – see below. At the south is the **Feldherrnhalle** (Field Marshalls' Portico), erected in the 1840s as a copy of the Loggia dei Lanzi in Florence, Italy. It has statues of General Tilly (Thirty Years' War) and General Wrede (Napoleonic Wars), guarded by Bavarian lions.

HITLER'S BEER HALL PUTSCH

In 1923, Adolf Hitler, the leader of a minor right-wing political party, decided to take over power in Munich. After a spirited speech in a beer hall – contrary to popular belief, it was the Bürgerbräukeller and *not* the Hofbräuhaus – he and his followers marched through the old city in what was supposed to have been the start of a Fascist march on Berlin similar to Mussolini's earlier successful march on Rome. When troops opened fire on the marchers in Odeonsplatz, Hitler threw himself into the gutter with such force that he dislocated his shoulder and was unable to flee.

Unfortunately, Hitler learned from this experience that grabbing power illegally was not a good idea – a decade later he would still employ illegal means but became dictator legally. As the Feldherrnhalle bore testimony to the 1923 event, a guard of honor was installed here in the Residenzstraße after the Nazis took power. Passersby, who wanted to avoid the Nazi salute, took a slight detour through the Viscardigasse to pass on the guard-free Theatinerstraße side of the monument.

The **Theatinerkirche** (Theatine Church, or officially, St Kajetan), Theatinerstraße 22, is an excellent example of Late Baroque architecture. It was built in 1663-88, with the Rococo façade added a century later by Cuveliés. The interior is mostly white and well lit with a cupola 71 m (240 feet) high. The stuccowork is particularly fine. The crypt contains the graves of 25 members of the Wittelsbach dynasty.

North of the Odeonsplatz is the monumental **Ludwigstraße**, commissioned by King Ludwig I in the early 19th century when he made Munich a major European cultural center. The huge Neo-Renaissance and Neo-Byzantine buildings are interesting but add no life to area. Once past the Siegestor (Triumph Arch), the street becomes alive as Leopoldstraße, lined with cafés and the good life expected from the Schwabing neighborhood (see next page).

Residenz: The Wittelsbach family, who ruled Bavaria for 700 years, built the massive **Residenz** (Residence) complex from 1385 onwards. It has examples of all building styles with large sections in the Renaissance and Classical styles. The interior, inevitably, also has many Baroque and Rococo rooms. The palace is one of the most important in Germany and, although severely damaged during World War II, it has been restored to its original condition. The complex houses several museums – if time is limited give preference to the Treasury.

The **Schatzkammer der Residenz** (Treasury in the Residence) contains the treasures of the Wittelsbach family collected over a period of 300 years. It is spread over eight rooms and is one of the

Residenz Grotto

most important collections of its kind in Europe. It includes the crown (1280) of Heinrich II, a bejeweled small statue of *St George Slaying the Dragon* (1597), and the royal insignia produced in 1807 after Napoleon had elevated Bavaria to a kingdom. Opening hours are daily from April to mid-October from 9 am to 6 pm, and from mid-October to March from 10 am to 4 pm. Admission is €6 and includes an excellent English audio guide. A combination ticket with the Residenzmuseum is €9.

The enormous **Residenzmuseum**, Max-Joseph-Platz 3, ☎ 089-290-671, www.schloesser.bayern.de, includes about 120 rooms of the former palace. The main attraction is the wall and ceiling decoration of the many rooms, as most are without furniture. The museum also has a large porcelain and silverware collection. Highlights include the **Antiquarium** (1570), which is the largest secular Renaissance hall north of the Alps. It is filled with Roman and Greek busts. Also popular are the **Reichen Zimmer** (Rich Rooms) in Rococo that were the state rooms during the 18th century, and the **Royal Apartments** constructed for King Ludwig I in the mid-19th century. The museum has no English signs, making an audio guide or guidebook essential. Opening hours are daily from April to mid-October, 9 am to 6 pm, and from mid-October to March, 10 am to 4 pm. Admission is €6. A combination ticket with the Treasury is €9.

The **Cuvilliés-Theater** (Altes Residenztheater/Old Residence Theater), Residenzstraße1, ☎ 089-290-671, is a magnificent Rococo theater built in 1751-3 by Francois Cuvilliés. It has four rows of boxes using different designs and decorations. The most lavish is the Prince Elector's box. The theater is still in frequent use. Opening hours are daily from April to mid-October, 9 am to 6 pm, and from mid-October to March, 10 am to 4 pm. Admission is €2.

Englischer Garten & Schwabing

The Renaissance **Hofgarten** (Royal Garden) is north of the Residenz complex. It is flanked by 19th-century arcades and the modern Staatskanzlei (State Chancellery). The octagonal temple in the middle of the garden is crowned by Huberd Gerhard's 1594 *Diana*.

In the south end of the Englischer Garten is the **Haus der Kunst** (House of Art), Prinzregentenstraße 1, ☎ 089-211-270, www.hausderkunst.de. It has no permanent collection but was commissioned by the Nazis to exhibit their ideas of real German art. Hitler opened the building in person (and broke the hammer with the first blow!). It currently houses temporary exhibitions and events.

Entartete Kunst (Degenerate Art)

In the summer of 1937, while Nazi kitsch went on display in the Haus der Kunst, a separate exhibition of *Entartete Kunst* (Degenerate Art) opened in the Hofgarten. This exhibition included 300 paintings, 25 sculptures, and 400 graphics that the Nazis considered as un-German. The exhibition toured Germany and drew huge crowds – two million in Munich alone. Thanks to the Nazis, large numbers of people suddenly showed an interest in modern art. A further 16,000 works were added to the list – many were destroyed, but some were saved by being sold secretly to private and international collectors. The artists themselves were banned from exhibiting, fired from academic posts, and many ended up in concentration camps or fled abroad.

Southeast of the Englischer Garten is the **Bayerisches Nationalmuseum** (Bavarian National Museum), Prinzregentenstraße 3, ☎ 089-211-2401, www.bayerisches-nationalmuseum.de. It focuses on local art and cultural items but many are world-renowned. The completion of restoration work by 2006 will see a reorganization and it is still uncertain which of the 800,000 items will be on permanent display. The excellent works by Tilman Riemenschneider are a sure bet, as are the vast collection of early medieval and Gothic works. Opening hours are Tuesday to Sunday from 10 am to 5 pm, closing at 8 pm on Thursday. Admission is €3, free on Sunday.

Nearby is the **Schack-Galerie**, Prinzregentenstraße 9, ☎ 089-2380-5224. It has a collection of 270 German 19th-century paintings. Opening hours are Tuesday to Sunday from 10 am to 5 pm. Admission is €2.50.

The **Englischer Garten** (English Garden) is Europe's largest city park. This huge park was laid out in the early 19th century and is a favored place to relax. In the south of the park is a Japanese Tea House (1972). Towards the middle of the park is a classical round temple, the Monopteros (1838). It is supposed to have great views of the old town skyline, but the number of drug users and undesirables that frequent the place lead many to prefer the view from the rolling lawns. The five-story Chinesischer Turm (Chinese Pagoda) of 1760 burned down during the Second World War but was reconstructed in 1952. In its shade is a 6,000-seat beer garden. Nude sunbathing is still practiced in many parts of the park, although students strolling around in the nude are much less common nowadays than they were in the 1970s and 1980s.

West of the Englischer Garten is the neighborhood of **Schwabing** – a mythical, nostalgic place for many Germans, a bit like Paris's Left Bank. It saw its golden age at the turn of the 19th century and early 20th century when the neighborhood was crowded by artists of all kinds. Although present Schwabing is not even a shadow of its former self, it is still the liveliest neighborhood with the most popular nightspots and small shops – clinging to its Bohemian tradition but very much bourgeois, with the trendiest cafés and "in" places. It is most easily reached by U-Bahn (station: Münchener Freiheit).

Deutsches Museum

The Deutsches Museum (German Museum), Museumsinsel 1, ☎ 089-21-791, www.deutsches-museum.de, is one of the largest technology museum in the world. It is on an island in the River Isar and has a vast collection, with 18,000 scientific and technology items on permanent display. Many working models and frequent demonstrations add further interest. Seeing it all will require a hike of some 16 km (10 miles). Particularly popular are the various transportation departments that include the first Benz automobile (the one in the Mercedes Museum in Stuttgart is a copy), the first German submarine, early trains and planes, boats, and missiles. Large sections are also devoted to pure science, with physical laws and chemical reactions explained. Further exhibitions include paper- and porcelain-making, photography, weather prediction, electronics, agriculture, and astronomy. Opening hours are daily from 9 am to 5 pm, with selected collections on Wednesday open until 9 pm. Admission is €7.50.

In contrast to the great formal museums in Munich is the **ZAM - Zentrum für Außergewöhnliche Museen** (Center for Unusual Museums), Westenriederstr. 41, ☎ 089-290-4121, www.zam-museum.de. It has seven small museums on offbeat items, including a collection of chamber pots (2,000!), guardian angels, pedal cars, Sisi (the Empress Elizabeth), Easter bunnies, bourdalous (traveling chamber pots), and scents. It is near the Isartor. Opening hours are daily from 10 am to 6 pm. Admission is €4.

Pinakotheken Viertel & Königsplatz

The **Pinakotheken Viertel** (Art Galleries' Quarter) is an informal name for the area a few blocks northeast of the Hauptbahnhof that houses several major art galleries. The most impressive are the three Pinakotheken that together present art from the Middle Ages to the present. The individual collections are among the best in Germany, with the Alte Pinakothek one of the best in the world.

THE PINAKOTHEKEN

Day tickets for all three Pinakotheken are €12 – a bargain for those visiting the Pinakothek der Moderne.

The **Alte Pinakothek** (Old Masters' Gallery), Barer Straße 27, ☎ 089-238-052, www.alte-pinakothek.de, is one of the world's greatest art collections of European painters from the Middle Ages to the early 19th century. It is housed in a large early 19th-century Neo Renaissance building rebuilt after World War II. The catalogue reads like a Who's Who of European painters, with excellent works by all the great masters. German, Dutch, and Flemish artists are particularly well represented. The Rubens collection is one of the largest in the world. Opening hours are Tuesday to Sunday from 10 am to 5 pm, closing at 8 pm on Tuesday. Admission is €5, free on Sunday.

Across the road is the **Neue Pinakothek** (New Art Gallery), Barer Straße 29, ☎ 089-2380-5195, www.neue-pinakothek.org. The post-modern building was only completed in 1981 to house the mainly 19th-century art collection that has been homeless since World War II. The sculptures and paintings cover all periods from Rococo to Art Nouveau. It has works by all the famous Impressionist artists but it is really the German works that come to the fore here. Opening hours are Tuesday to Sunday from 10 am to 5 pm, closing at 8 pm on Wednesday. Admission is €5, free on Sunday.

Adjacent is the **Pinakothek der Moderne** (Modern Art Gallery), Barer Straße 40, ☎ 089-2380-5118, www.pinakothek-der-moderne.de, opened in 2002. This glass and steel building houses four collections that together represent the largest modern art gallery in Germany. The exhibition comprises sections on modern art, industrial and graphic design, graphic art, and architecture. Opening hours are Tuesday to Sunday from 10 am to 5 pm, closing at 8 pm on Thursday and Friday. Admission is €9, free on Sunday.

Königsplatz: This area was destined to become the *Acropolis Germaniae* under the Nazis, but clever redesigning after the war left it with a less bombastic and still Classical appearance. Few visitors would associate the buildings here with the Nazi era, in stark contrast to what happened with the Party Rallying grounds in Nürnberg. The area houses several impressive museums to complement the nearby Pinakotheken.

At the north of the square is the Greek temple-like **Glyptothek**, Königsplatz 3, ☎ 089-286-100. This Ionic columned building was erected in 1816-30 to house one of Europe's largest collections of antique sculpture. Opening hours are Tuesday to Sunday from 10 am to 5 pm, closing at 8 pm on Tuesday and Thursday. Admission is €3, free on Sunday.

On the south side of the square, with a Corinthian colonnade, is the **Antikensammlungen** (Antiquities Collection), Königsplatz 1, ☎ 089-598-359, www.antikensammlungen.de. It has an impressive array of Greek ceramics, Etruscan art, small sculptures, bronzes, and jewelry. Opening hours are Tuesday to Sunday from 10 am to 5 pm, closing at 8 pm on Wednesday. Admission is €3, free on Sunday.

The **Städtische Galerie im Lenbachhaus und Kunstbau** (Municipal Gallery), Luisenstraße 33, ☎ 089-2333-2000, www.lenbachhaus.de, is in a Florentine-style villa constructed in the late 19th century for the artist Lenbach. A large part of the collection is by local painters or of regional subjects. However, the Avant-Garde Blaue Reiter collection is internationally famous, with many works by Kadinsky, Marc, Kubin, Klee, and Jawlensky. The attached Kunstbau is actually a former subway platform and is used to house temporary exhibitions. Opening hours are Tuesday to Sunday from 10 am to 6 pm. Admission is €6.

Olympiagelände & BMW

In the northern suburbs of Munich are the **Olympiagelände** (site of the 1972 Summer Olympic Games). The games then were much less elaborate than the current versions and the stadiums are still in everyday use. The 80,000-seat Olympic Stadium and the 14,000-seat multipurpose Olympiahalle are frequently used for sports and cultural events, while the Olympic swimming pool is open to the general public. Of particularly note is the enormous glass tent that was constructed to cover the main stadiums and large public areas. It was fabulously expensive and over-budget but now is much loved. Twelve pylons 81 m (260 feet) high and 36 smaller ones keep the glass roof in the air. The almost 60-m (195-foot) high Olympiaberg (Olympic Mountain) was created by rubble carted out of Munich after the Second World War. Most of the Olympiagelände is unfenced and freely accessible. It is a favored place for jogging, cycling, and inline skating.

The **Olympiaturm** (Olympic Tower, 1968), 290 m (950 feet) high, is the tallest television tower in Germany. A viewing platform and revolving restaurant at 190 m elevation (620 feet) attracts up to 700,000 annual visitors. The views of Munich are fine – it really is too high to see much detail – but the views of the Bavarian Alps are fantastic when weather is clear. The elevator costs €3 and operates from 9 am to midnight.

Adjacent to the Olympiagelände are the headquarters and a factory of Bayerischen Motoren Werken, better known by the acronym BMW. The headquarters are in a futuristic-looking silver building from the early 1970s. It looks as if four cylinders of 19 stories each are hanging from the support structures at the top. The **BMW-Museum**, Petuelring 130, ☎ 089-3822-3307, www.bmw.com, has an interesting exhibition of BMW cars, aircraft engines, and motorcycles, ranging from the 1928 Dixi to design studies. Factory tours are also possible – book well in advance for the limited number of English tours. Opening hours are daily from 9 am to 5 pm. Admission is €3.

The area is easily reached from the old town on U-Bahn U3, station Olympia-Zentrum.

Schloss Nymphenburg

Schloss Nymphenburg was erected originally from 1664 to 1674 as a small summer retreat west of the city for the ruling family. However, Prince Elector Max Emmanuel turned it into a lavish palace. For most of the 18th century, his successors added

more features and structures, until Nymphenburg became the largest palace in Germany. The garden was developed from 1700 onwards and eventually combined formal Italian and French elements with English landscape garden areas.

The huge palace – it is a km (.6 mile) long – can be visited without a tour. It is mostly Baroque and has a splendid interior. The huge **banqueting hall** has rich stuccos and frescoes by Johann Baptist Zimmermann. Several royal apartments are on display, including the Geburtzimmer (Birth Room) of mad King Ludwig II. Of special note is the **Schönheitengalerie** (Gallery of Beauties) – a huge collection of paintings by Joseph Stieler of beautiful women that caught the roving eye of King Ludwig. Especially of note is the painting of Lola Montez, the woman who cost him his throne.

The **Marstallmuseum mit Museum Nymphenburger Porzellan** (Carriage Museum with Porcelain Collection) is in the south wing of the palace. It includes the collection of lavish carriages owned by the Wittelsbach family. Of special interest are the coronation coaches of Karl VII (1741) and Max Joseph (early 19th century) as well as the luxurious sleigh of Ludwig II. On the second floor is the porcelain collection of 1,200 items from Rococo to Art Nouveau.

Of the structures in the garden, **Amalienburg** is the most interesting. Originally conceived as a simple hunting lodge, Cuvilliés created a simple exterior but a magnificent Rococo interior (1739). This pleasure pavilion served as inspiration for many others that were created all over Europe during the 18th century. It has lavish kennels for the royal hunting dogs, a hall of mirrors rotunda, and a kitchen tiled in blue and white Delft.

Three further early 18th-century structures in the garden are open to the public. The **Badenburg** contained the first heated swimming pool since Roman times. The **Pagodenburg** has an elegant French exterior but the interior is exotic Asian. It was used mainly as a teahouse. The **Magdalenenklause** is a folly of artificial ruins. It contains a chapel dedicated to Mary Magdalene.

Visitor Information: Schloss Nymphenburg, Amalienburg, and the Marstallmuseum with Porcelain Collection are open daily from April to mid-October, 9 am to 6 pm, and from mid-October to March, 10 am to 4 pm. Three Parkburgen (Badenburg, Pagodenburg, and Magdalenenklause) are only open during the summer season. Admission to the Schloss and Museum is €5 each and the Parkburgen €2 each. A combination ticket for the Parkburgen and Amalienburg is €4 and to all buildings in the complex €10 in summer and €8 in winter.

Admission to the park itself is free and daily opening hours long, if complex. From March to October, it opens at 6 am but closes at 6:30 pm in March, 7 pm in October, 8:30 pm in April and September, and 9:30 pm from May to August. From November to February, it opens at 6:30 am and closes at 6 pm, but 5:30 pm in December.

Contact: Schloss Nymphenburg, Eingang 1, ☎ 089-179-080, www.schloesser.bayern.de.

The area is now firmly within the city boundaries and six km (3.6 miles) west of the old town. It is most easily reached by Tram 17 or Bus 41.

Farther Afield

Dachau: In 1933, on orders from Heinrich Himmler, the Nazis' first concentration camp was created at Dachau near Munich. Those incarcerated here were mostly political prisoners. Although gas chambers were built, they were never used and it remained primarily a slave labor camp. By the time of liberation in 1945, 31,591 of the 206,000 prisoners had died, mostly of malnutrition and disease. At liberation, the camp had fewer than 70,000 prisoners, of which about a third were Jews. A local priest, Rupert Mayer, who was interned

Dachau gatehouse, 1945

there, was later declared a saint – see *Bürgersaal* for details.

The whole camp area is now a memorial site to those who diedl here, as well as to those who suffered under the Nazi regime elsewhere. Many parts of the camp have been restored or rebuilt. In the main building is the **KZ-Gedenkstätte Dachau Museum** (Concentration Camp Memorial), Alte Römerstraße 75, 85221 Dachau, ☎ 08131-669-970. It has photos and information about the tragic and disturbing events. An English information video is shown at 11:30 am and 3:30 pm. Opening hours are Tuesday to Sunday from 9 am to 5 pm. Admission is free. It is worth investing in the audio guide (€2.50) as explanatory signs are limited.

To reach the camp from the Hauptbahnhof, take S-Bahn S2 in the direction of Petershausen to Dachau Station. From here, it is a 10-minute walk, or take Bus 724 or 726. The train ride takes just over 20 minutes, but waiting for the bus can increase the total journey time to 50 minutes.

Mike´s Bike Tours, Discover Bavaria, Hochbrückenstraße, ☎ 089-2554-3987, www.mikesbiketours.com, assists with visits to Dachau. Although they do not include a guided tour of the site, they do provide all transportation (train/bus), a self-guided audio tour, and a guide, who is available to assist with orientation at the memorial. This tour departs Tuesday to Sunday from mid-April to October at 9:50 am from the main exit of the Hauptbahnhof in front of Yorma's Sandwich Shop.

Schleißheim: Prince Elector Max Emmanuel, who built large parts of

Schloss Nymphenburg, erected another magnificent Baroque palace north of Munich. **Neues Schloss Schleißheim** (New Palace) Max-Emanuel-Platz 1, ☎ 089-315-8720, www.schloesser.bayern.de, was to have been his Versailles. Debt and exile ruined his plans but one of the four planned wings of monumental proportions was eventually completed in 1719. The 335-m (1,000-foot) building has a Late Baroque and Rococo interior, which is partly the work of Johann Baptist Zimmermann and Cosmas Damian Asam. The art gallery includes a remarkable collection of European Baroque paintings, with three works by Rubens. About 50 rooms on two floors are open to the public. Opening hours are Tuesday to Sunday from April to September, 9 am to 6 pm, and October to March, 10 am to 4 pm. Admission is €4 – English audio guides are available. Combination ticket with Schloss Lustheim is €5.

The **Hofgarten** (Royal Garden) at Neues Schloss Schleißheim, is one of only two Baroque gardens in Germany that survived in an unaltered form. (The other one is Herrenhausen in Hanover.) It is in a French style with formal geometric design. The basic structures were already designed in 1684 and most of it completed early in the 18th century. A center canal leads to the end of the garden where a Baroque folly, the late 17th-century hunting palace of Lustheim, is encircled by smaller canals. Side-canals run the full length of the garden at the width of the main building and come together in a half-circle behind Lustheim. The fountains are operational daily from April to mid-September, 10 am to 4 pm. The gardens are freely accessible year-round.

Schloss Lustheim currently houses the most important early Meissen porcelain collection outside Saxony. The tiger shown at left is from 1732. Opening hours are the same as for the main palace. Admission is €3 or €5 when combined with the main palace.

The **Flugwerft Schleißheim** (Airport), Effnerstraße 18, ☎ 089-315-7140, is a dependence of the Deutsches Museum in the north of Munich. It has early aircraft and missiles on display. Opening hours are daily from 9 am to 5 pm. Admission is €3.50 or €10 when combined with the main museum.

Schleisheim is best reached by private car or S-Bahn line S1 to Oberschleißheim. It is a 15-minute walk to the palaces and the Flugwerft.

Cultural Events

Munich has a busy cultural calendar and offers everything from classical music to the latest pop stars. It is famous for its 50 theaters that perform works from all genres, but unfortunately for most foreign visitors, usually in German only.

There are three symphony orchestras and two opera houses. The **Bayerische Staatsoper** (Bavarian National Opera House) and **Bayerisches Staatsorchester** (Bavarian National Orchestra), www.staatsoper.de, are two of the oldest companies in Germany with the orchestra founded in 1523. Mozart raved over their talent. The orchestra first performed several Wagner operas in Munich and Bayreuth. The **Münchner Philharmoniker** (Munich Philharmonic), www.muenchner-philharmoniker.de, is just over a century old. With 16,000 subscribers, tickets are seldom available to outsiders. The symphony orchestra of the **Bayerischer Rundfunk** (Bavarian Radio), www.br-klassik.de, was founded in 1949 and has an international reputation for excellence.

A good source for tickets to all kinds of events is **München Ticket**, www.muenchen-ticket.de, ☎ 089-5481-8181. It has offices in the Rathaus next to the tourist information ofice, in the Gasteig, and in the Olympiapark at the Info-Pavillion. For the Bayerischen Staatsoper, reservations must be made at the **Staatsoper**, Max-Joseph-Platz 2, ☎ 089-2185-1920, www.staatsoper.de.

Festivals

Munich has a busy festival calendar that includes many originally Catholic holidays as well as purely secular merriments. The two largest festivals are described in more detail below.

Fasching (in other areas called Karneval or Fastnacht) starts in early January and last about two months. Particularly popular is the dancing of the market women at the Viktualienmarkt. After two weeks of fasting, usually at the end of March, comes the Starkbierzeit (Strong Beer Period) during which all local breweries brew a particularly strong beer.

This is followed by the first **Dult** festival (see below) and, in June, the city's **foundation day**. In summer, several festivals are held, including film and open-air music festivals. Two more Dult festivals are held at each end of Okotberfest, which is mostly in September. The year ends with the **Christkindlmarkte** (Christmas Market) held during Advent at several locations throughout the city.

Oktoberfest

Munich is world famous for the largest festival in the world – the annual 16-day Oktoberfest – actually held mostly in September and ending the first Sunday in October. It all started as a celebration of the wedding of Crown Prince Ludwig and Princess Therese of Saxony- H i ldburghausen in 1810. A commemorative medal from the time, above, shows the pair. But the celebration soon became an annual event and is now a firm part of Munich's cultural program. The festival is combined with an agricultural show every three years, but the main attractions to the millions of visitors are the beer tents, rides, and other entertainment.

Oktoberfest typically attracts over six million visitors, each of whom consumes at least a liter of beer as well as wine and non-alcoholic beverages. Half a million chickens and almost a hundred oxen are slaughtered and eaten, together with 110,000 lbs of fish and 400,000 of pork sausages. The total contribution to Munich's economy is estimated at around a billion euros.

The festival is held at a special terrain, about a 10-minute walk south of the Hauptbahnhof, known as the Theresienwiese, and Oktoberfest is therefore locally often referred to as the *Wies'n*. The show grounds are usually open from 10 am to midnight, with drinking stopping mostly at 10:30 pm. Beer tents close for new arrivals when full – on weekends that can be before noon! It is generally a good idea to leave before 10 pm both for safety reasons and to avoid the crowds on public transportation. Finding accommodations in Munich during Oktoberfest is problematic – expect to pay top dollar for even the simplest hotel.

Auer Dult Festivals

Auer Dult, www.auerdult.de, is another traditional Munich folk celebration. It is a combination market, flea market, and entertainment that lasts for nine days. Almost everything is sold at the market but it is particularly famous as the largest market in Europe for tableware, pots, and pans, although more people are drawn by the food, drink, and entertainment. Dating back to 1310, the festival is actually older than the more famous Oktoberfest. Three Dulten are organized annually – end of April, end of July, and mid-October. The market stalls are generally open from 9 am to 8 pm. The market is held at Mariahilfplatz – there is no parking in the area but Bus 52 connects to the Marienplatz and Tram 27 to Karlsplatz.

Shopping

Munich is a good city for shopping. The haute couture shops are in stylish **Maximilianstraße** as well as in streets near the **Residenz**. The pedestrian zone, especially **Neuhauser** and **Kaufingerstraße**, has the larger department stores. The largest and most famous store in Munich is the **Herties** department store, which spreads over several blocks between Karlsplatz and the Hauptbahnhof.

Buying a BMW

Probably the most desired souvenir to take home from Munich is a BMW car. Residents from the US (other areas need not apply), who are buying a BMW made in Germany can save, depending on the model, between $2,000 and $8,000 by taking personal delivery in Germany, rather than in the US. The car may be driven up to six months in Europe before being shipped to the US. Insurance for the first 30 days is included. The car can be dropped off at several cities in Europe at the end of the vacation and then shipped and delivered in the US through the normal channels. There is no catch, paperwork, or hidden costs, but do note that some options, including radios, are in some cases only fitted once the car arrives in the US. Contact any BMW dealer in the US, or www.bmwusa.com, for details on the European Delivery Program. (Other German car companies have similar schemes, but presently none offer such huge savings.)

Adventures

On Foot

Several companies offer guided walking tours of Munich. Munich Walking Tours uses native English-speaking guides, while the others are generally in German only.

- **Munich Walking Tours**, Discover Bavaria, Hochbrückenstraße, ☎ 089-2554-3987, www.mikesbiketours.com, conducts guided tours daily at 3:30 from mid-April to August. The tour departs from the Yorma Sandwich Shop at the main exit of the Hauptbahnhof. Participation is €9 for this three-hour walking tour that ends at the Hofbräuhaus, where Mike has a regular reserved table, known as a *Stammtisch*. (See also Dachau above** and Mike's Bike tours below.)
- **Munich Walks/Radius Bikes**, Arnulfstraße 3, ☎ 089-5502-9374, www.radius-munich.com, has several guided tours of Munich and Dachau. A fascinating two-hour tour is on Hitler and the Nazi period in Munich. It departs daily between April and October at 3 pm from the office at the Hauptbahnhof (near tracks 32-33).
- **Stattreisen München**, Frauenlobstraße 24, ☎ 089-5440-4230, www.stattreisen-muenchen.de, has an interesting range of tours – often of a specialist nature focusing on a special event, person, or neighborhood. Tours are available throughout the year but the schedule is busiest between April and October and over weekends.
- **Weisser Stadtvogel Münche**n, Utzschneiderstraße 4, ☎ 089-3846-4961, www.weisser-stadtvogel.de, has several thematic tours. The most frequent are of the old town, Schloss Nymphenburg, and the Pinakothek der Moderne.

On Wheels

Munich is a relatively flat city with 700 km (420 miles) of dedicated **cycling** routes, making for easy and safe cycling.

- **Mike's Bike Tours**, Discover Bavaria, Hochbrückenstraße, ☎ 089-2554-3987, www.mikesbiketours.com, is a pleasant way to discover Munich. From March to mid-November, one to four tours are available daily. The standard four-hour tour costs €22 and the extended seven-hour tour (in June and July only) costs €33 – both prices include bicycle rental. Bicycle rental without a tour is also available.
- Pedal-powered rickshaw taxis are available from the Marienplatz to many parts of the old town. Fares start at €3. They are operated by **Rikscha Mobil**, Oppenrieder Straße 28, ☎ 089-129-4808, www.rikscha-mobil.de, which also rents out rickshaws (€90 per day) and tandem bicycles (€30 per day) for self-peddling. Rentals on weekends are slightly more expensive.
- **Weisser Stadtvogel München**, Utzschneiderstraße 4, ☎ 089-3846-4961, www.weisser-stadtvogel.de, arranges two-hour cycling tours of the old town on Sunday at 3 pm from April to October. The fare of €14 includes bicycle rental. Departure point is the Feldherrnhalle at Odeonsplatz.

Munich has a surprising number of **cycle rental** options. In addition to the companies mentioned above, try any of the following:

Radius Tour and Bikes, In the Hauptbahnhof, Arnulfstr. 3, ☎ 089-596-113; **Radeldiscount GbR**, Benediktbeurerstr. 20-22, ☎ 089-724-2351; **Radsport Huber**, Friedrich-Eckard-Str. 56, ☎ 089-9393-0670; or **Spurwechsel**, Steinstr. 3, ☎ 089-692-4699.

Inline skating is popular in Munich, with many parks and the banks of the Isar River open to skaters. On Monday nights from May to August, **Münchner Bladenights** allow you to skate through the streets of Munich. It claims to be the biggest skating event in Europe. Information on routes is available from **Green City**, Klenzestraße 54, ☎ 089-8906-6833, www.muenchner-bladenight.de. The party starts at 7 pm, the actual skating is from 9 to 10:30 pm.

■ Sightseeing Tours on Wheels

Several companies operate traditional **bus sightseeing tours** of Munich and surrounding areas. Some include short walks and guided tours of castles. The buses generally depart from close to the Hauptbahnhof. Many hotels will make reservations at no charge. Prices are from €10 for one-hour tours. Some tours are in open-top double-decker buses.

Major operators include **Münchner Stadtrundfahrten**, Arnulfstrasse 8, ☎ 089-5502-8995, and **Yellow Cab**, Sendlinger-Tor-Platz 5, ☎ 089-2602-5183.

AutobusOberbayern, Heidemannstraße 220, ☎ 089-323-040, www.autobusoberbayern.de, operates city tours as well as daytrips to several destinations near Munich, including Rothenburg, Herrenchiemsee, Berchtesgaden, Salzburg, and Innsbruck. A particularly popular tour that departs daily at 8:30 am is to Schloss Neuschwanstein and Schloss Linderhof – using public transportation, it is virtually impossible to do both on the same day.

Taxi Guide München, Ganghoferstraße 63a, ☎ 089-3537-9808, www.taxi-guide-muenchen.de, uses taxis with drivers qualified as tour-guides. The price is €70 for the first hour and €20 for each additional hour. A full-day tour for up to eight persons, extending 300 km (180 miles), e.g. to Schloss Neuschwanstein or Berchtesgaden, costs just over €400.

With Horses

Hans Holzmann, Kutscherei, Schwere-Reiter-Strasse 22, ☎ 089-180-608, operates the only **horse-drawn carriage** in Munich. Trips from half an hour to two hours are possible daily in the afternoon from the Chinesischer Turm in the heart of the Englischer Garten. Prices are from €31 per half-hour for four to five persons.

Where to Stay & Eat

Luxury Hotels & Restaurants

The **Hotel Bayerischer Hof** is a privately managed luxury grand hotel close to the old town and the Pinakotheken Museums. Rooms are rustic, nostalgic, or modern but all are luxurious. The **Garden-Restaurant** (€€-€€€€) with terrace serves Mediterranean cuisine. **Trader Vic's** (€€-€€€€) serves Polynesian and Caribbean food. It is open for dinner only and reservations are recommended. The pleasant **Palais Keller** (€€-€€€) is a traditional Bavarian beer cellar and serves local specialties. Promenadeplatz 2-6, 80333 München, ☎ 089-21-200, fax 089-212-0906, www.bayerischerhof.de. (€€€€)

The **Mandarin Oriental Hotel** is close to the Hofbräuhaus just minutes from the Marienplatz. The hotel is luxurious with large rooms. The 19th-century building was originally a ballroom but successfully converted to a hotel in 1989. The manager reportedly told a famous British pop star, who demanded a discount recently, to stay elsewhere. The pool is on the roof and has fantastic views of the old town and Alps when weather allows. The dinner restaurant, **Mark's** (€€€-€€€€), serves international and nouvelle cuisine. **Mark's Corner** (€€-€€€) is open for lunch only. Neuturmstraße 1, 80331 München, ☎ 089-290-980, fax 089-222-539, www.mandarinoriental.com. (€€€€)

The **Königshof Hotel** is between the old town and the Hauptbahnhof at the Stachus intersection. It is an establishment in the grand hotel tradition with luxurious, individually furnished rooms and classic elegance. The **Königshof restaurant** (€€€-€€€€) is one of the best in Munich and serves nouvelle cuisine in stylish surroundings. Karlsplatz 25, 80335 München,

HOTEL PRICE CHART	
Rates per room based on double occupancy, including taxes.	
€	Under €50
€€	€50-€100
€€€	€101-€150
€€€€	Over €150

☎ 089-551-360, fax 089-5513-6113, www.koenigshof-muenchen.de. (€€€€)

The **Kempinski Hotel Vier Jahreszeiten** is on the Maximilianstraße close to the Opera – a grand hotel with a history dating back to the mid-19th century. Rooms combine traditional elements with modern comforts. The **Bistro Restaurant** (€€-€€€€) is good for people-watching. It serves international and nouvelle cuisine. Maximilianstraße 17, 80331 München, ☎ 089-21-250, fax 089-2125-2000, www.kempinski.com. (€€€€)

Old Town Area

Platzl Hotel is close to the Hofbräuhaus. It has comfortable, individually furnished rooms. The ones facing the courtyard are particularly pleasant. The **Pfistermühle** restaurant (€€-€€€) serves Bavarian specialties under a vaulted ceiling in an old-Munich atmosphere, but without the beer-hall effects. Pfisterstraße 4, 80331 München, ☎ 089-237-030, fax 089-2370-3800, www.platzl.de. (€€€-€€€€)

Hotel Torbräu is close to the Hofbräuhaus and within easy walking distance of the Deutsches Museum. The building dates back to the 15th century and claims to be the oldest hotel in Munich. Rooms are comfortably furnished and spacious. Tal 41, 80331 München, ☎ 089-242-430, fax 089-2423-4235, www.torbraeu.de. (€€€-€€€€)

Admiral Hotel is just a block from the Deutsches Museum. It is a small hotel with comfortable, large rooms furnished in an English country-house style. Some rooms are extremely large. Kohlstraße 9, 80469 München, ☎ 089-216-350, fax 089-293-674, www.hotel-admiral.de. (€€€-€€€€)

Domus Hotel is close to the Maximilianstraße at the edge of the old town. It has comfortable, tastefully decorated rooms, many with balconies. St-Anna-Straße 31, 80538 München, ☎ 089-221-704, fax 089-228-5359. (€€€)

Concorde Hotel is close to the Hofbräuhaus. It is a modern, family-run establishment with comfortable, individually furnished rooms. The ones facing the courtyard are quiet. Herrnstraße 38, 80539 München, ☎ 089-224-515, fax 089-228-3282, www.concorde-muenchen.de. (€€€)

Mercure Altstadt Hotel is two blocks from the pedestrian zone. It is a modern hotel with functionally furnished rooms. Hotterstraße 4, 80331 München, ☎ 089-232-590, fax 089-2325-9127, www.mercure.com. (€€-€€€)

Daniel Hotel is conveniently located at the Stachus, with an entry to the underground right next to the hotel. Rooms are pleasant, with modern furniture. Sonnenstraße 5, 80331 München, ☎ 089-548-240, fax 089-553-420, www.hotel-daniel.de. (€€-€€€)

The **Hotel Acanthus** is a small establishment at the Sendlinger Tor. Rooms are either in an English country-house style with some antiques or modern. All are furnished to high standards. An der Hauptfeuerwache 14, 80331 München, ☎ 089-231-880, fax 089-260-7364, www.achanthushotel.de. (€€-€€€)

Hauptbahnhof Area

As in most other major cities in Germany, the area around the Hauptbahnhof is not particularly inviting. The red light district, sex shops, and video booths are all close-by. The first three hotels listed here are all next to or directly across the road from the station and not in bad areas. The others are also close and in safe areas but a sex shop or two may be passed en route from the station.

Hotel Le Méridien opened in 2002 across the road from the Hauptbahnhof. It is unashamedly modern with well-equipped, stylish rooms. The restaurant **Le Potager** (€€€) serves international cuisine with strong French influences. Bayerstraße 41, 80335 München, ☎ 089-24-220, fax 089-2422-1111, www.lemeridien.de. (€€€-€€€€)

The **Excelsior Hotel** has a rustic décor. Rooms come with country-style furniture. The **Geisel's Vinothek** (€-€€€) serves German and Italian food to complement the wine list of 400 labels. Schützenstraße 11, 80335 München, ☎ 089-551-370, fax 089-5513-7121, www.excelsior-muenchen.de. (€€€-€€€€)

The **Intercity Hotel** is part of the station building and has been in operation since the early 1950s. Rooms are modern, well-equipped, and quiet. The room key gives free access to local transportation. Bayerstraße 10, 80335 München, ☎ 089-545-560, fax 089-5455-6610, www.intercity-hotel.de. (€€€-€€€€)

Hotel Drei Löwen is a block from the station. It is a modern hotel with individually furnished rooms using currently fashionable wood furniture. A pleasant option for the price. Schillerstraße 8, 80336 München, ☎ 089-551-040, fax 089-5510-4905, www.hotel3loewen.de. (€€-€€€)

The **King's Hotel First Class**, Dachauer Straße 13, 80335 München, ☎ 089-551-870, fax 089-5518-7300, www.kingshotels.de (€€€-€€€€), and the **King's Hotel Center**, Marsstraße 15, 80335 München, ☎ 089-515-530, fax 089-5155-3300, www.kingshotels.de (€€-€€€€), are two pleasant, modern hotels that use ample wood in the interior. All rooms have four-poster beds. They are two blocks north of the Hauptbahnhof and close to the Glyphothek.

The **Apollo Hotel** is on a side-street close to the station. Rooms come with mahogany furniture. The rooms in the back of the building are quieter. Mitterstraße 7, 80336 München, ☎ 089-539-531, fax 089-534-033, www.apollohotel.de. (€€-€€€)

Englischer Garten

The **Hilton München Park** opened for the 1972 Olympics and was completely renovated in 2000. It has large, luxurious rooms. The hotel is particularly popular for its location between the Isar River and the Englischer Garten. Am Tucherpark 7, 80538 München, ☎ 089-38-450, fax 089-3845-2588, www.hilton.com. (€€€€)

Schwabing

Schwabing is a pleasant, lively neighborhood to stay in and is within easy reach of all the sights.

The **Marriott** is a modern hotel, but stylish in the grand tradition. Rooms are luxurious, well-equipped, and typical Marriott, with floral prints. The **California Grill** (€€-€€€) serves international cuisine with strong American overtones. Berliner Straße 93, 80805 München, ☎ 089-360-020, fax 089-3600-2200, www.marriotthotels.com. (€€-€€€€)

Nearby is the **Renaissance Hotel** with syilish rooms. The **Bistro 47-47** (€€-€€€) serves Mediterranean cuisine. Theodor-Dombart-Straße 4, 80805 München, ☎ 089-360-990, fax 089-3609-6900, www.renaissanncehotels.com. (€€€)

Holiday Inn City Nord is a typical business hotel with functional rooms – many with balconies. The hotel is convenient to the Autobahn. Kistlerhofstraße 142, 81379 München, ☎ 089-780-020, fax 089-7800-2672, www.holiday-inn.com. (€€-€€€)

Four Points Hotel München Olympiapark is in the middle of the Olympiapark and an ideal location when attending sporting or cultural events. Rooms are functional. The restaurant **Bayern Stub'n** (€€) serves hearty local cuisine. Helene-Mayer-Ring 12, ☎ 089-35-75-10, fax 089-357-51755, www.arabellasheraton.com. (€€€-€€€€)

Hotel Cosmopolitan is in the heart of Schwabing, a few minutes from the U-Bahn and Leopoldstraße. Rooms are modern with designer furniture. Hohenzollernstraße 5, 80801 München, ☎ 089-383-810, fax 089-3838-1111, www.cosmopolitan-hotel.de. (€€€)

Mercure Hotel München-Schwabing is just north of the Münchner Freiheit, close to the Englischer Garten. Rooms are modern and functionally furnished. Leopoldstraße 120, 80802 München, ☎ 089-389-9930, fax 089-349-344, www.mercure.com. (€€-€€€€)

DINING PRICE CHART	
Price per person for an entrée, including water, beer or soft drink.	
€	Under €10
€€	€10-€20
€€€	€21-€35
€€€€	Over €35

Where to Eat

Spago, Neureuther Straße 15, ☎ 089-271-2406, a modern restaurant, serves nouvelle cuisine with strong Italian overtones. It is popular with local actors and artists. (€€-€€€)

Bistro Terrine, Amalienstraße 89, ☎ 089-281-780, is a popular French restaurant. Its décor has Art Nouveau and Art Deco elements. Reservations for dinner are recommended. (€€€)

The restaurant **Tantris**, Johann-Fichte-Straße 7, ☎ 089-361-9590, is considered by many to be the best in Munich. It serves classical dishes and nouvelle cuisine. The décor is Asian with straight lines, black and red furniture, and mythical figures. (€€€€)

The **Olympiaturm-Drehrestaurant** (Olympic Tower Revolving Restaurant), Spiridon-Louis-Ring 7, ☎ 089-3066-8585, has the best views in town. An elevator zooms guests up to 182 m (600 feet). A complete revolution usually takes 53 minutes, although the speed can be adjusted to either 35 or 72 minutes as well. Reservations are recommended for dinner. (€€-€€€).

Luxurious **Schuhbeck's in den Südtiroler Stuben**, Platzl 6-8, ☎ 089-216-6900, has wood-paneled walls and a Baroque ceiling. The food is first-class, with classical dishes and South Tyrolean specialties. (€€€-€€€€)

Nearby **Boettner's**, Pfisterstraße 9, ☎ 089-221-210, serves mostly classical dishes and nouvelle cuisine. It uses ample dark wood in its décor. Reservations are advisable. (€€€-€€€€)

Halali, Schönfeldstraße 22, ☎ 089-285-909, is an elegant-rustic spot that fits the hunting tradition its name recalls (halali means something akin to tally-ho). It is in between the Hofgarten and Englischer Garten. Food is classic international and regional dishes. Reservations are advisable. (€€€)

Hunsinger's Pacific, Maximiliansplatz 5 (enter from Max-Joseph-Straße), ☎ 089-5502-9741, is arguably the best-known fish restaurant in Munich. It serves a wide selection ranging from the standard to the exotic. The food is mostly international, but with an Asian touch. Meat is also served. (€€-€€€)

The **Restaurant Dallmayr**, Dienerstraße 14, ☎ 089-213-5100, in the famous Delicatessen Shop Dallmayr, is at the heart of the old town at the Marienplatz. The prices reflect the quality of the food rather than a tourist markup for the location. The restaurant is attractive and has a wide selection ranging from international cuisine to local specialties. (€€€)

Lenbach, Ottostraße 6, ☎ 089-549-1300, is between Stachus and Maximiliansplatz. It is an enormous restaurant designed by British architect Sir Terrance Conran, with a modern, stylish interior. The food is mostly international and Asian, with a separate sushi bar. Reservations are advisable. (€€-€€€)

The **Weinhaus Neuner** is a block from the Stachus in a mid-19th-century building claiming to be the oldest wine bar in Munich, ☎ 089-2603954. It has cross-vaulting and wall paintings. Hearty local dishes are featured. (€-€€)

Dukatz im Literaturhaus, Salvatorplatz 1, ☎ 089-291-9600, is in a former market hall close to the Theatinerkirche. It serves international cuisine with strong Mediterranean overtones in a modern restaurant with cross-vaulting. (€€-€€€)

Zum Alten Markt, Dreifaltigkeitsplatz 3, ☎ 089-299-995, is an attractive restaurant with wood paneling in a 400-year-old building at the Viktualienmarkt. It serves regional cuisine. (€-€€)

The **Ratskeller**, Marienplatz 8, ☎ 089-219-9890, is an enormous restaurant in the cellars of the old Town Hall. It has many rooms, niches, and hidden corners in a romantic, rustic style. Food is local, including Franconian specialties. Reservations are essential. (€-€€)

Close to the Asmankirche is the pleasant **Restaurant Prinz Myshkin**, Hackenstraße 2, ☎ 089-265-596, www.prinz-myshkin.com. It is the best vegetarian restaurant in town – granted, competition is limited. The modern restaurant is large, with a vaulted ceiling. It is hugely popular, making reservations for dinner advisable. (€€-€€€)

Another vegetarian option is the self-service **Restaurant Buxs**, Frauenstraße 9, ☎ 089-291-9550. Seven cookbooks have been published under the restaurant's aegis so far and it's good place to stop for a quick bite in the Marienplatz vicinity. (€-€€)

Beer Halls & Beer Gardens

The best-known building in Munich is the **Hofbräuhaus**, Platzl 6, ☎ 089-290-1360, www.hofbraeuhaus.de. Its best features are also its worst – the international fame and popularity of the place. It can be packed at night with international visitors, and barely a local in sight. Many seem to think that getting hopelessly drunk and singing out of tune is the way to have a good time. It can also be packed with locals. You take your chances. You may prefer to reserve a table at the more formal restaurants on upper levels, or visit for lunch. Even if not planning to eat or drink here, take a peak inside and especially at the upper floors. (€-€€€)

Beer Garden Etiquette

Munich is inevitably associated with beer and has several beer gardens and beer halls popular with locals and visitors alike.

Beer is usually served by *mass* (one liter), or if requested, *halb* (half liter). Ordering anything smaller will raise eyebrows. If not specified otherwise, the beer will be *helles* (clear). Colas are available in some, but non-drinkers will not be sniggered at when asking for an *Apfelschaftschorle* – apple juice and soda water mix. It is much healthier and more refreshing than cola. A *Radler* (literally "cyclist") is half-beer, half-lemonade. Beer mixed with cola and other drinks is currently fashionable in certain parts, but tastes as vulgar as it sounds.

The typical food in beer gardens is large, soft pretzels or sausages, served with potatoes and sauerkraut. A Munich favorite is Weißwurst (white sausage). It is traditionally only served in the morning; correct etiquette is to eat it by hand and not to eat the skin. It goes well with sweet Bavarian mustard and, of course beer. Payment is usually due at delivery. In some beer gardens, it is permissible to bring your own food, but never your own drink.

Tables are commonly shared with strangers in busy restaurants and beer gardens, with their long tables and bench seats, are no exception. Simply ask if there is free space - *Platz frei*. However, never sit down at a *Stammtisch* even if it is completely empty – it is a table reserved for members of a society or group and sitting there is by membership or invitation only.

The **Augustiner Gaststätten**, Neuhauser Straße 27, ☎ 089-2318-3257, is probably the most famous beer hall in Munich after the Hofbräuhaus. The Augustiner beer was brewed here up to 1885. Parts of the building are Art Nouveau, and the beer garden is particularly pleasant. (€-€€)

The **Paulaner im Tal**, Tal 12, ☎ 089-219-9400, is a nostalgic restaurant with terrace and beer garden serving local cuisine, including a reasonable vegetarian selection and some Austrian dishes. (€-€€)

The **Löwenbräukeller**, Nymphenburger Straße 2, ☎ 089-526-021, is close to the Hauptbahnhof and next to the brewery itself. It has a rustic locale and pleasant beer garden. The food is unapologetically Bavarian. It draws generally fewer foreign tourists than the breweries in the old town area. (€-€€)

Zum Franziskaner, Perusastraße 5, ☎ 089-231-8120, is a pleasant rustic restaurant with large beer garden. The cuisine is international, but includes regional specialties. (€-€€€).

The nearby **Spatenhaus and der Oper**, Residenzstraße 12, ☎ 089-290-7060, is a quieter, slightly upscale locale in a century-old building. It has a number of rooms and serves hearty local cuisine. (€€-€€€)

The **Weisses Bräuhaus**, Tal 7, ☎ 089-290-1380, serves regional cuisine in a building dating from the early 20th century. (€-€€€)

The **Bratwurstherzl**, Dreifältigkeitsplatz 1, ☎ 089-295-113, is a traditional bratwurst restaurant with homemade sausages grilled over beechwood fires. It is at the Viktualienmarkt. (€-€€)

A pleasant similar establishment is the **Nürnberger Bratwurst Glöckl am Dom**, Frauenplatz 9, ☎ 089-295-264. It serves Nürnberger Bratwurst (finger-size grilled sausages) and Bavarian cuisine. Ask for cola to receive the server's assurance, with a pained face, that no cola has ever fouled this fine establishment. (€-€€)

The second-largest beer garden in Munich is at the **Chinesischer Turm** (Chinese Pagoda) in the Englischer Garten. It seats 6,000! You can bring your own food, but not drinks! Several other smaller beer gardens are scattered through the park.

Camping

München Thalkirchen Campingplatz is conveniently located only four km (2.4 miles) from the old town in the Isar Valley. It can be reached in 15 minutes by public transportation and has space for 300 tents, plus 250 RVs or mobile homes. It is open from mid-March to October. Zentralländstrasse 49, 81379 München, ☎ 089-723-1707, fax 089-724-3177.

Campingplatz Nord-West is about two km (1.2 mile) from the Olympiagelände and convenient to both public transportation and Autobahns. There are many shady spots and three lakes for swimming within 800 m (half a mile). It is open year-round. Auf den Schrederwiesen 3, 80995 München, ☎ 089-150-6936, fax 089-1582-0463, www.campingplatz-nord-west.de.

Kapuzinerhölzl - The Tent has been in operation for 30 years. It is a campground for tents only but is best known for its large communal tent for backpackers and youth groups without camping equipment. The quiet location is in a park near Schloss Nymphenburg, but the Hauptbahnhof can be reached in 15 minutes by tram. Sleeping space in the big tent goes for €10. It is open from June to August. In den Kirschen 30, 80992 München, ☎ 089-141-4300, fax 089-175-090, www.the-tent.com.

■ Bavarian Alps

The Bavarian Alps are generally lower than the Austrian and Swiss counterparts but are equally beautiful. The Alps suddenly rise out of green meadows, making any approach from Munich or the north spectacularly beautiful. The mountains are easily reached from Munich by road or rail and are popular for daytrips. The east-west connections in the mountain areas themselves are less well developed and a private car makes traveling much simpler.

In addition to the mountains, the area teams with history and interesting buildings, many lakes and rivers, and countless hiking and cycling opportunities. Many ski resorts are popular with families as slopes are generally less challenging than in neighboring countries.

THE GERMAN ALPINE ROAD

Germany has 150 dedicated tourist vacation roads that crisscross the country supporting various themes. None of these offers more spectacular natural beauty than the German Alpine Road. It runs the full length of the Bavarian Alps from Berchtesgaden near Salzburg to Lindau on the Bodensee. In total, it is 460 km (276 miles) long, but it is possible to take shortcuts through Austria if time is limited. (Refuel when taking shortcuts – gas is currently much cheaper in Austria.) Highlights on this route include **Berchtesgaden**, **Garmisch-Partenkirchen**, **Füssen** with **Schwangau**, and **Lindau**. All of these places, with the possible exception of Lindau, are also easily reached from Munich on day-trips.

Information on the route is available from the **Deutsche Alpenstraße**, Nördliche Hauptstraße 1-3, 83700 Rottach-Egern, ☎ 08022-927-370, www.german-alpine-road.de.

Information Sources

Information on the area is available from two umbrella bodies. For Oberbayern, which includes most of the areas described in this section, contact the Tourismusverbad München-Oberbayern, Postfach 600320, 81203 München, ☎ 089-829-2180, www.oberbayern-toursimus.de. For Allgäu, which includes the areas at Füssen and Schwangau, as well as Lindau, which is described in the Baden-Württemberg chapter, contact the Tourismusverband Allgäu/Bayerisch-Schwaben, Fuggerstraße 9, 86150 Augsburg, ☎ 0821-450-4010, www.btl.de.

Chiemsee

Chiemsee is the largest lake in Bavaria. It is a popular vacation area but foreign visitors come mainly on day-trips from Munich to see King Ludwig's Schloss Herrenchiemsee.

Information Sources

Tourist Office: Chiemsee-Tourismus, Felden 10, 83233 Bernau, ☎ 08051-965-550, www.chiemsee.de.

Transportation

Chiemsee is easily reached by road or rail. Trains from Munich run hourly to Prien. From May to September, an original steam tram engine with wagons from 1887 operates between Prien train station and the boat landing. A shuttle bus operates on the same route all year.

The lake is next to the Autobahn A8, about an hour's drive from Munich or 30 minutes from Salzburg. Although ferry services are available from several towns, the most frequent and shortest rides to the islands are from Prien.

Sightseeing

The main attractions in the area are on the two largest islands in the lake: Herrenchiemsee (Men's) and Frauenchiemsee (Women's) islands. These are named after the monastery and nunnery that were originally on the islands. Both islands are traffic-free and easily reached by frequent boat from Prien.

■ Herrenchiemsee

The Herrenchiemsee Island is the more famous and popular because King Ludwig II erected the magnificent **Schloss Herrenchiemsee** (New Palace), 83209 Herrenchiemsee, ☎ 08051-68-870, www.herren-chiemsee.de, here in the late 19th century. Ludwig admired his French namesake Louis XIV. They were equally vain, but in contrast to the Sun King, Ludwig had no actual power and limited talent. His Schloss Herrenchiemsee was to be the new Versailles. It lacks none of the French palace's pomp or splendor and actually has a Great Hall of Mirrors larger than the original. Only 20 of the rooms were completed, but that alone cost more than Ludwig's two other follies – Schloss Linderhof and Schloss Neuschwanstein – together. Other highlights include the ambassadorial staircase, a huge bath, a dining table that was hoisted from a floor below so the King could eat in complete privacy, and a ceremonial bedroom with a bed of three x 2.6 m (10 x 8½ feet) .

The interior can only be seen on a 40-minute guided tour – frequent English tours are available. Opening hours are daily from April to October 3, 9 am to 6 pm, from October 4 to 31, 9:40 am to 5 pm, and from November to March, 9:40 am to 4 pm. The fountains in the park play daily from May to September, every 15 minutes between 9:35 am and 5:25 pm.

Inside the palace is the **King Ludwig II Museum**. It has exhibits on the king's life and plans. Several more castles were planned in addition to the ones he actually started. The museum also has a section on his friendship with Richard Wagner, with portraits and stage sets. Opening hours are daily from April to October 3, 9 am to 6 pm, from October 4 to 31, 10 am to 5:45 pm, and from November to March, 10 am to 4:45 pm.

In the **Altes Schloss** (Old Palace) is the Museum im Augustiner-Chorherrenstift Herrenchiemsee (Museum in the Augustinian Monastery), 83209 Herrenchiemsee, ☎ 08051-68-870, www.herren-chiemsee.de. A Benedictine monastery was founded on the island in the eighth century, but replaced in 1130 by an Augustinian Order. The current palace was later remodeled in a Baroque style. It was secularized in 1803 and King Ludwig stayed here after acquiring the island in 1873. The museum has an exhibition on the history of the island as well as the history of the German constitution – an early constitutional convention met here in 1948. An art gallery has 80 paintings by Munich artist Julius Exeter (1863-1939). Opening hours are daily from April to October 3, 9 am to 6 pm, from October 4 to 31, 10 am to 5 pm, and from November to March, 10 am to 4 pm. The Julius Exeter collection is closed from November to March. Admission is €2.50, but is included in the combination ticket with the New Palace.

VISITORS' INFORMATION

Admission to the island and parks is free. A combination ticket of €6.50 gives access to the Herrenchiemsee (New) Palace, King Ludwig II Museum, and the Museum in the Old Palace (Monastery). The latter can also be seen separately for €2.50.

The former Augustinian Monastery is right at the boat landing. It is now a hotel and has a large restaurant. The new palace is a pleasant 15-minute stroll from here. Cars and bicycles are banned from the island.

■ Frauenchiemsee

Frauenchiemsee has 300 inhabitants and is famous for both its nunnery and its smoked fish. The monastery was founded in 766 by the last Agilolfinger Duke Tassilo III. It became an Imperial Monastery during the reign of Charlemagne. Irmengard, daughter of German King Ludwig the German, once served as abbess. The monastery was secularized in 1803, but King Ludwig I later opened a new Benedictine Monastery. The monastery is still in operation, with the nuns running a popular conference center.

In addition to the Baroque monastery, the main sight on the island is the thousand-year-old Romanesque church. Its freestanding, onion-domed campanile was erected in the 11th century as the first high building in southern Bavaria. During the 1950s, frescoes dating back to 1130 were rediscovered. The nearby Carolingian **Torhalle** (Gate Portal, below), Frauenchiemseestraße 41, ☎ 08054-7256, is one of the oldest buildings in Bavaria and has an angel cycle painted in 860. There is an exhibition of mainly medieval art works and it's open daily from May to October, 11 am to 6 pm. Admission is €1.50.

Adventures

■ On Foot

Although the lake is in a relatively flat area, the Alps provide a beautiful backdrop. Many dedicated hiking paths exist but hiking on the two islands is particularly pleasant. Bicycles are not allowed on Herrenchiemsee.

■ In the Air

Hot-air balloon rides are available in the region from **Manfred Szemborski**, Mailinger Weg 5, 83233 Hittenkrichen-Bernau, ☎ 08051-4381, or from **Jonathan Ballooning**, Max-Kurz-Straße 3, Chieiming, ☎ 08664-927-614, www.jonathan-ballooning.de.

For tandem parachute jumps, contact **Flugschule Chiemse**e, Dreilindenweg 7, 83229 Aschau, ☎ 08052-9494, www.flugschule-chiemsee.de.

■ On Water

Wassersport Zentrum Seebruck, Ludwig-Thoma-Straße 1, 83358 Seebruck, ☎ 08667-8710, rents various kinds of boats, including canoes, kayaks, rowing, pedal, and electric motorboats.

Sailboats and yachts can be chartered from **Yachtenmeltl**, Chiemseestraße 65, 83233 Bernau, ☎ 08051-965-530, www.yachten-meltl.de.

Chiemsee Schifffahrt, Seestraße 108, 83209 Prien, ☎ 08051-6090, www.chiemsee-schifffahrt.de, operates ferries from Prien to the island of Herrenchiemsee and continues to Frauenchiemsee. Boats depart year-round every 20 minutes.

Where to Stay & Eat

■ Herrenchiemsee Island

It is possible to spend the night on King Ludwig's traffic-free island. Unfortunately, the opulent palace is not available, but the **Schlosshotel Herrenchiemsee** is in a mansion older than Ludwig's fantasy palace. Rooms are comfortable, but not particularly luxurious or spacious. The restaurant (€€-€€€) is famous for its fish dishes and is only a few minutes walk from the boat landing. The hotel is open from Easter to October; the restaurant is open all year. 83209 Herrenchiemsee, ☎/fax 08051-1509, www.schlosshotel- herrenciemsee.com. (€€-€€€)

■ Fraueninsel

Hotel zur Linde, on the car-free Fraueninsel, is one of the oldest hotels in Bavaria. It was long favored by artists and has simple, bright rooms. The historic restaurant **Fischerstüberl** (€€-€€€) serves mainly fish. 83256 Chiemsee-Fraueninsel, ☎ 08054-90-366, fax 08054-7299, hotel.linde.fraueninsel@t-online.de. (€€€)

■ Prien

The **Yachthotel Chiemsee** is idyllically located on the lake with views of the Herrenchiemsee Island. The small yacht harbor is directly in front of the hotel. Rooms are comfortably furnished and most have lake views. The honeymoon suite is spread over three floors. The hotel has several restaurant options but the **See-Restaurant** (€€-€€€) is the best, serving nouvelle cuisine with strong regional and French influences. The **Café** (€-€€), with a terrace, has pleasant views too. Yacht charters are available. Harrasser Straße 49, 83209 Prien-Harras, ☎ 08051-6960, fax 08051-5171, www.yachthotel.de (€€€-€€€€)

The **Hotel Bayerischer Hof** is in the heart of the town. It has a rustic ambience and comfortable rooms furnished with oak furniture. The restaurant (€-€€) serves hearty local cuisine. Bernauer Straße 3, 83209 Prien, ☎ 08051-6030, fax 08051-62-917, www.bayerischerhof-prien.de. (€€)

The **Mühlberger** restaurant, Bernauerstraße 40, ☎ 08051-966-888, serves nouvelle cuisine and regional dishes. It has wood-paneled walls and an elegant ambiance. The service and wine list are excellent, as befits a Michelin star establishment. (€€-€€€)

■ Camping

Various campgrounds are scattered around the lake and region. Two of the best are in Prien.

Panoramacamping Harras is quietly and beautifully located on a small peninsula near Prien. It has wonderful views of the lake. The site has 180 spaces, many with shade. Facilities are very good. The site is open from mid-April to mid-October. Harrasser Straße 135, 83209 Prien am Chiemsee, ☎ 08051-90-460, fax 08051-904-616, www.camping-harras.de.

Camping Hofbauer is at the southern edge of Prien, 1.5 km (.9 mile) from the lakeshore. It has excellent facilities and 120 spaces. Bicycle rental is available on-site. It is open from April to October. Bernauerstraße 110, 83209 Prien am Chiemsee, ☎ 08051-4136, fax 08051-62-657, www.camping-prien-chiemsee.de.

Berchtesgaden

The Berchtesgaden area is one of the most beautiful parts of Germany. The Alps are a constant presence, the towns are small and picturesque, and the natural beauty is serene. The area is very popular in the high season of July and August with families, in autumn for hikers and cyclists, and from December to March with winter sports fans.

In addition to outdoor pursuits, the area is also infamous as the favored retreat of Adolf Hitler. Although most of the buildings erected by the Nazis as holiday villas for the top leaders have been destroyed, some interesting sites survived, including bunkers and Hitler's Eagles Nest.

The **Watzmann peak**, at 2,713 m (8,899 feet) Germany's second-highest, forms the backdrop to many parts of Berchtesgaden. It is particularly impressive where it drops 1,800 m (5,900 feet) almost straight into the beautiful Königssee Lake.

Information Sources

Tourist Office: Berchtesgaden Tourismus, Königssee Straße 2, 83471 Berchtesgaden, ☎ 08652-967-270, www.berchtesgadener-land.com.

Transportation

Public transportation is available to all parts of the region, making non-circular hiking trips easy. In addition, many transportation modes are geared for easy connections, e.g., from bus to cable car to boat. Except for the high season, driving is a very pleasant option too, with ample parking lots at major attractions.

From Munich, at least hourly **trains** take 2½ hours and require a changeover at Freilassing, or change in Salzburg to a bus.

By **car**, the fastest way from Munich to Berchtesgaden is along the Autobahn A8 passing through Austria at Salzburg. However, do note that an Austrian highway vignette is required. This is a toll-sticker you must purchase in order to use the highway. Otherwise turn off at Bad Reichenhall and use the beautiful country road.

Sightseeing

■ Berchtesgaden

Berchtesgaden has a lovely old town with an interesting schloss and museum. However, the indoor sights here are best left for bad weather days. They are interesting, but the natural beauty of the area has much more to offer.

THE VACATION TICKET

Overnight guests in the Berchtesgaden area have to pay spa taxes. These allow some free and reduced admission prices. However, the best deal is the Urlaubsticket (Vacation Ticket) – it costs €15 and allows unlimited transportation for five days on the RVO local bus network. Included in this deal are buses to the Roßfeld area, Salzburg, Bad Reichenhall, and Schönau-Königssee, among others.

The **Königliches Schloss Berchtesgaden** (Royal Palace), Schlossplatz, ☎ 08652-947-980, www.haus-bayern.com, was a monastery from the 12th century up to secularization in 1803. Thereafter it became a royal residence and still has the art collection of Crown Prince Rupprecht. The interior can only be seen on a 50-minute guided tour that includes 30 rooms. Most are furnished with Renaissance or Baroque furniture and art. Opening hours are Sunday to Friday from Pentecost to mid-October, 10 am to noon and 2 to 4 pm. From mid-October to Pentecost, it is open weekdays only for tours at 11 am and 2 pm. Admission is €7 – steep when compared to the Residenz in Munich.

Very popular with children is the **Salzbergwerk** (Salt Mines), Bergwerkstraße 83, ☎ 08652-6002, www.salzbergwerk-berchtesgaden.de. The mine was in operation from 1517 and brought great wealth to the region. Tours include a barge ride on the lighted underground salt lake. Opening hours are daily from May to mid-October, 9 am to 5 pm. From mid-October to April, it is open from Tuesday to Saturday, noon to 3 pm. Admission is €12.50.

Maria Gern has a famous Wahlfahrtskirche (pilgrims church) seen on all postcards and brochures about the region. It was built in 1709 and has a rich interior. It is reached via narrow, but well-signposted, country roads. Parking at the church is limited, but it is the setting that attracts visitors more than anything else. The interior is rich but usually fenced of and can be seen in minutes.

■ Obersalzberg

In the 1920s, following release from prison for his attempted coup d'état in Munich, Adolf Hitler settled in Obersalzberg outside Berchtesgaden. After he came to power in 1933, the area became a second seat of government. His house, the Berghof, was enlarged and other senior party leaders acquired properties in the area. Locals, including party faithful, were forced off their land.

Virtually all the buildings were destroyed by the allies during or shortly after the war. However, a **Documentation Center Obersalzberg**, Salzbergstraße 41, 83471 Berchtesgaden, ☎ 08652-947-960, www.obersalzbergweg.de, opened in 1999 to explain the role of the area in the Nazi regime. Unfortunately, virtually all the information is in German only, although the photos and videos are graphic. English audio guides are available. Of more interest is the bunker complex that was constructed to protect the leadership during air raids. A vast complex of tunnels gave access to the outlying properties. Opening hours are Tuesday to Sunday from April to October, 9 am to 5 pm, and from November to March, 10 am to 3 pm. Admission is €2.50. A large parking lot is available at the center and Bus 38 from Berchtesgaden station stops here too.

Under the leadership of Martin Bormann, a "diplomatic house" was erected on the Kehlstein peak (1,834 m/6,000 feet) as a 50th birthday gift from the party to Adolf Hitler. In German this building, with absolutely stunning views, is known as the **Kehlsteinhaus**, www.kehlstein.info. In English, it is generally known as the **Eagle's Nest** – a term never used by the Nazis. Hitler never liked the place much – officially, he thought the elevator mechanism on top of the building would act as a lightening rod. Unofficially, some thought he suffered from vertigo, while there is also evidence that he thought the British might bomb it. Ironically, when the Berghof complex was bombed at the end of the war, it was apparently so small that they missed it.

It is possible to hike up to the top, but it is easier to take the shuttle bus from behind the Documentation Center. The access road, open only to the shuttle buses, is an incredible feat of engineering. From the bottom, it climbs 700 m (2,296 feet) over a distance of 6½ km (39 miles), making only a single turn in the process. From the upper bus station, a tunnel was carved 124 m (404 feet) though solid rock before an elevator sweeps visitors up another 124 m in 41 seconds. The elevator is the 1930s original. The whole project was completed in an impressive 13 months – Bormann never had to bother with accounting or budgets.

At the top, in the former diplomatic guesthouse, is a **restaurant**, ☎ 08652-2969, serving mostly local dishes. The views from here are magnificent and do not really improve on the short hike to the slightly higher peak. Note the absence of safety railing – in Germany *not* falling off a mountain remains the individual's responsibility.

It is necessary to make return reservations on arrival at the top bus station. Ignore the recommended times. Even if you have a drink at the top, it is hard to spend more than an hour. Opening hours are mid-May to October, but depend on snowfall. The bus and elevator round-trip cost €12.

The only sanctioned tour of the Kehlsteinhaus is in English and offered by **Eagle's Nest Tours**, Vorbergstrasse 12, 83471 Schönau, ☎ 08652-64-971, www.eagles-nest-tours.com. The tour usually departs daily at 1:30 pm from the Berchtesgaden Visitors' Center. Reservations are required.

■ Königssee

In 1978, the **Alpine National Park** was formed to protect the natural beauty of the area around the Königssee and Watzmann peak in Schönau. Nothing at the entrance to the park reveals any of the beauty that lies beyond the tollgate-like entrance, enormous parking lot, and the street of kitsch souvenir shops that leads to the lake.

Once at the water itself, things improve quickly. The **Königssee** (King's Lake) is Germany's cleanest, with water of drinking quality. This eight-km (6.4-mile) long, at most 1.2-km (.7-mile) wide, and up to 190-m (600-foot) deep lake is almost fjord-like and surrounded by mountains. The Watzmann rises 1,800 m (5,904 feet) straight up from the lake to form a wall on its eastern shore. It is impossible to hike around the lake, as much of the bank is sheer rock walls. Electric boats operate on the lake with a round-trip taking two hours.

The most popular stop is at the **St Bartholomä** enclave, about halfway down the lake. The first Wahlfahrtskirche St Bartholomä (Pilgrims Chapel) was erected in 1134. This Romanesque church was con-

verted to the present Baroque structure between 1698 and 1710. The triple apse is one of the most photographed buildings in Germany. It is best seen from the lake when all three round apses can be seen in equal proportion shortly before landing. You can also see it from several viewing points in the region such as Jenner and Kehlstein. This was a favored hunting area for the rulers of Berchtesgaden in the 18th century and the Bavarian royals in the 19th century. A popular hike is the two-hour round-trip to see the ice chapel. St Bartholomä can only be reached by boat or by hiking across the lake when it occasionally freezes over in winter.

At the far end of the lake is the **Salet** stop. From here, it is a 15-minute hike to see the spectacularly located, small **Obersee Lake**. Also visible from here are the 400-m (1,300-foot) **Röthbach waterfalls**.

Where to Eat: In the larger building attached to the chapel is the **St Bartholomä Historische Gaststätte**, 83471 Schönau am Königssee, ☎ 08652-964-937. It serves traditional hearty food. There is space for 370 with an additional 540 seats outdoors. (€-€€)

■ Ramsau

Ramsau is a lovely, traditional mountain village with wooden houses, guided streams, all set-off against the Alps. The **Kirche Ramsau** (Church) is beautifully located similar to Maria Gern and one of the most often photographed buildings in the region. However, this church dates from 1512 and parking is no problem.

The **Hintersee** just outside the town is a popular lake for swimming and rowing in summer. The area is particularly popular with hikers and the forest to the east of the lake is known as the **Zauberwald** (Enchanted Forest). In winter, wild animals of the national park are fed here.

These winter-feedings are particularly popular with children and take place at the Hintersee, a 15-minute walk from the parking lot. Exact dates and times are available from the tourism office.

Cultural Events & Festivals

A wide range of musical events are arranged to entertain visitors at night. They range from classical music to traditional folk music and can be either professional or local amateur performances. The tourism office has schedules and can usually make reservations.

Each spring, the cattle of the region still go up the mountain to special meadows, the Alms. A major event is the Almabtrieb, when the cows return to the valley. Cows are dressed in colorful headgear that can be up to 1.5 m (five feet) high. The headgear is a sign of good fortune. After a death or severe bad luck in the family, no decorations are used. The dates depend on the weather, but usually are between mid-September and the end of October.

Shopping

Lederhosen and other *Trachten* (traditional dress) items can be bought from **Franz Stanassinfer**, Marktplatz 10, 83471 Berchtesgaden, ☎ 08652-2685.

Schönauer Krippenställe, Vorbergstraße 23, 83471 Schönau, ☎ 08652-5375, www.weihnachtskrippen-online.de, produces and sells Christmas nativity scenes and other wood-carved items.

Adventures

■ On Foot

Berchtesgaden has about 200 km (120 miles) of marked hiking routes. Good hiking maps are available from the tourist office and hotels. On many routes are huts and restaurants – opening times are available from the tourist office or at www.huettenwirte.com.

Some of the most popular hikes are in the **Alpen National Park**, which includes the **Königssee** area and the **Watzmann peak**. The park has good hiking routes but note that it is strictly forbidden, and dangerous, to wander off the marked trails.

From the National Park parking lot in Schönau, a one-hour circular route leads to the **Malerwinkel** (Painter's Corner), from where beautiful panoramas of the lake as well as St Bartholomä can be enjoyed.

From St Bartholomä, it is a two-hour round-trip walk to the **Ice Chapel**. The shape and size of the chapel depends on the season.

Several interesting routes are available from the stops along the **Jennerbahn cable car route**. Hikes range from easy one-hour walks to challenging eight-hour hikes in the alpine peaks. Walking downhill from the middle station takes 90 minutes.

A popular long-distance hike is the 160-km (96-mile) **Alpen-Weitwanderweg**. It is divided into seven stages of between five and eight hours each. If the total route is done, an altitude difference of 5,200 m (17,056 feet) is overcome in 40 hours. The route is partly in Austria. It is open from May to October. Maps and other details are available from the tourism offices.

The tourism office in Schönau, Rathausplatz 1, ☎ 08652-1760, www.koenigssee.com, conducts guided hikes, usually on Tuesday mornings. Other guided hikes are also available – schedules are available from any tourist office in the region.

Bergschule Watzmann, Am Forstamt 3, 83486 Ramsau, ☎ 08657-711, www.bergschule-watzmann.de, offers a wide range of **mountain climbs and walks** in the region. Climbs for families and children are also available.

Outdoor Club, Am Gmundberg 7, 83471 Berchtesgaden, ☎ 08652-97-760, www.outdoor-club.de, offers guided climbs of the Watzmann and other peaks. Overnight hikes with sleeping in mountain huts are also available.

■ On Wheels

Most of the Berchtesgaden area is fantastic to **drive** in with marvelous views of the mountains. However, the **Roßfeld Panorama Straße** (Panorama Road) is in a class of its own. It reaches an altitude of 1,600 m (5,500 feet), making the Roßfeld road the highest public road in Germany. En route, ample parking areas allow drivers to enjoy safely the marvelous panoramas. It is open all year, but a small toll is payable. It starts a few km past the Documentation Center Obersalzberg and ends near Berchtesgaden.

The area is famous for its mountains and it should come as no surprise that **cycling** routes are available with altitude differences of up to 2,000 m (6,600 feet). However, it is also possible to enjoy cycling on relatively flat routes. Good cycling maps are available from the tourist information offices or bookstores.

Many hotels and holiday homes have bicycles for guests. Rentals are also available from **M&R Brandner**, Bergwerkstraße 52, Berchtesgaden, ☎ 08652-1434; **M& R Brandner**, Im Tal 64, Ramsau, ☎ 08657-790; and **BGD Radl Verleih**, Am Rehwinkl 3, Schönau, ☎ 08652-96-870, delivers to hotels. Bicycles may be taken for free on local trains.

Many a German spouse or partner with no interest in hiking, skiing, or other outdoor pursuits has been forced to accompany their better-halves to Berchtesgaden. People who tire of the mountains quickly will be happy to know that a wide range of **day-trips by bus** are available to alternative destinations. **Omnibus Biller**, Zentrale Schönau, ☎ 08652-95-660, and **Bus Schweiger**, Vorbergstraße 5, Schönau, ☎ 08652-2525, www.bus-schwaiger.de, operate day-trips with different destinations most days of the week. The most popular destinations include Salzburg, Munich, and Chiemsee, but trips to Vienna and even Venice are also possible.

Eagle's Nest Tours, Vorbergstrasse 12, 83471 Schönau, ☎ 08652-64-971, www.eagles-nest-tours.com, offers an English-language tour of Salzburg and the *Sound of Music* sights in the region. The tour is usually run Monday to Saturday from 8:30 am to 12:30 noon. Participation is restricted to eight persons and reservations are required.

■ In the Air

Hot-air balloon flights and tandem **paragliding** are offered by **Outdoor Club**, Am Gmundberg 7, 83471 Berchtesgaden, ☎ 08652-97-760, www.outdoor-club.de.

A popular **cable car** is the **Jennerbahn**, Jennerbahnstraße 18, Schönau, ☎ 08652-95-810, www.jennerbahn.de. In less than half an hour, two-seater gondolas lift passengers up to 1,800 m (5,900 feet) altitude. A 10-minute walk leads to the top of the plateau and affords a view that includes 100 German and Austrian Alpine peaks. Walking down from the halfway station requires about 90 minutes. The cable car operates daily from May to September, 9 am to 5 pm. The round-trip fare is €18.

The **Obersalzbergbahn**, ☎ 08652-2561, www.obersalzbergbahn.de, ascends to 1,000 m (3,280 feet) above sea level. At this point there are several marked hiking routes with little or no further variations in altitude. The car operates daily from 9 am to 5:20 pm. Round-trip journeys are €7.50.

The steep mountain cliffs make for excellent **paragliding**. Several companies offer tandem flights and **parachuting**: **Aero-Taxi Watzmann**, ☎ 0171-894-6394, www.aero-taxi.de; **Flieg mit Para-Taxi**, ☎ 08652-948-450; **Gleitschirm-Taxi**, ☎ 0171-314-2898; and **Tandem Flight Fun**, ☎ 0171-616-9048.

■ With Horses

Horse-drawn carriage rides are available from **Werner Zeininger**, Hochbahnstraße 13, 83471 Schönau, ☎ 08652-63-255, or from **Familie Koller**, Salzburger Straße 41, 83471 Berchtesgaden, ☎ 08652-2360, www.kilianhof.de. **Familie Maul**, Am Rehwinkl 1, 83741 Schönau, ☎ 08652-61-441, offers nighttime rides, usually on Wednesdays at 7 pm from the Schönau tourism office.

Horseback riding in the countryside for experienced riders is available from Monday to Saturday at **Reiter- und Lamahof-Phönix**, ☎ 08652-948-485, www.lamahof-phoenix.de.

■ On Water

Fishing is possible in certain streams and lakes. The **Hintersee** in Ramsau is particularly popular. The season is generally from May to September – fishing after dark is not allowed. Contact the tourist information office for details and permits.

Rowboats can be rented without reservation on the Königssee and Hintersee lakes.

Bayerische Seenschifffahrt, ☎ 08652-963-618, www.bayerische-seenschifffahrt.de, operates a fleet of 19 electric **motorboats** on the Königssee. Boats operate daily from May to late October, starting at 8 am and following at 30-minute intervals. From late October to April, boats depart at least hourly from 9:50 am onwards. Round-trip journeys to Salet are €13.80

and to St Barholomä €10.80. It is wise to take the earlier boats and, in summer, discounts are offered for departures before 9 am. Note the final return time of the day – missing it either means spending the night in the open, or paying an enormous fee to charter a special boat.

Occasionally, night cruises are available on the Königssee to St Bartholomä. They are combined with a dinner in the restaurant and a concert in the chapel. Exact dates and schedules are available from the Bayerische Seenschifffahrt.

■ On Snow & Ice

Skiing

The Berchtesgaden area has 50 km (30 miles) of Alpine skiing slopes at altitudes of 600-1,874 m (1,968-6,146 feet). For **cross-country skiers**, 61 km (36 miles) of trails are available, and **winter hikers** can enjoy up to 120 km (72 miles) of cleared winter hiking paths.

For updates on actual snow conditions, dial the **Schneetelefon** (snow telephone), ☎ 08652-967-297. The season is generally from December to April.

The **Königssee-Jenner** ski area, ☎ 08652-95-810, www.jennerbahn.de, in Schönau can transport up to 3,500 skiers per hour. 11 km (six miles) of prepared slopes are available with lengths up to 3.1 km (1.8 miles) and drops to 600 m (1,950 feet). Most slopes are classified as intermediate difficulty. A day ski-pass is €25, with cheaper options available for families and multiple days.

The **Roßfeld ski area**, ☎ 08652-3538, www.rossfeld.info, has the highest probability of natural snow of all skiing areas in the region. It is at 1,600 m (5,248 feet) and easily reached on public transportation. The area is popular with families, as it has just over seven km (4.2 miles) of beginners' level slopes and 2 km (1.2 miles) of intermediate. The lifts operate daily from 10 am to 4 pm, with floodlit skiing on Wednesday from 6:30 to 9:30 pm. Day-passes are €12.50.

The **Hochschwarzeck** ski area, ☎ 08567-368, www.jennerbahn.de/hsb.htm, in Ramsau is also popular with families. The four main slopes are between 500 and 2,500 m (1,640-8,200 feet) – all rated beginners' level. The long **tobogganing** course is also popular – rental equipment is available. The lifts operate daily from 9 am to 4 pm. Day-passes are €16.

In **Schönau**, four **cross-country skiing** courses are available ranging from two to four km (1.2-2.4 miles) each. **Ramsau** has five courses between one and six km (.6-3.6 miles) long. However, the best area for cross-country skiing is **Aschauer Weiher**, with eight courses ranging from two to nine km (1.2-5.4 miles) – some are classified very difficult and one is a skating route.

Several **ski schools** (downhill and snowboarding) operate in the area – all those listed below also rent out equipment. Five-day group courses cost €90 for adults for four hours per day. **Ski- und Snowboardschule Jenner-Königssee**, Franz Graßl, ☎ 08652-66-710; **Skischule Schönau**, Skilift Kohlhiasl, Oberschönauerstraße, ☎ 08652-948-406, www.skischoenau.de; **Skischule Berchtesgaden**, Schornstraße 34, ☎ 08652-61-197.

Bobsledding

The bobsledding course at Berchtesgaden was the world's first artificial ice course when it opened in 1969. It is 1,500 m (4,900 feet) long with 18 turns and is still considered one of the most challenging in the world.

It is possible to hurtle down this course in a Bob-Raft – less high-tech, and much less slick-looking than a real bobsled. In the Gästebob, three passengers join a professional for a 1,300-m (4,264-foot) downhill ride reaching speeds up to 85 km/h (50 mph). Each ride is €30. Information and reservations through the **Verkehrsamt Schönau**, Rathausplatz, Schönau, ☎ 08652-1760.

On most weekends from November to February, it is also possible to be a passenger in a real four-seater bobsled, with professional pilot and co-pilot supplied by **Rennbob-Taxi Königssee**, ☎ 08652-95-880. No running start, but everything else is the real thing. These rides cost €80.

Ice Skating

The **Eishalle Berchtesgaden**, An der Schießstätte, ☎ 08652-61-405, is open for ice skating during winter, from late September to April, on weekdays from 10 am to 12:30 pm and 2 to 4:30 pm, on weekends from 2 to 4 pm and 8 to 10 pm. Rental skates are available on-site. Admission is €3.

Ice skating is also allowed on the Hintersee and Böcklwieher lakes when sufficiently frozen.

Winter Hiking

Up to 120 km (72 miles) of **hiking routes** are cleared to allow safe hiking in winter.

Alpine tours in the upper mountain areas are possible for experienced mountaineers or in the company of mountain guides.

Where to Stay & Eat

■ Berchtesgaden

Hotel Vier Jahreszeiten is at the edge of town close to the station. Rooms are comfortable with dark and light wood furniture. South-facing rooms have excellent views of the mountains. The restaurant **Hubertusstuben** (€€-€€€) serves local and international dishes. Maximilianstraße 20, 83471 Berchtesgaden, ☎ 08652-9520, fax 08652-5029, www.berchtesgaden.com/vier-jahreszeiten. (€€-€€€)

Hotel Rosenbichl is quietly located outside the town in the National Park. The rooms are modern and have great views. The whole hotel is non-smoking. It operates its own ski school. Rosenhofweg 24, 83471 Berchtesgaden, ☎ 08652-94-400, fax 08652-944-040, www.hotel-rosenbichl.de (€€)

Alpenhotel Denninglehen is set quietly along the Roßfeld ring road and has spectacular views. (It is at 900 m/2,952 feet, as opposed to Berchtesgaden's altitude of 540 m/1,771 feet.) Rooms are spacious and partly furnished with traditional hand-painted furniture. The rustic dinner-only restaurant (€€) serves international cuisine. Am Priesterstein 7, 83471 Berchtesgaden-Oberau, ☎ 08652-5085, fax 08652-64-710, www.denninglehen.de. (€€-€€€)

■ Schönau am Königssee

Hotel Alpenhof is idyllically located at 700 m (2,296 feet) in a green area with meadows and forests. Most of the comfortable rooms have balconies and mountain views. Richard-Vos-Straße 30, 83471 Schönau, ☎ 08652-6020, fax 08652-64-399, www.alpenhof.de. (€€€-€€€€)

Hotel Zechmeisterlehen is at the edge of the town surrounded by a large meadow. Most rooms have balconies and mountain views. The hotel has an indoor and outdoor swimming pool. Wahlstraße 35, 83471 Schönau, ☎ 08652-9450, fax 08652-945-299, www.zechmeisterlehen.de. (€€-€€€)

The quiet **Stolls Hotel Alpina** is inside a large garden. It is a typical Alpine resort building. The rustic restaurant (€-€€) serves regional and international dishes. Dinner reservations are recommended. Ulmenweg 14, 83471 Schönau, ☎ 08652-65-090, fax 08652-61-608, www.stolls.hotl-alpina.de. (€€)

Restaurant Waldhauser-Bräu, Walshauserstraße 12, ☎ 08652-948-943, is a rustic spot with a wide-ranging menu from hearty local dishes to Chinese and Spanish favorites. On weekdays, it is open for dinner only, but on weekends is open from 10 am. (€-€€)

■ Bad Reichenhall

Some of the best accommodations in the region are in Bad Reichenhall. The open border with Austria means that it is only minutes from Salzburg and therefore staying here is also a good option for visitors to the Mozart City.

Hotel Steigenberger Axelmannstein is an excellent first-class grand hotel, beautifully located inside a large park with a small lake open to swimmers. Rooms are luxurious with all modern comforts. The elegant **Parkrestaurant** (€€-€€€), open for dinner only, serves international cuisine, while the more rustic **Axel-Stüberl** (€€) serves mainly local specialties. Salzburger Straße 2-4, 83435 Bad Reichenhall, ☎ 08651-770, fax 08651-5932, www.steigenberger.de. (€€€€)

The nearby **Parkhotel Luisenbad** is also in a park. It is a privately owned hotel with high service standards. Several dining options are available, with the restaurant **Luisenbad** (€€-€€€) praised for its creative regional cuisine. Ludwigstraße 33, 83435 Bad Reichenhall, ☎ 08651-6040, fax 08651-62-928, www.parkhotel.de. (€€€)

Kurhotel Alpina is at the edge of the town. It has comfortable rooms, with either cherry wood or oak furniture. Most have pleasant mountain views. Adolf-Schmidt-Straße 5, 83435 Bad Reichenhall, ☎ 08651-9750, fax 08651-65-393, www.bad-reichenhall.de/hotels/alpina. (€€)

In the Nonn part of town, idyllically located at the edge of the forest on an elevation with excellent views, is the **Hotel Neu-Meran**. It is a privately managed hotel with excellent service standards. The building is a typical Alpine hotel, its balconies filled with geraniums in summer. All rooms face south and have grand views of the valley and the Alps. The elegant, Alpine-style restaurant (€€-€€€) serves regional as well as international cuisine with strong Mediterranean influences. Nonn 94, 83435 Bad Reichenhall, ☎ 08651-4078, fax 08651-78-520, www.hotel-neu-meran.de. (€€€-€€€)

Five km (three miles) west of Bad Reichenhall, at the lovely Thumsee Lake, is the pleasant **Haus Seeblick**. It is a hotel with apartments that are spread over three buildings. Rooms are comfortably furnished. The area is peaceful and has many adventure options. Thumsee 10, 83435 Bad Reichenhall-Karlstein, ☎ 08651-98-630, fax 08651-986-388, www.hotel-seeblick.de. (€€)

■ Ramsau

The **Berghotel Rehlegg** has excellent views of the mountains from its location in the idyllic town of Ramsau. Rooms are nicely furnished with country-style furniture and all have balconies. The stylish restaurant (€€-€€€) serves creative regional dishes. Holzengasse 16-18, 83486 Ramsau, ☎ 08657-98-840, fax 08657-988-4444, www.rehlegg.de. (€€-€€€€)

A lovely place for lunch or coffee is just uphill along the main road from the church. **Gasthof Oberwirt**, Im Tal 86, ☎ 08657-225, is a traditional Alpine restaurant with solid wooden furniture. Hearty local specialties are served. The cakes are good too and the portions huge. (€-€€)

■ Camping

There are a surprising number of campgrounds in the Berchtesgaden vicinity. All the sites listed below are open year-round, but some require prior reservations in the winter season.

Camping Allweglehen is one of the best, with excellent facilities. It has 130 spaces on seven levels with marvelous views. 83471 Bechtesgaden-Salzberg, ☎ 08652-2396, fax 08652-63-503, www.alpen-camping-allweg.de.

Camping Grafenlehen also has excellent facilities and 180 spaces. It is at the beautiful Königssee. Königsseer Fußweg 71, 83471 Berchtesgaden-Königssee, ☎ 08652-4140, fax 08652-690-767, www.camping-grafenlahen.de.

In the same area is **Camping Mühlleiten** with good facilities and 100 spaces. 83471 Berchtesgaden-Königssee, ☎ 08652-4584, fax 08652-69-194, www.camping-muehlleiten.de.

Camping Simonhof in the beautiful village of Ramsau is idyllically located and has good facilities. It has 60 spaces for tourists and 40 for long-term campers. 83486 Berchtesgaden-Ramsau, ☎/fax 08657-284.

Garmisch-Partenkirchen

Garmisch-Partenkirchen is the most visited Bavarian Alpine resort. It became internationally famous after hosting the 1936 Winter Olympic Games and several international competitions since. The town of just under 30,000 is not particularly high – although its altitude is only 720 m (2,370 feet), it is surrounded by Germany's highest mountains. These allow for excellent skiing as well as summer-season hiking.

The town unified only in the early 20th century and the two parts still reflect some differences. Partenkirchen is on the eastern side of the railway line and has a history going back to Roman times. It was long an important station on the trade routes from Italy to Augsburg. Garmisch developed as a Germanic town. Its center is more modern and reflects much of what the modern city-slicker tourists expect of a ski-resort – first-class shopping.

The whole region is stunningly beautiful, with mountain panoramas. Interesting excursions include the amazing Baroque monastery in Ettal, Oberammergau with its woodcarving tradition, King Ludwig II's fabulous Linderhof palace, the Baroque Wieskirche, and, of course, the mountain peaks, including Zugspitze. The sights in Schwangau and Füssen are also easily accessible by car.

Information Sources

Tourist Office: Tourist Information, Richard-Strauss-Platz 2, 82467 Garmisch-Partenkirchen, ☎ 08821-180-700, www.garmisch-partenkirchen.de.

Transportation

Garmisch-Partenkirchen has a good bus system that connects to all sights and adventure areas. Driving is easy in the region and is the quickest way to get to several sights on the same day. It is often sensible to take short-cuts through Austria – where fuel is often significantly cheaper – but stay off the highways or purchase a vignette (a toll-sticker required for driving on the Autobahns.

Garmisch-Partenkirchen can be reached from Munich in 90 minutes on at least hourly trains. Driving along the Autobahn A95 can be slightly faster in light traffic.

Sightseeing

Garmisch-Partenkirchen is in such a lovely area that indoor sights are best left for rainy days. In addition, the excursions are generally more interesting than the sights in the town itself.

In the Garmisch part of town is the **Neue Pfarrkirche St Martin** (New Church), a single-nave church with two half-round chapels. It was erected in 1730-34 in a Rococo style with stuccos and wall paintings. The **Alte Kirche Garmisch** (Old Church) has a Romanesque core (1280), but was altered into a mainly Gothic structure during the 15th century. It has two equal naves with a single central column supporting the Gothic vaulting. Some 15th- and 16th-century wall paintings were preserved. Historic houses are in Loisach, Frühlings, and Kreuzstraße.

Ludwigstraße leads from the Bahnhof eastwards through Partenkirchen. It makes a sharp right turn to become the **Historische Ludwigstraße** (Historic Ludwigstraße) with many early buildings and painted facades. More such buildings are in Sonnenbergstraße and Ballengasse.

The **Werdenfels Museum**, Ludwigstraße 47, ☎ 08821-2134, has an interesting exhibition of masks, furniture and decorative items. It is in a former 17th-century grocer's house – the only building in the street that survived a town fire in 1865 intact. Opening hours are Tuesday to Friday, 10 am to 1 pm and 3 to 6 pm, weekends from 10 am to 1 pm only. Admission is €1.50.

■ Mittenwald

Mittenwald is 25 km (15 miles) east of Garmisch-Partenkirchen. It is generally considered the most picturesque of all Bavarian Alpine villages. Parts of it are straight from tourist brochures and post-cards. Goethe described the town as a living picture book and the attraction remains, despite the huge number of visitors.

The main attractions of Mittenwald are its beautiful location and the Alpine houses, many with painted façades. Hiking, cycling, and skiing are popular activities. The **Karwendel ski area** has Germany's second-highest cable-car route and a seven km (4.2-mile) downhill ski slope.

Mittenwald is also famous for violins. In 1684, Matthias Klotz, a former pupil of Stradivarius, settled here and started the violin-making industry that continues to the present. The **Geigenbau- und Heimatmuseum** (Violin and Local History Museum), Ballenhausgasse 3, ☎ 08823-2522, tells the story. It is open Tuesday to Friday from 10 am to 1 pm and 3 to 6 pm. On weekends, it is open from 10 am to 1 pm. Admission is €2.

■ Ettal

Ettal is a small village 15 km (nine miles) north of Garmisch-Partenkirche. The main sight is **Kloster Ettal** (Monastery), Kaiser-Ludwig-Platz 1, 82488 Ettal, ☎ 08822-740, which is next to the main through road.

In 1330, Emperor Ludwig the Bavarian founded a Benedictine monastery here. The original Gothic church has the only example in Germany of a figure-8 floor plan – it is still the basis of the present church. The monastery was relatively obscure in its first centuries, but became more prominent in the 18th century due to an increase in pilgrims and the foundation of a school. It was then that the monastery and especially the church was converted to a Baroque style. Following a major fire in 1744, the marvelous cupola was added. The interior is an excellent example of Bavarian Baroque excess with the cupola fresco by Johann Jakob Zeiller and some of the stuccos by Johann Baptist Zimmermann. The church is open daily from 8 am to 6 pm.

Part of the monastery is still functioning, brewing an excellent beer and a famous liqueur. Ettal also houses a prestigious private school.

■ Linderhof

Schloss Linderhof, Linderhof 112, 82488 Ettal, ☎ 08822-92-030, fax 08822-920-311, www.linderhof.de, is the only one of Mad King Ludwig's palaces that wasj actually completed. It is the smallest and least pretentious of them all. Still, it uses a wide range of conflicting styles and is over-decorated inside. It probably took the Petit Trianon in Versailles as inspiration. There are many references to French King Louis XIV, with whom King Ludwig became obsessed. Highlights of the interior include the sumptuous bedroom, a magnificent hall of mirrors, and King Ludwig's favorite: a table that could be hoisted from a floor below so he could eat his dinner in peace without servants hovering around.

The Schloss is inside a beautiful, large English-style landscape park with wonderful Alpine backdrops. There are several interesting features in the park. Directly in front of the Schloss is a fountain with a gilded Neptune that spouts water up to 30 m (99 feet) high. King Ludwig bought a Moorish Pavillion and a Moroccan House at world exhibitions in Paris. Several structures are reminiscent of Wagner operas: a grotto of Venus (*Tannhäuser*), a Hundingshütte pavilion (*The Valkyries*), and the Gurnemanzklause hermitage (*Parzifal*).

The Schloss is open daily from April to September, 9 am to 6 pm, and from October to March, 10 am to 4 pm. In winter, the structures in the garden are closed. Admission is €7 (€6 in winter) and includes a compulsory guided tour of the palace available in English . Advance reservations are possible in writing or by fax. Reservations require a small service fee, worth paying when visiting in the high season.

The Schloss is 10 km (six miles) west of Ettal on the B23. It can be reached by car, hiking, cycling, or bus. The B23 is a convenient shortcut through Austria to Füssen. The road is, however, one of the first in the region to close when weather is inclement.

■ Oberammergau

Oberammergau is a small village about 20 km (12 miles) north of Garmisch-Partenkirchen. It is most famous for its Passion Play, but is also a major woodcarving center. The village is pretty but at times commercial and full of religious kitsch.

The town has many painted façades in the local *Lüftlmalerei* style. The theme of the paintings is mostly religious, but some facades feature fairy tales and beer hall scenes. The **Pilatushaus**, Ludwig-Thoma-Straße 10, ☎ 08822-92-310, is a particular good example. It houses a gallery and workshops for carved wood items. Before buying woodcarvings from the wide range of shops in town, see what true skill can produce here. A shop next to the Pilatushaus sells the carvings. Opening hours are weekdays from May to October, 1 to 6 pm. Admission is free.

In 1633, the villagers of Oberammergau made a pledge to perform *Christ's Passion* if the approaching plague passed the town by. The first play was staged in 1634. Now, the ***Passion Play*** is performed every 10 years in a huge open-air theater built for the purpose. 2,000 performers are needed for the 100 performances between May and September. Each one lasts six hours. All actors are amateurs who were either born in Oberammergau or have lived here at least 20 years. The next performance is in 2010 and tickets will go on sale in 2008.

In recent years, the theater has been used in summer to stage major operas such as *Nabucco* and *Aida*. For details, contact **Oberammergau Tourismus**, Eugen-Papst-Straße 9a, 82487 Oberammergau, ☎ 08822-92-310, www.oberammergau.de.

■ Wieskirche

The magnificent Wieskirche (Church in the Meadow), Wies 12, 86989 Steingaden, ☎ 08862-932-930, www.wieskirche.de, is generally seen as the definitive Rococo church in southern Bavaria. This glorious construction in a meadow, literally in the middle of nowhere, is a UNESCO World Cultural Heritage site.

The Wieskirche was designed by master Rococo architect and stucco artist Dominikus Zimmermann (1685-1766). His equally talented brother Jean Baptiste Zimmermann (1680-1758) did much of the interior painting. The exterior is typical of a Rococo church – rather plain and serving mainly to keep the interior from falling apart. Approaching the Wieskirche, from the parking lot a few hundred yards down a gentle hill, the pale yellow exterior reveals nothing of the glorious interior. Inside, the church is oval-shaped with a narrow apse extension. The huge cupola is also oval and ideally suited for the Rococo painting of the Second Coming. The lower parts of the church, associated with earth, are sparsely decorated and mostly white. The upper reaches represent heaven and are typical Rococo with stuccos, paintings, and gilded decorations. The choir is a symphony of frescoes, gilded stuccos and statues, and marble balustrades. Large windows ensure ample light and the church is best appreciated on a sunny day. Opening hours are daily from 8 am to 7 pm, closing at 5 pm in winter. Admission is free.

It is hard to imagine today how so magnificent a church could have been financed by such a small agricultural community. It was all due to a statue of Christ that was considered too pitiful for use in processions. In 1738, a farming couple saw this *Christ in Tears*. Subsequent prayers were answered and the pilgrims and donations started to come in. It currently attracts a million visitors annually. Dominikus Zimmermann saw the church as his greatest accomplishment and spent the last 10 years of his life in a small house almost at its doorstep.

Several series of concerts are held in the church, especially in summer – each sponsored by different organizations. The details are available on the church's English-language website (www.wieskirche.de). The church itself does not have information on these concerts nor does it sell tickets. Entrance to many concerts is free and without reservations.

The Wieskierche is 50 km (30 miles) north of Garmisch-Partenkirchen on a small country lane near Steingaden. It can be reached from Füssen on the RVO bus lines 9715 and 1084.

Cultural Events

Kurkonzerte are held in the Garmisch Kurpark from May to September. The exact schedules are available from the tourist office but concerts are usually daily, except on Friday. The Kurpark Partenkirchen has concerts during summer, usually on Wednesday.

Richard Strauss died in Garmisch-Partenkirchen in 1949. The **Richard Strauss Institute**, Schnitzschulstraße 19, ☎ 08821-910-950, www.richard-strauss-insitute.de, frequently sponsors concerts where his and other composers' music is played.

Shopping

Shopping is a popular activity and the shops reflect what the visitors to the town expect. There are many small boutiques and jewelers for city slickers (in German referred to as *Schiki-Mickis*) and traditional souvenir shops for mainly foreign tourists.

Popular souvenir shops include the **Mall of Bavaria**, Chamonixstraße 6, ☎ 08821-943-467, which sells a wide range of traditional Bavarian products.

Käthe Wohlfahrt, the famous Christmas decorations shop from Rothernburg ob der Tauber, has a branch at Marienplatz 6, Garmisch Partenkirche, and in Obberammergau in Dorfstraße 6 and 25.

Adventures

■ On Foot

Garmisch-Partenkirchen is in a lovely area with many **hiking** opportunities. Popular starting points are at the mountain stations of cable cars. Often walks with spectacular views are possible without strenuous climbs. Excellent hiking maps are available from the tourist information office or any bookshop.

A popular walk is in the **Partnachklamm gorge**. This narrow gorge has bizarre rocks and arcades carved by the thundering Partnach Alpine stream. Take rain gear in summer. It is also open, but mostly frozen, during winter. A round-trip from the Partenkirchen ski area takes 90 minutes.

A similar walk is in the **Höllentalklamm** from Hammersbach towards Zugspitze. A small entrance fee is payable before entering the gorge, about a km (.6 mile) long, with tunnels, arcades, and bridges.

The tourist office arranges guided mountain hikes from mid-June to September on most Tuesdays and Thursdays. The route depends on the weather and details are only available a day prior to the walks.

Mountain guides are available through the **Bergsteigerschule Zugspitze**, Am Gudiberg 7, ☎ 08821-58-999, www.bergsteiger-schule-zugspitze.de. Guided trips from a few hours to several days are available and range from hiking to rock and ice climbing.

■ On Wheels

Bicycle rentals are available in Garmisch-Partenkirchen from **Trek-Pro-Shop**,Rathausplatz 11, ☎ 08821-79-528, www.trekproshop.de, and from **Multi Cycle**, Bahnhofstraße 6, ☎ 08821-948-994, www.multicycle.de. Mountain bikes only are available from **Sport Total**, Marienplatz 18, ☎ 08821-1425, www.agentursporttotal.de.

■ In the Air

Cable Cars

The mountains around Garmisch-Partenkirchen are divided for practical purposes into two main areas: Zugspitze and the Classic area, which includes Alpspitz, Kreueck, Hausberg, and Wank. All the cable cars are operated by Bayerische Zugspitzbahn Bergbahn, Olympiastraße 27, ☎ 08821-7970, www.zugspitze.de.

Zugspitze: At 2,962 m, Zugspitze is Germany's highest mountain with the only glacial skiing area in the country. It is a popular all-year destination.

Other than climbing, the peak can be reached in two ways: via the Bayerische Zugspitzbahn or the Eibsee-Seilbahn. The **Bayerische Zugspitzbahn**, ☎ 08821-7970, is a **cogwheel train** that runs from Garmisch-Partenkirchen via Eibsee to the Gletscherbahnhof (Glacier Station) at 2,590 m (8,500 feet). Part of the journey is in a tunnel carved through the mountain rock. The journey takes 75 minutes from Garmisch-Partenkirchen, or 40 minutes from Eibsee. From the Gletscherbahnhof, the 1,000-m (3,280-foot) **Gletscherbahn** cable car route goes to the Bergstation near the top at 2,950 m (9,676 feet) in four minutes. (€4 one-way if not used in conjunction with the Zugspitzbahn)

A much faster alternative is to take the **Eibsee-Seilbahn**, ☎ 08821-7970, from Eibsee directly to the Bergstation. The large cable car gondolas take only 10 minutes. (Due to the rapid changes in pressure, children under 18 months are not allowed in the gondolas)

Round-trip tickets are €43 in summer and €34 in winter. One-way tickets are €25. A combination of the cable car and train is allowed on the round-trip tickets. The service is available year-round from 8 am to 4:45 pm – longer hours in the high season.

A day ski pass is €34.

The Classic Area: The **Alpspitzbahn** cable car goes from Garmisch to the 2,050-m (6,700-foot) Osterfelderkopf peak in nine minutes. It operates daily from November to February, 8:30 am to 4:30 pm, from March to June, 8:30 am to 5 pm, and from July to October, 8 am to 5:30 pm. Round-trip journeys are €20, or €15 one-way.

The **Hochalmbahn** cable car goes from Hochalm to Osterfeldkopf in four minutes. It operates at the same times as the Alpspitzbahn and costs €4 one-way.

The **Kreuzeckbahn** cable car connects Garmisch and the 1,640-m (5,400-foot) high Kreuzeck in seven minutes. It operates year-round from 8:15 am, with the final ride 15 minutes after the Alpspitzbahn. Round-trip journeys are €16, or €11 one-way.

The **Hausbergbahn** cable car operates only in winter and connects Garmisch with the 1,340-m (4,400-foot) Hausberg in five minutes. Operation hours are daily from November to April, 8:30 am to 5 pm. Round-trip journeys are €11, or €8 one-way.

Combination tickets with hikes between the mountain stations are available. The Kreuzberg-Hausberg combination is €15.50 and requires an hour's hike. An Alpspitz-Rundfahrt combination includes the Alpspitz, Hochalm, and Kreuzeck cable cars with hikes of 30 minutes to an hour between the mountain stations. It costs €23.50.

A day ski pass valid on all Classic area cable cars costs €28.

The **Wankbahn** operates only in summer and connects Partenkirchen with the Bergstation (1,755 m/5,700 feet) on the Wank in 18 minutes. It operates daily from May to November, 8:45 am to 5 pm (4:30 pm in October and November). Round-trip journeys are €16.50, or €11.50 one-way.

HOLIDAY PASS

During the summer season, the Holiday Pass allows free entry to some sights and local transportation as well as one cable car per day in the Classic area. The train or bus can be taken to Eibsee but the final assault on Zugspitze itself is not included. It costs €35 and is available from the tourism office.

Hangliding & Paragliding

Tandem flights are arranged by **Sport Total**, Marienplatz 18, ☎ 08821-1425, www.agentursporttotal.de; **Gleitschirmschule Garmisch-Partenkirchen**, Am Hausberg 8, ☎ 08821-74-260, www.gleitschirmschule-gap.de; and **Aerotaxi**, Beim Gerber, 82481 Mittenwald, ☎ 0171-281-9199, www.aerotaxi.de. Winter and summer flights are available from various peaks in the region.

■ With Horses

Horse-drawn carriage and sleigh rides can be arranged at ☎ 08821-942-920. The postal carriage rides run daily June to September from Richard-Strauss-Platz to the Badersee – reservations through the tourist information office.

■ On Water

During summer, **rowboats** are available for rent without reservations at several lakes, including the Riessersee, Badersee, Eibsee, and Pflegersee.

Wildwasserschule Sprenzel, Alpspitzstraße 16, ☎ 08821-52-033, www.sprenzel-sport.de, arranges white-water **rafting**, canyoning, and kayak trips on the streams in the region (often in Austria).

On Wednesday and Sunday, **Bavaria Raft**, ☎ 08841-676-9870, www.bavariaraft.de, operates three-hour guided rafting trips on the River Loisach from Farchant to Murnau. Reservations are essential. Boat rentals are also available for do-it-yourself trips.

■ On Snow

The ski season is long and lasts from November to May, with Zugspitze's snow usually guaranteed. For actual snow conditions call the snow telephone, ☎ 08821-797-979.

Alpine Skiing

Garmisch-Partenkirchen is one of Germany's premier Alpine skiing areas with 118 km (70 miles) of downhill slopes. Zugspitze is the only glacial skiing area in Germany. The *Kandahar* is Germany's only downhill run with a World Cup License.

If the adjacent Austrian slopes are added, 210 km (126 miles) of downhill runs, serviced by 105 ski lifts and cable cars are available. The **Holiday Pass**, from €83 for three days, gives access to the whole area. Up to 120,000 people per hour can be transported, meaning few lines and short waiting times.

Cross-Country Skiing

For cross-country skiers, 110 km (66 miles) of trails (*Loipen*), both traditional and freestyle, are available for free. Kainzenbad has a floodlit trail.

Ice Skating

Ice skating is possible in the Olympia-Eissport-Zentrum, ☎ 08821-52-578, www.gemeindewerke-garmisch-partenkirchen.de. It is open to the public from July to Easter.

Rental Equipment & Ski Schools

Garmisch-Partenkirchen has many ski schools – all also rent out equipment. Alpine and cross-country ski schools include:

- **Skischule Alpin**, Reintalstraße 8, ☎ 08821-945-676, www.skischulealpin.de.
- **Skischule Garmisch-Partenkirchen**, Am Hausberg 8, ☎ 08821-4931, www.skischule-gap.de.
- **Ski and more 3 – Profiskischulen**, Alpspitzstraße 16, ☎ 08821-58-300, www.ski-and-more3.com.
- **Skischule Sport Total**, Marienplatz 18, ☎ 08821-1425, www.agentursporttotal.de.
- **Skischule Vivalpin**, Hauptstraße 36-38, ☎ 08821-943-0323, www.vivalpin.de.
- **Skischule Flori Wörndle**, Am Hausberg 4, ☎ 08821-58-300, www.skischule-woerndle.de.
- **Erste Skilanglaufschule Garmisch-Partenkirchen**, Olympia-Skistadion, Osteingang, ☎ 08821-1516, www.skilanglauf-schule.de, is a school for cross-country skiing only.
- **Snowboardschule Erwin Gruber**, Mittenwalder Straße 47d, ☎ 08821-76-490, www.snowboard-schule.de, is a school for snowboarding only.

The following companies rent out skiing equipment:

Skiverleih Ostler, at the Hausbergbahn, ☎ 08821-3999; **Welt des Sports**, Fürstenstraße 20, ☎ 08821-72-601, www.skiverleih-garmisch.de; and **Snowboard & Skicenter Zugspitzplatt**, on Zugspitze, ☎ 08821-74-505

Snowshoes can be rented from **Schneeshuh Verleih**, Reintalerstraße 8, ☎ 08821-945-676, www.schneeschuh-verleih.de.

Snowboarding

Some 21 km (12 miles) of slopes are open to snowboarders. The most popular area is on the Zugspitzeplatte. The area is a freestyle paradise with a super pipe, a line with four straight jumps and leaps, and a rail-combo.

Tobogganing

There are several challenging tobogganing courses in the area. **Rodelbahn am Kainzenbad** (1,060-m/3,400 feet long with a 180-m drop) is a natural tobogganing course, Partnachalm and St. Martin am Grasberg are on streets that are not cleared in winter. The longest course with the highest drop is on the Hausberg (3,900 m/12,870 feet and 650-m/2,100-foot drop). First ascend the peak with the cable car and then use the summer hiking trail, which is prepared as a tobogganing course in winter. On Wednesdays from 5 to 8 pm, the cable car is €9 for unlimited rides. Skiverleih Ostler next to the Hausbergbahn rents out equipment, or contact any of the ski schools

Where to Stay & Eat

■ Partenkirchen

Reindl's Partenkirchner Hof is a luxury country-style hotel in the heart of town close to the station. Rooms are romantic, with solid wood furniture. Some are luxurious. Many have balconies with views of the Wetterstein Mountain. The restaurant (€€-€€€) serves local as well as international cuisine and has a long wine list. Reservations are advisable. Bahnhofstraße 15, 82467 Garmisch-Partenkirchen, ☎ 08821-943-870, fax 08821-9438-7250, www.reindls.de. (€€-€€€€)

Post-Hotel Partenkirchen is in the heart of the old town. It has a Baroque façade and the interior combines antiques with modern furniture. Rooms are comfortable and some have great mountain views. Four restaurants (€-€€€) on the premises serve international and regional cuisine. Ludwigstraße 49, 82467 Garmisch-Partenkirchen, ☎ 08821-93-630, fax 08821-9363-2222, www.post-hotel.de. (€€-€€€)

The nearby **Mercure Hotel** is in a small park. It was renovated in 2001 and has modern rooms with typical Alpine wooden furniture. The rustic restaurant (€-€€) serves regional specialties. Mittenwalder Straße 2, 82467 Garmisch-Partenkirchen, ☎ 08821-7560, fax 08821-74-268, www.mercure.de. (€€-€€€)

■ Garmisch

Hotel Zugspitze is a typical Bavarian Alpine hotel with balconies. Rooms have country-style furniture. The hotel is halfway between the station and the Kurpark. Klammstraße 19, 82467 Garmisch-Partenkirchen, ☎ 08821-9010, fax 08821-901-333, www.hotel-zugspitze.de. (€€-€€€€)

Staudacherhof Hotel is a pleasant spot close to the center of town. Some rooms are quite luxurious and spacious. The fitness area is large, with many options. The rustic restaurant (€€-€€€) serves regional cuisine. Höllentalstraße 48, 82467 Garmisch-Partenkirchen, ☎ 08821-9290, fax 08821-929-333, www.staudacherhof.de. (€€€-€€€€)

Clausings Posthotel is in the heart of Garmisch at the edge of the major shopping street. Rooms are individually furnished. Many have views of the Zugspitze. The restaurant (€-€€€) serves regional as well as international cuisine. It has a pleasant terrace as well as a historic bar area. Marienplatz 12, 82467 Garmisch-Partenkirchen, ☎ 08821-7090, fax 08821-709-205, www.clausings-posthotel.de. (€€-€€€)

The small **Aschenbrenner Hotel** is in a quiet 19th-century villa next to the Loisach stream only minutes from the Kurhaus. The comfortable rooms are stylishly furnished and most have good views of the mountains. Loisachstraße 46, 82467 Garmisch-Partenkirchen, ☎ 08821-95-970, fax 08821-959-795, www.hotel-aschenbrenner.de. (€€-€€€)

Hotel Vier Jahreszeiten is a block from the station. It has rooms with solid wood furniture. All rooms have mountain views and some have balconies. The large restaurant (€-€€) is decorated with hunting trophies and serves hearty local dishes. Bahnhofstraße 23, 82467 Garmisch-Partenkirchen, ☎ 08821-9160, fax 08821-4486, www.vierjahreszeiten.cc. (€€)

Restaurant Alpenhof, Am Kurpark 10, ☎ 08821-59-055, serves hearty local dishes as well as Mediterranean cuisine. (€-€€)

■ Oberammergau

Hotel Wittelsbach is a typical Alpine-style building in the center of the town. Rooms are comfortable, with solid wood furniture. The restaurant **Ammergauer Stub'n** (€-€€) serves international cuisine and local specialties. Road noise can be a problem in some rooms. Dorfstraße 21, 82487 Oberammergau, ☎ 08822-92-800, fax 08822-928-0100, www.hotelwittelsbach.de. (€€)

The **Parkhotel Sonnenhof** is at the edge of town and away from the crowds. It is modern, with stylish rooms – each with a balcony. The restaurant (€€-€€€), open for dinner only, serves regional cuisine. König-Ludwig-Straße 12, 82487 Oberammergau, ☎ 08822-9130, fax 08822-3047, www.parkhotel-sonnenhof.de. (€€€)

Hotel Alte Post is in the heart of the town in a 350-year-old building. Rooms are simple but furnished with solid wood furniture and have wooden or stucco ceilings. The restaurant (€-€€) serves Bavarian food. Road noise can be a problem. Dorfstraße 19, 82487 Oberammergau, ☎ 08822-9100, fax 08822-910-100, www.altepost.ogau.de. (€€)

Hotel Landhaus Feldmeier is outside Oberammergau on the road to Ettal. It is in two typical Upper Bavarian buildings with typical geraniums on the balconies. Rooms are furnished in pine and all have either balconies or access to terraces. The restaurant (€€-€€€), open for dinner only, serves regional and seasonal specialties. Ettaler Straße 29, 82487 Oberammergau, ☎ 08822-3011, fax 08822-6631, www.hotel-feldmeier.de. (€€)

■ Ettal

The huge **Hotel Ludwig der Bayer** is run by the Benedictine order. Although there are plenty of carved wooden religious objects in the hotel, life here is anything but monastic. Rooms are comfortably furnished in solid wood furniture. The hotel has a huge restaurant (€€) popular with bus parties, which can mean serious waiting times for service. Kaiser-Ludwig-Platz 10, 82488 Ettal, ☎ 08822-9150, fax 08822-74-480. (€€)

The much smaller **Hotel Zur Post** is on the same square. It is a typical Alpine guesthouse with flowers on the balconies and ample unpainted wood in the interior. The hotel is popular with families. The restaurant (€-€€€) is open for dinner only and serves regional cuisine. Kaiser-Ludwig-Platz 18, 82488 Ettal, ☎ 08822-3596, fax 08822-6399, www.posthotel-ettal.de. (€€)

■ Ettal-Linderhof

Schlosshotel Linderhof is in a quiet location right next to the grounds of Schloss Linderhof and has welcomed guests for well over a century. Rooms are stylishly furnished in typical country style with all modern comforts. The restaurant (€-€€) serves regional specialties. Linderhof 14, 82488 Ettal-Linderhof, ☎ 08822-790, fax 08822-4347, www.schlosshotel-linderhof.de. (€€)

■ Camping

Camping Zugspitze is on the road to Grainau. It has many shady spots but can be noisy. Facilities are rather basic. It has 130 spaces for tourists and 50 for long-term campers. Reservations are required in winter. It is open year-round. Griesener Straße 4, 82491 Garmisch-Grainau, ☎ 08821-3180, fax 08821-947-594.

Much more pleasant are the two campsites near Mittenwald. **Alpen Caravanpark Tennsee** is a five-star site with excellent facilities. It bills itself as the campground with hotel flair. In winter, there is a shuttle bus to the ski areas. It has 267 spaces and is open from mid-December to early November. 82494 Mittenwlad-Klais-Krün, ☎ 08825-170, fax 08825-17-236, www.camping-tennsee.de.

Equally well located, only three km (1.8 miles) outside Mittenwald, is **Naturcamping Isarhorn**. It is in a natural setting with excellent facilities, including 200 spaces for tourists and a further 130 for long-term campers. It is open from mid-December to October. Isarhorn 4, 82481 Mittenwald, ☎ 08823-5216, fax 08823-8091, www.camping-mittenwald.de.

Schwangau & Füssen

Schwangau near Füssen is a small town in an idyllic location that caught the eye of the Bavarian royals during the 19th century. First King Maximilian II built a hunting castle here and then Mad King Ludwig erected the fantasy castle Schloss Neuschwanstein. Visitors come from all over the world to see this magical folly.

Schloss Neuschwanstein attracts 1.3 million visitors annually, making it one of the most popular tourist destinations in Germany. Then there is Schloss Hohenschwangau, where Ludwig spent much of his youth. Although much of the small town near the castles is geared to mass tourism, the area has some outstanding natural beauty, making it worth staying longer than the flood of day-trippers usually do.

Visitors arriving by rail have to pass through the town of Füssen, which has an interesting historical center. It is also generally a good place to spend the night in.

Information Sources

Tourist Office: Tourist Information Schwangau, Münchener Straße 2, 87645 Schwangau, ☎ 08362-81-980, www.schwangau.de.

Transportation

Hourly **trains** connect Munich Hauptbahnhof with Füssen in just over two hours. Some trains require transfers at Buchloe. Hourly trains from Augsburg take just under two hours and often require transfers at Buchloe. From Füssen train station, take **Bus 9713** (marked Königschlösser) to Schwangau. Alternatively, it is a five-km (three-mile) hike from Füssen to Hohenschwangau, or a **taxi** would cost €10.

Limited buses are also available from Füssen and Schwangau to the Wieskirche, Oberammergau, Ettal, and Garmisch-Partenkirchen.

From Munich, a good option would be to consider a guided **bus tour**. It cuts out the hassle of getting tickets in advance and some tours include both Schloss Neuschwanstein and Schloss Linderhof – something that is impossible to do in one day on public transportation. **AutobusOberbayern**, Heidemannstraße 220, www.autobusoberbayern.de,

☎ 089-323-040, offers day-tours that include both castles or just Schloss Neuschwanstein. A more active tour is offered by **Discover Bavaria**, Hochbrückenstraße, ☎ 089-2554-3987, www.mikesbiketours.com. It includes a hike up the Pöllat Gorge, a visit to Schloss Neuschwanstein, a bike tour, and a swim in the lake if weather allows. The tour is available most days from mid-April to September.

By **car**, Füssen is a just over 100 km (60 miles) from Munich and an hour's drive from Garmisch-Partenkirchen.

Sightseeing

■ Schwangau

Visitor Information for the Castles: For decades, visitors to Schloss Neuschwanstein had to walk up to the castle to buy tickets and then line up for hours to join a tour. In the late 1990s, it finally dawned on someone that it would be better to sell tickets in the village with specific tour times and allow visitors to spend more time and money there rather than waiting idly at the castle itself. The clever visitor skips the lines altogether and makes prior reservations.

Tickets can be bought in person or online from **Ticketcenter Neuschwanstein–Hohenschwangau**, Alpseestr. 12, 87645 Hohenschwangau, ☎ 08362-930-830, fax 08362-930-8320, www.ticket-center-hohenschwangau.de. Reserved tickets cost €1.60 extra but are worth it. The tickets need to be picked up at the ticket center but a special counter is set apart for reserved tickets.

Both Schloss Neuschwanstein and Schloss Hohenschwangau are open daily, April to September from 9 am to 5 pm and October to March, 10 am to 4 pm. Admission to each is €9 or €17 for both on the same day.

Schloss Neuschwanstein: This was the ultimate fantasy castle of Mad King Ludwig and was built between 1869 and 1886. It was supposed to resemble a medieval knights' castle and thus follows the Romanesque style to a large extend. It looks magical, high on a hill with it mostly white exterior against the Alpine background. The briefest of glances explains where Disney's castle came from.

The interior, which can only be seen on a guided tour, calls to mind scenes from Wagnerian operas such as *Tannhäuser* and *Lohengrin*. The Singers' Hall is a smaller copy of the one in the Wartburg near Eisenach and its walls are decorated with scenes from *Parzival*. Only about 20 rooms are on view, as the castle was never completed and King Ludwig spent less than six months here.

Several routes lead to the top of the hill where Schloss Neuschwanstein is perched. The most interesting route goes up through the **Pöllatschlucht** (Pöllat Gorge). Others go more directly and are less strenuous. Walking up requires from 20 to 45 minutes depending on the route chosen. It is also possible to take a minibus or horse-drawn carriage to the top.

The best views of the castle are from the **Marienbrücke** (Mary Bridge), which is 45 m (148 feet) above the Pöllat waterfall, and absolutely worth the 15-minute walk from the castle. (Note that the hike that continues on the far side of this bridge is beautiful but takes several hours.)

Schloss Hohenschwangau: The other royal castle in Schwangau, Schloss Hohenschwangau, shown below, was built by Maximilian II in 1832-36. It is a Neo-Gothic building with wall paintings of German sagas. Ludwig spent happy childhood years here and was almost certainly influenced by what he saw between and on these walls. He also first met Richard Wagner here. The interior can only be seen on a guided tour, which generally is less fully

booked than those for Neuschwanstein. To reach the castle follow the narrow pedestrian street or the more interesting route through the forest.

■ Füssen

Füssen has an interesting historic town center. The **Hohes Schloss** is a well-preserved Late Gothic castle that once was the seat of the Bavarian dukes. It was mortgaged to the bishop of Augsburg who used it as summer residence until secularization in the early 19th century saw it returned to the Bavarian state.

Below the castle is the huge former Benedictine **Kloster St Mang** (Monastery). The buildings date primarily from the 18th century and are used by the city government. The church is mostly Baroque, but the oldest parts, including the tower and crypt, are from the 10th and 11th centuries.

Reichenstraße has many elegant gabled houses and is the main shopping street. It was once part of the Roman Via Claudia that led to Augsburg farther north.

Cultural Events & Festivals

Concerts are held each September in the Sängersaal in Schloss Neuschwanstein. Tickets go on sale the first Monday in February and the program is available from the tourist office from January.

Alphorns are blown at the Alpsee from May to September on Monday at 8 pm.

St Coloman is a lovely pilgrim's church just outside Schwangau. It sees several colorful annual parades. The two most spectacular are on Fronleichnam and the second Sunday in October when 200 colorfully dressed horses attend a horse-blessing ceremony.

Adventures

■ On Foot

The natural beauty of the area invites **hiking**. A popular hike is from Schwangau up the Pöllat Gorge, over the Marienbrücke with views of Schloss Neuschwanstein, and then onwards through the mountains to the Bergstation of the Tegelberg cable car. From here, take the cable car or, more interestingly, follow the Schutzengel (Guardian Angel) route back to the valley. The walk takes three to five hours.

The tourism office in Schwangau arranges frequent guided walks in the region. These walks are free for visitors sleeping in the town but there is a minimal charge for others. The walks cover both the town area as well as mountain hikes.

■ On Wheels

A popular **cycling** route is the 32 km (19 miles) around the Forggensee. You can take bicycles on the lake boats. Cycling to the Wieskirche is also popular.

Many hotels have bicycles available for guests but otherwise try at **Aktiv Flugschule**, An der Tegelbergbahn-Talstation, ☎ 08362-921-457; **Auto Köpf**, Münchner Straße 11, ☎ 08362-930-271; or **Campingplatz Bannwaldsee**, ☎ 08362-93-000.

■ In the Air

The **Tegelbergbahn**, 87645 Schwangau, ☎ 08362-98-360, www.tegelbergbahn.de, uses an enclosed **cable car** to hoist passengers from Schwangau's 820 m (2,690 feet) altitude to the Tegelberg peak at 1,720 m (5,641 feet). The Bergstation is the starting point of many popular hikes. In winter, a downhill skiing slope is available. It operates daily from 9 am to 4:30 pm. A round-trip ticket is €15 or €9 one-way. Day tickets are available for skiers.

Balloon flights are arranged by **Bavaria Ballonfahrten**, Hitzleriederstraße 15, 87637 Seeg, ☎ 08364-986-068

For tandem **paragliding** flights from the Tegelberg, contact **Aktiv Flugschule**, Tegelbergstraße 33, 87645 Schwangau, ☎ 08362-921-457, www.flugschule-aktiv.de.

■ With Horses

Horse-drawn carriage rides are available from **Josef Kotz**, Seestraße 74, Brunnen, ☎ 08362-8581, or from **Otto Kotz**, Unterdorf 5, ☎ 08362-8094.

■ On Water

Fishing is allowed in many of the waters in the area. Permits and exact details are available from the tourist office.

Rowboats and **pedal boats** can be rented without reservations at the **Bootsverleih Alpsee**, ☎ 08362-8782, or from the **Campingplatz Bannwaldsee**, ☎ 08362-93-000. A larger selection, including **sailboats**, **canoes**, and family-size **kayaks**, is available from **Surfschule Forggensee** in Brunnen, ☎ 08362-924-386.

Windsurfer courses and equipment are available from **Surfschule Forggensee**, ☎ 08362-924-386.

Städtische Forggensee-Schifffahrt, ☎ 08362-921-363, www.fuessen.de, operates lake boats on the Forggensee from mid-June to early October. Excursions last from 50 minutes to two hours.

■ On Snow & Ice

Alpine Skiing

The **Allgäu-Tirol Vitales Land**, www.vitalesland.com, ski area encompasses not only the area around Füssen, but also other mountains in the region, including some in Austria. A total of 82 ski lifts and 145 km (87 miles) of downhill slopes are available. In Schwangau, in addition to the Tegelbergbahn, a further four ski lifts operate near the Talstation. A Vitales Land ski pass costs €48 for two days.

Cross-Country Skiing

The Füssen area is considered one of the best in Germany for cross-country skiers. In Füssen alone, 60 km (36 miles) of cross-country trails are open at no charge.

An interesting trail is at an altitude of 1,150 m (3,772 feet) on the **Buchenberge**. It allows cross-country skiing at a high altitude with wonderful views and guaranteed snow while the lower regions are still green.

Ice Skating

Ice skating is possible at the indoor rink in Füssen. The **Eisstadion**, ☎ 08362-50-750, is open daily but closed from end April to end June.

Tobogganing

A summer tobogganing course is available at the Tegelberg-Talstation. It operates daily from 10 am to 6 pm if weather allows.

Ski Schools

Schischule Tegelberg, Unterdorf 12, ☎ 08362-8455, has courses in downhill and cross-country skiing as well as in snowboarding.

Cross-country skiing courses are also available from **Skilanglaufschule Ostallgäu**, Weidachstraße 54, Füssen, ☎ 08362-6464.

Snowboarding courses are available from **Snowboardschule Xaver Henke**, Forggenseestraße 15, Hablech, ☎ 0177-466-6416.

Equipment Rentals

In addition to the ski schools, equipment rentals are also available from:

Armin's Sporthäusle, Füssener Straße 20, ☎ 08362-81-198; **Ski-Luggi**, An der Tegelberg-Talstation, ☎ 08362-983-651; **Sport-Roman**, Münchner Straße 12, ☎ 08362-8963.

Where to Stay & Eat

■ Hohenschwangau

Most visitors to Hohenschwangau are day-trippers, but there are a few hotels in town.

Lisl Schlosshotel und Jägerhaus are close to Schloss Hohenschwangau. The Jägerhaus is by far the more luxurious but both are comfortable. Many rooms have views of the castle. The **Wittelsbacher Restaurant** (€-€€) serves international cuisine and hearty local dishes at pleasantly low prices. Neuschwansteinerstraße 1, 87645 Hohenschwangau, ☎ 08362-8870, fax 08362-81-107, www.lisl.de. (€€€-€€€€)

The early 20th-century **Hotel Müller** is directly below Schloss Hohenschwangau. Most of the individually furnished rooms have balconies or terrace access. Some suites are quite luxurious. Alpseestraße 16, 87645 Hohenschwangau, ☎ 08362-81-990, fax 08362-819-913, www.hotel-mueller.de. (€€€-€€€€)

Alpenhotel Meier is a small, 12-bedroom pension. Rooms are comfortable and some have balconies. The rustic restaurant (€-€€) serves international cuisine as well as hearty local specialties. Schwangauer Straße 37, 87645 Hohenschwangau, ☎ & fax 08362-81-889, www.alpenhotel-allgaeu.de. (€€)

■ Füssen

Füssen offers an attractive alternative to staying in Schwangau itself. However, you can easily carry on to other towns such as Garmisch-Partenkirchen if preferred.

In 1995, **Treff Hotel Luitpoldpark** opened in the center of town, a block from the station. It has modern, elegant rooms with marble baths. The restaurant **Kurfürst von Bayern** (€€-€€€) serves international and local specialties. **El Bandito** (€-€€) serves Tex-Mex food. The **Wiener Café** (€-€€) has a piano bar and terrace. Luitpoldstraße, 87629 Füssen, ☎ 08362-9040, fax 08362-904-678, www.luitpoldpark-hotel.de. (€€€-€€€€)

Hotel Sommer is at the edge of the town and has spectacular views of Schloss Neuschwannstein and the Algäu Alps. Rooms are mostly spacious, modern, and comfortable. The restaurant (€-€€) serves local and international cuisine. Weidacherstraße 74, 87629 Füssen, ☎ 08362-91-470, fax 08362-917-714, www.landhaus-sommer.de. (€€€-€€€€)

The rustic **Restaurant Zum Schwanen**, Brotmarkt 4, ☎ 08362-6174, is in the heart of the old town close to the former monastery. It serves excellent regional specialties. (€-€€)

The **Restaurant Alpenschlößle** serves regional specialties as well as international dishes with strong French influences. It is at the edge of the forest in the Bad Faulenbach part of town and is primarily a restaurant, but it also has 12 individually furnished rooms (€€). Alatseestraße 28, 87629 Füssen, ☎ 08362-4017, fax 08362-39-847, hotel-alpenschloessle@t-online.de. (€-€€€)

■ Camping

Campingplatz Bannwaldsee is beautifully located next to the Bannwald Lake. It has on-site bicycle and boat rentals. There is a natural beach and it's close to ski areas. It has 520 spaces for tourists and a further 190 for long-term campers. Open year-round. Münchner Straße 151, 87645 Schwangau, ☎ 08362-93-000, fax 08362-930-020, www.camping-bannwaldsee.de.

Camping Brunnen is right next to the Forggensee Lake, only four km (2.4 miles) from Neuschwanstein. It has excellent facilities and many shady spaces, with 230 spaces for tourists and 70 for long-term campers. It is open from late December to early November. Seestraße 81, 87645 Schwangau, 8273, fax 08362-8630, www.camping-brunnen.de.

Camping Hopfensee is a first-class campground with excellent facilities. It is open from mid-December to early November, with its own ski lift and direct access to 60 km (36 miles) of cross-country skiing trails. There are 380 spaces. 87629 Füssen, ☎ 08362-917-710, fax 08362-917-720, www.camping-hopfensee.com.

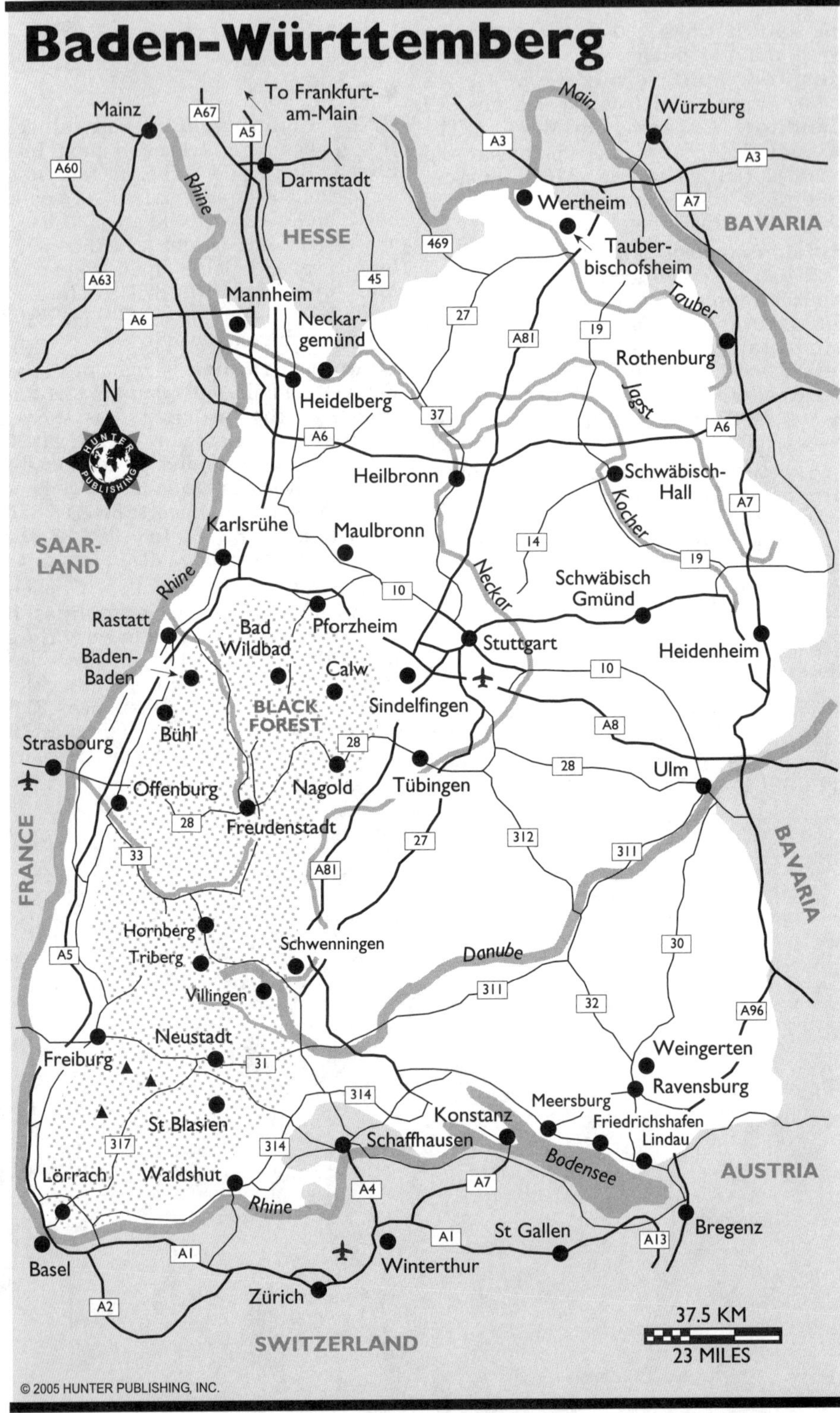
Baden-Württemberg
To Frankfurt-am-Main
Mainz
Würzburg
Main
Darmstadt
Rhine
HESSE
Wertheim
Tauber-bischofsheim
BAVARIA
Tauber
Mannheim
Neckar-gemünd
Rothenburg
Heidelberg
Jagst
Heilbronn
Schwäbisch-Hall
Kocher
Karlsrühe
Maulbronn
SAAR-LAND
Neckar
Schwäbisch Gmünd
Rastatt
Bad Wildbad
Pforzheim
Stuttgart
Heidenheim
Baden-Baden
Calw
Sindelfingen
BLACK FOREST
Bühl
Strasbourg
Offenburg
Nagold
Tübingen
Ulm
Freudenstadt
FRANCE
BAVARIA
Hornberg
Triberg
Schwenningen
Danube
Villingen
Neustadt
Freiburg
Weingerten
Ravensburg
Meersburg
Konstanz
Friedrichshafen
Lindau
St Blasien
Schaffhausen
Bodensee
Lörrach
Waldshut
AUSTRIA
Rhine
Bregenz
St Gallen
Basel
Winterthur
Zürich
SWITZERLAND
37.5 KM
23 MILES
N
HUNTER PUBLISHING
A67
A5
A60
A3
A7
469
45
A63
A6
27
A81
19
37
14
10
28
27
312
311
33
30
A96
31
314
317
A4
A1
A13
A2

Baden Württemberg

In this Chapter

After Bavaria, Baden-Württemberg is Germany's favorite holiday destination. It offers a combination of culture and nature that is hard to find elsewhere. In addition, Baden is famous for its good food – the French influence from across the Rhine certainly rubbed off – and parts of the state are among the sunniest in Germany.

Heidelberg, long the capital of the Palatinate, is one of the most popular destinations for foreign visitors. It is a romantic student town with marvelous ruins of a large castle towering over the town and the Neckar Valley.

Stuttgart is the state capital and home of major industries, including Mercedes-Benz and Porsche. It is an attractive city that attracts fewer foreign tourists than it should. **Ulm** is not particularly attractive, but worth a short stop to see the highest church spire in the world.

The **Black Forest** is a popular year-round tourist destination. It has incredibly beautiful areas and is a haven for outdoor enthusiasts. The spa town **Baden-Baden** is one of the most elegant and richest towns in Germany. Freiburg has the loveliest church spire in Christendom.

The **Bodensee (Lake Constance)** is another popular destination. In addition to the largest lake in Germany, the Swiss and Austrian Alps provide a constant impressive backdrop. **Konstanz** is a particularly lovely and interesting city.

■ History

In the early 19th century, Napoleon redrew the map of Germany and combined several small states to create the Grand Duchy of Baden and the Kingdom of Württemberg as part of his plan to reduce the number of independent political entities in Germany. Opportunistic coalition switching by both allowed them to keep the newly added territories.

During the 1866 Austrian-Prussian War, the two states sided with Austria. Victorious Prussia concluded a secret treaty with Austria's former allies and in the Franco-Prussian war these south German states joined on Prussia's side against the French. Both Baden and Württemberg became part of the German Empire in 1871. Following World War II, the two states, as well as other entities, united into Baden-Württemberg and became part of the Federal Republic of Germany.

■ Transportation

By Rail: The major cities of Baden-Württemberg are easily reached by rail from other centers in Germany. Trains run at least hourly from Munich to Stuttgart (two hours, 20 minutes). Frankfurt am Main can be reached in 90 minutes on at least two trains each hour. At least three trains per hour connect Frankfurt and Heidelberg in less than an hour. Trains run between Frankfurt and Basel hourly as well, stopping in Karlsruhe after an hour, and an hour later in Freiburg.

By Road: Although most parts of Baden-Württemberg can be reached by train, it is easier to see the beautiful countryside by car. Major Autobahns cross through the state and allow for fast connections. The A5 runs parallel to the Rhine from Switzerland past Freiburg, Baden-Baden, Karlsruhe, Heidelberg, Frankfurt and beyond. The A8 runs from Karlsruhe to Munich via Stuttgart and Ulm.

In rural areas, roads are much more scenic and, although generally in good condition, the going can be much slower. Do not expect to do much more than 60 km/h (36 mph) on most Black Forest roads, even during the quiet season.

By Air: Stuttgart Airport, ☎ 0711-9480, www.stuttgart-airport.de, is the largest in the state. It has connections to domestic and European destinations. S-Bahn lines S2 and S3 connect every 10 to 20 minutes to the Hauptbahnhof in under 30 minutes.

Baden-Württemberg has several airports, but often **Frankfurt International** (see *Hesse* chapter) is the most convenient. Most destinations in Baden-Württemberg can easily be reached by train, either directly from the airport or via Frankfurt or Mannheim. Special services are available to Heidelberg and Stuttgart.

A **Lufthansa Airport Bus** (☎ 0180-583-8426), open to all travelers, runs between Frankfurt International Airport's Terminal 1 (Halle B) and the Crowne Plaza Hotel in **Heidelberg**. The journey takes 75 minutes. Fares are €19 one-way or €35 round-trip. (It is possible to check luggage in at Heidelberg for most Lufthansa and SAS flights - ☎ 06221-653-256 for specific details.) **TLS**, ☎ 06221-770-077, www.tls-heidelberg.de, has an airport-to-door shuttle service between Heidelberg and the airport. Fares are about €30 one-way.

It is also possible to check-in at **Stuttgart Hauptbahnhof** for Lufthansa flights departing from Frankfurt International. This service is available for six ICE trains per day – the train journey takes 75 minutes. Check-in closes 20 minutes before train departure and arrivals at the airport should be at least 45 minutes prior to scheduled take-off.

Several budget airlines, including Ryanair to London-Stansted, use the rather inconveniently located **Frankfurt-Hahn Airport**. **Hahn-Express**, ☎ 01805-225-287, www.hahn-express.de, operates six buses daily between the airport and Heidelberg Hauptbahnhof. The two-hour journey costs €16. Ryanair also flies to Baden-Baden and Friedrichshafen.

■ Information Sources

Information on the whole state is available from **Info und Prospektservice Baden-Württemberg**, Yorckstraße 23, 79110 Freiburg, ☎ 0761-8979-7979, www.tourismus-baden-wuerttemberg.de.

■ Heidelberg

Heidelberg is popular with tourists and during July and August can be uncomfortably crowded. However, during the quieter months, it is a pleasant town, which can be enjoyed without having to wander into any of the formal museums.

For five centuries, Heidelberg was the principal residence of the Prince Electors of the Kurpfalz. It was therefore an important political center and its position was enhanced by the foundation of the first German university here in 1386. The castle was damaged in 1537 by a thunderbolt but soon after rebuilt as one of the most beautiful Renaissance palaces north of the Alps.

In 1619, Prince Friedrich V, married to Princess Elizabeth Stuart, daughter of James I of England, was elected King of Bohemia, although a family member of the Emperor already held the position. The resulting defenestration (throwing out the window!) of an imperial delegation in Prague was a direct cause of the Thirty Years' War and made Heidelberg an immediate target of the Imperial Army. In the 1620s, both Heidelberg and its castle were destroyed. The famous library, the Biblioteca Palatina was taken as war booty and is still currently in the Vatican. The region lost three-quarters of its population during the war but both town and castle were rebuilt soon afterwards.

During the War of the Palatinate Succession, French troops of King Louis XIV occupied and eventually destroyed the town and castle in 1688, 1689, and 1693. As a result, Heidelberg's old town has no buildings from the Middle Ages. A religious dispute between the Elector and the town saw the residence moved to nearby Mannheim and the castle was never completely rebuilt. Most of the restored parts of the castle date from the 19th century when Heidelberg castle became the focus of romantic movements. The town suffered only minor damage during World War II – the town council handed it over to the advancing American Army but the retreating Nazis blew up the Old Bridge.

Information Sources

Tourist Office: The Tourist Information Office, Willy-Brandt-Platz 1, ☎ 06221-19-433, www.cvb-heidelberg.de, is inside the main train station. It is open from April to October on weekdays, 9 am to 7 pm, weekends from 10 am to 6 pm, and from November to March, Monday to Saturday, 9 am to 6 pm.

HEIDELBERG CARD

The Heidelberg Card gives unlimited access to all public transportation in Heidelberg, including the funicular to the Castle and Königstuhl. It also allows free or reduced entry into many sights. The cost is €12 for two days or €20 for four days. It comes with a city map and guide.

Transportation

The main train station is in the newer part of town, about 20 minutes walk from the old town. It is more convenient to use public transportation departing from in front of the station.

Heidelberg has several parking garages and an electronic display system showing the number of unoccupied parking spaces. Street parking is limited with severe restrictions making garages a more sensible option. The tunnels have camera-enforced speed restrictions. It is possible to drive up to the peak of Königstuhl, but on a busy day, the funicular would be safer than the narrow, winding road.

Sightseeing

Schloss

The Heidelberg skyline is dominated by the ruins of the Schloss (Castle). It was for five centuries the principle residence of the Prince Electors of the Kurpfalz. However, since its destruction by the French in the late 17th century, it has been Germany's most famous ruin. Parts have been restored but most are still in ruins.

Much of the remaining castle follows a Renaissance style, but older parts are Gothic and a small section is in an English style built by the ill-fated Friedrich V. He also laid out the large garden behind the castle.

To the left of the main entrance is the Old Battery, with great views over the roofs of the old town. A closer inspection of the **Dicker Turm** (Fat Tower), 1533, is possible before passing through the **Elisabeth Gate** – a gate erected overnight by Friedrich V as a surprise birthday present to his wife.

Access the inner courtyard and buildings via the mighty **Torturm**. A small museum with paintings and models is housed in the former library. The main draw is, however, the **Großes Fass** (Great Vat). This huge cask, which could hold 58,000 gallons, was installed in 1751 and connected to the banqueting hall via pipes and a hand pump. It is possible to climb to the small dance and wine-tasting platform on top of the cask. A statue of Perkeo, the famous court jester, guards the cask. According to legend, Perkeo could consume astonishing amounts of liquor but died when he drank a glass of water by mistake.

Across the courtyard is the surprisingly interesting **Deutsches Apothekenmuseum** (German Pharmacy Museum). On display is mainly pharmaceutical equipment from the 18th and 19th centuries, including complete pharmaceutical shops.

The rest of the castle interior can only be seen on a guided tour.

The gardens offer good views of the castle and the Neckar Valley. The gardens are free of charge and especially pleasant in the late afternoon. Little of the original splendor remains, but a few statues, grottos, and fountains survive.

The Schloss, ☎ 062 21-538-422, is open daily from 8 am to 5:30 pm (the Apothekenmuseum from 10 am to 5 pm). Admission is €2.50. Guided tours, ☎ 06221-538-421, sometimes available in English, are an additional €3.50. The Schloss is about 15 minutes walk, mostly stairs, or a few minutes funicular ride from the old town.

Old Town

Most of Heidelberg's old town consists of Baroque buildings, often erected on top of Gothic foundations that remained after the demolition efforts by the French. Most sights are also in a narrow strip on either side of the pedestrians-only Hauptstraße.

The **Kornmarkt** (Wheat Market), at the east end of town, is an open square with a statue of the Madonna dating back to 1718. The main reason to visit the square is for the clear view it affords of the Schloss towering above.

Adjacent to this square is the larger and more impressive **Marktplatz** (Market Square). The **Heiliggeistkirche** (Holy Ghost Church), 1398-1441, is 60 m (195 feet) long and, rare for a Gothic church, consistently 20-m (66 feet) wide although architectural techniques create the optical illusion that it gets wider toward the choir. It once housed the largest single library in the world, the Bibliotheka Palatina, until the books were carted off to the Vatican, never to return, during the Thirty Years' War. The church, with the graves of the Prince Electors, was destroyed by the French at the end of the 17th century, but rebuilt shortly after. It was used by both the Lutheran and Roman Catholic congregations and a dividing wall remained in place until 1936. A dispute between the Lutheran community and the Catholic prince, who wanted sole use of the church as mausoleum for his family, ended with the prince moving his residence to nearby Mannheim in the early 18th century.

On the Hauptstraße side of the square is the famous **Hotel Haus zum Ritter**. It is the only Renaissance building in Heidelberg to have escaped the wrath of the French. Ironically, it was erected in 1592 by a French Huguenot who fled prosecution in France. It has been a guesthouse since 1703 and is still a popular place to sleep and eat.

On the northern side of the Heiliggeistkirche is the Fischmarkt (Fish Market) with a fountain. Also note the small stalls built into the walls of the church as was common since at least medieval times. From here, Steingasse leads to the Neckar River and the **Alte Brücke** (Old Bridge), which is guarded by the **Brückentor** (Bridge Gate). Prince Carl Theodor had the stone bridge erected in 1788 to replace earlier wooden ones – high-water levels are indicated on the second arch. Several statues adorn the bridge, including one with Carl Theodor surrounded by the water gods of the Rhine, Danube, Neckar, and Mosel. The bridge is a good place to view and photograph the castle and old town. For even better views, cross the bridge and follow the steep Schlangenweg to Philosophenweg (Philosophers' Way), which, halfway up Heilgenberg, runs parallel to the Neckar River.

The Baroque **Alte Universität** (Old University), Universitätsplatz 1, was erected in 1711 to bring all the different parts of the university together in a central location. Nowadays the university has 30,000 students but, apart from the humanities, all faculties have relocated to the newer parts of town. The 19th-century aula (hall) is decorated in grand, Historicist style typical for the period.

Most popular with tourists, however, is the graffiti-filled **Studentenkarzer** (Students' Prison), Augustinergasse 2, ☎ 06221-543-554. From 1778 until 1914, it was used to imprison students up to two weeks, mostly for small offenses such as public drunkenness. The first couple of days the prisoners had to survive on bread and water but, after that, visits and better food were possible. The cells are open from April to September, Tuesday to Sunday, 10 am to 6 pm, in October from 10 am to 4 pm, and November to March. Tuesday to Saturday from 10 am to 4 pm. Admission is €2.50.

The eclectic collection of the **Kurpfälzisches Museum** (Electoral Palatinate Museum), Haupstraße 97, ☎ 06221-583-402, is well worth seeing. A cast of the jaw of *Homo Heidelbergensis*, who roamed the region 600,000 years ago, is a star attraction. Notable art works include the Windsheim altarpiece of the *Twelve Apostles* by Tilman Riemenschneider and a large collection of Romantic period paintings featuring Heidelberg. Opening hours are Tuesday to Sunday from 10 am to 6 pm. Admission is €2.50.

Excursions from Heidelberg

■ Königstuhl

Königstuhl is a 568-m (1,864-ft) peak five km (three miles) southeast of Heidelberg. It can be reached by car, bus, or most easily by the Bergbahn (funicular) that runs from Heidelberg old town via the castle and Molkenkur. Molkenkur was the site of a castle that was destroyed by lightning in the early 16th century and never rebuilt. It currently has a restaurant with great views.

At the top of Königstuhl are several restaurants, a TV tower, and a fairy tale theme park. It is also the start of at least 12 marked hiking trails – see *Adventures* below. The funicular, which runs every 10 minutes in summer and every 20 minutes in winter, takes just over 15 minutes and costs €4 one-way or €6 round-trip.

MÄRCHENPARADIES

At the top of Königstuhl is Märchenparadies (Fairy Tale Paradise), www.maerchenparadies.de, ☎ 06221-23-416. It is a theme park, very much aimed at children, illustrating famous fairy tales. Some rides are also available. It is open daily from March to November, 10 am to 6 pm (7 pm on Sundays as well as in the months of July and August). Admission is €3 for adults, €2 for children between two and 12 – some rides and activities require additional charges.

■ Burgenstraße

The Burgenstraße (Castles Road), www.burgenstrasse.de, is one of Germany's most popular tourist routes. It connects Mannheim and Prague but en route goes through Heidelberg, the Neckar Valley, Rothenburg ob der Tauber, and Nürnberg, among others. The total route is almost 1,000 km (600 miles) and passes castles, fortified towns, and exciting landscapes. The Neckar Valley, upriver from Heidelberg, is particularly exciting for its castles and natural beauty.

Deutsche Touring, Am Römerhof 17, 60486 Frankfurt am Main, ☎ 069-790-350, www.deutsche-touring.de, has a daily bus from May to September on the stretch between Mannheim and Rothenburg.

Cultural Events & Festivals

Heidelberg has several cultural festivals – contact the tourist office for specific dates and details.

The **Spring Festival** stretches over three weeks in March and April. It features mainly classical music.

More famous, and stretching over two months in summer, is the **Schlossfestpiele** (Castle Festival). Many events, ranging from operettas to theater, are staged in the castle grounds. Sigmund Romberg's *The Student Prince*, performed in English, is a perennial favorite.

Three times a year, huge fireworks shows are staged with the Schloss as backdrop.

At the end of November, the **International Film Festival Mannheim-Heidelberg** is held, featuring non-Hollywood productions. It encourages new talent and independent producers.

Shopping

Most of Heidelberg's shops are concentrated in the pedestrian zone, especially in Hauptstraße. Shops here are increasingly the generic versions available in all German towns, but there are still some fine bookshops in town and antiques are reasonably priced, but true bargains are few and far between.

Adventures

On Foot

Heidelberg is best enjoyed on foot. The **old town** is compact and many streets are for pedestrians only. Brochures for self-guided tours are sold everywhere in town.

Guided walking tours of the old town take place daily from April to October at 10:30 am. On Friday and Saturday, the tour is also available in English. From November to March, the tour is only on Saturday and in German only. Meeting point is the information board at Universitätsplatz and the tour lasts 90 minutes.

A pleasant walk, with wonderful views of the old town and the castle, is along **Philosophenweg**, halfway up the hill on the opposite bank of the river.

Hiking opportunities abound in the immediate vicinity of Heidelberg. The Neckar Valley is best explored by bicycle or boat and the highlands on foot. Take the Bergbahn from the old town to **Königstuhl** from where 12 clearly marked hiking routes are available. The easiest walk, accessible to wheelchairs as well, is a 2½-km (1½-mile) circular route along the highest points of the mountain. Routes back to the old town are five km (three miles) long and to the other side of the mountain mostly eight km (4.8 miles) and always ending at bus stops, which allows easy returns to Heidelberg.

On Wheels

The Neckar Valey and the Odenwald areas around Heidelberg are ideal **cycling** territory. As with boat trips, Heidelberg is more often the destination rather than the starting point.

In Heidelberg itself, bicycles can be rented from **Fahrrad-Verleih Per Bike**, Bergheimer Str. 144, ☎ 06221-161-108, www.perbike.de.

Near Heidelberg, **Rudi's Radladen**, Mühlgasse 2, 69151 Neckargemünd, ☎ 06223-71-295, www.rudis-radladen.de, rents out quality bicycles of all types.

From April to September, on the third Monday of the month, TSG78, ☎ 06221-160-563, www.tsg78-hd.de, organizes an **inline skating** parade through the streets of Heidelberg. Start is at 7:30 pm from Tiergartenstraße 9. Participation ranges from 500 to 2,000 per session.

Inline skating is also possible on the Hockenheim Formula 1 racing circuit. During summer, four-hour events, attracting up to 4,000 participants, are scheduled in the evenings. Rental equipment and safety courses are available. Schedules and information are available from **Inline Skating am Hockenheimring**, ☎ 06205-104-820, www.skate-hockenheimring.de.

Hockenheim **auto racing** circuit, ☎ 06205-152, www.hockenheim.de, just south of Heidelberg, hosts the annual German Formula 1 Grand Prix. On most Thursday nights, April to October, from 5 to 8 pm, they welcome anyone interested in racing their own cars. Admission is €4 per person and €12 per 15 minutes on the circuit. "Racing" is done in groups of up to 40 cars and safety regulations must be followed. Double-check your insurance policy *prior* to participating!

In the Air

Heidelberg Ballon, Hauptstr. 24, 69253 Heiligkreuzsteinach, ☎ 06220-922-227, www.heidelberg-ballon.de, starts their hot-air balloon excursions from various locations around Heidelberg. A maximum of six persons are allowed per balloon. Flights cost from €230 upwards.

On Water

The Neckar Valley, especially upriver from Heidelberg, is a great area for both cycling and **canoeing**. For tours ranging from a few hours to several days, **100% Kanu+Bike**, Holderstraße 2, 74196 Neuenstadt-Kochertürn, ☎ 07139-934-900, www.kanu-bike.de, can arrange cycling and canoe combinations on the Neckar as well as its Kocher and Jagst tributaries.

In Heidelberg, **Kiwi Paddle**, Waldweg 15, ☎ 06221-136-388, www.kiwi-paddel.de, rents out easily transportable inflated canoes and **kayaks**. The minimum rental period is one week.

From around Easter to October, **Rhein-Neckar-Fahrgastschifffahrt**, ☎ 06221- 20181, www.rnf-schifffahrt.de, offers **cruises** on the Neckar River from Heidelberg. Roundtrips to Neckarsteinach take three hours and cost €10. Shorter 40-minute trips along the Heidelberg riverfront cost €3.50. Commentary is in German and English and food is available on all boats.

Wildlife

The **Deutsche Greifenwarte** (German Birds of Prey Station), Burg Guttenberg, 74855 Haßmersheim-Neckarmühlbach, ☎ 06266-388, www.burg-guttenberg.de, is an interesting venue about 60 km (36 miles) up the Neckar Valley from Heidelberg. This castle hosts a hundred eagles, falcons, and owls. It is open from April to October, 9 am to 6 pm, with flights at 11 am and 3 pm. In March and November it is open from noon to 5 pm, with flights at 3 pm. Admission is €8.

The Burg Guttenberg fortress itself was built around 1200 during the Staufen era. It has been the residence of the Gemmingen family for the past 550 years and the current owner, the 17th generation, often conducts guided tours of the castle himself. The castle museum is open April to October from 10 am to 6 pm and admission is €4. The restaurant **Burgschäncke** (€-€€) offers a wide range of regional specialties at reasonable prices.

Golf

One of Germany's highest-rated golf courses is just south of Heidelberg at the **Golf Club St Leon & Rot**, Opelstraße 30, 68789 St Leon-Rot, ☎ 06227-86-080, www.golfclub-stleon-rot.de. Tourists, who are registered members of other golf clubs, are allowed to play on one of the two 18-hole courses if they have a handicap of 36 and on the nine-hole course with a handicap of 54.

Where to Stay & Eat

The best hotel in Heidelberg is **Der Europäische Hof – Hotel Europa** on the edge of the old town. The luxurious rooms are individually furnished. The public areas are equally elegant and use antique furniture. The restaurant **Die Kurfürstenstube** (€€€-€€€€) is highly regarded and serves classic and local cuisine. It has a rustic beauty, with wood paneling that dates from the 18th century. Friederich-Ebert-Anlage 1, 69117 Heidelberg, ☎ 06221-5150, fax 06221-515-506, www.europaeischerhof.com. (€€€€)

The **Marriott** is a new, modern hotel on the banks of the Neckar River close to the station. Rooms are modern. The best rooms, as well as the **Globetrotter** restaurant (€€), have views of the river. Vangerowstraße 16, 69115 Heidelberg,
... x 06221-908-698,
... €€-€€€€)

... s a modern hotel at
... wn. Although it has
... usiness travelers in
... ant place to stay for
... Rooms are spacious.
... taurant (€€-€€€)
... sine, while the more
... bar **Gaudiamus**
... y regional dishes to
... wine and beer.
Kurfürstenanlage 1, 69115 Heidelberg, ☎ 06221-9170, fax 06221-21-007, www.ichotels.com. (€€€-€€€€)

The **Hirschgasse Hotel** is on the opposite bank of the Neckar River from the old town and dates back to 1472. Rooms are furnished in Laura Ashley style. The restaurant **Le Gourmet** (€€€) serves international and nouvelle cuisine. The **Mensurstube** (€€-€€€) offers nouvelle cuisine and local specialties. It has a 200-year tradition and can count Otto von Bismarck as a former patron. Both restaurants are open for dinner only. Hirschgasse 3, 69120 Heidelberg-Neuenhaim, ☎ 06221-4540, fax 06221-454-111, www.hirschgasse.de. (€€€€)

Arguably, one of the most popular hotels with foreign tourists in Germany is the **Romantik Hotel Zum Ritter St. Georg**. Shown at right, it is in the center of the old town in a beautifully preserved building dating from 1592. A large statue of St George slaying the dragon stands guard over the façade. It is the only Renaissance building in Heidelberg that survived the three demolition sprees of the French armies of Louis XIV in the 16th century. Rooms are comfortable although the cheaper ones are a bit small. It is a romantic place to stay. The restaurants (€€-€€€) serve international cuisine as well as local specialties. Hauptstraße 178, 69117 Heidelberg, ☎ 06221-1350, fax 06221-135-230, www.ritter-heidelberg.de. (€€€-€€€€)

Also in the old town is the **Hotel Weisser Bock**. The half-timbered building has a simple, yet comfortable interior with wooden floors but modern amenities. The restaurant (€€-€€€) maintains the feeling of a student's inn. Regional specialties as well as Italian food are served. Große Mantelgasse 24, 69117 Heidelberg, ☎ 06221-90-000, fax 06221-90-099, www.weisserbock.de. (€€-€€€)

The **Hotel Acor** is in a small, Neo-Classical building at the edge of the old town. The rooms are functional and clean, with some offering views of the castle. Friederich-Ebert-Anlage 55, 69117 Heidelberg, ☎ 06221-654-070, fax 06221-654-0717, www.hotel.acor.de. (€€-€€€)

Hotel Am Schloss is in the heart of the old town close to the funicular leading to the castle. Some rooms and the roof terrace have views of the old town and castle. Rooms are comfortable and modern. It is on top of the Kornmarkt parking garage. Zwingerstraße 20, 69117 Heidelberg, ☎ 06221-14-170, fax 06221-141-737. (€€-€€€)

The **Restaurant Simplicissimus**, Ingimstraße 16, ☎ 06221-183-336, serves nouvelle cuisine in the heart of the old town. The restaurant has an Art Nouveau décor and a pleasant courtyard. Reservations are recommended. (€€€)

Schönmehls Schlossweinstube, Im Schlosshof, ☎ 06221-97-970, is inside the Heidelberg castle. It has five rooms, with styles ranging from medieval to stylishly modern. Food is classic regional dishes and the wine list is extensive. The restaurant is open for dinner only and reservations are recommended. (€€€-€€€€)

A pleasant and informal place in the old town is **Café Journal**, Hauptstraße 162, ☎ 06221-161-712. It serves international dishes but is also popular for coffee and cake. Newspapers and magazines from all over the world are available for reading and front covers decorate the walls. It is popular with tourists and locals alike. (€-€€)

The oldest coffee shop in town is **Café Knoesel**, Haspelgasse 20, ☎ 06221-22-345. The "Heidelberger Students' Kiss" was invented here – when physical contact between sexes was still taboo, students would present these chocolates instead. (€-€€)

Zum Roten Ochsen, Hauptstraße 217, ☎ 06221-20-977, is a traditional students' pub, which has been run by the Spengel family for six generations. Although currently students are far and few between, it is still atmospheric and the bare oak tables are full of carved initials. Mark Twain and Marilyn Monroe, among others, left their "marks" here. Food is simple home-style dishes. Reservations are recommended. (€-€€)

Camping

Camping Heidelberg is open from April to mid-October. Tents and bicycles can be rented on-site and cheap sleeps are available in rental caravans. Heidelberg old town is five minutes away by bus. Schlierbacher Landstraße 151, 69118 Heidelberg, ☎ 06221-802-506, www.camping-heidelberg.de.

■ Stuttgart

The capital of Baden-Württemberg, this is a major industrial center. Approaching the center of the city, the visitor passes a Who's Who of German industrial and engineering companies such as VDO, Siemens, and Bosch. However, the brightest stars are Mercedes-Benz and Porsche. Both have their headquarters here.

It therefore comes as a pleasant surprise that the center of Stuttgart is both interesting and beautiful. At the heart of the city is the large castle park, surrounded by historic buildings, museums, shops, and cafés. The center is circled by hills – some with lovely 19th-century villas, others forested or still covered by vineyards.

As befits a state capital, Stuttgart is also the cultural center of Baden-Württemberg with an astonishing variety of cultural offerings ranging from classical music to modern musicals – some straight from Broadway and the West End, but always sung in German.

Although the Neckar River flows through the outskirts of the city, Stuttgart has largely turned its back on the celebrated river. Water does, however, play a major role here – in Europe, only Budapest can claim stronger mineral springs.

Information Sources

Tourist Office: Tourist information is available from **i-Punkt**, Königstraße 1A, 70173 Stuttgart, ☎ 0711-22-280, www.stuttgart-tourist.de, which is across the road from the main train station. Apart from providing information, it can make reservations for accommodations, as well as for an astonishing range of events, ranging from musical performances to spa visits. The office is open weekdays from 9 am to 8 pm, Saturday from 9 am to 6 pm, Sunday and holidays from April to October, 11 am to 6 pm, and November to March, 1 to 6 pm.

THE STUTTCARD

As in many other German cities, the tourism office developed a card to give tourists free entry into many museums as well as discounts to other attractions and events. The Stuttcard costs €11.50 and is valid for three consecutive days. The Stuttcard Plus costs €17 and gives unlimited access to all public transportation within the city limits, including transportation to and from the airport.

Getting Around

Most of the sights in the center are within easy walking distance of the main train station. As befits a city with such an automobile tradition, outlying areas and sights such as Mercedes-Benz, Porsche, Bad Cannstatt, and the television tower are easily reached by car. However, public transportation is equally convenient and combines trains, trams, and buses.

Sightseeing

Stuttgart's history dates back to 950, when a horse-breeding farm was here. The city has been the principle residence of the Württemberg dukes (and kings after 1806) since the early 14th century. Most of the old city was destroyed during World War II, but parts, especially around the magnificent Schlossplatz, have been reconstructed.

The center is best explored on foot. Large areas are for pedestrians only and the huge Schlossgarden often offers a pleasant alternative to leaving the city. Sights listed under *Farther Afield* are not within walking distance of the center or of each other. Most can be reached easily by public transportation or private car.

The Center

The Stuttgart **Hauptbahnhof** (main station) was designed in the mid-1920s and its stark, functional lines are typical of the artisitic trend called *Neue Sachlichkeit* or "New Objectivity." Its 58-m (190-foot) tower is topped by a large Mercedes star. A huge urban development project is underway to move the train tracks north of the station underground and develop a new suburb in the regained 250 acres.

Königstraße leads from the station and is the most important shopping street in Stuttgart. It also claims to be the longest pedestrian-only street in Germany.

Central Stuttgart was virtually destroyed during World War II. However, three blocks down the street is the lovely **Schlossplatz** (Palace Square), showing some of the former glory of the town. Across the square is the **Neues Schloss** (New Palace), completed in 1807. It was severely damaged during the war but rebuilt and currently houses government offices. The **Jubiläumssäule** (Jubilee Column) in the center of the square was erected in 1841 to commemorate the 25th jubilee of King Wilhelm's reign. The Classical **Königsbau** (1860) on the Königstraße-side of the square, houses the Stuttgart Stock Exchange and other commercial enterprises.

At the far end of the square is the **Altes Schloss** (Old Palace), mostly dating from the late 15th century, although parts date back to 1320. It has a magnificently painted Renaissance courtyard. Most of the building is used as exhibition space by the **Württembergisches Landesmuseum**, (State Museum), Schillerplatz 6, ☎ 0711-2790, www.landesmuseum-stuttgart.de. The museum covers local history from 5 BC to the present. The eclectic collection ranges from tapestries and tableware to religious statuary and funerary objects. The crown jewels and the dukes' treasure troves are also on display. The museum's fine collection of musical instruments from the 16th century to the present is housed on four floors in the Fruchtkasten, Schillerplatz 1. Opening hours are Tuesday to Sunday from 10 am to 5 pm. Admission is €3.

The area around **Schillerplatz** is the oldest part of Stuttgart. The two-towered **Stiftkirche** (Collegiate Church), Stiftstraße 12, ☎ 0711-226-5581, www.stiftkirche-stuttgart.de, dates back to the 12th century, but was changed to the Late Gothic style in the 15th century. The choir has a collection of 11 statues of the ducal family sculpted by Simon Schlör (1576-1608). The church has been Protestant since 1534 and is the most important Protestant church in Baden-Württemberg. It was severely damaged during World War II but rebuilt in the mid-1950s and recently again renovated. The church has a magnificent organ and religious music concerts are held every Friday at 7 pm – admission is usually €6. The church is open daily from 9 am to 5:30 pm, but Thursdays only from noon.

On the opposite side of the Neues Schloss, the **Schlossgarten** (Palace Garden) stretches all the way to the Neckar River. It has several notable buildings, including the glass cube that houses the Baden-Württemberg Parliament, and the Neo-Classical Staatstheater.

Across the road is the **Haus der Geschichte Baden-Württemberg** (History Museum), Konrad-Adenaur-Straße 16, ☎ 0711-212-3989, www.hdgbw.de. It concentrates on the history of the region since 1815. The museum is new and has a large multimedia selection. Opening hours are Tuesday to Sunday from 10 am to 6 pm, Thursday until 9 pm. Admission is €3.

Nearby, is the impressive **Staatsgallerie Stuttgart** (National Gallery), Konrad-Adenauer-Straße 30, ☎ 0711-212-4050, www.staatsgalerie-stuttgart.de.

One of Germany's most visited and best galleries, it is housed in the Classical Alte Staatsgallerie, built in 1843 and combined with a Post Modern new gallery in 1984. There is a large medieval collection, with *Bathseba's Bath* by Hans Memling (1485), shown at left, considered the most valuable piece. The French collection illustrates the development from Realism to Post-Impressionism. The new building houses the excellent modern art collection as well as contemporary works. Particularly noteworthy are the 12 works by Picasso illustrating all his major creative periods. The special exhibitions are usually worth the surcharge. The gallery is open Tuesday to Sunday from 10 am to 6 pm, until 9 pm on Thursday. The first Saturday of the month is Kunstnacht (Art Night) and the gallery is open until midnight. Admission is €4.50.

Still within easy walking distance from the center, but in the opposite direction behind the university, is the **Linden-Museum**, Hegelplatz 1, ☎ 0711-20-223, www.lindenmuseum.de. It is an ethnological museum with a large collection and displays from all continents. Opening hours are Tuesday to Sunday from 10 am to 5 pm, Wednesday until 8 pm. Admission is €3; free on Wednesday after 5 pm. It is 10 minutes walk from the Hauptbahnhof, or use buses 40 or 42 that stop in front of the museum.

Farther Afield

■ Mercedes-Benz

Mercedes-Benz is the most famous company associated with Stuttgart. Its presence is everywhere from the large star on the roof of the station to its head offices and several factories. Note that the three attractions mentioned below are geographically quite a distance from one another.

The **Mercedes-Benz Museum**, Mercedesstraße 137, ☎ 0711-172-2578, www.daimlerchrysler.com, is popular. About 100 cars from the collection of this famous company are on display, including the fabulous Silver Arrows racing cars of the 50s, the first Mercedes, and cars owned by celebrities. Chrysler gets only a (grudging) mention on one of the information panels. The first Benz is a copy – the original is in the German Museum in Munich. The museum is open Tuesday to Sunday from 9 am to 5 pm. It is inside the Mercedes factory grounds; park outside Tor 1 (Gate 1) and wait for the special bus. By public transportation, it is easiest to reach by S-Bahn Line S1 to Gottlieb Daimler Stadion station. From there, it is a short walk to Gate 1. Admission is free. (A new, larger museum is under construction and should open by 2006. It will be located, more conveniently, outside Gate 1.)

A must for fans of classic cars is the **Mercedes-Benz Classic Center**, Stuttgarter Straße 90, 70736 Fellbach, ☎ 0711-178-4040, www.mercedes-benz.com. This center has a workshop where classic cars belonging to the museum and well-healed customers are serviced and restored. It also sells spare parts for classic cars and can provide information and advice on buying such models. The center is open weekdays from 9 am to 5 pm. It is best reached by car. Admission is free.

Mercedes-Benz conducts two-hour **factory tours** at its plant in Stuttgart-Sindelfingen. Reservations are required at least four weeks in advance from the Kundencenter Sindelfingen, Käsbrünnlestrasse, 71059 Sindelfingen, ☎ 07031-907-0403, werkbesichtigungen.w050@daimlerchrysler.com. Tours are often available in English. Customers picking up cars from the factory, and many Germans do that, have preference. Children under six and cameras of any kind are not allowed. On public transportation, the plant is reached by S-Bahn Line S1 from the main station in the direction of Herrenberg. Get off at Böblingen after 20 minutes and take the free commuter bus to the Kundencenter from Stop 19 in front of the station. The tours are free.

Saving $$$ on Car Rental

For US residents only – Canadians and others need not apply – it is possible to save on car rental in Europe if buying a Mercedes, BMW, or Porsche built in Europe for ultimate delivery in the US. You can take delivery in Europe from the respective factories, drive the car, and have it shipped back to the US from several points in Europe. It is then delivered to you back home through the normal channels. This service has no additional charge, and in fact, on some models you even get huge discounts. The only downside – some equipment, such as radios, are often only fitted in the States. Contact dealers in the US for information on the European delivery program.

■ Porsche

Stuttgart's second car company is much smaller but no less famous. The **Porsche Museum**, Porscheplatz 1, 70435 Stuttgart-Zuffenhausen, ☎ 0711-911-5685, www2.porsche.de, is disappointingly small. It has only 40 cars and is worth the effort only for dedicated fans. Porsche also has a Classic Center for the restoration of classic models. It can also provide information and advice, and it sells spare parts. Opening hours are weekdays from 9 am to 4 pm. The museum is also open weekends from 9 am to 5 pm. Visits to the plant are possible for customers collecting cars – children under 16 not allowed. Admission is free.

Porsche is best reached by S-Bahn Line S6 in the direction of Leonberg/Weil der Stadt – get off at stop Neuwirtshaus.

■ Fernsehturm

Stuttgart's Fernsehturm (Television Tower), Jahnstraße 120, ☎ 0711-232-597, was the first in the world built with reinforced concrete. Since its completion in 1956, it has been the symbol of the city and its viewing platform at 217 m (712 feet) still offers the best views of Stuttgart. It has an excellent restaurant – see below. The tower is open daily from 9 am to 10 pm.

■ Weißenhofsiedlung

In 1927, 16 architects from five European countries designed 21 model houses. Like the Bauhaus structures, these were long ignored in Germany, but are now considered some of the most influential architectural works of the 20th century. Eleven houses, including two by Le Corbusier and one by Mies van der Rohe, survived in their original form. Most can only be seen from the outside, but a museum has recently opened in a Le Corbusier house. Information is available from the **Weißenhof-Infozentrum**, Am Weißenhof 20. Opening hours are Tuesday to Friday from 11 am to 3 pm, and weekends from 10 am to 4 pm. Guided tours, in German, are held on Saturday at 11 am. The community is a few minutes walk from U-Bahn station Killesberg/Messe.

Ulm – The World's Highest Church Steeple

Ulm, halfway between Stuttgart and Augsburg, is not a particularly interesting city. However, it is on a major highway crossing and many travelers therefore pass by. It is worth stopping over, even if only briefly, to see the **Ulm Münster** – its 161.6-m (533-foot) steeple is the tallest in the world and can be seen from the Autobahn A8 a few miles north. The Gothic Münster was erected between 1377 and 1390 and is the second-largest Gothic structure in Germany. The *Last Judgment* fresco, painted in 1471, is the largest fresco north of the Alps. The 15th-century tabernacle is 26 m (85 feet) high and the largest in Germany. The wood-carved choir stalls are equally impressive and from the same period. The viewing platform at 143 m (469 feet) can be reached after 768 spiral steps – on a clear day the view is worth the effort and reaches to the Alps and Black Forest. The church is open daily from 9 am to 5 pm (last ascent of the tower at 4 pm). Admission is €2.50.

■ Wilhelma Zoological & Botanical Garden

The Wilhelma Zoological and Botanical Garden, Neckartalstraße, ☎ 0711-54-020, www.wilhelma.de, with more than 10,000 animals and a thousand species, is one of the largest in Germany. It was originally constructed in 1850 for King Wilhelm I and has several Moorish-style buildings. There are also 5,000 different types of plants, providing a cross-section of different climatic zones. Opening hours are daily from 8:15 am until dark – latest 8 pm. It can be reached by U-Bahn Line U14, stop Wilhelma. Admission is €10.20, but €7 after 4 pm and all day from November to February.

Cultural Events

As befits a German state capital, Stuttgart has a huge range of cultural offerings. The **Staatsoper Stuttgart** is a frequent winner of the German Opera House of the Year award. The **Staatsorchester** (National Orchestra), **Staatsopernchor** (State Opera Choir), and the **Stuttgarter Ballet** are frequent winners of domestic and international awards. The **Schauspielhaus Staatstheater** (State Theater) rounds off the Stuttgart high culture scene with plays in German. For the program and reservations contact the Staatstheater, Oberer Schlossgarten 6, ☎ 0711-202-090, www.staatstheater.stuttgart.de, or the tourist office. Prices range from €20 to €30 in the State Theater, and €60 to €110 in the Opera.

More modern music is the center of attention at the **ECLAT Festival of New Music**, held annually in February. Variety shows and musicals are performed almost daily.

Festivals

For one week in April, the **International Trickfilm-Festival Stuttgart** (Cartoon Film Festival), www.itfs.de, entertains the old rather than the young. More than a hundred films are shown in what is considered the second-largest festival of its kind in the world.

The **summer festival**, www.stuttgarter-sommerfest.de, takes place in August on the huge Schlossplatz and involves cultural events and major eating and drinking.

The last weekend of February sees the **Retro Classics**, a large exhibition and market for old cars, motor bikes, and spare parts. For those not in need of rare spare parts, the highlights are the display of *Oldtimers* (cars older than 30 years) and *Youngtimers* (cars between 25 and 30).

For 10 days each August and September, wine lovers swarm to the Markt and Schillerplatz at the Alte Schloss for the annual **Stuttgarter Weindorf** (Wine Village). Some 250 types of wine are on offer, from the local Trollinger red to the better-known Riesling. Suitable local specialties are also on offer for the hungry.

Less famous than Munich's Oktoberfest is the similar **Cannstatter Volksfest** held over 16 days in September and October. It has a tradition dating back to 1818 and draws millions to the beer gardens and rides. The largest beer tents can seat up to 5,000 guests and beer is served by Maß (one liter or about a quart).

The **Stuttgart Weihnachtsmarkt** (Christmas Market) is held annually from November 26 to December23. It claims to be the largest in Europe – although Frankfurt among others disputes this. It is beautiful and has open-air skating in front of the Neues Schloss – rental equipment is available.

Shopping

The best shopping district is the pedestrian zone in the town center. **Königstraße** claims to be the longest pedestrians-only street in Germany and **Calwer Straße** that runs parallel to it, also has glitzy shops and malls. Although Hugo Boss is based in Stuttgart, he has no dedicated store in town. However, brand-name clothes are available from several department stores as well as dedicated clothing stores such as **Holy's**, Königstraße 54, ☎ 0711-222-9444.

It is still possible to see vineyards on the hills around central Stuttgart and wine shops abound. Riesling is well known, but a more interesting buy is the local Trollinger red. It is best bought here as two-thirds of the production is consumed locally and very few bottles ever cross German borders.

Adventures

On Foot

From April to October, the tourist office arranges 90-minute **walks** through the center of Stuttgart. Tours departs daily at 11 am and Friday at 5 pm as well, from the i-Punkt shop in Königstraße 1a. Tours are often available in English. Prior reservations are required. Participation is €6 per person.

The tourist office has town walks to various viewing points. The three walks are each five km (three miles) and can easily be done in less than two hours. All three depart from the center and lead to interesting viewing platforms offering panoramic views of Stuttgart and the surrounding hills.

Stuttgart is beautifully located and several **hiking** opportunities in the region are available. A pleasant three-hour hike is along the 12-km (7.2-mile) **Stuttgarter Weinwanderweg** (Wine Hiking Trail), which leads through beautiful countryside via vineyards and wine cellars. A brochure with route description is available from the tourist office. From May to October, the tourist office arranges guided walking tours, in German, along this route on the first Sunday of the month. Participation is about €20 and includes a wine sampling and small meal.

On Wheels

Bicycles can be rented through the tourist office. Note that bicycles are not allowed on the S-Bahn before 8:30 am and between 4 and 6:30 pm, and are allowed on the U-Bahn only after 7:30 pm. On weekends these restrictions are relaxed.

The Tourist Office, ☎ 0711-22-280, arranges 2½-hour **bus tours** of Stuttgart. They depart daily from April to October, and from November to March on Friday, Saturday, and Sunday at 1:30 pm from the Hotel am Schlossgarten, Schillerstraße 23. Tours are conducted in German and English. The price is €17 and includes the elevator fee for the television tower. Reservations are required.

In the Air

For **hot-air ballooning** in the Stuttgart region contact **Ballonfahrten-Südwest**, Tulpenstraße 10, 73655 Plüderhausen, fax 07181-89-006, www.Ballonfahrten-Suedwest.de.

On Horseback

The name Stuttgart is derived from the term "Stutengarten" used to describe the horse stud farm located here around 950 AD. The city shield is a prancing horse, also used on the emblem of Porsche cars. Riding opportunities in the city itself are limited but the Tourist Information Office can provide information on ample riding options in the region.

On Water

Stuttgart is generally associated with industrial might, so it usually comes as a pleasant surprise that the city has 19 mineral water sources. Their capacity of 22 million liter per day is, in Europe, only exceeded by Budapest. The best-known **spa** is **Mineralbad Cannstatt**, Sulzerrainstraße 2, ☎ 0711-216-9240, which has an enormous parabolic glass roof. **Mineralbad Leuze**, Am Leuzebad 2, ☎ 0711-216-4210, has eight pools. Both spas have first-class facilities with many spa options such as saunas, indoor and outdoor pools, massages, and health restaurants.

Neckar-Personen-Schiffahrt, ☎ 0711-5499-7060, operates **boat tours** on the Neckar from March to October. The ships depart from Bad Cannstatt.

Where to Stay & Eat

The best temporary address in Stuttgart is the **Steigenberger Graf Zeppelin** across the road from the main train station. Behind its monolithic façade is a luxurious and stylish interior. Like the locally produced Mercedes cars, the rooms are available in classic, elegant, and avant-garde. Cheaper rooms are a bit cramped but still stylish and all have lovely white and stainless steel bathrooms. The restaurant **Olivio** (€€€-€€€€) has a Michelin star and serves Italian food in attractive surroundings. The wine list and service are first-class too. Home-style cooking and regional specialties are available in the **Zeppelin-Stüble** (€-€€€) Arnulf-Klett-Platz 7, 70173 Stuttgart, ☎ 0711-204-80, fax

0711-204-8542, www.steigenberger.com. (€€€-€€€€)

Am Schlossgarten is conveniently next to the large park and the main shopping district. Rooms are luxurious but with a less formal look compared to the Graf Zeppelin. The **Zirbelstube** (€€€€) is the best gourmet restaurant in town. Its décor is rustic but stylish and the food is classic with a touch of French. The wine list is superb. The **Schlossgartenrestaurant** (€€€-€€€€) serves equally good food but with a more regional flavor. The terrace is especially popular. Schillerstraße 23, 70173 Stuttgart, ☎ 0711-202-60, fax 0711-202-6888, www.hotelschlossgarten.com. (€€€€)

The **Intercontinental** is a typical international luxury hotel between the station and the park. It is often the choice of visiting VIPs and guests have included the Rolling Stones. Rooms are stylish. Willy-Brandt-Straße 30, 70173 Stuttgart, ☎ 0711-202-00, fax 0711-2020-2020, www.ichotels.com. (€€€€)

The **Intercity Hotel** is right next to the main station. Rooms have been designed with business travelers in mind and are functional, and relatively large. The room key allows free travel on public transportation. Arnulf-Klett-Platz 2, 70173 Stuttgart, ☎ 0711-225-00, fax 0711-225-0499, www.intercityhotel.de. (€€-€€€)

A good budget choice is the recently constructed **Ibis am Löwentor**. It is at S-Bahn station Nordbahnhof, allowing for easy access to the city center. Rooms are functional, clean and bright. Presslestraße 15, 70191 Stuttgerat, ☎ 0711-255-510, fax 0711-1206-4160, www.accor-hotels.com. (€€)

A restaurant in a television tower is usually a guarantee of dubious quality food, but **Weber's Gourmet im Turm**, Jahnstraße 120, ☎ 0711-2489-9610, www.fernsehturm.stgt.de, is a pleasant, if pricey, exception. The Mediterranean food and excellent wine list earned it a Michelin star. The view, from 144 m (475 feet), is the best in the region. It's open for dinner only and reservations are recommended. (€€€€)

At the entrance to the television tower is the more affordable **Primafila**, Jahnstraße 120, ☎ 0711-236-3155, www.primafila.de. It serves international food with strong Italian overtones. The restaurant is modern, with a terrace, beer garden, and cigar lounge. (€-€€€)

Camping

Cannstatter Wasen is conveniently ensconced in Bad Cannstatt on the right bank of the Neckar River. It has 150 spaces and is open all year. Mercedesstraße 40, 70372 Stuttgart, ☎ 0711-556-696, fax 0711-557-454.

■ Tübingen

The lovely small town of Tübingen has a lot in common with Heidelberg. It also has a famous university, a castle, and is on the River Neckar. However, its old town is older and more interesting and the throngs of tourists, especially foreign ones, are absent. It is unfortunately no longer a well-kept secret and is popular with German travelers, but it is never as crowded as Heidelberg.

Information Sources

Tourist Office: Information is available from the **Verkehrsverein Tübingen**, Tourist & Ticket Center, An der Neckarbrücke, 72072 Tübingen, ☎ 07071-91-360, www.tuebingen-info.de. They have handy maps for self-guided walking tours of the old town area.

Transportation

Tübingen is a 45-minute drive from Stuttgart. It can also be reached on twice-hourly trains in an hour.

Sightseeing

Tübingen is one of the loveliest towns in southern Germany. It escaped World War II undamaged and has a beautiful medieval town center with half-timbered buildings in narrow alleys. A large castle towers over the old town.

The best views of Tübingen are from the **Eberhardsbrücke** (Bridge) that spans the River Neckar between the station and the old town. From here, the interesting riverbank as well as the old town and castle can be seen. Note the yellow riverside building with a small tower and turret. This is the **Hölderlinhaus** (Hölderlin

House), Bursagasse 6, ☎ 07071-22-040, named after the popular German poet Friedrich Hölderlin, left. He became schizophrenic and lived here from 1807 until his death in 1843. It now houses a museum dedicated to Hölderlin and his work. Opening hours are Tuesday to Friday from 10 am to noon and 3 to 5 pm. On weekends, it is open from 2 to 5 pm. Admission is €2.

The **Bürgsteige** has some of the oldest buildings in town and terminates on the top of the hill at **Schloss Hohentübingen**. This castle dates partly from 1078, but most of it is from the 16th century. Most impressive is the early 17th-century Renaissance portal. The views of the Neckar and old town are magnificent. The castle is being used by the University and also houses the **Egyptology and Archeology Museum**, ☎ 07071-297-7384. It has quite an eclectic display of mostly private donations. Opening hours are Wednesday to Sunday from 10 am to 5 pm. Admission is €2.

The most picturesque part of the old town is the **Marktplatz** (Market Square). A fountain featuring Neptune is at the center of the square. The impressive **Rathaus** (Town Hall) dates from the 15th century, but the paintwork is late 19th century. Its astronomical clock, above, is from 1511.

The late 15th-century **Stiftkirche** (Collegiate Church), Am Holzmarkt, ☎ 07071-52-583, is Late Gothic and has the graves of many of the counts of Württemberg. The church has a rich Gothic and Renaissance interior. The tower has lovely views. Opening hours are daily from 9 am to 5 pm, closing at 4 pm from November to January.

Across the road from the main entrance is the **Cotta Haus**, home of Johann Friedrich Cotta, who first published the works of Schiller and Goethe. According to legend, Goethe vomited on the wall of the house next door after finding too much inspiration in the local inns. A sign claims "Hier Kotzte Goethe" (Goethe vomited here). Hermann Hesse worked in the nearby Heckenhauer bookshop (now housing a travel agency) at the end of the 19th century before taking up writing full-time.

Cultural Events & Festivals

With students making up a third of the town's population, the cultural calendar is naturally varied and busy. The information office has listings of what is on.

Three annual events warrant special mention. **Viva AfroBrasil**, www.viva-afro-brasil.de, is held on the third July weekend and claims to be the largest open-air Brazilian festival in Europe. The **Tübinger Sommer** is a three-week arts and cultural festival held in August throughout the town – events range from street performances to formal workshops arranged by the university. The **Jazz & Klassik Tage** (Jazz & Classics Days) are held in October in about 20 venues.

Adventures

On Foot

The tourism office arranges old-town walks from mid-March to early November, daily at 2:30 pm, except Wednesday at 10 am. The rest of the year, the walks are on weekends only. The walks start from the Rathaus on the Marktplatz.

On Water

Rowboats and **pedal boats** can be rented by the hour from the **Bootsvermietung Märkle**, Eberhardsbrücke 1, ☎ 07071-31-529, next to the tourist information office at the Eberhardsbrücke. Punting is also available.

Where to Stay & Eat

Most visitors to Tübingen are on day-trips and this is fortunate because the number of hotels is limited.

The **Krone Hotel** has been family-run since 1885. It is the best hotel in town and all rooms are air-conditioned. Rooms are stylish – some with Chippendale-style furniture. The hotel is on the left bank close to the Eberhardsbrücke. The restaurant (€€€) serves regional specialties as well as Mediterranean cuisine. Uhlanstraße 1, 72072 Tübingen, ☎ 07071-13-310, fax 07071-133-132, www.krone-tuebingen.de. (€€€)

Nearby is the modern **Hotel Domizil** on the banks of the Neckar. Rooms are nicely furnished. Wöhrdstraße 5, 72072 Tübingen, ☎ 07071-1390, fax 07071-139-250, www.hotel-domizil.de. (€€-€€€)

Simpler, but far more interesting accommodations are available inside the old town. **Hotel am Schloss**, in a lovely old building, is up a steep street and has lovely views. Most of the rooms are renovated and some rooms have views in up to four directions. The restaurant (€-€€) is famous for its Maultaschen (German ravioli) – 28 varieties are on offer. No parking is available at the hotel itself but staff will find you something nearby. Burgsteige 18, 72072 Tübingen, ☎ 07071-92-940, fax 07071-929-410, www.hotelamschloss.de. (€€)

As befits a tourist and student town there are many dining options scattered about. However, for gourmet food head to **Restaurant Rosenau**, Rosenau 15, ☎ 07071-68-866, near the New Botanical Gardens. This elegant restaurant is in a building with a glass roof. International cuisine and regional specialties are served. The vegetarian selection is also large. (€€€)

Closer to the old town itself, **Museum**, Wilhelmstraße 3, ☎ 07071-22-828, is a good option. The food is mostly international and the décor rustic. (€€-€€€)

■ The Black Forest

The Black Forest is one of Germany's most popular vacation areas. It is the largest forested area in the country and the pleasant weather makes it a popular year-round destination. The area is mountainous, with lovely valleys. It also has wonderful hot springs and spas. Despite claims by the Swiss, the Black Forest actually had both the first downhill skiing and the first cuckoo clocks.

Tourism is a major industry and the region continuously develops new activities to lure in travelers with diverse interests. It has culture in the form of numerous museums, ruins of monasteries, Baroque palaces, and frequent musical festivals. Much is done to keep the traditional Black Forest experience alive. *Trachten* (national dress) is often worn at numerous festivals. Hotels and vacation homes are in traditional style using lots of wood and covering balconies with blooming geraniums. Many small towns are picture-perfect. You will find it almost impossible to pick a road here that is not scenic. The area is popular with hikers and cyclists, the numerous rivers and small lakes offer watersports, and the reliable snow makes it a good winter sports destination.

Thousands of years ago, the River Rhine divided the Vosges Mountains in France from the Black Forest range. The two areas are similar in character. The accommodations, food and wine in both are excellent.

The Black Forest is famous for its cuisine and the extraordinary range of award-winning restaurants. France is just a river crossing away and its influence shows especially in the higher end restaurants. At the more rustic places in the deeper valleys, the food is more hearty and Black Forest ham, cured by cold smoke over a series of months, is always popular. It is carved very thin, not primarily because of the price but rather to let the full flavor develop.

The wines from Baden are famous and the vineyards facing the Rhine are an integral part of the landscape. Local beers also appeal and some, such as the Alpinsbacher Klosterbräu, are beloved throughout Germany. Stronger liquors, liqueurs, or *Schnapps*, are also local specialties.

For the purposes of this guide, the Schwarzwald or Black Forest is divided into a northern and southern section. The division line is the Kinzig Valley, which runs from Offenburg to Alpirsbach.

Black Forest Cake

The most famous food from the region is probably the Schwarzwälder Kirschtorte (Black Forest cherry cake) made of chocolate, cream, cherries, and Black Forest *Kirschwasser* (cherry liqueur). It is what the Germans call a *Kalorienbombe* – a calory bomb. The cake is popular and available all over Germany, but having at least one piece in the Black Forest is almost compulsory. No one in the region will volunteer this information, and few would even admit it, but it does not actually originate in the region. The first one was baked in the late 19th century at a café in Bad Godesberg, a sleepy town near Bonn. It was called Black Forest cake because of the Black Forest liqueur used to flavor the cream.

Many foreign visitors used to the lavishly decorated Black Forest cakes available back home, may find the local version a bit bland. In many tourist-oriented restaurants the cake will be rather dry and eating it will be uneventful. The best cakes can be found at a Konditorei – a bakery that specializes in cakes and pastries.

Information Sources

Tourist Information: The tourism information offices generally divide the Black Forest into three major areas, and then again into smaller units. It is best to contact one of the big three first, then narrow things down to a specific region or town.

For the northern area: **Touristik Nördlicher Schwarzwald**, Am Waisenhausplatz 26, 75172 Pforzheim, ☎ 07231-147-380, www.noerdlicher-schwarzwald.de.

For the middle: **Mittlere Schwarzwald Tourismus**, Gerberstraße 8, 77652 Offenburg, ☎ 0781-923-7777, www.schwarzwald-tourismus.de.

For the south: **Tourismus Südlicher Schwarzwald**, Stadtstraße 2, 79104 Freiburg, ☎ 0761-218-7304, www.schwarzwald-sued.de.

THE SCHWARZWALD CARD

The Schwarzwald Card (Black Forest Card), www.schwarzwaldcard.info, is an electronic chip card designed by the tourism industry to give free access to 130 attractions in the region. In the summer season, it is valid on three freely selected days and in the winter season on four days. It costs €42 for over 12 year olds and €34 for children aged four to 11. It is transferable but not on the same day. The card can pay for itself with three visits to some of the spas and it is available from most tourist offices and many hotels.

Adventures

The Black Forest, with its beautiful hills and forests, combined with generally fine weather and good infrastructure, makes for excellent adventures. Hiking and cycling are particularly popular during all seasons. In winter, cross-country skiing is the main draw but downhill skiing and snow hiking are also options. Adventures are listed under the nearest town below, but some hiking and cycling routes run the full stretch of the forest and are listed here.

Long-Distance Hikes

Three long-distance hiking routes run the full length of the Black Forest from Pzorzheim in the north. The **Westweg** (West Route) goes to Basel and, at 280 km (168 miles) is the longest. Usually split into 12 stages, it claims to be the most popular long-distance walking route in Germany and has been in use since 1900. The **Mittelweg** (Middle Route) to Waldshut is 230 km (138 miles). It is split into nine stages and passes down the beautiful Nagold Valley. The **Ostweg** (East Route) leads to Schaffhausen on the Rhine, is 244 km (146 miles), and is divided into 12 stages.

Several other multi-day routes are scattered through the region. Many tourism offices can make arrangements for hotel accommodations, and luggage forwarding.

Long-Distance Cycling Routes

The Black Forest has 17 major multi-day cycling routes in addition to many shorter ones listed below under individual towns. Some routes are easy one way, but with extremely challenging returns. Often it is possible to catch up on lost time by using trains for part of the route. Hotels usually rent bicycles to patrons but for multiple tours it is often better to rent equipment from specialists. Most tourism offices can supply information and cycling maps are available from bookstores all over Germany or from tourism providers in the region.

The **Mountainbikeweg Schwarzwald** is a 354-km (212-mile) route along the crest of the Black Forest. It is divided into six challenging stages. Information is available from the Schwarzwaldverein, ☎ 0761-380-530, www.schwarzwaldverein.de.

Part of the Bodensee-to-Heidelberg route runs for 51 km (30 miles) as the **Nagoldweg** through this beautiful valley. This part of the route is not particularly challenging, allowing full enjoyment of the beautiful surroundings.

The **Neckartal-Radweg** traces the flow of the River Neckar from its source at Villingen in the Black Forest to its confluence with the Rhine in Mannheim. The route does not always follow the river, making some parts more challenging, especially at the start of the route.

Fishing

Angling opportunities abound in the rivers and lakes of the Black Forest. A license is always required – German residents must also present their annual fishing license, but such requirements are usually waved for non-residents. For more information and rental equipment, contact the applicable tourism office. Fishing without permission is a criminal offence.

MONEY-SAVING TIPS

A quick glance at the prices of top hotels and restaurants in fashionable resort towns such as Baden-Baden can leave the average visitor out of breath. The Black Forest has many exclusive and expensive resorts, hotels, and restaurants but it can also be enjoyed inexpensively.

Hotels and spas in smaller towns are often significantly cheaper. Holiday homes and apartments are numerous and are reasonably priced if the high season is avoided. It is also possible to rent a room in a private house with a bed and breakfast setup. In some cases the price may drop to €10 per night – a big eater can make a profit on the breakfast alone! Tourist information offices in individual towns can provide information and often book accommodation at no additional charge.

The whole Black Forest invites picnicking, but do be careful where you light fires. It is forbidden more often than not. Local guesthouses and *Gaststätte* serve good hearty meals at reasonable prices. The main attraction of the region is its natural beauty and it is mostly available for free.

Northern Black Forest

The northern part of the forest stretches from the industrial cities of Karlsruhe and Pforzheim to the Kinzig Valley. In between, the hills and mountains are mainly covered by pine trees, while the slopes facing the Rhine Valley are covered by vineyards and orchards.

The area has several hot-water springs and spa resorts. None is more famous or illustrious than Baden-Baden – arguably the most elegant town in all of Germany. The Schwarzwald-Hochstraße runs along the crest of the mountains, with fantastic views. Several other holiday theme routes criss-cross the region. Most of these scenic routes follow the valleys, which seem to run arbitrarily in any direction, rather than in a fixed, logical pattern.

Hiking and cycling are especially popular activities. The reliability of snow allows for winter sports, especially cross-country skiing. Many areas are designated as a *Luftkurort* – areas where the air is clean and considered very healthy.

The region is also filled with reminders of the past. The margraves, and later grand dukes, of Baden built lavish, mostly Baroque, residences in Baden-Baden, Rastatt, and Karlsruhe. The magnificent monastery in Maulbronn and the remnants of monasteries in Hirsau and Alpirsbach among others bear testimony to the religious institutions that flourished here a thousand years ago. Baden-Baden has a hodge-podge of architectural styles, mostly beautiful, reminders of the town's role as summer capital of Europe in the 19th century.

Karlsruhe

Karlsruhe is a major industrial center just north of the hills of the Black Forest. The town's most striking feature is best appreciated from the air or a simple glance at a map – at its center is a Baroque palace and 32 streets fan out around it. It creates the impression of a fan or, if the full circle is taken into consideration, the rays of the sun. This layout was first dreamed up when Margrave Karl Wilhelm of Baden-Durlach took a nap while looking for his wife's lost fan. The sun comparison is not fanciful either – the palace was inspired by Versailles, seat of Louis XIV, the Sun King, who caused major destruction in the Rhinelands and Baden areas in the late 17th century. The destruction of the residence at nearby Durlach led to the foundation of Karlsruhe as a planned-from-scratch town in 1715.

Originally, the radiating roads ran through forests, but after the two Baden principalities were united and eventually elevated to a grand duchy by Napoleon, a pretty town grew up around the palace. Most of it was destroyed during World War II. Karlsruhe was rebuilt in mainly modern style and this left it with a rather anonymous cityscape. The town is a major industrial center and the seat of Germany's highest court, but tourists generally pass it by. The true Black Forest towns are more pleasant places to stay. The palace here and the few excellent museums can be seen on the way through.

■ Information Sources

Tourist Office: Am Festplatz 9, 76137 Karlsruhe, ☎ 0721-37-200, www.karlsruhe.de, is south of the pedestrian zone near the Marktplatz.

■ Transportation

Karlsruhe has excellent transportation links by road and rail to other parts of Germany. The local rail network is extensive and S-Bahn trains offer cost-efficient access to Black Forest towns such as Pforzheim, Bad Wildbad, Bad Herrenalb, and Baden-Baden. Schedules are available from www.kvv.de.

■ Sightseeing

The main sight in Karlsruhe is the Baroque **Schloss** (Palace) built in 1715. Only the tower is original – most of the rest was destroyed in World War II but reconstructed in the 1950s. The interior was not restored. It is worth ascending the tower for the wonderful

views of the city and surrounding countryside.

Most of the Schloss is used by the **Badisches Landesmuseum** (Baden State Museum), Schloss Karlsruhe, ☎ 0721-926-6514, www.landesmuseum.de, for a large exhibition on the region's past from prehistoric times to the present. Particularly noteworthy are the Turkish trophies – war booty that Margrave Ludwig Wilhelm (1677-1707) brought back from his campaigns against the Turks. Opening hours are Tuesday to Thursday from 10 am to 5 pm, and Friday to Sunday from 10 am to 6 pm. (The tower closes an hour earlier) Admission is €4.

The **Staatliche Kunsthalle** (State Art Gallery), Hans-Thoma-Straße 2, ☎ 0721/926 3355, www.kunsthalle-karlsruhe.de, has an impressive collection ranging from early German paintings to modern. It also has works by most famous painters of the Flemish and Dutch golden age, including a Rembrandt self-portrait. The nearby Orangery houses German and French paintings from 1890 to the present and most famous painters are represented, including Cézanne, Gauguin, Kandinsky, Klee, and Miró. Opening hours are Tuesday to Friday from 10 am to 5 pm, and weekends from 10 am to 6 pm. Admission is €4.

In a true swords-to-ploughshares story, a huge former ammunitions factory was converted in 1999 into a major arts center. The **Zentrum für Kunst und Medien-technologie (ZKM)** (Center for Art and Media Technology), Lorenzstraße 19, ☎ 0721-8100-1200, www.zkm.de, houses several museums, galleries, and workshops. The **Museum für Neue Kunst** (Contemporary Art), exhibits works from private collections. The emphasis is on American and European art from the 1960s to the present. The **Media Museum** is the world's first interactive museum and unites media art with painting, sculpture, and photography. It requires active participation by the visitor to illustrate the impact of modern technologies on art. Opening hours are Wednesday to Sunday from 10 am to 6 pm (8 pm on Wednesday). Admission is €5.10 for the Media Museum, €4.10 for the Contemporary Art Museum, or €7.70 for both.

The 6.5-m (21-foot) **Pyramid** on Marktplatz is the symbol of Karlsruhe. It marks the grave of the town's founder, Margrave Karl Wilhelm, who died in 1738. In 1807, shortly after Karlsruhe became the residence of the newly created Grand Duke of Baden, the memorial church for the town's founder was destroyed since it stood in the way of the new town plan. A temporary wooden pyramid was erected to protect the grave of the margrave, but this eventually became popular and was replaced by a permanent stone pyramid in 1825. Due to the shape of the pyramid, the shockwaves of the bombings of 1944 did it practically no damage, while most of the old town was destroyed.

■ Cultural Events

Germany has three major annual festivals dedicated to the composer George F Handel. While his birthplace, Halle (Saxony-Anhalt), was behind the iron curtain, the festivals in Karlsruhe and Göttingen (Hesse) were the more popular. Karlsruhe has a week of Handel in February during the Händel-Festspiele Karlsruhe, which is accompanied by a two-week specialized musical course at the International Händel Academy, Baumeisterstraße 11, ☎ 0721-376-557.

■ Adventures

On Foot

The tourism office arranges guided walks of the city. Alternatively, request a flyer with map and information for a self-guided tour of the inner city and Schloss park.

■ On Water

Although not on the Rhine itself, Karlsruhe has a river harbor connected to it by canal. **Boat trips**, including day-trips to Speyer and Strasbourg, are arranged by **KVVH GmbH**, Werftstr. 2, 76189 Karlsruhe, ☎ 0721-599-7424, www.rheinhafen.de.

■ Where to Stay & Eat

The **Dorint Kongress Hotel** is at the Congress Center, halfway between the main station and the Schloss. It is modern, with well-equipped, comfortable rooms. The **Majolika** restaurant (€€-€€€) serves regional and Mediterranean food. Festplatz 2, 76137 Karlsruhe, ☎ 0721-32-260, fax 0721-352-6100, www.dorint.de. (€€€-€€€€)

The **Schlosshotel** is across the road from the main station, about a mile from the Schloss itself. It is a tradition-rich establishment and the elevator dates from 1914. Rooms are individually furnished. The **Zum Großherzog** restaurant (€€€) serves mainly international cuisine and the more rustic **Schwarzwaldstube** (€€-€€€) has regional and hearty dishes. Bahnhofplatz 2, 76137 Karlsruhe, ☎ 072138-320, fax 0721-383-2333, www.schlosshotel-karlsruhe.de. (€€€€)

Also at the station is the small **Hotel Am Tiergarten**. Rooms are well-maintained. Bahnhofplatz 6, 76137 Karlsruhe, ☎ 0721-932-220, fax 0721-932-2244, www.am-tiergarten-karlsruhe.de. (€€)

The pedestrian zone is filled with shops and restaurants. However, two are worth going out of your way for. The **Dudelsack** (€€-€€€), Waldstraße 79, ☎ 0721-205-000, serves international and regional cuisine. The rustic **Hansjakob Stube** (€€-€€€), Ständehausstraße 4, ☎ 0721-27-166, has mostly local, seasonal dishes. It is in a cellar on a back street a block from the Markt.

Baden-Baden

Internationally, Baden-Baden is the most famous of all Black Forest towns. Its hot springs attracted visitors from Celtic times to the present and are the source of the town's fame, although the casino and excellent wines are also major contributors to its wealth.

Baden-Baden has more millionaires per capita than any other German city. There is a stylish elegance about this town, from the high-class shopping streets to the manicured lawns of public parks. It is an expensive town – hotel rooms above €300 per night are easy to find – but can also easily be enjoyed without spending a cent.

THE RUSSIAN CONNECTION

Baden-Baden became fashionable with Russian nobles during the 19th century and even the Czar himself visited frequently. The Russian author Dostoevsky, who made a fortune gambling in Wiesbaden, lost most of it in Baden-Baden, including the shirt off his back and his wife's wedding ring, then wrote several novels about his experience and misery. For most of the 20th century, Baden-Baden was off-limits to the Russians but they are back. In recent years, the Russian nouveaux riches rediscovered the joys of Baden-Baden and they visit in droves. It was rumored that the Russian mafia recently met in a luxury hotel – a connection the town does not want to promote. The shop owners love the Russians, though. One commented, "They are not like the Germans who try on a hundred pants and buy nothing. The Russians simply buy everything they try and like."

■ Information Sources

Tourist Office: Tourist information is available from **Kur & Tourismus**, Schloss Solms, Solmsstraße 1, 76530 Baden-Baden, ☎ 07221-275-266, www.baden-baden.com. The tourism office inside the Trinkhalle can also make reservations for accommodations and virtually any event staged in town.

■ Transportation

The main **train** station is in the Oos district, about two km (1.2 miles) east of the center. Public transportation in Baden-Baden is part of the Karlsruher Verkehrsverband (www.kvv.de).

When **driving**, note that two tunnels lead traffic on the main roads past the center of town. Pedestrian zones and other restrictions make it impossible to actually cross through the old town by car for most of the day. It is best to park in one of the garages at the edge of the pedestrian zone and approach sights on foot.

■ Sightseeing

Humans settled in Baden-Baden at least 10,000 years ago, but the area's written history started around 70 AD after the Romans evicted the Celts and took to the waters themselves.

Baden-Baden served as a residence town of the dukes of Baden until the French destroyed the city during 1689 and the dukes moved to Rastatt. Although the city is a mixture of architectural styles of all periods, the Neo-Classical and Gründerzeit villas from the 19th century are particularly attractive.

Baden-Baden has been a magnet for artists, especially during the romantic period of the 19th century. Dostoevsky, Goethe, Mark Twain, Johannes Brahms, Clara Schumann, and Franz Liszt, among others, were frequent guests.

It is easy to enjoy Baden-Baden by just strolling through the magnificent parks and streets. None of the museums or galleries is an absolute must-see – water and gambling remain the main sources of revenue and the stylish ambiance comes for free.

Left Bank of the Oos

The **Lichtentaler Allee** along the River Oos was the meeting point of the European nobles and diplomats during the 19th century. Originally just an oak-lined street, it was changed into a large English landscape park in 1850 by the owner of the casino. It currently has more than 300 types of trees and plants. The most popular part of the park is between Goetheplatz and Kleingolfplatz, but it is worth continuing to the more formal park at Gönneranlage, on the opposite bank of the River Oos, which has 300 different types of roses. Most of the right bank is fenced off, with the exclusive, luxury Brenner's Park Hotel using a large section.

The **Staatliche Kunsthalle** (National Art Hall), Lichtentaler Allee 8a, ☎ 07221-300-763, www.kunstahlle-baden-baden.de, houses temporary exhibitions of 19th- and 20th-century art. During exhibitions, it is open Tuesday to Sunday from 11 am to 6 pm (8 pm on Wednesday). Admission is €5.

The magnificent Neo-Classical **Kurhaus**, by Friedrich Weinbrenner, opened in 1824 as a Conversation House. The name was not far off – while Baden-Baden was the summer capital of Europe, it was here that nobles came to be seen and gossip. The four halls were decorated during the 1850s in the Neo-Baroque of the Belle Époque and have lost none of their illustrious, over-the-top styling since. It houses the **Spielbank** (Casino), Kaiserallee 1, ☎ 07221-21-060, www.casino-baden-baden.de, Germany's oldest and largest casino. Admission is €3, the minimum bet €5 and the maximum €10,000. The Casino operates daily from 2 pm for suitably dressed adults only – at least a jacket and tie for men. In the morning, you may turn up in whatever for guided tours of the building, sometimes in English. Tours are daily from April to September, 9:30 am to noon, and from October to March, 10 am to noon. Tours are €4.

North of the Kurhaus in the Kurgarten is the Neo-Classical **Trinkhalle**, Kaiserallee 3. The Trinkhalle opened in 1842 and has a 90-meter (295-foot) arcade with Corinthian columns and 14 frescos depicting local sagas. A free drinking fountain spouts water from the source that fills the Caracalla and Friedrichsbad spas. Apart from a small bistro-café, there is also a tourist information office, open Monday to Sunday from 10 am to 5 pm, and Sunday and holidays from 2 to 5 pm.

Right Bank

The **Neues Schloss** (New Palace), Schlossstraße 22, constructed in 1479, was the former residence of the Margrave of Baden. It was recently sold by his heirs and is being converted into a luxury hotel. The terrace offers lovely views of the old town, including, in the foreground, the mainly Gothic **Stiftkirche** (Collegiate Church), Marktplatz, which contains the graves of the Margraves of Baden from the 14th to 18th centuries. The monument of Ludwig the Turk (1753) is particularly opulent. The crucifix in the choir, at 6.5 m (21 feet, is one of the masterpieces of the Late Gothic period, carved from a single piece of stone by Nicolaus Gerhaert von Leiden in 1467.

In contrast to many other German towns, the Marktplatz in Baden-Baden is rather dull. The **Rathausplatz**, in front of the Rathaus (Town Hall) is much livelier and features several outdoor restaurants. It also has a large statue of Bismarck, creator of the German Empire in the 19th century and a frequent spa guest. A plaque thanks him for his services in ensuring a long period of peace.

The **Römischen Badruinen** (Ruins of the Roman Baths), Römerplatz 1, ☎ 07221-275-934, www.badruinen.de, are underneath the current Friedrichsbad. The floor and wall heating systems of this soldiers' bath are in excellent preserved condition and an exhibition explains the Roman bath culture. Opening hours are daily from 11 am to 5 pm. Admission is €2.

Both the historic Friederichsbad and the adjacent modern Caracalla Therme are open to the general public. See *Adventures* below.

The **Russische Kirche** (Russian Church), Lichtentaler Straße 76, ☎ 07221-390-634, was erected in the Byzantine style in the 1880s to serve as a place of prayer for the visiting Russian nobles. It is open daily from February to November, 10 am to 6 pm. Admission is 70¢.

Excursions - Rastatt

After the French destroyed Baden-Baden, Ludwig the Turk moved his residence 10 km (six miles) downhill and turned Rastatt into a stronghold. His new palace was Baroque and the first such large Baroque structure in Germany. Inspired by Versailles and designed by the Viennese court architect Domenico Egidio Rossi, it was completed in 1707, around the time Ludwig died.

The main sights at **Schloss Rastatt**, Herrenstraße 18, Rastatt, ☎ 07222-978-385, www.schloesser-und-gaerten.de, are the royal apartments and the Ahnensaal, used for balls. The interior can only be seen on guided tours. Opening hours are Tuesday to Sunday from April to October, 10 am to 5 pm, and from November to March, 10 am to 4 pm. Admission is €4.

Two more museums are housed on the ground floor of the palace. The **Wehrgeschichtliches Museum** (Military Museum), ☎ 07222-34-244, has exhibitions on German military history from the Middle Ages up to 1815. Admission is €2.50. The **Freiheitsmuseum** (Liberty Museum), ☎ 07222-771-390, explains the history of the German Liberation Movement of the 19th century with special emphasis on the region's role in the unsuccessful struggle for the 1849 Constitution of the Empire. Admission is free. Opening hours for both museums are Tuesday to Sunday from 9:30 am to 5 pm.

A few miles away, in Rastatt-Niederbühl/Förch, is the Romantic pleasure palace shown above, **Schloss Favorite**, ☎ 07222-41-207, www.schloesser-und-gaerten.de, built in 1710-12 for Sibylla Augusta, widow of Ludwig the Turk. This small, but opulent Baroque palace served as her summer residence and a place to house her magnificent porcelain collection. Much of this collection of tableware, vases, and figures is still on display. Opening hours are Tuesday to Sunday from mid-March to September, 10 am to 5 pm; from October to mid-November, 10 am to 4 pm. Admission is €4.50 and includes the compulsory guided tour.

■ Cultural Events

The **Festspielhaus**, Beim Alten Bahnhof 2, ☎ 07221-301-3101, www.festspielhaus.de, opened in 1998, incorporating part of the old station in its design. It was more than a century in the making and finally offered Baden-Baden a concert venue in keeping with its strong cultural tradition. It has two galleries and seats 2,500 – the second-largest opera house in Europe. The cultural calendar is very full, offering a wide range of events. It is 10 minutes walk from the Kurhaus and town center.

Festspielhaus tickets can be ordered from the tourism office, ☎ 07221-275-233, fax 07221-275-202, at no additional charge. Packages, including hotel accommodation and other services, are often available. Delivery of the tickets to hotels in Baden-Baden is also possible.

■ Shopping

Baden-Baden has many high-class shops selling brand-name clothes and other quality items favored by the wealthy shoppers frequenting this spa town. Some small shops are in front of the Spielbank and others are in Sophienstraße and the vicinity of Leopoldsplatz.

The Romans introduced wine to the region and Baden has been an important producing area ever since. Wine shops abound and many estates are open to visitors. The wines produced by **Schloss Neuweier**, Mauerbergstraße 21, ☎ 07223-96-670, www.weingut-schloss.neuweier.de, are highly praised and make excellent gifts.

■ Adventures

On Foot

The **fountains' walk** leads past more than 50 fountains scattered through the parks and streets of Baden-Baden, constantly reminding the visitor of the importance of water to this town. A map is available from the tourism office.

Hiking is very popular in the Black Forest and, with 500 km (300 miles) of marked paths, Baden-Baden, despite its stylish upmarket image, is no exception. The **Panoramaweg** is a 40-km (24-mile) circular route around the town, divided into five sections, making it easily adaptable to personal preferences. Several times per year the tourism office arranges special Forest and Experience weeks during which guided tours and special events are staged to sample the delicacies of the region while hiking from event to event.

The **Merkur** is a 668-m (2,200-foot) peak in Baden-Baden. It can be ascended via one of the steepest mountain railways in Europe – at an angle of 54°. Apart from the magnificent view and restaurant at the top, several hiking paths designed for spa guests lead to numerous panoramic points. The **Merkurbahn**, ☎ 07221-2771, operates daily from February to December, 10 am to 10 pm. The fare is €4 round-trip. The ground station can be reached by Bus 204 and 205.

The hills of the Black Forest are generally gentle, but in Baden-Baden there is no need to practice **rock climbing** indoors. The **Battertfelsen** rocks, www.batterfelsen.de, offer paths from beginner's level to Alpine-quality – all with views of Baden-Baden. For information, contact the Baden-Baden-Murgtal section of the **German Alpine Society**, Rathausplatz 7,

☎ 07221-17-200, www.alpenverein-baden-baden.de.

On Wheels

Baden-Baden has 300 km (180 miles) of marked **cycling** paths. Difficulties range from simply avoiding collisions with the well-heeled on the flat, but oh-so-grand shopping streets to professional endurance training up the Schwarzwald-Hochstraße. The routes in the Rhine plains are easier but the higher ones offer better views. On weekends, from May to October, the **VeloBus** transports cyclists with equipment from Baden-Baden to Sand and the Mummelsee in the Black Forest hills.

Bicycles can be rented at most hotels, usually for guests only, or from the parking garages of the Kurhaus, ☎ 07221-277-201; Vincenti, ☎ 07221-277-203; and Festspielhaus, ☎ 07221-277-298. Rental fee for two hours is €1 and €5 for 10 hours.

Two major holiday routes from Baden-Baden are easiest to explore by **car**. The **Badische Weinstraße** (Wine Route) runs from Baden-Baden through the local vineyards along the Rhine plains to Offenburg and back into the Black Forest. Several vineyards, cellars, and wine shops can be visited en route.

The **Schwarzwald-Hochstraße** (Crest Road) runs from Baden-Baden along the B500 to Freudenstadt. It follows the crest of the mountains and offers stunning views. It is a busy road with both commercial and holiday traffic. The 60-km (36-mile) route takes about three hours if sights en route are visited (see section below}.

Around 10 times a year, an old **steam train** operates in the Achertal, a valley about 25 km (15 miles) south of Baden-Baden. For information contact the **Achertalbahn**, Großmatt 15, 77883 Ottenhöfen, ☎ 07842-80-440, www.sveg.de. Round-trips between Achern and Ottenhöfen cost €8.

In the Air

Baden-Baden's location between the Black Forest hills and the wide-open Upper Rhine valley is ideal for all kinds of air adventures.

Europe's largest **balloon** fleet is stationed in Baden-Baden. **Ballooning 2000** Baden-Baden, Dr Rudeolf-Eberle-Straße 5, ☎ 07223-60-002, www.ballooning2000.de, flies up to 25 balloons per day in the region. Wheelchair users can also join some of the flights.

Paragliding is allowed from the Merkur peak in Baden-Baden. Tandem flights with experienced instructors are available – contact the tourism office for arrangements.

On Horseback

Baden-Baden has 150 km (90 miles) of marked trails for horseback riding. For riding opportunities, inquire from the **Reitclub Baden-Baden**, Buchenweg 42, ☎ 07221-64-666, www.reitclub-baden-baden.de.

In fine weather, a **horse-drawn carriage** is available for hour-long rides from the Theater along Licthentaler Allee and the center of Baden-Baden.

Twice yearly, the **International Club**, Lichtentaler Allee 8, ☎ 07221-21-120, www.baden-galopp.de, stages major **horse racing** events at Iffezheim. The Spring Meet is held late May and the *Großen Woche* (Grand Week) late August or early September. Both attract international competition and spectators. For those not interested in racing itself, these weeks are also a good opportunity to see the gathering of the largest and grandest chauffeur-driven cars and high-end fashion. The use of pantsuits became socially acceptable after they were worn here in 1907.

On Water

For a brief period during the mid-19th century, Baden-Baden was more famous for its casino and as a gathering place of the European nobles, than for its spas. However, as soon as the prudish Prussians had gambling banned throughout Germany in 1872, the balance of attention swung back to the waters that originally drew the Celts and Romans to the region. Daily, 800,000 liters/208,000 gallons of water bubbles from 23 springs at temperatures up to 68°C/154°F. Many hotels have their own spas, and several exclusive clinics offer medical water treatments, but two of the best **spas** are open to all and well worth the splurge.

The **Friederichsbad**, Römerplatz 1, ☎ 07221-275-920, www.roemisch-irisches-bad.de, is by far the classiest. The 125-year-old Friederichsbad combines the Roman bathing tradition of steam and thermal baths at different temperatures with Irish spa traditions. Visitors go through 16 basic steps and can add additional treatments and massages. The spa is open Monday to Saturday from 9 am to 10 pm and Sunday from noon to 8 pm. Sometimes the sexes are split for some of the facilities but still use the same main pools. The whole spa is nude. A basic three-hour stay costs €21. The minimum age for admission is 14.

Mark Twain on Baden-Baden

Mark Twain, who did not particularly like Baden-Baden, wrote, "At Friedrichsbad you lose track of time within 10 minutes and track of the world within 20..." Less kindly, he also observed that he lost his rheumatism in Baden-Baden and that the town was welcome to it.

The nearby **Caracalla-Therme**, Römerplatz 1, ☎ 07221-275-940, www.caracalla.de, is a far less highbrow, more accessible, and clothes-on facility in one of the loveliest spas in Germany. There are seemingly endless water facilities, including indoor and outdoor pools, whirlpools, and hot and cold water grottos. Seven different saunas and a range of massages, mudpacks, and other treatments are available. Childcare facilities, for children 18 months and older are available – children under three are not allowed in the pool area. Opening hours are daily from 8 am to 10 pm. Admission is €12 for two hours and €16 for four.

The Baden-Baden region is excellent for **fishing**, with the Rhine, the Altrhine, the Baggersee, and several other water sources open to anglers. An annual permit is required – for information contact the tourism office.

On Snow

Many winter sports opportunities are available along the Schwarzwald-Hochstraße, which leads from Baden-Baden to Freudenstadt in the heart of the Black Forest. More information is available from the tourist office for activities listed below without specific contact details.

Although the Feldberg region claims to be the original home of downhill skiing, **cross-country skiing** (*Langlauf*) is more popular in the Black Forest. The Northern Black Forest has over 1,000 km (600 miles) of marked trails and groomed tracks (*Loipen*).

The longest **downhill** (*Alpinski*) run is at Mehliskopf just outside Baden-Baden. The course is open daily from 9 am to 10 pm. It is floodlit from around 5 pm. Snow machines assure skiing most of the winter. About 20 additional runs are available along the Schwarzwald-Hochstraße towards Freudenstadt. For snow conditions: ☎ 07231-147-380 or www.noerdlicher-schwarzwald.de.

On weekends, if the snow conditions are right, "snow buses" run from Baden-Baden to Scherrhof at Lichtenthal. From here, a three-km (1.8-mile) **tobogganing** run goes through the forests to the bottom of the valley from where the buses provide transportation back to the top. Children of all ages are welcome.

From mid-December to late February, an outdoor **skating** rink at **Freiluft-Kunsteisbahn Wiedenfelsen**, ☎ 07226-722-6282, www.eisbahn-wiedenfelsen.de, is open daily from 10 am to 10 pm. Equipment can be rented on-site.

About 15 km (nine miles) along the Schwarzwald-Hochstraße is the **Mehliskopf Bobbahn**, ☎ 07226-1300, www.mehliskopf.de. Tandem **bobsleds** use gravity to reach speeds up to 40 km/h (24 mph) down the hillside, navigating 11 curves and several jumps en route. The facilities are open May to March and rides cost €3.

Archery

Archery can be practiced on the grounds of the **Heimbachtäler Schützen club**, ☎ 07221-681-686, from April to October. Equipment can be rented and instructions are available at a minimal charge.

Golf

The Baden-Baden area has some of Germany's best golf courses. The tourism office has a special bilingual brochure explaining the fares and availability to non-members. Proof of membership in another golf club is usually required to play on the better courses. Most have equipment for rent.

■ Where to Stay & Eat

Baden Baden has sufficient hotels to accommodate the well-healed travelers who frequent the spas, shops, and casinos. It has a rich hotel tradition: the Badischer Hof defined the concept of a grand hotel, the Europäischer Hof was the start of the Steigenberger group, and Cäsar Ritz ran the Minerva (now the Brenner's) before starting his own hotel chain. Most of the top hotels combine old-world charm with modern comforts. Lower-priced accommodations are available in the outskirts of town, but for significantly lower rates, it is best to stay in nearby towns.

If money is no object, the **Brenner's Park Hotel** is the natural choice – it is one of Germany's best hotels, in the grand tradition with service and décor to match. It has a large spa and beauty farm in addition to a private, fenced-off park along the River Oos. The restaurant (€€€€), with views of the Kurpark and the River Oos, serves international cuisine with strong Mediterranean influences. Schillerstraße 4, 76530 Baden-Baden, ☎ 07221-9000, fax 07221-38-772, www.brenners.com. (€€€€)

The **Schlosshotel Bühlerhöhe** is about 15 km (nine miles) outside Baden-Baden, but from its location 800 m (2,624 feet) higher than the city, it offers a view of the Rhine plains second-to-none. The service is outstanding too and many rate this Grand Époque hotel as the best in the region. Its spa and beauty centers rank among the most beautiful in Europe. The **Imperial** restaurant (€€€€) serves excellent French cuisine, a reminder that the French border is but a few minutes drive away. On weekdays, it is only open for dinner and reservations are recommended. The **Schlossrestaurant** (€€€) offers international and regional cuisine. Schwarzwald-Hochstraße 1, 77815 Bühl, ☎ 07226-550, fax 07226-55-777, www.buehlerhoehe.de. (€€€€)

The **Steigenberger Europäischer Hof** is another top hotel with an extravagant tradition and history. It was the hotel of choice of Queen Victoria, Russian nobles, and heads of state during the 19th century. The interior is elegant and rooms are luxurious. The restaurant (€€-€€€€), with bar and terrace, has international cuisine with regional specialties according to the season. Kaiserallee 2, 76530 Baden-Baden, ☎ 07221-9330, fax 07221-28831, www.steigenberger.com. (€€€€)

For 40 years, the **Dorint-Sofitel Maison Messmer** was the summer residence of Kaiser Wilhelm I. In 2001, the hotel reopened with a new wing to complement two historic buildings. It is a popular, luxury alternative to the other grand hotels in town and the closest to the Kurhaus. The **J.B. Messmer** restaurant (€€€-€€€€) serves international and nouvelle cuisine. The **Theaterkeller** (€€-€€€) is a more rustic wine cellar with regional specialties. Both restaurants are open for dinner only. Werdestraße 1, 76530 Baden-Baden, ☎ 07221-30-120, fax 07221-301-2100, www.dorint.com. (€€€€)

The **Belle Epoque** is a popular hotel in a restored 1870s villa inside its own private park. It is small compared to the competition – it has only 16 rooms and suites – but furnished with antiques from various eras. Maria-Viktoria-Straße 2c, 76530 Baden-Baden, ☎ 07221-300-660, fax 07221-300-666, www.hotel-belle-epoque.de. (€€€€)

Although in a former monastery, the **Steigenberger Badischer Hof** is luxurious and comfortable. It is at the northern edge of the pedestrian zone. The **Park Restaurant** (€€-€€€) offers regional and nouvelle cuisine. Lange Straße 47, 76530 Baden-Baden, ☎ 07221-9340, fax 07221-934-470, www.steigenberger.com. (€€€€)

The décor of the **Romantik Hotel Der Kleine Prinz** is a tribute to St Exupery's *The Little Prince*. Rooms are individually furnished. The restaurant (€€€) serves mainly French cuisine. Lichtentaler Straße 36, 76530 Baden-Baden, ☎ 07221-346-600, fax 07221-346-6059, www.derkleineprinz.de. (€€€-€€€€)

The third Steigenberger property in town, **Bad-Hotel Zum Hirsch**, is in a building dating back to 1689. Rooms are stylishly furnished. Hirschstraße 1, 76530 Baden-Baden, ☎ 07221-9390, fax 07221-38-148, www.steigenberger.com. (€€€)

Despite, or perhaps because of, all its style, class, and pomp, central Baden-Baden has only one Michelin star restaurant and it is not inside one of the top hotels. **Le Jardin de France**, Lichtentaler Straße 13, ☎ 07221-300-7860, not surprisingly, serves French cuisine. The restaurant is nicely furnished, with the terrace in the courtyard particularly popular. Reservations are recommended. (€€€-€€€€)

Despite its name, **Medici**, Augustuaplatz 8, ☎ 07221-2006, serves not only Italian food but also a wide range of international dishes, including sushi. Bill Clinton dined in this opulent fin de siècle building. It is open only for dinner and reservations are recommended. (€€-€€€€)

The **Kurhaus Baden-Baden**, ☎ 07221-9070, www.kurhausrestaurant.de, has a restaurant café with a pleasant terrace ideal for people-watching. International cuisine is served. The selection of cakes and ice creams is vast. (€-€€€)

Outskirts of Town

Although there are a few non-grand hotels in central Baden-Baden, they are unexciting and offer little charm at great expense. Far better deals can be found on the outskirts of town and in nearby villages.

The **Gasthaus Auerhahn**, is about five km (three miles) south of the town center on the B500. It is a typical Black Forest guesthouse with charming rooms and painted wooden furniture. It successfully combines the style of Baden-Baden with the more laid-back approach of the countryside. The rustic **Schwarzwaldstube** (€€-€€€) offers regional specialties. Geroldsauer Straße 160, 76534 Baden-Baden-Geroldsau, ☎ 07221-7435, fax 07221-7432, www.gasthaus-auerhahn.de. (€€)

Neuwier, 10 km (six miles) southwest of the center has a couple of pleasant hotels and restaurants. For more than 25 years, **Restaurant Zum Alde Gott**, Weinstraße 10, ☎ 07223-5513, has had Baden-Baden's second Michelin star. It serves regional and international cuisine, varying the menu according to the season. The wine list, which includes a large selection from Baden, is excellent. (€€€-€€€€)

The **Rebenhof**, in the wine mountains, has rooms with views of the vineyards and wide Rhine Valley. Rooms are comfortable, with wooden furniture. Both restaurants serve regional specialties. Weinstraße 58, 76534 Baden-Baden OT Neuweier, ☎ 07223-96-310, fax 07223-963-131. www.hotel-rebenhof.de. (€€-€€€)

Heiligenstein, even higher in the hills, offers equally good views and a quiet location. Rooms are individually furnished with ample use of wood. The restaurant serves local specialties. Heilgensteinerstraße 19, 76534 Baden-Baden OT Neuweier, ☎ 07223-96-140, fax 07223-961-450, www.hotel-heiligenstein.de. (€€)

Camping

Free parking is available for motor homes at the **Aumatt Stadium**, about two km (1.2 miles) east of the town center. Contact the tourism office for details.

The Schwarzwald-Hochstraße (Black Forest Crest Route)

One of the most popular drives in the Black Forest is along the Schwarzwald-Hochstraße (Crest Road) between Baden-Baden and Freudenstadt. The route mostly follows the B500, a major road from the Black Forest to the highways in the Rhine plains, and is usually busy with both commercial and holiday traffic. However, ample stopping points are available to safely enjoy the views. Driving the 60-km (36-mile) route takes about an hour, but plan on more than three hours if you want to stop along the way to take in the views.

■ Mummelsee

The Mummelsee is a small lake at the **Hornisgrinde**, the highest peak of the Northern Black Forest – a reminder of the time when most of the Black Forest was covered by an enormous lake. The Mummelsee is at 1,029 m (3,290 feet), allowing an ascent of the 1,164-m (3,818-foot) Hornisgrinde in less than 30 minutes. The area has a large restaurant, an even larger souvenir shop, and a huge parking lot somewhat out of proportion to the actual beauty of the lake itself.

Statistically, it rains here every second day, but when it's not raining, the lake is filled with vacationers. Paddleboats are available from April to October, 8 am to 9 pm, from **Tretbootfahrt Mummelsee**, ☎ 07842-99-286. Cost is €4 per person.

■ Allerheiligen

At Ruhestein, it is worth turning off the B500 towards Oppenau – but avoid this route during snowfall or heavy rain. A narrow, winding road leads downhill to the ruins of **Kloster Allerheiligen**. The monastery operated from the late 12th century up to 1803, but was destroyed by lightning weeks after the last monk left. Parts of the Gothic chapels and a vaulted porch are still standing. The monastery and a restaurant are five minutes walk from the parking area.

More impressive than the actual ruins is the surrounding area. The top destination is the **Allerheiligen Wasserfälle** (waterfall), which can be reached in a 15-minute walk from the monastery. Since the late 19th century, a series of flights of stairs have been built adjacent to the falls, opening them to the general public. A circular route leads down the 232 steps next to the waterfall and then uphill again along a gentler slope. It is also possible to drive two km (1.2 miles) down the road and approach the falls from the bottom. From here, it is less than 10 minutes walk to the bottom of the falls. The falls are not particularly big, but they are lovely, dropping 83 m (272 feet) in several steps.

■ Freudenstadt

Information Sources

The tourist information office is at Marktplatz 1, 72250 Freudenstadt, ☎ 07441-8900, www.freudenstadt.de. Opening hours in summer are weekdays from 9 am to 6 pm, weekends from 10 am to 5 pm; in winter, weekdays from 10 am to 5 pm, Saturday, 10 am to 1 pm, and Sunday, 11 am to 1 pm.

Sightseeing

In 1599, the Duke of Württemberg founded Freudenstadt in order to have a town on the crest of his Black Forest lands. He gave the town Germany's largest market square. The town center was extensively damaged during World War II, but rebuilt, mostly according to the original plan, immediately afterwards. Freudenstadt has excellent transportation links and its central location at the meeting point of several valleys makes it a major tourist town.

The main sights are at the huge **Marktplatz**, although the major roads that intersect at the square reduce the visible impact of its size. The square is surrounded by several arcaded buildings with shops and restaurants. The large water fountain changes shape frequently and children are allowed to play in it. At the center of the square is the town hall with the **Heimat Museum** (Local History), ☎ 07441-864-718. Opening hours are Sunday from 10 am to noon.

The **Evangelische Stadtkirche** (Protestant Church), Marktplatz, ☎ 07441-81469, dates from the early 17th century, but was mostly destroyed in the war. Of note is its odd shape: it has two naves at a right angle allowing half of the church congregation to attend services without seeing the other half. The carved lectern (1140) came from the monastery in Alpirsbach and the Romanesque baptismal font is from the same era. It is open daily from 10 am to 5 pm. Free guided tours in German are held on Friday at 2 pm. Admission is free.

Cultural Events

The **Schwarzwald Musikfestival** (Music Festival), Lauterbachstraße 5, 72250 Freudenstadt, ☎ 07441-864-732, www.schwarzwald-musikfestival.de, is held annually for about six weeks around May. Most events involve classical music and are staged at different venues in the region.

Adventures

The neighboring town of Dornstetten-Hallwagen has a unique **hiking** route. In the **Barfusspark (Bare Feet Park)**, www.barfusspark.de, visitors have to kick off their shoes and experience the therapeutic effects of different surfaces on the soles of their bare feet. Two circular routes are available: 1.4 km/.8 mile (25 minutes) for beginners and 2.5 km/1.5 miles (around an hour) for experienced barefoot walkers. It is open daily in summer from 9 am to 6 pm. Admission is free and shoe lockers are available.

There are 34 **cycling** routes ranging from six to 67 km (3.6-40 miles) available in the region. Information is available from the tourism office or consult appropriate cycling maps. Bicycles can be rented from **Rad & Sport Glaser**, Katharinenstraße 8, ☎ 07441-7985, or from the Kurhaus, ☎ 07441-864-732.

Paragliding and tandem flights are arranged by **MB Outdoor Sports**, ☎ 07441-952-139, www.mb-outdoorsports.de.

Seven **long-distance skiing routes** lead to, or from, Freudenstadt. Luggage forwarding services are available.

Another 11 shorter routes are available. These are mostly easy. And 15 more short routes are scattered along the Schwarzwald-Hochstraße on the way to Baden-Baden.

Equipment for all kinds of winter sports can be rented from **Sport Glaser**,

Katharinenstraße 8, ☎ 07441-7985, www.intersport-glaser.de.

Where to Stay & Eat

The hotel and restaurant facilities in Freudenstadt are not at the same elevated level as nearby Baiersbronn. However, it does have pleasant, mainly middle-class hotels.

Hotel Bären is a small hotel in the town center, close to the market square. Rooms are large and comfortably furnished. The rustic restaurant (€-€€) serves a wide range of international and local dishes of excellent quality at moderate prices. Langestraße 33, 72250 Freudenstadt, ☎ 07441-2729, fax 07441-2887, www.hotel-baeren-freudenstadt.de. (€€)

The **Kur & Sporthotel Lauterbach** is beautifully located with views across the valley. Rooms are comfortable and stylish. The spa facilities, upgraded in 1999, are extensive for a hotel of this price class. Amserlweg 5, 72250 Freudenstadt-Lauterbach, ☎ 07441-860-170, fax 07441-860-1710, www.lauterbach-wellnesshotel.de. (€€€)

The **Langenwaldsee Hotel** is right next to a small forest lake with terraces above the water. The public rooms are Black Forest rustic, while the comfortable rooms are mostly modern. Straßburger Straße 99, 72250 Freudenstadt, ☎ 07441-88-930, fax 07441-88-936, www.langenwaldsee.de. (€€-€€€)

Camping

Camping Langenwald has excellent facilities and space for 100 campers. Bicycles can be rented on site. It is open from Easter to October. Strassburger Straße 167, 72250 Freudenstadt, ☎ 07441-2862, www.camping-langenwald.de.

Königskanzel Hallwangen, in the nearby town of Dornstetten, is an equally excellent campground. It has 150 spaces and good facilities. Bicycles can be rented on site. The swimming pool is not particularly large, but is solar-heated. It is open year-round. Fam Eiermann, 72280 Dornstetten, ☎ 07443-6730, fax 07443-4574, www.camping-koenigskanzel.de.

RVs may park for free, but for one night only, at the **Panoramabad**, Ludwig-Jahn-Straße 60.

■ Baiersbronn

Baiersbronn is actually 12 small villages spread through the district to form the most popular winter sports area in the Northern Black Forest. It has many hotels, holiday homes, and some of the best restaurants in Germany – a convenient place to stay with easy access to all the attractions of the Northern Black Forest.

Information Sources

Tourist information is available from **Baiersbronn Touristik**, Rosenplatz 3, 72270 Baiersbronn, ☎ 0744284140, www.baiersbronn.de. Accommodations, including holiday homes, can be reserved on-line.

Adventures

Seven **walking** paths are scattered through the towns that make up Baiersbronn. These walks range in length from two to 10 km (1.2 to six miles); many are paved and accessible to wheelchairs and strollers. Although in town, many of the paths are so green they could equally qualify as country hikes. The tourism office has brochures about these walks.

Nordic walking – a hiking style from Finland with two sticks like ski poles – is currently fashionable in Germany. Baiersbronn took up the cause in a big way and has two dedicated **Nordic Fitness Parks** in addition to the normal hiking trails. The tourist office, as well as **Sport Klumpp**, Bildstöckleweg 27, ☎ 07442-84-250, www.sport-klumpp.de, rents out equipment. Guided Nordic walking tours are available on Thursday at 10 am and Wednesday at 6 pm.

Bicycles can be rented from **Sport-Frey**, Klosterreichenbach, ☎ 07442-6468, www.sport-frey.de. They can also arrange paragliding and tandem flights.

Baiersbronn is the center of winter sports activities in the Northern Black Forest and has many options for participants of all development levels. **Horse-drawn sleighs** are popular and operate as long as snow conditions permits.

For activities without specific contact details, get in touch with the tourism office. Equipment can be rented from **Sport-Frey**, Klosterreichenbach, ☎ 07442-6468, www.sport-frey.de; **Sport Klumpp**, Bildstöckleweg 27, ☎ 07442-84-250, www.sport-klumpp.de; or **Sport**

Faißt, Ruhensteinstraße 289, ☎ 07442-50-416, www.sport-faisst.de.

Baiersbronn has 10 **cross-country skiing** tracks. Most are relatively easy and some are floodlit. More tracks are available in nearby Freudenstadt and the Schwarzwald-Hochstraße.

Eight lifts for **downhill skiing** operate in Baiersbronn. Seven of the slopes are floodlit. A further 18 lifts operate along the Schwarzwald-Hochstraße, with the four at Mehliskopf (see Baden-Baden).

Skating is often possible on some ponds, but from mid-November until early April, the **Eislaufhalle** (Indoor Ice Skating Rink), ☎ 07442-7702, is in operation. It is open on weekdays from 2 to 9 pm, and weekends from 10 am to 7 pm.

Baiersbronn has two short **tobogganing** courses of 150 m (492 feet). Nearby Freudenstadt has three, including a 400-m (1,200-foot) course.

Where to Stay & Eat

The **Traube Tonbach Hotel** is one of the most famous in Germany. This luxury hotel is at the end of the road leading up the Tonbach Valley. Rooms are large, with stylish furniture. A large spa area adds to the appeal. In summer, red geraniums lavishly color the balconies. The hotel has four restaurants on site. Compiling a list of Germany's best restaurants by combining the ratings of seven gourmet guides, the Schwarzwaldstube here came out on top; the Köhlerstube ranked a creditable 69th. Chef Harald Wohlfard, has kept the **Schwarzwaldstube** (€€€€) at the top of the league and has been awarded a Michelin three-star rating for several decades. French food and the chef's own creations are served in luxurious surroundings. The **Köhlerstube** (€€€-€€€€) has a more country-house style and serves international dishes and nouvelle cuisine. The ambiance in the rustic **Bauernstube** (€€-€€€) is more relaxed. Regional specialties are served. All these restaurants have excellent wine lists and service. Reservations are advisable. Tonbachstraße 237, 72270 Baiersbronn-Tonbach, ☎ 07442-4920, fax 07442-492-692, www.traube-tonbach.de. (€€€€)

Things are equally opulent at the modern **Hotel Bareiss**. This luxury hotel has large, luxurious rooms with balconies and perfect views of the Black Forest. The huge spa area has an array of indoor and outdoor pools. The restaurant **Bareiss** (€€€€) has two Michelin stars, although some gourmets rate it higher than the Schwarzwaldstube. It serves French and Mediterranean cuisine in an elegant atmosphere. The **Kaminstube** (€€€-€€€€) has a country house décor and serves international cuisine. The **Dorfstube** (€€-€€€) is more rustic, with solid wood furniture. It serves regional specialties and is popular. All restaurants here have excellent service and superb wine lists. Reservations are recommended. Gärtenbuhlweg 14, 72270 Baiersbronn-Mitteltal, ☎ 07442-470, fax 07442-47-320, www.bareiss.com. (€€€€)

The **Romantik Hotel Sackmann** is beautifully located in a building typical of the region with many balconies and flowerpots. Rooms are comfortable and service excellent. The **Schlossberg** restaurant (€€€-€€€€) has a Michelin star and serves nouvelle cuisine but with strong Euro-Asian influences. It seats only 24 so reservations are advisable. Murgtalstraße 602, 72270 Baiersbronn-Schwarzenberg, ☎ 07447-2890, fax 07447-298-400, www.hotel-sackmann.de. (€€-€€€)

Hotel Forsthaus Auerhahn is beautifully located in a quiet, somewhat isolated valley inside a former forester's house. Rooms are well-equipped. The spa area is worthy of a much more expensive establishment. Fam Zepf, 72270 Baiersbronn-Hinterlangenbach, ☎ 07447-9340, fax 07447-934-199, www.forsthaus-auerhahn.de. (€€-€€€)

Pforzheim

Pforzheim, at the northern edge of the Black Forest, was virtually destroyed during World War II and the decision to rebuild in modern style left the town less attractive than others in the Black Forest. It is a major industrial center, but its true claim to fame is the jewelry industry that was founded in 1767 by Duke Karl Friedrich von Baden. Even today, 8,000 craftsmen in 350 factories produces 70% of all jewelry manufactured in Germany. Highlights of the local industry include the world's first battery-operated watches (1952) and the first quartz watches (1972).

■ Information Sources

Tourist Information: The Tourist Information Office is inside the Neues Rathaus, Marktplatz 1, ☎ 07231-145-4560, www.stadt-pforzheim.de. Opening hours are weekdays from 9 am to 6 pm, weekends from 10 am to 1 pm.

■ Sightseeing

Pforzheim has several museums dedicated to the jewelry industry. Most impressive is the **Schmuckmuseum Pforzheim** (Jewelry Museum), Im Reuchlinghaus, Jahnstraße 42, ☎ 07231-392-126, www.schmuckmuseum-pforzheim.de, which has a large permanent exhibition of European jewelry from the past 5,000 years. Locally manufactured jewelry and watches are also on display. Opening hours are Tuesday to Sunday from 10 am to 5 pm. Admission is free.

More specialized is the **Technisches Museum der Pforzheimer Schmuck- und Uhrenindustrie** (Technical Museum of the Pforzheim Jewelry and Watch Industry), Bleichstraße 81, ☎ 07231-392-869. It is inside a historic goldsmith factory and is mainly an exhibition of historic machines and equipment used by the industry. Opening hours are Wednesday from 9 am to noon and 3 to 6 pm; on the second and fourth Sunday of the month from 10 am to 5 pm. Admission is free.

Although far from the former internal border, Pforzheim has a **DDR Museum**, Hagenschiedtstraße 9, ☎ 07231-62-191, dedicated to life in the former German Democratic Republic. Around 3,000 displays ranging from everyday items to parts of an electric border fence are shown. Opening hours are limited to Sunday from 11 am to 1 pm, but exceptions can be made. Admission is free.

■ Shopping

Not surprisingly Pforzheim has many jewelry shops and design studios. English is generally spoken and personal designs are possible. The Tourism Office has a list of shops and studios open to casual visitors.

■ Adventures

Jewelry Making Courses

Several times a year, five-day courses are available to amateurs interested in designing their own jewelry. Arrangements are made by the Tourism Office.

Vintage Cars

Bertha Benz, wife of inventor Carl Benz, was born in Pforzheim. In 1888, she drove from Mannheim to Pforzheim, without her husband's permission, in his *Patentwagen* and thereby finally established the popularity of the internal combustion car he had patented several years earlier. The event is commemorated in even years on a weekend in August. On the Saturday, vintage cars are driven from Mannheim to Pforzheim and are on display in the Market Square until the return trip on Sunday morning. The dates of the **Bertha Benz Fahrt** are available from the tourist office.

■ Excursions - Maulbronn

Maulbronn is 20 km (12 miles) north of Pforzheim. Tourists head here to see the best-preserved medieval monastery complex north of the Alps, a UNESCO World Cultural Heritage Site.

The Cistercian monastery was founded in 1147 and in 1361 surrounded by walls that resemble those of a medieval German town. In this walled-off area, referred to as the **Klosterhof**, are a number of beautiful half-timbered houses – some dating from 1201. Most currently house restaurants or shops. The monastery dissolved after Württemberg introduced the Lutheran Reformation and a Protestant school was founded at the monastery in 1556. Famous students include Nobel literature laureate Hermann Hesse, German poet Friedrich Hölderlin, and famed mathematician and astronomer Johannes Kepler.

The original monastery was in a Romanesque style but most of the remaining buildings are Gothic. The triple-nave Romanesque basilica was consecrated in 1178 but Gothic elements were introduced mainly in the 15th century. The early 13th-century **Paradise Portal** is one of the earliest examples in Germany of a Gothic addition to the Romanesque. Equally impressive is the mid-15th-century carved monks' choir stalls that seat 93.

Several rooms off the cloisters are also open to the public. Most impressive is the **refectory**, completed in 1230. It has Early Gothic vaulting. Also impressive is the mid-14th-century **lavabo** that houses the fountain. The lay brothers' dormitory was rebuilt in the 19th century and is now often used for functions.

Concerts are frequently held in the monastery – sometimes by candle light.

Admission tickets for the monastery must be bought from the **Infozentrum**, Klosterhof 5, 75433 Maulbronn, ☎ 07043-926-610, www.schloesser-und-garten.de, which is across the courtyard next to the town hall. Opening hours are from March to October, 9 am to 5:30 pm, and from November to February, Tuesday to Sunday, 9:30 am to 5 pm. The Klosterhof area is always freely open. Admission to the monastery and church is €4.

From Pforzheim, Maulbron can be reached by Bus Line 734.

■ Where to Eat

There are several restaurants on the edges of the monastery complex. However, a pleasant traditional restaurant is inside the walled complex. The **Klosterschmiede**, ☎ 07043-40-000, www.klosterschmiede.de, is in a building that partly dates from 1201. Although a few international dishes are available, the local cuisine deserves the most attention. Local wine and beer are on offer. Service is fast and friendly. (€-€€€)

Bad Wildbad

After Baden-Baden, Bad Wildbad is the most visited spa resort in the Black Forest. The **Palais Thermal**, ☎ 07081-30-330, www.palaisthermal.de, is one of the most stylish spa baths in Europe. It was already popular with the nobles in the 19th century but recent restoration work brought the Neo-Classical exterior and Art Nouveau interior back to their former glory. The Moorish hall is particularly impressive. The natural temperature of the water is 41°C/106°F. All the usual spa extras are on available.

Not as opulent, but no less therapeutic is the **Thermalbad**, Bätznerstraße 85, ☎ 07081-303-253, www.staatsbad-wildbad.de. It is open daily from 9 am to 7 pm, but closes at 6 pm on Sunday, and at 9 pm on Tuesday and Thursday. The sauna opens only from 1 pm. Admission is €7.50.

■ Adventures

On the Sommerberg, near Bad Wildbad, is a special **Bikepark**, ☎ 07081-925-080, www.bikepark-bad-wildbad.de, with seven tracks for downhill racing. Lifts are available to take biker and bike up the hills. Bicycles and safety equipment can be rented on site.

■ Where to Stay

Campingplatz Kleinenzhof is an award-winning campground. It has excellent facilities and is beautifully sited. There are 320 spaces and it's open year-round. It has large indoor and outdoor swimming pools. 75323 Bad Wilbad, ☎ 07081-3435, fax 07081-3770, www.kleinenzhof.de.

Mobile homes may park for free, for one night only, at the parking lot of the **Sportplatz Bad Wildbad**.

Calw

Information Sources: Tourist Information, Marktbrücke 1, 75365 Calw, ☎ 07051-968-810, www.calw.de. Opening hours are weekdays from 9 am to 12:30 pm and 2 to 5 pm; May to September also on Saturday from 9:30 am to 12:30 pm.

■ Sightseeing

Calw is a pretty little town, idyllically located in the Nagold Valley. The tourism office fondly quotes Herman Hesse's words, "Many a pretty town have I seen between Bremen and Naples, between Vienna and Singapore... but the prettiest town of all that I know is Calw on the Nagold."

After the Thirty Years' War, the town was the most important commercial center in Württemberg. It was famous especially for its cloth and dyes; many of the large, half-timbered houses date from this period.

Marktplatz (Market Square) has several lovely half-timbered buildings. The **Neue Apotheke** was rebuilt after a major town fire in 1692. **Haus Schäbele** is the oldest building in the region and survived the fire almost intact. Herman Hesse was born in the adjacent Haus Schaber. The **Rathaus**, with round arch arcades, dates from 1673, while the upper stories were added 60 years later. It was altered in the 19th century and the figures date from 1929.

On the opposite end of the square is the **Hermann Hesse Museum**, Marktplatz 30, ☎ 07051-7522, dedicated to his life, work, and influence on literature and society in general. Opening hours are Tuesday to Sunday from 11 am to 5 pm (Thursday until 7 pm). Admission is €5.

Hermann Hesse

Hermann Hesse (1877-1962), Nobel Price winner for literature in 1946 and internationally the most read German writer of the 20th century, was born in Calw. It was only after his death that he became a literary idol during the 1960s and 1970s. His works reflect his humanity and open-mindedness – somethzing he found most lacking in pre-World War I Germany. As a result, he started to travel and finally settled in Switzerland, where he spent most of his adult life. His best-known works include *Steppenwolf* (1927) and *The Glass Bead Game* (1943)

The **Nikolausbrücke** (Nicolaus Bridge) across the Nagold is the oldest stone bridge across the river and the symbol of the town. On the old town side of the bridge is a rare bridge chapel. The Gothic masterpiece dates from around 1400.

The **Langer Turm** (Tall Tower), Im Zwinger 22, ☎ 07051-167-260, is the last remaining tower from the once mighty city walls. It has a small museum on the history of the town wall but the views from the top are more interesting. Opening hours are April to October on weekends from 2 to 5 pm. Admission is free.

Kloster Hirsau

About three km (1.8 miles) north, in the small town of Hirsau, are the ruins of two former monasteries. Kloster St Aurelius was erected in 1071 but parts of the church date back to 830. The **Aureliuskirche** (Church) is open daily from 10 am to 5 pm. The rest of the ruins are unfenced and open freely.

The **Klostermuseum Hirsau** (Monastery Museum), ☎ 07051-59-015, explains the life and history of the Benedictine monastery. It is open from April to October, Tuesday to Sunday, 2 to 5 pm (6 pm on Sunday), and from November to March on weekends only, 2 to 5 pm. Admission is €2.50.

On the opposite bank of the river, Kloster St Peter and Paul, more often referred to as **Kloster Hirsau**, was consecrated in 1092. At the time, it was one of the largest monasteries in Europe. Although now in ruins, the enormous size of the original triple-nave basilica, 100 m/330 feet long, is still evident. Particularly impressive is the **Eulenturm**, above, a Romanesque tower that survived the calamities of the centuries. During the investiture struggle, the monastery supported the Pope and gained importance during the 12th century. A major reformation of monastic life all over Germany was introduced here, including the appointment of lay staff and the return to a more spiritual life for monks. After the Reformation, the monastery became a Protestant school. Most of the buildings were destroyed by French troops in 1692 during the War of the Palatinate Succession. The ruins are unfenced and open for free.

■ Cultural Events

The three-week **Klosterspiele Calw-Hirsau** (Monastery Festival), ☎ 07051-968-844, www.calw.de, is held annually in July and August. Plays and concerts are performed on the open-air stage in the monastery ruins and inside the Aurelius Church.

■ Adventures

On Foot

The information office arranges a series of guided **walking tours** (in German) of Calw and vicinity. Tours are mainly scheduled on weekend afternoons from May to October. Reservations are recommended.

Many **hiking** trails lead from Calw into the lovely countryside for walks ranging from half an hour to several days. Consult the tourism office for detailed hiking maps.

On Wheels

In addition to the **Nagold Valley Cycling Route**, 17 more routes, ranging from 15 to 50 km (nine to 30 miles), are available in the region. Bicycles can be rented from **Maisenbacher Zweiräder**, Turnstraße 1, ☎ 07051-50-788.

A 12-km (seven-mile) **in-line skating** route stretches along the Kreisstraße in Altburg in the direction of Oberreichenbach/Würzbach.

On Horseback

Ponies and horses can be rented by the hour from **Spindlershof Reitbetrieb K Pfrommer**, Hausackerweg 8, OT Altburg, ☎ 0705-59-295.

■ Where to Sleep & Eat

The pleasant **Hotel Kloster Hirsau** opened in 1999 inside the 15th-century guesthouse of the monastery. Its location in between the two monastery sites allows easy access to both as well as to the rest of the region. Rooms are spacious and comfortable. The restaurant (€€-€€€) serves international cuisine as well as regional specialties. Wildbader Straße 2, 75365 Calw-Hirsau, ☎ 07051-96-740, fax 07051-967-469, www.hotel-kloster-hirsau.de. (€-€€)

Camping

The campground called **Terrassen-camping Schwarzwald-blick** is open year-round, although most of its 180 spaces are rented for long periods only. Facilities are rather basic, but the views are great. Weidensteige 54, 75365 Calw, ☎ 07051-12-845, www.camping-schwarzwaldblick.de,

Campingplatz Obere Mühle is a spacious, well-equipped site with good facilities and a large swimming pool. There are only 30 spaces for tourists and 80 for long-term campers. It is open year-round. 75365 Calw-Stammheim, ☎ 07051-4844, fax 07051-12-485, www.camp-obermuehle.de .

Free parking spaces are available for mobile homes next to the Alten Bahnhof, about 10 minutes walk from the town center.

Kinzig Valley

The Kinzig Valley forms the natural division between the southern and northern Black Forest regions. The upper parts of the valley are the most frequented, especially by travelers en route from the Freudenstadt area to Triberg and Titisee in the south. Highlights include the Monastery Alpirsbach and the open-air museum near Hausach in the Gutach Valley.

■ Information Sources

Tourist Information: Werbegemeinschaft Kinzigtal, Hauptstraße 41, 77709 Wolfach, ☎ 07834-835-353, www.kinzigtal.de, has information on all towns in the valley.

■ Alpirsbach

The Benedictine **Kloster Alpirsbach** (Monastery), Klosterplatz, ☎ 0744-951-6281, www.alpirsbach.de, was founded in 1095. The first church was consecrated in 1099 and the Torturm (Gate Tower) survived from this structure. The Romanesque parts of the St Nicolas Church date from 1130, while the Gothic parts are mainly late 15th century. The wall paintings in the middle altar niche in the east apses are original 13th century – the light switch is on the left of the niche. The sacristy is from the first part of the 13th century and one of the oldest Gothic works in Germany. The richly decorated Late Gothic cloisters south of the church

are surrounded by late 15th-century structures. The Reformation spelled the end for the Benedictine order here, but it was used as a Protestant institution up to 1807. Opening hours are mid-March to October daily from 9:30 am to 5 pm (Sundays only from 11 am), and from November to mid-March only, Sunday to Monday from 1 to 3 pm. Admission is €2.50.

Alpirsbach Klosterbräu beer is famous not only in town but across the region and beyond. The **Brauerei-Museum (Brewery Museum)**, ☎ 07444-67-146, is a block from the Monastery and guided tours of the facilities are available on weekends at 3 pm.

Cultural Events

Alpirsbacher Kreuzgangkonzerte (Cloister Concerts), www.kreuzgangkonzerte.de, ☎ 07444-951-6281, are held during summer. They attract orchestras from all over Europe and the focus is classical music. Other concerts are also held throughout the year, mostly in the church.

■ Schiltach

Schiltach is a small village at the confluence of the Kinzig and Schiltach Rivers. It has a beautiful town panorama with many half-timbered buildings in an outstanding state of preservation. The main road passes it by – turn off at either end of the tunnels.

The most beautiful area is the **Marktplatz** (Market Square), unusual in that it slopes steeply. It is surrounded by mostly half-timbered buildings as well as the painted Early Renaissance Rathaus (1593). The market fountain is from 1751 and the Gasthof Adler dates from 1604. The **Museum am Markt**, Marktplatz 13, ☎ 07836-5875, explores the history of the town. It is open daily from April to October, 11 am to 4 pm. Admission is free.

The **Gerberviertel** (Tanners' Quarter) has often been flooded in the past, but currently is in a good state of repair. The traditional industries were tanning and rafting. Trees were cut and bound together in rafts and then the local young men would raft merchandise down to the Rhine and often all the way to Amsterdam. It was a well-paid profession but risky. The **Schüttesägemuseum**, Haupstraße 1, ☎ 07836-5850, is housed in a former water-driven sawmill and recalls the industries from the past. The waterwheel is 7.2 m (23.6 feet) in diameter. It is open from Easter to October, Tuesday to Sunday, 11 am to 5 pm. Machines are demonstrated Friday afternoons from 3 pm. Admission is free.

Where to Eat

Café Kaffeebohne, Marktplatz, ☎ 07836-1200, is on the Market Square itself. It serves exquisite cakes and smaller meals. (€-€€)

■ Wolfach

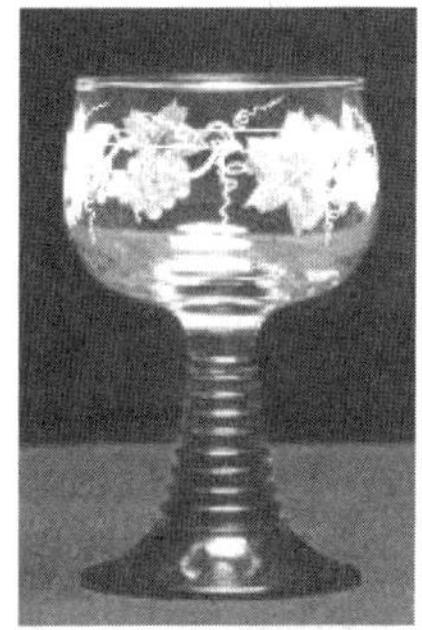

Glass blowing is a traditional industry of the Black Forest. However, nowadays most facilities are mere showplaces for tourists. The **Dorotheenhütte**, Glasshüttenweg 4, 77709 Wolfach, ☎ 07834-7834, www.dorotheenhuette.de, is the only remaining facility in the Black Forest that still primarily blows and etches glass for commercial sale rather than the tourism market. Tourists are still welcome to visit the glass museum, the workshops, and the factory shop. It is open daily from May to December, 9 am to 5 pm. Admission is €3.

■ Hausach

Near Hausach, in the Gutach valley is the **Schwarzwälder Freilichtmuseum Vogtsbauernhof** (Black Forest Open Air Museum), on the B33, 77793 Gutach, ☎ 07831-93-560, www.vogthauernhof.org. It is one of the most popular destinations in the region. At its center is the large, original farmhouse of the Vogt farm, dating from 1570 and surrounded by 25 other buildings, mostly farmhouses moved here from other parts of the Black Forest. The traditional life of the region is demonstrated in the museums, with different themes covered in each building. Opening hours are daily from end of March to early November, 9 am to 6 pm. Admission is €4.50.

■ Haslach

Haslach has a beautifully preserved, mainly 18th-century town center. However, most visitors come to see the **Schwarzwälder Trachtenmuseum** (Black Forest National Dress Museum), Im Alten Kapuzinerkloster, ☎ 07832-706-172. The museum aims to show the different *Trachten* (traditional clothes) worn in the various regions of the Black Forest. The most famous is the Bollenhut, below, the hats with red or black balls, worn by women in the Gutach area. It is open April to mid-October, from Tuesday to Saturday, 9 am to 5 pm, and Sundays from 10 am to 5 pm; mid-October to March, Tuesday to Friday from 10 am to noon, and 1 to 5 pm. Admission is €2.

Southern Black Forest

Freiburg im Breisgau

Freiburg is a beautiful city and a favored destination on any trip to the Black Forest. It has a population of 200,000 but somehow manages to maintain the unhurried charm of a small town. Its location between the Rhine plains and the western edge of the Black Forest assures a mild climate. Spring comes early; autumn comes late and drags. It claims the sunniest climate in Germany (although since re-unification that honor actually belongs to the island of Rügen).

Although the old town suffered severe damage during World War II, it has been beautifully restored to its original condition. The magnificent Gothic cathedral is the main sight but all of the old town invites you to wander and explore. Uniquely for a city of this size, many of the old town's streets still have "Bächle," little channels with water. In summer, children of all ages cool off in the water. According to legend, if you step in a Bächle by mistake you will return to Freiburg.

Freiburg is the main city in the Breisgau area. In contrast to most other parts of the Black Forest, Breisgau was ruled for almost 500 years by the Habsburg family – more famous for being the rulers of Austria, and frequently of the Holy Roman Empire of German States as well. Breisgau only became part of Baden after Napoleon created the Grand Duchy in the early 19th century.

■ Information Sources

Tourist Office: Information is available from Freiburg Wirtschaft und Touristik, Rotteckring 14, 79098 Freiburg, ☎ 0761-3881-880, www.freiburg.de. The office is halfway between the station and the minster. Opening hours are from June to September on weekdays, 10 am to 8 pm, Saturday, 10 am to 5:30 pm, and Sunday, 10 am to noon. From October to May, opening hours are weekdays, 10 am to 6 pm, Saturday, 10 am to 2:30 pm, and Sunday, 10 am to noon.

■ Transportation

In 2002, Freiburg became the first major German city to elect a member of the Green Party as mayor. In a city with such political leanings, it comes as no surprise that the public transportation system is superb. However, the average visitor will not use it much as all the sights in the old town are within easy walking distance. Most trams and buses depart from the main train station at the western edge of the old town, but a major tram line crossing point is in the heart of the old town where Bertold and Kaiser Josephstraße cross.

■ Sightseeing

The main sights are at Münster, Augustiner, and Rathausplatz – all in the old town.

Münsterplatz

Freiburg's best-known sight is the magnificent **Münster**, Münsterplatz. Although it has been the seat of a bishopric since 1827, the citizens continue referring to the church as a Münster rather than a Dom (cathedral) to confirm that the town paid for its construction. Small parts of the Romanesque church, built in 1200, survived, but most of the building is Gothic. Construction of the Gothic structure started in 1354, but it was only consecrated in 1513. Construction started in the east and culminated in the magnificent west tower. This belfry is housed in a delicately crafted openwork spire of stone. It has been described as the most beautiful tower in Christendom. The abundant use of gargoyles is a constant source of amuse-

ment – look for the one showing his rear to confirm that the medieval church was not as prudish as commonly thought. The interior is bright with several important art works, including a 13th-century Virgin (near the main entrance) and a 16th-century altarpiece by Hans Baldung Grien showing the coronation of the Virgin. Some of the windows in the south transept date from the 13th century. The 116-m (380-foot) south tower can be ascended via 328 steps to give wonderful views of Breisgau and the Vosges Mountains in France. The church is open Monday to Saturday from 10 am to 5 pm, and Sunday from 1 to 7:30 pm. The tower can be ascended up until 5 pm.

Several restaurants are housed in the buildings facing the church. The most beautiful of these is the arcaded, red **Historisches Kaufhaus** (Historic Department Store), erected in 1522-32. It was used by foreign traders in the city. The statues adorning the front of the building are Habsburg emperors. The building is only open for official functions.

The Baroque **Wetzingerhaus**, built in 1761 for the local artist Christian Wetzinger, currently houses the Museum für Stadtgeschichte (Local History). Apart from items related to local history, the magnificent Baroque staircase is well worth seeing. Opening hours are Tuesday to Sunday from 10 am to 5 pm. Admission is free.

Nearby is the 1733 **Alte Wache** (Old Guard House). It currently houses a wine shop where you can taste Baden wines.

At the south end of the square is the Baroque archbishop's palace and next to it the **Mittelalterliches Foltermuseum** (Medieval Torture Museum), Münsterplatz 12, ☎ 0761-292-1900, www.foltermuseum-freiburg.de, which takes a serious look at justice in the Middle Ages. Popular exhibits include chastity belts, a guillotine, and instruments of shame. Most descriptions are in English. Opening hours are daily from 11 am to 6 pm (opening at 10 am from June to August). Admission is €4.10.

Augustinerplatz

A former Augustine Monastery houses the **Augustinermuseum**, Augustinerplatz 1, ☎ 0761-201-2531, www.augustinermuseum.de. The museum has a significant collection of regional art from the ninth century to the present. The High Gothic cloisters are also worth seeing. Opening hours are Tuesday to Sunday from 10 am to 5 pm. Admission is free.

Nearby is the romantic **Schwabentor** (Swabian Gate, above), dating from the mid-13th century but restored in 1954. The statue above the arch reminded travelers that they were leaving Freiburg's juris-

Baden Württemberg

diction. Upper floors house the small **Zinnfigurenklause** (Tin Figures Collection), www.zinnfigurenklause.de, ☎ 0761-383-315. It has over 6,000 figures displayed in 17 dioramas, showing 24 castles from the region. It is open May to October from Tuesday to Friday, 2:30 to 5 pm, and weekends from noon to 2 pm. Admission is €1.20.

Rathausplatz

The Rathausplatz (Town Hall Square) is a lovely area of the old town with chestnut tress, outdoor cafés and, of course, the Rathaus itself. The **Neues Rathaus** (New Town Hall) was constructed in 1901 by connecting two 16th-century buildings that were previously used by the university. The small Glockenspiel (Carillon) plays daily at 12:03. The red, Late Gothic **Altes Rathaus** was destroyed in World War II but reconstructed to resemble its original mid-16th-century form.

Just north of the St Martin Church is the **Haus zum Walfisch** (Whale House). Most of this 1516 building where the humanist Erasmus once lived was destroyed in the War, but the oriel (bay window) and the richly ornamented Gothic doors are original

Schauinsland

Although not within the Freiburg city limits, the locals consider the 1,284-m (4,211-foot) Schauinsland peak as their own. The **Bergwelt Schauinslandbahn** (cable car), Im Bohrer 63, 79289 Horben bei Freiburg, ☎ 0761-292-930, www.bergwelt-schauinsland.com, takes visitors up to near the peak. At 3.6 km (two miles), it is the longest Umlaufbahn cable car in Germany and lifts visitors up 746 m (2,447 feet) in 15 minutes. From the mountain station, it is a short walk to the peak. Lovely views are available from the top. Many walks, scooter rides, and other adventures start from here.

The cable car operates daily from May to June, 9 am to 5 pm (6 pm on weekends), from June to September, 9 am to 6 pm, and from October to April, 9:30 am to 5 pm. Round-trips cost €10.20 for adults, €5.60 for children, bicycles, and dogs. Combination tickets with adventures are available.

By public transportation, it can be reached from Freiburg on S-Bahn 4; change at Günterstal to Bus line 21.

■ Cultural Events

Freiburg has a rich and varied cultural program. The town has seven theaters and four concert houses. The programs and schedules are available from the tourist office.

■ Shopping

Most of the old town is filled with shops of all kinds and sizes. The heart of the shopping area is the intersection of Kaiser Joseph and Bertoldstraße. The Markthalle (Market Hall) is in Kaiser Josephstraße just before the Martinstor – this area has many restaurants and specialty stores.

Next to the Münster in the Alten Wache is the **Haus der Badischen Weine**, Münsterplatz. It sells wine from the Baden region and tasting is available.

■ Adventures

On Foot

The tourist information office arranges a wide range of guided **city walks**. Tours are generally two hours long and are often available in English.

The more energetic can join a free guided **jog** through the city. The **Morgenlauf-Treff** (morning-run meeting), ☎ 0761-202-3426, www.morgenlauf-treff.de, meets on Monday, Wednesday, and Friday at 6:45 am at the main station for a five- or 10-km (three- or six-mile) guided jog through the city.

On Wheels

From the peak of Schauinsland, a very much adult-orientated eight-km (4.8-mile) downhill run can be done on 26-inch-wheel **scooters** – the minimum age is 12 years. It requires little effort, except for the hand-operated brakes. Combination tickets, including the scooter, safety equipment, and cable car ride up, are available from the bottom station of the cable car. For information contact **Bikers Paradise KG**, Im Bohrer 63, 79289 Horben, ☎ 07602-920-313, www.downhillrollerstrecke.de. Opening hours are from May to October on Friday and weekends, 10 am to 6 pm, and from June to early Septmeber daily at the same hours. The course is closed during heavy rain.

In the Air

Flugschule Dreyeckland, Freiburger Straße 5, 79199 Kirchzarten, ☎ 07661-627-140, www.flugschule-dreyeckland.de, arranges **hang gliding** and paragliding jumps in the region.

On Snow

The preferred site for **tobogganing** is on top of Schauinsland. From the top station of the cable car, it is about a 300-m (950-foot) walk to the Rodellift, ☎ 07602-920-313, www.rodellift.de, which pulls sleighs up to the start of the 200-m (650-foot) slope. Combination tickets, including the cable car and rental equipment are available. If snow permits, it is open Tuesday to Friday from 3 to 5 pm and weekends from 10 am to 5 pm.

On most Saturdays during the winter season, guided **snowshoe walks** are arranged by **Flugschule Dreyeckland**, Freiburger Str. 5, 79199, Kirchzarten, ☎ 07661-627-140, www.flugschule-dreyeckland.de. Walks range from three to five hours. Snowshoes and poles are available for rent.

■ Where to Stay & Eat

The top temporary address in Freiburg is the luxury **Colombi-Hotel**, halfway between the station and Münster. It is family-run and offers excellent service. Rooms are stylish and comfortable. The Michelin-star restaurant **Colombi** (€€€€) serves international cuisine in a luxurious setting. Reservations are recommended. The **Hans Thomas-Stube** (€€-€€€) serves nouvelle cuisine and regional sp;'ecialties in an original 18th-century wood-paneled setting. Rotteckring 16, 79098 Freiburg, ☎ 0761-21-060, fax 0761-31-410, www.colombi.de. (€€€€)

The **Ringhotel zum Roten Bären** claims to be the oldest guesthouse in Germany, with the building dating back to 1120 and the guesthouse tradition to 1311. It is in the old town between the Münster and the Schwabentor. The rooms are comfortable and adapted to the needs of the modern traveler. The restaurant (€€-€€€) serves local specialties. Oberlinden 12, 79098 Freiburg, ☎ 0761-387-870, fax 0761-387-8717, www.rote-baeren.de. (€€€)

The **Oberkirchs Weinstube** is next to the Münster and many rooms have views of the church and square. Rooms are comfortably furnished with either modern or country-style furniture. The popular, rustic restaurant (€€) serves hearty, regional cuisine. Münsterplatz 22, 79098 Freiburg, ☎ 0761-202-6969, fax 0761-202-6869, www.hotel-oberkirch.de. (€€€)

The **Intercity Hotel** is at the main train station. Like others in this group, the focus is on the business traveler, with well-equipped, modern rooms. The room key gives access to free public transportation. Bismarckallee 3, 79098 Freiburg, ☎ 0761-38-000, fax 0761-380-0999, www.intercityhotel.com. (€€€)

The **Schwarzwälder Hof** is a simple hotel and a good budget choice in the old town area. Rooms are mostly furnished in light wood. Herrenstraße 34, 79098 Freiburg, ☎ 0761-30-030, fax 0761-380-3135. (€€)

The best choice for food near the Münster is the Michelin star **Zur Traube**, Schusterstraße 17, ☎ 0761-32-190. The restaurant is rustic, yet elegant. Food is mainly light regional and Italian dishes. (€€€€)

Near the Colombi is the fashionably modern **Basho-An**, Am Predigertor 1, ☎ 0761-285-3405, serving sushi and other Japanese dishes. (€€)

The **Ganter Brauereiausschank**, Münsterplatz 18, ☎ 0761-34-367, is an informal restaurant in front of the Münster. It has rich wood paneling and serves local specialties. (€-€€)

Near Freiburg

Two small hotels, with excellent restaurants near Freiburg, offer a pleasant alternative to staying in the city itself. The **Hotel Zur Tanne** has been in business since 1786 and has stylish rooms. The restaurant (€€-€€€) uses ample wood in its decoration. The food is nouvelle cuisine. Altgasse 2, 79112 Freiburg-Opfingen, ☎ 07664-1810, fax 07664-5303, www.tanne-opfingen.de. (€€)

The **Schlegelhof** has only 10 rooms but they are comfortably furnished. Children are welcomed here. The roof suite is particularly attractive. The restaurant (€€-€€€) serves excellent local specialties. Höfener Straße 92, 79199

Kirchzarten-Burg-Höfen, ☎ 07661-5051, fax 07661-62-312, www.schlegelhof.de. (€€-€€€)

■ Excursions

Staufen in Breisgau

About 20 km (12 miles) south of Freiburg, at the end of the Münstertal Valley, is the pretty town of Staufen. It has a written history dating back to 770. From 1602, the area belonged to Austria, but in 1806 it became part of Baden.

DR FAUST

The most famous person connected to Staufen is Dr Johann Georg Faust. He was a doctor, alchemist, astrologer, and magician who, at the beginning of the 16th century, traveled widely through Germany – at least partly because he was never welcome anywhere for long. In 1540, he blew himself up by mistake while experimenting with chemistry. This happened in Room 5 on the third floor of the Guesthouse Zum Löwen – see Where to Stay below! Rumors soon spread that he was gruesomely killed by the devil at the end of their 24-year pact. The story of Faust is a recurrent theme in literature, with works on him by Marlow, Lessing, Heine, Thomas Mann and, most famously, by Goethe.

Staufen has a picturesque old town, especially along the pedestrian-only Hauptstraße. Most buildings are from the 17th and 18th century.

The **Rathaus** (Town Hall), Am Marktplatz, was erected in 1546 but was altered in the 19th century. The **Stadtmuseum** (City Museum), Am Marktplatz, is housed in the Stubenhaus, one of the oldest buildings in town. It has a small exhibition on the silver mining tradition that brought the town riches, on the Faust legend, and the Battle of Staufen, which ended the 1848 Baden revolution. Opening hours are weekends from 3 to 6 pm.

Nearby is the famous **Gasthaus Zum Löwen**, which dates back to at least 1407. The Catholic **St Martinkirche** was built in 1485 in a Gothic style on the foundations of a much older church. After a fire in 1690, the three naves were rebuilt with a flat ceiling. The modern high altar has a Late Gothic crucifix.

The ruins of the medieval **Burg Staufen** tower over the town. Although the castle's decline started soon after the extinction of the Staufen family line and the Austrian takeover, it was completely destroyed during the Thirty Years' War. It is worth climbing to the romantic ruins for the lovely views of the town and the Rhine plains.

Staufen makes a pleasant alternative to Freiburg for spending the night. Hotels are simple but well-maintained and hospitable.

Gasthaus Zum Löwen is in the heart of the old town. In 1539, according to legend, Dr Faust blew himself up, by mistake, in Room 5. The bedrooms were refurbished recently using light wood furniture. The restaurant **Fauststube** (€€-€€€) serves regional cuisine. Rathausgasse 8, 79219 Staufen, ☎ 07633-601-718, fax 07633-500-121. (€€)

Gasthof Kreuz-Post is a traditional restaurant with five neat rooms available for overnight guests. The restaurant (€€-€€€) serves regional specialties as well as a mix of international dishes. Haupstraße 65, 79219 Staufen, ☎ 07633-95-320, fax 07633-953-232, www.kreuz-post-staufen.de. (€€)

Europapark

Between Freiburg and Baden-Baden, along the Autobahn A5, is Europa Park, Rust, ☎ 01805-776-688, www.europapark.de, Gemany's largest entertainment complex. It is like a German-style Disneyland. Top attractions include Europe's highest and biggest rollercoaster, landmarks from 11 European countries, and 100 attractions and shows. It is open daily from April to early November, and in December from 9 am to 6 pm. Admission is €26.

Triberg Area

Triberg is Black Forest tourism central. It is full of souvenir shops and restaurants willing to dish out the *authentic* Black Forest experience. For independent travelers it is generally best to eat and stay elsewhere.

■ Information Sources

Tourist Office: The tourist information office is in the Kurhaus, Luisenstraße 10, 78098 Triberg, ☎ 07722-953-230, www.triberg.de.

■ Transportation

Although Triberg is a stop on the Intercity train line connecting Offenburg and Konstanz, trains are infrequent. The local bus network is better developed but it is generally easier to have private transportation in this area. A large number of visitors are on organized bus trips, which limits the need for better public transportation.

■ Sightseeing

Germany's **highest waterfall** is in Triberg. Three well-marked paths, usually crowded, lead from the town center to the falls, where the Gutach tumbles 163 m (534 feet) in seven cascades. The shortest route takes about half an hour from the bottom gate to the top of the falls and back. The falls attract a half-million visitors annually. From April to October the waterfalls are lit until midnight. During winter, two routes are lit up to 10 pm. Admission to the falls is €1.50.

Also in the heart of town is the **Schwarzwaldmuseum** (Black Forest Museum), Wallfahrtstraße 4, ☎ 07722-4434, www.schwarzwaldmuseum.de, with exhibitions of Black Forest stereotypes such as the cuckoo clock, mechanical instruments, and traditional dress. It is open from 10 am to 5 pm, daily from April to mid-November, and Tuesday to Sunday from mid-December to March. Admission is €3.

Maria in der Tanne, ☎ 07722-9532-3031, is a lovely Baroque church built around 1700. The high altar and pulpit are especially worth seeing. The church is at the edge of town on the road towards Furtwangen. It can also easily be reached on one of the walks from the waterfalls.

■ Shopping

Triberg is a good area to buy cuckoo clocks, and any other Black Forest kitsch. **Haus der 1000 Uhren**, An der B33, 78098, Triberg, www.houseof1000clocks.com, ☎ 07722-96-300, is one of the largest sellers of Black Forest clocks. It sells the complete range from around €15 to grandfather clocks costing several thousand euros. Worldwide shipping can be arranged and the prices quoted include all handling, customs, and delivery charges. The main shop is on the B33 near Triberg en route to Hornberg. A smaller shop is in Triberg itself at the crossing below the entrance to the waterfalls. Opening hours are Monday to Saturday from 9 am to 5 pm.

An alternative is **Eble Uhren-Park**, Schonachbach 27, ☎ 07722-96-220, www.uhren-park.de, an enormous souvenir and clock store. Opening hours are daily from 9 am to 6 pm (from 10 am on Sunday).

■ Adventures

On Wheels

The **Schwarzwaldbahn (Black Forest train)** runs from Offenburg to Konstanz on the Bodensee. The whole journey is beautiful but nowhere more so than the 26-km (16-mile) stretch between Hornberg and St Georgen. This segment has an altitude difference of 670 m (2,200 feet), a maximum gradient of up to 20%, and 39 tunnels. Normal trains use this line and cover the stretch from Hornberg to St Georgen via Triberg in 20 minutes. If planning a short round-trip, bear in mind that both Hornberg and Triberg stations are completely lifeless, with nothing to do if the round-trip connection is missed.

■ Where to Stay & Eat

Triberg

The **Romantik Parkhotel Wehrle** is an elegant establishment with its own private park. Rooms are individually furnished with modern or antique furniture. The **Ochsenstube** restaurant (€€-€€€€) serves international and regional cuisine in a stylish, wood-paneled setting. The rustic restaurant **Alte Schmiede** (€€) serves mainly local dishes. Gartenstraße 24, 78098 Triberg, ☎ 07722-86-020, fax 07722-860-290, www.parkhotel-wehrle.de (€€€-€€€€)

Best Western Schwarzwald Residenz uses light-colored, natural wood in the functional, yet comfortable rooms. All have balconies. The restaurant (€€-€€€) serves international and regional cuisine, but is open only for dinner. Bürgermeiseter-De-Pellegrine-Straße 20, 78098 Triberg, ☎ 07722-96-230, fax 07722-962-365, www.bestwestern.de. (€€)

Hornberg

Schloss Hornberg is in a former palace, an interesting alternative to the traditional Black Forest hotels in the region. Rooms are attractive; most have excellent views. Auf dem Schlossberg 1, 78132 Hornberg, ☎ 07833-6841, fax 07833-7231, www.schloss-hornberg.de. (€€)

Schönwald

A pleasant alternative to Triberg is staying in the nearby town of Schönwald.

The **Ringhotel Zum Ochsen**, quietly located at the edge of town, is a pleasant family-run sports and vacation hotel with a tradition dating back to 1796. The restaurant (€€-€€€) has wood-paneled walls, and serves local, Mediterranean and Alsatian dishes. Ludwig-Uhland-Straße 18, 78141 Schönwald, ☎ 07722-866-480, fax 07722-866-4888, www.ochsen.com (€€€)

The small **Hotel Dorer** impresses with attention to detail. The country house-style rooms are equipped with accessories usually only associated with pricier establishments. Schubertstraße 20, 78141 Schönwald, ☎ 07722-95-050, fax 07722-950-530, www.hotel-dorer.de. (€€)

■ Furtwangen

Furtwangen is a mainly industrial town but it is well worth stopping in to see the excellent **Deutsches Uhrenmuseum** (German Clock Museum), Robert-Gerwig-Platz 1, 78120 Furtwangen, ☎ 07723-920-117, www.deutsches-uhrenmuseum.de. It is one of the largest clock and watch collections in the world and is easy to enjoy even for non-enthusiasts. It also has an impressive collection of pre-electronic self-playing musical instruments. Opening hours are daily from April to October, 9 am to 6 pm, and from November to March, 10 am to 5 pm. Admission is €3.

The Origins of the Cuckoo Clock

Through the centuries, the watchmakers of the Black Forest produced many types of clocks, but none more famous or more often associated with the area than the cuckoo clock. The first clocks using the two-tone sound of the cuckoo were produced around 1730 – argument still rages whether it happened in Schönwald or Neukirch. The cuckoo clock in the form known today is more recent – it was first produced in 1850 after a competition to find a design that would be more popular.

Several places in the Black Forest claim to have the world's largest cuckoo clock – all of them best avoided. The Triberg area is a good place to buy cuckoo clocks but it is a case of buyer beware – a bargain almost inevitably means a cheap import rather than the real, locally crafted masterpiece.

Shopping

Furtwangen is not a particularly good place to buy watches. However, annually at the end of August, Europe's largest antique watch and clock exchange, www.antik-uhrenboerse.info, takes place in the school at the **Clock Museum**. Priority is given to Black Forest clocks, but all kinds of watches and clocks are exhibited and sold as long as they are not new.

Adventures

About six km (3.6 miles) north of Furtwangen is the **Bregquelle** (Breg Springs), the source of the mighty 2,888-km (1,780-mile) Danube River (*Donau* in German). Although other places claim the same honor, this is in fact the farthest point from the Black Sea. The start of the Danube proper is in Donaueschingen, about 30 km (18 miles) southeast. The Bregquelle and the small adjacent **St Martinskapelle** (St Martin's Chapel) are popular stops on hiking routes that crisscross the area.

Hoch Schwarzwald

■ Transportation

Special buses operate on weekends and vacation days to bring adventurers closer to the popular sights. Schedules are available from ☎ 07622-19-449, www.suedbahn.de. Bicycles on board are surcharged €2.50 per day. From May to October, buses for hikers and cyclists operate from Waldshut on the Rhine to St Blasien, from Freiburg to Wilhelmshöhe and Furtwangen, and along the Wutach Gorge. From December to April, the SGB bus line 7300 runs half-hourly, 9 am to 5 pm, from Titsee station to Feldberg's ski areas.

■ Titisee-Neustadt

Tourist Office: Tourist Information Titisee-Neustadt, 79815 Titisee-Neustadt, ☎ 07651-98-040, www.titsee.de. Opening hours are weekdays from 9 am to 6 pm and weekends from 10 am to 1 pm.

Snow telephone: ☎ 07651-980-428.

Sightseeing

The **Titisee** is a small, but beautifully located lake. It is at the crossing of many tourist routes and is popular. Serenity is not easily found here even in the off-season. In the high season, it can become unpleasantly crowded and is best avoided on summer weekends when seemingly no bus passes through the Black Forest without spewing its passengers out here for a while.

The Titisee was formed by a moraine barrier in the Ice Age. It is 40 m (150 feet) deep, but only two km (1.2 miles) long and 750 m (2,460 feet) wide – leading to the almost-true observation that the car park in summer is slightly bigger than the lake.

The **Alemannische Fastnach** is celebrated in Titisee with parades. It is usually held towards the end of February.

Adventures

The tourist office has information on the 150 km (90 miles) of **hiking** routes in the region. Around 50 km (30 miles) of winter hiking routes are also available.

Six walks of less than an hour each start from the Kurhaus in Titisee and a further six are available in Neustadt. A lovely walkway leads along the east bank of the lake – on the west side public roads must be used.

One of the most beautiful hikes in all of the Black Forest is in the **Wutachschlucht** (Wutach Gorge). This gorge has somehow managed to remain untamed and as a nature conservation area since the 1930s may succeed in remaining that way. The gorge itself is only accessible on foot, although crossroads make access by car and bus easy at various points along the route. The route is 33 km (19 miles) long, and generally divided into three equally long sections requiring three hours of hiking each.

An interesting, circular 95-km (57-mile) **cycling** route, taking five hours, starts from Titisee. It passes the Schlusee, St Blasien, Boll and Lenzkirchen at the edges of the unspoiled Wutach Gorge, before returning to Titisee via Neustadt. Shorter routes are of course also available.

Bicycles can be rented from **Ski-Hirt**, Wilhelm-Stahl-Straße 6, Neustadt, ☎ 07651-92280, www.ski-hirt.de; or in Titisee from **Bootsvermietung Drubba**, Seestraße 37, ☎ 07651-981-200, www.drubba.com.

Some 40 km (24 miles) east of Titisee is one of Germany's most interesting **train** journeys. The **Wutachbahn**, also known as the Sauschwänzle, covers 25 km (15 miles) from Blumberg-Zollhaus to Weizen, making four 180° turns and one 360° turn (mostly inside a tunnel), to cross the mountains. This strange track, of no economic value, was constructed at the end of the 19th century to allow the easier east-west movement of troops in southern Germany, without crossing the Swiss cantons north of the Rhine, in case of war with France. Although the track was used during both World Wars, in neither case did it contribute to troop movements as originally envisioned.

From May to October, steam and diesel engines pull museum trains along this track on a journey of just over an hour. Trains run at 10 am on Wednesday, Saturday, and Sunday. On most Sundays, afternoon trains run as well at 2 pm. During the high season afternoon trains also run on Saturday and Wednesday and occasionally on Thursday. The round-trip takes 90 minutes (€13, or €10 one-way). For reservations contact **Stadt Blumberg**, Postfach 120, 78170 Blumberg, ☎ 07702-51-200, www.sauschwaenzlebahn.de. Information is also available from the Wutachbahn supporter's club, www.ig-wtb.de.

Rowboats, pedal boats, and electrical **boats** can be rented from **Fa. Drubba**, Seestraße 37, ☎ 07651-981-200, www.drubba.com; or from **Firma Schweizer**, Seerundweg 1, ☎ 07651-8214, www.bootsbetrieb-schweizer-titisee.de. Boats are available for rent from 30 minutes or more and rates are lower in the mornings. Both companies also arrange 30-minute boat trips on the lake.

Fishing permits can be obtained from the Schwarzwaldhotel, ☎ 07651-8050.

Equipment for all winter sports activities can be rented from **Ski-Hirt**, Wilhelm-Stahl-Straße 6, Neustadt, ☎ 07651-92280, www.ski-hirt.de.

Ten **cross-country skiing** trails, ranging from a km (.6 mile) to 10 km (six miles), are in Titisee-Neustadt. A third of the nine-km (5.4-mile) **Moos Waldspur** in Titisee is floodlit.

Two **ski lifts** operate from 9 am to 5 pm in season at Waldau, ☎ 07669-690, www.schneeberglifte-waldau.de. A free shuttle bus is available from Titisee for holders of ski lift passes to the more challenging opportunities in Feldberg.

A kilometer-long *Rodelbahn* (**toboggan run**) goes downhill from Saig to Titisee. It is floodlit from 6 to 11 pm. A small course is available for children at the Bläsihof in Obertalweg.

Where to Stay & Eat

Treschers Schwarzwaldhotel am See is perfectly located right next to the Titisee. The large, comfortable rooms are furnished with country house-style furniture. The restaurant (€€-€€€) serves a wide range of international and regional dishes and offers a good view of the lake. The bistro-café also has lakeside seating and is arguably the best place in town to have a drink or light snack. Seestraße 10, 79822 Titisee, ☎ 07651-8050, fax 07651-8116, www.schwarzwaldhotel-trescher.de. (€€€-€€€€)

The **Maritim Titiseehotel** is another first-class hotel next to the lake. Rooms are comfortably furnished. The restaurant **Viertaler** (€€-€€€) has international cuisine and local specialties, with a marvelous panoramic view of the lake. Seestraße 16, 79822 Titisee, ☎ 07651-8080, fax 07651-808-603, www.maritim.de. (€€€)

The **Ringhotel Parkhotel Waldeck** is across the road from the Kurpark, about 100 m (330 feet) inland. It is a large, typical Black Forest building and has various categories of rooms. All are comfortable and service is friendly. The restaurant (€€-€€€) serves regional and Mediterranean cuisine. Parkstraße 4, 79822 Titisee, ☎ 07651-8090, fax 07651-80-999, www.parkhotelwaldeck.de. (€€-€€€)

Camping Bankenhof is on the banks of the Seebach stream, about 400 m (1,300 feet) from the edge of the lake. It has 190 spaces and is open year-round. There is a special section for youth campers about 300 m (1,000 feet) from the main site. Bicycle rental is available on site. Camping Bankenhof, Bruderhalde 31, 79822 Titisee, ☎ 07652-1351, fax 07652-5907, www.bankenhof.de.

Feldberg

■ Information Sources

Tourist Office: Tourist Information Feldberg, Kirchgasse 1, 79868 Feldberg, ☎ 07655-8019, www.feldberg-schwarzwald.de. Opening hours are weekdays from 8:30 am to 5:30 pm.

■ Transportation

Feldberg is on the B317 between Titsee and Lorrach. Visitors with a Gästekarte or Liftkarte can use free shuttle buses from Falkau, Altglashütten, and Neugalshütten to Feldberg-Ort.

■ Sightseeing

The highest peak in the Schwarzwald is the 1,493-m (4,900-foot) **Feldberg**. With a million and a half annual visitors, it is one of the most popular viewing points in the region and reasonably easy to reach. This is a nature conservation area and rules forbid wandering off the marked paths – in fact it was the first nature conservation area in Germany with a park ranger.

The **Feldbergbahn** (cable car/chair lift), ☎ 07655-8019, operates from Feldberg town to the 1,448-m Seebuck where there's a monument to Bismarck and a TV tower. A further easy 45-minute walk leads to the peak itself. From the top of Feldberg, the views are fantastic. On a clear day the Alps, including famous peaks such as Jungfrau, Pilatus, and Titlis, as well as the Vosges Mountains and Schwäbische Alb can be seen.

The Feldbergbahn operates daily from 9 am to 5 pm. In winter, it is a *Sesselbahn*, with six seats for skiers and in summer a *Kabinenbahn*, with a cabin for eight persons. In summer, bicycles, wheelchairs, and strollers can use the cable car as well. Even in summer, it is usually cool and windy at the top. In between seasons, the lift is closed for six weeks of maintenance work. Round-trips cost €7.

From the top, the almost perfectly round, small **Feldsee** lake can be seen. It is at 1,113 m (3,650 feet) and typical of lakes at the bottom of a glacial path. Many of the hikes in the Feldberg area pass along its shores.

Near the bottom station of the Feldbergbahn is the **Haus der Natur** (House of Nature), Dr-Pilet-Spur 4, ☎ 07676-933-610, www.naturschutzzentren-bw.de. It has information on hiking and cycling routes as well as exhibitions on the fauna and flora, geology, and land use of the Feldberg Nature Reserve. Opening hours are Tuesday to Sunday from 10 am to 5 pm. Admission is €2.

■ Adventures

On Foot

The tourist office arranges frequent **guided tours**, in German, of the town and local institutions.

Hiking is popular in this area, with the Feldberg itself offering excellent paths. Several walks originate from the top station of the Feldbergbahn (1,448 m/4,750 feet), ranging in length from 90 minutes to four hours. A popular walk is to the Feldberg peak itself. A round-trip walk takes 90 minutes. Most of the routes pass by *Hütten* (mountain huts) with restaurants serving hearty dishes. Walking down the mountain takes less than two hours but detours are more interesting and can take up to four hours.

Feldberg and Hinterzarten aim to be the most attractive area in Germany for **Nordic walking**. Currently, there are 13 marked trails totalling 101 km (60 miles) in the area. Luggage forwarding is possible for multi-day walks.

Guided Nordic walking tours are arranged mostly on Thursday mornings at 9:30 from the Feldberghall Altglashütten and on Wednesday at 10 from the Kurhaus Hinterzarten. Participation is free with a Gästekarte; otherwise it's €2.50. Details and rental walking sticks (€3 per day) are available from the Tourist Information office.

On Wheels

Mountain biking is allowed on paths wider than two m (6.56 feet) if not forbidden by specific signs. The 19-km (11-mile) circular route around the Feldberg is quite popular. It passes several country guesthouses, has wonderful views, and is mostly rated as difficult.

The **Bergbahn** transports bicycles as well, allowing for downhill riding from 1,448 m (4,749 feet) to Dreisamtal. The downhill rides are also suitable for families.

Bicycles can be rented from **MTB-Zentrum**, Benzenweg 3, Feldberg-Falkau, ☎ 07655-623.

In the Air

For **paragliding** and tandem flights in the Feldberg region, contact **Axel Plambeck**, Beim Steinernen Kreuz 10, 79798 Jestetten, ☎ 07745-308, www.air-power.de.

With Horses

Horse-drawn coach or sleigh rides are available from **Birlehof**, Schuppenhörn-lestraße 50, Feldberg-Falkau, ☎ 07655-778.

On Snow

The Feldberg area has the most reliable snowfall in the region and is popular for both downhill and cross-country **skiing**. For a snow report call 07676-1214.

Equipment can be rented from **Skiwerkstätte Lorenz**, Altglasshütten, ☎ 07655-278; **Skiverleih Schubnell**, Altglashütten, ☎ 07655-560; **Sporthaus**

Messerschmidt, Feldberg-Ort, ☎ 07676-229; **Skischule Thoma**, Feldberg-Ort, ☎ 07676-92688, www.thoma-sckischule.de.

Cross-country skiing is also popular in the Feldberg area. Some 120 km (72 miles) of marked trails (*Loipen*) are available at no cost.

It is locally claimed that downhill skiing originated in the Feldberg during the 19th century. It is still a popular skiing area with 29 ski lifts and 50 km (30 miles) of ski slopes.

DISCOUNT TICKETS

A combination day ticket for all lifts costs €22, but cheaper options are available for using fewer lifts, later in the day, or through multi-day tickets. Discounts are often available at the end of the season.

The Feldberger Snow Park at the Feldberg-Seeberg lift is specifically for **snowboarding**.

During the winter season **Skischule Thoma**, Feldberg-Ort, ☎ 07676-92688, www.thoma-sckischule.de, has daily skiing and snowboarding courses. It claims it can teach 95% of all students to ski in a day.

■ Where to Stay & Eat

The **Adler im Bärental** is a small hotel with apartments in a large farmhouse dating from 1839. Rooms are individually furnished, many with four-poster beds. The rustic restaurant (€€-€€€) serves mostly regional cuisine. Feldbergstraße 4, 79868 Feldberg-Bärental, ☎ 07655-230, fax 07655-930-521, www.adler-feldberg.de. (€€-€€€)

Haus Sommerberg is primarily a restaurant, but it does have seven rooms for rent as well. The restaurant (€€-€€€) serves international cuisine with strong local and Mediterranean accents. The service is excellent. Am Sommerberg 14, 79868 Feldberg-Altglashütten, ☎ 07655-1411, fax 07655-1640. (€€)

Hinterzarten

Near Feldberg, the town of Hinterzarten has several hotels offering a pleasant alternative to staying in the Feldberg area itself.

The **Parkhotel Adler** has been family-owned since 1446. It was completely renovated in 1999 and, in addition to comfortable, luxurious rooms, now also offers a large spa area. The restaurant (€€-€€€€) serves international cuisine as well as local specialties. Adlerplatz 3, 79856 Hinterzarten, ☎ 07652-1270, fax 07652-127-717, www.adler.de. (€€€€)

The **Thomahof** is a large, typical Black Forest hotel building. Rooms are comfortably furnished and a few apartments are available. The restaurant (€€-€€€) serves regional and Mediterranean cuisine. Erlenbrucker Straße 16, 79856 Hinterzarten, ☎ 07652-1230, fax 07652-123-239, www.hotel-thomahof.de. (€€€-€€€€).

Hotel Reppert impresses with stylish public rooms and comfortable bedrooms. The hotel has a large, beautiful spa area. The restaurant, open to hotel guests only, serves nouvelle cuisine with a large vegetarian selection. Adleweg 21, 79856 Hinterzarten, ☎ 07652-12-080, fax 07652-120-811, www.reppert.de. (€€€€)

Guesthouse Esche is in the quiet, small town of Alpersbach. Rooms are comfortable and well-equipped. The hotel has been managed by the same family for five generations. It is well-situated for forest hikes. The excellent restaurant (€-€€€) serves regional specialties. Alpersbach 9, 79856 Hinterzarten-Alpersbach, ☎ 07652-91-940, fax 07652-919-410, www.gasthof-esche.de. (€€-€€€)

Schluchsee

■ Information Sources

Tourist Office: Tourist Information, 79859 Schluchsee, ☎ 07656-7732, www.schluchsee.de. Opening hours are Monday to Thursday from 8 am to 6 pm and Friday from 9 am to 6 pm.

■ Sightseeing

The Schluchsee was originally a glacial lake but was dammed in the 1930s to become the largest single body of water in the Black Forest. It has a health resort on its shores, but most popular are activities on the water.

The lake is only seven km (four miles) long, but the height difference from here to the Rhine is 620 m (2,003 feet). As a result, several hydro-electrical plants have been installed between the lake and the Rhine. The villages on the northeastern bank of the lake are typical holiday towns with hotels, health clinics, and outdoor sports activities.

■ Adventures

On Foot

For information on **Nordic walking** routes in the region and pole rental, contact the tourist office. **Hotel Auerhahn, Aha**, ☎ 07656-542, offers guided tours and pole rental.

On Wheels

Bicycles can be rented from **G Müller**, Staumauer Blasiwald, ☎ 07656-850, or **Autohaus Rebman**, ☎ 07656-1027.

On Water

Boats of all kinds can be rented from several companies along the shores of the lake, including: **A Schlachter**, Wolfsgrundbucht and Strandbad Schluchtsee, ☎ 07656-512; **G Müller**, Staumauer Blasiwald, ☎ 07656-850; and **E Pohl**, Segelschule Aha, ☎ 07656-366. The latter also offers sailing courses and rents out windsurfing boards.

Already in the 19th century, when the Schluchtsee was still a small glacial lake, it was know for its good **fishing** and attracted anglers all the way from England to a rather forgotten corner of Germany. Fishing is still allowed but requires a permit (*Angelkarte*) – available from the tourist office, the kiosk at the dam wall, and several boat rental companies.

■ Where to Stay & Eat

The **Hotel Vierjahreszeiten** is a first-class hotel with modern, comfortable rooms. The spa and beauty treatment area is large and indoor golf is available too. The rustic restaurant **Am Kachelofen** (€-€€) serves regional specialties and the **Bella Vista** (€€), Mediterranean and especially Italian dishes. Am Reisenbühl 13, 79859 Schluchsee, ☎ 07656-700, fax 07656-70-323, www.vjz.de. (€€€€)

The pleasant **Parkhotel Flora** is high on the slopes and all rooms have balconies or access to the garden. Rooms are comfortable and stylish. The restaurant **St Georg** (€€-€€€) serves international cuisine. Sonnhalde 22, 79859 Schluchsee, ☎ 07656-97-420, fax 07656-1433, www.parkhotel-flora.de. (€€-€€€)

Wolfsgrund has 300 camping spaces and is directly on the banks of the lake with a beach in front of the site. It has good facilities and is open year-round. Campingplatz Wolfsgrund, Im Wolfsgrund, 79853 Schluchsee, ☎ 07656-7732, fax 07656-7759, www.schluchsee.de.

Mobile homes may park free for one night in the parking lot at Aqua Fun.

St Blasien

■ Information Sources

Tourist Information: Tourist Information St Blasien-Menzenschwand, Postfach 1140, 79829 St Blasien, ☎ 07672-41-460, www.st-blasien.de.

■ Sightseeing

The main reason to visit St Blasien is to see the third-largest dome in Europe. The **Dom Zu St Blasien** (Cathedral), ☎ 076272-678, was consecrated in 1781. Back then, as now, it was the largest dome in Germany and totally out of context with its surroundings. It overpowers the town from every direction.

The cathedral was erected in a Classical style to replace the Benedictine monastery's previous church that burned down in 1768. The prior at the time had visited Rome and Paris and wanted the new church to be like a Pantheon north of the Alps, along with some elements from Les Invalides.

Most of the church is under the enormous dome, with its 36-m (118-foot) diameter. The rectangular choir is the same length but appears smaller. The weight of the cupola rests on 20 Corinthian columns rather than on the outside walls. The interior is mostly white with a few light Baroque decorations.

Following secularization in 1806, the church was nearly destroyed for budgetary reasons. A fire in 1874 destroyed most of it, but it was rebuilt and restored in 1977 to its present form. **Kolleg St Blasien**, ☎ 07672-270, the school surrounding the cathedral, has massive proportions. It houses one of Germany's top private schools and is only open for a guided tour on Tuesday afternoons.

■ Cultural Events

The **St Blasien Klosterkonzerte** (Monastery Concerts), ☎ 07672-270, www.kloster-konzerte.de, are held mostly on Thursday evenings in the Festival Hall of the former monastery. Tickets are available from the monastery as well as from many tourism offices in neighboring towns.

■ Adventures

On Foot

The St Blasien area has 250 km (150 miles) of marked hiking routes. From May to October, guided hikes are arranged on Tuesday and Wednesday. An extensive bus network is also available to take hikers to and from starting points in the region.

On Wheels

A lovely, circular 90-km (54-mile), five-hour **cycling** route runs through St Blasien, to the Rhine River and then back via the Wehr Valley, Todmoos and Bernau. It passes through Bad Säckingen, which has the longest wooden bridge in Europe.

On Snow

Near St Blasien, in the small town of Todtmoos, international husky **sled dog races** are held each year, usually in February. Details on this Jack London experience in the middle of Europe are available from Todtmoos Tourist Information, Wehratalstraße 19, 79682 Todtmoos, ☎ 07674-90-600, www.todtmoss.net.

■ Where to Eat

Several restaurants face the cathedral, but for small meals and excellent cakes it is worth crossing the stream to **Café Ell**, Hauptstraße 15, ☎ 07672-2023. Although its interior is thoroughly modern, it has been in business for more than a century. (€-€€)

Belchen

■ Information Sources

Tourist Office: Belchenland Tourist Information, Gentnerstraße 2, Schönau, ☎ 07673-918-130, www.belchenland.com.

■ Sightseeing

Belchen, at 1,414 m (4,600 feet), is the third-highest peak in the Black Forest, but for many it is the most beautiful. The views from the stop are not bettered anywhere else, including from the higher Feldberg. It has been a nature conservation area since the 1940s and some of the flora are usually found only in the Alps.

Prior to December 2001, it was possible to drive to the top of the mountain. However, since then the road has been closed to private vehicles and the only ways up are on foot or, much easier, by cable car.

The **Belchen-Seilbahn**, ☎ 07673-888-280, www.belchen-seilbahn.de, lifts visitors up 262 m (859 feet) from the *Talstation* (Valley Station) to the *Bergstation* (Mountain Station) at 1,356 m (4,448 feet). The **Bergasthaus** (restaurant) here is the highest in Baden-Württemberg. From here it is a casual 15-minute stroll to the peak. The views are magnificent – on a clear day, even Mt Blanc can be seen.

The cable car operates daily from 9 am to 5 pm. The gondola takes eight passengers – wheelchairs, bicycles, and strollers are allowed. Round-trip tickets are €5.50.

The *Talstation* (Valley Station) can be reached by bus from Münstertal, with rail connections to Staufen, Freiburg, and Schönau.

■ Adventures

On Foot

Many popular **hikes** ranging from easy 30-minute walks to full-day hikes are available in the region. The most popular is the 30-minute walk from the Bergstation to the peak. A longer one-hour walk circles the mountain near the top with views in all directions. Walking from the Talstation to the peak takes just over two hours. Most of the way is easy but it gets steep close to the Bergstation.

Guided walking tours are arranged by the Tourist Information Office.

On Wheels

Bicycles can be rented from the Tourist Information Office.

On Snow

Belchen offers good winter sports opportunities. For snow conditions dial ☎ 07673-888-288. Equipment can be rented from **Jürgen's**

Sportladen, Friedrichstraße 20, Schönau, ☎ 07673-356.

More than 60 km (36 miles) of **cross-country skiing** paths are available in the region. The town of Aitern has more than 38 km (22 miles), including a floodlit route.

Downhill skiing is possible from Belchen, with slopes up to eight km (4.8 miles) long.

The most popular **tobogganing** run is at the Bergstation on Belchen. The former access road has been converted into a winter sports course. Some 4.5 km (2.7 miles) are available, with gentle slopes suitable for children's sledges and as hiking routes for adults.

■ Excursions

Bird Park in Steinen

About 40 km (24 miles) south of Belchen, near Lörrach is the Vogelpark Steinen (Bird Park), 79585 Steinen-Hofen, ☎ 07627-7420, www.vogelpark-steinen.de. The park has 300 kinds of birds, and other exotic animals such as kangaroos and monkeys. In the large tropical house, up to 200 birds fly freely. The birds of prey are the most popular and flight demonstrations take place daily at 11 am and 3 pm from the falconry. Opening hours are daily from March to October, 10 am to 6 pm, opening at 9 am from May to September. Admission is €12.

■ Bodensee (Lake Constance)

The Bodensee is the largest lake in Germany and the third-largest in Central Europe. It is 60 km (36 miles) long, 15 km (nine miles) wide, and up to 254 m (830 feet) deep. The lake is drained by the River Rhine into the North Sea.

In the Middle Ages important trade routes passed through this area. Several towns were free imperial cities for centuries, but by the Napoleonic era all had lost their independence – most became part of the Kingdom of Württemberg, although Bavaria claimed lovely Lindau.

The main attraction of the region is its natural beauty, but there are also many cultural landmarks here. Several Romanesque churches survive and Baroque masterpieces are found in seemingly unimportant, small towns. The wide variety of activities makes the Bodensee a favored holiday destination for people of all ages.

The region is best visited between late April and early October. Although winters are not particularly harsh, many attractions and hotels close during the winter season. Spring is particularly beautiful as the region is rich in blooming fruit trees. The snowcapped peaks of the Austrian and Swiss Alps form a lovely backdrop up to early summer. During July and August, the region get crowded, prices skyrocket, and traffic slows down to an unpleasant crawl. Autumn is also a good time to visit, with the large lake acting to moderate temperatures and ensuring generally pleasant weather up to late October.

Information Sources

Tourist Office: For information on the whole Bodensee area, including Austria and Switzerland, contact the **Internationale Bodensee Tourismus**, Insel Mainau, 78465 Konstanz, ☎ 07531-909-490, www.bodensee-tourismus.de. The tourism offices in many towns also stock information on neighboring areas.

BODENSEE DISCOUNT CARD

The Bodensee Erlebniskarte is a good deal for visitors to the region. It allows free entry to most major attractions in the region, to most open-air swimming pools, and to virtually all ships cruising on the lake. An added advantage is that it eliminates the need to queue for tickets at any of the almost 200 sites participating in the scheme. The one- and two-week cards are particularly good value. The cards cost €54 for three consecutive days, €67 for a week, and €93 for two weeks. They are available from most tourist offices in the region. All attractions listed in this section participate in the program unless otherwise noted.

Transportation

The most pleasant way to tour the region is by **boat**. The largest company is the **Bodensee Schiffsbetriebe**, Hafenstraße 6, ☎ 07531-281-389, www.bsb-online.com. It offers connections to and from most towns on the shores of the lake, with particularly good connections from Lindau,

Friederichshafen, Meersburg, and Konstanz. Lindau to Meersburg takes between two and three hours, depending on the number of stops along the way.

The **railway** is often the fastest way to travel. A rail line runs along the western shore of the lake, from Lindau to Ludwigshafen, but does not stop at Meersburg. **Bus** services are available where railways do not operate.

Although it is easy to drive the full length of the Bodensee from Lindau past Überlingen in a few hours, a **car** is a less than pleasant option most of the time. Even in the shoulder season, the going can be slow, with the stretch from Lindau to Meerburg taking well over an hour. Traffic is particularly problematic in Lindau and Friedrichshafen where the main road passes through the towns. An indecent number of speed trap cameras are also positioned along the B31. Adding insult to injury, for long stretches the lake is not even visible from the road.

Adventures

Germany's most popular long-distance **cycling** route, with 300,000 annual participants, is the **Bodensee Radweg**, www.bodensee-radweg.com. This 270-km (160-mile) route encircles Lake Constance and is usually done over a week, although it can also easily be handled in three days. A popular route is from Konstanz to Überlingen, 15 km (nine miles) plus a ferry ride, then 13 km (seven miles) to Meersburg, 17 km (10 miles) to Friederichshafen, 24 km (14 miles) to Lindau, and a further nine km (5½ miles) to Bregenz in Austria. Bicycles can be taken on the ships so it is easy to reduce cycling distances when desired. Bicycles and luggage forwarding services are available from most hotels.

Lindau

The tourism office likes to refer to Lindau as the happy end of Germany. It is the southernmost of the Bodensee towns, close to the border with Austria, and the only German part of the Bodensee that belongs to the state of Bavaria rather than to Baden-Württemberg.

Nestled on the small island of Lindau, it is a picturesque town with a lovely harbor and marvelous views of Alpine peaks across the water. The best things to do are walking around and enjoying the atmosphere, whiling away time in the harbor cafés, and leaving the few museums for a rainy day.

Information Sources

Tourist Office: Tourist information is available from **Verkehrsverein Lindau**, Ludwigstraße 68, 88131 Lindau, ☎ 08382-260-030, www.lindau-tourismus.de.

Transportation

Lindau has four **bus** lines running at 30-minute intervals but, once you are on the island, walking is the best option. Parking on the island is limited – during the high season a free shuttle bus operates between the island and some of the mainland parking spaces.

Lindau has good **rail** connections as well as good **boat** connections to other towns in the region. The station is on the island.

Sightseeing

Lindau Island **harbor** is arguably the loveliest on the lake and worth a journey in itself. It is the only harbor on the lake lit at night, but, even during the day, it is a beautiful and pleasant destination. Approached from the lake, the harbor walls are protected by a huge Bavarian lion and the 33-m (185-foot) **Neue Leuchtturm (New Lighthouse)**. Both were erected in the mid-19th century when the harbor was constructed – the lion serves as a reminder that this once-free imperial city has been under Bavarian rule since 1805. The lighthouse can be climbed for great views of the island and the lake. On the land side of the harbor is the **Altes Leuchtturm (Old Lighthouse)**, which dates from the 13th century. The **Seepromenade** is lined with luxury hotels and restaurants with pleasant terraces. The superb views of the harbor, lake, and Alpine peaks are factored into the price of the food and drink, but it is worth it.

Maximilianstraße is the island's grandest street and is lined with an array of shops in patrician houses. A major town fire destroyed much of the town in 1728, so most buildings are Baroque. The **Altes Rathaus**, Bismarckplatz, is a notable exception. It was built in Gothic style in 1422-36, but converted to Renaissance style in 1578. The painted façade illustrates the history of Lindau.

The **Haus zum Cavazzen** (1729) on Marktplatz is one of the loveliest patrician houses along the Bodensee. It currently houses the **Stadtmuseum** (Town Museum), Marktplatz 6, ☎ 08382-944-073, which focuses on furniture and cultural objects from the 15th century to the Art Nouveau. It also has a collection of mechanical instruments.

Two large churches form the east side of the Marktplatz. The Gothic **St Stephankirche** (St Stephan's) dates from 1180 but was converted in the late 18th century with light Rococo stuccos and decorations. The rather bare interior is the result of overzealous art destruction during the Reformation. The adjacent **Stiftkirche Maria Himmelfahrt** (Collegiate Church of Maria's Asuncion) was erected in 1752 for the local nunnery. The interior is richly decorated Rococo as could be expected from this period.

A third small church on the island is near the main station. The **Peterskirche** (Peter's Church, shown at left), Schrannenplatz, dates from about AD 1000 and was converted into a war memorial in 1928. Of special note are the 15th-century wall frescos – one is signed "HH" and may be the work of Hans Holbein.

Excursions

■ Bregenz

Bregenz, in Austria, is a popular excursion from Lindau. It is best reached by boat in about half an hour, although rail and road connections are also possible. Traffic can be heavy, with the 12 km (seven miles) taking more than an hour at times.

Bregenz itself is not a particularly attractive or interesting city, but it is popular for its Seebühne (Lake Stage) and the cable car to the top of **Mount Pfänder**. At 1,064 m (3,490 feet), this is the highest peak along the shore of the Bodensee and offers views second-to-none. On a clear day, the full length of the lake can be seen, along with 240 Alpine peaks. In addition to the views, a self-service restaurant and a falconry are at the top of the mountain. The **Pfänderbahn**, Steinbruchgasse 4, 6900 Bregenz, Austria, ☎ +43-5574-421-600, www.pfaenderbahn.at, operates cable cars daily from 9 am to 7 pm. Round-trip fares are €9.80. The valley station is about five minutes walk from the harbor.

■ Wasserburg

Six km (3½ miles) north of Lindau is the pretty, small town of Wasserburg. It has a beautiful peninsula into the harbor and a 14th-century castle – not open to the public. From 1592 to 1755, the castle belonged to the once fabulously rich Augsburg banker family, the Fuggers. A stone statue on the road to the mainland still reminds us of their time. The small St George Church and the castle are highly picturesque and one of the most often photographed scenes along the lake. It is best seen while approaching by boat from Lindau. Several restaurants with pleasant terraces have wonderful views of the lake and the Alpine peaks.

Adventures

■ On Foot

The tourism office arranges **guided tours** in German from April to September on Tuesday and Friday at 10 am.

■ On Wheels

Bicycles can be rented from **Farhrad Station**, Im Hauptbahnhof, ☎ 08382-21-261; or from **Unger's Fahrradverleih**, Inselgraben 14, ☎ 08382-943-688.

■ On Water

Boats of all kinds can be rented from **Grahneis**, An der Seebrücke im Kleiner See, ☎ 08382-5514; or from **Hodrius**, Bei der Inselhalle, ☎ 08382-297-771. Both companies can also arrange waterskiing.

Where to Stay & Eat

Although there are several fine hotels on the mainland, staying on the island when in Lindau is the most romantic option.

The **Bayerischer Hof** is conveniently located near the train station and across the promenade from the leisure boat harbor. Rooms are luxuriously furnished with all modern comforts. The restaurant (€€-€€€) serves international cuisine with a large vegetarian selection as well. Seepromenade, 88131 Lindau, ☎ 08382-9150, fax 08382-915-591, www.bayerischerhof-lindau.de. (€€€-€€€€)

Adjacent to, and under the same management as the Bayerischer Hof, is the Classical **Reutemann-Seegarten Hotel**. Rooms are comfortable and the views of the Alps are breathtaking. The restaurant (€€-€€€) serves international and local cuisine. Seepromenade, 88131 Lindau, ☎ 08382-9150, fax 08382-915-591, www.bayerischerhof-lindau.de. (€€€-€€€€)

The **Helvetia Hotel** is also on the lake promenade. Rooms are functionally furnished but comfortable, some with four-poster beds. The restaurant (€-€€€) serves local specialties including fish from the lake. Seepromenade 3, 88131 Lindau, ☎ 08382-9130, fax 08382-4004, www.hotel-helvetia.com. (€€€-€€€€)

A more rustic option, on the opposite end of the island, is the small **Hotel Brugger**. Rooms are simply furnished with unpretentious, light wood furniture but are reasonably comfortable. Bei der Heidenmauer 11, 88131 Lindau, ☎ 08382-93-410, fax 08382-4133, www.hotel-garni-brugger.de. (€€)

Camping

Park-Camping Lindau am See is on the shore of the lake just south of Lindau and close to the Austrian border. It is a comfortable site with good facilities. Bicycle rentals are available on site. It is open from December to October. Frauenhoferstraße 20, 88131 Lindau, ☎ 08382-72-236, fax 08382-976-106, www.park-camping.de.

Friedrichshafen

Friedrichshafen is a relatively young town, founded in 1811 by Friedrich I, the first king of Württemberg. Three companies played a major role in the town's development in the first half of the 20th century: Zeppelin, Dornier (aircraft manufacturer), and Zahnradfabriek (gears). The presence of the latter two made the town a major target during World War II and it was mostly destroyed in air raids. The town rebuilt in a modern and fairly ugly style, although some recent buildings are more attractive. It is primarily an industrial city, the second-largest near the Bodensee, but is worth visiting for its lakeside promenade and Zeppelin memorials.

Information Sources

Tourist Office: Tourist Information, Bahnhofplatz 2, 88045 Friedrichshafen, ☎ 07541-30-010, www.friedrichshafen.de.

Transportation

Driving in Friedrichshafen is fairly slow and a huge number of speed trap cameras on the B31 through-road ensure that it remains that way. Street-side parking is limited but parking garages are available near the main sights.

Good **boat** connections are available from Friedrichshafen. In addition to excursion cruises, a car ferry service is available to Romanshorn in Switzerland.

Sightseeing

The top attraction in Friedrichshafen is the **Zeppelin Museum**, Seestraße 22, ☎ 07541-380-010, www.zeppelin-museum.de. It is dedicated to the Zeppelins that were manufactured here prior to 1940. The number of actual Zeppelin pieces is limited and the largest part of the exhibition is photos and panels explaining the development of the Zeppelins. A major attraction is a huge, 108-foot reconstructed piece of the famous *Hindenburg*. It shows how grand and comfortable traveling in these marvels was. The top floor of the building has an art exhibition. The café is furnished in spacious Zeppelin retro-style and has a pleasant terrace with views of the harbor. Opening hours are Tuesday to Sunday from 10 am to 6 pm, closing at 5 pm from

The Hindenburg explodes, 1937

November to April. Admission is €7.50 (Bodensee Erlebnis cards not valid).

A pleasant stroll along the lakeside promenade is the **Schulmuseum** (School Museum), Friedrichstraße 14, ☎ 07541-32-622. It explains the development of schools from medieval to modern times. There are several classrooms and many exhibits may be touched and used. Opening hours are daily from April to October, 10 am to 5 pm, and Tuesday to Sunday, November to March, from 2 to 5 pm. Admission is €2.

Excursions

A worthwhile excursion, 20 km inland from Friedrichshafen, is to the towns of Weingarten and Ravensburg, which for all practical purposes have grown into one.

■ Weingarten

The main sight in the area is the huge **Weingarten St Martin Basilica**, Kirchplatz 6, ☎ 0751-561-270, www.st-martin-weingarten.de. It was constructed in 1715-24 as the largest Baroque church in Germany. The cupola was inspired by St Peter's in Rome and its façade by the Kollegienkirche in Salzburg. Its bright-colored stuccos were done by C D Asam and are complemented by other equally masterful stuccos and gilded works. The organ has 6,666 pipes and is popular for organ concerts. The church is part of a monastery complex founded by the Guelph (Welf) family in 940 and contains the graves of several members of this once-powerful family. A prize possession is the holy blood relic, claiming to contain blood from the wound in Christ's side mixed with earth from Golgotha. On the Friday after Asuncion, a religious procession attracting up to 3,000 horsemen takes place. On the night before, up to 10,000 pilgrims participate in a candle-light procession.

Cultural Events

The Weingarten Basilica is a wonderful venue for frequent musical events involving both the magnificent organ as well as five different choirs. Gregorian choir music accompanies services daily at 9 am and other choirs participate during services on special religious days. **Organ concerts** are held, May to October on Sunday at 3 pm and Thursday at 7:30 pm. International organ concerts are scheduled in July and August on Sunday at 5 pm. Schedules are available from www.st-martin-weingarten.de – tickets are only sold an hour before concerts and many concerts are free.

■ Ravensburg

Ravensburg is known to all German children and their parents as it lends its name to a large publisher and producer of children's games. The town itself has an interesting core, with 14 city gates and towers that survive from the Middle Ages.

Ravensburg was the seat of the Welfen in the 11th century and remained an important town up to the Thirty Years' War. It has been in decline since then, but some building still bear testimony to the glorious past.

The loveliest area is around **Marienplatz**. The 51-m (168-foot) **Blaserturm** was constructed in the 16th century as a fire watchtower. It can still be climbed from April to October on weekdays, 2 to 5 pm, and on Saturday from 11 am to 4 pm. Admission is €1. The **Lederhaus** (Leather House), now used by the post office, dates from the 16th century and parts of the adjacent **Seelhaus** are from 1408. Nearby is the Gothic **Rathaus** (Town Hall), dating from the 15th century. It is also worth following the former town walls to see the 14 surviving town gates and towers.

Traveling with Children

A few km south of Ravenburg is **Spieleland**, Am Hangenwald, 88074 Meckenbeuren, ☎ 07542-4000, www.spielenad.com, one of Germany's most popular amusement parks. It has 60 attractions and rides suitable for children from three to the early teens. Admission is €17 – Bodensee Erlebniskarte not valid.

Adventures

■ In the Air

A **zeppelin** in flight always causes some excitement among spectators. Even more exciting is actually flying in one. Flights in the Zeppelin NT, filled with safe helium rather than the hydrogen that did the Hindenburg in, are possible from Friedrichshafen. **Deutsche Zeppelin-Reederei**, Allmansweilerstrasse 132, ☎ 07541-59-000, www.zeppelinflug.de, has several flights per day ranging from €190 for 30-minute flights to €700 for two-hour flights. Weekdays are slightly cheaper than weekends and holidays.

■ On Water

Canoes and kayaks can be rented from **Sport Schmidt**, Scheffelstraße 4, ☎ 07541-23-531.

Where to Stay & Eat

The **Ringhotel Buchhorner Hof** is close to the Schulmuseum, with many rooms having lake views. Rooms are comfortable and well-equipped. The restaurant (€€-€€€) serves mainly international cuisine in a locale reminiscent of the early 1900s. Friedrichstraße 33, 88045 Friedrichshafen, ☎ 07541-2050, fax 07541-32-663, www.buchhorn.de. (€€-€€€€)

The **Seehotel** is in a modern building close to the station. Many of the modern, comfortable rooms have views of the lake. The restaurant **Uferlos** (€€-€€€) is in a modern bistro-style setting and serves international as well as regional dishes. Bahnhofplatz 2, 88045 Friedrichshafen, ☎ 07541-3030, fax 087541-303-100, www.seehotelfn.de. (€€€)

Best Western Goldenes Rad is close to the Zeppelin Museum in the heart of downtown Friedrichshafen. Rooms are modern. The restaurant (€-€€€) is one of the best in town and serves international and regional cuisine, including fish from the lake. Karlstraße 43, 88045 Friedrichshafen, ☎ 07541-2850, fax 07541-285-285, www.goldenesrad.de. (€€-€€€)

Hotel City Krone is in the heart of the town between the station and the Zeppelin Museum. The restaurant (€€-€€€) is open for dinner only and serves local dishes. Schanzstraße 7, 88045 Friedrichshafen, ☎ 07541-7050, fax 07541-705-100, www.hotel-city-krone.de. (€€€)

Meersburg

Meersburg is an attractive little town that attracts the highest number of Bodensee visitors. Most are day-trippers who come either to use the ferries to Konstanz or simply to see the lovely town. It has the oldest still inhabited castle in Germany, several beautifully restored medieval half-timbered houses, as well as a Baroque palace. It is best viewed from the lake, where the beauty of its buildings and the vineyards on the steep slopes of the lake can be appreciated.

Information Sources

Tourist Office: In the Oberstadt, at **Gästeinformation**, Kirchstraße 4, 88709 Meersburg, ☎ 07532-440-400, www.meersburg.de.

Transportation

Meersburg can only be discovered **on foot**. Although parts of the town are open to vehicles, no casual parking is allowed inside the town itself. The parking lot near the ferries is the most convenient although a second smaller site is available five minutes walk from the Oberstadt. The height difference between the Ober and Unterstadt makes for steep streets or stairs but the beauty of the town and the marvelous views are worth the effort.

Meersburg has good **boat** connections to all parts of the Bodensee. Half-day trips to Mainau Island are particularly popular. When facing the lake, the car ferries to Konstanz depart from the right side of the town and all passenger services on the lake are a few blocks to the left of the old town.

Sightseeing

For sightseeing purposes, Meersburg can be divided into two parts: the Oberstadt (upper town) and the Unterstadt (lower town). The Oberstadt has the best historic sights and views, while the main attractions in the

Unterstadt are the restaurants and small shops along the lakeside promenade.

■ Unterstadt

The Unterstadt has two main roads running parallel to the lakeshore. The **Unterstrasse** is lined with restaurants, hotels, vacation homes, and small shops and without lake views. The **Seepromenade** has similar attractions but with lovely views of the lake and prices reflect that. Some buildings in this neighborhood date back to the 16th century, with the ticket office for pleasure cruises in a former wheat warehouse erected in 1505.

■ Oberstadt

The Oberstadt can be reached via the stairs of Burgstraße or along the steep Steigstraße. Both routes are beautiful and rewarding. In the Steigstraße are several lovely half-timbered buildings and the Burgerstraße passes the huge waterwheel of the 1620 castle mill. The town is most picturesque at Marktplatz.

The **Alte Burg** (Old Fortress, shown in background above), Schlossplatz 10, ☎ 07532-80-000, www.burg-meersburg.de, is the most important sight here. The core of the castle was built by the Merovingian King Dagoberth I in the seventh century. It is thus the oldest still inhabitable castle in Germany. The prince-bishops of Konstanz used the castle as a summer residence from 1268 until it became their permanent residence after the introduction of the Reformation forced them out of Konstanz in 1526. A self-guided tour leads through 30 rooms and includes the rooms used by famous German poet Annette von Droste-Hülshoff, who frequently sojourned here in the mid-19th century. The tower can only be seen on a short guided tour. Splendid views of the lake are available from many vantage points but are most enjoyable from the small terrace of the castle café. Opening hours are daily from 9 am to 6:30 pm. Admission is €8.

For some of the best lake views, follow the Baroque staircase near the Alte Burg entrance to the terrace of the Neues Schloss. The **Neues Schloss** (New Palace), Schlossplatz, ☎ 07532-414-071, is entered from the Schlossplatz. It was built in the early 18th century when the Altes Burg was no longer thought suitable for the prince-bishops. Its Baroque interior, chapel, and museums are best reserved for rainy days – better examples are available elsewhere. Inside the palace is the Städtische Gallerie, with paintings by local artists, and the Dornier Museum with mainly photos and a few scale models of the famous Dornier planes of the early 20th century. The palace and museums are open daily from April to October, 10 am to 1 pm and 2 to 6 pm. Admission is €4.

Nearby in a small side street is the tiny **Weinbaumuseum Meersburg** (Viticulture Museum), Vorburggasse, ☎ 07532-440-400. It focuses on the local wine industry and is open from April to October on Tuesday, Friday, and Sunday, 2 to 6 pm. Admission is €2. Wine tasting and cellar tours are offered on most Wednesdays at 6 pm and Fridays at 7 pm from April to October – reservations via the tourism office are essential. Wine can be bought nearby in the Staatsweingut.

Cultural Events

The **Schlosskonzerte**, classical music concerts, are held throughout the year in the Neues Schloss. Information and tickets are available from the tourism offices in Meersburg and Konstanz.

Shopping

In its wine production, Meersburg has always valued quality over quantity and most wine is consumed locally. Although wine has been produced here at least since 1324, there is nothing stuffy or old fashioned about the **Staatsweingut Meersburg** (State Winery), Seminarstraße 6, ☎ 07532-357, www.staatsweingut-meersburg.de. The facilities are modern, as are the labels and products – the latest a white wine specifically to accompany asparagus (the Germans consume more asparagus than any other nation). The Staatsweingut sells wine and allows for tasting. A large selection of wines is also available from the **Haus der guten Weine**, Schützenstraße 1, ☎ 07532-49-450.

Omas Kaufhaus, Marktplatz, ☎ 07532-5788, has an incredible number of toys and gifts for sale. On the second floor of the shop is a wonderful exhibition of handmade model railways, boats on a water canal, aircraft, famous buildings, and dollhouses. The exhibition is open daily from 10 am to 6:30 pm and admission is €2.

Adventures

■ On Foot

From April to October, the tourist office arranges frequent **walks** in the town and region. Maps for self-guided walks are also available.

■ On Wheels

Bicycles can be rented from **Hermann Dreher**, Am Stadtgraben 5, ☎ 07532-5176; or from **Meersburger Hofladen**, Stettener Straße 44, ☎ 07532-414-227.

■ On Water

Boats of all kinds can be rented in Meersburg. Sailboats are available from the **Yachtschule am Waschplätzle**, ☎ 07532-5511. Canoes and smaller boats are available from **S Frey**, Anlegestelle am Stadtgarten, ☎ 07532-7732; or from **E Klingenstein**, Schifslandestelle, ☎ 07532-6630.

A larger selection of boats, including 10-m yachts with or without a skipper, is available from **Bodensee Motorboot-Charter**, Im Yachthafen, 88690 Unteruhldingen, ☎ 07556-455, www.bootscharter-weber.de. (Some boats require licenses.)

Despite the presence of beaches, the Bodensee is generally too cold for swimming even in the height of summer. Most towns, even tiny ones, have lovely solar-heated pool facilities generally open from mid-May to mid-September. However, **Meersburg Therme**, Uferpromenade 12, ☎ 07532-4460-2850, offers a full spa treatment. In addition to a heated 50-m (160-foot) outdoor pool and several children's pools and play areas, it also has a large indoor spa and sauna area.

Where to Stay & Eat

The **Romantik Hotel Residenz am See** is beautifully located a short distance out of town among vineyards and has a clear view of the lake. Rooms are comfortable and individually furnished. The restaurant (€€€-€€€€) is the best in the region, has a large wine selection, and serves nouvelle cuisine with a large vegetarian selection. Uferpromenade 11, 88709 Meersburg, ☎ 07532-80-040, www.romantikhotels.com. (€€€-€€€€)

In the upper part of town, behind a half-timbered façade, is the **Hotel 3 Stuben**. Rooms are modern and nicely furnished. The restaurant (€€-€€€) serves nouvelle cuisine in a modern setting. Kirchstraße 7, 88709 Meersburg, ☎ 07532-80-090, fax 07532-1367, www.3stuben.de. (€€€)

On the Market Square is the **Hotel Löwen**, with a 400-year tradition. Most rooms have pleasant views. The restaurant (€€€) serves international and regional dishes. Marktplatz 2, 88709 Meersburg, ☎ 07532-43-040, fax 07532-430-410, www.hotel-loewen-meersburg.de. (€€-€€€)

In the lower town, close to the Untertor, is the **Hotel Zum Schiff**. It is on the banks of the lake, with just the pedestrian lakeside promenade between the building and the water. Rooms are well-equipped. The restaurant (€-€€) is huge, but the terrace is particularly attractive with views of the lake. Bismarckplatz 5, 88709 Meersburg, ☎ 07532-45-000, fax 07532-1537. (€€)

Restaurant **Winzerstube zum Becher**, Höllgasse 4, ☎ 07532-9009, is in a side street close to the New Palace. It has a tradition dating back to 1610 and the décor evokes this long history. Regional cuisine is served. (€€-€€€)

Excursions

■ Überlingen

Überlingen is 13 km (7.8 miles) from Meersburg and a popular destination because of its pretty location and almost Mediterranean atmosphere. The town was a free imperial city from the 13th century onwards and seven city gates or towers survived. It is popular with artists and has an extraordinary number of small studios and galleries. Apart from the general town panorama, the Rathaus and Münster are well worth seeing.

The **Rathaus** (Town Hall), Münsterplatz, is a combination of two buildings from the 14th and 15th centuries. The main sight is the **Ratsaal** (Council Chamber, 1492), which is adorned with 41 carved wooden statues that represent the states of the Holy Roman Empire. The Ratsaal is open weekdays, 9 am to noon and 2:30 to 5 pm; from mid-April to mid-September also on Saturday, 9 am to noon. Admission is free.

The Gothic **Münster St Nikolaus** started out in the 13th century as a pillared basilica but was enlarged to a five-nave hall church in 1429 and eventually back to a basilica in the 16th century. The 78-m (250-foot) north tower has seven bells and the south tower, completed in 1444, has a bell weighing nearly 10 tons. An artistic highlight is the 1616 Renaissance high altar by Jörg Zürn – carved from wood it stands four stories high.

Where to Stay & Eat

The **Romantik Hotel Johanniter-Kreuz** is about four km (2.4 miles) outside the center of town. The rooms in the 300-year-old half-timbered farmhouse are furnished in a country-house style, while those in the new building are modern. The restaurant (€€-€€€) serves light, regional dishes. Johanniterweg 11, 88662 Überlingen, ☎ 07551-61-091, fax 07551-67-336, www.romantikhotels.com. (€€-€€€)

The **Bad-Hotel mit Villa Seeburg** is next to the Kurpark on the banks of the lake. Rooms are large and bright. The restaurant (€€-€€€) serves seasonal dishes and fish from the lake. Christophstraße 2, 88662 Überlingen, ☎ 07551-8370, fax 07551-837-100, www.bad-hotel-ueberlingen.de. (€€-€€€)

The **Bürgerbräu** is in the heart of the town above the city walls. It has 12 pleasant rooms furnished with painted pine furniture. The restaurant (€€-€€€) serves nouvelle cuisine and local dishes. Aufkircherstraße 20, 88662 Überlingen, ☎ 07551-92-740, fax 07551-66-017, www.buergerbraeu-ueberlingen.de. (€-€€)

■ Pfahlbaumuseum Unteruhldingen

An interesting stop en route to Überlingen is the **Pfahlbaumuseum** (Pile Dwellings Museum), Strandpromenade 6, 88690 Uhldingen-Hühlhofen, ☎ 07556-8543, www.pfahlbauten.de. It is an open-air museum with a reconstructed village representing life along the Bodensee in the stone and bronze ages (4000 to 850 BC). The village currently has 20 houses and an exhibition inside a museum. The village can only be seen on a guided tour. It is 25 minutes walk from the station and 15 minutes from the parking area – open daily from April to September, 8 am to 6 pm and in October from 9 am to 5 pm. In November and March, it is open on weekends from 9 am to 5 pm, and in January and February on Sunday from 10 am to 4 pm. Admission is €6 – Bodensee Erlebniskarte (discount card) not valid.

Konstanz (Constance)

Konstanz, with 80,000 inhabitants and the largest town on the Bodensee, is beautifully located on the southeastern shore of the lake where a narrow strip of land split the main body of the Bodensee from its Untersee prolongation. At this spot, the Rhine River leaves the Bodensee and starts its long journey to the North Sea. Although it has been an important city for centuries, Konstanz somehow managed to escape war damage – its close proximity to neutral Switzerland saved it from air raids during World War II.

Konstanz likes to claim that it was founded by Roman Emperor Constantius Chlorus around AD 300, but in truth, the city dates back to Celtic times. Its strategic location at the crossroads of major trade routes gave it prominence in the early Middle Ages. It received market rights in AD 900 and was a free imperial city from 1198 until 1548.

Its greatest moment came between 1414 and 1418 when the largest council during

the Middle Ages convened here to solve the problem of the three popes. Some 20,000 people participated in this council at a time when the town's total population was just 6,000. During the Council of Constance, Jan Hus was declared a heretic and burned at the stake. At the end of the conference, Martin V was elected Pope and thereby postponed the split in the Christian church by another century. It was also at this conference that "Lake Constance" became the English and French name for what is known in Germany as the Bodensee.

Following the Lutheran Reformation, Konstanz joined the Schmalkalden League and, after its defeat, was annexed by Austria and forcibly returned to Roman Catholicism. In 1805, Konstanz became part of Württemberg and has remained German ever since despite being on a small piece of land that logically should have been part of Switzerland.

Information Sources

Tourist Office: The Tourist Information, Postfach 102152, 78421 Konstanz, ☎ 07531-133-026, www.konstanz.de, is inside the main train station.

Getting Around

Most of Konstanz is easily explored on **foot**. The Bodensee ships arrive at the harbor in the heart of the old town near the main train station. The **car ferries** from Meersburg, however, dock in the northern suburbs of the town, several km from the old town. A frequent **bus** service is available from here to the main station.

Sightseeing

Despite being the largest city on the Bodensee, the old town of Konstanz is compact. Virtually all the major sights are south of the River Rhine, with a few notable exceptions on its northern shores. A pleasant walk starts from the station or harbor along the lakeside promenade.

Imperia, a voluptuous lady, is a nine-m (30-foot) sculpture by Peter Lenk that welcomes travelers to the harbor of Konstanz. It slowly turns on its pedestal so it can be appreciated from all angles. The sculpture is based on a character from Honoré de Balzac's similarly titled novel. In the novel, the lovely lady tempts both the religious and secular leaders; the sculpture holds a disdained pope in one hand and an equally weak emperor in the other. The controversy following its unveiling in 1993 has largely died down.

The huge **Konzilgebäude** (Council Building) was erected in 1388 as a warehouse for trade with southern Europe. It is, however, most famous for housing the Council of Constance. From November 8 to 11, 1417, the conclave of cardinals and envoys were locked into this building and finally emerged after electing Cardinal Otto Colonna as Pope Martin V. It currently houses a popular restaurant. Near the building are statues of Ferdinand Graf von Zeppelin, who was born in Konstanz in 1838, and Jan Hus, who was burned at the stake here in 1415.

The promenade leads through a shady park and via the island housing the Steigenberger Hotel to the River Rhine. Across the river is the lovely **Seestraße**. It has a row of 19th-century buildings. Luxury restaurants and hotels, as well as the casino, are in this street.

The oldest part of Konstanz is the **Niederburg** area between the Rhine and the Münster. The buildings in these narrow alleys date mostly from the 13th to

16th centuries. Many currently house specialty shops and restaurants.

The **Münster Unser Lieben Frau** (Minster of Our Dear Lady), Münsterplatz, ☎ 07531-90-620, www.kath-kirche-konstanz.de, was constructed over a period of several centuries and lacks the artistic unity of most other churches in the region. The Romanesque basilica, built in 1052-89 over a 10th-century crypt, still forms the core of the present building. Gothic side-chapels were added in the 14th century; the organ decorations are Renaissance; Baroque vaults were added to the central nave in 1680; and a Neo-Gothic top, as was popular in the mid-19th century, was added to the 76-m (250-foot) tower.

Although the Swiss reformer Ulrich Zwingli had many of the statues destroyed, the interior is still filled with art. Of particular note is the intricately carved spiral staircase turret (1438), the four large, gilded copper plaques from the 11th to 13th centuries housed in the crypt, and the marble Thomasaltar (1680). A door from the **Konradi Chapel**, to the left of the high altar, leads to the two remaining wings of the Late Gothic cloisters. From here, enter the 13th-century **Mauritius rotunda**. The wall paintings are Renaissance, but the true masterpiece is the huge 13th-century Holy Tomb, with three groups of statues – a rare example from this period.

In 1821, the church was downgraded from a Dom (cathedral) to a Münster (minster) when the bishopric moved to Freiburg. Ironically, Freiburgers were not that impressed – they still refer to their lovely Gothic church as a Münster, rather than a Dom. The church is open daily from 8 am to 6 pm.

The **Rathaus** (Town Hall), Kanzleistraße, constructed by combining several mostly medieval buildings, is worth seeing. The painted façade (1864), facing Kanzleistraße, illustrates events from the town's history. Enter through the Gothic arches to see the lovely Renaissance courtyard.

From the Rathaus, Hussenstraße leads to the 14th-century **Schnetztor**, one of only three remaining medieval city gates. Shortly before the gate is the **Hus Museum**, Hussenstraße 64, ☎ 07531-29-042, dedicated to the memory of the Prague church reformer Jan Hus. It was long thought that he actually lived here during his visit to the Council of Constance. (He actually stayed at Number 22 in the house Zur Roten Kanne.) Hus, who among other things questioned the authority of the Pope, was invited to explain himself at the Council of Constance. Emperor Sigismund assured him safe passage, but rescinded that in an effort to win favor with the church. In 1415, Hus was declared a heretic and burned at the stake outside the city gates.

The **Rosgartenmuseum**, Rosgartenstraße 3, ☎ 07531-900-246, www.stadt.konstanz.de, is the most important art collection along the Bodensee. Expositions explain the history of the region with special emphasis on Konstanz. A prized possession is the Paleolithic wall carving of a reindeer, made around 10,000 BC. The majority of the collection is artifacts from the Middle Ages to the 19th century. More recent items include a CARE packet, hugely sought-after food parcels sent from the US to Germany after World War II. Opening hours are Tuesday to Friday from 10 am to 6 pm, weekends from 10 am to 5 pm. Admission is €3, Bodensee Erlebniskarte not valid.

Sea Life Konstanz, Hafenstraße 9, ☎ 04531-128-270, is especially popular with children. At the lower end of the old town, a few minutes walk past the train station and virtually at the Swiss border, it takes visitors on an underwater tour of life in the Rhine from its source to where it flows into the North Sea. Open daily from 10 am, closing at 5 pm from November to April; at 6 pm on all weekends and in May, June, September, and October; at 7 pm from July to mid-September. Admission is €10.50. If visiting by car, park in the nearby Lago shopping center – a bridge from the second floor crosses the railway lines. (The seemingly free parking spots in front of Sea Life are only for buses and fines are dished out to parked cars.)

The **Bodensee Naturmuseum**, ☎ 07531-1287-3900, is above Sea Life. This hands-on museum explains the natural history of the Bodensee. Opening hours are similar to Sea Life and admission is free.

TRAVELING WITH CHILDREN

In front of Sea Life is a large free playing area called **Steine in Fluss** (Stones in the River). It explains the role of stones in life but is predominantly a play area with a small climbing wall, sand pits, and water features. The area is unfenced and always freely accessible.

Cultural Events

Konstanz has a busy cultural calendar with a wide range of offerings from popular music to religious organ concerts. Classical music generally features prominently.

Saturdays from 12:05 pm, free 15-minute organ recitals to encourage meditation are held in the Münster. Also in the Münster, but more lively, are international organ concerts scheduled annually from mid-July to mid-August. Tickets are available from the tourist office.

Shopping

The **Spitalkellerei Konstanz**, Brückengasse 16, ☎ 07531-128-760, www.spitalkellerei-konstanz.de, dates back to 1272 and is one of the oldest wine cellars in Germany. Selling quality wine and offering wine tasting and cellar tours, it is in the old Niederburg area, close to the Steigenberger hotel.

The old town is a shopper's paradise with about 400 shops. The Marktgasse is the commercial heart of the town but many shops are also found in side streets.

Adventures

■ On Foot

The tourist office arranges daily two-hour **town walks** from April to October at 10:30 am from Monday to Saturday and at 2:30 pm on Sunday. Thematic walks are available less often.

The tourist office also has handy leaflets on **self-guided walking tours** of the town. Audio sets with commentary can be rented for €7.50.

■ On Wheels

Bicycles can be rented from **Kultur-Rädle Radverleih**, Ladenzeile, Bahnhofplatz 29, ☎ 07531-27-310, www.kultur-raedle.de. The company also conducts guided cycling tours of the region.

■ On Water

Most of the Bodensee is calm. However, around Konstanz the effects of the Rhine River flowing out of the lake make clear why the bay is commonly referred to as the "Constance Funnel."

The largest **canoe rental** firm at the Bodensee is **La Canoa**, Robert-Bosch-Straße 4, ☎ 07531-959-595, www.lacanoa.com. It has branches in several Bodensee towns, including Friedrichshafen, Reichenau, and Überlingen. It arranges guided canoe tours and on Sundays special tours are available for beginners and families with small children.

On a less elaborate scale, **Zum Strandkörble**, at Strandbad Wallhausen, Uferstraße 39, ☎ 07533-998-813, rents canoes and kayaks. **Marc Fluck**, am Gondelhafen, ☎ 07531-21-881, rents out pedal, rowing, electrical, and solar powered boats.

Yachts and motor boats can be chartered, with or without skipper, from **Engert-Line**, Hafenstraße 10, 78462, ☎ 07531-26-075, www.bodensee-yachtzentrum.de.

In addition to the **car ferry** to Meersburg, and the regular pleasure boat **cruises** on the Bodensee, other interesting cruises are available from Konstanz.

The 1913 ***Hohentwiel***, Lindauerstraße 84, ☎ 01805-133-030, is the last remaining steamship operating on the Bodensee. It regularly offers excursions from Konstanz.

One of the loveliest cruises in Germany is the 3½-hour journey down the River Rhine from Konstanz to Schaffhausen near the Rhine falls. The **Schweizerische Schiffahrtgesellschaft**, Untersee und Rhein, Freier Platz 7, CH-8202 Schaffhausen, ☎ 052-4152-634-0888, www.urh.ch, operates along this route. Passports are required as the Swiss-German border is crossed frequently en route.

Where to Stay & Eat

Although Konstanz has pleasant hotels, most visitors prefer staying in smaller towns for the true relaxing Bodensee experience.

The **Steigenberger Inselhotel** is one of the best-known addresses along the Bodensee. It is inside a former Dominican monastery on a small privately owned island next to the harbor. As can be expected from a Steigenberger property, the hotel is luxurious, combining its historic location with the latest in modern comforts. Walls are adorned with oil paintings; the cloisters are an impressive public area. Many rooms and public areas have marvelous lake views. All three restaurants serve excellent food, with the **Seerestaurant** (€€€-€€€€), serving nouvelle cuisine and regional dishes, the best choice. Auf der Insel 1, 78462 Konstanz, ☎ 07531-1250, fax 07531-26-402, www.steigenberger.de. (€€€€)

The pleasant **Seehotel Siber** is best known for its Michelin-star restaurant (€€€-€€€€) but it also has 12 comfortable rooms. The hotel is in an Art Nouveau building on the northern banks of the River Rhine, next to the casino. The restaurant serves international, regional, and nouvelle cuisine – the terrace is particularly pleasant. Seestraße 25, 78462 Konstanz, ☎ 07531-996-6990, fax 07531-9966-9933, www.seehotel-siber.de. (€€€€)

The adjacent **Parkhotel am See** is in a villa-style building. All rooms have balconies or terraces with views of the lake. The restaurant (€€-€€€) serves international and regional cuisine. Seestraße 25a, 78462 Konstanz, ☎ 07531-8990, fax 07531-899-400, www.parkhotel-am-see.de. (€€€)

The **Mercure Halm** is across the road from the main station. The rooms are modern. Some have lake views. Bahnhofplatz 6, 78462 Konstanz, ☎ 07531-1210, fax 07531-21-804, www.accor-hotels.com. (€€€)

The **Bayrischer Hof** is in the heart of the old town close to the Rosgarten Museum. Behind the early façade is a hotel with pleasant, functionally furnished rooms. Request a room facing the garden or courtyard to avoid some street noise. Rosgartenstraße 30, 78462 Konstanz, ☎ 07531-13-040, fax 07531-130-413, www.bayrischer-hof-konstanz.de. (€€-€€€)

The Konzil-Gaststätten, Hafenstraße 2, ☎ 07531-21-221, is inside the huge Konzil building that was the setting for the famous meeting in the 15th century. It serves mainly regional dishes and fish. The large terrace with lake and harbor views is delightful. (€-€€)

Camping

Campingplatz Klausehorn is a lovely, award-winning campsite a few km north of Konstanz. On the banks of the lake opposite the town of Überlingen, it is run according to strict environmental standards. Cars must be parked on the periphery and all equipment carted to the dedicated spaces. Bicycle rental is available on site. The campground has 250 spaces and is open from April to September. Hornwiesenstraße, 78465 Konstanz-Dingelsdorf, ☎ 07533-6372, www.konstanz.de.

Excursions

■ Mainau

A highlight of any Bodensee vacation is a trip to the flower island of Mainau, 78465 Insel Mainau, ☎ 07531-3030, www.mainau.de. This 110-acre island, a mere seven km (four miles) north of Konstanz, is famous for its lush, subtropical vegetation and its flower displays, ranging from spring bulbs in April to roses in summer and dahlias in October.

Mainau belonged to the Teutonic Order from 1272 to 1805, during which time the Baroque castle and church were constructed. The fabulous gardens, the main attraction on the island, were created by the Grand Dukes of Baden and other owners since the mid-18th century and spread over most of the island. Meandering paths, fountains, creeks, and small buildings make the park more interesting. The Baroque palace and church were built in the mid-18th century – the Rococo church interior is especially worth seeing. The view from the palace terrace over the lake is particularly grand. The island also has Germany's largest butterfly house (*Schmetterlingshaus*), where some 25 species fly freely in a huge glass house. Several restaurants are available on the island, but picnicking is also allowed.

The island is best reached by boat, with good connections from Meersburg, Konstanz, and Überlingen especially. It can also be reached by Bus Line 4 from Konstanz. Parking is available on the mainland, a short stroll across the bridge to the island. The island is open daily from late March to late October, 7 am to 8 pm, and the rest of the year from 9 am to 6 pm. Admission is €11 in the summer season and €6 in winter. Set aside at least two hours plus transportation for visiting the island.

■ Reichenau

Reichenau, at six km (3.6 miles) northwest of Konstanz, is the largest island in the Bodensee. However, at only five by 1.5 km (three by .9 miles) it is still easily manageable even on foot. In contrast to Mainau, less glamorous vegetables are grown here. The main attractions are therefore not flora, but rather three superb Romanesque churches; all three are UNESCO World Cultural Heritage sites. The island is easiest explored by car, but most pleasantly by bicycle.

The first monastery on Reichenau was founded in 724 by Karl Martell. This first Benedictine monastery on German soil reached its zenith between the ninth and 11th centuries when the monks on Reichenau gained fame for the quality of their book copying and illustration skills. Decline set in from the 13th century onwards and the monastery was disbanded in the mid-18th century.

The late ninth-century **St Georg Kirche**, Oberzell, shown above, is clearly visible from the main road, with a small parking lot at the crossroad. Apart from the lovely Carolingian exterior, the main draw is the magnificent Romanesque painted interior – it is considered the best example north of the Alps. The crypt and oratorio can only be seen on guided tours, which take place in July and August on Monday at 5 pm.

The largest church on the island is another two km (1.2 miles) down the main road in Mittelzell. The **Münster St Maria und St Martin**, Pirminstraße 143, Reichenau-Mittelzell, ☎ 07534-999-5999, has a history dating back to the eighth century but the current Romanesque church is mainly 11th century with 15th-century additions. The 13th-century roof beams were left bare after a restoration project in the 1960s. The oak roof frame is a wonderful example of medieval craftsmanship and may be the oldest roof frame in Germany. The choir is only accessible when the treasury is open and has some relics and reliquaries, as well as 14th-century wall and ceiling paintings. The Schatzkammer (Treasury) has five Gothic reliquaries, sixth-century items, as well as a Roman crucifix from AD 170. It is open from May to September, Monday to Saturday, 11 am to noon and 3 to 4 pm. Admission to the treasury is €1. Guided tours take place in July and August on Tuesday at 5 pm.

Adjacent to church are the early 17th-century former monastery buildings. The road to the right of the church leads to the herb garden. Its design is based on the first botanical book in Germany – a work written between 830 and 840 by a former Reichenau abbot. Guided tours take place in July and August on Thursday at 5 pm.

The third church is the **Stiftkirche St Peter und Paul** in Niederzell. The Romanesque basilica, with two towers and three naves, dates mostly from the 11th and 12th centuries. However, the ceiling is mid-18th century, with Baroque stuccos. The church has some valuable Late Romanesque wall paintings. Guided tours take place in July and August on Friday at 5 pm. (If time is limited give preference to the first two churches.)

Information on the island and all three churches is available from **Tourist Information Reichenau**, ☎ 07534-92-070, www.reichenau.de

Index

ADVENTURE GUIDES from Hunter Publishing

This signature Hunter series targets travelers eager to explore the destination. Extensively researched and offering the very latest information, Adventure Guides are written by knowledgeable, experienced authors. Much more than just hiking, biking, canoeing and diving, the books also include cultural adventures, exploring the cuisine, the art, the theater, and meeting the people. The best local guides and other resources are listed, along with contact numbers, addresses, e-mail and website information, and recommendations. A comprehensive introductory section provides background on history, geography, climate, culture, when to go, transportation and planning. These very readable guides then take a region-by-region approach, plunging into the very heart of each area and the adventures offered, giving a full range of accommodations, shopping, restaurants for every budget, and festivals. All books have town and regional maps; some have color photos. Fully indexed.

Below are some of the most recent Adventure Guides. For a complete list of titles in this series, visit www.hunterpublishing.com or call ☎ 800-255-0343 to request a free catalog.

THE BAHAMAS

3rd Edition, Blair Howard

Fully updated reports for Grand Bahama, Freeport, Eleuthera, Bimini, Andros, the Exumas, Nassau, New Providence Island, plus new sections on San Salvador, Long Island, Cat Island, the Acklins, the Inaguas and the Berry Islands. Mailboat schedules, package vacations and snorkeling trips by Jean-Michel Cousteau.

6 x 9 pbk, 384 pp, $18.99, 1-58843-318-9

BELIZE

5th Edition, Vivien Lougheed

“Down-to-earth advice.... An excellent travel guide.”
– *Library Journal*

Extensive coverage of the country’s political, social and economic history, along with the plant and animal life. Encouraging you to mingle with the locals, Pariser entices you with descriptions of local dishes and festivals. Maps, color photos.

6 x 9 pbk, 400 pp, $18.95, 1-58843-289-0

ANGUILLA, ST. MARTIN, ST. BARTS, ST. KITTS, NEVIS, ANTIGUA, BARBUDA

2nd Edition, Paris Permenter & John Bigley

Far outdistances other guides. Recommended operators for day sails, island-hopping excursions, scuba dives, unique rainforest treks on verdant mountain slopes, and rugged four-wheel-drive trails. Previously called the *Adventure Guide to the Leeward Islands.*

6 x 9 pbk, 288 pp, $17.99, 1-55650-909-X

ARUBA, BONAIRE & CURACAO

Lynne Sullivan

By the author of our top-selling Virgin Islands Adventure Guide, here is the latest and most detailed guide to the three fascinating islands of the Dutch Caribbean. Diving, sailing, hiking, golf and horseback riding are excellent here. Enjoy gourmet cuisine, charming small inns and superb five-star resorts. Duty-free stores and unique island crafts makes the islands a shopper's delight. All of them are fully explored, with details on the history and culture that makes each one so appealing. Color photos.

6 x 9 pbk, 288 pp, $18.99, 1-58843-320-X

BERMUDA

3rd Edition, Blair Howard

Botanical gardens, pink sand beaches, historic houses, 17th-century forts, tennis clubs and a decidedly British air await! Bermuda retains much of its legendary charm even as a major tourist destination. Its golf courses are some of the best in the world, drawing an upscale crowd year-round.

6 x 9 pbk, 240 pp, $18.99, 1-58843-392-7

THE CAYMAN ISLANDS

2nd Edition, Paris Permenter & John Bigley

The only comprehensive guidebook to Grand Cayman, Cayman Brac and Little Cayman. Encyclopedic listings of dive/snorkel operators, along with the best sites. Enjoy nighttime pony rides on a glorious beach, visit the turtle farms, prepare to get wet at staggering blowholes or just laze on a white sand beach. Color photos.

6 x 9 pbk, 320pp, $18.99, 1-55650-915-4

COSTA RICA

5th Edition, Bruce & June Conord

"... most comprehensive... Excellent sections on national parks, flora, fauna & history."
– *CompuServe Travel Forum*

Incredible detail on culture, plants, animals, where to stay & eat, as well as practicalities of travel. E-mail and website directory.

6 x 9 pbk, 384 pp, $17.99, 1-58843-502-4

DOMINICAN REPUBLIC

4th Edition, Fe Liza Bencosme & Clark Norton

Virgin beaches, 16th-century Spanish ruins, the Caribbean's highest mountain, exotic wildlife, vast forests. Visit Santa Domingo, revel in Sosúa's European sophistication or explore the Samaná Peninsula's jungle. Color photos.

6 x 9 pbk, 360 pp, $17.99, 1-58843-402-8

DOMINICA & ST. LUCIA

Lynne Sullivan

An in-depth guide to these highly popular English-speaking Caribbean islands by the author of our top-selling Virgin Islands Adventure Guide. Dominica is unique in that it was never farmed over; it remains jungle-covered, mountainous and the only island still occupied by the original Carib Indians. St. Lucia is more developed, but is breathtaking in its beauty, with high peaks and azure-blue bays dotted with colorful boats. Town and regional maps, color photos, fully indexed.

6 x 9 pbk, 244 pp, $16.99, 1-58843-393-5

THE FLORIDA KEYS & EVERGLADES NATIONAL PARK

4th Edition, Bruce Morris

"... vastly informative, absolutely user-friendly, chock full of information..." – Dr. Susan Cropper

"... practical & easy to use." – *Wilderness Southeast*

Canoe trails, airboat rides, nature hikes, Key West, diving, sailing, fishing. Color.

6 x 9 pbk, 344 pp, $18.99, 1-558843-403-6

PUERTO RICO

4th Edition, Kurt Pitzer

"A quality book that covers all aspects... it's all here & well done." – *The San Diego Tribune*

"... well researched. They include helpful facts... filled with insightful tips." – *The Shoestring Traveler*

Crumbling watchtowers and fascinating folklore enchant visitors. Color photos.

6 x 9 pbk, 432 pp, $18.95, 1-558843-116-9

THE VIRGIN ISLANDS

5th Edition, Lynne Sullivan

Comprehensive coverage of both the US and British Virgin Islands, including St. Thomas, St. John, St. Croix, Tortola, Virgin Gorda, Jost Van Dyke, and more. Intriguing historical, ecological, and cultural facts bring the islands and their residents to life, while practical information smoothes the way for a stress-free vacation. Extensive coverage of the islands' protected natural areas both on land and underwater.

6 x 9 pbk, 400 pp, $19.99, 1-55650-907-3

THE YUCATAN, Cancún & Cozumel

3rd Edition, Bruce & June Conord

"This in-depth travel guide opens the doors to our enchanted Yucatán" – Mexico Ministry of Tourism
"A valuable resource." – *Travel & Leisure* magazine

Takes you to places not covered in competing guides. Take to the mountain trails, swim in hidden cenotes, watch the sun rise on a beach near the ancient Maya port of Polé (where the authors celebrated the dawn of the new millennium). Visit Bohemian Playa del Carmen, or history-rich Cozumel, where the Spanish first set foot on the North American continent.

6 x 9 pbk, 456 pp, $19.99, 1-558843-370-6

TAMPA BAY & FLORIDA'S WEST COAST

3rd Edition, Chelle Koster Walton

Visit vibrant cities, charming hometowns, nature preserves, wilderness areas and the famous white-sand beaches of Florida's Gulf shore. Covers all of Tampa Bay/St. Petersburg and north to Withlacoochee State Forest, and south to Sanibel Island, Naples and Everglades National Park. Canoeing the Everglades, fishing on Marco Island, biking in Boca Grande, diving with manatees in Crystal River, sailing along St. Pete Beach, theater-going in Sarasota, shopping the sponge markets of Greek-flavored Tarpon Springs, exploring the history of Tampa's Latin Ybor City - it's all here! Town and regional maps. Fully indexed. Color photos.

6 x 9 pbk, 320 pp, $18.99, 1-58843-350-1

TUSCANY & UMBRIA

Emma Jones

This history-rich region offers some of Italy's classic landscapes – pole-straight cypress trees lining dusty farm roads, rolling hills that stretch as far as the eye can see, fields of vibrant sunflowers, medieval villages perched on rocky spurs above crashing surf. Visit them all with this comprehensive guide that helps you explore the very best places. A largely untouched coastline and protected wild areas only add to the appeal of this top vacation destination. Town and regional maps, color photos, fully indexed.

6 x 9 pbk, 500 pp, $19.99, 1-58843-399-4

SWITZERLAND

Kimberly Rinker

With azure-blue lakes that shine brilliantly against the greenest slopes of the surrounding Alps, its picturesque villages and chic towns are accessible via high-speed trains, though many opt to travel by longboat on some of the country's tranquil waterways. It is one of the world's most advanced industrialized nations, yet its towns and cities are incredibly clean. Part-time Swiss resident Kimberly Rinker has lived and worked here for years. She tells of little-known attractions as well as major tourist draws and everything in-between. Color photos.

6 X 9 pbk, 528 pp, $17.99, 1-58843-369-2

ST. MARTIN & ST. BARTS

Lynne Sullivan

Half-French, half-Dutch, St. Martin offers Orient Bay; duty-free shopping in Philipsburg; Marigot, with chic French boutiques and superb food; and Restaurant Row in Grand Case, with great eateries in charming Creole houses. St. Barts has few buildings higher than one story, no large hotels, memorable food and 22 beautiful beaches along turquoise seas. Lynne Sullivan, author of our best-selling Adventure Guide to the Virgin Islands and several other guides, shows you how to discover and enjoy these islands to the fullest, with island tours, shopping tips, historic sightseeing, watersports and hundreds of places to stay and eat. Color photos. Maps. 6 x 9 pbk, 240 pp, $19.99, 1-58843-348-X

SPAIN

Kelly Lipscomb

A resident of Spain, the author delves into every province and town. He tells of the history and culture, and provides innumerableuseful traveling tips. Everything is explored – the cities, the parks, the islands, the mountains, the foods. Covers the entire country, from Ibiza to Granada, Andalucia, Barcelona, Madrid and Toledo. Town and regional maps, color photos, fully indexed. 6 x 9 pbk, 730 pp, $21.99, 1-58843-398-6

SCOTLAND

Martin Li

The definitive guide to every aspect of Scotland – the legends, the clans, the castles and romantic hotels, the Highland games and, of course, the whisky. This long-time Scotland resident takes us from Edinburgh to Glasgow, Argyll and the Isles, Loch Lomond, the Highlands and to the Outer Isles. Fascinating details on the Loch Ness monster, Shakespeare's "Macbeth" castle, Mary Queen of Scots, the Viking legacy, Burns Night and the royal castles. This book covers it all, and has color photos, maps and index. 6 x 9 pbk, 750 pp, $21.99, 1-58843-406-0

PANAMA

Mother nature has bequeathed Panama with some stunning spots, rich soils and a vast bio-diversity. White- and black-sand beaches alternate with mangrove mazes along the coast. Sparkling wild rivers overflowing with trout run through jungle-clad canyons filled with colorful flowers. Mist-crowned Baru Volcano towers above them all. This book explores every region from tip to toe, including the San Blas Islands, offshore Barro Colorado, and urban Panama City, gateway for visitors. Walking tours visit historic forts, gold museums, classic city parks and bustling crafts markets. Special attention is given to the national parks. 6 x 9 pbk, 360 pp, $19.99, 1-58843-368-4

MEXICO'S GULF COAST

Joanie Sanchez

The area of Veracruz, Tabasco and north to the US border is a throwback to Mexico of old. It has volcanoes, rainforests, Maya ruins and such abundant wildlife that you will see hundreds of toucans and an island filled with monkeys. Experience the dance and music of Veracruz (birthplace of La Bamba), the fabulous local foods of Xalapa, the local festivals, the miles of pristine coastline, Mexico's tallest mountain, the sheer beauty of the jungles. Town and regional maps, color photos, fully indexed.

6 x 9 pbk, 400 pp, $19.99, 1-58843-394-3

MEXICO'S PACIFIC COAST

Vivien Lougheed

The Pacific coast of Mexico is a playground for active travelers. Warm waves and sunny skies attract the beach crowd with watersports, while volcanoes, mountains and jungles appeal to hikers, naturalists and the culturally curious. Visit a pearl farm in San Carlos, ride a train through Copper Canyon, go crocodile hunting on La Tovara River, surf the big waves at Playa Las Islitas, or visit the village of Ajejic, where DH Lawrence once got inspiration. Town and regional maps, color photos, fully indexed.

6 x 9 pbk, 500 pp, $19.99, 1-58843-395-1

JAMAICA 5th Edition

Paris Permenter & John Bigley

This travel guide walks with the adventurous traveler to the heart of Jamaica, to the miles of sand beaches, to the rugged Blue Mountains, to the country villages that provide a peek at the real Jamaica. The authors focus on the adventures this popular Caribbean island has to offer: scuba diving along coral reefs, biking mountain trails, deep sea fishing, parasailing, windsurfing, horseback riding, and other adventures that range from mild to wild. Special sections include a look at Jamaica's Meet the People program, home visits, local nightspots, festivals, and more. Maps and photos enliven the down-to-earth text.

6 x 9 pbk, 360 pp, $18.99, 1-58843-504-0

NEW ZEALAND

Bette Flagler

Written by a local, this guide covers every region and town, with in-depth information on the Maori culture, the remarkable places to stay and eat, vineyard tours, cooking schools, thermal springs, albatross and whale encounters, scenic drives, and more. Canoe the Whanganui River, ride in a hot air balloon, hike the Waikaremoana Track, explore Whirikana Forest Park, take a glacier tour. There's even a section on how to talk Kiwi English! Color photos, maps and a thorough index.

6 x 9 pbk, 650 pp, $21.99, 1-58843-405-2

GRENADA, ST. VINCENT & THE GRENADINES

Cindy Kilgore & Alan Moore

Unspoiled islands at the southern end of the Caribbean chain just now being discovered by tourists. St. Vincent, with the oldest botanical garden in the Americas, is dominated by a huge volcano. The Grenadines include Bequia, Mustigue, Mayreau. Grenada, with its pristine reefs, is the source for a third of the world's nutmeg. Full details on accommodations and restaurants, getting around, sightseeing, climate, history and geography.

6 x 9 pbk, 352 pp, $18.99, 1-58843-349-8

GERMANY

Henk Bekker

Bavaria, the Mosel Valley, the Rhine region, the Black Forest, Dresden, Berlin, Hamburg – this highly detailed guide covers every part of the country in depth. The author, a German resident, shows you how to experience the best, through town walks, drives in the countryside and immersing yourself in the entertainment, the sights, the history and culture. Hundreds of hotel and restaurant reviews. Maps, color photos, index.

6 x 9 pbk, 550 pp, $19.99, 1-58843-503-2

IRELAND

Tina Neylon

Ireland is steeped in history, tradition and culture, making it one of the most popular vacation destinations worldwide. Its story is told in centuries-old castles (some of which now welcome overnight guests); stone circles strategically placed to shine in the winter solstice moon; and, of course, in its pubs, where local residents gladly share a pint and a tale. Its cities are a treat to explore, with winding streets packed with tiny antique stores. Trips along the coast take you to traditional fishing villages and past some of the world's best golf courses. This book, written by an Ireland native, tells it all. Color photos.

6 x 9 pbk, 624 pp, $18.99, 1-58843-367-6

PARIS & ILE DE FRANCE

Heather Stimmler-Hall

Written by a Paris resident, here is every neighborhood of the city, the forests and parks, plus recommended day-trips to majestic châteaux and authentic medieval villages. Shopping adventures, wine and food, dance and drama, language and literature, nightlife and entertainment – the author shows you how to get involved in it all, whether through cooking classes, dance lessons, language courses, luxury spas or wine festivals. Town and regional maps, color photos, fully indexed.

6 x 9 pbk, 448 pp, $19.99, 1-58843-396-X

All Hunter titles are available at bookstores nationwide or from the publisher. To order direct, send a check for the total of the book(s) ordered plus $3 shipping and handling to Hunter Publishing, 130 Campus Drive, Edison NJ 08818. Secure credit card orders may be made at the Hunter website, where you will also find in-depth descriptions of the hundreds of travel guides we offer.

ORDER FORM

Yes! Send the following *Adventure Guides*:

TITLE	ISBN #	PRICE	QUANTITY	TOTAL
SUBTOTAL				
SHIPPING & HANDLING (United States only) (1-2 books, $3; 3-5 books, $5; 6-10 books, $8)				
ENCLOSED IS MY CHECK FOR				

NAME:	
ADDRESS:	
CITY:	STATE: ZIP:
PHONE:	

Make checks payable to Hunter Publishing, Inc.,
and mail with order form to:

HUNTER PUBLISHING, INC.
130 Campus Drive
Edison NJ 08818
800-255-0343 / FAX 732-417-1744

www.hunterpublishing.com